INTERNATIONAL
Antiques
PRICE GUIDE

INTERNATIONAL
Antiques
PRICE GUIDE

Consultant
Judith Miller

General Editor
Elizabeth Norfolk

Introduction by
Lita Solis-Cohen

1998
Volume XIX

MILLER'S INTERNATIONAL ANTIQUES PRICE GUIDE 1998

Created and designed by
Miller's
The Cellars, High Street,
Tenterden, Kent, TN30 6BN
Tel: 01580 766411

Consultant: Judith Miller

General Editor: Elizabeth Norfolk
Editorial and Production Co-ordinator: Sue Boyd
Editorial Assistants: Jo Wood, Gillian Judd
Production Assistants: Gillian Charles, Nancy Charles
Advertising Executive: Elizabeth Smith
Advertising Assistants: Melinda Williams, Jill Jackson
Index compiled by: Hilary Bird
Design: Kari Reeves, Shirley Reeves, Matthew Leppard
Additional photography: Ian Booth, Roy Farthing, Dennis O'Reilly, Robin Saker

First published in Great Britain in 1997
by Miller's, an imprint of
Reed Books Limited,
Michelin House, 81 Fulham Road,
London SW3 6RB
and Auckland, Melbourne, Singapore and Toronto

Distributed in the USA by
Antique Collectors' Club Ltd
Market Street Industrial Park, Wappingers Falls
New York 12590
Reader enquiries: 914 297 0003
Distributed in Canada by McClelland & Stewart,
481 University Avenue, Suite 900, Toronto, Canada, M5G 2E9
Reader enquiries: 1 800 399 6858

© 1997 Reed International Books Limited

A CIP catalogue record for this book is
available from the British Library

ISBN 1-84000-039-2

Bromide output by Perfect Image, Hurst Green, E. Sussex
Illustrations by G.H. Graphics, St Leonard's-on-Sea
Colour origination by Scantrans, Singapore
Printed and bound in England by William Clowes Ltd,
Beccles and London

Front cover illustrations:
top l. *A Meissen group of Pantaloon and Columbine,
modelled by J. J. Kändler, c1741, 6½in (16cm) high.* **£9,000–9,500** *C*
top r. *An Ideal teddy bear, c1907.* **£2,000–2,500** *TED*
bottom. *A flame mahogany-veneered chest of drawers, c1770.* **£2,500–3,000** *S*

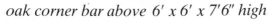

Apollo Antiques Ltd
EXPORT AND WHOLESALE

❋ ONE OF THE LARGEST STOCKS OF QUALITY FURNITURE
IN THE MIDLANDS

❋ 1½ HOURS FROM CENTRAL LONDON, VIA M40 JCT. 15

❋ 20 MINUTES FROM BIRMINGHAM INTERNATIONAL AIRPORT & NEC

❋ FREE DELIVERIES TO LONDON

We Stock 18th and 19th
Century English and
Continental Furniture,
also Arts and Crafts
Furniture and Decorative
items for the English,
European and American
Markets

Apollo Antiques Ltd.
The Saltisford
Warwick

TEL: 01926 494746

FAX: 01926 401477

Lloyd Williams Antiques

Anglo Am Warehouse

- Very competitive prices
- Full restoration service
- 15 years experience
- Containers loaded
- Large selection of smalls
- 5000 Pieces of Furniture
- All export market
- Buy one piece or a container
- Fax us your needs

Anglo Am Warehouse 2a Beach Road, Eastbourne BN22 7EX
Tel: 01323 648661 or Fax: 01323 648658 Eves: 01892 536627

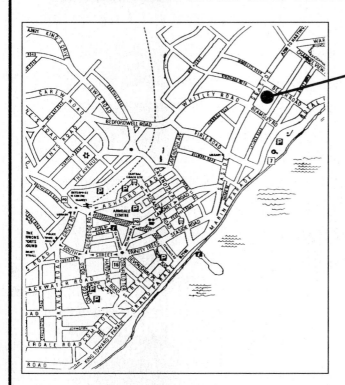

Anglo Am Warehouse

- *1 hr Dover* •
- *1½ hr Gatwick* •
- *1½ hrs London* •
- *½ hr Brighton* •

*We are open 9-5
Mon to Fri or by
appointment*

*Mainline station
customer collection*

CONTENTS

KEY TO ILLUSTRATIONS

Each illustration and descriptive caption is accompanied by a letter code. By referring to the following list of Auctioneers (denoted by *) and Dealers (•) the source of any item may be immediately determined. Inclusion in this edition in no way constitutes or implies a contract or binding offer on the part of any of our contributors to supply or sell the goods illustrated, or similar articles, at the prices stated. Advertisers in this year's directory are denoted by †.

If you require a valuation for an item, it is advisable to check whether the dealer or specialist will carry out this service and if there is a charge. Please mention Miller's when making an enquiry. Having found a specialist who will carry out your valuation it is best to send a photograph and description of the item to the specialist together with a stamped addressed envelope for the reply. A valuation by telephone is not possible. Most dealers are only too happy to help you with your enquiry; however, they are very busy people and consideration of the above points would be appreciated.

AAN	•	Appledore Antiques, 8 the Street, Appledore, Kent TN26 2BX Tel: 01233 758272
AAV	*	Academy Auctioneers & Valuers, Northcote House, Northcote Avenue, Ealing, London W5 3UR Tel: 0181 579 7466
ABC	•†	Academy Billiard Co, 5 Camp Hill Industrial Estate, West Byfleet, Surrey KT14 6EW Tel: 01932 352067
ACA	•	Acorn Antiques, Sheep Street, Stow-on-the-Wold, Glos GL54 1AA Tel: 01451 831519
ACC	•	Albert's Cigarette Card Specialists, 113 London Road, Twickenham, Middlesex TW1 1EE Tel: 0181 891 3067
AEF	•	A. & E. Foster, Little Heysham, Naphill, Bucks HP14 4SU Tel: 01494 562024
AG	*	Anderson & Garland (Auctioneers), Marlborough House, Marlborough Crescent, Newcastle-upon-Tyne, Tyne & Wear NE1 4EE Tel: 0191 232 6278
AH	*†	Andrew Hartley, Victoria Hall Salerooms, Little Lane, Ilkley, Yorkshire LS29 8EA Tel: 01943 816363
AHO	•†	Amanda House, The Barns, Twigworth Court, Twigworth, Glos GL2 9PG Tel: 01452 731296
AL	•†	Ann Lingard, Ropewalk Antiques, Ropewalk, Rye, Sussex TN31 7NA Tel: 01797 223486
ALB	•	Albany Antiques Ltd, 8-10 London Road, Hindhead, Surrey GU26 6AE Tel: 01428 605528
ALS	•†	Allan Smith Clocks, Amity Cottage, 162 Beechcroft Road, Upper Stratton, Swindon, Wiltshire SN2 6QE Tel: 01793 822977
AMH	•	Amherst Antiques, 23 London Road, Riverhead, Sevenoaks, Kent TN13 2BU Tel: 01732 455047
ANG	•†	Ancient & Gothic, PO Box 356, Christchurch, Dorset BH23 2YD Tel: 01202 478592
ANO	•†	Art Nouveau Originals, Stamford Antiques Centre, The Exchange Hall, Broad Street, Stamford, Lincolnshire PE9 1PX Tel: 01780 762605
AnS	•	The Antique Shop, 30 Henley Street, Stratford-upon-Avon, Warwickshire, CV37 6QW Tel: 01789 292485
ANT	•†	Anthemion, Bridge Street, Cartmel, Grange-over-Sands, Cumbria LA11 7SH Tel: 015395 36295
AP	*†	Andrew Pickford, The Hertford Saleroom, 42 St Andrew Street, Hertford, Herts SG14 1JA Tel: 01992 583508
APO	•†	Apollo Antiques Ltd, The Saltisford, Birmingham Road, Warwick, Warwicks CV34 4TD Tel: 01926 494746
ARE	•	Arenski, 185 Westbourne Grove, London W11 2SB Tel: 0171 727 8599
ARP	•	Arundel Photographica, The Arundel Antiques Centre, 51 High St, Arundel, Sussex BN18 9AJ Tel: 01903 882749
ASA	•†	A. S. Antiques, 26 Broad St, Pendleton, Salford, Greater Manchester M6 5BY Tel: 0161 737 5938
ASB	•†	Andrew Spencer Bottomley, The Coach House, Thongs Bridge, Holmfirth, Yorkshire HD7 2TT Tel: 01484 685234
ASP	•	John Aspley Antiques, Tel: 01538 373396
AWH	•	A. W. Hone & Son Oriental Carpets, 1486 Stratford Road (Robin Hood Island), Hall Green, Birmingham, West Midlands B28 9ET Tel: 0121 744 1001
AWT	•	Antique Associates at West Townsend, 473 Main Street, PO Box 129W, West Townsend, MA 01474 USA Tel: 508 597 8084
B	*	Boardman Fine Art Auctioneers, Station Road Corner, Haverhill, Suffolk CB9 0EY Tel: 01440 730414
B&F	•	Bears & Friends, 41 Meeting House Lane, The Lanes, Brighton, Sussex BN1 1HB Tel: 01273 202940

B&L	*	Bonhams and Langlois, Westaway Chambers, 39 Don Street, St Helier, Jersey JE2 4TR Tel: 01534 22441
BAD	•	Badgers Antiques, Tel: 01233 758337
BaH	•	Calamus, The Shambles, Sevenoaks, Kent TN13 1AL Tel: 01732 740603
Bar	•	Chris Barge Antiques, 5 Southside Place, Inverness, Scotland IV2 3JF Tel: 01463 230128
Bea	*	1 Southernhay West, Exeter, Devon EX1 1JG Tel: 01392 219040
Bea(E)*		Bearnes, St Edmund's Court, Okehampton Stt, Exeter, Devon EX4 1DU Tel: 01392 422800
BEL	•	Bell Antiques, 68A Harold Street, Grimsby, Humberside DN35 0HH Tel: 01472 695110
Ber	•	Berry Antiques, Berry House, 11-13 Stone Street, Cranbrook, Kent TN17 3HF Tel: 01580 712345
BERA	•†	Berry Antiques, 3 High Street, Moreton-in-Marsh, Glos GL56 0AH Tel: 01608 652929
BEV	•	Beverley, 30 Church Street, London NW8 8EP Tel: 0171 262 1576
BGA	•	By George Antique Centre, 23 George Street, St Albans, Herts AL3 4ES Tel: 01727 853032
BHa	•†	Judy & Brian Harden, PO Box 14, Bourton-on-the-Water, Cheltenham, Glos GL54 2YR Tel: 01451 810684
BIG	*	Bigwood Auctioneers Ltd, The Old School, Tiddington, Stratford-upon-Avon, Warwicks, CV37 7AW Tel: 01789 269415
BIL	•	Box in the Lanes, 1 Bartlett Street, Bath, Avon BA1 2QZ Tel: 0468 720338
Bon	*†	Bonhams, Montpelier Street, Knightsbridge, London SW7 1HH Tel: 0171 393 3900
Bon(C)*		Bonhams, 65-69 Lots Road, Chelsea, London SW10 0RN Tel: 0171 393 3900
BOR	•	Bed of Roses, 12 Prestbury Road, Cheltenham, Glos GL52 2PW Tel: 01242 231918
BR	*	Bracketts, 27-29 High Street, Tunbridge Wells, Kent TN1 1UU Tel: 01892 533733
BRA	•†	Billiard Room Antiques, The Old School, Church Lane, Chilcompton, Bath, Somerset BA3 4HP Tel: 01761 232839
Bri	*†	Bristol Auction Rooms, St John's Place, Apsley Road, Clifton, Bristol, Avon BS8 2ST Tel: 0117 973 7201
BRU	•	Brunel Antiques, Great Western Antiques Centre, Bath, Avon BA1 2QZ Tel: 01225 310388
BrW	•	Brian Watson, Antique Glass, The Grange, Norwich Road, Wroxham, Norwich, Norfolk NR12 8RX Tel: 01603 784177
BSA	•	Bartlett Street Antiques, 5-10 Bartlett Street, Bath, Avon BA1 2QZ Tel: 01225 446322/310457
BTA	•	Brian Taylor Antiques, 24 Molesworth Road, Plymouth, Devon PL1 5LZ Tel: 01752 569061
BWe	*	Biddle & Webb Ltd, Ladywood Middleway, Birmingham, West Midlands B16 0PP Tel: 0121 455 8042
ByI	•	Bygones of Ireland, Westport Antiques Centre, Lodge Road, Westport, County Mayo, Ireland Tel: 00 353 98 26132
C	*	Christie, Manson & Woods Ltd, 8 King Street, St James's, London SW1Y 6QT Tel: 0171 839 9060
C(Am)*		Christie's Amsterdam, Cornelis Schuystraat 57, Amsterdam, 1071 JG Tel: (3120) 57 55 255
C(G)	*	Christie's (International) SA, 8 Place de la Taconnerie, 1204 Geneva, Switzerland Tel: (41 22) 319 17 66
C(HK) *		Christie's Hong Kong, 2203-5 Alexandra House, 16-20 Chater Road, Hong Kong Tel: (852) 2521 5396
C(LA) *		Christie's, 342 North Rodeo Drive, Beverly Hills, Ca 90210, LA, USA Tel: (310) 275 5534
C(S)	*	Christie's Scotland Ltd, 164-166 Bath Street, Glasgow, Scotland G2 4TG Tel: 0141 332 8134
C(Sc)		

CAG *† The Canterbury Auction Galleries, 40 Station Road West, Canterbury, Kent CT2 8AN Tel: 01227 763337

CAT • Lennox Cato, 1 The Square, Edenbridge, Kent TN8 5BD Tel: 01732 865988

CB • Christine Bridge Antiques, 78 Castelnau, London SW13 9EX Tel: 0181 741 5501

CBC •† Cheshire Billiard Co, Springwood Lodge, Ermine Street, Appleby, Lincolnshire DN15 0DD Tel: 01724 852359

CBP * Comic Book Postal Auctions Ltd, 40-42 Osnaburgh Street, London NW1 3ND Tel: 0171 424 0007

CBu • Christopher Buck Antiques, 56-60 Sandgate High Street, Folkestone, Kent CT20 3AP Tel: 01303 221229

CCP • Campden Country Pine Antiques, High Street, Chipping Campden, Glos GL55 6HN Tel: 01386 840315

CDC * Capes Dunn & Co, The Auction Galleries, 38 Charles Street, Off Princess Street, Gt Manchester M1 7DB Tel: 0161 273 6060/1911

CEX • Corn Exchange Antiques Centre, 64 The Pantiles, Tunbridge Wells, Kent TN2 5TN Tel: 01892 539652

CHA • Chislehurst Antiques, 7 Royal Parade, Chislehurst, Kent BR7 6NR Tel: 0181 467 1530

CHR • Charnwood Antiques, Greystones, Coalville, Leicester, Leics LE67 4RN Tel: 0116 283 8530

ChS •† The Chair Set, 84 Hill Rise, Richmond, Surrey TW10 6UB Tel: 0181 332 6454

CMF • Childhood Memories, The Farnham Antique Centre, 27 South Street, Farnham, Surrey GU9 7QU Tel: 01252 724475

CNY * Christie, Manson & Woods International Inc, 502 Park Avenue, (including Christie's East), New York, NY 10022 USA Tel: 212 546 1000

CoA •† Country Antiques (Wales), Castle Mill, Kidwelly, Carms, Wales SA17 4UU Tel: 01554 890534

CoH *† Cooper Hirst Auctions, The Granary Saleroom, Victoria Road, Chelmsford, Essex CM2 6LH Tel: 01245 260535

COM • Combe Cottage Antiques, Castle Combe, Chippenham, Wiltshire SN14 7HU Tel: 01249 782250

CORO •† Coromandel, PO Box 9772, London SW19 3ZG Tel: 0181 543 9115

COT • Cottage Antiques, Bakewell & Woburn Antiques Centres, Bucks Tel: 01283 562670

COW •† Clive Cowell, Glassenbury Timber Yard, Iden Green, Goudhurst, Cranbrook, Kent TN17 2PA Tel: 01580 212022

CPA •† Cottage Pine Antiques, 19 Broad Street, Brinklow, Nr Rugby, Warwicks CV23 0LS Tel: 01788 832673

CPS • Country Pine Shop, Northampton Road, West Haddon, Northants NN6 7AS Tel: 01788 510430

CS •† Christopher Sykes, The Old Parsonage, Woburn, Milton Keynes, Bucks MK17 9QM Tel: 01525 290259

CSA • Church Street Antiques, 10 Church Street, Godalming, Surrey GU7 1EH Tel: 01483 860894

CSK * Christie's South Kensington Ltd, 85 Old Brompton Road, London SW7 3LD Tel: 0171 581 7611

CTO •† Collector's Corner, Tudor House, 29-31 Lower Bridge Street, Chester, Cheshire CH1 1RS Tel: 01260 270429

DA *† Dee, Atkinson & Harrison, The Exchange Saleroom, Driffield, Yorkshire YO25 7LJ Tel: 01377 253151

DaD * David Dockree, Cheadle Hulme Business Centre, Clemence House, Mellor Road, Cheadle Hulme, Cheshire SK7 1BD Tel: 0161 485 1258

DAF • Moderne, 14 Widcombe Parade, Bath, Avon BA2 4JT Tel: 01225 465000

DAN •† Andrew Dando, 4 Wood Street, Queen Square, Bath, Avon BA1 2JQ Tel: 01225 422702

DBA •† Douglas Bryan, The Old Bakery, St David's Bridge, Cranbrook, Kent TN17 3HN Tel: 01580 713103

DDM * Dickinson Davy & Markham, Wrawby Street, Brigg, Humberside DN20 8JJ Tel: 01652 653666

DFA •† Delvin Farm Antiques, Gormonston, Co Meath, Ireland Tel: 00353 1841 2285

DIC • D. & B. Dickinson, The Antique Shop 22 & 22a New Bond St, Bath, Avon BA1 1BA Tel: 01225 466502

DN * Dreweatt Neate, Donnington Priory, Donnington, Newbury, Berkshire RG13 2JE Tel: 01635 31234

Dns • Brian & Jenny Dennis, Bath, Somerset Tel: 01225 446574

DNW * Dix-Noonan-Webb, 1 Old Bond Street, London W1X 3TD Tel: 0171 499 5022

DOR •† Dorset Reclamation, Cow Drove, Bere Regis, Wareham, Dorset BH20 7JZ Tel: 01929 472200

DRA •† Derek Roberts, 24-25 Shipbourne Road, Tonbridge, Kent TN10 3DN Tel: 01732 358986

DRU •† Drummonds of Bramley, Birtley Farm, Horsham Road, Bramley, Guildford, Surrey GU5 0LA Tel: 01483 898766

DSP • David & Sarah Pullen, PO Box 24, Bexhill-on-Sea, Sussex TN39 4ZN Tel: 01424 848035

DUB • Dubey's Art & Antiques, 807 N. Howard Street, Baltimore, MD 21201, USA Tel: 001 410 383 2881

DW * Dominic Winter Book Auctions, The Old School, Maxwell Street, Swindon, Wiltshire SN1 5DR Tel: 01793 611340

E *† Ewbanks, Burnt Common Auction Rooms, London Road, Send, Woking, Surrey GU23 7LN Tel: 01483 223101

EH * Edgar Horn, Fine Art Auctioneers, 46-50 South Street, Eastbourne, Sussex BN21 4XB Tel: 01323 410419

EL * Eldred's, Robert C Eldred Co Inc, 1483 Route 6A, East Dennis, Massachusetts 02641, USA Tel: 001 508 385 3116

ELA • Eldreds, Auctioneers & Valuers, 13-15 Ridge Park Road, Plympton, Plymouth, Devon PL7 2BS Tel: 01752 340066

EP *† Evans & Partridge, Agriculture House, High Street, Stockbridge, Hampshire, SO20 6HF Tel: 01264 810702

FAG • Fagins Antiques, The Old Whiteways Cider Factory, Hele, Exeter, Devon EX5 4PW Tel: 01392 882062

FBG * Frank H. Boos Gallery, 420 Enterprise Court, Bloomfield Hills, Michigan 48302 USA Tel: 810 332-1500

FD • Frank Dux Antiques, 33 Belvedere, Bath, Avon BA1 5HR Tel: 01225 312367

FHA •† Flower House Antiques, 90 High Street, Tenterden, Kent TN30 6JB Tel: 01580 763764

FOX • Foxhole Antiques, Swan & Foxhole, Albert House, Stone Street, Cranbrook, Kent TN17 3HF Tel: 01580 712720

G&CC •† Goss & Crested China Ltd, 62 Murray Road, Horndean, Hampshire PO8 9JL Tel: 01705 597446

GAK *† G. A. Key, Aylsham Salerooms, 8 Market Place, Aylsham, Norfolk NR11 6EH Tel: 01263 733195

Gam * Clarke Gammon, The Guildford Auction Rooms, Bedford Road, Guildford, Surrey GU1 4SJ Tel: 01483 566458

GAS • Gasson Antiques, PO Box 7225, Tadley, Hampshire RG26 5YB Tel: 01189 813636

GAZE *† Thomas Wm. Gaze & Son, Diss Auction Rooms, Roydon Road, Diss, Norfolk IP22 3LN Tel: 01379 650306

GBr •† Breeze, Geoffrey Antiques, 6 George Street, Bath, Avon BA1 2EH Tel: 01225 466499

GD •† Gilbert & Dale, The Old Chapel, Church Street, Ilchester, Nr Yeovil, Somerset BA22 8LA Tel: 01935 840464

GeC •† Gerard Campbell, Maple House, Market Place, Lechlade, Glos GL7 3AB Tel: 01367 252267

GEM •† Gem Antiques, 28 London Road, Sevenoaks, Kent TN13 1AP Tel: 01732 743540

GH * Gardiner Houlgate, The Old Malthouse, Comfortable Place, Upper Bristol Road, Bath, Avon BA1 3AJ Tel: 01225 447933

Gle * Glendinings & Co, 101 New Bond Street, London W1Y 9LG Tel: 0171 493 2445

GLN • Glenville Antiques, 120 High Street, Yatton, Avon BS19 4DH Tel: 01934 832284

GLT • Glitterati, Assembly Antiques Centre, Saville Row, Bath, Avon BA1 2QP Tel: 01225 333294

GN •† Gillian Neale Antiques, PO Box 247, Aylesbury, Bucks HP20 1JZ Tel: 01296 23754

GOR *† Gorringes Auction Galleries, 15 North Street, Lewes, Sussex BN7 2PD Tel: 01273 472503

GOR(B) *† Gorringes Auction Galleries, Terminus Road, Bexhill-on-Sea, Sussex TN39 3LR Tel: 01424 212994

GRP •† Grayshott Pine, Crossways Road, Grayshott, Surrey GU26 6HF Tel: 01428 607478

GS • Ged Selby Antique Glass, Yorkshire
Tel: 01756 799673

GUN •† Gaby Gunst, 140 High Street, Tenterden,
Kent TN30 6HT Tel: 01580 765818

GV •† Garth Vincent, The Old Manor House,
Allington, Nr Grantham, Lincolnshire
NG32 2DH Tel: 01400 281358

GWA •† Great Western Antiques, Torre Station,
Newton Road, Torquay, Devon TQ2 5DD
Tel: 01803 200551

Hal *† Halls Fine Art Auctions, Welsh Bridge,
Shrewsbury, Shropshire SY3 8LA
Tel: 01743 231212

HALL • Hall's Nostalgia, 21 Mystic Street, Arlington,
MA 02174 USA Tel: 001 617 646 7757

HAM *† Hamptons Antique & Fine Art Auctioneers,
93 High Street, Godalming, Surrey GU7 1AL
Tel: 01483 423567

Har • Patricia Harbottle, Geoffrey Vann Arcade,
Portobello Road, London W11 2QB
Tel: 0171 731 1972

HB • Harrington Bros, The Chelsea Antique Market,
253 Kings Road, London SW3 5EL
Tel: 0171 352 5689/1720

HCC *† H. C. Chapman & Son, The Auction Mart,
North Street, Scarborough, Yorkshire
YO11 1DL Tel: 01723 372424

HCH * Hobbs & Chambers, Market Place, Cirencester,
Glos GL7 1QQ Tel: 01285 654736

HEL • Helios Gallery, 292 Westbourne Grove,
London W11 2PS Tel: 01225 336097

HEM •† Hemswell Antique Centre, Caenby Corner
Estate, Hemswell Cliff, Gainsborough,
Lincolnshire DN21 5TJ Tel: 01427 668389

HEY • Heytesbury Antiques, PO Box 222, Farnham,
Surrey GU10 5HN Tel: 01252 850893

HIG • Highcroft Antiques, Red Lion, 165 Portobello
Road, London W11 2DY Tel: 0171 221 7638

HOA •† Bob Hoare Pine Antiques, Unit Q, Phoenix
Place, North Street, Lewes, Sussex BN7 2DQ
Tel: 01273 480557

HOB • Hobday Toys, 44 High Street, Northwood,
Middlesex HA6 2XY Tel: 01923 820115

HOLL* Dreweatt Neate Holloways, 49 Parsons Street,
Banbury, Oxon OX16 8PF Tel: 01295 253197

HON •† Honans Antiques, Crowe Street, Gort, Co
Galway, Ireland Tel: 00 353 91 631407

HOW • Howards Antiques, 10 Alexandra Road,
Aberystwyth, Dyfed, Wales SY23 1LE
Tel: 01970 624973

HRQ •† Harlequin Antiques, 79 Mansfield Road,
Daybrook, Nottingham, Notts, NG5 6BH.
Tel: 0115 967 4590

HYD * HY Duke & Son, Dorchester Fine Art
Salerooms, Dorchester, Dorset DT1 1QS
Tel: 01305 265080

IHB • Imperial Half Bushel, 831 N. Howard Street,
Baltimore, MD 21201 USA
Tel: 001 410 462 1192

IW •† Islwyn Watkins, 1 High Street, Knighton,
Powys, Wales LD7 1AT Tel: 01547 520145

J&L *† James & Lister Lea, 1741 Warwick Road,
Knowle, Birmingham, West Midlands B93 0LX
Tel: 01564 779187

JAA * Jackson's Auctioneers & Appraisers, 2229
Lincoln Street, Cedar Falls, IA 50613 USA
Tel: 319 277 2256

JAd * James Adam & Sons, 26 St Stephen's Green,
Dublin 2 Ireland
Tel: 00 3531 676 0261/661 3655

JAK •† Clive & Lynne Jackson, Glos
Tel: 01242 254375

JBB • Jessie's Button Box, Bath, Avon BA1 2QZ
Tel: 0117 929 9065

JHa • Jeanette Hayhurst Fine Glass,
32a Kensington Church Street, London
W8 4HA Tel: 0171 938 1539

JHo •† Jonathan Horne (Antiques) Ltd,
66C Kensington Church Street, London
W8 4BY Tel: 0171 221 5658

JIL •† Jillings Antiques, 8 Halken Arcade,
Motcomb Street, London SW1X 8JT
Tel: 0171 235 8600

JM *† John Maxwell of Wilmslow, 133A Woodford
Road, Woodford, Cheshire SK7 1QD
Tel: 0161 439 5182

JP •† Janice Paull, PO Box 100, Kenilworth,
Warwicks CV8 1HY Tel: 01926 855253

JPr • Joanna Proops Antiques and Textiles,
Belvedere, Bath, Avon BA1 2QP

JRe • John Read, Ipswich, Suffolk IP5 7SA
Tel: 01473 624897

KEY •† Key Antiques, 11 Horsefair, Chipping Norton,
Oxfordshire OX7 5AL
Tel: 01608 643777

KW • Karel Weijand, Lion & Lamb Courtyard,
Farnham, Surrey GU9 7LL
Tel: 01252 726215

L * Lawrence Fine Art Auctioneers, South Street,
Crewkerne, Somerset TA18 8AB
Tel: 01460 73041

L&E *† Locke & England, Black Horse Agencies,
18 Guy Street, Leamington Spa, Warwicks
CV32 4RT Tel: 01926 889100

LAY * David Lay ASVA, Auction House, Alverton,
Penzance, Cornwall TR18 4RE
Tel: 01736 361414

LB • Lace Basket, 116 High Street, Tenterden, Kent
TN30 6HT Tel: 01580 763664

LCA • La Chaise Antiques, 30 London Street,
Faringdon, Oxfordshire SN7 7AA
Tel: 01367 240427

Lel * Leland's, 245 Fifth Avenue, Suite 902,
New York 10016, USA Tel: (212) 545 0800

LF • Lambert & Foster, 102 High St, Tenterden, Kent,
TN30 6HT Tel: 01580 762083

LHA * Lesley Hindman Auctioneers, 215 West Ohio
Street, Chicago, Illinois, IL 60610 USA
Tel: 001 312 670 0010

LHB * Les Hommes Bleus Gallery, Bartlett Street
Antique Centre, Bartlett Street, Bath,
Avon BA1 2QZ Tel: 01225 316606

LIB • Libra Antiques, 81 London Road, Hurst Green,
Etchingham, Sussex TN19 7PN
Tel: 01580 860569

LT *† Louis Taylor Auctioneers & Valuers,
Britannia House, 10 Town Road, Hanley,
Stoke-on-Trent, Staffordshire ST1 2QG
Tel: 01782 214111

M * Morphets, 6 Albert Street, Harrogate,
Yorkshire HG1 1JL Tel: 01423 530030

MAT * Christopher Matthews, 23 Mount Street,
Harrogate, Yorkshire HG2 8DQ
Tel: 01423 871756

MB •† Mostly Boxes, 93 High Street, Eton, Berkshire
SL4 6AF Tel: 01753 858470

MCA *† Mervyn Carey, Twysden Cottage, Benenden,
Cranbrook, Kent TN17 4LD
Tel: 01580 240283

ME • John Meredith, 36 The Square, Chagford,
Devon TQ13 8BB Tel: 01647 433474

MEG • Megarry's and Forever Summer, Jericho
Cottage, The Green, Blackmore, Essex
CM4 0RR Tel: 01277 821031

MER •† Mere Antiques, 13 Fore Street, Topsham,
Exeter, Devon EX3 0HF Tel: 01392 874224

MGC • Midlands Commemoratives, The Old
Cornmarket Antique Centre, 70 Market Place,
Warwick, Warwicks CV34 4SO
Tel: 01926 419119

MIC • Combesbury Antiques, Combesbury Farm,
Buckland St Mary, Chard, Somerset TA20 3ST
Tel: 01460 234323

Mit * Mitchells, Fairfield House, Station Road,
Cockermouth, Cumbria CA13 9PY
Tel: 01900 827800

MJW • Mark J West, Cobb Antiques Ltd, 39a High
Street, Wimbledon Village, London SW19 5YX
Tel: 0181 946 2811

ML • Magic Lantern (Josie Marsden),
By George Antique Centre, 23 George Street,
St Albans, Herts AL3 4ES
Tel: 01727 853032

MLa •† Marion Langham Tel: 0171 730 1002

MMo • Maureen Morris, Essex Tel: 01799 521338

MON • Monty Lo, Stand 369, Grays Antique Market,
58 Davies St, London W1Y 1AR
Tel: 0171 493 9457

MOP • Moseley Pianos, Birmingham Piano
Warehouse, Unit L, 68 Wirley Road, Witton,
Birmingham B6 7BH Tel: 0121 327 2701

MRT • Mark Rees Tools, Avon Tel: 01225 837031

MSB • Marilynn and Sheila Brass, PO Box 380503,
Cambridge, MA 02238-0503 USA
Tel: 617 491 6064

MSh • Manfred Schotten, The Crypt Antiques,
109 High Street, Burford, Oxfordshire
OX18 4RG Tel: 01993 822302

MSL *† Michael Stainer Ltd, St Andrew's Hall,
Wolverton Road, Boscombe, Bournemouth,
Dorset BH7 6HT Tel: 01202 309999

MSW *† Marilyn Swain Auctions, The Old Barracks,
Sandon Road, Grantham, Lincs NG31 9AS
Tel: 01476 568861

MUL •† Mullock & Madeley, The Old Shippon,
Wall-under-Heywood, Church Stretton,
Shropshire, SY6 7DS. Tel: 01694 771771

MUR •† Murray Cards (Int) Ltd, 51 Watford Way,
Hendon Central, London NW4 3JH
Tel: 0181 202 5688

NCA • New Century, 69 Kensington Church St, London W8 4BG Tel: 0171 376 2810

No7 •† No 7 Antiques, 7 Nantwich Road, Woore, Shropshire CW3 9SA Tel: 01630 647118

Nor • Sue Norman, L4 Antiquarius, 135 King's Rd, London SW3 5ST Tel: 0171 352 7217

NOST •† Nostalgia, 61 Shaw Heath, Stockport, Cheshire SK3 8BH Tel: 0161 477 7706

NWE •† North Wilts Exporters, Farm Hill House, Brinkworth, Wiltshire SN15 5AJ Tel: 01666 510876

Oli *† Olivers, Olivers Rooms, Burkitts Lane, Sudbury, Suffolk CO10 6HB Tel: 01787 880305

OLM/ WLD • The Old Mill, High Street, Lamberhurst, Kent TN3 8EQ Tel: 01892 891196

ONS * Onslow's, The Old Depot, The Gas Works, off Michael Road, London SW6 2AD Tel: 0171 371 0505

OO •† Pieter Oosthuizen, Georgian Village, Camden Passage, London N1 8DU Tel: 0171 376 3852

OT • Old Timers, Box 392, Camp Hill, PA 17001-0392 USA Tel: 001 717 761 1908

OTB •† Old Tackle Box, PO Box 55, Cranbrook, Kent TN17 3ZU Tel: 01580 713979

OTS • The Old Toy Shop, 7 Monmouth Court, Ringwood, Hants BH24 1H8 Tel: 01425 476899

P *† Phillips, 101 New Bond Street, London W1Y 0AS Tel: 0171 629 6602

P(B) * Phillips, 1 Old King Street, Bath, Avon BA1 2JT Tel: 01225 310609

P(Ba) * Phillips Bayswater, 10 Salem Road, London W2 4DL Tel: 0171 229 9090

P(C) * Phillips Cardiff, 9-10 Westgate Street, Cardiff, Wales CF1 1DA Tel: 01222 396453

P(Ch) * Phillips Chichester, Baffins Hall, Baffins Lane, Chichester, Sussex PO19 1UA Tel: 01243 787548

P(NE) * Phillips North East, St Mary's, Oakwellgate, Gateshead, Tyne & Wear NE8 2AX Tel: 0191 477 6688

P(NW) * Phillips North West, New House, 150 Christleton Road, Chester, Cheshire CH3 5TD Tel: 01244 313936

P(O) * Phillips, 39 Park End Street, Oxford, Oxfordshire OX1 1JD Tel: 01865 723524

P(S) * Phillips Fine Art Auctioneers, 49 London Road, Sevenoaks, Kent TN13 1AR Tel: 01732 740310

P(Sc) * Phillips Scotland, 207 Bath Street, Glasgow, Scotland G2 4HD Tel: 0141 221 8377

P(WM) * Phillips, The Old House, Station Road, Knowle, Solihull, West Midlands B93 0HT Tel: 01564 776151

PAO •† P. A. Oxley, The Old Rectory, Cherhill, Nr Calne, Wiltshire SN11 8UX Tel: 01249 816227

PCh *† Peter Cheney, Western Road Auction Rooms, Littlehampton, Sussex BN17 5NP Tel: 01903 722264/713418

PEN • Pennard House Antiques, 3-4 Piccadilly, London Road, Bath, Avon BA1 6PL Tel: 01225 313791/01749 860260

PEx •† Piano Export, Bridge Road, Kingswood, Bristol, Avon BS15 4PW Tel: 0117 956 8300

PF *† Peter Francis, The Curiosity Saleroom, 19 King Street, Carmarthen, South Wales SA31 1BH Tel: 01267 233456

PGH • Paris, 42A High Street, Tenterden, Kent TN30 6AR Tel: 01580 765328

PHA •† Paul Hopwell, 30 High St, West Haddon, Northants NN6 7AP Tel: 01788 510636

PIn • Postcards International, Vintage Picture Postcards, PO Box 2930, New Haven, CT 06515-0030 USA Tel: 001 203 865 0814

PNF •† Pinfold Antiques, 62 Rectory Road, Ruskington, Lincolnshire NG34 9AD Tel: 01526 832200

POA * Proud Oriental Auctions, Proud Galleries, 5 Buckingham St, London WC2N 6BP Tel: 0171 839 4942

POSH •† Posh Tubs, Moriati's Workshop, High Halden, Ashford, Kent TN26 3LZ Tel: 01233 850155

POT •† Pot Board, 30 King Street, Carmarthen, Dyfed, Wales SA31 1BS Tel: 01267 236623

PP • Poole Pottery, The Quay, Poole, Dorset BH15 1RF Tel: 01202 666200

PSA •† Pantiles Spa Antiques, 4, 5, 6 Union House, The Pantiles, Tunbridge Wells, Kent TN4 8HE Tel: 01892 541377

PSG • Patrick & Susan Gould, Stand L17, Gray's Mews Antique Market, Davies St, London W1Y 1AR Tel: 0171 408 0129

PT •† Pieces of Time, 1-7 Davies Mews, London W1Y 1AR Tel: 0171 629 2422

RA • Roberts Antiques, Lancashire Tel: 01253 827798

RAR *† Romsey Auction Rooms, 86 The Hundred, Romsey, Hants SO51 8BX Tel: 01794 513331

RBA • Roger Bradbury Antiques, Church Street, Coltishall, Norfolk NR12 7DJ Tel: 01603 737444

RBB *† Russell, Baldwin & Bright, Ryelands Road, Leominster, Hereford HR6 8NZ Tel: 01568 611122

RCh • Rayner & Chamberlain, London Tel: 0181 293 9439

RdeR •† Rogers de Rin, 76 Royal Hospital Road, London SW3 4HN Tel: 0171 352 9007

RECL • Reclamation Services Ltd, Catbrain Quarry, Painswick Beacon, Above Paradise, Painswick, Glos GL6 6SU Tel: 01452 814064

REN • Paul & Karen Rennie, 13 Rugby Street, London WC1N 3QT Tel: 0171 405 0220

RIT * Ritchie Inc, D. & J. Auctioneers & Appraisers, 288 King Street East, Toronto, Ontario, Canada M5A 1K4 Tel: (416) 364 1864

RKa • Richardson & Kailas, London Tel: 0171 371 0491

RP • Robert Pugh, PO Box 24, Carmarthen, Wales SA31 1YS Tel: 01267 236561

RPh •† Robert Phelps Ltd, 133-135 St Margaret's Road, East Twickenham, Middlesex TW1 1RG Tel: 0181 892 1778

RSch † R. O. Schmitt, 85 Lake Street, Salem, NH 03079 USA Tel: 603 893 5915

RTh •† The Reel Thing, 17 Royal Opera Arcade, Pall Mall, London SW1Y 4UY Tel: 0171 976 1830

RTw • Richard Twort, Somerset Tel: 01934 641900

RUM •† Rumours Decorative Arts, 10 The Mall, Upper Street, Camden Passage, Islington, London N1 0PD Tel: 01582 873561

RWB •† Roy W Bunn Antiques, 34/36 Church Street, Barnoldswick, Colne, Lancashire BB8 5UT Tel: 01282 813703

RYA •† Robert Young Antiques, 68 Battersea Bridge Road, London SW11 3AG Tel: 0171 228 7847

S * Sotheby's, 34-35 New Bond Street, London W1A 2AA Tel: 0171 493 8080

S(Am) * Sotheby's Amsterdam, Rokin 102, Amsterdam, Netherlands 1012 KZ Tel: 31 (20) 550 2200

S(G) * Sotheby's, 13 Quai du Mont Blanc, Geneva, Switzerland CH-1201 Tel: 41 (22) 732 8585

S(HK) * Sotheby's, Li Po Chun Chambers, 18th Floor, 189 Des Vouex Rd, Hong Kong Tel: 852 524 8121

S(LA) * Sotheby's, 9665 Wilshire Boulevard, Beverly Hills, California 90212 USA Tel: (310) 274 0340

S(NY) * Sotheby's, 1334 York Avenue, New York, NY 10021 USA Tel: 212 606 7000

S(S) * Sotheby's Sussex, Summers Place, Billingshurst, Sussex RH14 9AD Tel: 01403 783933

S(Z) * Sotheby's, Bleicherweg 20, Zurich, Switzerland CH-8022 Tel: 41 (1) 202 0011

SA • Somerville Antiques & Country Furniture Ltd, Moysdale, Killanley, Ballina, Co Mayo, Ireland Tel: 00 353 963 6275

SAF *† Saffron Walden Auctions, 1 Market Street, Saffron Walden, Essex CB10 1JB Tel: 01799 513281

SAS *† Special Auction Services, The Coach House, Midgham Park, Reading, Berkshire RG7 5UG Tel: 0118 971 2949

SAU •† Mary Sautter, Pine Furniture, c/o Churchill Antiques Centre, 6 Station Street, Lewes, Sussex BN7 2DA Tel: 01273 474842

SeH •† Seventh Heaven, Chirk Mill, Chirk, Wrexham County Borough, Wales LL14 5BU Tel: 01691 772622/773563

SEL • M. & D. Seligmann, 37 Kensington Church St, London W8 4LL Tel: 0171 937 0400

SER •† Serendipity, 168 High Street, Deal, Kent CT14 6BQ Tel: 01304 369165

SFL •† The Silver Fund, 139A New Bond Street, London W1Y 9FB Tel: 0171 499 8501

SHa •† Shapiro & Co, Stand 380, Gray's Antique Market, 58 Davies Street, London W1Y 1LB Tel: 0171 491 2710

SI •† Sound Instruments, Worth Farm, Little Horsted, Nr Uckfield, Sussex TN22 5TT Tel: 01825 750567

SK * Skinner Inc, The Heritage On The Garden, 63 Park Plaza, Boston, MA 02116, USA Tel: 001 617 350 5400

SK(B) * Skinner Inc, 357 Main Street, Bolton, MA 01740, USA Tel: 0101 508 779 6241

SLN * Sloan's, C. G. Sloan & Company Inc, 4920 Wyaconda Road, North Bethesda, MD 20852, USA Tel: 301 468 4911

SMI •† Janie Smithson, Hemswell Antiques Centre, Caenby Corner Estate, Hemswell Cliff, Gainsborough, Lincs, DN21 5TJ Tel: 01427 668389

SnA • Snape Maltings Antique & Collectors Centre, Saxmundham, Suffolk IP17 1SR Tel: 01728 688038

SO •† Samuel Orr Antique Clocks, 36 High Street, Hurstpierpoint, Nr Brighton, Sussex BN6 9RG Tel: 01273 832081

Som •† Somervale Antiques, 6 Radstock Road, Midsomer Norton, Bath, Avon BA3 2AJ Tel: 01761 412686

SOML • Somlo Antiques, No7 Piccadilly Arcade, London SW1Y 6NH Tel: 0171 499 6526

SPa •† Sparks Antiques, 4 Manor Row, Tenterden, Kent TN30 6HP Tel: 01580 766696

SpP * Specialised Postcard Auctions, 25 Gloucester Street, Cirencester, Glos GL7 2DJ Tel: 01285 659057

SPU •† Spurrier-Smith Antiques, 28, 30, 39 & 41 Church Street, Ashbourne, Derbyshire DE6 1AJ Tel: 01335 343669

SSW • Spencer Swaffer, 30 High Street, Arundel, Sussex BN18 9AB Tel: 01903 882132

STE • Stevenson Brothers, Ashford Road, Bethersden, Ashford, Kent TN26 3AP Tel: 01233 820363

SUC • Succession, 18 Richmond Hill, Richmond, Surrey TW10 6QX Tel: 0181 940 6774

SUF *† Suffolk Sales, Half Moon House, High Street, Clare, Suffolk CO10 8NY Tel: 01787 277993

SUS • Susannah, 142/144 Walcot Street, Bath, Avon BA1 5BL Tel: 01225 445069

SWA •† S. W. Antiques, Abbey Showrooms, Newlands, Pershore, Worcs WR10 1BP Tel: 01386 555580

SWB •† Sweetbriar Gallery, Robin Hood Lane, Helsby, Cheshire WA6 9NH Tel: 01928 723851

SWN • Swan Antiques, Albert House, Stone Street, Cranbrook, Kent TN17 3HG Tel: 01580 712720

SWO *† G. E. Sworder & Sons, 14 Cambridge Road, Stansted Mountfitchet, Essex CM24 8BZ Tel: 01279 817778

TAC • Tenterden Antiques Centre, 66-66A High Street, Tenterden, Kent TN30 6AU Tel: 01580 765655/765885

TAN •† Tanglewood Antiques, Tanglewood Mill, Coke Street, Derby, Derbyshire DE1 1NE Tel: 01332 346005

TAR • Lorraine Tarrant Antiques, 23 Market Place, Ringwood, Hants BH24 1AN Tel: 01425 461123

TAY * Taylors, Honiton Galleries, 205 High Street, Honiton, Devon EX14 8LF Tel: 01404 42404

TED •† Teddy Bears of Witney, 99 High Street, Witney, Oxon OX8 6LY Tel: 01993 702616

TH • Tony Horsley, Sussex Tel: 01273 732163

THOM • S. & A. Thompson, Stand V12 Antiquarius, 131/141 Kings Rd, London SW3 5ST Tel: 0171 352 8680

TMA *† Brown & Merry Tring Market Auctions, Brook St, Tring, Herts HP23 5EF Tel: 01442 826446

TMe • Thomas Mercer, (Chronometers) Ltd, 32 Bury Street, St James's, London SW1Y 6AU Tel: 0171 930 9300

TMi • Tim Millard Antiques, Stand 31-32 Bartlett Street Antique Centre, Bath, Avon BA1 2QZ Tel: 01225 469785

TPA • Times Past Antiques, 59 High Street, Eton, Windsor, Berkshire SL4 6BL Tel: 01753 857018

TPC •† Pine Cellars, 39 Jewry Street, Winchester, Hampshire SO23 8RY Tel: 01962 777546

TUR • W. F. Turk, London Tel: 0181 543 3231

TVM •† Teresa Vanneck-Murray, Vanneck House, 22 Richmond Hill, Richmond, Surrey TW10 6QX Tel: 0181 940 2035

UC •† Up Country, The Old Corn Stores, 68 St John's Road, Tunbridge Wells, Kent TN4 9PE Tel: 01892 523341

VCL • Vintage Cameras Ltd, 254 & 256 Kirkdale, Sydenham, London SE26 4NL Tel: 0181 778 5416

VH • Valerie Howard, 2 Campden Street, London W8 7EP Tel: 0171 792 9702

VS *† T. Vennett-Smith, 11 Nottingham Road, Gotham, Notts NG11 0HE Tel: 0115 983 0541

VSP * Van Sabben Poster Auctions, Oosteinde 30, 1678 HS Oostwoud, Holland Tel: 31 (0)229 202589

VSt • Vera Strange, 811 Christchurch Road, Boscombe, Dorset BH21 1TZ Tel: 01202 429111

W&W •† Walker & Walker, Halfway Manor, Halfway, Nr Newbury, Berkshire RG20 8NR Tel: 01488 658693

WAB • Warboys Antiques, Old Church School, High Street, Warboys, Cambridge, Cambs PE17 1NH Tel: 01487 823686

WAC • Worcester Antique Centre, Reindeer Ct, Mealcheapen St, Worcester WR1 4DF Tel: 01905 610680

WaH • The Warehouse, 29-30 Queens Gardens, Worthington Street, Dover, Kent CT17 9AH Tel: 01304 242006

Wai • Peter Wain, 7 Nantwich Road, Woore, Shropshire CW3 9SA Tel: 01630 647118

WAL *† Wallis & Wallis, West Street Auction Galleries, Lewes, Sussex BN7 2NJ Tel: 01273 480208

WBB •† William Bentley Billiards, Standen Manor Farm, Hungerford, Berkshire RG17 0RB Tel: 01488 681711

WDG * William Doyle Galleries, 175 East 87th Street, New York, NY 10128, USA Tel: 212 427 2730

WEE • Weedon Bec Antiques, 66 High Street, Weedon, Northants NN7 4QD Tel: 01327 349910

WeH • Westerham House Antiques, The Green, Westerham, Kent TN16 1AY Tel: 01959 561622

WEL • Wells Reclamation & Co, The Old Cider Farm, Coxley, Nr Wells, Somerset BA5 1RQ Tel: 01749 677087/677484

WELL •† Anthony Welling, Broadway Barn, High Street, Ripley, Woking, Surrey GU23 6AQ Tel: 01483 225384

WIM • Wimpole Antiques, Stand 349, Grays Antique Market, 58 Davies Street, London W1Y 1AR Tel: 0171 499 2889/624 7628

WL *† Wintertons Ltd, Lichfield Auction Centre, Wood End Lane, Fradley, Lichfield, Staffs WS13 8NF Tel: 01543 263256

WRe • Walcot Reclamations, 108 Walcot Street, Bath, Avon BA1 5BG Tel: 01225 444404

WSA •† West Street Antiques, 63 West Street, Dorking, Surrey RH4 1BS Tel: 01306 883487

WTA • Witney and Airault 20th Century Decorative Arts, The Lanes Gallery, 32 Meeting House Lane, Brighton, Sussex BN1 1HB Tel: 01273 735479

WW * Woolley & Wallis, Salisbury Salerooms, 51-61 Castle Street, Salisbury, Wiltshire SP1 3SU Tel: 01722 424500

YAG • The York Antiques Gallery, Route 1, PO Box 303, York, ME 03909, USA Tel: 207-363-5002

YC •† Yesterday Child, Angel Arcade, 118 Islington High St, London N1 8EG Tel: 0171 354 1601

ZEI • Zeitgeist, 58 Kensington Church Street, London W8 4DB Tel: 0171 938 4817

HOW TO USE THIS BOOK

It is our aim to make the Guide easy to use. In order to find a particular item, consult the contents list on page 19 to find the main heading, for example, Furniture. Having located your area of interest, you will find that larger sections have been sub-divided. If you are looking for a particular factory, designer or craftsman, consult the index which starts on page 796.

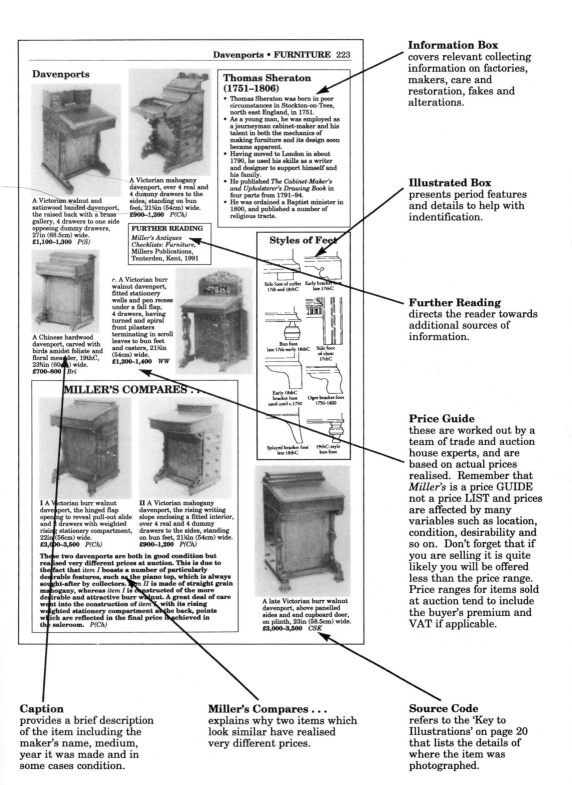

Information Box
covers relevant collecting information on factories, makers, care and restoration, fakes and alterations.

Illustrated Box
presents period features and details to help with indentification.

Further Reading
directs the reader towards additional sources of information.

Price Guide
these are worked out by a team of trade and auction house experts, and are based on actual prices realised. Remember that *Miller's* is a price GUIDE not a price LIST and prices are affected by many variables such as location, condition, desirability and so on. Don't forget that if you are selling it is quite likely you will be offered less than the price range. Price ranges for items sold at auction tend to include the buyer's premium and VAT if applicable.

Caption
provides a brief description of the item including the maker's name, medium, year it was made and in some cases condition.

Miller's Compares ...
explains why two items which look similar have realised very different prices.

Source Code
refers to the 'Key to Illustrations' on page 20 that lists the details of where the item was photographed.

ACKNOWLEDGEMENTS

**The publishers would like to acknowledge the great assistance given
by our consultants:**

OAK & COUNTRY FURNITURE : **Robert Young,** 68 Battersea Bridge Road, London SW11 3AG

FURNITURE: **Leslie Gillham,** Gorringes Auction Galleries, Lewes, East Sussex BN7 2PD

Allan James, The Chair Set, 84 Hill Rise, Richmond, Surrey, TW10 6UB

POTTERY & PORCELAIN: **John Sandon,** Phillips, 101 New Bond Street, London W1Y OAS

Mark Law, Dreweatt Neate, Donnington Priory, Newbury, Berks RG13 2JE

ORIENTAL CERAMICS & WORKS OF ART: **Peter Wain,** 7 Nantwich Road, Woore, Shropshire, CW3 9SA

GLASS: **Brian Watson,** The Grange, Norwich Road, Wroxham, Norwich, Norfolk, NR12 8RX

SILVER: **Richard Came,** Sotheby's, 34–35 New Bond Street, London W1A 2AA

CLOCKS: **John Mighell,** Strike One (Islington) Ltd, 48A Highbury Hill, London N5 1AP

WATCHES: **George Somlo,** Somlo Antiques, 7 Piccadilly Arcade, London SW1Y 6NH

BAROMETERS: **Alan Walker,** Halfway Manor, Halfway, Nr. Newbury, Berks RG20 8NR

DECORATIVE ARTS & TWENTIETH CENTURY DESIGN: **Paul Rennie,** 13 Rugby Street, London W1X 1RF

MOORCROFT: **John Donovan,** Rumours Decorative Arts, 10 The Mall, Camden Passage, Islington, London N1 OPD

LAMPS & LIGHTING: **Josie Marsden,** Magic Lanterns at By George, 23 George Street, St Albans, Herts AL3 4ES

RUGS & CARPETS: **Jacqueline Coulter,** Sotheby's, 34–35 New Bond Street, London W1A 2AA

JEWELLERY: **Freda Hacker and Lynn Lindsay,** Wimpole Antiques, 20 Upper Wimpole Street, London W1M 7TA

Michael Sinclair, Glitterati, Assembly Antique Centre, Saville Row, Bath, Avon BA1 2QP

ISLAMIC WORKS OF ART: **Deborah Freeman,** Christie's, 8 King Street, St James's, London SW1Y 6QT

ANTIQUITIES: **Peter A. Clayton, FSA,** Seaby Antiquities, 14 Old Bond Street, London W1X 4JL

DOLLS: **David Barrington,** Yesterday Child, Angel Arcade, London N1 8EG

EPHEMERA: **Trevor Vennett-Smith, FAAV,** 11 Nottingham Road, Gotham, Nottingham, NG11 OHE

SCIENTIFIC & MARINE INSTRUMENTS: **Jon Baddeley,** Sotheby's, 34–35 New Bond Street, London W1A 2AA

MARINE: **John Jefferies,** Great Western Antiques, Torre Station, Newton Road, Torquay, Devon, TQ2 5DD

CAMERAS: **David Larkin,** 38 High Street, Tenterden, Kent TN30 6AR

SPORT: **Mike Heffner,** Leland's, 36 East 22nd Street, 7th Floor, New York, NY 10010

*We would like to extend our thanks to all auction houses and dealers
who have assisted us in the production of this book.*

INTRODUCTION

The strong economy and soaring stock markets have pulled the antiques trade out of recession. The antiques market is still selective and more sober than in the late 1980s. 'There is a shift away from sparkling diamonds to more wearable gold jewelry,' said Joan Boening at James Robinson in New York. 'The trend is towards American-made jewelry; it is astonishing what was made in Newark, New Jersey, a hundred years ago. It is the focus of a special exhibition at the Newark Museum, with an accompanying catalog. American jewelry is the field to watch.'

'The stronger real estate market has driven the recovery,' suggests Larry Matlick at Macklowe Gallery in New York City, dealing in Art Nouveau and Art Deco furniture, Tiffany lamps, Art glass and jewelry of the period. 'People who buy and sell houses are furnishing again.' According to William Stahl, Sotheby's Decorative Arts chief, English furniture is enormously popular. 'Our English country house sales have gone way over estimates and the buyers are searching for pieces with few repairs.'

Miller's shows you which markets are moving upward and which are sliding downward and which are just spinning their wheels. For example, the market for Ming Dynasty hardwood furniture reached new heights in September 1996 when Christie's in New York sold the collection of the Renaissance California Museum of Classical Chinese Furniture. In March the highest quality pieces continued to soar above estimates. A pair of huanghuali wood yoke-back armchairs fetched $167,500 and a 17th century horseshoe-back chair sold for $244,500. 'Good things get more expensive,' says Marcus Flacks, at MD Flacks Ltd, who moved from London to New York in 1995 to deal in Chinese furniture. 'There is a hard core of collectors plus eclectic collectors who buy modern paintings and a Chinese table and a Roman bronze; as long as they are of like quality there is no aesthetic shift.' Flacks pointed out that provincial Chinese furniture also has a following: 'A 17th century chair made of the now nearly extinct huanghuali wood may cost $200,000; one made of yew wood 200 years later, in the early 19th century, which retains its design integrity, might cost $7,000.' There is also a huge amount of exotic late 19th and 20th century Asian furniture sold by the container load – a staple in the world antiques market. Explaining the booming market for Asian art and antiques, New York dealer Khalil Rizk says 'there is a good chance it forecasts the 21st century.' This is an area to watch.

English needlework as well as American schoolgirl embroideries continue to sell for higher prices ensuring an ample supply. On the other hand there has been a scarcity of good English silver. According to James McConnaughy at S. J. Shrubsole in New York, 'good things get more expensive, but average pieces you can't give away. You can sell useful candlesticks or flatware. It is hard to sell a teapot, though tea caddies are in demand because they can decorate any table.' When auctioneer Robert S. Brunt, of Asheville, North Carolina, sold a George II *épergne* for $32,000, twice its estimate, he had bids from all parts of the US and England. 'I reach my clientele in England and France on my web site. They depend on my accurate descriptions and never come to North Carolina.'

There are some people who want to live like 18th century English country gentlemen. Others prefer the lifestyle of early 19th century farmers and buy painted furniture, decorated earthenware and folk carvings. Still others have embraced the reform styles of the 20th century. 'The baby boomers who are collecting Arts and Crafts are looking for simplicity and wholesomeness in this wacky world,' says auctioneer David Rago, of Lambertville, New Jersey: 'The Arts and Crafts market is generally higher than ever, only spindle designs and Teco pottery have not reached the unrealistic prices paid in the late 1980s.'

Fifties furniture appeals to those who remember growing up with it. 'It can cost less than new furniture and it will keep its value,' Northampton, Massachusetts, dealer Chris Kennedy points out. 'There is great diversity: more formal designs by Dunbar and Widdecomb have a following and so does glass and steel furniture by well-known designers.'

That is why you will find *Miller's Antiques Price Guide* on the desks of dealers and auctioneers the world over. Computers and faxes connect the antiques world in an instant, and Miller's charts this international market for old things bought and sold to furnish houses or satisfy the passions of collectors. You can find everything in Miller's, from armchairs to wine coolers (even the wine for the cooler), drinking glasses, jugs, decanters and all the accoutrements for imbibing, together with the musical instruments, music boxes and phonographs to set the mood.

Our aim is to make this guide all inclusive and easy to use. In order to find a particular category consult the table of contents on page 19 where items like clocks, barometers, ephemera, fans, pottery, porcelain, snuff bottles and silver are listed. If you are looking for a particular factory, designer or craftsman, consult the index which begins on page 796.

Miller's is a price GUIDE not a price LIST. The prices are worked out by a team of dealers and auction house experts and based on actual prices paid, reflecting condition, quality and desirability. Don't forget: if you are selling you may well be offered less than the range of prices given, and what is popular in one region may not be as popular in another. Prices in a well publicised single-owner sale are generally higher, and higher still if the sale is held on the premises or if the owner is a celebrity.

We are always anxious to make this guide better. If we have left out what you collect or if you have any other comments, please let us know, we value your opinion.

Lita Solis-Cohen

FURNITURE

Anybody searching for the much-vaunted feel-good factor only had to observe the furniture market during the past twelve months. The cascade of record prices, many of them in provincial salerooms, made it quite clear that confidence was once more back in fashion.

One of the specific areas where there has been a notable increase in enthusiasm is in that of utilitarian 18th and 19th century English mahogany – often (and frequently unfairly) referred to disparagingly as 'brown' furniture. Added to this, the more unusual and rare items of the mid-18th century are attracting considerable premiums whether in the saleroom or in the antique shop. Any piece with a known maker or recorded provenance is likely to leave its auction estimate far behind, as is amply demonstrated in the following pages.

Seat furniture (the general term given to sofas, settees, bergères and so on) from the 18th and 19th centuries is particularly in demand, as are any good examples of Regency rosewood and mahogany. Interest has not just been confined to the larger items, however, since there has also been an increase in demand for small decorative pieces from the same period.

So what has driven this surge in interest? Not foreign money, it would seem, if our overseas trade statistics are to be trusted, since 1996 showed an apparent overall decrease in our exports of antiques. There is still a craving from across the water for the highest quality items but this is coming chiefly from the USA and, occasionally, from Russia where the rich appear to be getting richer. Not so in western Europe, however, where the painful process of aligning economies for the brave new world of the Euro is taking its toll. Therefore, in the absence of our European partners, the main force for recovery seems to have come from the home front and this has been particularly evident in the salerooms. It is likely that the long-awaited improvement in the housing market has affected both the supply and demand sides of the furniture market. Established modest collections are once more being broken-up or thinned, while new buyers are venturing into auction rooms and antique shops to satisfy their own appetites for furnishings. It is certainly tempting to think that at least a small percentage of those six-figure City bonuses we keep hearing about is being diverted into drawing room or dining room decor.

If there is any area which has lagged behind in this rush for the record books, it is that of oak. True, vintage pieces of good colour and proportion, untinkered with and in original condition can command very good prices; but you can still buy a perfectly reasonable looking coffer for somewhere in the region of $400 which is just about the same figure you would have paid for it twenty years ago. Why? Probably because oak tends to sit rather uncomfortably in the stylish affluence of the average town house. Of course, in the oak-beamed surroundings of the farmhouse it is as *de rigeur* as the new British Racing Green oil-burning Aga, but this limited potential market must go some way towards explaining the lack of performance of the less academic pieces.

So, what should you be looking for when you set about adding that bit of extra style and elegance to your own home? Of course, you must do all the mundane things like making sure that you can get your chosen item through the door and that it is not half an inch too large for that alcove next to the fireplace where it is going to look so fantastic. But most of all you should be absolutely certain that you want to share your home with it for the rest of your life. Never, ever, buy something you are not in love with even if you are convinced it is the greatest bargain since the Russians enquired if America would be interested in buying a little Alaskan real estate. Acquiring a bargain can sometimes seem like a breeze when compared with trying to get rid of it again.

Having established that you cannot live without the object of your desire inspect it very carefully. Look for repairs, replacements and additions. Be suspicious of tables when the tops are stained or coloured on the underside – it is usually hiding something. On 18th century furniture look for that rich, dark patina which cannot be faked. Lots of pieces have been over-restored over the years and have been stripped of this almost priceless asset. Admittedly, given another 250 years it will have developed again as a result of what is sometimes delightfully referred to as 'social wear' – your toddlers massaging their prunes and custard into the George III drop-leaf dining table for instance – but why wait 250 years when you can get the genuine thing now?

Finally, with an eye to future appreciation, what should you buy if you cannot afford the glorious examples of 18th century craftsmanship already recommended or if you are not fortunate enough to own that farmhouse with the Aga? You might well do worse than give some consideration to the products of the late Victorian and Edwardian era when fine work was still the order of the day despite the mass-production techniques which were by then the norm. In particular the Sheraton revival of this period produced much good furniture, light and delicate in design and rich in appearance with great use being made of veneers, banding and inlays. Fortunately, the proportions of these pieces often lend themselves to the smaller room sizes of modern homes, so you do not necessarily have to live in a Nash terrace or a small mansion to house them. Also, keep your eyes peeled for signed items. Always check the top of drawer fronts in particular – it is one of the most likely places to discover a maker's stamp. Although these signed examples should be more expensive than unsigned ones, you might just be lucky enough to find the Edwards & Roberts or Shoolbred mark which everyone else has missed.

Leslie Gillham

OAK & COUNTRY FURNITURE
Beds

An oak cradle, the canopy with serpentine-fronted folding lid, above fielded panelled sides and ends, on rockers, early 18thC, 36in (92cm) long.
$950–1,100 *P(Sc)*

A James I carved oak tester bed, inlaid with bog oak and holly, also inlaid with initials 'R.H.' and 'A.H.', c1620, 52in (132cm) wide.
$48,000–62,000 *PHA*

Factors which contribute to the value of a piece of furniture include fine craftsmanship, patina and original condition.

An oak tester bed, raised on foliate-carved and gadrooned posts, the headboard with 2 recessed arcaded panels flanked by male terms, above a further three-panel section centred with a double arcade, the lower panels of the headboard an addition but contemporary, feet raised in height, late 17thC, 63in (160cm) wide.
$30,000–35,000 *CSK*

Boxes

A churchwarden's oak box, c1620, 17in (43cm) wide.
$1,100–1,300 *COM*

An oak linen or lace box, with traces of original polychrome, c1650, 10in (25.5cm) wide.
$320–400 *COM*

A churchwarden's stripped oak box, c1650, 25in (63.5cm) wide.
$1,100–1,300 *COM*

A carved oak Bible box, early 19thC, 26in (66cm) wide.
$200–225 *GWA*

An oak Bible box, 17thC, 26in (66cm) wide.
$360–400 *WELL*

An oak Bible box, the front and sides carved with scrollwork flowers, leaves and mythical birds, with split-turned ornament, fitted with one drawer, on spool-turned legs united by plain stretcher rails, 17thC, 31in (79cm) wide.
$16,000–18,000 *LF*

This Bible box was bought 35 years ago for $80 in the same salerooms where it recently sold for over $16,000. It is a rare piece, originating from Lancashire or Anglesey, and was of particular appeal because it is still on its original stand. It attracted a great deal of interest in the saleroom, but the battle was finally fought between 2 telephone bidders.

A Charles II carved oak and elm boarded box, probably Devon, of nailed construction, the hinged lid above a front carved with stylised tulips amidst scrolling foliage, the top bearing an indistinct inscription, the rear with the branded initials 'TA', late 17thC, 16½in (42cm) wide.
$1,000–1,200 *S(S)*

An oak candle box, 19thC, 6½in (16.5cm) wide.
$275–300 *No7*

Bureaux

A Queen Anne oak bureau, the fall enclosing a fitted interior of drawers and pigeonholes over a well, with an arrangement of drawers below, on bracket feet, early 18thC, 33in (84cm) wide.
$3,500–4,000 *Bon*

A George III oak bureau, crossbanded with walnut, original brasses, c1800, 40½in (103cm) wide.
$6,800–8,000 *PHA*

An oak bureau, with walnut crossbanding to fall, fitted interior with 3 secret drawers, c1770, 37in (94cm) wide.
$4,500–5,000 *KEY*

An oak bureau, the interior with stepped fittings, a central cupboard and well, 4 drawers with later brass handles, on bracket feet, early 18thC, 40½in (103cm) wide.
$2,800–3,200 *DN*

A George I oak bureau, the fall enclosing a stepped interior with pigeonholes and drawers around a central door and well, above 4 drawers, with later brass handles, on bracket feet, 37¼in (95cm) wide.
$2,000–2,400 *DN*

A George II oak bureau in 2 parts, the upper stage with stepped interior fittings, including a central cupboard and 2 concealed compartments, on a stand with one long drawer above a shaped apron, on cabriole legs with pad feet, 34½in (87.5cm) wide.
$1,000–1,200 *DN*

An oak bureau, the fall enclosing a central cupboard flanked by drawers and pigeonholes above 3 long graduated drawers, on bracket feet, mid-18thC, 33¾in (86cm) wide.
$775–875 *Bon*

r. A George III oak bureau, with fitted interior above 4 long graduated drawers, shaped bracket feet, 36in (91.5cm) wide.
$2,500–2,800 *DN*

A Welsh oak bureau, with deep drawer and frieze, raised on square tapered legs, c1760, 43in (109cm) wide.
$4,000–4,400 *CoA*

A George III oak bureau, the sloping front enclosing a fitted interior with a Gothic carved central door, above 4 long drawers, on bracket feet, 40¾in (103.5cm) wide.
$2,000–2,200 *L*

Chairs

A set of 4 Charles II dining chairs, covered in nailed hide upholstery, the painted upholstered backs decorated in the manner of 17thC needlework with figures, flowers and foliage, on bobbin-turned legs joined by stretchers, restored.
$3,200–3,800 *S(S)*

A James II walnut and beech armchair, with caned back and seat, c1688.
$1,250–1,350 *MIC*

An American maple slat-back armchair, Delaware River Valley, restored, c1720.
$925–1,000 *SK(B)*

A joined oak school chair, c1670.
$620–720 *WELL*

Cross Reference
Oak & Country children's chairs can be found in our special feature on p106.

r. A Spanish walnut armchair, with leather upholstery and brass studs, 17thC.
$620–800 *ME*

An oak side chair, with carved cresting rail, c1690.
$1,100–1,300 *KEY*

A Welsh oak farmhouse carver chair, with shaped top-rail and centre splat, Caernarfonshire, c1780.
$925–1,000 *CoA*

Early Chairs
In Europe until the end of the Middle Ages the only types of seating were settles and benches. Early coffers doubled-up as seats and were the basis of the first true chair. The solid 'close' or 'joined' chair of coffer-like form with enclosed panelled sides was made from the end of the Medieval period until the end of the 16thC.

A lighter type of chair, known as a wainscot chair, was common from the mid-16thC until 1660. It had no panelling at the base and was made predominantly in oak, with carved and sometimes inlaid decoration. During the reign of Charles II a type of chair already popular on the Continent was introduced. Made from walnut with barley twist uprights, it had ornate carvings and caned back panels with upholstered seats. For the first time the chair was an object of comfort and fashion.

An ash and elm 'dug-out' chair, c1770.
$6,800–7,500 *ChS*

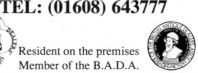

A Welsh primitive comb-backed Windsor armchair, c1780.
$1,700–2,000 *RYA*

A set of 4 fruitwood chairs, with drop-in rush seats, c1790.
$1,300–1,400 *WELL*

A roundabout rush seat chair, painted dark green, minor repairs, New England, 18thC.
$2,000–2,200 *SK(B)*

A braced bow-back Windsor side chair, with incised shaped seat, painted black, Massachusetts or Rhode Island, late 18thC.
$600–675 *SK(B)*

A Welsh oak farmhouse chair, with shaped and pierced wooden splat, c1780.
$400–450 *CoA*

A yew, fruitwood and oak ladderback armchair, c1780.
$1,000–1,200 *RYA*

A stick-backed armchair, signed 'Parham', c1800.
$640–720 *MIC*

A Norwegian carved birchwood chair, c1800.
$1,000–1,200 *RYA*

A harlequin set of 4 ash and elm ladderback chairs, with bar top rail, turned uprights, panelled seats with shaped apron, on turned supports joined by turned stretchers, with pad feet, Lancashire, early 19thC.
$775–900 *AH*

r. A harlequin set of 8 ash and spindle-backed chairs, the rush seats on turned legs with pad feet, tied by turned front stretchers, Lancashire, early 19thC.
$2,200–2,500 *Bon*

A spindle-backed armchair, c1800.
$880–960 *ChS*

A set of 6 elm and ash ladderback chairs, with rush seats, early 19thC.
$3,800–4,800 *SPU*

l. A Shaker turned-maple rocking chair, the back with 4 arched slats, woven fabric seat, on turned legs and rockers, 19thC.
$1,500–1,600 *S(NY)*

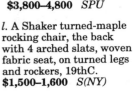

A fruitwood rocking nursing chair, with drawer under seat, c1820, 32in (81cm) high.
$530–620 *AAN*

A yew and elm low back armchair, c1830.
$780–950 *COM*

A yew Windsor elbow chair, c1840.
$1,900–2,200 *WELL*

A Lancashire beech ladderback armchair, c1840.
$320–400 *GWA*

l. A set of 5 fruitwood and elm chairs, including an armchair, c1850.
$640–720 *MIC*

A set of 6 red and black painted step-backed Windsor side chairs, each with a crest flanked by *faux* bamboo stiles centring 7 similarly turned spindles, the balloon-form plank seat signed 'W. Miller' on the underside, on *faux* bamboo legs joined by stretchers, Connecticut, c1840.
$1,600–1,900 *S(NY)*

An Irish primitive oak chair, c1830.
$450–500 *COM*

A Victorian yew and elm captain's chair, with turned supports, serpentine seat and turned legs tied by stretchers.
$520–580 *Bon(C)*

l. A miniature chair, c1840, 10in (25.5cm) high.
$560–620 *AEF*

A beech bar-backed chair, c1880.
$80–100 *HRQ*

A set of 8 yew and elm Windsor elbow chairs, with pierced vase-shaped splats, swept arms, on baluster-turned legs linked by stretchers, later repairs and replacements, 19thC.
$10,500–11,200 *WL*

A set of 6 French chairs, with rush seats, c1920.
$1,000–1,100 *RPh*

Chests & Coffers

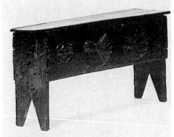

An oak plank chest, with hinged top, the front carved with a quatrefoil motif, a portrait medallion on its side and a spiral roundel, the sides extending to feet, front plank early 16thC, 45in (114cm) wide.
$2,200–2,500 *CSK*

An oak chest, the foliate carved front with inlaid panels depicting birds amongst flowers in urns, divided and flanked by term figures, with a drawer below, early 17thC, 52in (132cm) wide.
$2,400–2,800 *Bea(E)*

A Welsh oak coffer, with panelled lid and original free carving, Montgomeryshire, c1680, 43in (109cm) wide.
$3,500–4,500 *CoA*

An oak coffer, with panelled lid, original hinges and lockplate, 17thC, 54in (137cm) wide.
$1,600–1,900 *ME*

A Charles I oak arcaded coffer, c1640, 57in (145cm) wide.
$5,000–6,200 *PHA*

An oak coffer, with panelled front carved with 3 masks, c1630, 51in (129.5cm) wide.
$2,500–2,800 *MIC*

A panelled oak coffer, the front inlaid with holly and bog oak lines, the foliate lunette-carved frieze above 4 panels carved with stylised plants, on stile feet, one panel replaced, mid-17thC, 59½in (151cm) wide.
$1,000–1,200 *Bea(E)*

A six-plank oak coffer, with arcaded carving, c1670, 39in (99cm) wide.
$1,000–1,200 *WELL*

An oak plank chest, the front with a moulded channel and geometric pattern of scrolling motifs centred with rosettes and flanked by punched decoration, the sides extending to feet, hinges missing, early 17thC, 45in (114cm) wide.
$1,200–1,400 *CSK*

An oak coffer, with painted panels, Dorset, c1650, 44in (112cm) wide.
$3,200–4,800 *DBA*

A six-plank oak coffer, c1670, 38in (96.5cm) wide.
$1,200–1,300 *WELL*

An oak coffer, with a triple-panelled hinged lid, original wirework hinges, the panelled front with a lunette-leaf-carved frieze, an iron lockplate above vertical jambs, with scroll etched carving, the interior with candle box, one leg repaired, 17thC, 48in (122cm) wide.
$1,200–1,300 *WW*

l. An oak chest, with panelled sides, fitted with a frieze drawer, above a deep drawer with 2 moulded panels, the base with 3 long drawers enclosed by 2 doors with raised moulded panels above an associated fluted plinth, 17thC, 49in (124.5cm) wide.
$2,600–3,000 *DN*

A joined oak chest, the three-panelled hinged lid above a lunette-carved frieze and a pair of floral carved panels, on stile feet, late 17thC, 45in (114cm) wide.
$1,300–1,500 *Bon*

A Charles II carved oak coffer, the cleated top above a frieze and an arrangement of 3 carved panels and 4 plain panels, on stile feet, 17thC, cleating later, 59in (150cm) wide.
$1,100–1,300 *S(S)*

A black and gold japanned coffer, with twin-panelled hinged lid, above a conforming front decorated overall with birds, foliage and figures in landscapes, restored, c1700, 41¾in (106cm) wide.
$2,200–2,400 *Bon*

An oak coffer, the triple fielded panelled front inlaid with symmetrical cross motifs, early 18thC, 35½in (90cm) wide.
$1,400–1,600 *DN*

A Welsh oak coffer bach, with single drawer below, raised on eccentric cabriole legs, inlaid with a flowing holly and bog oak design, Pembrokeshire, c1740, 25in (63.5cm) wide.
$5,300–6,000 *CoA*

A joined oak mule chest, the hinged top enclosing a lidded compartment and 3 small drawers, the front with 4 fielded panels above 4 short drawers, flanked by fluted quarter pilasters, on bracket feet, mid-18thC, 43in (109cm) wide.
$1,100–1,300 *DN*

A panelled oak coffer, 18thC, 50in (127cm) wide.
$500–620 *GWA*

An oak corn hutch, late 18thC, 72in (183cm) wide.
$2,000–2,400 *ME*

A George III oak coffer bach, with drawer, Welsh, c1760, 23in (58.5cm) wide.
$4,000–5,600 *PHA*

MILLER'S COMPARES . . .

I A George III oak coffer bach, with shaped panels, on original bracket feet, Welsh, dated '1766', 24in (61cm) wide.
$3,200–5,400 *PHA*

II A George II inlaid oak coffer bach, with bog oak and holly decoration, on cabriole legs, Welsh, c1740, 24in (61cm) wide.
$6,200–7,800 *PHA*

A coffer bach of average quality with no decorative features will cost in the region of $2,400, but both these examples command a premium because of certain features. *Item I*, while of comparatively simple design, has the date '1766' inlaid contemporarily on either side of the brass key plate on the drawer, which enhances its value. *Item II* is worth quite considerably more, however, because of the waisted moulding, cabriole legs and fine inlays, and also because it is earlier and of a more compact design. *PHA*

A Welsh oak chest, with hinged lid over 5 'cupid's bow' panels, 4 fielded panels and 4 drawers beneath, on bracket feet, 18thC, 60in (152cm) wide.
$2,400–2,800 *RBB*

Chests of Drawers

A joined oak chest of drawers, the top with moulded edge above 4 geometric fielded panelled drawers, on later bracket feet, c1690, 33in (84cm) wide.
$1,300–1,400 *Bon*

A George III oak and mahogany-banded chest of drawers, with 2 short and 3 long drawers, on later shaped bracket feet, top and sides split, 40¼in (102cm) wide.
$740–840 *S(S)*

An oak chest of drawers, with 2 short and 3 long drawers, replacement handles, early 19thC, 35½in (90cm) wide.
$1,400–1,600 *No7*

An oak chest of drawers, with 3 long geometrically panelled drawers, on stile feet, late 17th/early 18thC, 33in (84cm) wide.
$3,100–3,300 *Bea(E)*

An oak chest of 3 drawers, c1790, 32in (81cm) wide.
$2,100–2,400 *WELL*

A Lancashire oak mule chest, with mahogany crossbanding and floral marquetry panels, raised gallery back over hinged top revealing till box, above an arrangement of 5 dummy and 4 real drawers with brass drop handles, fluted pilasters and ogee bracket feet, late 18thC, 68in (173cm) wide.
$2,100–2,400 *AH*

r. A grain-painted chest over drawers, with original red and black grained surface, replacement turned pulls, replacement top, northern New England, early 19thC, 36½in (92.5cm) wide.
$480–540 *SK(B)*

A George II oak tallboy, with original brasses, c1745, 38in (96.5cm) wide.
$8,000–9,600 *PHA*

A Georgian oak chest of drawers, with 2 short and 3 long drawers, on bracket feet, 38in (96.5cm) wide.
$640–780 *GAZE*

An oak chest, with small cupboard door flanked by 2 small drawers to either side, with 3 long drawers below, on bracket feet, formerly surmounted by a clothes press and in 2 sections, East Anglia, late 18thC, 31½in (80cm) wide.
$1,400–1,600 *CSK*

Chests-on-Stands

An oak chest-on-stand, with moulded cornice, 2 short drawers over 3 long drawers, the base with 6 drawers, brass drop handles, shaped frieze, on cabriole legs with pad feet, 18thC, 41in (104cm) wide.
$3,200–4,000 *AH*

An oak chest-on-stand, with moulded cornice and 4 long drawers, each with raised twin moulded panels, the stand with 3 small drawers and ogee apron, on turned legs joined by wavy stretchers, early 18thC, 46½in (118cm) wide.
$7,000–7,800 *CSK*

A joined oak chest-on-stand, with 5 fielded panelled drawers, the stand with 2 frieze drawers, on inverted baluster turned legs and bun feet tied by a wavy solid stretcher, late 17th/early 18thC, 38in (96.5cm) wide.
$6,750–7,400 *Bon*

An oak chest-on-stand, with 2 short and 3 long drawers, the stand with 3 short drawers, on baluster legs with shaped stretcher, late 18thC, 45in (115cm) wide.
$1,300–1,450 *B&L*

Cupboards

r. An oak primitive press cupboard, with carved frieze, initialled and dated '1640', North Wales or Westmorland, 61in (155cm) wide.
$12,500–14,800 *CoA*

> **Miller's is a price GUIDE not a price LIST**

l. A joined oak press cupboard, dated '1686', Lakeland district, 52in (132cm) wide.
$6,400–7,200 *KEY*

A George I oak tridarn, north Wales, c1720, 51½in (131cm) wide.
$19,200–22,400 *PHA*

A joined oak press cupboard, restored, mid-17thC, 50½in (128cm) wide.
$1,600–2,000 *Bon*

l. A Dutch Renaissance oak and ebony cupboard, the doors each with 6 moulded panels, flanked and divided by fluted stiles set with ebony ornaments, panelled sides, on stile feet, restored, early 17thC, 65in (165cm) wide.
$10,000–12,000 *S(Am)*

A George III oak hanging cupboard, with original brasses, c1760, 66½in (169cm) wide.
$8,000–9,600 *PHA*

An oak press cupboard, the frieze carved with initials 'IDR' and dated '1685', the recessed cupboards enclosed by doors carved with stylised flowerheads within lozenges, above cupboard with shelf enclosed by moulded panel doors, 17thC, 63in (160cm) wide.
$4,800–5,600 *Oli*

A French oak armoire, the moulded cornice above a pair of long panelled doors with steel hinges and pierced lockplates, on stile feet, 17thC, 49in (126cm) wide.
$1,000–1,200 *Bri*

Court & Press Cupboards

The piece of furniture which is commonly referred to these days as a court cupboard is strictly speaking a press or hall cupboard. True court cupboards date from the 12th or 13thC and consist of tiers of oak platforms separated by turned supports. The shelves were draped with carpets or fabrics and used to display valuables. The name probably originates from the French word for short and refers to the low height of the cupboard. Early examples of these are becoming increasingly rare.

Court cupboards were succeeded by press cupboards which first appeared in the latter part of the 16thC and continued to be made in the provinces until about 1800. These were effectively enclosed buffets and were intended for use in the dining hall or living room. The upper part of the cupboard often included turned or carved columns. From the mid-17thC larger versions of the cupboard, where the length was greater than the height, became more common in order to provide extra storage space. At about this time the splay-fronted canopy which had hitherto formed the upper part of the cupboard was replaced by a set of 3 flat-fronted cupboards.

A Dutch baroque oak and ebony low cupboard, the frieze divided by carved cherubs' heads above 2 doors with geometric and ebony panels, flanked and divided by carved lions' heads above a drawer carved with scoop pattern, above 2 doors with geometric and ebony panels, panelled sides, on stile feet, restored, 17thC, 68in (172cm) wide.
$7,500–8,800 *S(Am)*

A Charles II oak cupboard, with boarded top, a pair of panel doors above an apron drawer, the bobbin-turned legs joined by conforming peripheral stretchers, parts later, 33in (83cm) wide.
$2,500–2,800 *S(S)*

r. A Welsh joined oak low cupboard, with a pair of fielded panelled cupboard doors flanking twin central panels, the base with 3 fielded frieze drawers above a pair of fielded panelled doors, on stile feet, early 18thC, 60¼in (153cm) wide.
$4,800–5,300 *Bon*

An oak press cupboard, the upper section carved with foliage and rosettes, initialled and dated 'W.T.I, 1699', the lower section with 3 drawers and a pair of cupboard doors, on channelled stile feet, probably North West, late 17thC, 75in (190.5cm) wide.
$8,500–9,600 *CSK*

An oak court cupboard, the projecting frieze with turned finials above a fielded panel front with 2 doors, the base with 2 further panelled doors, panelled stiles and stile feet, late 17th/early 18thC, 56in (142cm) wide.
$2,000–2,200 *AH*

An oak press cupboard, with a pair of twin-fielded panel doors, the lower section with 3 horizontal panels and 3 frieze drawers, on stile feet, mid-18thC, 67in (170cm) wide.
$6,000–6,800 *CSK*

An oak corner cupboard, the 2 doors with fielded panels flanked by canted corners, on stile feet, mid-18thC, 32¾in (83cm) wide.
$2,100–2,400 *Bea(E)*

An oak corner cupboard, in 2 parts, with panelled doors, on bracket feet, west Wales, c1760, 31in (79cm) wide.
$4,800–5,400 *CoA*

A George III oak corner cupboard, with mahogany-banded panelled doors, 81in (205.5cm) wide.
$3,300–3,800 *L*

Beware!

When buying a corner cupboard it is wise to check that it will fit into the corner for which it is intended. Cupboards were often constructed *in situ* by a local craftsman as the angles of corners in period country cottages are rarely regular.

r. An oak and elm cheese cupboard, the upper section with panelled doors and central pierced panel, the base with 2 drawers and cupboard beneath, bone escutcheons and brass handles, 18thC, 42in (107cm) wide.
$3,200–4,000 *GH*

A northern French oak and
chestnut low cupboard, with
2 shaped fielded panelled
doors with steel lockplate
and tubular hinges, panelled
sides and corners, 18thC,
47¼in (120cm) wide.
$2,000–2,200 *DN*

A Dutch oak cupboard, the
panelled doors with foliate and
dolphin carved arches, applied
with ebonised strapwork, split
spindle mouldings and studs,
18thC, 65in (165cm) wide.
$2,400–2,800 *L*

| **Cross Reference** |
| Colour Review |

l. A George III oak standing corner
cupboard, with a pair of fielded
panel doors enclosing shaped
shelves, with 3 central drawers
above a further pair of panelled
cupboard doors enclosing a void
interior, restored, late 18thC,
43in (110cm) wide.
$2,600–3,200 *S(S)*

A George III oak standing
corner cupboard, with dentil
cornice and 4 doors with
marquetry fans within reeded
panels and 2 mahogany
bands, 46in (117cm) wide.
$2,500–2,800 *DN*

r. A provincial oak
and mahogany-
banded double
wardrobe, with
double panel doors,
each with 3 short
sham drawers
beneath enclosing
interior hanging rail,
shaped apron and
splay feet, late 18thC,
55in (140cm) wide.
$1,100–1,300 *L&E*

l. An oak deuddarn, c1790,
52½in (134cm) wide.
$4,800–5,400 *WELL*

r. An oak cwpwrdd
deuddarn, with a
pair of ogee-arched
fielded panelled
doors and 3 frieze
drawers, on bracket
feet, mid-Wales,
early 19thC,
43in (109cm) wide.
$4,800–5,300 *CSK*

Dressers

A George II oak dresser, with 3 frieze drawers above 2 panelled doors, the associated top with drop finials and open shelves, 57in (145cm) high.
$7,200–8,000 *HOLL*

A Welsh joined oak dresser, the shelf superstructure with 3 open shelves, the base with 2 long and one short frieze drawers, on bracket feet tied by a shelf stretcher, restored, late 18thC, 54in (137cm) wide.
$6,000–7,200 *Bon*

A George III Welsh oak cupboard dresser and rack, with spice drawers, c1780, 75in (190.5cm) wide.
$22,500–25,000 *PHA*

This dresser has a fine patina and is in excellent condition.

An oak dresser, the boarded rack with 2 moulded shelves, with a rectangular surface enclosing a pair of fielded panelled cupboards, on plain stile feet, north Wales, mid-18thC, 49in (125cm) wide,
$9,800–11,200 *P(NW)*

An oak dresser, with 3 open shelves flanked by fluted uprights, above a drawer and panelled door flanked by 3 drawers to either side, on bracket feet, repairs, the backboards replaced, possibly associated, North Wales, mid-18thC, 73½in (187cm) wide.
$6,000–6,800 *CSK*

FURTHER READING
Miller's Pine & Country Furniture Buyer's Guide
Miller's Publications 1995

r. A pale oak dresser, with plate rack and planked back, the base fitted with 3 frieze drawers above 3 further drawers, flanked by cupboards, on shaped bracket feet, 18thC, 61in (155cm) wide.
$4,800–5,400 *WL*

A George III oak dresser, the lower part fitted with an arrangement of 6 short drawers, flanked by panelled cupboards, 61½in (156cm) wide.
$5,600–6,200 *L*

A George III oak dresser, the base with 3 drawers, on turned supports and planked undertier, 67½in (172cm) wide.
$3,200–3,500 *DN*

An early George III oak dresser, the upper part with 3 shelves, the lower part with 3 fielded drawers, on pierced baluster legs joined by a potboard, 80in (203cm) wide.
$3,200–4,000 *L*

An oak dresser, with boarded rack and cupboards to base, c1790, 58in (147.5cm) wide.
$5,600–6,200 *WELL*

A late Georgian oak and mahogany crossbanded dresser, the upper stage with open plate rack, the base fitted with 3 drawers with oval stamped brass handles, on 4 block cabriole-shaped and tapering front legs, 73½in (187cm) wide.
$3,000–3,500 *WL*

An oak dresser, the open rack with a broad geometric fret pierced frieze, with 3 moulded shelves to each side and 4 small shaped headed shelves, the base enclosing 3 graduated cockbeaded drawers and a pair of cupboard doors, on a conforming moulded plinth base with bracket feet, early 19thC, 70½in (179cm) wide.
$4,400–5,000 *P(NW)*

An oak dresser, with 3 shelves to the upper section, 3 frieze drawers and 2 panelled doors below, on stile feet, early 19thC, 50½in (128cm) wide.
$6,000–6,800 *Bea(E)*

A William IV oak and walnut dresser, the raised back with an inlaid frieze and 3 shelves flanked by split mouldings, the base with 4 real and 2 dummy drawers and 2 panelled cupboard doors, on shaped bracket feet, mid-19thC, 63¾in (162cm) wide.
$3,000–3,500 *S(S)*

Dresser Bases

An oak dresser base, the 3 drawers with applied geometric mouldings, on turned legs joined by later peripheral stretchers, some damage, height reduced, late 17thC, 83½in (212cm) wide.
$4,300–5,000 *S(S)*

r. A joined oak dresser, the rectangular plank top with a moulded edge above 3 deep frieze drawers, on turned column legs with block feet, early 18thC, 83in (211cm) wide.
$3,800–4,200 *Bon*

A George III oak dresser base, crossbanded in mahogany, with cabriole legs, c1780, 73in (185.5cm) wide.
$12,000–14,000 *PHA*

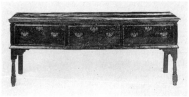

Miller's is a price GUIDE not a price LIST

An oak dresser base, with shaped gallery sides and 5 spice drawers, 3 shallow frieze drawers and 2 cupboard doors with fielded panelled centres flanking a central fielded panel, turned bun feet, 18thC, 65in (165cm) wide.
$6,700–7,400 *B*

Settles & Settees

An oak box settle, the back with 5 fielded panels, above a solid seat enclosing 2 hinged compartments, on stile feet, early 18thC, 82in (208cm) wide.
$4,800–5,200 *CSK*

A William & Mary two-seater walnut settee, c1695, 48in (122cm) wide.
$18,000–19,200 *PHA*

Many chairs of this style were made in the late 17thC, but settees were rare and few have survived. This piece is in exceptional condition with very little restoration.

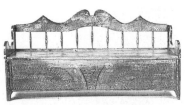

A Scandinavian paint-decorated settle/bed, the hinged seat opens to reveal a pull-out bed frame, grained in mustard and raw umber, some paint wear, c1830, 70¾in (180cm) wide.
$1,000–1,200 *SK(B)*

Umber is a yellow-brown pigment derived from ferric oxide which was applied to soft woods to imitate the colour of more expensive hard woods.

A George III panelled oak settle, the back with 3 fielded panels, rope-strung seat, on square and turned legs, restorations, 18thC, 55in (140cm) wide.
$1,600–2,000 *S(S)*

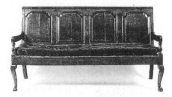

An oak settle, the back with carved and moulded arched panels, on cabriole supports and pad feet, 18thC, 72in (183cm) wide.
$3,000–3,200 *C(S)*

This settle was of a rich colour and in pristine condition.

An oak high-back settle, with panelled back, scrolled arms on square tapering supports, plank seat, square legs joined by stretchers, 18thC, 52in (132cm) wide.
$1,300–1,500 *AH*

Stools

A joined oak stool, with centre stretcher, c1630, 19in (48cm) wide.
$2,800–3,200 *ME*

A joined oak stool, c1670, 18in (46cm) wide.
$560–620 *WELL*

A Charles II walnut stool, carved legs and stretchers, c1680, 18in (46cm) wide.
$2,000–2,400 *MIC*

A James II ebonised beech wood stool, c1688, 15in (38cm) wide.
$3,500–4,000 *MIC*

A William & Mary oak upholstered stool, with turned legs and stretchers, c1690, 15in (38cm) wide.
$2,800–3,200 *MIC*

Stools

Stools were made in sets, but today it is rare to find them even in pairs as damp, woodworm and ill-use have taken their toll. Joint (or joined) stools often have tops that have been replaced or remade at a later date. The underside of an authentic top and inside the frieze will have a dry, untouched appearance. The outer edge will appear darker and slightly patinated after many years of human contact.

A country fireside stool, original painted surface c1800, 10in (25.5cm) wide.
$200–240 *RYA*

A slab-topped elm milking stool, c1780, 30in (76cm) wide.
$250–280 *RYA*

A lace maker's stool, 18thC, 7½in (19cm) high.
$720–800 *AEF*

A Welsh sycamore milking stool, with ash legs, early 19thC, 11½in (29cm) diam.
$200–240 *No7*

A slab-topped country stool, the top with old red-painted surface, c1820, 9½in (24cm) wide.
$200–240 *RYA*

An elm three-legged milking stool, c1830, 12½in (32cm) wide.
$50–65 *GRP*

A Welsh sycamore milking stool, with original painted surface, c1800, 10in (25.5cm) diam.
$280–320 *RYA*

A child's elm stool, c1830, 9in (23cm) wide.
$80–100 *COM*

A miniature walnut stool, 19thC, 6in (15cm) high.
$100–160 *SPU*

A beech stool, with original red paint, c1880, 8in (20.5cm) wide.
$30–40 *WLD*

An elm milking stool, with original paint, c1860, 11in (28cm) high.
$50–65 *TAN*

An elm stool, c1890, 12in (30.5cm) high.
$40–50 *TAN*

A cherry wood stool, bearing label 'Made from a cherry tree at St . . .', 19thC, 8½in (21.5cm) diam.
$720–800 *AEF*

Tables

A Charles II oak trestle gateleg table, c1670, 31in (79cm) long.
$8,000–9,500 *PHA*

An oak gateleg table, the oval twin-flap top above a frieze drawer, ball-turned and block legs with plain stretchers, on turned feet, some old restoration to top, late 17thC, 61in (155cm) long.
$1,200–1,400 *WW*

A Flemish oak refectory table, with cleated plank top, moulded friezes and square tapered legs joined by square section stretchers, replacements, late 17th/early 18thC, 92in (234cm) long.
$2,500–3,200 *CSK*

An oak lowboy, on turned tapered supports with pad feet, c1750, 29½in (75cm) long.
$2,000–2,200 *WELL*

r. An oak and burr-elm banded lowboy, with 3 drawers above shaped aprons, on cabriole legs with pointed pad feet, mid-18thC, 30in (76cm) long.
$2,000–2,200 *CSK*

A William & Mary oak side table, with original fretwork, on baluster-turned legs, c1695, 34in (86.5cm) long.
$9,500–11,000 *PHA*

Beware!

Floor boards and other old timber are often used to make up a new table top or to replace damaged parts of a refectory table. Replacement planks can be difficult for the inexperienced eye to detect, but certain signs may expose them:

- Circular saw marks indicate that the timber has been sawn since the early 20thC – hand saws leave straight marks.
- Refectory table tops sit on the base and are rarely fixed. If the top is lifted there should be marks where the heavy top has rested on the blocks of the legs and the frieze bearers.
- Pegs should be handmade and stand slightly proud of the surface.

An oak side table, with moulded edges to the top, on spiral-turned legs united by plain stretcher rails, early 18thC, 30½in (77.5cm) long.
$3,500–4,000 *LF*

A Charles II joined oak gateleg table, the hinged top above a pair of end frieze drawers, on ball and fillet-turned supports tied by stretchers, c1690, 60in (152.5cm) long.
$2,200–2,500 *Bon*

An oak side table, with frieze drawer, on bobbin legs, late 17thC, 34½in (88cm) long.
$900–1,000 *HOLL*

A walnut side table, c1700, 32in (81.5cm) long.
$2,300–2,800 *WELL*

An oak drop-leaf table, c1760, 24½in (62cm) long.
$2,100–2,400 *SPU*

A tavern serving table, with
2 frieze drawers, on an X-frame
supports, c1760, 20in (51cm) wide.
$5,400–6,000 *RYA*

A butternut tavern table, on
turned tapering legs ending in
pad feet, retains traces of blue
paint, lacking pegs to secure top
to base, probably Pennsylvania,
c1770, 80in (203cm) long.
$4,000–4,800 *S(NY)*

A Welsh oak fold-over table,
c1790, 36in (91.5cm) long.
$1,200–1,400 *CoA*

An oak refectory table, with
three-plank top, on chamfered
legs joined by rectangular section
stretchers, some restoration,
18thC, 105in (266cm) long.
$3,000–3,500 *DN*

An oak refectory table, with four-
plank top, cleated ends and a
fitted drawer to each end, on
square supports with H-stretcher,
c1800, 104in (264cm) long.
$7,500–8,000 *RBB*

l. A twin-pillar trestle tavern
table, with old painted
decoration, on original sledge
feet, c1830, 30in (76cm) high.
$1,300–1,400 *RYA*

A sycamore and beech cricket
table, c1800, 20in (50cm) diam.
$950–1,100 *COM*

Miscellaneous

A mahogany and oak spice cabinet,
c1840, 17½in (44.5cm) wide.
$720–800 *No7*

l. An oak two-division dough bin,
the hinged tops enclosing a two-
section interior, on a moulded base
with turned and block supports,
joined by stretchers, on turned feet,
early 18thC, 50½in (128cm) wide.
$500–600 *P(Sc)*

A Federal cherry cellaret,
replaced pulls, refinished and
restored, southern states,
c1780, 26in (66cm) wide.
$2,200–2,500 *SK(B)*

l. An oak commode, with
yew wood lid, Breconshire,
c1890, 19in (48cm) wide.
$760–840 *CoA*

A Charles II carved and silvered
oak looking glass, within a leaf-
carved and moulded frame
decorated with flowers and birds,
the arched cresting pierced and
carved with leaves and birds,
19in (48cm) wide.
$8,200–9,000 *S*

FURNITURE
Beds

A mid-Georgian mahogany metamorphic couch bedstead, the padded back rising to form canopy with curtain rail, the removable seat with hinged single bedstead under, 41in (105cm) wide.
$2,800–3,500 *Bri*

A Portuguese rosewood marquetry bed, the shaped headboard with banded scrolls and flowers centred by a padded cartouche and flanked by vase finials, on cabriole legs with ball-and-claw feet, and a conforming footboard, 18thC, 55in (140cm) wide.
$2,400–2,800 *DN*

A brass and cast iron bed, with central candy twist ring, supporting a brass gallery, c1880, 54in (137cm) wide.
$880–1,100 *SeH*

A Victorian brass bed, with spiral supports, 60in (152.5cm) wide.
$1,100–1,200 *GH*

l. A four-poster bed, with spiral turned columns and acanthus leaf decoration, the arched crossbanded canopy with a string inlay fascia, c1835, 60in (152.5cm) wide.
$8,000–9,500 *SeH*

r. A French oak panelled bed, the pillars surmounted by 2 carved owls on the foot, and a man and woman on the back, the broken pediment with coat-of-arms, decorative foliage and a sun face, c1830, 45in (114.5cm) wide.
$3,000–3,500 *SeH*

Miller's is a price GUIDE not a price LIST

l. A Victorian mahogany bed, with original side rails, 60in (152.5cm) wide.
$1,800–2,200 *SWA*

A Victorian mahogany bed, the moulded half-tester with turned drop finials linking the brass curtain rails, the arched and rectangular panelled footboard flanked by spiral twist pilasters on square section legs, 54½in (138cm) wide.
$2,800–3,200 *P(NW)*

An oak half tester bed, with curved footboard, 19thC, 60in (152.5cm) wide.
$3,500–4,000 *SWA*

A mahogany four poster-bed, the moulded cornice with arcaded pendant moulded frieze, the reeded front posts of baluster form with carved foliage, box spring, late 19thC, 60in (152.5cm) wide.
$2,000–2,400 *P(S)*

A pair of Louis XVI style gilt-bronze-mounted tulipwood parquetry beds, with original side rails, 19thC, 36in (91.5cm) wide.
$4,000–4,500 *SWA*

A Renaissance style walnut bed, with parquetry veneered panels and ormolu mounts, c1890, 60in (152.5cm) wide.
$2,000–2,200 *SWA*

A Louis XVI style rosewood bed, with fluted and turned column posts, c1890, 66in (167.5cm) wide.
$3,200–4,000 *SeH*

A French Empire style mahogany bed, with ormolu decoration and carved wooden winged harpies on the head pillars, c1890, 60in (152.5cm) wide.
$5,600–6,400 *SeH*

A Louis XV style walnut bed, with original wooden side rails, and a pair of pot cupboards, late 19thC, 60in (152.5cm) wide.
$2,800–3,200 *SWA*

A mahogany Louis XV style bed, with original side rails, late 19thC, 66in (167.5cm) wide.
$3,500–4,000 *SWA*

r. A French grey-painted bed, comprising a suspended canopy with shaped foliate rail centred by a shell, a padded headboard and footboard with overscroll top-rails centred by a shell and foliate boss, on scrolling foliate feet joined by similar side rails, stamped 'Gallet', late 19thC, 52½in (133.5cm) wide.
$1,400–1,500 *CSK*

l. A pair of Edwardian mahogany beds, each 36in (91.5cm) wide.
$1,600–2,000 *SWA*

Day Beds & Chaises Longues

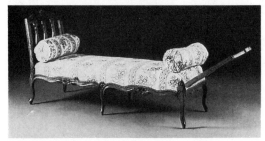

A Louis XV beechwood chaise longue, with serpentine moulded top-rails centred by a foliate cartouche above later baluster-shaped splats, upholstered seat raised on cabriole legs with a foliate-carved apron, one side fitted with ratchet mechanism to recline, restored, 74in (188cm) long. **$2,400–2,800** *S(NY)*

A north European cream and grey-painted day bed, the outswept panelled ends above squab cushions and a box spring, joined by side rails, on ring-turned legs, early 19thC, 77in (195.5cm) long. **$1,300–1,600** *CSK*

An early Victorian rosewood chaise longue, with overswept end and back arm rest with scroll terminal, on turned tapering legs, 61in (155cm) long. **$1,300–1,600** *CSK*

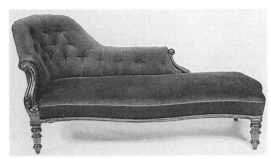

A Victorian rosewood-framed chaise longue, the buttoned back above a serpentine seat, on turned front legs, 75in (190cm) long. **$1,000–1,200** *P(Sc)*

Chaises Longues

The chaise longue, a fully upholstered chair with an elongated seat and inclined back open at one end, was first seen in the late 18thC and became popular throughout Europe and the US. Many Regency examples had painted, carved or stencilled decoration. The early Regency designs, although ornate, are relatively light and elegant with flowing lines incorporating scrolls, and with sabre legs.

By the George IV period they had become much heavier, with a renewed emphasis on carving. Designs of this period bordered at times on the bizarre, reflecting the Prince Regent's taste for the exotic: dolphins, sphinxes, crocodiles and Chinamen are among the motifs that appear during this 'high Regency' period.

Prices vary dramatically: the buying criterion is elegance, as chaises longues are essentially decorative pieces. Original decoration is an added bonus. Size is also a factor – many chaises longues are just too large for the average house.

A Regency brass-inlaid rosewood chaise longue, on turned tapered feet with gadrooned gilt-metal collars, the whole profusely inlaid with foliate-cut brasswork, c1820, 77½in (197cm) long. **$4,000–4,400** *Bon*

Bonheurs du Jour

A George III satinwood bonheur du jour, the superstructure with shaped gallery and with a pair of oval veneered panelled cupboards, the rosewood-banded flap above a frieze drawer, on square tapered legs, 65in (165cm) wide.
$4,000–4,800 *S*

Bonheurs du Jour

A bonheur du jour is a lady's small desk and dressing table combined. The origin of the name is obscure, but the design first appeared in the mid-18th century in France and quickly became popular in England.

The distinguishing feature of the bonheur du jour is the many small drawers and compartments which were incorporated into the design to provide the maximum amount of storage space for trinkets, toiletries and writing accoutrements in the limited space available.

A Victorian walnut and tulipwood crossbanded bonheur du jour, with gilt-metal mounts, the pierced brass gallery above a pair of ogee arched glazed panel doors and an apron drawer, on cabriole legs, some crossbanding lacking, c1870, 30¼in (77cm) wide.
$2,700–3,200 *S(S)*

A Colonial solid maple bonheur du jour, with ebony line inlay and an upper flower motif to the pediment, the stepped secretaire with one long concave central drawer, open shelves and 4 short drawers over a cupboard fitted with pigeonholes and enclosed by panelled doors, the table base with a fold-over writing surface, one long drawer and reeded shaped tapering legs with bronze paw feet, early 19thC, 25in (63.5cm) wide.
$3,400–4,000 *TMA*

A Victorian burr walnut and marquetry bonheur du jour, with boxwood and ebony stringing, the upper section with pierced brass three-quarter gallery and 2 panelled doors enclosing drawers and pigeonholes, the frieze drawer with leather-inset adjustable writing slope above a panelled door enclosing 3 shelves for sheet music, with fluted brackets, on plinth base with casters, 23¼in (59cm) wide.
$2,800–3,200 *DN*

r. An Edwardian inlaid mahogany bonheur du jour, with leather-inset top, on tapering legs with casters, 48in (122cm) wide.
$3,200–3,600 *GAZE*

A George III ebony-inlaid satinwood bonheur du jour, inlaid overall with ebony and boxwood lines, the sliding superstructure with a pair of doors crossbanded with kingwood, enclosing a fitted birch interior with 8 arcaded pigeonholes above 4 short drawers, one fitted, and 2 long mahogany-lined drawers, above a hinged green leather-lined writing surface, on square tapering legs, stamped 'Gillows Lancaster', minor restorations, 27in (69cm) wide.
$6,500–8,000 *C*

A Victorian marquetry-inlaid walnut bonheur du jour, with a central mirrored cupboard door above a drawer and flanked by 6 further drawers, the leather-inset serpentine top above a long frieze drawer, on gilt-metal-mounted cabriole legs inlaid with foliate scrolls, 41in (104cm) wide.
$4,000–4,400 *Bon*

Bookcases

A George II mahogany breakfront bookcase, with moulded cornice, a pair of glazed doors over a pair of raised and fielded panelled doors, on bracket feet replacing original plinth, original brass escutcheons, 75¼in (191cm) wide.
$12,000–13,000 *P*

A George III mahogany bookcase/collector's cabinet, the 2 sections each with 4 adjustable shelves with reeded edges above 2 pairs of panelled doors with a simulated drawer at the top, each enclosing 2 columns of 10 small drawers, losses to mouldings, the top Regency, 91¾in (233cm) wide.
$6,000–6,500 *C*

A George III mahogany bookcase, with dentil cornice, 2 thirteen-pane astragal glazed doors, 2 fielded panel doors below, 56in (142cm) wide.
$4,500–5,000 *Bea(E)*

l. A George III mahogany bookcase, the reeded moulded cornice above 4 glazed doors with astragals and panelled cupboard doors, restored, 113¼in (288cm) wide.
$13,500–15,000 *Bon*

l. A mahogany bookcase with ebony moulding and cockbeads, the upper part with a dentil cornice above shelves enclosed by 2 glazed astragal doors, the base with 2 short and 3 long drawers with later brass handles, on bracket feet, early 19thC, 47½in (121cm) wide.
$4,000–4,500 *DN*

A mahogany bookcase, the dentil-moulded cornice above a pair of astragal glazed doors enclosing shelves, above a projecting base with 2 panelled doors, on bracket feet, the glazed section 18thC, 50in (127cm) wide.
$2,000–2,400 *CSK*

A Regency mahogany bookcase, comprising 2 wings of a breakfront bookcase, each section with moulded cornice and crossbanded frieze above a glazed door with arched astragals enclosing 4 adjustable shelves, on a base of 5 graduated drawers with knob handles, 67in (170cm) wide.
$2,400–2,800 *P(Sc)*

A Regency mahogany boxwood and ebony-lined inverted breakfront bookcase, with arched ends, the shaped cornice above 2 glazed doors, flanked on each side by 2 arched glazed doors, the base fitted with a drawer above panelled doors flanked on either side by a secretaire fall flap above 2 doors, 136¼in (346cm) wide.
$24,000–26,500 *P(Sc)*

This is a good quality piece with unusual twin-domed tops.

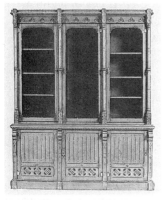

A mid-Victorian oak bookcase, of Gothic revival style in the manner of J. P. Seddon, the pierced carved frieze above glazed doors enclosing adjustable shelves, the base with 3 cupboard doors, enclosing adjustable shelves with fluted panels and blind fretwork frieze divided by pilasters, 78¾in (200cm) wide.
$2,500–2,800 *P(Sc)*

A George III style carved mahogany bookcase, with projecting moulded dentil and blind fret decorated cornice, above adjustable shelves enclosed by 3 astragal glazed doors, the base with 3 panelled doors with applied foliate motifs, 19thC, 72½in (184cm) wide.
$4,800–5,600 *P(NE)*

Alterations

Bookcases and display cabinets have sometimes been cut down to make them more saleable.
- Pediments may have been removed to reduce height, in which case there will be marks where the pediment once sat.
- The cabinet may have been reduced in depth by cutting through the sides and shelves and refixing the back; this is usually traceable by the obvious distressing of the newly cut surfaces.
- If the main carcase has been reduced in height, the slots for the adjustable shelves may appear too close to the top or bottom; there should be at least 8in (20cm) clear to accommodate books.

An inlaid-rosewood library bookcase, with turned pillar terminals, the upper section with 4 arched astragal doors enclosing adjustable shelves, above 4 panelled doors enclosing adjustable shelves, altered, c1835, 91¼in (232cm) wide.
$7,300–8,800 *S(S)*

A Victorian mahogany bookcase, the moulded cornice above 2 pairs of glazed doors enclosing shelves, on reeded bun feet, 31in (78.5cm) wide.
$2,400–2,700 *CSK*

> **Miller's is a price GUIDE not a price LIST**

A Victorian mahogany breakfront bookcase, the 8 geometrically glazed doors enclosing adjustable shelves, on a plain plinth, 2 panes cracked, with depository label to the cornice for Hampton & Sons Ltd, 80in (203cm) wide.
$9,500–11,000 *C*

l. A late Victorian oak bookcase, the arched glazed doors enclosing shelves, flanked by foliate corbels and fluted uprights, the projecting base with a pair of panelled doors, 52in (132cm) wide.
$1,900–2,200 *CSK*

A late Victorian mahogany
bookcase, with 2 geometrically
glazed doors enclosing shelves,
above a pair of panelled
cupboard doors,
50in (127cm) wide.
$2,500–2,800 · *C(S)*

A late Victorian mahogany library
bookcase, the angled cornice above
2 glazed doors and a single long
drawer with 2 cabinet doors below,
43¼in (110cm) wide.
$1,900–2,200 *B&L*

A oak library bookcase, with
divided adjustable shelves flanked
by fluted pilasters, above
3 panelled cupboard doors between
fluted pilasters, the interiors
grained, formerly with doors, late
19thC, 96in (243.5cm) wide.
$2,500–2,800 *CSK*

r. A late Victorian black walnut bookcase, in
the manner of Gillows of Lancaster, the
moulded and foliate-carved cornice fitted with
3 glazed doors enclosing shelves, above
3 panelled doors, on a shaped plinth with
turned bun feet, adapted, 78in (198cm) wide.
$4,400–4,800 *C(S)*

l. A George II style walnut
and parcel-gilt breakfront
bookcase, the 2 central
astragal glazed doors
flanked by a further pair of
arched astragal doors with
canted corners enclosing
shelves, on 'Braganza' feet,
c1920, 68in (173cm) wide.
$1,600–2,000 *S(S)*

r. An Edwardian
mahogany bookcase, the
astragal glazed doors
enclosing 4 adjustable
shelves with channelled
fronts, the lower section
fitted with a pair of
panelled doors, above a
scroll-decorated frieze, on
foliate-capped cabriole legs
with claw-and-ball feet,
40½in (103cm) wide.
$2,000–2,400 *CSK*

l. A French Transitional
style marquetry-inlaid
bookcase, the rounded
rectangular marble top
above a pair of brass
grille-filled and part-
panelled cupboard doors
inlaid with flower-filled
baskets, on fluted
tapering legs, c1900,
41⅛in (105.5cm) wide.
$1,200–1,300 *Bon*

Bureau Bookcases

A George II Irish mahogany bureau bookcase, the mirror-panelled doors enclosing 3 adjustable shelves, above a pair of short drawers, the lower section with a long drawer, enclosing a green leather-lined writing slide, concealing 3 wells and 4 mahogany-lined small drawers, above a shaped kneehole with 4 short drawers flanked to each side by 3 short drawers, on shaped bracket feet, lacking finial, restored, replacements to veneer on the top, 40½in (103cm) wide.
$15,000–17,500 *C*

A walnut bureau bookcase, with broken swan neck pediment above a pair of arched bevelled glazed doors, cross-banded fall enclosing a fitted interior, above 5 drawers, on bracket feet, restored, early 18thC, 35in (89cm) wide.
$5,500–6,300 *Bon*

A Scottish oak bureau bookcase, the upper section with swan-neck pediment, pierced thistle leaf fretting, a pair of astragal glazed doors with arched tracery, the base with fitted interior, 4 long graduated drawers under, on bracket feet, 18thC, 37in (94cm) wide.
$4,000–4,500 *RBB*

A George III mahogany bureau bookcase, the later dentil-moulded cornice above an inlaid frieze, with a pair of astragal glazed doors below, with fitted interior, above 4 graduated drawers, on ogee bracket feet, associated, 43in (109cm) wide.
$1,900–2,200 *CSK*

r. A George III mahogany bureau bookcase, the dentil cornice above astragal glazed doors and fall-front, opening to reveal a fitted interior, above 4 long graduated drawers, bracket feet, c1800, 42in (106.5cm) wide.
$4,800–5,200 *B&L*

A mahogany bureau bookcase, the dentil-moulded cornice above a pair of astragal glazed doors, the sloping fall enclosing a fitted interior of pigeonholes and short drawers, above 4 graduated long drawers, on bracket feet, the bureau George III, the bookcase 19thC, 41in (104cm) wide.
$2,800–3,200 *CSK*

A mahogany marine bureau bookcase, the upper section with bevelled glazed panelled doors, the fall enclosing a fitted interior, above 3 long drawers, on bracket feet, 19thC, 25¼in (64cm) wide.
$1,200–1,400 *P(NE)*

This bookcase had carrying handles for easy transportation. The 2 extra locks on the writing fall were for additional security. Its small dimensions enabled it to be placed in a cabin on board ship where it would be firmly secured to the cabin wall.

A Victorian mahogany cylinder bureau bookcase, the ogee cornice above a pair of glazed doors, the maple-veneered fitted desk with sliding adjustable leather-inset writing surface above 2 panelled doors, on plinth base, 46in (117cm) wide.
$2,400–2,700 *Bri*

An Edwardian mahogany and inlaid bureau bookcase, on shaped bracket feet, one glazed panel lacking, c1910, 45¼in (115cm) wide.
$2,000–2,400 *S(S)*

Low Bookcases

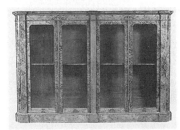

A mid-Victorian walnut and boxwood-inlaid dwarf bookcase, the rounded rectangular top fitted with 2 pairs of glazed doors enclosing adjustable shelves, adapted, 94in (239cm) wide.
$2,500–2,800 *C(S)*

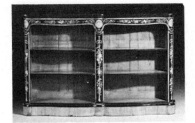

A walnut and marquetry serpentine-shaped open bookcase, the frieze and uprights inlaid with foliate marquetry, with 2 apertures each with 2 adjustable shelves, on a plinth base, late 19thC, 73¼in (186cm) wide.
$4,800–5,200 *C*

A satinwood dwarf breakfront bookcase, with brass grille back, the top with reeded rim above an ebonised line-inlaid frieze fitted with 2 astragal glazed doors flanked by 2 further astragal glazed doors enclosing shelves, late 19thC, 102in (260cm) wide.
$2,800–3,200 *CSK*

Open Bookcases

A late George III mahogany open cabinet bookcase, the raised gallery above 2 open tiers, the sides with brass carrying handles, the lower section with a slide above a pair of crossbanded doors and an apron drawer, on turned tapering legs ending in brass cappings and casters, 19in (48cm) wide.
$4,400–5,000 *S(S)*

A rosewood breakfront open bookcase, the raised back with 2 tiers and spiral-twist supports, the base including adjustable shelves and flanked by spiral-twist columns, c1840, 72in (183cm) wide.
$2,400–2,800 *S(S)*

A rosewood open bookcase, the frieze with 3 drawers, 3 divisions below between downscrolled corbels and reeded uprights, stamped 'Bell and Coupland, Preston', 19thC, 94¼in (239cm) wide.
$3,200–3,500 *CSK*

An Edwardian mahogany shallow bowfront four-tier open bookcase, the lower drawer crossbanded and with boxwood and ebonised stringing, on square tapered legs, 31in (79cm) wide.
$1,900–2,200 *DN*

Revolving Bookcases

l. A late Victorian oak revolving bookcase, the moulded rectangular top above 2 tiers of 4 open shelves, on a base, 18in (46cm) wide.
$520–560 *C(S)*

r. An Edwardian mahogany revolving bookcase, with marquetry and satinwood crossbanded top and boxwood-strung side panels with foliate scrolls, on quadruped base, 18in (46cm) wide.
$1,000–1,200 *HOLL*

An Edwardian mahogany revolving bookcase, the chequer-line-inlaid square top above open compartments and slatted sides, on splayed legs, 15in (38cm) wide.
$880–960 *C*

Secretaire Bookcases

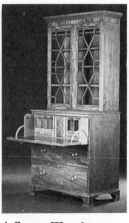

A George III mahogany secretaire bookcase, with moulded cornice above a pair of astragal glazed doors enclosing adjustable shelves, the lower part with ebonised stringing outline, the secretaire drawer with fitted interior, above 3 long graduated drawers, the brass handles with oval *repoussé* neo-classical backplates, on bracket feet, printed paper label of 'Bowen, Carmarthen', 42in (106.5cm) wide.
$4,400–5,000 *PF*

A George III mahogany secretaire bookcase, the upper section with a pair of lancet astragal glazed doors, the base with a secretaire drawer enclosing an arrangement of drawers and pigeonholes above 3 further graduated drawers, on splayed bracket feet, c1790, 39½in (100.5cm) wide.
$5,000–6,000 *Bon*

r. A George III mahogany secretaire bookcase, the inlaid moulded cornice above a pair of astragal glazed doors, the fall enclosing a fitted interior above 3 further drawers and bracket feet, 38¼in (97cm) wide.
$3,000–3,500 *Bon(C)*

A George III mahogany secretaire bookcase, the associated upper section with a pair of geometric astragal glazed doors, the fitted writing drawer simulating 2 drawers and 2 drawers below, shaped bracket feet, c1790, 43in (109cm) wide.
$2,200–2,500 *S(S)*

A George III satinwood and mahogany secretaire bookcase, the Greek key cornice above a pair of astragal glazed doors, the secretaire drawer enclosing an arrangement of drawers and pigeonholes with 3 long graduated drawers beneath, on bracket feet, restored, c1790, 41¾in (106cm) wide.
$6,200–7,200 *Bon*

A George III mahogany secretaire bookcase, the fret-filled broken swan neck cornice inlaid with a shell above a pair of astragal glazed doors, the double dummy secretaire drawer enclosing a fitted interior, above 3 long graduated drawers, on splayed bracket feet, 2 parts associated, restored, 42in (106.5cm) wide.
$6,500–8,000 *Bon*

A secretaire bookcase with simulated bamboo split-turned mouldings and astragals and painted throughout with trailing leaves, flowers and ribbons, enclosed by 2 glazed doors above 2 panelled doors, on turned feet, early 19thC, 39¼in (100cm) wide.
$11,000–12,000 *DN*

An inlaid mahogany secretaire bookcase, early 19thC, 42in (107cm) wide.
$7,000–8,000 *GAZE*

A mahogany, boxwood and ebony-strung secretaire bookcase, the pierced fretwork swan neck pediment above twin astragal glazed cupboard doors enclosing adjustable shelves, the lower section with secretaire drawer enclosing a fitted interior with central inlaid door, flanked by pilasters concealing secret drawers, the secretaire drawer with double dummy drawer front over 3 long graduated drawers, on splayed bracket feet, early 19thC, 48in (122cm) wide.
$6,400–7,000 *P(Sc)*

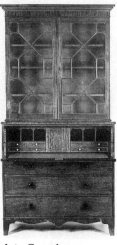

A mahogany line-inlaid secretaire bookcase, the moulded and chequer-banded cornice above a pair of astragal glazed doors, the projecting base with fall-front drawer enclosing an arrangement of 7 drawers amongst pigeonholes with 3 further long graduated drawers, on outswept feet, possibly associated, the cornice later, early 19thC, 42in (107cm) wide.
$3,800–4,400 CSK

Cross Reference
Colour Review

A late Georgian mahogany secretaire bookcase, the upper part with astragal glazed doors, above a secretaire drawer enclosing drawers and pigeonholes, above 3 long graduated drawers, on swept bracket feet, 45in (114cm) wide.
$2,700–3,000 WL

A mahogany secretaire bookcase, with reeded and partial spiral reeded Corinthian pilaster terminals, the pair of astragal doors enclosing adjustable shelves, the bowfront base with ebonised banding, the fitted writing drawer above 3 long graduated drawers, on carved claw feet, c1810, 49in (124.5cm) wide.
$7,500–8,500 S(S)

l. A late Regency mahogany secretaire bookcase, with astragal glazed doors, the base with fall-front drawer enclosing a fitted interior, above a pair of panelled cupboard doors, on turned feet, 47in (119.5cm) wide.
$3,500–4,000 CSK

A Regency rosewood secretaire bookcase, banded overall in satinwood and with ebony lines, the glazed doors with egg-and-dart moulding, enclosing 3 adjustable shelves, above the later secretaire drawer with green baize-lined writing surface, pigeonholes and 4 drawers, above 2 panelled doors enclosing one shelf and on a later mahogany plinth, adapted, the base section extended in depth, the upper section previously fitted, 42in (107cm) wide.
$8,800–9,600 C

A veneered and inlaid mahogany secretaire bookcase, the upper section with 2 six-light cupboard doors, the lower section with 2 short drawers, over a butler's fall-front drawer opening to an interior fitted with a baize-lined writing surface and a central drawer, all over a recessed case fitted with 3 graduated drawers, on tapering ring-turned and reeded legs, New York, c1830, 49½in (125.5cm) wide.
$4,000–4,800 CNY

A Victorian mahogany secretaire bookcase, the glazed doors with foliate carving enclosing shelves, the fall-front enclosing a leather-lined writing surface, drawers and pigeonholes, 2 doors below, 51in (129.5cm) wide.
$3,500–4,000 CSK

Buckets

An Irish mahogany turf bucket, the coopered moulded body with 2 brass bands and a brass loop handle, c1780, 15¼in (39cm) diam.
$4,000–4,500 *S*

A mahogany and brass-bound peat bucket, of tapering coopered form, with a brass swing handle, later oak base, c1780, 14¼in (36cm) diam.
$1,400–1,600 *S(S)*

A George III mahogany and brass-bound peat bucket, with ribbed tapered body and brass carrying handle, possibly Irish, 14in (35.5cm) diam.
$1,900–2,200 *Bon*

A George III mahogany and brass-bound peat bucket, adapted with a single door for storage, 14in (35.5cm) diam.
$1,300–1,450 *JAd*

A George II brass-bound mahogany plate bucket, with loop handle, now fitted with a brass liner, 14in (35.5cm) diam.
$1,400–1,500 *CNY*

A George III brass-bound mahogany peat bucket, with dipped rim, loop handle and brass liner, 13in (33cm) diam.
$1,500–1,600 *CNY*

A mahogany and brass-bound peat bucket, with brass carrying handle and 4 brass bands, later brass liner, c1790, 14¼in (36cm) diam.
$2,200–2,400 *S(S)*

l. A mahogany and brass oyster bucket, with raised moulded handles, later metal liner, c1780, 18in (46cm) wide.
$2,200–2,600 *S(S)*

Buffets

An early Victorian stained oak two-tier dining room buffet, the shelves with three-quarter galleries, supported by fluted columns, on acanthus-carved bar feet and turned bun supports with recessed brass caps and casters, 54in (137cm) wide.
$800–950 *C(S)*

An early Victorian mahogany three-tier buffet, the shelves supported by turned-baluster columns, the centre shelf fitted with 2 drawers, on fluted tapering supports with brass caps and ceramic casters, 42in (107cm) wide.
$1,700–2,000 *C(S)*

A mahogany three-tier buffet, incorporating a cartouche above a foliate frieze, the turned fluted supports with studded collars, on bun feet with ceramic casters, c1870, 51¼in (130cm) wide.
$3,500–3,800 *S(S)*

Bureaux

A George I walnut bureau, crossbanded and herringbone strung, the fall-front enclosing boxwood and ebony strung pigeonholes and drawers around a central door, above 3 short drawers and 3 long drawers, with brass handles, on bracket feet, restored with some later veneers and cockbeading, 39½in (100.5cm) wide.
$4,500–5,500 *DN*

A walnut and featherbanded bureau, the fall enclosing a stepped interior with pigeonholes and drawers, 4 graduated drawers below, on later bracket feet, c1720, 35in (89cm) wide.
$4,800–5,600 *S(S)*

A George III mahogany bureau, the sloping fall enclosing a fitted interior with an arrangement of drawers and pigeonholes, above 4 graduated drawers, on bracket feet, 36in (91.5cm) wide.
$2,000–2,400 *CSK*

A walnut-veneered bureau, with herringbone inlay and crossbanded, the fall-flap revealing a fitted interior, with central cupboard, flanked by secret pillar drawers, pigeonholes and short drawers, on shaped bracket feet, early 18thC, requires restoration, 30in (76cm) wide.
$4,800–5,800 *J&L*

A mahogany bureau, the fall enclosing an arrangement of drawers and pigeonholes above one long, 2 short and a further 2 long drawers, on bracket feet, c1760, 36in (91.5cm) wide.
$3,600–4,200 *Bon*

A George III mahogany, boxwood and ebony-strung bureau, the sloping fall inlaid with a central oval flowerhead patera and opening to reveal an interior fitted with drawers and pigeonholes, above 4 graduated satinwood banded drawers, on bracket feet, 41¾in (106cm) wide.
$1,900–2,400 *P(Sc)*

A walnut bureau, the sloping flap enclosing a stepped interior with a cupboard, drawers, pigeonholes and a well, 2 short and 2 long drawers below, on later bun feet, restored, early 18thC, 37¼in (94.5cm) wide.
$3,200–3,500 *Bea(E)*

A George III mahogany bureau, the fall-front with fitted interior, over 4 long drawers with brass drop handles, on bracket feet, 35½in (90cm) wide.
$2,000–2,500 *AH*

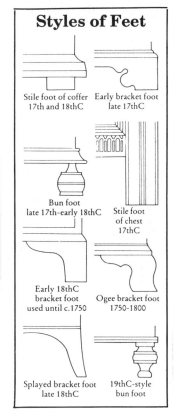

Styles of Feet

Stile foot of coffer 17th and 18thC

Early bracket foot late 17thC

Bun foot late 17th–early 18thC

Stile foot of chest 17thC

Early 18thC bracket foot used until c.1750

Ogee bracket foot 1750-1800

Splayed bracket foot late 18thC

19thC-style bun foot

A Georgian mahogany bureau, the fall-front enclosing a fitted interior of string-inlaid drawers and pigeonholes, over 4 long graduated drawers with later cast brass ring handles, on shaped bracket feet, 41½in (105.5cm) wide.
$1,600–1,900 *DA*

A Georgian mahogany bureau, with fitted interior, original handles, on bracket feet, 36in (91.5cm) wide.
$3,200–3,500 *RPh*

A walnut featherbanded bureau, the fall-front revealing a fitted interior, single long drawer below, over 2 short and 2 long drawers, brass drop handles and bracket feet, 18thC, 36in (91.5cm) wide.
$6,000–7,200 *AH*

A Chippendale birchwood reverse-serpentine fall-front bureau, the moulded hinged-lid opening to an interior with 3 short drawers flanked by 2 long drawers, above 3 valanced pigeonholes, with 4 graduated long drawers below, on ogee bracket feet, New England, c1795, 41½in (105.5cm) wide.
$3,500–4,000 *S(NY)*

l. A Chippendale cherry slant-lid bureau, with fitted interior, restored, northern New England, late 18thC, 36in (91.5cm) wide.
$2,000–2,400 *SK(B)*

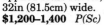

r. A Victorian walnut strung and inlaid *bureau de dame,* the three-quarter brass gallery over 2 short drawers and sloping fall, inlaid with flowers and with gilt-metal cast rim, opening to reveal fitted interior, on cabriole legs with applied brass sabots, 32in (81.5cm) wide.
$1,200–1,400 *P(Sc)*

An inlaid mahogany bureau, the sloping front enclosing a fitted interior, 4 graduated drawers below, on bracket feet, 19thC, 36¼in (92cm) wide.
$1,900–2,200 *Bea(E)*

A mahogany bureau, on cabriole legs, c1920, 30in (76cm) wide.
$560–640 *GBr*

An Edwardian inlaid mahogany bureau, crossbanded in satinwood, the fall with shell motif, 38in (96.5cm) wide.
$1,000–1,200 *GAZE*

An Edwardian mahogany roll-top bureau, with rosewood crossbanding and ebony and boxwood stringing, the top with three-quarter gilt-metal balustraded gallery, the cylinder-fall enclosing fitted interior and writing slide, with 4 graduated drawers, on bracket feet, 35¾in (91cm) wide.
$3,000–3,500 *P(Sc)*

Cabinets

A George II mahogany estate cabinet, the concave-cut cornered panelled doors enclosing a fitted interior with 33 pigeonholes and 3 small mahogany-lined drawers, the pigeonholes with ivory-inlaid letters of the alphabet, the lower section with a pair of panelled doors enclosing 2 compartments each with 3 adjustable shelves, on bracket feet, locks and 2 shelves replaced, restored, 2 letters missing, 48½in (123cm) wide.
$5,800–6,400 *C*

r. A Biedermeier mahogany and parcel-gilt cabinet, the stepped-top above a shaped frieze drawer, with recessed bowed door enclosing 2 shaped shelves, flanked by detached columns and above an inverted breakfront deep drawer with spreading base, north European, early 19thC, 27¾in (70.5cm) wide.
$2,500–2,800 *C*

A George IV mahogany cabinet, the raised back with 2 open bookshelves and a brass gallery, above 2 arched panelled doors and pilasters, 36¼in (92cm) wide.
$1,600–2,000 *DN*

A walnut and inlaid pier cabinet, with a panelled door enclosing a velvet-lined interior and 2 shelves, c1870, 31in (79cm) wide.
$2,800–3,200 *S(S)*

A red and gold lacquer cabinet, the 2 cupboard doors decorated with chinoiserie scenes, with brass escutcheon and lock, on a foliate-carved plinth base, 19thC, 34½in (87.5cm) wide.
$4,000–4,500 *C(S)*

A George III style inlaid satinwood and kingwood D-shaped cabinet, the hinged top revealing a well and a drawer, the tapered legs with knopped feet, c1900, 25¼in (64cm) wide.
$1,900–2,400 *S(S)*

r. An Edwardian inlaid rosewood music cabinet, with raised panelled back, decorated with musical instruments in boxwood and ivory, above a panelled door partially glazed, raised on shaped platform base, 21½in (54.5cm) wide.
$1,000–1,100 *JAd*

An Edwardian mahogany music cabinet, with shaped galleried top, fitted with 5 fall-front drawers, inlaid with crossbanding and stringing, on cabriole legs, some damage to top, 21½in (54.5cm) wide.
$450–520 *LF*

Bedside Cabinets

A Louis XV kingwood-veneered bedside cabinet, with marble-top and interior, brass side handles and foliate mouldings, on cabriole legs, 19in (48cm) wide.
$4,200–4,800 *Bea(E)*

An early George III mahogany bedside cabinet, with pierced raised border, an open recess and on turned tapering legs, with pad feet, 18½in (47cm) wide.
$1,500–1,700 *DN*

A pair of Italian marquetry-inlaid night tables, the crossbanded tops with a crossed quiver and flaming torch, above frieze drawers and cupboard doors, on husk-inlaid tapered square legs, c1790, 16in (40.5cm) wide.
$6,000–7,000 *Bon*

A George III mahogany tray-top bedside cabinet, the gallery with carrying handles, above a tambour slide and pull-out front with circular incision and cover, on chamfered legs, 20½in (52cm) wide.
$850–1,000 *C*

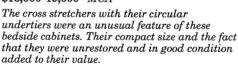

A pair of George III mahogany tray-top bedside cabinets, each enclosed by a crossbanded and line-inlaid panel door with brass handle, on turned tapered legs with cross stretchers and circular undertiers, 13in (33cm) wide.
$16,000–19,000 *MCA*

The cross stretchers with their circular undertiers were an unusual feature of these bedside cabinets. Their compact size and the fact that they were unrestored and in good condition added to their value.

A French brass-inlaid mahogany bedside cabinet, the white marble top above tambour door flanked by inlaid lozenges, with frieze drawer below, on square tapering legs with block feet, 19thC, 13¾in (35cm) wide.
$950–1,000 *CSK*

An inlaid mahogany bowfronted commode, with hinged lid and original chamber pot, c1820, 25¼in (64cm) wide.
$560–640 *GBr*

An Edwardian inlaid rosewood bedside cabinet, c1910, 14in (35.5cm) high.
$650–750 *RPh*

Don't Forget!

If in doubt please refer to the 'How to Use' section at the beginning of this book.

l. A George IV mahogany bowfronted bedside cabinet, with reeded three-quarter gallery and borders, on turned and reeded legs, 15½in (39.5cm) wide.
$1,900–2,200 *DN*

l. An Edwardian inlaid satinwood and chequer-lined pot cupboard, the moulded ledge back above a moulded crossbanded top and single cupboard door with inlaid neo-classical panel, on square tapering legs, 16¼in (41cm) wide.
$600–680 *P(Sc)*

An oak coffer, with carved front,
c1670, 44in (111.5cm) long.
$1,900–2,200 *WELL*

A joined oak carved chest, the hinged plank lid
enclosing a lidded candle box, above a foliate
strapwork carved frieze and a panelled arcaded
front, with strapwork carved apron, on stile
feet, mid-17thC, 56in (142in) wide.
$3,500–4,000 *Bon*

An Italian cedar wood cassone, with an inset lid, decorated
overall with carving of leaves, figures and animals, on
later bun feet, mid-17thC, 68½in (174cm) wide.
$2,400–2,800 *Bon*

An oak mule chest, with carved front
and 2 drawers with brass handles,
c1670, 44in (111.5cm) wide.
$2,000–2,300 *WELL*

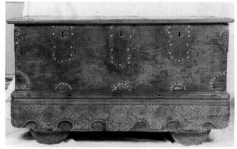

A Welsh oak coffer bach, with chequer inlay of
holly and bog oak, with drawer and shaped frieze,
on turned legs, c1760, 23in (58.5cm) wide.
$4,800–5,400 *CoA*

A Spanish walnut wheeled chest,
with ornate brass inlay and 3 locks,
late 17thC, 53in (134.5cm) wide.
$1,900–2,400 *ME*

An oak chest of drawers, with
geometric moulding, the 3 long
drawers with brass ring handles,
c1680, 36in (91.5cm) wide.
$2,500–3,000 *WELL*

A Queen Anne black and gold
japanned chest-on-stand, with
ogee moulded top, c1705,
40¼in (102cm) wide.
$4,800–5,400 *Bon*

An oak chest-on-stand, with
2 short and 3 long drawers,
on a stand with 2 drawers,
c1730, 40in (101.5cm) wide.
$4,500–4,800 *WELL*

Paul Hopwell Antiques

Early English Oak

Dressers, tables and chairs always in stock

A set of eight (four showing) early C19th ash and alder spindle back dining chairs. Excellent colour, condition and patina. English c1820.

A set of eight (four showing) Georgian ash wavyline ladderback dining chairs. Excellent colour, condition and patination. English c1800.

A small Queen Anne cherrywood cupboard dresser base.
English c1715

Paul Hopwell Antiques

A George III oak cupboard dresser
and rack with spice drawers.
Excellent colour and condition.
N. Wales c1780

A George III oak tridarn. The central
cupboard fitted with secret drawer
and pigeon hole. Exceptional colour
and patina. Original condition.
N. Wales c1760

A George III oak dresser base on
cabriole legs inlaid with walnut.
Excellent colour, condition and patina.
Engish c1780

Furniture restoration service available
30 High Street, West Haddon, Northamptonshire NN6 7AP
Tel: 01788 510636

WE WISH TO BUY 17TH & 18TH CENTURY OAK FURNITURE

A James I carved oak wainscot chair, c1620.
$3,200–3,600 *MIC*

A set of 4 oak armchairs, upholstered in leather, c1660.
$8,000–8,800 *WELL*

A joined oak chair, Yorkshire, c1660.
$1,200–1,300 *MIC*

A set of 4 ash and elm Windsor chairs, c1870.
$720–800 *GBr*

An ash comb-back Windsor chair, early 19thC.
$3,200–3,600 *CoA*

A walnut high-backed chair, c1695.
$1,600–1,800 *WELL*

A turned ash chair, Welsh or Cornish, 17thC.
$3,500–4,000 *CoA*

A Spanish walnut armchair, upholstered in leather, 17thC.
$880–960 *ME*

An oak armchair with splat back and drawer under seat, dated '1742'.
$2,700–3,000 *CoA*

An oak preacher's chair, mid-18thC.
$9,000–10,000 *CoA*

A Welsh primitive armchair, 1780.
$2,500–2,800 *COM*

A primitive comb-back Windsor armchair, with a shaped crest-rail above a stylised vase splat, c1760.
$3,500–4,000 *RYA*

A Scottish crofter's plank chair, c1840.
$1,300–1,450 *RYA*

A painted lambing chair, with drawer under seat, c1840.
$5,000–5,600 *ChS*

Cross Reference
Oak & Country Chairs page 33

An oak country box settle, with 4 fielded panels to the back and front, c1760, 72in (183cm) wide.
$1,300–1,500 *TAY*

Robert Young
Antiques

Fine Country Furniture & Folk Art

Robert and Josyane Young

68 Battersea Bridge Road London SW11 3AG
Tel: 0171 228 7847   Fax: 0171 585 0489

ENTHUSIASTIC BUYERS OF FINE
COUNTRY FURNITURE AND FOLK ART

A George III oak dresser, with open
shelves flanked by diamond inlay,
the base with crossbanded top,
73½in (187cm) wide.
$7,000–7,500 *S(S)*

An oak Welsh dresser, with
graduated rack above 6 fitted
drawers flanked by cupboards,
18thC, 66in (167.5cm) wide.
$6,000–6,500 *TAY*

A fruitwood breakfront dresser,
with boarded rack, 6 drawers
and 2 cupboard doors, c1810,
59in (150cm) wide.
$7,200–8,000 *WELL*

An oak dresser base, the back with 5 small
drawers, the base with 3 drawers, shaped apron
and turned legs, 18thC, 70in (178cm) wide.
$2,250–2,500 *AAV*

An oak refectory table, with plank top, carved
frieze, turned bulbous legs, stretcher altered
from side stretchers to single central stretcher,
17thC, 87in (221cm) long.
$9,600–11,200 *SPa*

An oak centre table, c1680,
17thC, 32in (82cm) wide.
$3,200–3,500 *MIC*

An oak cricket table, 17thC,
24in (61cm) diam.
$1,100–1,300 *ME*

An oak lowboy, with carved
knees and cabriole legs,
c1720, 33in (84cm) wide.
$3,500–4,000 *WELL*

A Queen Anne style oak
cricket table, c1740,
24in (61cm) high.
$3,200–3,500 *RYA*

An oak lowboy, with single
drawer, on cabriole legs,
c1790, 30in (76cm) high.
$3,200–3,500 *RYA*

An oak tray-top table,
on tripod base, c1770,
24in (61cm) diam.
$1,300–1,400 *WELL*

A pine bacon cupboard, with coffered seat, mid-18thC, 33in (84cm) wide.
$1,500–1,700 *Bon*

An oak corner cupboard, with astragal glazed doors over a panelled base, Glamorganshire, c1780, 45in (114.5cm) wide.
$5,600–6,200 *CoA*

A French carved walnut armoire, basically 16thC, 60in (153cm) wide.
$16,000–19,000 *Bon*

A Welsh oak wall cupboard, with raised and fielded panelled door, c1870, 26in (66cm) wide.
$850–950 *CoA*

A Welsh oak food cupboard, c1790, 55in (139.5cm) wide.
$7,500–8,500 *CoA*

A Flemish oak sideboard, late 19thC, 52¾in (134cm) wide.
$5,500–6,500 *TAR*

An oak court cupboard, the moulded cornice with strapwork carved frieze, dated '1686', 54½in (138cm) wide.
$3,800–4,400 *P(Sc)*

A George II oak dresser base, with 3 drawers above a shaped apron, on cabriole legs, c1745, 30in (76cm) wide.
$14,500–16,000 *PHA*

A George III oak dresser, with 3 drawers, and an under shelf, 72in (183cm) wide.
$3,600–4,200 *TMA*

An oak dresser, with 3 drawers above 2 panelled doors flanking 3 small drawers, c1740, 54in (137cm) wide.
$12,800–14,200 *CoA*

A George III oak dresser, the associated raised back with shaped apron and 3 shelves, 66½in (169cm) wide.
$8,800–10,000 *S(S)*

A Regency inlaid rosewood bonheur du jour, with a pair of glazed doors enclosing shelves, 30½in (77.5cm) wide. **$11,200–12,800** *C*

A serpentine-shaped inlaid rosewood bonheur du jour, with ormolu mounts, c1870, 28in (71cm) wide. **$6,400–8,000** *BERA*

An Edwardian painted satinwood bonheur du jour, the 2 doors decorated with putti, 26½in (67.5cm) wide. **$8,000–8,800** *C*

A walnut bureau, on bracket feet, early 18thC, 28in (71cm) wide. **$4,800–5,200** *MAT*

A George I crossbanded burr walnut bureau, on later bracket feet, 38in (96.5cm) wide. **$8,500–9,000** *DN*

A George I figured walnut and feather-banded bureau, with fitted interior, bracket feet, 35½in (90cm) wide. **$9,600–10,400** *P*

An ash bureau, the fall revealing a cupboard, pigeonholes and drawers, c1760, 36in (91.5cm) wide. **$5,700–6,400** *FHA*

A Queen Anne style walnut bureau, with cabriole legs, c1920, 19in (48.5cm) wide. **$1,800–2,200** *RPh*

An Italian rococo giltwood bed, the headboard and footboard carved with C-scrolls and rocaille decoration, mid-18thC, 63in (160cm) wide.
$21,000–22,500 *S(NY)*

An Empire ormolu-mounted plum-pudding mahogany *lit en bateau*, some restoration, c1800, 83in (211cm) long.
$11,200–12,000 *C*

A walnut half tester bed, with serpentine footboard, c1850, with later drapes, 60in (152cm) wide.
$7,200–8,000 *SWA*

A Japanese style bronze-mounted giltwood bed, the mirrored headboard formed as a pagoda carved with vines and applied with crests of 2 Russian houses of nobility, the footboard with a bronze mounted panel flanked by mirrors, late 19thC, 61in (155cm) wide.
$35,000–39,000 *C*

A Spanish giltwood and white painted single bed, the inscribed headboard with pierced arched foliate scroll cresting, 19thC, 44in (112cm) wide.
$2,500–2,800 *C*

A George III style mahogany and chequer-lined four-poster bed, early 20thC, 65in (165cm) wide.
$4,200–4,800 *C(S)*

A Breton oak wedding bed, with heavily carved headboard, footboard and side rails, late 19thC, 54in (137cm) wide.
$2,200–2,400 *SWA*

A Louis XV style walnut bed, with carved headboard and footboard, c1900, 60in (152cm) wide.
$1,700–2,000 *SWA*

An early Victorian carved rosewood day bed, with button-upholstered seat and scrolled end with scroll and foliate carved facings, 84in (214cm) long.
$4,400–5,200 *S*

A George IV ormolu-mounted rosewood day bed, the waved crest-rail above a padded back, arms and seat, the frieze with lappeted brass bands, on reeded tapering legs with brass caps and casters, restored, 92in (233.5cm) long.
$4,800–5,600 *C*

A Victorian walnut day bed, with outswept drop-end and downswept back, upholstered in buttoned cotton, on ring-turned legs, 72in (183cm) long.
$1,600–2,000 *C*

A carved mahogany
bookcase, New York State,
c1820, 55in (140cm) wide.
$6,400–7,200 *S(NY)*

A mahogany breakfront bookcase,
with astragal glazed doors, early
19thC, 98in (248cm) wide.
$8,500–9,000 *P(Sc)*

A Victorian mahogany breakfront
bookcase, with moulded cornice,
72in (183cm) wide.
$8,800–9,600 *CAG*

A Victorian walnut bookcase,
with floral and leaf-carved
crestings, 54in (137cm) wide.
$3,600–4,200 *CAG*

An Edwardian mahogany breakfront
bookcase, 80in (203cm) wide.
$12,000–13,500 *P(Sc)*

An 18thC style mahogany
breakfront library bookcase,
19thC, 100½in (255cm) wide.
$13,000–14,500 *DN*

A red walnut bureau bookcase,
c1750, 44in (112cm) wide.
$17,000–18,500 *S*

A Regency mahogany secretaire
bookcase, 39in (99cm) wide.
$8,800–9,600 *RBB*

r. A George III mahogany,
ebony and fruitwood secretaire
bookcase, 43in (109cm) wide.
$27,500–30,500 *C*

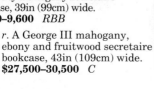

A mahogany bureau bookcase,
with satinwood-inlaid fan and
stringing, 19thC, 48in (122cm) wide.
$5,000–5,700 *RBB*

A Regency mahogany open bookcase, cross-banded in kingwood, attributed to Gillows, 25in (63.5cm) wide.
$16,000–17,500 *C*

A George IV mahogany open bookcase, with adjustable shelves, 40¾in (103.5cm) wide.
$2,400–2,800 *DN*

An Edwardian revolving bookcase, on original casters, 18¼in (46cm) wide.
$1,900–2,400 *BERA*

A mahogany revolving bookcase, c1910, 20in (51cm) wide.
$1,900–2,400 *S*

A mahogany canterbury, with a drawer, on turned legs, 19thC, 21in (53.5cm) wide.
$2,400–2,800 *MAT*

A Victorian walnut canterbury, with carved scrolling divisions and drawer below, 22in (56cm) wide.
$1,200–1,400 *APO*

An ebonised and gilt canterbury, with divisions and drawer below, c1890, 23in (58.5cm) wide.
$480–520 *RPh*

A mahogany two-door cabinet, with a single drawer, early 19thC, 23in (58.5cm) wide.
$3,200–3,600 *CAT*

A *faux* rosewood and brass cabinet, early 19thC, 30¼in (76.5cm) wide.
$5,000–5,600 *S*

A French Louis XVI style ormolu-mounted kingwood and trellis parquetry cabinet, with bowfronted marble top above a frieze drawer, late 19thC, 53in (134.5cm) wide.
$10,000–11,000 *C*

A George III tray-top commode, with 2 short and 3 long drawers, 26in (66cm) wide.
$7,200–8,000 *SPU*

A mahogany tray-top bedside cabinet, alterations to drawers, c1790, 18¾in (47.5cm) wide.
$1,300–1,600 *FHA*

A walnut purdonium, with central carved panel, c1875, 38in (96.5cm) wide.
$560–640 *GBr*

A George I walnut
bureau cabinet, with
mirrored doors, restored,
41in (104cm) wide.
$10,500–12,000 *C*

A crossbanded figured walnut
bureau cabinet, with moulded
double-domed cornice, on later ball
feet, c1705, 40½in (103cm) wide.
$23,000–25,500 *S*

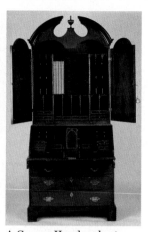

A George II red walnut
bureau cabinet, the arched
doors and fall enclosing
fitted interior, 4 long
drawers below, on bracket
feet, 40½in (103cm) wide.
$10,500–12,000 *P(NW)*

A walnut feather-banded
escritoire, with fitted
interior, the drawers with
cockbeading, on bun feet,
c1700, 43½in (110cm) wide.
$10,500–12,000 *S*

A Chinese export
mahogany bureau
cabinet, with monogram
'JCRD', late 18thC,
39in (99cm) wide.
$4,600–5,400 *C*

A George II miniature
bureau cabinet, with
cavetto cornice,
on bracket feet,
16⅝in (42cm) wide.
$7,000–8,000 *Bon*

A George III mahogany bureau
cabinet, with dentil cornice,
40½in (103cm) wide.
$4,800–5,400 *Bea(E)*

A William & Mary seaweed-
marquetry walnut escritoire,
with banded foliate border,
restored, 44⅝in (113cm) wide.
$8,500–9,500 *C*

A George III mahogany
secretaire tallboy, with fitted
interior, on bracket feet,
c1790, 45½in (115.5cm) wide.
$4,000–4,500 *Bon*

A Regency ormolu-mounted and
brass-inlaid rosewood secretaire
cabinet, on scrolled feet with casters,
restored, 43½in (110.5cm) wide.
$18,500–20,000 *C*

A japanned serpentine-shaped corner cupboard, early 18thC, 23in (58.5cm) wide. **$7,200–8,000** *DN*

A Dutch carved mahogany corner cupboard, mid-18thC, 55¼in (140cm) wide. **$12,000–13,500** *S(Am)*

A mahogany corner cupboard, with shaped interior shelves, c1775, 42½in (107cm) wide. **$7,200–8,000** *Bon*

A mahogany glazed bowfronted hanging corner cupboard, c1780, 41in (104cm) high. **$7,000–8,000** *S*

A George III mahogany freestanding corner cabinet, line-inlaid along the top, the arched panelled doors enclosing shaped interior shelves, c1790, 45in (114.5cm) wide. **$6,000–6,500** *RPh*

A figured mahogany corner cabinet, with ebony inlay, and shaped interior shelves, on splay feet, c1820, 37¾in (36cm) wide. **$3,800–4,500** *GBr*

A mahogany corner cupboard, the interior with 2 shelves, fitted with Gothic style brass hinges, c1860, 26in (66cm) wide. **$320–400** *GWA*

A mahogany corner cabinet, with 2 pairs of bowed doors, c1795, 45⅜in (116cm) wide. **$8,500–9,500** *S*

A marquetry-inlaid mahogany corner cabinet, c1890, 41in (104cm) wide. **$3,000–3,600** *Bon*

An oak corner cupboard, the single door with inlaid design, early 19thC, with later back, 33in (34cm) wide. **$1,300–1,400** *No7*

An Edwardian mahogany glazed corner cabinet, 80in (203cm) high. **$1,200–1,300** *GAZE*

A mahogany and rosewood-banded chiffonier, c1830, 37in (94cm) wide.
$2,200–2,600 *S(S)*

A kingwood and porcelain side cabinet, the painted panels with gilt-bronze borders, c1860, 44⅛in (113cm) wide.
$7,300–8,000 *S*

A Victorian marquetry and ivory-inlaid satinwood side cabinet, c1870, 70in (178cm) wide.
$43,500–48,000 *Bon*

A Victorian burr walnut side cabinet, the moulded top above an inlaid frieze, the central panel door flanked by glazed doors, 70¼in (178cm) wide.
$7,500–8,500 *S(S)*

An ebonised and amboyna-inlaid inverted breakfront side cabinet, c1870, 52in (132cm) wide.
$2,000–2,400 *S(S)*

A late Victorian ebonised and brass-inlaid side cabinet, 57in (145cm) wide.
$3,600–4,200 *C(S)*

A French marquetry-inlaid and gilt-metal-mounted side cabinet, c1890, 43⅛in (110.5cm) wide.
$3,200–3,500 *Bon*

An Edwardian painted satinwood side cabinet, 36in (91.5cm) wide.
$5,600–6,400 *Bon*

A Louis XV style quarter-veneered and marquetry credenza, with Sèvres panels and ormolu beading, late 19thC, 74in (188cm) wide.
$12,800–14,400 *JM*

A William & Mary oyster-walnut-veneered cabinet-on-stand, the doors enclosing an arrangement of 7 holly-banded drawers and cupboard door, 31in (79cm) wide.
$6,400–7,000 *DN*

A black japanned cabinet-on-stand, with a pair of panelled doors enclosing 6 drawers to either side, c1815, 49in (124.5cm) high.
$1,900–2,200 *Bon*

A mahogany and rosewood lady's writing cabinet, inlaid with brass and tortoiseshell, with fitted interior, 19thC, 20in (51cm) wide.
$6,400–7,200 *S*

A George II mahogany Windsor armchair, with shaped bowed front and balustrade splats, on cabriole legs, c1750. $7,500–8,500 *Bon*

A mahogany armchair, the carved and scroll moulded cabriole legs with French scroll toes, arms associated, c1765. $4,500–5,000 *S*

A George III mahogany open armchair, the foliate-carved arms with flowerhead terminals, restored. $4,700–5,300 *C*

A pair of pale blue painted armchairs, with upholstered backs and floral-painted top-rails, the arms with painted beads continuing to square tapered legs, c1790. $17,000–18,500 *Bon*

A mahogany armchair, the centre rail carved with gadroons, c1830. $720–800 *SPU*

A rosewood chair, with upholstered seat, on cabriole legs, c1860. $1,000–1,200 *GBr*

A William IV mahogany open elbow armchair, with upholstered seat. $950–1,100 *SPa*

A pair of American painted and gilded carver chairs, c1930. $1,100–1,200 *RPh*

A Regency bronzed and parcel-gilt bergère, with caned back, sides and seat, with squab cushion, on sabre legs headed by drapery and terminating in paw feet, restored.
$5,800–6,400 *C*

A Regency mahogany library armchair, with caned back, arms and seat, cushions upholstered in red hide, raised on turned legs with casters.
$5,000–5,600 *CAT*

A French carved mahogany framed library armchair, the arms terminating with lions' heads, c1850.
$3,200–4,000 *CAT*

A mahogany-framed armchair, upholstered in green, on turned legs and on casters, c1880.
$1,400–1,550 *RPh*

A pair of mahogany armchairs, with original oilcloth upholstery, the padded arms with turned spindle supports, c1860.
$1,600–1,800 *GBr*

A rosewood-framed slipper chair, with upholstered buttoned back, on carved cabriole legs terminating in casters, c1870.
$680–760 *RPh*

A pair of French Louis XVI style giltwood bergères, with arched foliate-carved and beaded frames, on square tapering legs, late 19thC.
$6,500–7,200 *C*

A George III style mahogany library bergère, the turned arm supports above turned tapering legs, on brass casters, c1900.
$4,000–4,500 *S*

A leather open armchair, with leaf-carved frame, the back, arms and seat covered in red hide and raised on fluted turned supports, c1920.
$720–800 *RPh*

A pair of red walnut dining chairs, with cabriole legs, c1720.
$5,600–6,400 *SPU*

A set of 4 George III mahogany dining chairs, the top-rails with brass inlay, turned tapering front legs, c1810.
$2,250–2,500 *ChS*

A set of 8 mahogany dining chairs, c1810.
$16,000–17,500 *CAT*

A set of 6 Flemish carved rosewood dining chairs, c1830.
$7,200–8,000 *BERA*

A set of 4 *faux* rosewood dining chairs, c1835.
$2,000–2,250 *ChS*

A set of 6 Victorian Cuban mahogany dining chairs, with hide seats, carved backs, on cabriole front legs.
$6,000–7,000 *LCA*

A Victorian walnut dining chair, c1850.
$240–300 *SPU*

A set of 6 rosewood dining chairs, c1850.
$4,200–4,700 *ChS*

A set of 6 mahogany dining chairs, c1860.
$3,200–3,500 *ChS*

A pair of rosewood dining chairs, c1870.
$720–800 *RPh*

A set of 4 Victorian satinwood chairs, with boxwood inlay.
$1,700–1,900 *ChS*

A set of 10 mahogany Sheraton style dining chairs, including 2 carvers, by Morrison & Co, Edinburgh, late 19thC.
$5,000–5,800 *P(Sc)*

A set of 10 mahogany Chippendale style dining chairs, c1900.
$15,200–16,800 *GAZE*

A set of 6 Edwardian dining chairs, with gilt highlighting, c1905.
$3,500–4,000 *RPh*

A walnut crossbanded bachelor's chest, with one long and 4 short drawers, the sides with carrying handles, c1710, 35⅜in (91cm) wide.
$12,000–13,500 S

A walnut chest of drawers, 18thC, 37in (94cm) wide.
$4,000–4,500 MIC

A burr walnut crossbanded chest of drawers, with slide and 4 drawers, on bracket feet, restored, c1720, 30¼in (77cm) wide.
$15,000–17,500 S

A walnut chest, top inlaid with chequer stringing, c1740, 30¼in (77cm) wide.
$4,800–5,400 Bon

A burr walnut chest of drawers, the quarter-veneered moulded top above a later mahogany slide, restored, c1720, 29¼in (74cm) wide.
$20,000–22,500 S

A George II walnut cross-banded chest of drawers, inlaid with stringing, 33½in (85cm) wide.
$7,000–8,000 C

A George II figured-walnut writing chest, with hinged top and 2 later candle slides, on shaped bracket feet, restored, 36½in (92.5cm) wide.
$58,000–64,000 C

An early Louis XV kingwood and tulipwood commode, by Pierre Roussel, with bombé front, 57in (145cm) wide.
$23,000–25,500 Bon

A mahogany demi-lune commode, the top crossbanded with satinwood, c1770, 48in (122cm) wide.
$25,500–28,500 B&L

A George III mahogany serpentine-fronted commode, on ogee bracket feet, with later brass handles, 44in (112cm) wide.
$6,000–6,500 CAG

A George III mahogany serpentine dressing commode, with green baize-lined writing slide concealing a fitted interior, on shaped bracket feet, 47in (119.5cm) wide.
$18,500–20,000 C

A mahogany bachelor's chest, with crossbanded top over a brushing slide, and 4 graduated long drawers, 18thC, 36in (91.5cm) wide.
$2,200–2,600 RBB

An Italian marquetry rosewood commode, the top inlaid with fan segments and central decorative panel, late 18thC, 49in (124.5cm) wide.
$20,000–22,500 P

A mahogany clothes press, the panelled doors enclosing an arrangement of trays and drawers, c1760, 41in (104cm) wide. **$3,800–4,200** *S*

A George III mahogany clothes press, the panelled doors enclosing 5 oak slides, 56in (142cm) wide. **$12,000–13,500** *C*

A German black and gilt-japanned walnut armoire, the panelled doors enclosing 3 shelves, on paw feet, 18thC, 59½in (151cm) wide. **$4,500–5,500** *C*

A George III mahogany clothes press, with a pair of doors enclosing 4 trays, 47in (119.5cm) wide. **$7,500–8,000** *C*

A mahogany and cross-banded linen press, on bracket feet, c1800, 48½in (123cm) wide. **$4,200–4,600** *Bon*

A mahogany linen press, with panelled doors, c1880, 53in (134.5cm) wide. **$3,400–4,000** *RPh*

A French carved oak cupboard, c1890, 55in (139.5cm) wide. **$950–1,300** *GWA*

A Breton fruitwood armoire, 19thC, back feet replaced, 36in (91.5cm) wide. **$2,800–3,200** *C*

A burr walnut davenport, with galleried top, and a pen and ink drawer, c1835, 21in (53.5cm) wide. **$9,000–10,400** *S*

A Regency brass-inlaid calamander davenport, with pierced brass gallery, restored, 14½in (37cm) wide. **$8,500–9,000** *C*

A George III mahogany partners' pedestal desk, the boxwood strung top with leather-inset, 6 frieze drawers, 3 drawers opposing panelled cupboard doors, c1800, 59in (150cm) wide. **$5,600–6,200** *Bon*

A rosewood and satinwood harlequin davenport, c1850, 24in (61cm) wide. **$8,000–9,000** *BERA*

A Georgian mahogany kneehole desk, with an arrangement of 8 drawers around the kneehole cupboard, on ogee bracket feet, c1760, 31½in (80cm) wide. **$4,000–4,500** *PSA*

A mahogany pedestal desk, by Gillows, with 2 frieze drawers opposing 3 false drawers and a slide, c1840, 60in (152.5cm) wide. **$8,000–8,800** *Bon*

A George III mahogany pedestal desk, with 3 frieze drawers each side, the kneehole flanked by 4 drawers and 2 doors to the reverse, on a moulded plinth and later bracket feet, restored, 62¾in (159.5cm) wide. **$7,500–8,500** *C*

A Victorian walnut kidney-shaped desk, with 2 short drawers and panelled cupboard to one side, the other with 3 short drawers, 48in (122cm) wide. **$14,400–16,000** *DN*

A mahogany partners' pedestal desk, the moulded leather-lined top above an arrangement of 18 opposing drawers, on a pair of moulded plinths, early 19thC, 60in (152cm) wide. **$8,500–9,000** *S*

A mahogany partners' pedestal desk, the moulded leather-inset top above an arrangement of 18 opposing drawers, on a pair of moulded plinths, 19thC, 59½in (151cm) wide. **$14,000–16,000** *S*

A Queen Anne walnut looking glass, c1710, 37½in (95cm) high.
$10,000–11,200 *S*

A George I gilt gesso looking glass, c1720, 39in (100cm) high.
$7,000–7,500 *S*

A Régence giltwood mirror, the crest with acanthus-carved cartouche, c1725, 72in (183cm) high.
$7,000–8,000 *Bon*

A walnut and parcel-gilt looking glass, the moulded frame with swan neck cresting, c1730, 52in (132cm) high.
$9,000–10,000 *S*

A George II carved giltwood looking glass, c1755, 55⅛in (141cm) high.
$4,800–5,200 *S*

A George III giltwood mirror, restored, c1765, 55in (140cm) high.
$6,000–6,500 *Bon*

A George III giltwood mirror, the later plate in gadrooned border, possibly altered, 48½in (123cm) high.
$4,800–5,200 *C*

A Federal inlaid and figured mahogany wall mirror, with polychrome-decorated *églomisé* panel and parcel-gilt decoration, New York, minor repairs, c1795, 55in(140cm) high.
$10,500–11,500 *S(NY)*

A giltwood, gesso and porcelain mirror, c1840, 77in (195cm) high.
$10,200–12,000 *S*

A gilt, composition and porcelain wall mirror, c1860, 52in (132cm) high.
$5,600–6,500 *S*

A Louis XVI carved and gilded mirror, the pierced crest surmounted by garlands of leaves and berries, 114in (291cm) high.
$6,500–8,000 *C*

l. A Venetian rococo style polychrome and etched glass mirror, replacements, late 19thC, 68in (173cm) high.
$9,000–10,400 *S(NY)*

A George III style mirror, with divided plate within shaped frame, late 19thC, 84in (213cm) high.
$5,600–6,500 *C*

A mahogany serpentine sideboard, the crossbanded top above a central frieze drawer, a cellaret drawer and 2 short drawers, c1780, 78½in (199.5cm) wide.
$9,500–11,200 *Bon*

An inlaid mahogany bowfronted sideboard, on tapered legs, c1790, 54in (137cm) wide.
$14,000–15,200 *S*

A George III mahogany serpentine-fronted sideboard, crossbanded and inlaid with boxwood and ebonised lines, the arch with fan spandrels, restored, 71⅛in (181.5cm) wide.
$12,000–13,500 *C*

A mahogany serpentine-fronted sideboard, the top fitted with a later brass rail with urn finials, inlaid throughout with boxwood stringing, on square tapered legs, c1790, 72in (183cm) wide.
$14,500–16,500 *S*

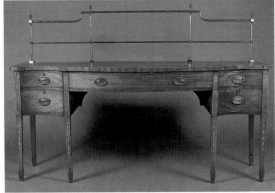

A Scottish George III mahogany serpentine-fronted sideboard, inlaid with chequer and boxwood lines, with brass superstructure, 84½in (214.5cm) wide.
$8,000–8,700 *C(S)*

A Federal figured mahogany sideboard, the D-shaped top with chequer inlay and fluted edge, Massachusetts, c1810, 60in (152.5cm) wide.
$9,500–10,500 *S(NY)*

A Scottish Regency mahogany breakfront sideboard, with quadrant ends, boxwood stringing and later inlaid urn panels, on 6 square tapering legs, 71¾in (182cm) wide.
$5,400–6,200 *P(Sc)*

An Edwardian Adam style mahogany sideboard, decorated with satinwood inlay and marquetry panels, with carved open balustrade, the glazed cabinet enclosing 2 shelves, 75¼in (191cm) wide.
$14,500–16,000 *P(Sc)*

Bureau Cabinets

A Venetian painted and silvered bureau cabinet, decorated overall with C-scrolls, foliate cartouches and sprays of flowers, the 2 cartouche-shaped doors enclosing a shelf, above a fall-front with 2 short drawers, 2 long drawers, on scrolling foliate feet, redecorated, mid-18thC, 45in (114.5cm) wide.
$11,200–12,800 *C*

A mahogany bureau cabinet, the moulded panelled doors with candle slides below, enclosing a fitted interior above 4 drawers, on bracket feet, c1750, 40¼in (102cm) wide.
$5,000–6,000 *S*

A Dutch walnut and oyster-veneered bureau cabinet, with fitted interior with drawers, on bun feet, 18thC and later adapted, 34in (86.5cm) wide.
$2,000–2,400 *CSK*

l. A Georgian mahogany bureau cabinet, with panelled doors enclosing adjustable shelves, the fall-front revealing numerous pigeonholes and small drawers, below 4 long graduated drawers, on bracket feet, 39in (99cm) wide.
$6,400–7,000 *RBB*

A south German ivory-inlaid walnut, marquetry and parquetry bureau cabinet, the central door with strapwork and engraved figure of a putto, the interior with 2 long and 6 short drawers, flanked by 2 rows of 6 drawers, the sides banded with satinwood, above a writing slope, enclosing a fitted interior, with later bracket feet, the cornice partially replaced and previously shaped, the top section with later back, minor losses, mid-18thC, restored in the 19thC with later ivory inlay, 45½in (115.5cm) wide.
$8,800–9,600 *C*

A Biedermeier mahogany cylinder bureau cabinet, the central bowed cupboard door flanked by column pilasters and serpentine doors, the cylinder enclosing a writing slide with wells and an arrangement of drawers and cupboards above 3 long drawers with flanking acanthus-carved scrolls, on reeded bracket feet, c1830, 51¾in (131.5cm) wide.
$4,800–5,000 *Bon*

r. A Dutch walnut bureau cabinet, the 2 arched panelled doors enclosing a fitted interior, the *bombé* base fitted with a fall-flap enclosing a well and a fitted interior, on claw-and-ball feet, 19thC, 49¼in (125cm) wide.
$5,800–6,400 *P(Sc)*

> **Cross Reference**
> Colour Review

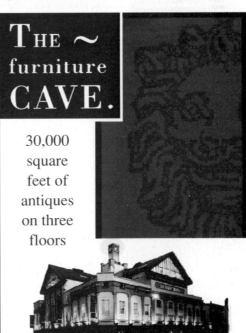

Cabinets-on-Stands

A Victorian Oriental style red painted and gilt-lined cabinet-on-stand, the doors painted with floral sprays and parrots enclosing a fitted interior, on a floral painted stand fitted with a drawer, on square section floral painted legs, joined by an X-shaped stretcher, 16¼in (41cm) wide.
$1,300–1,400 *P(Sc)*

A pair of Chinese export black and gilt-lacquer cabinets-on-stands, the doors enclosing a fitted interior, the stand with pierced apron, on a stand with on square chamfered legs with pierced arched brackets and joined by a pierced C-scroll X-shaped stretcher, later top to both stands, late 18thC, 14in (36cm) wide.
$6,000–7,200 *C*

A William and Mary black-japanned cabinet-on-stand, decorated with raised japanning depicting a landscape setting, a pair of doors enclosing a plain interior with an arrangement of 10 various drawers, on a carved giltwood stand with a pierced apron composed of scrolling acanthus leaves, flowers and strapwork, centred by Hercules, between 2 putti, the corners headed by further putti, the sides centred with a shell, on scrolled cabriole legs with trailing leaves, regilt, traces of original silvering, the cabinet re-mounted and re-japanned on a veneered surface, 43½in (110.5cm) wide.
$6,000–7,200 *C*

A Spanish ebonised and *verre églomisé vargueño*, with a central architectural door flanked by a bank of 10 drawers, on turned feet, 19thC, the associated stand with pierced frieze, on square tapering legs with spade feet, 28½in (72.5cm) wide.
$3,200–3,500 *CSK*

MILLER'S COMPARES . . .

I An Italian walnut and burr walnut cabinet-on-stand, the frieze drawers with supportive putti and a central cartouche, with a fall-front enclosing a central cupboard, flanked by a pair of drawers and cupboards with a long drawer below with flanking pilasters carved with figures, the associated later stand with barley-twist legs and bun feet, 17thC, 26in (66cm) wide.
$3,600–4,400 *Bon*

II An Italian walnut and burr walnut cabinet-on-stand, the frieze drawers with supportive putti and a central armorial cartouche, above a central recessed cupboard door, carved with a niche and an arrangement of drawers with flanking pilasters carved with figures, the associated later stand with barley-twist legs and bun feet, 17thC, 25¼in (64cm) wide.
$2,400–2,800 *Bon*

These 2 cabinets came from the same source. When they sold, however, there was a $1,600 difference in the prices they achieved. This was due to the fact that *item II* was lacking its fall-front, although in other respects it was in similar condition to *item I*. This example shows very clearly how a factor such as this can affect the value of a piece. *Bon*

r. A Dutch ebonised line-inlaid walnut cabinet-on-stand, the doors enclosing shelves and 4 short drawers, the stand with one long frieze drawer, on spiral-turned legs joined by flattened stretchers, 19thC, 66in (167.5cm) wide.
$2,800–3,200 *CSK*

Cabinets-on-Stands

Late 17thC and 18thC cabinets-on-stands were often opulent display pieces exhibiting the finest skills of cabinet making and decoration.
 As they are not the most practical of pieces, cabinets have sometimes had their fitted interiors removed to convert them into drinks cabinets.
 Legs, being of fragile construction, are quite often replaced. Look for colour differences and signs of artificial distressing on the vulnerable surfaces, and for appropriate wear to the feet.

Corner Cabinets

A George III mahogany standing corner cupboard, the painted interior with serpentine-fronted shelves and a hinged flap, the doors with later stringing, the base with a shelf enclosed by a pair of panel doors, also with later stringing, on ogee bracket feet, 42½in (108cm) wide.
$2,800–3,200 *WW*

A George III mahogany bowfront corner cabinet, the Gothic lancet headed glazed doors opening to reveal an interior of 3 shelves, the lower part with central slide above one real and 2 false drawers, with 2 lower oval flame-veneered doors, opening to reveal a single shelf, 37¾in (96cm) wide.
$6,400–7,200 *P(NW)*

A George III oak and mahogany crossbanded corner cabinet, the scrolled pediment above a moulded cornice fitted with a pair of panelled cupboard doors, the base fitted with a further pair of panelled cupboard doors, on a moulded plinth, with bracket feet, 42in (106.5cm) wide.
$3,200–3,500 *C(S)*

r. A mahogany corner cupboard, the line-inlaid arched pediment above an astragal glazed door enclosing 3 shaped shelves, fitted with a drawer above a panelled door, early 19thC, 31in (78.5cm) wide.
$1,700–2,000 *CSK*

FURTHER READING
Miller's Furniture Antiques Checklist
Miller's Publications, 1991

A Victorian ebonised and boulle ormolu-mounted corner cabinet, the shaped top above a foliate inlaid frieze and a similar glazed door enclosing a shelf flanked by fluted angles, on a shaped base, 31in (79cm) wide.
$1,600–1,900 *P(Sc)*

A mahogany bowfront corner cabinet, with a moulded cornice and enclosed by a pair of panelled doors, on later bracket feet, 19thC, 30in (76cm) wide.
$1,000–1,100 *CSK*

A late Victorian mahogany corner cabinet, with a pair of glazed panelled doors enclosing lined shelves, flanked by canted corners, decorated with fielding and acanthus carved scrolls, raised on cabriole legs with claw-and-ball feet and subsidiary bracket supports, 37½in (95.5cm) wide.
$680–720 *AG*

A late Victorian Gothic carved oak corner cupboard-on-stand, fitted with a panelled cupboard door applied with stylised flowerheads, arches and floral cruciform motifs, enclosing 3 fitted pine shelves, on square supports and block toes joined by a shaped-triangular undertier, 33in (84cm) wide.
$1,000–1,100 *C(S)*

An ebonised brass-inlaid and scarlet-tortoiseshell bowfront corner cabinet, applied with gilt-metal mounts, the marble top above a foliate frieze and panelled door decorated with scrolling arabesques, on shaped plinth base centred with a grotesque mask, the panelled door partly distressed, late 19thC, 36in (91.5cm) wide.
$1,500–1,600 *CSK*

A satinwood and kingwood crossbanded corner cabinet, the boxwood and ebony strung top above a boxwood inlaid fluted frieze, over glazed cupboard doors, enclosing a shelf, on toupie feet, late 19thC, 35½in (90.5cm) wide.
$2,800–3,500 *P(Sc)*

l. An Edwardian mahogany serpentine corner display cabinet, the fretwork dentil cornice above twin-glazed astragal doors, revealing twin-shaped fitted shelves, the cupboard base with panelled doors, on shaped ogee bracket feet, 75½in (192cm) high.
$2,200–2,500 *BWe*

Cross Reference
Colour Review

Display Cabinets

A George I kingwood miniature or picture cabinet, with a pair of panelled doors enclosing a green velvet-lined interior with miniature hooks, losses to veneer, 26½in (67cm) wide.
$11,200–12,800 *C*

This cabinet was almost certainly supplied to Sir Andrew Fountaine (d.1753) for his London home.

A Victorian figured-walnut display cabinet, with ebonised mouldings, boxwood marquetry inlay and ormolu beading and mounts, enclosed by a single glazed door, on turned bun feet, 29in (74cm) wide.
$1,200–1,300 *JM*

A Victorian mahogany display cabinet, the grey marble top above a moulded cornice and plain frieze, with a pair of glazed doors below flanked by foliate scrolling corbels, on a plinth base, 32½in (82.5cm) wide.
$580–680 *CSK*

A Victorian figured-walnut and floral marquetry display cabinet, with gilt-brass mouldings and mask pattern mounts, the front inlaid with leaf and floral sprays, 2 fitted velvet-covered shelves enclosed by single door with shaped glazed panel, 33in (84cm) wide.
$2,400–2,800 *CAG*

A mahogany display cabinet, the dentil-moulded cornice above a blind fret-carved frieze, with a pair of astragal doors below, enclosing 4 adjustable shelves, the stand with a fluted frieze, on cabriole legs with claw feet, 19thC, 50in (127cm) wide.
$2,000–2,200 *CSK*

A Victorian walnut pier cabinet, 48in (122cm) high.
$800–880 *GAZE*

A late Victorian mahogany display cabinet, the moulded serpentine top above a frieze drawer and an open cupboard, flanked on either side by a glazed door, on acanthus-carved cabriole supports and scrolled toes, joined by a shaped serpentine undertier, 54in (137cm) wide.
$1,200–1,600 *C(S)*

A French mahogany and gilt-metal mounted corner display cabinet, the pierced gallery top above a glazed panel door enclosing velvet-lined shelves with Vernis Martin style panels of lovers in a landscape, on shaped legs, 19thC, 34in (86cm) wide.
$2,500–3,200 *P(Sc)*

A walnut and inlaid display cabinet, the bevelled astragal doors enclosing lined shaped shelves and a mirror back, the doors with lower fielded panels incorporating roundels, on bun feet, c1890, 47in (120cm) wide.
$1,500–1,800 *S(S)*

A Victorian ebonised and gilt-decorated cabinet, with canted corners and glazed door, fluted side columns and turned feet, 47in (119.5cm) high.
$640–760 *SAF*

An inlaid mahogany cabinet, with leaded glass door, c1890, 25¼in (64cm) wide.
$950–1,100 *GBr*

A late Victorian mahogany and satinwood inlaid display cabinet, with a pair of glazed doors, the breakfront base with a pair of panelled doors, flanked by similar bowed panels, stamped 'Edwards and Roberts', 58in (147.5cm) wide.
$17,600–19,200 *C(S)*

This piece was in excellent condition with fine quality inlay made by a respected manufacturer.

A late Victorian gilt-metal mounted and marquetry breakfront display cabinet with 3 glazed doors and plinth with bracket feet, 60in (153cm) wide.
$2,400–2,800 *CSK*

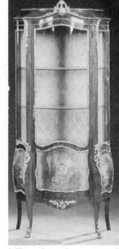

A French mahogany and Vernis Martin vitrine, on cabriole legs, c1890, 31½in (80cm) wide.
$6,400–7,200 *S*

A satinwood mahogany and inlaid vitrine, the chequer-banded cornice above a harebell and ribbon-decorated frieze, with central mirrored recess above a pair of panelled doors flanked by 2 astragal glazed doors enclosing glass shelves, on foliate-lappeted turned supports joined by a serpentine undertier, on turned feet, late 19thC, 61in (155cm) wide.
$3,500–4,000 *CSK*

An Edwardian mahogany display cabinet, the moulded cornice above astragal-glazed doors centred by foliate-carved oval panels, the shelved base on pad supports, 48¾in (124cm) wide.
$2,400–2,700 *Bri*

l. An Edwardian mahogany, satinwood-banded and inlaid display cabinet, the astragal glazed door enclosing 2 shelves, the lower section with projecting top over tablet frieze and twin panel inlaid doors, on square tapering legs with spade feet, 32in (81cm) wide.
$6,200–7,200 *P(Sc)*

An Italian carved giltwood vitrine, with a glazed door and canted sides, the velvet-lined interior with carved gilt supports to the shelves, scroll and foliate borders with a shell and foliate crest and foliate scroll feet, late 19thC, 24¼in (61.5cm) wide.
$5,000–6,000 *DN*

An Edwardian mahogany display cabinet, decorated with inlaid satinwood crossbanding and boxwood stringing, the small raised back above a glazed panel door decorated with ribbon motifs and concave glazed panel sides enclosing lined shelves, the corners with open shelves and decorated with turned and inlaid pilaster supports, on splay feet, 44½in (113cm) high.
$2,700–3,200 *AG*

An Edwardian mahogany display cabinet, with satinwood crossbanding fitted glazed door with tracery centred by an urn marquetry plaque, flanked by concave glazed sides, the shelved base on squared tapering legs, 49in (124.5cm) wide.
$3,500–4,000 *RBB*

An Edwardian mahogany display cabinet, with boxwood stringing and satinwood crossbanding, the astragal glazed doors enclosing 3 velvet-lined shelves, above 2 short drawers, on 4 square section tapering legs with spade feet, 41¾in (106cm) wide.
$1,200–1,300 *P(Sc)*

l. An Edwardian mahogany line-inlaid display cabinet, with moulded cornice above a scroll-decorated frieze and central astragal glazed door enclosing 2 shaped shelves, on square legs and spade feet, 42in (106.5cm) wide.
$1,700–1,900 *CSK*

An Edwardian mahogany display cabinet, with satinwood marquetry medallion and stringing, bowfront glass-panelled door, glass side and end panels, squared tapering supports, 46in (117cm) wide.
$2,500–2,800 *RBB*

A George II style carved mahogany display cabinet, the pierced latticework cornice above a blind arcaded frieze and astragal door incorporating ribbon ties, a pair of doors below with applied foliate mouldings above a shaped apron with short cabriole legs ending in claw-and-ball feet, reverse bearing incised marks and ivorine label, 'C. Baker', one astragal panel lacking, one bowed glazed panel cracked, splits to carcase, early 20thC, 65¾in (167cm) wide.
$8,300–9,000 *S(S)*

Secretaire Cabinets

A William and Mary walnut and burr walnut escritoire, the cushion frieze fitted with a drawer, the fall-front opening to an arrangement of drawers and compartments and fitted with a leather inset, the chest with 2 short and 2 long drawers, on later shaped bracket feet, 42in (107cm) wide.
$10,800–11,800 *S*

A walnut secretaire cabinet with an arrangement of pigeonholes, small drawers, a central cupboard and concealed drawers, enclosed by 2 doors, the base with a fitted drawer above 2 long drawers veneered in ash, crossbanded and herringbone strung, engraved brass handles and hinges, on bun feet, alterations, the top and base associated, early 18thC, 45in (114cm) wide.
$4,400–4,800 *DN*

A walnut secretaire, the upper part with moulded cornice and moulded cushion-fronted frieze drawer, the fall-front inlaid with quarter-veneered panel, stringings and bandings and crossbanded, enclosing fitted interior with pigeonholes, central cupboard and 11 small drawers, on base with 2 short and 2 long drawers, on later bracket feet, possibly associated and with later cross-grained mouldings and feet, early 18thC, 41in (104cm) wide.
$4,400–5,000 *CAG*

A walnut escritoire, with a cushion-moulded frieze drawer, the featherbanded fall-front enclosing a fitted interior with pigeonholes and drawers around a central drawer, 2 hidden secret compartments and hinged writing slope, fitted with 4 drawers on later turned bun feet, early 18thC, 45in (114cm) wide.
$6,400–7,000 *CSK*

A George III mahogany secretaire cabinet, the later detachable lattice-work superstructure with an open tier and Vitruvian scroll gallery, the fitted writing drawer above 2 short and 2 long drawers, on later shaped bracket feet, restorations, 25½in (65cm) wide.
$4,000–4,800 *S(S)*

l. A Continental burr walnut *secrétaire à abattant*, the frieze drawer and quarter veneered feather-banded fall-front opening to reveal a fitted interior with drawers, above 3 feather-banded long drawers, standing on later turned feet, late 18thC, 38½in (98cm) wide.
$1,600–1,900 *B&L*

A mid-Georgian walnut and herringbone-banded secretaire cabinet, fitted with a pair of arched bevelled mirrored doors, enclosing an interior fitted with 11 variously sized drawers, the base fitted with 2 candle slides, above a sliding secretaire drawer, restorations, 42in (107cm) wide.
$13,800–15,200 *C(S)*

A French brass-bound mahogany *secrétaire à abattant*, the frieze drawer above a panelled fall-front enclosing a writing surface, short drawers and pigeonholes, with 2 panel doors below flanked by fluted stiles, on turned feet, some brass fitments detached, early 19thC, 36in (91.5cm) wide.
$2,800–3,000 *CSK*

A walnut and rosewood escritoire, veneered on an oak carcase, the moulded rounded cornice with a drawer, the fall-front with satinwood border and writing surface, with mirror back and drawer inlaid with boxwood stringing, latticed base, wrythen solid rosewood columns and 6 small drawers and 3 long drawers, on squat turned feet, early 19thC, 38½in (98cm) wide.
$4,200–4,800 *DN*

A Regency brass-mounted rosewood secretaire cabinet, decorated overall with spirally-twisted lines, the lower section with a fitted sectraire drawer and writing surface, above a pair of mahogany-panelled doors, the mahogany panels later, originally with pleated material panels to top and bottom section, 36¾in (93cm) wide.
$7,600–8,200 *C*

A Regency mahogany secretaire cabinet, with line-inlaid panelled doors, above a twin dummy drawer fall-front enclosing a fitted interior of drawers and pigeonholes around a central cupboard, with 3 further drawers below, on bracket feet, 45in (114cm) wide.
$2,400–2,600 *CSK*

A Dutch marquetry inlaid mahogany *secrétaire à abbatant*, the stepped top above a long frieze drawer and a fall enclosing a central cupboard flanked by drawers and pigeonholes with a pair of cupboard doors below, inlaid overall with flower-filled urns and foliate sprays, on turned bun feet, c1830, 39⅜in (101cm) wide.
$6,400–7,000 *Bon*

A Dutch marquetry *secrétaire à abattant*, with frieze drawer and counter-balanced fall-front enclosing 6 drawers and a shelf, above a pair of doors, on sharply tapering square section feet, 19thC, 37¾in (96cm) wide.
$4,200–4,800 *P(Sc)*

A Russian mahogany secretaire, with marble top, inlaid with pale wood and brass, a single frieze drawer above leather inset fall-front, with fitted interior, 3 long drawers under enclosed by a pair of doors, turned front brass feet, 19thC, 41in (104cm) wide.
$26,400–29,600 *E*

The price which this piece achieved reflects the trend of the past few years where items in exceptional condition attract eager bidding in the salerooms.

r. A Transitional style marquetry-inlaid *secrétaire à abattant*, the serpentine marble top above a conforming front with a bombé fall enclosing 4 short drawers with 3 further drawers beneath, on short outsplayed legs with gilt-metal sabots, inlaid overall with foliate scrolls, c1880, 26½in (67.5cm) wide.
$2,000–2,400 *Bon*

l. A French ormolu-mounted kingwood and foliate marquetry *secrétaire à abattant*, with marble top above a drawer with hinged drop-flap, with fitted interior, above 4 long drawers, on shaped legs with foliate-cast sabots, c1900, 35¼in (89.5cm) wide.
$5,800–6,400 *C*

Side Cabinets

A George III mahogany serpentine-fronted side cabinet, the moulded top including a green leather-inset writing slide above a pair of crossbanded doors enclosing an adjustable shelf on a plinth base, splits to doors, 30¾in (78cm) wide.
$8,000–8,800 *S(S)*

A mahogany chiffonier, the upper part with 2 graduated shelves on slender turned spindle supports, the rectangular surface enclosing a pair of cockbeaded frieze drawers above a pair of doors opening to reveal a single adjustable shelf, on short turned feet, early 19thC, 30in (76cm) wide.
$3,800–4,200 *P(NW)*

A satinwood secretaire chiffonier, with dummy drawer concealing secretaire and 2 doors with 5 long drawers within, early 19thC, 38in (96.5cm) wide.
$22,000–24,000 *SPU*

l. A Dutch marquetry side cabinet, with floral/leafage panels and borders, with fitted frieze drawer and a pair of doors flanked by 2 pairs of pilasters with gilt-metal mounts and later marble top, early 19thC, 36in (91.5cm) wide.
$2,400–2,800 *RBB*

A George IV rosewood display cabinet, c1825, 42in (107cm) wide.
$5,200–6,200 *RPh*

Side Cabinet Conversions

Many side cabinets started life with wooden panels to the doors and have subsequently been replaced with glass, brass grilles or pleated silk to give a less solid appearance. Provided the conversion has been skilfully carried out it should not adversely affect the appearance of the piece and may well enhance it.

A mid-Victorian ebonised credenza, with satinwood floral marquetry panels, ormolu figurative mounts and leaf-cast banding, the central shelved cupboard enclosed by a glazed door, flanked by bowed side display cupboards enclosed by glazed doors, on turned bun feet, 71½in (181.5cm) wide.
$3,500–4,000 *TMA*

A Victorian mahogany chiffonier, the raised panel back with scrolled crest and shelf on turned and reeded supports, carved frieze drawer over 2 panelled cupboard doors, flanked by square pilasters, 34in (86cm) wide.
$1,900–2,200 *AH*

An early Victorian goncalo alves chiffonier, with raised panelled back and shelf with turned supports, a bolection moulded frieze drawer, above 2 doors with bevelled mirrors, 36in (91.5cm) wide.
$1,100–1,200 *DN*

Goncalo alves is a Brazilian timber sometimes mistaken for rosewood.

A pair of Victorian mahogany side cabinets, each with a cushion-moulded frieze above a bank of 4 drawers, flanked by 2 panelled doors enclosing sliding trays, on ogee bracket feet, some mouldings and 2 feet missing, 72in (183cm) wide.
$2,700–3,200 *C*

A rosewood chiffonier, the arched mirrored-back with shelf on scrolled supports, single carved frieze drawer, on leaf-carved scrolled supports, shaped undershelf and turned feet, 19thC, 44in (112cm) wide.
$3,800–4,400 *AH*

A Victorian walnut marquetry inlaid and gilt-metal-mounted side cabinet, the shaped frieze inlaid with scrolling foliage, a hinged glazed door below, enclosing a velvet-lined interior fitted with 2 shelves, 32¼in (82cm) wide.
$1,300–1,400 *C(Sc)*

r. An Edwardian satinwood, ebony-lined and inlaid bowfront side cabinet, the twin doors enclosing shelf and centred with oval panels, each inlaid with stained and specimen woods depicting 'Diana' and 'Actaeon', detailed in penwork, on outswept bracket feet, 35½in (90.5cm) wide.
$3,000–3,300 *P(Sc)*

A late Victorian mahogany-veneered chiffonier, 41in (104cm) wide.
$400–480 *GWA*

A late Victorian mahogany chiffonier, c1900, 37in (94cm) wide.
$1,800–2,000 *RPh*

Canterburies

A mahogany music canterbury, the 4 divisions with slender ring-turned columns and supports, above a drawer, on turned tapering legs with brass casters, early 19thC, 21in (53.5cm) wide.
$2,200–2,400 *DN*

A George III mahogany canterbury, the 3 concave divisions with shaped splat supports above 2 graduated drawers, on ring-turned feet with brass casters, c1810, 20in (51cm) wide.
$2,700–3,000 *S*

A Federal inlaid mahogany canterbury, the upper section with 5 slightly arched transverses, the centre divider fitted with a hand-hold, a single drawer below, on square tapering legs ending in brass caps, c1810, 17½in (44.5cm) wide.
$1,400–1,600 *S(NY)*

A Regency rosewood canterbury, with 4 slatted divisions, baluster-turned corner supports, a drawer below, on toupie feet with brass casters, 21¼in (54cm) wide.
$2,400–2,600 *Bea(E)*

A William IV rosewood music canterbury, the curved divisions with a central handle, the mahogany-lined frieze drawer with turned knob handles, the turned ribbed legs on brass casters, 21½in (55cm) wide.
$3,800–4,400 *WW*

A William IV rosewood three-division canterbury, with turned supports and button finials, above a drawer, on turned legs with unusual gilt-brass collars and brass casters, 17¾in (45cm) wide.
$5,000–5,400 *S(S)*

A Victorian walnut three-division canterbury, with turned spindles and side columns, full width drawer with turned knobs, on original white porcelain casters, 24in (61cm) wide.
$740–800 *GH*

A Victorian walnut oval canterbury, the 3 folio sections with pierced carved supports and turned supports above a convex single frieze drawer and turned legs, 25in (63.5cm) wide.
$1,800–1,900 *Bon (C)*

l. A Victorian rosewood canterbury, the foliate-carved three-section magazine rack above a frieze drawer and turned tapered supports, fitted caps and casters, 20in (51cm) wide.
$1,500–1,800 *BWe*

A walnut canterbury with 3 divisions to the lower section, fretted sides, single drawer under, on turned, gadrooned and shaped legs, missing casters, 19thC, 37in (94cm) wide.
$2,200–2,600 *L&E*

Open Armchairs

A George II walnut open armchair, with pierced and interlaced splat and moulded supports, the arms with carved eagle head terminals, padded seat in needlework, on leaf-and-shell carved cabriole legs with claw-and-ball feet,
$1,900–2,200 *DN*

A George II walnut armchair, with carved and pierced vase-shaped splat, the drop-in seat flanked by scrolled arm supports, with leaf-carved knees and scroll brackets ending in claw-and-ball feet, c1745.
$4,000–4,500 *S*

A George III mahogany carver, the serpentine top-rail above pierced interlaced splat and scrolled outswept arms, with drop-in seat above square section chamfered legs with H-stretchers.
$480–550 *P(Sc)*

An early George III mahogany open armchair, the shaped moulded top-rail above a pierced splat and outscrolled arms with a drop-in seat, on chamfered square section legs tied by block stretchers, c1770.
$1,100–1,300 *Bon*

A George III mahogany open armchair, with a trellis splat, on slender turned and fluted legs headed by leaves and rosettes.
$1,400–1,600 *DN*

What's Inside a Chair?

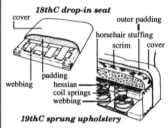

18thC drop-in seat

cover
outer padding
horsehair stuffing
scrim   cover
webbing
padding
hessian
coil springs
webbing

19thC sprung upholstery

Before c1830 the upholstery on chairs was made from thin layers of horsehair and padding supported by webbing covered with fabric. Upholstery using coiled metal springs covered with padding and webbing was made from c1830.

A George III mahogany shield-back carver, with stuffover seat on square section tapering legs and H-stretcher.
$320–360 *P(Sc)*

A French carved giltwood and upholstered chair, the carved and beaded frame with padded arms, on turned foliate and fluted legs, early 19thC.
$1,900–2,300 *B&L*

A mahogany elbow chair, the Gothic style back with pierced lattice and carved strapwork top-rail, the seat and arm pads upholstered in damask, raised on square section deeply carved blind fret style front legs, with pierced and carved corner brackets and stretchers, early 19thC.
$2,000–2,400 *P(NW)*

A pair of Regency mahogany elbow chairs, with carved and pierced horizontal splats. $1,400–1,600 *GAZE*

A Regency mahogany open armchair,the spoon-shaped back with shaped padded panel, reeded frame and scroll arms with oval paterae on reeded sabre legs and casters. $2,800–3,200 *DN*

A Regency open armchair, with carved decorated top-rail, 33in (84cm) high. $640–720 *ChS*

A Regency mahogany open armchair, with reeded frame and scroll arms, the centre rail carved with leaf scrolls, drop-in seat, sabre legs, and a matching side chair. $320–400 *DN*

A pair of early Victorian mahogany rail-back open armchairs, the centre rails carved with lotus leaves and rosettes, arms with scroll terminals and turned supports, padded seats and turned legs. $1,500–1,700 *DN*

A pair of George IV mahogany rail-back armchairs, the open arms with scroll supports above dralon overstuffed seats, on turned and reeded legs, one top-rail detached, c1820. $2,700–3,200 *S(S)*

A William IV mahogany elbow chair, with scroll arms and turned legs. $420–480 *HOLL*

A pair of early Victorian mahogany open elbow chairs, with rounded top-rails above a lower scroll rail, with outswept down-scrolled open arms, upholstered in woven horsehair, on turned and facetted tapering legs, with toupie feet, the underside of one bearing the label of 'W. Constantine & Co'. $1,300–1,500 *P(NW)*

A pair of Victorian carved walnut open armchairs, with a carved top-rail, the arms with moulded supports and cabriole legs, on ceramic casters, c1860. $3,400–4,200 *S(S)*

A Victorian gentleman's walnut parlour armchair, the back with buttoned squab above low scrolled open arms, on leaf-carved cabriole legs with scroll toes and casters.
$1,000–1,100 *P(Sc)*

A George III style carved walnut armchair, with a pierced vase-shaped back, scroll arms and drop-in seat, on cabriole legs ending in pointed pad feet, early 20thC.
$800–950 *S(S)*

An Edwardian Sheraton revival satinwood open armchair, painted with leaves, beads, drapery and patera, the oval back with a feather splat tied with a ribbon, caned seat and square tapering legs.
$1,100–1,300 *DN*

A Victorian walnut and gilt decorated open arm commode armchair, in the French style, the back with bold leaf-carved cresting, leaf-capped double scroll arms and with cane panelled seat and back, on cabriole front legs with leaf capped toes and casters.
$800–950 *CAG*

A pair of Louis XVI style beech fauteuils, upholstered in needlework, each with channelled frame, on paterae-headed stop-fluted tapering legs, late 19thC.
$1,300–1,600 *C*

l. An Edwardian painted satinwood elbow chair, the caned oval back with painted centre panel featuring a cherub with garland, caned seat and turned tapering front legs, the whole painted with trailing flowers.
$680–800 *AH*

A Victorian mahogany bobbin-turned armchair, the ratchet adjustable slat-back with turned finials, the tapering square legs joined by turned stretchers and ending in brass cappings and casters, front stretcher lacking, designed by Philip Webb, probably by Morris and Co, late 19thC.
$2,000–2,400 *S(S)*

The design of this chair is based on an 18th/early 19th century original seen in a Sussex workshop by Warington Taylor. He sketched this in a letter to the architect designer Philip Webb in 1866. Webb adapted this design with the addition of bobbin turning and William Morris's company, Morris, Marshall, Faulkner & Co, put the chair into production. A chintz-covered version retailed for $12.

A Carolean style armchair, c1920, with caned back and tapestry seat.
$430–480 *RPh*

Upholstered Armchairs

A Queen Anne walnut easy chair, the conical tapering arms centring bowfront seat, on cabriole legs joined by block and vase-turned stretchers ending in pad feet, patches to 3 feet, Boston, Massachusetts, c1740.
$5,600–6,400 *S(NY)*

For American furniture 'Queen Anne' refers to style rather than period.

A George I walnut wing armchair, the padded back, sides and scrolled arms above a squab cushion seat, on cabriole legs and pad feet.
$2,200–2,600 *CSK*

r. A mid-Georgian walnut wing armchair, with curved padded back, out-scrolled armrests and seat on cabriole supports and pad feet with brass barrel caps and casters.
$6,400–7,000 *C(Sc)*

Upholstered Armchairs

Armchairs in England enjoyed popularity in the Queen Anne and George I periods. French influence became apparent in the latter half of the 18thC, and can be seen in the basic form of the bergère – an armchair with upholstered sides. An 18thC overstuffed (thick upholstered) armchair can be difficult to distinguish from a 19thC reproduction without lifting the over-canvas and examining the construction. The wing chair appeared in the Queen Anne period, and subsequently showed little change.

A George II mahogany wing armchair, the upholstered back, seat and outward scrolling arms with a cotton slip, on club legs and pad feet.
$2,200–2,600 *P(Sc)*

A mahogany wing armchair, upholstered in floral crewel-work, on cabriole legs with pad feet, parts 18thC.
$1,900–2,200 *CSK*

A Chippendale mahogany easy chair frame, the serpentine crest with pointed ears flanked by ogival wings and outscrolled arms on square moulded legs joined by stretchers, requires upholstering, New England, c1805.
$4,800–5,300 *S(NY)*

A George IV armchair, covered in crimson velvet, the mahogany-faced U-shaped front carved with reeds, leaves and rosettes, on turned and reeded leaf-carved legs with gilt-brass caps and casters.
$2,200–2,600 *DN*

An early Victorian mahogany button-back upholstered armchair, the arms with carved lion heads, the channelled and scrolled frame raised on small lobed legs and casters.
$2,200–2,600 *Bon(C)*

A Victorian walnut-framed armchair, with padded arms on pierced and scrolled supports, on reeded turned tapering front legs with brass caps and casters.
$1,000–1,100 *AH*

A Victorian oak easy chair, the back with bold leaf-carved cresting and with turned, fluted and leaf-capped uprights, the arms with moulded scroll terminals and leaf-capped front supports, on turned lobed and carved front legs with casters, upholstered in cut moquette.
$800–850 *CAG*

A Victorian walnut armchair, the back with floral cresting above out-curved arms with scrolling terminals, on cabriole legs.
$750–880 *CSK*

A Louis XV style carved giltwood fauteuil, with giltwood frame carved in rococo style with pair of birds, leafage and C-scrolls, upholstered in petit-point, on slender supports, late 19thC.
$3,300–3,600 *RBB*

A mahogany tub armchair, with turned legs, original porcelain casters and legs stamped 'Trollope & Sons', c1870, 35in (89cm) high.
$1,600–2,000 *LCA*

A Victorian mahogany armchair, c1860.
$2,400–2,800 *BERA*

A Victorian iron frame chair, upholstered, c1880, 32in (81.5cm) high.
$1,200–1,350 *RPh*

l. A Victorian walnut and button upholstered low armchair, covered in patterned blue damask, the arms with turned supports, on turned legs ending in brass cappings and casters, casters stamped 'Cope & Collinson' and rear leg stamped '247 609', c1870.
$400–480 *S(S)*

A Victorian mahogany spoon-back armchair.
$750–800 *GAZE*

Bergère Chairs

A Louis XV walnut bergère, with cabriole legs, c1750.
$5,600–6,400 *FHA*

A pair of Regency mahogany bergères, with reeded frames and cane-filled backs and arms, baluster-turned supports and reeded sabre legs, one with a brass bracket to take a reading stand, both now with padded seats and cushions, repairs to the legs.
$10,000–11,000 *DN*

A pair of French Louis XVI style carved giltwood bergères, with an acanthus-carved frame, the arms terminating in spirally fluted and acanthus decorated balusters, c1870.
$6,500–7,500 *S*

r. A pair of late Victorian satinwood and floral-painted bergères, the seats with loose squab cushions, the downswept armrests on square tapering supports painted with graduated harebell chains.
$7,500–8,000 *C(S)*

l. A French Louis XVI style giltwood bergère, the scrolled arms on stop-fluted baluster supports, on turned fluted tapering legs headed by a rosette, losses to decoration, previously with casters, 19thC.
$1,600–1,900 *C*

MILLER'S COMPARES . . .

I A William IV mahogany and cane bergère, with carved scrolling arms, on reeded baluster legs with ceramic casters, c1830.
$2,200–2,600 *S(S)*

II A William IV mahogany and cane bergère, with carved scrolling arms, on turned tapering legs with stylised lotus leaf moulding, on brass cappings and casters, c1835.
$1,600–1,800 *S(S)*

When these two pieces were catalogued it was expected that *Item II* would fetch slightly more than *Item I*. The legs of *Item II* were considered to be more attractive in design than those of *Item I*, and even more so due to the brass cappings and casters, which are more of a 18th/early 19th century feature than the ceramic casters of *Item I*, usually associated with Victorian pieces. When the chairs were offered for sale, however, it was obviously their overall appearance which was the important factor and *Item I* fetched the higher price. *Item I* had more presence as a piece of furniture than *Item II* because of the rounder profile of the arms, the scrolling on the arm supports and top-rail, and its more elegant proportions, being larger and slightly higher than *Item II*. *S(S)*

A pair of Edwardian Sheraton revival satinwood and painted bergères, the crests decorated with putti, the frames with ebonised stringing, the turned supports to the arms and legs with leaves, drapery and pendant husks.
$6,400–7,000 *DN*

A mahogany bergère armchair, with a cane panelled back, sides and seat, on turned tapering legs, brass casters, early 20thC,
$520–560 *Gam*

Children's Chairs

The first seat furniture for children was developed from stools and benches in medieval times, with the earliest high chairs being Elizabethan. These rarely had a restraining bar at the front, no doubt because they were meant to be placed against the dinner table at meal times. In the seventeenth century, versions of oak nursing chairs were made for children's use with a hole being placed in the seat with a pewter or earthenware pot underneath. These were the early potty chairs, often with rockers.

Children's chairs subsequently followed the same styles as those for adults. Chippendale, Hepplewhite and Sheraton designs are seen in later chairs as well as some wonderful examples of the Windsor chair being developed for children in both high and low chair varieties. An eighteenth century Windsor high chair is basically a miniature version of an adult Windsor chair with lengthened legs and the addition of a footrest. The early nineteenth century brought about the correction chair, the invention of a surgeon called Astley Cooper – a typical example is shown on page 107. When seated at the table the upright back gave the child support, discouraging leaning forward.

Victorian children spent more time in the company of adults and their furniture developed accordingly with beautiful miniature versions of whole suites being produced. The two-part chair as shown (page 107) was a development of the high chair, the upper part being an elbow chair with a restraining bar and often a footrest, the lower part being a small table. The high chair could then be used as a table and chair when the upper and lower parts were detached. Later developments had sprung supports between the chair and table allowing a bouncing motion, and a hinged detachable dining tray. This type of chair was made well into the twentieth century with many features recognisable in high chairs of today.

Children's chairs can be split into two types – low and high chairs. A good quality child's low chair should not be an obvious miniaturised version of its adult counterpart. A quality child's chair would have been made by a top craftsman, as getting the proportions exact is an extremely difficult task. Children's versions of Windsor and other country chair types have become increasingly popular with collectors and doting grandparents. Prices for these are generally higher than their adult equivalent, whereas earlier town chair types tend to be considerably lower priced than fine adult versions.

Children's high chairs should be judged by how successfully the craftsman has heightened and adapted the piece while remaining sympathetic to the style of the period. Prices are also affected by the presence of footrests and restraining bars if originally fitted. Evidence of their attachment is usually present even if they have been lost.

Allan James

A child's oak bobbin-turned chair, dated '1602', 27in (69cm) high. **$2,200–2,600** *COM*

A child's oak chair, with carved panelled-back, c1670, 28in (71cm) high. **$1,100–1,300** *MIC*

A child's patinated pine rocking chair, early 18thC, 24in (61cm) high. **$600–680** *SPU*

A child's oak wainscot highchair, the rectangular back panel with a crowned rose flanked by tulips, on turned underframe, initialled 'I.E.' and dated '1691', restorations. **$3,000–4,000** *L*

r. A George III child's mahogany armchair, with serpentine crest, pierced splat and moulded shaped arms, drop-in seat and straight legs with X-stretcher on conforming stand, lacking the foot rest, damaged, 35in (89cm) high. **$640–720** *DN*

A child's fruitwood chair, 18thC, 28in (71cm) high. **$880–960** *SPU*

A Welsh child's oak chair, 18thC, 26in (66cm) high. **$1,100–1,200** *AEF*

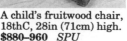

A child's maple slat-back armchair, needlepoint cushion, old refinish, minor height loss, New England, 18thC, 28in (71cm) high.
$480–550 *SK(B)*

A green-painted and turned cherrywood bow-back Windsor highchair, on splayed *faux* bamboo turned legs, repaired, New England, early 19thC.
$1,000–1,200 *S(NY)*

A child's chair, red and cream painted with green leather seat and back, designed by Gerrit Rietveld c1921, made by G. A. van de Groenekan c1938.
$22,000–24,000 *S*

Gerrit Rietveld's work is highly sought after today, and commands high prices.

A child's beech, ash and elm Windsor chair, early 19thC, 26in (66cm) high
$760–860 *SPU*

A child's elm and beech chair, c1930, 18in (46cm) high.
$50–65 *TAN*

A child's beech and elm chair, c1930, 20in (51cm) high.
$45–50 *AL*

l. A George III child's brass-inlaid mahogany chair-on-stand, the floral inlaid top-rail above a railed back and padded seat, on square section legs, the stand with boxwood strung square section legs, c1800, 55½in (141cm) high.
$1,200–1,400 *Bon*

A Regency mahogany deportment chair, with cane seat, 38in (96.5cm) high.
$640–720 *AAN*

A turned beech Phoenix Kinderstuhl high chair, with original transfer trademark, early 20thC, 48in (122cm) high.
$270–320 *AP*

A child's mahogany chair, base unscrews to form table, c1830, 35in (89cm) high.
$1,300–1,400 *ChS*

A child's potty chair, with rush seat, c1820, 20½in (52cm) high.
$550–630 *ChS*

A Victorian simulated rosewood correction chair, 48in (122cm) high.
$350–400 *GAZE*

l. A pair of French children's chairs, possibly fruitwood, c1950, 24in (61cm) high.
$100–115 *TAC*

Corner Chairs

A George I walnut corner chair, the curved moulded and shaped back with solid scroll-carved splat, the outset moulded arms with columnar supports and a shaped moulded seat-rail, on cabriole legs, the centre leg now carved with a shell and acanthus leaf, c1720.
$24,500–26,500 *S*

The design of this chair is unusual. The fine craftsmanship is endorsed by the fact that a related corner chair is recorded in Ralph Edwards and Percy Macquoid, The Dictionary of English Furniture, *Vol I, 1954.*
Another chair of this type forms part of the Frederick Poke Collection in Coventry Museum.

A Chippendale carved mahogany corner chair, with moulded armrests, on turned columnar supports centring pierced strapwork splats, slip-in seat within a moulded frame carved with pendant shells, on square tapering legs, the front cabriole leg with claw-and-ball foot, c1760.
$1,800–2,200 *S(NY)*

A pair of Victorian carved oak Renaissance revival corner chairs, decorated with carved putti masks, foliate scrolls and carved griffin form scroll splats, drop-in seats raised on turned legs.
$800–900 *JAd*

A George III walnut corner chair, top-rail and splats with foliate carving.
$550–630 *GAZE*

A mahogany corner armchair, the curved back and arms with turned and tapering 'cannon' supports, the drop-in seat on square section legs, alterations, early 19thC.
$600–680 *P(Sc)*

Dining Chairs

A pair of Chippendale style mahogany dining chairs, pierced with Gothic arches and Chinese fretwork, the seat-rails and square section legs with moulded edges, mid-18thC.
$3,000–3,500 *LAY*

A pair of George I red walnut dining chairs, the shaped cresting rails carved with a scallop shell motif over pierced splats, slip-in seats over shaped friezes, on cabriole legs terminating in paw feet to the front.
$2,000–2,300 *P*

A pair of Chippendale mahogany dining chairs, mid-18thC.
$7,200–8,000 *SPU*

l. A set of 6 George III mahogany dining chairs, the serpentine crests carved with foliate sprays, pierced interlaced splats and moulded frame, restored and replacements.
$3,300–3,800 *DN*

Sets of Chairs

Sets of 8 or more chairs, including 2 elbow, or armchairs, have become increasingly sought-after in the last twenty years and today command a premium. Sets of 4 or 6 are more modestly priced. Each chair of a set should be examined carefully as sets have sometimes been completed by taking some chairs apart and replacing one or 2 parts of each chair with new members, using the replaced parts to make up an extra chair, a practice known as 'scrambling'.

A set of 6 mahogany dining chairs, the reeded frame arcaded crest backs with pierced plumed crested splats, with drop-in seats, on front square tapering legs with H-stretchers, c1800.
$2,500–2,800 WW

A set of 6 George III mahogany dining chairs, c1800.
$4,000–4,500 ChS

A set of 6 Regency mahogany dining chairs, the reeded frames with bowed rectangular top-rails, narrow crossbars, drop-in seats, on sabre legs, repairs and restorations.
$1,400–1,600 Bea(E)

A set of 12 Regency mahogany dining chairs, including 2 armchairs, the gadrooned scrolled toprails with scrolled foliate-carved angles, above moulded horizontal splats, the drop-in seats on moulded sabre supports, Scottish.
$22,500–24,000 C(S)

A set of 5 George IV mahogany rail-back dining chairs, the scroll top-rail above 'Trafalgar' seats covered in cream moiré fabric, on sabre legs, one chair with loose joints, c1820.
$1,000–1,200 S(S)

l. A set of 6 George IV dining chairs, with rush seats and drop-in cushions, on turned and reeded legs, c1830.
$3,800–4,400 ChS

A set of 4 George IV mahogany dining chairs, the ebony strung top-rails with anthemion carved crests, pierced leaf and anthemion centre rails, flanked by spiral reeding, with drop-in seats, on sabre legs.
$1,400–1,600 DN

A set of 4 George IV simulated rosewood rail-back dining chairs, the top-rail with brass inlay and paterae above a carved mid-rail and slip-in seats, on turned and reeded legs, faults, c1820.
$1,000–1,100 S(S)

A set of 8 dining chairs, with *faux* rosewood graining, stencilling and gilt highlights, paint wear, slight damage, c1830.
$2,500–2,800 SK(B)

A set of 6 George IV mahogany dining chairs, with plain cresting rails above carved and turned mid-rails, the seats covered in olive green moquette, on turned tapering legs.
$2,500–3,000 *AG*

A set of 4 early Victorian mahogany dining chairs, each with a shaped scrolling tablet top-rail above a pierced C-scroll carved splat, with green damask upholstered drop-in seat, on gadrooned and baluster-turned legs.
$750–880 *CSK*

A set of 6 William IV rosewood dining chairs, the down-curved crestings with carved roundels and leaf swags over carved back bars, slip-in seats covered in green ground floral needlework, on turned tapering lappet-carved legs to the front, each stamped 'G.T.'.
$3,500–4,000 *P*

A set of 4 walnut balloon-back chairs each with scroll-ended back-rail and cabriole front legs, c1850.
$2,200–2,400 *ChS*

A set of 4 Victorian mahogany balloon-back dining chairs, c1860.
$1,700–2,200 *ChS*

A set of 6 Victorian rosewood dining chairs.
$3,500–4,000 *SPa*

A set of 4 Victorian mahogany dining chairs, each with a waisted back with paterae and scratch-carved splat above a leatherette upholstered serpentine seat, on turned and fluted legs.
$640–720 *CSK*

A set of 4 dining chairs, with cabriole legs, c1870.
$1,100–1,200 *GBr*

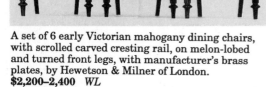

A set of 6 early Victorian mahogany dining chairs, with scrolled carved cresting rail, on melon-lobed and turned front legs, with manufacturer's brass plates, by Hewetson & Milner of London.
$2,200–2,400 *WL*

r. A set of 6 Victorian walnut dining chairs with cabriole legs, c1870.
$2,800–3,200 *RPh*

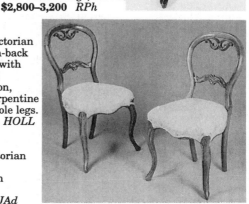

r. A set of 6 Victorian walnut balloon-back dining chairs, with carved pierced scroll decoration, overstuffed serpentine seats, on cabriole legs.
$1,200–1,400 *HOLL*

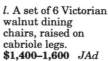

l. A set of 6 Victorian walnut dining chairs, raised on cabriole legs.
$1,400–1,600 *JAd*

A set of 6 late Victorian walnut and burr-walnut dining chairs, with boxwood inlay, c1890. **$3,500–4,000** *ChS*

A set of 4 Georgian style mahogany dining chairs, by Gane of Bristol, c1890. **$1,700–2,200** *GBr*

A set of 8 mahogany dining chairs, including a pair of armchairs, the top-rail incorporating a carved floral frieze, on bulbous turned and multi-faceted legs, c1880. **$2,200–2,400** *S(S)*

A set of 8 George III style mahogany dining chairs, including 2 open armchairs, each with vertical splats and arched top-rail, on square legs joined by stretchers, 19thC. **$2,500–3,200** *CSK*

A set of 4 Continental mahogany dining chairs, the broad crest rails with pierced C-scroll borders, padded seats and turned faceted legs, 19thC. **$1,000–1,200** *DN*

A set of 10 late Victorian oak dining chairs, the moulded waisted open backs above stuffover seats, on turned and studded front legs. **$2,500–3,200** *P(Sc)*

A set of 12 late Victorian George III style mahogany dining chairs, including 2 pairs of armchairs, on moulded square supports joined by square stretchers. **$8,800–9,600** *C(S)*

A set of 6 Victorian rosewood dining chairs, on cabriole legs, c1900. **$2,700–3,200** *RPh*

r. A set of 8 Edwardian George III style mahogany dining chairs including a pair of armchairs, with pierced vase-shaped splats above floral upholstered slip-in seats, on tapered square legs joined by an H-shape stretcher, bearing the trade label 'Cranston and Elliot Ltd', c1910. **$1,900–2,300** *S(S)*

A set of 4 Edwardian mahogany dining chairs. **$500–650** *GWA*

Hall Chairs

A set of 4 late George II mahogany hall chairs, the curved solid backs with shaped outline, rounded dished seats on cartouche-shaped supports with recessed roundels at the front and joined by rectangular section stretchers.
$6,500–6,750 *DN*

A Regency mahogany hall chair, with a carved back, saddle seat with reeded rails terminating in roundels, on splayed legs carved with reed and leaf design, c1820.
$4,000–4,400 *DN*

A pair of George IV mahogany hall chairs, the incised decoration incorporating C-scrolls and horns above a solid seat and reeded sabre legs, one leg repaired, c1820.
$560–680 *S(S)*

An early Victorian ash hall chair, with roundel-shaped back.
$160–180 *AL*

A pair of William IV mahogany hall chairs, c1835.
$1,900–2,200 *CAT*

A pair of Victorian mahogany hall chairs, the cartouche-shaped backs with paper scroll carving, solid seats and cabriole legs with scroll toes and a shaped and moulded rear support.
$1,200–1,300 *DN*

Hall Chairs

Most hall chairs date from the late 18th/early 19thC and are made of plain, polished wood as they were intended for use by messengers in rough and probably dirty outdoor clothes. Common features are a slightly dished seat and a flat back often with a crest or cipher.

A pair of Victorian oak hall chairs, with pierced and moulded cartouche-shaped backs and solid seats, on turned front legs.
$160–200 *LF*

A pair of Victorian faded-mahogany hall chairs, the cartouche-shaped backs with a carved griffin crest to a raised shield above scrolling foliage, tapering seats, on cartouche-carved cabriole front legs.
$880–960 *WW*

A late Victorian brass-mounted oak hall chair, the top-rail with a brass balustraded gallery, the downswept arms mounted with brass stylised leaf sprays meeting roundels centred with a brass roundel, on 4 square tapering cabriole legs, joined by stretchers, with 2 registration marks for 13 December 1883, and metal plaque inscribed 'Evans & Owen Ltd'.
$4,800–5,500 *C*

Library Chairs

A George III mahogany library armchair, the downswept arm supports carved with motifs, on stop-fluted chamfered square legs joined by H-shaped stretchers, with later brass casters.
$6,500–7,000 *S*

A George III mahogany library armchair, with downswept foliate-carved styles, on blind fretwork-carved square supports, headed by pierced scrolled angle brackets and joined by foliate and pendant-carved square stretchers, some carving later.
$4,500–5,000 *C(S)*

A George III mahogany open arm library chair, with rosette-carved arms, later studded leather upholstery, on chamfered moulded legs and stretchers.
$3,600–4,200 *MCA*

A George III carved mahogany library armchair, covered in green silk damask, the arms with rosette-carved and reeded supports, moulded and chamfered square legs joined by stretchers, and leather casters.
$3,500–4,000 *AH*

A Regency mahogany library armchair, with a reeded frame and X-shaped splat, brass-nailed green leather upholstery, on square tapering legs.
$1,900–2,200 *DN*

A Georgian mahogany library chair, c1820.
$4,200–4,800 *FHA*

A William IV mahogany library chair, upholstered in burgundy leather.
$4,000–4,500 *ChS*

A William IV leather upholstered library armchair, the arms with leaf-carved, scrolled and panelled supports, on turned tapered and fluted legs ending in brass casters, c1835.
$6,500–7,500 *S*

l. A pair of William IV simulated rosewood library chairs, with leaf-clasped arms, on turned and tapering legs with leaf-carved feet and inset brass casters.
$8,800–9,600 *P(Sc)*

A William IV padouk library armchair, with leather-covered arms, seat and back cushions, cane-filled seat and back, the crest carved with flowers and foliate scrolls, the arms faced with S-scrolls, stylised lotus and anthemion, turned and reeded legs with casters, possibly Anglo-Indian.
$1,600–2,000 *DN*

A pair of early Victorian oak library armchairs, each upholstered in buttoned black leather, with foliate and cabochon-carved terminals to arms, on reeded tapering legs.
$4,200–4,600 *CSK*

A mahogany library armchair, the bowed top-rail with acanthus-carved terminals, above an interlaced channelled support with Greek key motifs, on fluted tapering legs, 19thC.
$420–480 *CSK*

A pair of George III style mahogany and upholstered library armchairs, covered in ivory hide, the arms with carved acanthus, on cluster-turned splayed legs joined by an H-shaped stretcher, c1910.
$2,800–3,200 *S(S)*

Nursing Chairs

A Victorian mahogany nursing chair, with cabriole legs and casters, c1870.
$720–800 *RPh*

An early Victorian carved walnut nursing chair, with balloon-back, carved panels and cabriole legs, c1860.
$2,800–3,200 *BERA*

A Victorian beech nursing chair, with cane seat.
$110–130 *SPU*

r. A mid-Victorian rosewood nursing chair, the back flanked by spirally-turned columns, with acanthus-carved pierced scrolled cresting centred by a stylised shield, upholstered in *gros point* needlework, on spirally-turned tapering supports with brass caps and casters joined by spirally-turned stretchers.
$880–960 *C(S)*

An upholstered nursing chair, on turned legs with brass casters, c1900.
$120–140 *RPh*

Salon Chairs

A set of 16 Louis XVI style giltwood salon chairs, upholstered in claret and white-ground velvet, each with an arched top-rail centred by a shell, the curved tapering back with pierced central upright carved with foliage and tassels, on square tapering legs, 6 with differently upholstered seats, late 19thC.
$6,500–7,500 *C*

A Victorian rosewood salon chair, with acanthus-carved and scrolled top-rail, on cabriole legs, re-upholstered.
$280–320 *PSA*

A set of 6 late Victorian mahogany marquetry and line-inlaid salon chairs, with pierced shield-shaped backs, on square tapering supports ending in spade feet, and a matching open armchair, the out-scrolled armrests on square tapering supports and spade feet headed by inlaid oval medallions.
$2,500–2,800 *C(S)*

Side Chairs

An early Chippendale carved-mahogany side chair, the serpentine crest with moulded ears above a pierced splat, on cabriole legs joined by stretchers, ending in pad feet, one knee return replaced, Boston, Massachusetts, c1760.
$1,700–2,000 *S(NY)*

A pair of George III mahogany side chairs, on scroll-carved moulded cabriole legs with scroll toes, c1780.
$4,000–4,800 *S*

Side Chairs

Side chairs, particularly those associated with the 18thC, are quality pieces intended for display against the walls of libraries, halls, salons and so on. They normally have wider seats and higher backs than dining chairs.

An elm and Dutch marquetry side chair, the arched top-rail above a vase splat and serpentine drop-in seat, on shell-headed cabriole legs with pad feet joined by shaped stretchers, early 19thC.
$650–720 *CSK*

A pair of yellow-painted and japanned side chairs, each with foliate-carved top-rail and solid splat above a padded seat upholstered in crimson watered silk, on cabriole legs joined by stretchers, with pointed pad feet, re-decorated, possibly Spanish, late 18thC.
$1,100–1,500 *CSK*

A pair of late George III floral-painted side chairs, each with double-curved X-frame splats above a button-down padded seat, on turned tapering legs, with painted mark 'Burley' under seat-rail.
$900–1,000 *CSK*

An American Chippendale mahogany side chair, with voluted ears, fan crest and pierced splat-back, slip-in seat and square legs, 18thC.
$780–880 *EL*

A Victorian papier-mâché and mother-of-pearl inlaid chair, with painted floral decoration and cane seat, cabriole legs, faults, underside stamped 'F', c1860.
$480–540 *S(S)*

A pair of Renaissance revival walnut side chairs, with shell-carved crest, tufted upholstery, 19thC.
$450–520 *FBG*

A pair of mahogany side chairs, each with C-scrolled and bellflower carved corners, above a reeded swag and anthemion-carved splat flanked by scrolled stiles, on sabre legs, Boston, Massachusetts, c1815.
$2,000–2,400 *CNY*

An Edwardian mahogany inlaid side chair, c1910.
$240–280 *RPh*

A set of 4 mahogany carved side chairs, c1910.
$1,300–1,500 *RPh*

Chests of Drawers & Commodes

A Charles II marquetry chest, the top with oval central floral- and bird-inlaid panel between floral quarter-corner panels, above 2 short and 3 long graduated and inlaid drawers, raised on later turned feet, 37¾in (96cm) wide.
$9,500–10,500 *B&L*

A George III mahogany chest of drawers, with 3 drawers, on bracket feet, 28in (71cm) wide.
$850–1,000 *E*

A Dutch rococo walnut and burr walnut commode, the top inlaid with fishtail banding, with chamfered corners, above 4 shaped drawers, the concave corners inlaid with banding, on bracket feet, restored, c1730, 33⅞in (86cm) wide.
$5,500–6,500 *S(Am)*

A George III mahogany chest of drawers, crossbanded in walnut with satinwood line inlay, the top with moulded edge, with 4 long graduated drawers, on carved bracket feet, 31½in (80cm) wide.
$850–1,000 *TMA*

A Queen Anne walnut and inlaid chest of drawers, the crossbanded top above an arrangement of 2 short and 3 long graduated drawers, on later shaped bracket feet, 39in (99cm) wide.
$2,400–2,800 *S(S)*

A Chippendale cherry chest of 4 drawers, brasses replaced, restored, New England, late 18thC, 34½in (87.5cm) wide.
$1,900–2,.200 *SK(B)*

A mahogany bowfronted chest of drawers, early 19thC, 40½in (103cm) wide.
$1,100–1,400 *SPa*

MILLER'S COMPARES . . .

I A serpentine mahogany chest, the moulded top above a baize-lined brushing slide and 4 graduated drawers, with blind fret-carved canted corners, on shaped bracket feet, c1765, 41in (104cm) wide.
$28,800–32,000 *S*

II A serpentine mahogany chest, the moulded crossbanded top above a frieze drawer fitted with a slide, above 3 graduated drawers, on ogee bracket feet with canted fluted corners, c1755, 39in (99cm) wide.
$12,000–13,000 *S*

These two chests were expected to fetch similar prices at auction, but in the event *Item I* far outstripped *Item II*. The most obvious difference in *Item I* is the fine fretwork carving at the corners. This is a classic Chippendale feature and pinpoints the period in which it was made, very much a 'plus' in the eyes of the prospective purchaser. Further desirable features of *item I* are the brushing slide, the original colour and the depth which, being rather less than that of *Item II*, gives it a slightly more elegant look. *S*

A bowfronted chest of drawers, with 3 long drawers, inlaid with fan quadrants, on splayed bracket feet, early 19thC, 29¾in (75.5cm) wide.
$1,600–1,900 *L*

A mahogany chest of drawers, with pine sides, original key, lock and brass handles, early 19thC, 36½in (93cm) wide.
$1,400–1,550 *GBr*

A central European walnut and part-ebonised commode, the crossbanded top above 3 drawers, on square tapering legs, 19thC, 48½in (123cm) wide.
$1,500–1,800 *CSK*

A mahogany chest of drawers, c1810, 45in (114cm) wide.
$1,600–1,900 *RPh*

A late George III mahogany dressing chest, the hinged boxwood-lined top inlaid with an oval panel of crossbanding and enclosing a fitted interior containing a pottery part wash-set, above a writing slide, 4 drawers and a panelled cupboard door, on square tapering supports, 28in (71cm) wide.
$2,500–2,800 *C(S)*

A Federal birch- and mahogany-veneered chest of drawers, replaced brasses, New England, c1810, 39½in (100cm) wide.
$950–1,100 *SK(B)*

A Regency mahogany bowfronted chest of drawers, with crossbanded and boxwood-strung top, above 2 short and 3 long graduated drawers with brass drop handles and cockbeading to the fronts, on bracket feet, 43in (109cm) wide.
$1,900–2,200 *Mit*

A French flame-mahogany veneered commode, c1830, 50in (127cm) wide.
$3,500–4,000 *FHA*

A mid-Victorian walnut chest, in the style of A. W. N. Pugin, with moulded top, 2 short and 4 long graduated drawers, on shaped feet, 40½in (103cm) wide.
$1,600–1,900 *P(NE)*

A mid-Victorian bowfronted chest of drawers, with walnut-veneered drawers and mother-of-pearl inlay on handles, 46in (117cm) wide.
$800–950 *GWA*

A mahogany serpentine chest of drawers, with 3 drawers, 19thC, 45in (114.5cm) wide.
$2,000–2,400 *AAV*

A Victorian mahogany military chest, 39in (99cm) wide.
$2,000–2,400 *SPU*

A French Louis XV style commode, the 3 drawers veneered in kingwood, floral marquetry panels to top, sides and drawer fronts, cast ormolu mounts, the cabriole supports fitted with leafy sabots, 19thC, 33½in (85cm) wide.
$2,200–2,700 *J&L*

Chests-on-Chests

A Queen Anne walnut and crossbanded chest-on-chest, with 3 short and 3 long graduated drawers, the base with a slide above a pair of cupboard doors, and applied dummy drawers enclosing 2 adjustable slides, on later shaped bracket feet, restored, c1710, 46¾in (119cm) wide.
$4,000–4,500 *S(S)*

A George I walnut chest-on-chest, with moulded cornice over 3 short and 3 long feather-banded drawers, the base with brushing slide over 3 long drawers, on bracket feet, 42in (107cm) wide.
$17,600–19,000 *BR*

This piece was of superb craftsmanship and in exceptional original condition. Coming from a private source, it attracted feverish bidding both in the saleroom and over the telephone until it finally sold for about 5 times its pre-sale estimate.

A George II mahogany chest-on-chest, the 2 short and 3 long drawers with canted fluted corners, the lower part with a brushing slide above 3 long drawers, on bracket feet, c1755, 44¼in (112cm) wide.
$4,500–5,500 *S*

A George III mahogany tallboy, the upper part with moulded and dentil cornice, the 2 short and 3 long drawers with fluted canted corners, the base fitted with a brushing slide and 3 long drawers, all with oval handles embossed with Trafalgar memorial, on bracket feet, 42in (106.5cm) wide.
$3,500–4,000 *CAG*

A mahogany-veneered chest-on-chest, the upper section with shaped canted cornice, above 2 short and 3 long cockbeaded drawers, flanked by canted reeded corners, the base with 3 graduated cockbeaded drawers, all with brass drop handles, on shaped bracket feet, late 18thC, 46½in (118cm) wide.
$2,800–3,200 *BWe*

A George III mahogany bowfronted chest-on-chest, handles replaced, on swept bracket feet, 43¼in (110cm) wide.
$4,000–4,500 *Bri*

A figured and carved mahogany scroll-top chest-on-chest, the removable pediment centring a carved bust of Milton, above 5 short and 3 graduated long drawers flanked by fluted quarter-columns, the base with 3 long drawers, similarly flanked, on ogee bracket feet, restored and altered, Philadelphia, c1780, 47in (119.5cm) wide.
$11,200–13,600 *S(NY)*

A George III mahogany tallboy, with blind fret-carved frieze and canted corners, 2 short and 3 graduated drawers to the upper section, a brushing slide and 3 further long drawers below, on bracket feet, 43½in (110.5cm) wide.
$2,200–2,600 *Bea(E)*

r. A George III mahogany chest-on-chest, the upper section with Greek key cornice over a blind fret frieze, the 2 short and 3 long graduated drawers flanked by canted fluted corners, the base with 3 drawers, on bracket feet, 44½in (113cm) wide.
$2,200–2,600 *LAY*

Chests-on-Chests

Chests-on-chests, or tallboys, were first made in the late 17th/early18thC, usually in walnut with feather-banding, overlapping drawer mouldings and bun or bracket feet. They were often in 2 sections with a cornice. A few had a concave inlaid sunburst set into the bottom drawer and these are particularly sought-after today.

From the mid-1730s they were usually made in mahogany, although a few exist in other timbers, such as yew, and country versions were made in oak throughout the period.

The most desirable tallboys belong to the early 18thC and the Chippendale period. Chests-on-chests were far less common after c1780 and had virtually ceased to be made after the first quarter of the 19thC.

Chests-on-Stands

A William and Mary walnut and simulated mulberry chest-on-stand, the upper part with 2 short and 3 long crossbanded drawers, the stand with 3 frieze drawers, on spiral-twist supports and ebonised bun feet, stand restored, 41½in (105cm) wide.
$6,000–7,000 *P(NW)*

A George I walnut chest-on-stand, with cabriole legs and pad feet, with additions and alterations, 37½in (95cm) wide.
$1,200–1,400 *P(NE)*

A walnut and herringbone-crossbanded chest-on-stand, the base with 3 variously sized drawers, on turned baluster supports and bun feet, basically 18thC, 43in (109cm) wide.
$4,500–5,500 *C(S)*

A walnut-veneered chest-on-stand, with 2 short and 3 long crossbanded drawers, the stand with 3 drawers, on cabriole legs, sides re-veneered, early 18thC, stand later, 40in (101.5cm) wide.
$2,700–3,200 *Bea(E)*

A walnut and crossbanded chest-on-stand, the drawers with brass drop handles, the base with 3 drawers, shaped apron, cabriole legs and pointed pad feet, 18thC, 40in (101.5cm) wide.
$3,200–3,500 *AH*

A walnut feather-banded chest-on-stand, with 3 short and 3 long drawers above a further long drawer and a shaped apron, on cabriole legs with pad feet, chest basically 18thC, 41½in (105cm) wide.
$3,200–3,500 *CSK*

A walnut inlaid chest-on-stand, with 2 short and 3 long drawers, on bun feet, stand restored, c1705, 40½in (103cm) wide.
$14,000–16,000 *S*

This chest has beautiful graining and veneer, and its stand is original.

A George II inlaid walnut chest-on-stand, with 3 short and 3 long drawers, the stand fitted with 2 short and one long drawer, on cabriole legs with pad feet, 40in (101.5cm) wide.
$4,500–5,500 *CNY*

A walnut quarter-panelled chest-on-stand, c1910, 43in (109cm) wide.
$900–1,000 *GWA*

Secretaire Chests

A George II Cuban mahogany secretaire chest, with fall-front fitted drawer above 3 long graduated drawers with original brass open plates and escutcheons, some with broken handles, on bracket feet, slight damage, 33in (84cm) wide.
$5,700–6,400   *WW*

A George III mahogany secretaire chest, with a central secretaire drawer flanked by 2 double-fronted drawers, above 3 long drawers, all with boxwood stringing, later brass handles and bracket feet, 48½in (123cm) wide.
$2,200–2,800   *DN*

Condition

Condition is absolutely vital when assessing the value of any item. Damaged pieces appreciate much less than perfect examples. However, a rare, desirable piece may command a high price even when damaged.

A Regency mahogany secretaire chest, with fall-front in the form of 2 dummy drawers, enclosing a fitted interior with leather-lined writing surface, pigeonholes and drawers, on outswept bracket feet, 45in (114.5cm) wide.
$1,400–1,550   *CSK*

A George III mahogany secretaire chest, the top drawer with twin astragal panelled mouldings enclosing pigeonholes and 6 drawers, 4 long graduated drawers below, with brass carrying handles to sides, on bracket feet, 34in (86.5cm) wide.
$1,600–1,900   *CAG*

A mahogany secretaire chest, with boxwood stringing, the fitted writing drawer including 4 small sycamore-veneered drawers, flanked by 4 short drawers, above 2 long drawers and a valanced apron, on splayed bracket feet, c1790, 48½in (123cm) wide.
$2,400–2,800   *S(S)*

A Regency mahogany secretaire chest, the secretaire drawer with fitted interior, 3 further drawers under, each with gilt-brass foliate handles, on bracket feet, 40½in (103cm) wide.
$1,900–2,200   *Bri*

r. A teak and figured walnut military secretaire chest, in 2 parts, the fitted writing drawer flanked by a short drawer, 3 long drawers below, c1870, 42in (106.5cm) wide.
$1,900–2,200   *S(S)*

A George III mahogany secretaire chest, the panelled-fall enclosing a fitted interior of drawers and pigeonholes, above a pair of panelled cupboard doors, enclosing 2 short drawers and shelves, 48in (122cm) wide.
$1,700–2,000   *Bon(C)*

A mahogany secretaire chest, the fitted drawer with applied mouldings, pigeonholes and drawers, above 3 long drawers, on splayed bracket feet, early 19thC, 37in (94cm) wide.
$1,300–1,500   *DN*

A Victorian walnut campaign secretaire chest, in 2 parts, with fitted fall-front writing drawer flanked by 2 short drawers, above 3 long drawers, with brass-inset handles and strapwork, raised on ball feet, stamped 'Brown Bros Piccadilly', 39in (99cm) wide.
$3,800–4,600   *JAd*

Wellington Chests

A Louis XVI ormolu-mounted tulipwood, amaranth and green-stained *semainier*, the mottled-grey marble top above 7 banded quarter-veneered drawers, the canted angles headed by foliate and berried tapering mounts, the sides veneered as 2 panels, on bracket feet, restored, re-mounted, 2 drawers re-lined and originally with drawers to the sides, 20½in (51cm) wide.
$5,600–6,200 C

A Louis XV style gilt-bronze-mounted marquetry *semainier*, the shaped marble top above concave corners, fitted with foliate scrolls continuing to 7 inlaid drawers fitted with cartouche-shaped escutcheons, raised on scrolled feet, fitted with gilt-bronze sabots, impressed metal label 'Mati. Paris', late 19thC, 20in (51cm) wide.
$7,200–8,000 S(NY)

A satin maple Wellington chest, the 7 graduated drawers with moulded cockbeading and turned handles, early 19thC, 19⅜in (50cm) wide.
$2,500–2,800 P(Sc)

A mahogany Wellington chest, with an arrangement of 8 drawers enclosed by locking pilasters with carved corbels, on a plinth base, c1840, 23¼in (59cm) wide.
$4,000–4,800 S(S)

r. A late Victorian mahogany Wellington chest, the satinwood-crossbanded and boxwood-lined top above 7 drawers, inlaid with graduated floral swags and ribbon-tied harebell chains, with boxwood-lined angles, one drawer with a hinged flap, 24in (61cm) wide.
$7,800–8,500 C(S)

A William IV rosewood Wellington chest, comprising 7 drawers flanked by scrolling corbel-headed uprights, on a plinth base, 19in (48cm) wide.
$1,600–1,900 CSK

An early Victorian rosewood Wellington chest, the moulded top above 6 drawers, on a plinth base, 21½in (54.5cm) wide.
$2,000–2,200 Bon(C)

Wellington Chests

Wellington chests are a type of English early 19thC single-tier chest of drawers. They are most commonly produced in mahogany, but were made in a variety of other woods, such as maple and sycamore and, in the Victorian period, veneered-walnut. The decoration tends to be minimal, although walnut examples often have some inlay. These chests were often locked by means of a narrow hinged flap down one side of the drawers.

A Victorian mahogany secretaire Wellington chest, with 2 drawers, a secretaire drawer with fitted interior and 3 further drawers, within stile supports, 49¼in (125cm) high.
$2,200–2,700 P(NE)

An Edwardian mahogany crossbanded Wellington chest, with 7 drawers, flanked by bell-flower-inlaid stiles, one locking, on plinth base, 23¾in (60cm) wide.
$2,500–2,800 C

Cupboards

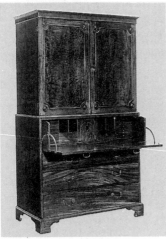

A mahogany secretaire clothes press, the interior with sliding trays, enclosed by fiddle-back panelled doors, the fall-front with 2 dummy drawers revealing a fitted interior, a pull-out mirrored compartment with square parquetry and secret compartments, a door with a peep-hole flanked by drawers and pigeonholes, above 3 graduated drawers, with brass swan neck handles, on bracket feet, c1780, 46in (117cm) wide.
$3,800–4,800 *WW*

A mahogany linen press, by Gillow's, the central panelled doors enclosing slides, flanked by an arrangement of 8 short drawers, stamped, c1800, 86½in (220cm) wide.
$3,500–4,000 *S(S)*

A mahogany breakfront cupboard, the 4 panelled doors with applied mouldings enclosing adjustable shelves, the lower part with conforming doors, the central section enclosing a pair of drawers, c1780, 84in (214cm) wide.
$4,800–5,400 *S(S)*

A George III mahogany linen press, the ogee-arched panelled doors with applied leaf carving enclosing hanging space, over 2 short and 2 long graduated drawers, on ogee feet, 45¾in (116cm) wide.
$2,400–2,800 *P(Sc)*

A mahogany linen press, the panelled doors enclosing hanging space, the lower section fitted with 2 long drawers, on bracket feet, restored and altered, late 18thC, 51in (130cm) wide.
$880–1,000 *CSK*

A late George III mahogany linen press, with panelled doors, 2 frieze drawers and 2 graduated long drawers, on bracket feet, 52½in (133.5cm) wide.
$2,500–2,800 *Bea(E)*

A William IV mahogany linen press, the moulded top above 2 short and one long drawer, a pair of panelled cupboard doors enclosing sliding trays, on black-painted cast-iron hairy paw feet, 49in (124.5cm) wide.
$1,700–2,200 *C(S)*

A mahogany, boxwood and ebony-lined linen press, with a pair of cupboard doors, the base fitted with 2 short and 2 long drawers, on bracket feet, 19thC, 52in (132cm) wide.
$2,000–2,400 *C(S)*

A 17thC style oak and marquetry cupboard, the cornice with drop finials above a central panel, above a carved apron frieze, on stile feet with pierced angle brackets, c1910, 54½in (138cm) wide.
$1,400–1,600 *S(S)*

Davenports

A George IV yew-veneered davenport, the sliding top with a chased-brass gallery, a leather-inset slope and a hinged pen drawer, the base with a slide to each side and 3 drawers enclosed by a panelled door to the right, on turned feet with casters, 20¼in (51.5cm) wide.
$2,400–2,800 DN

A Victorian figured-walnut and inlaid davenport, by T. H. Filmer & Sons, London, boxwood-inlaid with stringing and scrolled leafage, the upper part opening to reveal fitted stationery rack, leather-lined slope, fitted with 4 real and 4 dummy drawers, carved leaf scroll brackets to front, 22in (60cm) wide.
$2,200–2,600 CAG

A Victorian walnut davenport, with raised ormolu gallery, interior with bird's-eye maple fitted drawer, secret drawer, serpentine front, and 4 drawers, on carved cabriole supports, 22in (56cm) wide.
$2,500–2,800 RBB

An early Victorian mahogany davenport, the leather-lined hinged top opening to drawers, above 4 drawers opposed by 4 dummy drawers, 21½in (54.5cm) wide.
$1,600–1,900 CSK

A rosewood davenport, with a pierced-brass gallery and leather-inset writing slope, above a sliding pen tray, the pedestal base with an arrangement of 4 drawers and turned supports, c1850, 21¼in (54cm) wide.
$1,400–1,800 S(S)

A Victorian walnut davenport, the raised back with pierced grille and hinged lid opening to reveal fitted stationery compartment, the hinged slope with fitted drawers, on foliate scroll supports, 4 side drawers, 21in (53cm) wide.
$2,000–2,400 AH

r. A Victorian walnut davenport, with hinged domed pencil box, leather-lined writing surface, 4 drawers to one side, with panelled front, 21in (53cm) wide.
$1,450–1,600 C(S)

An early Victorian oak davenport, with tooled leather insert to the sloping flap, a hinged pen drawer and slides, side door enclosing 4 drawers, C-scroll front supports, on lobed bun feet with casters, 20½in (52cm) wide.
$1,200–1,300 Bea(E)

A mid-Victorian walnut and boxwood strung davenport, the hinged top with gilt-metal three-quarter gallery opening to reveal a fitted interior of compartments, with hinged moulded sloping-fall opening to reveal a satinwood-lined interior with 2 faux and 2 real drawers, on spiral-turned supports and scroll base, the right-hand side with 4 drawers fitted with patent locks, the left-hand side with 4 false drawers, 21¼in (54cm) wide.
$1,600–1,900 P(NW)

A mid-Victorian burr walnut davenport, with satinwood-line inlay, the top opening compartment fitted with 2 short drawers and 2 pigeonholes, enclosed by double-mirrored doors, the hinged writing slope reveals a maple-lined interior, the base with 4 short drawers and 4 opposing dummy drawers, with twisted roundel carved pilasters, 21in (53.5cm) wide.
$1,600–1,900 TMA

A Victorian mahogany davenport, with pen compartment over leather-inset sloping top, the concave front opening to reveal a fitted interior, the serpentine front supports with flowerhead decoration, the sides with 4 real and 4 dummy drawers, 22⅜in (58cm) wide.
$1,300–1,450 B

A Victorian walnut davenport, with scroll inlay and cross-banding, fitted gallery to the pen box, and 4 drawers to one side, 21in (53cm) wide.
$1,300–1,450 RBB

Desks

A walnut and feather-banded kneehole desk, the quarter-veneered top above 9 drawers, the rear with 4 long graduated drawers, on later shaped bracket feet, sides split, faults, c1715, 37½in (95cm) wide.
$8,300–9,600 *S(S)*

A George I walnut kneehole desk, the crossbanded top fitted with an arrangement of one long and 8 short drawers around a recessed cupboard door, on bracket feet, restored, 30in (76cm) wide.
$2,800–3,200 *L*

A George II mahogany kneehole desk, with long cockbeaded frieze drawer, above a shaped apron drawer with lower recessed cupboard, flanked to each side by 3 cockbeaded drawers, on moulded base with short bracket feet, 28¾in (73cm) wide.
$1,600–1,800 *P(NW)*

A mahogany kneehole desk, the long drawer fitted with a hinged surface enclosing further drawers, above a central recessed fielded panelled cupboard door, flanked by columns of 3 graduated drawers with fluted quarter-column pilasters, on ogee bracket feet, c1750, 47in (119.5cm) wide.
$5,800–6,800 *Bon*

An early George III mahogany kneehole desk, fitted with an arrangement of 7 drawers around a recessed kneehole cupboard, 30in (76cm) wide.
$1,900–2,400 *L*

A late George III mahogany tambour writing desk, the domed top with a fall enclosing a fitted interior with drawers and pigeonholes, sliding writing compartment with a hinged ratcheted slope, fitted with 2 frieze drawers, on square tapered legs ending in brass caps and casters, 43in (109cm) wide.
$7,000–7,600 *CSK*

A mahogany kneehole desk, the leather-lined crossbanded top above 3 frieze drawers with 3 drawers to each pedestal flanking a moulded cupboard, c1780, 48in (122cm) wide.
$8,000–9,600 *S*

A mahogany double-sided library desk, the inverted breakfront top with a tooled-leather inset above an arrangement of 6 drawers, the cupboard doors flanked by fluted and reeded pilasters enclosing an arrangement of drawers and shelves, on shaped bracket feet with blind fret decoration, faults, c1770, 65in (165cm) wide.
$5,600–6,600 *S(S)*

l. A late George III mahogany kneehole desk, with 3 frieze drawers above an apron drawer and shaped recessed cupboard, flanked by 3 drawers to either side, on bracket feet, 36in (91.5cm) wide.
$1,400–1,600 *CSK*

A late George III mahogany and inlaid roll-top desk, the tambour shutter enclosing a fitted interior of drawers and pigeonholes, pull-out leather-lined writing surface, with central ratcheted section, above 2 frieze drawers and square tapering legs inlaid with bell-flowers, drawers re-lined, restored, 36½in (93cm) wide.
$2,400–2,800 *CSK*

Pedestal Desks

Pedestal desks were produced in large quantities from the mid-18thC, although a few exist from the early 18thC. They enjoyed a long period of popularity and continued to be produced throughout the 19thC and into the Edwardian period.

In the 18th and early 19thC they are most commonly found in mahogany and are usually veneered. They were made in a wider variety of woods in the late 19thC.

Pedestal desks are usually constructed in 3 sections with 3 frieze drawers along the top and 3 graduated drawers to each pedestal. In the second half of the 19thC large quantities were made as office desks, and the quality of these varies considerably. Most pedestal desks have replacement leather tops – original leather is very rare.

An early Victorian mahogany desk, the raised back with a moulded cornice above a baize-lined fall with 3 arched panels enclosing pigeonholes, drawers and recesses, above a long frieze drawer and a kneehole flanked by 2 further arched panelled doors, each enclosing 4 drawers with turned wood handles, 50in (127cm) wide.
$3,600–4,400 *DN*

l. A Victorian lady's French style figured-walnut desk, with gilt-brass mouldings and mounts, the superstructure fitted with 5 drawers, above a leather-lined writing surface, the frieze drawer inset with a floral decorated porcelain plaque, on square cabriole supports with gilt-brass mounts and sabots, 43in (109cm) wide.
$4,400–5,000 *CAG*

A walnut twin-pedestal desk, the top with ebonised edges and 3 moulded drawers above a lower moulded edged shelf and sloping-fall opening to reveal a fitted interior, with baize-inset surface, pigeonholes and drawers, the lower part with central frieze drawer, flanked to each side by 4 moulded panelled drawers, mid-19thC, 43in (109cm) wide.
$1,400–1,800 *P(NW)*

A Victorian mahogany partners' desk, the top with leather writing surface, above 3 opposing frieze drawers and twin pedestals each with 3 opposing drawers with panelled sides, 72in (183in) wide.
$4,200–4,800 *P(Sc)*

r. A Victorian mahogany pedestal desk, the embossed leather-inset top above a single frieze drawer, flanked by a pair of panelled cupboard doors, each enclosing 4 further drawers, 48½in (123cm) wide.
$2,200–2,800 *Bon(C)*

l. A mahogany pedestal desk, the top inset with old tooled-leather, the front frieze with 3 drawers and each pedestal with 3 drawers, the reverse with dummy drawers, on steel casters, mid-19thC, 48in (122cm) wide.
$4,400–4,800 *WW*

r. A Victorian pollard oak-veneered and ebonised pedestal desk, with tooled-leather top, an arrangement of 9 drawers with brass handles and escutcheons, on plinth base, 51¾in (131.5cm) wide.
$2,800–3,200 *Bea(E)*

A Victorian bamboo-framed and red lacquered pedestal desk, with an arrangement of 5 drawers, 38in (96.5cm) wide.
$1,000–1,200 *Bea*

A mahogany and inlaid kneehole desk, with moulded top and frieze drawer above an arched apron and recessed cupboard, flanked by 3 drawers to either side, on bracket feet, 19thC, 36½in (93cm) wide.
$2,400–2,800 *CSK*

A Victorian mahogany partners' desk, the leather-lined top above 3 drawers to each side, each pedestal fitted with 3 drawers with an opposing panelled door, locks stamped 'Hobbs & Co, London', 66in (167.5cm) wide.
$4,000–4,400 *CSK*

A Victorian burr walnut pedestal desk, the green leather inset top above 3 frieze drawers, each pedestal including 3 further drawers, with concealed casters, some veneers lacking, 54¼in (138cm) wide.
$6,400–7,000 *S(S)*

A Continental double-sided walnut *secrétaire de dame*, with ebony and boxwood string inlay and marquetry decoration of acanthus leaves, flowers and vases, one side fitted with 2 small drawers and a fall-front writing surface enclosing a mahogany and satin birch-lined interior with drawers, pigeonholes and letter racks, the other fitted with a top hinged adjustable writing slope, on pierced double-lyre ends and splay feet, 19thC, 28in (71cm) wide.
$1,400–1,600 *JM*

A mahogany roll-top pedestal desk, the moulded shelf above panelled drum, enclosing pigeonholes and drawers above sliding desk with leather-inset writing slope and further drawers, 3 false drawers to front, on pedestals with 3 graduated drawers, 19thC, 53½in (136cm) wide.
$2,400–2,800 *P(Sc)*

A French walnut pedestal writing desk, the top with green leather-inset, above 3 frieze drawers, the fronts with guilloche moulding, 3 short drawers in each pedestal, on tapered feet with gadrooned collars, labelled 'S & H Jewell, 26 Parker Street, London', locks stamped 'Mon Krieger, Ameublement, Paris', 19thC, 57in (145cm) wide.
$2,800–3,200 *Oli*

A French kneehole desk, parquetry-veneered in kingwood with satinwood stringing, with brown leather-inset top, over 9 drawers to the front and dummy drawers to the reverse, with rococo style ormolu mounts, 19thC, 52in (132in) wide.
$5,600–6,400 *RBB*

A late Victorian walnut twin-pedestal partners' desk, the leather-lined top above a frieze fitted with 3 drawers to either side, the kneehole flanked on either side by 3 short drawers and a panelled cupboard door, similarly fitted to the reverse, the lockplate stamped 'Hobbs & Co, London', 60in (152.5cm) wide.
$4,000–4,400 *C(S)*

A late Victorian lady's marquetry inlaid cylinder writing desk, the upper section with a pierced gilt-metal three-quarter gallery above a bevelled glazed cupboard door, the cylinder fall inlaid with a fan patera, husk chains and scrolling foliage, enclosing pen trays above 3 short drawers, the similarly inlaid hinged writing slope above a long frieze drawer, on square tapered legs with spade feet, tied by a shelf stretcher, 29¾in (75.5cm) wide.
$6,200–7,200 *Bon*

An oak roll-top desk, with fitted interior, above 8 drawers on plinth bases, the brass lockplate marked 'Derby Desk, London', late 19thC, 66in (167.5cm) wide.
$1,200–1,400 *E*

A Chippendale style mahogany partners' pedestal desk, the top with a leather-inset and gadrooned drawers, the pedestals raised on acanthus-carved bracket feet, c1905, 59½in (151cm) wide.
$3,200–3,500 *Bon(C)*

A French brass-mounted mahogany lady's writing desk, the superstructure with a mirror and canopied shelf with gallery and supported on fluted columns, with 2 drawers and galleried shelves to either side, the roll-top with a vignette of figures, enclosing a fitted interior and pull-out writing surface, with a frieze drawer and fluted tapering legs, late 19thC, 31½in (80cm) wide.
$2,200–2,600 *CSK*

An Edwardian mahogany bowfronted desk, crossbanded with string inlay, the arched back with 2 drawers, 2 frieze drawers with brass drop handles, on square tapering supports, with spade feet and brass casters, 48in (122cm) wide.
$2,400–2,800 *AH*

An Edwardian mahogany desk, the top with leather-inset writing surface, pen rest and recesses for ink pots, 9 drawers to the kneehole with brass leaf-tied reeded drop handles, the top drawer fronts and sides with crossbanding in walnut and strung in ebony and boxwood, stamped 'Maple & Co Ltd', 48in (122cm) wide.
$4,000–4,800 *HAM*

An Edwardian inlaid mahogany twin-pedestal desk, the satinwood crossbanded top with tooled-leather writing surface above centre frieze drawer and 8 moulded pedestal drawers with ebonised handles, 48in (122cm) wide.
$2,800–3,200 *JAd*

An Edwardian mahogany, boxwood-lined and inlaid twin-pedestal desk, the top above central bowed drawer inlaid with a *faux* fluted frieze flanked by drawers above pedestals of 3 graduated drawers each with boxwood beading, 53½in (136cm) wide.
$5,000–5,600 *P(Sc)*

Dumb Waiters

A George III mahogany dumb waiter, the circular tiers with vase-turned supports, on tripod base with pointed pad feet, 23½in (60cm) diam.
$2,400–2,700 *Bri*

A George III mahogany two-tier dumb waiter, each moulded tier with hinged flap on a baluster-turned stem and tripod base with brass casters, c1790, 24in (61cm) diam.
$3,400–4,000 *S*

A Regency mahogany dumb waiter, with 2 octagonal hinged graduated tiers held by ring-turned columns and 3 outswept supports, early 19thC, 23½in (60cm) diam.
$1,400–1,600 *Bon*

A Regency mahogany two-tier dumb waiter, each circular graduated revolving tier supported on a lobed baluster column, on reeded outswept and down-curved legs, c1815, 42½in (108cm) high.
$2,500–3,200 *Bon*

A Regency mahogany two-tier dumb waiter, the round trays with reeded borders and joined by 3 slender turned-brass columns, on a ring-turned pillar with 3 downswept legs with brass caps and casters, 22in (56cm) diam.
$3,200–3,500 *DN*

A matched pair of Edwardian two-tier dumb waiters, one in satinwood, the other mahogany, each with a circular pierced brass gallery above a chequer line inlaid circular top, on splayed cabriole legs, 18in (46cm) diam.
$2,700–3,200 *C*

Etagères

l. A Victorian Louis XV style satinwood and rosewood crossbanded étagère, the top with a shallow frieze drawer, with gilt-metal mounts, the slender cabriole legs ending in sabots, polish partially lacking to upper and central tier, c1880, 18½in (47cm) wide.
$2,800–3,500 *S(S)*

An Edwardian mahogany étagère, crossbanded with string and floral marquetry inlay, the oval tray top with gilt loop handles, on turned supports with brass casters joined by shaped stretchers and galleried undershelf, 31½in (80cm) wide.
$2,400–2,800 *AH*

A parquetry and gilt-metal two-tier étagère, with pineapple finials and columnar supports, on casters, late 19thC, 14½in (37cm) wide.
$1,300–1,500 *Bon*

l. A late Victorian bamboo and black japanned étagère, with 2 hinged rectangular shelves, decorated with exotic birds, 22in (56cm) wide.
$600–660 *C*

An Edwardian mahogany and inlaid square-shaped étagère, with shaped upper cresting formed into a turned finial, splay feet, 40in (102cm) high.
$720–800 *L&E*

Frames

A Louis XIV carved and gilded frame, the corners with anthemia in high relief, flanked by pierced scrolling foliage, c1800, 17½ x 25in (44.5 x 63.5cm). $1,000–1,200 CSK

A French carved and gilded oval frame, with leaf sight edge, acorn, oak leaf and flower running between flowerhead centres and corners, late 17thC, 23¾ x 19½in (60.5 x 50cm). $680–740 Bon

A Spanish carved and gilded reverse profile frame, the corners with cartouches flanked by scrolling leaves, the centres with scrolling foliage in high profile, bead course at sight edge, early 18thC, 13¾ x 9¾in (35 x 25cm). $2,800–3,200 C

A carved and décapé frame, the pierced corners and centres with anthemia flanked by scrolling foliage and flowers, cavetto sight edge, 18thC, 29 x 23¾in (74 x 60.5cm). $1,100–1,300 C

A carved pierced and gilded frame, of Grinling Gibbons influence, with scrolling leaves and flowers, berry and corn trophies to scrolling foliate crest, c1800, 10½ x 14¼in (27 x 36cm). $1,300–1,500 Bon

A Florentine carved pierced and gilded frame, carved with scrolling acanthus, with stepped sight, 19thC, 17½ x 15¼in (44.5 x 39cm). $420–480 Bon

Jardinières

A George III oak and brass-bound jardinière, on square legs, 25½in (65cm) wide. $840–1,000 P(Sc)

A Continental walnut jardinière, c1835, 17¾in (45cm) wide. $1,300–1,600 FHA

A pair of Continental satinwood and ebony planters, early 19thC, 21in (53.5cm) wide. $5,600–5,800 SPa

l. A Louis XVI style walnut and brass-inlaid jardinière, the top with pierced-brass gallery surrounding a torch and trophy-inlaid lid enclosing a tin liner, on turned tapering fluted legs joined by a wavy and baluster-turned stretcher, on turned feet, 19thC, 24in (61cm) wide. $880–1,000 CSK

r. An Edwardian inlaid satinwood jardinière, with ebony stringing and decorated with bell-flowers raised on square tapering legs with lower shelf, on spade feet, 12¾in (33cm) wide. $1,000–1,200 JAd

Lowboys

A mahogany lowboy, the central drawer flanked by 2 deep drawers with moulded angles over a shaped apron, on square section chamfered moulded legs, restored, early 18thC, 25¼in (64cm) wide.
$1,000–1,200 *P(Sc)*

A George I walnut lowboy, with central drawer flanked by 2 short drawers, on cabriole legs, c1725, 19½in (49.5cm) wide.
$5,000–5,800 *FHA*

Lowboys

Originally used as dressing tables, lowboys are among the most classic types of early 18thC English furniture. The veneered examples are the most sought-after. They were also made in solid oak and other country woods and during the Chippendale period in Virginia walnut and mahogany. Some lowboys are found with straight legs: examples from the Chippendale period in mahogany with carved spandrels are often of very fine quality. Those of a similar quality but with cabriole legs tend to fetch higher prices.

A George I walnut lowboy, the top and drawer crossbanded and herringbone strung, above a shaped arch, on cabriole legs, original brass handles with disc backplates, 32in (81.5cm) wide.
$7,200–8,000 *LAY*

A carved and figured walnut lowboy, with one long drawer carved as 3 short drawers with 2 short drawers and a shaped apron below, on shell-carved cabriole legs with trifid feet, top reset, all knee returns restored, patch to rear left foot and long drawer, both short drawers restored, c1750, 36in (91.5cm) wide.
$6,000–6,600 *S(NY)*

A walnut lowboy, the crossbanded top above a long drawer with shaped apron below, flanked by 2 short drawers, on cabriole legs with pad feet, 18thC, 30in (76cm) wide.
$1,800–2,100 *CSK*

> *r.* A George III mahogany lowboy, with shaped frieze, 30in (76cm) wide.
> **$3,600–4,200** *CNY*

l. A mahogany lowboy, with one long and 3 short drawers, shaped apron and lappeted turned tapering legs with pad feet, mid-18thC, 30in (76cm) wide.
$2,700–3,000 *CSK*

A Dutch walnut serpentine lowboy, with a long frieze drawer and 2 further small drawers, shaped apron, on cabriole legs with pointed pad feet, c1715, 33in (84cm) wide.
$8,000–8,800 *Bon*

A carved walnut lowboy, with one long and 3 short drawers, shaped scrolling apron below, on cabriole legs with trifid feet, repairs to drawer lips and top detached, Pennsylvania, c1760, 36½in (93cm) wide.
$9,600–10,600 *S(NY)*

A walnut lowboy, the base with one long drawer over 3 narrow drawers, with fan-carved and central lower drawer, turned drop handles, cabriole legs and pad feet, brasses not original, New England, 18thC, 36in (91.5cm) wide.
$9,000–10,000 *EL*

Miniature Furniture

A Queen Anne miniature walnut chest-on-chest, the crossbanded top above 2 short and 2 long drawers, the lower part with 3 long drawers, on shaped bracket feet, c1710, 10in (25cm) wide.
$4,800–5,200 *S*

A George III miniature bowfronted mahogany chest of drawers, the 4 graduated drawers outlined with boxwood stringing above a shaped apron and bracket feet, c1800, 12in (30.5cm) wide.
$1,400–1,500 *S*

A mahogany miniature chest of drawers, with 3 short drawers and 3 long graduated drawers, on turned legs flanked by barley-twist columns, 19thC, 11¾in (30cm) wide.
$760–860 *P(Sc)*

A Chippendale miniature figured-maple and pine slant-front desk, opening to 6 small drawers, the case fitted with 3 graduated long drawers, straight bracket feet, patches and repairs where hinge broken, feet reduced in height, New England, c1760, 17½in (44.5cm) wide.
$1,900–2,200 *S(NY)*

A miniature spirit or medicine box, in the form of a miniature chest of drawers, the hinged top incorporating a dummy drawer and enclosing 6 divisions above 3 further dummy drawers, inlaid with brass stringing and flanked by gilt-metal-mounted ebonised columns, on brass ball feet, early 19thC, 10¼in (26cm) wide.
$1,400–1,500 *S*

A Swedish miniature walnut commode, of bombé outline, with 3 drawers and gilt bronze mounts, 19thC, 11¾in (30cm) high.
$700–760 *CSK*

r. A Victorian style miniature mahogany chest of drawers, c1935, 12in (30.5cm) high.
$640–800 *DUB*

A George III miniature carved giltwood looking glass, the arched mirror plate in a moulded scrolled and leaf-carved frame, c1760, 10½in (27cm) wide.
$1,200–1,300 *S*

A Victorian miniature walnut and ebonised Wellington chest, with breakfront top, over 6 satin-crossbanded and string-inlaid drawers, all with ebonised turned handles, 14¾in (37.5cm) wide.
$800–920 *DA*

A mahogany and ash miniature wheelbarrow, the shaped sides painted with a cypher and with scrolled handles and spoked wheels, outlined in black with red highlights, 19thC, 40in (102cm) wide.
$8,800–9,600 *S*

Cheval Mirrors

MILLER'S COMPARES . . .

A George IV mahogany
cheval mirror, the
square and turned
supports with beehive
finials joined by turned
stretchers, on moulded
sabre legs ending in
brass cappings and
casters, now lacking
candle sconces, c1830,
28¼in (72cm) wide.
$2,400–2,700 *S(S)*

A Victorian mahogany
cheval mirror, supported
by turned baluster
columns, on acanthus-
carved arched bar feet
ending in scrolled toes,
27½in (70cm) wide.
$850–950 *C(S)*

I A George III mahogany
cheval mirror, the
rectangular mirror
plate within reeded
turned uprights fitted
with adjustable candle
arms, the turned double
crossbars on reeded
splayed legs with
brass casters, c1800,
30in (76cm) wide.
$6,400–7,000 *S*

II A George IV mahogany
cheval mirror, the
rectangular plate within
a reeded frame, the
ring-turned and square
supports surmounted by
turned finials and on
reeded splayed legs
ending in brass caps
and casters, c1820,
30¼in (77cm) wide.
$2,500–2,800 *S*

**These 2 cheval mirrors were made within
twenty years of each other but** *item I*
realised more than twice the price of
item II **at auction. Top quality pieces
usually command a premium, and a
seemingly small feature such as the
reeded detail extending up the entire
length of the uprights made** *item I* **more
desirable. It has also retained its original
colour, whilst** *item II* **has been repolished
and, therefore, stripped of much of its
colour. However, for an item to realise so
much over the saleroom estimate it
usually needs to have a particularly
special feature; in this case the original
candle arms which are rare. This is almost
certainly one of the most important
factors which contributed to the elevated
price of** *item I.* **S**

A French ormolu-
mounted and ebonised
cheval mirror, the
frame surmounted by
a female mask and
shell, the sides each
with a scrolled volute
below a foliate boss
finial, on twin-scrolled
legs joined by a
stretcher, late 19thC,
48¾in (124cm) wide.
$8,800–10,400 *C*

An Edwardian mahogany
cheval mirror, the line-
inlaid frame flanked by
down-scrolled uprights
with gadrooned finial
mounts and paterae inlay,
on down-curved bracket
feet, 30½in (77.5cm) wide.
$1,000–1,100 *CSK*

r. A mahogany cheval
mirror, with shaped top, the
stand with turned finials,
brass side screw knobs, on
shaped legs with carved
knees and claw pad feet,
c1900, 60in (152.5cm) high.
$320–400 *GH*

Cheval Mirrors

Cheval mirrors, or 'horse dressing glasses',
so-called because of their four-legged frame, were
introduced during the last decade of the 18thC,
when it became possible to cast single mirror
plates more than 10 feet (3m) in height. Most
examples date from 1790–1830, but they were
still being made as late as 1910. Some cheval
mirrors have adjustable candle holders, which are
usually a sign of quality and increases the value.

A German mahogany
cheval mirror,
surmounted by a
cabochon and foliate
scrolling cresting
between scrolling
uprights, on
serpentine-fronted
plinth base, 19thC,
56in (142cm) wide.
$1,500–1,600 *CSK*

Dressing Table Mirrors

A Queen Anne walnut and parcel-gilt dressing mirror, with later mirror plate, c1710, 17in (43cm) wide.
$4,000–4,500 *S*

A mahogany toilet mirror, on original marble base, c1835, 54in (137cm) wide.
$480–560 *GBr*

A mahogany dressing table mirror, 19thC, 20in (51cm) wide.
$200–220 *No7*

A Georgian mahogany toilet mirror, with single frieze drawer and original ivory knobs and escutcheon, c1810, 18in (47cm) wide.
$400–450 *RPh*

A George IV carved-mahogany dressing table mirror, after a design by George Smith, with leaf scroll cresting and conforming scroll-carved corners, on a stepped and cavetto-moulded plinth with S-scroll feet, 33½in (85cm) wide.
$1,100–1,300 *S*

A late Victorian mahogany and satinwood crossbanded toilet mirror, the serpentine base fitted with 3 drawers, on bracket feet, 23in (58.5cm) wide.
$480–620 *C(S)*

l. An East European burr sycamore veneered toilet mirror, with inlaid stringing and 3 drawers, on short bracket feet, 19thC, 15¼in (39cm) wide.
$650–750 *WW*

A Regency mahogany swing dressing table mirror, the original plate with thumbnail moulding between channelled scrolled arms and shaped platform, c1820, 19in (48.5cm) wide.
$400–450 *RPh*

A Victorian mahogany toilet mirror, c1870, 24in (61cm) wide.
$500–560 *RPh*

A Victorian toilet mirror, with scolled crest, 19in (48.5cm) wide.
$320–440 *SPU*

A Queen Anne style walnut mirror, c1910, 23in (58.5cm) wide.
$480–550 *SPa*

Wall Mirrors

A George I looking glass, the giltwood frame carved in shallow relief with leaves and flowers, on a scale ground, the shaped crest with a shell and leaves, 18in (46cm) wide.
$2,700–3,200 *DN*

An early George III giltwood and gesso-framed looking glass, the later rectangular plate enclosed by a frame, of open scrolls and leafy flowering branches, some restoration, 27in (68cm) wide.
$1,600–2,000 *Bea(E)*

A George II gilt-gesso mirror, the later rectangular plate surmounted by a scrolled broken pediment centred by a shell motif, the moulded apron with foliate and acanthus decoration, originally with candle branches to the centre of the apron, the gilding refreshed and with some later gold painting, 22in (56cm) wide.
$3,500–4,000 *C*

A Regency giltwood convex mirror, the circular ball-decorated frame with a reeded ebonised slip, the carved eagle surmount with a scroll plinth flanked by foliage, the base with foliage sprays and a fruiting pendant, 19in (48.5cm) wide.
$650–800 *WW*

l. A Gothic revival pier glass, with 2 rectangular bevelled mirror plates within a crystoline and gilt border and moulded gilt frame with fleur-de-lys, some pieces of the frame detached, early 19thC, 30in (76.5cm) wide.
$3,200–3,600 *DN*

An Italian looking glass, the carved giltwood and mirrored frame with borders of entwined scrolls and leaves, the shaped C-scroll crest enclosing a vase of fruits, 18thC, 19¾in (50cm) wide.
$1,400–1,600 *DN*

l. A carved giltwood wall mirror, decorated with acanthus scrolled designs, late 18thC, 31in (79cm) wide.
$1,900–2,200 *DN*

A pair of Venetian giltwood girandoles, the engraved mirror panels depicting figures, within scroll and flower-carved frames, candle branches lacking, mid-18thC, 30½in (77.5cm) high.
$5,000–6,000 *Bon*

Girandoles are always popular, and this pair are in good original condition.

A Regency giltwood framed girandole, surmounted by an anthemion, double eagle-head and acanthus cresting, 2 candle arms to each side and an acanthus pendant apron below, 55in (140cm) wide.
$5,600–6,300 *Bea(E)*

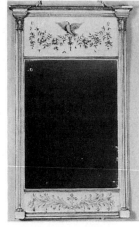

A Regency gilt looking glass with a *verre églomisé* panel and leaf-capped column sides with leaves and flowers at the base, 28¼in (72cm) wide.
$1,900–2,200 *DN*

A George IV gilt-gesso *verre églomisé* overmantel mirror, the moulded cornice above a frieze depicting cherubs and swans, above a mirror plate flanked by reeded columns and blind trellis work panels, on bun feet, c1820, 45½in (115.5cm) wide.
$950–1,200 *S(S)*

An American convex mirror, with shell-form pediment flanked by 2 dolphins, 2 candle arms, leaf-carved drop, c1820, 29in (73.5cm) high.
$4,400–4,800 *EL*

An early Victorian carved giltwood and gesso overmantel, the pierced frame carved with vine leaves and bunches of grapes, with slightly overhanging carved scrolled pediment, 45in (114.5cm) wide.
$1,600–1,800 *C(S)*

A rococo style gilt framed girandole, c1850, 19in (48cm) wide.
$1,200–1,400 *RPh*

A Victorian giltwood and gesso girandole, with three-tiered open shelves, the sides supporting vase stands and a pair of candle sconces, the whole decorated with C- and S-scrolls and fruiting vines, 27in (69cm) wide.
$2,700–3,000 *P(Sc)*

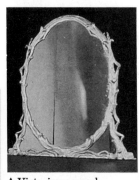
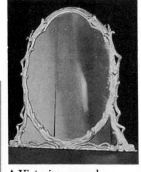

A Victorian carved-giltwood overmantel mirror, the oval plate within a naturalistically-carved pierced branch surround, the splayed base flanked by a pair of triangular shaped mirror plates, late 19thC, 68in (173cm) wide.
$1,200–1,400 *S(S)*

A Continental giltwood mirror, the shaped bevelled plate within a bead-moulded inner frame, the mirrored surround to scrolling foliage main frame with leaf spray surmount, 19thC, 30in (76cm) wide.
$2,000–2,400 *WW*

A late Victorian giltwood and composition mirror, the arched rectangular plate surmounted by a foliate cresting supported by putti and draped with floral swags, with opposed C-scroll foliate apron, some damage, 38in (96.5cm) wide.
$1,400–1,600 *C*

r. A George II style giltwood pier mirror, the foliate surmount incorporating husk motifs, the shaped-bevelled mirror in 2 parts with conforming margin plates, mid-20thC, 35½in (90cm) wide.
$4,400–4,800 *S(S)*

Screens

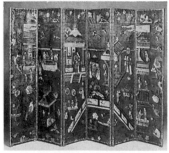

A Dutch painted and parcel-gilt leather screen, depicting figures in period costume within a later gilded border, painted in tones of iron-red, olive-green, cream, brown and black, highlighted with gilding, late 18th/early 19thC, each leaf 20¼in (51.5cm) wide.
$4,500–5,000 *S(NY)*

A French painted seven-panel screen, depicting country folk in native costume dancing, with 2 gentlemen hunters looking on, painted *en grisaille*, within an applied brown Greek key border, now fitted onto a hardwood backing, some tearing to screen, restorations, 19thC, 78in (198cm) high.
$2,800–3,500 *S(NY)*

An Edwardian gilt gesso screen, the foliate surmounts incorporating scallop shells above a segmented glazed panel and woven fabric panel, with a blind fretwork base, c1910, each panel 24in (61cm) wide.
$6,000–6,500 *S(S)*

Fire Screens

A George III mahogany fire screen, the needlework banner worked in petit and gros point depicting a musician, on a turned tapered and fluted column and moulded over-scrolled tripod, c1765, 63in (160cm) high.
$10,200–11,200 *S*

A George III carved mahogany pole screen, the adjustable rectangular framed panel with a needlework picture of an urn of flowers on a gold ground, the pole with a turned finial and baluster-turned stem, on a leaf-carved tripod base, c1760, 52½in (133.5cm) high.
$3,200–3,500 *S(S)*

A George II mahogany pole screen, with a Soho tapestry depicting a heron beside a lake, within a ribbon-tied border of summer flowers and foliage, the back of the panel lined with Chinese floral wallpaper, on a turned and fluted stem, cabriole legs with claw-and-ball feet, c1755, 58½in (148.5cm) wide.
$18,500–20,000 *S*

A Chippendale carved mahogany pole screen, with an adjustable English canvas-work panel, monogrammed 'HG', the standard on 3 cabriole legs and claw-and-ball feet, slight damage, c1770, 60in (152.5cm) high.
$22,500–27,000 *S(NY)*

Good quality American furniture is highly sought after by American collectors.

r. An Empire ormolu-mounted mahogany firescreen, the needlepoint panel depicting a pastoral landscape, flanked by columnar supports with ormolu capitals and terminals, raised on trestle supports and fitted with a foliate apron mount, early 19thC, 50½in (128.5cm) high.
$2,800–3,500 *S(NY)*

Fire Screens

Because wax was used in the production of many cosmetics in the 18thC, pole screens were designed as a way of protecting complexions from the heat of the fire. Consisting of an adjustable screen attached to a wooden or metal pole supported on a tripod base they were developed during the first half of the 18thC. The screen itself, usually oval, rectangular or shield-shaped, was attached to the pole by a ring and screw. Pole screens became more decorative rather than functional pieces by the 19thC.

A pair of Regency pollard oak fire screens, with table tops, original gilt bronze casters, c1820, 32½in (83cm) high.
$7,200–8,000 *BERA*

A pair of Victorian giltwood screens, each with foliate cartouche glazed frame with foliate embroidered silk panel, on gilt-brass upright, 3 slender legs and scroll feet, the reverse of one silk panel with inscription 'worked by Viscountess Strathallan 1856' within a ribbon, 55¼in (140.5cm) high.
$4,000–4,500 *C*

Miller's is a price GUIDE not a price LIST

A pair of satinwood inlaid pole screens, the oval frames enclosing coloured prints, 19thC, 60in (152.5cm) high.
$1,700–2,000 *GAZE*

A mid-Victorian rosewood and simulated rosewood fire screen, with an oval floral woolwork panel within a moulded frame, under a leaf-carved crest supported on a turned tapering column with carved cabriole legs, 56½in (143.5cm) high.
$800–950 *TMA*

A pair of pole screens, with turned columns, the glazed screens with floral embroidered inserts, mid-19thC, 57in (145cm) high.
$480–560 *GH*

A Victorian rosewood pole screen, with needlework banner depicting a garden scene, in an acanthus-carved scrolled frame on a barley-twist column and arched scrolled tripod legs, 59in (150cm) high.
$600–680 *P(Sc)*

A Victorian mahogany-framed silk-embroidered fire screen, with William Morris inspired silk embroidery in silver and pale rose tones on a blue ground, within a mahogany frame capped with urn finials, on downswept legs joined by a turned stretcher, late 19thC, 46¼ x 24in (117.5 x 61cm).
$400–450 *RIT*

l. An Edwardian mahogany-framed fire screen, with floral tapestry panel, 33½in (85cm) high.
$200–220 *PSA*

r. A mahogany and beaten copper fire screen, c1890, 33in (84cm) high.
$160–240 *GBr*

A Victorian carved and scrolled mahogany-framed and glazed fire screen, with tapestry and woolwork roses, together with matching tripod pedestal base, no centre column, 28 x 23in (71 x 58.5cm) overall.
$500–560 *SAF*

A late Victorian rosewood screen, 40in (101.5cm) high.
$160–200 *PSA*

Settees & Sofas

A George II mahogany sofa, with upholstered square back, downswept arms and stuffover seat, on cabriole front legs with pad feet and club rear legs, 57in (145cm) wide.
$1,100–1,400 *P(Sc)*

A George III mahogany and upholstered settee, covered in gold damask, with a 'camel' back and scrolled arms, on square legs joined by stretchers, with loose seat cushions, one cushion cover lacking, c1770, 86½in (220cm) wide.
$7,200–8,000 *S(S)*

A mahogany sofa, with bird's head scrolls at back, scrolled arms with acanthus carving, green and white chequered upholstery, on paw feet, 19thC, 70in (178cm) wide.
$2,200–2,400 *EL*

A Federal carved mahogany settee, the crest rail centering a ribbon and swag-carved panel flanked by reeded panels, reeded sloping arms, reeded and ring-turned baluster arm supports, cylindrical tapering reeded legs with compressed ball feet and socket casters, restorations to legs, c1800, 77¾in (196cm) wide.
$2,200–2,700 *CNY*

An early Victorian rosewood settee, the curved top-rail with central floral and foliate cresting above a buttoned-back, with incurved arms and scrolled terminals, on cabriole legs with scroll feet, 66in (168cm) wide.
$1,300–1,500 *CSK*

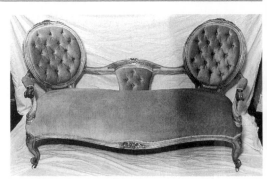

A Victorian walnut sofa, with deep-buttoned double chair-back and serpentine seat, raised on cabriole legs, c1860, 71in (180cm) wide.
$3,200–3,500 *GBr*

A Victorian rosewood-framed settee, carved with flowers, leaves and fruit, upholstered in floral embossed velvet, on cabriole legs and knurled feet, 75in (190.5cm) wide.
$2,000–2,400 *JM*

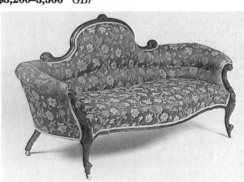

A mid-Victorian walnut sofa, with central arched section and foliate cresting, rounded ends with scroll terminals, serpentine seat and cabriole legs, 78in (198cm) wide.
$1,400–1,600 *CSK*

Settees & Sofas

The earliest form of seat furniture to accommodate 2 or more people was the settle, which dates back to c1500. The more comfortable chair-back settee evolved from this in the late 17thC, and this developed into the fully-upholstered long seat or settee, where the wood was exposed.

Sofas are similar in construction and style to settees, but are larger and more comfortable. However, in 18thC and 19thC catalogues of furniture the terms are often interchangeable.

Victorian sofas and settees are characterised by ornate carving and bold curvaceous designs with deep-buttoned upholstery, often using rich velvets and patterned fabrics. This period also saw the development of the chesterfield, one of the first settees to be entirely upholstered.

A mid-Victorian walnut sofa, upholstered in blue fabric, the buttoned-down padded back with cross-splat supports and a central roundel, on ring-turned and fluted legs, 49in (124.5cm) wide.
$600–720 *CSK*

A brass and iron collapsible campaign couch, c1860, 35¾in (91cm) high.
$950–1,100 *GBr*

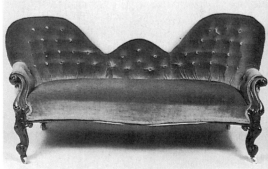

A Victorian rosewood settee, with button-upholstered padded back, covered in a salmon pink velvet, on acanthus-carved cabriole supports, with scrolled toes and pottery casters, 66in (168cm) wide.
$1,200–1,400 *C(S)*

A Victorian mahogany sofa, the serpentine upholstered back and seat flanked by entwined curving carved arms, on cabriole legs ending in scroll toes, 73½in (187cm) wide.
$1,900–2,400 *P(Sc)*

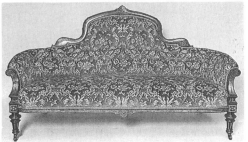

A Victorian ebonised and burr-walnut sofa, with satinwood floral scroll inlay, floral buttoned cut-brocade, on fluted turned legs with casters, 73in (185.5cm) wide.
$1,400–1,800 *M*

A French provincial mahogany and cane canape, with leaf-carved moulded crest-rail and caned back with shaped leaf-carved arms and shaped serpentine seat-rail, caned seat, with button tufted cushion, raised on leaf-carved cabriole legs with scrolled toes, late 19thC, 49½in (126cm) long.
$450–550 *RIT*

A late Victorian Louis XVI style beechwood canapé, the curved padded back in a lotus and acanthus-carved and moulded frame, with floral cresting, upholstered seat on acanthus-carved and stop-fluted tapering supports, 48in (122cm) wide.
$1,100–1,300 *C(S)*

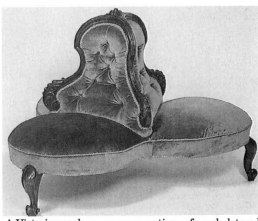

A Victorian mahogany conversation sofa, upholstered in buttoned old-gold velvet, the spoon-backs enhanced with acanthus scrolls, raised on cabriole legs, 49¼in (125cm) wide.
$1,600–1,800 *J&L*

An Edwardian inlaid mahogany settee, with roll back and arms, upholstered in green dralon, on square tapered legs with brass castors, 73in (185.5cm) wide.
$950–1,100 *MAT*

Sideboards

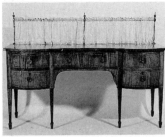

A George III mahogany and line-inlaid sideboard, with brass rail above the bow and serpentine outlined top, the drawers and door with brass ring handles, on square tapering supports with spade feet, 72¾in (185cm) wide.
$2,000–2,400 *Bri*

A George III mahogany sideboard, crossbanded with tulipwood and inlaid with boxwood lines, the serpentine-fronted top above 2 short drawers and one cellaret drawer, simulated as 2 drawers, on turned tapering legs with spade feet, the cellaret drawer previously with removable liners, 36¼in (92cm) wide.
$5,800–6,400 *C*

Miller's is a price GUIDE not a price LIST

A mahogany breakfront sideboard, with ebonised line inlay, the raised reeded panelled-back centred with a stellar medallion above an associated top and bowed frieze drawer flanked by cupboard doors and reeded chevron uprights, on spiral-turned legs and foliate-decorated pad feet, restorations, early 19thC, 70in (178cm) wide.
$1,900–2,400 *C*

A George III mahogany small bowfronted sideboard, crossbanded and with boxwood stringing, on square tapering supports with spade feet, 49¼in (125cm) wide.
$4,300–4,800 *Bri*

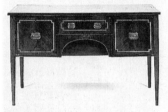

A George III mahogany and satinwood-banded sideboard, with central frieze drawer and arched apron drawer, flanked by deep drawers, on line-inlaid square tapering legs, apron drawer later, 59in (150cm) wide.
$1,700–2,200 *CSK*

A Federal inlaid mahogany sideboard, the bowed top with line-inlaid edge above a line-inlaid cockbeaded long drawer over a pair of bowed cupboard doors flanked by short drawers over a cupboard, on square tapering legs with inlaid cuffs, New York, c1800, 70¼in (178.5cm) wide.
$6,000–7,000 *CNY*

A mahogany bowfronted sideboard, with central frieze drawer and an arch with shaped apron, flanked by a deep drawer to each side, on square section tapering legs ending in spade feet, early 19thC, 43¾in (111cm) wide.
$950–1,100 *P(Sc)*

A George III bowfronted mahogany sideboard, the central drawer between 2 deep drawers on turned tapered legs, 48in (122cm) wide.
$2,700–3,000 *Oli*

A Georgian mahogany-veneered breakfront sideboard, with central single drawer above spandrels and flanked on one side by a deep curved drawer and on 2 curved drawers, the whole with inlaid lines, on square section legs, 76½in (195cm) wide.
$3,800–4,400 *LAY*

An ebony and boxwood line bowfronted mahogany sideboard, the frieze drawer above 2 small drawers flanking an arch, on diamond section tapering legs with brass caps and casters, early 19thC, 39¼in (100cm) wide.
$2,000–2,400 *P(Sc)*

A mahogany bowfronted sideboard, with a central drawer flanked to either side by 2 short drawers, with sunburst spandrels, on turned and fluted tapering legs, the legs and top later, early 19thC, 74in (188cm) wide.
$1,250–1,600 *CSK*

A mahogany bowfronted sideboard, the frieze drawer and doors applied with beading, the uprights inlaid with ebonised motifs, on tapering turned legs, early 19thC, 60¼in (153cm) wide.
$4,200–4,800 *Bea(E)*

A late George III mahogany D-shaped breakfront sideboard, with rosewood crossbanding, fitted with a short drawer flanked by 2 drawers and a cupboard, on square tapering legs, 63in (160cm) wide.
$5,800–6,400 *L*

A Regency mahogany sideboard, with brass inlay, the gadrooned edge top with a central bow fronted drawer, flanked by a smaller drawer each side, above pedestal cupboards, fitted with shelves enclosed by panelled doors, flanked by leaf-plumed capped rope-twist pilasters on tassel feet, 62in (157.5cm) wide.
$4,800–5,300 *WW*

l. A George III Scottish mahogany serpentine sideboard, with rosewood crossbanded stepped superstructure and later brass gallery, incomplete, 90¼in (229cm) wide.
$7,500–8,500 *C(S)*

r. A Regency mahogany pedestal sideboard, the central section with a frieze drawer and narrow raised back, each pedestal support with a moulded top above a drawer and tapered cupboard on shaped bracket feet, restored, 69in (175cm) wide.
$1,200–1,350 *S(S)*

A George IV mahogany pedestal sideboard, the raised back centred by a carved scallop shell motif with paterae and acanthus-scrolled leaves, fitted with 4 short drawers to the frieze, each pedestal enclosed by a panelled door with pilaster mount and carved scrolled claw-and-ball feet, 90in (228.5cm) wide.
$1,200–1,300 *AG*

A Regency mahogany breakfront sideboard, with central drawer above an arched apron drawer, flanked by 2 deep drawers, on ring-turned reeded tapering legs, 60in (152.5cm) wide.
$1,600–1,900 *CSK*

A Federal carved mahogany and mahogany-veneered sideboard, old refinish, replaced brasses, stretcher added, other damage, possibly New York City, c1815, 38½in (98cm) wide.
$3,600–4,400 *SK(B)*

A mahogany and crossbanded bowfronted sideboard, with boxwood stringing, the top with a narrow satinwood band, above 2 deep drawers flanking a false drawer and an arched centre, on square tapering legs, 19thC, 46in (117cm) wide.
$1,400–1,550 *DN*

A George IV mahogany inverted breakfront sideboard, the ebony-strung front with an arched centre, 2 drawers and a door, with brass lion mask handles, on square tapering legs, 50¼in (128cm) wide.
$2,400–2,800 *DN*

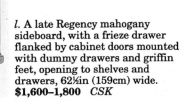

l. A late Regency mahogany sideboard, with a frieze drawer flanked by cabinet doors mounted with dummy drawers and griffin feet, opening to shelves and drawers, 62½in (159cm) wide.
$1,600–1,800 *CSK*

An early Victorian mahogany pedestal sideboard, with fitted cellaret in right pedestal and raised door panels, mid-19thC, 67in (170cm) wide.
$2,000–2,300 *RPh*

A William IV Scottish mahogany sideboard, the top with ledged back and scrolled pediment, carved with oak foliage, scrolling acanthus, vine leaves and bunches of grapes, above 3 bowed frieze drawers supported by a pedestal flanked by acanthus-carved scrolled demi-columns, centred by a further drawer carved with acanthus scrolls and oak foliage, the lockplate stamped 'Patent', with panelled back, 84in (213cm) wide.
$6,500–8,000 *C(S)*

An early Victorian mahogany pedestal sideboard, with arched mirror-back flanked by pierced carved scrolls and flowers and with similar cresting, the central frieze drawer with rosette, flanked by panelled pedestals with foliate scrolling corbel-headed pilasters, 84in (214cm) wide.
$1,700–2,200 *CSK*

A Victorian mahogany mirror-back breakfront sideboard, the raised back surmounted by a cartouche with foliate supports, 3 frieze drawers incorporating vine leaf carving centred by a ram's head, the pedestals incorporating masks flanked by carved pilasters, the interiors with cellaret divisions and opposing slides, 96½in (245cm) wide.
$4,400–4,800 *S(S)*

A Victorian rosewood mirror-back sideboard, with marquetry inlay, the base with central bowfront cupboard and frieze drawer, flanked on either side by a drawer, open shelf and cupboard, on turned legs, 60in (152.5cm) wide.
$3,300–4,000 *JM*

A late Victorian oak and walnut serpentine-front sideboard, the back with 3 small mirrors flanked by carved figures of putti, the front supports carved as leafage and putti, the back panel carved with fruiting vine and fir cones flanked by goat mask and leafage brackets, 114in (289.5cm) wide.
$13,000–14,500 *RBB*
This sideboard is of particular appeal owing to the fine quality of the carving.

A late Victorian rosewood and inlaid sideboard, the broken arch pediment above mirrored and shelved back with central door, the base with glazed and panel doors and shelves, 54in (137cm) wide.
$1,600–1,800 *Bri*

A mahogany breakfront pedestal sideboard, with a silvered gallery, the fluted frieze drawer flanked by cupboards with applied mouldings incorporating musical trophies, swags and ram's heads, the interior with an arrangement of drawers including a cellaret, early 20thC, 66¼in (168cm) wide.
$2,400–2,700 *S(S)*

An Edwardian mahogany and marquetry pedestal sideboard, inlaid overall with scrolling foliage and ribbon-tied swags, crossbanded in satinwood and with a swan neck ledge back, the serpentine central drawer flanked by pedestals each with a drawer and a panelled cupboard door, on bracket feet, 58in (147cm) wide.
$2,800–3,200 *CSK*

Stands

A gilt-bronze and thuya *guéridon*, on simulated bamboo legs, triform base, centred by a tazza, on splay feet, Paris, c1890, 29½in (75cm) high. **$10,000–12,000** *S*

This table is inspired by those produced by one of the finest Parisian ébénistes, Adam Weisweiler (1744–1820). In the late 18thC, he supplied a predominantly noble French clientele with furniture in a very elegant and delicate style, made from the finest exotic woods and gilt-bronze mounts.

A Venetian carved wood blackamoor *guéridon*, painted in black and gilt, on an ebonised, gilded and painted child figure S-scroll column, on 3 splayed scroll-carved legs, 19thC, 35½in (90cm). **$1,200–1,400** *DN*

r. A pair of French mahogany and gilt-metal *guéridons*, each with a pierced gallery and onyx top, on turned fluted legs, with a platform stretcher, c1890, 20in (51cm) wide. **$6,400–7,000** *S*

An Edwardian mahogany inlaid plant stand, c1910, 13½in (34.5cm) diam. **$320–360** *RPh*

An Edwardian mahogany cake stand, 33in (84cm) high. **$400–480** *SPU*

Folio & Reading Stands

A mahogany reading stand, the rectangular hinged and adjustable top with a moulded bookrest and 2 candle-stands, on a rising stem and plain turned column with 3 splayed legs, mid-18thC, 23in (58cm) wide.
$1,600–1,900 DN

A George III mahogany reading stand, the adjust-able top with ebonised inlay, on a turned baluster support and quatreform base with downswept legs incorporating leaf carving, 17in (43cm) wide.
$1,900–2,200 S(S)

A Regency mahogany reading stand, with rectangular adjustable top, book rest and candle arm, on ring-turned column with 3 splayed legs, 21in (53cm) wide.
$1,200–1,400 DN

A William IV reading stand, the hinged folio rest above a lobed baluster pillar and quatreform plinth base, on scroll feet, 22in (56cm) wide.
$1,600–1,900 S(S)

A Victorian oak folio stand, decorated overall with short fluted lines and imbrocated bands, on vase-shaped end standards and hipped downswept legs, with ceramic casters, stamped 'Cope/Patent', lacking 4 turned paterae, restorations, 28¼in (72cm) wide.
$2,700–3,000 CSK

A William IV walnut reading table, the top with a pair of ratcheted slopes to one end, on acanthus-carved octagonal faceted column with foliate collar and concave-sided platform base, with gadrooned feet, one book rest missing, 36in (91.5cm) wide.
$1,200–1,300 CSK

A Victorian mahogany reading and writing table, with gilt-tooled leather insert and removable book rest to the rising and ratcheted top, the square end supports with foliate-carved brackets and trestle feet, 33in (84cm) wide.
$950–1,200 Bea(E)

A Victorian walnut folio stand, bearing a paper label with 'J. J. Helston', the adjustable folio section raised on scroll-carved end supports and over-scrolled downswept legs, 28½in (72.5cm) wide.
$3,200–3,500 Bon(C)

This type of stand was used as a rack for folios of prints, watercolours, etc.

Steps

A set of Regency rosewood two-tread steps, the padded steps covered in close-nailed light-green suede, on baluster legs, 4 legs restored, 18½in (47cm) wide.
$2,700–3,000 C

A set of George IV mahogany library steps, with leather-lined treads, turned feet and brass casters, c1825, 28in (70cm) wide.
$5,500–6,500 S

A set of George III mahogany metamorphic library steps, in the form of a stool, the hinged bowed seat with pierced carrying handles, on chamfered square legs, the interior re-fitted, 28in (71cm) wide.
$2,200–2,700 C

Stools

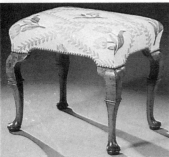

A Queen Anne walnut stool, the seat covered with modern crewelwork, on shaped cabriole legs with pad feet, c1710, 16½in (42cm) wide.
$3,400–3,800 *S*

A late George III mahogany rectangular stool, the solid saddle seat with moulded edge, boxwood-strung seat rails and square tapering legs, 20in (51cm) wide.
$800–880 *DN*

An early Victorian mahogany duet stool, on roundel-decorated scrolled X-frame supports joined by later ring-turned stretchers, 35½in (90cm) wide.
$720–800 *CSK*

A satinwood gout stool, with a buttoned green-leather ratcheted footrest, 19thC, 21in (53.5cm) wide.
$320–400 *CSK*

A George II walnut stool, with woolwork-covered drop-in seat, shaped frieze, on foliate-carved cabriole legs with claw-and-ball feet, 20in (51cm) wide.
$3,800–4,000 *Bea(E)*

A George IV simulated rosewood beech framed long stool, the front seat rail with a brass marquetry panel of foliate scrolls, on moulded splayed legs carved with acanthus, on brass paw terminals and casters, 45in (114cm) wide.
$1,700–1,900 *DN*

A late Victorian ebonised stool, upholstered in burgundy fabric, the bowed seat on ring-turned legs, 22in (56cm) wide.
$1,000–1,200 *C*

A pair of French beadwork and giltwood stools, each with a padded top worked with a dragon and scrollwork, on turned carved legs, c1860, 13½in (34.5cm) diam.
$2,800–3,200 *S*

A footstool, painted mustard yellow with freehand sepia and black decoration, minor paint wear, New England, early 19thC, 18in (46cm) wide.
$1,600–1,800 *SK(B)*

A George IV rosewood footstool, on turned tapered reeded legs with a turned crossover stretcher and central boss, on turned toes, c1825, 20½in (52cm) wide.
$2,500–2,700 *S*

A mahogany stool, the upholstered top above a moulded and shell-carved frieze, on cabriole supports and scrolled toes, 19thC, 19½in (49.5cm) wide.
$850–950 *C(S)*

A walnut X-frame stool, the turned arm supports surmounted by animal masks, on foliate splayed legs terminating in paw feet, one arm support detached, c1900, 20½in (52cm) wide.
$750–880 *CSK*

Bedroom Suites

A Hungarian ash bedroom suite, comprising: wardrobe, pedestal dressing table, marble-topped washstand and writing table, all bearing ivorine trade labels for 'Collinge and Co Ltd, Burnley', c1880, wardrobe 101in (256.5cm) wide.
$5,000–6,000 *S(S)*

A brass bedroom suite, comprising: three-section wardrobe with mirrored doors, kidney-shaped dressing table, a pair of bowfront pot cupboards, double bed, the arched headboard above a glazed gilt-metal insert, a pair of footstools, side chair, coat stand and a crucifix, all decorated with foliate and acanthus-cast scrolling swags and ribbons, c1890, dressing table 36in (91.5cm) wide.
$22,500–25,500 *Bon*

A walnut Louis XV style bedroom suite, comprising: bed, wardrobe and a pair of bedside tables, late 19thC, bed 78in (198cm) long.
$7,200–8,000 *SWA*

Salon Suites

r. An Edwardian mahogany three-piece bedroom suite, comprising: wardrobe with bowfront centre section, bowfront dressing table and a bedside cupboard, raised on square tapering legs, wardrobe 84in (213.5cm) wide.
$3,800–4,400 *AG*

A Louis XVI style ebonised mahogany salon suite, with foliate carved crest-rails, padded backs and seats, Aubusson upholstery, on cabriole legs, 19thC.
$2,600–2,800 *SLN*

A Victorian Louis XV style ormolu-mounted rosewood salon suite, comprising: a sofa, 8 armchairs and a pair of side chairs, repolished and restored, the sofa 75½in (192cm) wide.
$12,000–14,500 *C*

A Victorian walnut seven-piece drawing room suite, comprising: settee, lady's chair, gentleman's chair and 4 occasional chairs.
$2,800–3,200 *Mit*

A late Victorian inlaid-mahogany salon suite, comprising: a sofa, a pair of armchairs and a set of 4 single chairs, the shield-shaped backs with ribbon crests carved with swags and acanthus, inlaid with satinwood ovals, on inlaid square tapered legs with spade feet, c1890.
$6,000–7,000 *Bon*

A Victorian carved mahogany nine-piece salon suite, comprising: chair-back settee with scrolled crest, 3 pierced and waisted splats, cabriole front legs with peg feet, 2 armchairs and 6 single chairs, settee 54in (137cm) wide.
$2,400–2,800 *AH*

A set of 8 Victorian rosewood parlour chairs, comprising an armchair with a carved floral crest above an upholstered back and seat, flanked by arms on floral-carved moulded cabriole legs, ending in scroll toes, a nursing chair, and 6 balloon-backed chairs.
$4,000–4,400 *P(Sc)*

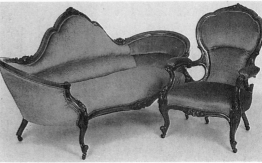

A walnut-framed part salon suite, comprising: a sofa, and a gentleman's armchair, upholstered in green plush dralon, the sofa with shaped headed cartouche carved moulded back descending to rounded hand supports and continuing to scroll-carved stylised foliate-hipped cabriole legs, late 19thC, 83½in (212cm) wide.
$2,000–2,400 *P(NW)*

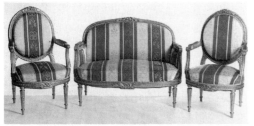

A Louis XVI style three-piece salon suite, comprising: a sofa and 2 oval-backed armchairs, the seats and back panels upholstered in red and cream Regency stripe, with carved and gilded frames, scrolled arms and circular tapering legs, regilded, late 19thC.
$780–940 *JM*

A Louis XV style giltwood salon suite, comprising: a canapé and 4 fauteuils, each upholstered in Aubusson tapestry, with arched top-rail above a padded rectangular back, on cabriole legs joined by an X-stretcher, damaged, late 19thC, canapé 63½in (161.5cm) wide.
$5,000–6,000 *C*

A French Empire revival style ormolu-mounted mahogany salon suite, comprising: a canapé, a pair of fauteuils and a pair of side chairs upholstered in a green silk damask, the canapé with a scrolled top-rail, above armrests, with eagle-head terminals, on shaped square tapering legs, c1900, canapé 61½in (156cm) wide.
$6,400–8,000 *C*

An Edwardian rosewood salon suite, comprising: a settee, the foliate-carved undulating top-rail centred with a foliate and urn-inlaid panel, above a pierced vase-shaped inlaid splat, flanked by 2 padded chair-backs, on ring-turned tapering legs, 2 matching open armchairs and 2 side chairs, settee 52½in (133cm) wide.
$1,400–1,800 *CSK*

A late Victorian eight-piece mahogany salon suite, comprising: a pair open tub armchairs, 4 single chairs and a pair of nursing chairs, inlaid in satinwood with urns, foliate scrolls and florets, pierced fern vertical splats, upholstered backs and serpentine seats, on turned legs.
$1,600–1,800 *M*

A mahogany three-piece bergère suite, c1920.
$1,100–1,300 *GWA*

A three-piece bergère suite, c1920.
$2,800–3,200 *RPh*

l. An Edwardian two-seater settee, with painted top-rail of amorini, floral and pierced splats to side, pierced trellis panels with caned panel, painted husk details to the 3 square tapering supports, and a pair of armchairs with similar decoration, on square tapering supports with spade feet, settee 48in (122cm) wide.
$4,000–4,800 *RBB*

Architects' Tables

A George III mahogany architect's table, the adjustable leather inset top above one false and one true drawer to the back, raised on square section tapering supports, 28½in (72.5cm) wide.
$1,200–1,450 *Bon(C)*

An early George III mahogany architect's table, with a hinged rising top above a drawer enclosing a slide with a divided interior and drawers, a candle slide to either side, on moulded square section legs with quadrant pilasters to the insides, c1760, 35½in (90cm) wide.
$5,500–6,500 *Bon*

A George III mahogany draughtsman's table, the hinged rectangular top rising on an adjustable trestle support, above a cockbeaded frieze drawer, on chamfered square section legs with pierced brackets, 28¼in (72cm) wide.
$1,000–1,200 *P(Sc)*

Breakfast Tables

A George III mahogany breakfast table, the rounded rectangular top crossbanded in partridge wood and inlaid with boxwood lines, on a ring-turned spreading baluster support and 4 reeded downswept square tapering legs, the locking mechanism stamped 'Bullock Patent', 60in (152.5cm) wide.
$9,000–10,000 *C*

An early Georgian mahogany breakfast table, the hinged top on a ring-turned spreading support with 3 cabriole legs and pointed pad feet, previously with casters, restored, 47½in (121cm) diam.
$6,400–7,200 *C*

An American cherry tip-top breakfast table, with vase-shaped turned pedestal, 18thC, 36½in (92.5cm) diam.
$880–1,000 *EL*

A Regency rosewood breakfast table, the circular top with split-reel moulding, on a bold turned column and concave plinth with 4 paw feet, 50in (127cm) wide.
$3,800–4,600 *L*

A stained walnut-veneered and inlaid breakfast table, the hinged top centred with a floral marquetry roundel within boxwood-strung edge, on turned and faceted column, quadripartite base with turned feet, early 19thC, 48¾in (124cm) diam.
$3,400–4,000 *P(Sc)*

A Regency mahogany breakfast table, the rounded rectangular tilt-top on a baluster-turned shaft and 4 hipped foliate-carved downswept reeded legs with claw feet, 48in (122cm) wide.
$1,200–1,600 *CSK*

Don't Forget!
If in doubt please refer to the 'How to Use' section at the beginning of this book.

A Regency mahogany breakfast table, the rounded oblong tip-up top with reeded edge on ring-turned stem, 4 reeded downswept legs with brass toes and casters, 53¼in (135.5cm) wide.
$1,700–1,900 *AH*

A George IV mahogany breakfast table, the moulded tilt-top above a turned columnar pillar and quadruple splayed legs ending in brass cappings and casters, restored, 47½in (121cm) wide.
$1,600–1,900 *S(S)*

A William IV rosewood circular breakfast table, on cylindrical column with lobed bands on circular base with 3 paw feet, 51in (130cm) diam.
$2,500–2,800 *DN*

A William IV rosewood breakfast table, with tip-up top and beaded frieze, on hexagonal column with gadrooned collar, concave-sided platform with foliate scroll-carved paw feet, some mouldings missing, 48in (122cm) diam.
$3,200–3,500 *CSK*

A William IV rosewood breakfast table, the tilt-top above a fluted frieze on a concave triangular support with a triform plinth base, on acanthus-scrolled feet incorporating concealed casters, c1835, 51in (129.5cm) diam.
$3,500–3,800 *S(S)*

A William IV rosewood breakfast table, the tip-up top with bead-and-reel edging, leaf-carved turned stem, on trefoil platform base with paw feet and casters, 49¾in (126.5cm) diam.
$3,400–3,600 *AH*

A William IV rosewood breakfast table, on a faceted shaft and concave-sided tripartite base, with gadrooned feet, 49in (124.5cm) diam.
$1,200–1,600 *CSK*

A William IV Scottish mahogany breakfast table, the top with egg-and-dart moulded border and similar frieze, on a slightly concave rectangular shaft, with fluted splayed supports, brass caps and casters, 48in (122cm) diam.
$3,400–3,800 *C(S)*

An early Victorian rosewood breakfast table, with octagonal bulbous column and concave-sided platform with paw feet, the top now affixed, 48in (122cm) diam.
$1,800–2,000 *CSK*

An early Victorian burr-yew veneered breakfast table, the tilt-top with radiating veneers, on a faceted column and concave trefoil platform, with bun feet, 49¾in (126cm) wide.
$2,200–2,700 *CSK*

> **Cross Reference**
> Colour Review

An early Victorian mahogany breakfast table, the tilt-top on tripartite concave-sided column with scrolling corners and conforming base, 60in (152.5cm) diam.
$5,000–5,600 *CSK*

A rosewood tip-top breakfast table, supported on a turned and carved centre column with quatrefoil base, scroll feet and casters, mid-19thC, 48in (122cm) diam.
$3,200–4,000 *GH*

A Victorian rosewood breakfast table, with an oval tilt-top on a turned and carved knopped column, on 4 leaf-carved splayed legs with scrolled terminals, 57in (145cm) wide.
$4,000–4,500 *DN*

Card Tables

A George II walnut triple-top card table, the quarter-veneered leaf and baize-lined leaf with counter wells, on husk-carved cabriole legs with hairy paw feet, c1730, 32in (81cm) wide.
$5,800–6,400 *Bon*

A George II mahogany card table, the folding top baize-lined and enclosing counter wells, on cabriole legs with pointed pad feet, 36¼in (92cm) wide.
$2,700–3,000 *DN*

A George II walnut card table, the fold-over top with projecting rounded corners revealing a green baize-lined interior, counter wells and candle stands, with a gateleg action, on turned tapering legs ending in pad feet, faults, restored, c1750, 33½in (85cm) wide.
$2,400–2,700 *S(S)*

A George III mahogany card table, the line-inlaid hinged top above a crossbanded frieze, on square tapering collared legs, 30½in (77.5cm) wide.
$720–880 *CSK*

l. A George III inlaid mahogany card table, the twin-divided hinged top inlaid with urns, above a frieze drawer, on square tapered legs, c1790, 17¼in (45cm) wide.
$1,700–1,900 *Bon*

A Sheraton style mahogany card table, with parquetry top of mulberry, tulip, yew-wood and rosewood divided by chequerwork stringing, single gate action, on 4 square tapering moulded legs, late 18thC, 36in (91.5cm) wide.
$3,400–4,000 *L&E*

MILLER'S COMPARES . . .

I A George III inlaid mahogany card table, with kingwood crossbanded fold-over top and frieze, on square tapering legs headed by ovals, 38¼in (97cm) wide.
$3,200–3,500 *Bea(E)*

II A George III inlaid mahogany card table, with kingwood crossbanding, the top later inlaid with an oval reserve, the tapering square legs inlaid with husk chains headed by fan medallions, on block feet, 36¼in (92cm) wide.
$1,400–1,600 *Bea(E)*

The appearance of an item is often the most important factor when determining its value. These 2 card tables were expected to sell for similar amounts, but the price achieved by *item I* was more than double that of *item II*, which sold within the auctioneer's estimate. *Item I* attracted particular interest because of its good colour and the slightly unusual elliptical shape when opened out. *Item II* is a standard shape and the inlay was noted in the catalogue as not being contemporary with the table. Although inlay is usually regarded as a desirable feature, the fact that it was executed later may have deterred prospective purchasers from bidding too highly. *Bea(E)*

A Dutch marquetry demi-lune card table, the fold-over top inlaid with an urn and flowers above a floral-inlaid frieze, on 4 square tapered legs, late 18thC, 31½in (80cm) wide.
$1,400–1,800 *B&L*

A mahogany and boxwood-lined fold-over card table, the hinged top opening to reveal a baize-lined interior, on square-section tapering legs, early 19thC, 39¾in (101cm) diam.
$880–1,000 *P(Sc)*

A Federal inlaid and figured mahogany and birchwood card table, with drawer, on reeded tapering legs ending in elongated vase-form feet, minor repair to inlay, New Hampshire, c1810, 37in (94cm) wide.
$9,000–10,000 *S(NY)*

An early Victorian rosewood-veneered card table, with fold-over top, octagonal baluster stem and on concave-sided platform with reeded bun feet, 35¼in (91cm) wide.
$650–780 *Bea(E)*

A Regency mahogany card table, the lined folding top crossbanded in rosewood and tulipwood, with boxwood and ebony stringing and a tulipwood banded frieze, on turned tapering legs, headed by spool-and-reed decoration, 36¼in (92cm) wide.
$2,800–3,200 *DN*

A Federal inlaid mahogany bowfront card table, the hinged top with diamond and chequer-inlaid edge above an inlaid frieze on square double-tapering line-inlaid legs, slight damage, c1815, 34⅛in (87cm) wide.
$4,200–4,800 *S(NY)*

A Victorian inlaid burr walnut card table, the hinged top inlaid with a continuous band of ivy leaves, on a fluted and floral-carved baluster column on similarly moulded outscrolled legs, c1860, 36½in (92.5cm) wide.
$2,000–2,500 *Bon*

l. An Edwardian mahogany and satinwood-banded card table, the fold-over top revealing a green baize interior above a rear frieze drawer, on tapered square legs and spade feet ending in casters, top warped, 35¾in (91cm) wide.
$1,100–1,450 *S(S)*

A Regency mahogany card table, with hinged top, on square sectioned pedestal, with a concave-sided platform base, on hipped downswept legs with claw feet, 35in (89cm) wide.
$950–1,100 *CSK*

A William IV rosewood card table, with fold-over top, on tapering stem with leafage-carved collar, the concave platform with 4 carved paw feet, 36in (91.5cm) wide.
$1,350–1,500 *RBB*

A Victorian burr walnut card table, the semi-elliptical folding swivel top lined in baize, on a pierced baluster column with 4 carved splayed legs, 39in (99cm) wide.
$1,600–1,800 *DN*

An Edwardian mahogany card table, the fiddle-back top inlaid with acanthus foliage, on square tapering legs, 36in (91.5cm) wide.
$4,000–4,400 *L*

Centre Tables

A George II Irish mahogany centre table, the dished top above a plain frieze, on cabriole legs headed by shells and foliage, on claw feet, 30in (76cm) wide.
$9,000–10,500 *C*

A Regency satinwood centre table, supported by a gun barrel column, raised on swept base with brass-capped casters, c1810, 27in (68.5cm) wide.
$4,800–5,400 *CAT*

A brass-bound and inlaid centre table, the segmental birch-veneered top with kingwood crossbanding above frieze with 4 quarter-veneered and crossbanded drawers, on 4 square section tapering legs and brass caps, possibly Swedish, early 19thC, 37¼in (95cm) diam.
$1,400–1,600 *P(Sc)*

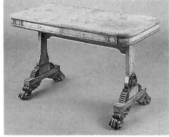

A Regency ormolu-mounted parcel-gilt rosewood centre table, the top inlaid with satinwood lotus flowers, the frieze mounted with ribbon-tied oak leaf wreaths, on a simulated rosewood turned shaft with lappeted and gadrooned band, on a tripartite base with scrolled paw feet, restored, remounted, 42in (107cm) diam.
$8,400–9,800 *C*

A pollard oak centre table, the rounded rectangular top above a pair of shallow frieze drawers, on solid vase-shaped end supports carved with scallop shells, on claw feet, c1825, 48in (122cm) wide.
$11,400–12,800 *Bon*

Centre Tables

Centre tables were used predominantly as decorative pieces in halls or large drawing rooms from the 18thC onwards. Their design was based on architectural forms, and early 19thC examples often had marble tops. Inlaid floral designs began to appear during the mid-1820s and by Victorian times the tables were of grand proportions, ornately decorated and often embellished with ormolu mounts in the 'French' taste.

A rosewood-inlaid carved and figured mahogany centre table, the crossbanded and veneered top tilting above a pineapple, leaf and fruit-carved standard with a gadrooned collar, the leaf-carved plinth on acanthus-carved paw feet, slight damage, Philadelphia, c1825, 48in (122cm) diam.
$14,500–16,000 *S(NY)*

This table is of exceptional quality with an unusual carved column.

A mahogany centre table, with serpentine-shaped top over shaped and carved frieze, supported by 2 turned and carved columns with carved scrolled feet, c1850, 47in (120cm) wide.
$4,000–4,800 *BERA*

A George IV rosewood and fossil stone centre table, the reel-moulded top on turned supports with gadroon-carved collars, the reel-moulded tricorn base with lion paw feet, c1825, 27⅜in (70cm) diam.
$8,800–9,600 *S*

r. A mid-Victorian burr walnut centre table, the serpentine oval top inlaid with foliate scrolls and with a crossbanded border, above a central frieze drawer, on gilt-metal-mounted square section cabriole legs, c1860, 46in (117cm) wide.
$2,500–3,000 *Bon*

A burr walnut centre table, with fully carved double roll edge over 2 turned and carved columns and carved cabriole legs and stretcher, southern Ireland, c1850, 57in (145cm) wide.
$10,500–11,000 *BERA*

A veneered centre table, with solid walnut shaped edgings, supported by 2 turned and carved columns joined by a stretcher, on carved cabriole legs, c1870, 39¼in (100cm) wide.
$3,200–4,000 *BERA*

A Louis XV style walnut and marquetry centre table, the serpentine top with a rosewood-banded border above a transverse frieze drawer and shaped apron, on cabriole legs, c1880, 40½in (103cm) wide.
$2,500–3,000 *S(S)*

A French giltwood centre table, the inset serpentine yellow mottled marble top with a foliate-carved border, the frieze centred with floral cartouches, on foliate-headed cabriole legs joined by conforming X-frame stretcher, late 19thC, 42in (106.5cm) wide.
$1,700–2,000 *CSK*

A Victorian mother-of-pearl and marquetry-inlaid walnut centre table, the inset tooled red leather inlaid with a broad band depicting birds, butterflies and scrolling foliage, above a foliate-carved shaped frieze with a central drawer on dolphin carved supports, tied by an inlaid solid stretcher, on acanthus-carved feet, c1870, 60½in (154cm) wide.
$5,600–6,300 *Bon*

A Louis XV style parquetry centre table, the shaped rectangular top above a long frieze drawer, on slender cabriole legs with gilt-metal sabots, c1880, 29½in (75cm) wide.
$1,300–1,500 *Bon*

A French Empire mahogany centre table, with grey veined marble slab top, on hexagonal bulbous centre column and 3 splayed supports carved with anthemion ornament, and on paw pattern feet, 19thC, 32in (81cm) diam.
$1,700–2,200 *CAG*

l. A satinwood oval centre table, the quadrant-veneered top with a central painted panel depicting cherubs, with a further 6 painted panels of children, above a frieze with foliate scrolls, on tapered square legs incorporating husk decoration, ending in spade feet, faults, early 20thC, 41½in (105cm) wide.
$3,500–4,000 *S(S)*

A Victorian walnut centre table, the shaped oval quarter-veneered top with leaf-carved edge, the underside with 4 scrolled stretchers to 4 foliate-carved cabriole legs linked by a central platform, 58¾in (149cm) wide.
$4,000–4,800 *WL*

A North African centre table, inlaid with ivory, 19thC, 41in (104cm) wide.
$1,700–2,000 *SPa*

A French ormolu-mounted boulle and ebonised centre table, the serpentine top inlaid with cut-brass foliate marquetry, above an undulating frieze with central drawer, the cabriole legs each headed by a caryatid, on scroll sabots, late 19thC, 51¼in (130cm) wide.
$3,000–3,400 *C*

An Edwardian mahogany and satinwood rococo-style centre table, the shaped circular top with satinwood veneer, scrolled marquetry decoration and moulded rim, above a carved foliate frieze and 4 similar carved cabriole legs, joined by scrolled stretchers supporting an inlaid platform, 36¼in (92cm) diam.
$1,500–1,600 *P(Sc)*

Console & Pier Tables

A Louis XVI ormolu-mounted mahogany console table, with a galleried white marble top and stretcher, on turned tapered fluted legs with brass caps, c1785, 43in (109cm) wide.
$7,500–8,500 *Bon*

A Regency mahogany and giltwood console table, with later simulated pale green marble top, on lappeted capitals resting on lion monopodiae, decorated with an anthemion motif, the back with 3 later mirror plates, restorations, regilt, the backboards replaced, adapted, 73½in (187cm) wide.
$3,400–4,000 *C*

A George IV rosewood and giltwood console table, the veined white marble top above a gadrooned ogee moulded frieze, on acanthus and foliate-carved scrolled front supports, with a mirrored back, on a plinth base, c1825, 50¼in (127.5cm) wide.
$5,700–6,700 *Bon*

A Louis XV style carved giltwood pier table, the Carrara marble top above a shaped frieze, carved with scrolling acanthus foliage and flowerheads, on cabriole supports and acanthus-carved stretcher, bearing a paper label printed 'Ciceri & Co, Edinburgh', late 19thC, 75in (191cm) wide.
$2,700–3,300 *C(S)*

A George III carved oak console table, the later pine top above a serpentine frieze incorporating pierced roundels and foliate motifs, the cabriole legs with acanthus leaf and bell-flower motifs joined by a pierced stretcher, formerly painted or gilded, faults, c1770, 34⅜in (88cm) wide.
$3,200–3,500 *S(S)*

A George IV rosewood and gilt gesso console table, now in the form of a radiator grille, the white marble top above a gadrooned frieze and reeded supports with leaf-form lappets, c1820, 62¼in (158cm) wide.
$4,000–4,500 *S(S)*

A William IV bird's-eye maple console table, with an inlaid frieze and acanthus-carved and turned tapered pilasters, with a mirrored back, c1835, 42in (107cm) wide.
$5,500–6,000 *Bon*

A pair of giltwood console tables, each with a grey-veined white marble top above a guilloche and beaded frieze, draped with floral swags, on tapering legs joined by a stretcher surmounted with a floral-filled and swag-draped urn, 19thC, 24½in (62cm) wide.
$5,000–5,600 *C*

Console & Pier Tables

Console or pier tables were designed to be placed against a pier, which is the wall space between windows in formal Queen Anne and Georgian rooms. They were often surmounted by a tall mirror in an elaborate gilded frame. These tables were made throughout Europe in the 18th and 19thC, often with marble tops and ornate gilt bases. They were not popular in America until the early 19thC, when Parisian Empire designs were followed by many New York cabinet makers.

A George IV rosewood pier table, the top above carved scroll supports and rear mirror panel, c1825, 62in (158cm) wide.
$5,500–6,000 *S(S)*

A Victorian giltwood and gesso console table, the marble top with shaped and pierced frieze modelled with scrolling leaves and fruits, on cabriole legs, united by ornate scrollwork stretcher, 80¼in (204cm) wide.
$1,200–1,600 *P(Sc)*

A giltwood console table, of serpentine outline, the streaky pink marble top above a rocaille and pierced lattice pendant apron, on carved downscrolled legs with a pierced scrolling stretcher, some restoration, 19thC, 35in (89cm) wide.
$2,700–3,200 *CSK*

Dining Tables

A George II mahogany drop-leaf dining table, on turned tapering supports incorporating gateleg action, on pad feet, c1750, 55¾in (142cm) wide extended. **$5,600–6,300** *S*

A George III mahogany D-end dining table, with string inlay, on square tapering supports, 114½in (291cm) wide. **$6,500–7,000** *AH*

Cross Reference
Colour Review

A George III mahogany triple section D-end dining table, with one extra leaf, formerly with an additional leaf to the centre section, on square tapering legs, 83½in (212cm) extended. **$3,200–3,500** *CSK*

A Regency mahogany dining table in 3 parts, the 2 D-ends inlaid with central shells and a central section, all crossbanded in satinwood and on turned fluted legs with brass casters, lacking some crossbanding, some decoration later, and 2 later leaves, 76½in (194cm) wide. **$1,600–2,000** *HOLL*

A Regency mahogany dining table, with reeded rounded rectangular ends, telescopic action, together with 4 extra leaves, on lobed turned tapering legs, 140¼in (356cm) wide. **$8,000–9,500** *L*

An early Victorian mahogany extending dining table, including 3 extra leaves, on gadrooned and octagonal tapering legs, some moulding to frieze lost, some colour differences, 128in (325cm) extended.
$3,500–4,500 *CSK*

An early Victorian mahogany dining table, the top above an undulating frieze with scrolling border, on a boldly-carved base with foliate-carved scrolled feet, 55in (140cm) diam.
$3,200–4,000 *CSK*

A Victorian mahogany extending dining table, the top opening to enclose 2 extra leaves, on turned and fluted tapering supports, 94in (239cm) extended.
$3,200–4,000 *C(S)*

A Victorian mahogany mechanical dining table with a patent wind-out ratchet and beech bearer action, incorporating 2 sets of 4 rectangular loose leaves, on a turned and carved column with 4 splayed scroll legs carved with acanthus and shell terminals and casters, with label of 'T.H. Filmer's cabinet manu-facturers', with a mahogany cabinet to hold the leaves, 89¾in (228cm) wide extended.
$31,000–34,000 *DN*
This exceptionally large and unusual table was found recently in a Victorian house in very original condition.

A William IV mahogany dining table, the well-figured crossbanded circular top with ebony line inlay over a cross-grained frieze with moulded edge, on a reeded tapering pedestal with wreath form mount, quadrant base and carved lion paw feet, 47¾in (121.5cm) wide.
$4,200–4,800 *P*

A mahogany extending dining table, on five ring-turned legs with brass casters, mid-19thC, 3 extra leaves of later date, 121½in (308.5cm) wide extended.
$3,600–4,200 *Bea(E)*

A late Victorian mahogany extending dining table, with panelled friezes, on boldly-gadrooned and fluted tapering legs, including one extra leaf, 82in (208cm) extended.
$2,200–2,800 *CSK*

An Edwardian mahogany extending dining table, with cabriole legs ending in ceramic casters, 2 leaf insertions and a winding handle, c1910, 95¼in (242cm) extended.
$1,600–2,000 *S(S)*

r. A George III style mahogany twin pedestal dining table, including a leaf insertion, on baluster supports with tripod bases, the reeded legs ending in brass casters, early 20thC, 74¾in (190cm) extended.
$1,600–2,000 *S(S)*

An early Victorian mahogany extending dining table, with 2 loose leaves, on turned legs carved with stylised leaves and casters, 95in (241cm) wide.
$4,500–5,000 *DN*

An early Victorian oak telescopic extending dining table, with 4 extra leaves, leaf-clasped turned and tapering legs with turned feet on brass caps and casters, 148in (376cm) extended.
$3,500–4,000 *P(Sc)*

A Victorian mahogany extending dining table, including 3 leaf insertions, on turned and reeded tapering legs ending in brass cappings and casters, together with a winding handle, 104in (264cm) extended.
$4,400–4,800 *S(S)*

A Victorian mahogany extending dining table, with 3 leaf insertions and a winding handle, the top with a carved border, on cabriole legs with acanthus form lappets ending in claw-and-ball feet, c1900, 108in (274.5cm) extended.
$4,400–4,800 *S(S)*

Display Tables

A Victorian ebonised and brass-inlaid display table, the double-hinged glazed top above a frieze inlaid with trailing foliage, on fluted and foliate-carved baluster legs joined by cross stretchers, with a central raised finial, damages, 71½in (181.5cm) wide extended.
$2,800–3,500 C

A rosewood and marquetry bijouterie table, with glazed top and sides, on cabriole legs, united by serpentine rectangular undertier, the whole with gilt-metal mounts and sabots, 19thC, 34¼in (87cm) wide.
$4,200–4,800 P(Sc)

A mahogany display table, the glazed hinged top and sides with brass stringing, on square tapering legs with casters, 19thC, 25in (63.5cm) wide.
$2,800–3,400 DN

A gilt-metal-mounted mahogany vitrine table, the hinged glazed top above glazed sides, on cabriole legs trailing to gilt sabots, late 19thC, 18in (45.5cm) wide.
$1,200–1,500 C

A gilt-metal-mounted mahogany vitrine table, the hinged glazed top above glazed sides, on cabriole legs trailing to gilt sabots, late 19thC, 23¼in (59cm) wide.
$1,200–1,500 C

An Edwardian line-inlaid mahogany heart-shaped vitrine table, on cabriole legs joined by a triangular stretcher, 16¾in (42.5cm) wide.
$875–1,000 C

Dressing Tables

A Victorian mahogany demi-lune dressing table, the mirror with carved floral supports, the base with moulded top, central drawer and turned handles, on turned supports with metal casters, 48in (122cm) wide.
$900–1,000 GH

A Dutch Empire mahogany toilet table, the black marble top and frieze drawer set with gilt palmets, on columnar legs with gilt brass capitals and bases, 19thC, 32¼in (82cm) wide.
$3,000–3,500 S(Am)

An Edwardian mahogany and floral marquetry dressing table, crossbanded in satinwood with a central frieze drawer and fan-inlaid spandrels, flanked by 3 drawers to either side, on square tapering legs, labelled 'Edwards & Roberts, London', 48in (122cm) wide.
$2,200–2,600 C

Drop-leaf Tables

A George II mahogany drop-leaf table, the moulded gateleg action club legs ending in claw-and-ball feet, 51½in (130.5cm) extended.
$650–800 *P(Sc)*

An American Empire mahogany-veneered drop-leaf table, turned pedestal, hairy paw feet, requires restoration, c1830, 72in (183cm) wide extended.
$270–320 *EL*

A George III mahogany drum table, the octagonal gilt-tooled leather-inset top with 8 frieze drawers, on a ring-turned column and fluted outswept legs, restored, 46½in (118cm) wide.
$5,000–6,000 *Bon*

A George III mahogany revolving drum table, the top with an arrangement of real and dummy drawers, on a later associated pedestal support with quatreform base, the reeded lobed sabre legs ending in claw feet, restored, 45¼in (115cm) diam.
$4,500–5,500 *S(S)*

A George III oval mahogany drop-leaf table, on cabriole legs ending in claw-and-ball feet, faults, c1760, 56in (142cm) extended.
$1,400–1,600 *S(S)*

A George IV mahogany table, with 2 drop leaves and one drawer opposing a false drawer, on a baluster-turned column with 4 moulded splayed legs, with chased brass terminals and casters, 42in (107cm) wide.
$1,200–1,600 *DN*

A George III mahogany drum table, with a leather-lined top, the frieze fitted with alternate real and false drawers, on a turned column and 4 down-curved legs, 33in (84cm) diam.
$4,500–5,500 *L*

A Regency *faux* rosewood drum table, the gilt-tooled circular leather-inset top above 4 true and 4 false drawers to the frieze, on a turned column and 4 outswept supports with brass cap casters, c1810, 48in (122cm) diam.
$11,000–12,500 *Bon*

An American Hepplewhite circular drop-leaf table, with 2 extra leaves, pine top and walnut base, late 18thC, 73in (185.5cm) wide extended.
$1,100–1,300 *EL*

Drum Tables

A George III mahogany drum rent table, the rotating leather-inset top above an arrangement of 12 frieze drawers with ivory inlaid index letters, the square base with a cupboard door flanked by canted blind fretwork corners, on reduced carved bracket feet, faults to top, splits to base, 42in (107cm) diam.
$6,000–7,000 *S(S)*

Drum Tables

Although most drum tables are veneered in mahogany or rosewood, exceptionally fine examples are sometimes found in more exotic woods such as satinwood and kingwood and these usually command higher prices.

A Regency mahogany drum table, the green leather writing surface within a crossbanded border, the frieze having 4 drawers alternating with 4 matching dummy drawers with gilt-brass knobs, on a tapering stem and concave triform platform base with turned feet, 29⅜in (75.5cm) diam.
$2,800–3,200 *P(Sc)*

Games Tables

A George II mahogany triple-top games table, the baize-lined leaf with guinea wells, on plain turned tapered legs with pad feet, 32in (81cm) wide.
$3,800–4,800 *Bon*

A George III mahogany games table, inlaid overall with boxwood lines, the crossbanded reversible top with a boxwood and mahogany chessboard to the reverse, above a boxwood and ebony-inlaid backgammon board with red leather-lined playing surface, above 2 drawers simulated as 3 drawers, with a slide on each side, on square tapering legs with spade feet, one slide replaced, 22in (56cm) wide.
$5,000–5,500 *C*

An Edwardian rosewood folding top games table, the inner leaves revealing a chessboard and backgammon board, the front frieze with single drawer and fitted compartments within, marquetry inlay to drawer and the under drawer, raised on 4 tapering legs with line inlay, pierced centre stretcher with marquetry detail, 24in (61cm) wide.
$1,500–1,700 *GAK*

A Dutch rococco burr walnut games table, the velvet-lined hinged top above a frieze drawer, on cabriole legs carved with rocailles, ending in claw-and-ball feet, mid-18thC, 27in (69cm) wide.
$5,700–6,300 *S(Am)*

A George IV rosewood games table, the inlaid sliding chequer-board top with a well and backgammon board, drop-flaps, with turned legs and stretcher, on square block feet, inset with plain brass roundels, part restored, 33in (84cm) wide.
$4,000–4,500 *DN*

A Victorian walnut games table, the top inlaid for chess, raised on lyre-shaped end supports and linked by a turned central stretcher, 36in (91.5cm) wide.
$1,200–1,400 *GAZE*

A Chippendale mahogany games table, with 4 pierced brackets and moulded legs, some damage, c1780, 35½in (90cm) wide.
$2,000–2,500 *SK(B)*

An early Victorian rosewood games table, the top reversing to show inlaid chessboard, with side-flaps and on octagonal pedestal to platform base, 28¼in (72cm) extended.
$1,100–1,200 *Bri*

A Victorian burr walnut and boxwood inlaid games/work table, the hinged top with an inlaid border of flowers and trailing foliage opening to reveal a burr walnut work surface with inlaid chess, backgammon and cribbage board of boxwood, ebony and kingwood above a single frieze drawer and a wool bin, on ring-turned baluster trestle supports and carved cabriole legs joined by a turned stretcher, with scroll feet and casters, 27in (69cm) wide.
$3,200–3,500 *P(Sc)*

l. An Edwardian rosewood and marquetry-inlaid folding top games table, on tapering legs with line inlay, pierced centre stretcher with marquetry detail, 24in (61cm) wide.
$1,500–1,650 *GAK*

Library Tables

A George III mahogany and ebonised octagonal library table, the green leather-lined top above 4 panelled drawers and 4 simulated drawers, each lined in mahogany and cedar, 2 with fitted compartments and a pen-tray, on ring-turned baluster shaft and reeded downswept tripod legs with brass caps and casters, restorations to top of shaft, the top and bottom possibly associated, 41½in (105.5cm) wide.
$11,000–13,000 *C*

A Regency rosewood library table, attributed to Gillows, with turned spindle-filled end supports and square section outswept legs with foliage brass caps, c1815, 44in (112cm) wide.
$2,600–3,200 *Bon*

A Victorian mahogany library table, with a frieze drawer, square baluster end supports incorporating acanthus leaf carving joined by a turned stretcher, on scroll feet with concealed casters, 56in (142cm) wide.
$2,200–2,600 *S(S)*

A George III mahogany double-sided library writing table, the leather-lined top having end drawers fitted with hinged slides and above dummy drawers, the turned reeded legs carved with pointed lappets, 62¼in (158cm) wide.
$12,000–14,500 *S*

A George IV rosewood library table, with 2 frieze drawers flanked by scroll-carved brackets, on rectangular end supports with turned lotus-carved stretcher, the scroll and leaf-carved feet with brass casters, 57¼in (145.5cm) wide.
$3,500–4,000 *DN*

A Victorian mahogany library table, with a leathercloth-inset top above an arrangement of 4 opposing frieze drawers, on turned and fluted legs ending in brass cappings and casters, c1860, 57½in (146cm) wide.
$4,400–4,800 *S(S)*

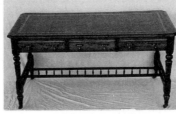

An Edwardian library table, with leather tooled top, c1910, 56in (142cm) wide.
$950–1,300 *GWA*

A Regency rosewood library table, with a pair of frieze drawers, raised on lobed reeded turned end supports, 51½in (131cm) wide.
$2,200–2,700 *Bon(C)*

A Victorian mahogany library table, the moulded leather-inset top above an arrangement of 6 frieze drawers, on turned baluster supports with a gadrooned base, c1840, 66in (168cm) wide.
$4,400–4,800 *S(S)*

A mid-Victorian oak library table, with leather-lined top above 2 end frieze drawers, on fluted column supports with platform base and scrolling frieze, leading to foliate scroll-carved downswept legs, 67in (170cm) wide.
$2,800–3,500 *CSK*

A late Victorian mahogany partners' library table, with moulded leather-lined top and 6 frieze drawers, on ring-turned tapering legs, stamped 'Maple & Co', 72in (183cm) wide.
$2,800–3,200 *CSK*

r. A walnut library table, attributed to Daniel Pabst, the 3 frieze drawers with floral carving and animal mask handles, raised on a trestle-form base with columnar and foliate-carved supports, joined by a stretcher centred by a stylised rosette, Philadelphia, late 19thC, 90in (228.5cm) wide.
$18,500–20,000 *S(NY)*

The price that this piece achieved when sold at auction reflected that it was attributed to a named maker.

Occasional Tables

A George III mahogany tilt-top occasional table, on birdcage turned baluster and triple splay support, c1760, 31in (79cm) wide.
$800–900 *MCA*

A William IV rosewood occasional table, the bifurcated end supports with scroll brackets, joined by a lotus-carved pole stretcher, on chamfered down-turned splayed feet with brass casters, 19¾in (75.5cm) wide.
$3,500–4,000 *Bea(E)*

A pair of Louis XV style ormolu-mounted tulipwood and marquetry occasional tables, each top, front and side inlaid with a flower-filled vase, above a pull-out leather-lined writing slide, with a drawer to the side and a further pair of drawers to the front, on slender cabriole legs with foliate-cast sabots, late 19th/early 20thC, 12¼in (31cm) wide.
$12,000–13,500 *C*

A William IV rosewood occasional table, the top veneered with a rolled edge and scalloped frieze, over turned and shaped column, on a triform base and bun feet, c1830, 17in (43cm) diam.
$1,300–1,500 *BERA*

An octagonal rosewood and pietra dura occasional table, the top inlaid with white roses and insects and a lapis lazuli border, above a baluster support, on paw feet, c1860, 25¾in (65.5cm) wide.
$9,000–10,000 *S*

An Edwardian satinwood occasional table, the top with ivy and husk decoration, above a frieze of swags, on 3 square section cabriole legs joined by a Y-shaped stretcher, 12in (30.5cm) diam.
$270–320 *P(Sc)*

A William IV pollard oak occasional table, the stepped top with beaded moulding, on a rectangular column divided by a collar, on a stepped and beaded base, 19¾in (50cm) wide.
$2,400–2,800 *P(Sc)*

A kingwood marquetry and gilt-bronze occasional table, the oval top crossbanded and centred by a spray of flowers, the drawer stamped 'Grohe Paris', c1870, 24in (61cm) wide.
$6,400–7,200 *S*

A gilt-metal and porcelain-mounted occasional table, the Sèvres-style dished top above a decorated frieze on fluted turned tapering legs and casters, united by stretchers and mounted with an urn, restored, late 19th/early 20thC, 20¼in (51.5cm) diam.
$1,400–1,600 *P(NE)*

r. A mahogany two-tiered occasional table, with scalloped edge, c1910, 24in (61cm) diam.
$130–160 *GWA*

An early Victorian burr walnut occasional table, the top above a scallop frieze, on a column and circular base with scroll feet, 24in (61cm) wide.
$1,000–1,200 *CSK*

A papier-mâché and gilt tilt-top occasional table, painted with flowers, the chamfered pillar above a triform base, on bun feet, reduced in height, c1860, 20½in (52cm) diam.
$750–900 *S(S)*

An Edwardian painted satinwood occasional table, crossbanded with string inlay, on square tapering supports joined by shaped stretchers supporting a small oval under shelf, 29¾in (75.5cm) wide.
$1,000–1,200 *AH*

Pembroke Tables

A kingwood veneered Pembroke table, with single drawer, c1790, 19in (48.5cm) wide.
$4,800–5,400 *CAT*

A mahogany Pembroke table, the twin-flap top above a frieze drawer, on turned tapering legs with pad feet, 18thC, 36in (91.5cm) wide.
$750–800 *CSK*

A Hepplewhite mahogany Pembroke table, with banded inlay to top, one real and one false drawer, original oval brasses, American, late 18thC, 38½in (98cm) wide.
$2,200–2,600 *EL*

An oval-shaped satinwood Pembroke table, with decorated border, raised on 4 square legs, replaced handles and casters, some wear, 18thC, 36½in (93cm) wide.
$13,000–16,000 *CAT*

A George III mahogany Pembroke table, the top and frieze with satinwood crossbanding, boxwood and ebony stringing, the frieze with a drawer, the boxwood-strung tapering square legs headed by shell medallions, on brass casters, 38½in (98cm) wide.
$3,800–4,200 *Bea(E)*

A George III Pembroke table, the top veneered in figured satinwood and crossbanded in mahogany, an oak-lined frieze drawer with later brass knob handles, on square chamfered legs, the centre later banded to cover a repair, 22in (56cm) wide.
$1,000–1,100 *WW*

l. A mahogany Pembroke table, with turned and reeded legs, c1835, 38in (96.5cm) wide.
$800–900 *RPh*

A George III mahogany oval Pembroke table, the top with a central marquetry fan and rosewood crossbanding, above one drawer, on square tapering legs with leather-covered casters, lacking 3 brass ring handles, 35½in (90cm) wide.
$1,200–1,300 *DN*

A Federal inlaid mahogany Pembroke table, with line-inlaid top, blind frieze drawer, on bellflower-inlaid square double-tapering crossbanded legs, New England, c1800, 37½in (95.5cm) wide.
$2,000–2,400 *S(NY)*

A Sheraton mahogany Pembroke table, with one drawer, turned and reeded legs, Northshore, Massachusetts, c1820, 61in (155cm) extended.
$1,200–1,500 *EL*

A William IV mahogany Pembroke table, with spiral twist legs, 19½in (50cm) long.
$1,400–1,800 *SPa*

Serving Tables

A George II mahogany marble top serving table, the associated top above a frieze incorporating bead-and-reel beading, on carved cabriole legs with acanthus leaf-carved angle brackets, on hairy paw feet, formerly a centre table, some parts missing, restored, 56¾in (144cm) wide.
$7,500–8,000 *S(S)*

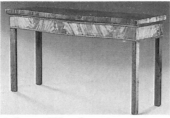

A George III mahogany serpentine-fronted serving table, on square chamfered legs, restored, 60½in (154cm) wide.
$2,400–2,700 *S(S)*

A George III style mahogany serpentine serving table, fitted with 3 drawers to the frieze, on boxwood-lined square tapering supports headed by oval boxwood paterae and block toes, c1890, 66in (167.5cm) wide.
$4,400–4,800 *C(S)*

A Regency mahogany serving table, on square tapering legs previously with gallery, replacements to bottom of front drawer, 60in (152cm) wide.
$4,000–4,500 *C*

A George III style carved mahogany serving table, the top above a foliate scroll-carved frieze, centred by cherubs with a shield, on cabriole legs, c1890, 54in (137cm) wide.
$1,300–1,600 *S(S)*

A Louis XV style ormolu-mounted two-tier *serviteur*, by P. Sormani, the top tier with a glass-bottomed tray on pierced acanthus-cast supports above a conforming top, on cabriole legs and sabots, c1900, 39¼in (100cm) wide.
$9,500–10,500 *Bon*

Side Tables

A William and Mary walnut side table, the quarter-veneered top with cross-banded border above a frieze drawer, on later spirally-turned legs and bun feet, restorations and replacements, the top possibly associated, 31in (79cm) wide.
$8,500–9,500 *C*

l. A George III mahogany side table, with a frieze drawer, on moulded chamfered legs with pierced brackets, 33⅜in (86cm) wide.
$6,400–7,200 *S*

A George II walnut side table, the moulded top above an arrangement of 2 short and one long drawer, on chamfered square legs, c1750, 32in (81cm) wide.
$1,400–1,600 *S(S)*

A pair of George III mahogany side tables, on square tapered legs with squared collars and block feet, 42in (107cm) wide.
$7,500–8,000 *S*

A George III mahogany single drawer side table, c1800, 28in (71cm) wide.
$3,200–3,500 *CAT*

A mahogany side table, c1815, 30in (76cm) wide.
$1,100–1,300 *GBr*

A mahogany side table, with turned stretcher, c1850, 48in (122cm) wide.
$400–500 *GWA*

Silver Tables

A Dutch marquetry inlaid mahogany silver table, the top inlaid with foliate scrolls, above a similarly inlaid long frieze drawer, on slender tapering legs with pad feet, mid-18thC, 31¼in (79.5cm) wide.
$2,400–2,800 *Bon*

A George III figured mahogany side table, the top crossbanded, with ebony and boxwood line inlay and moulded and carved rim, 4 short oak-lined drawers with original gilded-brass swan-neck handles with relief decorations, on square tapering moulded legs, 34½in (87.5cm) wide.
$2,200–2,700 *JM*

A Dutch walnut marquetry side table, the top centred by an inlaid vase of flowers flanked by a flower-filled cornucopia with exotic birds, the front with 2 frieze drawers, raised on cabriole claw-and-ball feet, 19thC, 30in (76cm) wide.
$3,300–4,000 *P(NW)*

> **Cross Reference**
> Colour Review

r. A gilt side table with decorated marble top, c1920, 22in (56cm) wide.
$380–430 *RPh*

A mahogany silver table, the square tapered moulded legs with pierced brackets, joined by a chamfered X-shaped stretcher, on block feet, c1765, 30¼in (77cm) wide.
$12,000–13,500 *S*

A George III mahogany bowfronted side table, decorated with ebony stringing and crossbanding, with 2 short drawers to the frieze and brass knob handles, on turned tapering legs, 42in (107cm) wide.
$900–1,000 *AG*

A Dutch mahogany and inlaid side table, the top with chequerbanded frieze, fitted with a drawer above a shaped apron, on square tapering legs, 19thC, 34in (86cm) wide.
$1,400–1,550 *CSK*

An Edwardian mahogany silver table, the serpentine top and undertier with fretwork galleries, on foliate-carved cluster column legs, with block feet, damaged, 42½in (108cm) wide.
$2,400–2,800 *C*

Sofa Tables

A late George III mahogany and satinwood crossbanded sofa table, centred by a flowerhead in an oval above 2 frieze drawers, on turned twin-end supports, with splayed legs ending in carved block terminals, 53¼in (135cm) extended.
$2,500–3,200 *P(Sc)*

A late George III mahogany sofa table, the boxwood-strung frieze with 2 cedar-lined drawers with brass handles, on tapering end supports, reeded splayed legs with brass caps and casters and a high arched stretcher, one leg repaired, 61in (155cm) wide.
$5,800–6,400 *DN*

A George IV rosewood and brass-inlaid sofa table, the figured top inlaid with brass bandings of scrolled leafage within brass stringings, with 2 real and 2 dummy drawers, on twin-turned reeded and gilt decorated central columns and swept-in rectangular base with cast brass toes and casters, 59in (150cm) wide.
$6,400–7,200 *CAG*

A George IV rosewood sofa table, with a frieze drawer and nulled borders, on a turned column with 4 splayed legs having roundels and brass paw feet with casters, 56in (142cm) wide.
$1,500–1,800 *HOLL*

A Regency rosewood line-inlaid crossbanded and tulipwood inlaid sofa table, with real and dummy drawer, on octagonal tapering pedestal with inlaid swept legs, on brass casters, 25¼in (64cm) wide.
$11,000–12,000 *P*

This table is of unusual size and proportion with a single frieze drawer.

A late Regency rosewood crossbanded sofa table, with a frieze drawer, on trestle ends, joined by an arched stretcher on splayed legs, ending in lotus leaf-cast brass casters, 58in (147cm) wide.
$2,400–2,700 *P(Sc)*

A late George III mahogany sofa table, with 2 frieze drawers on end supports with splayed reeded legs, brass paw terminals and casters, joined by a central stretcher, 61¾in (157cm) wide.
$4,000–4,400 *DN*

A late Regency mahogany sofa table, with 2 frieze drawers and raised on turned twin-end supports, brass paw terminals and hipped outswept legs linked by a pair of turned stretchers, 55in (140cm) wide.
$4,200–4,800 *GAZE*

A Regency rosewood sofa table, line-inlaid and crossbanded having 2 frieze drawers with Greek key inlay and 2 opposing dummy drawers, on a square tapering column and rectangular platform base, with 4 hipped downswept legs and claw feet, 40in (101.5cm) wide.
$4,000–5,000 *CSK*

A Scottish mahogany sofa/dressing table, the frieze fitted with 5 variously sized drawers, on squat trestle-end supports and splayed bar feet with brass caps and casters, c1800, 52in (132cm) wide.
$2,500–2,800 *C(S)*

A George IV mahogany sofa table, crossbanded in tulipwood above one frieze drawer, fitted with a leather-lined writing slide and pen compartments, with brass flower-chased handles on twin-turned end supports, with a turned stretcher and splayed legs with chased brass terminals, 64¼in (163cm) wide.
$3,200–4,000 *DN*

A George IV mahogany sofa table, with one frieze drawer, on twin-baluster turned end supports, moulded splayed legs, brass paw terminals and a turned and reeded stretcher, lacking casters, 59in (150cm) wide.
$2,000–2,500 *DN*

Sutherland Tables

A Victorian walnut Sutherland table, the oval top on lobed baluster trestle legs, 35in (89cm) wide.
$750–800 *L*

A Victorian ebonised, amboyna, kingwood and marquetry Sutherland table, each leaf incorporating a floral motif within a parquetry border, the top with a gilt-metal border, on a turned fluted support and quatreform base, the cabriole legs ending in ceramic casters, leaves warped, c1860, 53½in (136cm) wide.
$6,000–6,500 *S(S)*

An Edwardian crossbanded mahogany Sutherland table, c1905, 31½in (80cm) wide.
$480–520 *RPh*

Tea Tables

A figured mahogany tea table, on turned tapering legs ending in pad feet, patches to top, underside of top distressed, restored, Rhode Island, c1750, 35½in (90cm) wide.
$11,200–12,400 *S(NY)*

A George II mahogany gateleg action tea table, the hinged top above a frieze with a long drawer, on cabriole legs with scrolled angles and claw feet, lacking 4 angle-brackets, Irish, 34½in (87.5cm) wide.
$4,400–4,800 *C*

A George II mahogany tea table, the hinged top with gateleg action, on cabriole legs with carved scroll ears ending in claw-and-ball feet, restored, c1750, 33in (84cm) wide.
$1,400–1,600 *S(S)*

A mid-Georgian mahogany tea table, with hinged top, on club supports and pad feet, restorations, 32in (81cm) wide.
$1,400–1,600 *C(S)*

A George III mahogany breakfront tea table, with boxwood-strung borders, folding top and one frieze drawer, on square tapering legs with spade feet, 38¼in (97.5cm) wide.
$1,400–1,600 *DN*

Tea Tables

Towards the mid-18thC the many tea gardens in and around London came to be regarded as vulgar and disreputable and it thus became customary for fashionable people to invite their friends to drink tea in each other's homes. It was at this time that cabinet-makers turned their attention to designing suitable ornamental tables for the occasion.

A Georgian mahogany spider-legged drop-leaf tea table, with 2 drawers and brass ring handles, 33in (84cm) wide.
$2,500–3,000 *AP*

A George III mahogany triple folding top tea/games table, with spiral-turned banding, raised on chamfered square supports, 32in (81.5cm) wide.
$2,400–2,800 *JAd*

A George III mahogany and crossbanded tea table, the fold-over top enclosing a hinged lockable centre section with adjustable support, the frieze with satinwood and ebony stringing, on square tapering block legs terminating with brass caps and casters, 33¾in (86cm) wide.
$2,800–3,500 *WL*

A George III mahogany tea table, the serpentine fold-over top above a frieze with fan paterae, supported on square tapered legs, late 18thC, 34¼in (87cm) wide.
$1,700–2,200 *B&L*

A late George III mahogany and boxwood-lined tea table, with hinged top above a frieze drawer, on square tapering supports and elongated spade feet, 40in (102cm) wide.
$1,500–1,600 *C(S)*

A mahogany D-end tea table, on a turned pedestal with 4 anthemion-carved hipped supports with cast brass cup casters, c1830, 36in (91.5cm) wide.
$1,100–1,200 *Bri*

A George III satinwood and rosewood-crossbanded tea table, inlaid with stringing, the fold-over top supported on twin gatelegs, the tapering square legs ending in brass cappings and casters, restored, c1800, 36in (91.5cm) wide.
$3,600–4,300 *S(S)*

A late George III mahogany satinwood and burr-elm crossbanded fold-over tea table, with boxwood-strung top over a single frieze drawer, standing on square section tapering legs and spade feet, 38½in (98cm) wide.
$1,900–2,200 *P(Sc)*

A William IV mahogany tea table, with folding swivel D-shaped top, on reeded and collared turned tapering stem, concave base and lion paw feet with casters, 36in (91.5cm) wide.
$1,400–1,600 *AH*

l. A William IV mahogany metamorphic tea table and dumb waiter, banded overall with beading, the hinged top enclosing a quarter-veneered interior, above 2 conforming shelves on an octagonal extending shaft and concave-sided quadripartite base with scrolled serpentine feet, the top and interior probably re-veneered, 31in (79cm) wide.
$4,800–5,800 *C*

A mahogany fold-over tea table, on turned and fluted column, the quatrefoil base with 4 scroll feet and casters, early 19thC, 30in (76cm) wide.
$850–1,000 *JM*

A late Regency mahogany fold-over top tea table, standing on tapered reeded legs, 37½in (95cm) wide.
$1,500–1,600 *Mit*

A George IV mahogany tea table, with rounded rectangular top, beaded mouldings to the frieze and square stem, on a concave-sided platform with bun feet and casters, 36in (91.5cm) wide.
$880–960 *Bea(E)*

An early Victorian mahogany tea table, with an acanthus-carved apron, raised on a turned and carved column with 4 splay legs and brass casters, 33½in (85cm) wide.
$1,000–1,100 *AG*

Tripod Tables

An early George III circular mahogany tip-up tripod table, changes to top and possible later carving to feet, c1770, 29in (74cm) diam.
$2,400–2,800 *FHA*

A oak tripod candle stand, on cabriole legs and club feet, 33in (84cm) high.
$1,200–1,400 *SPa*

An early Victorian mahogany tripod table, the solid top with a dish edge, on a barley-twist tailored column with 3 cabriole legs, c1850, 19in (48cm) diam.
$1,100–1,400 *BERA*

A Chippendale carved mahogany tilt-top bird-cage tea table, the hinged top tilting and rotating above a ring-turned baluster-form standard, on cabriole legs ending in claw-and-ball feet, restored, probably New Bern, North Carolina, c1775, 31in (79cm) diam.
$5,600–6,200 *S(NY)*

l. A George III mahogany tripod table, with a spindle-moulded gallery to the circular tilt top, the turned stem with a spiral-cut bowl, on cabriole legs and club feet, 24in (61cm) diam.
$2,400–2,800 *WW*

A circular mahogany tilt-top table, c1860, 20in (50.5cm) diam.
$400–550 *GWA*

r. A red lacquered Chinese design wine table, early 20thC, 12in (30.5cm) diam.
$190–220 *PSA*

A circular flame mahogany tripod wine table, on cabriole legs and club feet, 18thC, 22½in (57cm) diam.
$1,900–2,400 *SPU*

A George III mahogany tilt-top table, with a turned support and a tripod base, the reeded downswept legs ending in spade feet, one leg repaired, c1800, 39¼in (100cm) diam.
$1,400–1,550 *S(S)*

A Dutch marquetry tripod table, the top with central urn of flowers surrounded by a band of foliage, on a hexagonal baluster column and 3 scroll legs, c1830, 30in (76cm) diam.
$1,800–2,200 *B&L*

Two-Tier Tables

A mahogany marquetry-inlaid two-tier tray table, by Shoolbred of Tottenham Court Road, c1890, 35in (89cm) high.
$4,000–4,800 *BERA*

A George III mahogany two-tier bedside table, 42in (107cm) high.
$650–750 *GAZE*

A two-tier table, with ormolu mounts, late 19thC, 27in (68.5cm) wide.
$680–750 *RPh*

An Edwardian mahogany two-tier table, crossbanded with satinwood, boxwood and ebony line-stringing, c1900, 24in (61cm) diam.
$1,600–2,000 *BERA*

Work Tables

A Federal mahogany work table, with 2 drawers, on tapering legs, New England, c1800, 16½in (42cm) wide.
$950–1,100 *CNY*

A George III rosewood-veneered work table, with boxwood and ebony-stringing, a satinwood-banded top, rising firescreen panel, frieze drawer with divisions and pull-out work bag, on slender tapering square legs joined by an X-undertier and later brass casters, 21in (53.5cm) wide.
$2,400–2,800 *Bea(E)*

A George III mahogany and rosewood banded work table, with 2 drawers including a writing slope and compartments, on ring-turned legs ending in brass cappings and casters, c1800, 21in (53cm) wide.
$2,700–3,000 *S(S)*

A Regency amboyna and cut-brass-inlaid work table, with brass-inlaid frieze and fitted tapering work basket, the square supports incorporating a foliate motif joined by a stretcher, on short sabre legs, faults, c1810, 21¾in (55cm) wide.
$12,800–14,200 *S(S)*
The burr effect of the amboyna veneer and the extensive brass inlay made this piece desirable.

A Regency mahogany drop-leaf pedestal work table, with 2 real and 2 false drawers, U-shaped support to the shaped flat pedestal, on 3 reeded S-scrolled legs with brass paw caps and casters, 30¼in (77cms) wide.
$2,400–2,700 *Bea(E)*

A Regency mahogany work table, inlaid overall in ebony and boxwood, the twin-flap top over a mahogany-lined frieze fitted drawer and a further drawer, above a work basket slide, on square splayed tapering legs with brass caps and casters, restorations, the work basket missing, originally fitted with baize-lined writing surface, 40in (101.5cm) wide.
$4,000–4,800 *C*

A Regency ormolu-mounted rosewood work table, inlaid overall with boxwood lines, the top crossbanded in tulipwood above a cedar-lined frieze drawer and workbox slide, on lyre-end supports joined by a ring-turned stretcher and splayed legs with brass casters, lacking workbox, restorations on top, 20in (51cm) wide.
$6,000–6,500 C

A Regency mahogany crossbanded and boxwood-lined canted rectangular sewing table, the hinged top above a shaped fitted drawer, on square section tapering legs joined by an arched and shaped stretcher, 20½in (52cm) wide.
$1,100–1,300 P(Sc)

A Regency brass-mounted rosewood and Vincennes porcelain work table, the top with a porcelain tray and central landscape scene, above a spring-loaded frieze drawer flanked by shell roundels, on lyre-end supports and scrolled serpentine square tapering legs joined by a turned baluster stretcher, the porcelain with date letter 'A' for 1753, previously with casters, lacking 2 brass rosettes, 18in (45.5cm) wide.
$8,800–9,600 C

A Federal flame birchwood and carved mahogany sewing table, the drawer and sewing slide hung with a fabric bag, flanked by leaf-carved and star-punched capitals, reeded tapering legs and peg feet ending in brass caps and casters, minor patches to veneer and mouldings, bottom board of sewing bag replaced, Salem, Massachusetts, c1810, 22in (56cm) wide.
$11,000–13,500 S(NY)

A figured mahogany sewing table, the top flanked by hinged leaves fitted with a frieze drawer and a sewing basket on 4 flaring columnar supports, the concave-sided plinth below on bun feet and casters, retains old surface, losses and damage to veneer, Boston, Massachusetts, c1820, 37in (94cm) wide extended.
$2,200–2,700 S(NY)

A Federal mahogany-veneered astragal-ended work table, the top lifts to a fitted interior above 2 drawers, the lower one with tambour reeding, on ring-turned legs ending in turned feet, original brass, slight damage, Philadelphia or New York, c1810, 23¾in wide (60.5cm) wide.
$5,500–6,500 SK(B)

A Regency mahogany octagonal top work table, raised on 4 swept legs, c1820, 17½in (44.5cm) diam.
$3,200–3,600 CAT

An American Empire mahogany two-drawer work table, bamboo turned columns to all 4 corners, on acanthus carved pedestal and scroll-carved base with 4 brass feet, c1820, 18½in (47cm) wide.
$650–800 EL

A carved and figured mahogany two-drawer work table, the bottom drawer bearing the stencilled inscription 'Geo. W. Miller, Cabinetmaker', raised on acanthus-carved urn-form standard and leaf-and-feather-carved animal legs ending in paw feet on casters, patches to top and drawer fronts, c1825, 22¼in (56.5cm) wide.
$2,000–2,400 *S(NY)*

A William IV rosewood work table, c1850, 25in (63.5cm) wide.
$1,300–1,500 *RPh*

A Napoleon III papier mâché ebonised and mother-of-pearl inlaid work table, the hinged top centred by a chinoiserie landscape with figures, enclosing a line interior, the frieze with gilt-painted flower decoration within mother-of-pearl borders, on double scroll feet, with an X-form stretcher surmounted by an urn, c1850, 23¼in (59cm) wide.
$5,500–6,500 *S*

A mahogany Pembroke work table, with fitted drawer above a deep pleated well, on turned tapering legs with casters, c1830, 19¾in (50cm) wide.
$3,200–4,000 *BERA*

A William IV mahogany drop-leaf work table, with plain top, 3 real and 3 dummy drawers, on central turned column and swept-in rectangular base with bun feet, 17in (43cm) wide.
$750–850 *CAG*

A Napoleon III walnut work table, the hinged crossbanded top with a gilt-bronze foliate border, enclosing a mirrored interior and a tray, on cabriole legs, the lock stamped 'Nettlefoli Patent', c1865, 21¾in (55cm) wide.
$8,000–9,000 *S*

A north European mahogany end-supported single-drawer work table, raised on small lion paw feet, c1830, 18½in (47cm) wide.
$3,500–4,000 *CAT*

A Victorian ormolu-mounted tulipwood and kingwood work table, the hinged top quarter-veneered and crossbanded with boxwood outlines, with compartmented interior, on slender cabriole legs with foliate-cast clasps, on foliate sabots, 23¼in (59cm) wide.
$2,400–2,800 *C*

A French rosewood work table, the hinged top enclosing a fitted interior, the shaped sliding frieze applied with foliage, on moulded cabriole supports and scrolled toes, the brass lockplate stamped 'Tahan à Paris', late 19thC, 23in (58.5cm) wide.
$1,200–1,400 *C(S)*

Writing Tables

A George III mahogany writing table, the reeded top above a frieze fitted with a single drawer enclosing pen and ink compartments, on ring-turned tapered legs and brass casters, drawer stamped 'Gillows Lancaster', c1800, 28in (71cm) wide.
$6,000–6,500 *S*

A mahogany writing table, the top with reeded rim above a frieze drawer with beaded surround, on associated turned column supports and carved platform base with scrolled hairy paw feet, early 19thC, 42½in (108cm) wide.
$1,700–2,000 *CSK*

r. A Regency mahogany writing table, the square top with brass and ebonised inlay, the frieze drawer with adjustable writing surface, on turned and fluted tapering supports and casters, 20½in (52cm) wide.
$1,400–1,550 *RBB*

A mahogany writing table, the top with solid gallery above 3 frieze drawers on reeded tapered legs with brass casters, early 19thC, 47½in (120cm) wide.
$2,400–2,700 *Oli*

A Regency satinwood and parcel-gilt writing table, the old leather within a crossbanded surround with flowerhead-carved edge mould, over a frieze fitted with 2 drawers to one side and 2 dummy drawers to the reverse and flanked by acanthus scrolls, on twin-end supports of pillar form flanked by gilded leaf-scroll supports on trestle-form ends and gilt leaf scroll and paw feet incorporating casters, 54¼in (138cm) wide.
$2,500–3,200 *P*

A George III rosewood writing table, with original leather, shallow drawer, turned and reeded columns, on sabre feet with gilt-bronze casters, c1810, 37in (94cm) wide.
$8,000–9,500 *BERA*

A late Regency rosewood-veneered and simulated rosewood writing table, with pierced brass three-quarter gallery, 2 frieze drawers opposing 2 false drawers, baluster end supports, trestle bases and bun feet, 45in (114.5cm) wide.
$2,500–3,000 *Bea(E)*

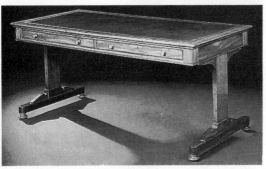

A George IV mahogany double-sided library writing table, the crossbanded and leather-lined top above one real and one dummy drawer to each side, c1820, 57in (176cm) wide.
$4,800–5,800 *S*

A mahogany writing table, the top with 2 frieze drawers, on turned and vase-shaped supports, and reeded platform bases with elaborately carved scrolled and hairy paw feet, early 19thC, 52in (132cm) wide.
$2,800–3,200 *CSK*

A Regency rosewood writing/work table, the flap top above a frieze drawer with writing surface, above a further fitted drawer and sliding drum well, on U-shaped support with column uprights and quadripartite concave platform on scroll feet, 34in (86.5cm) wide.
$2,500–2,800 *CSK*

A George IV mahogany metamorphic writing/dressing table, enclosed by 2 outward-hinging covers with hinged compartments, a false drawer fall with an adjustable writing slope, above a drawer fitted with recesses and a further drawer with brass lion mask handles, on turned and reeded legs, brass casters, 52½in (133.5cm) wide.
$5,000–5,600 *DN*

A Victorian walnut kidney-shaped writing table, with inset leather surface and floral marquetry inlay, on 2 leaf-carved baluster-turned end standards with cabriole legs, scrolled feet and china casters, joined by a pole stretcher, 36½in (93cm) wide.
$1,500–1,700 *AH*

A mid-Victorian figured mahogany writing table, with 2 drawers, on turned and tapering moulded legs raised on casters, 49in (124.5cm) wide.
$1,100–1,200 *DA*

A Victorian ebonised and bone-inlaid writing table, the raised superstructure incorporating 4 drawers above an inset leather writing surface, 2 frieze drawers on turned and fluted legs ending in brass sabots, joined by an X-form stretcher, some bone and brass lifting, c1880, 40in (102cm) wide.
$3,600–4,400 *S(S)*

A Louis XV style ormolu-mounted marquetry *bureau-plat*, the velvet-inset serpentine top above one long and 2 short drawers, standing on 4 cabriole legs, late 19thC, 44½in (113cm) wide.
$7,000–8,000 *B&L*

An Edwardian mahogany writing table, decorated with crossbanding and stringing, the top with inset leather writing surface, one long drawer and 4 short drawers, with brass handles, raised on square tapering legs and under-stretcher, 44½in (113cm) wide.
$700–800 *AG*

l. A George III style mahogany cheveret, the detachable top section with bentwood handle above a gallery with wire mesh back panel, 2 short and one long drawer, the lower section fitted with a deep frieze drawer, all with bone handles, on square tapering legs joined by a cross stretcher, early 20thC, 16in (41cm) wide.
$1,700–2,000 *CSK*

The cheveret is a small writing table intended for ladies' use, and is often fitted with a handle to allow it to be moved around. It originated in the 18thC and is distinguished by the sets of drawers at the back or underneath the top. The upper galleried shelf was intended as a bookshelf.

An Edwardian satinwood cross-banded and boxwood-strung lady's mahogany writing table, the hinged top opening and projecting the sliding writing surface to reveal a morocco leather-fitted interior, the edge stamped 'English Patent No 6425 AD1902' on slender tapered legs, with out-turned feet, united by a segmental stretcher, 31in (79cm) wide.
$1,200–1,400 *P(NW)*

Teapoys

A Regency mahogany teapoy, of sarcophagus shape, on a turned column and three-hipped down-curved legs, 16½in (42cm) wide.
$1,000–1,100 *L*

A Regency rosewood teapoy, the hinged top with stiff-leaf-cast ormolu rim revealing a pink velvet-lined fitted interior with 2 hinged foil-lined caddies and 2 mixing bowl apertures, raised on a pair of fluted Ionic style columns, on a pair of ormolu-mounted platforms and scroll feet, 19in (48cm) wide.
$3,500–4,000 *AP*

A Regency mahogany and ebony-lined teapoy, the hinged top enclosing 4 lidded pull-out caddies and 2 lined circular recesses, above 2 ring-turned baluster columns and a leaf-carved quadruped base ending in turned finials, with pointed feet, caps and casters, 15¾in (40cm) wide.
$3,500–4,000 *P(Sc)*

A William IV rosewood teapoy, with a moulded rising top enclosing 2 cylindrical caddies, each with a hinged cover and 2 glass sugar bowls, on a tapering octafoil column, on scroll feet, 19in (48.5cm) diam.
$1,200–1,400 *Gam*

Trays

A papier mâché tray/coffee table, on separate modern base, c1810, 30in (76cm) wide.
$3,200–3,800 *CAT*

A mahogany butler's tray, on a folding stand, c1840, 20in (50cm) wide.
$640–720 *RPh*

A Regency papier mâché tray, with a red ground, raised on a simulated bamboo stand, 30in (76cm) wide.
$3,200–3,500 *CAT*

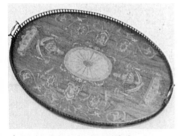

A marquetry tray, with brass gallery and handles, inlaid with Classical urns, mask heads and scrolling foliage around a central fan medallion, slight damage to gallery, 19thC, 27½in (70cm) wide.
$880–960 *Bea(E)*

A papier mâché tray, decorated in green and gilt on a maroon ground, on a later stand, 19thC, 32in (81.5cm) wide.
$2,800–3,200 *DN*

An Edwardian mahogany kidney-shaped butler's tray, with brass handles, boxwood-strung and inlaid in the centre with a shell motif, 26in (66cm) wide.
$190–215 *GAK*

Wall Brackets

A set of 4 giltwood wall brackets, each with a serpentine top and lambrequin pendant frieze, 19thC, 15in (38cm) wide.
$1,700–2,000 *C*

A pair of carved pine giltwood wall brackets, with a shelf, above a phoenix flanked by and perched upon carved scrolls, leaves and ruffles, one bracket lacking a wing, chips to gilding, minor repairs, 18thC, 8in (20.5cm) wide.
$5,700–6,300 *S(NY)*

A pair of George III carved giltwood wall brackets, the D-shaped carved moulded shelf supported by gathered acanthus leaves, c1800, 12in (30cm) high.
$11,000–12,000 *S*

Wardrobes

A George III mahogany and crossbanded breakfront wardrobe, with a pair of panel doors enclosing sliding trays above 2 short and 3 long graduated drawers, flanked on both sides by a cupboard enclosing hanging space and 2 further drawers, c1800, 96in (244cm) wide.
$10,500–11,500 *S(S)*

The figuring of the mahogany on this impressive wardrobe was extremely decorative.

A Victorian mahogany three-door wardrobe, 70in (178cm) wide.
$3,200–3,600 *RPh*

A Victorian mahogany wardrobe, the cornice with carved scroll supports beneath, the arched panelled doors with turned knobs, above 2 drawers, 60in (152.5cm) wide.
$800–1,000 *GH*

A Dutch East Indies hardwood armoire on stand, with panelled doors and sides, shaped brass strap hinges, the stand with 2 drawers, on carved cabriole legs with claw-and-ball feet, 18thC, 52in (132cm) wide.
$6,000–7,000 *Bea(E)*

A figured walnut two-door wardrobe, c1860, 55½in (141cm) high.
$2,000–2,400 *GBr*

An Edwardian mahogany and floral marquetry wardrobe, the central arched mirrored door flanked by panelled doors, inlaid with floral sprays and bellflower swags, enclosing hanging space and drawers, 75in (190.5cm) wide.
$1,700–2,000 *C*

A figured mahogany ormolu-mounted wardrobe, the fielded and panelled doors opening to 3 long shelves, 2 short shelves and a large compartment flanked by engaged pilasters, on turned tapering legs and ball feet, New York, c1815, 41in (104cm) wide.
$3,500–4,500 *S(NY)*

A George IV mahogany and rosewood-banded four-door wardrobe, the central section with a pair of frieze drawers above later-mirrored panel doors enclosing slides, flanked by a pair of cupboards, with void interiors, 110¼in (280cm) wide.
$1,400–1,800 *S(S)*

An Edwardian mahogany triple wardrobe, with moulded cornice, arched bevelled mirrored side doors, central upper cupboard and drawers, on bracket feet, 78in (198cm) wide.
$1,400–1,600 *GH*

Whatnots

A William IV rosewood three-tier whatnot, 53in (134.5cm) high.
$3,500–4,000 *GAZE*

A William IV mahogany whatnot, the 4 shelves supported by 4 turned and carved columns with reeded finials, drawer at base, on original casters, c1830, 20in (51cm) wide.
$3,200–4,000 *BERA*

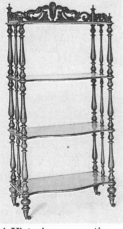

A Victorian serpentine walnut four-tier whatnot, with baluster-turned uprights, the top tier with foliate carved gallery, 22in (56cm) wide.
$1,250–1,400 *Oli*

A Regency mahogany whatnot, with 2 caned shelves above a cupboard with a panelled door enclosing an adjustable shelf, with ring-turned supports on turned legs with casters, 18in (46cm) square.
$2,400–2,800 *DN*

A burr walnut, satinwood and ebony inlaid whatnot, c1850, 19in (48.5cm) wide.
$1,000–1,200 *PSA*

A Victorian rosewood canterbury whatnot, with turned finials and spirally turned supports, concave drawer with turned handles, the legs with brass casters, 22in (56cm) wide.
$1,000–1,200 *DN*

A William IV mahogany whatnot, the rising top on an easel ratchet, with a book rest, the base undertier fitted with a drawer with brass knob handles, the turned legs on brass casters, 20½in (52cm) wide.
$1,700–2,000 *WW*

r. A mahogany four-tier whatnot, the top with fringed adjustable book rest, ring-turned supports and a drawer with turned handles, on bun feet, early 19thC, 18in (46cm) wide.
$2,000–2,500 *DN*

A whatnot, with 3 mahogany shelves, bamboo sides, raised on original cup brass casters c1825, 16in (40.5cm) wide.
$4,500–5,500 *CAT*

Window Seats

A mahogany window seat, original frame with the exception of one rail, on H-stretcher base and square chamfered legs, c1790, 41in (104cm) wide.
$2,000–2,400 *LCA*

A French giltwood window seat, the squab cushion between 2 overscrolled ends with a floral and foliate-moulded frame, on beaded scrolling supports joined by a pierced wavy stretcher, on turned and paterae-carved feet, 19thC, 80in (203cm) wide.
$3,200–3,600 *CSK*

A George III mahogany window seat, the scrolled ends and serpentine seat on moulded cabriole legs, c1780, 38in (97cm) wide.
$4,500–5,000 *S*

Wine Coolers

A George III mahogany wine cooler, the oval top section with brass binding, 2 brass swing handles, on a stand with gouge-carved frieze and carved paterae, on chamfered square splay supports with fluted fronts, 27in (69cm) wide.
$4,000–4,500 *RBB*

A George III oval brass-bound wine cooler, with tin liner and 3 brass bands, lion mask handles, the base with a plain frieze, on square tapering collared legs, 28½in (72.5cm) wide.
$1,600–2,000 *CSK*

A mahogany rectangular wine cooler, with hinged lid and fitted interior, on a stand with square tapering legs, early 19thC, 20in (51cm) wide.
$1,200–1,350 *CSK*

A George IV yew-wood cellaret, of sarcophagus form, 25½in (65cm) wide.
$3,000–3,500 *L*

A Regency mahogany sarcophagus-shaped wine cooler, the domed hinged top with cavetto-moulded sides above an ebonised line-inlaid tapering body with lion mask handles and fluted frieze, on later turned feet, 27in (68cm) wide.
$1,500–1,600 *CSK*

A Victorian inlaid mahogany and boxwood-strung wine cooler, of sarcophagus form, the hinged top and front with inlaid boxwood decoration within harewood ovals, on lobed bun feet, 26in (66cm) wide.
$2,200–2,600 *P(Sc)*

A mahogany cellaret, on claw-and-ball feet, c1890, 32¼in (82cm) wide.
$3,800–4,200 *GBr*

An Anglo-Indian carved hardwood wine cooler, the hinged lid with a trellis pattern of leaves, a bunch of grapes and vine leaves to the knop, the ogee sides decorated with bunches of grapes and vines, with a brass lock, the paw feet on china casters, 19thC, 28in (71cm) wide.
$2,500–2,800 *WW*

An oak brass-bound wine cooler on stand, by R. A. Lister & Co Ltd, with inset metal tray, the stand with cross stretchers, c1900, 26in (66cm) wide.
$480–560 *GH*

PINE
Beds & Cradles

A Mennonite painted pine settle bed, with hinged seat opening to a storage cupboard, turns to form a bed, raised on shaped bracket base, with plank supports, distressed mustard and green/black finish, Ontario, 19thC, 73½in (187cm) wide.
$1,000–1,200 *RIT*

A pine doll's cradle, Pembrokeshire, c1870, 20in (51cm) long.
$350–400 *COA*

A European pine sleigh bed, 1920s, 72in (183cm) long.
$350–400 *TPC*

Benches

An Irish pine child's form, c1800, 16in (40.5cm) long.
$40–50 *TAN*

An Irish pine form, c1850, 22in (56cm) long.
$50–65 *TAN*

A pine sheep slaughtering bench, c1890, 50in (127cm) long.
$300–350 *AL*

A pine bench, c1880, 104in (264cm) long.
$640–720 *AL*

A Scottish pine bench, c1880, 88in (223.5cm) long.
$675–725 *AL*

A pine pig bench, c1880, 25in (63cm) long.
$200–240 *AL*

An east European pine bench, 19thC, 61in (155cm) long.
$880–1,000 *GRP*

A pine bench, c1900, 73in (185.5cm) long.
$80–100 *HRQ*

Bookcases

A pine glazed
bookcase, c1860,
51in (129.5cm) wide.
$800–1,000 *HRQ*

An Irish Gothic style
pine bookcase, part-
glazed, c1860,
45in (114.5cm) wide.
$1,450–1,600 *TAN*

l. A pine bookcase, with
glass door, 2 drawers,
replacement pillars,
c1860, 39in (99cm) wide.
$800–1,000 *NWE*

r. A pine bookcase, on a
kneehole desk, the
associated base with writing
surface and ribbon-carved
frieze drawer, with recessed
urn-carved door below,
flanked by 4 graduated
drawers to each side,
19thC, 40½in (103cm) wide.
$4,000–4,500 *CSK*

A Welsh pine bookcase,
part-glazed, c1860,
45in (114.5cm) wide.
$1,300–1,450 *GRP*

A pine bookcase, with
arched top glazed door
and single drawer, c1860,
36in (91.5cm) wide.
$800–1,000 *NWE*

A mid-Victorian pine
bookcase, with
mahogany mouldings
to doors, c1860,
46½in (118cm) wide.
$950–1,100 *POT*

Cross Reference
Colour Review

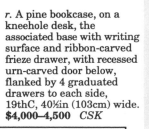

A pine glazed bookcase,
c1890, 39in (99cm) wide.
$350–420 *AHO*

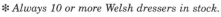

A pine standing bookcase,
with boarded back,
c1890, 37in (94cm) wide.
$280–320 *AL*

A two-piece pine
bookcase, with part-
glazed doors enclosing
adjustable shelves, c1880,
47½in (121cm) wide.
$1,600–2,000 *AL*

Boxes

A grained pine painted ditty box, c1780, 14½in (37cm) wide.
$320–360 *RYA*

A ditty box is a small box in which sailors kept their personal belongings, such as love letters, penknife, comb etc.

An elm and sycamore box, with candle box, c1860, 35in (89cm) wide.
$320–370 *AL*

An elm box, with pine top, c1860, 25¾in (65.5cm) wide.
$280–320 *AL*

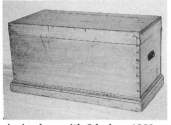

A pine box, with 2 locks, c1880, 39in (99cm) wide.
$240–320 *AL*

A pine box, c1890, 15½in (39.5cm) wide.
$70–80 *AL*

An elm box, Devon, c1860, 26in (66cm) wide.
$160–200 *COW*

A pine box, c1860, 43½in (110.5cm) wide.
$370–420 *AL*

An elm box, Devon, c1870, 35in (89cm) wide.
$200–225 *COW*

A painted pine box, c1887, 23in (58.5cm) wide.
$175–200 *AL*

A pine box, c1900, 28in (71cm) wide.
$80–90 *AL*

A pine box, with candle box, c1860, 29in (74cm) wide.
$280–320 *AL*

A pine box, with candle box, c1860, 36in (91.5cm) wide.
$320–400 *AL*

A Scottish pine blanket box, with original varnish, 1870s, 44½in (113cm) wide.
$200–225 *TAN*

A pine tuck box, with metal hinges, c1890, 19¾in (50cm) wide.
$120–140 *AL*

A pine box, c1900, 29in (74cm) wide.
$80–90 *AL*

l. A craftsman's pine work box, with name plate, Devon, c1910, 30in (76cm) wide.
$130–150 *COW*

A George III mahogany camel-back settee, the shaped back and scrolled arms with padded cushion seat, on square chamfered legs joined by stretchers, on moulded block feet, c1765, 62¾in (159cm) wide.
$8,000–8,800 *S*

An Italian giltwood settee, upholstered in damask, with arched foliate-carved top-rail and serpentine-shaped seat, late 19thC, 93½in (237.5cm) wide.
$7,200–8,500 *C*

A Regency rosewood sofa, with reeded back, the scroll ends carved with acanthus and grapes, on turned and reeded legs, c1820, 86in (218cm) wide.
$5,600–7,200 *BERA*

A Victorian chesterfield, with deep-buttoned back and plain seat, finished with brass nails and cord, on turned walnut legs and original porcelain and brass casters, c1870, 72in (183cm) long.
$2,400–2,800 *LCA*

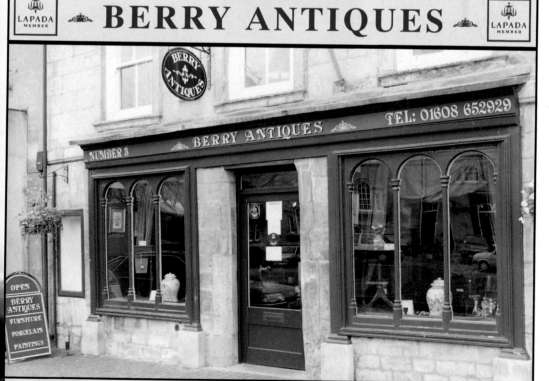

A pair of walnut stools, with padded drop-in seats, on plain cabriole legs, c1710, 19½in (49.5cm) wide.
$16,000–17,500 *S*

A pair of Chippendale style mahogany hall stools, with arched stretchers, c1765, 23in (58.5cm) wide.
$40,000–44,000 *S*

A pair of Regency ebonised and parcel-gilt stools, each with eagle head terminals joined by baluster stretchers, with silk-upholstered seats, on paw feet, redecorated, 31in (79cm) wide.
$24,000–26,500 *C*

A Regency walnut dressing stool, with X-frame, turned stretcher and floral tapestry upholstered seat, 19in (48cm) wide.
$680–750 *PSA*

A Regency mahogany X-framed stool, attributed to Gillows, with caned seat, 22in (56cm) wide.
$8,000–8,800 *C*

A George IV rosewood footstool, the scrolled padded top with moulded carved sides, roundels and turned gadroon-carved feet, c1825, 15in (38cm) wide.
$1,200–1,400 *S*

A pair of mahogany upholstered footstools, on bun feet, c1850, 14in (36cm) wide.
$480–560 *GBr*

A Victorian elm upholstered piano stool, c1890, 20in (51cm) high.
$350–400 *RPh*

An Edwardian inlaid rosewood piano stool, c1910, 21in (53.5cm) wide.
$800–880 *RPh*

A Georgian style walnut stool, on cabriole legs, c1920, 21¼in (54cm) wide.
$320–400 *GBr*

A burr walnut pedestal table, with lions' paw feet and fluted column, early 19thC, 56in (145cm) wide.
$9,600–11,200 *SPa*

A Regency mahogany and rosewood breakfast table, restored, 53½in (136cm) diam.
$5,600–6,000 *C*

A Regency mahogany table, on a carved column, tripod base and scroll feet, 48in (122cm) diam.
$720–800 *GAZE*

A George IV mahogany breakfast table, with brass paw feet and casters, 1820, 43in (109cm) wide extended.
$2,250–2,850 *FHA*

A William IV bird's-eye maple breakfast table, with floral scrolled decoration, on a reeded turned column and bun feet, c1835, 52½in (133.5cm) diam.
$13,600–14,500 *Bon*

A Victorian rosewood breakfast table, on a foliate carved turned baluster stem, 56in (142cm) wide.
$5,000–5,600 *C(S)*

A mahogany centre table, on a spiral-turned column and acanthus-carved legs, original casters, c1840, 35in (89cm) diam.
$4,000–4,800 *BERA*

A William IV rosewood centre table, with marble top and moulded frieze, on S-scroll supports, 34½in (87.5cm) diam.
$12,800–14,000 *CSK*

A Victorian walnut centre table, with moulded shaped top and inlaid border, frieze drawer, on cabriole legs and gilt-metal sabots, later writing surface, 72in (183cm) wide.
$7,500–8,000 *S*

A Victorian burr walnut veneered and marquetry centre table, inlaid with floral sprays on an ebonised ground, on acanthus and scroll-carved splayed legs, 50½in (128cm) diam.
$10,000–10,500 *Bea(E)*

A Louis XV style marquetry inlaid centre table, the frieze and ebonised serpentine top inlaid with a floral spray and foliate strapwork, with a central drawer, on gilt-metal-mounted cabriole legs, c1880, 49in (124.5cm) wide.
$2,400–2,800 *Bon*

An Italian beechwood centre table, the black marble top inlaid with pietra dura, the H-stretcher with central shield panel, on bun feet, dated '1928', 31¼in (79.5cm) wide.
$11,200–12,500 *C*

A walnut card table, with drawers, c1710, 31in (78.5cm) wide.
$5,600–6,400 *S*

A walnut card table, with a frieze drawer, c1710, 34in (86.5cm) wide.
$5,000–6,400 *S*

A George I burr walnut card table, restored, 32in (81.5cm) wide.
$4,800–5,600 *C*

A rosewood and satinwood card table, with ormolu mounts, c1810, 36in (91.5cm) wide.
$4,800–5,400 *FHA*

A pair of George III mahogany and satinwood crossbanded card tables, with canted corners, on boxwood strung tapered legs, 37¼in (95cm) wide.
$14,500–16,000 *Bon*

A pair of mahogany card tables, with tulipwood banding and stringing, c1780, 36in (92cm) wide.
$12,800–14,400 *S*

A pair of mahogany crossbanded card tables, on square tapered legs headed by inlaid panels, c1790, 35¼in (90cm) wide.
$18,400–20,800 *S*

A satinwood card table, c1795, 18in (45.5cm) wide.
$4,400–5,000 *S*

A rosewood card table, c1830, 36in (91.5cm) wide.
$4,400–4,800 *RPh*

A pair of George III crossbanded card tables, with a ribbed frieze, c1810, 38in (96cm) wide.
$19,200–20,800 *S*

A pair of Regency rosewood, ebonised and parcel-gilt card tables, each swivel twin-flap top concealing a well, restored, regilt, 35½in (90cm) wide.
$7,500–8,800 *C*

A pair of Victorian rosewood, walnut, marquetry and ebonised card tables, 34¾in (88cm) wide.
$8,000–9,600 *C*

A Victorian rosewood inlaid envelope card table, with fretted second tier, c1890, 21½in (54.5cm) wide.
$3,500–4,000 *PSA*

A Victorian card table, quarter-veneered in burr walnut, inlaid with ebony, satinwood and tulipwood, c1850, 36in (91cm) wide.
$4,800–5,600 *BERA*

A French ormolu-mounted tulipwood and foliate marquetry card table, top repaired, late 19thC, 33½in (85cm) wide.
$8,000–8,800 *C*

A mahogany twin pedestal dining table, altered, c1770, 75½in (192cm) long.
$14,000–16,800 *S*

A George III mahogany pedestal dining table, with later brass paw feet, restored, 148in (376cm) long extended.
$15,500–18,500 *C*

A mahogany campaign dining table, with telescopic action, including 4 extra leaves, c1825, 122in (309cm) long extended.
$11,800–14,400 *S*

A George III mahogany and rosewood-inlaid breakfront serving table, c1790, 85in (216cm) long.
$4,200–5,000 *Bon*

A Regency mahogany serving table, with acanthus-carved scrolled back, c1825, 85⅛in (217cm) long.
$10,000–12,000 *Bon*

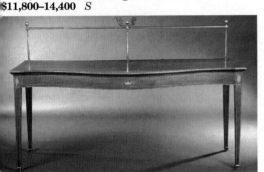

A late George III mahogany serpentine-fronted serving table, later inlaid, 79in (201cm) wide.
$5,000–5,600 *P(Sc)*

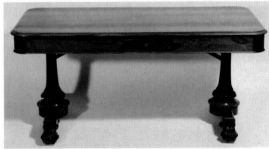

A Victorian rosewood library table, with 2 frieze drawers, on reeded supports, 60in (152cm) long.
$2,000–2,400 *Bri*

A rosewood library table, inlaid with satinwood crossbanding, c1825, 54in (137cm) long.
$8,800–11,200 *S*

A Victorian oak library table, with leather-lined top above 8 frieze drawers and 4 dummy drawers, 96in (244cm) long.
$2,250–2,750 *C*

A George IV oak committee table, by Alexander Norton, with simulated leather-lined top, each end with painted inscription 'Kesteven', with 4 leaves, 216in (548.5cm) long.
$11,200–12,500 *C*

An American carved mahogany occasional table, the top inlaid with flowerheads and lozenges, the downswept legs with moulded snake feet, c1795, 16in (40.5cm) wide.
$15,000–17,500 *S(NY)*

A Victorian walnut kidney-shaped burr walnut table, with crossbanded edge, turned and carved cross-rail, on cabriole legs, c1870, 26in (66cm) wide.
$2,250–2,750 *BERA*

A Victorian occasional table, with a parquetry top, the carved column support on a tripod base, c1870, 21¾in (55.5cm) diam.
$1,900–2,200 *CAT*

A walnut occasional table, on a turned column support and splayed legs, c1860, 24in (61cm) diam.
$650–800 *APO*

A pair of walnut wine tables, the tops with floral marquetry inlay, on turned column supports, c1880, 15in (38cm) diam.
$1,600–1,900 *GBr*

A Victorian mahogany oval occasional table, with barley-twist column and scroll feet, 24in (61cm) wide.
$720–800 *PSA*

An Edwardian rosewood octagonal occasional table, the top and undertier with marquetry inlay, c1910, 28in (71cm) diam.
$750–850 *RPh*

An Edwardian painted satinwood occasional table, the frieze with swag decoration, the legs joined by stretchers, 15in (38cm) diam.
$720–800 *SPU*

A French walnut table, with marble top and single drawer above a shaped apron, on turned tapering legs, c1910, 19in (48.5cm) wide.
$720–800 *RPh*

A George III mahogany butterfly Pembroke table, the satinwood crossbanded top with serpentine leaves above an end drawer, c1780, 35in (89cm) wide.
$2,400–2,600 *Bon*

A harewood and mahogany Pembroke table, the top with 3 oval panels, crossbanded in rosewood, c1780, 36in (91cm) wide.
$11,200–12,500 *S*

A George III mahogany Pembroke table, the top inlaid with sycamore parquetry, c1790, 37½in (95cm) wide.
$7,000–8,500 *S*

A Federal mahogany Pembroke table, the line-inlaid top above a single drawer, the legs inlaid with bellflowers, c1800, 21in (53.5cm) wide.
$19,000–20,800 *S(NY)*

A mahogany side table, with concave front, crossbanded in kingwood, above a pair of drawers, c1790, 39½in (100cm) wide.
$8,800–9,600 *S*

A mahogany side table, attributed to Gillows, on lobed tapering legs, c1820, 39¾in (101cm) wide.
$2,400–2,800 *Bon*

A giltwood side table, the marble top above a carved frieze, on cabriole legs with pad feet, late 19thC, 56in (142cm) wide.
$8,500–9,000 *C(S)*

A rosewood and kingwood sofa table, with brass line inlay, on lyre-shaped supports, c1810, 33½in (85cm) wide.
$5,000–6,400 *S*

A Regency mahogany and rosewood sofa table, the top inlaid with boxwood lines, with 2 frieze drawers, restored, 55¾in (142cm) wide.
$8,500–9,000 *C*

A brass-inlaid and gilt-metal-mounted rosewood sofa table, on U-shaped support with foliate brass inlay, c1815, 60in (152.5cm) wide.
$6,000–7,200 *Bon*

A Regency ebony-inlaid satinwood sofa table, crossbanded in tulipwood, with one drawer and one simulated drawer on each side, with brass caps and casters, restored, 59in (150cm) wide.
$7,500–8,000 *C*

A Regency mahogany sofa table, with reeded mouldings, 2 real and 2 dummy drawers, the baluster end supports with splayed feet, 28¾in (73cm) wide.
$4,400–5,000 *Bea(E)*

A brass-inlaid rosewood teapoy, with 4 later bowls, c1810, 15½in (39.5cm) wide.
$3,000–3,600 *Bon*

A mahogany teapoy, with lotus-carved stem on bun feet, c1840, 16in (41cm) wide.
$1,600–1,800 *S(S)*

A mahogany tray-on-stand, with brass-inlaid waved gallery, brass handles, c1770, on a modern stand, 31½in (80cm) wide.
$7,000–7,300 *S*

A mahogany tray-on-stand, with waved gallery, brass-inlaid, c1790, on a modern stand, 30½in (77cm) wide.
$2,500–3,200 *S*

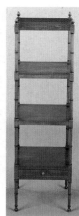

A mahogany and satinwood crossbanded washstand, with concave cupboard doors, c1790, 26in (66cm) wide.
$1,750–2,000 *Bon*

A Georgian mahogany corner wash-stand, c1800, 24½in (62cm) wide.
$720–800 *RPh*

A mahogany whatnot, the top tier with a drawer, above 3 galleried tiers, c1790, 19½in (50cm) wide.
$8,500–9,000 *S*

A mahogany whatnot, with a drawer, c1800, 16in (40.5cm) wide.
$2,500–2,750 *Bon*

A rosewood whatnot, with galleried tiers, 2 drawers in base, on turned supports and bun feet, c1835, 20½in (52cm) wide.
$3,250–3,500 *S(S)*

An inlaid mahogany and brass-bound wine cooler, c1780, 27½in (70cm) high.
$2,500–2,800 *Bon*

A George III mahogany and brass-bound wine cooler, on tapering supports, late 18thC, 24½in (62cm) wide.
$2,000–2,400 *Bon*

A George III mahogany wine cooler, the top with canted corners, with a panelled tapering body, on lion's paw feet, 32½in (82.5cm) wide.
$2,000–2,500 *Bon*

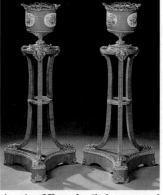

A Regency mahogany sarcophagus-shaped cellaret, with ebony scroll-banding, 24¾in (63cm) wide.
$3,250–3,500 *HOLL*

A pair of French gilt-bronze and porcelain wine coolers, painted with children and flowers, on tripods, c1880, 43¾in (111cm) high.
$7,500–8,800 *S*

A mahogany bidet, on turned tapering legs, together with fitted top, c1830, 13in (33cm) wide.
$480–520 *RPh*

A Scottish pine and mahogany chest of drawers, with a secret drawer, c1780, 46in (117cm) wide.
$720–880 *TAN*

A Scottish pine chest of drawers, on a plinth base, c1860, 48in (122cm) wide.
$880–960 *AL*

A pine chest of drawers, with porcelain handles, c1870, 44in (112cm) wide.
$450–520 *TAN*

A pine miniature chest of drawers, on a flat base, c1880, 19in (48.5cm) wide.
$145–180 *SA*

A pine miniature chest of drawers, 19thC, 12in (30.5cm) wide.
$100–120 *No7*

A pine chest of drawers, on a plinth base, c1880, 30in (76cm) wide.
$560–640 *BOR*

A Victorian pitch pine chest of drawers, with 2 long and 2 short drawers, c1880, 44in (112cm) wide.
$480–520 *GWA*

A Victorian pine tray-top chest of drawers, 36in (91cm) wide.
$520–640 *HRQ*

A pine chest of drawers, with shaped gallery back, 3 long drawers, on bun feet, 19thC, 41in (104cm) wide.
$550–620 *No7*

An Edwardian chest of drawers, with 2 short and 3 long drawers, brass handles, on bracket feet, 36in (91.5cm) wide.
$480–560 *HRQ*

An Edwardian pine dressing chest, with mirror and side drawer, on bracket feet, 36in (91.5cm) wide.
$450–560 *HRQ*

A Victorian pine flight of graduated short and long drawers, 30in (76cm) wide. **$560–620** *SPU*

r. A late Georgian bank of drawers, 34in (86.5cm) wide. **$640–800** *HRQ*

A pine box, with candle box and 2 drawers, together with 2 handles, c1860, repaired, 36½in (93cm) wide. **$160–190** *AL*

A pine box, fitted with 2 drawers and a candle box, c1890, 31in (78.5cm) wide. **$240–280** *COW*

A pine military chest of 3 drawers, c1880, 37½in (95cm) wide. **$550–620** *AL*

A pine winged armchair, with a
seat drawer, on rockers, c1800.
$3,200–3,500 *CoA*

An Irish pine and elm country
chair, 1850s.
$55–65 *TAN*

A beech and mahogany campaign
folding chair, c1870.
$290–320 *BOR*

An elm high-backed chair, with
turned arm supports, c1870.
$225–255 *ASP*

A Victorian shop's chair, the
back advertising Nubolic Soap.
$400–480 *SMI*

An Austro-Hungarian pine
chair, c1900.
$80–95 *HRQ*

An Austro-Hungarian
pine chair, with shaped
top-rail, c1900.
$80–95 *HRQ*

A pine folding fishing
chair, c1920.
$50–60 *AL*

A beech folding chair, with open
back, 1940s.
$15–30 *TAN*

A pine two-piece corner cupboard, c1850, 40½in (103cm) wide. **$1,800–2,000** *AL*

A Dutch pine display cabinet, on bun feet, 37in (94cm) wide, c1880. **$880–960** *COW*

A pine and elm housekeeper's cupboard, 19thC, 44in (112cm) wide. **$1,200–1,350** *No7*

A pine cupboard, the upper part with glazed doors, c1880, 46in (117cm) wide. **$1,900–2,400** *BOR*

A Continental pine wardrobe, with interior drawer, 1880s, 43in (109cm) wide. **$650–800** *HRQ*

A pine and fruitwood dresser, with raised panelled back, the base with 3 drawers, a pair of cupboard doors and 3 dummy drawers, on stile feet, early 19thC, 60in (152.5cm) wide. **$2,250–2,750** *S(S)*

A Welsh two-piece dresser, the top with open shelves, above 3 drawers and 2 cupboard doors, c1880, 74in (188cm) wide. **$3,200–3,500** *AL*

A French pine dresser, the back with shaped top, above one long drawer and 2 cupboard doors, c1890, 50in (127cm) wide. **$1,500–1,600** *GRP*

An Irish pine dresser, with 5 shelves above 2 drawers and 2 panelled doors, 1860s, 51in (129.5cm) wide. **$800–960** *TAN*

A pine hanging corner cupboard,
19thC, 28in (71cm) wide.
$190–240 *HRQ*

A Welsh pine glazed
hanging cupboard, c1860,
26in (66cm) wide.
$400–450 *GRP*

A Victorian pine corner cupboard,
with one drawer, 31in (79cm) wide.
$380–480 *HRQ*

A pine corner cupboard,
with carved shelves,
19thC, 27in (68.5cm) wide.
$520–560 *No7*

A Victorian pine cupboard,
with 2 figured panelled doors,
c1880, 37in (94cm) wide.
$320–400 *HRQ*

A Welsh pine dog kennel dresser
base, with 7 drawers, c1860,
42in (106.5cm) wide.
$600–680 *TAN*

A pine bureau, with central flap, c1795, 42in (106.5cm) wide. **$1,000–1,300** *WLD*

A pine bureau, with original knobs, c1900, 37in (94cm) wide. **$950–1,000** *HRQ*

A pine and elm estate desk, c1795, 30½in (77.5cm) wide. **$560–720** *WLD*

A pine desk, with 2 short drawers, c1840, 29in (73.5cm) wide. **$560–640** *FAG*

A late Victorian pitch pine clerk's desk, 33in (84cm) wide. **$160–200** *GWA*

A pine desk, with 4 short drawers, c1860, 35in (89cm) wide. **$400–480** *SAU*

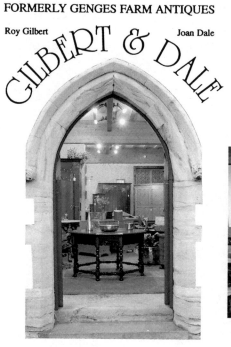

ANN LINGARD

ROPE WALK ANTIQUES, RYE, SUSSEX
TEL: 01797 223486 FAX: 01797 224700

**10,000 square feet of hand-finished
ENGLISH ANTIQUE PINE FURNITURE
KITCHEN SHOP
and
COMPLEMENTARY ANTIQUES**

A Victorian Gothic style pine buffet,
c1860, 50in (127cm) wide.
$560–640 *BOR*

A Georgian pine serving table, with 2 short and one
long drawer, brass handles, c1800, 42in (106.5cm) wide.
$480–560 *HRQ*

A pine work table, with 2 drawers, the legs
joined by a stretcher, c1870, 72in (183cm) wide.
$950–1,100 *AL*

A pine lowboy, with a shaped and carved
apron, c1780, 29in (73.5cm) wide.
$880–960 *MIC*

A pine table, with a single drawer, on
turned legs, c1880, 44in (112cm) wide.
$320–350 *AL*

A pine side table, with one central drawer,
on turned legs, c1870, 37in (94cm) wide.
$190–225 *GWA*

A pine table, with turned legs,
c1880, 34½in (87.5cm) wide.
$190–220 *AL*

A pine side table, with straight legs,
c1870, 48in (122cm) wide.
$400–440 *AL*

A pine cricket table, with triangular undertier, c1820, 30in (76cm) diam.
$380–420 *TAN*

A pine cricket table, with sycamore top, c1860, 31½in (80cm) diam.
$430–480 *AL*

A pine side table, with a single drawer and tapering legs, c1870, 28in (71cm) wide.
$340–380 *AL*

A pine tripod table, c1880, 31in (78cm) high.
$200–230 *AL*

A Hungarian pine folding games table, c1900, 27in (68.5cm) wide.
$480–560 *HRQ*

A pine table, with turned legs, cut down, c1900, 42in (106.5cm) wide.
$320–350 *AL*

A pine tavern table, the overhanging top above a drawer, beaded apron, on block vase and ring-turned legs joined by box stretchers, old red painted surface, Massachusetts, early 18thC, 30in (76cm) wide.
$5,500–6,000 *SK(B)*

A Regency painted pine tripod table, 22in (56cm) wide.
$400–480 *HRQ*

A pine baker's table, with marble top and one deep drawer, c1870, 39in (99cm) wide.
$900–1,000 *AL*

A pine serving table, with 2 drawers above a shaped apron, on turned legs, c1870, 48in (122cm) wide.
$640–700 *AL*

A pine table, with a single end drawer, on turned legs, cut down, c1880, 53in (134.5cm) wide.
$370–420 *AL*

An Irish pine washstand, with gallery back, one small central drawer, 1840s, 39in (99cm) wide.
$160–190 *TAN*

A pine washstand, with marble top and tiled back, 1880s, 40in (102cm) wide.
$250–300 *TAN*

A Victorian pine washstand, with shaped back, one small drawer, on turned legs, 36in (91.5cm) wide.
$320–400 *HRQ*

A pine double pedestal washstand, with shaped back, a central drawer and 4 drawers each side, c1880, 43in (109cm) wide.
$1,300–1,600 *BOR*

A pine washstand, with plain gallery back, 2 drawers, on turned legs, c1880, 40in (102cm) wide.
$230–260 *DFA*

A French fruitwood washstand, with gallery back, shaped undertier, c1900, 32in (81.5cm) wide.
$320–400 *HRQ*

A Welsh painted pine cradle, c1800, 30in (76cm) long.
$680–750 *CoA*

An Irish painted pine cradle, Co Clare, c1850, 36in (91.5cm) wide.
$560–640 *COM*

An Irish 'súgan' chair, with rush seat, c1800.
$200–240 *COM*

A painted beech stick-back kitchen chair, c1900.
$50–60 *TAN*

A Welsh painted pine hanging corner cupboard, c1820, 25in (63.5cm) wide.
$1,100–1,300 *CoA*

A Continental painted pine marriage chest, c1829, 28in (71cm) wide.
$800–880 *RPh*

A pine blanket chest, painted in brown and decorated with panels of flowers, signed by Johannes Rank (or Ranck), Jonestown, Pennsylvania, c1795, 51½in (131cm) wide.
$9,600–10,500 *S(NY)*

A pine chest of drawers, with 4 drawers and original paint, c1880, 41in (104cm) wide.
$350–380 *TAN*

A Romanian pine linen chest, with original paint, c1897, 47in (119.5cm) wide.
$480–560 *TAN*

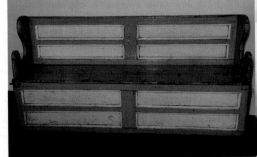

An Irish bed settle, opening to a double bed, with original paint, c1850, 72in (183cm) wide.
$600–720 *TAN*

An eastern European painted pine box, with original paint, c1850, 30in (76cm) wide. $400–480 FOX

A Continental painted pine blanket chest, the frame and top painted with flowers, on square bracket feet, signed and dated '1843', 49in (124.5cm) wide. $2,500–2,800 LHA

An eastern European painted pine chest, on bun feet, c1820, 32in (82cm) wide. $480–560 CPA

An Austrian primitive painted pine chest, the top above a pair of doors painted with hearts and flowers, on block feet, c1800, 52½in (133.5cm) wide. $760–820 LHA

A Welsh oak salt box, c1790,
9in (23cm) wide.
$640–720 *CoA*

A carved wood butter dish, with
liner, c1900, 8in (20cm) diam.
$50–60 *SMI*

A pair of George III brass flour
dredgers, 4½in (11cm) high.
$350–400 *No7*

Two tin and copper jelly moulds, c1850,
largest 8in (20cm) wide.
$120–150 *SMI*

A copper knife sharpener,
c1880, 2½in (6.5cm) diam.
$65–75 *SMI*

A copper ice cream bombe
19thC, 5¼in (13.5cm) high.
$90–100 *No7*

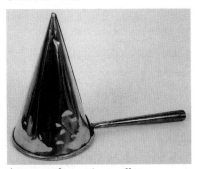

A copper ale or wine muller,
19thC, 10¼in (26cm) high.
$100–120 *No7*

A miniature copper kettle,
19thC, 8in (20cm) high.
$115–125 *No7*

A treacle dispensing tin,
c1850, 9in (23cm) wide.
$320–400 *SMI*

A miniature enamel teapot, cup and saucer,
c1900, teapot 3in (7.5cm) high.
$90–105 *SMI*

A set of enamel storage jars,
c1900, 5½in (14cm) high.
$25–35 each *SMI*

A set of storage jars for sugar, by T. G. Green,
black shield mark, 1930s, 5¾in (14.5cm) high.
$50–65 each *AL*

A set of 5 dairy cans, with brass handles,
c1880, largest 7in (18cm) high.
$80–135 each *SMI*

Chairs

A pair of beech famine chairs,
County Mayo, c1840.
$640–720 *HON*

A pine scroll-back Windsor
chair, c1860.
$64–72 *WaH*

An Irish elm rocking chair, c1860.
$320–400 *ByI*

*Many chairs popularly termed
'pine' are, in fact, made of
more durable woods such
as elm or beech.*

A pine fiddle-back chair, c1880.
$80–100 *AL*

A pine farmhouse chair, c1880.
$140–180 *ByI*

A *faux* bamboo chair, 19thC.
$70–100 *FOX*

Pine Furniture

The diverse origins of pine furniture, and numerous types of pine
trees, all contribute to its varied repertoire. Pine, or deal as it
was known in early times, was partly grown in Great Britain,
with some imported from Scandinavia and North America.
This accounts for its wide variety of colour and grain. Pitch pine,
another variety, is a dark, grainy wood and, although very hard,
is not as popular since its unique colour does not mix well with
other woods.

A pine park chair, c1900.
$50–60 *AL*

A pair of pine country chairs, c1920.
$200–215 *Ber*

A pine folding fishing
chair, c1920.
$50–60 *AL*

Chests

A German pine marriage chest, dated '1614',
68in (172.5cm) wide.
$2,400–2,800 *CCP*

A pine blanket chest, painted red,
green and yellow, the hinged top
opening to a lidded till, with
2 short drawers below, the feet
restored, Pennsylvania, c1790,
43in (110cm) wide.
$5,600–7,200 *S(NY)*

A red-painted pine six-board
chest, with moulded top and
shaped ends, New England,
18thC, 39½in (100.5cm) wide.
$500–600 *SK(B)*

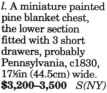

A poplar and pine blanket box,
painted green and brown,
with one drawer, original cotter
pin hinges, the feet restored,
Long Island, New York,
c1720, 41½in (105.5cm) wide.
$8,000–9,000 *S(NY)*

*Good quality American pieces
such as this are highly sought after.*

l. A miniature painted
pine blanket chest,
the lower section
fitted with 3 short
drawers, probably
Pennsylvania, c1830,
17½in (44.5cm) wide.
$3,200–3,500 *S(NY)*

A red-painted pine chest-over-
drawers, with lidded top and
2 drawers below, replaced
brasses, New England, late
18thC, 42in (107cm) wide.
$1,100–1,300 *SK(B)*

A blue-painted pine six-board chest, with lidded
till, some damage, probably New York State,
early 19thC, 47¼in (120cm) wide.
$560–640 *SK(B)*

A red-painted pine blanket chest, carved with
leaf tips, florettes and paterae, feet reduced in
height, New England, c1800, 48in (122cm) wide.
$3,500–4,000 *S(NY)*

Cross Reference
Pine boxes, page 184

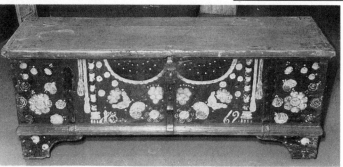

A Romanian pine marriage chest, painted with flowers, dated '1869',
59in (150cm) wide.
$480–560 *TAN*

An Austro-Hungarian pine
marriage chest, dated '1852',
33in (84.5cm) wide.
$200–220 *HRQ*

Chests of Drawers

A pine chest of drawers, with 4 thumb-moulded drawers, the bottom drawer false, original finish, lacks brass pulls, New England, late 18thC, 37½in (95.5cm) wide.
$520–640 *SK(B)*

A pine chest of drawers, with 2 short and 2 long drawers, c1830, 34in (86.5cm) wide.
$320–480 *HRQ*

A pine chest of drawers, with splash-back, on turned feet, c1850, 34in (86.5cm) wide.
$320–400 *HRQ*

A chest of drawers, with 3 long drawers, the central one with inset panel, c1860, 40in (101.5cm) wide.
$480–560 *CPS*

A pine chest of drawers, with 2 short and 3 long drawers, new trim, c1820, 43in (109cm) wide.
$1,000–1,200 *AL*

A Scottish pine chest of drawers, with 2 short and 3 long drawers, c1840, 46in (117cm) wide.
$900–1,150 *AL*

A pine chest of drawers, with 3 long drawers, c1850, 42in (106.5cm) wide.
$480–560 *CPS*

A pine chest of drawers, with 4 long drawers, c1860, 42in (106.5cm) wide.
$560–640 *CPS*

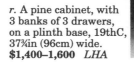

r. A pine cabinet, with 3 banks of 3 drawers, on a plinth base, 19thC, 37¾in (96cm) wide.
$1,400–1,600 *LHA*

A pine watchmaker's chest of drawers, early 19thC, 18in (45.5cm) wide.
$280–320 *TPC*

A pine chest of drawers, with 6 short drawers and one long drawer, c1840, 40in (101.5cm) wide.
$800–950 *TPC*

A pine chest of drawers, with shaped back and cotton-reel columns, c1860, 38in (96.5cm) wide.
$800–1,000 *TPC*

A pine chest of drawers, with 3 drawers, on turned legs, c1860, 42in (106.5cm) wide.
$720–800 *CPS*

A pine chest of drawers, with
2 short and 3 long drawers,
on bracket feet, c1870,
37½in (95cm) wide.
$500–560 *WEE*

A miniature pine chest of
drawers, Cardiganshire, c1880,
18in (45.5cm) wide.
$680–780 *CoA*

A Victorian chest of drawers,
with 2 short and 3 long drawers,
41in (104cm) wide.
$560–680 *CPS*

A Victorian chest of drawers,
with 2 short and 3 long drawers,
37in (94cm) wide.
$520–600 *CPS*

Don't Forget!

*If in doubt please refer to
the 'How to Use' section at
the beginning of this book.*

A Victorian pine chest of
drawers, with 2 short and
3 long drawers, c1860,
41in (104cm) wide.
$640–760 *CPA*

A Victorian pine chest of
drawers, with hat and glove
drawer, 51½in (131cm) wide.
$1,100–1,300 *AHO*

A Victorian chest of drawers,
with 2 short and 2 long drawers,
41in (104cm) wide.
$400–480 *CPS*

A Victorian chest of drawers,
with 2 short and 3 long drawers,
37½in (95cm) wide.
$440–520 *CPS*

r. A pine chest of drawers, with
simulated bamboo columns,
c1900, 37in (94cm) wide.
$640–680 *WEE*

An east European pine chest of
drawers, with 3 long drawers,
c1880, 45in (114.5cm) wide.
$620–700 *GRP*

A Victorian pine chest of drawers,
with 2 short and 3 long drawers,
37in (94cm) wide.
$570–640 *GRP*

A Victorian chest of drawers,
with 2 short and 2 long
drawers, 41in (104cm) wide.
$400–480 *CPS*

A pine chest of drawers, with
2 short and 3 long drawers,
c1890, 41½in (105.5cm) wide.
$480–520 *WEE*

A Michelangelo. Only in Florence.

A Van der Tol. Only in Almere.

We carry one of the world's finest collections of antique pine furniture.

Available in unstripped, stripped and finished & painted versions. Plus pine

reproductions and decorative items. We offer quality, quantity & profit and

full packing service. Please visit our 75,000 sq.ft. warehouse

in Almere and enjoy the personal and friendly service.

Jacques van der Tol
unique antique pine furniture

Jacques van der Tol wholesale BV. (20 min. from Schiphol Airport)
Antennestraat 34, 1322 AE Almere‑Stad, Holland. Industrial Estate 'Gooise Kant'
Tel.:(0)36‑5362050. Fax:(0)36‑5361993

Cupboards

A Spanish primitive pine
aumbry, with a pair
of part-lattice pierced
doors and solid panels
beneath, possibly c1600,
32in (81.5cm) wide.
$950–1,000 *RBB*

A Continental pine
cupboard, with 2 raised
and fielded panelled
doors, 18thC,
34in (86.5cm) wide.
$1,000–1,300 *TPC*

A pine cupboard, with
2 drawers over raised and
fielded panelled doors,
18thC, 50in (127cm) wide.
$2,800–3,200 *TPC*

A Georgian pine
panelled cupboard, with
2 drawers in the base,
68in (172.5cm) wide.
$2,200–2,600 *TPC*

An ochre-painted pine
cupboard, the door
opening to 3 shelves,
appears to retain the
wrought-iron H-hinges
and rosehead nail door
handle, probably original,
some damage to cornice
and moulding, probably
New York State, c1750,
39in (99cm) wide.
$4,000–4,500 *S(NY)*

A Georgian pine food
cupboard, with
original paint, c1780,
58in (147.5cm) wide.
$1,400–1,500 *TAN*

A Continental painted
pine cabinet, the upper
part with a pair of glazed
doors enclosing 2 shelves,
the lower part with
moulded segmental arch
above a pair of panelled
doors flanked by a further
pair of recesses with
glazed panels, late 18thC,
88¼in (224cm) high.
$4,800–5,600 *P(NW)*

A pine cupboard,
the 2 raised panelled
doors opening to
4 shelves, original red
and grey paint, appears
to retain wrought-iron
H-hinges, c1750,
54in (137cm) wide.
$2,500–3,000 *S(NY)*

A Welsh pine
housekeeper's cupboard,
c1780, 59in (150cm) wide.
$1,600–2,200 *TAN*

A pine clothes press,
Carmarthen, c1800,
38in (96.5cm) wide.
$3,200–3,600 *AHO*

A pine spice cupboard,
with 3 shelves and
2 drawers, with original
paint, early 19thC,
20in (51cm) wide.
$680–760 *No7*

A Chippendale pine
corner cupboard, the
glazed mullioned doors
opening to 3 scalloped
shelves, the centre one
pierced for cutlery,
the lower section
with fielded-panelled
cupboard doors, opening
to a shelf, originally
painted green,
Pennsylvania, c1780,
53in (134.5cm) wide.
$3,200–3,500 *S(NY)*

A pine cupboard,
restored, some damage,
New England, late 18thC,
38in (96.5cm) wide.
$2,500–2,800 *SK(B)*

A Georgian pine corner
cupboard, with shaped
shelves, and 2 fielded
panelled doors below,
48in (122cm) wide.
$2,800–3,500 *TPC*

A pine corner cupboard, with recessed panelled doors enclosing 2 shelves, restored, New England, early 19thC, 54½in (138.5cm) wide.
$1,600–2,000 *SK(B)*

A pine cupboard, the top doors with cranberry and etched glass panels, 2 drawers and 2 doors below, 19thC, 48in (122cm) wide.
$2,000–2,400 *TPC*

A pine food cupboard, with part-glazed doors, c1840, 44in (112cm) wide.
$800–1,000 *TAN*

A pine housekeeper's cupboard, with glazed top doors enclosing shelves, c1860, 46in (117cm) wide.
$560–720 *AHO*

A Continental pine cupboard-on-cupboard, with ornate pierced carving, c1840, 40in (101.5cm) wide.
$2,000–2,300 *TPC*

A pine housekeeper's cupboard, with panelled doors, Hampshire, c1860, 48in (122cm) wide.
$2,400–2,800 *TPC*

An Irish pine food cupboard, c1840, 64in (162.5cm) wide.
$1,300–1,500 *HOA*

A pine livery cupboard, County Antrim, c1840, 57in (145cm) wide.
$1,200–1,400 *TAN*

A Hungarian pine and woven osier smoke cupboard, c1860, 24in (61cm) wide.
$1,200–1,400 *UC*

A pine cupboard, with brass handle, on ball feet, c1860, 21½in (54.5cm) wide.
$350–400 *AL*

A Victorian pine skirting corner cupboard, 18in (45.5cm) wide.
$200–240 *HRQ*

A French pine linen press,
19thC, 50in (127cm) wide.
$2,000–2,300 *TPC*

A Victorian linen press,
with 2 long and 2 short
drawers, the top part
fitted with slides,
46½in (118cm) wide.
$1,400–2,000 *AHO*

A pine four-door
cupboard, c1880,
48in (122cm) wide.
$860–960 *AL*

A pine cupboard, with
2 panelled doors, c1880,
26in (66cm) wide.
$520–600 *TPC*

A pine two-door cupboard,
with enclosed drawer,
c1880, 50in (127cm) wide.
$950–1,100 *AL*

A pine cupboard, with
a single door, c1880,
36in (91.5cm) wide.
$750–850 *AL*

A Victorian pine glazed
bookcase, with arched
doors over ogee drawers
and panelled doors, c1880,
42in (106.5cm) wide.
$1,300–1,450 *TPC*

A pine food cupboard,
with 4 doors and
2 short drawers, c1880,
36in (99.5cm) wide.
$800–950 *TAN*

A pine wall cupboard,
with open shelf above,
c1880, 15in (38cm) wide.
$140–160 *AL*

A grained pine estate
cabinet, with a pair of
panelled doors, above
6 fall-front flaps,
variously inscribed,
19thC, 50in (127cm) wide.
$2,800–3,200 *CSK*

A pine pot cupboard, c1880,
15½in (39.5cm) wide.
$280–350 *AL*

A pine wall cupboard,
with shelf above, c1880,
24½in (61.5cm) wide.
$280–320 *AL*

Furniture Proportions

The proportions of a piece of furniture, such as
a wardrobe which is too narrow for a coat hanger,
or a table with insufficient leg-room, have a bearing
on price, as they are therefore less practical.

l. A pine cupboard, with
a single door, c1880,
25in (63cm) wide.
$240–280 *AHO*

r. A pine pot cupboard,
with a marble top,
c1880, 13in (33cm) wide.
$200–260 *AL*

A pine cupboard, with 2 doors, c1880, 29½in (75cm) wide. **$430–480** *AL*

A pine cupboard, with a single door, c1890, 31in (78.5cm) wide. **$350–380** *AL*

A pine cupboard, with 2 doors, c1890, 53½in (136cm) wide. **$430–480** *AL*

A pine bedside cupboard, with one drawer, on bun feet, c1880, 18in (45.5cm) wide. **$160–200** *ByI*

A pine cupboard, with a single door, c1890, 25½in (65cm) wide. **$220–260** *AL*

A pine cupboard, with 2 panelled doors, c1870, 49in (124.5cm) wide. **$800–900** *AL*

A Continental pine pot cupboard, with a moulded drawer, c1880, 15in (38cm) wide. **$200–250** *HRQ*

r. A pine linen press, by Heal's of London, c1900, 50in (127cm) wide. **$1,600–2,000** *GRP*

A pitch pine corner cupboard, c1900, 35in (89cm) wide. **$280–350** *GWA*

A pine hanging cupboard, enclosed by a pair of doors with stencilled decoration, c1900, 45in (114cm) wide. **$480–560** *DN*

A pine cupboard, with a table and 2 short drawers, c1950, 30in (76cm) wide. **$720–800** *COW*

Desks

An auctioneer's/farmer's
pine desk, 19thC,
39½in (100.5cm) wide.
$320–400 *SPa*

A Danish pine five-drawer kneehole
desk, c1870, 44in (112cm) wide.
$1,600–1,800 *UC*

A Victorian pine writing desk,
48in (122cm) wide.
$1,400–1,600 *TPC*

A Victorian pine pedestal desk,
with kneehole cupboard,
54in (137cm) wide.
$2,000–2,250 *TPC*

A painted pine school desk,
c1950, 24in (61cm) wide.
$50–65 *TAN*

l. An oak double school desk,
c1920, 40in (101.5cm) wide.
$160–200 *WaH*

Dressers

A pine and walnut dresser,
with potboard, early 18thC,
72in (183cm) wide.
$2,700–3,000 *TPC*

A Georgian pine and elm dresser,
72in (183cm) wide.
$2,200–2,600 *TPC*

r. A George III pine dresser,
the base with 3 drawers above
panelled cupboard doors and
3 dummy drawers, faults, early
19thC, 62½in (159cm) wide.
$2,500–2,800 *S(S)*

A painted pine and poplar
panelled dresser, the cupboard
doors opening to a two-shelved
interior, old dark green paint,
lowered, damaged, New England
or Canada, 18thC,
71½in (181.5cm) wide.
$5,500–6,200 *SK(B)*

> **Don't Forget!**
> *If in doubt please refer to
> the 'How to Use' section at
> the beginning of this book.*

l. A pine and elmwood dresser,
with traces of red and grey paint,
one backboard replaced, repairs to
mouldings, possibly Continental,
mid-18thC, 64in (163cm) wide.
$3,700–4,500 *S(NY)*

An Irish pine dresser, with original sledge feet, c1820, 47in (119.5cm) wide. $1,000–1,150 *TAN*

A stained pine dresser, with recessed panelled doors opening to a three-shelved interior, old red stain, restored, New England, c1830, 56in (142cm) wide. $1,600–1,800 *SK(B)*

An Irish pine dresser, the lower part with 2 drawers and 2 cupboards under, c1830, 54in (137cm) wide. $950–1,150 *TAN*

A pine dresser, with open shelves, bull's-eye and reeded columns, Hampshire, c1840, 84in (213.5cm) wide. $2,500–3,000 *TPC*

An Irish fiddle-front pine dresser, c1840, 62in (157.5cm) wide. $1,200–1,400 *TAN*

An Irish pine dresser, c1860, 52in (132cm) wide. $1,000–1,150 *TAN*

An Irish pine dresser, c1850, 59in (150cm) wide. $1,100–1,200 *TAN*

A Victorian stripped pine dresser, 30in (76cm) wide. $800–1,000 *BTA*

A Victorian pine dresser, c1870, 80in (203cm) wide. $2,200–2,700 *TPC*

A Victorian pine dresser, with 2 glazed doors, and split turned columns, 48in (122cm) wide. $1,300–1,600 *TPC*

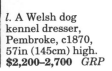

l. A Welsh dog kennel dresser, Pembroke, c1870, 57in (145cm) high. $2,200–2,700 *GRP*

An Irish glazed pine
dresser, c1880,
48in (122cm) wide.
$880–1,000 *TAN*

A Scottish pine
dresser, c1880,
52in (132cm) wide.
$1,200–1,400 *AL*

An Austro-Hungarian
glazed pine
dresser, c1880,
40in (101.5cm) wide.
$800–1,000 *HRQ*

A Scottish pine dresser,
c1880, 57in (145cm) wide.
$2,000–2,300 *AL*

An Irish pine dresser,
with sycamore slab,
original paint, c1880,
61in (155cm) high.
$1,300–1,450 *TAN*

An Irish pine dresser,
County Galway, c1890,
59in (150cm) high.
$1,200–1,400 *TAN*

An Irish two-piece
glazed pine dresser,
with scratch-carved
door panels, c1890,
48in (122cm) wide.
$640–720 *TAN*

A Canadian pine open
dresser, the upper section
with moulded cornice and
dentil frieze over 3 open
shelves, the lower with
2 long and one short frieze
drawer over 2 panelled
cupboard doors, raised
on a shaped bracket base,
Maritime Provinces, 19thC,
49in (124.5cm) wide.
$1,700–2,000 *RIT*

An American brown and
blue-painted pine dresser,
19thC, 60in (152cm) wide.
$8,000–9,000 *S(NY)*

A Victorian pine
dresser, the
upper part with
3 cupboards, the
lower part with
3 frieze drawers above
2 panelled doors and
4 central drawers,
62in (157.5cm) wide.
$2,000–2,300 *TPC*

r. A bleached beech and
pine dresser, c1890,
73in (185.5cm) high.
$1,100–1,300 *TAN*

Dresser Bases

A pine dresser base, stained
black, Somerset, mid-19thC,
66½in (169cm) wide.
$2,400–2,800 *CSK*

A pine dresser base, with
3 drawers and a cupboard, on bun
feet, c1870, 49½in (126cm) wide.
$560–640 *AHO*

A Romanian pine dresser base,
with original paint, c1840,
35in (89cm) wide.
$380–440 *TAN*

A Victorian pine pot board dresser
base, 62in (157.5cm) wide.
$800–960 *GRP*

A pine dresser base, with
2 doors and 2 drawers, c1880,
49in (124.5cm) wide.
$960–1,100 *AL*

A Scottish pine dresser base,
c1880, 48in (122cm) wide.
$1,400–1,600 *AL*

Plant Stands

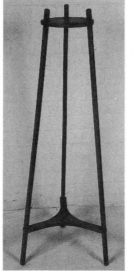

A pine plant stand, with
round lower shelf, c1890,
26in (66cm) high.
$80–90 *AL*

A pine plant stand, with
square lower shelf, c1890,
42in (106.5cm) high.
$100–110 *AL*

A Contintental pine
plant stand, c1900,
39½in (100.5cm) high.
$70–100 *ASP*

Racks & Shelves

A pine wall rack, c1860,
60in (152.5cm) wide.
$580–640 *AL*

A green-painted pine
wall rack, c1860,
46in (117cm) wide.
$580–640 *AL*

A small pine wall shelf,
c1890, 17in (43.5cm) wide.
$120–140 *AL*

A Victorian beech and
pine whatnot, with cotton
reel turned supports,
26in (66cm) wide.
$320–400 *GRP*

A French pine plate
rack, c1900,
18in (45.5cm) wide.
$120–140 *TAN*

A French pine
plate rack, c1880,
58in (147.5cm) wide.
$320–400 *GRP*

Settles & Settees

A pine settle, with bow back,
early 18thC, 60in (152.5cm) wide.
$1,000–1,300 *TPC*

A George III painted pine box-
seat settle, the plank seat above
a panelled cupboard door, late
18thC, 54¼in (138cm) wide.
$960–1,200 *S(S)*

A pine and fruitwood high back
settle, 18thC, 82in (208.5cm) wide.
$1,800–2,300 *SPa*

A European pine box settle,
c1900, 60in (152.5cm) wide.
$620–720 *TPC*

An Irish pine settle table,
original paint, c1860,
48in (122cm) wide.
$640–800 *TAN*

l. A French painted pine chairback
settee, with rush seat, the turned
legs joined by multiple stretchers,
late 19thC, 72in (183cm) wide.
$640–800 *CSK*

Beware!

When buying pine furniture,
be wary of any items which
need repairing: it is difficult
to match woods for invisible
restoration, particularly as it
may have mellowed with the
passing years. Pieces which
have been used in a
workshop and have oily
patches are also problem
areas – oil is very difficult to
remove, and produces a
sticky finish when waxed.

Side Cabinets

A Scottish pine
sideboard, c1870,
48in (122cm) wide.
$1,100–1,300 *AL*

An Irish pine chiffonier,
c1890, 54in (137cm) wide.
$560–640 *TAN*

A pine chiffonier, c1880,
54in (137cm) wide.
$1,600–2,000 *BOR*

An Irish pine chiffonier,
with scratch-carved
decoration, and central
mirror, c1900,
48in (122cm) wide.
$360–420 *TAN*

Stools

A joined beech and pine stool,
c1680, 18in (45.5cm) wide.
$1,100–1,300 *COM*

r. A pine stool, c1890,
15½in (39.5cm) wide.
$60–65 *AL*

A pine milking stool,
c1850, 20in (51cm) wide.
$240–320 *COM*

A pine stool, original paint,
c1890, 12in (30.5cm) wide.
$40–50 *TAN*

r. A pine folding stool,
c1920, 9½in (24cm) high.
$30–35 *AL*

A carved and painted pine foot
stool, some cracks and wear,
Pennsylvania, mid-19thC,
14in (35.5cm) wide.
$620–680 *S(NY)*

A pine stool, with original paint,
c1890, 14in (35.5cm) wide.
$30–50 *TAN*

A pine rush-seated stool,
c1890, 18in (45.5cm) wide.
$50–65 *ASP*

Tables

A pine and maple tea table,
New York State, c1780,
25½in (65cm) wide.
$2,800–3,500 *S(NY)*

A painted pine and birch
chair table, with hinged seat,
on turned legs, minor traces
of original paint, repairs,
New England, early 19thC,
47½in (120.5cm) wide.
$2,000–2,400 *SK(B)*

r. An Irish pine table,
with stretchers, original
paint, cut down, c1860,
44in (112cm) wide.
$200–220 *TAN*

l. A pine side server, with
fruitwood top, early 19thC,
66in (167.5cm) wide.
$1,400–1,600 *CPA*

A Federal turned maple and
red-stained pine harvest table,
appears to retain old and
possibly original finish, slight
damage, New England, early
19thC, 71in (180cm) wide.
$3,400–3,600 *S(NY)*

A tilt-top breakfast table, c1860,
48in (122cm) diam.
$720–780 HOA

A Scandinavian farmhouse
pine kitchen table, on an old
blue-painted base, c1830,
28in (71cm) wide.
$2,400–2,600 RYA

A pine serving table,
with 3 drawers, c1860,
53½in (136cm) wide.
$1,200–1,300 AL

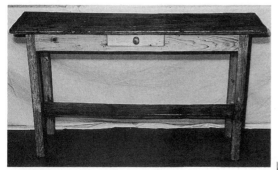

An Irish pine sofa table, with single drawer,
on elm legs, c1860, 52in (132cm) wide.
$240–270 TAN

An Irish pine table, with a single drawer and
twin stretcher, c1840, 31in (78.5cm) wide.
$640–800 WEE

r. A pine refectory table, c1850,
122in (310cm) wide.
$1,100–1,300 HOA

An Irish pine table, with stretchers, original multi-coloured paint, c1870, 42in (106.5cm) wide.
$200–240 *TAN*

A pine cricket table, c1870, 31½in (80cm) diam.
$720–800 *AL*

A pine writing table, with a single drawer, c1870, 42in (106.5cm) wide.
$370–420 *AL*

An Irish pine drop-leaf table, with original paint, c1870, 47in (119.5cm) diam.
$260–280 *TAN*

r. An Irish pine table, with double stretchers, original paint, cut down, c1870, 48in (122cm) wide.
$200–240 *TAN*

> **Don't Forget!**
> *If in doubt please refer to the 'How to Use' section at the beginning of this book.*

r. A Victorian pine kitchen table, 48in (122cm) wide.
$350–400 *GRP*

l. A pine side table, with a single drawer, c1880, 38in (96.5cm) wide.
$320–350 *AL*

A pine table, with turned legs, c1880, 41in (104cm) wide.
$350–380 *AL*

A pine table, with straight legs, c1880, 89in (226cm) wide.
$800–950 *AL*

A pine table, with a single drawer, on turned legs, c1880, 72in (183cm) wide.
$680–780 *AL*

A pine table, with turned legs, c1880, 72in (183cm) wide.
$1,000–1,200 *AL*

A pine ship's table, with turned legs and stretchers, c1880, 108in (274.5cm) long.
$1,300–1,600 *TPC*

19th Century Pine

A great deal of pine furniture was made in the second half of the 19thC as inexpensive furniture for kitchens and servants' quarters. It would usually be painted to make it more attractive and it is only since the 1960s that stripped pine has become fashionable.

r. A pine folding table, with original varnish, c1880, 71in (180.5cm) wide.
$240–320 *TAN*

l. A Welsh pine cricket table, with original paint, c1880, 31in (79cm) diam.
$280–320 *TAN*

A pine table, with a drawer, on straight legs, c1880, 72in (183cm) wide.
$1,000–1,200 *AL*

A pine pub table, c1880, 60¾in (154.5cm) wide.
$520–560 *AL*

A pine drop-leaf table, c1880,
46in (107cm) wide.
$430–480 *AL*

An Irish pine table, with
stretchers, original paint,
c1880, 48in (122cm) wide.
$220–250 *TAN*

A pine side table, with turned
legs, c1880, 36in (91.5cm) wide.
$350–400 *AL*

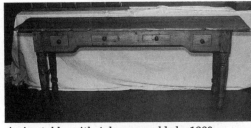

A pine table, with tapered legs, c1880,
95in (241.5cm) wide.
$1,000–1,200 *AL*

A pine table, with 4 drawers added, c1880,
78in (198cm) wide.
$400–480 *TAN*

l. An Irish pine
table, with
mahogany top
and green base,
cut down, c1880,
48in (122cm) wide.
$200–220 *TAN*

r. A pine tripod
table, late 19thC,
18¼in (46.5cm) wide.
$430–480 *AL*

A pine table,
with a drawer,
on straight legs,
drawer bottom
replaced, c1890,
54in (137cm) wide.
$580–640 *AL*

r. A pine side table,
with a drawer, on
turned legs, c1890,
36in (91.5cm) wide.
$280–320 *AL*

A pine writing table, with single drawer, on turned legs, original paint, c1890, 42in (107cm) wide. **$260–280** *TAN*

A pine table, with straight legs, c1890, 47½in (120.5cm) wide. **$400–450** *AL*

A pine table, c1890, 30in (76cm) diam. **$350–400** *AL*

A pine draw-leaf table, with original casters, c1900, 53in (134.5cm) wide. **$320–400** *TAN*

A pine drop-leaf table, with a single drawer, on turned legs, c1890, 32½in (83cm) wide. **$350–380** *AL*

A pine table, with turned legs, drawer replaced, c1890, **$370–420** *AL*

r. A Victorian pine table, with original paint, 37in (94cm) wide. **$350–400** *GRP*

l. A pine work table, with 2 drawers, c1920, 71in (180.5cm) wide. **$720–800** *AL*

A pine work table, c1920, 72in (183cm) wide. **$580–640** *AL*

A pine folding table, with slatted shelf below, marked 'J. Ryans & Co, Hire Dept', c1920, 40in (101.5cm) diam. **$220–260** *TAN*

Wardrobes

A Continental pine wardrobe, with 2 drawers, c1810, 63in (160cm) wide.
$1,100–1,200 *BEL*

A pine and oak wardrobe, c1820, 53¼in (135cm) wide.
$640–720 *BEL*

A pine armoire, Normandy, c1850, 52in (132cm) wide.
$3,500–4,000 *PEN*

A pine wardrobe, with a single drawer, c1880, 42in (106.5cm) wide.
$900–1,000 *AL*

A pine single wardrobe, c1880, 36½in (92.5cm) wide.
$700–780 *AL*

A painted pine wardrobe, with original painted decoration, c1880, 43in (109cm) wide.
$480–560 *TAN*

Miller's is a price GUIDE not a price LIST

A Victorian pine single wardrobe, with drawer under, 76in (193cm) wide.
$480–560 *AHO*

A Dutch pine knock-down wardrobe, c1880, 51¼in (130cm) wide.
$800–950 *AHO*

An east European pine wardrobe, with carved arch top, 2 doors and one drawer, c1880, 41in (104cm) wide.
$640–800 *NWE*

An east European pine wardrobe, with 2 doors and single drawer, c1880, 43¼in (110cm) wide.
$480–560 *NWE*

An east European two-piece pine wardrobe, the carved panelled doors with green frosted glass panels, above 2 drawers, c1880, 42½in (108cm) wide.
$480–560 *NWE*

A Continental triple-door pine wardrobe, c1890, 55½in (141cm) wide.
$1,100–1,200 *ASP*

Washstands

A Regency pine washstand, 40in (101.5cm) wide.
$1,100–1,300 *TPC*

A pine washstand, with single drawer, c1820, 15in (38cm) wide.
$200–240 *AL*

A pine washstand, with single drawer and bamboo turned legs, c1830, 24in (61cm) wide.
$320–400 *HRQ*

r. A painted pine washstand, with original paint, c1840, 34in (86.5cm) wide.
$200–220 *TAN*

Stripping pine

If a piece of pine furniture has not already been stripped down to the natural wood, then it may still be covered with paint, or black or brown varnish. To find out what the bottom layer is, remove part of the paint or varnish in a concealed place with the edge of a coin, for example, taking care not to damage the wood itself. If you want to buy a piece to strip down and not repaint, avoid pine which has a red stain – this will have been caused by the pigment of an old paint or brown stain. Do not forget, however, that pieces with their original paint, particularly when elaborately decorated, can be valuable.

A painted pine washstand, with *faux* marble top, painted with blue and black bands and leaves on a cream ground, mid-19thC, 31in (79cm) wide.
$1,100–1,250 *DN*

An early Victorian lyre-ended washstand, with gallery back and central kneehole drawer, 44in (112cm) wide.
$1,100–1,300 *TPC*

A pine washstand, with
2 short drawers, c1870,
35½in (90cm) wide.
$520–640 *AL*

A pine washstand, with marble
top, tiled splashback and
single cupboard under, c1880,
42in (106.5cm) wide.
$900–1,000 *AL*

A pine tray-top washstand,
with 2 drawers, c1890,
38in (96.5cm) wide.
$480–560 *BOR*

r. An Irish pine washstand,
with single drawer, c1880,
26½in (67.5cm) wide.
$200–240 *DFA*

> **FURTHER READING**
> *Miller's Pine & Country
> Furniture Buyer's Guide*
> Miller's Publications, 1995

l. A pine double washstand,
with fitted enamel bowls,
c1890, 43¼in (110cm) wide.
$320–400 *AHO*

A pine washstand, with single drawer. *(pictured at right is a tray-top washstand)*

Miscellaneous

r. A painted pine
boot remover,
original paint, c1840,
20in (51cm) long.
$25–30 *TAN*

l. A Continental pine peg rack,
c1860, 48in (122cm) wide.
$30–40 *ASP*

A red-painted carved pine wall
mirror, appears to retain its
original mirror plate, backboard
and finish, New England, c1740,
12in (30.5cm) wide.
$6,400–7,000 *S(NY)*

l. A carved pine carousel
cockerel, by Spooner, late
19thC, 55in (140cm) wide.
$5,000–5,500 *SPU*

A Regency pine seat commode,
the front with simulated
drawers, 27in (68.5cm) wide.
$320–400 *COT*

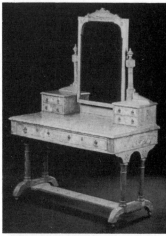

A Victorian Gothic revival style
pine bedroom suite, comprising
a mirror-back dressing table,
and a wardrobe, with 3 panelled
doors, one with a mirror plate,
the interior fitted with an
arrangement of slides and
3 short and 2 long drawers,
Oregon, c1870, wardrobe
48in (122cm) wide.
$1,800–2,000 *S(S)*

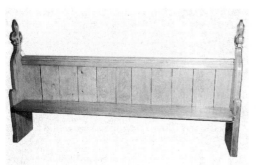

A pine church pew, c1880, 89in (226cm) wide.
$480–560 *COW*

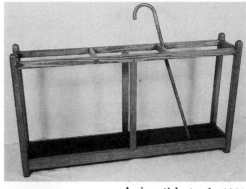

A pine stick stand, c1880,
49in (124.5cm) wide.
$200–260 *AL*

A pine writing slope, c1880,
16in (40.5cm) wide.
$50–60 *ASP*

A Victorian pine towel rail,
c1890, 27in (68.5cm) wide.
$100–110 *HRQ*

l. A pine barrel bench, c1890,
18in (45.5cm) wide.
$50–60 *AL*

A pine towel rail, c1880,
27in (68.5cm) wide.
$60–70 *ASP*

KITCHENWARE

A leaded bronze cauldron, bearing the chiselled date '1610', 13¾in (35cm) diam.
$1,300–1,500 *CSK*

A bronze cauldron, the body inscribed 'MG 1658', 17¾in (45cm) diam.
$6,000–6,400 *Bea(E)*

A treacle-glazed roasting brick, c1860, 15in (38cm) long.
$200–240 *RYA*

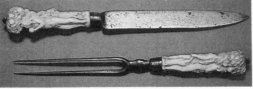

r. Two brass iron trivets, one heart-shaped and one spade-shaped, c1850, 9in (23cm) long.
$70–80 each *SMI*

Three knives with carved handles, c1920, cake knife 10in (25.5cm) long.
$40–50 each *SMI*

A set of 6 pieces of wooden-handled steel cutlery, c1760, knife 13in (33cm) long.
$400–450 *RYA*

A pewter serving spoon, c1780, 13in (33cm) long.
$100–120 *RYA*

An ivory-handled steel knife and fork, each carved with the figures of Adam and Eve, the silver collars incised with the owner's initials, the blade with cutler's stamp 'Douvre', the ivory handles French, 17thC, the steel blade, fork and silver collars associated, knife 8¼in (21cm) long.
$1,800–2,000 *CSK*

A Welsh elm spoon rack, 19thC, 20in (51cm) wide.
$1,000–1,100 *SMI*

A painted pine salt box, with brass fittings, 19thC, 8½in (21.5cm) wide.
$100–110 *No7*

An oak spoon rack and spice chest, 18thC, 9½in (24cm) wide.
$640–720 *SPU*

An oak knife box, the shaped top inlaid with knife on front, c1780, 19in (48.5cm) high.
$400–480 *RYA*

r. An oak spoon rack, with a lidded box, fret-carved back and end panels, 18thC, 12in (30.5cm) wide.
$740–800 *TMA*

r. A Welsh pine spoon rack, 19thC, 11in (28cm) wide.
$350–400 *COA*

Spice Containers

Special spice containers were first made in the 17th century, often in the form of wooden cabinets with drawers or as small chests that stood on a table or hung on the wall. By the 1840s, stacking spice columns had begun to appear – these were small round boxes that fitted on top of each other to form a 'tower'.

A yew-wood spice pot, in the shape of a beehive, c1720, 5in (12.5cm) high.
$880–960 *RYA*

An oak spice box, 19thC, 9in (23cm) high.
$350–400 *No7*

A boxwood four-piece spice tower, c1880, 7in (17.5cm) diam.
$200–240 *SMI*

A set of Hungarian fruitwood spice drawers, with 4 small drawers and one long drawer, wooden handles, c1880, 8in (20.3cm) wide.
$100–115 *HRQ*

An American butternut spice cabinet, refinished, 19thC, 20¼in (51.5cm) wide.
$1,000–1,100 *SK(B)*

A Lightning steel chopper, Newhaven, USA, 19thC, 6in (15cm) wide.
$30–35 *No7*

FURTHER READING
Christina Bishop,
Collecting Kitchenware,
Miller's Publications, 1995.

A beechwood mortar grater, c1780, 8in (20.5cm) high.
$600–640 *RYA*

This item is equivalent to a pestle and mortar. Herbs, salt and pepper would be ground together in it and caught in the small, perforated tray. They would then be put on the table as a condiment.

An elm chopping board, 19thC, 19in (48cm) wide.
$40–50 *No7*

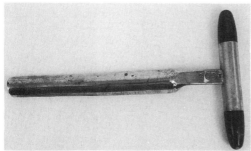

A brass, steel and ivory cheese tester, 6¾in (17cm) long.
$100–120 *No7*

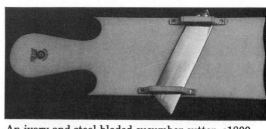

An ivory and steel-bladed cucumber cutter, c1800, 9in (23cm) long.
$800–960 *DIC*

A set of weights and scales, with brass pans, labelled 'J. & J. Siddons, West Bromwich', early 20thC, 14in (35.5cm) wide.
$90–100 *No7*

A set of kitchen weights and scales, with enamelled pan, early 20thC, pan 8in (20cm) diam.
$55–60 *No7*

A Salters butter balance, for weighing up to 2lbs, c1930, 10in (25.5cm) high.
$90–100 *SMI*

Two Victorian sycamore and ceramic pastry wheels, largest 7in (18cm) long.
$40–55 *SMI*

A set of Victorian brass pastry jiggers, 5in (13cm) long.
$25–30 each *SMI*

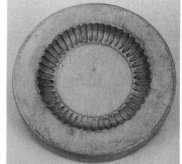

A ceramic jelly mould, 19thC, 7½in (19cm) diam.
$30–40 *No7*

A ceramic shortbread mould, advertising Raisley raising powder, c1920, 8in (20cm) diam.
$55–70 *SMI*

A yew-wood shortbread mould, 20thC, 8½in (21.5cm) diam.
$25–30 *No7*

A wooden confectionery roller, 19thC, 15in (38cm) long.
$90–100 *SMI*

A tin grater mounted on a sycamore base, c1890, 16¼in (41cm) long.
$25–30 *No7*

A Holt's egg beater, c1890, 13in (33cm) long.
$40–60 *SMI*

A Victorian round embossed copper jelly mould, and two oval moulds, largest 7in (17.5cm) wide.
$400–440 *DN*

A copper chocolate mould, with rooster pattern, c1880, 4in (10cm) wide.
$120–130 *SMI*

A copper ring mould, 19thC, 5½in (14cm) diam.
$180–200 *No7*

Three tin ice cream moulds, 19thC, largest 8½in (21.5cm) high.
$30–50 each *No7*

A Grimwade's ceramic pudding basin, c1920, 5½in (14cm) diam.
$70–80 *SMI*

The Patent Quick Cooker, c1910, 4½in (11.5cm) wide.
$100–115 *SMI*

A Shelley ceramic mould, in the form of a swan, c1930, 10in (25cm) wide.
$440–480 *BEV*

Five Welsh sycamore butter stamps, c1830, largest 6in (15cm) wide.
$110–160 each *COM*

A wooden butter stamp and bowl, stamp designed with picture of cow, 19thC, bowl 5in (12.5cm) diam.
$120–140 *No7*

Three sycamore butter stamps, depicting various birds, 19thC, largest 4in (10cm) diam.
$90–100 each *SMI*

A wooden butter mould, with handle, 19thC, 7½in (19cm) long.
$60–75 *No7*

An elm butterpat, 19thC, 15in (38cm) long.
$25–30 *No7*

Butter Stamps

Butter stamps were used mainly in the 19thC to decorate butter with attractive designs. Surplus butter was sold by farmers' wives at market and butter stamps also acted as a trademark, identifying the different farms where the butter was made. Stamps and moulds often depicted appropriate farm animals, crops and plants found on farms. Thus, a farm set in a valley might use a swan and bulrushes, while a farmer with a good herd of cattle might have a stamp with a portrait of his prize cow.

r. Three stoneware storage jars, c1880, largest 9in (23cm) high.
$55–70 each *SMI*

A stoneware banded lentil jar,
c1890, 6in (15cm) high.
$30–40 *AL*

A yellow and white
Cornish ware butter dish,
by T. G. Green, 1950s,
6in (15cm) diam.
$50–55 *SMI*

**Miller's is a price
GUIDE not a price LIST**

Cornish Ware

Cornish ware pottery was produced
from 1926 by T. G. Green & Co,
makers of household pottery since
the mid-1860s. The traditional
colour was blue and white, and the
range consisted of both table and
kitchenware. It was extremely
popular, and other colours began to
make an appearance towards the end
of the 1950s, in particular 'sunlit
yellow', and the buff-bodied range
later known as Cornish Gold. Some
black and white items were made,
and are quite difficult to find today.
In the late 1960s the shapes were
redesigned and some new items
added to the range, while more
recently pieces have been produced
in navy blue and teal green.

A Domino ware muffin dish and butter dish, by
T. G. Green & Co, c1930, largest 6½in (16.5cm) wide.
$40–55 each *SMI*

A set of blue and white Cornish ware, by T. G.
Green & Co, comprising: a flour sifter, sugar sifter,
tea jar and cover, 2 pudding basins with pouring
lips, and an egg separator, c1930, flour sifter
5in (12.5cm) high.
$160–200 *E*

A blue and white Cornish ware rolling pin,
by T. G. Green, c1950, 18in (45.5cm) long.
$70–80 *SMI*

Two black and white Cornish
ware salt and pepper shakers,
by T. G. Green, c1960,
5in (12.5cm) high.
$30–40 each *SMI*

A ceramic mixing jug,
advertising Borden's Malted
Milk, by Woods & Sons,
c1940, 8in (20cm) high.
$55–65 *SMI*

A green speckled enamel bread tin and cake
tin, c1900, bread bin 12in (30.5cm) high.
$40–55 each *SMI*

A horn beaker, scoop and spoon,
19thC, spoon 9in (23cm) long.
$15–25 each *No7*

A McVitie's biscuit tin with
Beatrix Potter pattern,
c1938, 4in (10cm) square.
$55–65 *WAB*

A copper and brass scoop,
with wooden handle, 19thC,
7in (18cm) long.
$50–55 *No7*

A pewter ladle, 19thC, 12½in (32cm) long
$30–35 *No7*

A fruitwood skimmer, 19thC,
9in (23cm) diam.
$45–50 *No7*

A baker's pine peel, c1850,
35in (89cm) long.
$240–320 *COM*

A Victorian banister brush,
55in (140cm) long.
$40–50 *SMI*

A chinoiserie-decorated
toleware plate warmer, in
the form of a miniature oven,
c1835, 26in (66cm) high.
$1,600–2,000 *RYA*

American coffee grinder,
'The Enterprise' model,
with original paint and
eagle, drawer replaced,
19thC, 10in (25cm) wide.
$560–640 *SMI*

A brass-bottomed box iron,
c1880, 4in (10cm) wide.
$130–150 *SMI*

A Norwegian chip-carved mangle board,
with original polychrome decoration,
c1780, 23½in (60cm) long.
$640–700 *RYA*

*Wet clothes were wrapped around a mangle
board and rolled backwards and forwards
to get the water out. The better carved
ones were often given as love tokens.*

A sleeve iron, by W. Bullock & Co,
c1900, 15in (38cm) long.
$90–100 *SMI*

A wicker picnic basket,
with 2 place settings,
c1920, 29in (74cm) wide.
$240–320 *GBr*

A Victorian ten-gallon
milk dilvery churn,
with measures,
24in (61cm) high.
$560–640 *SMI*

A syrup barrel tap, 19thC,
8½in (21.5cm) wide.
$80–90 *No7*

A brass-banded milk
delivery bucket, with
milk measures, c1900,
10in (25.5cm) diam.
$200–240 *SMI*

POTTERY & PORCELAIN

Considering how breakable old pottery and porcelain is, I remain astounded by the quantity that is about. Every year there seems to be more and more crowding into antiques fairs and markets. What used to remain at home as mere ornaments and crockery are now actively traded as collectable ceramics and there is something new every year. London auction houses are now holding specialised sales of Chintz ware, Beswick and Wade, and I have just catalogued Phillips' first auction of Quimper, a situation I would not have dreamt of 20 years ago. Yet collectors are keen, and 20th century ceramics are no less enjoyable than my own beloved early Worcester. Dealers in traditional pre-1850 ceramics have been quoted at length this year bemoaning the present shortage of anything worthwhile to buy, unlike the old days. But was there really more about 20 years go? Could it be that, in the absence of interest in later goods, everyone traded in the same kind of porcelain, buying and selling the same pieces and collections over and over? I believe there are more ceramics sales today than ever before; it is just that Doulton and Clarice Cliff have taken over from New Hall and Staffordshire flatbacks as fashionable pieces to collect.

There does seem to be less early Worcester and Sèvres about, but Royal Worcester and decorative later Sèvres style vases sell instead. More Meissen is sold now than ever before, but it is the 19th century pieces that cause excitement and fly out of shops and auction rooms faster than anything else.

A Meissen teapot and cover, probably by Johann Georg Funke, crossed swords mark, minor damage, c1723, 5in (12.5cm) high.
$14,500–16,000 *S*

Meanwhile, 18th century Meissen is actually much harder to sell. American and Japanese bidders compete with English and German collectors for 19th century Meissen, while 18th century items remain largely the domain of Germans alone. The best and most decorative Meissen will always sell well, thankfully, regardless of condition. A damaged rare piece is full of interest, but a standard object with damage is not so desirable.

I am glad that later porcelain is more valuable, for much of it deserves our full attention. I grew up at the Royal Worcester factory and have great admiration for 20th century workmanship. But we have reached a very odd situation. New collectors naturally follow fashion. They seek later Meissen or Royal Crown Derby, or Belleek, or whatever – always clearly marked and easy to look up in a price guide. At the same time there are not so many enthusiasts for early pottery and porcelain. Eighteenth century Derby figures or early Staffordshire models do not have a convenient serial number to look up the rarity in a book, so some experience is essential. Early marks on German or French tewares are commonly faked and most early English porcelain is unmarked. Collecting is much more difficult, but for those willing to persist and learn there are wonderful opportunities about. Eighteenth century English delft or French faience plates can cost less than Quimper examples. Bow figures can be cheaper than Doulton. I have even seen some 18th century Worcester and Chelsea sell for the same price as Samson copies which strikes me as crazy.

All is not gloom – far from it. Many spectacular prices have been paid for early English and German rarities – notice the prices of some of the German fayence on the following pages. The smaller numbers of collectors are all chasing the same scarce items – the best that is available in their field. I can only praise their actions, for these fine rarities will give a great deal of pleasure and should continue to hold their value. On the other hand, the pieces which these serious collectors regard as 'ordinary' can be very difficult to sell. There is no doubt these were overvalued in the past and fashions do change.

Observant readers will find some pieces in the *Miller's Antiques Price Guide* worth less than in old editions of 10 years ago. Many uninteresting and unattributable pieces deserve to have fallen in value, but there is another side to the coin. I believe there are great opportunities at the moment to begin collections of 18th and 19th century ceramics. Avoid poor, damaged specimens – pieces that are cheap for a good reason. Shop around and develop an eye for quality, and then be prepared for bargains as dealers reduce the prices on stock that no-one else is buying. It is easy for me as an expert to write this; I realise many new collectors still want the confidence of easy, clearly marked collectables. That is fine – but it is nearly impossible to know which of these are still rising markets and for how long – I do believe, though, that traditional pre-1850 ceramics are unlikely ever to fall much in value, and some may never be as reasonably priced as they are now.

John Sandon

POTTERY
Baskets

A delft blue and white basket, by Henry Delamain, Dublin, decorated with a landscape beneath a border of pierced interlocking circles, footrim pierced for suspension, slight damage, c1755, 6½in (16.5cm) diam.
$10,800–12,000 *C*

A pair of Spode pearlware baskets, with transfer-printed underglaze blue border with overglaze decoration and gilding, with a central floral spray, c1820, 8in (20.5cm) wide.
$640–800 *DAN*

A Magdeburg two-handled basket, with manganese and green decoration, marked 'M', small hairline crack, c1765, 10¼in (26cm) wide.
$3,500–4,000 *C*

The Magdeburg factory copied the work of the Hannoversch-Münden factory, making items painted in high temperature colours, and produced excellent floral decoration.

A Wemyss basket, painted with sweet peas, c1900, 11¾in (30cm) wide.
$1,100–1,200 *RdeR*

Items in the Pottery section have been arranged in date order within each sub-section.

A pearlware basket and stand, moulded with basketwork panels, the basket with flared sides linked by scroll bands, and picked out in underglaze blue, c1800, 12in (30.5cm) wide.
$520–640 *DN*

A Quimper basket, decorated with a blue rim, 1920s, 4¾in (12cm) wide.
$200–220 *VH*

Bowls & Dishes

A sgraffito stemmed conical bowl, decorated with a band of strapwork and flowers streaked in green and ochre, the interior with a stylised figure within a band of leaves similarly streaked, on a flared domed spreading foot, perhaps Bologna, slight damage, c1480, 4¾in (12cm) high.
$2,200–2,400 *C*

An English delft punchbowl, decorated in blue, green, yellow and iron-red with a chinoiserie figure in a landscape, c1760, 12in (30.5cm) diam.
$9,600–10,600 *JHo*

The colours used on this bowl are rare for a delft piece.

r. A Bristol delft polychrome bowl, c1750, 8¾in (22cm) diam.
$2,200–2,400 *JHo*

A Dutch Delft blue and white porringer, c1740, 8½in (21.5cm) wide.
$200–240 *IW*

A Sceaux faience leaf dish, naturalistically moulded and picked out in yellow and green, fleur-de-lys mark in brown, c1770, 14¾in (37.5cm) wide.
$1,600–1,900 *S*

An English delft dish, painted
blue, decorated with a cottage
within chainlink border and
stylised flower rim, 18thC,
13in (33cm) diam.
$420–480 *BR*

18thC English Delftware

There were several potteries in and around London in the 17thC,
making tin-glazed earthenware known as delftware. The tradition
spread in the late 17thC and early 18thC to other parts of the British
Isles – Brislington, Bristol, Wincanton, Liverpool, Glasgow and
Dublin. While it is possible to attribute some pieces to particular
towns, it is difficult to distinguish London ware from Bristol or
Liverpool in the 18thC. The material, with some slight variations, is
the same and identification depends more on the decoration and the
patterns on the undersides of dishes. Unfortunately this is not
accurate as both potters and designers copied one another.

After 1720 English delftware is distinct from its Continental rivals.
Designs have a character of their own, whether they are Oriental or
European in inspiration: patterns are looser and less complex, scenes
and figures are cruder and less meticulous than those produced in
mainland Europe.

A Wedgwood creamware
commemorative punchbowl,
decorated in Liverpool, the interior
inscribed 'Capt Joseph Anthony,
Ship St Ann with her two Prizes Le
Pelerin & Consalateur', the exterior
printed in black with sporting
scenes, extensively damaged,
restored, c1785, 12½in (32cm) diam.
$640–780 *C*

*This punchbowl commemorates the
capture of 2 French ships, the frigate
Pelerin and the merchantman
Consalateur, by the privateer St
Ann, captained by Joseph Anthony,
off the West Indies in 1762.
The price reflects the fact that it is
badly damaged, and would be
considerably higher if it was in
good condition.*

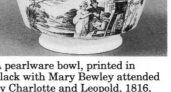

A pearlware bowl, printed in
black with Mary Bewley attended
by Charlotte and Leopold, 1816,
6¼in (16cm) diam.
$320–400 *SAS*

*Mary (called Goody) Bewley lived in
a small cottage within the grounds
of Claremont, the residence of
Princess Charlotte and her husband
Prince Leopold, who were her
frequent visitors. Goody Bewley used
to read a fine print Bible, and the
Princess is seen here presenting her
with a large print Bible.*

Maiolica/Majolica

Maiolica is tin-glazed
earthenware produced in
Italy from the 15th–18thC,
and although tin-glazed
ware was made earlier it
was not truly developed until
the Renaissance.

Majolica is a heavily-potted,
moulded ware covered in
transparent glazes in
distinctive, often sombre,
colours developed by the
Minton factory in the middle
of the 19thC. A number of
other factories in England,
France and north America
also produced majolica.

A Wedgwood majolica strawberry
dish, with loop handle, moulded
in relief with a sunburst mask,
on turquoise ground, within blue
ground flowerhead moulded
borders, cracked, impressed
marks, c1870, 15¾in (40cm) wide.
$1,100–1,250 *DN*

Two Quimper dishes, in the
shape of leaves, one decorated
with a lady and coloured in blue
and yellow, the other with a
man and coloured green,
mustard and orange, c1910,
10in (25.5cm) long.
$150–160 *PSA*

A maiolica bowl, by Richard Ginori,
painted with a band of masks, birds
and flowers, on 4 mermaid, mask
and scroll feet, slight damage,
painted mark and No. 409-845, late
19thC, 13in (33cm) wide.
$720–780 *HOLL*

r. A pottery dish, moulded with
Prince of Wales' feathers
encircled by a crown, and
ribboned inscription 'Ich Dien'
in gilt, 1958, 5in (12.5cm) diam.
$100–115 *SAS*

*Prince Charles was created Prince
of Wales in 1958, and his
subsequent investiture was at
Caernarfon in 1969.*

A Wemyss ewer and basin,
painted with yellow irises,
c1910, 9in (23cm) high.
$1,400–1,600 *RdeR*

Buildings

A pair of Staffordshire pearlware cottages, 1820, 3½in (9cm) high.
$320–340 *JHo*

A Staffordshire souvenir money box, modelled as a house, inscribed 'A Present from Scarborough', c1850, 5in (12.5cm) wide, I546, 55, 105.
$240–270 *RWB*

A Scottish pottery cottage money box, slight restoration, c1840, 5in (12.5cm) wide.
$680–800 *DAN*

Staffordshire Models

The reference numbers included in some captions refer to the cataloguing system used by P. D. Gordon Pugh in his book *Staffordshire Portrait Figures*, published by Antique Collectors' Club, 1970. This book only refers to identified portrait figures and allied subjects of the Victorian period, with no animals or early figures.

A Staffordshire model of Potash Farm, c1849, 5½in (14cm) wide, G482, 23, 44(b).
$270–300 *RWB*
Potash Farm was the location of a notorious Victorian murder, and many variations of the model were made.

A Staffordshire pastille burner, c1860, 8¼in (21cm) high.
$350–400 *TVM*

A Staffordshire model of a castle, with simulated clock face, c1860, 7½in (19cm) high.
$160–200 *SER*

A Staffordshire model of a castle, with green and rust decoration on a tan ground, c1860, 8½in (21.5cm) high.
$220–240 *EL*

A Staffordshire model of a house, decorated with a blue roof, c1860, 7in (18cm) high.
$200–220 *SER*

A Maling model of the old castle, Newcastle-upon-Tyne, made for the North East Coast Exhibition, May 1929, 5in (12.5cm) high.
$640–700 *AG*

Busts

A pair of documentary busts of Admirals Duncan and St Vincent, modelled by Pierre Stephan, c1797, largest 9in (23cm) high.
$2,000–2,400 *S*

Pierre Stephan worked independently, and was most celebrated for his work at the Derby factory which included a series of standing Admirals and Generals, some of which are signed. He also briefly produced work for the Wedgwood and Coalport factories.

A Staffordshire pearlware bust of Zingara, enamel decorated, possibly by Enoch Wood, 1800, 10½in (26.5cm) high.
$1,300–1,400 *JRe*

A Wedgwood black basalt bust of Winston Churchill, by Arnold Machin, commemorating the centenary of his birth, limited edition of 750, 1974, 7in (18cm) high.
$160–200 *MGC*

Candlesticks

A pair of Wemyss candlesticks, c1890, 12½in (32cm) high.
$280–320 *RdeR*

Only a few were made after 1900, when electric lights became popular in the home.

r. A Dutch Delft candlestick, after a silver example, decorated in enamel colours with scrolling foliage and scaled bands, slight damage, etched 'C' to base, mid-18thC, 6in (15cm) high.
$7,000–7,500 *S(Am)*

A pair of Mason's beaded candlesticks, decorated in iron-red and blue with Japan pattern, line impressed mark, c1815, 3½in (9cm) high.
$1,400–1,600 *JP*

Covered Dishes

A pair of Dutch Delft butter dishes, painted in blue, manganese, red and shades of green, the cover modelled as a plover, the dish as a duckweed bird's nest, slight damage and restoration, marked, c1765, 6in (15cm) wide.
$14,000–15,500 *S(Am)*

r. A pair of Dutch Delft two-handled butter dishes and covers, decorated with chinoiserie scenes, gilt ball finials replaced, marked, 18thC, 4½in (11.5cm) high.
$5,400–6,400 *S(Am)*

A Dutch Delft butter dish and cover, the cover decorated with a Chinese lady and surmounted by a finial in the shape of a yellow apple surrounded by green leaves, glaze chipped, marked, 18thC, 5in (12.5cm) wide.
$1,300–1,400 *S(Am)*

A Proskau fayence leaf-shaped dish, with 3 covers, formed as a melon resting on a leaf flanked by a bunch of grapes and a rose, damaged, marked, c1775, 12¾in (32.5cm) wide.
$7,200–8,000 *C*

A blue majolica sardine dish, with gilt decoration, the cover with a sardine finial, c1860, 8in (20.5cm) wide.
$440–480 *SSW*

A George Jones majolica cheese dish and cover, modelled as a cylindrical tower, with banner finial, naturalistically coloured, the interior in pale blue, slight damage, impressed factory and registration mark for 1873, 12¾in (32.5cm) wide.
$2,700–3,200 *CSK*

A George Jones majolica game pie dish, relief-decorated in colours with geese, ducks and sporting trophies on a turquoise ground, the fern leaf strewn cover with a fox and a dead goose, cover repaired, No. 2267, c1875, 7½in (19cm) high.
$3,800–4,400 *MCA*

A majolica butter dish, in the form of an artichoke, decorated in green and yellow, the cover with a bird finial, c1880, 7½in (19cm) wide.
$200–240 *SSW*

Locate the Source
The source of each illustration in Miller's can be found by checking the code letters below each caption with the Key to Illustrations.

A Victorian cheese dish, transfer-printed in brown, cream and blue, c1890, 8½in (21.5cm) wide.
$80–100 *TAC*

A Burleigh Ware cheese dish, with sloping cover, decorated with the Briar pattern, printed marks, c1900, 9in (23cm) wide.
$160–200 *GAK*

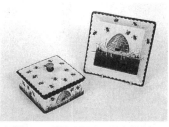

A Wemyss box, cover and dish, painted with bees and a beehive, designed by Thomas Goode & Co, c1910, dish 8in (20.5cm) wide.
$560–640 *RdeR*

Cow Creamers

A Staffordshire cow creamer, 1790, 6in (15cm) wide.
$1,400–1,800 *JHo*

A West Country earthenware cow creamer and cover, modelled with a milkmaid, the cow sponged in pale blue and brown colours on a buff ground, c1800, 5in (12.5cm) wide.
$700–800 *HYD*

A North Country cow creamer, modelled with a milkmaid, the cow sponged in black with a green-lined base on a cream ground, the tail forming a handle, early 19thC, 5½in (14cm) wide.
$700–850 *HYD*

A pearlware cow creamer, on a green-lined slab base, sponged in red and black glazes on a cream ground, c1800, 5½in (14cm) wide.
$450–520 *HYD*

A Pratt ware cow creamer, restored, c1800, 5½in (14cm) wide.
$1,100–1,300 *DAN*

r. A cow creamer, decorated with red, possibly Swansea, slight restoration, c1830, 5½in (14cm) wide.
$520–620 *DAN*

Cups & Saucers

A miniature pearlware cup and saucer, hand-painted with floral sprays and brown rims, c1820, saucer 3¾in (9.5cm) diam.
$160–200 *DAN*

A Quimper cup and saucer, marked 'HR', c1885, saucer 4¾in (12cm) diam.
$300–320 *VH*

A Wedgwood coffee can and saucer, sprigged in white with swags of flowers and fruit suspended from rams' masks between lilac oval cameos and trophies against a green jasper dip ground, slight damage, marked, early 19thC, saucer 4in (10cm) diam.
$1,000–1,100 *S(S)*

A coronation cup and saucer, decorated with a photographic portrait of Princesses Elizabeth and Margaret, and a blue-lined rim, 1937, saucer 3in (7.5cm) diam.
$80–90 *SAS*

A Coronetware cup and saucer, by Parrot & Co, commemorating the Coronation of George VI nd Queen Elizabeth, 1937, 3½in (9cm) diam.
$55–65 *SAS*

Figures

A Dutch Delft figure of a monk, wearing a manganese headdress and habit, 18thC, 5in (13cm) high.
$480–520 *S(Am)*

r. A Staffordshire figure group, entitled 'Rural Pastime', enamelled in colours, on a square base, c1800, 7½in (19cm) high.
$950–1,000 *JRe*

l. A Hannoversch-Münden figure of a grape harvester, seated with a basket on his back, some damage and repairs, c1760, 8in (20cm) high.
$7,400–8,800 *C*

A Pratt ware figure of Mercury, c1790, 8in (20.5cm) high.
$320–350 *TVM*

A Staffordshire figure of a boy, c1810, 5½in (14cm) high.
$580–640 *JHo*

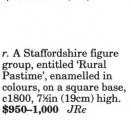

FURTHER READING
Gordon Lang, *Miller's Pottery Antiques Checklist*, Miller's Publications, 1995.
Gordon Lang, *Miller's Pottery & Porcelain Marks*, Miller's Publications, 1995.

A Staffordshire figure of a girl at a pump, c1820, 6in (15cm) high.
$1,200–1,400 *JHo*

A Yorkshire figure of a man on a horse, restored, early 19thC, 10½in (26.5cm) high.
$4,800–5,200 *JHo*

In the 19thC the Yorkshire factories mainly produced models of cows, consequently figures on horseback are extremely rare.

A Staffordshire figure of a woman holding a bird, with painted decoration, standing on a square base, c1810, 4in (10cm) high.
$120–140 *RBB*

r. A Staffordshire pottery Walton-type group, entitled 'Rualere', modelled as a rustic male musician and his female companion, painted in enamel colours, c1820, 7in (18cm) high.
$520–580 *HYD*

A pair of Staffordshire pearlware figures, entitled 'Jobson' and 'Nell', enamelled in colours, slight damage, 1820, 6½in (16.5cm) high.
$720–800 *JRe*

This is an early example of named figures, which became common later in the century.

l. A Staffordshire pearlware figure, entitled 'Elijah', by John Walton, enamelled in colours, impressed strap mark, 1820, 12in (30.5cm) high.
$520–580 *JRe*

A Staffordshire clock face group, portraying Mrs Siddons as Lady Macbeth, and John Philip Kemble as Hamlet, c1845, 8in (20.5cm) high, E7, Fig 19.
$320–400 *RWB*

A Staffordshire porcellaneous figure of a Scotsman and a dog, c1845, 8½in (21.5cm) high.
$400–450 *DAN*

A Staffordshire candlestick, modelled as Queen Victoria and Prince Albert, with the Prince of Wales sculling in a boat, c1848, 9½in (24cm) high, A55, Fig 165.
$560–640 *RWB*

A Staffordshire spill holder, modelled as a shepherd and shepherdess, with a dog and sheep, c1850, 9¾in (25cm) high.
$270–300 *RWB*

Staffordshire Figures

The reference numbers included in some captions refer to the cataloguing system used by P. D. Gordon Pugh in his book *Staffordshire Portrait Figures*, published by Antique Collectors' Club, 1970. This book only refers to identified portrait figures and allied subjects of the Victorian period, with no animals or early figures.

l. A Staffordshire group, entitled 'Turkey, England and France', portraying Abd-ul-Medjid, Queen Victoria and Napoleon III, restored, c1854, 11in (28cm) high.
$650–720 *SER*

A Staffordshire spill vase group, depicting a boy, a girl and a dog, c1860, 8½in (21.5cm) high.
$160–200 *DAN*

A Staffordshire circus group, depicting Mazeppa bound naked to his horse being pursued by wolves, with a spill vase behind, c1860, 9½in (24cm) high.
$1,100–1,300 *TVM*

A Staffordshire group, entitled 'Robin Hood', c1860, 14¾in (37.5cm) high.
$120–140 *EL*

A Staffordshire group, entitled 'Dog Tray', the man wearing a green cape, the dog with red spots, restored, c1860, 12¼in (31cm) high.
$120–140 *EL*

A Quimper handbell, in the form of a lady, her leg acting as the bell clapper, marked, c1920, 5in (12.5cm) high.
$300–320 *VH*

A Wedgwood figure of a cherub, c1920, 22½in (57cm) high.
$450–480 *No7*

This was a trial figure, and never went into production.

Flatware

A Gubbio dish, decorated in blue, brown, green, gold and red lustre, with cupid poised to shoot an arrow in the centre, the rim with berried scrollwork on a blue ground, hairline crack, c1525, 8¾in (22cm) diam.
$12,000–13,000 *S*

An English delft blue-dash charger, decorated in blue with an equestrian portrait, probably General Monck, on an alternate green, yellow/manganese ground, slight damage, c1710, 13¼in (33.5cm) diam.
$13,800–15,200 *Bon*

Even though General Monck died in 1670, he remained a celebrated figure on chargers after his death for his assistance in the restoration of the Monarchy.

Blue-dash Chargers

Among the most idiosyncratic of English delft is the blue-dash group of chargers. Decorated with blue dashes around the rim, hence the name, they are painted with a variety of subjects including tulips, oak leaves, geometrical patterns, Biblical themes, portraits of English monarchs or generals.

Blue-dash wares are painted in a simple but vigorous manner within a flattened rim embellished with dashes. This group spans a period of a little over a century until about 1740, when chargers seem to disappear altogether.

r. A delft blue and white dish, painted with a scene of the Greek poet Arion holding a lyre, astride a dolphin, probably Bristol, slight damage, mid-18thC, 13in (33cm) diam.
$3,200–3,500 *S(S)*

A Castel Durante dish, lustred at Gubbio, the centre with a seated putto with a staff and a bag, and a skull and crossbones, the border reserved with martial trophies heightened with lustre on a blue ground, damaged and restored, c1530, 8¼in (21cm) diam.
$10,400–11,200 *C*

A Rouen faience blue and white dish, decorated with deer, with scattered birds and insects, c1720, 19in (48.5cm) diam.
$5,200–5,800 *C*

A Dutch lead-glazed maiolica dish, the centre decorated in blue with rustic flowers, the border decorated with pomegranates and blue bands, damaged, early 17thC, 16¾in (42.5cm) diam.
$1,100–1,200 *S(Am)*

A Dorotheenthal fayence blue and white dish, the centre painted with a concentric strapwork tassel and Cupid medallion, slight damage, c1735, 16¾in (42.5cm) wide.
$10,200–12,000 *C*

Faience/Fayence

Tin-glazed earthenware was known as 'faience' in France and 'fayence' in Germany. The name is derived from Faenza, one of the biggest pottery making centres in Italy.

l. A Liverpool delft plate, painted in Fazackerley palette with a central spray of flowers and leaves, the rim with scattered flowers, slight damage, c1750, 9¼in (23.5cm) diam.
$800–880 *DN*

A Bristol delft plate, painted in blue with a fisherman within a *bianco-sopra-bianco* flower border, slight damage, c1760, 9in (23cm) diam.
$320–380 *DN*

The term bianco-sopra-bianco *means white-on-white.*

A Liverpool delft plate, decorated
with blue floral sprays, c1760,
7in (18cm) diam.
$160–180 *JHo*

A Les Islettes plate, decorated in
green, red and yellow with a
Chinaman fishing, late 18thC,
9in (23cm) diam.
$320–350 *VH*

A Mason's plate, decorated
with a prunus bush, pattern
No. 2588, printed mark and
'Higginbotham & Son, Dublin',
c1830, 10in (25.5cm) diam.
$180–200 *JP*

A Staffordshire alphabet plate,
the centre decorated with a picture
entitled 'The Village Blacksmith',
c1840, 7in (18cm) diam.
$40–50 *SER*

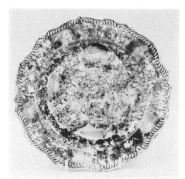

A Whieldon-type moulded plate,
decorated with sponged underglaze
colours, c1760, 9½in (24cm) diam.
$400–480 *DAN*

A Spode New Stone two-handled
dish, applied with moulded branch
handles, decorated in Imari colours
with the Oriental pattern, incised
marks and pattern No. 3875,
c1825, 10½in (26.5cm) wide.
$350–400 *GAK*

A Staffordshire pottery miniature
plate, printed in dark brown with
the head and shoulders of Queen
Victoria, commemorating her
Coronation, restored, 1838,
3¼in (8.5cm) diam.
$180–200 *SAS*

A pottery plate, by Dixon Phillips
& Co of Sunderland, the border
moulded with daisies, the centre
printed in mauve with 2 full-
length Oriental dancing figures,
entitled 'Chinese Polka', 1844,
7¾in (19.5cm) diam.
$380–420 *SAS*

A Dutch Delft plate, decorated
with a central vase of flowers and
edged with Ming-style peonies,
1760, 9¾in (25cm) diam.
$160–200 *BRU*

A William Mason earthenware
plate, transfer-printed in
underglaze blue with coloured
enamel border, beaded frame,
marked 'Linlithgow', c1820,
9½in (24cm) diam.
$300–320 *JP*

An Alcocks Indian Ironstone
meat plate, the centre decorated
with peonies in a vase,
with combed back, c1840,
18in (45.5cm) wide.
$320–370 *BRU*

An ironstone plate, by Charles
Meigh & Son, decorated with
green flowers, c1850,
9in (23cm) diam.
$80–100 *BRU*

A Mason's plate, decorated with Vase pattern, printed crown mark, c1835, 10in (25.5cm) diam.
$180–200 *JP*

A majolica oyster plate, c1860, 9½in (24cm) diam.
$200–240 *SSW*

A Belleek earthenware meat dish, transfer-printed in blue and white with a thorn branch, First Period, 1865–90, 23in (58.5cm) wide.
$320–480 *MLa*

Two Powell, Bishop & Stonier satin ware plates, decorated with vignettes, the centres with a landscape and a coastal sailing scene, on a foliate printed off-white ground, printed marks, late 19thC, 9½in (24cm) diam.
$150–160 *GAK*

A Belleek earthenware plate, hand-decorated in red with crest, First Period, 1865–90, 10in (25.5cm) diam.
$250–320 *MLa*

A Wedgwood majolica plate, decorated with Japanese Fan design, late 19thC, 9in (23cm) diam.
$160–200 *SSW*

A Wemyss plate, decorated with thistles, c1910, 8½in (21.5cm) diam.
$280–320 *RdeR*

A Wemyss miniature plate, decorated with raspberries, c1910, 3½in (9cm) diam.
$160–240 *RdeR*

A Wemyss miniature early morning plate, decorated with oranges, c1910, 3½in (9cm) diam.
$160–240 *RdeR*

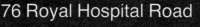

Inkstands & Inkwells

A Staffordshire pearlware inkwell, in the form of a shoe, enamel-decorated over the glaze, c1820, 2½in (6.5cm) long.
$560–620 *JRe*

> **Miller's is a price GUIDE not a price LIST**

r. A Wemyss inkwell, decorated with green leaves and ships in a sunset, c1900, 10in (25.5cm) wide.
$500–550 *RdeR*

A Mason's Ironstone inkstand, painted in black and enamelled with lakeside pavilions and Oriental flowers on a deep blue ground, restored, black printed mark, c1835, 13in (33cm) wide.
$1,200–1,300 *S(S)*

An Italian maiolica inkwell, in the form of a winged griffin attendant, polychrome coloured on an oval base, late 19thC, 4in (10cm) wide.
$200–225 *GAK*

Jardinières

A Stockelsdorf fayence jardinière and stand, the sides painted with estuary scenes, the stand painted in shades of blue with flower sprays, slight damage and repair, c1775, stand 14½in (37cm) wide.
$18,500–20,000 *C*
Works by this German maker are rare.

A Renaissance revival glazed coloured earthenware jardinière, by W. Schiller & Sons, Bodenbach, Bohemia, restored, late 19thC, 8in (20.5cm) high.
$320–350 *RIT*

A Doulton Burslem flower pot, printed in brown with portraits and inscribed 'Australian Federation' and with quotation from Joseph Chamberlain, 1901, 4¾in (12cm) high.
$160–180 *SAS*

Jars

r. A Derbyshire salt-glazed handled jar, with rouletted decoration, c1800, 6¼in (16cm) high.
$100–115 *IW*

A Castelli albarello, painted with a portrait bust of a young woman, above a drug label inscribed 'dia. olibano', the reverse blue with stylised foliage, damaged and repaired, c1530, 9¾in (25cm) high.
$5,500–7,000 *S*

A Montelupo syrup jar, painted in blue, yellow, green and manganese with foliage, loop handle and straight spout above an armorial shield enclosing monogram 'CAR', slight damage, 17thC, 9in (23cm) high.
$950–1,100 *S(Am)*

A Spanish maiolica albarello, painted in blue with a hound encircled by a laurel wreath, slight damage, 17thC, 8½in (21.5cm) high.
$950–1,100 *S(Am)*

A north Midlands black glazed handled jar, c1800, 5½in (14cm) high.
$100–130 *IW*

A salt-glazed preserve jar, with incised inscription 'J. C. Hoffmann, Redcurrant Jelly', probably London, early 19thC, 5½in (14cm) high.
$55–75 *IW*

A Yorkshire handled jar, with flattened sides, early 19thC, 9½in (24cm) high.
$120–150 *IW*

A Staffordshire British Lion tobacco jar, late 19thC, 7in (18cm) high.
$260–300 *SER*

A Wemyss preserve jar, painted with greengages, c1900, 4in (10cm) high.
$320–400 *RdeR*

Jugs

A Liverpool delft puzzle jug, with typical inscription, fire crack, c1760, 8in (20.5cm) high.
$1,600–2,000 *JHo*

A Davenport ironstone jug, with bright Imari pattern, printed anchor mark, early 19thC, 8½in (21.5cm) high.
$400–450 *GAK*

A Mocha ware jug, with inlaid coloured clay borders, banding and trees, early 19thC, 13½in (34.5cm) high.
$500–560 *GAZE*

A Yorkshire creamware jug, painted in underglaze blue, dated '1778', 8in (20.5cm) high.
$4,000–4,500 *JHo*

A Ralph Wood type creamware Bacchus mask jug, with loop handle, picked out in green and brown, on scroll-moulded round base, damaged and repaired, c1780, 4½in (11.5cm) high.
$280–320 *HOLL*

r. A creamware milk jug and cover, with ball knop, decorated with combed slip tortoiseshell bands, the reeded borders picked out in green, on 3 short feet, c1780, 6in (15cm) high.
$1,750–2,000 *DN*

A tavern jug, in white salt-glaze with scratch blue decoration, late 18thC, 6¼in (16cm) high.
$100–150 *SAS*

Slipware

Slipware is probably the earliest identifiable type of pottery made in Staffordshire, although it was also made elsewhere in England, most notably at Wrotham in Kent, c1612–1710. It is composed of red or buff-coloured clay, decorated in brown and white coloured slip, (clay mixed with water), which is then covered in a thick, glassy, clear lead glaze. There is a small amount of iron present in the lead glaze which gives a slightly yellowish cast to the underlying white slip.

As well as trailed and dotted slip decoration, *sgraffito* or scratched decoration and applied moulding were also used to decorate slipware.

Favourite subjects on slipware include Adam and Eve, mermaids, cockerels, royal portraits, crests, coats-of-arms and abstract designs. Items were made for the local market, and included large dishes and flatware, honey pots, salt pigs, loving cups and other domestic vessels.

A pearlware commemorative jug, printed in blue with a portrait of Admiral Lord Nelson, and with a view of HMS *Victory*, within military emblems, battle honours and leaf scrolls, inscribed, slight damage, c1810, 5½in (14cm) high.
$950–1,100 *DN*

A Bristol jug, painted with red and yellow flowers and green leaves, dated '1815', 6¾in (17cm) high.
$480–560 *DAN*

A white stoneware jug, moulded with a hunting scene, the ground blue glazed to imitate jasper, c1815, 5½in (14cm) high.
$160–200 *DAN*

A lustreware jug, decorated with leaves and berries, c1815, 5¼in (13.5cm) high.
$200–250 *PCh*

A Staffordshire moulded jug, well coloured, entitled 'Lord Wellington' and 'General Hill', c1820, 5¼in (13.5cm) high.
$500–600 *TVM*

A Mason's jug, decorated with Red Scale pattern, c1835, 5¼in (13.3cm) high.
$280–340 *VH*

A John and William Ridgway stoneware covered jug, printed Ironstone mark, c1814, 7½in (19cm) high.
$400–450 *JP*

A Mason's moulded jug, with vine stock handle, printed crown mark, c1835, 8in (20.5cm) high.
$430–480 *JP*

A Staffordshire 2 gallon tavern pitcher, the earthenware body printed and hand-coloured, c1825, 12in (30.5cm) high.
$320–350 *WL*

An Albion white jug, with hinged pewter lid and vine twist handle, moulded with heraldic panels, coats-of-arms and Prince of Wales' feathers, 1863, 7½in (19cm) high.
$100–120 *SAS*

A Minton majolica jug, moulded with reserves of 17thC soldiers drinking, on a deep maroon ground, the neck blue and border and handle ochre, slight damage, 1870, 14¼in (36cm) high.
$2,400–2,800 *Bri*

A Staffordshire earthenware moulded jug, with Celtic style design, c1875, 13½in (34.5cm) high.
$135–150 *TVM*

A Victorian pottery wine jug, with plated mounts, handle and hinged lid, the body decorated with flowers, 8½in (22cm) high.
$200–240 *Gam*

r. A Quimper jug, c1875, 5¼in (13.5cm) high.
$160–180 *VH*

l. A Doulton jug, decorated with Lord Nelson and his captains, c1905, 8½in (21.5cm) high.
$800–875 *TVM*

A majolica jug, modelled as an owl, c1880, 9in (23cm) high.
$320–350 *SSW*

A Wemyss jug, decorated with green grass and a black cockerel, inscribed 'Bon Jour', c1900, 2¾in (7cm) high.
$240–320 *RdeR*

A Doulton Lambeth brown stoneware jug, commemorating the Relief of Ladysmith, the body decorated with the standing figure of a sailor with rifle above an inscribed scroll and portraits of Captain H. Lambton and Captain P. M. Scott, impressed marks, 1900, 8in (20.5cm) high.
$320–350 *Oli*

A Royal Doulton jug, commemorating the Coronation of 1953, decorated with a picture of Windsor, 6¼in (16cm) high.
$85–100 *SAS*

Models – Animals

A Whieldon-type model of a
pigeon, enriched with a mottled
brown tortoiseshell glaze, slight
damage, c1765, 6¼in (16cm) high.
$2,200–2,700 *C*

A Staffordshire model of a lion
with a lamb, decorated in
underglaze Pratt-type colours,
c1800, 7in (18cm) wide.
$5,000–6,000 *JHo*

A Staffordshire pearlware model
of a lion, its front paw resting on
a ball, decorated in brown, on a
base with stiff leaf moulded
band, marbled in blue, brown,
yellow and orange, damaged,
c1810, 12½in (32cm) wide.
$950–1,100 *DN*

Whieldon-type Wares

Auctioneers use the generic term
'Whieldon-type wares' to describe
lead-glazed pottery with a cream
coloured body and underglaze
colouring of green, grey, brown
and slate blue. Although it is
named after the Staffordshire
manufacturer Thomas Whieldon,
he was, in fact, just one of several
makers of this type of pottery,
which was also produced in
Yorkshire, Devon, Scotland
and even as far afield as Belfast.

A Staffordshire pottery model
of an eagle, decorated in yellow
on a black and green base with
a pink and white flower, c1810,
7¾in (19.5cm) high.
$1,100–1,300 *DAN*

A Yorkshire group of a cow, calf and
a lady, c1820, 5½in (14cm) high.
$1,700–2,000 *JHo*

l. A Staffordshire group of a ewe
and a lamb, with bocage support
and rustic base, painted in
colours, c1810, 5½in (14cm) high.
$270–320 *RBB*

A Dutch Delft model of a
recumbent cow, decorated in
blue, with floral garlands, the
horns painted in yellow, slight
restoration, marked, 18thC,
11½in (29cm) wide.
$750–800 *S(Am)*

l. A Staffordshire pearlware model
of a recumbent hound, picked out
in brown, the green ground base
modelled with an ochre
flowerhead, damaged and
repaired, c1810, 3½in (9cm) high.
$720–800 *DN*

A Staffordshire pottery game spill
vase, c1815, 8¾in (22cm) high.
$350–450 *DAN*

A Staffordshire model of a
deer, with bocage behind,
c1820, 7in (18cm) high.
$640–700 *JHo*

A pearlware model of a swan, c1825, 6½in (16.5cm) high.
$1,400–1,800 *DAN*

A Staffordshire porcellaneous model of a black and white cow, restored, c1830, 2¼in (5.5cm) high.
$400–500 *DAN*

A Staffordshire hound's head stirrup cup, picked out in black and brown, on a bright cream ground, c1830, 6⅝in (17cm) wide.
$1,200–1,400 *DN*

A Brampton salt-glazed model of a spaniel, decorated in brown, c1830, 3in (7.5cm) high.
$550–650 *SPU*

A pair of Derbyshire Brampton salt-glazed models of spaniels, with incised brown decoration, c1830, 14in (35.5cm) high.
$4,800–6,200 *SPU*

A Staffordshire porcellaneous model of a poodle, seated upright on a scroll base, c1835, 5in (12.5cm) high.
$320–400 *DAN*

A pair of Staffordshire porcellaneous models of deer, c1830, 4½in (11.5cm) high.
$320–360 *SER*

l. A Staffordshire dog spill vase, c1835, 4in (10cm) wide.
$440–560 *DAN*

A pair of Staffordshire porcellaneous models of spaniels, with both front legs separated, c1840, 4¾in (12cm) high.
$640–720 *RWB*

A pair of Staffordshire porcellaneous models
of a cow and a bull, decorated with red,
restored, c1840, 2¾in (7cm) high.
$720–880 *DAN*

A pair of Staffordshire porcellaneous models of
seated spaniels, each picked out in brown and
wearing a gilt collar, one impressed 'CS', c1840,
7in (18cm) high.
$1,300–1,400 *DN*

A Staffordshire pottery spill vase,
in the form of a standing and a
recumbent greyhound, before a
fence and a tree trunk, decorated
in coloured enamels, restored,
c1850, 11in (28cm) high.
$450–520 *DN*

A Staffordshire model of
a greyhound with a rabbit,
c1850, 11in (28cm) high.
$240–270 *SER*

A pair of Staffordshire models of
cockerels, c1850, 4½in (11.5cm) high.
$160–200 *SER*

*The models illustrated above
and below were recovered from
a ship which was wrecked in
the mid-19thC.*

A pair of Staffordshire models of recumbent
lambs, c1850, 3½in (9cm) high.
$160–200 *SER*

A pair of flint-enamelled pottery lions, with mottled
green, rust and cream glaze, each standing on a
plinth, damaged and repaired, Bennington,
Vermont, c1849, 11in (28cm) wide.
$7,200–8,000 *S(NY)*

*American pottery is quite rare and is
enthusiastically collected in the United States.
The damage mentioned above is not serious enough
to make any great difference to the price.*

A Staffordshire model of a cat, sponge decorated in brown and black, mid-19thC, 5½in (14cm) high.
$320–370 *SER*

A pair of Staffordshire porcellaneous models of seated poodles, each wearing a gilt collar, with granitic decoration, one restored, c1850, 5½in (14cm) high.
$270–300 *DN*

A Staffordshire model of a leopard and a cub, on a shaped plinth base, c1840, 5in (12.5cm) wide.
$750–800 *RBB*

Don't Forget!
If in doubt please refer to the 'How to Use' section at the beginning of this book.

A Staffordshire lustre hen on a nest, c1860, 5½in (14cm) high.
$130–150 *SER*

A pair of Staffordshire models of black spaniels, with traces of gold paint and glass eyes, c1880, 13¼in (33.5cm) high.
$350–400 *EL*

A Staffordshire watch holder, modelled as 2 whippets chasing a hare, c1855, 8¾in (22cm) high.
$550–600 *RWB*

A pair of Staffordshire lop-eared rabbits, each eating a leaf, one damaged, c1860, 3¾in (9.5cm) high.
$1,100–1,300 *TMA*

A pair of Scottish pottery models of seated spaniels, each sponged in black and wearing an ochre collar, 19thC, 9¼in (23.5cm) high.
$480–540 *DN*

Mugs & Tankards

A London salt-glazed stoneware commemorative mug, applied with a portrait of Queen Anne, figures hunting and flowerhead roundels, inscribed, handle missing, rim chips, dated '1722', 8¼in (21cm) high.
$950–1,000 *DN*

A Mason's Ironstone mug, decorated with Japan pattern, with printed crown mark, c1825, 3in (7.5cm) high.
$320–400 *JP*

> **Cross Reference**
> Colour Review

A Staffordshire mug, commemorating the Coronation of Queen Victoria, the scroll handle with pinched decoration and printed in black with 2 portraits centred by a crown, the inner rim with trellis and floral panel border, inscribed, 1838, 3¼in (8.5cm) high.
$1,200–1,400 *SAS*

A Mocha ware mug, the green ground decorated with a blue stripe and applied excise stamp 'Quart', c1820, 6in (15cm) high.
$190–230 *RYA*

A pottery mug, commemorating the Champions of Reform, with portraits of Baron Brougham and Earl Grey, inscribed, c1830, 4in (10cm) high.
$950–1,000 *TVM*

The design on this mug was commemorating the 1831 Great Reform Bill of which Brougham and Grey were two supporters in the House of Lords.

A pearlware mug, the brown ground decorated in green and ochre with bands, inscribed 'A Trifle for Ann', c1820, 2¾in (7cm) high.
$350–400 *HOLL*

A pottery mug, commemorating the Coronation of King William IV & Queen Adelaide, printed in purple with half-length portraits centred by a crown and flanked by flowers of the union, restored, inscribed, dated '1831', 4in (10cm) high.
$350–400 *SAS*

l. A William of Orange commemorative mug, printed with red Orange Order decoration, mid-19thC, 4in (10cm) high.
$200–220 *TVM*

A pottery mug, commemorating the marriage of the Prince and Princess of Wales, with twin portraits surmounted by the Prince of Wales' feathers, inscribed, dated '1863', 4in 10cm) high.
$220–250 *SAS*

l. A Mocha ware pint mug, possibly Edge, Malkin & Co, c1880, 5¼in (13.5cm) high.
$110–150 *IW*

A Maling Mocha ware
pint mug, late 19thC,
5in (12.5cm) high.
$110–130 *IW*

Plaques

A Doulton Burslem pottery mug,
commemorating Queen Victoria's
Jubilee, printed in brown with
young and old portrait
medallions, inscribed ribbon and
crown, 1887, 3¾in (9.5cm) high.
$150–170 *SAS*

A pottery mug, commemorating the
visit to Bournemouth by the Prince
and Princess of Wales, printed in
brown with oval portraits, centred
by a view entitled 'Royal Victoria
Hospital, Bournemouth', gilt rim,
dated '1890', 2¾in (7cm) high.
$130–150 *SAS*

A Castelli plaque, painted in
the Grue workshop, with a dog
flanked by a boy and a seated
lady in an extensive landscape,
within a manganese and
ochre-lined rim, broken in
half and restored, early 18thC,
8 x 11in (20 x 28cm).
$1,400–1,700 *C*

A North Country Pratt-type plaque,
relief moulded with Prometheus
and the Eagle, cracked, c1810,
10in (25.5cm) diam.
$240–270 *RWB*

A majolica plaque, moulded in
relief with putti playing musical
instruments beneath a tree, on a
blue ground, in wooden frame,
late 19thC, 18¾in (47.5cm) wide.
$620–680 *HOLL*

r. A Pratt ware pottery
plaque, depicting 2 sleeping
lions in relief, painted in
brown, green and yellow
underglaze colours, c1790,
11in (28cm) wide.
$720–800 *AH*

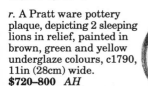

l. An Urbino istoriato
plaque, painted in the
workshop of Francesco
Durantino, with
The Holy Family in
the stable, slight
damage, dated '1544',
5¾in (14.5cm) square.
$5,000–5,500 *C*

A pair of Dutch Delft wall plaques, with polychrome
decoration, the central panel depicting harbour
scenes, contained within a marbled blue and white
fluted border, one riveted, 19thC, 14⅛in (36cm) high.
$570–640 *EH*

Pot Lids

'Trafalgar Square', framed,
c1845, 4in (10cm) diam.
$240–270 *TVM*

'The Outs', No. 16, slight damage,
c1850, 3in (7.5cm) diam.
$225–250 *SAS*

'The Eastern Repast', No. 98,
c1850, 3in (7.5cm) diam.
$160–200 *BHa*

'A Letter from the Diggings',
No. 360, c1855, 4in (10cm) diam.
$140–160 *BHa*

'The Listener', No. 363, with
gold-lined border, small chip,
c1855, 4in (10cm) diam.
$110–130 *SAS*

'Pegwell Bay Shrimpers',
No. 31, no ships, chipped rim,
c1855, 4¾in (12cm) diam.
$120–140 *SAS*

'Belle Vue Tavern, Pegwell Bay',
No. 29, domed lid, white cliffs,
with base, c1855, 4in (10cm) diam.
$800–900 *SAS*

'Lobster Fishing at Pegwell Bay',
No. 24, restored, c1855, 4in
(10cm) diam.
$125–150 *SAS*

'The Maid Servant', No. 343,
c1860, 3¾in (9.5cm) diam.
$300–380 *BHa*

Sauce Boats

A Staffordshire salt-glazed
stoneware sauce boat, cast with
lions and birds, above a fluted
band, and splashed in blue,
on 3 lion mask and paw feet,
restored, c1750, 6¼in (16cm) long.
$400–500 *DN*

A Staffordshire salt-glazed
stoneware sauce boat, with
C-scroll handle, brightly
painted in coloured enamels
with sprays of flowers and
leaves, the handle, gadrooned
rim and foot picked out in
green, c1760, 7⅝in (19.5cm) long.
$800–1,000 *DN*

A creamware sauce boat, with
figure handle, the sides moulded
with the fable of the fox and the
stork, c1790, 8in (20cm) wide.
$1,400–1,600 *JHo*

Services

A Wedgwood composite Queensware part dinner service, comprising 68 pieces, the borders painted in green with oak leaves and acorns, minor damage, impressed marks and painted pattern No. 819, late 18th/early 19thC.
$4,800–5,600 C

A Wedgwood composite Queensware part dinner service, comprising 53 pieces, the borders painted with a band of blue daisies, extensive damage, impressed marks and painted pattern No. 937, late 18th/early 19thC.
$2,400–2,800 C

A Wedgwood pearlware part dessert service, comprising 26 pieces, each piece decorated with a band of passion flowers and leaves, on a buff border, some damage, impressed marks and pattern No. 1145, early 19thC.
$1,500–1,700 DN

A Herculaneum pottery part dinner service, comprising 27 pieces, each printed in sepia and enamelled with flowers and shells, minor damage, impressed Liverbird mark, pattern No. 1917, c1830.
$1,700–2,000 S(S)

A stone china dinner service, comprising 105 pieces, each piece printed in Chinese style in blue with sprays of flowers and emblems, picked out in iron-red and gilt, probably Charles Meigh, slight damage, printed Chinese style mark, pattern No. 147, c1835.
$1,500–1,700 DN

A Staffordshire John Ridgway dinner service, comprising 61 pieces, painted in gilt and blue with stripes to a central disc and the border, marked 'Victoria stoneware J.R.' in underglaze blue, c1840.
$2,200–2,600 S(Am)

A Mason's Ironstone dessert service, comprising 66 pieces, decorated with Chinese Mountain pattern, c1835.
$5,600–6,400 JP

A Minton stone china part dinner service, comprising 24 pieces, decorated in underglaze blue enamels and gilt with the Hindostan Japan pattern, a central spray of flowers inside a complex border, minor damage, impressed and blue printed marks, pattern No. 5150, mid-19thC.
$850–950 S(S)

A Bishop and Stonier Bisto ware pottery part dinner service, comprising 61 pieces, printed and painted in underglaze blue, iron-red and gilt with flowers and scrolls inside a gadroon-moulded border, minor repair and damage, printed marks, c1900.
$1,600–1,800 S(S)

Spirit Flasks & Barrels

A salt-glazed stoneware spirit flask entitled 'Lord Nelson', c1820, 8½in (21.6cm) high.
$350–380 *TVM*

Salt-glazed Stoneware

John Dwight, founder of the Fulham Pottery, patented the technique of producing salt-glazed stoneware in 1693, and the process was soon being copied by other factories. Originally developed in Germany, salt-glazing involves throwing common salt into the kiln when the furnace reaches its maximum temperature of $2,500°F$ ($1,300–1,400°C$). The salt then separates into chlorine, which was passed out through the kiln chimney, and sodium, which combined with the silicates in the clay to form a thick glass-like glaze. Salt-glaze is a thick ceramic glaze, and the surface has a granular, 'orange-peel' appearance.

A Bourne's Pottery salt-glazed stoneware spirit flask, incised 'Success to Reform', c1830, 8in (20.3cm) high.
$480–520 *TVM*

A salt-glazed stoneware spirit flask, in the shape of a fish, c1830, 7in (18cm) long.
$250–280 *TVM*

A salt-glazed stoneware spirit flask, in the shape of a pistol, by Smith, Lambeth, mid-19thC, 8in (20.5cm) long.
$550–580 *TVM*

A Bristol pottery barrel, painted with flowers and initialled 'JC', c1830, 4¾in (12cm) high.
$400–550 *DAN*

Tea & Coffee Pots

A Staffordshire salt-glazed stoneware teapot and cover, in the form of a recumbent camel, moulded with birds and leaf scrolls, the neck with profiles within rectangular panels, some damage, c1750, 4¼in (11cm) high.
$1,800–2,000 *DN*

A Staffordshire Jackfield glazed coffee pot, with traces of original oil gilding, c1750, 10in (25.5cm) high.
$620–680 *JRe*

A glazed redware teapot, with engine-turned decoration, c1760, 5½in (14cm) high.
$520–560 *JRe*

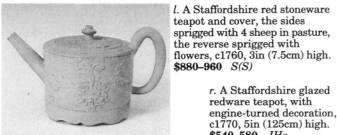

l. A Staffordshire red stoneware teapot and cover, the sides sprigged with 4 sheep in pasture, the reverse sprigged with flowers, c1760, 3in (7.5cm) high.
$880–960 *S(S)*

r. A Staffordshire glazed redware teapot, with engine-turned decoration, c1770, 5in (125cm) high.
$540–580 *JHo*

A creamware teapot and cover, with ear-shaped handle and flower knop, decorated in coloured enamels with flowers and leaves, the cover with a landscape, some damage, c1780, 5¼in (13.5cm) high.
$600–640 *DN*

A basalt unglazed teapot, with fine engine-turned fluting and spaniel finial, c1800, 3in (7.5cm) high.
$280–350 *JRe*

A majolica teapot, with bamboo-shaped pot, spout and handle, c1880, 7½in (19cm) high.
$280–320 *SSW*

A majolica teapot, Japanese shape, c1875, 7½in (19cm) high.
$280–320 *SSW*

An Ashworths chocolate/coffee pot, with printed mark and pattern No. 2865, c1880, 9¾in (25cm) high.
$520–560 *VH*

A General Household Utilities pottery teapot and cover, modelled in the form of a crown, printed in sepia with portraits and inscriptions commemorating the Coronation of King George VI and Queen Elizabeth, gilt lining, c1937, 5in (12.5cm) high.
$200–220 *SAS*

Tiles

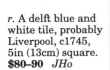

l. A delft tile, painted with a Dutch landscape and unusual spider-head corners, probably London, late 17thC, 4¾in (12cm) square.
$80–100 *IW*

r. A delft blue and white tile, probably Liverpool, c1745, 5in (13cm) square.
$80–90 *JHo*

l. A Liverpool polychrome tile, painted in yellow, blue, red, green and brown, c1760, 5¼in (13.5cm) square.
$2,400–2,600 *JHo*

This tile is decorated with a very rare subject and is exceptional in these colours.

A Dutch Delt tile, decorated with a fisherman and boats, c1750, 5¼in (13.5cm) square.
$55–75 *IW*

A Bristol delft tile, painted in blue with a horse amongst buildings and trees, c1760, 5¼in (13.5cm) high.
$140–150 *JHo*

A blue and white delft tile, painted with a flower, c1770, 3in (7.5cm) square.
$60–70 *PHA*

A London delft tile, with powdered manganese ground, blue carnation corners, c1760, 5in (13cm) high.
$120–140 *JHo*

r. Four Minton transfer-printed tiles, designed by William Wise, signed, c1870, 6in (15cm) square.
$320–350 *SSW*

l. A set of hand-painted Doulton faience tiles, signed by Florence Barlow and Isabel Lewis, c1890, 6in (15cm) square.
$220–240 each *HIG*

A set of Copeland tiles, designed by Lucien Besche, depicting the months of the year, c1870, 6in (15cm) square.
$140–180 each *Nor*

A Minton & Hollins transfer-printed tile, Shakespeare series, c1890, 6in (15cm) square.
$30–35 *HIG*

A Minton transfer-printed tile, Idylls of the King series, designed by John Moyr Smith, c1890, 6in (15cm) square.
$40–50 *HIG*

A Maw & Co tile, Children's Pastimes series, c1890, 6in (15cm) square.
$70–80 *HIG*

A Makkum tile picture, consisting of 12 tiles, painted in colours, depicting a large galleon, late 19thC, 20 x 15¼in (51 x 38.5cm).
$1,400–1,500 *S(Am)*

A pottery tile, designed by Bernard Leech, St Ives, white glazed with blue decoration, c1930, 4in (10cm) square.
$220–250 *IW*

Toby Jugs

A pearlware Toby jug, depicting a man seated wearing a blue coat, with a jug of ale on his knee, on a sponged octagonal base, slight chips, possibly Scottish, c1830, 7½in (19cm) high.
$520–560 *CAG*

A pearlware Toby jug, depicting a man seated wearing a blue coat and brown and yellow hat, a speckled jug on his knee, on sponged octagonal base, some damage, possibly Scottish, c1830, 7¾in (20cm) high.
$520–560 *CAG*

A pearlware Toby jug, decorated in blue, yellow, black and ochre, in the form of a seated red-faced man holding a flagon, on black and ochre sponged base, hat restored, 19thC, 10in (25.5cm) high.
$540–600 *DN*

A stoneware Toby jug, the gentleman wearing a hat and taking snuff, with foliate handle and raised base, mid-19thC, 10in (25.5cm) high.
$140–150 *AG*

A Doulton Lambeth stoneware Toby jug, the gentleman wearing a tricorn hat, seated astride a barrel of beer, late 19thC, 10in (25.5cm) high.
$280–320 *HYD*

l. A Staffordshire Toby jug, entitled 'Hearty Good Fellow', modelled as a standing gentleman holding a clay pipe and mug of ale and wearing a tricorn hat, painted in enamelled colours, on a rustic base, inscribed, c1900, 11in (28cm) high.
$240–270 *HYD*

r. A Johnnie Walker Toby jug, modelled as a huntsman wearing a red coat, boots, top hat and holding a monocle, inscribed, limited edition by Ashtead Potters, c1930, 14½in (37cm) high.
$200–240 *HYD*

Tureens

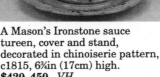
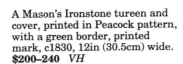

A Mason's Ironstone sauce tureen, cover and stand, decorated in chinoiserie pattern, c1815, 6¾in (17cm) high.
$420–450 *VH*

A Hicks & Meigh stone china tureen and cover, c1815, 12½in (31.5cm) wide.
$1,400–1,500 *JP*

A Mason's Ironstone sauce tureen and cover, decorated in Scroll pattern, c1815, 7½in (19cm) wide.
$320–370 *JP*

A Mason's Ironstone tureen and cover, printed in Peacock pattern, with a green border, printed mark, c1830, 12in (30.5cm) wide.
$200–240 *VH*

Mason's Ironstone

Patented in 1813, Mason's Ironstone was the most successful of the 'stone chinas' – heavy earthenwares made with feldspar.

Mason's wares are nearly always marked. Their products include jugs, massive vases, dinner services and fireplace surrounds. They were often transfer-printed with enamels applied on top. Strong blues, reds and greens are typical, sometimes with gilding. Blue and white wares were also made in quantity.

A Mason's Ironstone sauce tureen, cover and stand, c1815, 8in (20.5cm) wide.
$580–640 *GAZE*

A Mason's Ironstone tureen, cover and stand, printed in blue and overpainted in colours, c1820, 8in (20.5cm) wide.
$640–680 *JP*

A Minton blue and white soup tureen, cover and stand, decorated in Chinese Marine pattern, with moulded handles, on 4 pad feet, marked, c1830, 15in (38cm) diam.
$680–780 *M*

Tygs & Loving Cups

A Bristol salt-glazed stoneware loving cup, c1766, 5¾in (14.5cm) high.
$4,800–5,200 *JHo*

A Wemyss three-handled loving cup, painted with wild roses, c1900, 9¼in (23.5cm) high.
$1,200–1,400 *RdeR*

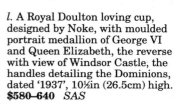

A pottery tyg, printed in turquoise with portraits of the King and Queen, Bishop of Bath and Glastonbury Abbey, inscribed, dated '1909', 4in (10cm) high.
$50–60 *SAS*

A Staffordshire three-handled tyg, inscribed with 'The Farmers Arms' and verse 'God Speed the Plough', c1860, 5in (12.5cm) high.
$120–140 *SER*

A Copeland tyg, retailed by Thomas Goode, decorated in bright colours with portraits of Queen Victoria, Roberts and Salisbury and panel depicting Britannia, gilt decoration, inscribed and dated '1900', 5¾in (14.5cm) high.
$1,400–1,500 *SAS*

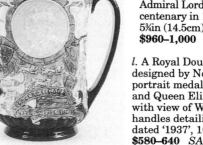

A loving cup, with scroll handles, printed in black with portraits of Queen Victoria and Prince Albert, the reverse with scenes of agriculture, industry and trade above the ribboned inscription 'True blue principles Fear God and Honour the Queen', restored, dated '1844', 4¾in (12cm) high.
$380–440 *SAS*

A Doulton two-handled loving cup, with moulded portrait of Admiral Lord Nelson, for his centenary in 1905, 5¾in (14.5cm) high.
$960–1,000 *TVM*

l. A Royal Doulton loving cup, designed by Noke, with moulded portrait medallion of George VI and Queen Elizabeth, the reverse with view of Windsor Castle, the handles detailing the Dominions, dated '1937', 10½in (26.5cm) high.
$580–640 *SAS*

Vases & Urns

A maiolica two-handled vase and cover, probably Savona, painted with flowers and shrubs and a stylised shell, early 18thC, 21¼in (54cm) high.
$4,500–5,000 *S*

A Frankfurt blue and white vase, painted with 4 panels of Oriental figures in river landscapes, the footrim with a band of stiff leaves, minor damage and restoration, c1720, 16½in (42cm) high.
$6,400–7,000 *C*

A Spode pearlware vase, with scrolled handles, decorated with blue fleur-de-lys and coloured flowers, on a red ground of fish roe pattern, c1800, 5in (12.5cm) high.
$400–440 *GAK*

An Ironstone vase and cover, with sepia printed country scene overpainted in colours, c1815, 9¼in (23.5cm) high.
$1,200–1,400 *JP*

r. A pair of Mason's pot pourris, with mazarine blue ground, painted with gilded flowers, c1820, 8½in (21.5cm) high.
$2,400–2,800 *JP*

A pair of Mason's vases, applied with birds, insects and flowers, on mazarine blue ground, profusely gilded, c1815, 16¼in (41cm) high.
$5,000–6,400 *JP*

A Mason's vase, decorated with a Japan pattern in the Imari palette, with Chinese scroll handles picked out in gilt, minor wear to gilding, c1820, 14¾in (37.5cm) high.
$900–1,000 *Bon*

Cross Reference
Colour Review

A Mason's Ironstone vase, in Japan fence pattern, c1815, 4⅜in (11cm) high.
$560–640 *JP*

An Ironstone vase, gilded with chinoiserie figures, possibly Davenport, c1820, 25¼in (64cm) high.
$2,400–2,500 *JP*

A pair of Mason's Ironstone vases, with reserved panels, c1830, 8in (20.5cm) high.
$1,300–1,400 *JP*

A Staffordshire copper lustre vase, decorated with handpainted cottage scene on a yellow ground, c1825, 5in (12.5cm) high.
$130–140 *BRU*

l. An Ironstone vase, probably Mason's, modelled in relief with flowersprays and butterflies, picked out in gilt, within keyfret and *ruyi* head bands, on a lime green ground, hairline crack to rim, c1830, 21¼in (54cm) high.
$1,000–1,100 *DN*

A Swansea Pottery Dillwyn's Etruscan Ware vase, c1855, 13in (33cm) high.
$1,800–2,000 *RP*

A majolica urn and cover, by Brown-Westhead, Moore & Co, twin handles applied with husking, on a square plinth base, enriched in blue, brown, yellow and green glazes, c1875, 20½in (52cm) high.
$800–900 *WL*

A country slipware vase, with sgraffito decoration, c1890, 12in (30.5cm) high.
$200–250 *IW*

A pair of Quimper bud vases, monogrammed 'HB', c1885, 4½in (11.5cm) high.
$140–180 *VH*

A James Kent chintz ware vase, decorated in Apple Blossom pattern, c1930, 5in (12.5cm) high.
$130–140 *BEV*

l. An Adams blue and white vase, c1915, 12in (30.5cm) high.
$130–160 *SSW*

Wall Brackets & Vases

A pair of Pratt ware wall cornucopiae, each moulded with Cupid and a quiver of arrows, one depicting him drinking from a flask, the other holding a flaming vase, damaged and restored, probably Scottish, c1810, 12in (30.5cm) high.
$800–900 *Bon*

A pair of Royal Worcester majolica wall brackets, each supported by a pair of putti within a frieze of fruiting vines above a single cherub mask, restored, c1870, 9¾in (25cm) high.
$2,700–3,000 *CSK*

r. A pair of mazarine blue wall brackets, modelled as faces of young women wearing acorns and oak leaves in their hair, late 19thC, 12in (30.5cm) high.
$1,300–1,500 *Bon*

A pair of Cantagalli maiolica wall brackets, each supported on a putto astride a mythical sea creature, c1900, 17in (43cm) high.
$1,000–1,300 *TMA*

Blue & White Transfer Ware

A Spode pierced basket stand, decorated with Greek pattern, c1810, 9in (23cm) wide.
$350–380 *Nor*

A cheese cradle, attributed to Bathwell & Goodfellow, decorated in Palladian Porch pattern, c1820, 11in (28cm) wide.
$1,600–2,000 *GN*

A slop bowl, transfer-printed in underglaze blue, inscribed 'Battle of Austerlitz', hairline crack, marked 'C. J. Mason', c1830, 6¾in (17cm) diam.
$160–180 *JP*

A blue and white meat plate, possibly Elkin, Knight & Co, decorated with the Domestic Cattle pattern, within a floral border, also with grease reservoir, early 19thC, 21in (53.5cm) wide.
$520–560 *GAK*

A blue and white transfer-printed bowl, the interior inscribed 'John Abrahams Commercial Inn, Newton', damaged, c1840, 11in (28cm) diam.
$160–180 *PCh*

A J. & W. Ridgway footbath jug, decorated with Indian Temple design, c1825, 12in (30.5cm) high.
$1,600–1,800 *GN*

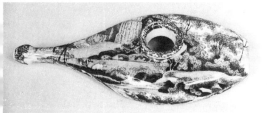

An infant's feeding bottle, by Pountney & Allies, Bristol, decorated in Abbey pattern, c1825, 6in (15cm) wide.
$640–800 *GN*

An eye bath, decorated in Willow pattern, c1810, 2½in (6.5cm) high.
$1,200–1,400 *GN*

A Rogers blue and white plate, decorated with Elephant pattern, c1815, 10in (25.5cm) diam.
$160–200 *Nor*

r. A Mason's platter, transfer printed in underglaze blue, with a view of King's College Chapel, Cambridge, impressed and printed crown mark, c1815, 6½in (16.5cm) wide.
$280–320 *JP*

A Don Pottery transfer-printed
plate, impressed mark, c1830,
8¼in (21cm) diam.
$180–200 *JP*

A Spode pearlware dish, printed
with Lucano pattern, within a vine
and leaf band, in original mahogany
tray, with 2 scroll handles, c1820,
18½in (47cm) wide.
$2,000–2,400 *DN*

A W. Ridgway & Son Co
platter, decorated with Catskill
Moss, Boston & Bunker's Hill
pattern, some damage, dated
'1844', 19in (48cm) wide.
$520–620 *SK(B)*

A Bristol Alkalon China dinner
service, comprising 53 pieces,
printed in flow blue in Chinese
style with Mandarin pattern,
impressed marks, c1900.
$2,000–2,000 *HOLL*

A pair of Spode two-handled footbaths, printed
in blue Lucano pattern, within floral borders,
one damaged, mid-19thC, 20½in (52cm) wide.
$3,200–4,000 *S(S)*

r. A blue and white platter,
decorated with Ponterotto
pattern, c1820,
16½in (42cm) wide.
$320–400 *GN*

l. A Spode spitoon,
with fixed top,
decorated in Tower
pattern, c1820,
4in (10cm) high.
$480–640 *GN*

r. A Davenport sauce
boat on stand, c1830,
7½in (19cm) wide.
$170—200 *Nor*

l. A chamber pot,
commemorating the
marriage of Victoria
and Albert, c1840,
6½in (16.5cm) diam.
$2,400–2,600 *TVM*

A Dutch Delft *doré* basket, with double scroll handles, the base decorated with a courting couple, 18thC, 9½in (24cm) wide.
$9,600–11,200 *S(Am)*

A pottery basket and stand, decorated with Piping Shepherd pattern, c1820, 10in (25.5cm) wide.
$560–720 *GN*

A Davenport footed bowl, decorated with Heron pattern and gilding, c1810, 10½in (27cm) diam.
$720–800 *JP*

A Dutch Delft dish, painted with a building and a tree, mid-18thC, 11¼in (28.5cm) wide.
$2,400–2,800 *S(Am)*

A George Jones majolica punchbowl, the holly-moulded bowl supported by a figure of Mr Punch, cracked, marked, c1872, 13¾in (35cm) diam.
$7,500–8,500 *DN*

A spongeware bowl, with polychrome decoration, c1870, 13in (33cm) diam.
$280–320 *RYA*

l. A Mason's Ironstone pot pourri bowl, with 2 covers, painted with enamel and gilt sprays on a lilac ground, one cover restored, marked, c1820, 14¾in (37.5cm) diam.
$800–960 *Bon*

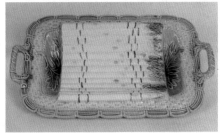

A French majolica asparagus cradle, late 19thC, 16in (40.5cm) wide.
$200–240 *SSW*

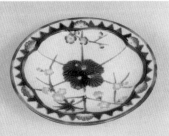

A Wedgwood majolica comport from a dessert service, c1880, 9in (23cm) diam.
$160–200 *SSW*

A Mason's Ashworth punchbowl, decorated in Flying Bird pattern, marked, c1880, 18½in (47cm) diam.
$2,000–2,300 *JP*

A Wemyss Audley bowl, painted by James Sharp, c1900, 7in (18cm) diam.
$1,000–1,200 *RdeR*

A Mason's dessert dish, decorated in Scroll pattern with relief gilding, marked, c1814, 11in (28cm) wide.
$520–560 *JP*

A Wemyss quaiche, decorated with strawberries, c1900, 7½in (19cm) diam.
$400–480 *RdeR*

A Carlton Ware Hydrangea pattern hors d'oeuvres dish, c1930, 13in (33cm) diam.
$160–200 *CSA*

A pottery model of a cow, decorated in underglaze colours, possibly Bovey Tracey, Devon, horns restored, c1770, 8in (20.5cm) wide.
$3,800–4,200 *JHo*

A Pratt ware model of a lion, painted in ochre, with acanthus leaves around base, c1800, 7½in (19cm) wide.
$4,800–5,200 *JHo*

A Pratt ware model of a ram, restored, c1800, 6½in (16.5cm) wide.
$1,600–1,900 *DAN*

A pair of Staffordshire models of zebras, with separate and raised legs, flowing manes and wearing bridles, on gilt-lined bases, c1850, 8in (20.5cm) wide.
$1,200–1,400 *TVM*

Two Staffordshire models, depicting a lion and a unicorn, marks for John Walton, some restoration, c1820, 6½in (16.5cm) wide.
$6,400–7,000 *JHo*

A Staffordshire model of a seated cat, wearing a collar, c1860, 3½in (9cm) wide.
$320–400 *DAN*

A pearlware cow creamer, with a milkmaid, the cow sponged in blue/grey on a cream ground, c1800, 5½in (14cm) wide.
$750–800 *HYD*

A creamware cow creamer and cover, with a milkmaid, the cow sponged in ochre and brown, c1800, 6in (15cm) wide.
$520–600 *HYD*

A Staffordshire pearlware model of a lion, decorated in red/brown enamel, c1810, 5½in (14cm) wide.
$1,400–1,500 *JRe*

A Wemyss blue-glazed cat, impressed marks, c1900, 13in (33cm) high.
$21,000–22,500 *S*

A cow creamer and cover, painted red and black on a cream ground, early 19thC, 5½in (14cm) wide.
$480–520 *HYD*

A pair of Staffordshire figures of a shepherd and shepherdess, each standing with a dog, she wearing a striped dress, he wearing yellow breeches and a brown jacket, with bocage, on green and brown mound bases, c1820, 5¼in (13cm) high.
$850–900 *TVM*

A Staffordshire figure of a Scottish gamekeeper, wearing a kilt, standing with his dog, c1820, 8in (20.5cm) high.
$5,000–6,000 *JHo*

A Staffordshire figure of Minerva, on an inscribed square base, c1790, 12in (30.5cm) high.
$880–960 *TVM*

A Staffordshire figure of Lord Byron, base inscribed, c1845, 7½in (19cm) high, H7, 17.
$480–560 *RWB*

A Staffordshire figure of a female gardener, seated on a branch holding a watering can, c1850, 7½in (19cm) high.
$200–240 *SER*

A Staffordshire figure depicting William Tell, restored, c1850, 10½in (26.5cm) high.
$265–300 *SER*

A Staffordshire figure of Andromache, standing beside an urn, bocage missing, c1820, 9½in (24cm) high.
$400–480 *DAN*

A Staffordshire group of 2 seated figures below an arbour, possibly Jessica and Lorenzo, mid-19thC, 9in (23cm) high.
$550–600 *TVM*

A Staffordshire figure of a shepherd, wearing a blue coat, with a sheep at his feet, c1860, 13½in (34cm) high.
$350–450 *DAN*

A Staffordshire group of Princess Alice and Prince Louis of Hess, c1862, 14in (35.5cm) high, A70, 218.
$720–800 *RWB*

A Dutch Delft jug, mark for
Adriaan Koecks, c1700, later gilt-
metal mount, 10in (25.5cm) high.
$12,800–13,600 *C*

A Sunderland pink lustre jug,
decorated with a ship and a
verse, c1810, 8¼in (21cm) high.
$480–540 *IW*

A Swansea Bonaparte jug,
the figures with speech bubbles
c1815, 6¾in (17cm) high.
$2,000–2,250 *TVM*

A Pratt ware jug, decorated
with Admiral Lord Nelson,
c1790, 6in (15cm) high.
$800–900 *TVM*

A Mason's Ironstone jug,
decorated in Japan pattern,
c1820, 9¼in (23.5cm) high.
$720–800 *JP*

A Staffordshire copper lustre
jug, with a blue band
decorated with raised cherub
c1830, 7in (18cm) high.
$125–135 *SER*

A Scottish commemorative
jug, by Bell & Co, 1863,
8¾in (22cm) high.
$200–220 *SAS*

A Staffordshire jug,
decorated in red and green
enamel on a yellow ground,
c1820, 4½in (11.5cm) high.
$320–400 *HOW*

A pottery commemorative jug, depicting
Queen Victoria and Prince Albert, damage
and restored, 1840, 5⅝in (14.5cm) high.
$200–250 *SAS*

A Wedgwood jasper
vase, with snake
handles, minor
restoration, c1790,
15¾in (40cm) high.
$6,400–7,200 *C*

A Mason's Ironstone
vase, enamelled and
gilt with insects,
lid missing, c1820,
7¾in (20cm) high.
$560–640 *JP*

A pair of Mason's
Ironstone vases and
covers, marked,
restored, c1830,
8¾in (22cm) high.
$580–640 *JP*

A Mason's Ironstone vase,
probably painted by Samuel
Bourne, slight damage, marked,
c1820, 27¼in (69cm) high.
$9,600–1,200 *C*

A Staffordshire Pratt ware
type Toby jug, modelled as a
orpulent gentleman holding
jug of foaming ale,
1820, 10½in (26.5cm) high.
880–960 *HYD*

A Staffordshire Toby jug, decorated
with underglaze Pratt type colours,
c1820, 10in (25.5cm) high.
$640–720 *RWB*

A copper lustre pottery mug,
with raised flower decoration,
c1835, 3in (7.5cm) high.
$65–80 *GLN*

A north country pottery
jug, modelled with a
satyr's face mask, c1830,
4½in (11.5cm) high.
$130–150 *RWB*

A Thomas Rathbone two-handled
frog mug, decorated with Milkmaid
pattern, c1820, 5in (12.5cm) high.
$640–720 *GN*

Staffordshire Toby jug,
odelled as a gentleman holding
flagon of ale, with figural
odelled handle, mid-19thC,
0in (25.5cm) high.
150–200 *HYD*

A Staffordshire two-handled mug,
painted in Imari colours, c1835,
4½in (11.5cm) high.
$200–240 *BSA*

A Staffordshire pearlware mug,
printed with a chinoiserie
scene, c1825, 4¾in (12cm) high.
$400–450 *DAN*

Mason's Ironstone mug,
ainted with Japan pattern,
825, 5¼in (13cm) high.
520–640 *JP*

A Wemyss three-handled mug,
painted with mallard ducks,
c1900, 9½in (24cm) high.
$2,800–3,200 *RdeR*

A Wemyss mug, decorated
with lilac blossoms, c1900,
5¾in (14.5cm) high.
$680–800 *RdeR*

A Belleek earthenware plate, First Period, 1865–90, 10¾in (27cm) diam. **$240–320** *MLa*

A Staffordshire salt-glazed plate, with moulded edge, the centre decorated with a flower spray, c1750, 10in (25.5cm) diam. **$240–280** *BRU*

A Dutch Delft dish, painted in blue, green and yellow, with the initials 'WR', broken and repaired, c1690, 11½in (29cm) diam. **$1,000–1,200** *SAS*

A Davenport stone china oval platter, with shaped rim, decorated with sprays of flowers, pattern No. 145, c1825, 11in (28cm) wide. **$160–200** *BSA*

A Mason's Ironstone plate, transfer-printed with blue and white Bird and Peony pattern, initialled 'G.P.', impressed circle mark, c1820, 9½in (24cm) diam. **$140–160** *JP*

A Mason's Ironstone soup plate, decorated in Mogul pattern, impressed mark, c1815, 9½in (24cm) diam. **$180–200** *JP*

A pearlware plate, the centre depicting Queen Caroline, enamel colouring faded, c1820, 6½in (16.5cm) diam. **$160–190** *SAS*

A pottery platter, by Charles Meigh, painted with central spray of flowers, edged with single flowers within quatrefoil vignettes, c1840, 11in (28cm) wide. **$160–175** *BRU*

A Staffordshire Indian Ironstone plate, by Samuel Alcock, decorated with central spray of flowers, edged with vignettes, c1840, 10in (25.5cm) diam. **$65–80** *BRU*

A Staffordshire Pratt ware plate, inscribed 'The Queen – God Bless Her', c1860, 7in (18cm) diam. **$50–65** *SER*

A pair of Quimper faience plates, one hand-decorated with a bagpiper, the other with his companion, signed Henriot Quimper, early 20thC, 10in (25.5cm) diam. **$240–265** *BRU*

A Wemyss plate, decorated with oranges and with a green rim, c1930, 8½in (21.5cm) diam. **$240–320** *RdeR*

A London delft tile,
c1740, 6in (15cm) square.
$640–720 *JHo*
*London delft tiles of this
size are very rare.*

A Liverpool delft tile,
c1760, 5¼in (13.5cm) square.
$2,400–2,700 *JHo*
*The design and colours of this
tile are very unusual.*

A Liverpool delft tile,
polychrome decorated with
a pot of flowers, c1760,
5¼in (13.5cm) square.
$520–580 *JHo*

A pair of Dutch Delft tile pictures, manganese
painted with Biblical scenes, some damage,
late 18thC, 19½ x 14½in (50 x 37cm), framed.
$2,000–2,400 *Bri*

A Minton transfer printed tile,
hand-coloured design by
L. T. Swetnam, c1886,
6in (15cm) square.
$70–80 *HIG*

A hand-painted tile,
by W. B. Simpson, c1890,
8in (20.5cm) square.
$70–80 *HIG*

A Carter & Co Dutch series
tile, hand-painted design
by J. Roulelants, c1930,
5in (12.5cm) square.
$45–55 *HIG*

A Wemyss comb tray,
decorated with violets,
c1900, 10in (25.5cm) wide.
$560–640 *RdeR*

A Wemyss plaque,
decorated with plums,
c1920, 5¾in (14.5cm) wide.
$240–320 *RdeR*

A Rouen faience tray, with
rope-twist handles, decorated
with chinoiserie figures in
a landscape, slight damage,
c1730, 19in (48.5cm) wide.
$5,000–5,600 *S*

A Cantagalli Della Robbia wall plaque,
decorated with the Virgin Mary and
Child between winged putti, within a
garland of lemons and vines, marked,
late 19thC, 31in (79cm) diam.
$3,200–3,500 *CSK*

A Bow figure, representing Earth, holding a bunch of flowers and resting on a lion, restored, c1758, 7½in (19cm) high.
$1,600–1,900 *DAN*

A Royal Dux porcelain figure of a lady, holding a bowl and lying at the edge of a shell-shaped dish, c1895, 11in (28cm) wide.
$2,000–2,250 *SHa*

A Naples group of children, the boy asleep on a rocky outcrop, slight damage, c1790, 5¾in (14.5cm) high.
$9,000–11,200 *S*

A French porcelain scent bottle, in the form of a figure, by Jacob Petit, c1840, 11½in (29cm) high.
$620–720 *DAN*

A Doccia figure of Plenty, slight damage and restoration, c1760, 5¾in (14.5cm) high.
$7,000–8,000 *C*

A Chelsea model of a duck, minor restoration, marked, c1751, 4½in (11.5cm) high.
$40,000–44,000 *C*

A Meissen chinoiserie figure group, by J. J. Kändler, P. Reinicke and F. E. Meyer, slight damage, marked, c1755, 6¼in (16cm) high.
$4,400–5,000 *Bon*

r. A Derby porcelain model of a pug dog, late 18thC, 2½in (6.5cm) high.
$440–560 *DAN*

A Meissen model of a turkey, slight damage, marked, c1880, 4¼in (11cm) high.
$850–900 *MER*

A Meissen group of figures harvesting apples, minor restoration, marked, c1870, 11½in (29cm) high.
$3,200–4,000 *MER*

A Volkstedt group of a fisherman holding a fish, and his companion, with trees and rockwork, some damage, c1775, 8¼in (21cm) high.
$12,500–13,500 *C*

A Derby group of a sheep with a lamb lying at its feet, on a green base decorated with flowers, c1785, 5in (12.5cm) high.
$560–720 *DAN*

A Chelsea four-sided bowl, painted with a battle scene, damaged, raised red anchor mark, c1750, 7½in (19cm) wide. **$17,600–19,200** *S*

A Derby punchbowl, painted with bands of flowers, gilt borders, minor crack, marked in red, c1820, 13in (33cm) diam. **$12,000–13,000** *S*

A French porcelain and gilt-bronze centrepiece, painted with country scene on a *bleu celeste* ground, c1870, 15in (38cm) high. **$14,500–16,000** *S*

A Naples sugar bowl and cover, minor damage, marked, c1790, 5¾in (14.5cm) diam. **$5,600–6,400** *C*

A German porcelain comport, in Dresden style, the pedestal supported by 4 figures, c1900, 12in (30.5cm) high. **$1,100–1,200** *PSA*

A pair of Coalport porcelain ice pails, with gilt handles, c1830, 15½in (40cm) high. **$7,000–7,800** *AH*

A Wedgwood lustre bowl, decorated with butterflies and central Moorish motifs, c1920, 9in (23cm) diam. **$350–400** *BRU*

A Belleek shell-moulded bowl, with blue-painted decoration of coral, First Period, 1865–90, 7in (18cm) wide. **$600–680** *MLa*

A Chamberlain's Worcester ice pail, with liner, the side handles with grapes and vines, script mark to cover, c1820, 13in (33cm) high. **$3,200–4,000** *MER*

An English porcelain basket and pierced lid, encrusted with flowers, 1835, 7in (18cm) wide. **$720–800** *DAN*

A garniture of 3 Derby bough pots and covers, painted with rural scenes, possibly by John Brewer, damage to one cover, wear to gilding, red painted marks, c1820, 9in (23cm) wide. **$9,000–9,600** *Bon*

A Belleek plate, Third
Period, 1926–46,
6¾in (17cm) diam.
$320–350 *MLa*

A Chelsea-Derby saucer dish,
pink ground with neo-classical
panels and swags, c1770,
7in (18cm) diam.
$720–880 *DAN*

A pair of John Ridgway dessert
plates, pattern No. 8214, c1840,
9½in (24cm) diam.
$225–250 *BSA*

A Worcester saucer dish,
Flight & Barr Period, painted
with blue flowers and gilt leaves,
c1795, 8in (20.5cm) diam.
$120–135 *BSA*

A Worcester dish, enamelled
with floral sprays on a blue
scale ground, underglazed
mark in blue, c1770,
11¼in (28.5cm) wide.
$1,400–1,600 *CAG*

A Worcester plate, Flight, Barr
& Barr period, the claret border
with flowers and insects, c1820,
8in (20.5cm) diam.
$640–800 *DAN*

A Chamberlain's Worcester plate,
painted with Venus and the Graces,
probably painted by Humphrey
Chamberlain, minor rubbing to gilt
rim, c1815, 9½in (24cm) diam.
$4,200–4,800 *DN*

A Royal Worcester plate,
painted with flowers,
signed by E. Phillips, c1908,
8½in (21.5cm) diam.
$240–280 *VSt*

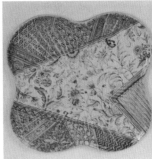

A Wileman & Co porcelain
cabaret tray, printed in
Japanese style, c1888,
9½in (24cm) wide.
$40–50 *WAC*

A Paris plate, depicting Venus
and Diana, with a border of
fruit, printed marks, restored,
c1820, 8¾in (22cm) diam.
$430–480 *S*

A Russian dish, painted with view
of Palermo, Imperial Porcelain
marks, Alexander 1st Pavlovich
period, c1801, 9¾in (25cm) wide.
$5,200–6,000 *S*

A Minton visiting card tray, painted in the
centre with a view of Windsor Castle and
gilded, c1840, 11½in (29cm) wide.
$1,600–1,800 *BSA*

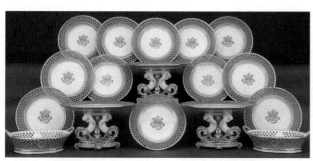

A Minton 30-piece dessert service, monogrammed to the centres, impressed marks, date codes and marks for T. Goode & Co, some damage and restored, late 19thC.
$2,400–2,800 *C*

A Spode cream bowl and stand, the bowl with butterfly handles, c1820, 7½in (19cm) diam.
$520–600 *BSA*

A Dresden 148-piece dinner service, by Adolph Hamman & Co, painted with scattered flowersprays and bouquets within gilt scroll borders, marked, early 20thC.
$6,400–7,000 *C*

A Vienna *tête à tête*, painted after Nicklaus Berchem, some damage and restoration, marked, c1775, tray 12½in (32cm) wide.
$20,000–24,000 *C*

A Sèvres cabaret set, incised marks, c1763, tray 9¼in (23cm) diam.
$7,000–7,800 *S*

A Derby sauce tureen and stand, c1810, stand 9in (23cm) long.
$880–1,000 *DAN*

A Coalport 36-piece part tea and coffee service, painted in coloured enamels with sprays of flowers and leaves, impressed marks, c1820.
$1,200–1,400 *HOLL*

A Meissen teapot, with Imari decoration, incised Johanneum mark, c1730, 3¼in (8.5cm) high.
$20,000–24,000 *S*

A Meissen porcelain part tea set, encrusted with flowers, some chips and restoration, c1880.
$5,600–6,400 *S(Am)*

A Cookworthy, Plymouth or Bristol teapot, c1770-75, 6½in (16.5cm) high.
$1,250–1,500 *S*

An Aynsley cream jug, decorated with floral sprays within gilt bands, c1895, 5½in (14cm) high.
$135–150 *BSA*

An H. & R. Daniel shell-shaped teapot, with scroll handle, on 4 shell feet, spout restored, c1830, 6in (15cm) high.
$430–480 *BSA*

A Worcester jug, decorated with portrait of George III, c1792, 6¾in (17cm) high.
$3,500–4,000 *Bon*

A Coalport fluted cup and shaped saucer, decorated with green leaves on a white ground, gilt rims, green mark, c1900, cup 1¾in (4.5cm) high.
$190–240 *MER*

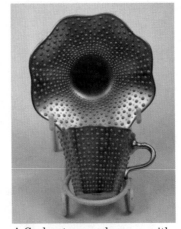

A Coalport cup and saucer, with graduated turquoise jewelling on a gilt ground, green mark, c1900, cup 1¾in (4.5cm) high.
$800–880 *MER*

A Coalport cup and saucer, decorated with birds on a blue and gilt ground, green mark, cup 2in (5cm) high.
$175–200 *MER*

A Copeland-Spode coffee cup and saucer, c1937, cup 2⅛in (5.5cm) high.
$55–65 *BEV*

A Worcester tea bowl, coffee cup and saucer, painted in green, blue, iron-red and gilt with Hop Trellis pattern on a pink ground, c1775.
$1,300–1,450 *DN*

A Berlin coffee can and saucer, blue and gilt decorated with *en grisaille* portrait of Paul Petrowitz, late 18thC.
$3,200–3,500 *E*

A pair of Worcester flared beakers, Flight & Barr period, gilding worn, marked, c1800, 3¾in (9.5cm) high.
$1,800–2,000 *C*

A Royal Doulton coffee cup and saucer, hand-painted with views of Kenilworth Castle, signed 'C. Hart', c1930, saucer 4in (10.5cm) diam.
$240–265 *WAC*

A Royal Worcester cup and saucer, decorated with the inside of a flower, puce mark, c1923, cup 1¾in (4.5cm) high.
$480–560 *MER*

A Meissen Hausmaler tea bowl and saucer, decorated by Abraham Seuter, from the Berne service, restored, c1725.
$7,000–7,800 *S*

A Naples coffee can and saucer, painted with the 3 Muses, handle repaired, slight rubbing to gilding, indistinct incised marks, c1790.
$3,500–3,800 *C*

A Vincennes tea bowl, painted in Meissen style with flowersprays, chip to rim, marked, c1750.
$1,500–1,700 *S*

A Meissen gold-mounted snuff box, the interior of the cover decorated with a scene from the Commedia dell'Arte, c1745, 3in (7.5cm) wide. **$7,500–8,000** *C*

A Belleek jardinière, decorated with shamrocks, with fluted rim, Second Period, 1891–1926, 9½in (24cm) diam. **$2,400–3,200** *MLa*

A Meissen box and cover, painted in the manner of J. G. Höroldt, marked, c1735, 4½in (11.5cm) diam. **$3,500–3,800** *EH*

A Belleek diamond flower pot, Third Period, green mark, 1965–81, 3in (7.5cm) diam. **$240–270** *MLa*

A Doccia gilt-metal mounted snuff box, inscribed with verses from Dante's *Inferno*, some damage, c1760, 3½in (9cm) wide. **$15,000–17,500** *C*

A Sèvres jardinière, painted with rural scenes by André-Vincent Vielliard, minor restoration, marked, c1760, 7½in (19cm) high. **$15,000–16,000** *S*

A Spode basket weave inkstand, decorated with landscapes within cartouches on a pastel blue and pink ground, with double cover, marked in red, c1815, 5in (12.5cm) wide. **$4,800–5,600** *MER*

A pair of Chamberlain's Worcester miniature pots and lids, decorated with fruit, with gilt rims, one chipped, c1830, 2½in (6.5cm) high. **$560–720** *DAN*

A French tray, painted in Sèvres style with portraits of Henri IV and 8 portraits of ladies, 19thC, 19in (48.5cm) diam. **$1,500–1,700** *S*

A pair of French porcelain candlesticks, decorated with flowers in cartouches, with gilt-metal mounts, c1870, 9½in (24cm) high. **$800–960** *GEM*

A Spode scent bottle and stopper, gilt-decorated in relief on a cobalt blue ground, red mark, c1815, 4in (10cm) high. **$1,100–1,200** *MER*

A John Bevington vase, encrusted with flowersprays, damaged and restored, c1875, 11¼in (28.5cm) high. **$450–550** *DN*

A pair of Chelsea vases, with gilt-metal mounts c1760, 11in (28cm) high. **$2,800–3,500** *S*

A Derby vase, with floral panel on a blue ground, c1830, 8¼in (21cm) high. **$880–1,000** *DAN*

A Derby vase, possibly by John Brewer, damaged, c1810, 12½in (32cm) high. **$3,200–4,000** *Bon*

A pair of Sèvres style ormolu-mounted vases and covers, painted in the manner of Watteau, late 19thC, 19¾in (50cm) high. **$11,200–12,800** *C*

A Royal Worcester seven-piece garniture, by Harry Davis, painted with castle views, printed marks in gilding, c1960, vases 14in (35.5cm) high. **$22,500–24,500** *S*

A pair of Samson *famille rose* jars and covers, decorated with exotic birds and flowers, 19thC, 21½in (54.5cm) high. **$7,200–8,000** *AH*

A pair of Sèvres vases and covers, on ormolu bases, c1770, restored, marked, 10¼in (26cm) high. **$14,500–16,000** *S*

A Berlin vase, painted with named views, marked, c1835, 19in (48.5cm) high. **$34,000–38,000** *S*

A pair of French ormolu-mounted vases and covers, early 20thC, 21in (54cm) high. **$8,500–9,600** *C*

A German ormolu-mounted garniture, possibly Dresden, comprising a pair of vases and covers and a bowl, decorated with figures in landscapes, late 19thC, vases 27in (69cm) high. **$21,500–25,500** *C*

A marbled bowl, with a clear yellow glaze, encircled by a narrow filet, on a slightly splayed low cut foot, Tang Dynasty, 4in (10cm) high.
$15,000–16,000 S(HK)

A famille verte stem bowl, the interior painted with parrots on a tree peony above rockwork, Kangxi period, 6¼in (16cm) diam.
$7,000–8,000 C(HK)

A famille verte enamelled bowl and cover, with floral knop finial, minor damage, Kangxi period, 9in (23cm) diam.
$5,600–6,000 C

A famille verte deep bowl and cover, enamelled with flowers, minor enamel flakes, Kangxi period, 9¼in (23.5cm) diam.
$3,200–3,500 C

A wucai bowl, decorated with a dragon and phoenix, the interior with a dragon roundel, chips to rim, mark and period of Yongzheng, 5in (15cm) diam.
$4,800–5,600 S

A doucai bowl, the interior decorated with a flower, rim ground, six-character Yongzheng mark, 4½in (11.5cm) diam.
$3,400–4,000 S(NY)

A Chinese export bowl, painted in the tobacco leaf palette with peonies, chrysanthemums and other flowers in a fenced garden, Qianlong period, 16in (40.5cm) diam.
$3,200–3,500 Bea

An underglaze blue and copper-red bowl, the exterior decorated with the eight Immortals, Qing Dynasty, 5in (12.5cm) high.
$2,800–3,500 S(HK)

A famille rose bowl, painted with a butterfly, bamboo and fruit on flowering vines, seal mark and period of Qianlong, 4½in (11.5cm) diam.
$9,000–10,000 S(HK)

A poem tea bowl, with iron-red decoration, the exterior enamelled with an Imperial poem, Qianlong seal mark and of the period, 4¼in (11cm) diam, boxed.
$5,600–6,400 C(HK)

A sanduo stem bowl, decorated in underglaze copper-red, minor restoration, Xuande six-character mark, 5¾in (14.5cm) diam.
$6,000–6,400 C(HK)

A wucai bowl, painted with a dragon pursuing flaming pearls, the interior with a red dragon roundel, seal mark and period of Daoguang, 6¼in (16cm) diam.
$4,400–5,600 S

A yellow-ground famille rose bowl, the interior painted with 5 iron-red bats, Daoguang seal mark and of the period, 7¼in (18.5cm) diam.
$10,000–11,200 S(NY)

A turquoise-ground bowl, with iron-red seal of the Empress Dowager, mark and period of Guangxu, 5in (12.5cm) diam.
$4,400–5,000 S(HK)

A *sancai* tripod dish, incised with central floret, one leg restored, Tang Dynasty, 10½in (26.5cm) high.
$3,800–4,200 *S*

A pair of yellow-ground saucers, incised with dragons, marks and period of Kangxi, 5¼in (13cm) diam.
$8,800–9,600 *S(HK)*

A *famille verte* dish, decorated with birds, Kangxi period, 13¾in (35cm) diam.
$2,800–3,200 *S(Am)*

A *famille rose* dish, Qianlong period, 14in (36cm) diam.
$1,100–1,200 *S(Am)*

A pair of Chinese Imari La Dame au Parasol plates, 18thC, 9¼in (23.5cm) diam.
$4,000–4,800 *C*

A Judgement of Paris dish, hair crack, Qianlong period, 14in (35.5cm) diam.
$5,600–6,400 *S*

A pair of *famille rose* plates, each enamelled with a gentleman beside an admiring lady companion, with a pair of dogs at their feet, beneath bands of spearheads and baroque shell scrolls, early Qianlong period, 9in (23cm) diam.
$5,600–6,400 *C*

A *famille rose* dish, painted with figures, 18thC, 13¼in (33.5cm) diam.
$4,400–4,800 *S(NY)*

A *famille rose* octagonal plate, decorated with a bird and flowers, c1760, 9in (23cm) diam.
$480–640 *DAN*

A *famille rose* saucer dish, mark and period of Qianlong, 6¼in (16cm) diam.
$3,200–3,500 *Wai*

A pair of dishes, seal marks and period of Daoguang, 5¼in (13.5cm) diam.
$12,000–13,000 *S(HK)*

A blue ground saucer dish, enamelled in yellow, Tongzhi six-character mark and of the period, 10in (25.5cm) diam.
$4,000–4,800 *C*

A pair of saucer dishes, painted over the rim, Hongxian *nian zhi* mark, c1916, 6½in (16.5cm) diam.
$1,600–1,900 *Wai*

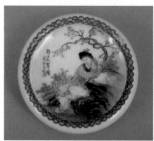

A brush washer, signed by the artist, seal mark, 1930s, 3½in (9cm) diam.
$480–640 *Wai*

A pair of grey-painted pottery figures of horses, the riders seated with hands pierced for reins, their faces with flesh-coloured pigment and detailed moustaches and eyebrows, Han Dynasty, 11¼in (28.5cm) high.
$9,600–10,400 *S(NY)*

A brown-glazed pottery horse, head and legs restored, tail missing, Tang Dynasty, 14in (35.5cm) high.
$4,800–6,400 *C*

A *sancai*-glazed pottery figure of an official, restored, Tang Dynasty, 36in (91cm) high.
$3,500–3,800 *C*

A painted stucco bust of a woman, her patterned robes over a white undergarment, pigment flaking, Tang Dynasty, 15½in (40cm) high.
$16,800–18,400 *CNY*

Two painted stucco heads of female attendants, some pigment loss, late Sung/early Ming Dynasty, 13⅓in (34.5cm) high.
$19,200–20,800 *CNY*

A Chinese export *famille rose* group of 4 boys at play, 18thC, 3in (7.5cm) high.
$960–1,200 *Wai*

A blue and white figure of a crane, standing astride rockwork, beak restored, 19thC, 10in (25.5cm) high.
$8,800–9,600 *C*

A *sancai*-glazed figure of a seated monk, restored, late Tang/Liao Dynasty, 15in (38cm) high.
$3,600–4,400 *C*

A Shiwan ware flambé-glazed figure of Guanyin, seated with her left hand on her knee, Guangdong Province, 18th/19thC, 9½in (24cm) high.
$3,200–3,500 *CNY*

A *sancai* figure of an attendant, Tang Dynasty, 23in (59cm) high.
$4,800–5,600 *S*

A pair of *famille verte* models of kylins, late 19thC, 7½in (19cm) high.
$280–400 *DAN*

A pair of turquoise-glazed models of kylins, c1900, 14in (35.5cm) high.
$480–640 *DAN*

A Chinese water dropper, modelled as a carp, from the *Diana* cargo, c1816, 4in (10cm) high.
$800–880 *DAN*

A green-glazed vase, the foliate mouth resting on a phoenix head, restored, Liao Dynasty, 17in (43cm) high.
$5,000–5,800 *S*

A baluster-shaped vase, decorated with figures in a landscape, Kangxi period, 18in (45.5cm) high.
$4,000–4,400 *S*

A yellow-ground *famille rose* altar vessel, top and base joined, Jiaqing period, 17in (43cm) high.
$11,200–12,500 *S(NY)*

A *famille verte* baluster-shaped vase, painted with dragons, Kangxi period, 15½in (39.5cm) high.
$11,200–12,200 *S(NY)*

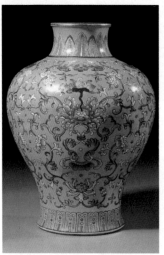

A *famille rose* lime-ground baluster vase, base drilled, some scratching, Qianlong mark and of the period, 8½in (21.5cm) high.
$12,800–14,000 *C*

An underglaze blue vase, painted in copper-red pigment with 9 dragons, 19thC, 21½in (54.5cm) high.
$11,400–12,000 *S(NY)*

A pair of blue and white bottle vases, one with rim crack, Kangxi period, 11½in (29cm) high.
$4,400–5,600 *C*

A *famille rose* celadon-ground oviform vase, 18thC, 11½in (29cm) high.
$5,000–5,800 *C*

An underglaze blue vase, decorated with scaly dragons, Qing Dynasty, 11¼in (28.5cm) high.
$7,500–8,500 *S(HK)*

A baluster-shaped *famille rose* vase, Hongxian mark, c1916, 19in (48.5cm) diam.
$800–960 *Wai*

A vase, painted with a hunting scene, seal mark, c1912, 13in (33cm) high.
$1,600–1,900 *Wai*

A *fencai* enamel-decorated vase, attributed to Wang Yeting, Qianlong mark, c1920, 8½in (21.5cm) high.
$2,200–2,600 *Wai*

A Japanese E-Shino dish, small repair, slight damage, Momoyama period, 6¼in (16cm) wide.
$7,500–8,000 *C*

A Japanese Nabeshima porcelain dish, decorated in underglaze blue with flowers on a celadon ground, the exterior with scrolling peony sprays, early 18thC, 8in (20cm) diam.
$80,000–88,000 *S(NY)*

A Japanese flask, Dutch-decorated with European scenes, slight damage, c1720, 6½in (16.5cm) high.
$3,200–3,500 *S*

A Japanese Arita ewer, in Kutani style, decorated in coloured enamels and gilt, 18thC, 5½in (14.5cm) high.
$3,500–4,000 *C*

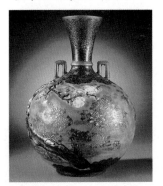

A Japanese Satsuma earthenware vase, by Kinkozan, painted by Matsuyama, Meiji period, 14in (36cm) high.
$3,500–4,000 *S*

A Korean celadon lobed cup and stand, the petals inlaid with chrysanthemum heads, small chips, Koryo Dynasty, 12thC, stand 5¼in (13cm) diam.
$12,500–13,500 *S(NY)*

A Japanese Satsuma carved and inlaid vase, Kinkozan Studio, black seal mark, c1890, 4in (10cm) high.
$4,000–4,500 *MER*

A pair of Japanese Satsuma earthenware covered vases, decorated in imitation brocade cloth with folds moulded in relief, one restored, impressed mark, 19thC, 13½in (34cm) high.
$16,800–18,400 *S*

A Korean iron-brown decorated celadon vase, Koryo Dynasty, 13thC, 10½in (26.5cm) high.
$43,000–48,000 *CNY*

A Korean inlaid celadon bowl, decorated with a central chrysanthemum, Koryo Dynasty, 14thC, 5¼in (13cm) diam.
$2,200–2,700 *CNY*

A Korean white porcelain water dropper, slight chips, Choson Dynasty, 18th/early 19thC, 4½in (11.5cm) long.
$16,800–18,400 *CNY*

A Korean blue and white bowl, inscribed on base in underglaze blue, Choson Dynasty, 19thC, 3½in (9cm) high.
$4,000–4,800 *CNY*

A pair of blue decanters, inscribed in gilt 'R Wine', 'W Wine' and 'RH', c1790, 12in (30.5cm) high.
$3,500–4,000 *BrW*

A pair of amber spirit bottles, the bodies with slice, flute, diamond and printy cutting, and star cut bases, possibly Irish, c1840, 11⅝in (29.5cm) high.
$1,100–1,200 *Som*

A red glass decanter, overlaid with white, c1850, 14½in (37cm) high.
$800–880 *MJW*

An engraved blue glass decanter, c1860, 13⅓in (34.5cm) high.
$520–600 *MJW*

A pair of brandy carafes, c1840, 9in (23cm) high.
$640–720 *CB*

A shaft and globe decanter, c1860, 12in (30.5cm) high.
$640–720 *MJW*

A decanter/claret jug, with clear barley-twist handle, c1880, 10in (25.5cm) high.
$240–280 *CB*

A scent bottle, with red on white overlay and gilt decorated panels, c1860, 4¾in (12cm) high.
$1,100–1,200 *Som*

Three red glass scent bottles, with vinaigrette bases: *l. & r.* with silver-gilt mounts by Samson Mordan, c1880, 3¾in (9.5cm) high. **$1,200–1,350 each** *c.* with finger ring and chain, c1880, 2⅜in (6cm) high.
$960–1,100 *Som*

A Victorian cameo glass scent bottle, by Thomas Webb, with a silver mount and stopper, c1880, 5in (12.5cm) long.
$2,400–2,600 *THOM*

A glass decanter, with red overlay, c1840, 12in (30.5cm) high.
$400–480 *CB*

A pair of green glass decanters, with stoppers, c1850, 12in (30.5cm) high.
$680–800 *CB*

A blue glass cream jug and sugar basin, each with a band of gilt navette decoration, probably by Jacobs, Bristol, c1810, jug 3in (8cm) high. **$1,600–1,900** *Som*

A cranberry glass jug, with white trailed decoration, c1880, 9in (23cm) high. **$400–480** *MJW*

A cranberry glass jug, with amber trailed neck, c1820, 5½in (14cm) high. **$280–350** *ARE*

A glass jug, with purple overlay, c1900, 8in (20.5cm) high. **$520–560** *MJW*

A vaseline glass jug, with white spiral decoration and plain loop handle, c1900, 7⅞in (20cm) high. **$280–320** *ARE*

A cranberry ice glass jug, with moulded handle, c1890, 9in (23cm) high. **$280–320** *CB*

A glass sugar basin, the body cold-enamelled with a floral band, c1820, 4¼in (11cm) high. **$350–400** *Som*

An amethyst glass rib-moulded finger bowl, c1830, 3½in (9cm) high. **$270–320** *MJW*

A green glass bonbon dish, with a silver-plated stand, c1910, 7in (18cm) high. **$240–270** *CB*

A vaseline glass basket, with pincer feet, c1900, 6in (15cm) high. **$200–240** *CB*

A glass bowl and cover, with gilded decoration, c1800, 6in (15cm) high. **$800–880** *CB*

A glass finger bowl, with green overlay, c1880, 5in (12.5cm) diam. **$240–270** *MJW*

A blue-green wine glass, with plain stem, c1830, 5in (13cm) high. **$80–100** *BrW*

Four wine glasses, with knopped, facet-cut stems, c1830, 5¼in (13.5cm) high. **$880–960** *Som*

A Richardson engraved glass goblet, c1850, 6in (15cm) high. **$1,800–2,000** *MJW*

An Osler glass goblet, with white overlay, c1860, 7in (18cm) high. **$1,000–1,100** *MJW*

A Bohemian blue glass beaker, with pink overlay, c1860, 5½in (14cm) high. **$520–560** *MJW*

A cranberry glass roemer, c1880, 5in (12.5cm) high. **$270–320** *MJW*

A Bohemian goblet, with panel-cut body, 19thC, 6½in (16.5cm) high. **$120–160** *CAG*

A pair of engraved purple wine glasses, c1870, 5½in (14cm) high. **$320–380** *MJW*

l. A cranberry glass carafe and tumbler, c1910, carafe 7in (18cm) high. **$160–175** *AnS*

A set of 4 Fritz Heckert hock glasses, late 19thC, 7½in (19cm) high. **$1,000–1,100** *MJW*

A set of 8 St Louis hock glasses, c1890, 7in (18cm) high. **$1,200–1,300** *MJW*

A Lobmeyr Islamic style gilt and enamel beaker, after a design by Franz Schmoranz, c1880, 7½in (19cm) high. **$5,500–6,500** *C*

A Bohemian red overlay goblet, with double series twist stem, c1860, 8in (20.5cm) high. **$720–800** *CB*

A French glass jug and 2 tumblers, with paste gilt decoration, c1890, jug 7in (18cm) high. **$1,100–1,200** *MJW*

A Clichy paperweight, the tightly packed canes resting on a basket of dark blue and white staves, c1850, 3in (7.5cm) diam.
$3,600–4,200 *SWB*

A Clichy paperweight, with scattered millefiori 'sodden snow' ground, with 3 'C' canes for Clichy, c1850, 3in (7.5cm) diam.
$3,200–3,500 *SWB*

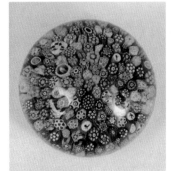

A Baccarat paperweight, with close millefiori canes and 4 silhouettes, polished flat base, dated '1848', 3in (7.5cm) diam.
$2,000–2,400 *MLa*

A Baccarat paperweight, with millefiori and filigree rods, c1855, 3in (7.5cm) diam.
$640–720 *MLa*

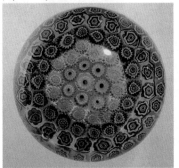

A Bacchus paperweight, with close-concentric millefiori, slight wear, late 19thC, 3½in (9cm) diam.
$3,500–3,800 *C*

A Bohemian paperweight, with scattered millefiori on muslin, 19thC, 2¾in (7cm) diam.
$520–560 *SWB*

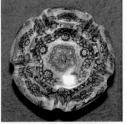

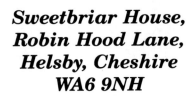

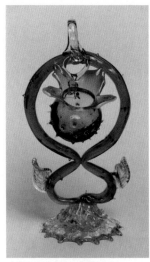

A Victorian posy bowl, supported on a glass stand, c1900, 8in (20.5cm) high.
$280–320 *CB*

A vaseline opalescent glass vase, on green leaf-moulded foot, c1890, 5in (12.5cm) high.
$130–160 *CB*

A pair of Stourbridge yellow glass and gilt enamel vases, c1880, 5in (12.5cm) high.
$520–600 *MJW*

A pair of Lobmeyr opalescent glass vases, c1885, 9½in (24cm) high.
$8,500–9,000 *S*

A pair of Northwood glass vases, with intaglio cut decoration, c1880, 9in (23cm) high.
$4,800–5,200 *MJW*

A pink and green vaseline glass Jack-in-the-pulpit vase, c1890, 10in (25.5cm) high.
$520–600 *MJW*

An opaline glass vase, with enamel decoration, c1870, 11in (28cm) high.
$190–240 *CB*

A late Victorian cranberry glass vase, 13¾in (35cm) high.
$270–300 *SPU*

A cranberry glass vase, with applied leaves, c1890, 8in (20.5cm) high.
$280–330 *ARE*

A cranberry glass *épergne*, c1880, 21in (53.5cm) high.
$960–1,100 *CB*

A French opaline glass hand-painted casket, c1870, 4in (10cm) high.
$1,350–1,550 *CB*

A Stevens & Williams overlay vase, c1910, 6in (15cm) high.
$640–720 *MJW*

A French opaline glass and enamelled night light, c1900, 5in (13cm) high.
$640–720 *Som*

PORCELAIN

As has been the trend in recent years, demand for good porcelain continues to grow whilst the supply remains static. At auction buyers seek those items fresh to the market and the gulf between pieces in the 'first division' and lesser examples continues to widen.

Ingredients to add special appeal to a piece include scarcity, decorative merit, provenance and condition; although damage is now more acceptable on uncommon pieces as perfect examples are frequently not available. This is shown by the New Hall documentary teapot, dated 1798, sold by Dreweatt Neate for $4,000, despite some damage, and the two Meissen Marcolini period lobster-shaped tureens, which although restored made $14,720 at Christie's. Here the combination of rarity and decorative appeal was the great attraction. A noticeable recent change is the growing enthusiasm for pieces of academic interest. As more research is carried out on English porcelain in particular, attributions tend to change, pieces are reassessed and values can rise accordingly. Many pieces once attributed to the Liverpool factories have now been reassessed and correctly attributed to the London manufactories of Vauxhall and Limehouse. Consequently prices paid for reattributed pieces can be surprising as demonstrated by the $22,400 paid for a wonderful Limehouse tureen and cover at Sotheby's which would have been an unthinkable result a few years ago.

A trend that continues apace is the division of tea, dinner and dessert services. As the value to collectors and decorators of individual pieces in a service rises, so the temptation to both dealers and auctioneers to divide them increases. As a result it is becoming more uncommon to find services intact, and in years to come those that survive will be at a considerable premium.

Continental ceramics of all periods have performed well in recent years, with particular demand for Meissen wares. Prices for Meissen and other Continental porcelain, such as figures, have risen and 18th century English porcelain figures seem very under-valued. Decorative Derby figures of the 1770s and '80s can still be found relatively easily for prices in the low hundreds, in many cases for less than the cost of buying a good quality modern figure.

With little to indicate that the supply of traditional mainstream ceramics will increase, auctioneers and dealers are placing greater relevance on areas that twenty years ago would not have been considered. Sales in fields such as blue printed earthenware, commemoratives and Doulton figures have the current advantage of ready availability, and also of remaining affordable to many collectors. It is this combination of supply and demand that the market needs to survive, as there is little satisfaction to collectors in a field where only one example appears every few years.

Mark Law

Baskets

A Belleek three-strand basket, c1865–90, 12½in (32cm) long.
$3,200–4,000 *MLa*

Three-strand means the centre is woven from three-ply strands of porcelain. Later examples are four-ply or four-strand.

A Belleek basket, with 2 twig handles, the border applied with roses and shamrock, marked, c1900, 9in (23cm) diam.
$1,200–1,300 *HOLL*

> Items in the Porcelain section have been arranged in factory order within each sub-section.

A Belleek four-strand heart-shaped basket, c1945, 5in (13cm) wide.
$400–480 *MLa*

A Bow pierced basket, the interior painted in underglaze blue with flowers and leaves, the exterior moulded with flowerheads picked out in blue, firing crack, c1765, 6¾in (17cm) diam.
$350–400 *DN*

Five Worcester shallow baskets, with gilt rims, on pale-green grounds, one restored, marked c1820, 5½in (14cm) wide.
$2,200–2,800 *C*

A Worcester pierced quatrefoil two-handled stand for a chestnut basket, decorated in the atelier of James Giles, the centre with 2 exotic birds among trees, the handles applied with flowers and foliage, chips to flowers, c1770, 10in (25.5cm) wide.
$1,200–1,300 *C*

Bowls

A Chelsea blue-ground bowl, painted with exotic birds bordered by flowers and foliage in tooled gilding on the mazarine-blue ground, the interior with cut lemons and lemon blossom, gold anchor mark and inscribed 'N.1' in gilding, rim cracks, c1765, 15in (38cm) diam.
$13,000–14,000 *S*

A Worcester bowl, decorated in coloured enamels with a version of the Stag Hunt pattern, within flower and scroll-moulded cartouches, on a pleated ground, c1756, 6¼in (16cm) diam.
$2,800–3,000 *DN*

A German Dresden style figural bowl, painted and encrusted with flowers flanked by standing putti, c1900, 7½in (19cm) diam.
$480–520 *AH*

A Wedgwood Fairyland lustre bowl, designed by Daisy-Makeig Jones, the interior decorated with the Ship and Mermaid pattern, within arched panels, the exterior with the Fiddler in Tree pattern, c1920, 7¾in (19.5cm) wide.
$4,000–4,400 *HOLL*

A Frankenthal chinoiserie slop-bowl, painted in a bright palette with Oriental figures, below a band of puce and gilt umbrellas, bells and hatched decoration, the interior with scattered butterflies and other insects, slight damage, marked, c1772, 6¾in (17cm) diam
$11,500–13,500 *C*

Fairyland Lustre

Fairyland lustre wares were produced at Wedgwood by Daisy Makeig-Jones from c1910 until her retirement in 1931. The name was derived from prints she had designed, which featured fanciful palaces and landscapes peopled by fairy folk. These prints were filled in a full range of underglaze colours, a lustre glaze was applied and then the pattern was picked out with a gold print. Each subject was given a name and bears a 'Z' and a pattern number on the base. The range was a great commercial success, despite the painstaking work that went into it. Prospective purchasers should be aware that damage and restoration are difficult to detect in Fairyland pieces due to the complexity of the decoration.

Sugar & Covered Bowls

A Belleek sugar bowl, in the shape of a thistle, First Period, 1865–90, 3in (7.5cm) high.
$160–200 *MLa*

A Meissen punchbowl and cover, painted with sprays of flowers, the finial formed as a kneeling putto, damaged and restored, marked, c1765, 11¾in (30cm) diam.
$3,000–3,200 *CSK*

A Worcester sugar bowl with cover, decorated in blue, rust and gilt pattern, First Period, c1770, 5in (12.5cm) high.
$900–1,100 *DAN*

l. A two-handled *écuelle*, cover and stand, by Helena Wolfsohn, slight damage, 'AR' monogram, late 19thC, 6¾in (17cm) high.
$800–960 *DN*

During the 19th century, a considerable number of German factories produced excellent imitations of Meissen. One of the best was Carl Thieme's factory in Potschappel, and another was the Dresden factory of Helena Wolfsohn who copied Meissen wares of the 1740s and even added the Augusta Rex mark, until Meissen obtained an injunction against her, forcing her to change the mark to a crown above the word Dresden.

Boxes

A Frankenthal gold-mounted snuff box, moulded with floral scrollwork cartouches enclosing on the side and base vignettes of figures in park settings, the cover by a different hand with figures in a wooded landscape, the mounts chased with scrollwork, c1770, 3in (7.5cm) wide.
$10,200–11,200 *S*

A Meissen porcelain gold-mounted snuff box, painted in colours, the exterior and base decorated with floral sprays and sprigs, the interior of the hinged cover painted with a basket of summer flowers, mid-18thC, 2½in (6.5cm) long.
$3,500–3,800 *S(Am)*

A Meissen porcelain snuff box, the cover with a scene of a female figure and putti, a similar scene to the interior, the base painted with a parrot on a table by a basket, the interior gilded, with white metal mounts, marked, later decorated probably by Franz Ferdinand Mayer, c1723, 2¾in (7cm) wide.
$3,500–3,800 *Bon*

Franz Ferdinand Mayer decorated Meissen porcelains from the 1720s, often using pieces which had previously been rejected by the factory as substandard. He worked in Pressnitz, Bohemia, c1745–78.

A Royal Copenhagen box, painted with dragonfly and iris, c1895, 4¼in (11cm) diam.
$180–200 *SUC*

l. A Minton box and cover, to commemorate the Coronation of Edward VIII, with central white moulded head, on a pale blue ground, the border inscribed in gilt, the base with flowers of the union in gilt, the base inscribed and numbered '5 of 300', slight damage, 1937, 2½in (6.5cm) diam.
$300–320 *SAS*

A Sèvres style casket, the cover painted with figures in 18th century style attire, within a cobalt blue border and gilded with scrolling vines, the sides similarly decorated with views of lovers and arcadian landscapes, gilt-metal mounts, lined interior, signed Cottinet, marked, c1900, 16in (40.5cm) wide.
$13,000–14,000 *Bon*

This casket is particularly large in size which contributed to the high price achieved when sold at auction.

Busts

A biscuit bust of the Duke of Wellington as a Roman emperor, by Samuel Alcock, printed marks, dated '1828', 9½in (24cm) high.
$450–520 *DN*

A Copeland bust of Nelson, c1850, 13¼in (33.5cm) high.
$2,400–2,600 *TVM*

r. A Copeland Parian ware bust, entitled 'Lesbia', sculpted by W. C. Marshall RA for the Crystal Palace Art Union, inscribed and dated, c1870, 16½in (42cm) high.
$1,200–1,400 *HAM*

A Copeland Parian ware bust, entitled 'The Veiled Bride', by Rafaello Monti, c1861, 15½in (39.5cm) high.
$2,800–3,500 *JAK*

A Copeland Parian ware bust of Autumn, by Owen Hale, c1881, 18in (46cm) high.
$2,400–2,800 *JAK*

A Parian ware bust of Dr Samuel Johnson, by W. H. Goss, c1880, 7½in (19cm) high.
$640–720 *G&CC*

A Sèvres biscuit bust of Napoleon Bonaparte as First Consul, after the model by Boizot, inscribed marks, c1809, 11in (28cm) high.
$2,200–2,800 *C*

A Parian ware bust of Shakespeare, unmarked but probably by Wedgwood, c1860, 13½in (34cm) high.
$560–640 *JAK*

Copeland Parian ware

The Copeland factory in Staffordshire was one of the first to develop Parian, a form of porcelain simulating marble. From 1844 onwards it produced a wide range of figures and busts after the leading sculptors of the day. Almost every piece was marked with the sculptor's name.

l. A Continental porcelain bust of Diana, after the antique known as 'Diana Chasseresse', lilac pad 'VB' mark, firing cracks and wear, late 19thC, 28¼in (72cm) high.
$800–960 *CSK*

The mark on this piece is of Vion and Baury, who continued the Gille factory after 1868. They were the most important makers of bisque in Paris in the 19thC.

A pair of German porcelain busts, in Dutch style dress of pink, green, gold and brown colours, c1920, 6in (15cm) high.
$120–140 *AnS*

Centrepieces

A Worcester First Period porcelain tripart centrepiece, c1765, 5in (12.5cm) high.
$720–800 *LHA*

A Dresden dessert comport, the bowl with pierced shaped rim with painted and encrusted sprays of flowers, figures in 18thC costume encircling a central pedestal, marked, late 19thC, 13¾in high.
$950–1,000 *HYD*

A Sèvres style porcelain and gilt-bronze centrepiece, with a central figural panel, the opposing side and interior with musical trophies and floral decorations on a lustre ground, flanked by gilt-bronze figural handles, signed Collet, late 19thC, 15¾in (40cm) high.
$5,500–6,000 *S(NY)*

r. A Sèvres style gilt-metal mounted porcelain centrepiece, painted by Cantin, with foliate-cast feet each headed by a ram's mask and joined by a foliate swag, late 19thC, 18in (45.5cm) diam.
$1,900–2,200 *C*

Clocks

A Meissen porcelain clock, the brass dial above a landscape vignette, the scroll-moulded body applied with flowers and 4 putti emblematic of the seasons, on 4 scroll feet, with flower cluster finial, minor damage, c1880, 16¾in (42.5cm) high.
$7,500–8,000 *S(Am)*

A porcelain mantel clock, by Jacob Petit, the dial possibly signed 'Leitzmani', surmounted by a horseman being attacked by tigers, some damage, mid-19thC, 22in (56cm) high.
$1,900–2,000 *S(NY)*

A German porcelain clock case, the clock with French 8-day movement, c1880, 39in (99cm) high.
$1,800–2,000 *TPA*

Coffee & Teapots

A Derby faceted teapot and cover, with hexagonal loop knop, decorated in coloured enamels with floral garlands, interlinked with gilt leaf scrolls, minor crack, crowned crossed baton mark in puce and pattern number, c1790, 6¾in (17cm) high.
$640–800 *DN*

A New Hall teapot and flat cover, with baluster-shaped knop, inscribed in puce and decorated in *famille rose* with flowers and leaves, pattern No. 195, tip of spout chipped, dated '1798', 5¾in (14.5cm) high.
$4,000–4,400 *DN*

The inscription and date make this a valuable item.

A Lowestoft teapot and cover, painted in underglaze blue with chinoiserie buildings, c1765, 6in (15cm) high.
$900–960 *HYD*

A Spode miniature teapot, richly gilded, slight repair, c1820, 2in (5cm) high.
$560–640 *JP*

r. A German porcelain teapot and cover, to commemorate the Coronation of Edward VII, printed with portraits in colours upon a ground of flags, inscribed and dated, the reverse with floral panel, gilt decoration, 1902, 7in (18cm) high.
$140–150 *SAS*

l. An H. & R. Daniel teapot, cover and stand, with leaf-moulded handle, spout and feet, decorated in coloured enamels with flowers, on a blue ground, some restoration, c1825, 6¼in (16cm) high.
$450–520 *DN*

A Meissen coffee pot and cover, painted with a chinoiserie scene heightened in gilding, the scroll handle with Oriental flowers and gilt scrollwork, spout restored, marked, c1725, 8¼in (21cm) high.
$13,000–14,500 *S*

Coffee & Tea Services

A Caughley 22-piece part tea and coffee service, each piece printed in blue with flower, butterfly and diaper bands in Chinese style, picked out with gilt, some damage, blue printed SX marks, c1785.
$850–950 DN

A Coalport 63-piece tea and coffee set, decorated with the Batwing pattern with cobalt blue floral panel and gilt decoration, early 20thC.
$800–900 PCh

A Copeland blue and white combination 'Lazy Susan' coffee urn and 14 piece coffee service, printed with Willow pattern within gilt line rims, damages, c1860.
$1,300–1,400 CSK

l. A Pinxton 39-piece part tea and coffee service, each piece painted in green, black and iron red, with a leaf and berry band, within gilt line borders, 3 items cracked, c1800.
$3,200–3,500 DN

A Royal Crown Derby Imari pattern 18-piece tea service, printed marks and painted with pattern No. 3788, minor wear, date codes for 1892.
$1,200–1,300 CSK

A Staffordshire 26-piece pink lustre teaset, decorated with leaves and berries, edged with swags, c1850, teapot 7½in (19cm) high.
$300–340 BRU

A Sèvres style 10-piece cased tête-à-tête, each piece painted with figures in a landscape and trophies within a tooled-gilt frame on a turquoise-blue ground, with fitted leather-bound case, marked, slight damage.
$4,400–5,000 S

A Spode 37-piece part tea and coffee service, printed in iron-red with a band of roses and gilt, minor damage, painted iron-red marks, pattern No. 786, early 19thC.
$1,900–2,000 C

A Worcester composite 13-piece part tea service, painted with loose sprays of flowers among scattered sprigs within gilt line rims, minor chips and repairs, c1775.
$950–1,100 CSK

A Royal Worcester 22-piece porcelain tea service, by Mildred Hunt and Ethel Spilsbury, with garden roses on an ivory ground within a gold line rim, minor glaze damage, printed mark and date code for 1926.
$800–960 Bea

A Chamberlain's & Worcester 35-piece tea set, c1820, tea pot 7in (18cm) high.
$1,800–2,000 ALB

Cups

A Belleek heart-shaped cup and saucer, painted with shamrock design, Third Period, 1926–46, 2¼in (6cm) high.
$160–200 *MLa*

A Caughley blue and white coffee can, with fence pattern, c1785, 2½in (6.5cm) high.
$180–200 *DAN*

A Coalport spiral-fluted coffee can, c1805, 2½in (6.5cm) high.
$90–100 *BSA*

A Coalport cup and saucer, the cobalt-blue ground with heavy gilt decoration, gilded well to saucer and interior of cup, green mark, c1900, 1¾in (4.5cm) high.
$240–320 *MER*

A Derby coffee can, decorated with blue, gilt and orange flowers with buds, c1815, 2½in (6.5cm) high.
$120–150 *AnS*

A pair of Du Paquier Hausmaler teabowls and saucers, painted possibly in Bohemia in iron-red, the saucers each with a landscape scene of figures and buildings, the figures heightened in yellow and black, the teabowls with vignettes of buildings in wooded landscapes, slight damage, c1725, cup 2½in (6.5cm) high.
$3,200–3,500 *S*

A Hammersley coffee cup and saucer, decorated with a pink and green festooned border, gilded, c1920, 2¼in (6cm) high.
$40–50 *AnS*

A Meissen Marcolini blue-ground chocolate cup, cover and saucer, the body painted with a portrait of Pius VI within a gilt circular laurel-wreath cartouche, the saucer with the keys of St Peter on a cloud, the cover with a papal tiara, palm branch and lilies on a cloud within a gilt myrtle leaf cartouche, with gilt pierced laurel-wreath finial, c1780, saucer 5½in (12.5cm) high.
$5,600–6,000 *C*

r. A Minton trio, decorated with rococo revival scenes, c1835, plate 5¾in (15cm) diam.
$110–130 *BSA*

r. A New Hall Imari pattern coffee can, blue and gold with fruiting trees and foliage, orange fruit, pattern No. 466, c1800, 2¼in (6cm) high.
$160–180 *AnS*

A New Hall trio, decorated with a chinoiserie scene, c1815, saucer 5½in (14cm) diam.
$180–200 *JP*

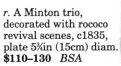

A Sèvres coffee can and saucer, painted with flowers and fruit, the rims with gilt scrollwork borders, painter's marks, c1772, cup 2½in (6.5cm) high.
$3,500–4,000 *S(Z)*

Bat Printing

Bat printing is a type of transfer printing used to produce fine detail on porcelain and bone china by English factories in the early 19thC. The design was conveyed from an engraved copper plate to a glazed surface by means of slabs of glue or gelatin (bats). Tiny dots of oil were transferred to the porcelain and a fine coloured powder was then dusted on to the surface of the glaze. This powder stuck to the oil, rendering the design onto the article.

A Spode coffee can, with cobalt ground, bat printed in gold with a castellated building, from the Ancient Buildings series, pattern No. 1695, c1810, 2½in (6.5cm) high.
$560–640 *AnS*

A Spode bat printed coffee can, c1810, 2½in (6.5cm) high.
$80–90 *BSA*

r. A Staffordshire porcelain trio, attributed to Yates & Co, decorated with gilt foliage pattern and flowers, c1830, saucer 5¾in (14.5cm) diam.
$160–180 *BSA*

Cross Reference
Colour Review

A Vauxhall coffee cup, with simple loop handle, painted in underglaze blue with a Chinese woman and child in a continuous landscape, slight damage, c1756, 2¼in (5.5cm) high.
$1,400–1,800 *DN*

A porcelain mug, by Wileman, commemorating the wedding of George V and Mary of Teck, enamelled with heraldic shield, flags and ribboned inscription, gilt rim, 1893, 2¾in (7cm) high.
$110–130 *SAS*

A Staffordshire porcelain pink lustre banded cup and saucer, printed in black and inscribed 'HRH Princess Charlotte, died Nov 6 1817', 2¼in (6cm) high.
$180–200 *SAS*

A Worcester cup and cover, enamelled in colours with floral spray within royal blue and gilt panels, pierced loop handles, the domed cover with flower pattern finial, lacking saucer, c1770, 4¼in (11cm) diam.
$580–620 *CAG*

A Victorian Royal Worcester tea cup and saucer, decorated in apricot, green and gold, etched 'ER' for Edward Raby, cup 2in (5cm) high, c1885.
$90–100 *AnS*

A Worcester, Flight and Barr period cup and saucer, decorated with gilt leaves and blue flowers, c1795, saucer 5½in (14cm) diam.
$180–200 *BSA*

Dessert & Dinner Services

A Coalport part dessert service, comprising 8 pieces, painted in the manner of John Plant and Edward Ball with vignettes of river and lake views, each titled on reverse, on a dark blue ground, printed marks, slight damage, early 20thC.
$2,800–3,000 *CSK*

r. A Royal Crown Derby porcelain dessert service, comprising 16 pieces, with floral decoration and gilding on a white ground, 1905.
$800–880 *GH*

l. A Royal Crown Derby dessert service, comprising 15 pieces, painted in coloured enamels with flowers and leaves within blue and gilt borders, pattern No. 2028, printed marks, c1889.
$1,000–1,300 *DN*

A Grainger & Co part dessert service, comprising 11 pieces, painted in coloured enamels with wild flowers, grasses and insects within blue and gilt borders, impressed marks and pattern No. 2443, c1875.
$900–960 *DN*

A Limoges dinner service, comprising 67 pieces, decorated in iron-red, orange and blue with flowering branches and floral sprays, marked, c1900.
$1,200–1,300 *S(Am)*

A Meissen part dessert service, comprising 10 pieces, moulded with seeds and radiating bands of leaves, naturalistically coloured and in bright and matt gilt, damaged and repaired, blue crossed swords marks, c1900.
$2,000–2,200 *CSK*

A Meissen blue and white Onion pattern dessert service, comprising 11 pieces, with pierced basket pattern borders, the shaped and moulded cartouches decorated with floral sprays, crossed swords mark in underglaze blue, c1900.
$1,800–1,900 *CAG*

A La Courtille, Paris, part dessert service, comprising 35 pieces, London decorated with flowers and gilt vases, anthemion, vine wreath and scroll borders, gilt line rims, slight damage, incised and blue crossed arrow marks, c1810.
$4,800–6,400 *C*

A Staffordshire dinner service, comprising 77 pieces, decorated with Chinese Tree pattern No. 1959, some damage and repair, c1830.
$2,200–2,500 *WL*

A Royal Worcester dessert service, comprising 18 pieces, painted in coloured enamels with a spray of flowers and leaves, the pink ground borders decorated with stylised flowers and leaves within gilt dentil bands, some restoration, impressed marks, pattern No. 9035, c1870.
$1,200–1,300 *DN*

Ewers & Jugs

A Belleek jug, with harp handle, First Period, 1865–90, 8¼in (21cm) high.
$1,200–1,300 *MLa*

A Coalport white Goat and Bee jug, c1860, 4in (10cm) high.
$200–280 *ALB*

A Liverpool cream jug, of Chelsea Ewer shape, by Pennington's, decorated in coloured enamels with sprays of flowers and leaves, above a stiff leaf band picked out in green, yellow and puce, the interior with a puce band, c1775.
$640–720 *DN*

A Minton milk jug, decorated with gilt flowers, leaves and scrolls, pattern No. 4278, c1845, 7½in (19cm) high.
$90–100 *BSA*

A pair of Minton Pembroke ewers, probably by Thomas Steel, the high loop handles with satyr mask terminals, each decorated in coloured enamels, with fruit within a gilt scroll and diaper cartouche, on a green ground, c1830, 8¾in (22cm) high.
$2,400–2,500 *DN*

A New Hall cream jug, with scroll handle, printed in underglaze blue with figures in a Chinese landscape, on 3 short feet, repaired, c1785, 5in (12.5cm) high.
$1,300–1,400 *DN*

> **Don't Forget!**
> *If in doubt please refer to the 'How to Use' section at the beginning of this book.*

A Wallendorf porcelain hot water jug and cover, the slightly ribbed body applied with scroll handle, painted with an orange cartouche enclosing script, with scattered floral sprigs, gilt-edged rim, the cover similarly decorated and surmounted by bud finial, slight damage, underglaze mark in blue, late 18thC, 8in (20.5cm) high.
$480–550 *S(Am)*

A Worcester jug, with scroll handle and mask spout, decorated in puce monochrome with an urn within a gilt scroll and flower cartouche, decorated in coloured enamels with flowers and leaves, beneath a blue and gilt band, marked, c1775, 5¾in (14.5cm) high.
$680–800 *DN*

A Chamberlain's Worcester jug, painted in coloured enamels with The Chase, within a gilt panel, on a grey marble ground with gilt leaf and C-scroll bands, restored, painted mark, c1815, 6¼in (16cm) high.
$1,300–1,400 *DN*

A Royal Worcester ewer, with gilt and rust floral decoration on an ivory ground, lizard handle with gilt jewel work, slight damage, c1889, 7in (18cm) high.
$250–280 *GAK*

Fairings

A fairing, 'An Awkward Interruption', late 19thC, 4in (10cm) wide.
$200–200 *SAS*

A fairing, 'Who is Coming?', late 19thC, 3½in (9cm) wide.
$100–110 *SAS*

Fairings

Fairings are small porcelain figure or animal groups made in Germany in the late 19thC, which were sold in fairs as cheap souvenirs. They often portrayed bedroom scenes with humorous inscriptions in English on the base. Rare specimens, such as those which feature unusual items like velocipedes, can fetch high prices.

A fairing, 'To Epsom', restored, cycle frame detached in firing, late 19thC, 10in (25.5cm) wide.
$1,100–1,200 *SAS*

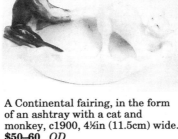

A Continental fairing, in the form of an ashtray with a cat and monkey, c1900, 4½in (11.5cm) wide.
$50–60 *OD*

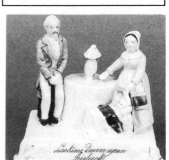

A fairing, 'Looking Down upon his Luck', late 19thC, 3½in (9cm) wide.
$110–130 *SAS*

A fairing, modelled as a green fallen fence with pigs playing, late 19thC, 4¼in (11cm) wide.
$110–130 *SAS*

A fairing, modelled as a car with pig passengers, painted green, slight damage, late 19thC, 4¾in (12cm) wide.
$60–70 *SAS*

A fairing, 'Five o'clock Tea', restored, late 19thC, 3½in (9cm) wide.
$140–160 *SAS*

Figures

A Berlin figure group of Paris and Helen, a dog and a lamb, late 19thC, 10in (25.5cm) high.
$420–480 *AH*

A Bow figure of a hunter, in front of bocage, on a scroll base, slight restoration, c1765, 7¼in (18.5cm) high.
$1,000–1,300 *DAN*

A Parian group, designed by Gibson for the Art Union of London, by Bates, Brown-Westhead and Moore & Co, depicting Cupid and Psyche, c1858, 18in (45.5cm) high.
$1,600–2,000 *JAK*

A Bow figure of a male flautist, seated on a mound and wearing a yellow jacket and flower-decorated breeches, restored, c1756, 3¾in (9.5cm) high.
$800–950 *DN*

A Copeland Parian group, entitled 'Go To Sleep', by J. Durham, c1862, 18in (45.5cm) high. **$1,300–1,600** *JAK*

A Chelsea Derby group, depicting a boy and girl playing musical instruments, c1775, 6¾in (17cm) high. **$1,400–2,000** *DAN*

A Copeland parian figure of Narcissus, adapted by E. B. Stephens from Gibson's marble statue, c1847, 13in (33cm) high. **$950–1,100** *JAK*

A Parian figure, entitled 'Cupids Contending', after Fiamingo for Copeland, c1860, 15in (38cm) high. **$1,400–1,800** *JAK*

r. A pair of Bow figures depicting Spring and Autumn, the man with a goblet and bunch of grapes, the lady with baskets and bunches of flowers, both seated among flowers on high rococo scroll bases picked out in gilding, marked, c1765, 6¾in (17cm) high. **$1,900–2,200** *S*

A set of 4 Derby figures, entitled 'The French Seasons', after the Tournai models by Gauron and based on designs by Boucher, Spring holding flowers, Summer a corn sheaf, Autumn with a basket of grapes, and Winter carrying faggots, painted with coloured enamels and rich gilding, Spring restored, unmarked, c1770, 9½in (24cm) high. **$4,000–4,400** *WW*

r. A pair of Derby figural candlesticks, each in the form of a kneeling cupid, in front of floral bocage, beside a pierced sconce, a quiver and arrows at their feet, the shell and scroll moulded bases picked out in turquoise, puce and gilt, c1770, 7½in (19cm) high. **$800–960** *DN*

A Derby figure of Dr Syntax, marked 'S & H' for Sampson Hancock, c1875, 5½in (14cm) high. **$400–480** *DAN*

A Derby figure group, entitled 'Time Clipping the Wings of Love', some damage, c1770, 12¾in (32.4cm) high. **$750–800** *PCh*

A Royal Doulton group, 'The Flower Seller's Children', HN1206, modelled as a young boy and his sister on a bench with a large basket of flowers, printed and painted marks, 1926–49, 7¼in (18.5cm) high.
$400–480 *HYD*

A Royal Doulton figure, 'Gay Morning', HN2135, modelled as a young lady in a flowing pink dress holding a blue shawl, 1954–67, 7½in (19cm) high.
$180–200 *HYD*

A pair of Royal Dux figures, depicting a girl and boy sitting on basketweave bowls, painted in pastel shades and highlighted with gilding, marked, early 20thC, 5in (12.5cm) high.
$380–420 *HYD*

r. A Höchst group of a boy with pet animals, modelled by J. P. Melchior, damaged and restored, incised wheel mark flanked by 'T' and 'SP', c1775, 6¾in (17cm) high.
$5,000–5,800 *C*

A pair of Royal Dux figures of grape harvesters, painted in pastel shades and highlighted with gilding, marked, c1900, 10in (25.5cm) high.
$560–640 *HYD*

A Ludwigsburg miniature group of figures gambling, in coloured clothes enriched with gilding, restored, faint black interlaced 'C' mark, c1765, 2½in (6.5cm) high.
$5,500–6,500 *C*

A Meissen figure of a girl with a doll, modelled by Hentschel, blue crossed swords mark, incised 'W124', *Pressnummer* 48, early 20thC, 5¼in (13.5cm) high.
$5,000–5,600 *CSK*

These charming Meissen figures modelled by Hentschel are particularly sought-after.

r. A Meissen figure of Cupid, a tricorn hat under his right arm and a sword tucked under his tailcoat, slight damage, c1755, 3¾in (9.5cm) high.
$650–800 *Bon*

A pair of Minton biscuit figures, the man holding a basket of fruit, the woman holding flowers in her apron, slight restoration, c1840, 7½in (19cm) high.
$560–640 *DAN*

A Minton Parian group, by A. Carrier-Belleuse, entitled 'Mother and First Born', c1855, 13in (33cm) high.
$1,300–1,500 *JAK*

A Meissen figure of a boy holding a staff and a cockerel, restored, c1760, 6in (15cm) high.
$2,200–2,500 *DAN*

A Samson figure of Neptune, after a Derby original, a stylised dolphin at his feet, on a pierced scroll-moulded base applied with shells and leaves, gold anchor mark, c1900, 13½in (34.5cm) high.
$350–450 *CSK*

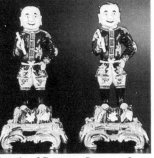

A pair of Samson figures of Chinamen, 19thC, on 18thC rococo gilt-bronze bases, 13¼in (34cm) high.
$2,500–2,800 *S(Z)*

Edmé Samson of Paris started his career in 1845 as a decorator of white porcelain from various factories. In the 1850s he set up a hard paste factory in Montreuil and produced copies of Chinese, Japanese, German, French and English porcelain of earlier periods. Some Samson pieces bore his mark, the letter 'S'. However, the Samson mark has often been removed.

A figure of a young woman in 18thC dress, by Vion & Baury, Paris, entitled 'The Broken Pitcher', blue anchor printed mark, 19thC, 26in (66cm) high.
$640–700 *CAG*

A Sèvres biscuit figure of a boy seated on a tree stump, damaged, incised mark, c1760, 4¾in (12cm) high.
$950–1,100 *C*

A miniature figure of Punchinello, holding a basket of pretzels, by Le Nove, restored, c1780, 2½in (6.5cm) high.
$2,200–2,800 *C*

l. A pair of Royal Worcester figures of a satyr and a bacchante, by James Hadley, printed marks with year codes for 1891 and 1897, 29¼in (74.5cm) high.
$4,500–5,000 *Bon*

r. A Chamberlain's Worcester figure of one of the Rainer brothers, c1828, 6in (15cm) high.
$800–960 *DAN*

A Bohemian bisque group, depicting fishermen, c1860, 10½in (26.5cm) high.
$130–150 *SER*

A pair of chinoiserie groups, by Carl Thieme, one depicting a seated woman, a girl with a basket, and an infant, the other a man fishing by a pool, and a woman holding a basket of fish, both on mounds applied with flowers, slight damage, printed blue marks, early 20thC, each 17½in (44.5cm) wide.
$3,400–4,000 *CSK*

Flatware

A Belleek tray, the raised shaped rim with gold edging repeated to the central panel depicting a scaled dragon, with surrounding raised star and swirled patterns, First Period, 1863–90, 15in (38cm) diam.
$1,350–1,550 HCC

A Chelsea plate, painted with floral sprays within a red/brown lined border, red anchor mark, c1760, 8in (20cm) diam.
$280–320 HYD

A pair of Copeland plates, in Sèvres style, painted in coloured enamels, the turquoise border with flowers, within raised paste gilt cartouches and scroll and diaper bands, printed marks in gilt, pattern No. C1237, retailer's mark for T. Goode & Co, c1900, 9½in (24cm) diam.
$550–620 DN

A Belleek ring-handled bread plate, with gilt family crest and decoration, First Period, 1863–90, 10¼in (26cm) diam.
$400–480 MLa

A Coalport plate, the centre painted in coloured enamels with a figure before a ruin in a landscape, the broad orange ground border decorated in puce and gilt with panels and garlands of leaves and patera, c1810, 9½in (24cm) diam.
$400–480 DN

A Derby soup plate, centrally decorated en grisaille with an urn, the rim with laurel garlands, within blue and gilt flowerhead and anthemion borders, crowned 'D' mark in blue, c1775, 9in (23cm) diam.
$480–520 DN

l. A Derby plate, decorated by John Brewer with the fable of the Lion and the Goat, within a broad blue band with gilt decoration, marked, c1790, 7½in (19cm) diam.
$1,100–1,300 DN

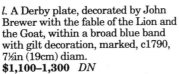

r. A Derby octagonal dish, c1780. 9in (23cm) wide.
$320–400 ALB

A Berlin pierced dessert plate, from a service made for Frederick the Great, the centre painted en grisaille with a scene from Ovid, slight wear, blue sceptre mark, c1784, 10¾in (27.5cm) diam.
$6,400–7,200 C

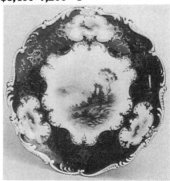

A pair of Coalport plates, painted by P. Simpson, with coastal landscape scenes within a cobalt blue ground rim decorated with gilt within a scrolling edge, printed marks in green, red Waring & Gillow Ltd retailer's mark, c1910, 9in (23cm) diam.
$480–560 EH

A pair of Derby shell-shaped dishes, each painted in coloured enamels, the borders picked out in gilt, crowned crossed baton marks in red, c1825, 9¾in (25cm) wide.
$780–520 DN

A Frankenthal dish, the centre painted with a large flowerspray, scattered leaves and flowers, edged in iron-red, marked, c1759, 17¼in (44cm) diam.
$8,000–8,800 *S*

A set of 17 Mintons *pâte-sur-pâte* dinner plates, decorated by A. Birks, each with 3 blue-ground panels decorated with Classical figures, the border with gilt acanthus swags and ribbons on a pale cream ground, signed and retailed by Ovington's New York and Chicago, c1921, 10¼in (26cm) diam.
$6,000–6,500 *S(NY)*

Alboin Birks devised the process of semi-moulded pâte-sur-pâte *panels on plates which had particular appeal in the USA.*

l. A Meissen Dulong-moulded dish, the centre painted with travellers in a wooded landscape, the border with wooded landscape vignettes within gilt scroll and foliate cartouches, marked, c1745, 13in (33cm) diam.
$3,200–4,000 *C*

> ### Don't Forget!
> *If in doubt please refer to the 'How to Use' section at the beginning of this book.*

l. A Meissen leaf-shaped dish, moulded as 3 overlapping vine leaves with a stalk handle, painted in enamels, the leaves with green borders, marked, c1750, 10½in (26.5cm) wide.
$1,600–2,000 *WW*

A Meissen plate, with gilt-scalloped rim, c1780, 9½in (24cm) diam.
$280–320 *ALB*

A Naples plate, painted with a spray of flowers within a border of sprigs and a lobed black line rim, late 18thC, 16¼in (41.5cm) diam.
$750–800 *CSK*

A Nantgarw plate, painted in coloured enamels with pink roses and a butterfly, with scroll, flower and ribbon-tie moulded border, impressed mark, c1820, 8½in (21.5cm) diam.
$800–880 *DN*

MILLER'S COMPARES . . .

A Worcester, Barr, Flight and Barr fluted two-handled dish, painted in coloured enamels with a view entitled 'Ponty Pair, near Llanrwst', within a gilt leaf scroll and cornucopia band, the pale pink ground with gilt dentil rim, marked, c1807, 13½in (34.5cm) wide.
$1,400–1,800 *DN*

A Worcester, Barr, Flight and Barr fluted dish, painted in coloured enamels with a view entitled 'Kilgarren Castle', within a gilt leaf scroll and cornucopia band, the pale pink ground with gilt dentil rim, marked, c1807, 11in (28cm) wide.
$720–880 *DN*

Size was a major factor contributing to the very different prices achieved by these two dishes at auction. Dessert services would normally contain only one dish as large as *item I***, but would include several of the slightly smaller dimensions of** *item II***, which creates the comparative rarity of** *item I***. The appeal of** *item I* **was further enhanced by the 2 gilt decorated handles, the overall fine gilding and its pristine condition.** *DN*

A Paris plate, with a printed panel of a mother and children, c1820, 9in (23cm) diam.
$130–160 *DAN*

A Sèvres plate, decorated with bouquets of flowers, c1770, 9½in (24cm) diam.
$240–320 *ALB*

A set of 6 Spode feldspar plates, each decorated in enamels with flowers and leaves, the lime-green ground moulded in relief and picked out in gilt, printed marks, c1825, 9in (23cm) diam.
$800–880 *DN*

A Wedgwood Fairyland lustre plate, painted and printed in gilding with a version of the Imps on a Bridge pattern, within a border of fruit and flowers on a grey-brown ground, printed mark in gilding, c1920, 10½in (26.5cm) diam.
$4,800–5,000 *S*

A Worcester plate, the scalloped border painted with puce and coloured flowers within a blue and gilt border, crescent mark, c1780, 8½in (21.5cm) diam.
$450–380 *HYD*

r. A Chamberlain's Worcester Regent China cabinet plate, painted with a view of the Government House and Council Chambers at Madras, within a pale lilac border, the rim moulded with gadroon shell and stiff-leaf edge, gilt highlight, marked, restored chip, c1811, 9½in (24cm) diam.
$1,400–1,600 *Bon*

In the early 19thC, Chamberlain developed a fine, hard, white, and very translucent porcelain covered in a glassy Paris-type glaze. Known as 'Regent China', it was used almost exclusively for dinner and dessert services.

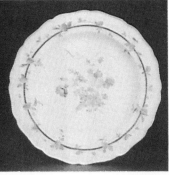

l. A Worcester plate, decorated in the London studio of James Giles, in coloured enamels with a spray of flowers and leaves, within a vine and brown ribbon band, dentil rim, gilding slightly rubbed, c1770, 8¾in (22cm) diam.
$430–560 *DN*

A Royal Worcester ice dish, decorated in the style of Edward Raby, with floral sprig bouquets on an ivory ground, shaped scalloped and gilded borders, c1892, 8in (20cm) wide.
$640–720 *GAK*

Edward Raby designed a series of etchings of flower subjects which were coloured in by juniors. Some etchings included his initials 'ER'.

Inkstands

A Samuel Alcock two-handled inkstand, fitted with a taperstick and 2 wells with covers, painted and encrusted with flowers and leaves, within green and gilt scroll-moulded borders, some damage, c1840, 14in (35.5cm) wide.
$880–1,000 *DN*

A Derby inkstand, painted with scattered flowers and with 3 wells set with baluster ink and pounce pots with covers, flanking a knopped column candlestick, the tray on 5 shell feet, restored, c1760, 10in (25.5cm) wide.
$2,200–2,500 *S*

A Ludwigsburg inkstand, after a design by G. F. Riedel, heightened in green and edged in purple, on paw feet, surmounted by 2 putti, modelled by J. C. W. Beyer, interlaced Cs in underglaze blue, c1760, 8in (20.5cm) wide.
$4,800–5,600 *S*

Jardinières

A Belleek low jardinière, decorated with naiads, First Period, 1863–90, 11in (28cm) high.
$1,600–2,000 *MLa*

A pair of Coalport cachepots, in Sèvres style, each painted with vignettes of Cupid, with leaf-moulded scroll handles, some wear, c1860, 4¼in (10.5cm) high.
$1,000–1,200 *CSK*

A Coalport jardinière, with rams' head handles, the reserve depicting exotic birds on gilded deep blue ground, late 19thC, 7¾in (20cm) high.
$1,300–1,500 *AH*

A Meissen jardinière, with 2 shell and scroll handles, painted in underglaze blue with the Onion pattern, marked, late 19thC, 6¾in (17cm) high.
$320–360 *HOLL*

A Royal Worcester jardinière, with pierced flared rim, painted pink rose panels by Ethel Spilsbury, on gilt and ivory leaf and scroll-moulded ground, c1910, 8in (20.5cm) high.
$2,200–2,600 *AH*

A pair of Sèvres style gilt-bronze cachepots, each painted with a reserve of lovers in a landscape opposed by similar reserves filled with flowers, with a *bleu celeste* ground, with mask handles, on scroll feet, c1870, 12¼in (31cm) high.
$8,200–8,800 *S*

Lamp Bases

l. A pair of Continental porcelain lamp bases, each decorated in coloured enamels with figures, flowers and leaves, within gilt borders on a green ground and with pierced flower cast gilt metal mounts, probably French, mid-19thC, 14in (35.5cm) high, later fitted as table lamps.
$1,100–1,300 *DN*

l. A pair of Royal Worcester figural lamp bases, modelled by James Hadley, shape No. 25, 1896 and 1912, 31½in (80cm) high.
$4,800–5,500 *Bon*

r. A Vienna style porcelain vase/lamp, with opposing figural panels, bordered by a rouge ground, flanked by scrolled handles ending in female busts, signed 'Kreyson', late 19thC, 17in (43cm) high.
$5,500–6,000 *S(NY)*

Models – Animals

A Belleek model of a greyhound, Second Green Period, 1955–65, 6½in (16.5cm) high.
$240–280 *MLa*

A Capodimonte model of a boar, with light-brown markings, pink snout, iron-red mouth and black hooves, on a rockwork base, c1755, 2¼in (5.5cm) high.
$7,500–8,800 *C*

A Chelsea fable candlestick group, in the form of 2 foxes before floral bocage, decorated in coloured enamels, the sconce and scroll-moulded base decorated with insects and picked out in turquoise and gilt, some damage and restoration, c1765, 12¼in (31cm) high.
$1,100–1,300 *DN*

r. A Derby porcelain model of a squirrel, ears restored, c1775, 3in (7.5cm) high.
$1,300–1,500 *DAN*

A pair of Bow white lions, lying outstretched on a rocky outcrop, with stippled and incised details, some firing cracks filled, c1750, 11¾in (30cm) long.
$8,400–8,800 *S*

A Capodimonte miniature group of a pug and her puppy, modelled by Guiseppe Gricci, with light-brown coat, black and grey ears and muzzle, wearing a blue collar and bow with gilt bells, on a dark-red cushion with gilt tassels at the angles, repaired, c1755, 2½in (6.5cm) high.
$10,400–11,200 *C*

A Meissen model of a cockatoo, modelled by J. J. Kändler, the crest, wings, tail and claws with yellow and black striped markings, one leaf chipped, c1745, 3in (7.5cm) high.
$3,200–4,000 *C*

A pair of Capodimonte white candlesticks, each modelled with a recumbent horse on a rocky mound with a palm tree and a branch forming the handle, the bases applied with leaves and flowers, some damage and restoration, marked, c1750, 5½in (14cm) high.
$4,000–4,800 *S*

A pair of Chelsea models of leverets, after the Meissen originals, their white fur dappled with touches of brown, their eyes and whiskers picked out in black, restored, c1750, 4¼in (11cm) wide.
$21,000–22,500 *S*

A Meissen model of a recumbent cow, modelled by J. J. Kändler, naturalistically coloured in shades of brown, the base applied with leaves and flowers, restored, c1745, 6¼in (16cm) long.
$2,000–2,400 *S(Z)*

Two Meissen partridge tureens and covers, after models by J. J. Kändler, on basketwork nests edged with naturalistically coloured twigs and corn, their plumage coloured in grey, brown and black, restored, marked, c1745 and early 19thC, largest 5¾in (14.5cm) wide.
$5,500–6,500 *C*

Two Meissen Marcolini lobster tureens, one in orange and red, the other in shades of brown, the covers with branch and foliage finials, restorations and minor chipping, marked, c1780, 8¾in (22cm) long.
$15,000–16,500 *C*

These tureens are desirable because of their unusual shape.

A Meissen white box and cover, modelled as a ewe, restoration to cover, cancelled blue crossed swords and star mark, c1780, 6in (15cm) long.
$2,400–2,700 *C*

l. A Meissen model of a heron, naturalistically modelled standing above rushes, the plumage painted in shades of grey and black, the foliage in green, on a mound base moulded with water lilies, extensively damaged and restored, marked, late 19thC, 20¼in (51.5cm) high.
$1,700–2,000 *CSK*

A pair of Meissen models of magpies, each perched on a tree trunk, on rockwork bases, late 19thC, 20in (51cm) high.
$1,900–2,300 *AH*

A Meissen model of a swan, c1900, crossed swords mark, 3½in (9cm) high.
$1,300–1,450 *MER*

A Royal Dux model of a standing horse, with green saddle and pink rug, on a rustic base, c1920, 7½in (19cm) wide.
$600–680 *AH*

A Royal Worcester model of a black and tan King Charles spaniel, on a turquoise cushion with gold tassels, c1910, 1½in (3.5cm) wide.
$650–800 *TH*

A Royal Worcester model of spotted deer, by Doris Lindner, decorated in coloured enamels, on a pale blue glazed base, printed marks, 1938, 4¾in (12cm) high.
$520–560 *DN*

A porcelain dog whistle, c1830, 2in (5cm) wide.
$380–480 *DAN*

A Parian model of a group of dogs, after the picture by Landseer, restored, unmarked, c1860, 12½in (31.5cm) wide.
$520–560 *SER*

l. A Continental bisque model of a fish, incised 'G' on base, c1880, 9½in (24cm) long.
$50–60 *SER*

Mugs

An Aynsley commemorative porcelain mug, printed in sepia and enamelled in colours with portrait panels, ribbons, flowers of the union, scenes from the Empire and shield, gilt rim, 1911, 3in (7.5cm) high.
$70–80 *SAS*

A Belleek mug, inscribed 'Stigo' in a central cartouche, Second Period, 1891–1926, 2¾in (7cm) high.
$160–200 *MLa*

A Coalport commemorative loving cup, each side decorated with a head and shoulders silhouette of George III, inscribed in gilt 'Long May the King Live' and on the reverse 'Token from Windsor', the rim gilded, 1810, 3¾in (9.5cm) high.
$1,400–1,600 *SAS*

It is likely such pieces were produced in celebration of the Jubilee for retailers in several of the royal towns.

A Worcester mug, decorated in Beckoning Chinaman pattern, with loop handle, enamelled in *famille rose* colours, unmarked, c1758, 3¾in (9.5cm) high.
$3,200–3,500 *CAG*

A Lowestoft mug, with scroll handle, printed in underglaze blue with Chinese style river landscape, the interior with a diaper band, slight damage, c1775, 5¾in (14.5cm) high.
$350–400 *DN*

A Worcester, Flight, Barr & Barr mug, painted with flowers, c1815, 3¼in (8cm) high.
$570–630 *TVM*

Plaques

A set of porcelain plaques, probably Coalport, each painted in coloured enamels with floral sprays to a lavender blue ground, early 19thC, largest 13¼ x 10¼in (33.5 x 26cm).
$6,500–8,000 *WW*

A Berlin porcelain plaque, painted in coloured enamels with Tannhauser and Venus, marked, 19thC, 9 x 11¼in (23 x 28.5cm), in a pierced giltwood Florentine frame.
$3,200–4,000 *DN*

A Berlin plaque, painted with John the Baptist as a child, a staff in his left hand, a lamb to his right, in a dark landscape with waterfall for background, marked 'KPM' with sceptre, 19thC, 15½ x 12½in (39.5 x 32cm).
$6,500–8,000 *Bon*

A Rockingham plaque, painted by Thomas Steel, with fruit and flowers, slight damage, 1830, 4¾ x 6½in (12 x 16.5cm).
$8,500–9,500 *C*

r. A German porcelain plaque, decorated with a girl wearing a grey skirt, a black cap and bodice and proferring flowers to a stone image of the Virgin, late 19thC, 12½ x 6½in (32 x 16.5cm), in a Florentine carved giltwood frame.
$1,900–2,200 *HOLL*

Sauce Boats

A Bow sauce boat, applied with flowerheads, leaves and branches, picked out in coloured enamels, the interior decorated with sprays of flowers and leaves, on 3 lion mask and scroll feet, the scroll handle picked out in blue, some damage, c1747, 6¾in (17cm) long.
$4,800–5,500 *DN*

A Derby lobed sauce boat, with S-scroll handle, decorated in coloured enamels with sprays of flowers, leaves and scattered flowers, beneath a brown line rim, c1758, 8¼in (21cm) long.
$520–560 *DN*

A Caughley lobed cream boat, with C-scroll handle, painted in coloured enamels with flowers and leaves, within gadrooned and iron-red line borders, c1785, 2¼in (5.5cm) long.
$240–320 *HOLL*

A Worcester cream boat, of Chelsea ewer type, the scroll handle with bird's head terminal, decorated in puce, purple, iron-red and gilt with scattered flowers and leaves, the interior with a pendant flower and puce diaper band, c1780, 2½in (6.5cm) high.
$650–800 *DN*

A pair of Derby sauce boats, with gadrooned borders, moulded with pendant fruits picked out in blue, the interiors decorated with sprays of flowers and leaves, within flower panelled cell diaper bands, some damage and repair, c1758, 7in (18cm) long.
$450–520 *DN*

A Liverpool sauce boat, from Samuel Gilbody's factory, with double scroll handle, the exterior painted with chinoiserie vignettes of a lady leading a horse in a landscape, the interior with a lady seated on a grassy knoll teasing a dog beneath a *grisaille* scroll border, chip to rim, c1754, 6½in (16.5cm) wide.
$16,000–17,500 *C*

All Gilbody pieces are rare and individual and many are the only known examples.

Tea Canisters

l. A Meissen tea canister and cover, painted in the manner of J. G. Höroldt with a chinoiserie scene, crossed swords mark, cover chipped, c1730, 4¼in (10.5cm) high.
$8,000–9,000 *S*

A Meissen tea canister and cover, painted in purple with landscape and harbour scene, the angles with gilt lines and the shoulder entirely gilt, the cover with interlocking gilt scrollwork about a quatrefoil, slight damage, marked, c1735, 4in (10cm) high.
$6,400–8,000 *C*

r. A Worcester tea canister, printed in underglaze blue with Obelisk and Vase pattern, the reverse with a European landscape group view, within gilt borders, lacking cover, hatched crescent mark, c1775, 5¼in (13cm) high.
$400–480 *DN*

A Worcester ribbed tea canister and domed cover, with flower knop, decorated in coloured enamels with an exotic bird in a branch and scattered flowers, c1775, 6¼in (16cm) high.
$720–880 *DN*

Tureens

A pair of Caughley dessert tureens with stands, decorated in blue and gilt, c1785, stands 9¼in (23.5cm) wide.
$1,100–1,350 *DAN*

A pair of Derby sauce tureens with stands, red marks, c1820, stands 10in (25.5cm) wide.
$4,400–5,600 *DUB*

A Davenport soup tureen, stand and ladle, decorated in blue and white, highlighted with gilding, c1840, 12in (30.5cm) high.
$320–360 *BRU*

A Limehouse tureen and cover, with twin scroll-moulded handles, painted in a greyish underglaze blue with Arcadian water scenes, some cracks, restored, c1746, 9½in (24cm) high.
$22,500–27,000 *S*

Limehouse (c1746–48)

Although one of the least known of the London factories, Limehouse was one of the pioneers of English porcelain manufacture and was probably the first factory in England to make blue and white porcelain. Many wares previously thought to have been made by William Reid of Liverpool are now known to have been made at Limehouse. Their output included shell-shaped dishes, wavy-edged sauce boats with tripod feet shaped like lions' heads or cherubs, teapots in a variety of shapes and chinoiserie pickle dishes.

A Meissen soup tureen and cover, the knop modelled as a sliced lemon, the sides with entwined stem handles, the whole painted with *Deutsche blumen* and with a gilt line rim to the cover, marked, c1750, 13¾in (35cm) high.
$3,200–4,000 *WW*

A Meissen tureen, cover and stand, the knop in the form of a putto, decorated in 17thC Dutch style in coloured enamels with figures and animals, one handle riveted, marked, late 18thC, 15¼in (38.5cm) wide.
$3,000–3,500 *HOLL*

A Nymphenburg lobed tureen and cover, with scroll handles and sliced lemon knop, decorated in coloured enamels, on scroll-moulded feet picked out in gilt, impressed mark, late 19thC, 11½in (29cm) diam.
$880–960 *DN*

A Sèvres porcelain gilt-bronze-mounted tureen and cover, decorated with exotic birds reserved on a green ground flanked by winged dragon and scroll handles continuing to gilt-bronze dolphin feet, the cover similarly decorated, with mushroom finial, marked, porcelain 18thC, mounts 19thC, 13½in (34.5cm) high.
$12,500–13,500 *S(NY)*

A Worcester, Barr, Flight & Barr dessert tureen and cover, in Japan style, decorated in iron-red, puce, blue and gilt with flowerhead and stiff-leaf bands, impressed marks, c1810, 8¼in (21cm) high.
$950–1,100 *DN*

A Chamberlain's Worcester sauce tureen, cover and stand, with leaf-moulded handles and flower knop, painted in coloured enamels with flowers on a pale yellow ground, within gilt cartouches, on a blue printed leaf and berry ground, marked, c1835, 9in (23cm) wide.
$320–400 *DN*

Vases

A Belleek spill vase, decorated in Cleary pattern, First Period, 1863–90, 5in (12.5cm) high.
$240–320 *MLa*

A Bow porcelain vase and cover, with pierced shoulders and mask-head handles, applied with flowers and painted with insects, the domed cover surmounted by a yellow bird, slight damage, mid-18thC, 12in (30cm) high.
$600–750 *Bea*

A pair of Coalbrookdale porcelain vases, with rustic loop handles, the white ground painted with exotic birds within flower encrusted surrounds, mid-19thC, 9in (23cm) high.
$480–560 *AH*

A Coalport vase, with scroll handles, painted and encrusted with coloured flowers and leaves, the green ground decorated in gilt with flowers and leaves, scroll-moulded foot, painted mark in blue, restored, c1825, 12¼in (31cm) high.
$850–950 *HOLL*

A pair of porcelain two-handled pot pourri vases and covers, of rococo form, probably Coalport factory, enamelled in bold colours with sprays of exotic flowers within yellow and gilt borders and with leaf scroll handles, the pierced covers with leaf finials, each on leaf scroll feet, repairs, c1835, 17¼in (44cm) high.
$1,200–1,500 *CAG*

A pair of Copelands 'jewelled' two-handled vases and covers, each painted with a lady, the reverse with a gilt geometric pattern, between gilt fluting highlighted with gilt seeds, the domed cover with bud finial, some damage and repairs, signed 'S. Alcock', c1895, 10¾in (27.5cm) high.
$3,600–4,200 *S*

Samuel Alcock specialised in delicate figure subjects at Copelands, and examples of his work are always in demand.

r. A pair of Derby 'frill' vases and covers, with pierced arcaded rims, each moulded with 2 female mask handles and applied with flowers and foliage above a basal collar of leaves, the pierced domed flower-encrusted covers with canary finials, some chips, restored and repaired, c1765, 10in (25.5cm) high.
$3,000–3,500 *C*

A pair of Paris porcelain vases, in the Empire style, the gilt scroll side handles with mask terminals, each painted with a panel of flowers and buildings, on a *bleu de roi* ground with gilt flower heads, repaired, printed mark, early 19thC, 12¼in (31cm) high.
$2,400–2,700 *WW*

r. A Royal Doulton vase, hand-decorated with garlands of flowers with gilt embellishments to the shaped rim, scrolled handles, signed 'C. B. Brough', late 19thC, 7½in (19cm) high.
$280–320 *HCC*

A pair of pot pourri vases and covers on stands, by Carl Thieme's factory Potschappel, Dresden, each with scrolled panels joined by encrusted flowers forming a garland the reverse with figural landscape scenes, each with a pierced lid with flower encrusted finial, marked, late 19thC, 23in (58.5cm) high.
$3,500–4,000 *S(NY)*

A pair of baluster vases and covers, by Carl Thieme, Potschappel, painted with hunting scenes, the finials formed as plumed helmets above rolled-up maps, the twin handles as warriors' heads, some damage, late 19thC, 18¼in (46cm) high.
$1,900–2,400 CSK

A pair of Samson porcelain vases, copies of Chelsea, decorated in pink, green, blue and red with peacocks and other birds among foliage, with a pair of scrolled handles, one with restored rim, late 19thC, 11¼in (28.5cm) high.
$360–480 C

A Grainger & Co, Worcester, pot pourri vase, pierced cover and inner cover, printed and painted with flowers and leaves within leaf and flowerhead moulded borders picked out in gilt, on a blush ivory ground, printed mark in green, c1895, 10½in (26.5cm) high.
$950–1,000 DN

A pair of Worcester two-handled pot pourri vases and covers, painted with insects and flowersprays, the female mask handles suspending ribbon-tied flower garlands, the high domed covers pierced and applied with flowers and rose finials, severe damage, c1770.
$4,800–5,500 C

A Worcester, Flight, Barr & Barr spill vase, the blue ground with gilt vermiculi, full script marks, c1820, 4¼in (11cm) high.
$1,900–2,400 MER

A Worcester, Flight, Barr & Barr vase, with pierced cover, decorated with a view of Warwick Castle, restored, full script marks, c1830, 5½in (14cm) high.
$3,200–4,000 MER

A Royal Worcester reticulated two-handled vase, by George Owen, the body with pierced bands of honeycomb and stylised motifs, the neck with gilt angular handles, the whole enriched with gilt seeding and 'jewelled' borders, haircrack in neck, printed and incised marks, c1880, 6¼in (16cm) high.
$4,000–4,800 S

l. A French porcelain vase, with apple green ground and Egyptian revival polychrome painted decoration, mounted as a lamp, c1860, 15½in (39.5cm) high.
$320–400 FBG

r. A porcelain spill vase, with floral decoration, c1825, 4in (10cm) high.
$350–450 DAN

A Royal Worcester spill vase, formed as a hand clutching a Grecian urn, polychrome colouring with jewelled bracelet, c1890, 6in (15cm) high.
$640–720 GAK

Known as 'Mrs Hadley's Hand' and said to be modelled by James Hadley after his wife's hand.

A pair of Royal Worcester spill vases, painted with pink roses on an ivory ground with gilt edging, one signed 'Spilsbury', c1905, 9in (23cm) high.
$960–1,000 AH

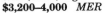

Focus on Belleek

A Belleek thorn sugar basin, First Period, 2¼in (5.5cm) high.
$160–200 *MLa*

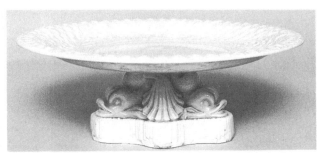

A Belleek comport, the pedestal of dolphins and sea shells, on a serpentine base, First Period, 10½in (26.5cm) diam.
$320–350 *HCC*

A Belleek breakfast cup and saucer, First Period, saucer 6¾in (17cm) diam.
$240–320 *MLa*

A Belleek shell-shaped dessert plate, First Period, 7in (18cm) wide.
$160–240 *MLa*

Belleek Dates

First Period:	1863–90
Second Period:	1891–1926
Third Period:	1926–46
First Green Period:	1946–55
Second Green Period:	1955–65
Third Green Period:	1965–81
First Gold Period:	1981–

A Belleek salt, in the shape of a lily, Second Period, 2¼in (5.5cm) high.
$100–110 *MLa*

A Belleek photograph frame, encrusted with lily of the valley flowers, First Period, 6 x 5in (15 x 12.5cm).
$1,300–1,400 *MLa*

A Belleek cauldron, decorated with shamrocks, Second Period, 5in (12.5cm) high.
$480–560 *MLa*

A Belleek trinket box, decorated with shamrocks, Second Period, 4in (10cm) wide.
$200–240 *MLa*

A Belleek Tridacna muffin dish, Second Period, 9in (23cm) diam.
$800–880 *MLa*

A Belleek limpet coffee cup and saucer, with green tinted and gilt edging, Second Period, saucer 4¼in (10.5cm) diam.
$250–280 *MLa*

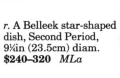

r. A Belleek star-shaped dish, Second Period, 9¼in (23.5cm) diam.
$240–320 *MLa*

A Belleek sycamore leaf dish, Second Period, 5½in (14cm) wide.
$120–160 *MLa*

A Belleek cream jug, decorated with a shell pattern, Second Period, 2¾in (7cm) high.
$160–200 *MLa*

A pair of Belleek Aberdeen jugs, encrusted with flowers, Second Period, 6in (15cm) high.
$880–960 *MLa*

A Belleek bread plate, decorated with a lace pattern, Second Period, 10¼in (26cm) diam.
$560–640 *MLa*

A Belleek rock spill vase, decorated with green shading, Second Period, 5½in (14cm) high.
$350–400 *MLa*

A Belleek dish, modelled as a swan, Second Period, 4in (10cm) high.
$200–240 *MLa*

A Belleek beaker, Second Period, 4½in (11.5cm) high.
$160–240 *MLa*

A Belleek sea horse spill vase, Second Period, 5in (12.5cm) wide.
$480–560 *MLa*

An American Belleek thimble, painted with sprays of roses and forget-me-nots within gilt borders, c1900, ¾in (2cm) high.
$720–800 *CSK*

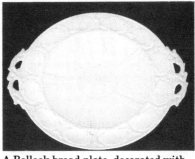

A Belleek bread plate, decorated with shells, Third Period, 10¼in (26cm) wide.
$250–320 *MLa*

A Belleek flying fish spill vase, decorated with green shading, Second Green Period, 5in (12.5cm) high.
$200–270 *MLa*

A Belleek Tridacna kettle, decorated with pink and gilt edging, Second Green Period, 7in (18cm) high.
$440–480 *MLa*

A Belleek trinket box, decorated with shamrocks, Third Period, 4in (10cm) wide.
$160–200 *MLa*

r. A Belleek cream jug and sugar basin, decorated with a shamrock pattern, Second Green Period, 3¾in (9.5cm) high.
$70–90 *MLa*

Chinese Dynasties and Marks

Earlier Dynasties

新石器時代	Neolithic	10th – early 1st millennium BC		唐	Tang Dynasty	AD 618 – 907
商	Shang Dynasty	16th Century – c1050 BC		五代	Five Dynasties	AD 907 – 960
周	Zhou Dynasty	c1050 – 221 BC		遼	Liao Dynasty	AD 907 – 1125
秦	Qin Dynasty	221 – 206 BC		宋	Song Dynasty	AD 960 – 1279
漢	Han Dynasty	206 BC – AD 220		北宋	*Northern Song*	AD 960 – 1127
三國	Three Kingdoms	AD 220 – 265		南宋	*Southern Song*	AD 1127 – 1279
晉	Jin Dynasty	AD 265 – 420		西夏	Xixia Dynasty	AD 1038 – 1227
南北朝	Southern & Northern Dynasties	AD 420 – 589		金	Jin Dynasty	AD 1115 – 1234
隋	Sui Dynasty	AD 581 – 618		元	Yuan Dynasty	AD 1279 – 1368

Ming Dynasty Marks

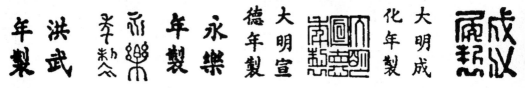

Hongwu	Yongle	Xuande	Chenghua
1368–1398	1403–1424	1426–1435	1465–1487

Hongzhi	Zhengde	Jiajing	Longqing	Wanli	Tianqi	Chongzhen
1488–1505	1506–1521	1522–1566	1567–1572	1573–1620	1621–1627	1628–1644

Qing Dynasty Marks

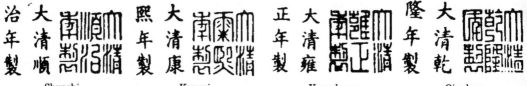

Shunzhi	Kangxi	Yongzheng	Qianlong
1644–1661	1662–1722	1723–1735	1736–1795

Jiaqing	Daoguang	Xianfeng	Tongzhi
1796–1820	1821–1850	1851–1861	1862–1874

Guangxu	Xuantong	Hongxian
1875–1908	1909–1911	1916

CHINESE CERAMICS
Animals

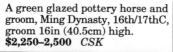

A Yueyao olive glazed model of a recumbent lion, with snarling expression, Song Dynasty, 5in (12.5cm) wide.
$780–850 *CSK*

A pair of figures on horseback, old wear and damaged, Ming Dynasty, 15¾in (40cm) high.
$2,500–2,800 *CSK*

A green glazed pottery horse and groom, Ming Dynasty, 16th/17thC, groom 16in (40.5cm) high.
$2,250–2,500 *CSK*

Two Chinese export models of hounds, Qianlong period, 3in (7.5cm) high.
$1,300–1,600 *Wai*

Two *blanc-de-chine* models of cockerels, small chips, Kangxi period, largest 8¼in (21cm) high.
$4,800–5,600 *C*

A pair of *famille verte* Buddhistic lions, one with a cub, the other with a ball, seated on bases decorated with cartouches and flower sprays, slight damage, 19thC, 17in (43cm) high.
$3,800–4,500 *C*

Bowls

A Kinrande bowl, the interior decorated with a fisherman, Jiajing period, 5in (12.5cm) diam.
$2,250–2,500 *Wai*

Kinrande, named after the Japanese word for gilding, has an iron-red wash on the outside with added gilded decoration.

An Anhua decorated white-glazed stem bowl, the interior decorated in low slip relief with a lotus scroll, Jiajing, 4½in (11.5cm) diam.
$5,600–5,400 *S*

A pale green rice bowl and cream-coloured spoon, Kangxi period, bowl 4¼in (11cm) diam.
$130–140 *SPU*

These items were rescued c1990 from the Chinese trading vessel, Vung Tau, wrecked off the coast of Vietnam in about 1696. The ship was on its way to the Dutch trading post of Jakarta, with a cargo of Chinese items bound for the great houses of Europe.

A blue and white bowl and saucer, from the *Vung Tau* cargo, c1690, bowl 3½in (9cm) diam.
$640–720 *RBA*

A *famille verte* bowl, decorated with panels of beasts on a plain ground, slight damage, Chenghua mark, Kangxi period, 6¼in (16cm) diam.
$600–720 *DN*

Much Kangxi porcelain bears the retrospective six-character mark of the Chenghua period (1465–87). The Kangxi mark often appears on late 19th and early 20thC export wares, especially ginger jars.

A large blue and white fish basin, painted overall with various fish, Kangxi, 21in (53.5cm) diam.
$7,500–8,000 *S*

A blue and white bowl, the exterior decorated with panels of flowers beneath a diaper border, the interior with a central panel of a deer, crane and other longevity symbols, artemisia mark, Kangxi, 10¼in (26cm) diam.
$640–720 *WW*

A *famille rose* Mandarin palette bowl, the exterior decorated with figures at various pursuits in a landscape, the interior with a panel of figures, some damage, Qianlong, 14in (35.5cm) diam.
$1,200–1,300 *WW*

A Chinese export bowl, with floral decoration, hairline crack, 18thC, 9in (23cm) diam.
$350–380 *EL*

A *famille rose* bowl, the exterior decorated with phoenix and flower and leaf sprays, hairline crack to rim, Daoguang seal mark and of the period, 8¼in (21cm) diam.
$1,100–1,300 *WW*

A pair of bowls, decorated with incised dragons under yellow glaze, the interior turquoise, Guangxu mark and of the period, 8in (20cm) diam.
$2,500–2,800 *Wai*

Traditionally, only the Imperial household was allowed to use the colour yellow.

A bowl, the coral ground reserve-decorated with scrolling lotus, the interior glazed white, seal mark and period of Qianlong, 5in (13cm) diam.
$8,800–10,400 *S(HK)*

A Chinese export *famille rose* bowl, c1740, 11in (28cm) diam.
$800–880 *DUB*

When tea and dinner services were imported into Britain in the 18thC, the service would include a table 'washing bowl', which was normally about 11in (28cm) diam. This was for the lady of the house to wash the teabowls at the table, as the porcelain was far too expensive to be left for the servants to wash.

A *doucai* flaring bowl, painted with scrolling branches within bands of *ruyi* heads and stylised foliage, slight damage, Chenghua six-character mark, 18thC, 7½in (19cm) diam.
$750–880 *CSK*

A *famille rose* bowl, with ribbed exterior, painted and gilt with figures, the interior turquoise, iron-red Daoguang seal mark and of the period, 6in (15cm) diam.
$640–720 *CSK*

r. A green enamelled yellow-ground bowl, incised with a pair of dragons, the interior with yellow glaze, Guangxu six-character mark and of the period, 5¾in (14.5cm) diam.
$1,800–2,000 *C(HK)*

A pair of *famille rose* bowls, enamelled in rich tones of pink, yellow, green, blue and white, on a dark pink ground of cherry-red tone, gilt rims, seal mark and period of Qianlong, 4¼in (11cm) diam.
$7,200–8,800 *C(HK)*

A Chinese export porcelain bowl, the exterior with 4 reserves, small edge chip, hairline crack, 18thC, 9in (23cm) diam.
$320–400 *EL*

A blue and white bowl, from the *Diana* cargo, decorated with Starburst pattern, c1816, 5½in (14cm) diam.
$160–200 *DAN*

A Canton *famille rose* punch-bowl painted with shaped panels of figures on terraces, rim chipped, 19thC, 14in (35.5cm) diam.
$1,300–1,600 *C(S)*

Boxes

A seal paste box, painted with roses, c1930, 2in (5cm) diam.
$560–640 *Wai*

A carved box and cover, decorated with radiating vertical lines, the top carved with a lotus spray, Yuan Dynasty, 5in (12.5cm) diam.
$6,000–7,200 *S(HK)*

A *famille rose* covered box, the cover enamelled with a fruiting peach tree with *lingzhi* and flowers, the base with camellia, peony and prunus, late 19thC, 10¼in (26cm) diam.
$1,000–1,100 *RIT*

Brush Pots

A brush pot, painted in iron-red and black with groups of men, gilt highlights, wear to pigments, Kangxi period, 6¾in (17cm) diam, and a wood stand.
$5,000–5,600 *CNY*

A biscuit brush pot, by Chen Guozhi, with carved and moulded chickens gazing at a butterfly, slight chip, 19thC, 5½in (14cm) high.
$2,800–3,200 *S*

Transitional Period

Transitional describes the period between the death of Wanli in 1619 and the accession of the first Qing emperor in 1662.

r. A Transitional blue and white brush pot, painted with 2 scholars admiring the moon and stars, with an attendant carrying lanterns, c1650, 7½in (19cm) high.
$2,800–3,500 *C(HK)*

A blue and white brush pot, decorated with a continuous river landscape, on 3 cloud scroll feet, Kangxi period, 8in (20cm) high.
$2,700–3,000 *DN*

Censers

An iron-red and underglaze blue censer and cover, the cover surmounted by a lion dog, slight damage, late Ming Dynasty, 5½in (14cm) high.
$2,800–3,500 *S*

A *famille rose* tripod censer, decorated on a pink ground with lotus heads, the cover with a lion finial, restored, 19thC, 14½in (37cm) high.
$1,600–2,000 *S(Am)*

A blue and white lobed tripod censer, with S-shaped handles, painted with panels of seated Immortals, Ming Dynasty, 4¼in (11cm) high.
$750–880 *CSK*

r. A blue and white tripod censer, painted with figures in mountainous landscapes, rim chipped, Ming Dynasty, 10in (25.5cm) diam.
$800–880 *CSK*

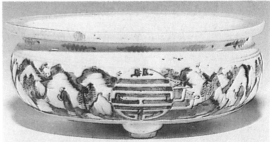

Cups

A stem cup, the exterior covered in a celadon glaze, the interior with underglaze blue decoration, Kangxi period, 3in (7.5cm) diam.
$480–640 *Wai*

A Transitional blue and white stem cup, painted with a bird on a peony branch, insects and a butterfly, with an incised foliate band below the rim, c1650, 5¼in (13.5cm) high.
$6,200–7,200 *C*

A *famille rose* tea bowl and saucer, 18thC, saucer 4½in (11.5cm) diam.
$620–720 *DAN*

A tea bowl and saucer, with a marriage cipher, hairline crack, 18thC, saucer 4¼in (11cm) diam.
$400–560 *DAN*

These are probably part of a service ordered specifically for use at a wedding.

A tea bowl and saucer, decorated in orange and blue with a country house scene, c1790, saucer 5½in (14cm) diam.
$240–320 *DAN*

A blue and white tea bowl and saucer, from the *Nanking* cargo, c1750, saucer 4¾in (12cm) diam.
$150–200 *DAN*

r. A gilt-decorated cup, decorated with scrolls and peony sprays, bats and *shou* characters, on a blue ground, the interior and base glazed turquoise, iron-red seal mark and period of Jiaqing, 3¼in (8.5cm) diam.
$22,000–22,500 *S(HK)*

Figures

A pottery figure of a lady, with traces of orange and white pigment, the head detachable, Han Dynasty, 29½in (75cm) high.
$2,400–2,500 *S(Am)*

A red-painted pottery figure of a guardian, remains of black, grey and brown pigment over white slip, slight damage, Tang Dynasty, 22¾in (58cm) high.
$10,500–12,800 *S(NY)*

Although guardian figures are common, it is unusual to find one with such expressive facial features and wearing this type of helmet.

A red-painted pottery figure of a court lady, her robe slit at the sides to show pointed shoes, the hair, belt and further details picked out in black, some restoration, Tang Dynasty, 12¾in (32.5cm) high.
$11,200–12,200 *S(NY)*

A Yingqing glazed standing figure, the arms, eyes and hair unglazed, slight damage, Song/Yuan Dynasty, glaze crackled, 8in (20cm) high.
$560–640 *CSK*

A pair of green and ochre glazed models of attendants, traces of red and black pigment, Ming Dynasty, largest 19½in (49.5cm) high.
$1,600–1,800 *CSK*

A *blanc de chine* figure of Guanyin, 17thC, 20in (51cm) high.
$2,000–2,250 *Wai*

A *blanc de chine* figure of Guanyin, holding a *ruyi* sceptre, a boy attendant at her side, slight damage, Qing Dynasty, 10½in (26.5cm) high.
$600–720 *S(S)*

A *blanc de chine* model of Guanyin, standing beside a deer on a rockwork base, slight restoration, 18thC, 8in (20cm) high.
$2,000–2,400 *CSK*

A *blanc de chine* figure of Guanyin, standing on a swirling base, marked, 18thC, 16in (40.5cm) high.
$5,500–6,000 *S(NY)*

Blanc de Chine

Blanc de chine is a white, or near white, porcelain with a thick, rich glaze. It was used in the Dehua area of China from the late Ming Dynasty, particularly in the manufacture of figures for export during the 17thC and 18thC.

A *blanc de chine* figure of Budai Heshang, laughing, holding prayer beads in his left hand, and a flask in his right, small chip, 18th/19thC, 6½in (16.5cm) high.
$2,800–3,200 *CNY*

A *blanc de chine* figure of the Virgin Mary, holding a child in her arms, on a cloud scroll base, 18thC, 14¼in (36cm) high.
$2,500–2,800 *CSK*

Two *famille rose* figures of dignitaries, holding a *ruyi* sceptre and a peach spray, slight damage and restoration, Jiaqing period, 9¼in (23.5cm) high.
$1,100–1,200 *CSK*

A *blanc de chine* figure of Budai, holding a peach in one hand, surrounded by 5 boys, restored, 19thC, 10¼in (26cm) high.
$4,500–5,000 *C(HK)*

A *blanc de chine* figure of Wenshu, seated on the back of a Buddhistic lion, restored, marked, 18th/19thC, 15½in (39.5cm) high.
$5,000–5,600 *CNY*

l. A pair of *blanc de chine* figures, one modelled as Guanyin seated cross-legged on a lotus petal base, the other as an emaciated Immortal carrying a basket of fish, slight damage, 18th/19thC, 13in (33cm) high.
$5,000–5,600 *CSK*

Flatware

A celadon saucer, carved with a recumbent ox gazing at the moon, within a foliate quatrefoil, under an olive glaze, Jin Dynasty, 7in (18cm) diam.
$8,500–9,000 *S(NY)*

An octagonal dish, carved and moulded in the centre with a peony spray, the exterior lightly carved with leaves, with pale celadon glaze, slight wear, Ming Dynasty, 15thC, 13½in (34.5cm) diam.
$5,000–5,600 *S(HK)*

A *kraak porselein* blue and white charger, decorated with birds, fruits and flowers, restored, Wanli period, 18½in (47cm) diam.
$1,200–1,300 *S(Am)*

A Swatow dish, painted in white slip on a light blue ground with flowers and leaves, the well with 4 floral motifs with a floral scroll, Ming Dynasty, 16thC, 15¾in (40cm) diam.
$3,800–4,000 *S*

A Swatow dish, painted in blue and white with phoenix and foliage within a border of scattered flowers, slight damage, 16thC, 11in (28cm) diam.
$480–560 *CSK*

A set of 6 Chinese export blue and white dishes, Kangxi period, 5in (12.5cm) diam.
$1,100–1,300 *Wai*

A blue and white saucer-dish, the interior painted with a five-clawed dragon, the reverse with 2 similar striding dragons, Qianlong seal mark and of the period, 6½in (16.5cm) diam.
$4,800–5,600 *C(HK)*

A *famille rose* export armorial plate, painted and gilt with panels depicting a European village scene, the rim with a floral crest and inscription, slight damage and restoration, Qianlong period, 9in (23cm) diam.
$640–720 *CSK*

A *rose verte* charger, enamelled with a coat-of-arms and inscribed 'Uytrecht', restored, Yongzheng period, 19in (48.5cm) diam.
$7,500–8,800 *S*

Chinese Export Wares

During the reign of the Emperor Qianlong (1736–95), vast quantities of porcelain were shipped to Europe and America. For the most part these wares were painted not with traditional Chinese designs but with motifs requested by the shippers and their clients – Biblical scenes, coats-of-arms, commemorative images with inscriptions, and so on. Most pieces were underglaze blue, but a substantial quantity were decorated in coloured enamels dominated by a distinctive rose-pink – the *famille rose* palette, or *en grisaille* (monochrome). Increasingly, European shapes were copied.

A pair of *famille rose* European subject plates, enamelled in the centre with a man seated at a table and a beer barrel, Qianlong period, 9in (23cm) diam.
$3,800–4,000 *C*

A *famille rose* fluted dish, the centre painted with a lakeside pavilion beside fruit trees in a fenced garden, within bands of peony and bamboo, Qianlong period, 12½in (32cm) diam.
$700–800 *S(S)*

A *Nanking* cargo dish, with rosette and keyhole border, the centre decorated with a scene of pagodas and a figure on a bridge, 18thC, 16½in (42cm) wide.
$380–430 *GAK*

A blue and white *shou* character dish, with the 8 Daoist emblems, Jiaqing mark and of the period, 5½in (14cm) diam.
$800–1,000 *Wai*

These emblems are the attributes of the 8 Immortals, which often appear on Qing Imperial porcelain. They are the Fan, the Sword, the Gourd, the Castanets, the Flower basket, the Bamboo tubes and rods (a kind of drum), the Flute and the Lotus.

A blue and white Nanking plate, c1760, 13½in (34.5cm) diam.
$560–640 *Wai*

Currently known as Nanjing, Nanking was the port on the Yangzi river from where the porcelain was shipped. It was not made in Nanjing, but in Jingdezhen. Nanking refers to a particular type of export porcelain, and is the type that was found on the Nanking *cargo ship. This plate is not from the Nanking cargo.*

A Chinese export *famille rose* dish, the centre decorated with a seated figure and attendants, with a gilt highlighted border of floral sprigs, 18thC, 13½in (34.5cm) wide.
$1,500–1,600 *CNY*

A pair of *famille rose* leaf-shaped dishes, painted and gilt with cartouches of European figures, slight chip, c1800, 8½in (21.5cm) long.
$680–750 *CSK*

l. A pair of saucer dishes, one decorated with plum blossom, the other with apple blossom, both signed by Tian Hexian, c1930, 5½in (14cm) diam.
$1,600–2,000 *Wai*

A Nanking platter, decorated in blue with a river scene, c1760, 13in (33cm) wide.
$250–280 *BRU*

A Ming blue and white saucer dish, the exterior painted with a frieze of boys at play, the interior with similar theme, slight damage, Jiajing six-character mark and of the period, 5¾in (14.5cm) diam.
$7,000–7,800 *C(HK)*

A dish from the *Diana* cargo, decorated with Starburst pattern, c1816, 11in (28cm) diam.
$200–240 *DAN*

A Rose Medallion platter, painted in *famille rose* palette with cartouches, c1840, 18in (45.5cm) diam.
$950–1,000 *EL*

'Rose Medallion' is a type of pattern, popular in the USA throughout the 19thC.

Garden Seats

A reticulated garden seat, the top carved with a roundel of a floral spray, the tapering sides pierced to simulate basketwork, covered with a translucent pale celadon coloured crackled glaze, Ming Dynasty, 16thC, 15¾in (40cm) high.
$4,500–5,000 *S(HK)*

It is unusual to find a celadon garden seat in the form of a wickerwork stool.

A blue and white garden seat, painted with a continuous leafy lotus scroll in early Ming style, 18thC, 7½in (19cm) high.
$3,800–4,200 *S(NY)*

A pair of *famille rose* barrel-shaped garden seats, with phoenix, birds, cranes and flower decoration, 19thC, 19in (48.5cm) high.
$3,200–3,500 *EL*

The pierced work on the side of these seats is based upon the design of Chinese cash coins.

l. A blue and white hexagonal garden seat, with foliate decoration, late 19thC, 18½in (47cm) high.
$750–800 *DA*

A pair of Cantonese hexagonal garden seats, 19thC, 24in (61cm) high.
$4,000–4,400 *GAZE*

A pair of *famille rose* barrel-shaped garden seats, the panels enamelled with birds, on a flower-decorated ground, the top and sides with pierced 'cash' decoration, late Qing Dynasty, 18¼in (46.5cm) high.
$1,600–2,000 *CNY*

A pair of *famille rose* barrel-shaped garden seats, decorated with *shou* characters on a yellow ground with enamelled peach sprays and bats, late Qing Dynasty, 18¼in (47cm) high.
$850–1,000 *CNY*

Jardinières

A *famille verte* jardinière, decorated in iron-red with a broad band of scrolling, leafy stems, with drainage hole in base, minor damage, Kangxi period, 20¾in (52.5cm) diam.
$5,000–5,600 *CNY*

A blue and white jardinière, with everted rim, decorated with figures in a mountainous river landscape, marked, Kangxi period, 7¼in (18.5cm) diam.
$2,800–3,200 *S(Am)*

l. A Chinese blue and white jardinière, with everted rim, painted with birds perched on rockwork among peonies and bamboo, Daoguang seal mark and of the period, 10in (25.5cm) wide.
$2,800–3,200 *CSK*

A *famille rose* reticulated hexagonal jardinière, painted with roundels of flowers and river landscapes, damaged, Yongzheng, 7½in (19cm) high.
$950–1,000 *CSK*

Jars

A *sancai* moulded tripod jar, on cabriole legs with paw feet, splashed with straw, chestnut and green glaze over buff, some repainting, Tang Dynasty, 5in (12.5cm) high.
$2,400–2,800 *S(NY)*

A Chinese export *famille rose* ginger jar, cover damaged and repaired, Yongzheng period, 8in (20cm) high.
$1,100–1,300 *Wai*

A blue and white *Vung Tau* cargo jar and lid, containing a pebble from the sea-bed, c1690, 7¼in (18.5cm) high.
$2,200–2,400 *SPU*

Kendi

A blue and white *kendi*, painted with scrolling lotus flowers and foliage, below a band of stiff leaves, the shoulder with stylised foliate bands, slight damage, Ming Dynasty, 6¼in (16cm) high.
$1,600–1,800 *CSK*

An Annamese polychrome *kendi*, decorated in underglaze blue, iron-red and green enamels with mythical beasts amidst fire and cloud scrolls, restored, 16thC, 8in (20cm) wide.
$3,200–4,000 *C*

A *famille rose kendi*, painted with a broad band of scrolling peonies below a lappet collar of flowers and within bands of stiff leaves, the neck and spout with entwined lotus and peonies, 18thC, 8in (20cm) high.
$1,000–1,100 *CSK*

Kendi

Probably originating in India, Kendi are globular-shaped drinking vessels. They are filled through the neck and the liquid is drunk through the spout.

Jugs

An ewer, carved with peony blossoms above a lotus petal border, covered with a green glaze with dark brown splashes, the glaze burning to a rusty orange around the foot, Ming Dynasty, 6¼in (16cm) high.
$7,000–8,000 *S(HK)*

A Chinese clobbered jug and domed cover, painted and gilt with tables, jardinières and censers in gardens, handle restored, porcelain 18thC, 10in (25.5cm) high.
$400–440 *CSK*

Clobbered is the term given to Chinese export blue and white ceramics which have had enamel decoration added in Europe, usually in Holland.

A Chinese blue and white barrel-shaped cider jug and cover, with Buddhistic lion finial, painted with fishermen and pavilions in a rocky river landscape, damaged, 18thC, 11¼in (28.5cm) high.
$1,400–1,600 *CSK*

Mugs

A Chinese Imari mug, decorated in underglaze blue, red and gilt with peonies and chrysanthemums within diaper borders, Kangxi period, 5¾in (14.5cm) high.
$380–480 *HYD*

A Chinese export blue and white mug, painted in underglaze blue with chrysanthemums and peonies beneath a cloud scroll border, Kangxi period, 5¼in (13.5cm) high.
$800–880 *HYD*

A Chinese export porcelain mug, with underglaze blue and polychrome figural decoration, repaired, 18thC, 5½in (14cm) high.
$240–280 *EL*

Snuff Bottles

A porcelain snuff bottle, decorated in iron-red over yellow enamel with 5 bats round a *shou* medallion on each side, the neck and shoulders in blue and white with a brocade pattern, Qianlong mark and of the period, 2¼in (55mm) high.
$800–880 *S(NY)*

A *famille rose* porcelain snuff bottle, moulded and highlighted in bright colours with iron-red and gilding with the 18 Lohan, Qianlong four-character seal mark, 3in (75mm) high.
$840–960 *S*

Lohan is the term for priests.

A porcelain double snuff bottle, decorated with birds and dogs, Daoguang two-character mark, 2in (50mm) high.
$80–90 *POA*

A moulded porcelain snuff bottle, in the form of a corn on the cob, on a circular footrim, covered overall in blue, Daoguang period, 2¾in (70mm) high.
$400–480 *S(NY)*

l. A Chinese porcelain blue and white snuff bottle, with carved dragon decoration on white ground, inscribed seal mark, 19thC, 3in (75mm) high.
$540–640 *LHA*

Teapots

A *famille verte* barrel-shaped teapot and cover, with bands of studs and Buddhistic lion finial, painted and gilt with a phoenix among peonies and rockwork and a mandarin duck among lotus, the cover with entwined flowers and foliage, metal handle, Kangxi, 4½in (11.5cm) high.
$320–400 *CSK*

r. A Yixing teapot, with gold mounts, 18thC, 2½in (65mm) high.
$1,400–1,600 *Wai*

The Intellectuals or Scholar class would hold the lid with their hand and drink from the spout of the teapot.

A Chinese teapot, with English floral decoration, c1750, 5in (12.5cm) wide.
$640–800 *DAN*

A Chinese export porcelain drum-shaped teapot, decorated in blue, white and gilt, monogrammed, 18thC, 6in (15cm) high.
$240–280 *EL*

Tureens

A *famille verte* tureen and cover, with butterfly-shaped handles, painted and gilt with chrysanthemum sprays, the interior with a cluster of peonies, damaged and repaired, Kangxi period, 4¾in (12cm) wide.
$2,500–2,800 *CSK*

A tureen and cover, decorated with a lady and boys fishing, flanked by flowers, the handles in the form of rabbits, slight damage, Qianlong period, 13¾in (35cm) wide.
$4,000–4,400 *S*

A Chinese blue and white tureen and domed cover, the handles modelled as masks with feathered headdresses, the tureen painted with pomegranates and flowers, Qianlong period, 14¼in (36cm) wide.
$3,200–4,000 *CSK*

A Chinese export blue and white porcelain tureen, with gilt decoration and monogrammed armorial-type shields, 18thC, 14½in (37cm) wide.
$1,800–2,000 *EL*

A Chinese blue and white lobed tureen and cover, with pierced finial and boars' head handles, painted with lotus flowers and foliage within whorl pattern borders, cover restored, 18thC, 11¼in (28.5cm) wide.
$1,300–1,400 *CSK*

A Chinese blue and white tureen and domed cover, with fruit spray finial and hare's head handles, painted with stags in river landscapes, the cover with peonies, 18thC, 11¾in (30cm) wide.
$750–800 *CSK*

Vases

A pair of vases, with angular handles, moulded with characters, prunus, rockwork and cloud scrolls, damaged, Ming Dynasty, 12½in (32cm) high.
$900–1,000 *CSK*

Two Chinese blue and white vases, decorated with figures in landscapes, 19thC, 12½in (32cm) high.
$280–320 each *BRU*

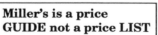

Miller's is a price
GUIDE not a price LIST

r. A blue and white vase, decorated in the Ming style, Qianlong period, 13in (33cm) high.
$2,500–2,800 *Wai*

l. A pair of Chinese porcelain vases and covers, of archaistic bronze form, the sides decorated with panels of figures and flowering branches, the neck and foot with panels of antiques, finials missing, damaged, Kangxi period, 15in (38cm) high.
$7,200–8,000 *DN*

A Chinese *famille rose* porcelain vase, moulded with vases of flowers on a white ground, Qing Dynasty, 23in (58.5cm) high.
$440–540 *SLN*

l. A pair of Chinese *famille rose* vases, decorated with birds and flowers on a yellow ground, c1920, now mounted as lamps, 17in (43cm) high.
$780–820 *RIT*

JAPANESE CERAMICS

Japanese Chronology Chart

Jomon period (Neolithic)	circa 10,000 – circa 200 BC	Muromachi (Ashikaga) period	1333 – 1573
Yayoi period	circa 200 BC – circa 200 AD	Momoyama period	1573 – 1614
Tumulus (Kofun) period	200 – 552	Edo (Tokugawa) period	1614 – 1868
Asuka period	552 – 645	Meiji period	1868 – 1911
Nara period	645 – 794	Taisho period	1912 – 1926
Heian period	794 – 1185	Showa period	1926 –
Kamakura period	1185 – 1333		

Animals

A Japanese model of a piebald rabbit, with ears pricked, slight damage, 18thC, 3½in (9cm) high.
$1,200–1,300 *CSK*

Bottles

An Arita model of a cockerel, perched on a rockwork base applied with flowers and fungus, painted in underglaze blue, iron-red, enamels and gilt, restored, early 18thC, 9¾in (25cm) high.
$5,000–5,600 *S*

A Kutani porcelain jar and cover modelled in the form of a brown and white cat, wearing a brocade collar, with a kitten, signed 'Kanzan', Meiji period, 9¼in (23.5cm) high.
$3,200–3,500 *S(S)*

A Japanese earthenware bottle, in the form of a pilgrim's flask, decorated in enamels and gilt, gilt rubbed, late 19thC, 5in (12.5cm) high.
$2,500–2,800 *S(NY)*

An Imari blue and white sake bottle, painted with chrysanthemum and peony sprays restored, early 18thC, 8¾in (22cm) high.
$1,300–1,400 *CSK*

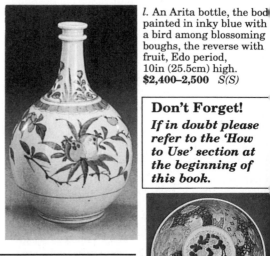

l. An Arita bottle, the body painted in inky blue with a bird among blossoming boughs, the reverse with fruit, Edo period, 10in (25.5cm) high.
$2,400–2,500 *S(S)*

Don't Forget!

If in doubt please refer to the 'How to Use' section at the beginning of this book.

Bowls

A Satsuma bowl and cover, decorated with flora in relief, c1860, 4½in (11.5cm) diam.
$2,200–2,500 *MER*

A Ninsei teabowl, decorated with panels imitating cloth, late 18th/early 19thC, 4¾in (12cm) diam.
$14,000–15,000 *C*

A floriform earthenware punchbowl, with a dragon in the central roundel, the exterior enamelled with flowers and similar decoration, Meiji period, 8¼in (21cm) diam.
$1,300–1,600 *CNY*

An Imari bowl, painted with a central floral panel within radiating panels incorporating trellis, floral scrolls, panels of prunus, pine and bamboo, dragons and landscapes repeated on the exterior, Meiji mark and of the period, 14in (35.5cm) wide.
$1,100–1,200 *S(S)*

A Japanese porcelain fishbowl, with painted hawk and tiger decoration and blue and white floral landscape motif, late 19thC, 24in (61cm) diam.
$480–640 *LHA*

An earthenware teabowl, decorated in enamels and gilt, the interior with scattered butterflies and chrysanthemums, the exterior with butterflies in flight on a ground of gilt lattice, signed 'Shizan', late 19thC, 5¼in (13cm) diam.
$6,000–6,500 *S(NY)*

An earthenware bowl, the exterior decorated with figures with floral medallions around the foot, the interior centred with a chrysanthemum among butterflies, signed 'Yabu Meizan', c1905, 3¼in (8cm) diam.
$3,500–4,000 *S(NY)*

Censers

A Satsuma earthenware censer, decorated in iron-red, blue and turquoise enamels and gilt with a *ho-o* bird among chrysanthemum and paulownia, with a silver pierced cover, signed 'Ippo Zo', 19thC, 5½in (14cm) diam.
$3,000–3,200 *S(NY)*

A Satsuma earthenware censer, decorated in iron-red, blue, turquoise and black enamels and gilt, with a silver metal wire-form cover, signed by 'Satsuma Yaki', 19thC, 5in (12.5cm) diam.
$3,200–3,500 *S(NY)*

A Kakiemon style censer, with ormolu mounts, late Meiji period, 4in (10cm) diam.
$1,400–1,600 *Wai*

Figures

A Satsuma earthenware figure of a small boy, seated holding a glove puppet of a dog with both hands, his robe painted in enamels and gilt with scattered clouds and formal designs, early Meiji period, 9½in (24cm) high.
$2,800–3,200 *S*

An Imari model of a *bijin*, wearing flowing robes and holding a bunch of flowers in her right hand, hair damaged, c1700, 6½in (16.5cm) high.
$480–560 *CSK*

Flatware

A Kakiemon dish, with blue and white floral and bamboo decoration, Edo period, 8in (20.5cm) diam.
$1,300–1,600 *Wai*

A blue and white porcelain charger, the interior decorated with a mountainous landscape, the exterior with insects among flowers, 18thC, 17¾in (45cm) diam.
$3,200–3,500 *S(NY)*

An Imari porcelain charger, painted with 4 reserves of figures and birds in 4 colours and gilt, 19thC, 18½in (47cm) diam.
$520–560 *RBB*

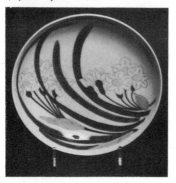

A Nabeshima saucer-dish, decorated with the Narcissus pattern, Meiji period, 8in (20.5cm) diam.
$2,000–2,400 *Wai*

Nabeshima was the most famous kiln in Japan. They produced some of the first porcelain ever made in the world. 18thC examples can fetch up to £200,000.

An Imari porcelain saucer dish decorated with central wheel motif and flanked with floral panels, c1880, 12in (30.5cm) diam.
$270–300 *BRU*

An Imari charger, with a dragon on blue ground, the central plaque with an Oriental lady holding a fan, blue and white decoration on reverse, 19thC, 18½in (47cm) diam.
$840–940 *WeH*

Satsuma Wares

To a Japanese, the term 'Satsuma' refers to the output of kilns located in and around Nayeshirogawa, which were first established by Korean potters in the early 17thC. Famous for their tea ceremony wares, these kilns flourished until 1868 when political turmoil, loss of patronage and a disastrous fire all contributed to their demise. In 1875 the official kiln of Tauno, Satsuma, was reorganised as a modern industrial company. Amongst their output they developed a highly decorated white ware which proved popular in the West and has become known in England as Satsuma ware. It is light, porous earthenware of a soft, crackled, cream colour profusely decorated with enamels, and although some was made at Satsuma, the majority was produced in Kyoto, Kobe or Tokyo.

A Satsuma earthenware dish, by Kyoto Shoun, painted with figures near the temple at Nikko in the autumn, the angled rim with flowers, Meiji period, 9¼in (23.5cm) long.
$3,800–3,500 *S*

A Satsuma dish, decorated in various coloured enamels and gilt with a *ho-o* bird among clouds and foliage, the rim with a repeating foliate motif, signed, late 19thC, 12¾in (32cm) diam.
$2,400–2,500 *C*

A pair of Imari chargers, decorated with a scroll shaped panel of birds, flowering branches and rockwork, on an emblem and flower panelled ground, late 19thC, 21in (53cm) diam.
$1,000–1,200 *HOLL*

Jars

A Satsuma jar, with cover and mythical dragon finial, c1880, 23in (58.5cm) high.
$1,100–1,300 *ALB*

An Arita clobbered jar, the shouldered sides painted with peonies and rocks beneath a band of shell and flowerhead motifs, the neck with foliate scrolls, overpainted and gilt in iron-red, green, pink and yellow, Edo period, 19in (48cm) high.
$2,400–2,500 *S(S)*

A Satsuma earthenware jar and cover, by Seikozan, painted in enamels and gilding with a continuous band of chrysanthemums and hedges, signed, Meiji period, 5¼in (13.5cm) high.
$4,000–4,800 *S*

An earthenware jar and cover, decorated in coloured enamels and gilt with a band depicting assorted tea articles and writing implements, reserved on a cobalt blue ground with scattered flying geese, gilt rubbed, signed 'Kyoto Kinkozan Zo Sozan', late 19thC, 5in (12.5cm) high.
$3,400–3,800 *S(NY)*

Jugs & Ewers

Two Arita blue and white ewers and covers, one body decorated with tree peonies, the cover with a phoenix, a flowerhead and scrolling foliage, the other similarly decorated with a mountainous water landscape, damaged, late 17thC, largest 8½in (21.5cm) wide.
$4,500–4,800 *C*

An Arita blue and white jug, with loop handle and pinched spout, painted with a band of birds and butterflies among flowers issuing from rockwork, restored, c1700, 7¾in (19.5cm) high.
$550–650 *CSK*

An earthenware miniature ewer, decorated in coloured enamels and gilt with cherry blossoms encircling the shoulder, panels of flowers surrounding the waist, restored, signed 'Yabu Meizan', c1905, 3½in (9cm) high.
$5,600–6,200 *S(NY)*

Koros

A koro and cover, painted and gilt with a coiled dragon above foaming waves, the sides with floral medallions, signed 'Kinkozan zo', late 19thC, 2in (5cm) high.
$320–350 *CSK*

A Satsuma earthenware koro and cover, painted with a panel of peonies, chrysanthemums and dianthus among clouds, supported on 3 bracket feet, the cover pierced and surmounted by a bud finial, 19thC, 7in (18cm) high, with wooden stand.
$5,600–6,200 *S(S)*

A Satsuma koro and cover, on 3 elephant-head feet, decorated in enamels and gilt with panels of warriors, ladies, birds and flowers, some damage, Meiji period, 36½in (93cm) high.
$5,600–6,000 *S*

Vases

A Bizen *ikebana* vase, reddish brown to one side, the other with a yellow and light brown glaze, with 2 lug handles, marked, mid-Edo period, 9¼in (23.5cm) high.
$2,200–2,500 *C*

A pair of Japanese lacquered ceramic vases, c1820, 24in (61cm) high.
$1,600–2,000 *SSW*

> **Cross Reference**
> Colour Review

A pair of Arita blue and white vases, decorated with landscapes, c1880, 16in (40.5cm) high.
$400–480 *BRU*

A pair of Kutani vases, decorated with female figures and flowers, c1880, 18in (45.5cm) high.
$720–800 *BRU*

A Kinkozan earthenware vase, decorated with scenes of *geisha* and *samurai* in a garden, between brocade borders, the neck with landscape border, signed and marked, 19thC, 12¼in (31cm) high.
$9,600–10,400 *S(Am)*

A Satsuma bud vase, with 5 cylindrical spouts, encircled with pointed lappet collars, decorated in iron-red, blue turquoise and white enamels and gilt with chrysanthemums, signed 'Satsuma Yaki', 19thC, 6½in (16.5cm) high.
$5,000–5,600 *S(NY)*

A Satsuma miniature vase, decorated with figures to lower body and neck, with diaper bands, black seal mark, c1900, 3¾in (9.5cm) high.
$1,400–1,800 *MER*

A pair of Satsuma vases, decorated with panels of figures, c1900, 9¼in (23.5cm) high.
$220–250 *PCh*

A Satsuma vase, decorated with 4 fan-shaped panels, one of a *shishi*, 2 with vases of flowers and another with a phoenix, on a diaper ground, slight damage, Meiji period, 9⅞in (25cm) high.
$1,600–1,800 *WW*

A Satsuma vase, painted with a landscape and figural panels, marked, Meiji period, 12in (30.5cm) high.
$4,500–5,000 *GOR(B)*

A Satsuma double gourd vase, decorated with figures and gilt, c1890, 4in (10cm) high.
$1,600–2,000 *MER*

A porcelain vase, by Makuzu Kozan, painted in underglaze blue, highlighted in transparent enamels and gilt, c1930, 11¼in (28.5cm) high.
$3,800–4,400 *S*

GLASS

Why are so many people fascinated by antique glass? Perhaps it has to do with the way glass reflects the light, or perhaps the fact that a material which appears so fragile and ephemeral is in reality so enduring. Whatever the reason, glass has been collected since before Roman times and is still highly popular with collectors today.

Eighteenth century wine glasses have always been popular with British collectors and that market remains strong: unexceptional examples have maintained their price while rarer pieces have risen in value. Recently there has been more activity at the top end of the market, and buyers with spending power are facing increased competition in their search for new pieces.

Interest in 19th century glass is also growing. Recent exhibitions in Manchester and London have helped raised awareness of the high-quality glass made by James Powell & Sons at the Whitefriars Glass Works in London, but the fine quality of other contemporary glass has not been ignored, and Victorian engraved glass in particular is becoming increasingly popular. The engraving is generally less restrained than that found on 18th century glass, and the surfaces of jugs, goblets and vases may be covered with intricate detail. Even acid-etched pieces, once despised, are now desirable as collectors have discovered some of the finer pieces with freehand line work and polishing rather than the most common mass-produced geometric designs.

Coloured Victorian glass is now appreciated much more than it was a few years ago, and prices have risen accordingly. By the mid-19th century, glass makers were producing every colour imaginable, and those collectors who had the foresight to begin buying such glasses a few years ago now have displays that can only be described as kaleidoscopic.

If you want to build a collection it is wise to develop a relationship with an established dealer who is likely to offer advice based on experience. He can also advise you about buying at auction, another important source, or may bid for you.

On the whole, it appears that the market in glass is looking up. However, no-one should buy with a view to making a quick profit. Such profit may come in time, but the real value of a glass lies in how much it means to you. Buy what you like and the best you can afford; one good example is always going to be more satisfactory than many poor ones.

But be warned, glass collecting is an obsession. One fine example will in time become two and then three, and before you know it you will be seeking some way of displaying your collection more effectively in order to share its appeal with others. By then you might even be part way to providing an answer to my opening question, but you will probably be more interested in finding your next glass.

Brian Watson

Bottles, Decanters & Flasks

l. A mallet-shaped green glass decanter, with a gilt label, c1790, 9in (23cm) high.
$280–320 *CB*

A glass ale decanter, the neck with 3 rings, engraved with hops and barley, c1790, 10¼in (26cm) high.
$720–800 *BrW*

A tapered glass decanter, engraved 'W Wine', with a cartouche containing a hatched rose and fruiting vine, and a lozenge stopper, c1780, 9¾in (25cm) high.
$1,200–1,300 *Som*

r. A central European Masonic glass flask, enamelled with instruments in a basket, the shoulders with dash decoration, slight wear, dated '1791', 4¼in (10.5cm) high.
$1,600–2,000 *C*

A blue glass mallet-shaped brandy decanter, with gilt decoration and a lozenge stopper, c1790, 10in (25.5cm) high.
$280–320 *CB*

A Cork Glass Co
engraved decanter
and stopper,
decorated with hatch
pattern and stars
within a band of loops,
the lower part and
base with hammered
flutes, with a moulded
bull's-eye stopper,
stopper chipped,
marked, early 19thC,
10¼in (26cm) high.
$820–900 *C*

An Anglo-Irish mould-
blown and cut-glass
decanter, with 3 milled
neck rings, c1800,
9¾in (25cm) high.
$520–580 *BrW*

r. Two blue glass spirit
bottles, with wrythen-
moulded decoration,
c1840, tallest
12¼in (31cm) high.
$350–380 each *Som*

Two wrythen spirit bottles,
one amber, one blue, c1830,
10½in (26.5cm) high.
$480–520 *FD*

A red glass carafe,
c1850, 9½in (24cm) high.
$520–600 *MJW*

A green glass serving
bottle, with a silver
mount, c1830,
14in (35.5cm) high.
$420–480 *CB*

Don't Forget!
*If in doubt
please refer
to the 'How to
Use' section at
the beginning
of this book.*

A green glass decanter,
with single neck ring
and spire stopper, c1840,
13¼in (34cm) high.
$440–480 *BrW*

A Baccarat glass flask,
cut with arches beneath
a faceted neck and string
rim, enclosing a double
sulphide portrait of Helen
of Troy and Aeneas and
another of Madame de
Sévigné, slight damage,
c1840, 8¼in (21cm) high.
$520–600 *C*

An amber glass
decanter, with a
single neck ring
and spire stopper, c1840,
14½in (36.5cm) high.
$760–860 *MJW*

A cobalt blue glass
bottle, engraved with
vine leaves, c1860,
10in (25.5cm) high.
$280–320 *Har*

An amber glass miniature globe and shaft decanter and 4 champagne glasses, c1870, decanter 1¾in (4.5cm) high.
$130–140 *BrW*

A glass decanter, with spire stopper, c1860, 13in (33cm) high.
$900–1,000 *MJW*

A Victorian green glass decanter, with concave sides and floral engraving, silver mounts, Chester 1898, 9½in (24cm) high.
$350–380 *L*

Locate the Source

The source of each illustration in Miller's can be found by checking the code letters below each caption with the Key to Illustrations.

Bowls

A glass patty pan, with folded rim, c1800, 3in (7.5cm) diam.
$55–60 *BrW*

A Sowerby pressed glass caramel-coloured two-handled bowl, c1880, 3½in (9cm) wide.
$160–180 *MJW*

A vaseline glass bonbon dish, with fluted edge and silver-plated holder, c1890, 6in (15cm) diam.
$280–320 *ARE*

l. An Irish glass fruit bowl, with turnover rim cut with geometric slices, the body cut with a band of alternate prisms, on a knopped stem and square domed lemon squeezer foot, c1800, 9¼in (23.5cm) diam.
$1,300–1,500 *Som*

A hexagonal cut glass dish, the diamond-cut body with crenellated rim and star-cut base, c1800, 8¾in (22cm) wide.
$350–400 *Som*

Drinking Glasses
Beakers & Tumblers

An armorial beaker, enamelled in ochre, blue, pale blue, brown and white with a coat-of-arms surmounted by a crest, the lower part and the base gadrooned, possibly Bohemian or Brandenburg, restored, dated '1696', 3¼in (8.5cm) high.
$190–220 *C*

A Venetian *latticinio* tumbler, in *vetro a reticello*, late 17th/18thC, 3½in (9cm) high.
$1,600–1,800 *C*

The term vetro a reticello *means criss-cross or network pattern.*

A barrel-shaped tumbler, with Lynn rings, c1770, 3½in (9cm) high.
$320–360 *BrW*

Lynn glass was made during the late 18th and early 19thC, and is recognised by horizontal grooved rings around the bowls or bodies of vessels. Every type of vessel was made, from wine glasses and tumblers to jugs, decanters and bowls. Lynn glass was believed to have been made at Kings Lynn, although many examples have been found in Norfolk.

A naval commemorative tumbler, engraved with pendant anchors and drapery festoons, inscribed 'Duncan, 11th October 1797, Nelson, 1st August 1778, Howe, 1st June 1794, St Vincent, 14th February 1797', with flute-cut base, c1800, 4⅜in (12cm) high.
$1,000–1,100 *Som*

Three whisky tumblers, with flute-cut conical bowls, c1850, 4in (10cm) high.
$100–110 *Som*

r. A glass tumbler, engraved 'M. Parkin' within a floral cartouche, c1810, 4¼in (10.5cm) high.
$140–160 *BrW*

A glass tumbler, engraved with flora, fauna and the initials 'J. M.', c1890, 4½in (11.5cm) high.
$55–60 *JHa*

A Historismus beaker, enamelled with a coat-of-arms, German or Bohemian, c1880, 4in (10cm) high.
$240–280 *MJW*

In the second half of the 19thC there was great interest in the Renaissance which led to a demand for reproduction items. In consequence, Venetian styles of the past were copied across Europe. In Germany and Bohemia glassmakers also produced their versions of 17th and 18thC German glasses. It can often be difficult to tell Historismus glasses, as they are known, from the originals.

l. A Bohemian amber glass beaker, engraved 'Anne Pertina' and with cameo views of buildings, on a petal foot, late 19thC, 4¾in (12cm) high.
$130–160 *P(O)*

A Bohemian beaker, transfer-printed and painted in transparent colours with a portrait of the Archduke Charles of Austria, the reverse with a map, beneath a border of red lozenge, amber-flash and gilt decoration, the cogwheel foot and star-cut base stained in amethyst, gilding rubbed, mid-19thC, 4¼in (11cm) high.
$1,100–1,300 *C*

r. A glass tumbler, engraved with a Masonic symbol within a floral cartouche, c1900, 4¼in (11cm) high.
$100–125 *BrW*

A footed tumbler, engraved with birds on branches and fencing, c1890, 5¼in (13cm) high.
$130–150 *JHa*

Wine Glasses & Goblets

A Venetian wine glass, the bell-shaped bowl with a light blue trail around the rim, set on a collar above a hollow inverted baluster stem with wide conical foot, 16th/early 17thC, 6in (15cm) high.
$2,800–3,200 *S*

A Dutch *façon de Venise* winged goblet, the bowl with spiked gadroons to the lower part, the stem with a hollow knop between mereses above a hollow tapering section applied with opposing scroll ornament with pincered decoration, on a folded conical foot, late 17thC, 8¼in (21cm) high.
$1,800–2,000 *C*

In a drinking glass a merese is a flat disc of glass which links the bowl and stem and sometimes the stem and foot.

A Dutch *façon de Venise* goblet, the wrythen-moulded coiled serpent stem with a central figure-of-eight and applied with opaque-white pincered decoration, on a basal knop and conical foot, 17thC, 7in (18cm) high.
$560–680 *C*

r. A balustroid wine glass, with central knop and tear in stem, c1745, 5¾in (14.5cm) high.
$400–430 *FD*

A flammiform ale glass, c1740, 4½in (11.5cm) high.
$130–150 *FD*

A gin glass, with shoulder and base knopped stem, on a folded foot, c1745, 4¾in (12cm) high.
$240–280 *GS*

A goblet, with an ogee bowl and plain stem, engraved with a sunflower and a moth, c1750, 6¼in (16cm) high.
$350–430 *BrW*

l. A wine glass, the funnel bowl engraved with 2 carnations and a bee, on a shoulder knopped multiple series air-twist stem, c1750, 5¾in (14.5cm) high.
$800–950 *JHa*

An ale glass, engraved
with hops and barley,
the stem with multiple
spiral air-twist and
swelling knop, on
plain conical foot, c1750,
7¼in (18.5cm) high.
$1,300–1,400 *Som*

An ale glass, engraved
with hops and barley,
on slice cut stem, c1810,
6in (15cm) high.
$70–80 *JHa*

Air-twist Stemmed Glasses

Air-twists were formed by denting a gather
of molten glass and placing another gather
on top, thereby creating air-bubbles. The
pattern made by the air was elongated and
twisted by drawing and rotating the molten
glass until it assumed the length and breadth
needed for a stem.

Air-twist stemmed glasses proliferated
between 1750–60, as craftsmen sought
to find a way to produce drinking glasses that
were both light in weight and sufficiently
decorative to have consumer appeal. Early air-
twists were made in two pieces, with the twist
extending into the bowl.

A soda glass toasting
glass, the conical bowl
on slender stem and
conical foot, possibly
Continental, c1720,
9¾in (25cm) high.
$1,100–1,200 *Som*

An armorial rummer,
engraved with the coat-
of-arms of the Earl of
Cadogan, on a lemon
squeezer base, c1800,
5½in (14cm) high.
$560–600 *GS*

l. A pair of Georgian
panel-cut rummers,
with bucket bowls,
c1810, 5½in (13cm) high.
$190–200 *FD*

A toasting glass, with
teared stem, mid-
18thC, 7in (18cm) high.
$320–370 *FD*

A wine glass, engraved
with a single rose bud
and a jay in flight, the
rim with swags, the
stem cut with
diamond facets, c1770,
5¼in (13.5cm) high.
$350–400 *GS*

r. A Continental cut-glass
goblet and cover, with
stylised leaf decoration
beneath a gilt rim, on a
faceted double-knopped stem
and domed foot, the faceted
spire finial with gilding,
slight rubbing, late 18thC,
12¾in (32.5cm) high.
$900–1,000 *C*

A double series opaque-
twist miniature dram
glass, with funnel bowl,
on a heavy foot, c1750,
3¾in (9.5cm) high.
$640–720 *BrW*

A wine glass, with bell
bowl, the stem with an
air-twist gauze spiral
entwined with a single
brick-red thread, on a
conical foot, c1765,
6¾in (17.5cm) high.
$2,500–2,800 *C*

An ale flute, the conical bucket bowl cut with flutes, c1820, 5¼in (13.5cm) high.
$55–70 *GS*

l. A green wine glass, with bell-shaped bowl, knopped stem and plain foot, c1830, 5¼in (13cm) high.
$110–130

r. A light green wine glass, the conical bowl engraved with a band of rose decoration, on a knopped stem, c1840, 5¼in (13cm) high.
$100–110 *Som*

A set of 5 port glasses, the double ogee bowls cut with arches and fans, c1835, 3¾in (9.5cm) high.
$190–210 *GS*

Lobmeyr

The Lobmeyr glassworks was founded in Vienna in 1822 by Josef Lobmeyr. Later he was joined in the company by his sons Louis and Josef Jr. By the late 19thC, under the leadership of Josef Jr, the factory had become internationally famous for the design and beauty of their products.

Lobmeyr brought together the best Bohemian and Austrian craftsmen and designers to create glassware which reflected the contemporary mood but used earlier techniques such as enamelling, gilding and engraving. Much of their work was influenced by Islamic art or the intricate rococo designs of the 17th and 18thC.

Lobmeyr's introduction of iridescent glass at the 1873 International Exhibition in Vienna led to its use by Thomas Webb in England and Tiffany in the USA. Pieces by Lobmeyr were sometimes signed, but signatures may be hard to find as they are often worked into the pattern.

A white opaline glass, with blue and white cane rim, c1850, 7in (18cm) high.
$700–780 *MJW*

A Lobmeyr opaline glass, with polychrome enamelling, c1890, 5¾in (14.5cm) high.
$1,300–1,400 *MJW*

Cross Reference
Colour Review

r. A champagne glass, engraved with fruiting vine, on cut baluster stem, c1870, 5in (12.5cm) high.
$50–60 *BrW*

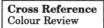

A pair of goblets, engraved with passion flowers, c1870, 6¾in (17cm) high.
$320–350 *JHa*

A set of 6 wine glasses, with orange bowls, clear stems and feet, c1870, 5in (12.5cm) high.
$380–430 *MJW*

A pair of goblets, with acid-etched and engraved floral decoration, c1875, 7in (18cm) high.
$350–400 *JHa*

l. A champagne glass, the bucket bowl engraved with a geometric pattern and stars, c1880, 4¾in (12cm) high.
$30–40 *BrW*

Jugs

A decanter jug and cover, the lower part moulded with gadroons beneath a trailed triple-ply chain band, the ribbed loop handle with thumb-rest and scrolling terminal, the cover with knob finial, some damage, c1685, 11½in (29cm) high.
$4,400–5,400 *C*

A blue cream jug, the angular body diamond moulded, with loop handle, on a solid conical foot, c1790, 4in (10.5cm) high.
$480–560 *Som*

A cut glass claret jug and stopper, the body cut with strawberry diamonds, ovals and prisms, heavy strap handle, c1825, 8½in (21.5cm) high.
$800–880 *Som*

A decanter jug, the gadrooned lower part below a band of applied chain ornament, with applied scroll handle, later silver mount to footrim, damaged, c1680, 9¼in (23.5cm) high.
$1,800–2,000 *C*

A pillar-moulded engraved jug, c1830, 7in (18cm) high.
$190–200 *FD*

A Webb cameo glass claret jug, with silver-plated mounts, the body of pale yellow glass overlaid in opaque white, etched and carved with arum lilies, the engraved mount repeating the design, remounted, late 19thC, 8¾in (22cm) high.
$2,000–2,200 *S(S)*

A rib-moulded jug, north of England, c1790, 3¼in (8.5cm) high.
$560–640 *MJW*

A wrythen-moulded cream jug, of bellied shape, with folded rim and loop handle, c1800, 2¾in (7cm) high.
$130–140 *Som*

A 'Nailsea' jug and pitcher, with olive green bottle glass bodies and opaque white marvered inclusions, loop handles, c1810, largest 7½in (19cm) high.
$550–600 each *Som*

Nailsea Glass

The group of glass articles known as 'Nailsea' gain their name from the glass company started in 1788 by John Robert Lucas in Nailsea near Bristol. Until its closure in 1869 this glasshouse produced green tinted bottle or window glass which was used to make a variety of domestic and garden articles, as well as novelty items in the shape of walking sticks, pipes and hats.

Much of the output was plain glass but some had coloured glass worked into it. Looped white, blue, red or pink designs are traditionally known as Nailsea. The name is often applied to any article with splashes of colour marvered into its surface. In fact, there is strong evidence to show that a great deal of Nailsea was made elsewhere in the country and was probably more likely to have come from the north of England. Similar wares were also made in New England, USA.

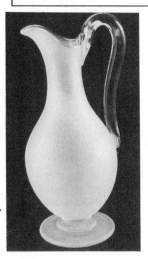

r. A frosted glass water jug, with clear loop handle, c1870, 11¾in (29.5cm) high.
$320–350 *BrW*

A miniature water jug, c1870, 1¼in (3cm) high
$20–30 *BrW*

Lustres

A pair of table lustres, each with baluster-shaped stems, cut with diamond and faceted bands, hung with 2 tiers of faceted drops, on stepped square bases, some damage, early 19thC, 11in (28cm) high.
$600–720 *DN*

l. A lustre, the cut baluster stem on a square cut pedestal foot, the sconce with crenellated rim, c1820, 10in (25.5cm) high.
$800–900 *Som*

r. A turquoise opaque candle-stick, with clear lustre drops, on a black base, c1840, 9in (23cm) high.
$640–800 *CB*

Mugs & Tankards

A south German or Bohemian enamelled blue-tinted mug, painted in opaque white with 4 panels of dots enclosing applied glass beads flanked by curlicues, restored, early 17thC, 4in (10cm) high.
$2,000–2,200 *S*

A central European opaque mug, the flared thistle-shaped white body with iron-red pulled decoration, with applied opalescent loop handle and crimped footrim, c1750, 5½in (14cm) high.
$520–600 *C*

A Continental *milchglas* mug, painted in coloured enamels with a portrait of a gentleman, within a roundel and flower and scroll cartouche, flanked by flowers and leaves, late 18thC, 7¼in (18.5cm) high.
$900–1,000 *HOLL*

l. A Continental *milchglas* mug, painted in coloured enamels with a young man within a scroll cartouche, flanked by flowers and leaves, late 18thC, 5½in (14cm) high.
$560–640 *HOLL*

Cross Reference
Colour Review

Milchglas

Milchglas – milk glass (or *lattimo* in Italian) – is an opaque white glass made with oxide of tin. Invented in Italy in the 15thC, it was used to make drinking vessels and bottles in an attempt to imitate porcelain wares imported from the East. In the 18thC *Milchglas* was made at the Bristol glass-houses as well as in Germany, Bohemia and Holland.

A mug, engraved with the arms of the Duke of Bridgwater above an inscription, with heavy strap handle, c1820, 5¼in (13cm) high.
$720–880 *Som*

A Bohemian ruby flashed tankard, engraved with The Academy, Edinburgh, c1850, 5in (12.5cm) high.
$780–820 *MJW*

Paperweights

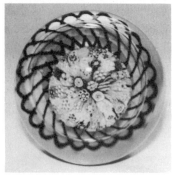

A Baccarat mushroom paperweight, with fine canes in red, white and blue, encircled by a spiralling translucent blue torsade, on star-cut base, c1845, 3in (7.5cm) diam.
$2,400–2,500 *SWB*

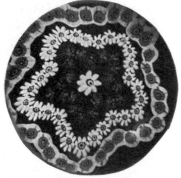

A Clichy patterned millefiori paperweight, set with 3 star-shaped garlands, on a translucent red ground, repolished, 19thC, 3in (7.5cm) diam.
$900–1,000 *S(NY)*

A Paul Ysart 'basket' paperweight, with 'PY' cane, c1960, 2¾in (7cm) diam.
$640–720 *SWB*

A Baccarat faceted sulphide paperweight, depicting Louis XIV within a garland of green and white and pink and white canes, on a star-cut base, mid-19thC, 3in (7.5cm) diam.
$820–900 *C*

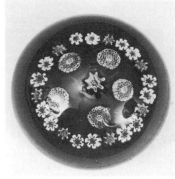

A Clichy paperweight, with coloured 'pastry mould' canes on a turquoise ground, mid-19thC, 2½in (6.5cm) diam.
$1,100–1,300 *MLa*

Canes

A cane is a glass rod made up from concentric layers of coloured glass and fused by heating. They are then cut across the grain to form the flowers in millefiori work.

l. A St Louis faceted paperweight, with 3 stylised millefiori cane flowerheads on green leaves, within a circle of canes, on a flat base, mid-19thC, 2¾in (7cm) diam.
$1,200–1,350 *MLa*

A Perthshire close-pack paperweight, from an edition of 400, dated '1973', 2½in (6.5cm) diam.
$400–480 *SWB*

A Baccarat millefiori paperweight, with coloured canes forming garlands, c1850, 3in (7.5cm) diam.
$1,600–2,000 *MLa*

A Clichy patterned millefiori paperweight, set with a cinquefoil garland, repolished and slight damage, 19thC, 2½in (6.5cm) diam.
$1,100–1,300 *S(NY)*

A St Louis bouquet paperweight, with 3 bundled canes representing flowers, with 5 yellow-green leaves, in clear glass, on a strawberry-cut base, c1845, 2½in (6.5cm) diam.
$800–880 *SWB*

A St Louis faceted paperweight, with blue, yellow and white flowers and green leaves, mid-19thC, 3in (7.5cm) diam.
$720–800 *MLa*

Pictures

A picture transferred on to glass, depicting a memorial to Admiral Lord Nelson, c1808, 13 x 17in (33 x 43cm).
$1,800–2,000 *TVM*

A painting on glass, depicting a young lady in a blue dress holding a basket of flowers, c1750, 15 x 12½in (38 x 32cm).
$3,500–4,000 *CAT*

This painting is of exceptional quality.

A pair of south German reverse glass paintings, depicting The Virgin Mary and Child, and The Holy Trinity, each in circular panels hung with drapery, one damaged, c1800, 9½ x 7in (24 x 18cm).
$400–440 *S(Am)*

r. A picture on glass, depicting Admiral Lord Nelson, c1808, 12 x 10in (30.5 x 25.5cm).
$1,200–1,300 *TVM*

Scent Bottles

A clear glass scent bottle, with cut decoration, the silver plaque with gilt inscription, silver cap, c1790, 4in (10.5cm) long.
$1,300–1,500 *Som*

A blue scent bottle, with gilt diaper decoration, and wrythen gold screw cap, c1760, 2¼in (5.5cm) high.
$1,300–1,400 *Som*

l. A novelty cut glass scent bottle, with hinged silver-gilt lid modelled as a fish's head, opening to reveal a cut glass stopper, c1880, 6½in (16.5cm) long.
$450–520 *WeH*

A Webb citron-coloured icicle scent bottle, with opaque-white cameo decoration, silver stopper marked London 1884, 6in (15cm) long.
$1,400–1,600 *Som*

A blue glass scent bottle, c1850, 9½in (24cm) high.
$520–550 *MJW*

A scent bottle, with gilt and cranberry overlay, silver top, by S. Mordan, c1880, 3½in (9cm) high.
$1,000–1,100 *THOM*

Cameo glass

Cameo glass was first produced in Roman times, but the technique fell into disuse until the beginning of the 19thC. It is produced from 2 or more layers of different coloured glass, which are cut away from the base vessel leaving the subject standing out in relief. Most cameo glass comprises a body with a white overlay, although up to 4 layers of different colours may occur. The major British manufacturers of cameo in the 19thC were Thomas Webb, W. H., B. & J. Richardson, and Stevens & Williams, who were all based in the Midlands.

Vases

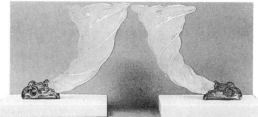

A pair of Regency glass cornucopia, on gilt-metal rams' mask mounts and white marble bases, 8in (20.5cm) high.
$580–640 *HYD*

A James Powell vaseline glass jardinière, c1900, 4½in (11.5cm) diam.
$200–240 *MON*

A cranberry ribbed-glass vase, with turnover rim, c1890, 6in (15cm) high.
$160–200 *CB*

A James Powell lustre glass vase, c1900, 4in (10cm) high.
$210–250 *MON*

A Bohemian trumpet-shaped vase, ruby flashed and overlaid in white with 6 diamond-cut panels above a flattened faceted knop, on a circular base, decorated with gilt borders and vermiculation, slight rubbing, mid-19thC, 15½in (39.5cm) high.
$850–950 *WW*

r. An iridescent threaded glass vase, deep purple with overall spider-web threading, early 20thC, 11¾in (30cm) high.
$100–120 *RIT*

A pair of James Powell vaseline glass Iris vases, c1900, 10in (25.5cm) high.
$250–280 *MON*

r. A cranberry glass vase, c1880, 12in (30.5cm) high.
$240–280 *CB*

A pair of posy vases, with blue glass ribbons, c1890, 2in (5cm) high.
$400–450 *MJW*

A pair of Bohemian glass vases, with knopped stems, flared feet, overlaid with alternating panels in gilt and white on a cranberry glass ground, the gilt panels painted with flowers, c1880, 11in (28cm) high.
$1,400–1,600 *WL*

Silvered Glass

Silvered glass was made with double walls which were silvered in the middle with mercury and then sealed in the base to prevent oxygen from turning the silvering black. Sometimes the outside was layered with coloured glass which was engraved or cut to reveal the silver underneath. Because of their bulk it was difficult to produce articles which were elegant in shape. However, several important presentation pieces were made.

Although silvered glass may have been made as early as the late 18thC, it is often called 'Varnish' glass after Edward Varnish who, together with Frederick Hale Thomson, took out the British patent for the technique in 1849. Actual Varnish pieces are usually marked as such on a glass disc placed over the plug. Examples of this glassware were exhibited in the Great Exhibition of 1851. In America, silvered glass was produced from 1855 and was popular in Europe at the end of the 19thC.

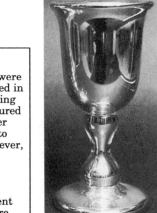

A pair of Varnish vases, with mercury discs sealed into their bases, c1870, 9in (23cm) high.
$480–560 *ARE*

SILVER

Recently a Louis XV royal soup tureen, cover, liner and stand made by Thomas Germain in Paris in 1733 sold for over $9,500,000 at Sotheby's in New York, a world record price for any piece of silver. Although made as a piece of functional silver, its quality, together with that of valuable other royal pieces in the same sale, meant that it escaped the melting pot during the many crises that France experienced in the 18th century, culminating in the Revolution of 1789, which saw the destruction of so much beautiful French silver and many other works of art.

Britain, however, benefited from the turmoil in France. After the Revocation of the Edict of Nantes in 1685, a flood of French Huguenot craftsmen emigrated, many to London, and brought the prevailing French designs and styles with them. English silversmithing was transformed by such distinguished names as Pierre Platel, Paul de Lamerie, John Le Sage, Augustine Courtauld, Abraham Buteux, among others, and the many surviving pieces from the reigns of William & Mary, Queen Anne, George I and George II display French-inspired skills.

Fine silver from the late 17th to mid-18th century has always fetched high prices and the market in this area is buoyant, with exceptional objects continuing to make very high prices indeed. More mundane domestic silver of the 1750s and '60s, such as utilitarian coffee pots and cast candlesticks (many made for instance by the specialist producers John and William Café), which must have been made literally in their tens of thousands, have remained on something of a plateau for many years, but there are indications that most silver is fetching substantially more at auction than it was a couple of years ago.

As always it is the fine and rare object which is most difficult to find and the easiest to sell. The common complaint in the trade is the difficulty of finding pieces of real quality that are new to the market. That apart, the market for small, collectable silver has never been more buoyant. The ease with which such objects as wine labels, caddy spoons, vinaigrettes, boxes, card cases and similar pieces can be displayed and stored is, of course, an attraction, and prices can be reasonable, although even in this collecting field unusual or rare items can bring startlingly high sums.

It seems probable that the perceptible increase in silver prices at all levels of collecting is likely to continue for the time being. The silver market has become very international, and although many European economies are still struggling out of a recession, across the Atlantic the market is improving. English silver has always had a cachet of its own, thanks to its longstanding and consistent system of hallmarking.

London still remains the centre of the silver trade; no other capital has such a high number of specialist dealers in the field, or can boast four major auction houses with regular sales of silver. All specialists in the auction rooms will advise potential buyers and will point out any defects, repairs or restoration. Many dealers also specialise in various fields of collecting and after many years in the trade can be very knowledgeable. Some auction buyers prefer to get a professional dealer's opinion and in addition possibly ask him or her to bid for them. The dealer will levy a small charge but it can be prudent to get a second opinion.

Although sadly the number of specialist silver dealers outside London can almost be counted on the fingers of one hand today, there are a number of auctioneers nationwide holding specialist well-illustrated art sales, including silver, which certainly was not the case thirty years ago.

The interest in house contents sales has also never been greater. In general though it is wiser to buy from a dealer or at regular silver auctions as specialist buyers at country house auctions can get carried away by the occasion and often pay particularly high prices.

However, thanks to increasingly popular radio and television programmes covering the decorative arts and the large number of extremely well written and illustrated books on every aspect of collecting, the silver enthusiast is probably better informed than ever before.

Richard Came

Baskets

A German parcel-gilt silver basket, the basket-weave body applied with 4 enamel plaques, with foliate and fruit chased handles, by Samuel Schneeweiss, Augsburg, c1690, 27¼in (69cm) wide, 39oz.
$7,500–8,000 *S(G)*

A George II silver cake basket, with trellis pierced sides, rope edge, pierced plaited handle, maker's mark 'W.P.', London 1757, 12in (30.5cm) wide, 22oz.
$1,700–1,900 *GAK*

A George III silver dessert basket and stand, with 2 medallions engraved with coats-of-arms, rams' heads and ring handles, on 4 bud feet, maker's mark of John Wakelin and William Taylor, London 1790, 15½in (39.5cm) wide.
$28,000–32,000 *C(G)*

A silver basket, with ruby glass liner, crested, pierced with leaves and scrolls, swing handle, marked 'II' over 'DM', London 1768, 4¾in (12cm) high, 2.5oz.
$720–800 *S(Am)*

A silver pierced basket, by Richard Mills, London 1772, 5in (13cm) wide.
$5,600–6,400 *DIC*

A silver pierced bonbon dish, London 1774, 6in (15cm) wide.
$800–950 *DIC*

A George III fruit basket, with reeded swing handle, the rim with pierced leaf pattern, London 1791, 7in (18cm) wide, 21oz.
$760–840 *JAd*

A George III Irish silver sugar basket, with reeded border and swing handle, by George West, Dublin 1795, 7in (18cm) wide.
$450–550 *DN*

A George III silver cake basket, with pierced fret border, the swing handle with reeded moulding, by William Allen III, London 1801, damaged, London 1801, 15in (38cm) wide.
$1,400–1,600 *WW*

A George III silver cake basket, the interior with floral and foliate engraved border, by Thomas Wallis, London 1803, 13¾in (35cm) wide, 23.5oz.
$1,400–1,600 *Oli*

A George III silver cake basket, the reeded swing handle with raised hinges, cast shell and gadrooned border, by Rebecca Emes and Edward Barnard, London 1811, 14in (35.5cm) wide, 32oz.
$1,400–1,600 *GAK*

A Victorian silver-gilt quatrefoil sugar bowl, with pierced and cast swing handle, flat chased foliate engraving, the handle chased with rosettes and a leaf, by William Smith, Chester 1876, 6in (15cm) wide, 5.5oz, and a matching sifter spoon.
$550–620 *DN*

A George III silver cartouche-shaped cake basket, the roll handles with rosettes, engraved with crests and initial 'M', inscribed, London 1807, 14¼in (36cm) wide.
$2,000–2,400 *DN*

Miller's is a price GUIDE not a price LIST

A pair of French silver baskets, pierced with foliage, on silver-plated stands, 19thC, 10in (25.5cm) wide.
$5,600–6,000 *S*

l. A silver-gilt neo-classical style dessert basket, the pierced sides with cast and applied ribbon-tied paterae swags, by Thomas William and Henry Holmes Dobson, London 1881, 11½in (29cm) wide, 18oz.
$1,200–1,300 *WW*

An Edwardian silver cake basket, the body with Classical patera and husk garlands on a pierced band, the leaf-capped swing handle with a band of husks within rope twist border, by Thomas Bradbury & Sons, 1903, 11½in (29cm) wide, 19oz.
$840–960 *C(S)*

An Edwardian silver cake basket, with pierced swing handle, the border with moulded edge, on acanthus scroll feet, by Goldsmiths & Silversmiths Company, London 1905, 12in (30.5cm) wide, 20.5oz.
$400–480 *DN*

A Victorian silver and silver-gilt sugar basket, with beaded swing handle, chased and engraved with a wreath cartouche, by Martin & Hall, Sheffield 1866 and 1867, 6½in (16.5cm) wide, 8.25oz, with matching sifter spoon and morocco-covered case.
$800–880 *P(S)*

r. A silver bread basket, by R. Martin & E. Hall, Sheffield 1906, 12in (30.5cm) long.
$880–960 *THOM*

Beakers

A pair of Russian silver beakers, chased with strapwork, with gilt interiors, by Timofej Filippow Silujanow, assay master AK, Moscow 1761, 3¼in (8.5cm) high, 5oz.
$1,900–2,200 *S(Am)*

A George III beaker, with engraved with concentric bands, by Henry Chawner, 1788, 4in (10cm) high, 6oz.
$640–740 *P(WM)*

A parcel-gilt silver beaker, nielloed with views of boats on the river Neva and scrolling foliage, maker's mark indistinct, assay master A. Kovalsky, Moscow 1844, 2in (5cm) high.
$2,500–2,800 *S(G)*

Bowls

A William III bleeding bowl, the flat pierced scroll handle with engraved shield, by Benjamin Braford, 4in (10cm) diam, 4oz.
$5,500–6,300 *DN*

Many bowls of this type have had a lot of use. However, this example is engraved with contemporary arms, excellent marks, and is in very good condition. In America they are described as porringers.

An American silver porringer, monogrammed 'SC', by Moody Russell, Barnstable, Massachusetts, c1730, 5in (12.5cm) diam, 7.5oz.
$4,000–4,400 *EL*

A George IV lobed sugar bowl, with gadrooned border, acanthus and reeded handles, on 4 acanthus and shell cast paw feet, 1824, 4¼in (11cm) wide, 11oz.
$280–320 *P(WM)*

l. A Dutch silver brandy bowl, the centre raised and chased with flowers, pierced handles, traces of gilding, maker's mark 'LA', Zwolle, 1670, 9in (23cm) wide, 5.5oz.
$2,200–2,700 *S(Am)*

A late Victorian monteith, with
scroll borders, the sides with
cartouche panels within scale
borders, cast lion's mask and ring
handles, by Martin & Hall, Sheffield
1890, 15in (38cm) diam, 98oz.
$5,500–6,200 *P(WM)*

An American silver punchbowl,
the bowl and foot with floral
repoussé decoration and applied
floral and shell cast border, by
James R. Armiger of Baltimore,
c1892, 12in (30.5cm) diam, 66oz.
$4,800–5,600 *IHB*

A silver-mounted palisander
bowl, the silver rim chased with
anthemion and the girdle
decorated with silver acanthus
leaves, marked 'Fabergé', Moscow
c1910, 3⅓in (8.5cm) diam.
$2,200–2,700 *CNY*

A Victorian sugar bowl, with bead
borders, and a frieze of animals,
by John & Edward Barnard,
1876, 4½in (11.5cm) diam, 5oz.
$200–240 *P(WM)*

A late Victorian silver-gilt bowl,
with an applied Islamic style
frieze of flowers and foliage,
part fluted sides, 2 lions' mask
handles, on a round fluted foot,
London 1898, 8¼in (21cm) diam.
$700–800 *DN*

A Chinese silver punchbowl,
the filigree sides decorated
with entwined snakes, c1880,
15½in (39.5cm) diam.
$8,800–10,400 *SFL*

A Fabergé silver kovsh, the
prow with the crowned Imperial
eagle, angular handle, gilt
interior, work-master
A. Nevalainen, St Petersburg,
c1910, 4¾in (12cm) long.
$2,500–2,800 *S(G)*

A Dutch 18thC style silver fruit
bowl, pierced and engraved with
foliage, flowers, beading and
trelliswork, on lions' paw feet,
import marks for Birmingham
1902, 11½in (29cm) wide, 16.25oz.
$1,200–1,300 *CSK*

An Edwardian presentation bowl,
partly fluted with embossed
and chased panels and enamelled
with arms of Hartlepool, inscribed
by The Goldsmiths & Silversmiths
Co Ltd, London 1911,
12¼in (31cm) diam, 105oz.
$5,000–5,600 *P(NE)*

Covered Bowls

A George II silver sugar
bowl, with slightly domed
cover and spreading foot, by
John Gamon, London 1735,
3½in (9cm) high, 7oz.
$3,600–4,200 *C*

A Continental silver *écuelle* and cover,
the raised partly fluted cover chased
with swirling flutes, applied rocaille
and flower finial, inscribed, on 3 shell
and hoof feet, maker's mark 'SH' and
coronet, c1750, 9in (23cm) wide, 14oz.
$3,500–4,000 *C(G)*

A George III two-handled sucrier,
with part ribbed decoration,
engraved with a crest, the cover
with a reeded loop handle, the
interior gilded, on a knopped
stem and square foot, by Robert
& Samuel Hennell, London 1805,
6½in (16.5cm) wide, 15.5oz.
$1,200–1,350 *WW*

Boxes

A Dutch silver tea box, the cover applied with laurel swags and portrait medallions, swing handle, by B. Swierink, Amsterdam, 1780, 5½in (14cm) wide, 28.3oz.
$5,000–6,000 *S(Am)*

A Victorian silver heart-shaped box, with floral repoussé decoration, central medallion of Salisbury Cathedral, Birmingham 1887, 3¼in (8.5cm) high, 3oz.
$320–380 *SLN*

A silver dressing table box, the top pierced with floral and foliate designs, Chester 1910, 6in (15cm) wide.
$450–550 *GAK*

A Regency Irish silver box, the hinged cover with bright-cut engraved foliage, thistles, harps and crowns, the centre with the Cork coat-of-arms and Freedom motto, inscribed, maker's mark of Carden Terry & Jane Williams, Cork, 1820, 3in (7.5cm) wide.
$3,500–4,000 *CNY*

A silver double stamp box, Birmingham 1897, 2¼in (5.5cm) wide.
$240–260 *PSA*

A Fabergé silver bonbonnière, embossed with a battlefield scene and enamelled with a red cross on a white field, the flange inscribed in Cyrillic with 'M.V. Steiger' and '10th November, 1916', marked 'A.R.' for Anna Ringe, St Petersburg, c1910, 1¾in (4.5cm) diam.
$1,900–2,400 *S(NY)*

l. A George III silver tea caddy, with urn finial, engraved with bright-cut borders of formal ornament and monogram, by Aldridge & Green, 1778, 4½in (11.5cm) high, 13oz.
$3,200–3,500 *C(S)*

A German silver box, with hinged cover, embossed with a panel depicting a naval engagement with borders of military trophies and cornucopia, the sides with winged putti and birds, imported by Bertold Muller, Chester 1905, 7in (18cm) wide, 35oz.
$1,800–2,000 *DN*

An Edwardian silver dressing table box, the hinged cover with a tortoiseshell panel decorated with ribbons and festoons, by H. Matthews, Birmingham 1909, 5in (12.5cm) wide.
$370–400 *Bea*

Caddies

A Belgian tea caddy, the pull-off cover with a knop finial, gadrooned borders, traces of gilding, maker's mark of Pieter van Sychen, Bruges c1710, 5¼in (13cm) high, 8.5oz.
$14,500–16,000 *Bon*

l. A George III silver tea caddy, decorated with bands of foliage, crested within a floral wreath, by Henry Chawner and John Emes, London 1796, 6in (15cm) high, 10.7oz.
$1,200–1,450 *Bea*

Candlesticks & Chambersticks

A Queen Anne taperstick, the faceted baluster stem on a welled moulded square base with canted corners, by Thomas Merry I, London 1706, 4½in (11.5cm) high, 4oz.
$3,600–4,200 *WW*

A George II silver taperstick, the hexagonal base shell-moulded at the angles, double knopped and faceted stem, spool-shaped sconce, by James Gould, London 1752, 5in (12.5cm) high.
$750–850 *S*

A George II silver taperstick, on shaped square base cast with shells at the angles, knopped baluster stem, detachable nozzle, by William Cafe, 1747, 5½in (14cm) high, and matching extinguisher, maker's mark 'TW', 9oz.
$880–1,000 *C(S)*

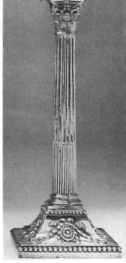

A pair of George III pillar candlesticks, with fluted columns, Corinthian capitals and acanthus leaf designs, on square bases, by John Carter, London 1773, 12½in (32cm) high.
$3,200–3,500 *RBB*

A pair of silver candlesticks, with loose sconces, knopped columns, saucer-shaped bases with cast shell feet, by John Cafe, London 1748, 9in (23cm) high, 43oz.
$2,700–3,200 *L&E*

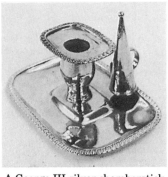

A George III silver chamberstick and snuffer, with gadrooned edges and loop handle, by T. Jones, London 1808, 4½in (11.5cm) wide.
$560–640 *GAK*

A pair of silver candlesticks, London 1896, 4in (10cm) wide.
$800–870 *PSA*

l. A pair of silver candlesticks, by Hawkesworth & Eyre, Sheffield 1896, 9in (23cm) high.
$1,900–2,200 *THOM*

A pair of rococo candlesticks, by Kirkby Waterhouse & Co, Sheffield 1816, 8in (20.5cm) high.
$2,400–2,800 *DIC*

r. A pair of silver bedroom candlesticks, on shaped square bases, embossed with anthemions and fluted designs, with reeded columns and detachable sconces, Birmingham 1901, 5in (12.5cm) high.
$560–640 *GAK*

An Edwardian silver chamberstick and snuffer, with detachable nozzle, oblong handle all with gadrooned borders, by Thomas Bradbury & Sons, 1904, 5in (12.5cm) wide, 10.5oz.
$640–700 *C(S)*

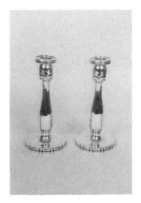

Card Cases

A silver card case, with pierced designs depicting Kenilworth and Warwick Castles, by Nathaniel Mills, Birmingham 1825, 4in (10cm) long.
$1,400–1,600 *DIC*

A Victorian silver 'castle-top' card case, decorated with a view of the Royal Exchange within foliate scrolls, the reverse with foliate scrolls and cartouche, inscribed, slight damage, maker's mark of Nathaniel Mills, Birmingham 1845, 4in (10cm) high.
$880–960 *Bon*

A silver card case, depicting Kenilworth and Warwick Castles, by Nathaniel Mills, Birmingham 1838, 4in (10cm) long.
$2,000–2,400
A silver card case, depicting Windsor and Warwick Castles, by Taylor & Perry, Birmingham 1843, 4in (10cm) long.
$1,600–1,900 *THOM*

A silver card case, depicting St Paul's Cathedral, by David Pettifer, Birmingham 1848, 4in (10cm) long.
$2,200–2,400
A silver card case, depicting Westminster Abbey, by Hilliard & Thomson, Birmingham 1868, 4in (10cm) long.
$3,200–3,500 *THOM*

A Victorian card case, decorated in relief with St Paul's Cathedral with chased scroll and foliage decoration to a scrolling border, the reverse with initials engraved in a cartouche, Birmingham 1844, 4in (10cm) long.
$2,000–2,400 *WW*

A silver card case, decorated in high relief with a stag, maker's mark 'C&N', Birmingham 1906, 4in (10cm) long.
$400–480 *DIC*

l. A silver card case, with scrolling foliate decoration, Chester 1911, 4in (10cm) long.
$190–210 *PSA*

Centrepieces

An Edward VII silver centrepiece, by J. W. D., Sheffield 1902 and London 1903, 15½in (39.5cm) high, 126oz.
$5,500–6,200 *LT*

A silver centrepiece, the bowls with shell and scroll borders, on 4 scroll legs with shell feet, maker's mark of James Dixon & Sons, Sheffield 1910, 13¾in (35cm) high, 106oz.
$3,800–4,400 *Bon*

A silver centrepiece, by J. & W. Dixon, Sheffield 1911, 15in (38cm) high, 34oz.
$1,400–1,600 *PSA*

Coffee Pots & Teapots

A George I silver teapot, the cover with part wood finial, the body engraved with a coat-of-arms within a foliate scroll cartouche, maker's mark 'JP' possibly for John Penfold, London, c1720, 4¼in (11cm) high, 15oz.
$3,200–3,500 *C*

A George II coffee pot, with moulded swan neck spout, the hinged bun cover with turned finial, hardwood scroll handle, by John Pero, London 1737, 9in (23cm) high, 25.5oz.
$1,300–1,600 *WW*

A silver teapot, with bright-cut panelled decoration, by George Smith and Thomas Hayter, London 1797, 4in (10cm) high.
$2,400–2,800 *DIC*

Bright-cutting was popular at the end of the 18thC. It employs the same method as engraving, but uses a burnished steel tool to cut the metal, which polishes the silver as it cuts, producing a sharp design which reflects the light.

Regency coffee pot, with epoussé rococo floral scroll chasing, engraved with an armorial in a cartouche, a chased moulded leaf-capped swan-neck spout, the domed cover with an asparagus finial, the wood handle with dolphin head terminal, by Joseph Angell, London 1816, 10½in (26.5cm) high, 25.5oz.
$1,500–1,700 *WW*

A George III silver coffee pot, crested with 2 arms holding a dog below a gadrooned rim, the spout chased with acanthus leaves and anthemions, with ivory finial and scroll handle, by Paul Storr, London 1818, 8¾in (22cm) high, 29.5oz.
$3,200–4,000 *S*

A George III silver bullet-shaped teapot, with wooden handle and knop, 4in (10cm) high.
$720–880 *PSA*

George IV silver teapot, with half-fluted decoration, gadrooned rim and foot, leaf-capped scrolled handle, London 1827, 4¾in (12cm) high, 20oz.
$500–560 *GAK*

A William IV silver teapot, embossed with panels of flowers and leaves, the domed cover with cast flower finial, leaf-chased handle and spout, on 4 feet, probably by Edward Barton, London 1833, 5in (12.5cm) high, 28.5oz.
$1,000–1,200 *DN*

A Victorian silver teapot, with chased scrolled border, scroll and foliate engraved panels and crest, by Joseph and George Angell, London 1849, 6½in (16.5cm) high.
$950–1,000 *DN*

miniature silver teapot, engraved with leaves and ferns, with wooden handle and finial, London 1881, 4in (10cm) high.
$520–600 *DIC*

A pair of silver George II style *café au lait* pots, with domed covers with baluster finials and fruitwood scroll handles, engraved with a crest, by Tessier, 1915, 8in (20.5cm) high, 33oz.
$1,200–1,300 *C(S)*

An Austro-Hungarian lobed coffee pot, the domed cover with cast flower knob with a simulated ivory handle, on 4 leaf-chased feet, Vienna 1856, 6½in (16.5cm) high.
$530–580 *DN*

Cruets

A William IV silver cruet stand and fittings, the stand on 4 acanthus and shell feet, supporting 8 reeded glass bottles, 2 with silver mounts, some damage to glass, by Joseph and John Angell, London 1831, 37.5oz.
$1,400–1,600 *Bea*

A silver thistle-shaped cruet set, with original spoons, by Fenton Bros Ltd, Sheffield 1922, 6in (15cm) high.
$1,100–1,300 *THOM*

Cups & Goblets

A James II porringer cup, chased with chinoiserie decoration, depicting 2 standing figures amongst foliage and birds, scroll and head handles, maker's mark 'PM', c1686, 4in (10.5cm) diam, 8oz.
$1,900–2,400 *L*

A George III silver pepper pot, by Thomas Shepherd, c1778, chased later, 5in (13cm) high.
$320–400 *PSA*

A Victorian silver cruet stand, with pierced foliate sides and a central scroll-chased loop handle, supporting 8 cut-glass bottles, by Robert Harper, with marks for London 1863, 11in (28cm) high, and with fiddle pattern mustard spoon, Exeter 1861.
$2,200–2,600 *DN*

l. A pair of George III goblets, with part-fluted bowls with gilt interiors, on gadrooned footrims, by Robert & Samuel Hennell, London 1806, 6½in (16.5cm) high, 17¾oz.
$1,000–1,250 *P(S)*

A George III silver cruet, with carrying handle, on 4 ogee feet and wooden base, hallmarked London 1803, 8in (20.5cm) high, and 7 flute-cut bottles with silver tops.
$1,100–1,200 *GAK*

A mid-Victorian silver novelty pepper pot, modelled as a standing owl with red glass eyes, maker's mark of George Richards and Edward Brain, London 1864, 3in (7.5cm) high.
$520–560 *Bon*

l. A silver-mounted carved coconut cup, London 1802, 6in (15cm) high.
$1,400–1,600 *DIC*
Items such as this would probably have been imported by sailors who carved the coconut shells themselves. The cups would then be mounted in silver and sold in the UK.

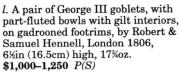

A German silver stirrup cup, modelled as a fox's head, c1880, 6in (15cm) high.
$2,000–2,300 *SFL*

Cutlery

A Henry VII silver slip-top spoon, engraved with Gothic initial 'M', London 1506, 6¾in (17cm) long, 1oz.
$9,600–10,600   CNY

The unique uninterrupted system of marking silver in London since 1478 at Goldsmiths' Hall ensures that the buyer of a spoon like this knows that it was made in 1506. However, because silver was melted down in times of crisis and with changes of fashion, the few early examples which have survived have done so because of their fairly low silver value. Nevertheless today they are highly prized by specialist collectors, and spoons of Henry VII's reign are very rare.

A set of 6 William and Mary silver trefid tablespoons, by Jonathan Bradley, engraved with contemporary initials 'AT', London 1694, 9oz.
$2,200–2,400   S(NY)

A silver feather-edged gravy straining spoon, London 1775, 12in (30.5cm) long.
$650–800   DIC

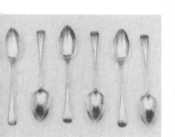

A set of 6 George III silver Old English and thread pattern dessert spoons, crested above motto, by George Smith and William Fearne, London 1795, 7oz.
$240–280   Bea

A George III silver Old English pattern table service, comprising 60 pieces, by Eley, Fearn & Chawner, c1807, 73oz.
$5,600–6,400   C(S)

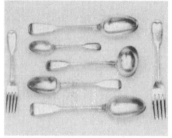

A Victorian silver fiddle and thread pattern part table service, comprising 54 pieces, London mid-19thC, 112oz.
$2,400–2,700   Bea

A Victorian silver Prince's pattern table service, comprising 28 pieces, engraved with monogram, the majority by George Adams, 1849, 296oz.
$6,500–8,000   Gam

A sterling silver King's pattern flatware service, comprising 144 pieces, by Dominick & Haff, monogrammed, 1880, 221oz.
$2,800–3,500   SK(B)

A gold-washed sterling silver Francis I pattern flatware set, comprising 39 pieces, by Reed & Barton, 1907, 58oz.
$1,400–1,600   SK(B)

A set of 12 Edward VII silver fiddle pattern coffee spoons, initialled 'G', by J. Round & Son, Sheffield 1908, ?oz, in fitted case.
$320–350   Bea

> **Don't Forget!**
> *If in doubt please refer to the 'How to Use' section at the beginning of this book.*

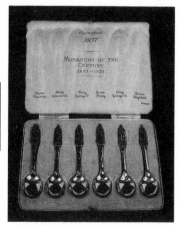

r. A set of 6 sterling silver teaspoons, entitled 'Monarchs of the Century, 1837–1937', made for the Coronation 1937, in a fitted case, 7½ x 6in (19 x 15cm).
$200–235   WeH

Dishes & Comports

A pair of American silver comports, partly pierced with foliate designs, the handles modelled as demi-putti, openwork bases applied with leaf-tailed monsters, one with gilt interior, marked and No. 355, by Gorham Mfg Co, Providence, RI, 1869, 14¼in (36cm) long, 60oz.
$2,500–2,800 *S(NY)*

A Victorian silver-gilt dish, with a repoussé figure of a maiden amongst a border of flowers and bulrushes, on 4 scroll feet, by Edward Brown, London 1892, 8in (20.5cm) long, 6.5oz.
$750–800 *WW*

An oval silver dish, pierced and decorated with scrolling foliage and gadrooned edge, by D & A, Birmingham 1892, 8¼in (21cm) long, 11oz.
$320–350 *Bea*

r. A silver dish, with twin snake handles, c1911, 10in (25cm) wide, 65oz.
$1,900–2,400 *PSA*

A pair of Victorian parcel-gilt dishes, embossed with foliate scrolls, winged putti and flowers, by W. Gibon and J. L. Langman, London 1893, 6¾in (17cm) diam, 9oz.
$480–540 *DN*

A pair of silver bonbon dishes, by Nathen & Hayes, Chester 1907, 6in (15cm) diam.
$600–680 *PSA*

Covered Dishes

A George III silver entrée dish, the cover with turned wood finial and beaded borders, the base engraved with crests, by Charles Hougham, London 1783, 14¾in (37.5cm) long.
$1,400–1,600 *DN*

A Victorian silver-plated butter dish, in the form of a boater, c1860, 3in (7.5cm) high.
$650–800 *SFL*

A Victorian silver butter dish, cover, stand and knife, engraved with fern sprays, by E. & J. Barnard, London 1875/6, stand 7½in (19cm) diam, together with a cut-glass dish, in a fitted leather case.
$640–720 *Bea*

A pair of George III silver entrée dishes, with covers and handles, the covers engraved with armorials, the fluted and foliate-decorated handles on gadrooned circular bases, by T. & J. Guest & Joseph Cradock, London 1808, 11½in (29cm) long, 124.25oz.
$2,800–3,200 *CSK*

A pair of late Victorian silver entrée dishes, the covers engraved with monograms, with detachable handles, by Atkin Brothers, Sheffield 1896, 11in (28cm) long, 113.5oz.
$2,400–2,700 *WW*

Inkstands & Wells

A George III silver inkstand, with 2 pen wells, on anthemion cast scrolling feet, 3 original cut-glass and silver topped bottles for pounce, quills and ink, by John Emes, London 1806, 10in (25.5cm) long, 20oz.
$1,400–1,600 *J&L*
Pounce is a fine powder used for drying ink.

A George IV silver standish, on 4 leaf-scrolled feet, with 2 pots for ink and pounce, together with taperstick, snuffer and stand, by Rebecca Emes and Edward Barnard, London 1821, 9¾in (25cm) wide, 25oz.
$1,900–2,200 *J&L*

A Victorian silver inkstand, of scallop shell form with mermaid figure handle, shell finial and rocky base, London 1848, 5in (13cm) wide.
$2,000–2,400 *RBB*

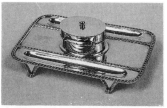

A silver inkstand, with original cut-glass bottles, by George Fox, London 1882, 9½in (24cm) wide.
$3,500–4,000 *THOM*

A silver inkwell, with gadrooned edge, by Barnard Bros, London 1905, 5in (13cm) wide.
$1,200–1,300 *THOM*

A silver presentation inkstand, the stamp box flanked by square cut-glass ink bottles, on ball-and-claw feet, London 1913, 11in (28cm) wide, 13oz.
$1,000–1,100 *AH*

Jugs & Ewers

An early Georgian silver cream jug, with scroll handle, 3½in (9cm) high.
$400–450 *PSA*

A George III silver hot water jug, crested and with gadroon edging, the domed hinged cover with reeded finial, by Charles Wright, London 1770, 10½in (27cm) high, 21oz.
$640–720 *Bea*

A George III silver hot water jug, with ivory knop, chased shell oak leaf and gadrooned border, and fruitwood handle, by John Page, London 1814, 8in (20cm) high, 18oz.
$450–520 *DN*

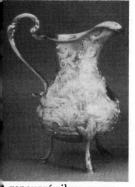

> **Cross Reference**
> Colour Review

A repoussé silver cream pitcher, with chased decoration, on hoof feet, by R. & W. Wilson, Philadelphia 1825, 6½in (16.5cm) high, 8oz.
280–320 *SK(B)*

l. A Victorian Scottish silver claret jug, set with engraved panels of flowers and coats-of-arms, with scrolling handle, by J. Mitchell, Glasgow 1852, 14in (36cm) high, 29oz.
$2,400–2,700 *C(S)*

A pear-shaped silver hot water jug, with domed lid and wooden handle, London 1905, 6in (15cm) high, 7oz.
$160–200 *DN*

Mirrors

A Victorian silver-mounted mirror, the pierced surround decorated with cherubs, masks, birds and foliage, by William Comyns, London 1887, 14¾in (37.5cm) high.
$480–540 *Bea*

A French rococo style silver-mounted dressing table mirror, stamped and pierced with scrolling foliage, enclosing a cartouche with engraved initials, on velvet-backed easel stand, by Walker & Hall, Sheffield 1901, 18in (45.5cm) high.
$1,000–1,200 *C(S)*

An Edwardian 17thC style silver dressing table mirror, in pierced frame of cherubs among floral scrollwork, mounted on velvet, by Goldsmiths & Silversmiths Co, 1902, 27½ x 21½in (70 x 55cm).
$2,700–3,200 *L*

Mugs & Tankards

A Charles II tankard, the cover with a cast scroll thumbpiece, engraved with a coat-of-arms, possibly by George Day, London 1664, 4¼in (11cm) high, 8.5oz.
$4,400–5,400 *Bon*

A Charles II tankard, engraved with a coat-of-arms within a laurel wreath, the scroll handle engraved with initials, maker's mark 'R.H.', crowned, London 1680, 6in (15cm) high, 24oz.
$10,200–11,200 *MAT*

This piece is in excellent condition with original armorials, full marks on body and cover, maker's mark on the handle, and is clearly a first rate piece.

A George II silver provincial tankard, with scroll handle, open-work scroll thumbpiece and hinged domed cover, maker mark 'R.F.', Exeter 1736, 7in (18cm) high, 24oz.
$4,400–4,800 *C*

> **Miller's is a price GUIDE not a price LIST**

A George II silver baluster mug, with leaf-capped scroll handle, c1745, 4¾in (12cm) high, 11oz.
$280–350 *P(WM)*

A George III silver quart tankard, with pierced thumbpiece, domed lid and scroll handle, engraved with initials 'L.T.A.', maker 'C.W.', London 1776, 9in (23cm) high, 27oz.
$2,200–2,700 *RBB*

A George III silver mug, later chased with scrolls and foliage, with leaf capped double scroll handle, by Peter, Ann and William Bateman, London 1799, 5in (12.5cm) high, 10.5oz.
$420–480 *Bea*

A George III silver tankard, with a pierced scrollwork thumbpiece, engraved with presentation inscription, possibly by Thomas Chawner, London 1784, 8½in (21.5cm) high, 24oz.
$3,500–4,000 *Bon*

A Scottish provincial silver christening mug, with plain scroll handle, the body embossed and chased with a band of thistles and foliage centred by a scrolled cartouche engraved with a monogram, by John Sellar, Wick, c1830, 3¼in (8cm) high, 5oz.
$7,300–8,000 *C(S)*

A William IV silver christening mug, the body embossed and engraved with flowers within double-reeded reserve, with acanthus scroll handle, by Reily & Storer, London 1833, 5in (12.5cm) high, 6oz.
$330–370 *EH*

An American silver mug, with double C-scroll handle, by Andrew Ellicott Warner, Baltimore, Maryland, c1850, 3¼in (8cm) high, 6.5oz.
$220–260 *RIT*

r. A Victorian octagonal silver mug, engraved with panels of scrolls and flowers and 'Lucy', with shaped borders and scroll handle, by George Angell, London 1856, 4in (10cm) high.
$350–380 *DN*

A Victorian silver christening mug, the body embossed and engraved with a parrot amongst vine leaves, on a rocaille base, with scroll handle, by Roberts & Briggs, London 1857, 6in (15cm) high, 5oz.
$360–400 *EH*

An American silver repoussé floral pattern mug, with double C-angle handle, by Samuel Kirk & Son, Baltimore, Maryland, 1850, 4in (10cm) high, 8.5oz.
$380–430 *RIT*

A Victorian silver christening mug, the sides panelled with embossed bulrushes and a cartouche, beaded scroll handle and circular foot, Birmingham 1862, 3½in (9cm) high, 3oz.
$140–160 *DN*

An Egyptian style silver-gilt christening mug, by RMEH, London 1873, 3½in (9cm) high.
$880–960 *DIC*

A Victorian silver mug, with engraved bird and geometric decoration, monogrammed 'H', by William Hunter, London 1879, 4in (10cm) high, 6oz.
$400–450 *SLN*

A silver christening mug, Birmingham 1898, 3in (7.5cm) high.
$110–130 *PSA*

Salvers & Trays

A George II silver waiter, with moulded shell and scroll border, on 3 hoof feet, by John Langlands, Newcastle, c1756, 7in (18cm) diam.
$950–1,100 *C(S)*

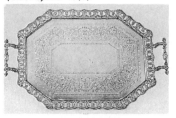

A late Victorian silver twin-handled tray, bright-engraved with harebell festoons, leafy scrolls and anthemion motifs, on bun feet, by Daniel and John Wellby, Sheffield 1896, 27½in (70cm) diam, 170oz.
$4,800–5,500 *P(WM)*

The unusual design of the handles and pierced octagonal borders contributed to the high price achieved.

A Victorian silver salver, the body engraved with arabesque and rocaille scrolls enclosing a vignette of hounds, inscribed 'Ballybourney Coursing Meeting', maker's mark of William K. Reed, London 1845, 18in (45.5cm) diam, 80oz.
$1,600–1,800 *EH*

An Edwardian silver salver, with central armorial, on 4 plain feet, by Charles Stuart Harris, London 1903, 8¼in (21cm) square, 14oz.
$270–320 *DN*

A silver tray, London 1870, 7in (18cm) diam.
$430–480 *THOM*

Don't Forget!

If in doubt please refer to the 'How to Use' section at the beginning of this book.

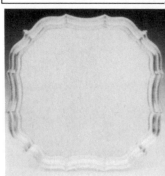

A George V silver salver, on 4 hoof feet, maker's mark B.B.S. Ltd, Birmingham 1928, 17¾in (45cm) square, 66oz.
$950–1,100 *Bea*

Sauce Boats

l. A late George II silver cream boat, with card-cut rim, leaf-capped flying scrolled handle, later embossed with foliate design, standing on 3 shell and hoof feet, London 1758, 5in (13cm) long.
$160–180 *GAK*

A pair of George III silver sauce boats, with punch-beaded borders, a flying leaf-capped scroll handle, on applied shell legs with hoof feet, by Elizabeth Munns, London 1768, 7¼in (18.5cm) long, 15.5oz.
$2,200–2,700 *WW*

Sauce Boats

The earliest English and American sauce boats date from the reign of George I. At first they had simple waved borders, but soon acquired gadrooned edges that predominated until the 1770s, when punched or beaded borders appeared. With the turn of the century and the onset of Regency influence the sauce boat became more elaborate with massive borders and feet, and the handles became a major feature, as they occasionally were in the mid-18thC. Design stagnated during the 19thC and later examples follow the style of their predecessors. Sauce boats were usually made in pairs and single ones are, therefore, less desirable.

A pair of Edwardian silver sauce boats, each with a rising scroll handle, engraved with crest and motto, on 3 hoof feet, by Elkington & Co, Birmingham 1902 and 1903, 7in (18cm) long, 11oz.
$1,100–1,250 *C(S)*

Services

A George III silver three-piece tea service, with floral and leaf engraving, on ball feet, makers SH & IT, London 1814.
$1,300–1,450 *RBB*

An American silver four-piece tea service, with key pattern borders and urn finials, engraved with initial 'W', made by Bogert for Tiffany & Co, New York, c1860, 78oz.
$3,500–4,000 *S(NY)*

l. A silver three-piece tea service, of ribbed pear shape, engraved monogram, by J. & W. Moir, New York 1845, 54.5oz.
$950–1,100 *SK(B)*

A Victorian silver-gilt three-piece tea service, embossed with flowers, scroll and diaper panels, the teapot with a domed cover and rose finial, cast bird's head spout with a bearded mask, on mask and scroll feet, by Robert Harper, London 1879, 27.5oz.
$1,000–1,100 *DN*

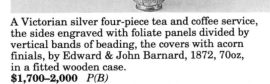

A Victorian silver four-piece tea and coffee service, the sides engraved with foliate panels divided by vertical bands of beading, the covers with acorn finials, by Edward & John Barnard, 1872, 70oz, in a fitted wooden case.
$1,700–2,000 *P(B)*

An Edwardian silver three-piece tea service, by James Dixon & Sons, teapot Sheffield 1905, milk jug Sheffield 1909, sugar bowl 1902, 18oz, in a fitted case.
$680–800 *EH*

A Scottish Regency style silver four-piece tea service, with partly fluted bodies, foliage and gadrooned rims, by Sorley, Glasgow 1902/3, 35oz.
$600–720 *C(Sc)*

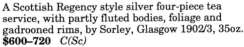

A silver four-piece half-fluted boat-shaped tea service, the teapot and hot water jug with domed covers, ivory button finials, angular scroll handles, gadrooned and shell borders, on ball feet, by Walker & Hall, Sheffield 1936, 70oz.
$2,200–2,700 *WL*

r. An Edwardian three-piece tea service, the teapot of bombé oblong form, the domed lid with ivory finial, all with double scroll handles, embossed foliate bodies and spouts, on bun feet, Birmingham 1906, 25oz.
$1,300–1,400 *AH*

A neo-classical style silver three-piece tea service, the medallions with maidens and cherubs linked by engraved ribbon-tied husk swags and florets, teapot with ebony handle and pineapple finial, by Stewart Dawson Ltd, London 1912, 37.5oz.
$1,000–1,100 *WW*

Snuff Boxes

A Victorian silver 'castle-top' snuff box, the hinged lid depicting a view of Kenilworth Castle, the sides with engraved chevron decoration, by Nathaniel Mills, Birmingham 1837, 3½in (9cm) wide.
$1,600–1,800 *Bon*

'Castle-top' items, such as snuff boxes, card cases and vinaigrettes, have always been popular with collectors. With the advent of the railway during the early years of Queen Victoria's reign, the population became more mobile and people were keen to buy souvenirs of the places they visited. Nathaniel Mills of Birmingham was the first person to recognise the commercial aspect of this interest. His output of small silver objects was prolific, and is enthusiastically collected today.

A Victorian silver snuff box, the hinged cover with presentation inscription within an engraved and chased border of scrolls and foliage, by Nathaniel Mills, Birmingham 1846, 3¼in (8.5cm) wide, 4oz, in a fitted leather case.
$800–880 *Bea*

A silver snuff box, with inscription, Birmingham 1907, 3in (7.5cm).
$180–200 *PSA*

A silver snuff box, Birmingham 1894, 2½in (65mm) wide.
$200–225 *PSA*

A Victorian silver table snuff box, London 1899, 2¾in (70mm) diam.
$80–130 *PSA*

As these boxes are airtight they were also used for tobacco.

A Scottish silver-mounted horn snuff mull, the foliate repoussé-decorated cover with replaced paste gem, the tail with Cairngorm stone, 19thC, 9in (23cm) wide.
$770–850 *CSK*

Sugar Casters

A George III silver caster, with shaped bun top and reeded borders, by Crispin Fuller, London 1808, 4in (10cm) high.
$270–320 *DN*

A pair of Austro-Hungarian silver cylindrical casters, the detachable tops with urn finials, and decorative borders, Vienna 1806, 3½in (9.5cm) high, 5.75oz.
$460–560 *DN*

> **Cross Reference**
> Colour Review

A Queen Anne silver sugar caster, the lid pierced with flowerheads and leaves, the base and top of the lid with repoussé lobed horizontal bands and with a sleeve, by Jonathan East, London 1703, 5½in (14cm) high, 5.5oz.
$2,200–2,700 *RIT*

r. An Edwardian silver sugar caster, with embossed design, 8½in (21.5cm) high.
$200–240 *PSA*

l. A George III silver sugar caster, the body decorated with reeded bands, the cover with a ball finial, London 1800, 6½in (16.5cm) high, 3.75oz.
$400–440 *CSK*

l. A Victorian 18thC style silver sugar caster, the pierced cover with bayonet fittings and baluster finial, by George Fox, London 1881, 8½in (21.5cm) high, 13.25oz.
$1,200–1,300 *CSK*

Vases

A pair of late Victorian silver vases, cast in the form of rams' masks with foliate cornucopiae on mossy plinths, with opaque glass shell-moulded liners, by Elkington & Co, 12½in (32cm) high.
$2,700–3,000 *P(WM)*

A pair of Dutch silver flower vases, the bodies chased with classical figures, with angel caryatid handles and crimped tops, c1880, 6in (15cm) high, 15oz.
$550–600 *GAK*

A pair of silver flower vases, with fluted rims, by Samson Mordan & Co, London 1902, 7in (18cm) high.
$640–720 *THOM*

A silver replica of the Warwick vase, applied with lions' pelts below masks, vines and beaded tongue-and-dart rim, with bifurcated vine handles, by Edward Barnard & Sons, London 1908, 8¼in (21cm) high, 62oz.
$4,800–5,400 *S(S)*

The original Warwick vase, of massive size, was excavated in Italy in 1771 and was eventually sold to the then Earl of Warwick. It is now in the Burrell collections in Glasgow. Silver versions took the form of wine coolers, cups and even a tea set is recorded. Paul Storr was a prolific user of this design, and there are also examples in Sheffield plate. This piece is modelled after the antique, and they always seem to attract brisk bidding.

Vinaigrettes

A silver vinaigrette, Birmingham 1806, 1in (25mm) long.
$150–170 *PSA*

A silver-gilt vinaigrette, with embossed top, the grille pierced with musical instruments, by George Tye, Birmingham 1834, 2in (50mm) wide.
$640–720 *DIC*

A George III silver vinaigrette, engraved with stylised branded and prick dot decoration, the interior fitted with a pierced grille with ferns and foliate decoration, by William Eley I, London 1811, 1½in (40mm) wide.
$380–480 *Bon*

A William IV silver vinaigrette, with engine-turned decoration, the interior fitted with a pierced grille with foliate and flowering cornucopia, by Gervase Wheeler, Birmingham 1832, 1¼in (35mm) diam.
$450–520 *Bon*

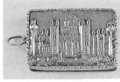

An early Victorian silver 'castle-top' vinaigrette, chased in low relief on one side with Windsor castle and foliate border, the other side with engine-turned engraving, ring attachment, by Nathaniel Mills, Birmingham 1837, 2in (50mm) wide, 1oz.
$680–760 *P(B)*

FURTHER READING

John Bly, *Miller's Silver & Sheffield Plate Marks*, Miller's Publications, 1993.

l. A mid-Victorian silver 'castle-top' vinaigrette, the top engraved with a view of St Paul's Cathedral, fitted with a pierced floral grille, by R. Thornton, Birmingham 1868, 1½in (35mm) long.
$560–680 *Bon*

A Victorian silver 'castle-top' vinaigrette, the hinged cover with a view of Abbotsford House, foliate scroll borders, reeded sides, with a dependent loop, the interior fitted with a pierced foliate scroll grille, by Nathaniel Mills, Birmingham 1839, 1½in (40mm) wide.
$600–680 *Bon*

An early Victorian silver vinaigrette, engraved with a scroll border and swirl decoration and a vacant cartouche, the interior fitted with a pierced scrolled grille, by Edward Smith, Birmingham 1846, 1½in (35mm) long.
$280–350 *Bon*

SILVER PLATE

A set of 4 Sheffield plate candlesticks, the candleholders with detachable nozzles, early 19thC, 11¾in (30cm) high.
$640–720 *WW*

A pair of Old Sheffield plate candlesticks, c1800, 11½in (29.5cm) high.
$400–480 *PSA*

A pair of silver-plated candlesticks, late 19thC, 12¼in (31cm) high.
$400–480 *SPU*

A pair of Regency Sheffield plate sauce tureens, with flowering bead and shell ring handles, the covers with a shell applied to each corner, detachable reeded and shell handles, on paw feet, some repair, 7½in (19cm) long.
$450–520 *WW*

A pair of William IV Sheffield plate dishes and covers, the panelled sides with shell and foliage scrolling borders, the covers with detachable handles decorated with acanthus leaves, scrolls and flowerheads, 14¼in (36cm) long.
$280–350 *WW*

A Victorian silver-plated coffee pot, engraved with arabesque and scroll patterns, scroll handle, greyhound finial to lid, c1850, 8½in (21.5cm) high.
$175–190 *GAK*

A Victorian silver-plated breakfast dish, the revolving cover with floral decoration, on scroll feet, 15½in (39.5cm) long.
$370–400 *Gam*

A William IV silver-plated meat dome and warming stand, with loop handle and gadrooned borders, on ball feet, 19thC, 16in (40.5cm) wide.
$730–800 *LHA*

A Victorian silver-plated revolving tureen, in Renaissance revival style, with plain and pierced liners, on foliate scroll legs with lion's masks and paw feet, by Mappin & Webb, Sheffield/London, late 19thC, 13in (33cm) long.
$280–350 *RIT*

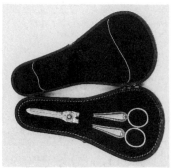

A pair of late Victorian silver-plated grape scissors, 7in (17.5cm) long, in original box.
$190–240 *GEM*

A pair of Victorian Sheffield plate communion flagons, the hinged lids with urn knops, by Martin Hall & Co, 16in (40.5cm) high.
$520–560 *DA*

r. A Sheffield plate inkstand, with shell and gadroon chased borders and handle, on winged paw feet, with 2 square glass pots, early 19thC, 5in (13cm) wide.
$280–320 *DN*

A set of 5 silver-plated fruit spoons, by
Mappin & Webb, c1890.
$480–560 *DIC*

Electroplating

This method was used from c1840 and
gradually replaced Sheffield plate which,
after the Great Exhibition of 1851, became
increasingly rare. Electroplating creates a
film of pure silver which is white and harsher
in appearance than the soft glow of Sheffield
plate. The process involves covering one
metal with a thin layer of silver by electro-
deposition. The base metal was initially
copper, but later nickel was used, hence the
term EPNS (electro-plated nickel silver).
Styles followed those that were most popular
in silver.

A Victorian silver-plated shell-
form spoon warmer, the chased
shell with hinged cover, mounted
on foliate, shell and rock base
with shell thumbpiece, by Atkin
Bros, Sheffield, late 19thC,
6¼in (6cm) long.
$440–480 *RIT*

A late Victorian silver-plated
spoon warmer, by Mappin &
Webb, 7in (18cm) wide.
$420–480 *GAZE*

A silver-plated spoon warmer,
in the form of a buoy on a rocky
base, c1880, 8in (20cm) wide.
$560–640 *DIC*

FURTHER READING
John Wilson, *Miller's Silver
& Plate Antiques Checklist,*
Miller's Publications, 1994

A Regency style silver-plated tea
urn, the upturned foliate scroll
handles and spigot with ivory
knob, chased all-over with foliate
scroll motifs centering vacant
cartouches, probably Sheffield,
c1830, 14¾in (37.5cm) high.
$560–640 *RIT*

A silver-plated tray, with
gadrooned border and 2 foliate
handles, engraved in the centre
with an armorial, on chased feet,
19thC, 27in (69cm) wide.
$700–800 *DN*

A George III Sheffield plate tea
urn, the body engraved with a
contemporary armorial, the tap
with an ivory handle, the
crested cover with a ball finial,
c1785, 22in (60cm) high.
$400–480 *WW*

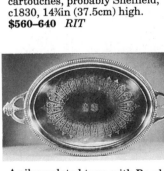

A silver-plated tray, with Bacchus
mask figural decoration, the
interior with engraved and
chased geometric decoration,
monogrammed, by Gorham,
19thC, 36in (91.5cm) long.
$750–880 *FBG*

A pair of Sheffield plate wine
coolers, with foliage and shell
rims, 2 reeded handles issuing
from grapevines, detachable
liner and collar, c1810,
11in (28cm) high.
$1,200–1,400 *SLN*

WINE ANTIQUES

A three-piece moulded whisky flask, engraved, 19thC, 8in (20.5cm) high.
$480–530 *C(S)*

This type of flask was handmade in 3 pieces and then moulded together.

A spirit flask, with iridescent surface, c1800, 5in (12.5cm) high.
$70–80 *Har*

r. A Victorian Mannerist style silver-gilt and glass claret jug, with lidded grotesque mask spout over acanthus and strapwork neck, the body engraved with flowers, bell husk swags and maidenhair fern, with anthemion and grotesque mask scroll handle, Sheffield 1865, 12in (30.5cm) high.
$2,400–2,700 *EH*

MILLER'S COMPARES . . .

I A dark brown mallet-shaped wine bottle, with a seal inscribed 'I Rumbo Calne 1731', minor chips, 6¼in (16cm) high.
$3,200–3,500 *C*

II A dark brown onion-shaped wine bottle, with a seal inscribed 'I Warren 1764', minor chips, 7½in (19cm) high.
$1,500–1,800 *C*

The fact that *item I* bears a seal of a much earlier date than *item II* makes it immediately more desirable to a collector. As the seals are all initialled and relate to particular cellars, bottles from a cellar for which comparatively few bottles were made or, alternatively, survive, will command a premium. A further factor is that the mallet shape of *item I* is much scarcer than the onion shape of *item II*.   *C*

r. A George III brandy warming saucepan and cover, with engraved crest, hinged spout cover, stained ivory finial and turned wooden handle, by Henry Chawner and John Emes, London 1796, 6in (15cm) high, 10.5oz.
$950–1,100 *Bea*

A mahogany bottle carrier, with turned legs and casters, early 19thC, 17¼in (44cm) wide.
$3,500–4,000 *S*

A Victorian glass claret jug, wheel-engraved with grapevine detail, with engraved silver-plated mounts and scrolled handle, c1875, 11in (28cm) high.
$370–420 *GAK*

r. A Victorian silver-mounted glass claret jug, with star-cut tapering glass body, engraved 'Rangoon Boat Club Regatta, 1891', Sheffield 1890, 9in (23cm) high.
$950–1,100 *C(S)*

A late Victorian cut glass diamond-engraved claret jug, with re-plated mount and handle, 12in (30.5cm) high.
$140–160 *GAK*

A Victorian silver-mounted plain glass claret jug, by Latham and Morton, Birmingham 1900, 8in (20.5cm) high.
$450–520 *Bea*

r. A silver-mounted claret jug, the clear glass etched with flowers, possibly Portuguese, mid-20thC, 11½in (29cm) high.
$880–960 *WeH*

A japanned gilt-metal-mounted trefoil-shaped decanter stand, with 3 blue glass bottles, decorated in gilt with cartouches, one stopper damaged, c1800, 10in (25.5cm) high.
$800–880 *S(S)*

A Sheffield plate decanter stand, with 4 cut-glass spirit decanters, c1820, 10½in (26.5cm) high.
$900–1,000 *SSW*

A pair of George III Sheffield plate decanter stands, the sides with pierced engraved paterae linked by bands of foliage, with turned mahogany bases, 5½in (14cm) diam.
$420–480 *WW*

A Victorian rosewood serpentine-fronted decanter box, the hinged lid and panel front brass-inlaid with a cartouche of scrolling foliage, enclosing 4 decanters and 16 glasses, in a gilt stand, 5 pieces later, 11in (28cm) high.
$950–1,100 *P(Sc)*

A toleware trefoil-shaped liqueur stand, enamelled in red with gilt flowering foliage, the central column and handle with a bronzed classical figure, containing 3 cut-glass decanters, early 19thC, 11½in (29cm) high.
$880–960 *P(S)*

A silver-plated stand, with 3 spirit decanters, c1840, decanters 6¼in (16cm) high.
$720–800 *Som*

A silver bottle holder, by W. Hutton & Sons, Sheffield 1899, 4¾in (12cm) diam.
$720–800 *THOM*

r. A Victorian burr walnut tantalus box, with a hinged folding cover, hinged side opening doors and a lift-out tantalus frame with 4 decanters and 11 glasses, slight damage, 12¾in (32.5cm) wide.
$680–750 *TMA*

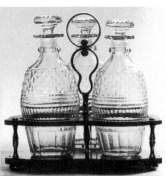

An ormolu and papier mâché decanter stand, containing 3 cut-glass spirit decanters, c1815, 9in (23cm) high.
$770–870 *FD*

A silver-plated tantalus, containing 3 glass decanters, c1890, 13½in (34.5cm) high.
$1,100–1,300 *JIL*

A George III Sheffield plate wine cooler, with 4 reeded bands and loop handles, engraved with a crest, detachable liner and rim, c1800, 8¾in (22cm) high.
$1,000–1,200 *WW*

A George III toddy ladle,
with whalebone handle,
14in (35.5cm) high.
$180–220 *PSA*

A set of 3 wine labels,
inscribed 'Claret',
'Madeira' and 'Sherry',
possibly by John Russell,
c1760, 2in (5cm) wide.
$200–240 *P(B)*

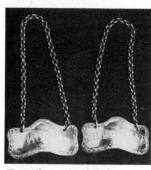

Two silver wine labels,
inscribed 'Champagne'
and 'Hock', London,
c1790, 2in (5cm) wide.
$320–350 *DIC*

A silver vine leaf label, pierced
with 'Madeira', London 1852,
2½in (6.5cm) wide.
$160–240 *DIC*

A silver shell and foliate wine label,
London 1827, 2½in (6.5cm) wide.
$240–280 *DIC*

A set of 5 inscribed silver bottle collar labels,
by Matthew Fenton & Co, Sheffield 1794,
3½in (9cm) diam.
$1,200–1,300 *DIC*

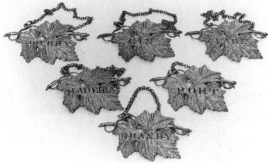

Six pierced silver vine leaf labels, with chains, by
Joseph Willmore, Birmingham 1827–32, 2in (5cm) wide.
$720–800 *WW*

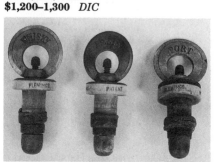

Three bottle stoppers, inscribed 'Port',
'Whisky' and 'Brandy', with Sheffield
plate tops, late 19thC, 3¼in (8.5cm) high.
$95–105 *SPU*

A George III silver
two-part wine funnel,
with beaded edges,
by S H, London 1794,
6in (15cm) high.
$560–600 *GAK*

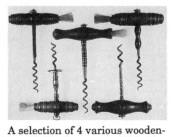

A selection of 4 various wooden-
handled corkscrews, c1830–80,
longest 6¼in (16cm).
$15–25 each
bottom left. A walnut-handled
corkscrew, with brass shank
and button, inscibed 'Wilmot
& Roberts Patent', c1825,
5¼in (13cm) long.
$100–140 *CS*

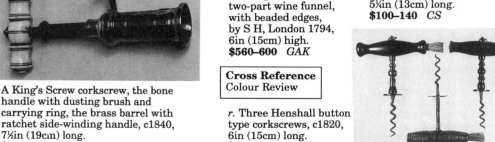

A King's Screw corkscrew, the bone
handle with dusting brush and
carrying ring, the brass barrel with
ratchet side-winding handle, c1840,
7½in (19cm) long.
$520–560 *Har*

Cross Reference
Colour Review

r. Three Henshall button
type corkscrews, c1820,
6in (15cm) long.
$40–60 each *CS*

A metal corkscrew, 19thC, 4¾in (12cm) long. $90–100 *SPU*

A Henshall patent mahogany-handled corkscrew, with turned brass shaft and button, c1840, 5¼in (13cm) long. $100–120 *Har*

An open-framed corkscrew, 19thC, 6½in (16.5cm) long. $100–115 *SPU*

A Farrow & Jackson style open-framed brass corkscrew, c1850, 7¼in (18.5cm) long. $130–145 *Har*

Two corkscrews, *l.* with wooden handle, *r.* of eyebrow type, 19thC, longest 5in (12.5cm). $15–20 each *No7*

Two corkscrews, with brushes, 19thC, longest 5½in (14cm). $70–100 each *SPU*

A brass corkscrew, with two-pillar frame and rosewood handle, c1870, 4¼in (11cm) long. $80–90 *Har*

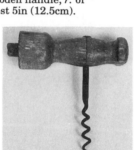

A Victorian corkscrew, with wooden handle, 4¼in (11cm) long. $40–50 *SPU*

Two two-part lever type corkscrews, *l.* inscribed 'The Tangent Lever' *r.* inscribed 'Lund', c1880, longest 8in (20.5cm). $55–70 each *CS*

A wooden-handled corkscrew, with sliding screw action, brush missing, 19thC, 5in (12.5cm) long. $3,500–4,000 *E*

This corkscrew, having been estimated at $80–130, attracted great interest in the saleroom as it was an unrecorded example, finally selling for over $3,200.

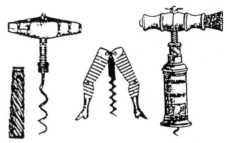

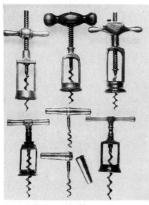

A selection of all-steel corkscrews, late 19thC, longest 6½in (16.5cm).
$15–70 each *CS*

A cellarman type all-metal corkscrew, with button on shaft, c1880, 4¾in (12cm) long.
$30–40 *Har*

A wooden-handled corkscrew, with lever, 19thC, 5½in (14cm) long.
$80–100 *SPU*

An A1 all-steel double lever corkscrew, by James Heeley & Sons, c1890, 6in (15cm) long.
$95–105 *Har*

Three all-steel corkscrews, late 19thC, 6½in (16.5cm) long.
$15–40 each *CS*

An all-metal corkscrew, by James Heeley & Sons, Weir's Patent 1884, extended 12½in (32cm) long.
$110–130 *Har*

An Excelsior steel open-framed corkscrew, with bone handle, c1900, 5½in (14cm) long.
$120–140 *Har*

An American wooden-handled 'T' bar corkscrew, c1890, 5in (12.5cm) long.
$30–40 *Har*

An Italian four-pillar brass corkscrew, late 19thC, 6in (15cm) long.
$105–120 *Bar*

A cellarman type all-metal corkscrew, c1900, 5½in (14cm) long.
$20–25 *Har*

A German all-metal perpetual corkscrew, c1900, 6¾in (17cm) long.
$80–100 *Bar*

r. A brass bottle opener, inscribed 'Lands End', 1930s, 5½in (14cm) long.
$15–25 *BGA*

l. A silver-plated champagne tap, c1910, 5in (12.5cm) long.
$65–80 *TAC*

Four French cork pullers, 1930–60, longest 4in (10cm).
$15–25 each *Bar*

Vintage Wines & Spirits

r. A half case of Cockburn's vintage port, 1950.
$240–280 *WL*

A bottle of Boutillier G. Briand Grande Fine Champagne Cognac, vintage 1906.
$200–240 *Bon(C)*

A bottle of W. & J. Graham & Co vintage port, embossed wax seal, 1945.
$350–380 *Bon(C)*

Three bottles of Chambertin Clos de Bèze vintage Burgundy wine, 1945.
$320–350 *Bon(C)*

A bottle of Château Latour Premier Grand Cru Classé, 1959.
$1,100–1,200 *S*

Vintage Wines
When buying vintage wines remember there is always a risk of cork failure, as corks over 20 years old begin to lose their elasticity.

Twelve bottles of Château Margaux Premier Grand Cru Classé, vintage 1970.
$850–900 *Bon(C)*

A bottle of Ballantine's Liqueur Blended Scotch Whisky, c1934.
$400–440 *C(S)*

A bottle of Château Lafite Rothschild Premier Cru Classé Pauillac, vintage 1978.
$110–130 *Bon(C)*

A bottle of Special Purest and Oldest Whiskey, from N. Glen Williams' Estate, Williams, N.C., 1890.
$560–620 *C(S)*

r. A bottle of Hill Thomson & Co Something Special Liqueur, c1940.
$320–350 *C(S)*

A bottle of The Distiller's Company King George IV Liqueur Whisky, early 20thC.
$560–620 *C(S)*

CLOCKS
Bracket Clocks

An ebony-veneered striking spring clock, by Aylwood of Guildford, with pull quarter repeat on 2 bells, c1710, 12½in (32cm) high.
$19,000–24,000 *DRA*

A mahogany bracket clock, with 8in (20cm) silvered convex dial signed Willm Addis, London, the twin fusee movement with signed and engraved backplate, restored verge escapement, 18thC, 19½in (49cm) high.
$6,500–8,000 *P*

An ebonised bracket clock, the break-arch 7in (18cm) dial with silvered chapter ring and signed A. J. Austen, subsidiary dials in the arch, the 3 train fusee movement with anchor escapement, chiming on 8 bells or 4 gongs and striking on a further gong, c1880, 19⅜in (50cm) high, with a matching bracket.
$2,200–2,400 *S(S)*

A figured walnut four-glass bracket clock, by Barraud & Lund, London, striking on a gong, c1850, 12in (30.5cm) high.
$8,000–9,500 *DRA*

A Victorian ebonised bracket clock, the silvered dial signed Barraud & Lund, the twin chain fusee movement with anchor escapement and strike on gong, 15in (38cm) high.
$1,600–1,900 *CSK*

A William and Mary ebonised bracket timepiece, the dial with silvered alarm disc and silvered chapter ring, by William Cattell, the 6 ringed pillar gut fusee movement with knife-edge verge escapement and Webster backcock, pull quarter repeat on 2 bells and alarm on a further bell, 13½in (34cm) high.
$7,500–8,500 *C*

A boulle bracket clock, by Martin Benoist, Paris, with verge escapement, c1750, 50in (127cm) high.
$13,500–16,000 *DRA*

A Regency mahogany bracket clock, the white painted dial signed by Edward Bird, the twin wire fusee movement with anchor escapement and strike on bell, pull trip repeat, damaged, 20¼in (51.5cm) high.
$775–850 *CSK*

r. A mahogany bracket clock, the arched engraved silvered dial with date aperture, signed by John Bryan, Shadwell, the 5 pillar twin fusee movement now converted to anchor escapement, 18thC, 20½in (52cm) high.
$3,200–3,500 *P*

A Regency mahogany bracket clock, the white-painted dial signed Ja's Cattlin, London, the twin fusee movement with anchor escapement and strike on bell, 15in (38cm) high.
$1,200–1,400 *CSK*

A Georgian mahogany bracket clock, the 7in (18cm) brass dial with strike/silent to arch, signed James Chater, London, the brass movement bell striking, 14½in (37cm) high.
$3,500–4,500 *Bri*

A rosewood bracket clock, the painted arch dial signed G. J. Clerke, London, the twin train fusee movement with anchor escapement and striking on a bell, c1840, 27¼in (69cm) high.
$1,100–1,300 *S(S)*

A Regency mahogany bracket clock, the dial signed Goodhugh, London, with strike/silent lever, 2 train bell striking and trip repeating fusee chain movement, anchor escapement and mahogany wall bracket, c1810, 20½in (52cm) high.
$4,400–5,000 *S*

A Regency ebonised and brass-mounted 8-day bracket clock, by Grant of London, with convex dial and strike/silent facility, with anchor escapement and striking the hours on a bell with repeat, c1810, 21in (53.5cm) high.
$7,000–8,000 *PAO*

A George III ebonised bracket clock, the dial signed Thos Hill, London, the matted centre with mock pendulum and calendar apertures, the 5 pillar twin fusee movement with original verge escapement, early 18thC, 15¾in (40cm) high.
$6,400–7,200 *C*

A late George III bracket clock, the dial signed Grant, London, with strike/silent ring in the arch, the 4 pillar triple chain fusee movement chiming on 8 bells via 8 hammers, anchor escapement, late 18thC, 13¼in (33.5cm) high.
$10,200–11,200 *C*

A leaf-carved mahogany 8-day bracket clock, by Hudson of Otley, with white enamel dial, early 19thC, 20½in (52cm) high.
$1,300–1,600 *AH*

A Victorian carved walnut bracket clock, the white painted dial signed Hills, Sudbury, the twin fusee movement with anchor escapement and strike on gong, slight damage, 16½in (42cm) high.
$800–1,000 *CSK*

A William and Mary walnut marquetry 8-day bracket clock, by Nathaniel Hodges of London, with pull repeat striking on the hour, 14¼in (36cm) high.
$17,000–19,000 *J&L*

HINTS ON DATING BRACKET CLOCKS

Dials	Date	Period
Square dial	to c1770	pre-George III
Break-arch dial	from c1720	George I or later
Round/painted/silvered	from c1760	George III or later

Case finish		
Ebony veneer	from c1660 to c1850	Carolean to mid-Victorian
Walnut	from c1670 to c1870	Carolean to Victorian
Marquetry	from c1680 to c1740	Carolean to early Georgian
Rosewood	from c1790	from mid-Georgian
Lacquered	from c1700 to c1760	Queen Anne to early Georgian
Mahogany	from c1730	from early Georgian

A Regency mahogany bracket clock, the white enamel dial inscribed John Jeffries, Biggleswade, with 2 train fusee movement and repeater mechanism, 19in (48cm) high.
$2,000–2,400 *RBB*

A mahogany 8-day bracket clock, by Thomas Langford of London, the brass dial with engraved and silvered centre with date and strike/silent feature, striking the hour on a bell and repeating at will, c1775, 20in (51cm) high.
$14,000–15,500 *PAO*

An ebonised bracket timepiece, the silvered dial engraved with foliate decoration, signed on backplate A. Mitchell, Glasgow, the fusee movement with pendulum, 19thC, 8¾in (22cm) high.
$1,000–1,200 *P(Sc)*

A George II ebonised miniature bracket clock, the dial signed Marwick Markham, London, the movement with 7 baluster pillars, twin chain fusees, knife-edge verge escapement, strike on bell and now lacking pull quarter repeat, possibly associated, 11¼in (28.5cm) high.
$8,800–9,600 *C*

A George III ebonised 8-day bracket clock, the brass dial with silvered chapter ring, by Thomas Reid, Edinburgh, bell strike, converted to anchor escapement, 17in (43cm) high.
$4,800–5,600 *J&L*

A Regency mahogany 8-day bracket clock, by George Lowe of Gloucester, with brass foliate inlaid front panel, 8in (20cm) silvered dial, engraved brass double fusee movement, striking on bell and hour repeater attachment, 17in (43cm) high.
$1,450–1,800 *GH*

A William and Mary ebonised and gilt-metal-mounted bracket clock, the dial signed Henry Massy, London, with silvered chapter ring, the 6 ringed pillar twin fusee movement now with anchor escapement, strike on bell, pull quarter repeat train and strike/silent lever removed, 16in (41cm) high.
$7,000–8,000 *C*

A George III mahogany bracket clock, the engraved chapter ring signed Thos Simpson, Hertford, with strike/silent and pendulum rings to the arch, the twin wire fusee movement now with anchor escapement, strike on bell and pull trip repeat, 16¾in (42.5cm) high.
$5,000–6,000 *CSK*

A George III mahogany bracket clock, the arched brass dial with silvered chapter ring and date aperture signed by James Smith, London, with strike/silent subsidiary dial, the twin fusee movement with verge escapement and engraved backplate, 19½in (49.5cm) high.
$4,000–4,800 *P*

A mahogany and ormolu-mounted bracket clock, by A. & H. Rowley, late 19thC, 20in (51cm) high.
$1,000–1,100 *GAZE*

r. An ebonised and fruitwood 8-day bracket clock, the arched silvered dial signed Nathaniel Tranter, London, with strike/silent dial to arch and calendar dial, striking and repeating movement with verge escapement, 18thC, 18in (45.5cm) high.
$2,800–3,200 *CAG*

A late Victorian ebonised gilt-brass bracket clock, by S. Smith & Son, London, the movement with 9 bells and one gong, 29in (74cm) high.
$2,700–3,200 *Bea(E)*

A rosewood bracket clock, the enamel dial signed J. Thwaites & Reed, London, the twin fusee movement striking on a bell, signed and engraved backplate, c1840, 19½in (49cm) high.
$2,700–3,200 *Bon*

A mahogany bracket clock, by James Warne, London, with strike/silent feature to the arch, 8-day movement with verge escapement, striking the hours on a bell, c1765, 21in (53cm) high.
$15,500–17,000 *PAO*

A Victorian mahogany and brass-inlaid bracket clock, the white painted dial signed Webster, London, the twin chain fusee movement with anchor escapement and strike on gong, 19½in (49.5cm) high.
$1,500–1,800 *CSK*

A William IV mahogany bracket clock, the white painted dial signed Wither, Bristol, the twin wire fusee movement with strike on bell, 17in (43.5cm) high.
$950–1,100 *CSK*

A George III mahogany and brass-inlaid bracket timepiece, 15in (38cm) high.
$1,200–1,600 *DaD*

A George III ebonised bracket clock, signed Thos Wright, London, the 8-day 2 train fusee movement with 5 ringed pillars, with hour strike and pull repeat on a bell, 16in (41cm) high.
$5,000–6,000 *DN*

Wright's clocks are rare. He was a maker of all sorts of scientific instruments and sundials, and invented a number of watch and chronometer escapements. In 1783 Wright patented a form of detent escapement and was appointed watchmaker to the King.

A Regency mahogany and brass-inlaid bracket timepiece, with cream enamel dial and single fusee movement, 16½in (42cm) high.
$1,500–1,900 *C(S)*

A mahogany bracket clock, with painted dial, calendar aperture, strike/silent and rise/fall regulator in the arch, 5 pillar twin fusee movement, verge escapement, striking on a bell, c1780, 24in (61cm) high.
$3,600–4,200 *Bon*

An ebonised bracket timepiece with silvered dial, French single-barrel movement with anchor escapement, c1910, 14in (36cm) high.
$400–500 *CSK*

A late Victorian mahogany bracket clock, by John Moore, London, the silvered and engraved dial with subsidiaries, chimes on 4 and 8 gongs, the 3 chain fusee movement with anchor escapement, 29½in (75cm) high.
$2,200–2,700 *CSK*

r. A late Victorian carved oak bracket clock, the brass dial with silvered chapter ring, subsidiary dials, the musical movement with 5 hammers striking on 5 coiled gongs, 25in (64cm) high.
$1,900–2,200 *C(S)*

A French brass 8-day bracket clock, by Japy Frères, c1880, 16in (40.5cm) high.
$850–950 *OT*

MILLER'S COMPARES . . .

A French ebonised and red boulle bracket clock, with brass dial, the movement striking on a gong, some damage, 19thC, 24in (61cm) high. **$950–1,000** *Bea(E)*

A painted bracket clock, the movement repeating and striking on 3 bells, late 18thC, 43¼in (110cm) high, and conforming bracket. **$5,000–5,600** *S(Z)*

I An ormolu and shell boulle bracket clock, the dial signed Charles Le Roy, Paris, the 5 pillar movement now with a half deadbeat escapement, some repairs, mid-18thC, 35in (89cm) high, together with a matching bracket. **$5,000–5,800** *Bon*

II A French gilt, ormolu and boulle bracket clock, with enamel dial, signed Jean Prévost, the movement with 5 vase-shaped pillars, later anchor escapement, mid-18thC, 22½in (57cm) high, together with a matching under-curved bracket. **$2,800–3,500** *Bon*

Both these clocks are attractive pieces, but *Item I* **fetched twice as much as** *Item II* **in the saleroom because it was in more original condition. Both clocks had later escapements but** *Item II* **also had regilded mounts. Moreover, the Le Roy family are considered by most horologists to be one of the best French clock makers and** *Item I* **was sold complete with a letter from Charles Le Roy.** *Bon*

l. A rosewood and inlaid bracket clock, the dial with silvered chapter ring, regulation, chime/silent and chime selection dials, the 3 train fusee W & H movement chiming on a nest of 8 bells or 4 gongs and striking on a further gong, c1900, 22¾in (58cm) high. **$2,400–3,200** *S(S)*

A Louis XV ormolu-mounted boulle bracket clock, with shell cast dial, striking movement signed Viger à Paris, the cartouche-shaped case cast with a seated figure of Diana, chinoiserie supports and scroll feet, 52in (132cm) high, on an ogee-shaped bracket. **$10,500–11,500** *Bon*

A George III style rosewood and walnut 8-day bracket clock, with arched brass dial with foliate scroll spandrels, and subsidiary dials for strike/silent and seconds, inverted bell-top case, brass urn and flame finial, foliate scroll and paw feet, c1900, 28¾in (73cm) high. **$2,400–2,800** *WL*

Carriage Clocks

A French brass-cased 8-day carriage timepiece, the dial signed S. Krakauer, Barnsley, within a *champlevé* enamel mask, early 19thC, 6in (15cm) high.
$880–1,000 *HOLL*

A French gilt-bronze *grande sonnerie pendule d'officier* alarm carriage clock, the enamel dial signed LeRoi & Fils, 3 train movement with fusee and chain for the going train and verge escapement, c1800, 8½in (21.5cm) high.
$9,600–10,400 *S*

A one-piece carriage clock, the strike/repeat alarm on a bell, c1845, 6¼in (16cm) high.
$2,000–2,300 *DRA*

A gilded carriage clock, with engraved and silvered dial, signed by Jas McCabe, Royal Exchange London, striking and repeating, c1850, 10in (25.5cm) high.
$27,000–29,500 *DRA*

Carriage Clocks

Carriage clocks originated in France from the *pendule de voyage*, literally 'travel clock', made by Abraham-Louis Bréguet (1747–1823). Paul Garnier (1801–69) then introduced a simple basic design, making it possible to produce these clocks more cheaply. Many carriage clocks were exported to England at the time of manufacture.

A French gilt-brass repeating carriage clock, with enamel dial, bell striking movement, with club-tooth lever escapement, c1850, 5¼in (13cm) high, with leather travelling case.
$1,500–1,800 *S*

An Austrian *grande sonnerie* alarm carriage clock, the enamel dial signed Ad Uhlig in Wien, the gong striking repeating movement with cylinder escapement and 4 standing barrels, c1860, 5in (12.5cm) high, with leather travelling case.
$3,200–4,000 *S*

A French gorge-cased carriage clock, enamel dial with subsidiary alarm dial, repeating bell striking movement signed by retailer Black-Murray, Hastings Street, Calcutta, with club-tooth lever escapement, c1870, 4½in (11.5cm) high, with red leather travelling case.
$1,900–2,200 *S*

An oval porcelain-panelled striking carriage clock, by Brunelot, c1870, 6½in (16.5cm) high.
$8,000–8,800 *DRA*

A French gilt-brass gorge-cased carriage clock, with white enamel dial, the silvered lever platform with bimetallic balance, strike on bell, c1870, 5½in (14cm) high.
$880–1,100 *CSK*

A Victorian brass striking carriage clock, the silvered dial with seconds ring intersecting the chapter ring, signed Thos Earnshaw London, with lever escapement, 5¾in (14.5cm) high.
$1,100–1,200 *CSK*

Cross Reference
Colour Review

r. A French gorge-cased carriage clock, by H. Jacot, with white enamel dial, repeating bell striking movement with lever platform escapement, c1865, 5¼in (13.5cm) high.
$1,600–1,900 *S(S)*

A French miniature gilt-brass-cased carriage timepiece, with 1in (2.5cm) enamel dial, engine-turned gilt surround, movement with cylinder escapement, marked with characters for Beijing retailers Henlida, c1875, 3½in (9cm) high.
$1,500–1,900 *S*

A French corniche-cased carriage clock, with pale blue enamel dial, the gong striking movement with ratchet-tooth lever escapement, c1880, 6in (15cm) high.
$800–950 *S*

A French engraved and porcelain-panelled carriage clock, the dial with floral decorated centre, the movement with lever escapement and striking on a gong, in a gilt corniche style case, c1880, 7in (18cm) high.
$6,500–7,200 *Bon*

A French gilt-brass carriage timepiece, c1880, 7in (18cm) high.
$400–550 *GEM*

r. A French brass gorge-cased *grande sonnerie* carriage clock, with white enamel dial, the repeating movement striking on 2 gongs, lever platform escapement, strike selection lever in the base, c1880, 5¾in (14.5cm) high.
$2,400–2,800 *S(S)*

A French brass *anglaise riche* carriage clock, striking on the hour and half-hour, c1880, 10½in (26.5cm) high.
$3,800–4,200 *PAO*

A French gilt-brass corniche-cased carriage clock, with white enamel dial, silvered lever platform to the bimetallic balance, strike/repeat on gong to backplate, c1880, 5½in (14cm) high.
$1,000–1,100 *CSK*

A French *mignonette* corniche-cased 8-day carriage clock, with enamel dial and cylinder platform escapement, c1880, 2¾in (7cm) high.
$1,400–1,500 *JIL*

A French corniche-cased 8-day repeater carriage clock, c1880, 6¾in (17cm) high.
$960–1,100 *TPA*

A French brass *grande sonnerie* carriage clock, with alarm dial, the silvered lever platform with bimetallic balance, strike/repeat/alarm on 2 gongs, with *anglaise* case, c1890, 6in (15cm) high.
$1,600–1,900 *CSK*

A French brass carriage clock, c1890, 8in (20.5cm) high, with original carrying case.
$1,900–2,200 *PAO*

A French miniature enamelled carriage clock, c1900, 3¼in (8cm) high, with original presentation box.
$1,600–1,900 *GEM*

A French brass *anglaise riche* carriage clock, the gilt-metal mask dial with subsidiary alarm dial, silvered lever platform to the bimetallic balance, strike/repeat/alarm on gong, c1890, 6½in (16.5cm) high.
$950–1,100 *CSK*

A French miniature gilt-brass carriage timepiece, with enamel dial, club-tooth lever escapement, c1890, 3in (7cm) high, with red leather travelling case.
$720–800 *S*

A French gilt-brass corniche-cased repeating carriage clock, with enamel dial, gong striking Pons movement with ratchet-tooth lever escapement, alarm bell in the base, c1890, 8½in (21.5cm) high.
$2,800–3,000 *S*

The large size of this clock contributed to its high price.

A French gilt-brass *anglaise riche* carriage clock, with silvered mask to chapter ring, platform lever escapement, strike/repeat on gong to backplate, c1890, 6¼in (16cm) high.
$600–680 *CSK*

r. A French gilt-brass carriage clock, with arched dial and recessed chapter ring, platform escapement, strike/ repeat on gong, c1900, 5½in (14cm) high.
$1,000–1,200 *CSK*

l. A gilt-brass *champlevé* carriage timepiece, the off-white dial within foliate enamel mask signed by Benetfink & Co, London, with platform escapement, c1900, 5¼in (13cm) high, with leather travelling case.
$650–800 *CSK*

A French brass and enamelled carriage clock, with brass dial, the twin train movement with lever platform escapement, striking the hours and half-hours on a gong with repeater mechanism, 19thC, 6in (15cm) high, with leather travelling case.
$2,000–2,400 *P(Sc)*

A French gilt-brass corniche-cased carriage clock, with white enamel dial and retailer's signature Manoah Rhodes & Sons Ltd, Bradford, silvered lever platform to the bimetallic balance, strike/repeat on gong to the backplate, c1900, 4¾in (12cm) high.
$400–480 *CSK*

A repeating carriage clock, signed by T. H. Smith & Sons, Paris, c1890, 4¾in (12cm) high.
$1,300–1,450 *GEM*

A French carriage timepiece, the off-white dial within *champlevé* enamel mask, with subsidiary alarm ring, platform escapement, c1900, 4¾in (12cm) high. **$1,000–1,200** *CSK*

A French brass corniche-cased carriage clock, with gilt mask to enamel chapter ring, the silvered lever platform with bimetallic balance, strike/repeat on gong, c1900, 5¾in (14.5cm) high. **$560–640** *CSK*

A French gilt-brass corniche-cased carriage clock, with white enamel dial, the silvered lever platform with bimetallic balance, strike/repeat on gong, c1900, 5¾in (14.5cm) high. **$750–850** *CSK*

A French gilt-brass carriage clock, the dial signed Ramsay, Dundee, gong striking movement with repeater, c1900, 7in (18cm) high, with leather case. **$1,000–1,200** *AP*

A Swiss miniature 8-day enamelled carriage clock, by Zenith, c1920, 2½in (5.5cm) high, with original box. **$1,100–1,300** *GEM*

A French gilt-brass *anglaise riche* carriage timepiece, the white enamel dial with gilt-metal mask signed by retailer H. Greaves, platform cylinder escapement, c1900, 5½in (14cm) high. **$280–360** *CSK*

A French *mignonette* 8-day carriage clock, with enamel dial, silver by William Comyns, London 1903, 2¾in (7cm) high. **$2,200–2,600** *JIL*

A Swiss nickel 8-day repeating carriage clock, the enamel dial signed by Henri Blanc, Genève, with lever escapement and striking on 2 gongs, c1910, 3¼in (8cm) high. **$4,000–4,800** *S*

A Louis XV style brass carriage timepiece, the white enamel dial signed J. C. Vickery, silvered platform to the lever escapement, c1910, 5¼in (13cm) high. **$240–320** *CSK*

Cartel Clocks

A Louis XVI gilt-
bronze cartel clock
and barometer,
signed Chevallier
à Paris, mid-19thC,
25½in (65cm) high.
$5,000–5,600 *S(Z)*

A giltwood cartel clock,
by John Green, London,
the silvered dial with
Roman and Arabic
numerals, verge
escapement, c1760,
40in (101.5cm) high.
$8,800–10,400 *DSP*

A French Louis XV
ormolu cartel clock,
the enamel dial signed
Harel à Paris, 5 pillar
plated movement with
anchor escapement,
silk suspension and
top mounted bell with
vertical hammer, c1770,
25½in (65cm) high.
$5,600–6,400 *S*

A Swedish neo-classical
giltwood cartel clock,
the enamel dial
signed Hovenschold,
Stockholm, early 19thC,
20in (51cm) high.
$3,200–4,000 *S(NY)*

Cartel Clocks

The word 'cartel' probably originates from the
Italian *cartella*, or wall bracket. Introduced in
the 18th century in France, cartel clocks are
decorative gilt, spring driven, usually with verge
escapements. Only a few English cartel clocks were
made from 1730–70, and are highly collectable,
especially if the case is in good condition.

An ormolu cartel
timepiece, the
enamel dial signed
Louis Montjoye à
Paris, with pierced
gilt hands, narrow
anchor escapement,
silk suspension and
quarter repeating on
a single bell, c1780,
20½in (52cm) high.
$2,700–3,700 *S*

Cross Reference
Colour Review

A French gilt-bronze
cartel clock, the enamel
dial signed Julien Le
Roy à Paris, 5 pillar
plated movement with
silk suspension, anchor
escapement and outside
countwheel with top
mounted bell, c1775,
28¼in (72cm) high.
$4,800–5,600 *S*

r. A French bronze cartel
clock, by Marti et Cie,
bronze by Charpentier,
Paris, c1870,
29in (73.5cm) high.
$8,800–10,400 *DRA*

A French gilt-bronze
cartel clock, the enamel
dial signed Julien
Le Roy à Paris, verge
escapement with silk
suspension, strike
work with trip repeat
mounted on the back-
plate, restored, c1785,
16¼in (40.5cm) high.
$5,000–6,000 *S*

A Louis XV 8-day
cartel clock, striking
on 2 bells, mid-18thC,
20in (51cm) high.
$4,000–4,500 *S(Z)*

A French gilt-bronze
cartel clock, with
convex enamel dial,
bell striking movement,
c1890, 17in (43cm) high.
$2,200–2,700 *TUR*

Garnitures

A French ormolu clock garniture, the enamel dial signed Charuyer, 19thC, clock 12¼in (31cm) high, with matching candelabra.
$950–1,100 *WL*

A French gilt-bronze and porcelain clock garniture, the movement stamped Japy Frères, striking on a bell, clock 21¼in (54cm) high, together with a matching pair of twin-handled urns.
$8,000–9,500 *P*

A French gilt-bronze clock garniture, the enamel dial inscribed Balthazard à Paris, the 8-day movement striking on a bell, the case with a pair of classical figures above porcelain panels, 19thC, clock 10in (25.5cm) high, and a pair of matching candelabra.
$9,000–10,000 *WW*

A French ormolu-mounted red marble clock garniture, the white enamel dial inscribed Maple & Co, à Paris, striking on a bell, late 19thC, clock 15¼in (38.5cm) high.
$4,800–6,200 *C(S)*

A French red shell and brass-inlaid clock garniture, with gilt mounts, the enamel dial signed A. Mesnard, Bordeaux, the drum movement striking on a bell, c1880, clock 19¼in (49cm) high, with a pair of matching candelabra.
$2,200–2,700 *Bon*

A French ormolu and bronze-mounted white marble clock garniture, the 8-day countwheel movement striking on a bell, c1855, clock 15in (38cm) high.
$11,200–12,200 *JIL*

A French gilt-mounted and red tortoiseshell clock garniture, c1900, clock 10in (25.5cm) high.
$2,800–3,200 *TUR*

A French gilded spelter clock garniture, the clock and urns with porcelain panels and surmounted by putti, late 19thC, clock 18in (45.5cm) high.
$1,450–1,600 *DaD*

A Thomas Hope style bronze timepiece and garniture, c1860, clock 15½in (39.5cm) high, with a pair of matching candlesticks.
$4,000–4,500 *ARE*

A French ormolu and grey marble 8-day clock garniture, c1890, clock 13in (33cm) high, with a pair of matching candelabra.
$1,000–1,200 *TPA*

Lantern Clocks

A brass lantern clock, the dial signed John Aylward, Brentford, with silvered chapter ring, now with 19thC twin fusee movement with anchor escapement and ting tang quarter-chime, surmounted by a bell, c1700, 15in (38cm) high.
$1,400–1,600 *P*

A miniature gilt-brass lantern clock, the chapter ring with central alarm disc and single steel hand, movement with verge escapement and short bob pendulum, alarm striking on bell above, c1650, 8½in (21.5cm) high.
$6,400–7,200 *C*

A brass lantern clock, the dial signed Jno Hill, London, with verge escapement, c1700, 14½in (37cm) high.
$3,200–3,600 *S(S)*

A brass lantern clock, the dial signed Humphrey Marsh, Highworth, with single hand, 2 train weight driven posted movement with verge escapement, late 17thC, 14½in (37cm) high.
$5,600–6,200 *S*

r. A brass lantern timepiece, with replaced fusee movement, passing strike on the hour, 18thC and later, 15½in (39cm) high.
$800–880 *Bon*

A miniature lantern clock, the front signed Peter Closon, London, the movement with verge escapement and short bob pendulum, countwheel strike on bell, within galleried frets, later doors, c1640, 8¾in (22cm) high.
$4,800–5,400 *C*

A brass lantern clock, the engraved silvered chapter ring signed Smorthwait, Colchester, twin fusee movement striking on a bell mounted above, c1800, 15in (38cm) high.
$1,000–1,300 *Bon*

r. A brass lantern clock, the twin fusee movement striking on a bell mounted above, pierced and engraved front fret, 19thC, 14¾in (37.5cm) high.
$800–880 *Bon*

A brass lantern clock, signed Thos Kefford, Royston, the later movement with lever escapement, striking on bell above, early 18thC, 9¾in (24cm) high.
$580–640 *Bon*

A brass lantern clock, the dial signed Jno Wimble, Ashford, with single hand 2 train posted rope and weight driven movement with anchor escapement, lacking side frets and doors, early 18thC, 12¾in (32.5cm) high.
$2,800–3,200 *S*

silver-gilt basket, by
Mappin & Webb, the scroll
supports headed by busts of
Ceres, London 1919,
15½in (39.5cm) wide, 98oz.
8,800–9,600 S(S)

A silver-plated cake basket, with
pierced border and reeded handle,
c1875, 9in (23cm) wide.
$130–150 SSW

A sterling silver sweetmeat
dish, with handle, Sheffield
1895, 7¼in (18.5cm) wide.
$280–320 WeH

late Victorian silver-plated
stand, with cranberry glass
ner, 6in (15cm) high.
200–230 SPU

A set of 6 George IV silver salt cellars, by Thomas Death, chased with
flowers and scrolls, on rocaille and mask supports, London c1820,
4in (10cm) diam, 37oz.
$4,000–4,400 S

pair of George IV spool-shaped salt
cellars, by Jonathan Hayne, London
828, 3½in (9cm) wide, 4oz.
1,500–1,800 DN

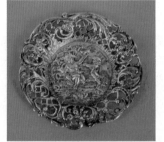

A silver dish, by James Dudley,
with trelliswork border,
the base embossed with putti,
London 1895, 4in (10cm) diam.
$190–220 WeH

A silver-gilt salt cellar,
by William Comyns & Sons,
on a dolphin base, London
1960, 4½in (11.5cm) high.
$350–400 WeH

l. A pair of silver
salt cellars, with
spoons, by Jas
Dixon & Sons,
with foliate rims,
on pad supports,
Sheffield 1909/10,
2½in (6.5cm) diam.
$350–380 WeH

A Napoleon III silver jardinière, on 4 scroll and
foliage feet, with plated liner, probably French,
c1860, 25½in (65cm) wide, 96oz.
$7,500–8,500 C(G)

set of 3 Victorian silver rose bowls, by Horace Woodward & Co,
chased with trailing foliage, the centre bowl crested with a demi-
leopard gorged with a ducal coronet, London 1890,
largest 12in (30.5cm) wide.
6,000–6,500 S

A late Victorian silver rose
bowl, by Martin, Hall & Co,
with drop handles, London
1892, 16in (40.5cm) diam, 75oz.
$4,500–5,500 S(S)

A silver wine cup, the rim prick-engraved 'ETIH 55', maker's mark 'ET', c1655, 6in (15cm) high, 11oz.
$5,500–6,500 *C*

A Scandinavian silver tankard, c1690, 6¼in (16cm) high, 17oz.
$5,600–6,200 *C*

A silver tankard, with presentation inscription, by Robert Cooper, London 1697, 6½in (16.5cm) high, 22oz.
$8,500–9,500 *C*

A silver salver, unmarked, c1720, 17⅛in (44cm) diam.
$2,200–2,700 *DN*

A pair of Russian silver-gilt and *cloisonné* enamel water jugs, by Pawel Akimow Ovchinnikov, maker's mark below the Imperial warrant, Moscow 1879, 10in (25cm) high, 88.5oz.
$6,600–7,200 *S(Am)*

A silver salver, engraved with coat-of-arms, by William Eaton, London 1816, 11¾in (30cm) diam, 44oz.
$4,000–4,800 *C*

A silver-gilt polo challenge cup trophy, engraved with winners' names 1890–98, by Robert Hennell, 1871, 19in (48cm) high, 138oz.
$5,000–5,600 *C(S)*

A silver tankard, with domed cover, by William Shaw II and William Priest, London 1752, 7½in (19cm) high, 29oz.
$2,800–3,200 *DN*

A pair of French silver three-light candelabra, the armorial-engraved detachable candle branches with flame finials, the bases raised on paw and leaf supports, by Jacques-Florent-Joseph Beydel, Paris, c1800, 18½in (47cm) high, 135oz.
$12,000–13,000 *S*

A set of 4 leaf-chased silver candlesticks, by Elkington & Co Ltd, Birmingham 1904, 12¾in (32cm) high.
$3,200–3,500 *DN*

rosewood bottle stand,
825, 10in (25cm) diam.
50–1,100 *GBr*

An oak tantalus, with 3 cut-glass
decanters, c1880, 13½in (34cm) wide.
$680–750 *WeH*

An oak, silver-plated and
brass-bound tantalus,
c1900, 16in (40.5cm) high.
$3,200–3,500 *CSK*

glass sherry
canter, c1870,
¼in (36cm) high.
20–400 *MJW*

A silver-mounted oak
tantalus, Sheffield 1908,
14in (35.5cm) wide.
$2,400–2,700 *S(S)*

A silver wine label,
Birmingham 1843.
$140–160 *DIC*

A silver port bottle
label, London 1873.
$100–120 *PSA*

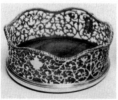

Three Danish silver wine ladles,
19thC, 17in (43cm) long.
$640–720 *AEF*

A King's Screw corkscrew, with bronze
barrel, the bone handle with brush and
carrying ring, c1830, 7½in (19cm) long.
$430–480 *Har*

vo silver wine coasters,
ndon, c1807, 6in
5cm) diam.
,000–4,400 *S(S)*

A pair of silver coasters,
c1768, 5in (12.5cm) diam.
$4,700–5,500 *DIC*

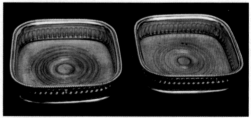

Two Sheffield plate wine coasters, with fluted
sides, c1810, 5in (12.5cm) square.
$720–880 *DIC*

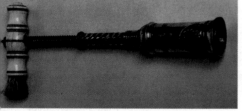

Thomason Patent 1802 bone-handled
rkscrew, with brass barrel, dusting brush and
rrying ring, c1840, 7½in (19cm) long.
80–320 *Har*

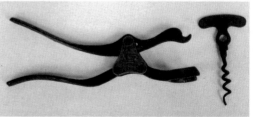

A Lund's London patent lever
and corkscrew, mid-19thC,
8in (20cm) long.
$100–120 *SPU*

A mahogany 8-day bracket clock, by Bennett, London, striking the hours on a bell, with brass lions' mask handles, c1820, 17in (43cm) high.
$5,600–6,200 *PAO*

A Regency mahogany bracket clock, signed Thos Gibbs, Stratford-on-Avon, 17½in (44.5cm) high.
$3,600–4,500 *CSK*

A Regency mahogany bracket clock, by Goodhugh, London, c1820, 18in (45cm) high.
$5,000–5,800 *DRA*

A mahogany bracket clock, signed Jn Grant, London, c1810, 17in (43cm) high, with original wall bracket.
$6,400–7,200 *TUR*

A mahogany 8-day bracket clock, by Hollister, London, with double fusee movement and anchor escapement, c1845, 14in (35.5cm) high.
$4,400–4,800 *PAO*

A Regency ebonised fruitwood bracket clock, by N. Hart & Son, c1830, 20in (51cm) high.
$6,200–7,000 *JIL*

An early George III ebonised fruitwood bracket clock, by William Owen, London, with brass carrying handles, c1775, 20in (51cm) high.
$7,500–8,500 *JIL*

A mahogany 8-day bracket clock, by John Taylor, London, the dial with centre date, the 5 pillar verge movement striking the hours on a bell, c1770, 18in (45.5cm) high.
$12,800–14,400 *PAO*

A mahogany 8-day bracket clock, by William Seymour, London, with 5 pillar verge movement, c1770, 19in (48.5cm) high.
$11,200–12,200 *PAO*

Derek Roberts

25 Shipbourne Road, Tonbridge, Kent TN10 3DN
Tel: 01732 358986   Fax: 01732 771842

MUSIC BOXES   **FINE ANTIQUE CLOCKS**   BAROMETERS

We carry a very extensive range of fine clocks of all types including over 60 carriage clocks, a few of which are seen above.

Also shown are:
Left: A month duration walnut longcase by John Faver, London, c.1715.

Right: A fine Georgian mahogany longcase by Godfrie Poy, London.

Below: A very rare grande sonnerie striking bracket clock with skeletonised chapter ring by Joseph Knibb.

Stock lists and details of books written and supplied by us are available on request.

A satinwood bracket timepiece,
by William Williams, London,
c1808, 11in (28cm) high.
$4,000–4,500 *JIL*

A Regency ebonised and inlaid
bracket clock, with finely
engraved backplate,
brass handle and feet,
15in (38cm) high.
$5,600–6,400 *SPU*

A carved oak 8-day bracket
clock, with gilt spandrels,
mid-19thC, 16in (40.5cm) high.
$250–350 *CAT*

An Austrian ebonised bracket clock,
made for the Turkish market, with
brass floral carrying handle, 2 train
movement, verge escapement,
mid-18thC, 16in (40.5cm) high.
$800–950 *TMA*

A Regency figured mahogany 8-day
bracket clock, by C. J. R. Ardouin,
Quebec, with twin fusee movement
and anchor escapement, c1825,
16in (40.5cm) high.
$5,000–5,600 *JIL*

An ebonised bracket clock
with fusee movement and
anchor escapement, striking
on 8 bells and a gong,
c1880, 24½in (62cm) high.
$2,400–2,700 *CSK*

A French Louis XV style boulle 8-day
bracket clock, with gilt-bronze mounts,
c1850, 17in (43cm) high.
$5,000–6,000 *JIL*

A boulle striking bracket clock,
by Gilles Martinot, Paris,
c1715, 24in (61cm) high.
$1,900–2,400 *CSK*

A Swiss bracket clock, by
E. Huguenin, with bracket,
mid-18thC, 44in (112cm) high.
$8,000–8,800 *S(Z)*

Samuel Orr
Antique Clocks

36 High Street, Hurstpierpoint
West Sussex BN6 9RG

Telephone:
Hurstpierpoint (01273) 832081
(24 Hour Answerphone)

The Pantiles Spa Antiques
Tunbridge Wells
(01892) 541377
Car Phone: 0860 230888

ANTIQUE CLOCKS · BAROMETERS
RESTORATION CLOCKS PURCHASED

**FINE SELECTION OF ANTIQUE CLOCKS
FOR SALE**

Exhibitor at Olympia

OVER 200 CLOCKS ALWAYS IN STOCK

A carriage clock, retailed
by Mappin & Webb,
c1900, 8in (20cm) high.
$2,800–3,500 *GEM*

A French 8-day
carriage clock, c1910,
5¾in (14.5cm) high.
$2,000–2,300 *JIL*

A French 8-day
carriage clock, with
lever escapement, c1855,
4½in (11.5cm) high.
$3,500–4,000 *JIL*

A French 8-day carriage
timepiece, by Ferdinand
Duvinage, c1870,
4¾in (12cm) high.
$3,000–3,500 *S*

A carriage clock,
by Lucien, Paris,
restored, c1870,
8½in (21.5cm) high.
$11,200–12,800 *S*

A French *grande
sonnerie* and calendar
carriage clock, c1875,
8in (20cm) high.
$14,000–15,000 *S*

A French Japanese style carriage
clock, c1885, 5½in (14cm) high.
$7,200–8,000 *DRA*

A carriage clock, by
Richard of Paris, with
enamel chapter ring,
c1900, 6¼in (16cm) high
$1,000–1,200 *TPA*

A porcelain-mounted clock garniture, by
Japy Frères, c1855, clock 12in (30.5cm) high.
$6,400–7,200 *JIL*

A French bronze and gilt-bronze clock garniture,
by Japy Frères, clock 18½in (45.5cm) high.
$10,000–11,000 *S*

An 8-day skeleton
timepiece, c1860,
11½in (29cm) high.
$1,100–1,300 *TPA*

A brass lantern clock,
by Wm Rayment, c1720,
16in (41cm) high.
$3,500–4,500 *Bea(E)*

A Japanese brass
lantern clock, 17thC,
17¾in (45cm) high.
$5,600–7,000 *C*

A French timepiece, mounte
in a stirrup and horseshoe
c1910, 9in (23cm) high.
$320–400 *TPA*

An oak longcase
clock, c1780,
83in (211cm) high.
$3,000–3,500 *S(S)*

A walnut longcase clock, by
J. Allsop, c1705, 86in (218cm) high
$25,500–28,000 *PAO*

A mahogany longcase
clock, by John Alker,
Wigan, c1790,
94in (239cm) high.
$4,800–5,600 *S*

A mahogany 8-day longcase clock,
by Jn Boner, 18thC, 85in (216cm) high.
$10,000–11,000 *DRA*

A mahogany 8-day
longcase clock, by
George Bartle, Brigg,
with subsidiary dials,
c1825, 84in (213cm) high.
$5,600–6,400 *PAO*

A mahogany longcase clock,
c1830, 77in (196cm) high.
$3,800–4,200 *ALS*

A walnut month going
longcase clock, by Simon
de Charmes, c1715,
104in (264cm) high.
$12,800–16,000 *S*

An oak longcase cloc
early 19thC,
96in (244cm) high.
$2,400–2,700 *HOL*

A walnut 8-day longcase clock,
by John Clowes, London, with
5 pillar movement, c1710,
95in (241cm) high.
$15,200–16,800 *PAO*

An oak longcase
clock, by Deykin,
c1720, 88in
(223.5cm) high.
$6,000–7,000 *PNF*

A walnut longcase
clock, by Ellicot,
London, c1755,
96in (244cm) high.
$28,000–31,000 *PAO*

A lacquered longcase clock,
by Samuel Eny, London,
with 5 pillar movement,
c1740, 109in (277cm) high.
$15,500–17,500 *PAO*

A japanned longcase clock, by Esaye Fleureau, with 12in (30.5cm) dial, restored, c1705, 95in (241cm) high. **$4,800–5,400** *S*

A mahogany longcase clock, by D. Forbes, Leith, with glazed trunk door, c1850, 79in (201cm) high. **$5,800–6,400** *PAO*

A mahogany longcase clock, late 18thC, 87in (221cm) high. **$10,000–11,200** *ALS*

An inlaid mahogany longcase clock, by James Glass, c1840, 87in (221cm) high. **$5,000–6,000** *PAO*

An oak longcase clock, by George Goodall, 18thC, 82in (208cm) high. **$2,700–3,200** *M*

A mahogany longcase clock, by Harrison, c1775, 91in (231cm) high. **$6,400–7,000** *S*

A George III walnut 8-day longcase clock, by Emmanuel Hopperton, altered, 88in (224cm) high. **$2,700–3,200** *Bea(E)*

A mahogany longcase clock, by W. Jones, c1785, 91in (231cm) high. **$6,400–7,000** *S*

A walnut longcase clock, by John Jullion, c1762, 74in (188cm) high. **$8,500–9,500** *RIT*

r. A walnut 8-day longcase clock, by Thomas Kefford, Royston, with 5 pillar movement, c1735, 85in (217cm) high. **$12,800–14,000** *PAO*

l. An oak 8-day longcase clock, by Jenkins, Cardigan, the 13in (33cm) painted dial with moonphases to the arch, seconds and date dial, with swan neck pediment, mid-19thC, 88in (223.5cm) high. **$4,800–5,600** *ALS*

A mahogany longcase clock, by Samuel Kendall, Liverpool, with *verre églomisé* panels, c1800, 96in (244cm) high. **$5,600–7,000** *S*

A longcase clock,
by P. Miller, c1870,
85in (216cm) high.
$4,800–5,400 *ALS*

A longcase clock,
by I. Moses, c1810,
92in (234cm) high.
$5,600–6,200 *PAO*

A mahogany
longcase clock,
by Thomas Nevitt,
c1775, 93in
(236cm) high.
$4,000–4,800 *S*

A longcase clock, by
Daniel Paillet, c1760,
87in (221cm) high.
$9,500–10,500 *PAO*

A mahogany
longcase clock,
by Reid & Auld,
Edinburgh,
c1800, 90in
(230cm) high.
$8,000–9,500 *S*

A longcase clock,
by John Scott, 18thC,
87in (221cm) high.
$10,000–11,000 *ALS*

A longcase clock, by
John Seymour, c1730,
83in (210cm) high.
$6,000–7,000 *ALS*

A longcase clock,
by A. Staurenghi,
c1850, 91in
(231cm) high.
$5,000–6,000 *PAO*

A walnut longcase
clock, by William
Speakman,
restored, c1700,
94in (238cm) high.
$10,000–11,000 *S*

An oak longcase
clock, c1770,
75in (190cm) high.
$2,500–2,800 *PNF*

A mahogany musical
longcase clock,
by William Withers,
London, c1775,
107in (271cm) high.
$28,000–31,000 *PAO*

A mahogany
longcase clock,
by John Wreghit,
c1835, 89in
(226cm) high.
$6,300–7,000 *M*

A mahogany long-
case clock, rack-
and-bell striking,
c1785, 89in
(226cm) high.
$5,600–6,200 *S*

A mahogany
tubular chiming
longcase clock,
c1910, 94in
(238cm) high.
$6,000–6,500 *S*

A walnut striking
longcase clock, by
Ary van Winden,
c1730, 108in
(274cm) high.
$5,800–7,200 *S*

A mahogany longcase clock, by William Kirk, Stockport, with 13in (33cm) dial, painted moon in the arch, c1780, 94in (238cm) high.
$8,500–9,500 *S*

A walnut and floral marquetry longcase clock, by Daniel Lecount, London, with 11in (28cm) dial, seconds dial and date aperture, the trunk with glazed lenticle, restored, c1705, 80in (203cm) high.
$7,300–8,000 *C(S)*

A mahogany longcase clock, by William Logan, Glasgow, the 12in (30.5cm) painted dial showing the 4 continents and Britannia, c1810, 88in (224cm) high.
$5,000–6,000 *ALS*

A mahogany longcase clock, by William Loof, the dial with seconds, date and moon-phases, striking the hours on a bell, c1820, 96in (244cm) high.
$8,800–10,000 *PAO*

A gilt and ebony timepiece, by Bell,
London, c1820, 14in (35.5cm) high.
$3,200–4,800 *GEM*

An ormolu and
white marble
mantel clock, 1855,
14in (35.5cm) high.
$1,600–1,800 *C*

A Regency ormolu and white marble
mantel clock, attributed to Thomas
Weeks, 15¼in (38.5cm) wide.
$4,000–4,800 *C*

A Louis XVI marble and
gilt-bronze mantel clock,
18thC, 15½in (39cm) high.
$4,300–4,800 *S(Z)*

A French ormolu-mounted
mantel clock, late 19thC,
25¼in (64cm) high.
$7,000–8,000 *C*

A French boulle and
gilt-bronze mantel clock,
c1850, 35in (89cm) high.
$17,500–19,000 *S*

A French calendar
mantel clock, c1865,
19¼in (49cm) high.
$5,000–5,600 *S*

A French Bontemps
mantel clock, inlaid with
porcelain plaques, late
19thC, 21in (53cm) high.
$22,500–25,000 *S*

A French ormolu and bronze mantel clock, by
Deniere, Paris, late 19thC, 18¾in (47.5cm) high.
$7,300–8,800 *C*

A French four-glass regulator
mantel clock, by Elkington,
c1890, 18in (45.5cm) high.
$7,500–8,500 *PAO*

A French quarter striking
mantel clock, with alarm,
4 train movement, c1805,
16½in (42cm) high.
$12,000–13,500 *S*

A boulle mantel clock,
by Marti, with 8-day
French movement, c1890
12in (30.5cm) high.
$2,400–2,700 *JIL*

A white marble and ormolu mantel
clock, by Raingo Frères, surmounted
by 2 figures of maidens, c1870,
19in (48cm) high.
$3,200–3,500 *TUR*

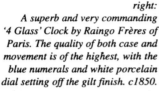

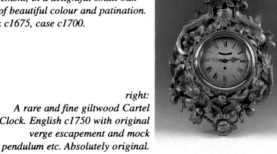

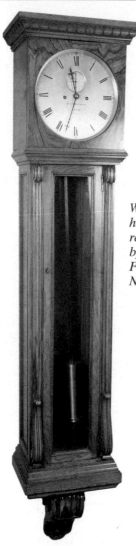

A French mantel clock,
c1880, 20in (51cm) high.
$9,000–10,000 *S*

A French marble 8-day
mantel clock, c1860,
31in (79cm) high.
$1,000–1,200 *TPA*

An ormolu and Sèvres mantel
clock, c1860, 15in (38cm) high.
$1,600–2,000 *GEM*

A French gilt-bronze
and porcelain mantel
clock, c1870,
34in (87cm) high.
$27,500–30,500 *S*

A French boulle mantel clock,
c1880, 12in (30.5cm) high.
$2,400–2,700 *TUR*

A French mantel clock,
c1880, 15in (38cm) high.
$1,100–1,300 *TPA*

A French mantel clock,
c1900, 12in (31cm) high.
$320–350 *TPA*

A French mantel clock,
c1880, 18in (45cm) high.
$2,000–2,200 *TPA*

A month going mahogany regulator, by Schonberg, Vienna, c1830, 60in (152.5cm) high.
$55,000–60,000 *GeC*

A walnut wall regulator, by Charles Frodsham, with mercury compensated pendulum, date code for 1850, 55in (140cm) high.
$40,000–45,000 *DRA*

A Scottish mahogany 8-day longcase regulator, by D. Doig, with 12in (30.5cm) silvered dial, c1850, 84in (213.5cm) high.
$11,000–12,500 *PAO*

A mahogany and maple-strung month going Viennese regulator, by Loeffler, with Huygens method of winding, c1840, 74in (188cm) high.
$50,000–56,000 *GeC*

l. A mahogany regulator, by Alex Simmons, Warwick, with 11½in (29cm) silvered dial, deadbeat escapement, maintaining power, mid-19thC, 63in (160cm) high.
$11,000–12,000 *ALS*

A gold duplex quarter repeating pocket watch, by John Cross, London, 1824, 45mm diam.
$2,000–2,400 *S*

A gilt-metal and underpainted horn pair cased pocket watch, by J. Williamson, London, c1770, 56mm diam.
$1,100–1,200 *PT*

A silver keyless Masonic fob watch, by Golay, the mother-of-pearl dial painted with inscription, nickel-plated bar movement, bimetallic balance and cabochon winder, 1940s, sides 51mm long.
$2,200–2,700 *C*

A Jacquemart quarter repeating pocket watch, early 19thC, with later cylinder escapement, 50mm diam.
$2,200–2,600 *CSK*

l. A 14ct gold hunter pocket watch, by A. Lange & Söhne, with gilt three-quarter plate movement, gold lever escapement, c1930, 51mm diam.
$2,500–3,000 *S(G)*

An enamel brooch watch, decorated with gold and silver stars, c1900, 32mm long.
$640–720 *AnS*

An 18ct pink gold hunter watch, by A. Lange & Söhne, with nickel lever movement, gold lever escapement, c1890, 54mm diam.
$10,500–11,200 *S(G)*

A Swiss gold quarter repeating musical pocket watch, the centre with enamel miniature of a shepherd, slight damage, c1820, 57mm diam.
$6,400–7,000 *S*

A 18ct gold open face pocket watch, by Patek Philippe, with 24-hour dial, subsidiary seconds dial, gilt lever movement, c1920, 56mm diam.
$9,500–10,500 *S(G)*

A Swiss automaton musical watch, by C. Reuge St Croix, playing 2 tunes, the centre decorated with a miniature of a violinist, c1880, 56mm diam.
$9,500–11,000 *PT*

A Cartier gold wristwatch, signed European Watch & Clock Co, 1920s, 23mm square.
$11,200–12,800 *C*

A Patek Philippe platinum wristwatch, with circular nickel lever movement jewelled to the centre and with wolf's tooth winding, 18 jewels adjusted to 8 positions, 1921, 37mm long.
$14,000–15,200 *S*

A Longines 14ct gold wristwatch, with gilt lever movement, c1925, 34mm diam.
$2,000–2,300 *S(G)*

A Glycine 18ct gold jump hour digital wristwatch, with tonneau nickel lever movement, signed, c1930, 37mm long.
$4,800–5,400 *S(G)*

A Patek Philippe lady's platinum and diamond set wristwatch, signed, c1930, 14mm wide.
$12,000–13,500 *C*

A Rolex stainless steel water-resistant wristwatch, with silvered dial, signed, 1938, 29mm diam.
1,500–1,700 *Bon*

A Universal Tricompax gold triple calendar moonphase chronograph wristwatch, with monometallic balance, signed, 1950s, 34mm diam.
$2,800–3,200 *C*

A Patek Philippe gentleman's gold wristwatch, 1940s, 26mm wide.
$8,500–9,500 *C*

A Rolex 18ct gold Oyster Perpetual wristwatch, with *cloisonné* enamel dial, centre seconds and lever movement, signed, 1956, bezel 32mm diam.
$70,000–80,000 *S*

A Rolex lady's gold and diamond set wristwatch, signed, 1950s, 20mm wide.
4,500–5,500 *C*

A Jaeger LeCoultre 18ct gold wristwatch, with nickel level movement signed, c1960, 34mm wide.
$2,000–2,400 *S*

A Patek Philippe 18ct gold self-winding perpetual calendar wristwatch, c1965, 37mm diam.
$30,500–33,500 *S(G)*

A Piaget lady's gold, diamond and malachite set wristwatch, 1970s, 25mm wide.
$6,000–7,000 *C*

A Rolex 18ct gold and diamond set automatic wristwatch, 1970s, 36mm diam.
$7,500–8,000 *C*

A flame mahogany stick barometer, with thermometer, by Barwise, London, with swan neck pediment, flat-to-the-wall case and urn-shaped cistern cover, c1820, 38in (96.5cm) high.
$10,000–11,500 *W&W*

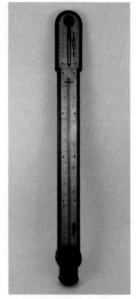

A mahogany barometer, signed J. Ayscough, London, with concealed tube and large scale thermometer, c1750, 36in (91.5cm) high.
$4,000–5,500 *GEM*

r. A Victorian table barometer, with engraved and silvered dial, framed by ormolu scrolling mounts and supported by 2 putti, on a glass crystal base, by Baccarat, c1880, 12in (30.5cm) high.
$2,700–3,000 *JIL*

A George III inlaid mahogany wheel barometer, clock and thermometer, c1820, 47¼in (120cm) high.
$7,500–8,500 *Bea(E)*

A mahogany stick barometer, c1790, 40in (101.5cm) high.
$3,000–3,500 *P*

A spelter-cased aneroid barometer and thermometer, with Bourdon-type movement, decorated with classical figures and fruiting vines, c1870, 28in (71cm) high.
$3,500–4,500 *W&W*

A mahogany and fan-inlaid wheel barometer, by P. Gally, Cambridge, with engraved silvered brass dials, c1790, 37in (94cm) high.
$2,700–3,500 *W&W*

A rosewood and mother-of-pearl-inlaid stick barometer, by Joseph Somalvico & Co, c1860, 38in (96.5cm) high.
$4,700–5,500 *PAO*

A walnut and mulberry stick barometer, with inverted pear-shaped cistern cover, c1715, 41in (104cm) high.
$14,500–16,000 *S*

Longcase Clocks

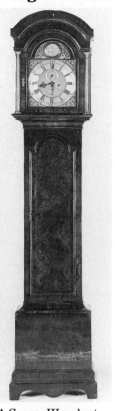

A George III walnut 8-day longcase clock, the arched dial with silvered chapter ring inscribed William Andrews, London, damage to base, 95in (241cm) high.
$5,000–6,000 *L&E*

A George III mahogany 8-day longcase clock, by J. Ashton, Tideswell, with brass dial, 88in (223.5cm) high.
$3,000–3,500 *DaD*

A Scottish mahogany 8-day longcase clock, by Ballantyne, Edinburgh, with silvered dial, c1790, 85in (216cm) high.
$5,600–6,200 *PNF*

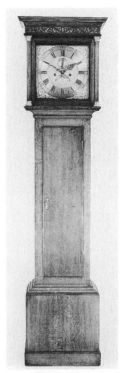

An oak 8-day longcase clock, by Baker & Miles, Chippenham, the 12in brass dial with silvered brass chapter rings, c1790, 78in (198cm) high.
$7,200–8,000 *PAO*

A mahogany 8-day longcase clock, by George Berry, Whitby, with 12in (30.5cm) painted arch dial, mid-19thC, 87½in (222cm) high.
$1,100–1,300 *DN*

A Charles II walnut longcase clock, brass dial signed Johannes Beale Londini, 5 latched ringed pillar movement with anchor escapement and outside countwheel strike, altered and restored, 73¾in (187cm) high.
$5,600–7,000 *CSK*

An oak 8-day longcase clock, by Richard Comber, Lewes, with brass dial, strike/silent, subsidiary seconds and date dials, c1770, 82in (209cm) high.
$8,800–9,600 *PAO*

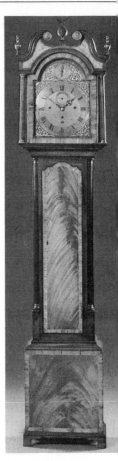

r. A mahogany and satinwood-inlaid longcase clock, the 12in (30.5cm) dial signed William Brooke, London, with seconds dial and calendar aperture, strike/silent dial, 3 train movement with anchor escapement, 8 bells with further hour bell, restored, 18thC, 88in (223.5cm) high.
$7,200–8,000 *S*

An oak 8-day longcase clock, by George Brand, Howden, the white dial showing both date and seconds, c1800, 82in (208cm) high.
$3,300–3,600 *PAO*

A George III oak 8-day longcase clock, the 11½in (29cm) dial inscribed James Brown, Matlock, 77½in (197cm) high.
$1,700–2,200 *WL*

A chinoiserie-decorated 8-day longcase clock, by Benjamin Cox, London, with 12in (30.5cm) brass dial, 5 pillar movement striking the hours on a bell, c1725, 87in (221cm) high.
$8,500–9,500 *PAO*

r. A stained maple longcase clock, the brass dial signed Payton Dana, Providence, Rhode Island, the case Goddard-Townsend School, foot restored, c1750, 82in (209cm) high.
$18,500–20,000 *S(NY)*

The identity of the maker of the case contributed to the high price of this American clock.

A mahogany 8-day longcase clock, by William Crawshaw, the 12in (30.5cm) brass dial with seconds and date aperture, c1750, 76in (193cm) high.
$5,000–6,000 *ALS*

A mid-Victorian mahogany and rosewood-crossbanded musical 8-day longcase clock, by Thomas Cross, Manchester, with 13in (33cm) brass dial, 3 train movement with detachable 5in (13cm) diam cylinder, possibly playing several tunes on a multi-pipe organ, 100in (254cm) high.
$6,500–7,200 *P(NW)*

A mid-Georgian oak and mahogany-crossbanded 8-day longcase clock, the 12in (30.5cm) brass dial signed Henry Deykin, 84¼in (214cm) high.
$2,200–2,400 *Bri*

A George III oak 30-hour longcase clock, by Francis Eck, Northampton, with brass dial, 82in (208cm) high.
$950–1,100 *DaD*

l. An oak crossbanded 30-hour longcase clock, the arched dial inscribed Dixon, Pickering, painted with birds, fruit and flowers, 86¼in (219cm) high.
$1,400–1,600 *MSW*

A Welsh mahogany and boxwood-strung 8-day longcase clock, by John Edward, Merthyr Tydfil, the white dial with subsidiary seconds and date apertures, painted hunting scene to the arch, c1845, 87in (221cm) high.
$5,000–6,000 *PAO*

A mahogany longcase clock, the 13in (33cm) dial with silvered chapter ring signed Elliott, London, painted moonphase, 4 pillar movement with deadbeat escapement and maintaining power, striking on 4 coil gongs and single hour gong, 99in (246cm) high.
$3,800–4,200 *Bon*

A figured mahogany 8-day longcase clock, by W. Evens, Totnes, the 12in (30.5cm) painted dial with moonphases, seconds and date, c1830, 83¾in (213cm) high.
$7,200–8,000 *ALS*

r. An oak 8-day longcase clock, with mahogany and satinwood inlay, by Flather, Halifax, the white enamelled dial painted with a charioteer, late 18thC, 90in (228.5cm) high.
$1,300–1,500 *M*

A walnut-veneered 8-day longcase clock, by William Greene, Maidstone, the 12in (30.5cm) brass dial with strike/silent, seconds and date apertures, the arch with automaton figure of Father Time, 18thC, 91in (231cm) high.
$5,000–6,000 *Oli*

l. A mahogany longcase clock, the 12in silvered dial signed John Gibson, Edinburgh, the 4 pillar movement with deadbeat escapement and rack-and-bell striking, c1780, 76in (193cm) high.
$2,700–3,200 *Bon*

A George III mahogany longcase clock, by Geo Graham, Cockermouth, the 13½in (34cm) painted dial with moonphase, date and second hand, 86in (218cm) high.
$5,000–6,000 *Mit*

An oak and mahogany-crossbanded 30-hour longcase clock, by Gugeri, Blandford, with 12in (30.5cm) painted dial, early 19thC, 29¾in (192cm) high.
$1,900–2,200 *ALS*

A mahogany longcase clock, by Osbertus Hamley, London, with inset brass-capped pillars, c1773, 82½in (210cm) high.
$10,400–11,200 *DSP*

A Georgian oak 8-day longcase clock, by Thomas Harben, Lewes, the 12in (30.5cm) brass dial with lunar aperture, 80in (203cm) high.
$2,400–3,200 *TAY*

An oak and mahogany crossbanded 8-day longcase clock, by Hickman, Stamford, the white enamel dial with subsidiary seconds dial and date arch, early 19thC, 35¼in (89.5cm) high.
$2,700–2,900 *Oli*

An oak and mahogany 8-day longcase clock, by J & G Holt, Newark, the painted arched dial with a lady in a landscape, subsidiary seconds dial and date aperture, early 19thC, 88in (224cm) high.
$1,300–1,450 *MSW*

An oak 30-hour longcase clock, by Hornby, Oldham, the 12in (30.5cm) brass dial with penny moon and date aperture, c1765, 83in (211cm) high.
$3,500–4,000 *ALS*

l. An oak and mahogany-crossbanded 8-day longcase clock, by Horden Kidderminster, with white enamel dial, subsidiary seconds dial and date indicator, mid-19thC, 90in (228.5cm) high.
$1,600–2,000 *GH*

An oak 8-day longcase clock, by Thomas Loftus, Wisbech, the 12in (30.5cm) brass dial with matted centre and silvered brass chapter ring, 5 pillar movement with countwheel striking on a bell, c1725, 82in (208cm) high.
$6,500–7,500 PAO

Early country clocks such as this have now become quite rare.

l. A Victorian oak and mahogany-crossbanded 8-day longcase clock, with 14in white enamelled and painted dial signed William Jones, Llanrwst, centred by a seconds ring and date aperture, 88½in (225cm) high.
$1,300–1,450 P(NW)

An oak 8-day longcase clock, the 13in (33cm) dial signed Lawson, Newton, with subsidiary date and moonphase indicators, c1780, 87¾in (223cm) high.
$2,500–2,800 S(S)

A walnut and marquetry-inlaid 30 day longcase clock, by Peter King, London, early 18thC, 97in (246.5cm) high.
$14,500–16,000 AH

l. A lacquered chinoiserie-decorated 8-day longcase clock, the brass dial inscribed Samuel Pearse, Honiton, the arch inscribed High Water, Topsham Barr, the trunk with painted scene of figures drinking, 18thC, 91in (231cm) high.
$4,800–6,400 *RBB*

A mahogany 8-day longcase clock, by John Petrie, New Deer, Aberdeenshire, the 12in painted dial with scene of 2 anglers, river and church, some satinwood detail, c1846, 81in (205cm) high.
$5,600–6,400 *ALS*

An oak 8-day longcase clock, the 12in (30.5cm) dial signed Thos Richardson, subsidiary seconds dial and date aperture, striking on a bell, c1790, 83¾in (213cm) high.
$1,600–1,900 *S(S)*

A George II oak 30-hour longcase clock by William Porthouse of Penrith, with 11in (28cm) brass dial and silvered chapter ring, 87in (221cm) high.
$1,400–1,600 *Mit*

An olivewood veneered longcase clock, the 12in (30.5cm) dial with silvered chapter ring, matted centre with subsidiary seconds and calendar aperture, signed on a silver plaque Step Rimbault, London, strike/silent lever, 5 pillar rack-and-bell striking movement, c1760, 87in (221cm) high.
$6,200–7,200 *Bon*

r. A late Georgian mahogany 8-day longcase clock, the dial with brass bezel and raised chapter seconds and date ring, inscribed Edward Radford, Shelton, 80in (203cm) high.
$1,200–1,400 *L&E*

A mahogany 8-day longcase clock, by W. Self, Frome, with 12in (30.5cm) white dial and matching steel hands, c1830, 86in (218.5cm) high.
$5,600–6,200 *PAO*

A George III oak 8-day longcase clock, by G. Saunders, Atherstone, the 13in (33cm) dial painted with figures fishing in park grounds, with calendar aperture, subsidiary seconds dial, striking on a bell, 86¼in (219cm) high.
$1,300–1,500 *WL*

An oak 8-day longcase clock, by William Robb of Montrose, with 12in (30.5cm) painted dial, c1800, 86in (218.5cm) high.
$3,200–3,500 *PNF*

A Victorian mahogany and oak 8-day longcase clock, by Thomas Robinson, Sheffield, with satinwood banding, the painted dial with religious scene in the arch, 88in (223.5cm) high.
$800–950 *MSW*

An oak 30-hour longcase clock, with marquetry inlay and mahogany crossbanding, by Lawrence Shakeshaft, Preston, 19thC, 87in (221cm) high.
$4,500–5,500 *AH*

A mahogany 8-day longcase clock, by David Somerville, St Ninians, Scotland, the 13in (33cm) brass dial with engraved centre, c1790, 88½in (225cm) high.
$5,600–6,400 *ALS*

r. A mahogany and line-inlaid 8-day longcase clock, by Tucker, Coleford, the 13in (33cm) white dial with moonphase, seconds dial and date aperture, early 19thC, 87½in (222cm) high.
$2,800–3,200 *Bri*

A mahogany longcase clock, by Swinburn of Hexham, with brass dial, c1760, 76in (193cm) high.
$9,600–11,200 *SO*

A mahogany and rosewood-crossbanded 8-day longcase clock, the 14in (35.5cm) dial painted with figures in rural settings and signed Jos Taylor, Great Hampton, 4 pillar movement, early 19thC, 97in (247cm) high.
$1,900–2,200 *DN*

A George III oak and mahogany-crossbanded 8-day longcase clock, by Samuel Whalley, Manchester, 84in (213.5cm) high.
$2,500–2,900 *DaD*

r. An early Victorian 8-day mahogany drum head longcase clock, the gilt dial inscribed L. O. White, Glasgow, with subsidiary seconds dial, twin train movement with anchor escapement, 86¼in (219cm) high.
$3,000–3,500 *P(Sc)*

A mahogany 8-day longcase clock, by Taylor, Manchester, the arched dial with moonphase and painted with allegorical figures representing 4 continents, 19thC, 93in (236cm) high.
$3,200–3,500 *AH*

An oak and mahogany-inlaid 8-day longcase clock, by J. Winstanley, Holywell, the 13in (33cm) painted dial with moonphases and painted corners, early 19thC, 87in (221cm) high.
$5,600–6,400 *ALS*

Cross Reference
Colour Review

---

r. A figured mahogany and boxwood-strung 8-day longcase clock, by Wood, Stroud, the 12in (30.5cm) dial with moonphase, seconds and date aperture, c1810, 80¾in (205cm) high.
$7,200–8,000 *ALS*

A flame mahogany-veneered 8-day longcase clock, by William Withers, Bristol, the 13in (33cm) white dial with seconds and date dial, painted country scene to the arch, c1845, 90in (229cm) high.
$4,700–5,400 *PAO*

An American inlaid maple longcase clock, with subsidiary seconds dial, 8-day brass movement, double weight driven, striking the hour on bell, c1800, 84in (213cm) high.
$3,500–4,200 *FBG*

Mantel Clocks

A rosewood four-glass mantel clock, signed Aldred & Son, Yarmouth, with gilt dial, double fusee movement and anchor escapement, striking the hours on a gong, with repeat, on brass bun feet, c1870, 9½in (24cm) high.
$9,500–11,000 *PAO*

A Louis XVI ormolu-mounted white and black marble mantel clock, the enamel dial inscribed Courvoisier à Paris, surmounted by an eagle and hung with swags, restored, 25in (63cm) high.
$3,200–4,000 *C*

A Danish mahogany and fruitwood mantel clock, with white enamel dial, German movement, decorated with neo-classical penwork and signed N. Hummeldaand, dated '1813', 22½in (57cm) high.
$5,000–5,600 *S(NY)*

An ebony-veneered mantel clock, inlaid with ivory and mother-of-pearl, the enamel dial signed Baltazard à Paris, bell striking movement, 19thC, 25in (63cm) high.
$3,200–4,000 *Bon*

An inlaid mahogany mantel clock, by Dent, with striking fusee movement, c1880, 19in (48.5cm) high.
$2,400–2,800 *SO*

A French gilt-metal and rouge marble mantel clock, by Japy Frères, with white enamel dial, 8-day striking movement, late 19thC, 21¼in (54cm) high.
$2,400–2,800 *CAG*

A French electric mantel timepiece, the silvered dial signed Bulle-Clock, coil pendulum over a fixed bar magnet, supported by a brass cylinder concealing the battery, c1920, 15in (38cm) high, with a brass and mahogany glazed cover.
$900–1,000 *S*

An electric mantel clock, by The Eureka Clock Co Ltd, London, the coil with a large balance wheel with screwed weights, c1900, 12in (30.5cm) high, with glass dome.
$1,100–1,200 *HOLL*

A French four-glass mantel clock, probably by Japy Frères, with porcelain columns and panels decorated with pink roses and cherubs, c1890, 19½in (49.5cm) high.
$4,000–4,800 *SO*

A gilt-brass tripod mantel timepiece, by Thomas Cole, with thermometer and barometer, movement with going barrel, split backplate and deadbeat escapement, damaged, mid-19thC, 20in (51cm) high.
$5,600–6,400 *P*

A George IV marble mantel timepiece, by James Gorham, London, the gilt dial with a snake bezel, 8-day single train fusee movement, 11¼in (28.5cm) high.
$1,300–1,450 *DN*

A French red tortoiseshell and gilt-mounted mantel clock, by Japy Frères, Paris, with striking movement c1880, 16½in (42cm) high
$1,900–2,200 *SO*

A French gilt-brass mantel clock, by Japy Frères, Paris, with white enamel dial, 8-day striking movement, surmounted by a putto reading a book, 19thC, 12¾in (32.5cm) high. **$750–850** *CAG*

A mahogany mantel clock, the dial signed T. Leeming, Settle, the 2 train fusee movement with anchor escapement striking on a bell, c1870, 17¾in (45cm) high. **$1,000–1,200** *S(S)*

Mantel Clocks

Mantel clocks were made in France in large numbers from 1780 to 1880, in a wide range of highly decorative cases with figural decoration. Those of the 1830s to 1850s are usually a little more subtle and of better quality. As with the garnitures of that period, the movements are of a fairly standard type and not therefore of great importance. Mantel clocks are abundant and widely available, being second in popularity to the carriage clock, but quality and condition do vary. Most European countries have produced them in large quantities since the mid-19th century.

A French gilt-bronze mantel clock, by Samuel Marti, Paris, with striking movement, c1840, 14in (35.6cm) high. **$2,400–2,800** *SO*

A French Empire marble and bronze-mounted mantel clock, c1820, 19¾in (50cm) high. **$2,200–2,400** *TPA*

A French inlaid rosewood mantel clock, by Henri Marc, Paris, with striking movement, c1840, 9in (23cm) high. **$2,000–2,400** *SO*

A French bronze and gilt-bronze mantel clock, by Raingo, c1840, 27½in (70cm) high. **$17,000–20,000** *DRA*

This clock was made to commemorate Quentin Durwood *by Walter Scott.*

A mahogany mantel timepiece, with silvered dial signed Vulliamy, London, fusee movement with anchor escapement, steel rod pendulum with roller suspension and two-prong locking device, c1840, 10¼in (26cm) high. **$4,800–5,600** *S*

This clock would have been made by Benjamin Lewis Vulliamy, 1780–1854. He held the Royal Warrant and was the grandson of the company founder, Justin Vulliamy.

A Regency black marble mantel timepiece, the silvered dial with black-painted chapters, single fusee movement with anchor escapement, signed on the backplate G & W Yonge, London, surmounted by a bronze model of a sphinx, 10½in (26.5cm) high. **$880–1,100** *CSK*

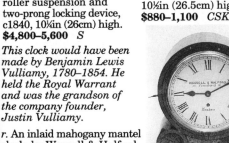

r. An inlaid mahogany mantel clock, by Wassell & Halford, with 8-day fusee movement, c1875, 13in (33cm) high. **$1,200–1,300** *TPA*

A satinwood mantel timepiece, with engine-turned gilt dial, fusee and chain movement with anchor escapement, ogee moulded plinth and ebony trim around top and base, c1840, 9in (23cm) high.
$2,200–2,700 S

A French gilt-metal and porcelain mantel clock, the dial painted in gilt and coloured enamels on a pink ground, twin train movement striking the half-hours on a bell, lacking pendulum, 19thC, 13in (33cm) high.
$1,200–1,300 P(Sc)

l. A gilt-metal and porcelain-mounted mantel clock, with Vincenti movement, over 3 porcelain plaques depicting 18thC figures, on gadrooned base raised on toupie feet, mid-19thC, 14½in (37cm) high.
$850–950 LHA

A Victorian ebonised mantel clock, the enamel dial on a gilt metal ground engraved with scrolls, 6¾in (17.5cm) high.
$380–450 HYD

A French gilt-bronze mantel clock, the twin train movement with countwheel strike on a bell, the case depicting a classical figure, 19thC, 24in (61cm) high.
$1,100–1,300 P

A French inlaid mahogany mantel clock, by Russells Ltd, with striking movement, brass columns and finials, on brass feet, c1900, 11½in (29cm) high.
$950–1,100 SO

A French gilded spelter mantel clock, the movement with countwheel strike on a bell, with inset pink porcelain panels, mid-19thC, 21in (53.5cm) high.
$950–1,100 TMA

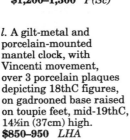

A French ormolu mantel clock, with floral casting, c1880, 12in (30.5cm) high.
$2,500–2,800 TUR

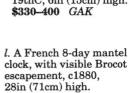

A red boulle mantel clock, with 8-day movement, on gilt-metal scroll moulded feet, late 19thC, 6in (15cm) high.
$330–400 GAK

l. A French 8-day mantel clock, with visible Brocot escapement, c1880, 28in (71cm) high.
$440–520 TPA

A French black marble mantel clock, the enamelled dial with exposed Brocot escapement, subsidiary dial for calendar, with 8-day movement, late 19thC, 23¾in (58cm) high. **$1,600–1,800** *AH*

A French black slate and gilt-brass perpetual calendar clock, with visible Brocot escapement, surmounted by an urn and dragons, late 19thC, 22in (56cm) high. **$1,200–1,500** *DaD*

A French tortoiseshell and gilt-mounted mantel clock, with 4¾in enamel dial, c1890, 13in (33cm) high. **$1,700–2,200** *Bon*

A French carved pine striking mantel clock, with a glazed panel below the white enamel dial, late 19thC, 13in (33cm) high. **$640–800** *CSK*

A French ormolu mantel clock, with 8-day drum silk suspension movement, surmounted by a classical figure, 19thC, 24½in (61cm) high. **$1,600–1,800** *AH*

An oak mantel timepiece, with single fusee movement, c1900, 14in (35.5cm) high. **$800–950** *SO*

l. A Napoleon III gilt-bronze striking mantel clock, with white enamel dial, twin barrel movement with countwheel strike on bell, the case surmounted by a swag-hung urn finial, lion mask and tassle handles, on fluted block feet, 18¼in (46.5cm) high. **$1,100–1,300** *CSK*

A French gilt-bronze mantel clock, late 19thC, 13½in (34cm) high. **$1,300–1,500** *DaD*

A solid silver guilloche enamel mantel clock, the ivory dial with gold hands and painted with cherry blossom in the centre, with striking movement and lever escapement, the panel decorated with a scene of possibly the Rhone, Swiss hallmark, c1910, 8½in (21.5cm) high. **$16,000–20,000** *DRA*

This is a superb example of the Genevan enamellers' art.

l. A late Victorian brass 8-day mantel clock, decorated with winged griffins and scroll leafage, on claw feet, 22in (56cm) high. **$1,300–1,600** *LT*

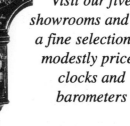

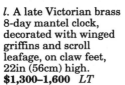

Portico Clocks

A Victorian pink marble and brass portico clock, with French drum case striking movement, decorative dial, flambeau and crossed arrow finials, 15in (38cm) high.
$320–380 GAK

An Austrian porcelain and gilt-metal portico clock, with enamelled dial on drum movement, painted with scenes from classical mythology on a blue ground, signed Schular, 19thC, 13½in (34cm) high.
$2,400–2,800 AH

A Louis XVI ormolu-mounted white and black marble portico clock, the enamelled dial with pierced gilt-metal hands, with twin barrel movement, silk suspension and countwheel strike on bell, signed to the blackplate Antoine François à Paris, 18¾in (47.5cm) high.
$1,500–1,800 CSK

A French Empire mahogany and gilt-bronze portico clock, with silvered dial, movement striking on a bell, gridiron pendulum, slight alterations, 21¾in (55cm) high, with glass dome.
$800–960 Bea(E)

Skeleton Clocks

A brass skeleton clock, the silvered chapter ring signed Barr, London, 2 train fusee movement with anchor escapement and striking on a bell, mounted on a mahogany base with glass dome, c1850, 13¼in (33.5cm) high.
$2,500–2,800 S(S)

A brass skeleton clock, by Bennett, London, with a silvered chapter ring, twin fusee chain movement with repeat and striking on an overhead bell, on a rosewood stand, 19thC, 14½in (37cm) high.
$1,700–2,200 Bea(E)

A Regency 8-day skeleton timepiece, by Druce & Co, London, with fusee movement c1820, 12½in (32cm) high, with glass dome.
$2,000–2,300 GUN

An early Victorian skeleton timepiece, by J. Homes Junior, London, the fusee movement with anchor escapement, in a steeple frame on a mahogany plinth, with spirit level, 14½in (36cm) high, glass dome damaged.
$1,100–1,400 J&L

A triple-plated Arabesque skeleton clock, by Evans of Handsworth, c1860, 17½in (44.5cm) high.
$5,000–6,000 DRA

A brass skeleton timepiece, with silvered chapter ring, the fusee movement with anchor escapement, scroll and rosette frame with plaque engraved Mosley, Waterford, on a marble base, c1850, 14¼in (36cm) high, with glass dome.
$800–1,000 S(S)

A brass skeleton timepiece, with engraved silver chapter ring, fusee and chain movement, anchor escapement, 6 spoke wheels, shaped pallets and wood rod pendulum with cylindrical zinc bob, on marble plinth, c1860, 15in (38cm) high, with replacement dome.
$1,100–1,400 S

A French skeleton table regulator, quarter striking month duration, c1800, 21½in (54.5cm) high.
$25,500–29,500 DRA

Table Clocks

A quarter striking boulle and brass-inlaid table clock, with enamelled dial, 7 pillar 3 train movement signed Louis Baronneau à Paris, with later Brocot escapement, late 17thC, 21¾in (55.5cm) high.
$7,500–8,500 *S*

A mahogany 8-day table clock, by Frederick Miller, London, the silvered brass dial with strike/silent feature and centre date, 5 pillar movement and anchor escapement, c1795, 15½in (39.5cm) high.
$8,000–9,500 *PAO*

r. A mahogany timepiece, with convex dial and fusee movement, c1820, 14in (35.5cm) high.
$2,000–2,400 *SO*

A Louis XV style table clock, the dial with enamelled numerals, the ormolu case with cherub surmounts, the base with 2 reclining cherubs, on scroll feet, 19thC, 25in (63.5cm) high.
$3,200–3,800 *RBB*

A mahogany table clock, by Thomas Howard, London, with fusee striking movement, c1810, 14in (35.5cm) high.
$5,600–6,400 *SO*

A gilt-brass-mounted fruitwood table clock, the dial signed E. G. Parker, Altrincham, 3 train fusee and chain movement with anchor escapement, chiming on 8 bells and 4 gongs, c1895, 27in (68.5cm) high.
$3,200–4,000 *S*

A French mahogany 8-day table clock, with striking movement, c1900, 12in (30.5cm) high.
$1,300–1,450 *SO*

A mahogany pad top table clock, with enamel dial signed Arnold, London, brass pierced hands, twin fusee movement with half deadbeat escapement, c1780, 16¼in (42cm) high.
$6,000–6,500 *Bon*

l. An ebony-veneered table clock, with white enamel dial signed Wm Sharpe, Holborn, subsidiary strike/silent and regulation dials, the 2 train fusee movement with verge escapement and striking on a bell, c1785, 16¾in (42.5cm) high.
$6,500–7,500 *S(S)*

A mahogany-veneered table clock, with chamfered top, the engraved silvered dial inscribed Joseph Merrick, Windsor, with wire fusee movement, on a plinth with pad feet, c1840, 10½in (26.5cm) high.
$3,200–3,500 *JIL*

Tavern Clocks

A George III mahogany tavern timepiece, the 25in (63.5cm) painted wood dial signed Simon Cavit, Bedford, with 8-day weight driven movement and 5 wheel train, c1800, 47¾in (121cm) high.
$5,000–5,600 S

An Act of Parliament clock, the silvered dial with Roman numerals inscribed Thos Sharp, Stratford-upon-Avon, the case now painted brown, 18thC, 53½in (136cm) high.
$2,500–2,800 BWe

A George III tavern clock, the white dial with Roman and Arabic chapters, a printed tavern scene on the door, signed Moore, Ipswich, with anchor escapement, adapted, case redecorated, 56½in (143cm) high.
$2,400–2,700 CSK

A George III black and gold lacquered chinoiserie-decorated Act of Parliament clock, the dial signed Edward Webb, Bristol, with arched door and moulded base, case restored, 59in (150cm) high.
$3,300–4,000 CNY

FURTHER READING
Miller's Clocks & Barometers Buyer's Guide, Millers Publications, 1997.

l. A George III tavern clock, with chinoiserie-lacquered trunk, gilt Roman and Arabic chapters against a black ground, the movement with anchor escapement, adapted, case redecorated, 55in (140cm) high.
$1,500–1,900 CSK

Tavern Clocks or Act of Parliament Clocks

Tavern or Act of Parliament clocks were made for taverns and coaching inns throughout England from c1740 to 1800. Their main purpose was to provide accurate local time, and in particular to regulate the arrival and departure of stage coaches, which kept to very reliable schedules.

The name Act of Parliament clock arose from the Act which was passed in 1797 putting a tax on all clocks and watches. The result was that people stopped buying clocks and watches and concealed those they already had, thus producing an increased need for public clocks. Because of the dramatic fall in the sale of clocks and watches, many makers faced bankruptcy. King George III was petitioned and within a year of its introduction the Act was repealed.

Travel Clocks

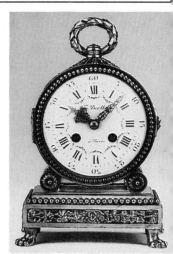

An Austrian gilt-bronze travel clock, with white enamel dial, the engine-turned drum case on claw-and-ball feet, with ring suspension, twin barrel movement with platform escapement and quarter strike on 2 gongs, mid-19thC, 5¾in (14.5cm) high.
$2,000–2,400 CSK

An Austrian ormolu *grande sonnerie* travel clock, with enamel dial, chased bezel, the movement with verge and balance escapement, striking on 2 gongs, the going train with fusee and chain, the case surrounded by gilt-bronze lion's pelt, c1830, 6¼in (16cm) high.
$3,500–4,000 S

A French gilt-bronze *pendule d'officier*, the white enamel dial signed Fd Berthoud à Paris, twin barrel movement with platform escapement and strike on bell, on stepped base with beaded border, early 19thC, 9½in (24cm) high.
$2,400–2,700 CSK

Wall Clocks

An oak hooded wall clock, by Obadiah Body, Battle, with striking birdcage movement, c1740, 27½in (70cm) high.
$2,800–3,200 *DSP*

r. A Regency walnut and rosewood-inlaid drop dial wall clock, with painted dial and 8-day movement striking to bell, the brass bezel within an octagonal inlaid surround over a shaped brass-framed pendulum window and cushion base, 27in (68.5cm) high.
$1,100–1,250 *DA*

A mahogany brass-inlaid drop dial wall clock, with 12in (30.5cm) enamelled dial and 8-day fusee movement, c1860, 19in (48cm) high.
$880–1,000 *TPA*

An oak dial timepiece, by Camerer Cuss & Co, London, the single fusee movement in a case with turned surround and pegged back, c1910, 15in (38cm) diam.
$560–640 *Bon*

A mahogany drop dial wall clock, by Henry Crew, Ledbury, the 4 pillar fusee movement with anchor escapement, c1870, 14in (35.5cm) high.
$2,400–3,200 *PAO*

A mahogany and ebony 8-day pendulum wall clock, with white enamel dial, the case with circular top on scroll brackets, glazed trunk and shaped base, 19thC, 70in (178cm) high.
$1,900–2,200 *AH*

American Clocks

An enamelled cast iron mechanical ship's wheel shelf clock, by Ansonia Clock Co, New York, c1905, 12in (30.5cm) high.
$1,600–1,800 *OT*

A walnut King model shelf clock, by Ansonia Clock Co, Connecticut, c1895, 14in (35.5cm) high.
$400–450 *OT*

A late Federal gilt-stencilled mahogany shelf clock, by Jeromes & Darrow, Bristol, Connecticut, with Roman chapter ring, c1830, 34½in (87.5cm) high.
$350–400 *C(NY)*

A terrestrial globe timepiece, by Louis P. Juvet, with 18in (46cm) globe, c1880, 55in (138cm) high.
$12,500–13,500 *RSch*

Juvet lived in Glen Falls, New York and patented this globe clock design. He formed a partnership with James Arkell of Canajoharie, New York, where they manufactured clocks with both 12in and 18in globes.

A Federal style stained oak wall clock, by Sessions Clock Co, 8-day movement with coil gong striking on the hours, c1905, 20in (51cm) high.
$350–380 *OT*

A walnut double dial parlour calendar clock, by Seth Thomas, c1880, 20in (51cm) high.
$480–600 *RSch*

r. A rosewood-veneered World model long drop octagon timepiece, by Seth Thomas, with 15-day double spring movement, c1890, 32in (81cm) high.
$480–560 *RSch*

A walnut perpetual calendar wall clock, with painted dials, by Seth Thomas, c1880, 26in (66cm) high.
$1,600–1,900 *S*

An oak globe clock, by Theodore Timby of Baldwinsville, c1865, 27in (68.5cm) high.
$4,800–5,600 *RSch*

A light oak double dial calendar clock, by Waterbury, with time strike and alarm, gong replaced, c1895, 24in (61cm) high.
$720–880 *RSch*

r. A Federal giltwood and mahogany banjo clock, the white dial inscribed David Williams, Newport, the box door with *églomisé* panel depicting 3 women dancing on a stage, c1815, 40in (102cm) high.
$3,400–4,000 *S(NY)*

A black-enamelled and ormolu parlour clock, with white dial, 8-day half hour cathedral gong strike, early 20thC, 11in (28cm) high.
$160–200 *RIT*

English Regulators

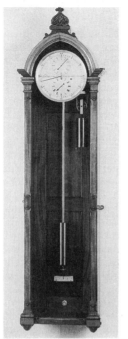

A mahogany weight driven longcase regulator, with 6 ringed screwed pillar movement, deadbeat escapement, maintaining power, beat adjustment, steel rod pendulum with a mercury-filled glass bob, mid-19thC, 71in (180cm) high.
$5,000–5,500 *Bon*

A mahogany month duration wall regulator, by Dent, London, with deadbeat escapement and maintaining power, c1878, 67½in (171.5cm) high.
$28,000–32,000 *DRA*
This unusual month duration regulator was made by the firm of Dent, who were responsible for the manufacture of Big Ben.

A George III mahogany regulator, by Earnshaw, London, the 5 pillared movement with shaped plates, maintaining power and deadbeat escapement with cranked crutch, 74½in (189cm) high.
$15,200–16,800 *P*

A flame mahogany 8-day regulator, by Handley & Moore, London, with 5 pillar movement with shaped plates, deadbeat escapement, maintaining power, c1800, 86in (33¾in) high.
$11,000–12,000 *PAO*

Viennese Regulators

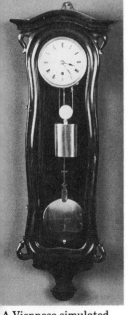

A Viennese simulated rosewood miniature wall regulator, with 8-day weight driven movement, c1855, 27in (68.5cm) high.
$5,000–5,600 *DRA*

A Viennese mahogany *grande sonnerie* 8-day regulator, with maple stringing, gilded engine-turned dial centre and ring, spring driven, c1835, 38in (96cm) high.
$29,000–35,000 *GeC*

WATCHES

The watch market is currently experiencing a period of growth. Last year a total of 80% of lots entered at auction were sold, and watch auctioneers overall saw a substantial increase in turnover. Noteworthy auction successes have been the thematic sales such as the Magical Art of Cartier, the Art of Patek Philippe and the Art of Breguet, but watch sales in general have produced numerous records with a recent world record for a wristwatch of $1.7 million.

The two main types of watch are the wristwatch and the pocket watch that, despite a certain amount of overlapping, maintain very separate identities and attributes, effectively forming two separate markets.

The pocket watch market is by far the oldest of the two main sectors of the watch market. Prices have risen steadily in recent years, but in terms of the quality of workmanship values remain relatively low and it is possible to purchase a fine Swiss or English example for a very reasonable price.

Within the watch market, value depends on three factors, maker, age and condition. There are many examples of pocket watches in circulation with little or no market value, something which anybody hoping to purchase or sell a pocket watch is well advised to bear in mind. In terms of value for money and potential growth, however, the pocket watch represents a good prospect at the moment.

In comparison to the pocket watch the wristwatch is a fairly new phenomenon. The market is dominated by the Swiss companies and examples by Patek Philippe,

Vacheron Constantin, Cartier or Rolex from the 1920s to the '50s continue to rise in value. Many other Swiss-made watches from that period are collectable, these depend much more on the individual model than those companies previously mentioned. The wristwatch market in general is much more fluid than the pocket watch market and the boundaries are less well-defined. Prices tend to be higher and more varied over the short term.

It is impossible to over-estimate the importance of the condition, both internal and external, of any type of watch. The internal condition is, of course, the most difficult aspect to assess. The expertise needed to properly repair and service a vintage watch is rare and it is not uncommon for the cost of repair to exceed the value of the watch itself. With watches, as with any vintage mechanical purchase, there is usually a hidden cost and some form of guarantee, though rare, is worth its weight in gold.

The most popular victims of the forger's art are of course Cartier and Rolex, being the most widely known makers of high value watches. However, most collectable watches have been targets of the forger's art at one time or another. Even the most experienced of dealers has been taken in by good copies and, particularly when seeking a bargain, it is often a case of *caveat emptor* (buyer beware). To avoid undue stress the less-experienced buyer is advised to seek a reputable retailer.

George Somlo

Pocket Watches

A tortoiseshell pair cased verge pocket watch, signed Jn Edmonds, Salop, with square baluster pillars, pierced and engraved winged balance cock in a plain case, mid-18thC, 48mm diam.
$400–550 *Bon*

Cross Reference
Colour Review

A silver pair cased verge pocket watch, by David Lestourgeon, London, with silver *champlevé* dial and blue steel regulator, engraved parcel-gilt silver cartouche with a portrait of Queen Anne, late 17thC, 58mm diam.
$5,600–6,400 *PT*

r. A gold and enamel keyless minute repeating triple calendar hunter pocket watch, signed Henry Lewis, the white enamel dial with blued steel hands, the front cover with painted enamel crest, 1887, 48mm diam.
$5,000–6,500 *C*

A George III gold pair cased pocket watch, by John Ellicott, London, with fusee verge movement, the repoussé outer case decorated with a court scene, 1770, 50mm diam.
$1,400–1,600 *DN*

A gilt pocket watch, by Jean Martinot, Paris, with frosted gilt chain fusee verge movement, later white enamel dial, minute hand, glass and pendant ring missing, late 17thC, 57mm diam.
$1,900–2,200 C

A 9ct gold pocket watch, by Omega, with 17 jewels, 1929, 50mm diam.
$400–480 PSA

A quarter repeating verge pocket watch, by George Prior, London, made for the Turkish market, with full plate fire gilt movement, triple 18ct gold and enamel cases, 1813, 52mm diam.
$13,500–15,000 PT

The Prior family specialised in making watches for export to Turkey, and this is a particularly fine example.

A gold and enamel pear-shaped pocket watch, the shaped movement with cylinder escapement, signed on front plate Recordon, London, the dial with pierced gold hands, the case with visible diamond set balance above the dial, enamel restored, early 19thC, 85mm high.
$9,500–10,500 P

A stainless steel military open faced watch, by Rolex, the black dial with luminous painted Arabic numerals and subsidiary seconds, the jewelled lever movement in a case marked 'GS MK.II' with government arrow, c1910, 46mm diam.
$250–300 Bon(C)

A silver-cased pocket watch, by Rolex, the movement with 17 jewels, 1926, 50mm diam.
$400–480 PSA

A 14ct gold engraved hunter pocket watch, by Tavannes Watch Co, with silvered dial and Swiss 17 jewelled movement, c1930, 50mm diam.
$620–720 PSA

A gold and enamel duplex pocket watch, made for the Chinese market, the case with a border of pearls, c1840, 60mm diam.
$24,500–27,000 SOML

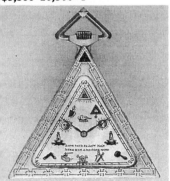

A Swiss gilt-metal pocket watch, by Solvil Watch Co, the mother-of-pearl dial with Masonic symbols, blued steel hands, club foot lever escapement, the back hinged to form an easel stand, c1920, 54mm wide.
$2,000–2,400 PT

l. A Swiss silver-cased split chronograph pocket watch, recording 60 minutes, c1930, 50mm diam.
$600–720 PSA

Wristwatches

A Breitling Chronomat Co-Pilot steel chronograph wristwatch, with adjustable calculating scale, the nickel-plated bar movement with monometallic balance, 1950s, 36mm diam.
$1,200–1,400 *C*

An Ebel gold-plated triple calendar and moonphase wristwatch, c1950, 34mm diam.
$600–700 *Bon*

A Le Coultre and Vacheron & Constantin 14ct white gold and diamond Galaxy mystery wristwatch, the silvered matt dial set with single cut diamonds, with rotating central disc set with diamond hour indicator and second glass disc, with diamond set minute indicator, c1960, 33mm diam.
$1,900–2,200 *S(G)*

l. A Cartier lady's platinum and diamond set wristwatch, the nickel-plated movement signed European Watch Co Inc, with 19 jewels, adjusted to temperature and 6 positions, bimetallic balance, 1920s, 13mm wide.
$15,500–17,500 *C*

A Cartier gentleman's gold Tank wristwatch, the cream dial with Roman numerals, the nickel-plated movement with 17 jewels and gold alloy balance, cabochon set winding crown, 1970s, 30mm diam.
$2,400–2,700 *CSK*

A Heuer stainless steel chronograph wristwatch, the black dial with Arabic numerals, subsidiary dials for seconds and 30 minute recording, c1960, 34mm diam.
$500–575 *Bon*

An Omega asymmetric stainless steel water resistant wristwatch, the silvered dial with Arabic numerals, nickel-plated bar movement, 1930s, 21mm wide.
$1,200–1,400 *C*

A Longines stainless steel aviator's chronograph wristwatch, with black enamel dial, nickel movement, c1940, 48mm diam.
$2,800–3,200 *Bon*

r. An Omega 18ct gold centre seconds wristwatch, the silvered dial with Arabic and baton numerals, the pink gilt 17 jewel movement in a polished case stamped with Birmingham hallmark for 1952, 35mm diam.
$800–950 *Bon*

A Cartier 18ct gold automatic centre seconds wristwatch, with silvered dial, nickel 21 jewel movement, c1960, 38mm diam.
$1,200–1,400 *Bon*

An Omega stainless steel chronograph wristwatch, the silvered dial with Breguet numerals, the nickel-plated bar movement jewelled to the centre with 17 jewels, bimetallic balance, 1930s, 37mm diam.
$1,400–1,550 *C*

A Patek Philippe stainless steel chronograph, in a waterproof case, c1950, 30mm diam.
$58,000–64,000 *SOML*

It is very unusual to find a Patek Philippe wristwatch in a stainless steel case.

A Patek Philippe lady's 18ct gold wristwatch, the silvered dial with Arabic numerals, the nickel lever movement with 18 jewels adjusted to 5 positions, and associated bracelet, c1955, 24mm diam.
$2,800–3,200 *S*

Locate the Source
The source of each illustration in Miller's can be found by checking the code letters below each caption with the Key to Illustrations.

A Piaget 18ct yellow and white gold wristwatch, with black dial, nickel finished lever movement, 18 jewels, monometallic balance, with tapering bracelet and clasp, c1980, 25mm wide.
$4,700–5,200 *C*

l. A Swiss 9ct gold half hunter wristwatch, with 15 jewel movement, c1905, 37mm diam.
$600–720 *PSA*

A Girard Perregaux 18ct gold chronograph wristwatch, with white enamel dial, register and pulsemeter, nickel lever movement, monometallic compensation balance, 2 subsidiary dials for seconds and register for 30 seconds, c1925, 32mm diam.
$3,000–3,400 *S(G)*

An Audemars Piguet 18ct pink gold wristwatch, with silvered matt dial, black baton numerals, nickel lever movement, bimetallic compensation balance, 18 jewels, c1955, 27mm wide.
$2,000–2,300 *S(G)*

r. A Rolex 9ct gold wristwatch, the engine-turned silvered dial with Arabic numerals, subsidiary seconds dial, blued steel hands, nickel-plated movement, late 1920s, 24mm wide.
$1,600–1,900 *C*

BAROMETERS
Stick Barometers

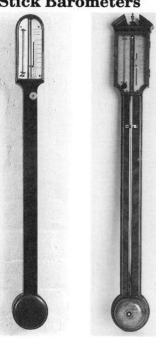

l. A mahogany stick barometer, by H. Andrews, Royston, the silvered plate with mercury thermometer, c1810, 38⅜in (98cm) high.
$2,400–2,700 *S(S)*

r. A mahogany stick barometer, chevron-veneered with chequer stringing, by D. Barreta, London, with silvered register plate and thermometer, cistern cover replaced, c1800, 38¼in (97cm) high.
$1,200–1,300 *HOLL*

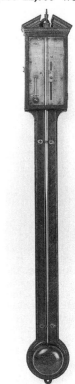

A rosewood and tortoiseshell-veneered flat-to-the-wall bowfronted stick barometer, by Thos Blunt, London, c1810, 39in (99cm) high.
$10,500–12,000 *W&W*

A mahogany stick barometer, by A. E. Abraham, Exeter, with arched top above ivory plates, 19thC, 35⅜in (91cm) high.
$1,100–1,300 *BWe*

A George III mahogany stick barometer, by Aiano, with steel dial and chequerwork inlay, 38in (96.5cm) high.
$1,500–1,800 *LT*

A mahogany stick barometer, the silvered dial signed J. Gilbert, London, with gilt-brass door frame, c1770, 39¾in (101cm) high.
$3,000–3,400 *CSK*

A George III mahogany stick barometer, by Thos Blunt, London, with silvered scale and thermometer, c1810, 39in (99cm) high.
$4,400–4,800 *LAY*

A mahogany and chequer-strung stick barometer, by Bossi, Lynn, with silvered brass scale, c1810, 39in (99cm) high.
$2,800–3,400 *PAO*

A George III mahogany and chequer-banded stick barometer, inscribed P. Galley & Co, London, with broken pediment and turned cistern cover, 38in (96.5cm) high.
$1,700–2,000 *AP*

A George IV mahogany stick barometer, signed Donegan & Co, Newcastle, thermometer damaged, 39in (99cm) high.
$1,600–1,800 *LT*

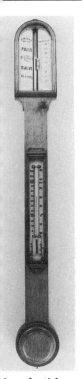

r. A French mahogany stick barometer, the bowfronted case inlaid with panels of contrasting wood inscribed with scales, signed J. & A. Molteni, Paris, early 19thC, 41¾in (106cm) high.
$1,200–1,500 *S*

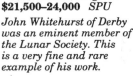

A mahogany angle barometer, by Whitehurst of Derby, with silvered scale and original mercury reservoir, 1766, 40in (101.5cm) long.
$21,500–24,000 *SPU*

John Whitehurst of Derby was an eminent member of the Lunar Society. This is a very fine and rare example of his work.

An oak stick barometer, by J. Hicks, London, c1880, 38in (96.5cm) high.
$1,300–1,500 *PAO*

A mahogany stick barometer, the paper register inscribed Charles Howorth, Halifax, early 19thC, 41in (104cm) high.
$775–875 *AH*

An oak 'sea-coast' barometer, by Negretti & Zambra, London, c1870, 41¼in (105cm) high.
$1,700–2,200 *Bon(C)*

Admiral Fitzroy Barometers

Admiral Robert Fitzroy (1805–65), formerly captain of Darwin's ship, *Beagle*, developed techniques for weather forecasting. The barometers associated with his name are usually of oak, with scales invariably of paper bearing his remarks on forecasting. An interesting variant is the Royal Polytechnic barometer, produced by Joseph Davis of London.

A brass-cased Fortin barometer, by Negretti & Zambra, London, on a mahogany backboard, c1900, 40in (101.5cm) high.
$1,300–1,600 *W&W*

A carved mahogany marine stick barometer, by A. H. Ross, with 'Improved Sympiesometer', 19thC, 37in (94cm) high.
$4,200–4,800 *AP*

An oak Royal Polytechnic barometer, with Admiral Fitzroy's remarks on paper scales, c1890, 45in (114.5cm) high.
$1,200–1,350 *GAZE*

An oak Royal Polytechnic barometer, by J. Davis, London, with silvered paper scales bearing Admiral Fitzroy's remarks, c1890, 41¼in (105cm) high.
$875–1,000 *P(Sc)*

An oak Admiral Fitzroy's barometer, with moulded arched pediment and flanked by fluted Corinthian columns, c1890, 46in (117cm) high.
$1,600–2,200 *W&W*

Wheel Barometers

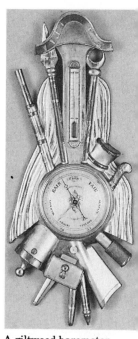

A flame mahogany and boxwood-strung wheel barometer, by J. Beal, Oundle, with silvered brass 8in (20.5cm) dial, c1830, 37in (94cm) high.
$1,100–1,250 PAO

A flame mahogany wheel barometer, by Blachford & Imray, London, silvered brass 10in (25.5cm) dial, with applied mouldings, c1830, 41in (104cm) high.
$1,600–2,000 W&W

A mahogany and boxwood-strung 'onion-top' banjo barometer, by J. Boyall, Spilsby, with silvered main dial and thermometer, c1860, 37in (94cm) high.
$350–380 GAK

A giltwood barometer, in the form of a martial trophy, the 9½in (24cm) dial signed C. Brestbarta, Northampton, with thermometer above, c1830, 45¼in (115cm) high.
$1,900–2,400 S

A mahogany five-dial wheel barometer, by Della Torre, Perth, c1840, 39in (99cm) high.
$950–1,100 W&W

A mahogany wheel barometer, the dial engraved Dollond, London, c1840, 37in (94cm) high.
$770–870 BR

A rosewood 'onion-top' wheel barometer, the silvered dial signed A. Intross & Co, Strood, c1870, 40in (101.5cm) high.
$480–550 HOLL

A mahogany combination wheel barometer with timepiece, the 12in (30.5cm) engraved silvered dial with Masonic symbols and level signed Giobbio, Devizes & Trowbridge, c1830, 46¾in (119cm) high.
$1,500–1,650 P

A Regency giltwood and gesso barometer, by Mantica, London, with crossed torch and quiver cresting, bellflower swags and floral bouquet finials to the sides, the thermometers with stiff leaf borders, 41¾in (106cm) high. **$2,700–3,100** *CSK*

A rosewood wheel barometer, inlaid with mother-of-pearl, the 10in (25.5cm) dial signed F. Lemiere, London, c1835, 43¾in (111cm) high. **$1,250–1,350** *S*

A Victorian carved oak hall barometer, in Gothic style, by Negretti & Zambra, c1880, 26in (66cm) high. **$320–380** *RTw*

A rosewood and kingwood-crossbanded wheel barometer, with ebony and boxwood inlay, by J. King, Bristol, c1830, 37in (94cm) high. **$2,700–3,000** *PAO*

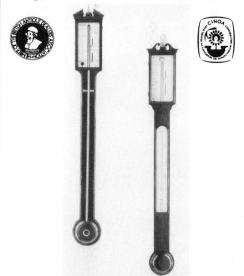

A mahogany and boxwood-strung wheel barometer and clock, by John Pensa & Son, London, the clock movement by George Barlow, London, c1840, dial 10in (25.5cm) diam. **$3,500–4,000** *PAO*

A mahogany four-dial wheel barometer, signed H. M. Shaw, Lymington, with square base, c1840, 39in (99cm) high. **$1,000–1,200** *W&W*

A Louis XVI painted and parcel-gilt barometer, the dial flanked by fruit-filled cornucopia, late 18thC, 49in (124.5cm) high.
$2,500–2,800 *S(NY)*

l. A mahogany and line-inlaid wheel barometer, with 10in (25.5cm) silvered dial, 19thC, 43in (109cm) high.
$620–680 *Bri*

Aneroid Barometers

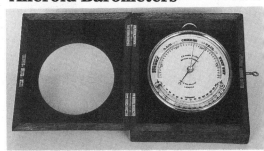

A mahogany and brass aneroid barometer, by C. W. Dixey, the enamel dial with a curved thermometer, blued steel hands, c1870, dial 4in (10cm) diam.
$1,600–1,800 *JIL*

Care of Barometers

A barometer can be placed anywhere in the home, as long as it is away from the sun, open fires and radiators. Care should be taken when moving a mercury barometer, and it is important to ensure that the cistern containing the mercury at the bottom is always lower than the top of the tube, otherwise the mercury may spill or air may enter the tube.

Before being transported some barometers may be plugged with a specially designed stopper, but if this is not possible the barometer should be carried at an angle around 45° from the vertical. Aneroid barometers can be moved without difficulty, but should always be handled with care.

A brass-cased aneroid barometer, by E. Ducretet, Paris, with thermometer, on a simulated marble stand, c1880, 10in (25.5cm) high.
$450–550 *W&W*

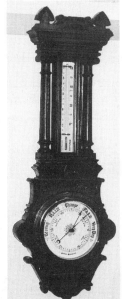

l. An aneroid barometer, with moulded pediment, the thermometer flanked by fluted Corinthian columns, moulded below with foliage, late 19thC, 38in (96.5cm) high.
$520–620 *GAK*

A floral marquetry-inlaid aneroid banjo barometer, with arched pediment, and exposed mechanism, late 19thC, 31in (78.5cm) high.
$480–540 *GAK*

An oak aneroid barometer, with a ceramic dial, c1890, 35in (89cm) high.
$370–400 *RTw*

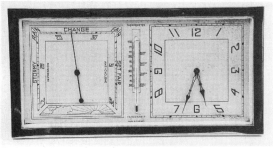

An Art Deco aneroid desktop barometer, thermometer and clock, in a polished chrome case, c1935, 9½in (24cm) wide.
$200–225 *RTw*

Don't Forget!
If in doubt please refer to the 'How to Use' section at the beginning of this book.

Barographs

An oak barograph, by C. W. Dixey & Son, with chart drawer and lacquered movement, c1912, 15in (38cm) wide.
$880–960 *RTw*

A mahogany box-type barograph, by Richard Frères, Paris, with ivory scaled thermometer, c1895, 11in (28cm) wide.
$560–640 *RTw*

A mahogany barograph, by Dollond, London, with 8-day movement and cylinder escapement, chart drawer, hand lacking, c1900, 8in (20.5cm) high.
$1,600–1,800 *S*

An oak barograph, by Negretti & Zambra, London, with mercury thermometer and seven-section chamber, early 20thC, 14in (36cm) wide.
$640–780 *Bea(E)*

r. An oak barograph, with circular scale and chart drawer, c1915, 15in (38cm) wide.
$1,600–1,800 *RTw*

l. A mahogany barograph, signed Negretti & Zambra, London, with chart drawer, c1910, 13¾in (35cm) wide.
$880–1,000 *Bon(C)*

An oak barograph, by Negretti & Zambra, London, the movement with ancillary signed dial and thermometer, c1910, 15in (38cm) wide.
$1,900–2,200 *W&W*

An oak barograph, by Short & Mason, London, c1930, 13in (33cm) wide.
$720–800 *W&W*

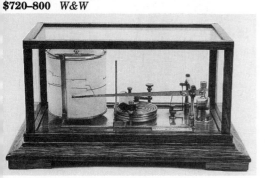

An oak barograph, by James Woolley & Sons, Manchester, c1910, 14in (35.5cm) wide.
$640–720 *RTw*

DECORATIVE ARTS
Arts & Crafts Furniture

An Arts and Crafts oak buffet, c1890, 50½in (128cm) high.
$1,100–1,300 *GBr*

An Arts and Crafts cabinet, the 2 leaded glass doors mounted with copper hinges, damaged, c1910, 76½in (194.5cm) high.
$950–1,100 *SK*

A Gothic revival oak cabinet-on-stand, with linenfold carved panels, fitted interior with single shelf, early 20thC, 37in (94cm) wide.
$750–850 *L&E*

An Arts and Crafts inlaid mahogany armchair, with pierced back and outswept arms above a padded seat, the back inlaid with stylised foliate motifs, on square tapering legs joined by stretchers, c1900, ex-Britt Ekland collection.
$900–1,000 *CSK*

r. A pair of Belgian oak armchairs, the back and sides carved with whiplash motifs, the legs with foliate motifs, drop-in velvet covered seats, c1900.
$3,200–4,000 *C*

An armchair, by Pál Horti, the back and armrests carved with stylised lotus flowers, upholstered seat, c1900, 54⅜in (139cm) wide.
$2,000–2,500 *S*

An American Arts and Crafts oak chair, by Gustav Stickley, with ladderback and hide seat, c1900.
$600–700 *P(Ba)*

A beech side chair, by Henry van de Velde, with woven cane back and seat, c1904.
$5,000–5,600 *S*

FURTHER READING
Eric Knowles, *Victoriana to Art Deco* Miller's Publications, 1993.

Josef Hoffmann (Austrian 1870–1956)
Originally trained as an architect, Hoffmann was influenced by Charles Rennie Mackintosh and the Glasgow School. In 1897 he founded the Vienna Secession, an association of artists and architects who were disillusioned with the work of the Viennese Society of Visual Artists, and very influential at that time. Inspired by the more abstract and purer forms of design of the Vienna Secessionists, he went on to found the Wiener Werkstätte (Vienna Workshops) in 1903. Hoffmann designed all kinds of furniture, much of it having a severe, geometric form, rather than the sinuous forms of other Art Nouveau designers. The majority of his designs were executed by Jacob and Josef Kohn and the Thonet brothers, both large Viennese firms. Unlike many Wiener Werkstätte designers, Hoffmann took advantage of mass-production techniques.

A stained beech and laminated wood *sitzmachine,* with adjustable back, upholstered seat cushion and headrest, c1905.
$9,600–11,200 *S*

A wicker armchair, designed by Benjamin Fletcher, the back terminating in armrests constructed to hold a drinking glass and magazines, c1907, 42¾in (108.5cm) wide.
$2,800–3,200 *S*

An Arts and Crafts chair, with rush seat, c1920.
$190–240 *OLM*

A tiger maple chest of drawers, by Gustav Stickley, designed by Harvey Ellis, the top inlaid in copper, ebony and tulipwood with stylised Art Nouveau foliate designs, the 9 drawers with original brass knobs, damaged, c1902, 36in (91.5cm) wide.
$7,000–8,000 *S(NY)*

A Gothic revival carved oak cradle, decorated with foliate and lancet arch panels flanking central panels with a coat-of-arms, on hexagonal supports with later acorn finials, the stretcher inscribed and dated 'HLS 1841', 62¼in (158cm) long.
$4,000–4,800 *Bon*

The arms carved on the sides would appear to be those of Hamon le Strange born in 1840.

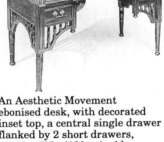

An Aesthetic Movement ebonised desk, with decorated inset top, a central single drawer flanked by 2 short drawers, c1880, 47¼in (120cm) wide.
$850–950 *P(Ba)*

An Arts and Crafts oak dresser, with a central astragal glazed cupboard, the base with a serpentine top over 2 frieze drawers and 3 panelled doors, the hinges and handles embossed in copper, c1900, 74in (188cm) wide.
$1,600–1,900 *SWO*

l. A Gothic revival oak hall stand, the panelled back decorated with quatrefoils and lancet arches and with scrolled hooks, above a central column of 3 panelled drawers flanked by stick stands, late 19thC, 74in (188cm) wide.
$2,600–3,200 *Bon*

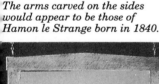

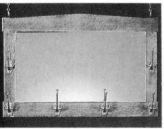

An oak hall mirror, by Gustav Stickley, with 6 wrought-iron coat hooks, c1909, 42½in (108cm) wide.
$2,500–2,800 *CNY*

An oak writing table, the top with leather insert, the 2 drawers with brass drop handles, c1870, 42in (107cm) wide.
$550–650 *L&E*

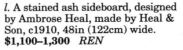

l. A stained ash sideboard, designed by Ambrose Heal, made by Heal & Son, c1910, 48in (122cm) wide.
$1,100–1,300 *REN*

An oak side table, designed by A. W. N. Pugin, the bevelled top above a pair of frieze drawers, on sledge feet with brass casters, c1845, 42in (107cm) wide.
$2,400–2,700 *Bon*

This table was probably made by J. G. Crace after Pugin's designs for Adare Manor.

Art Nouveau Furniture

A mahogany *Clématite* bed, by Louis Majorelle, the pierced headboard carved with clematis blossoms, vines and leaves, c1900, 71½in (181.5cm) wide.
$5,000–5,600 *S*

An Art Nouveau satin walnut side cabinet, the 2 central glazed doors enclosing fitted shelves, inlaid with neo-classical floral designs, c1905, 47½in (120.5cm) wide.
$640–720 *GAK*

An Art Nouveau mahogany display cabinet, with inlaid copper floral bracket motifs above an open shelf with shaped mirrored back panel, over a pair of leaded glass cupboard doors with green stained glass inserts and central floral copper inlaid design, c1900, 47in (119.5cm) wide.
$2,400–2,800 *C(S)*

A music cabinet, by Louis Majorelle, the back panel inlaid in various fruitwoods, set above shelves, c1900, 31¼in (79.5cm) wide.
$5,500–6,500 *S*

A white-painted pine bedside cabinet, by Henry van de Velde, with brass handle, on casters, c1902, 15½in (39.5cm) wide.
$3,500–4,000 *S*

An Art Nouveau mahogany music cabinet, c1910, 20in (51cm) wide.
$430–480 *RPh*

r. A French Art Nouveau mahogany and marquetry-inlaid secretaire, attributed to Louis Majorelle, the drop-front opening to a fitted interior above a shaped lower shelf backed by fabric, c1900, 28½in (72.5cm) wide.
$3,700–4,500 *S(NY)*

A pearwood side chair, designed by Hector Guimard, the open back with padded top, carved with fine tendrils and pierced with foliate scrolls, original upholstery, c1903.
$38,000–43,000 *C*

This museum quality piece is by one of the masters of Art Nouveau design.

A white painted wood side chair, by Peter Behrens, with original tapestry seat cover, 1903.
$4,400–4,800 *S*

This chair was designed by Behrens for the poet Richard Dehmel, Hamburg. An identical chair from this same source is in the collection of the Kunstgewerber-museum, Hamburg.

A set of 3 French Art Nouveau oak chairs, each shaped back inlaid with a stylised animal or bird, with rounded upholstered seats, c1905.
$560–720 *RIT*

A stained bentwood and plywood side chair, by Josef Hoffmann for Jacob & Josef Kohn, Vienna, with studded black leather upholstery, 1904.
$18,500–20,000 *S*

This important chair is of museum quality.

An Art Nouveau inlaid
mahogany corner chair,
c1910, 24in (61cm) wide.
$520–560 *RPh*

An Art Nouveau mahogany-framed
tub chair, c1920, 25in (63.5cm) wide.
$680–760 *RPh*

An Art Nouveau mahogany
fire screen, with leaded
lights, glass replaced,
c1890, 24in (61cm) wide.
$400–480 *GBr*

An Art Nouveau carved
giltwood and gesso wall mirror,
the pierced surround of
entwined floral stems with
floral roundels below, c1905,
79 x 54in (200.5 x 137cm).
$5,600–6,400 *CSK*

A cast iron fireplace surround, by
Hector Guimard, cast with stylised
floral designs and swirling flower
motifs in relief around the central
recess, c1904, 39¼in (99.5cm) wide.
$8,800–9,800 *CNY*

A mahogany and fruitwood two-
tier tea table, by Louis Majorelle,
inlaid in various woods with
irises and leafage and fitted
with 2 whiplash ormolu handles,
raised on moulded legs, c1900,
32½in (82.5cm) wide.
$3,800–4,800 *S(NY)*

A French carved walnut sideboard,
the upper section with a glazed
centre door flanked by doors
carved with berries and leafage,
raised on 4 carved legs, the lower
section with frieze drawer and
3 cupboard doors, Nancy School,
c1900, 70in (178cm) wide.
$4,800–5,600 *S(NY)*

An Art Nouveau mahogany piano,
the upper section with pierced
lattice work enclosing 3 inlaid
panels, the side and lower panels
with floral decoration, c1890,
60in (152.5cm) wide.
$5,600–7,000 *S(NY)*

Emile Gallé (1846–1904)

Gallé was the principal force
in a group of French Art
Nouveau artists and
designers working in and
around Nancy. In 1890 they
formed a school to promote
naturalism in design. Known
equally for his exquisite glass
wares, Emile Gallé's
furniture is considered to be
pure Art Nouveau. His
inventive furniture designs
heralded the rise of more
floral decorative forms. He
drew his inspiration from
nature, particularly the flora
and fauna of his native
Lorraine. Gallé's work also
led to a revival of marquetry.

l. A Gallé fruitwood marquetry
dressing table, the hinged top
and underside inlaid in
various woods with clematis
blossoms and leafage, opening
to a fitted interior, c1900,
27in (68.5cm) wide.
$2,800–3,500 *S(NY)*

Arts & Crafts Metalware

An Arts and Crafts metal bowl, the embossed, pierced and chased foliate rim enhanced with berries, c1900, 11¼in (28.5cm) diam.
$320–400 *P*

An Arts and Crafts copper inkstand, c1900, 9in (23cm) wide.
$280–350 *WAC*

A pair of Arts and Crafts bronzed-brass and copper candlesticks, designed by Albin Müller, with 4 opalescent glass cabochons at the base, 10½in (27cm) high.
$2,000–2,400 *P*

An Arts & Crafts silver jug, with hinged cover and cane handle, c1900, 9in (23cm) high.
$1,300–1,450 *ASA*

An American Gothic revival silver ice pitcher, chased with stylised foliate arches and floral motifs, with a fruiting grapevine handle, maker's marks for Jacob Wood & Jasper W. Hughes, and John & William Moir, New York, c1860, 10in (25.5cm) high, 78.5oz.
$2,800–3,200 *RIT*

l. A Secessionist copper-cased glass vase, c1900, 10in (25.5cm) high.
$1,400–1,500 *ARE*

r. An electroplated and ebony tureen, cover and ladle, by Christopher Dresser for J. W. Hukin & J. T. Heath, registered mark for 28th July 1880, tureen 8in (20.5cm) high.
$11,500–13,000 *S*

Cross Reference
Colour Review

Art Nouveau Metalware

A Jugendstil glass and silver posy vase, c1900, 7in (18cm) diam.
$320–350 *SUC*

An Orivit pewter bowl, c1900, 13in (33cm) wide.
$140–155 *WAC*

Orivit pewter was produced by the Rheinische Bronzegeisserei from c1901.

r. A Kayserzinn fruit bowl, c1900, 7½in (19cm) diam.
$1,000–1,100 *SUC*

Kayserzinn

J. P. Kayser & Söhne (1885–c1904) was established at Krefeld-Bochum, near Düsseldorf, and was one of the first German foundries to produce art pewter, manufactured under the name Kayserzinn (Kayser pewter) from 1896. Unlike WMF (Württembergische Metallwarenfabrik), Kayser did not electroplate their wares, which were more akin to ordinary pewter. High standards of casting were achieved using a strong, malleable alloy of tin, copper and antimony, which gave a fine silvery shine when polished.

The majority of wares, which included ashtrays, dishes and vases, were in Jugendstil (the term for German and Austrian design in the Art Nouveau style), although some wares show a French influence. In turn, Kayserzinn was the inspiration for Liberty's Tudric range.

A WMF white metal bottle coaster, with pierced and cast classical figures, c1900, 4in (10cm) diam.
$80–100 *TMA*

A silver box, decorated with the head of a lady, c1900, 4in (10cm) diam.
$1,000–1,200 *SHa*

An Orivit pewter dish, c1900, 9in (23cm) wide.
$220–240 *ZEI*

A green glass silver overlay vase, by Alvin & Co, c1905, 12in (30.5cm) high.
$3,200–4,000 *SFL*

r. An Art Nouveau silver photograph frame, by Davenport, Birmingham 1904, 5 x 3½in (12.5 x 9cm).
$450–550 *THOM*

A WMF pewter desk set, marked, c1900, 16in (40.5cm) wide.
$5,500–6,500 *SHa*

r. A Bohemian glass liqueur set, c1910, tray 17in (43cm) wide.
$550–600 *WAC*

An Art Nouveau silver water jug, by William & John Barnard, repoussé-decorated with flowerheads and tendrils, the tendrils forming the handle, hinged cover, London 1900, 10in (25.5cm) high, 9oz.
$600–650 *L&E*

A French Art Nouveau pewter ewer, signed T. Jean, c1905, 19¾in (50cm) high.
$1,200–1,400 *ANO*

Arts & Crafts Glass

l. A Bohemian Art glass engraved punch set, the bowl and undertray of frosted colourless glass with red glass 'jewels' centring gold enamelled swags and medallions, dated '1875', 11in (28cm) high.
$350–400 *SK*

FURTHER READING
Miller's Art Nouveau Antiques Checklist, Miller's Publications, 1992.

An Arts and Crafts stained glass panel, painted with birds, animals and mythical beasts, c1900, 16½ x 21¼in (42 x 54cm).
$560–640 *CSK*

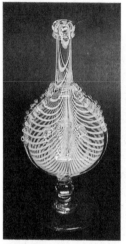

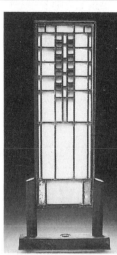

A Nailsea glass vase, in the shape of a pair of bellows, c1880, 14in (35.5cm) high.
$480–540 *ARE*

A pair of vaseline glass vases, c1860, 10in (25.5cm) high.
$640–720 *ARE*

A Loetz red and white glass vase, by Jutta Sika, c1905, 8½in (21.5cm) high.
$16,000–17,500 *S*

Art glass items by the Bohemian firm of Loetz are always particularly sought-after.

A leaded glass panel, by Frank Lloyd Wright, decorated with opaque white and iridescent glass segments, and a single yellow glass segment, c1902, 12¾in (32.5cm) high.
$4,800–5,400 *CNY*

Art Nouveau Glass

l. A Harrasche Glashütte vase, the green-flashed clear glass wheel-carved with geometric banding, foliage, fruit and flowers, heightened with gilding, c1900, 8¾in (22cm) wide.
$370–420 *P*

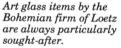

l. An iridescent glass vase, by H. Copillet et Cie, the milky amber/green glass overlaid with lustrous copper pink and etched with sprays of creeper, c1905, 16in (40.5cm) high.
$5,500–6,500 *C*

A Daum cameo glass vase, the yellow ground overlaid in orange and brown, carved with a riverscape with trees and plants, small chip, c1890, 13in (33cm) high.
$1,100–1,200 *TMA*

r. A Daum etched and enamelled glass vase, with inclusions of vitrified powdered glass, c1900, 9½in (24cm) high.
$2,400–3,200 *PSG*

A Gallé enamelled smoky-grey glass vase, with trefoil neck, decorated with pink, green, yellow and blue dragonflies and flowering waterlilies, signed, c1880, 8¾in (22cm) high.
$2,800–3,200   P

A Gallé cameo glass vase, rim chipped, c1890, 13¾in (35cm) high.
$1,200–1,400   DaD

A Gallé glass vase, decorated in brown with trees in a landscape, c1900, 6½in (16.5cm) high.
$1,600–1,800   SUC

A Gallé cameo glass vase, etched with blossoms and leaves, enamelled in pink, white, green, grey and orange, heightened in gilt, c1900, 9in (23cm) high.
$1,700–2,200   S(NY)

A French glass vase, by Eugène Rousseau and E. Leveille, c1890, 7¾in (19.5cm) high.
$950–1,100   SUC

A Gallé cameo glass vase, brown and green overlaid on pink, c1900, 4¾in (12cm) high.
$2,200–2,700   PSG

A Loetz iridescent glass vase, designed by Koloman Moser, with silver oil spot motif against wavy lines, 3 applied drop-shaped feet, hairline crack, c1902, 6¾in (17cm) high.
$8,500–9,500   CNY

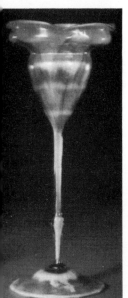

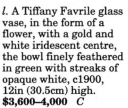

A Gallé glass vase, decorated with flowers and leaves, c1900, 4¼in (11cm) high.
$1,200–1,400   SHa

l. A Tiffany Favrile glass vase, in the form of a flower, with a gold and white iridescent centre, the bowl finely feathered in green with streaks of opaque white, c1900, 12in (30.5cm) high.
$3,600–4,000   C

A Palme-König & Habler Art glass vase, in iridescent red with bronze mount, c1905, 15¼in (39cm) high.
$1,100–1,300   ANO

Palme-König, established in 1786, were Bohemian glassmakers who produced fine quality Art Nouveau iridescent glass wares and table glass in forms popularised by Loetz.

A Loetz internally decorated glass vase, with iridescent blue spotting, cased in cranberry-coloured glass with applied gilt decoration to the rim, c1895, 6¾in (17cm) high.
$640–780   P

Art Nouveau Ceramics

A pair of Doulton pottery beakers, made to simulate leather, with silver rims, c1900, 4¼in (11cm) high.
$160–200 SPU

A Burmantofts pottery jardinière, decorated with blue and green flowers and leaves, c1890, 12in (30.5cm) diam.
$400–550 ASA

A Meissen porcelain plate, decorated by Henry van de Velde, in underglaze blue, maker's mark, c1903, 10½in (27cm) diam.
$850–900 S

A Doulton stoneware three-handled tyg, sgraffito decorated with blue foliage on a buff ground, silver-plated rim, repaired, signed 'Louisa Davis', date mark for 1880, 6¼in (16cm) high.
$110–130 WL

Boch Frères

Boch Frères was founded in 1767 at Sept Fontaines in the Saarland in Germany. By the mid-19thC, following a split, part of the firm established Boch Frères, Keramis, in Belgium, to produce mainly earthenware vases, some tableware and candlesticks.

l. A bronze lustre vase, by Boch Frères, Keramis, decorated with irises, c1905, 15¾in (40cm) high.
$1,100–1,300 ANO

A Doulton Lambeth pottery claret jug, by Hannah Barlow, incised with a frieze of cattle on a blue and green fluted ground, applied flowerhead banding, loop handle and silver hinged cover, late 19thC, 10½in (26.5cm) high.
$1,000–1,100 AH

A Martin Brothers ewer, decorated with aquatic creatures, late 19thC, 5¼in (13.5cm) high.
$1,200–1,350 HYD

r. A salt-glazed stoneware pitcher, designed by Peter Behrens, made by Simon Peter Gerz I, incised with stylised linear decoration heightened with blue, with hinged cover, c1903, 12½in (32cm) high.
$1,400–1,500 S

Teco

William Day Gates established Gates Potteries at Terra Cotta, Illinois, in 1881, to manufacture architectural terracotta, tiles and bricks. He introduced Teco stonewares in 1902, the name being derived from the location. Unlike other American pottery of the period, Teco wares were mass-produced in large industrial kilns using sophisticated slip casting and glazing methods. The wares, which include garden ornaments, pots and vases, designed by local architects, tend to be heavily walled, with good, crisp outlining. Some display complex moulding, with protruding structural elements.

A Martin Brothers vase, incised with birds on a buff ground, 1903, 5¾in (14.5cm) high.
$320–350 *HYD*

A Mettlach pottery vase, designed by Hans Christiansen, decorated with the head of a maiden and pink, white and blue irises on a blue ground, maker's marks, c1900, 10in (25.5cm) high.
$2,000–2,400 *P*

A Della Robbia Persian style vase, signed 'C.A.W.', c1903, 15in (38cm) high.
$430–480 *ZEI*

A Doulton Lambeth vase, by Rosina Harris, c1890, 7in (18cm) high.
$190–215 *SnA*

Cross Reference
Colour Review

r. A vase, by N. S. A. Brantjes & Co, Holland, c1900, 8¼in (21cm) diam.
$800–880 *OO*

An earthenware vase, by Hugh M. G. Garden, for Teco, with fluted vertical bands and rings at the top, in a matt green glaze, c1903, 12in (30.5cm) high.
$5,600–6,400 *CNY*

A Zuid Holland pottery vase, the shoulders painted with mauve flowers and green leaves, marked, c1900, 6in (15cm) high.
$280–320 *P*

l. Two Barum fish wall pockets, signed 'C. H. Brannam', and 'A. Lauder', 1886, largest 12in (30.5cm) long.
$140–180 *PCh*

Moorcroft

One of the most important names in the history of British art and studio pottery, Moorcroft this year celebrates its centenary. William Moorcroft (1872–1945) developed his own style of slipware design whilst employed at the Staffordshire firm of James MacIntyre & Co. Drawing on designs inspired by William Morris, his colourful Aurelian ware quickly became successful, followed by Florian and Flamminian ware. He drew and controlled the design of each pattern that was made in his department, and was also responsible for the shapes, many of which reflect his interest in both Eastern and Art Nouveau designs.

In 1913 William Moorcroft opened his own works in Burslem, Staffordshire. Although he continued to produce colourful and delicate items of natural form, his patterns evolved to keep up with the contemporary styles of the 1920s and '30s, the 'Jazz Age' and the more severe Art Deco style. In 1920 Queen Mary bought an item from the Moorcroft stand at the British Industrial Arts Exhibition in London, which resulted in the company being awarded a Royal Warrant in 1928. All wares made from then until 1945 bear the symbol as part of their mark.

William remained in control of production until his death in 1945 when his son, Walter, took over and continued to produce high quality art pottery. Using many of his own designs, he was able to experiment with a new range of colours and methods of firing.

Sally Tuffin became the new designer after Walter Moorcroft retired in 1986, and for the first time in the company's history a member of the family was not responsible for design. However, Sally maintained the Moorcroft tradition in both style and quality until 1993 when she left the company, and Rachel Bishop became the new designer under the leadership of Walter's half-brother, John, who is today the Managing Director.

Moorcroft pottery has been collected enthusiastically over the years. The past year has seen a dramatic rise in interest of both new and earlier pieces, and an increase in value of items made by both William and Walter. Illustrated in the following pages are examples of Moorcroft design, from the early intricate Florian ware to the Landscape and Toadstool designs of the 1920s, as well as the ever-popular Pomegranate, Pansy and Wisteria patterns, and the floral designs produced in the 1950s and '60s.

When looking at Moorcroft pottery it must be remembered that each piece is unique, as it is hand-painted. No two pieces are the same, and old designs are never reproduced. Prices range from around $240 to $16,000, thus ensuring a varied and secure market.

John Donovan & Angela Stones

A Moorcroft Florian ware vase, decorated with acanthus and floral scrolls, picked out in 2 tones of blue with white piping,, signed, c1898, 3¼in (8.5cm) high.
$750–800 *J&L*

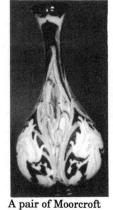

A pair of Moorcroft Florian ware vases, decorated with Iris pattern in yellow and green on a blue ground, c1898, 9in (23cm) high.
$1,500–1,800 *MSW*

A Moorcroft Florian ware vase, decorated with Peacock design, c1900, 12in (30.5cm) high.
$2,500–3,000 *RUM*

A Moorcroft Florian ware ewer, decorated with Peacock design, c1902, 8in (20.5cm) high.
$2,000–2,400 *RUM*

A Moorcroft bowl, painted and piped with red capped fungi on a blue green ground, signed, c1910, 9in (23cm) diam.
$950–1,100 *L*

l. A Moorcroft vase, decorated with late Florian design, c1916, 8in (20.5cm) high.
$2,800–3,500 *RUM*

r. A Moorcroft MacIntyre twin-handled vase, decorated with Florian ware pattern on a mottled green and blue ground, marked, c1912, 8in (20.5cm) high.
$3,500–4,000 *LAY*

A Moorcroft Claremont vase, decorated with Toadstool pattern, on a shaded blue/green ground, maker's mark and initials, c1918, 7in (18cm) high.
$1,100–1,200 *RIT*

A Moorcroft vase, decorated with Wisteria pattern, signed, c1918, 3½in (9cm) high.
$430–480 *CEX*

A Moorcroft vase, decorated with Wisteria pattern, c1925, 6in (15cm) high.
$560–640 *RUM*

l. A Moorcroft Flambé vase, decorated with Ochre Poppy design on a blue/grey ground, c1920, 6½in (16.5cm) high.
$1,600–1,800 *RBB*

r. A Moorcroft vase, decorated with leaves and berries on a woodsmoke ground, signed, c1927, 6¼in (16cm) high.
$680–760 *CEX*

A Moorcroft slender baluster vase, decorated with Pomegranate pattern, c1940, 12½in (32cm) high.
$400–550 *WW*

A Moorcroft vase, decorated with Pomegranate pattern, signed, c1928, 3½in (9cm) high.
$400–450 *CEX*

A Moorcroft vase, decorated with Hibiscus pattern, 1950s, 3¾in (9.5cm) high.
$250–280 *CEX*

A Moorcroft vase, decorated with Anemone pattern on a woodsmoke ground, c1950, 4½in (11.5cm) high.
$320–350 *CEX*

Arts & Crafts and Art Nouveau Jewellery

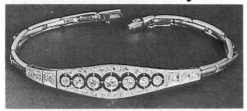

An 18ct white gold and diamond bracelet, with an open graduated setting bordered by small stones and flexible links, early 20thC.
$1,600–1,800 *RBB*

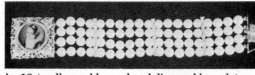

An 18ct yellow gold, pearl and diamond bracelet, the centre set with a miniature portrait painting set with 2 diamonds, suspending 4 strands of pearls with 3 yellow gold cross bars set with 5 small diamonds, early 20thC, 6¾in (17cm) long.
$1,200–1,300 *FBG*

An Art Nouveau emerald, diamond and enamel brooch, the diamond collet centre forming a pear-shaped *plique-à-jour* enamel river scene with cabochon emerald centre, French assay marks, c1900, 3¼in (8.5cm) high.
$8,800–10,400 *C*

A gold, diamond, ruby, sapphire and emerald butterfly brooch, late 19thC.
$1,700–1,800 *Bea*

Plique-à-Jour

Plique-à-jour, or open braid, is an enamelling method whereby a structure of metal strips laid on a metal background forms enclosed areas that are then filled with translucent enamels. When the backing is removed, a transparent 'stained glass' effect is achieved. The method was developed in Russia during the 17thC, and was adopted by French and English jewellers of the Art Nouveau period for use in pendants and brooches.

An emerald and diamond quatrefoil brooch, c1910, 1¼in (33mm) wide.
$11,200–12,200 *C*

A silver-gilt and enamel ornament, by George Frampton, with bright green trees and flowers on a blue ground, for use as a buckle, pendant or brooch, 1898, 3¼in (8.5cm) diam.
$15,500–17,500 *C*

A French Art Nouveau silver-gilt enamelled brooch, with freshwater pearl drop, c1900.
$240–320 *ANO*

A French Art Nouveau gold and enamelled silver belt buckle, c1900, 2in (55mm) wide.
$3,200–3,500 *S(NY)*

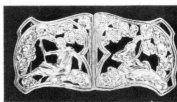

An Art Nouveau silver buckle, c1910, 4in (10cm) wide.
$280–320 *ASA*

A set of 6 silver and paste coat buttons, c1900, 1¼in (30mm) diam.
$100–120 *JBB*

A set of 6 Art Nouveau buttons, each embossed with a maiden's head, Birmingham 1903, 1in (25mm) wide
$220–250 *AH*

A carved horn and turquoise hair comb, by Henri Vever, pierced and carved at the top with a row of blossoms, one turquoise missing, impressed mark, c1900, 5in (12.5cm) long.
$1,400–1,600 *S(NY)*

An Arts and Crafts necklace, with 3 openwork plaques, the cruciform wirework panels centred with opal cabochons and linked by 3 rows of chains, c1895, 19¼in (48.5cm) long.
$320–350 *P*

An Arts and Crafts necklace, by Arthur and Georgie Gaskin, the wirework pendant set with mother-of-pearl, pink tourmalines and green stained chalcedony, centred by a heart-shaped mother-of-pearl plaque, suspended from a plaque similarly decorated, on a chain, c1914, pendant 2¼in (5.5cm) long.
$2,800–3,200 *P*

An Arts and Crafts necklace, the wirework pendant set with carnelian cabochons, with carnelian drop, suspended on chains, c1900, 11in (28cm) long.
$280–320 *P*

An Art Nouveau gold, turquoise and pearl pendant, c1900, 2in (50mm) long.
$560–720 *ASA*

FURTHER READING

Miller's Art Nouveau & Art Deco Buyer's Guide, Miller's Publications, 1995.

A gold, enamel and baroque pearl pendant, by Edouard Colonna, enamelled in green, c1901, 2½in (64mm) high.
$5,600–7,000 *S(NY)*

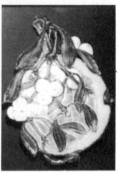

An enamelled silver pendant, by André Fernand Thesmar, c1900, 2¾in (70mm) long.
$4,500–5,500 *S(NY)*

r. A pair of French Art Nouveau gold, enamel, baroque pearl and diamond pendants, c1900, 2¼in (54mm) long.
$5,000–6,000 *S(NY)*

An Art Nouveau gold pendant, chased with a swan on pink and blue *plique-à-jour* enamel sunburst sky set with a rose-cut diamond, with a gem-set and pearl detail, c1910.
$5,600–6,400 *CSK*

A silver-coloured metal locket, by Bertold Löffler for the Wiener Werkstätte, the swivel cover with repoussé design and beaded border, c1910, 1¼in (32mm) diam.
$1,400–1,600 *S*

A French gold and platinum openwork pendant, the central shaped petals set with diamonds and pearls, c1910, 1½in (37mm) high.
$3,200–3,500 *DN*

A gold, opal and diamond bat ring, by Georges Fouquet, designed by Charles Desrosiers, c1900, 1½in (37mm) high.
$5,600–6,400 *S(NY)*

Tiffany Lighting

An opal and iridescent glass and twisted wire ornamental hanging shade, attributed to Tiffany, late 19thC, 18in (45.5cm) high.
$2,800–3,200 *SK*

A Tiffany Favrile glass and bronze hall light fitting, composed of yellow and white opalescent glass brickwork tiles, c1899, 19in (48cm) high.
$11,000–12,500 *S(NY)*

A Tiffany Favrile glass and gilt-bronze turtleback tile chandelier, composed of iridescent amber glass tiles, c1899, 18½in (47cm) high.
$5,500–6,500 *S(NY)*

A Tiffany Poppy leaded glass and bronze table lamp, shade and base impressed, c1900, 24¼in (62cm) high.
$29,500–33,500 *FBG*

A Tiffany Favrile Peacock lamp base, the green glass decorated with iridescent feathering and silvery-blue eyes, mounted on a beaded bronze base, c1892, 16¾in (42.5cm) high.
$13,500–15,500 *S(NY)*

A Tiffany Favrile seven-light Lily lamp, on a gilt-bronze base, c1920, 20in (51cm) high.
$7,300–8,000 *S*

r. A Tiffany Wisteria leaded glass and bronze table lamp, impressed, c1900, 16¾in (42.5cm) high.
$50,000–55,000 *FBG*

A Tiffany Favrile glass and bronze counterbalance weight lamp, c1899, 16in (40.5cm) high.
$3,200–3,600 *S(NY)*

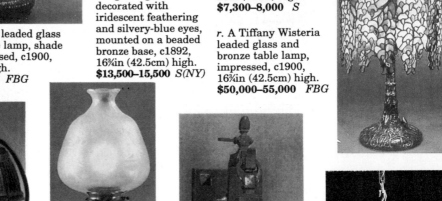

A Tiffany Favrile glass and bronze Linenfold lamp, the ten-sided shade with emerald green glass panels, c1899, 19in (48.5cm) high.
$5,000–5,600 *S(NY)*

A Tiffany Favrile glass and bronze lamp, decorated with amber and white leaves, c1899, 21in (53.5cm) high.
$7,200–8,000 *S(NY)*

A Tiffany leaded glass and bronze sconce, the square tapered shade set with amber glass panels, and another with shade lacking, c1914, 12in (30.5cm) high.
$2,000–2,500 *CNY*

A Tiffany brass ceiling fixture, formed as 6 flattened arms with hexagonal light sockets suspended by a chain, c1914, 47in (119.5cm) high
$1,100–1,300 *CNY*

Lighting

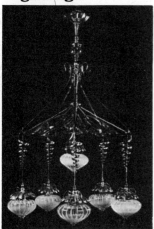

A brass ceiling light, by W. A. S. Benson and James Powell, with 6 onion-shaped opalescent glass shades, c1880, 51in (129.5cm) high.
$21,000–22,500 S

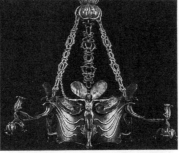

A wrought iron, bronze, silver and silvered metal hanging light, possibly designed by Alexander Fisher or Walter Gilbert, the central wrought iron band applied with 3 figures, the wings inset with panels of mother-of-pearl, c1900, 24in (61cm) wide.
$6,000–7,000 C

A Loetz iridescent glass and bronze chandelier, the shades decorated with peach oil spots and emerald green stringing, c1900, 24in (61cm) high.
$12,800–14,200 S(NY)

A Daum lamp, the grey glass streaked with yellow and peach/pink, overlaid with green and etched with a wooded lakeside scene, marked, c1900, 16½in (42cm) high.
$10,500–11,200 S

A pewter table lamp, attributed to Orivit, with 2 stems on a black marble base, the green glass shade decorated with red, c1900, 17½in (44.5cm) high.
$5,500–6,500 S

An Art Nouveau brass lamp, the shade inset with coloured glass berries and leaves, on a curved stem and lily pad base set with an illuminated frog, early 20thC, 20in (51cm) high.
$4,800–5,400 DN

A gilt-bronze and glass ceiling light, by Hector Guimard, the central support with 4 curved arms joining a square framework with pierced organic motif suspending alternating glass and bronze rods, c1908, 21½in (54.5cm) high.
$5,600–7,000 CNY

An Arts and Crafts beaten copper lantern, with vaseline glass and turquoise inserts, c1910, 19in (48.5cm) high.
$950–1,100 CHA

A Gallé cameo glass table lamp, decorated in chinoiserie style, internally mottled with lemon and overlaid in red, ex-Britt Ekland collection, c1910, 10in (25.5cm) high.
$18,500–20,000 CSK

An Art Nouveau three-light electrolier, with green frosted glass shades, c1910, 20in (51cm) high.
$1,000–1,200 CHA

A copper table lamp, by Gustav Stickley, the wicker shade lined with fabric, stamp mark, c1909, 25½in (65cm) high.
$7,200–8,000 CNY

A frosted glass hanging lamp, by René Lalique, moulded with leaves, engraved mark, after 1914, 19½in (49.5cm) high.
$7,500–9,000 S

l. An obverse-painted scenic lamp, the glass shade with textured hand-painted surface, mounted on a gilt-metal lamp base with handles, dated '1913', 13½in (34.5cm) high.
$1,100–1,300 SK

A silver-plated and glass table lamp, on a silver-plated base signed 'Empire Lamp Mfg Co, Chicago, 6.30.14', early 20thC, 22in (56cm) high. **$600–680** *FBG*

l. A Pairpoint Puffy glass and patinated metal lamp, the shade moulded and painted with red roses and yellow and blue butterflies, on a dark green ground, dated '1907', 15¼in (38.5cm) high. **$11,000–12,000** *S(NY)*

In the early 20thC, the Pairpoint Corporation of New Bedford, Massachusetts, made a range of innovative, reverse-painted and moulded table and boudoir lamps called Puffy lamps, with uneven glass shades. Bases vary; some simulate bronze, some are designed to resemble tree trunks, or are ribbed, and others are made from gilt-metal.

A wrought iron and alabaster torchère, by Edgar Brandt, the shade with grey veining, restored, c1925, 67in (170cm) high. **$5,500–6,500** *S(NY)*

A copper and mica table lamp, by Dirk van Erp, the shade with 4 sections set in a riveted hammered copper base, c1918, 11¼in (28.5cm) high. **$9,600–10,400** *CNY*

l. A *pâte-de-verre* lamp, by G. Argy-Rousseau, the grey glass moulded with stylised flowerheads, shaded with blue, green and purple, on an illuminated iron base, c1928, 7in (18cm) high. **$9,500–10,500** *S(NY)*

A wrought iron chandelier, the shade with 12 scrolling applications terminating in acorn-shaped finials, with hammered finish, c1930, 40in (101.5cm) high. **$3,600–4,800** *CNY*

A brown enamelled metal and Bakelite table lamp, by Poul Henningsen for Louis Poulsen, Copenhagen, with opalescent glass shade, c1927, 16¾in (42.5cm) high. **$16,000–17,500** *S*

This is an early form of the well-known Poul Henningsen table lamp 'PH'. Several variations on the design were shown in Paris in 1925, each conforming to the principle that lighting fixtures should illuminate without generating glare from the naked bulb.

A nickel-plated and opaque and frosted glass ceiling light, by W. H. Gispen, c1927, 23½in (59.5cm) diam. **$880–1,100** *S*

Cross Reference
Colour Review

A French Art Deco table lamp, c1930, 18in (45.5cm) high. **$550–650** *SUC*

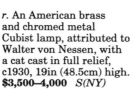

r. An American brass and chromed metal Cubist lamp, attributed to Walter von Nessen, with a cat cast in full relief, c1930, 19in (48.5cm) high. **$3,500–4,000** *S(NY)*

A bronze lamp, by Fayral, in the form of a figure carrying a vase, c1920, 22in (56cm) high. **$5,600–6,400** *ASA*

Art Deco Furniture

An Art Deco display cabinet, with walnut glazing bars, 1930s, 44½in (113cm) diam.
$720–880 *DAF*

A pair of Art Deco burr walnut bedside cabinets, each with demi-lune top and a single frieze drawer above 2 doors opening to a finished interior, c1930, 14¾in (37.5cm) wide.
$3,200–3,800 *S(NY)*

A pair of oak-veneered chairs, by Hille, with mock leather backs, arms and seats, on block front legs, 1930s.
$1,200–1,400 *P(Ba)*

A set of 6 French Art Deco rosewood and gilt-bronze dining chairs, c1935.
$7,000–8,000 *S(NY)*

An Art Deco fluted cocktail cabinet, veneered in burr maple, 1930s, 42in (107cm) wide.
$2,800–3,500 *DAF*

A pair of Macassar ebony upholstered club chairs, the backs with gilding on the top, probably French, c1925, 29½in (75cm) high.
$6,500–8,000 *CNY*

A pair of Art Deco walnut-veneered salon chairs, with stuff-over seats, on tapering legs, c1930.
$750–850 *P(Ba)*

r. An Art Deco birch three-door cupboard, the central door with bevelled glass, enclosing shelves with birch and ebony-strung edges, 1930s, 69¾in (177cm) wide.
$480–560 *P(Ba)*

An Art Deco walnut-veneered display cabinet, 1930s, 60⅛in (153cm) wide.
$950–1,100 *DAF*

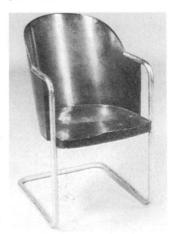

A set of 4 Art Deco walnut-veneered tub chairs, on tubular metal supports, with leather seats, 1930s.
$720–880 *P(Ba)*

A pair of Art Deco black lacquered and stained wood upholstered armchairs, 1930s.
$2,200–2,700 *S(NY)*

A velvet-covered day bed, on rounded supports enclosed by velvet-covered bracket feet, 1930s, 60in (153cm) long.
$480–560 *P(Ba)*

An oak-panelled desk, designed by Gordon Russell, made by H. Allway, 1929, 36in (91.5cm) wide.
$950–1,100 *HOLL*

A Dominique burr elm desk, the tambour top opening to a writing surface, c1930, 38in (96.5cm) wide.
$6,400–7,800 *S(NY)*

A silvered-bronze wall mirror, by Jacques-Emile Ruhlmann, with green silk hanging cord, c1925, 19¾in (50cm) high.
$5,000–5,800 *CNY*

A silvered-bronze table mirror, by Jacques-Emile Ruhlmann, on a base modelled as antelope horns, the back with adjustable stand, c1923, 18in (45.5cm) high.
$5,000–5,800 *CNY*

Jacques-Emile Ruhlmann (French, 1879–1933)

Initially a painter, Ruhlmann became the best known French cabinet-maker of his day. He designed for a rich and exclusive clientele, using exotic woods and other expensive materials. After WWI he took over his father's successful building firm, Ruhlmann et Laurent, and expanded it with workshops devoted to furniture and other aspects of interior design.

Ruhlmann designed a wide range of furniture, including dining tables and chairs, beds, desks, secretaires, mirrors, upholstered armchairs and so on. He also designed all manner of other items for interiors including textiles, light fixtures and even wastepaper baskets.

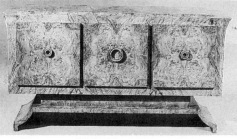

A French Art Deco walnut settee, incorporating shelves and drawers, 1930s, 103in (262cm) wide.
$950–1,100 *DAF*

An Art Deco walnut dining room suite, comprising: a sideboard, table, and a set of 6 chairs, c1930, sideboard 72in (183cm) wide.
$1,900–2,200 *P(Ba)*

A Rowley Gallery bedroom suite, comprising: a corner unit, wardrobe, pedestal cupboard and an electric fire, each piece painted and combed in predominantly silver, c1935, wardrobe 60in (153cm) wide.
$650–800 *P(Ba)*

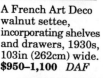

A French Art Deco limed oak sideboard, with central plaster figure of a mermaid flanked by 2 carved doors, opening to drawers and shelves, on dark stained oak legs and scrolled feet, c1940, 72in (183cm) wide.
$4,800–5,500 *S(NY)*

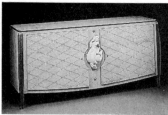

A French Art Deco sideboard, with marble top and chrome supports, some damage and repairs, c1935, 68½in (174cm) wide.
$1,250–1,350 *S(NY)*

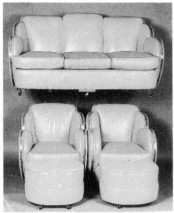

An Art Deco five-piece 'cloud'
suite, upholstered in red
leather, with walnut trim,
c1930, sofa 70in (178cm) wide.
$1,400–1,550 *SWO*

A French Art Deco wrought-
iron and marble console table,
in the manner of Raymond
Subes, with marble top,
on 2 double scroll-and-ball legs
joined by a ribbon stretcher,
c1925, 39¼in (99.5cm) wide.
$4,800–5,600 *S(NY)*

A French Art Deco mahogany draw-leaf
dining table, on vertical supports and
D-form plinths, trimmed in bronze, leaves
missing, c1930, 79in (200.5cm) wide.
$2,400–2,800 *S(NY)*

An Art Deco bentwood serving
trolley, with frieze drawer,
hinged handle, disc wheels
with rubber tyres, 1930s,
28½in (72.5cm) wide.
$1,300–1,450 *CSK*

A French Art Deco mahogany
and marquetry-inlaid table,
c1930, 23in (58.5cm) wide.
$5,600–6,400 *S(NY)*

A French Art Deco wrought-
iron and marble console table,
the central frieze with stylised
flowerheads and leafage, on a
reeded urn-form standard
above a shaped foot, c1925,
48½in (123cm) wide.
$6,500–8,000 *S(NY)*

A nest of 3 lacquered tables, by
J. Leleu, impressed mark, c1930,
largest 15¾in (40cm) wide.
$5,000–5,600 *S(NY)*

FURTHER READING
Eric Knowles, *Miller's
Victoriana to Art Deco*,
Miller's Publications, 1993.

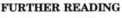

A mahogany table, by René Prou,
the top with *verre églomisé*
roundel, reverse-painted in gold
and white with signs of the
zodiac, c1935, 35½in (90cm) diam.
$4,000–4,800 *S(NY)*

An Art Deco shagreen bedside
table, with 2 drawers, one with a
book rest, and a circular sliding
ledge, 1930s, 14½in (37cm) wide.
$1,900–2,200 *CSK*

A mahogany and marble console
table, by Christian Krass, on
pedestal legs with reeded lower
portions, the feet ending in bronze
cylindrical toes, impressed mark,
c1928, 59½in (151cm) wide.
$10,500–11,500 *S(NY)*

A birch wardrobe, by
Gio Ponti, with a pair of
serpentine doors, with
Lucite knobs, on tapering
X-frame supports, c1940,
47in (119.5cm) wide.
$1,000–1,100 *CSK*

An Art Deco walnut whatnot,
manufactured and retailed by
Bowman Bros, Camden, 1930s,
20½in (52cm) wide.
$320–400 *DAF*

Art Deco Carpets & Textiles

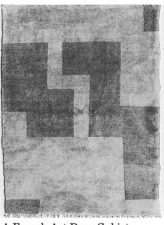

A French Art Deco yellow, orange and black carpet, c1930, 160 x 119in (406 x 302cm).
$15,500–18,500 *S(NY)*

An Aubusson woven wool tapestry, entitled 'Le Masque', designed by L. M. Jullien, with a puce and lavender patchwork ground surrounded by stylised foliage, woven signature, c1930, 56½ x 44in (143.5 x 112cm).
$4,000–5,000 *S(NY)*

A French Art Deco Cubist wool carpet, c1930, 77 x 56in (196 x 142cm).
$2,400–2,800 *S(NY)*

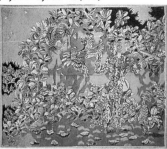

A tufted wool carpet, designed by René Crevel, with a formalised design of Cypress trees in a landscape in shades of purple, brown and beige, with a purple border, c1940, 102 x 80in (259 x 204cm).
$5,600–7,000 *C*

An Aubusson wool tapestry, entitled 'L'Homme avec l'Oiseau', designed by Jean Lurçat, depicting a man and various birds amidst vivid foliage, in shades of tan, brown, red, yellow, black, blue and grey, woven signature, c1945, 112½ x 97in (286 x 246cm).
$7,200–8,000 *S(NY)*

An Aubusson wool tapestry, entitled 'L'Oiseleur', designed by Jean Picart-le-Doux, depicting a man holding a bird cage surrounded by birds in flight, in shades of yellow, red, maroon, tan, brown, green, grey and ochre, c1946, 68 x 58in (173 x 147.5cm).
$4,500–5,500 *S(NY)*

Art Deco Metalware

l. A silver footed bowl, by Georg Jensen, c1930, 4in (10cm) diam.
$1,100–1,300 *ASA*

A pair of WMF silver-plated candlesticks, c1910, 8in (20cm) high.
$560–640 *WAC*

r. A Ronson enamelled cigarette case and lighter, c1930, 4in (10cm) long.
$400–480 *ASA*

A Bruford's Devon silver-plated kettle, on a stand with burner, c1910, 12in (15cm) high.
$320–360 *MSW*

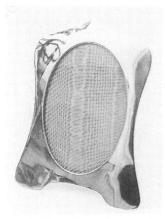

An Art Deco silver photograph frame, by L. Emmanuel, Birmingham 1915, 7¼ x 5⅜in (18.5 x 14.5cm).
$520–560 *THOM*

An Art Deco bronze inkwell, with raised side wells centred by 2 bear cubs, c1930, 11½in (29cm) wide.
$680–760 *WeH*

An Art Deco bronze paperknife, by Chiparus for Martin's Bank, with verdigris-coloured finish, c1930, 4¾in (12cm) long.
$560–640 *ANO*

A silver toast rack, marked 'MN & Co', Birmingham 1921, 6in (15cm) wide.
$55–65 *WAC*

A French silver tea and coffee set, by Tétard Frères, Paris, with octagonal wooden knops, c1930, coffee pot 5in (12.5cm) high, 39.5oz.
$2,200–2,700 *S(NY)*

l. A silver three-piece tea service, by Edward Spencer for the Artificers' Guild, the teapot with ivory scroll handle and knop, 1933, teapot 5in (12.5cm) high.
$2,800–3,200 *S*

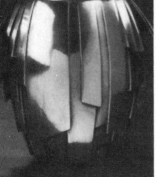

A silvered-bronze vase, by Albert Cheuret, cast with a geometric overlapping leaf motif forming 2 handles, c1925, 8in (20.5cm) high.
$10,500–11,500 *CNY*

An Art Deco silver three-piece tea set, the teapot with ebonised wooden handle, Birmingham 1937, 6½in (16.5cm) high.
$2,500–2,800 *SWO*

l. A French enamelled copper vase, decorated in blue, white, green and gilt, signed 'Leclaire', 1930s, 9in (23cm) high.
$560–640 *P*

Art Deco Glass

A green glass bowl, decorated with American Indians, c1920, 17½in (44.5cm) diam.
$430–480 *WeH*

A frosted glass bird, by René Lalique, 1920s, 5in (12.5cm) high.
$400–480 *ASA*

An opalescent glass bowl, by René Lalique, entitled 'Ondines Ouverte', moulded with a frieze of sirens, after 1921, 8in (20.5cm) diam.
$1,200–1,450 *S*

A brown cloud glass vase, 1930s, 8in (20.5cm) high.
$50–60 *BEV*

A green glass vase, by René Lalique, entitled 'Perruches', moulded with lovebirds and prunus blossom, c1925, 10in (25.5cm) high.
$7,300–8,000 *P*

An amber-tinted water jug and 4 glasses, by René Lalique, 1928, jug 7in (18cm) high.
$1,600–1,900 *ANO*

A glass fruit bowl, c1925, 6½in (16.5cm) high.
$280–320 *SUC*

Cross Reference
Colour Review

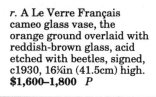

A Steuben yellow and green jade acid-cut glass vase, designed by Frederick Carder, decorated with Acanthus pattern, c1925, 9¼in (23.5cm) high.
$6,400–7,200 *S(NY)*

An opalescent glass bowl, by René Lalique, decorated in deep relief with trailing vine and bunches of grapes, slight chips, signed, c1925, 7in (18cm) high.
$950–1,100 *MCA*

A Worth Dans la Nuit perfume bottle, by René Lalique, decorated with stars on a royal blue enamelled ground, c1924, 4in (10cm) high.
$1,100–1,400 *RIT*

r. A Le Verre Français cameo glass vase, the orange ground overlaid with reddish-brown glass, acid etched with beetles, signed, c1930, 16¼in (41.5cm) high.
$1,600–1,800 *P*

Steuben Glass Works (American, 1903–present)

The company was founded in 1903 by an Englishman, Frederick Carder, and became a division of Corning in 1918. In the United States its work is regarded as the epitome of elegance in Art Deco glass. Before 1930 Carder designed many items himself, but from 1930 onwards the company employed a number of leading designers such as Sidney Waugh and Walter Dorwin Teague.

GALERIE MODERNE

Since 1982

THE WORLD'S LEADING SPECIALIST GALLERY FOR RENÉ LALIQUE GLASS

Since its inception in 1982 Galerie Moderne has become recognised as the only gallery dedicated exclusively to the works of René Lalique. Working closely with the world's leading museums, corporate collectors and private collectors, Galerie Moderne offers its clients unrivalled expertise and enthusiasm, as well as professional gallery advice and support. Apart from a varied stock of fine René Lalique pieces at all price levels, Galerie Moderne is usually able to source specific pieces required by its clients, and a full valuation service without obligation. Please contact us with your requirements.

Hours of business: Monday - Friday 10.00 - 18.00 hours, other times by appointment.

10 Halkin Arcade, Motcomb Street, Belgravia
London SW1X 8JT

Tel: 0171 245 6907   Fax: 0171 245 6341

Art Deco Ceramics

A Gouda pottery humidor and cover, decorated with Westland design, c1920, 8in (20.5cm) high.
$480–560 *OO*

A Susie Cooper jug, decorated with Dresden Spray pattern, c1935, 4¾in (12cm) wide.
$50–60 *WAC*

A Royal Cauldon hand-painted dinner service, 1920s, small plate 8in (20.5cm) diam.
$240–320 *SnA*

A Rosenthal porcelain part coffee service, decorated by Adolf Geigenmüller, enamelled with a stylised foliate pattern, in shades of green, pink, blue, magenta, yellow and gold, stamped mark, c1924, coffee pot 9in (23cm) high.
$4,400–4,800 *S(NY)*

A Burleigh Ware flower jug, decorated with Highwayman design, c1933, 8in (20.5cm) high.
$400–450 *WTA*

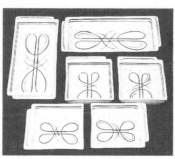

A Susie Cooper six-piece hors d'oeuvre set, painted with a scroll motif on a cream ground, painted mark '2226', c1930.
$110–160 *HYD*

An 11-piece tea service, by Josef Hoffmann, decorated with ribs of white and green, marked, c1930, teapot 6½in (16.5cm) high.
$1,400–1,500 *SK*

A Belgian pottery vase, decorated with cream flowers on a brown ground, c1925, 9¾in (25cm) high.
$550–630 *SUC*

A Susie Cooper hot water jug, decorated in sgraffito with crescent motifs, c1936, 6in (15cm) high.
$80–90 *WAC*

A Myott hand-painted jug, c1930, 7in (18cm) high.
$100–110 *WAC*

A Shelley 36-piece tea set, decorated in colours with sunrise design and trees, restored, printed marks, c1930.
$200–250 *GAK*

A Crown Devon vase, decorated with trees and flowers on a brown ground, 1930s, 5¼in (13.5cm) high.
$200–240 *WAC*

A Royal Doulton vase, decorated in blue, orange and yellow, 1930s, 4¾in (12cm) high.
$65–80 *TAC*

A ceramic vase, designed by Gio Ponti for Richard Ginori, decorated with figures playing musical instruments, c1925, 8½in (21.5cm) high.
$1,700–1,900 *S*

A Gouda pottery vase, decorated with yellow and green design, c1930, 8½in (21.5cm) high.
$100–115 *CSA*

A Gouda pottery vase, decorated with Shinski design, c1924, 10½in (26.5cm) high.
$320–400 *OO*

l. A Poole Pottery vase, 1920s, 7½in (19cm) high.
$70–80 *WAC*

l. A Ruskin high-fire pottery vase, with 4 applied vertical lobes, covered in a deep flambé glaze fired to reveal purple hues, and green and black spotting, marked, 1933, 16½in (42cm) high.
$8,500–9,500 *P*

r. A Poole Pottery vase, painted with flowerheads, berries and scrolling foliage, impressed mark, c1927, 9½in (24cm) high.
$120–150 *HYD*

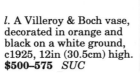

A Ruskin high-fired vase, c1933, 6½in (16.5cm) high.
$800–880 *SUC*

l. A Villeroy & Boch vase, decorated in orange and black on a white ground, c1925, 12in (30.5cm) high.
$500–575 *SUC*

Clarice Cliff

A Clarice Cliff Bizarre bowl, decorated with Diamonds pattern, factory marks, interior worn, c1930, 8¼in (21cm) diam.
$450–520 *CSK*

A Clarice Cliff Bizarre Havre bowl, decorated with Shark's Teeth pattern, factory marks, c1930, 8¼in (21cm) diam.
$450–550 *Bon*

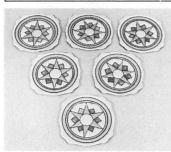

A Clarice Cliff two-handled Lotus jug, decorated with Melon pattern, Fantasque mark, c1930, 11½in (29cm) high.
$1,500–1,800 *Bon*

Miller's is a price GUIDE not a price LIST

A set of 6 Clarice Cliff Bizarre tea plates, each painted in orange, green and black with a star shaped medallion, on a yellow ground, printed and impressed marks, 1930s, 6¼in (16cm) square.
$1,400–1,700 *DN*

A Clarice Cliff Bizarre Holborn bowl, decorated with Orange V pattern, marked, 1930s, 9¼in (24cm) diam.
$550–650 *Bon*

A Clarice Cliff Bizarre bowl, decorated with Swirls pattern, factory marks, small chip, c1930, 8¼in (21cm) diam.
$550–620 *CSK*

A Clarice Cliff Lotus jug, decorated with Idyll pattern, c1932, 5½in (14cm) high.
$880–960 *WTA*

A Clarice Cliff Bizarre plate, decorated with Blue W pattern, c1930, 6in (15cm) diam.
$480–560 *WTA*

A Clarice Cliff Bizarre bowl, decorated with Mondrian pattern, hairline crack, factory marks, c1930, 7¾in (19.5cm) diam.
$550–650 *CSK*

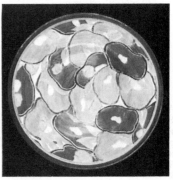

A Clarice Cliff Bizarre Havre bowl, decorated with May Avenue pattern, lithograph mark, c1932, 8½in (21.5cm) diam.
$2,500–3,000 *Bon*

A Clarice Cliff charger, decorated with Blue Chintz pattern, lithograph Fantasque mark, c1930, 18in (45.5cm) diam.
$1,400–1,600 *Bon*

A Clarice Cliff plate, decorated with Delecia pattern, c1932, 7in (18cm) diam.
$160–200 *BEV*

l. A Clarice Cliff Bon Jour bachelor tea set, consisting of 7 pieces, designed by Eva Crofts, painted with a bird, trees and sun, in shades of red, green black and yellow, factory marks, c1934, teapot 5¼in (13cm) high.
$2,400–2,700 *CSK*

A Clarice Cliff Le Bon Dieu tea set, consisting of 9 pieces, decorated with an orange and green glaze, c1932.
$1,100–1,200 *CSK*

One of Clarice Cliff's most controversial lines, this 1932 shape was far removed from her Art Deco shapes produced at the same time. This full early morning set is in the original Le Bon Dieu colours of mossy brown and green. Later examples were issued in the softer colours of her Nasturtium design.

A Clarice Cliff Stamford shape 'tea for two' set, decorated with Sunshine pattern, marked, c1934, teapot 5in (12.5cm) high.
$880–960 *AG*

A Clarice Cliff dinner service, decorated with Sungleam Crocus pattern, comprising 48 pieces, marked, 1930s.
$2,000–2,500 *AG*

A Clarice Cliff Conical sugar sifter, decorated with Pastel Autumn pattern, marked, c1932, 5½in (14cm) high.
$1,400–1,600 *WTA*

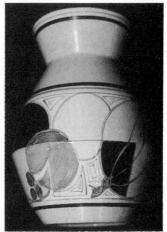

A Clarice Cliff Fantasque vase, decorated with Melon pattern, c1932, 8½in (21.5cm) high.
$1,300–1,600 *WTA*

A Clarice Cliff Newport Bizarre vase, decorated with Rudyard pattern, painted in pastel colours, marked, 1930s, 3in (7.5cm) high.
$720–800 *GAK*

r. A Clarice Cliff wall pocket, Pan, modelled as a youth, with flowers and foliage in his hair, factory marks, slight damage, c1930, 8¼in (21cm) high.
$280–320 *CSK*

A Clarice Cliff vase, decorated with Forest Glen pattern, c1936, 12in (30.5cm) high.
$1,000–1,200 *WTA*

A Clarice Cliff Bizarre vase, decorated with Caravan pattern, marked, c1931, 8in (20.5cm) high.
$4,800–5,600 *WTA*

The Caravan pattern is very rare.

Figures & Models

An Italian Art Nouveau white marble bust, entitled 'Iris', by E. Battiglia, c1900, 22in (56cm) high.
$2,300–2,600 *Bea(E)*

An alabaster and ivory female figure, entitled 'Dancing Grisette', by E. Seger, marked, c1910, 11½in (29cm) high.
$1,500–1,800 *S*

A boxwood figure of a nude female, by Kisfaludi Strubben, c1930, 15in (38cm) high.
$2,000–2,500 *S*

A porcelain biscuit figural group, by Agathon Léonard, 1890s, 14¾in (37.5cm) high.
$3,500–4,000 *S(NY)*

A Goldscheider glazed earthenware figure of a female dancer, restored, c1925, 17½in (44.5cm) high.
$1,900–2,400 *S(NY)*

A plaster female figure, by Leonardi, c1930, 15in (38cm) high.
$220–260 *DAF*

A Lenci pottery figure, by Essevi, entitled 'Oriental Dancer', with a drawer, signed and dated '20.7.32', 18in (45.5cm) high.
$2,700–3,200 *P*

A German porcelain figure of a female nude holding a serpent, by Fraureuth, on a base enamelled in gold, orange, blue, black and gilt, factory marks, slight damage, early 20thC, 14in (35.5cm) high.
$3,200–3,600 *S(NY)*

> **Miller's is a price GUIDE not a price LIST**

l. A French marble model of a dove, by Joel Martel, c1920, 10in (25.5cm) wide.
$3,500–4,000 *SUC*

A pair of Royal Dux male and female figures, wearing robes and carrying a pitcher, basket and melons, marked, c1910, tallest 18in (45.5cm) high.
$1,300–1,500 *AG*

A Goldscheider porcelain figure, c1940, 6in (15cm) high.
$320–400 *WTA*

Bronze

Joseph Lorenzl (Austrian)

One of the leading sculptors of the Art Deco period, Lorenzl produced a range of figures in bronze, ivory, and occasionally in chryselephantine (an expensive and highly desirable combination of bronze and ivory).

Lorenzl's sculptures usually depict figures of women and tend to be fairly small – up to 12in (30.5cm) without the pedestal. Lorenzl, unlike other sculptors of the period, seldom depicted figures from antiquity. His figures have the 1920s and '30s look, with bobbed or cropped hair. They tend to be very streamlined figures and small breasts and are usually idealised, although the facial features are realistic, with serene, calm expressions. The nudes often hold a scarf, fan or other accessory.

An Art Nouveau bronze bust, by Müller, c1900, 7in (18cm) high. $1,000–1,200 *ASA*

A gilt-bronze figure of Loie Fuller, by H. Levasseur, with swathes of material billowing over her head, c1900, 15in (38cm) high. $4,800–5,400 *S*

A bronze and ivory figure, by Lorenzl, 1930s, 10in (25.5cm) high. $1,600–1,900 *ASA*

An Austrian bronze and ivory dancing figure, entitled Castanets, by Blacz, mounted on a black marble revolving plinth, signed, c1920, 11in (28cm) high. $1,600–1,800 *FBG*

A patinated bronze figure of a dancer, by J. Lorenzl, with ivory face and hands, on an onyx plinth, inscribed, 1920s, 13½in (34.5cm) high. $1,300–1,500 *DN*

An Italian gilded and silvered-bronze figure, entitled 'La Danse Orientale', by Fatori, mounted on a mottled marble plinth, c1920, 27½in (70cm) high. $1,500–1,600 *FBG*

A bronze and ivory figure, cast and carved from a model by R. Marquet, entitled 'Egyptian Piper', on an onyx base, signed, c1920, 17in (43cm) high. $3,500–4,000 *P*

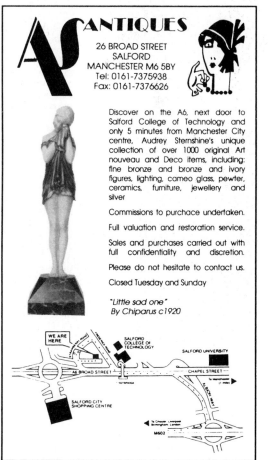

Art Deco Jewellery

A diamond and green paste bracelet, with 9 calibré-cut green paste and diamond *bombé* sections with diamond buckle connections, c1925, 6¾in (17.5cm) long.
$4,800–5,400   C

An emerald and diamond jewel, probably part of a bracelet, 1920s.
$6,400–7,200   S

A sapphire and diamond dress clip, set with baguette and cushion-shaped diamonds, c1920.
$1,700–1,900   S(S)

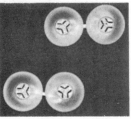

A Sibyl Dunlop clip brooch, with a central plaque of carved and pierced jadeite, mounted with leaves and tendrils with moonstones, lapis lazuli, pink tourmalines and chrysoprase fruits, c1925, 2in (50mm) high.
$1,300–1,450   P

A pair of Art Deco rock crystal diamond and calibre onyx cuff links, c1930.
$1,900–2,400   DN

> *r*. A diamond brooch, c1925, 2in (50mm) wide.
> $5,600–6,400   C

An emerald and diamond bracelet, c1925, 6¾in (17.5cm) long.
$4,000–4,500   C

A diamond and synthetic sapphire bracelet, c1930, 7in (18cm) long.
$7,200–8,600   Bon

A brooch and bracelet, the brooch with oval carved amethyst cameo, designed as a female bust, bracelet with green/blue enamelled panels alternating with blister pearls on a snap clasp, c1920.
$480–560   S(S)

A Sibyl Dunlop clip brooch, in the form of scrolling tendrils, vine leaves and fruits, the upper section set with dark green tourmalines, the lower part with peridots, c1925, 2in (50mm) high.
$1,100–1,200   P

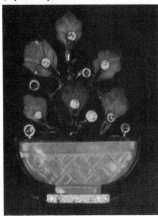

A turquoise and gem-set brooch, with ruby, emerald and multi-coloured diamond collet, c1925, 1¾in (45mm) high.
$5,600–6,200   C

A collection of 6 pieces of lacquered metal jewellery, by Jean Dunand, marked, c1922
$6,000–6,500   S

A Dorrie Nossiter gem-set brooch, with central aquamarine and brilliant-cut diamonds, encircled with blue zircons, pearls, amethysts, emeralds and paste, and 7 pearl drops, c1935, 1¾in (45mm) wide.
$3,800–4,600   P

A diamond brooch, designed as a scrolled fan, c1930.
$7,300–8,000   S

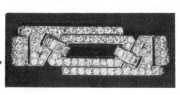

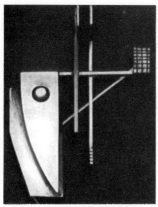

A steel, brass, copper and
ebony brooch, designed by
Peter Macchiarini, marked,
c1940, 2¼in (55mm) wide.
$1,600–1,900 *S*

A pair of
diamond ear
pendants, c1925.
$16,000–17,500 *C*

A pair of French aventurine
quartz, enamel and diamond
cuff links, c1925.
$1,500–1,600 *S*

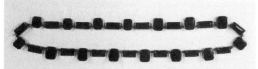

A Sibyl Dunlop necklace, comprising 15 opal
doublet plaques with cut corners, alternating with
green-stained chalcedony, c1935, 14½in (37cm) long.
$1,400–1,600 *P*

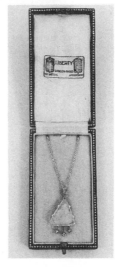

r. An 18ct gold and
platinum set opal and
diamond pendant, with
silver chain, c1920.
$560–640 *PSA*

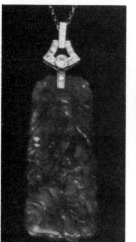

A jade pendant, carved
as birds and foliage,
with diamond
articulated geometric
panel suspension.
$1,000–1,200 *CSK*

A diamond dress ring,
in a platinum mount,
early 20thC.
$5,000–6,000 *DN*

Cross Reference
Colour Section

An Art Deco platinum
and diamond pendant,
set with 2 collet-set
diamonds, c1930,
14in (35.5cm) long.
$10,000–11,000 *SK*

A diamond and ruby
clip/pendant, with chain,
c1930, 15in (38cm) long.
$2,400–2,800 *GEM*

An aquamarine dress
ring, mounted with
alternately set circular-
cut diamond and
calibré-cut sapphire
stepped shoulders.
$1,900–2,200 *Bon*

A gold and citrine ring,
1930s, cased.
$400–480 *ASA*

A platinum, diamond,
ruby and sapphire
ring, c1935.
$1,900–2,400 *CSK*

A lady's diamond
wristwatch, the
jewelled lever
movement with
cabochon gem winder,
black moiré straps with
diamond twin two-
stone collars, 1930s.
$1,600–1,900 *CSK*

l. A lady's diamond
bracelet watch, 1930s.
$12,000–13,500 *CSK*

Posters

A set of 5 lithographs in colour, Poster Calendar 1897, by Louis Rhead, each depicting a maiden in a seasonal setting, signed, 18¼ x 13in (46.5 x 33cm), framed separately.
$1,300–1,400 *CNY*

A lithograph in colours, for Canuto Berea y Cia, La Coruña, by M. Miguel, on 3 sheets, c1890, 27 x 59in (69 x 150cm).
$1,300–1,400 *CSK*

A lithograph in colours, entitled 'Tour the Empire at Wembley', by F. Newbould, backed on linen, fold marks, c1920, 35 x 45in (89 x 114.5cm).
$850–950 *CSK*

A railway poster, by Geo Francois, c1920, 40 x 30in (101.5 x 76cm).
$850–950 *MUL*

A lithograph in colours, entitled 'Winter Sports in the French Alps', by R. Broders, c1929, 40 x 25½in (101.5 x 65cm), framed.
$1,500–1,900 *CNY*

A colour lithograph Olympic Games poster, Stockholm 1912, 37 x 27in (94 x 69cm).
$1,600–1,900 *P(NW)*

Cross Reference
Ephemera

A lithograph in colours, for Great Western Railways, by E. M. Kauffer, backed on linen, restored, c1932, 39½ x 24in (100 x 61cm), framed.
$2,400–2,700 *CSK*

A lithograph in colours, for Cacao, A. Driessen, by P. Livemont, backed on old linen, slight damage, c1900 30 x 16in (76 x 40.5cm).
$1,900–2,200 *CSK*

A lithograph in colours, for Ford, minor defects, c1930, 35 x 25½in (89 x 65cm).
$720–800 *CSK*

A Yorkshire Coast poster, by Frank H. Mason, printed by Jarrold, 1937, 40 x 50in (102 x 127cm).
$1,100–1,300 *ONS*

r. A lithograph printed in colours, entitled 'Normandie', by A. J. M. Cassandre, some repairs, c1938, 39¾ x 24¼in (100 x 62cm), framed.
$5,000–5,600 *S(NY)*

Art Nouveau & Decorative Arts
(1860 to the present day)

A Liberty & Co Tudric pewter timepiece designed by Archibald Knox, 36cm high. Sold for £13,200

Danseuse Cosaque, a bronze and ivory figure by D.H. Chiparus, signed, 58cm high. Sold for £12,100

An early Edward Barnsley Chest of Drawers, in Chestnut, 93.5cm wide, commissioned in 1927. Sold for £3,190

An elaborate Arts & Crafts necklace by Arthur and Georgina Gaskin, length of pendant 5.5cm. Sold for £1,815

At Phillips in London we hold eight specialised auctions of Art Nouveau and Decorative Arts a year, which not only include items of sculpture and British art pottery as illustrated here, but also the full range of disciplines, from glass, ceramics, silver, metalwares and jewellery to furniture, books, graphics, textiles and carpets.

"The Combat", a large and spectacular Royal Doulton "Sung" Exhibition vase, 56cm high. Sold for £24,200

Items for inclusion in these sales are accepted thoughout the year. For a free valuation either call into our London salerooms or send an adequate photograph with a brief description. Home visits can also be arranged by appointment.

For further information on buying or selling at auction please contact Keith Baker on (0171) 468 8381 or (0171) 629 6602.

http://www.phillips-auctions.com

LONDON

Phillips
INTERNATIONAL
AUCTIONEERS & VALUERS

101 New Bond Street, London W1Y 0AS

An Aesthetic Movement upholstered chair, c1870. **$2,400–2,700** *ARE*

An Arts and Crafts oak reclining armchair, c1880. **$1,200–1,400** *APO*

An Arts and Crafts oak armchair, c1900. **$560–640** *APO*

An Arts and Crafts rocking chair, with original upholstery, c1890 **$720–800** *GBr*

An Art Nouveau inlaid open armchair, c1890. **$1,200–1,350** *ARE*

An Art Nouveau mahogany chair, c1900. **$800–900** *AAN*

An Arts and Crafts oak piano stool, with padded seat, c1890, 22in (58cm) wide. **$95–115** *GBr*

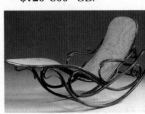

A Thonet brothers bent stained beech and cane rocking chair, probably designed by August Thonet, c1880. **$9,000–11,500** *S*

A Richard Riemerschmid armchair, by Dresdener Werkstätten, c1902. **$5,600–6,400** *S*

A carved fruitwood settee, by Georges de Feure, c1900, 62in (157.5cm) wide. **$13,500–16,000** *S(NY)*

A pair of Art Nouveau mahogany chairs, with upholstered seats, c1910. **$680–760** *RPh*

An inlaid birch armchair, designed by Mackay Hugh Baillie Scott, c190 **$7,200–9,500** *C*

A pair of carved walnut chairs, by Hector Guimard, with original tooled-leather upholstered seats, c1900. **$64,000–72,000** *S*

A mahogany salon suite, by Louis Majorelle, comprising settee and 4 side chairs, c1900. **$8,000–8,800** *C*

An Art Nouveau mahogany bed and a pair of bedside cabinets, by Carlo Zen, c1900, bed 58in (148cm) wide.
$6,000–6,500 *S*

Two wooden panelled beds, by Gustav Serrurier-Bovy, c1900, 48in (122cm) wide.
$1,900–2,400 *S*

A walnut glazed bookcase, attributed to J. G. Grace after a design by A. W. N. Pugin, carved with flowers and foliate motifs, c1852, 74in (188cm) wide.
$19,000–22,500 *C*

An oak bookcase, inlaid with Masonic motifs, c1870, 35in (89.5cm) wide.
$17,000–18,500 *C*

A stained oak corner vitrine, by Gustav Serrurier-Bovy, c1900, 47in (119cm) wide.
$3,800–4,800 *S*

A pine cabinet, probably American, stencilled with floral motifs, 1870s, 36in (91.5cm) wide.
$3,500–5,000 *C*

An Art Nouveau vitrine, inlaid with fruitwood and metals, c1910, 50in (127cm) wide.
$5,500–6,200 *S*

An Art Nouveau vitrine, the leaded glass doors decorated with stylised leaves, c1905, 60in (152cm) wide.
$6,000–6,500 *S*

A carved giltwood three-panel screen, by Georges de Feure, c1900, 41in (104cm) wide.
$8,500–9,500 *S(NY)*

A carved mahogany desk, by Louis Majorelle, with 2 tambour doors opening to a fitted interior, flanked by cabinets, the reverse with drawers and cupboards, c1905, 78in (200cm) wide.
$21,500–24,000 *S(NY)*

A fruitwood two-tier table, by Louis Majorelle, c1900, 30in (76cm) high.
$4,500–5,500 *SUC*

A hammered-metal mirror, by the Wiener Werkstätte, c1925, 26in (66cm) high.
$8,800–9,600 *C*

An oak sideboard, by Gustav Stickley, the top with plate rack, 3 central drawers and one long drawer under, branded mark and paper label, c1921, 66in (167.5cm) wide.
$5,500–6,500 *CNY*

An upholstered oak club chair, by Jean-Michel Frank, with curved back and loose squab cushion, raised on tapered oak feet, c1930, 29½in (75cm) wide.
$8,800–9,600 *CNY*

A pair of wrought iron chaises longues, by Chad Topassier Beranger, with sloping caned backs and seats, c1930, 72in (183cm) long.
$25,500–29,000 *S(NY)*

An Art Deco cabinet by Siegel, c1925, 90in (228cm) high.
$5,000–5,600 *CSK*

A French pearwood cabinet, by Robert Mallet-Stevens, with narrow hinged cupboards along top and bottom centering an open shelf, with attached geometric open shelves at one end, on narrow plinth, c1932, 92in (233.5cm) wide.
$29,500–32,000 *CNY*

A Continental parcel-gilt and mirrored glass mounted cabinet, c1940, 42in (107cm) wide.
$2,400–2,700 *CSK*

An oak desk, by Charles Dudouyt, one end curved, 3 drawers to one side, branded with artist's logo, c1940, 70in (178cm) wide.
$7,500–8,500 *CNY*

A Macassar ebony kneehole desk, by Sanyas et Popot, with 2 drawers either side of the kneehole, on tapering legs, c1940, 71in (180cm) wide.
$6,500–8,000 *S(NY)*

A blonde wood dressing table and stool, with black painted trim, by Betty Joel, c1935, 76in (193cm) wide.
$5,600–6,400 *S*

A dining room suite, by E. Gomme, comprising 13 pieces, monogrammed mark, c1930, table 71in (180cm) long.
$6,000–7,000 *S*

An Art Deco bird's-eye maple table and 4 small tables, 1930s, 36in (91.5cm) diam.
$1,400–1,550 *AAV*

A Martin Brothers grotesque bird, with removable head, c1900, 14in (35.5cm) high.
$21,000–24,000 C

A William de Morgan Persian footed bowl, painted with Damascus floral designs, the interior with a dragon within a scroll border, painted by Joe Juster, signed, c1900, 13in (33cm) diam.
$5,600–7,000 S

An Austrian amphora bowl, with symbolist heads either side and a band of stylised flowers, c1890s, 10in (25.5cm) diam.
$850–950 SUC

A cup and saucer, by Wassily Kandinksy for the Imperial Russian Porcelain Factory, c1921, saucer 6in (15cm) diam.
$56,000–62,000 S

A pair of glazed earthenware figural jardinières, by Delphin Massier, restored, c1900, 55in (140cm) high.
$19,000–22,500 S(NY)

An Aesthetic Movement majolica jug, c1875, 7in (18cm) high.
$160–200 SSW

A Wedgwood Arts and Crafts wall plate, with platinum lustre, designed by Louise Powell, c1905, 18in (46cm) diam.
$1,300–1,600 ANO

A Minton blue and white toilet jug, c1900, 9in (23cm) high.
$200–225 BRU

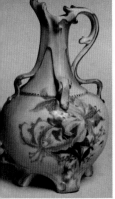

A pair of Royal Vienna porcelain ewers, c1900, 8½in (22cm) high.
$500–560 ANO

A Doulton Lambeth tankard, c1881, 4¼in (10.5cm) high.
$130–145 WAC

A porcelain tea service, designed by Josef Hoffmann, manufactured by Pfeiffer & Lowenstein, unglazed factory marks, c1910, teapot 7in (18cm) high.
$28,000–32,000 C

A William de Morgan glazed earthenware vase, decorated in Isnik palate with flowers, possibly an experimental piece, c1885, 15in (38cm) high. **$1,300–1,450** *C*

A Doulton Lambeth vase, c1890, 7½in (19cm) high. **$135–150** *WAC*

A Doulton Lambeth bottle, with silver stopper, 1920s, 9in (23cm) high. **$320–355** *GAZE*

A French porcelain silver-gilt and enamel vase, late 19thC, 10in (25.5cm) high. **$6,400–7,200** *SHa*

A Gebrüder Heubach *pâte-sur-pâte* porcelain vase, with silver overlay, decorated with figures, c1890, 6¾in (17cm) high. **$560–720** *ANO*

An Austrian porcelain vase, by Amphora, decorated with a bird, c1900, 12⅛in (32cm) high. **$480–520** *SUC*

A Clement Massier lustre vase, French, c1900, 11in (28cm) high. **$950–1,100** *SUC*

A Martin Brothers vase, the washed ground incised with lizards, marked, c1898, 11⅛in (29cm) high. **$3,200–3,500** *HYD*

A Doulton stoneware vase, by Hannah Barlow, c1900, 27in (68.5cm) high. **$950–1,000** *GAZE*

An Austrian Art Nouveau style pottery vase, decorated with flowers, c1900, 16in (40.5cm) high. **$4,300–4,800** *SHa*

A Clement Massier lustre vase, with stylised flower, French, c1900, 6¾in (17cm) high. **$800–880** *SUC*

A Shelley salad drainer and saucer, c1935, 7½in (19cm) diam.
$55–65 *WAC*

A Gouda pottery jug, c1920, 9½in (24cm) high.
$140–160 *WAC*

A Gray's pottery jug, hand-painted with a flower, 1930s, 4in (10cm) high.
$55–65 *WAC*

A Wade Heath pottery jug, 1930s, 6¾in (17cm) high.
$70–80 *WAC*

A Myott jug, c1930, 7¾in (20cm) high.
$30–50 *CSA*

A Royal Lancastrian double-handled lustre vase, c1920, 6½in (16.5cm) high.
$800–950 *ASA*

A Beswick jug, c1935, 7½in (19cm) high.
$110–130 *WTA*

A Wilkinson charger, designed by Frank Brangwyn, painted with a jungle scene, c1933, 17¼in (43.5cm) high.
$3,200–4,000 *C*

A Burleigh tea set, decorated with orange flowers, c1930s, teapot 5in (13cm) high.
$110–120 *WAC*

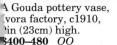

A Gouda pottery vase, Ivora factory, c1910, 9in (23cm) high.
$400–480 *OO*

A Gouda pottery vase, with butterfly design, c1920, 11¼in (29cm) high.
$400–550 *OO*

A Gouda pottery vase, Regina factory, c1920, 13in (33cm) high.
$400–480 *OO*

A Villeroy and Boch vase, c1923, 12¾in (32.5cm) high.
$480–520 *SUC*

A Longwy vase, decorated
with stylised leaves, c1925,
10½in (26.5cm) high.
$950–1,100 *SUC*

A Myott waisted square-shaped
vase, 1920s, 8½in (21.5cm) high.
$135–150 *BEV*

A French Primavera vase, c1925,
12½in (32cm) high.
$640–720 *SUC*

A pair of Royal Doulton stoneware vases,
designed by Nicki Webb, impressed mark,
1926, 16in (40.5cm) high.
$7,500–8,000 *HYD*

A Shelley Chintz ware vase,
1930s, 8in (20.5cm) high.
$130–160 *BEV*

A Ginori glazed earthen-
ware vase, designed
by Gio Ponti, c1925,
10½in (26.5cm) high.
$9,500–10,500 *C*

A Myott diamond-shaped graduated and
stepped vase, 1920s, 10¾in (27.5cm) wide.
$90–100 *BEV*

A French pottery double vase, designed by Jean
Lurçat, St Vincent, 1940s, 10½in (26.5cm) high.
$1,600–2,000 *SUC*

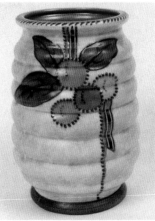

A James Kent hand-painted vase,
1930s, 6¼in (16cm) high.
$110–160 *WAC*

A Charlotte Rhead vase, c1935,
7in (18cm) high.
$160–200 *WAC*

A Shelley vase, c1935,
6in (15cm) high.
$40–50 *WAC*

A Moorcroft bowl, decorated with Waving Corn pattern, signed, late 1930s, 8in (20.5cm) wide.
$680–760 *CEX*

A Moorcroft bowl, decorated with Hibiscus pattern, c1950, chip restored, 6in (15cm) diam.
$300–340 *CEX*

A Moorcroft bowl, with Spring Flowers pattern, 1947–57, 4¼in (11cm) diam.
$260–300 *CEX*

A Moorcroft candle-stick, c1913, 10½in (26cm) high.
$600–640 *CEX*

A Moorcroft jug, c1996, 9½in (24cm) high.
$200–240 *CEX*

A Moorcroft ewer, with Pansy pattern, c1916, 12in (30.5cm) high.
$2,200–2,600 *RUM*

A Moorcroft coronation mug, signed, 1902, 4in (10cm) high.
$675–750 *CEX*

A Moorcroft Florian ware teapot, 1902, 5½in (14cm) high.
$1,600–2,000 *RUM*

A Moorcroft salt-glaze wall plaque, with African Lily pattern, c1930, 12in (30.5cm) diam.
$880–1,000 *RUM*

A Moorcroft Florian ware vase, with Peacock pattern, c1902, 12in (30.5cm) high.
$4,800–5,600 *RUM*

A Moorcroft vase, with Pansy pattern, c1915, signed, 10in (25.5cm) high.
$900–1,000 *CEX*

A Moorcroft vase, with Cornflower pattern, c1912, 8in (20.5cm) high.
$2,200–2,700 *RUM*

A Moorcroft vase, with Bougainvillea pattern, c1955, 10in (25.5cm) high.
$880–1,000 *RUM*

A Moorcroft vase, with Waratah pattern, c1930, 9in (23cm) high.
$8,000–8,800 *RUM*

A Clarice Cliff beehive honey pot and cover, decorated with a landscape on a turquoise and blue ground, 1930s, 4½in (11.5cm) high.
$250–300 *HYD*

A Clarice Cliff honey pot, with Crocus pattern, 1930s, 4in (10cm) high.
$250–300 *HYD*

A Clarice Cliff Bizarre dish, decorated in Blue Japan design, marked, c1933, 10in (25.5cm) wide.
$1,100–1,300 *WTA*

A Clarice Cliff Bizarre Conical shape tea-for-two service, painted in blue, green, black and orange with stylised leaves, printed marks in black, 1930s.
$2,500–2,800 *DN*

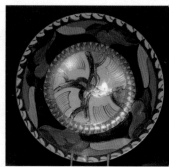

A Clarice Cliff Persian design charger, c1928, 10in (25.5cm) diam.
$950–1,100 *WTA*

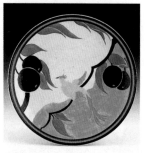

A Clarice Cliff Applique Bird of Paradise charger, marked, 1930s, 13in (33cm) diam.
$4,400–4,800 *Bon*

A Clarice Cliff teapot, decorated with raised wheat, poppies and fruit design, early 20thC, 7in (18cm) high.
$330–370 *GAZE*

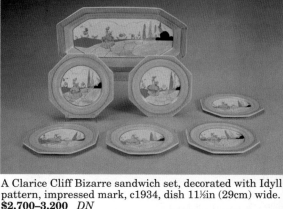

A Clarice Cliff Bizarre sandwich set, decorated with Idyll pattern, impressed mark, c1934, dish 11½in (29cm) wide.
$2,700–3,200 *DN*

A Clarice Cliff Gardenia Red wall charger, marked, 1930s, 18in (45.5cm) diam.
$6,000–7,000 *Bon*

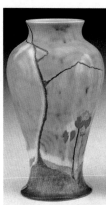

A Clarice Cliff Inspiration Garden Meiping vase, 1930s, 12in (30.5cm) high.
$1,200–1,400 *Bon*

A Clarice Cliff House and Bridge Meiping vase, 1930s, 16¼in (41.5cm) high.
$12,000–13,500 *Bon*

A Clarice Cliff flanged vase, decorated with Windbells pattern, marked, c1933, 8½in (21.5cm) high.
$2,400–2,700 *WTA*

A Clarice Cliff Sunray pattern Bizarre vase, shape No. 186, rubber stamp mark, 1930s, 5⅓in (14cm) high.
$1,300–1,600 *Bon*

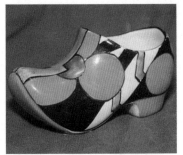

A Clarice Cliff Bizarre sabot, decorated with Orange Flower design, printed marks, c1930, 4in (10cm) long.
$400–500 *WTA*

A Clarice Cliff Bizarre fluted sandwich plate, decorated with Blue W pattern, stamped mark, 1930s, 9⅖in (24cm) diam.
$1,100–1,300 *Bon*

A Clarice Cliff vase, decorated with Broth pattern, shape No. 372, marked, 1930s, 8in (20.5cm) high.
$775–875 *Bon*

A Clarice Cliff matched part tea service, decorated with Autumn Crocus pattern, comprising: teapot and cover, milk jug, sugar basin, 2 bread and butter plates, 5 tea cups, 6 saucers and 6 tea plates, 1930s.
$1,300–1,450 *Bea*

A Clarice Cliff Linton coffee service, decorated with Blue Firs pattern, comprising: coffee pot and cover, cream jug, sugar basin, and 6 cups and saucers, 1930s.
$4,000–4,500 *Bea*

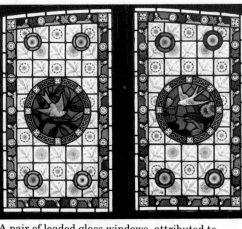

A pair of leaded glass windows, attributed to Donald MacDonald, decorated with stencilled flowerheads and leafage, the central medallions with birds, dragonflies, sunflowers and foliage, c1890, 39½ x 21½in (100.5 x 54.5cm), framed.
$4,800–5,600 *CNY*

A landscape 'blow-out' vase, by Daum, mould-blown with trees and a village, c1900, 11½in (29cm) high.
$8,800–9,600 *S*

A cameo glass vase, by Daum, overlaid and etched with sunflowers, with tapered rim, marked, c1900, 23¼in (59cm) high.
$13,000–14,000 *C*

A pair of stained glass panels, attributed to Loetz c1900, 50in (127cm) high.
$4,800–5,500 *S*

A wheel-carved cameo glass Crocus vase, signed 'Daum/Nancy', c1900, 11¾in (30cm) high.
$13,000–15,000 *S(NY)*

A wheel-carved cameo glass vase, with magnolias, signed 'Daum/Nancy', c1900, 19½in (49.5cm) high.
$16,000–19,000 *S(NY)*

A two-piece praying mantis vase, by Emile Gallé, c1880, 11¾in (30cm) high.
$16,800–18,400 *S*

A cameo glass vase, by Gallé, red and brown overlaid on amber, signed, c1900, 7½in (19cm) high.
$3,600–4,400 *PSG*

A cameo glass vase, by Gallé, with long slender neck, decorated with a leaf, 7in (18cm) high.
$1,000–1,200 *ANO*

A pair of enamelled glass vases, by Legras, Pantin, Paris, c1910, 13in (33cm) high.
$680–800 *ANO*

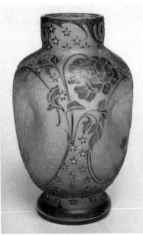

An Art Nouveau cameo glass vase, by Mountjoy, Blue Flower design with gilded stars, c1900, 8in (20.5cm) high.
$1,000–1,200 *ANO*

A Steuben Aurene glass scent bottle, by Frederick Carder, inscribed, c1910, 6¾in (17cm) high.
$21,500–25,000 *S(NY)*

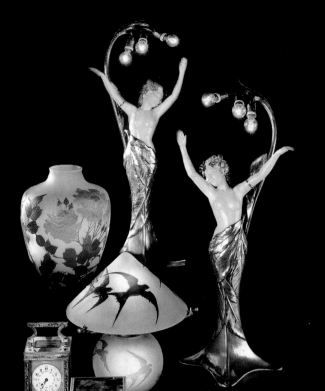

ARTEMIS
D E C O R A T I V E   A R T S   L T D

Dealers in varied selection of fine 19/20th Century Decorative Arts
Galle, Daum, Lalique, Bronzes, Marble, Clocks, Lighting, Art Deco and Art Nouveau

ガレ，ドーム，ルネ・ラリック

36 Kensington Church · London W8 4BX · Tel/Fax: 0171-376 0377

An American parcel-gilt, silver and metal Japanese style tray, by Gorham, in the form of a trompe l'oeil still life, marked, 1882, 11in (28cm) wide.
$16,000–19,000 *S(NY)*

An Arts and Crafts copper and brass inkwell, with coloured enamel, c1890, 6¼in (16cm) wide.
$480–640 *ANO*

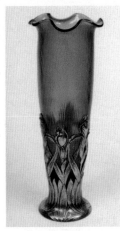

A German Art Nouveau vase, with pewter base, c1900, 11½in (29cm) high.
$520–580 *WAC*

A metal and enamel plate, engraved by the Vaughton brothers and Gilbert Marks, c1890, 8in (20.5cm) diam.
$4,000–4,400 *SHa*

A pair of gilt-bronze models of peacocks, with onyx bases, c1890, 27in (68.5cm) wide.
$12,800–14,000 *ARE*

A WMF Art Nouveau silver-plated jug, with figural handle, c1900, 14in (35.5cm) high.
$1,350–1,500 *WAC*

An American silver-gilt and cut-glass decanter, by Gorham, c1893, 14¾in (37.5cm) high.
$4,400–5,000 *S(NY)*

An Arts and Crafts hammered copper letter box, c1900, 10in (25.5cm) wide.
$640–800 *ASA*

An Austrian brass and fruitwood inlaid jewellery box, c1900, 6in (15cm) wide.
$400–550 *ASA*

A Tiffany Favrile glass and bronze candlestick, c1900, 14¾in (37.5cm) high.
$16,500–18,500 *S(NY)*

An Orivit gilt-metal mounted vase, Germany, c1900, 16½in (42cm) high.
$950–1,000 *SUC*

An Arts and Crafts copper box, with Ruskin pattern mount, c1900, 6¾in (17cm) wide.
$100–120 *WAC*

An Arts and Crafts silver serving bowl, by Middleton & Heath, London 1902, 10in (25.5cm) diam.
$8,000–8,800 *SHa*

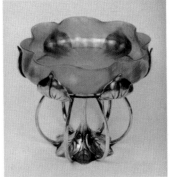

An Austrian silvered-metal and Loetz glass bonbon dish, c1900, 10in (25.5cm) high.
$1,100–1,250 *SUC*

An Art Nouveau embossed copper tea kettle and burner, with brass handles, on a brass stand, c1900, 15in (38cm) high.
$400–560 *ASA*

An Austrian enamel cigarette case, in the style of Mucha, c1900, 3½in (9cm) high.
$4,000–4,400 *SHa*

A Limoges enamel vase, signed 'Camille Fauré', c1925, 10in (25.5cm) high.
$960–1,000 *SUC*

A pewter dish, by Osiris, with fluted rim, c1900, 11½in (29cm) wide.
$135–155 *WAC*

An Art Nouveau pewter-mounted wine jug, 1901, 15in (38cm) high.
$1,000–1,200 *TAY*

A Liberty Tudric tobacco jar, by Archibald Knox, with enamel inlay, c1903, 5in (12.5cm) high.
$800–960 *ZEI*

A Fouquet enamelled silver-gilt cup, designed by Alphonse Mucha, in the shape of a beaker, c1902, 2in (5cm) high.
$3,200–4,000 *S(NY)*

A pair of Art Nouveau silver vases, c1905, 4in (10cm) high.
$350–400 *PSA*

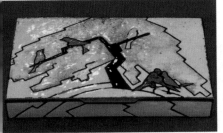

A metal box, by Jean Goulden, the enamelled white ground decorated with a stylised tree and birds, 1930, 6½in (16.5cm) wide.
$5,600–6,400 *CNY*

A silver-coloured metal and rosewood tea service, designed by Louis Tardy, c1935, teapot 5in (12.5cm) wide.
$4,400–4,800 *S*

A metal candle-stick, by Josef Hoffmann, 1925, 8½in (22cm) high.
$6,800–7,200 *S*

A French terracotta figure, 'Après le Bain', signed by Bruyas, c1900, 24½in (62cm) high.
$1,300–1,500 *ANO*

A French gilt-metal figure, holding a thermometer, c1900, 13½in (34cm) high.
$640–720 *ANO*

An Art Deco Goldscheider pottery figure, 1920s, 15in (38cm) high.
$1,600–1,900 *ASA*

A patinated bronze figure, by Franz von Stuck, entitled 'Amazon', poised to throw a spear, c1900, 24½in (62cm) wide, on a bronze base.
$13,500–15,200 *S*

A gilt-bronze and marble figural centrepiece, by Paul-Eugène Breton, inscribed, c1910, 26in (66cm) wide.
$16,000–17,500 *S(NY)*

An Italian silvered-copper figure of a Japanese girl, c1920, 12½in (32cm) high.
$550–600 *WeH*

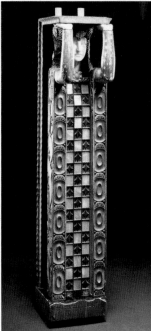

A gilded wood caryatid figure, by Czeschka and Hoffmann, with mother-of-pearl and ivory, c1908, 19in (48.5cm) high.
$34,000–37,000 *S*

A Lorenzl silvered-bronze and ivory figure, c1925, 17in (43cm) high, on an onyx base.
$5,000–5,600 *S(S)*

A Lorenzl spelter dancing figure, c1925, 11in (28cm) high.
$600–640 *WeH*

A bronze and ivory figure of Ayouta, by Chiparus, 1920s, 11in (28cm) high.
$12,800–14,400 *ASA*

A pair of bronze and ivory figures, of a Dutch boy and girl, c1920, 6½in (16.5cm) high.
$1,100–1,200 *WeH*

A Lorenzl bronze figure of a dancing girl, 1920s, 14in (35.5cm) high.
$1,100–1,200 *AAV*

A bronze and ivory figure, by Gilbert, 1920s, 8½in (21.5cm) high.
$5,600–6,400 *ASA*

A bronze figure, after Le Faguays, c1925, 30¾in (78cm) high.
$9,000–10,000 *C*

A pair of Loetz iridescent glass and bronze sconces, hanging from mounts cast as open-mouthed winged dragons, c1900, 23in (58.5cm) high.
$14,400–16,000 *S(NY)*

A glass and brass chandelier, designed by Koloman Moser, the white glass spheres decorated with blue spots, c1902, 14in (35.5cm) diam.
$22,000–24,000 *CNY*

A glass and brass chandlier, designed by Koloman Moser or Jutta Sika, glass by Loetz, the glass decorated with blue and gold lustre on a pink and gold ground, c1903, 43½in (100.5cm) high.
$27,500–30,000 *C*

A silver-plated brass and enamel wall light, possibly designed by Alexander Fisher, c1905, 26 x 12in (66 x 30.5cm).
$4,400–4,800 *C*

A Loetz iridescent glass and bronze lamp, with dark brown patina, unsigned, c1900, 21½in (54.5cm) high.
$4,000–4,800 *S(NY)*

A Daum landscape lamp, decorated with a lake at sunset and trees, marked, c1900, 31⅛in (80cm) high.
$13,000–14,400 *S*

A Loïe Fuller gilt-bronze lamp, by Larche, c1900, 12¾in (32.5cm) high.
$16,000–17,600 *S(NY)*

A bronze and glass ceiling light, by Hector Guimard, hung with bronze rods, glass beads and tubing, c1908, 20in (51cm) long.
$11,200–13,600 *CNY*

A cast-bronze cobra lamp, by Brandt and Daum, with inverted bell-shaped shade, marked, c1925, 20in (51cm) high.
$21,000–24,000 *S(NY)*

A butterfly lamp, by Emile Gallé, the base with chrysanthemums, marked, c1900, 22¼in (56.5cm) high.
$11,200–12,800 *S*

An acid-etched glass and silvered wrought iron and metal lamp base, by Daum, c1925, 39in (99cm) high.
$12,800–14,400 *S(NY)*

A Tiffany Favrile glass
and silvered wirework
chandelier, c1990,
48in (122cm) high.
$8,000–9,600 S(NY)

A Tiffany Favrile glass and
bronze chandelier, mounted
with a pierced bronze frame,
c1900, 12in (30.5cm) diam.
$24,500–27,200 S(NY)

A Tiffany brass
chandelier, supported
by 3 linked arms, c1914,
36in (91.5cm) high.
$9,000–10,000 CNY

A Tiffany Favrile
glass lantern, c1914,
13in (33cm) high.
$17,000–19,000 S(NY)

A Tiffany Favrile glass
and bronze lamp, c1900,
27in (69cm) high.
$21,500–24,000 S(NY)

A Tiffany Favrile glass
and bronze counter-
balanced desk lamp,
c1900, 14½in (37cm) high.
$10,400–11,000 CNY

A Tiffany bronze and
iridescent glass lamp,
c1900, 16in (40.5cm) high.
$8,800–9,600 C

A Tiffany Favrile glass
and bronze lamp, c1910,
24in (61cm) high.
$25,500–30,000 S(NY)

A Tiffany leaded glass
and bronze table lamp,
c1900, 31in (80cm) high.
$30,000–32,000 FBG

A Tiffany Favrile and
bronze lamp, c1900,
25in (63.5cm) high.
$14,000–15,000 S

A Tiffany floral lamp,
c1900, 24in (61cm) high.
$30,000–32,000 S

A Tiffany Favrile glass
and enamelled copper
Daffodil lamp, c1910,
18½in (47cm) high.
$11,500–13,500 S(NY)

A Tiffany glass
and bronze table
lamp, c1900,
15in (38cm) high.
$6,500–7,500 CNY

A Tiffany Favrile
glass and bronze
Apple Blossom lamp,
c1910, 23in (58.5cm) high.
$17,000–19,000 S(NY)

A Tiffany Favrile glass
and bronze reticulated
lamp, c1910,
24in (61cm) high.
$26,500–29,000 S(NY)

A Tiffany Favrile glass
and bronze Lotus Bell
lamp, c1910,
20in (51cm) high.
$25,000–27,000 S(NY)

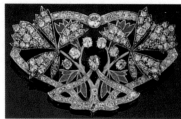

An Art Nouveau diamond and
enamel brooch, with 2 diamond
sprays and *plique-à-jour* enamel
leaves, mounted in gold, c1890,
60mm wide.
$8,000–9,500 *C*

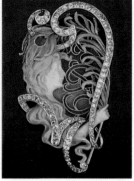

An Art Nouveau *plique-à-
jour* enamel and diamond
brooch, by Louis Aucoc,
c1900, 62mm high.
$33,500–36,500 *C*

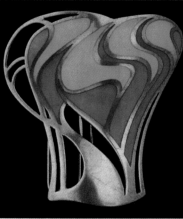

A gilt and enamel buckle, by
Georg Anton Scheid, designed
by Koloman Moser, c1900,
70mm high.
$6,500–8,000 *C*

An Art Nouveau brooch, by Murrle
Bennet, with 2 opal cabochons,
a central opal, and 2 opal drops,
marked, c1910, 30mm wide.
$680–780 *P*

A gold and enamelled pendant,
by René Lalique, depicting
Romeo and Juliet, c1900,
50mm wide, in original case.
$10,000–11,000 *S*

A Maison Vever hair comb, th
amber horn carved as a spray
of Queen Anne's lace, set with
turquoise cabochons, stamped
c1900, 4in (10cm) high.
$4,500–5,500 *S(NY)*

An Art Nouveau opal, diamond
and enamel grasshopper brooch,
mounted in silver and gold,
c1905, 53mm wide.
$13,500–15,500 *C*

An Arts and Crafts ring, by
Bernard Instone, the bezel
with a faceted amethyst and
2 peridots amidst foliage, with
florets on the shanks, 1920s.
$800–950 *P*

An Art Nouveau silver, enamel
and mother-of-pearl necklace,
possibly by Liberty, c1920.
$1,600–2,000 *ASA*

A Theodor Fahrner silver-
coloured metal, topaz and
marcasite pendant and
chain, stamped, c1930,
14⅛in (37cm) long.
$3,600–4,000 *S*

An Art Deco ruby and diamond bracelet, the ribbon bow with central diamond and ruby detail,
the ruby bracelet with diamond spacers, openwork diamond buckle clasp, c1925, 7in (18cm) long.
$6,400–7,200 *C*

A silver boudoir carriage timepiece, marked 'GB', London 1892, 2½in (6.5cm) high.
$1,100–1,200 *WeH*

A Liberty pewter and enamelled clock, c1900, 16in (40.5cm) high.
$4,000–4,800 *ASA*

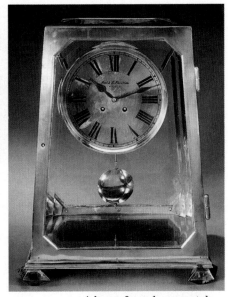

A brass four-glass mantel clock, designed by Adolf Loos, Budapest, c1902, 20in (50cm) high.
$16,000–17,500 *S*

A mantel clock, possibly designed by J. M. Olbrich, Darmstadt, with brass face, c1905, 20½in (52cm) high.
$4,800–5,200 *C*

An Art Deco 8-day clock, Westminster chiming, 1930s, 11in (28cm) wide.
$280–320 *TPA*

l. A Zenith 18ct gold and enamel cushion-form open face watch, signed, c1920, 42mm wide.
$2,400–2,500 *S(G)*

A Berlin Secessionist clock case and stand, painted with a forest view, marked, c1910, 23½in (59.5cm) high.
$13,000–14,000 *S*

A Swiss silver-gilt and enamel desk clock, by Henri Capt, c1910, 4in (10cm) high.
$2,500–3,000 *SHa*

A copper and plastic digital clock, 'The Zephyr', by Kem Weber for Lawson Time Inc, California, marked, c1934, 8in (20cm) wide.
$2,000–2,400 *S*

An Art Deco enamel and gilt-metal clock, the dial decorated as a vase of flowers in a gilt-metal frame, 1920s, 4½in (11.5cm) high.
$1,400–1,500 *SHa*

An opalescent glass clock, Sirènes, by René Lalique, the moulded nude mermaids with flower hair swirling around the clock face, marked, after 1928, 11in (28cm) square.
$15,000–16,500 *S*

A design for a textile, Seven Sisters, by Charles A. Voysey, watercolour on paper, c1893, 23 x 15in (58 x 38cm), framed and glazed.
$52,000–58,000 *C*

A French Art Deco wool carpet, attributed to Paul Poiret for Atelier Martine, c1925, 127 x 77in (323 x 196cm).
$4,500–5,000 *S(NY)*

An Arts and Crafts penwork tea caddy, decorated with fruit and leaves, c1900, 6in (15cm) wide.
$200–240 *ANO*

A Tiffany Studios watercolour on paper, entitled 'Peach Blossoms', c1910, framed, 27½ x 25in (70 x 63.5cm).
$2,800–3,200 *S(NY)*

An Art Nouveau Limoges enamel wall plaque, depicting a naked woman dancing with a draped scarf, c1900, 5½ x 4in (14 x 10cm), framed.
$1,100–1,300 *ANO*

A lacquered wood, mother-of-pearl and moulded glass figural plaque, by Lucien Gaillard, c1900, 24in (61cm) high.
$22,500–25,000 *S(NY)*

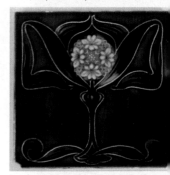

An Art Nouveau moulded tile, decorated with pink flowers and green stylised leaves on a purple ground, c1900, 6in (15cm) square.
$25–35 *HIG*

An Art Nouveau leather work mirror, decorated with painted flowers, 1930s, 18in (46cm) high.
$160–200 *SUS*

An Omega Workshops painted wood toy chest, decorated by Roger Fry, with hinged top, the front and sides painted with bowls of fruit, marked, c1917, 36in (91.5cm) wide.
$4,400–5,000 *S*

A printed silk costume, textile by the Wiener Werkstätte, printed with a geometric design, c1915.
$6,400–7,200 *C*

A Marcel Breuer chair, probably or Thonet, with chromium-plated ubular steel frame, rattan seat, c1928.
$30,000–32,000 S

A 'Mouseman' panelled oak single wardrobe, by Robert Thompson, 1930s, 41in (104cm) wide.
$6,400–7,200 S

A set of six office chairs, by Gio Ponti, made for the Montecatini Building, Milan, with aluminium frames and red upholstery, 1936.
$12,000–12,800 S

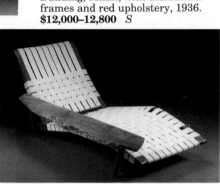

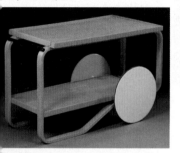

An Alvar Aalto bent laminated and solid birch, plywood tea cart, fter 1936, 35½in (90cm) wide.
$5,600–6,200 S

A plywood dining chair, designed by Frank Lloyd Wright, c1955.
$3,500–4,000 CNY

A walnut lounge chair, by George Nakashima, with one free-form armrest and adjustable back, webbed seat and black cushions, c1971, 58½in (149cm) long.
$7,000–7,500 CNY

A walnut desk and chair, by George Nakashima, he chair with woven grass seat, 1960s.
$8,000–8,800 S(NY)

A floral pin brooch, set with rhinestones and crystals in a gilt setting, 1950s, 3in (7.5cm) high.
$80–120 PGH

An electroplated metal and ebony tea service, by Peter Macchiarini, c1950, teapot 6½in (16.5cm) high.
$3,200–4,000 S

An Aubusson wool tapestry, entitled 'Exotic Morn', designed by Russell Cowles, depicting a woodland scene and various birds, c1962, 94in (240cm) wide.
$11,500–12,500 S(NY)

An American pin brooch, by Hollywood, 1950s, 3in (7.5cm) high.
$100–120 PGH

A shelf unit, attributed to Raymond Subes, c1940, 60in (152cm) wide.
$2,800–3,500 C

A ruby and diamond bracelet and ear clips, c1950, bracelet 7¼in (18.5cm) long.
$18,500–22,500 C

A blue stoneware tea caddy, by Bernard Leach, 'BL' and St Ives seal marks, c1924, 6in (15cm) high.
$1,000–1,100 *Bon*

A stoneware covered box, by Shoji Hamada, with light grey and iron glaze brushwork, c1946, 4¼in (11cm) wide.
$4,800–5,200 *Bon*

A stoneware grey and blue slab bottle vase, by Bernard Leach, decorated with tree motifs, c1958, 8in (20.5cm) high.
$1,000–1,200 *Bon*

A bottle vase, by Hans Coper the cylindrical neck with disc top, the body richly textured, impressed 'HC' seal, c1965, 11in (29cm) high.
$11,200–12,800 *Bon*

A porcelain beaker vase, by Dame Lucie Rie, impressed 'LR' seal, c1968, 5¼in (13cm) high.
$1,600–1,800 *Bon*

An 'American' yellow porcelain bowl, by Dame Lucie Rie, impressed 'LR' seal, c1970, 6½in (16.5cm) diam.
$3,200–4,000 *Bon*

An Aureliano Toso Oriente glass vase, designed by Dino Martens, entitled 'Geltrude', the clear glass internally decorated, c1954, 11¾in (30cm) high.
$9,500–10,500 *S(NY)*

A glass vase, by Ingeborg Lundin for Orrefors, entitled 'Applet', engraved on the underside 'Orrefors Expo du 32-57 Ingeborg Lundin', designed 1955, executed 1957, 13¾in (35cm) high.
$5,500–6,500 *S*

An Aureliano Toso Oriente glass vase, designed by Dino Martens, internally decorated with patches of various colours and gold aventurine inclusions, c1951, 24in (61cm) high.
$10,500–11,500 *S(NY)*

A Ferro and Lazzarini sand-engraved and enamelled black glass bowl, after a design by Jean Arp, marked, c1955, 14¾in (37.5cm) high.
$5,500–6,500 *S(NY)*

A glass Seaform set, by Dale Chihuly, composed of 7 nested blown glass elements in pink with white rims and various motifs, 1984, largest 17¾in (45cm) diam.
$8,500–9,000 *CNY*

An Ariel glass vase, designed by Edvin Ohrstrom, manufactured by Orrefors, 1951, 6½in (16.5cm) high.
$4,500–5,000 *C*

A glass vase, design attributed to Fulvio Bianco made by Venini, marked, 1960s, 9in (23cm) high.
$3,000–4,000 *C*

TWENTIETH CENTURY DESIGN
Metal Furniture

Metal furniture is both strong and hard wearing, consequently it survives in great abundance. Both of these characteristics have tended, in the antiques market at least, to work against our taking metal furniture seriously. This has changed in the last couple of years in auction rooms and collectors have worked hard to establish a more sophisticated twentieth century market founded on the social, economic and industrial contexts of design. Within this process metal furniture and especially tubular steel furniture is bound to emerge as significant.

Nineteenth century engineers dreamt of tubular steel as a wonder material of enormous strength allied to incredible lightness. The manufacture of steel tubes was perfected during the 1880s and the new product had an immediate and profound impact in technological terms and quickly became a staple material of industrial economies. The bicycle craze of the 1890s was made possible by the advent of the safety diamond frame which was mass-produced from steel tubes. It was no accident that the first powered flight was made by the Wright brothers who had a background in bicycle engineering. Within a few years tube manufacturers were supplying the nascent aircraft industry with tube sets for airframe assemblies.

World War I accelerated the development of the aircraft industry and expanded the manufacturing capacity of tube makers. The natural consequence of this was that by 1920 tubular steel was about the only building material easily available in great quantity. The political and social context of post-war rebuilding was very different in Britain and Germany. In Britain the garden suburbs were extended to accommodate the returning servicemen,

whilst in Germany a new urban environment was created amidst the turmoil of social and political instability. The resulting modernism was functional, spare, egalitarian and associated with the ideas of the Bauhaus school. The furniture for this was all made of tubular steel.

The new designs for cantilever chairs by Marcel Breuer, Mart Stam and Mies van der Rohe were exhibited internationally. Everywhere they appeared the German designs were adopted by the artistic avant-garde. The Austrian firm of Thonet was the first to exploit the new designs commercially. Thonet opened shops throughout Europe and for ten years tubular steel was the epitome of modernism. Pel was the major manufacturer in Britain. Both makers produced a range of interchangeable designs that were pioneers of system and office furniture.

The Festival of Britain in 1951 was probably the last time, in England at least, where metal furniture, designed by Ernest Race and others, was presented in a modernist context rather than as a purely functional choice. For most of the post-war period metal furniture has been associated with village halls, schools, hospitals and mean office environments. This kind of public use has tended to give metal furniture a battering. Much of it is broken and badly worn and any qualitative assessment of old metal furniture is made much harder for this.

Many of the classic designs of the 1920s and '30s are still in production. This has given the designs a modernist credibility, whilst at the same time diminishing the status of all but the very earliest examples.

Paul Rennie

Furniture

Two chromium-plated tubular steel B5 side chairs, designed by Marcel Breuer, c1927.
$8,800–10,400 *S*

l. A chromium-plated tubular steel and canvas chaise longue, by W. H. Gispen, Rotterdam, c1929, 74½in (189cm) long.
$1,500–2,000 *S*

An LC104 chaise longue, designed by Le Corbusier, Pierre Jeanneret and Charlotte Perriand, on a welded iron painted frame, c1964.
$1,600–1,800 *Bon*

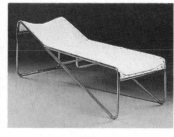

A pair of brass plated tubular steel armchairs, by Marcel Breuer, each with brown leather back and seat on cantilever frame, with ebonised armrests, designed 1932.
$3,500–4,000 *CSK*

A pair of chromed-steel and leather B301 Basculant armchairs, designed by Le Corbusier, Pierre Jeanneret and Charlotte Perriand, manufactured by Heidi Webe, each with welded tubular frames with leather strapwork arms and pony-skin back and seat, designed 1928.
$7,300–8,000 *S(NY)*

A walnut gateleg tea table, designed by Edward Barnsley, with stepped carved flange feet, c1930, 40in (101.5cm) wide.
$4,300–4,800 *C*

A 'Mouseman' oak stool, by Robert Thompson, with faceted legs joined by stretchers, the top with brown leather seat, c1930, 17½in (44.5cm) wide.
$950–1,100 *S*

A nickel-plated metal chaise longue, designed by René Herbst, the wood-framed seat with original interwoven rattan cover, set on tubular steel frame, c1936.
$1,200–1,300 *CSK*

A Cotswold School walnut bureau, with panelled drop-front enclosing compartments and leather inset, 2 drawers below, on tapering supports, c1950, 31in (78.5cm) wide.
$400–480 *P(Ba)*

Robert 'Mouseman' Thompson

Thompson followed the principles adopted by the Cotswold School. His work is largely undecorated, except for panelling and the occasional use of wrought-iron fixtures. The carved figure of a mouse, usually in relief but sometimes carved into a niche, became his trademark. Pieces are all made in oak, and are given a sculpted, hand-made look by use of an adze. Although Robert Thompson died in 1955, Mouseman furniture is still made today, but modern examples usually have a smooth finish. Commissions from the 1930s tend to be the most sought-after by collectors.

A 'Mouseman' oak table, by Robert Thompson, the octagonal top with adzed surface, c1930, 19¾in (50cm) diam.
$2,200–2,600 *S*

A set of 6 beech and teak stacking chairs, by Hans Wegner, and a matching dining table, c1949, table 47½in (120.5cm) wide.
$1,200–1,300 *CSK*

A black stained birch 'harp chair', by Jørgen Hovelskov, Denmark, the frame strung with flag line, c1958.
$640–800 *Bon*

The Harp chair shape is based on the bow section of Viking sailing ships.

A pair of Scandinavian beech laminated open armchairs, designed by Alvar Aalto, c1935.
$1,700–1,900 *M*

A Heal's rosewood pedestal desk, attributed to A. J. Milne, the curving top with inset leather writing surface, above 2 frieze drawers, over a bank of 3 graduated drawers, c1955, 96in (244cm) wide.
$1,600–1,900 *CSK*

A walnut day bed, by George Nakishima, with plank back and green vinyl cushion, c1957, 91in (231cm) wide.
$6,400–7,200 *SK*

A black tubular metal and wire rod frame chair, by Martin Eisler, with upholstered back and adjustable seat, on brass feet, c1959, 39½in (100.5cm) wide.
$4,800–5,500 *S*

A pair of upholstered steel armchairs, designed by Warren Platner in 1966, constructed of continuous vertical wires, silver-nickel type finish, upholstered in wool maroon fabric, c1980.
$880–1,100 *RIT*

A black painted table, attributed to Robin Day for Hille, raised on angled and tapering supports, united by a stretcher, c1960, 30in (76cm) wide.
$250–320 *P(Ba)*

A set of 5 GF40/4 chairs, by David Rowland, USA, the chromium-plated steel leg frame with black seat and back stamped out of vinyl-covered sheet metal, c1964.
$400–480 *Bon*

This chair took from 1956 to 1964 to develop and the result was a chair which could be stacked 40 high but was only 4 feet high. It can link in rows and was available in 6 colours. The design won gold medals at exhibitions in Vienna, Milan and the US.

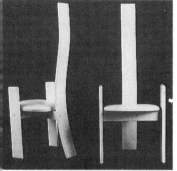

A set of 4 Golem dining chairs by Vico Magistretti, Italy, the white lacquered wood with white padded leather seats, c1970.
$640–800 *Bon*

Vico Magistretti commented that the Golem was a homage to Charles Rennie Mackintosh's designs.

A pair of laminated cardboard stools, by Frank Gehry, each of compressed scroll form and constructed of laminated corrugated cardboard sections with fibreboard ends, c1972, 17in (43cm) wide.
$2,800–3,500 *CNY*

A Lemon Sole easy chair, by Kwok Hoi Chan, Japan, the chrome frame with black vinyl upholstered seat and back pads, c1970.
$1,000–1,200 *Bon*

A conversation sofa, by Andrea Branzi, Italy, with segmented seat and gently sloping back/armrests to either end, upholstered in turquoise, purple and cream fabric, raised on cylindrical cream lacquered legs, c1986.
$2,800–3,200 *Bon*

This piece was designed for the 17th Milan Triennale Exhibition. The sofa was placed in the centre of the 'Remote Controlled House' where a couple would sit and summon objects by remote control.

A red painted metal, black wood, plastic and brass Bambi chair, by Borek Sipek, covered with blue fabric, c1983.
$4,800–5,400 *S*

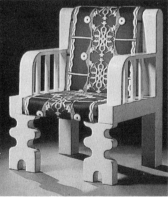

A white lacquered wood Denise armchair, by Nathalie du Pasquier, with coloured fabric upholstery, c1987, 39¾in (101cm) high.
$2,200–2,700 *S*

A steel Tankette table, with metal springs, by Paolo Pallucco & Mireille River, aluminium wheels and black epoxy powder finish, c1987, 49½in (125.5cm) long.
$2,800–3,200 *S*

l. A prototype steel and rubber S-shaped chair, by Tom Dixon, the metal frame bound with re-cycled inner-tube rubber, on domed pedestal, c1986.
$1,400–1,600 *CSK*

Ceramics

A bulbous stoneware pot, by Charles Vyse, with red rust, black and green glaze, incised 'CV 1933', 5in (12.5cm) high.
$250–280 *Bon*

A pottery dish, by Stig Lindberg for Gustavesberg, Sweden, c1940, 10½in (26.5cm) long.
$65–75 *RCh*

A porcelain cup and saucer, by Bernard Leach, the celadon cup with oblique fluting, the saucer with combed pattern on the outside, c1953, 5½in (14cm) diam.
$1,400–1,600 *Bon*

A Bernard Leach pottery bud vase, St Ives, c1950, 3¼in (8.5cm) high.
$65–100 *IW*

r. A Rye pottery pot, in white, grey and yellow, c1950, 6½in (16.5cm) high.
$50–65 *NCA*

A cut-sided stoneware teapot, by Shoji Hamada, with thrown handle, *tenmoku* glaze, small repair to spout, c1935, 10¾in (27cm) high.
$1,900–2,200 *Bon*

Studio Potters

The 20thC saw the rise of Studio potters, craftsmen who modelled or turned, glazed, decorated and fired their own wares. Bernard Leach is probably the best known of the early Studio potters, and his Chinese and Japanese-influenced pieces are widely collected, together with those of his colleague Shoji Hamada. William Staite Murray and Michael Cardew are other key figures.

Modern, post-war ceramics are dominated by the work of Dame Lucie Rie and Hans Coper. These two potters worked closely together for many years, experimenting widely with forms, glazes and materials, and produced highly individual wares that have become very popular.

A Crowan Pottery (Harry & May Davis) celadon stoneware bowl, c1950, 6¼in (16cm) diam.
$65–75 *SnA*

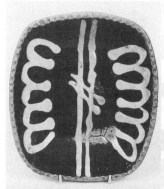

A Winchcombe Pottery slipware dish, c1940, 10in (25.5cm) wide.
$140–160 *IW*

A ceramic model of a peacock, by Albert Schild, c1950, 25in (63.5cm) long.
$90–110 *RCh*

A blue-grey stoneware lidded bowl, by Bernard Leach, with white sgraffito design based on the dual sun pattern from South America, the lid with brown finial, derived from the roof of the Temple of the Moon in Peking, c1950, 13½in (34cm) diam.
$8,000–9,500 *Bon*

This is an outstanding piece by this sought-after Studio potter.

A pottery plate, by Jean Lurçat, St Vincent, c1952, 19½in (49.5cm) wide.
$1,400–1,600 *SUC*

A Poole Pottery vase, c1950,
7¾in (20cm) high.
$70–80 *WAC*

A stoneware bowl, by Hans Coper,
with buff exterior, black interior and
shiny white sgraffito semi-abstract
face, c1955, 6in (15cm) diam.
$5,800–7,200 *Bon*

A ceramic plate, by Jean Cocteau,
entitled 'Chevre-pied au Long
Cou', No. 13 of an edition of 40,
signed, c1958, 12½in (31.5cm) diam.
$1,600–1,900 *Bon*

A St Ives stoneware pottery
tankard, with scroll handle,
c1950, 4in (10cm) high.
$55–75 *SnA*

A green stoneware vase, by Dame
Lucie Rie, the pitted glaze revealing
dark brown, c1960, 5¾in (14.5cm) high.
$2,500–2,800 *Bon*

A stoneware slab bottle
vase, by Bernard Leach,
the rust glaze with
running olive and combed
sgraffito vertical design,
c1965, 7¾in (20cm) high.
$2,500–2,800 *Bon*

A footed stoneware dish, by
Gordon Baldwin, with matt white
glaze and incised linear decoration
to well, flared foot, painted
'GB '73', 14in (35.5cm) long.
$200–250 *Bon*

l. A stoneware moon ring,
by Ian Godfrey, pale green with
carved decoration of houses, a
donkey, hills and a half-moon,
c1974, 5¼in (13cm) high.
$720–800 *Bon*

A Rye pottery plate, designed
by Walter Cole, c1980,
11in (28cm) diam.
$320–350 *NCA*

A Poole Pottery calendar plate,
'May', designed by Tony Morris,
decorated by T. D. Trapp, from a
perpetual calendar published in
the 15thC showing the
agricultural cycle month by month,
decorated with coloured glazes
within a black wax-resist outline
and red glazed border,
No. 140/1000, issued in 1974.
$160–200 *PP*

A porcelain 'Light Gatherer'
vessel, by Rudolf Staffel, the
hand-built translucent body
of flared cylindrical form with
applied vitreous elements,
c1979, 6¾in (17.5cm) high.
$4,800–5,600 *CNY*

Glass

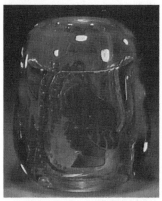

An Ariel glass vase, designed by Edvin Ohrstrom, manufactured by Orrefors, the heavy cased glass internally decorated with pale blue heads, one of a girl seen full face, the other of a boy in profile, c1939, 8¼in (21cm) high.
$5,600–6,200 *C*

A glass bowl, by Vicke Lindstrand for Kosta, c1952, 17¼in (43.5cm) diam.
$4,000–4,800 *S*

A set of 6 Smoke crystal drinking glasses, by Joe Colombo, Italy, the glass with asymmetrical shaped stem ending on a circular foot, each with manufacturer's and designer's labels to body, c1964, 6¼in (16cm) high.
$950–1,100 *Bon*

The Smoke glass moved away from the traditional shape by placing the stem asymmetrically, thus enabling the glass to be held by the thumb alone, leaving the other fingers free to hold, for example, cigarettes. Winner of 7 awards including the 1969 and 1971 Marcf Award, Milan.

A Venini Fazzoletto glass handkerchief vase, in clear glass, decorated with white latticinio stripes alternating with solid pink ribbons, c1950, 12in (30.5cm) diam.
$800–880 *S(NY)*

A Fascia Murrina vase, by Riccardo Licata for Venini, the 2 parts of opal lattimo glass divided by a band of murrinas, c1953, 7¼in (18cm) high.
$7,000–8,000 *S*

This design was first presented at the 1956 Venice Biennale.

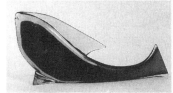

An Italian glass model of a fish, attributed to Venini, the green glass enhanced with blue, c1950, 15½in (39.5cm) long.
$340–400 *P*

A glass Seaform set, by Dale Chihuly, comprising 6 nested, blown glass elements in pink, lavender and white, 4 elements decorated with dotted stripes of white, one with dotted stripes of beige and one with waves, c1980, largest element 16in (40.5cm) diam.
$4,400–4,800 *CNY*

A clear mould-blown crystal 'iceberg' vase, by Tapio Wirkkala for Iittala, c1950, 8in (20cm) high.
$4,000–4,500 *S*

A Composizione Latticinio vase, by Archimede Seguso, the clear glass internally decorated with irregular white thread patterns, c1954, 8¾in (22cm) high.
$5,800–6,400 *S*

An Orrefors glass bowl, the thick compressed oval sides of amethyst and white encased in clear glass, c1958, 11in (28cm) wide.
$320–380 *WeH*

A set of 4 Paro drinking glasses, by Achille Castiglioni, Italy, the double-ended glasses with bottle green glass to one side and clear glass to other, c1983, tallest 4¼in (11cm) high.
$320–400 *Bon*

Jewellery

A silver-coloured metal bracelet, by Sam Kramer, c1935, 3in (7.5cm) diam.
$320–400 *S*

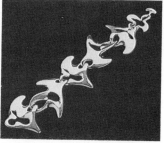

A silver-coloured metal bracelet, by Henning Koppel for Georg Jensen, stamped marks for post 1945 production and 'Sterling Denmark, 89' and 'HK', c1947, 8¾in (22cm) long.
$950–1,000 *S*

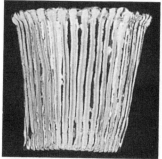

A ceramic silver glazed bracelet, by Dame Lucie Rie, with incised decoration inlaid with cream glaze, wavy rim to wider side, 2 slits for ribbon, 1980s, 3½in (9cm) long.
$2,000–2,500 *Bon*

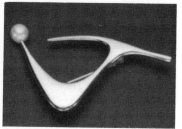

A gold brooch with a pearl, by Ed Wiener, c1951, 2in (5cm) wide.
$720–800 *S*

A silver-coloured metal brooch, by Harry Bertoia, c1946, 2½in (6.5cm) wide.
$4,000–4,500 *S*

A gilt-brass brooch/pendant, with hand-crafted floral design, c1950, 2½in (6.5cm) diam.
$110–130 *PGH*

An American gilt-brass cornucopia brooch, by Trifari, c1950, 3in (7.5cm) wide.
$110–130 *PGH*

A pewter brooch, by Georg Jensen, Denmark, c1950, 2in (5cm) wide.
$40–60 *RCh*

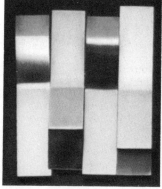

A silver-coloured metal brooch, by Betty Cooke, c1959, 3in (7.5cm) wide.
$950–1,100 *S*

A silver-coloured metal ring, by Friedrich Becker, with moonstone cabochons, c1960, 1½in (3.5cm) diam.
$1,200–1,500 *S*

A cast bronze and gold brooch, by Salvador Dali, after a design by Chagall, signed and dated '1965'.
$1,000–1,200 *SHa*

l. A ceramic silver and gold glazed neckpiece, by Dame Lucie Rie, 1980s, 6in (15cm) long.
$7,200–8,000 *Bon*

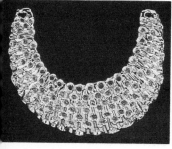

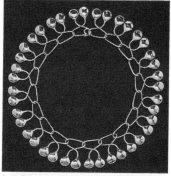

A gold-coloured metal necklace, by Nanna Ditzel for Georg Jensen, stamped with manufacturer's marks for post 1945 production, c1966, 14¾in (37.5cm) long.
$4,800–5,500 *S*

Lighting

A French phenolic Bolide desk lamp, by Jumo, with adjustable canopy on chromed and copper-plated hinged metal support, resting in shaped well, c1945, 6½in (16.5cm) long.
$1,200–1,300 *CSK*

A Scandinavian desk lamp, the red painted aluminium shade raised on a C-shaped arm, on a metal 'talon' foot with on/off button, stamped 'EWA', c1950, 15¾in (40cm) high.
$200–250 *Bon*

r. A bulb lamp, by Ingo Maurer, of black, yellow and white plastic, with original bag and label, c1980, 24in (61cm) long.
$370–400 *S*

A chandelier, by Verner Panton, with blue, turquoise and purple spheres, c1967, 18½in (47cm) high.
$1,600–1,800 *S*

A metal table lamp, by Arredoluce, of shiny and white metal, with gunmetal 'eye', c1950, 24½in (62cm) high.
$950–1,000 *S*

A white plastic and metal Dahlia lamp, by Gino Marotta, with circular fluorescent tube inside, c1968, 21in (53.5cm) diam.
$1,200–1,400 *S*

A Fibonacci lamp, by Sophus Frandsen, Denmark, with polished metal graduated concentric rings, c1968, 19in (48cm) diam.
$175–200 *Bon*

A brass and metal table lamp, by Pierre Paulin, France, for Philips, the black enamelled metal shade on brass stylised base, c1955, 14¼in (36cm) high.
$450–520 *Bon*

A Paramount UFO lamp, by Carlo Bachi, Lapo Binazzi, Patrizia Cammeo, Riccardo Foresi and Titti Maschietto, with red and green ceramic base, chrome, stretched black fabric, grey cable, 2 brass and ceramic bulb holders with small bulbs, designed 1969, 31in (78.5cm) high.
$8,800–9,600 *S*

This piece was retailed by Alchimia for the Bauhaus Collection 1979.

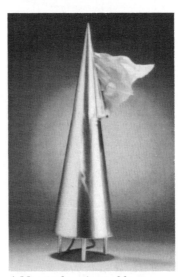

A Maestrale animated lamp, by Denis Santachiara, with cast aluminium cone, internal light and fan to create an artificial internal wind which moves the pink silk flag, c1982, 27in (68.5cm) high.
$2,400–2,700 *S*

An On Taro stone and glass table lamp, by Keith Haring and Toshiyuki Kita for Kreon, c1988, 21in (53.5cm) high.
$1,600–2,200 *CNY*

Posters

An offset lithograph poster, by Jean Colin, entitled '2eme Salon de la Vie Collective', on paper, c1958, 61in (155cm) long.
$1,400–1,800 *S*

A lithograph in colours, entitled 'Cannes', by Pablo Picasso, printed by Henri Deschamps, some foxing and slight staining, c1950, 39in (99cm) high.
$1,100–1,300 *CSK*

A lithograph in colours, entitled 'Klosters', printed by Fretz Frères SA, Zurich, backed on linen, minor restored defects, c1954, 39½in (100cm) high.
$400–480 *CSK*

A lithograph poster in colours, by Bernard Villemot, for Orangina, backed on linen, c1980, 24in (61cm) wide.
$450–520 *CSK*

l. An offset lithograph poster in colours, by V. Karakashev, entitled 'We have opened the Cosmos Era, Gagarine', printed by The Soviet Art, Moscow, minor creases and tears, c1972, 35½in (90cm) high.
$400–480 *CSK*

An offset lithograph in colours, by David Hockney, entitled 'Parade', printed by Petersburg Press, inscribed and signed by the artist in pen and black ink, framed, minor defects, c1981, 36½in (93cm) high.
$950–1,100 *CSK*

Textiles

A machine-woven Mimosa wool carpet, by Henri Matisse, of Axminster construction, monogrammed in the weave 'HM', c1949, 59in (150cm) long.
$12,000–13,500 *S*

This is the only carpet design by Matisse. The reverse has a printed label 'This rug designed by H. Matisse and named Mimosa by him, has been woven by Alexander Smith in a limited edition of 500 of which this is number 212'.

A Thea Porter couture kaftan, woven with gold lamé circles, trimmed with turquoise velvet, and pieced silk side panels, c1960, ex-Britt Ekland collection.
$110–130 *CSK*

A Judith Lieber evening bag, with green, red, blue, white and gold geometric diamanté decoration, suspended from a woven gold rope, tassel bottom, signed and dated 1980, 3½in (9cm) diam.
$880–1,100 *FBG*

LAMPS & LIGHTING

More and more people are discovering the beauty and charm of old lamps and light fittings. The market has picked up considerably over the last year especially in the area of large chandeliers which are much sought-after by interior designers. Good quality wall lights and ceiling lights are in great demand. The area which has increased most in value is that of original glass shades, large bowls and small hand-painted shades – those made of cranberry and vaseline glass have doubled and even trebled their value. The overseas market has not been buoyant, with less sales to Germany and Japan, but more to the USA.

As with most antiques, it is the quality of lamps and lighting which is important. The price of quality items and those of named designers and makers have continued to increase. Prices of Arts and Crafts, Art Nouveau and Art Deco pieces have risen dramatically. The media coverage of the William Morris centenary created a huge demand for Arts and Crafts lighting.

All forms of oil lamps have increased in value especially fine examples with original glassware; even the smaller domestic and workmen's lamps are more difficult to find.

When buying oil lamps for practical use, check:
• The reservoir is not damaged as the oil could leak.
• The wick is the right size for the burner. There should be about 2in (5cm) of wick in the reservoir, and it should wind up and down smoothly.
• The burner is complete and the funnel holder is unbroken.
• The funnel is the correct size for the lamp or it will not burn efficiently.
• Parts for oil lamps are notoriously difficult to find, so check there is nothing missing.
• Always try to buy the original glass.

Most purchasers of antique lighting buy items they want to put to practicable use. Recent changes to the Electrical Safety Regulations, relating particularly to second-hand electrical goods (antique light fittings fall into this category), means that they must be rewired to conform to current safety standards. Fulfilling these conditions can be difficult and costly. Some auction houses and traders have chosen to sell lighting fixtures as *decorative items* only. To do this the item must be without wire and plug and have a permanent label stating that it is only a decorative item and must be wired by a qualified electrician before use. Buyers of lamps sold as decorative objects risk buying something that has parts broken or missing with no guarantee that they can use it for the purpose it was originally made.

Josie A. Marsden

Table Lamps & Lamp Standards

A pair of Regency cast plaster lamp figures, with bronze patination, by H. Hoppner, London, stamped 'Dec 1 1809', 35in (89cm) high.
$9,000–10,500 *WW*

A gilt-bronze and overlay glass lamp, enclosing a mercury coloured interior, on a foliate and berry-cast base, mid-19thC, 31in (78.5cm) high.
$1,800–2,000 *S(NY)*

l. A pair of Louis Philippe ormolu and marble storm lamps, on white marble base, mid-19thC, 12½in (32cm) high.
$4,500–4,800 *S(NY)*

l. An Italian silver oil lamp, by Antonio Cappelletti, Rome, with berried heart-shaped foliate handle and a reflector modelled as a moth, c1830, 34in (36.5cm) high.
$7,500–8,000 *S(G)*

A carved and giltwood Venetian gondola lantern, the sides with oval glazed panels flanked by putti, fitted for electricity, 19thC, 78in (198cm) high.
$600–700 *AH*

A Victorian brass oil lamp, with floral decorated font and amber glass etched shade, c1890, 33in (84cm) high.
$1,250–1,450 *CHA*

Safety Regulations

Following changes to electrical safety regulations, the most important message from the Department of Trade and Industry is that all electric lighting supplied for sale must be safe, and anyone supplying unsafe products is liable to prosecution.

Antique and second-hand lighting does not need to be CE marked (the European safety regulation mark), but suppliers must guarantee and confirm its safety. The most effective way to ensure this is to have it independently tested by a qualified electrician.

- Table and floor lamps must be wired and have a 3 amp fused and sleeved plug.
- Wiring must be effectively insulated and capable of carrying the correct voltage.
- Metal lights or lights with metal fittings must be earthed.
- There must be no exposed wires or access to live parts.
- Porcelain insulation in lamp holders should not be chipped or broken.
- It is not sufficient that the lamp is in working order as it may still be unsafe.

A Victorian bronzed-spelter figure of an angel, the lamp with flame-shaped opaque glass shade, 21in (53.5cm) high.
$320–400 *PCh*

A gilt and patinated bronze lamp, with a figural group of a satyr seated astride a panther and supporting a cornucopia, signed 'E. F. Caldwell & Co Inc, New York', late 19thC, 26in (66cm) high.
$4,800–5,500 *S(NY)*

A late Victorian gilded table light, by Palmer & Co, 22½in (57cm) high.
$400–450 *DN*

A blue opaline and clear glass oil lamp, on a dolphin base, lamp converted to electricity, shade chipped, late 19thC, 24in (61cm) high.
$440–480 *SK*

An Edwardian gas table lamp, with vaseline glass shade, fitted for electricity, 19in (48.5cm) high.
$1,100–1,300 *CHA*

A French bronze lamp, with painted metal shade, above a base with three nozzles, c1900, 17¼in (44cm) high.
$880–960 *CSK*

A twin branch brass desk lamp, with glass shades, fitted for electricity, c1910, 27in (68.5cm) high.
$800–880 *CHA*

A gilt-bronze six-light candelabrum, supported by a seated putto, 19thC, 26in (66cm) high.
$1,100–1,200 *CSK*

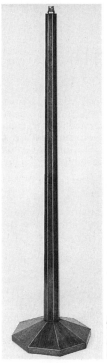

l. An inlaid mahogany lamp standard, c1920, 65in (165cm) high.
$400–450 *RPh*

A pair of Louis XVI style silvered-bronze and cut glass four-light candelabra, fitted for electricity, c1900, 14in (36cm) high.
$800–880 *S(Am)*

Ceiling and Wall Lights

A George IV bronze hanging lantern, each corner with a foliate satyr mask, divided by 4 handles, lacking lights and hanging chains, 23in (58.5cm) wide.
$4,800–5,200 C

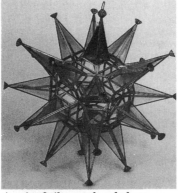

A pair of gilt-metal and glass lanterns, c1860, 18in (45.5cm) high.
$400–450 SSW

A pair of Italian polychrome-decorated and parcel-gilt three-light girandoles, with pierced outer border carved with foliage and flowerheads, distressed, 19thC, 49in (124.5cm) high.
$6,400–7,200 C

A Victorian brass hanging lantern, the brass-moulded and glazed sides with double scroll supports, centred by a later six-arm light fitment, c1850, 16½in (42cm) diam.
$5,000–5,600 S

A Continental three-branch gasolier, with cranberry glass shades, fitted for electricity, c1870, 34in (86.5cm) high.
$2,000–2,400 CHA

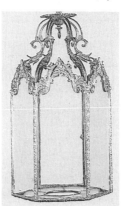

A mid-Victorian hexagonal brass hall lantern, with arched panels, pierced foliate crestings and conforming scroll supports, 22in (56cm) high.
$2,400–2,700 CSK

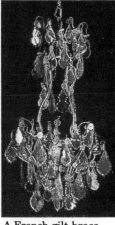

A French gilt-brass eight-light chandelier, with scrolling branches, petal-cut drip pans and urn-shaped candle sockets, fitted for electricity, 19thC, 44in (112cm) high.
$2,200–2,500 CSK

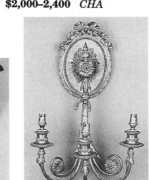

A pair of gas wall lights, with a gilt mermaid support, fitted for electricity, c1880, 13in (33cm) high.
$1,400–1,600 CHA

A pair of gilt-bronze wall lights, with 3 scrolling acanthus cast arms, late 19thC, 17in (43cm) high.
$950–1,000 P

A French gilt-bronze hanging Colza lamp, the foliate cast girdle hung with drops, one reservoir stamped 'Miller & Sons, 179 Piccadilly London', 19thC, 25¼in (65cm) high.
$2,250–2,500 P

A set of 3 French gilt-metal wall lights in Louis XV style, with 3 candle arms cast with acanthus, fitted for electricity, 19thC, 25in (63.5cm) high.
$1,000–1,200 AH

A centre light fitting, the glass bowl formed with diamond-cut radiating bands, secured by a gilt-bronze and brass ring, the centre with a pomegranate, 19thC, 29¼in (74.5cm) high.
$9,500–10,500 P(S)

A French cut-glass and gilt-bronze lantern, the corona modelled with fleur-de-lys decoration, the terminal with a fruiting finial, late 19thC, 24in (61cm) high.
$1,800–2,200 *CSK*

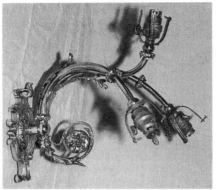

A set of 8 brass wall sconces, c1895, 15in (38cm) high.
$3,500–4,200 *DRU*

An alabaster ceiling light, with inverted dome carved in relief, and an acanthus cast corona, c1900, 18in (45.5cm) diam.
$2,800–3,200 *CSK*

A pair of Italian wall lights, with 2 arms of foliate candle cups issuing from a pierced foliate cast backplate, late 19thC, 10¼in (26cm) high.
$900–1,000 *P*

A French ormolu hall lantern, after the Alhambra model, with a pierced Moorish foliate design, supporting 4 candle branches, the lower part supporting the moulded glass shade, fitted for electricity, c1900, 26⅜in (68cm) high.
$4,800–5,600 *C*

An Edwardian brass and copper lantern, with bevelled glass panels, each centred with a sunburst motif below a scrolling corona, 30in (76cm) high.
$1,100–1,200 *CSK*

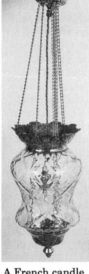

A French candle lantern, with cranberry glass shade, fitted for electricity, c1900, 16in (40cm) high.
$650–800 *CHA*

A French gilt-bronze and cut-glass ceiling light, the inverted dome with hob-nail and starburst decoration, the frame cast with lattice decoration and applied with scallop shell mounts, c1900, 12⅜in (32.5cm) diam.
$4,400–5,000 *CSK*

> **Cross Reference**
> Colour Review

A forged steel gas lantern, with cranberry glass shade, fitted for electricity, c1900, 35in (89cm) high.
$1,100–1,200 *CHA*

An Edwardian cast brass three-branch electrolier, with cranberry glass shades, 18in (45.5cm) high.
$1,200–1,350 *CHA*

A six-light brass chandelier, the well and column applied with satyr and goat masks, and foliate swags, the suspension loop stamped 'F & S', early 20thC, 30in (76cm) high.
$2,000–2,400 *CSK*
It has been suggested the stamp F & S is the mark of Farraday & Sons.

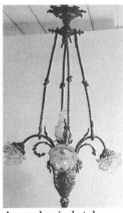

A neo-classical style gilt-brass five-light electrolier, the urn-shaped centre cast with swags and female masks, flambeau pattern glass centre shade and 4 branches with frosted glass flowerhead pattern shades, early 20thC, 31in (78.5cm) high.
$800–960 *CAG*

RUGS & CARPETS

The carpet market can be said to fall into three broad categories: the decorative market, that is pieces bought primarily for furnishing; the collector market, covering fine quality Persian and Turkish rugs, including silks, 19th century and earlier tribal pieces from the Caucasus, Turkey, Persia and Central Asia, and the Classical carpet market, that is pieces from the 17th century and earlier.

In all areas auctions in the past year proved the continuing trend for good examples of a type in good condition to make strong prices, but conversely, poor examples or those in poor condition were difficult to sell or unsaleable.

Provenance, as always, carries a premium and an interesting lineage will make a substantial difference to the price achieved for a piece. A prime example of the effect of provenance was the Bernheimer Family Collection of Carpets, (a collection formed by a family of German dealers), sold at Christie's recently, which realised just over $3,200,000 in 200 lots. Primarily consisting of classical and collectors' pieces, strong prices were reached across the board. The Cassirer Ushak Medallion carpet, dating from the late 16th century, and from the collection of Baroness Gabrielle Bentinck-Thyssen, sold at Sotheby's for $146,000 and the 17th century Esfahan carpet from the British Rail Pension Fund, sold for $217,500, also at auction. However, the effect of provenance is not limited to the market in classical pieces. A Russian carpet from Leeds Castle in Kent, reputedly made for Catherine the Great, sold at auction for $253,500 against a pre-sale estimate of $100,000–130,000.

The auction market for carpets, of course, does not only consist of pieces worth hundreds of thousands of dollars. Many, many examples are available from as little as a few hundred dollars, particularly amongst the commercially produced tribal and town weavings of the late 19th and 20th centuries.

In the area of decorative carpets, shifts of emphasis have been apparent. Increasing interest in Ushak carpets of the late 19th and early 20th centuries was seen in the past year. These carpets, produced for the western market, often have bold overall designs in colours atypical of Oriental carpets, ie coral oranges, turquoise, pale green, yellow and pale pink. In appearance they can resemble the highly sought-after Ziegler carpets. Prices for these have risen dramatically, from the high hundreds 3 to 5 years ago, to several thousand dollars today. Conversely the market for Heriz carpets, which was extremely strong in the late 1980s and early 1990s, has seen a distinct cooling down. Whilst good examples still make prices in the $15,000–30,000 range, less unusual or later examples are now making between $1,500–6,500, a fall of 50–80%.

Other types of decorative carpets that have seen increases include turn of the century Tabriz carpets (often referred to as Hadji Jallili, after a weaver). These are generally paler in colour than the post-1930s examples. A carpet with an overall design in pale colours and in good condition, 257 x 171in (652 x 434cm), sold at Sotheby's New York for $120,000. But even those with central medallions, if pale coloured, have seen an increase of 30–50%. Another type to watch is turn of the century Kerman carpets, again particularly the pale coloured examples. The changing fortunes of decorative carpets is most often the result of the changing tastes of decorators, the impetus usually coming from the US and migrating eastwards.

In the collector market, less subject to the vagaries of fashion, the prime considerations continue to be age, rarity, condition and colour. A Kazak rug in full pile, with natural dyes, from the 1870s or '80s, with good drawing and colour can achieve $13,000–20,000 at auction, whereas a rug of similar date, but in worn condition and with some chemical dyes, may make only $1,300–2,000.

Jacqueline Coulter

An English carpet, with an overall design of floral stems, in a green border of floral vine, late 19thC, 153 x 96in (388.5 x 244cm). **$9,500–10,500** *C*

A Napoleon III Aubusson rug, the pale green field decorated with a bouquet of flowers surrounded by classical scrolls interspersed with flowers, within a burgundy surround, France, 91 x 80in (231 x 203cm). **$4,000–5,000** *P*

A *rya* rug, with a vase with a leafy stem, flowerheads and perching birds, in an ivory border, Finland, 19thC, 108 x 77in (274 x 196cm). **$1,400–1,600** *C*

An Anatolian *yastik*, with
3 diamonds and 4 octagons in
red, blue, apricot and green on a
gold field, red spandrels, apricot
double triangle and bar border,
rewoven to one end, late 19thC,
36 x 17in (91.5 x 43cm).
$1,000–1,200 *SK(B)*

Yastik *is a piled cushion cover,
being Turkish for cushion or pillow.*

A Caucasian rug, the dark blue
field with a blue cruciform
medallion enclosing flowers,
similar flanking terracotta
medallions, pale blue and rust
L-shaped brackets, saffron zigzag
vine border, Armenia, c1920,
52 x 45in (132 x 114.5cm).
$3,200–4,000 *KW*

An Anatolian rug, with an overall
design formed of 3 columns of
polychrome palmette vine and
stylised plant motifs, probably
missing main border, areas of
re-weave and old repair,
possibly Ushak, 18th/early
19thC, 61 x 47in (155 x 119cm).
$15,000–17,000 *C*

A Gendje rug, the camel
field with offset rows of
serrated and ivory
polychrome diamond *guls*,
south west Caucasus, c1880,
96 x 36in (244 x 91.5cm).
$8,000–9,000 *KW*

The rugs in this section have
been arranged in geographical
sequence from west to east, in the
following order: Europe, Turkey,
Anatolia, Caucasus, Persia,
Turkestan, China and India.

l. A Chi Chi rug, with alternating
rows of octagons and hooked
polygons in red, rust, royal blue,
gold, and dark blue-green on a
midnight blue field, blue rosette
and diagonal bar border, north
east Caucasus, late 19thC,
72 x 50in (183 x 127cm).
$2,200–2,700 *SK(B)*

*Chi Chi is one of the most famous
rug weaving centres in the Kuba
region of Azerbaijan, which
produced some of the best made
rugs in the Caucasus.*

A Kazak Loripambak rug,
the terracotta field with
3 polychrome hooked *gul*
medallions, overall dice, stars,
animals and people, ivory
stylised flowering vine border,
south west Caucasus, c1890,
85 x 58in (216 x 147.5cm).
$8,800–9,600 *KW*

A Daghestan prayer rug, the ivory
diamond lattice field of stylised
flowers beneath the *mihrab*,
enclosed by terracotta hooked motif
borders, north east Caucasus,
c1880, 52 x 42in (132 x 106.5cm).
$800–950 *P*

A Zakatala rug, the walnut brown
field with a large hooked red
medallion, overall polychrome
hooked motifs, ivory border of red
arabesques, north Caucasus,
c1900, 86 x 72in (218 x 183cm).
$5,500–7,000 *S*

A Lenkoran rug, the dark brown field with 3 horned ivory ground medallions, each with a pale green hexagon central medallion on a pale brick medallion, narrow ivory main border, south east Caucasus, late 19th/early 20thC, 97 x 49in (246 x 125cm).
$2,000–2,500 WW

A Shirvan rug, the medium blue field with 3 rows of 4 shield design palmettes within a red ground floral border and 3 pairs of blue and ivory guard borders, east Caucasus, late 19th/early 20thC, 59 x 40in (150 x 101.5cm).
$1,400–1,600 RIT

A Heriz carpet, the brick-red field around charcoal-black medallion containing palmette cartouches encircling similar brick-red and ivory double medallion with flowerhead centrepiece, in an indigo border of polychrome flowerheads and serrated leaf vine, north west Persia, c1910, 158 x 121in (401 x 307cm).
$1,500–1,800 CSK

A Marasali prayer rug, the ivory *mihrab* with animals and stylised flowering shrubs, indigo main border with double headed brackets and medallion bars, repaired, east Caucasus, late 19thC/early 20thC, 61 x 59in (155 x 150cm).
$2,400–2,600 WW

A Heriz rug, the terracotta field with a green cruciform medallion issuing angular vines, serrated leaves and palmettes, dark blue turtle palmette and flower border, north west Persia, c1900, 70 x 58in (178 x 147.5cm).
$6,000–7,000 KW

A Tabriz rug, the plain ivory field with a terracotta and dark blue flower-filled lobed pole medallion, issuing flower sprays, dark blue lyre palmette and flower spandrels, terracotta flower spray border, north west Persia, c1900, 74 x 56in (188 x 142cm).
$3,600–4,200 KW

A Shirvan prayer rug, with flower and lattice design, stylised plants, 3 borders, on a pale field, east Caucasus, c1875, 50½ x 44in (128 x 112cm).
$3,300–3,800 DN

A Heriz carpet, the rust field with angular vine around a yellow medallion, with a stylised pink flowerhead centrepiece, the ivory, pink and green spandrels similar, in an indigo border of palmettes and flowerhead vine, north west Persia, c1900, 124 x 90in (314 x 228.5cm).
$2,800–3,500 C

A Persian rug, the dark mushroom-brown field woven with a floral trellis, the honey main border with flowering plants, possibly Tabriz, c1920, 82 x 50½in (208 x 128cm).
$650–800 L

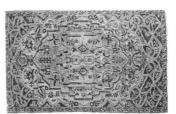

A Ziegler rug, the terracotta medallion on an ivory field, overall angular vines and palmettes, green and terracotta vine spandrels, narrow floral border, north west Persia, c1900, 42 x 57in (106.5 x 145cm).
$1,400–1,600 *Dns*

A Malayer rug, with a column of palmette motifs flanked by flower buds and rosettes in midnight and royal blue, red, gold, brown and blue-green on the rose-red field, royal blue floral meander border, slight moth damage, west Persia, early 20thC, 80 x 54in (203 x 137cm).
$1,600–1,900 *SK(B)*

r. A Karaja carpet, the brick field with indigo centre medallion, indigo and ivory spandrels, all-over angular flowers and foliage, repeated in the wide indigo main border, indigo and brick outer border, north west Persia, late 19thC, 148 x 99in (376 x 251cm).
$4,000–5,000 *WW*

A Ziegler carpet, the shaded blue field with polychrome palmettes linked by scrolling floral vine around a central shaded red medallion, north west Persia, c1880, 163 x 128in (414 x 325cm).
$6,400–7,200 *C*

Ziegler & Co

Messrs Ziegler & Co, a British/Swiss firm, opened offices in the Sultanabad area of Persia in the late 19thC to cater for the increased demand for room-sized carpets from the rapidly expanding upper and middle-classes of Europe and north America. By the late 1880s, in response to specific requests from European clients, they became actively involved in the production of carpets, employing local carpet designers to create new designs. Traditional patterns were adapted, and more carpets of the large format, so much in demand in the west, were woven. Ziegler carpets are distinguished by their all-over, large scale, lattice vine patterns often based on classical Persian designs of the 17thC. Medallions are rarely seen.

MILLER'S COMPARES . . .

A Serapi carpet, the pale terracotta field with an ivory medallion, pale yellow spandrels, ivory border of palmettes, north west Persia, c1875, 156 x 121in (401 x 306cm).
$38,000–42,000 *S*

A Serapi carpet, the terracotta field with blue and ivory medallion pendant palmettes, ivory spandrels, terracotta border of palmettes, north west Persia, c1890, 144 x 107in (366 x 272cm).
$6,500–7,500 *S*

Although these two carpets are from the same area, the Heriz region in north west Persia, one fetched almost five times more at auction than the other.
Item II **was made slightly later than** *Item I* **and shows the influence of more commercialised production – a more crowded field, stiffer drawing and heavier colouring.**
Item I, **in contrast, has an open field with well-spaced motifs and is generally much paler including, importantly, a light coloured border.**
Pale yellow, apricot and ivory hues are more sought-after in the decorative market and always command a premium over the stronger reds and blues. *S*

An Isfahan rug, the field with a lobed floral medallion, overall scrolling vines and arabesques, surrounded by a border of palmettes and flowering vines, silk warps, c1930, central Persia, 87 x 57in (221 x 145cm).
$3,500–4,000 *SLN*

A Kashan silk rug, the ivory field containing an overall multi-coloured floral pattern surrounded by mustard-yellow main border with palmette design, central Persia, c1920, 84 x 50in (213.5 x 127cm).
$1,300–1,450 *GH*

A Feraghan rug, comprising terracotta field with multi-coloured *herati* pattern surrounded by 3 borders, the main border in green and comprising flower and leaf design, west Persia, c1860, 78 x 47in (198 x 119.5cm).
$1,700–1,900 *GH*

r. A Hamadan rug, the terracotta field with small flower medallion issuing floral sprays, reciprocal surround, 3 narrow borders, west Persia, c1930, 86¾ x 50in (220 x 127cm).
$640–720 *AWH*

Borders

Almost all rugs have at least one main border. The narrow, minor borders are known as 'guard stripes'. The earlier the rug, the fewer the borders; early rugs usually have one main border and a tiny guard stripe. A proliferation of borders is not uncommon on rugs specifically intended for the western market.

A Bubukabad rug, with flowers and trellis on a blue field, with one wide and 2 narrow borders, west Persia, c1890, 71½ x 53½in (181.5 x 136cm).
$550–650 *DN*

A Ghom part-silk rug, the mid-indigo field decorated with leafy vines and flowers, enclosed by similar borders between ice-blue guard stripes, central Persia, c1930, 81 x 54in (205.5 x 137cm).
$4,000–5,000 *Bon*

A Feraghan rug, the dark blue field woven with rows of small *boteh* within narrow multiple borders, west Persia, c1920, 80 x 63in (203 x 160cm).
$1,700–1,900 *L*

A Sarouk rug, the rose-red field with overall flowering vine sprays, dark blue flowerhead and vine border, west Persia, c1920, 80 x 52in (203 x132cm).
$6,500–7,500 *KW*

A Sarouk rug, the field with opposing stylised flowering vases and overall floral sprays, narrow similar border, west Persia, c1920, 58 x 42in (147.5 x 106.5cm).
$1,000–1,200 *SLN*

A Sarouk rug, the terracotta field with overall flowersprays, dark blue border of palmettes and flowers, west Persia, c1930, 79 x 50in (200.5 x 127cm).
$5,500–6,500 *KW*

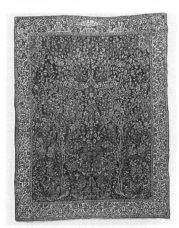

A Bakhtiyari carpet, the dark blue field with a design of blossoming trees and exotic birds, within an ivory flowering shrub and bird border, inscribed cartouche with 'Order of Hani Ghaffari, 1344', west Persia, c1925, 189 x 143in (480 x 363cm). **$7,300–8,800** *S*

A Kashgai rug, the copper rust field decorated with birds, vases issuing flowers and rosettes, centred by a mid-blue and ivory medallion, within charcoal spandrels and triple borders, south Persia, c1910, 82 x 60in (208.5 x 153cm). **$1,000–1,200** *P*

An Afshar rug, the polychrome diamond lattice field enclosed by narrow borders, south east Persia, c1900, 65 x 52in (165 x 132cm). **$850–1,100** *Bon*

A Bakhtiyari rug, the red lozenge with a European floral design cartouche in brick red, teal, deep and medium blue framed by a blue ground floral border, west Persia, c1900, 99 x 67in (251.5 x 170cm). **$1,900–2,200** *RIT*

A Belouch prayer mat, the camel filled *mihrab* with stylised hands in the spandrels, multiple borders, south east Persia, c1930, 72 x 49in (183 x 124.5cm). **$500–575** *AWH*

A Laver Kirman rug, with *herati* central medallion with guards on a floral field surrounded by a floral border with palmette and rosette guard stripes, south east Persia, late 19thC, 83 x 51½in (210 x 131cm). **$3,000–3,500** *AWH*

The term Laver is a corrupt spelling for a village north of the City of Kirman known as Raver, where ultra fine rugs are produced. They were quite often pictorial.

An Abadeh carpet, the fox-brown field with polychrome *herati* pattern around charcoal-black medallion containing flowerheads and birds, with similar spandrels, in shaded indigo border of polychrome palmettes, flowerheads and leaves, outer ivory palmette vine and plain stripes, south west Persia, c1930, 132 x 89in (335 x 226cm). **$1,500–1,800** *CSK*

A Belouch rug, the field with offset rows of serrated *guls,* panelled stylised flower border, banded kelim *elems,* south east Persia, late 19thC, 73 x 39in (185.5 x 99cm). **$750–800** *SLN*

Elems are the end panels or skirts of Turkoman carpets.

A Kirman rug, with rosette medallion and floral sprays in midnight blue, cochineal, tan and light blue-green on an ivory field, midnight blue border, south east Persia, late 19thC, 80 x 50in (203 x 127cm). **$880–1,100** *SK*

A Yomud *chuval,* with a red ground central panel with overall rows of 5 latched cross-form *guls* and diamond *guls* in ivory, rose, deep and medium blue within an ivory *ashik gul* border above a plain lower *elem*, central Asia, late 19thC, 49 x 28in (125 x 70cm).
$880–1,100 *RIT*

A Chodor *chuval,* the purple-brown ground with rust, ivory and deep indigo Ertmen *guls* within an ivory lightning lattice, all within a border of latch hooked squares and serrated diamond *elem*, some damage, north Turkestan, late 19thC, 33 x 49in (84 x 124cm).
$3,500–4,000 *S(NY)*

FURTHER READING
Andrew Middleton,
Rugs & Carpets
Mitchell Beazley, 1996.

A Beshir *chuval*, the lattice field of apple blossom design, enclosed by indigo borders of flowerheads and serrated leaves, central Turkestan, c1900, 75 x 43in (191 x 118cm).
$650–800 *Bon*

A pair of Tekke saddle bags, the pink fields with narrow centre panels, each with 2 *guls*, trellised medallion skirts, piled centre band with 3 *guls*, central Turkestan, c1910, 37in (94cm) wide.
$160–200 *WW*

A Ningxia carpet, with yellow ground depicting 2 monks blowing conch shells flanking a large incense burner, China, 19thC, 71½ x 182in (78 x 198cm).
$5,500–7,000 *CNY*

A Tekke carpet, the terracotta field with 15 rows of 3 *guls*, terracotta border of sunburst *guls*, hooked leaf *elems*, central Turkestan, c1910, 101 x 66in (256.5 x 168cm).
$6,000–7,000 *KW*

A Chinese carpet, the plain ivory field with a central roundel of angular stylised blue vine flowerheads around a tomato-red and blue circular panelled roundel, in an ivory border, moth damage, old repairs, late 19thC, 197 x 150in (499 x 382cm).
$6,500–8,000 *C*

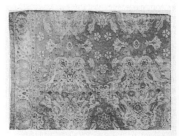

An Indian carpet, with flowers on a pastel coloured field with one main border, c1930, 142 x 109in (360.5 x 276.5cm).
$1,700–1,900 *DN*

l. An Amritzar carpet, the shaded light-blue field with diagonal rows of pine cone *boteh* in a blackcurrant-red meandering vine border, India, late 19thC, 204 x 157in (518 x 299cm).
$3,500–4,500 *C*

An Indian cotton *dhurrie,* the white field with pale green floral sprays around an open lozenge medallion, in a green border of stellar flowerheads, pink meandering flowering vine border with outer ivory flowerhead and zigzag stripe, an indigo cross-panel at each end, Rajasthan, c1880, 84 x 47in (213 x 119cm).
$1,900–2,400 *C*

TEXTILES
Covers & Quilts

An appliqué remembrance quilt, the central patch embroidered 'Edwin, Mary, Bloomfield 1850' within a flowerhead of printed cottons and chintz, bordered by squares with pious verses, and birds, flowers and crosses, 90 x 96in (229 x 244cm).
$3,200–3,600 *CSK*

An American pieced cotton quilt, the calico stars on red and green hexagonal bands on a white background, with a red calico border, c1860, 82 x 76in (208 x 193cm).
$560–720 *SLN*

A coverlet of 2 joined lengths of commemorative printed cotton, depicting a family within a floral medallion interspersed with an eagle motif, with filet trimming, 19thC, 61 x 87in (155 x 221cm).
$1,600–1,800 *C*

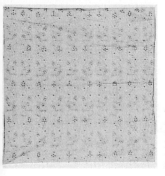

A Continental coverlet, embroidered with pale silks and gilt threads, with a central vacant cartouche, the corners with exotic birds, 18thC, 112 x 88in (284.5 x 223.5cm).
$850–950 *CSK*

A printed cotton cover, in light blues within leafy borders, with machine lace trimming, 19thC, 84 x 67in (213.5 x 170cm).
$400–450 *C*

A pieced quilt, in a connected multi-coloured sunburst pattern on a white ground, 19thC, 113 x 114in (287 x 290cm).
$430–480 *EL*

l. An ivory silk cover, with applied gold thread, designed with panels of fruit, seeds, pods and leaves, padded and lined, early 20thC, 89 x 87in (226 x 220cm).
$250–280 *P*

A silk and velvet patchwork coverlet, with a central flowerhead surrounded by a star, c1860, 102 x 90in (259 x 229cm).
$800–900 *CSK*

A Jacquard coverlet, depicting George Washington in the corners and the White House, in red, blue, deep green and ivory, signed 'Made by Phillip Schum, Lancaster, PA, 1869', 80 x 74in (203 x 188cm).
$640–720 *RIT*

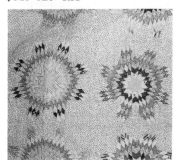

An American quilt, with yellow, red, grey and blue star patterns, Pennsylvania, c1900, 80 x 92in (203 x 234cm).
$320–350 *LB*

A Welsh quilt, with a floral design, blanket-lined, c1900, 90 x 84in (229 x 213.5cm).
$480–560 *LB*

Embroidery & Needlework

A needlework picture, depicting Adam and Eve in the Garden of Eden, in a moulded frame, 17thC, 14½ x 24½in (37 x 62cm).
$2,800–3,200 *S*

A needlework picture, the coloured wools and silk worked in tent stitch, depicting a tobacco seller and an Eastern figure, unfinished, early 18thC, 11¼ x 9½in (28.5 x 24cm).
$1,000–1,300 *WW*

A tapestry cushion, with bobble braiding, 18thC, 15 x 22in (38 x 56cm).
$380–420 *JPr*

A painted silkwork picture, depicting a lady beneath a palm tree, edged with imitation pearl glass beads and a chenille floral border, c1790, 12 x 11¼in (30.5 x 28.5cm), framed.
$550–650 *WW*

A needlework portrait of Catherine of Braganza, worked in long and short stitches on a cream silk ground surrounded by metallic lace, mid-17thC, 11 x 9¼in (28 x 23.5cm).
$1,000–1,200 *WW*

A silkwork picture, worked in coloured silks in stem stitch, couching and French knots, depicting a cavalier and his companion, beneath an arch of flowers and flanked by exotic birds, a lion and a stag, late 17thC, 8 x 12¼in (20 x 31cm).
$1,300–1,600 *DN*

An embroidered pillow, the linen ground with a silk and gold thread flower to the centre, within a scrolling cartouche border, button opening to one side, c1710, 13½ x 9in (34 x 22.5cm).
$900–1,000 *S*

r. A George III framed linen map of England and Wales, embroidered in black, green and yellow silks and bordered with a garland of flowers, with 'Eliza Lamborn, Islip, Novbr 18 1799', 19 x 17½in (48.5 x 44.5cm).
$1,100–1,200 *DN*

Embroidery

For many centuries sewing was an important pastime for women and young girls. Some multi-patterned embroideries served as a visual recipe book of different stitches. In general, the finer the stitching and the brighter the colours the more desirable the piece will be. Silk embroideries are usually more valuable than those sewn in wool. Nineteenth century textiles are relatively abundant but it is best to avoid badly damaged pieces unless they are particularly unusual.

A needlework panel, worked in petit point with coloured silks, depicting a lady looking into a mirror, and oval landscape cartouche spandrels, probably Dutch, c1700, 40 x 22in (101.5 x 56cm).
$3,200–3,500 *Bon*

A silk needlework picture, depicting royal figures beneath swagged drapery, flanked by flowering plants, butterflies and birds, initialled 'EA', dated '1728', 10¾ x 14¾in (27.5 x 37.5cm).
$5,600–6,200 *L*

A Regency woolwork picture, worked in satin stitch, depicting a boy seated on a hill looking at a bird in a tree, c1820, 17 x 23½in (43 x 60cm).
$850–950 *S(S)*

A lace box, covered in silk embroidery, with Bartolozzi prints mounted in the lid, c1850, 18in (45.5cm) wide.
$520–560 *RA*

A Victorian Berlin woolwork and beadwork panel, depicting Little Red Riding Hood, with painted features, 23 x 21in (58.5 x 53cm).
$140–160 *DN*

A needlework panel, worked in coloured silks and wools, with a fruit-filled urn at the centre, bordered by scrolling acanthus leaves with fruit, flowers and birds worked in petit point, cut down, reworked, 19thC, 18 x 71in (46 x 180.5cm).
$480–560 *CSK*

A collection of 34 Victorian needlework panels, worked in petit point, depicting flowers, fruit, landscapes and figures, each panel with the needlewoman's name, all dated '1845', each 12 x 9in (30.5 x 23cm), mounted as a set in 6 giltwood frames.
$3,800–4,400 *MSW*

A Victorian tapestry beadwork cushion, 10in (25.5cm) diam.
$95–115 *LB*

A Victorian beaded cushion, minor repairs, 10in (25.5cm) high, in a glass dome.
$240–280 *MEG*

FURTHER READING

Katrin Cargill, *Traditional Needle Arts: Embroidery*, Mitchell Beazley, 1996.

A beaded tapestry cushion, c1880, 16in (40.5cm) square.
$160–200 *JPr*

A German floral embroidered tapestry cushion, with ruched velvet border, 1920s, 20 x 26in (51 x 66cm).
$55–65 *JPr*

A white watered silk chasuble, the front embroidered in silk and gold thread with a column and panels of flowers, the reverse embroidered in the shape of a cross with a representation of the Last Supper, with pink satin lining, c1900.
$1,400–1,600 *E*

Two joined needlework hangings, worked in wools and silks in cross stitch in shades of green, red and blue against a gold-coloured chequered silk ground, late 19thC, largest 64 x 39in (162.5 x 99cm).
$1,200–1,300 *CSK*

Lace

An Italian filet lace panel, worked with a design of birds, mythical beasts, corona and foliate sprays, c1640, 9¾ x 68in (25 x 173cm).
$350–380 *Bon(C)*

A whitework sampler, of linen and linen thread with cutwork and drawn threadwork with needlepoint fillings and detached buttonhole stitch, late 17thC, 13 x 6½in (33 x 16.5cm).
$2,200–2,400 *CSK*

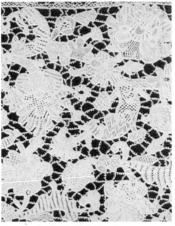

A panel of needlepoint lace, depicting branches, petals and leaves, late 17thC, 9½ x 119in (24 x 302cm).
$1,400–1,550 *S*

A Brussels lace handkerchief, c1890, 12½in (32cm) wide.
$65–80 *LB*

> **Miller's is a price GUIDE not a price LIST**

A wedding dress of mixed Brussels Duchesse and needle laces, the skirts with needle lace vignettes, slightly trained, the composite bodice with bib front, laces 19thC, made up in 20thC.
$2,000–2,400 *CSK*

A flounce of Brussels *point de gaze* lace, with raised flower petals, c1900, 24¾ x 122in, (63 x 310cm).
$1,600–1,900 *E*

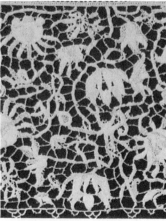

A panel of *punto in aria* needlepoint lace, worked with sprays of tulips and vases, monogrammed to one end with interlocking Cs, c1650, 7½ x 152in (19 x 387cm).
$1,600–1,900 *S*

A panel of *gros point de Venise* needlepoint lace, with a design of parrot-head tulips, lilies and acanthus scrolls, late 17thC, 10½ x 122½in (27 x 311cm).
$650–800 *S*

An Irish lace collar, c1890, 32in (81.5cm) wide.
$140–160 *LB*

A linen tablecloth, with lace insertions, c1900, 84 x 60in (213.5 x 152.5cm).
$170–200 *LB*

Samplers

A linen sampler, embroidered in coloured silks in a variety of stitches, with spot motifs, a boxer and fragmented bands, marked 'M.W.', early 17thC, 22½ x 9½in (57 x 24cm).
$4,000–4,800 *MMo*

A band sampler, by Jane Bradford, dated '1683', worked in bright red, pale green, coral and blue silks in a variety of stitches with rows of stylised flowers, acorns and foliate sprays, 21½ x 8½in (54.5 x 21.5cm).
$1,400–1,600 *Bon(C)*

A band sampler, worked in green, red, blue and ivory silks in a variety of stitches, unfinished, 17thC, 38 x 8in (96.5 x 20.5cm).
$3,000–3,600 *Bon(C)*

A band sampler, by Mary Crimbaldson, dated '1740', worked in blue, red, brown, green and cream silks in various stitches, with bands of alphabets and stylised flowers, and a verse, 18½ x 8½in (47 x 21.5cm).
$3,600–4,000 *CSK*

A sampler, by Elizabeth Oxley, dated '1754', worked in coloured silks, with an angel, shepherds and their flock, with alphabets, numerals, verses and spot motifs, 21½ x 20in (54.5 x 51cm).
$5,600–6,200 *CSK*

A sampler, by Edith Coombs, dated '1785', worked in green, pink, blue and brown silks, with a verse, surrounded by a leafy meander with flowers and spot motifs, 17 x 12½in (43 x 32cm).
$1,000–1,100 *CSK*

A sampler, by Mary Morley, dated '1796', worked in red, green and brown with alphabets, spot motifs, verses and prayers, within a stylised floral border, 16 x 20in (40.5 x 51cm).
$560–640 *CSK*

Sampler care

l. A sampler, worked in coloured silks, listing the Ten Commandments, bordered by floral spot motifs, late 18thC, 16½ x 9½in (42 x 24cm).
$480–530 *CSK*

A sampler, by Sarah Appleton, dated '1799', worked in coloured silks with a verse, flowers and birds, within a stylised floral border, 18½ x 15½in (47 x 39.5cm).
$1,400–1,600 *CSK*

A sampler, by Miss Eliza Beth Yater, dated '1802', worked in coloured silks with spot motifs, a stag, vases of flowers, a peacock, butterflies, and a verse, within a stylised floral border, 17 x 12in (43 x 30.5cm).
$1,100–1,200 *CSK*

A sampler, by Ann Mercer, worked in coloured silks with a verse, alphabet and numerals, a house, birds and spot motifs, c1811, 18½ x 14in (46 x 35.5cm).
$750–800 *CSK*

A sampler, by Mary Ann Frost, dated '1825', worked in cross stitch on wool gauze with a poem, tree of life, flowers and animals, within a floral border, 19 x 12in (48.5 x 30.5cm).
$1,700–1,900 *S*

A sampler, by Ann Taylor, aged 10, depicting the Return of the Spies from Canaan, surrounded by trees, figures and a verse within a floral border, early 19thC, 25½ x 26in (65 x 66cm).
$1,300–1,500 *Bon(C)*

A sampler, by Christian Baive, aged 11, dated 'March 9, 1812', worked in silk and wool on linen, with a verse, alphabet, buildings, flowers and trees, 20 x 15in (51 x 38cm).
$950–1,000 *RIT*

A sampler, by Sarah Young, dated '1815', worked in coloured silks with spot motifs, a verse, 2 floral bands, and a stylised border of brown flowers, 19 x 15in (48.5 x 38cm).
$1,200–1,300 *CSK*

r. A sampler, by Reb*ª* Cons*ª* Worrell, aged 9, dated '1825', worked in bright silks, within a stylised honeysuckle border, 17¾ x 14in (45 x 35.5cm).
$1,200–1,300 *Bon(C)*

A sampler, by Jane Cooper, aged 10, dated 'Nov 15 1809', worked in blue, ochre and green silk and wool on linen, with a verse, a house, animals, birds and trees within a meandering floral border, 19¾ x 17in (50 x 43cm).
$1,100–1,300 *RIT*

An American sampler, depicting the Dickinson family tree and a verse, early 19thC, 14½ x 13½in (37 x 34.5cm).
$850–1,000 *SK(B)*

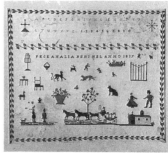

An American cross stitch sampler, by Analia Beni, dated '1817', with animals, motifs and figures, 19¾ x 23½in (50 x 59.5cm).
$640–720 *LHA*

A sampler, by Harriet Burry, dated '1827', worked in coloured silks with a house and garden, a verse, birds, animals and trees, within a stylised floral border, 19½ x 16in (49.5 x 40.5cm).
$480–560 *CSK*

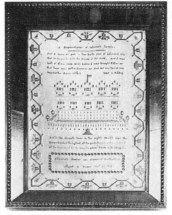

A sampler, by Elizabeth Barker, Cromford, Derbyshire, dated '1838', worked in green, blue and brown silks with Solomon's Temple, and a verse, within a border of stylised carnations and birds, 27 x 22in (68.5 x 56cm).
$900–1,100 *CSK*

A sampler, by Eliza Gibbons, dated '1839', worked in silk with a church, Biblical quotations, angels, fruit, trees and birds, 17 x 12½in (43 x 32cm).
$1,000–1,200 *DN*

Cross Reference
Colour Review

An American sampler, by Hannah K. Ansell, dated '1840', depicting a verse, and a hunter with his gun, surrounded by a flower and vine border, in a mahogany-veneered frame, 22in (56cm) square.
$1,100–1,200 *EL*

A sampler workbag, the wool ground worked in cross stitch with russet silk patterns, and a verse, c1840, 8½in (22cm) wide.
$1,600–1,900 *S*

A sampler, by Ellen Young, dated 'Aug 30th 1840', worked in cross stitch with a stag, flowers and birds, within a honeysuckle border, 18½ x 14¾in (47 x 37.5cm).
$380–480 *Bon(C)*

A sampler, by Hannah Elizabeth Ling, dated '1842', worked in blue, green and brown silks with a verse, flower urns and vases, within a border of stylised carnations, 18½ x 13½in (47 x 34.5cm).
$800–880 *CSK*

A sampler, by Jane Ann Ellwood Thompson, dated '1867', worked in coloured silks with alphabets and numerals, a house and farm animals, and a verse, 19½ x 18½in (49.5 x 47cm).
$400–480 *CSK*

Miller's is a price GUIDE not a price LIST

A Bristol sampler, by M. Russell, aged 17, dated '1884', with bands of alphabets, numerals, houses, flowers and coronets, some staining, 15½ x 13½in (39.5 x 34.5cm).
$1,900–2,200 *Bon(C)*

Tapestries

A Flemish mythological tapestry, depicting Diana and her maidens after the hunt, with a deer carried by 2 attendants, 17thC, 88 x 192in (223.5 x 488cm).
$14,500–16,000 *Bon*

A Flemish tapestry, woven in wools and silks, depicting a wooded landscape with a river, within a foliate and floral border and later blue outer slip, cut and reattached, 17thC, 118 x 150in (300 x 381cm).
$10,500–12,000 *C*

A French tapestry panel, woven in coloured silks and wools, depicting a man with a bassoon and a lady in a garden, cut down, restored, late 18thC, 57 x 60in (145 x 152.5cm).
$2,800–3,200 *CSK*

A Brussels tapestry panel, woven in coloured wools with silk highlights, depicting a mother and child amongst a crowd, cut down and reworked, 17thC, 22 x 29in (56 x 74cm).
$1,300–1,500 *CSK*

A Flemish tapestry, depicting an ornamental fountain, pheasants in a wooded landscape, bordered with flowers, rosettes and leaves, restored, early 18thC, 102 x 116in (260 x 295cm).
$4,800–5,400 *S(Z)*

An Aubusson tapestry panel, the central pale yellow cartouche with a floral arrangement, bordered with pale green, within a strapwork border with flowers in each corner, early 20thC, 108 x 72in (274.5 x 183cm).
$6,400–7,200 *CSK*

l. A pair of tapestry pictures, woven in coloured wools, depicting a peasant boy and girl, 19thC, 35 x 28in (89 x 71cm).
$950–1,100 *CSK*

A Flemish tapestry, depicting a landscape with a chateau, 17thC, 101 x 71in (256.5 x 180.5cm).
$4,800–5,400 *SLN*

A Flemish tapestry fragment, depicting a pair of exotic birds within a landscape with a building, 17thC, 89 x 60in (226 x 152.5cm), in a giltwood frame.
$4,000–4,800 *LHA*

Four Aubusson tapestry panels, depicting figures in 18thC dress celebrating the 4 seasons, 19thC, 57 x 38½in (145 x 98cm), in rococo style frames.
$9,000–10,500 *Bon(C)*

COSTUME

A linen coif or cap, embroidered in coloured silks and gilt threads, in detached buttonhole and plaited braid stitch, with spangles, early 17thC, 16½ x 9½in (42 x 23.5cm).
$3,200–3,500 *CSK*

A purse, the silver embroidered ground worked with pink strawberries, late 17thC.
$750–800 *CSK*

A gentleman's ivory taffeta silk waistcoat, the facings and pocket flaps embroidered with flowers and sprigs in pastel shaded silks, c1760.
$320–350 *P*

Locate the Source

The source of each illustration in Miller's can be found by checking the code letters below each caption with the Key to Illustrations.

r. A shield-shaped green silk purse, embroidered with roses on coiled silver thread stems, 18thC.
$640–700 *CSK*

A drawstring purse, embroidered with a leopard beneath a tree, the reverse with a hind and fawn, 17thC.
$8,500–9,500 *CSK*

A purse, with gilt embroidered ground worked with an urn of flowers, early 18thC.
$320–400 *CSK*

A George III gentleman's cream silk waistcoat, embroidered with floral border to the front and pocket flaps in green, brown, purple and pink coloured silks, with silk embroidered covered buttons, c1770.
$250–320 *DN*

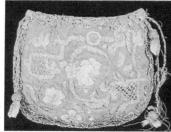

A wallet, embroidered in silk flame stitch, bound in silver braid and lined in blue silk, late 17thC, 8in (20.5cm) wide.
$880–1,000 *CSK*

A silk sack-backed open robe, known as 'The Suffield Dress', the ivory silk brocaded with silver and gold metal threads, with flowers in purple and pink silks, c1750.
$1,300–1,600 *S*

A gentleman's silk waistcoat, embroidered in coloured silks with flowers and foliage to the collar, front edges and shaped pocket flaps, scattered floral motifs to the ivory silk ground, the buttons worked with cupid's arrows, c1785.
$480–560 *WW*

A pair of lady's cream kid leather shoes, the heel covered in olive green kid, the pointed toe with matching silk embroidery and ruched silk ribbon trim, c1790.
$1,200–1,300 *P*

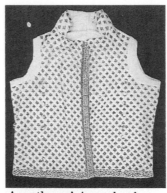

A gentleman's ivory shawl cloth waistcoat, woven with a blue leaf sprig pattern, c1800.
$240–280 *CSK*

A French boy's indigo woollen double-breasted dress coat, early 19thC.
$640–800 *CSK*

A pair of lady's canary yellow shoes, with pointed toes, low black leather heels, trimmed with black ribbon and fringes, c1790.
$1,600–1,900 *S*

l. A lady's ivory silk dress, cloak trimmed with ivory silk tassels, shawl and later bonnet, c1815.
$1,900–2,200 *CSK*

r. A white cotton dress, with drawstring waist and fall-fronted bodice, the front with whitework flower border, slightly trained, c1810.
$560–640 *CSK*

r. A white cotton divorce corset, the sides and back corded, with lacing over the hips, 1820s.
$800–880 *CSK*

A divorce corset is an early 19thC style of corset which separated the breasts.

A dark brown felt beaver top hat, with a braid hatband, lined with bronze silk, possibly a lady's hat, c1810, 7in (18cm) high, with original shaped box.
$4,800–5,500 *CSK*

A Regency white embroidered muslin dress, the train with Lille lace insertions, cream ribbon trim and handmade buttons.
$2,000–2,400 *WW*

l. A lady's cotton corset, with 2 detachable metal busks to the centre front, reinforced quilted zig-zags, back-laced, repaired, c1830.
$1,300–1,450 *S*

A child's white cotton dress, with puffed sleeves, printed with a mauve Maltese cross motif, 1830s.
$320–350 *CSK*

Paisley Shawls

These became popular because the voluminous crinoline skirts which were fashionable in the mid-19thC made it impossible for ladies to wear coats. Named after the town of Paisley in Scotland, these shawls were also produced in Edinburgh, Norwich and France.

A paisley shawl, in shades of red, blue, green and ivory, 19thC, 119¾ x 60in (304 x 152cm).
$520–560 *RIT*

A folding carriage parasol, with green painted metal shaft, tilting face shield in the form of a cream petalled flower with green silk sepals, carved bone handle, c1860, 20½in (52cm) long.
$250–320 *P*

A pair of child's black braces, embroidered in gold thread, mid-19thC, 16in (40.5cm) long.
$560–640 *LB*

A pair of Victorian silk wedding shoes, with silver-backed paste buckles, c1890.
$250–280 *LB*

A Victorian cotton lawn floral print dress, 57in (145cm) long.
$280–350 *LB*

A grey taffeta two-piece dress, the bodice with ruching to the yoke and tight sleeves, the trained skirt with triple flounce to the hem with bands of ruching above, c1870.
$1,100–1,300 *P*

A lady's black taffeta outfit, comprising a moiré skirt, petticoat and cape, with embroidered and bead decoration, an additional organdie cape with crimped tiers, each with silver stripe and frill, c1900, together with an unfinished striped black velvet long skirt.
$160–190 *GH*

l. An Afghan silk woman's robe, the bodice embroidered and encrusted with glass beads, late 19thC.
$200–250 *CSK*

A purple silk two-piece costume, lined, the coat with mandarin collar and embroidered floral decoration, together with a matching skirt and petticoat, c1900.
$200–250 *GH*

A Hungarian black sheepskin wedding coat, with appliqué and embroidered floral decoration, c1900.
$1,200–1,300 *CSK*

An Ayrshire cotton christening gown, c1900, 41in (104cm) long.
$280–320 *LB*

A chiffon gown, the black chiffon ground printed with roses and foliage, and trimmed with black spotted velvet and ivory lace, c1905.
$190–240 *S*

An Edwardian baby's lawn dress, with slip, c1910, 20in (51cm) long.
$100–115 *LB*

A pair of baby's cream kid leather shoes, c1920.
$65–75 *LB*

A black sequinned opera cloak, lined in pale blue satin, 1920s, ex-Britt Ekland collection.
$320–400 *CSK*

A baby's cotton and lace dress, c1920, 15in (38cm) long.
$65–80 *LB*

A dress, with panels of cream and black silk chiffon and black lace over cream, together with a black silk chiffon jacket, probably Austrian, 1920s.
$2,800–3,500 *C*

A blue plush velvet opera cape, lined in ivory silk, c1920, ex-Britt Ekland collection.
$280–320 *CSK*

A knitted ivory silk jersey tunic top, embroidered by Kitmar with Art Deco style arabesques and flowers, labelled 'Chanel', 1925.
$1,300–1,800 *CSK*

A black tulle cocktail dress, embroidered with a seaweed design in silver bugle beads, mid-1920s.
$520–560 *CSK*

A raspberry plush velvet opera cape, lined in black and gold lamé, c1925, ex-Britt Ekland collection.
$110–130 *CSK*

A pair of lady's silver leather shoes, labelled 'Cammeyer, Fifth Avenue, New York', c1920.
$100–115 *LB*

A French hat, by Mercedes, c1920, 13in (33cm) diam.
$70–80 *LB*

An orange straw hat, by Mitzi Laurens, decorated with roses on the headband, c1920.
$80–100 *LB*

A straw hat, decorated with yellow flowers, c1920.
$65–80 *LB*

A peer's crimson velvet coronation robe and coronet, trimmed with ermine, by Ede and Ravenscroft, c1937.
$480–560 *DN*

l. A pair of child's kid gloves, c1920, 5in (12.5cm) long.
$15–25 *LB*

A beaded shawl, decorated with yellow and orange roses, 1920s, 30¼in (77cm) square.
$65–75 *SUS*

A black crepe dress, with diamanté studs, late 1930s, ex-Britt Ekland collection.
$160–190 *CSK*

A peach chiffon negligee, with ivory tulle overlay, embroidered in coloured silks, 1930s, ex-Britt Ekland collection.
$280–320 *CSK*

A midnight blue chiffon evening dress, embroidered with sequins, labelled Alice Thomas, Paris, mid-1930s.
$220–250 *CSK*

A black silk jersey cocktail dress, labelled 'Holt Renfrew Canada', c1950.
$280–320 *CSK*

FANS

A Japanese fan leaf, painted in colours and gilded, with a scene depicting a dancer before a figure seated on a throne in a garden landscape, early 18thC, 17½in (44.5cm) wide, framed.
$480–560 *DN*

A fan, with floral carved and pierced ivory sticks, the paper leaf painted with a river scene and figures, the reverse with a landscape vignette, slight damage, c1770, 11⅛in (29cm) wide.
$280–320 *WW*

A Chinese export silver and gilt metal filigree brisé fan, with blue and green *cloisonné* decoration, designed with houses, trees and flowers, the guardsticks with dignitaries and scholars, slight damage, late 18thC, 11½in (29cm) wide.
$2,200–2,700 *P*

A fan, the silk leaf painted with 4 vignettes, 3 in shades of pink, grey and blue, the reserves painted to simulate wood, the verso painted with villages on islands, with ivory sticks carved and pierced with figures, c1890, 12in (30.5cm) wide, boxed.
$1,000–1,200 *CSK*

r. A fan, the silk leaf painted with the nursery rhyme 'Lavender's Blue', in shades of blue, silver and gold, 1917, 16in (40.5cm) wide, framed and glazed.
$560–640 *CSK*

A French fan, the leaf painted with figures in a landscape, each holding a Claude glass, the reserves painted with ribbons and flowers, the verso with a spray of flowers, the bone sticks pierced and painted with pink and blue flowers, upper guardstick repaired, c1760, 11in (28cm) wide.
$640–720 *CSK*

A Claude glass, named after the French painter Claude Gelée, is a convex mirror used for viewing landscapes.

A carved ivory fan, the leaf painted with a classical scene of Neptune and Amphitrite, with pierced and carved ivory sticks, the guardsticks carved with figures and scallop shells, some damage, 18thC, 11in (28cm) wide.
$550–650 *Hal*

A Cantonese carved ivory fan, with painted leaf and ivory set with a Thousand Faces pattern to both sides, the guardsticks carved with figures on terraces, some damage, mid-19thC, 9in (23cm) wide.
$320–350 *Hal*

A French fan, the paper leaf painted with a central cartouche of a lady playing a lute, the reserves with medallions of a gentleman and his lady, with mother-of-pearl sticks, c1760, 10½in (26.5cm) wide, in glazed case.
$1,200–1,300 *P*

A fan, with ivory brisé guardsticks and sticks decorated with flowers and hunting dogs, the paper leaf painted with a central circular scene of a goddess in a golden chariot, with 4 panels of grotesques on a blue and black ground, gilded, repaired, late 18thC, 19in (48cm) wide, in gilt frame.
$600–680 *DN*

> **Miller's is a price GUIDE not a price LIST**

l. A fan, the canepin leaf painted with a scene of a gentleman proposing to a lady, with mother-of-pearl sticks, signed by Cecil Chenneviere, c1890, 12in (30.5cm) wide.
$1,000–1,100 *CSK*

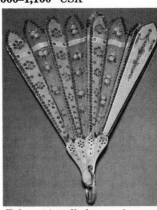

A Fabergé jewelled two-colour gold and enamel-mounted fan, the mother-of-pearl guardsticks inlaid with *piqué* discs, the gauze leaf embroidered with spangles, rosettes and painted pink roses, the front guard mounted with an outer guard enamelled and applied with swags and rosettes picked out with rose diamonds, marked, workmaster H. Wigström, St Petersburg, 1903–08, 6¼in (16cm) wide.
$13,700–15,200 *S(G)*

JEWELLERY

Victorian jewellery is one of the most collectable of antiques. Walk around any antiques market and one can find a veritable Aladdin's cave of desirable jewellery, much of which is surprisingly modestly priced.

During the reign of Queen Victoria (1837–1901) many people started to travel and brought back souvenirs from the cities of Europe, thus influencing jewellery and fashion styles at that time. Initially, romantic jewels incorporating flowers, insects and tiny animal motifs were made into small and delicate pieces. Later in mid-Victorian times rather larger, heavier jewellery was worn.

Queen Victoria herself influenced many different fashions including, of course, mourning jewellery, inspired by the death of her beloved consort, Albert, and which is widely collected today. Many pieces of mourning jewellery were made from black or blue enamel and often contained hair from the loved one in the locket back. The buckle brooch (page 541) was also made popular by Queen Victoria who was so modest that she did not wish to wear the Order of the Garter as a real garter below the knee, as originally intended. Instead she transferred the buckle emblem of the Order to brooches, bangles and rings.

An effect popularised in Victorian gold jewellery was achieved by dipping an item into an acid bath. The process known as 'blooming' created a dull finish, but was soon made illegal because of the danger to the craftsmen caused by the acid fumes.

Although diamond jewellery had always been popular, at this time semi-precious stones were also mounted into beautiful necklaces, bracelets and rings. Peridot, amethyst, citrine, topaz, aquamarine and garnet were amongst the popular stones of the day. When buying stone-set jewellery the depth of colour is very important, and with all antique jewellery the back of the piece should be carefully checked for solder or repairs. Condition will, of course, affect its value.

The best places to look for good quality, competitively priced jewellery is either a reputable antiques market or a vetted antiques fair. Auctions are another good source, but it is wise to obtain professional advice before placing your bids. Always ask for a receipt with a full description of the article.

Antique jewellery usually appreciates in value and there is also the added knowledge that you are buying a piece of history as well as an interesting, beautiful and wearable item.

Freda Hacker and Lynn Lindsay

Bangles & Bracelets

A Victorian 15ct gold slave bangle, with rams' heads, c1860, 3in (7.5cm) diam.
$1,900–2,200 *WIM*

An Edwardian turquoise set bracelet, with oval link connections to a matching clasp, 6in (15cm) long.
$800–960 *CSK*

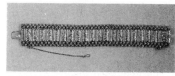

A Victorian silver bangle, with gold-inlaid circles engraved with birds, c1870, 32mm high.
$430–480 *WIM*

An Edwardian 15ct gold chain bracelet, with heart-shaped padlock fastener, c1903, 7½in (19cm) long.
$1,300–1,500 *WIM*

A 15ct gold and turquoise bangle, c1870, 25mm wide.
$1,400–1,600 *DIC*

A Victorian silver gilt bracelet, c1880, 6½in (16.5cm) long.
$880–960 *WIM*

A Fabergé jewelled two-colour gold bracelet, the sliced and attenuated navette-shaped bars articulated by points set alternately with diamonds and rubies, workmaster A. Hollming, St Petersburg, c1910, 7¾in (19.5cm) long.
$4,400–4,800 *S(G)*

l. A 15ct gold gate bracelet, c1918, 7in (18cm) long.
$1,300–1,500 *WIM*

Brooches

A gold foiled amethyst and
pearl cross brooch, c1820.
$800–880 *DIC*

A diamond set crescent brooch,
with cut down silver setting and
gold back, c1860, 38mm diam.
$2,800–3,200 *PSA*

A gold and foiled emerald
brooch, with applied wirework
decoration, 19thC.
$640–700 *CSK*

A Victorian 15ct gold brooch,
with raised centre and enamel
design, with central pearl,
c1870, 38mm long.
$880–960 *WIM*

Brooches

Collecting Victorian brooches
can be bewildering for all but
the expert. Many pieces are
unmarked, and few are
signed, except for those from
very important makers. Any
marks that do exist are
usually well hidden, and it
pays to check the hooks and
fittings carefully. Check also
that fittings are original to
the piece, otherwise the
marks may well have nothing
to do with the brooch itself.

A diamond and enamelled
brooch, designed as an open
flowerhead, the centre set with
a cluster of rose diamonds, the
petals with pink highlighted
matted enamelled decoration,
probably French, late 19thC.
$1,100–1,250 *S(S)*

A Victorian 15ct gold and seed
pearl mourning brooch, c1870,
30mm diam.
$400–480 *GEM*

A late Victorian diamond and
pearl cluster brooch, mounted
in silver and gold, with a pearl
at the centre, one small
diamond missing.
$3,500–4,000 *Bon*

A gold jewelled brooch, retailed
by Nicholls & Plincke, of Greek
cross form with trefoil terminals,
set with 5 garnets interspersed
with diamonds, maker's mark
'A.S.', St Petersburg, c1856,
40mm wide, in original fitted case.
$5,000–5,600 *S(G)*

A Victorian gold, pearl and
diamond brooch/pendant, with
detachable brooch harness and
hinged pendant loop.
$750–800 *C(Sc)*

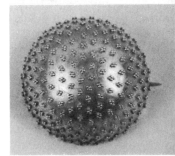

A Victorian 15ct gold domed
brooch, c1870, 32mm diam.
$560–630 *WIM*

A Victorian 18ct gold Etruscan
style brooch, c1880.
$400–480 *PSA*

A Victorian 15ct gold brooch, in the form of a buckle, 38mm wide.
$550–600 *WIM*

A 15ct gold double heart thistle brooch, set with amethysts, citrines and pearls, c1880, 38mm long.
$1,100–1,300 *DIC*

A Victorian 15ct gold brooch, with diamond centre, c1880, 32mm diam.
$680–760 *WIM*

A late Victorian diamond brooch, designed as an openwork scroll, mounted in silver and gold, c1890.
$2,800–3,200 *Bon*

A sapphire, diamond and pearl crescent and bee brooch, c1890.
$2,800–3,200 *DIC*

A Fabergé gold brooch, with rose-cut diamond border, on an openwork, floral, three-colour gold ground, the centre set with a triangular cabochon amethyst, marked, St Petersburg, c1890.
$3,200–4,000 *C*

A pearl and diamond dragonfly brooch, mounted in silver and gold, late 19thC.
$5,600–7,000 *Bon*

An opal and diamond bar brooch, c1900, 60mm wide.
$1,100–1,200 *GEM*

l. An Edwardian brooch, mounted with an octagonal peridot within a border of half pearls.
$580–640 *P(WM)*

A gold pearl and turquoise lizard brooch, c1900, 64mm long.
$1,400–1,500 *DIC*

A Fabergé gold and pearl brooch, maker's mark, St Petersburg, 1908–17, 50mm wide.
$2,000–2,400 *S(G)*

l. An Edwardian diamond brooch/pendant, with detachable brooch fitting and diamond set suspension loop, in a fitted case stamped 'The Goldsmiths & Silversmiths Company Ltd'.
$5,000–6,000 *CSK*

An Edwardian diamond brooch, the pierced, shaped oval plaque set with old brilliant-cut diamonds, c1910.
$4,200–4,800 *Bon*

A jade, enamel and rose diamond brooch, c1920.
$3,200–3,500 *S*

An American bow brooch, with amethyst crystals and pink paste rhinestones, set in gilt cord, c1930, 75mm wide.
$80–110 *PGH*

A chrome-plated flowerspray brooch, by Elsa Schiaparelli, set with blue glass crystals, signed, c1940.
$320–400 *GLT*

FURTHER READING
Stephen Giles, *Miller's Jewellery Antiques Checklist* Miller's Publications, 1997

An American floral brooch, with dark green paste on gilt setting, c1940, 64mm diam.
$70–100 *BaH*

An emerald, diamond and onyx bow brooch, c1925.
$3,800–4,400 *Bon*

A 18ct white gold bar brooch, set with sapphires and diamonds, c1935, 64mm wide.
$880–1,100 *GEM*

Costume Jewellery

The 'golden age' for the production of costume jewellery, usually made of glass crystals and electroplated base metals, was from the 1930s to the 1960s. It was mainly manufactured in the US by companies such as Kenneth Lane and Schiaparelli, although costume jewellery was also produced in Europe, particularly France, by leading designers such as Chanel and Dior. British manufacturers include Attwood & Sawyer and Butler & Wilson.

A kingfisher blue rhinestone and crystal brooch, on rhodium mount, c1950, 25mm diam.
$50–80 *PGH*

r. A brooch, by Garrard, designed as a bird-of-paradise with ruby, diamond and turquoise plumage and 18ct yellow gold tails, signed, 1960s.
$1,600–2,000 *Bon*

An American brooch and earrings set, with emerald paste rhinestones set in gold plate on silver mounts, signed, c1930, brooch 50mm wide.
$140–200 *BaH*

A 18ct diamond set fly brooch, c1935, 25mm wide.
$520–580 *GEM*

A Hollycraft pin and earring set, with multi-coloured crystals in gilt setting, signed, c1950.
$240–320 *GLT*

Cameos

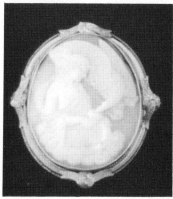

An Italian shell cameo, carved with Zeus in the form of an eagle accepting a libation from Ganymede, set in a gold brooch mount applied with scrolls and wirework, mid-19thC, 65mm high.
$1,400–1,600 *DN*

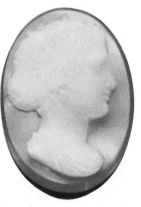

A sardonyx cameo, depicting a female classical profile, 19thC, 57mm high.
$1,100–1,300 *S*

A Victorian shell cameo brooch, depicting Bacchante, in a gold frame with scrolling leaf motif decoration.
$1,600–1,800 *C(Sc)*

. A carved cameo and gold oval brooch, depicting a profile bust of a classical young maiden, within a chased gold acanthus leaf surround, 19thC, 50mm high.
$320–350 *MCA*

An oval agate cameo brooch, depicting a female profile, the gold mount with applied wirework decoration, c1870.
$1,400–1,550 *CSK*

A shell cameo brooch, the oval panel depicting a mythological romantic scene, in a gold pierced and scrolled frame, 19thC.
$1,100–1,200 *P(S)*

A Victorian shell cameo brooch, depicting Hercules sitting with Hebe and Cupid in the background, with chased and scrolled gold border, 3in (7.5cm) wide.
$1,200–1,300 *P(S)*

A gold and shell cameo brooch, carved with the profile of Athena within a gold frame, with Greek key-fret border of black *champlevé* enamel, late 19thC.
$1,300–1,450 *S(NY)*

A shell cameo, depicting the head of Medusa, to a bead and wirework decorated brooch mount, 19thC, 55mm high.
$800–880 *DN*

An oval shell cameo brooch, depicting the Three Graces with attendants, the gold frame with applied wire and ropework decoration, 19thC.
$1,600–1,800 *CSK*

A shell cameo brooch, depicting a classical scene, with a gold mount, late 19thC, 70mm high.
$1,400–1,550 *WL*

Cuff Links

A pair of Victorian 9ct gold heart-shaped cuff links, for men or ladies, 20mm long.
$430–480 WIM

A pair of 18ct gold cuff links, c1900, 12mm diam.
$550–600 WIM

A pair of white enamel cuff links, with gold mounts, each with 2 gold-bordered studs enamelled over engine-turning around a central rose diamond, maker's mark 'A.A.', St Petersburg, c1908.
$1,700–1,900 S(G)

A pair of 18ct gold and blue enamel cuff links, c1920.
$480–520 WIM

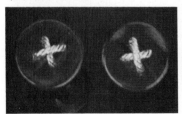

A pair of malachite cuff links, by Webb, with twisted wirework thread, French import mark, c1950.
$640–720 C

A pair of Fabergé gold, enamel and jewelled cuff links, each disk applied with a gold eagle grasping a diamond in its claws, marked with maker's initials, workmaster Knut Oskar Pihl, Moscow, c1890, 25mm wide.
$8,500–9,500 S(NY)

A set of 4 diamond and chrysoberyl cat's-eye dress buttons convertible to cuff links, c1900.
$1,300–1,600 PSA

A pair of gold and enamel cuff links, the blue enamel sunburst reserve centred with a diamond and framed by a chased husk border, maker's mark 'IM', Kiev, 1908–17.
$2,800–3,200 S(G)

l. A pair of 18ct gold and emerald cuff links, c1915.
$1,300–1,450 WIM

A pair of Cartier 18ct gold cuff links, with rubies, in original box, c1930.
$2,000–2,300 WIM

A pair of Fabergé gold and diamond cuff links, each cast and chased as the head of an elephant curling a cushion-shaped diamond in its trunk, workmaster E. Kollin, St Petersburg, c1896, 25mm wide.
$5,000–5,600 S(G)

A pair of two-colour gold cuff links, each formed as a sky blue enamelled disc centred by a rose diamond, slight damage to enamel, maker's mark 'A.A.', St Petersburg, c1908, 17mm diam.
$2,200–2,700 S(G)

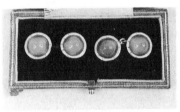

A pair of Edwardian 18ct gold enamel and chalcedony cuff links, c1910.
$980–1,100 WIM

A pair of rock crystal and enamel presentation cuff links, with the crown and cipher of King George V and Queen Mary, signed Benzie Cowes, in original fitted case.
$2,200–2,700 Bon

Presented to Sir Godfrey Thomas, Private Secretary to the Duke of Windsor, by King George V and Queen Mary, on the occasion of his marriage, 1924.

l. A pair of sapphire cuff links, by Van Cleef & Arpels, each with calibré cut sapphire central line, signed, c1950.
$3,200–4,000 C

Earrings

A pair of Victorian 15ct gold and banded agate earrings, 50mm long.
$1,300–1,500 *WIM*

A pair of hardstone cameo earrings, each depicting a classical bearded male profile, the gold mount with bead and wirework decoration, 19thC.
$1,600–1,900 *CSK*

Pendant Earrings

Pendant shapes were the most popular form of earrings in the 19thC. They tend to be long in design and almost always incorporate a drop in some form. Most settings of large pendant earrings tend to be lightweight in order not to pull the wearer's ears. This has meant that earrings in perfect condition are fairly rare, owing to their delicacy.

A pair of 15ct gold earrings, c1870, 32mm long.
$1,300–1,500 *WIM*

A pair of Victorian 15ct gold earrings, with original fringing, 45mm long.
$1,900–2,200 *WIM*

A pair of Victorian 15ct gold earrings, with converted screw tops which can be reverted to swan fittings, c1880, 25mm long.
$720–800 *WIM*

A pair of Victorian gold earrings, c1890, 18mm diam.
$750–850 *WIM*

A pair of foiled amethyst pendant earrings, the drop-shaped amethyst in a scrolled filigree mount, 19thC.
$1,300–1,450 *DN*

Cross Reference
Colour Review

A pair of Austro-Hungarian silver gilt pendant earrings, part enamelled and set with a square, step-cut, green beryl, rose-cut garnets and half-pearls, late 19thC.
$280–350 *DN*

A pair of Fabergé gold, diamond and sapphire earrings, each mounted with a cabochon sapphire surrounded by diamonds, marked with maker's Cyrillic initials, workmaster Michael Perchin, St Petersburg, c1900, 13mm diam.
$8,000–8,800 *S(NY)*

A pair of earrings, by Kenneth J. Lane, the red and green cabochon crystals set with diamanté, with blue cut-glass drop and metal settings, signed 'K.J.L.', c1960.
$160–240 *GLT*

A pair of earrings, by Kenneth J. Lane, with pink and green cut-glass crystals, *faux* pearl fringe and metal settings, signed, c1960.
$160–240 *GLT*

A pair of American earrings, with white rhinestones on rhodium-plated mounts, c1960, 50mm long.
$100–115 *PGH*

Necklaces

A Victorian 15ct gold
collar necklace, c1870,
17½in (44.5cm) long.
$5,600–6,400 *WIM*

A gold filigree necklace,
with moss agate, c1820.
$1,900–2,200 *DIC*

A gold necklace, set with
5 Wedgwood panels, c1860.
$3,600–4,400 *DIC*

r. A Christian Dior necklace,
composed of iridescent
blue/green cut crystals, cabochon
foil beads and *faux* pearls, set
in gilt-plated mounts, 1950s.
$1,600–1,800 *GLT*

l. A gold-mounted half-
pearl necklace, c1900.
$2,200–2,700 *DIC*

*In the Victorian and Edwardian
period pearls were often split in
half because the
flat backs were
easier to set
in jewellery.*

Pendants

A Victorian emerald
set pendant, c1860,
25mm diam.
$950–1,100 *PSA*

A Georgian mourning
pendant, with pen and ink
design on ivory and lock of
hair behind glass at back,
c1800, 12mm high.
$130–160 *PSA*

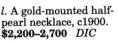

A Fabergé miniature
egg, commemorating the
coronation of Nicholas II
in 1895, workmaster's
mark of August
Hollming, St Petersburg.
$3,200–4,400 *SHa*

An Edwardian diamond
pendant necklace, the
pale blue enamel panel
with locket back and
applied rose diamond
and seed pearl floral
motif, platinum chain,
in a fitted case.
$1,300–1,450 *CSK*

An Edwardian
diamond pendant, the
central brilliant-cut
diamond of 0.7cts.
$2,200–2,400 *P(B)*

An Edwardian opal and
diamond pendant
necklace, on fine link
neck chain, c1910,
pendant 40mm high.
$7,400–8,800 *C*

A Fabergé gold and
enamel pendant, the
oval enamel plaque
decorated with the
Tolga Mother of God,
maker's mark,
workmaster
Henrik Wigström,
St Petersburg, the
reverse with inscription
dated 1914, 34mm high.
$3,800–4,400 *S(G)*

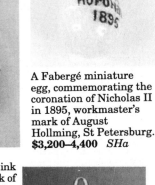

An Edwardian diamond
pendant, designed as a
snowflake, the central
brilliant-cut diamond with
4 further similarly cut
stones, each within an
openwork surround, c1910.
$2,000–2,400 *Bon*

An Edwardian tourmaline and enamel pendant, with central cushion-cut green tourmaline and matching pear-shaped drop, with later neck chain, c1910.
$750–800 *CSK*

An Edwardian emerald and diamond pendant, the central cabochon emerald within a diamond two-row surround, with bow surmount, c1910, 48mm high.
$20,800–22,400 *C*

A Fabergé gold and emerald cross pendant, work-master Henrik Wigström, St Petersburg, marked with initials and standard, 41mm long, c1910, with gold chain.
$5,000–5,600 *S(NY)*

A heart-shaped sapphire and diamond pendant, the pavé set diamond heart with calibré-cut sapphire striped detail and central diamond collet, mounted in platinum, on fine link chain, c1930, pendant 37mm high.
$13,600–15,200 *C*

Rings

l. An 18ct gold, turquoise and pearl cluster ring, c1830.
$280–320 *DIC*

r. A black opal, diamond and 18ct gold cluster ring, platinum set with gold undersetting and shank, c1910, 25mm long.
$1,400–1,600 *PSA*

An 18ct gold cluster ring, with small carved turquoise, rose-cut diamond and flowers, with beaded borders, mid-19thC.
$600–675 *DN*

A Victorian 18ct gold ring, with 3 central diamonds bordered by turquoise cabochons, 2 stones later replaced.
$240–280 *DN*

A late Victorian diamond and synthetic ruby ring, of Indian style, vertically collet set with an old-cut diamond flanked by synthetic rubies, within a frame of rose-cut diamonds, French control marks.
$1,000–1,200 *P(WM)*

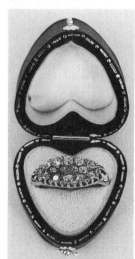

A Carré diamond full eternity ring, platinum set, c1940.
$1,900–2,400 *PSA*

An old cut diamond cluster ring, c1920.
$1,000–1,200 *GEM*

GOLD

A vari-coloured gold snuff box, the hinged cover chased and engraved with a basket of flowers and foliage, the sides with rabbits, birds, flowers and an insect, the base with a trelliswork pattern and vacant cartouche, unmarked, c1750, 2½in (6.5cm) wide.
$4,400–4,800 *C*

A gold and enamel box, formerly containing a musical movement, the exterior cut-out and embellished in dark blue *champlevé* enamel with fruiting and flowering sprays between flaming torches, some enamel loss, maker's mark rubbed, Geneva, c1810, 3¼in (8.5cm) wide.
$2,000–2,400 *S*

A gold musical toothpick box, the hinged cover chased with foliate and floral decoration and flowerheads set with turquoises and a diamond, the sides and base engine-turned within trailing foliate decoration, Swiss movement, with key, c1820, 2½in (6.5cm) long.
$5,000–5,600 *Bon*

A two-colour gold and lacquer powder box, by André-Louis Cassé, striped in scarlet lacquer between narrow gold bands, the borders stamped with interlaced leaves and ribbons, charge and discharge marks of Julien Alaterre, Paris, 1773, 3in (7.5cm) diam.
$3,500–4,000 *S*

An Austro-Hungarian gold Masonic snuff box, engraved with the 'All Seeing Eye' within an eternal snake motif, the whole with engraved interwoven decoration and trailing foliate border, the base engraved with an ear within similar decoration, maker's mark 'D. F.', c1825.
$6,400–7,200 *Bon*

A Swiss gold snuff box, by Bautte & Cie, Geneva, engine-turned, the borders chased with scrolls, shellwork and leaves, the hinged cover mounted with a faceted topaz quartz surrounded by pearls and flanked by 2 citrine quartz hearts, c1830, 2½in (6.5cm) long.
$2,200–2,700 *S(NY)*

l. A Continental gold cigarette case, mounted with a diamond-set crowned monogram, with cabochon push button lock, the inside with presentation inscription 'from William II, Emperor of Germany, 1889', 3¼in (8.5cm) high.
$3,400–3,800 *Bon*

r. A gold and citrine revolving seal, c1900.
$400–480 *DIC*

An early George III gold snuff box, the lid embossed and chased with 'The Judgement of Paris', 2½in (6.5cm) long.
$5,700–6,400 *WW*

A French gold box, by Louis-François Tronquoy, the lid and base engine-turned with a pattern formed by concentric discs, within borders of trailing foliage, marked, Paris, 1819-38, 1¾in (47mm) diam, 39gr.
$1,900–2,200 *C(G)*

A gold foliate seal, with split ring, c1830, 2in (5cm) long.
$950–1,100 *DIC*

ENAMEL

A German enamel snuff box, with gilt-metal mounts, the lid decorated with a boar hunt, the sides and base with pastoral views, the lid interior with a landscape in blue tones, c1730, 3½in (9cm) wide.
$2,500–2,800 *S*

An enamel snuff box, the cover printed and painted with an Italian scene, after Sebastien le Clerc, the sides with flowersprays, the interior cover with an insect, with engraved gilt-metal mounts, Birmingham, c1765, 2½in (6.5cm) wide.
$1,300–1,500 *C*

An enamel *étui*, painted with allegorical subjects and putti representing the Arts and Sciences, gilt-metal mounts, slight damage, Staffordshire, c1760, 3¾in (9.5cm) high.
$6,000–6,400 *S*

An enamel *bonbonnière*, brightly painted as a parrot perched over a blue and white bowl filled with fruit on a dark brown ground, reeded gilt-metal mounts, Birmingham, c1765, 3in (7.5cm) wide.
$13,000–14,500 *S*

An enamel snuff box, the lid painted with Rinaldo and Armida in her palace garden, with Cupid poised behind, the sides with pastoral landscapes and ruins, wavy gilt-metal mounts with corded thumbpiece, base with some restoration, Bilston, c1765, 3¼in (8cm) wide.
$2,800–3,500 *S*

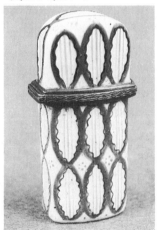

An enamel scent bottle *étui*, with original bottle, Bilston, c1780, 2in (5cm) high.
$1,200–1,300 *BHa*

An enamel *étui*, complete with tools, minor restoration, Staffordshire, c1770, 3½in (9cm) high.
$3,200–4,400 *BHa*

A French enamel and gilt-metal box, the dark blue ground painted with figures and landscapes within gilt reserves, the hinged cover rising to reveal an interior lined with embroidered panels, 18thC, 3½in (9cm) wide.
$600–650 *TMA*

r. An enamelled patch box, depicting scene of Cheltenham Wells, with original mirror, Birmingham, c1780, 2in (5cm) diam.
$560–640 *BHa*

A Swiss enamelled gold snuff box, made for the Oriental market, the body and sides chased with scrolling foliage on an enamelled green ground, the body edged by bands of white enamelled Greek key pattern on red enamelled ground, the cover painted with a flower bouquet, c1840, 2¾in (7cm) wide.
$4,400–4,800 *C(G)*

A silver and enamel perfume bottle, by Horton & Allday, Birmingham, c1886, 3in (7.5cm) long.
$1,400–1,550 *THOM*

A French enamelled and gilt-metal casket, the lid and sides with Sèvres style 'jewelled' panels on a pink ground, late 19thC, 7¼in (18.5cm) wide.
$1,100–1,300 *Bea(E)*

An Imperial Russian *cloisonné* enamel purse, by Maria Semenova, c1890, 3in (7.5cm) wide.
$3,200–3,600 *SHa*

An enamel and silver case, with sporting scenes, London 1896, 2in (5cm) wide.
$3,200–3,500 *SHa*

l. An enamel and silver cigarette case, with concealed compartment depicting Leda and the Swan, c1900, 3 x 2in (7.5 x 5cm).
$1,600–2,000 *SFL*

A French enamelled vesta case, c1890, 2¾in (7cm) high.
$3,200–3,600 *SHa*

An enamel plaque, signed T. Sayer and entitled 'Cavalier', depicting a gentleman admiring himself in a mirror, late 19thC, 10½in (26.5cm) high.
$2,200–2,600 *S(NY)*

l. A silver and enamel cigarette case, the lid depicting a lady with Cupid, Russian inscription, c1903, 3 x 3¼in (7.5 x 8.5cm).
$2,000–2,400 *SFL*

A silver and enamel photograph frame, bordered in opaque white enamel enclosing translucent chartreuse over sunray reeding, by I. Britzin, St Petersburg, c1908–17, 3¾in (9.5cm) high.
$7,200–8,000 *S(G)*

A Fabergé light blue enamelled silver-gilt compact, the 3 compartments enclosed by hinged covers with rose diamond mounted catches, the centre cover with interior mirror, with a gold lipstick holder to match, maker Henrik Wigström, 1908–17, 3¼in (8.5cm) wide.
$4,500–5,500 *AG*

A pair of *basse taille* enamel candlesticks, by Thomas Company, the transparent peach enamel with opaque white banding, gold washed, c1920, 8in (20cm) high.
$1,600–1,800 *SK(B)*

Basse taille *is a process of enamelling where an object is engraved and then flooded with translucent enamel so that the colour is strongest where the enamel is deepest.*

ORIENTAL
Cloisonné

A pair of Chinese *cloisonné* bowls, decorated with lotus flowers and scrolling foliage, the undersides with cracked ice pattern designs, 18thC, 5¼in (13.5cm) diam.
$1,200–1,400 *CSK*

A pair of Chinese *cloisonné* enamel plaques, decorated with peony, chrysanthemum and lotus flowers, issuing from ornamental rockwork, beneath a magnolia tree, gilded rims, late 18thC, 23⅝in (60cm) diam.
$1,400–1,600 *Bon*

A pair of Chinese *cloisonné* enamel quail censers and covers, with white breast and turquoise bodies, the wings with multi-coloured feathers forming detachable covers, Qing Dynasty, 18thC, 5in (12.5cm) high.
$3,200–3,600 *S*

A Chinese *cloisonné* tripod dish, decorated with entwined flowers and foliage on a turquoise ground, Ming Dynasty, late 16th/early 17thC, 5¾in (14.5cm) diam.
$1,000–1,200 *CSK*

A Chinese *cloisonné* enamel octagonal stand, the top decorated with figures on a terrace, supported by the gilt body of the stand, on 8 scrolling legs joined at the feet, some enamel losses and gilding rubbed, 17thC, 13in (33cm) diam.
$3,700–4,500 *C*

A Japanese *cloisonné* enamel vase, by Inaba Nanaho, decorated with songbirds amongst maple on a midnight blue ground, Meiji period, 4¾in (12cm) high.
$2,800–3,200 *S(S)*

A Japanese *cloisonné* vase, depicting a hen and a cockerel on a light green ground, Meiji period, 7in (18cm) high.
$330–370 *SK*

A Japanese *cloisonné* vase and cover, decorated with 2 doves sitting amid an autumnal vine on a light blue ground, Meiji period, 5¼in (13.5cm) high.
$520–600 *SK*

A Japanese *cloisonné* enamel vase, worked in copper wire within a ground of alternating ox-blood and mottled *café au lait* vertical bands with butterflies, Meiji period, 5in (12.5cm) high.
$2,000–2,400 *S*

l. A pair of Japanese *cloisonné* vases, the green ground inlaid in wire and coloured enamels portraying bamboo shoots among leaves and stones, silvered mounts, slight damage, late 19thC, 12¼in (31cm) high.
$3,600–4,000 *C*

l. A Japanese *cloisonné* vase, decorated in opaque and translucent enamels with shaped panels enclosing stylised birds and insects, with carved wood stand, early 20thC, 7¼in (18.5cm) high.
$1,600–1,900 *S(NY)*

Enamel

A Japanese vase, decorated in coloured enamels in relief with 3 goldfish swimming below overhanging wisteria, silver fittings, late Meiji period, 7¼in (18.5cm) high.
$950–1,100 *SK*

A pair of Chinese enamel bowls, painted in *famille rose* against a lemon-yellow ground with dragons, the interior similarly decorated against a white ground with a central double peach spray, one restored, 18thC, 6in (15cm) diam.
$3,300–4,000 *CNY*

l. A Chinese gilt-metal *cloisonné* bottle vase, the body enamelled with lotus flowers and tendrils, later mounted with a shaped gilt-metal openwork panel with 2 dragons, the base possibly later, Qing Dynasty, 17th/18thC, 4¾in (12cm) high.
$2,700–3,200 *S*

A Chinese *cloisonné* enamel censer and cover, decorated with birds, surmounted by a pierced dragon knop on a platform with raised petal border, on 4 dragon-form legs, marked, Kangxi period, 14¾in (37.5cm) high.
$2,800–3,500 *CNY*

Glass

A Peking red overlay Snowflake glass cup, with a band of dragons beneath a cloud collar border, Qianlong period, 2½in (6.5cm) high.
$2,200–2,400 *SK*

A Peking midnight blue glass dish, supported on a wide foot, Qianlong mark and of the period, 6½in (16.5cm) diam.
$1,400–1,600 *S(HK)*

A pair of Chinese opaque turquoise glass bottle vases, Qianlong marks and of the period, 6½in (16.5cm) high.
$5,000–5,600 *CNY*

A Peking red and yellow overlay glass vase, carved with flowers and birds with a rockwork ground, 18thC, 6in (15cm) high.
$2,200–2,600 *S(NY)*

A Chinese reverse glass painting, depicting a maiden holding an oar, in a boat with vases of flowers, Qing Dynasty, 19thC, 17½ x 12½in (44.5 x 32cm), framed.
$1,000–1,200 *S(S)*

A pair of Peking red overlay Snowflake glass vases, decorated with 2 dragons and 2 phoenix, Qianlong period, 7½in (19cm) high.
$4,500–5,500 *SK*

A pair of Peking red overlay white glass vases, each decorated with female figures in a garden, early 19thC, 8in (20.5cm) high.
$1,900–2,000 *SK*

Jade

A Chinese celadon jade elephant group, surmounted by a boy holding a crop, the opaque green stone with tan skin highlights, Ming Dynasty, 3¾in (9.5cm) high.
$2,200–2,600 *S(NY)*

A Chinese carved spinach jade brush pot, late 19thC, 4in (10cm) high.
$1,100–1,200 *LHA*

A Chinese celadon jade vase, carved in relief around the shoulder with a sinuous dragon in pursuit of a flaming pearl, 18thC, 10in (25.5cm) high, wood stand.
$3,600–4,000 *C*

A Chinese yellow-green jade lion dog, with teeth bared below the thick eyebrows and single short horn, tail curled-up, mid-Qing Dynasty, 4in (10cm) long.
$3,200–4,000 *C*

A Chinese pierced jade *coupe*, the sides carved and pierced with handles, late Ming Dynasty, 17thC, 5¼in (13cm) diam.
$2,500–2,800 *S*

A Chinese jadeite figure, modelled as Lan Caihe, dressed in a coat and skirt, holding a flower basket, her celestial scarf draped over shoulders, 19thC, 8½in (21.5cm) high.
$3,200–3,600 *S(NY)*

Lan Caihe was one of the 8 immortals.

A Chinese celadon jade oval plaque, pierced and carved with a phoenix among peonies, Ming Dynasty, early 17thC, 3½in (9cm) wide.
$2,000–2,400 *CSK*

A Chinese carved spinach jade bowl, with inscription, late 19thC, 2½in (6.5cm) diam.
$800–880 *LHA*

A pair of Chinese jade joss-stick holders and gilt-metal stands, pierced with a trellis diaper border, Qing Dynasty, 18thC, 6in (15cm) high.
$4,000–4,400 *S*

Two Chinese jade dragon finials, each carved and pierced in the form of a dragon emerging from the top of flowers and foliage in pursuit of a flaming pearl, Ming Dynasty, tallest 2½in (6.5cm) high.
$3,600–4,000 *S*

A Chinese white jade pendant, carved as a pair of catfish, 18th/19thC, 2¼in (5.5cm) long.
$1,900–2,400 *C(HK)*

Lacquer

A Japanese *lac burgauté* metal ground bottle, shaped as an open-winged butterfly, inlaid in mother-of-pearl, silver and gold with a fisherman in a river landscape on one side and a solitary figure on the other, Qianlong mark and of the period, 19thC, 2½in (6.5cm) high.
$2,500–2,800 *CNY*

Lac burgauté is inlaid lacquer, usually with gold and precious stones.

A Japanese lacquer desk box, raised on 4 bracket feet, the lid designed with a flowering peony with a butterfly above, gold *hiramakie* on a black ground, 18thC, 10¾in (27.5cm) wide.
$640–720 *SK*

Hiramakie *means sponged gold.*

A Japanese lacquer box and cover, decorated with Tokugawa symbols, scrolling foliage and diaper panels on a red ground, the sides on a raised and textured ground, the interior fitted with one tray, late 19thC, 11in (28cm) wide.
$800–880 *DN*

A Japanese lacquer covered bowl, decorated with 7 *Toyama* and possibly 7 *Osagawara/Karatso* symbols, restored, mid-Edo period, 8½in (21.5cm) diam.
$1,100–1,300 *SK*

A Japanese lacquer and burr elm calligraphy box, the cover decorated with a mountainous landscape, the underside of the lid with a design of flowering branches, the base fitted with compartments, an ink slate and a gilt-bronze scroll paperweight in the form of a chrysanthemum, with a bamboo brush, some damage, 19thC, 9 x 8½in (23 x 22.5cm).
$720–800 *Bea(E)*

A Japanese export lacquer chest, the cover decorated in gold and inlaid in mother-of-pearl with birds and flowers, the sides and front with decorated panels, 2 drawers, damaged and restored, Edo period, 17thC, 17½in (44.5cm) wide.
$3,200–4,000 *C*

Please refer to pages 324 & 336 for Chinese and Japanese chronology charts.

A Chinese cinnabar lacquer box and cover, the cover carved with 2 gentlemen standing beneath a pine tree, the sides with a band of scrolling chrysanthemums, Qianlong mark and of the period, 2¾in (7cm) diam.
$5,000–5,600 *C(HK)*

A Chinese red lacquer lobed box and cover, carved with a central chrysanthemum medallion within concentric circles of stylised petals enclosing lotus flowerheads, slight chips to rim, 18thC, 7in (18cm) diam.
$1,500–2,000 *C*

A Chinese inlaid mother-of-pearl lacquer dish, decorated with a pair of birds amidst flowering peony branches issuing from rockwork, enclosed by a trellis pattern band, the exterior decorated with a band of floral scrolls, Ming Dynasty, 16th/17thC, 8¾in (22cm) diam.
$4,800–5,600 *C*

l. A Japanese lacquer charger, decorated with carp, octopus, squid, lobster and other fish with embedded glass eyes, on a black ground, Meiji period, 27¼in (69cm) diam.
$5,600–6,200 *SK*

Metalware

A Chinese bronze bell, with double intertwined dragon handle, decorated with various miscellaneous objects, 17/18thC, 17½in (44.5cm) high, with beater and wooden stand.
$1,600–1,900 *CSK*

A pair of Chinese bronze candlesticks, in the form of 2 boys holding lotus-shaped torches, riding on an elephant and a mythical lion, 18th/19thC, 12½in (32cm) high.
$1,700–2,200 *S(NY)*

A Japanese bronze lantern, modelled as an owl, the hollow body with stylised pierced feathers, slight damage, late 19thC, 14½in (37cm) high.
$3,200–3,600 *C*

A Chinese bronze footed bowl, with loose ring handles and animal masks, Han Dynasty, 10in (25.5cm) diam.
$1,100–1,200 *WW*

A Chinese bronze censer and joss-stick holder, with handles modelled as boys standing on rockwork above mythical deers, Ming Dynasty, 16thC, 5in (12.5cm) high.
$900–1,000 *CSK*

r. A Chinese silver-inlaid bronze tripod censer, with elephant-head ring handles, decorated on a key-fret pattern ground, above flowersprays, wood cover, 18thC, 6¼in (15.5cm) wide.
$500–560 *CSK*

A Chinese bronze censer and pierced cover, modelled as a mythical horned beast, 19thC, 8¼in (21cm) high.
$1,100–1,250 *CSK*

A Japanese bronze bowl, with 3 panels depicting interior scenes with figures, silvered mounts, raised on 3 silver feet, 19thC, 5in (12.5cm) high.
$1,500–1,600 *FBG*

A Chinese bronze *bombé* censer, moulded with twin Buddhistic lion handles, 18thC, 5½in (14cm) high.
$250–300 *CSK*

A Chinese gilt-bronze figure of a Bodhisattva, Ming Dynasty, 9in (23cm) high.
$1,400–1,600 *Bon*

l. Two Japanese bronze models of quails, probably by Yukiyasu, Meiji period, 5in (12.5cm) wide.
$7,000–8,000 *WW*

A Japanese bronze figural group, Meiji period, 18in (45.5cm) high.
$950–1,000 *SK*

Okimono

Okimono are purely ornamental, finely sculptured objects for display and admiration of skill alone. From the 18thC onwards, bronze okimono were made for the tokonoma (display alcove) in the form of insects, reptiles, animals and legendary characters. It was not until the late 19thC that a huge and sudden foreign demand for these ornamental objects saw an increase in the styles and mediums used for okimono, the best often using a mixture of wood, ivory, metal and fine inlay. Those pieces produced during the golden age of okimono (1880–1920) often reflect two cultures, the West in style and influence and the East in technical skill.

A Japanese bronze okimono of an archer, by Seiko, Meiji period, 16in (40.5cm) high.
$4,000–4,500 *S*

A Japanese bronze group, with a tripod vase, figure of a *bijin*, a fan and a dove, on a table-form stand, Meiji period, 17in (43cm) high.
$770–850 *S(S)*

A Chinese gilt-splashed bronze vase, moulded with 2 scrolls, the neck flanked by dragon loop handles, Qing Dynasty, 18thC, 4¾in (12cm) high.
$2,200–2,600 *S(HK)*

A Chinese bronze vase, with 2 animal mask loose ring handles, the body with raised mask and cloud collar designs, the base of the neck with a band of stylised dragons, 19thC, 21½in (54.5cm) high.
$200–225 *SK*

A pair of Japanese silver presentation vases, each with chrysanthemums above a butterfly and lilies, Meiji period, 11¾in (30cm) high.
$3,400–4,000 *Bon*

A Japanese copper vase, carved and decorated with insects among plants and flowers over the band of shaped panels, the neck with cherry blossom on a stream, signed Shob Sei, late 19thC, 7½in (19cm) high.
$1,700–2,200 *C*

A Japanese bronze vase, with bird-shaped handles, moulded and gilded with birds, late Meiji period, 18in (45.5cm) high.
$4,000–4,500 *LHA*

Stone

A Chinese greystone head of Damo, carved bald with a furrowed brow, pronounced eyes, moustache, sideburns and beard, teeth exposed, his ears with distended lobes, Song Dynasty, 10½in (27cm) high.
$3,200–4,000 *C(HK)*

A Chinese hardstone mountain, carved on one side with a bearded sage walking along a mountain path, the reverse carved with a monkey carrying another on his back, 19thC, 7¼in (18.5cm) high, wooden stand.
$6,400–7,200 *CNY*

A pair of Chinese soapstone seal stones, with 20thC mounts, c1850, 8in (20.5cm) high.
$1,300–1,600 *HEY*

Wood

A Chinese export painted wooden tea box, c1830, 12in (30.5cm) wide.
$250–400 *Wai*

A Chinese wooden mirror stand, with a hinged cover pierced and carved with panels of scrolling dragons and foliate motifs, 17thC, 5in (38cm) wide.
$7,500–8,000 *S(NY)*

A Japanese two-piece kiri wood kimono storage chest, c1880, 40in (101.5cm) wide.
$2,400–2,700 *POA*

A Japanese wooden model of a mythical lion dog, by Nobukatsu, late 18thC, 1¾in (4.5cm) high.
$1,300–1,600 *S*

A Japanese lacquered wood and ivory okimono, modelled as a courtesan and a servant, late 19thC, 11½in (29cm) high.
$3,400–4,000 *S(NY)*

A Tibetan carved wooden figure, depicting Nahakala, with lacquer and gilt highlights, 17thC, 20⅝in (52.5cm) high.
$1,700–2,200 *LHA*

l. A Japanese carved boxwood and ivory okimono, depicting a seated man cutting green and stained bamboo, a group of baskets to one side, a cabinet to the other, minor damage, Meiji period, 4in (10cm) high.
$1,200–1,400 *Bea(E)*

A Korean damascened iron and shagreen decorated wood saddle, Choson Dynasty, repaired, 18thC, 18in (45.5cm) long.
$4,000–4,800 *S(NY)*

In the Choson Dynasty, the materials used for making saddles were distinguished by the rank of the rider. Sharkskin (shagreen) was reserved for the high ranking officials, with antlers for the lower ranking officials.

Arms & Armour

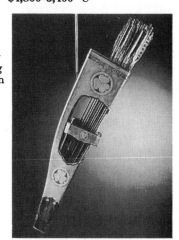

A Korean silver-mounted iron helmet, the 4 panels conjoined with rivets, the front rib mounted with a shaped silver medallion decorated with a leafy floral spray, the lower section set with a band of pins originally for leather or fur ear flaps, the peak pierced at the top, Choson Dynasty, 16th/17thC, 12in (30.5cm) high.
$6,500–7,500 *S(NY)*

A Japanese iron *myochin* helmet bowl, the gilt peak carved with peonies, late 16th/17thC.
$4,800–5,400 *C*

r. A Japanese leather quiver, bow and arrows, the quiver containing 2 removable inner containers with 20 arrows, the bow lacquered black and bound in red lacquered rattan, 19thC, quiver and arrows 35½in (90cm) long.
$6,500–7,500 *S*

A Japanese lacquered helmet, decorated with dragonflies, 19thC.
$4,800–5,400 *C*

A pair of Japanese matchlock guns, decorated in silver and brass with foliate designs, some parts missing, signed, early 19thC, barrels 12in (30.5cm) long.
$6,400–7,200 *S*

A Japanese *katana* blade, possibly 13th/14thC, 27in (69cm) long.
$2,500–3,000 *C*

A Japanese matchlock pistol, the iron barrel decorated with a gold dragon, brass matchlock mechanism, 19thC, barrel 4½in (11.5cm) long.
$3,200–3,600 *GV*

A Japanese *koto katana* blade, ascribed to Kanesada, 16thC, 27½in (69.5cm) long.
$2,800–3,200 *S*

A Japanese *shinto wakizashi* blade, ascribed to Omi (no) Kami Tadatsugu, 18thC, 20¾in (52.5cm) long.
$1,400–1,600 *S*

A Japanese *aikuchi koshirae*, decorated with trailing *kiri* leaves and *karakusa* in Higo Kumagai style, 18thC, 18½in (47cm) long.
$2,500–3,200 *S*

A Japanese *shin-shin to wakizashi*, in a *same* scabbard inlaid with the moon and flowers, late 18thC, blade 16in (40.5cm) long.
$1,400–1,600 *C*

A Japanese *shin-shin to tanto*, in a black lacquer mounting sprinkled with gold, 19thC, blade 8½in (21.5cm) long.
$2,800–3,200 *C*

A Japanese *shakudo kozuka*, attributed to Goto Kenjo, inlaid in silver, copper and gold with a monkey and his trainer, 17thC, 3¾in (9.5cm) long.
$1,500–1,600 *S(NY)*

A Japanese lacquered wood
sword stand for 3 swords,
decorated with chickens and
pheasants in gold and coloured
takamakie, chipped and faded,
19thC, 20½in (52cm) wide.
$2,500–3,000 *S*

A Japanese *nashiji* ground sword
rack, decorated in gold and silver
with cranes, the reverse
decorated with *aoi mon*, some
wear, 19thC, 20in (51cm) wide.
$5,600–6,400 *C*

A Japanese lacquered wood sword
stand, decorated with peonies and
butterflies among rockwork in gold
and silver, 2 hinged side plates for
3 swords, old wear and damage,
19thC, 16¾in (42.5cm) wide.
$3,200–3,600 *C*

Tsuba

An *owari or kyo-sukashi tsuba*,
carved and pierced within the
half-pipe rim, late Muromachi
period, 16thC, 2⅞in (7.5cm) diam.
$1,200–1,300 *S*

An iron *tsuba*, the plate pierced
and decorated in brass, the
ground with vine leaves,
17thC, 3¼in (8.5cm) wide.
$4,800–5,400 *C*

An iron *mokume tsuba*, signed
'Kuminaga', probably 18thC,
3in (7.5cm) wide.
$560–640 *POA*

An *akasaka tsuba*, carved and
pierced with birds, within a
slightly rounded rim, mid-Edo
period, 18thC, 3in (7.5cm) diam.
$1,400–1,500 *S*

A *shakudo tsuba*, by Akiyoshi,
the rim inlaid with cherry
blossoms and petals in gold and
silver, signed, Edo period, 19thC,
3in (7.5cm) wide, with a box.
$2,500–2,800 *S*

An iron *tsuba*, by Otaka
Masateru, decorated with figures
beneath a pine tree, details in
copper, silver, *shakudo* and gold
nunome, signed, late Edo period,
19thC, 3in (7.5cm) wide.
$350–400 *Bon*

A *shakudo ishimeji tsuba*,
pierced with 3 gold and
silver *mon*, 19thC,
2½in (6.5cm) wide.
$480–540 *POA*

An iron *tsuba*, decorated with
peonies and a *karashishi* in
iron, silver and gilt, 19thC,
3in (8cm) wide.
$1,100–1,200 *C*

A gilt-copper *tsuba*, in the form
of 4 open fans, carved in relief,
Meiji period, late 19th/early
20thC, 2¾in (7cm) wide.
$1,900–2,200 *S*

Furniture

A Chinese hardwood four-poster canopy bed, with applied bone figural decoration and overall bat and peach blossom motifs, 19thC, 81in (206cm) long.
$2,200–2,700 *CSK*

A Chinese bamboo bookcase, with latticework back and sides, Shanxi Province, 18th/19thC, 24in (62cm) wide.
$5,600–6,400 *S(NY)*

A Japanese cabinet, decorated in shades of gilt with figures, birds and houses in garden landscapes, with elaborate brass hinges, the 2 front doors enclosing 11 small drawers, 18thC, 37¼in (94.5cm) wide.
$1,200–1,500 *P(S)*

A Chinese hardwood cabinet, early 19thC, 40½in (103cm) wide.
$950–1,100 *SLN*

A Chinese table cosmetic cabinet, the hinged cover opening to an arrangement of short drawers, the exterior with bright metal mounts, 18thC, 14¼in (37cm) wide.
$4,500–5,500 *S(NY)*

Table cosmetic cabinets generally have a flat or domed hinged cover which opens to a recessed area designed to accommodate a hinged mirror stand. The front contains a pair of doors which open to an arrangement of short drawers.

A Japanese hardwood, mother-of-pearl and bone inlaid and gilt-embellished stage cabinet, the frieze fitted with 2 sliding doors above open shelves, centred by a fenced temple, a shelf below fitted with 2 short drawers above a single long drawer and flanked by a pair of panelled cupboard doors, late 19th/early 20thC, 51in (130cm) wide.
$4,800–5,400 *C(Sc)*

A Japanese export black lacquer coffer, decorated in mother-of-pearl and gilt with trailing flowers and grasses issuing from rockwork, gilt-bronze carrying handles, foliate hinged clasp and lockplate, 18thC, 24in (61cm) wide, on a black lacquered wooden stand.
$850–1,000 *CSK*

l. A pair of Chinese horseshoe-shaped back chairs, each splat carved with a central cloud form medallion, restored, 18th/19thC.
$2,500–2,800 *SK*

r. A pair of Chinese black lacquer armchairs, each with a scrolled crest-rail with a bowed, panelled splat and panelled seat, Shanxi Province, 18thC.
$2,800–3,200 *S(NY)*

A Chinese mandarin chair, 17thC.
$1,200–1,300 *AWH*

A Chinese coromandel screen, the 12 leaves forming a continuous scene with pavilions, trees, figures and animals within a fenced garden, the border panelled with fantastic animals, birds, flowers and utensils, late 17thC, 108in (274.5cm) high.
$13,000–14,500 *DN*

A pair of Chinese crimson lacquer hexagonal stands, decorated in gilt, c1900, 38in (96cm) high.
$1,000–1,200 *S(S)*

A Japanese black lacquered temple table, with gold floral design, incised foliate scrolling on metal mounts, restored, 17th/18thC, 36in (91.5cm) wide.
$2,500–2,800 *SK*

A Chinese table, top damaged, late 19thC, 21in (53.5cm) wide.
$800–900 *CAT*

A Chinese two-fold screen, mounted with a bas-relief design of birds amongst flowering branches carved with ivory, bone, wood and mother-of-pearl, on black lacquer, within a carved frame of dragons, late 19thC, 73in (185.5cm) high.
$1,000–1,200 *RBB*

A Chinese polychrome hardwood altar stand, with pierced foliate carved apron, the foliate carved backplate over 3 graduated shelves above a drawer, 18thC, 52in (132cm) high.
$1,300–1,500 *SLN*

A Japanese lacquered table, c1900, 23½in (60cm) diam.
$320–400 *TAR*

A Japanese six-panel screen, depicting the 4 seasons, each panel painted with figures contemplating a landscape, ink and colour on silk, Meiji period, 19thC, 38¾in (98.5cm) high.
$2,500–3,200 *SK*

A pair of Chinese garden stools, 17thC, 18in (45.5cm) high.
$7,200–8,000 *C(NY)*

A pair of Chinese tables, with panelled tops and stylised scroll pierced friezes, on moulded straight legs with stretchers, 19thC, 15½in (39.5cm) wide.
$600–700 *DN*

> **Miller's is a price GUIDE not a price LIST**

A Chinese export black lacquered and gilt work table, the interior fitted with compartments and removable trays above a well, mid-19thC, 25½in (65cm) wide.
$2,000–2,400 *S(S)*

Inro

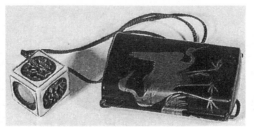

A Japanese black lacquer four-case inro, gilt decorated with 3 storks with pewter tail feathers, 19thC, 2¾in (7cm) high, and a carved and pierced ivory cube-shaped netsuke.
$350–400 *CDC*

A brown lacquer five-case inro, decorated in gold and coloured *takamakie*, with monkeys perched on a tree branch, cracked, 19thC, 3½in (9cm) long.
$680–740 *S(Am)*

A four-case brown lacquer inro, decorated in gold and inlaid with mother-of-pearl with 3 *karako* carrying another, the reverse with musical instruments, 19thC, 3½in (9cm) long.
$2,500–3,000 *C*

Inro

Inro are multi-compartmental medicine or seal containers, carried suspended from the sash of a kimono. Usually made of lacquered wood, they display the full range of lacquer techniques and are almost a form of functional jewellery.

A gold lacquer three-case inro, decorated with a wasp on a plant, 19thC, 2½in (6.5cm) long.
$1,600–1,800 *S*

A black lacquered four-case inro, by Kajikawa Hidetaka, decorated with a cockerel and chicks by a large water ladle, late 18thC, 3in (7.5cm) long.
$3,200–3,500 *S*

A cherry-bark three-case inro, inlaid in ivory, horn and mother-of-pearl with various fish, 19thC, 3¼in (8cm) long.
$1,900–2,400 *C*

A lacquer three-case inro, decorated with quails under bushes, damaged, 19thC, 3in (7.5cm) long.
$950–1,100 *SK*

A gold lacquer five-case inro, decorated with flowering prunus and rockwork, 19thC, 3¾in (9.5cm) long, and a netsuke of Hotei.
$2,200–2,400 *S(Am)*

Netsuke

A wooden netsuke of Jurojin and a deer, signed Shoko, 19thC, 1¾in (4.5cm) wide.
$1,600–1,800 *C*

A wooden netsuke, depicting the priest Kensu, gaping at a prawn in one hand, the eyes inlaid in dark horn, prawn chipped, 19thC, 2in (5cm) high.
$1,600–1,800 *C*

A stag antler netsuke, carved as an insect-eaten lotus leaf, an iron and gilt spotted frog perched in the leaf's hollow centre, 19thC, 4in (10cm) diam.
$900–1,000 *S(NY)*

Snuff Bottles

A soapstone snuff bottle, carved with 2 archaistic dragons in pursuit of a flaming pearl, the reverse with bats and clouds, early 18thC, 2¾in (6.5cm) high.
$680–800 *S(NY)*

A red single overlay glass snuff bottle, carved to the snowflake ground with 2 *chilong* chasing a flaming pearl on one side, the reverse with a further *chilong*, small chips, Qianlong period, 2¼in (5.5cm) high.
$450–550 *S(NY)*

Chilong are mythical dragon type lizards.

A jasper bottle, depicting an ochre monkey chasing a butterfly with a stick, small chip, late 18thC, 2¾in (6.5cm) high.
$4,500–5,000 *S*

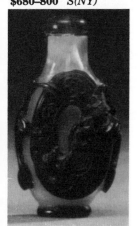

A double overlay glass snuff bottle, carved with stylised discs, and a pair of glass *chilong*, chipped, Qing Dynasty, 2⅛in (6.5cm) high.
$2,200–2,700 *S*

A faceted red glass snuff bottle, carved with shaped polygonal facets, Qing Dynasty, 2¾in (7cm) high.
$850–1,000 *S*

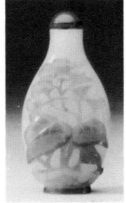

A multi-overlay semi-opaque white glass snuff bottle, carved with a begonia and rockwork, and a praying mantis on pea pods, foot chipped, late 18thC/early 19thC, 2⅛in (6.5cm) high.
$1,500–1,600 *CNY*

An enamelled snuff bottle, painted on a blue ground in bright enamels with a magpie perched on a blossoming prunus tree, Daoguang period, 3¼in (8cm) high.
$1,000–1,200 *S(NY)*

A coral snuff bottle, in the form of a tree trunk, carved in relief with a bird in a tree and a bear underneath, 19thC, 2¼in (5.5cm) high.
$1,400–1,600 *S(NY)*

A carved jade snuff bottle, the vessel well hollowed and carved in low relief overall with a fruiting double gourd vine, Qing Dynasty, 19thC, 2⅛in (5.5cm) high.
$2,400–2,700 *S*

Cross Reference
Colour Review

A Chinese glass overlay snuff bottle, with blue incense burner decoration cut to clear glass, 19thC, 3in (7.5cm) high.
$270–320 *LHA*

An inside-painted glass snuff bottle, by Ye Zhongsan, with a continuous scene of boys dressed in bright colours, playing in a tree-lined field, signed and dated, 1914, 2¼in (6cm) high.
$1,600–1,900 *S(NY)*

Robes

A Chinese dragon robe, of chestnut-brown silk gauze worked with 9 dragons chasing flaming pearls, in couched metal thread amidst cloud bands above a deep sea wave border, Qing Dynasty, 19thC.
$850–1,000 *Bon(C)*

A Chinese silk priest's robe, with 7 gold couched dragons in shaped cartouches, the reverse with a Buddha on a lotus throne, the base bordered with dragons and phoenix, the neck with floral roundels, 19thC, 51in (129.5cm) long.
$1,300–1,500 *SK*

A Chinese semi-formal robe, the pale brown satin embroidered in coloured silks and couched gilt-metal threads, with cicada among scrolling stems of lotus and peach sprigs, over a sea wave border, lined in blue silk damask, 19thC.
$140–160 *CSK*

A Chinese couched and embroidered silk robe, with 8 dragons surrounded by double fish, symbols and clouds, 19thC.
$5,000–6,000 *SK*

This robe is inscribed on the interior '1868 Gift of Chin Hsuen-Pin'.

A Chinese aubergine silk jacket, embroidered with flower-filled baskets, the borders with figures, 19thC, 38in (96.5cm) long.
$800–900 *S(NY)*

A Chinese informal robe, the lilac silk damask trimmed with a cutwork collar and woven ribbons, late 19thC.
$640–720 *CSK*

A Chinese lady's informal robe, the pale green silk woven with prunus and butterflies, late 19thC.
$720–800 *CSK*

A Chinese informal quilted jacket, the sky blue silk damask woven with bats and other emblems, trimmed with embroidered ivory satin bands with ladies flying kites, c1900.
$580–640 *CSK*

A Chinese informal robe, the mauve satin embroidered with pheasants, crickets and flowers, trimmed with ivory satin sleevebands, collar and hem embroidered with blue and white, c1900.
$520–580 *CSK*

Textiles

A Chinese brocade canopy, the sienna ground woven in yellow with a central lotus wheel enclosed by the 8 Buddhist symbols on scrolling lotus, Ming Dynasty, 16thC, 70in (178cm) square.
$3,500–4,000 *S(NY)*

A Japanese ivory satin coverlet, embroidered with a central tree peony, pheasant and other birds, 19thC, 110 x 71in (280 x 180cm).
$720–800 *CSK*

A Korean embroidered silk badge, made for a civil official of first to third rank, with a pair of white cranes above foaming waves and rockwork, worked in shades of blue, green, white and purple on a green silk ground, Choson Dynasty, late 19thC, 9½ x 8¼in (24 x 21cm).
$1,400–1,600 *S(NY)*

ISLAMIC

Islamic art is a general term for an enormous range of artefacts produced over more than 1,300 years and from any country where Islam is the dominant faith. In practice this has meant the Arab world, India, Iran and Turkey, but works of art from such other Muslim areas as Malaysia and China are also becoming sought after by collectors. Applied arts are perhaps most numerous, with all types of ceramics, metalwork, carved ivory, woodwork, hardstones, textiles and carpets readily available on the market. However, the more esoteric arts of the book – calligraphy, Qur'ans and illuminated manuscripts and miniatures – have always played an important part in Muslim cultural life and no collection would be complete without examples of them. Prices range from $160 to hundreds of thousands of dollars.

The Islamic art market has been fairly steady in the past twelve months, with excellent prices achieved for top quality items, especially for fine ceramics, manuscripts and arms and armour. There has been a steady increase in the prices paid for Iznik pottery in particular, although the market has still not recovered the levels of the late 1980s. Sixteenth century Iznik vessels in good condition are now realising between $16,000–130,000 at auction. As a result, more Iznik pottery is coming onto the market, and 17th century and repaired pieces can be found from $400–8,000.

The appearance on the market of a number of intact early 13th century Kashan lustred fritware bowls has also stimulated prices, and these items achieve between $16,000–82,000 at auction. However, Islamic medieval pottery generally remains inexpensive, and repaired items of Persian and Syrian pottery can still be bought for a few hundred dollars. The same is true of medieval metalwork: Iranian and Egyptian or Syrian lampstands, oil lamps, boxes and bowls of the 11th–15th centuries can be readily found in the $800–8,000 range, but the best engraved and inlaid pieces achieve prices in the range of $11,000–115,000.

Prices of 19th century Iranian art continue to be firm, with Qajar oil paintings and fine manuscripts making very good prices at auction, although lacquer pen boxes, once highly valued, can now be bought for a few hundred dollars. Other undervalued items include mould-blown glass, both of the early period (10th to 13th centuries) and later pieces from India and Iran; early cut glass remains more highly priced. Indian miniatures also remain modestly priced, particularly those of the 18th and 19th centuries, which continue to appear on the market in great quantities.

Deborah Freeman

A post-Sassanian turquoise glazed storage jar, the 4 handles linking the shoulder and neck, repaired small hole to body, Persia, circa 8th century, 19¼in (49cm) high.
$3,200–3,600 *C*

An Abbasid lustre bowl, the interior painted with a golden lustre ground around 3 roundels each containing the figure of a bird, the exterior with dot and dash motifs around 3 concentric circles, restored, Mesopotamia, 9th century, 4½in (11.5cm) diam.
$3,200–4,000 *C*

A Kashan turquoise glazed tapering oviform vase, with 3 lug handles and slightly everted rim, damage to rim, 14thC, 8½in (21.5cm) high.
$250–300 *CSK*

l. An Iznik pottery dish, painted in underglaze cobalt blue, green and relief red with black outline, with carnations surrounded by 2 leaves forming an inverted arch flanked by tulips, Turkey, c1580, 12in (30.5cm) diam.
$9,000–10,000 *S*

r. An Iznik pottery dish, painted in underglaze cobalt blue, relief red and green with black outline, with a geometric design, Turkey, c1600, 13in (33cm) diam.
$6,400–7,200 *S*

An Iznik pottery dish, the white interior painted in green, blue, black and red with tulip, carnation and hyacinth blooms, rim chips, Ottoman Turkey, c1600, 10½in (26.5cm) diam.
$3,200–3,600 *C*

An Iznik pottery tile, the white ground painted with an octafoil red central medallion, surrounded by 8 inverted blue palmettes divided by green leaves, in a wooden frame, Ottoman Turkey, c1620, 9¾in (25cm) square.
$1,600–1,800 *C*

An Iznik pottery dish, the white interior painted in red, blue, green and black with rose, hyacinth and *saz* leaf border, with simple floral motifs, exterior similar, rim chips, Ottoman Turkey, c1640, 8in (20cm) diam.
$1,300–1,500 *C*

A Safavid blue and white soft paste porcelain ewer, the body with a band of drop-shaped cartouches containing floral sprays, the spout scattered with linear floral motifs, probably Kirman, south east Persia, late 17thC, 7½in (19cm) high.
$8,500–10,500 *C*

An Iznik pottery dish, painted with stylised flowers around a large central figure of a peacock, the underside with simple blue motifs, rim chips, Ottoman Turkey, c1650, 9¾in (25cm) diam.
$7,000–8,000 *C*

A Persian blue and cream *huqqa* base, painted with bands of stylised stiff leaves and flowering grasses, c1700, 8½in (21.5cm) high.
$450–520 *CSK*

A huqqa is a hubble-bubble pipe.

l. A Kütahya pottery covered bowl, the cover with a pear-shaped finial, painted in cobalt, with swirling sprays and floral motifs, Turkey, mid-18thC, 9¼in (23.5cm) diam.
$11,500–12,500 *S*

A Qallaline pottery tile panel, comprising 45 tiles, decorated in blue, green, yellow and purple, with a mosque within an arch supported on 2 columns, another mosque above with 4 corner towers, with a border of black rectangular tiles, Tunisia, 18thC, 32¾in (83cm) high mounted.
$6,400–7,200 *S*

A Kütahya pottery dish, painted in cobalt blue, yellow, green, manganese purple and red, with a long-haired courtesan dressed in a long kaftan, striped pantaloons and a floppy hat, holding a spray of flowers, flanked by larger sprays, Turkey, mid-18thC, 6¼in (16cm) diam.
$11,000–12,000 *S*

A Persian blue and black glaze Qajar bottle, decorated with flowerheads and scrolling vines, base slightly ground, c1800, 11in (28cm) high.
$550–700 *SK*

A pale green glass flask, cut with 3 rows of slightly concave oval medallions, Persia, 7th/8th century, 4½in (11cm) high.
$17,000–18,500 *S*

A Safavid engraved brass magic bowl, extensively engraved with signs of the zodiac and magic script, all contained within cartouches, one small repair, Persia, c1645, 8¾in (22cm) diam.
$1,600–1,900 *C*

A magic bowl is used for mixing medicines. The astrological, Koranic inscriptions and lucky numbers are intended to convey good luck.

A gilded copper jug and cover, the body with deep-cut swirling flutes below a plain band with inscription, considerable loss of gilding, Ottoman Turkey, 18thC, 14½in (37cm) high.
$17,000–18,500 *C*

Turkish items such as this are currently very popular.

A post-Sassanian bronze ewer, the S-shaped handle with palmette thumbpiece and stylised animal-head terminal, strong blue patination, Persia or Mesopotamia, 7th/8th century, 11¾in (30cm) high.
$14,000–15,500 *C*

This ewer has a beautiful and unusual blue patination and, therefore, realised well in excess of its estimate at auction.

A pair of gold *zarfs*, engraved and pierced with scrolling interlaced serrated leaves and stems rising from a band of radiating leaves, Ottoman Turkey, late 19thC, 2in (5cm) high.
$2,800–3,200 *C*

Zarfs are receptacles to hold porcelain coffee cups.

A gold-mounted banded agate inkwell, the hinged lid domed with a pointed knop, the interior with gold collar and stopper, with openwork handle, probably Turkey, 19thC, 2¼in (6cm) high.
$3,200–3,600 *Bon*

A Timurid gold and silver inlaid brass jug, the handle with upper dragon-head terminal, the body with a band of inlaid scrolling vine around inscription cartouches with Persian verses alternating with arabesque medallions, handle probably associated, Persia, late 15thC, 5in (12.5cm) high.
$10,500–11,500 *C*

A copper-gilt bowl and cover, decorated with floral swags, the domed lid with an acorn finial, Turkey, c1800, 6¾in (7.5cm) high.
$7,500–8,500 *S*

A Qajar papier mâché pen box, decorated with a courtesan in a landscape, the sides with portrait roundels and hunting scenes, some restoration, mid-19thC, 8¾in (22cm) long.
$240–300 *DN*

A pair of eastern Mediterranean gold earrings, each in the form of a camel, decorated with granulation, circa 8th century, 32mm wide.
$5,600–6,400 *S*

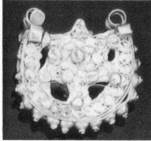

A Fatimid gold earring, the centre formed of a six-pointed star, the surface on both sides decorated with wire-work twists and with applied beading, Egypt or Syria, 12thC, 31mm wide.
$1,200–1,400 *C*

A gold eight-pointed star, of box construction, probably from a necklace, with granulated decoration around 4 inset stones, the central turquoise only remaining, probably 12thC, 27mm wide.
$1,300–1,600 *C*

A Qajar enamelled gold pendant of Fath 'Ali Shah, wearing a red robe and kneeling on a carpet, a curtained opening visible behind, on associated gold chain, Persia, c1830, 22mm diam.
$5,000–6,000 *C*

A Qajar enamelled gold medallion, decorated in polychrome enamel with a cockerel amidst a spray of flowers and foliage including roses, fringed with a row of pearls, modern gold clasp, Persia, mid-19thC, 52mm diam.
$13,000–14,500 *S*

A Qajar enamelled gold Qur'an case, a star-shaped medallion of calligraphy on the lid, decorated with polychrome enamelled birds and roses, a sunburst with human face on the underside, Persia, 19thC, 45mm diam.
$4,000–4,500 *S*

r. An Ottoman embroidered wrapping cloth, the linen gauze ground worked in silk couched stitch, ground mainly replaced, mounted, 17thC, 58in (147cm) wide.
$11,000–12,000 *S*

A painted parcel-gilt wood turban stand, the back carved with 2 pairs of columns flanking a vase of flowers below a foliate arch, painted on a green ground, the carving gilded and with polychrome details, Turkey, 19thC, 35in (89cm) high.
$4,000–4,500 *S*

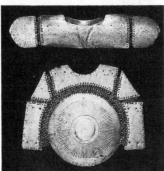

A steel chest plate, composed of a circular convex plate decorated with radiating flutes, 5 plaques attached with lengths of mail, and a gorget, with a pair of epaulettes attached with mail, Turkey, 16thC, 17in (43cm) diam.
$2,000–2,500 *S*

An Ottoman barber's apron, the wool ground worked in silk chain stitch and flat silver metal thread strip, Istanbul, Turkey, 18thC, 83in (211cm) long.
$17,000–18,500 *S*

This apron would have formed part of a set of matching embroideries, including a cloth to drape over the back and several hand towels, called the tras takim, *used for the shaving ritual of the Sultan, or those who followed his example.*

An Ottoman sword, the blade inscribed in the name of Sultan Sulayman the Magnificent, the spine with inlaid gold inscriptions, associated steel sheath with steel fittings, originally cloth-covered, some loss of gold decoration and inlay, Turkey, Sultan Sulayman Period, 1522–66, 33¼in (85cm) long.
$5,000–5,600 *C*

ARCHITECTURAL ANTIQUES

Brass

A brass air vent, c1930, 9in (23cm) wide.
$100–110 *DRU*

l. An Indian brass jardinière, with a lobed bowl on a knopped stand, with foliate decoration, the base pierced and chased with foliage, 19thC, 63in (160cm) high.
$1,100–1,300 *S(S)*

A pair of brass air vents, c1875, 6in (15cm) high.
$200–225 *DRU*

Iron

A pair of cast iron gatepost finials, 19thC, 24in (61cm) high.
$1,900–2,300 *SUF*

A Victorian cast iron jardinière, 26in (66cm) wide.
$370–440 *DOR*

A Regency wrought iron garden seat, decorated with reeding, the seat bars with hourglass shaping, 61½in (156cm) wide.
$550–650 *LAY*

A French decorated cast iron radiator, early 20thC, 32in (81.5cm) high.
$700–800 *POSH*

A French cast iron radiator, c1920, 38in (96.5cm) high.
$1,400–1,600 *POSH*

A cast iron gas radiator, from Chilham Castle, early 20thC, 41in (104cm) high.
$700–800 *POSH*

r. A Regency wrought iron garden seat, with white painted rails, slatted seat, on paw feet, 59in (150cm) wide.
$1,100–1,300 *WL*

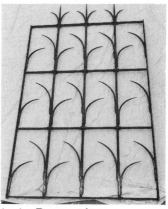

An Art Deco cast iron railing panel, c1930, 77in (195.5cm) high.
$100–115 *RECL*

A Victorian Gothic style cast
iron bench, 48in (122cm) wide.
$850–950 *GAZE*

A Coalbrookdale cast iron bench,
with Fern and Blackberry pattern,
c1894, 42½in (108cm) wide.
$1,700–2,200 *DRU*

A cast iron bench, the wooden
slatted seat and overscrolled back
on 2 supports, the end supports
cast with scrolling foliage, late
19thC, 74in (188cm) wide.
$1,000–1,150 *P*

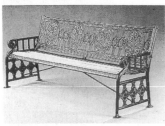

A Coalbrookdale cast iron seat,
with wooden slatted seat, the
back with oval panels of flowering
plants flanked by paterae,
overscrolled arms, registration
stamp for 5th May 1883,
75in (190.5cm) wide.
$1,400–1,600 *S(S)*

r. A Victorian cast iron three-
cornered umbrella stand, based on a
Coalbrookdale design, the front panel
decorated with entwined ferns, on a
stepped plinth and with scrolling
bracket feet, 23¼in (59cm) high.
$320–400 *P*

A Shaker cast iron stove, the front
fitted with hinged door and
locking device, with moulded
convex hearth below, on tapering
legs, 19thC, 30in (76cm) wide.
$2,000–2,400 *S(NY)*

l. A Victorian painted cast iron
slatted plant stand, with scrollwork frieze, 56¼in (143cm) high.
$950–1,150 *P*

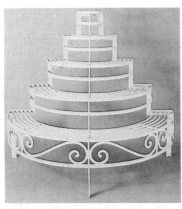

A pair of cast iron urns, raised on
baluster stems, with foliate
decorated circular and hexagonal
plinths, 19thC, 38½in (98cm) high.
$4,400–4,800 *P*

A pair of cast iron urns, the
shallow fluted bowls with
gadrooned borders, raised on flared
feet with stepped square plinths,
19thC, 42½in (108cm) high.
$2,200–2,700 *P*

A Victorian cast iron vase,
with scroll handles, on a metal
base, 33in (84cm) high.
$700–800 *GAZE*

A bell, on original headstock and
with cast iron clapper, dated
'1842', 21in (53.5cm) high.
$800–1,000 *DOR*

Lead

A Georgian lead cistern, the panelled front cast with initials 'WIF', dated '1773', flanked by figures in classical dress, 35in (83cm) wide.
$9,000–10,000 *S(S)*

A lead cistern, with panelled front depicting a domestic scene, 19thC, 25in (63.5cm) wide.
$450–520 *GAZE*

A lead birdbath, modelled as a child holding a bowl, with a bird on the side, c1860, 28in (71cm) high.
$3,500–4,300 *DRU*

r. A lead figure, of a winged angel holding a torch, 19thC, 55in (140cm) high.
$850–950 *GAZE*

r. A lead figural fountain of a mermaid, by Wheeler Williams, dated '1939', 62in (157.5cm) high, with a lead basin.
$3,500–4,000 *S(NY)*

A lead two-tier garden fountain, decorated with 3 putti, on a dolphin triform base, 19thC, 33in (84cm) high.
$1,600–1,800 *GAZE*

A lead figure, depicting a farmer, c1938, 43in (109cm) high.
$1,600–1,800 *DRU*

l. A French lead group, depicting Commerce, the man seated on a rocky outcrop, with a boat, an anchor and a wheel, 19thC, 20in (51cm) wide.
$950–1,000 *S(S)*

A lead urn, the body moulded with a frieze of classical figures beneath a fruiting vine frieze, swan handles, domed lid with finial, late 19thC, 30in (76cm) high.
$1,400–1,600 *S(S)*

A pair of lead planters, with lion mask decoration, late 18thC, 20in (51cm) high.
$850–950 *GAZE*

l. A lead fountain, the bowl mounted with a seated frog, on a square column, the base decorated with foliage, flowerheads and rope twist borders, early 20thC, 38in (96.5cm) high.
$6,000–6,500 *S(S)*

A lead planter, moulded in relief with fruiting vines and snails, early 20thC, 18in (45.5cm) wide.
$1,000–1,150 *S(S)*

Marble

A marble Roman style double basin, carved with a roundel and central cross, framed within foliage borders, c1900, 42in (107cm) wide.
$3,500–4,000 *S(NY)*

An Italian white marble bowl-on-stand, the inside carved with fluted decoration centred with a dragon and with egg-and-dart moulded rim, above loop and flowerhead handles, late 19thC, 31½in (80cm) wide.
$2,000–2,200 *S(S)*

An Italian marble carving of a young girl, by Pietro Negro, signed and dated 'Milan 1873', 34½in (87.5cm) high.
$10,500–11,500 *LAY*

A white marble bust of Piety, by William Frederick Woodington, the young girl with long flowing hair and wearing a shift, inscribed and dated '1870', 18in (45.5cm) high.
$1,500–1,900 *S(S)*

A white marble portrait bust of a lady, wearing a low-cut dress with puffed sleeves, on a shaped socle carved with trailing foliage, c1880, 28in (71cm) high.
$3,200–4,000 *S(S)*

r. A white marble figure of a young boy, seated cross-legged and holding a bird, a bird's nest at his feet, late 19thC, 26in (66cm) high.
$1,700–2,200 *S(S)*

A pair of white marble urns, the bodies with gadrooned sections, on turned socles and square plinths, 19thC, 30in (76cm) high.
$7,200–8,800 *S*

Pottery

A French glazed stoneware bust, of a Neapolitan fisher boy, after Jean Baptiste Corpeaux, 19thC, 29½in (75cm) high.
$480–540 *GAK*

A pair of Compton pottery jardinières, with moulded lobed sides and everted rim, early 20thC, 13½in (34.5cm) high.
$1,100–1,300 *S(S)*

l. A French glazed pottery water filter, c1880, 24in (61cm) high.
$140–160 *DOR*

Stone

A carved stone model of a reclining lion, on a rectangular base, 19thC, 45in (114.5cm) wide.
$3,500–4,000 *S(S)*

A pair of stone jardinières, decorated on all sides with allegorical panels, damaged and restored, c1900, 15½in (39.5cm) high.
$2,800–3,500 *S(NY)*

A pair of staddle stones, 18thC, 36in (91.5cm) high.
$720–800 *DRU*

A pair of sandstone urns, with pineapple finials, swag-carved faceted tapered bodies on rising leaf-carved feet, 19thC, 49in (125cm) high.
$1,400–1,600 *P(NW)*

A weathered limestone rustic garden bench, c1930, 45in (114.5cm) wide.
$175–225 *RECL*

A pair of limestone door or window pediments, c1900, 44in (112cm) wide.
$1,400–1,600 *RECL*

A stone trough, mid-19thC, 34in (86.5cm) wide.
$720–880 *DOR*

A composition stone gargoyle, 19thC, 27in (68.5cm) high.
$480–530 *GAZE*

A set of Cotswold stone spiral barn steps, mid-19thC, 55in (140cm) high.
$2,400–2,700 *RECL*

A composition stone birdbath, with baluster support, 19thC, 43in (109cm) high.
$130–150 *GAZE*

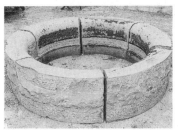

A late Victorian York stone pond, 69in (175.5cm) diam.
$1,600–1,900 *RECL*

Bathroom Fittings

A zinc collared bath, early
19thC, 57in (145cm) long.
$480–640 *DOR*

A slipper bath, c1850, 50in (127cm) long.
$720–800 *POSH*

*The slipper, or boot, bath allowed the occupant to
bathe in warmth and privacy. It is filled by means
of a small funnel at the front and emptied through
a draincock at the bottom.*

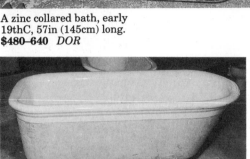

A late Victorian glazed earthenware
bath, 66in (167.5cm) long.
$1,900–2,400 *WRe*

A copper bath, c1890, 65in (165cm) long.
$6,500–8,000 *DRU*

> **Miller's is a price GUIDE
> not a price LIST**

r. A hip bath, c1880,
42in (107cm) long.
$280–320 *POSH*

An enamelled cast iron sitz
bath, c1910, 43in (109cm) long.
$1,000–1,150 *DOR*

A Shanks canopy bath with
shower, in original condition,
c1900, 78in (198cm) long.
$2,200–2,400 *POSH*

An Edwardian roll-top bath,
with soap dish and plunger,
84in (213.5cm) long.
$1,900–2,400 *WRe*

A French cast iron sitz bath,
with tapering legs, 1930s,
41in (104cm) long.
$400–500 *DOR*

A cast iron bath, with swivelling taps, integral soap
dishes and bowl, 1920s, 66in (168cm) long.
$1,900–2,100 *DOR*

A skirted roll-top enamelled cast iron bath, 1930s,
72in (183cm) long.
$1,600–1,900 *WRe*

A blue and white washbasin, the interior decorated with an urn and a landscape, the border with flowers and leaves, c1830, 9½in (24cm) high.
$575–675 *DRU*

A Victorian 'thunder box' lavatory bowl, the interior decorated with flowers, 17in (43cm) diam.
$400–500 *WRe*

A Twyford's washbasin and pedestal, with fittings, 1930s, 22in (56cm) wide.
$400–500 *WRe*

A hairdresser's washbasin, 1930s, 21in (53.5cm) wide.
$480–560 *WRe*

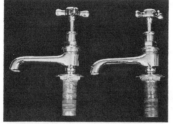

A Victorian pair of nickel-plated long reach bath taps, by Alex Ritchie & Co, London, c1900, 5½in (14cm) wide.
$240–320 *DOR*

A pair of nickel-plated globe taps, with ceramic tops, c1910, 6in (15cm) high.
$160–180 *DOR*

A pair of brass hot and cold water taps, 1920s, 6in (15cm) high.
$70–80 *LIB*

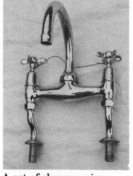

A set of chrome mixer taps, 1920–30, 12in (30.5cm) high.
$350–400 *DRU*

r. A set of brass bath mixer taps, c1930, 6in (15cm) wide.
$160–200 *HEM*

Two nickel taps, 1930s, 4in (10cm) wide.
$15–20 each *LIB*

A pair of brass pillar taps, c1930, 11in (28cm) high.
$200–250 *HEM*

A Shanks cast iron high level two-gallon cistern, c1890, 19in (48.5cm) wide.
$140–160 *DOR*

A Victorian blue and white urinal, decorated with flowers, c1890, 11½in (29cm) high.
$1,100–1,200 *DRU*

A white lavatory pan, 1930s, 16in (40.5cm) high.
$280–320 *WRe*

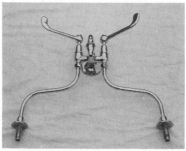

A set of chrome mixer taps, c1930, 16in (40.5cm) high.
$480–560 *DRU*

A Shanks combination washdown lavatory, with mahogany seat and cistern cover, c1894, 24in (61cm) wide.
$2,800–3,200 *POSH*

A Twyfords Zone lavatory pan, decorated with brown leaf patterns, c1910, 15½in (39.5cm) high.
$720–800 *POSH*

A white bidet, 1930s, 15in (38cm) high.
$350–400 *POSH*

r. A chromium-plated combination towel rail and radiator, c1950, 37in (94cm) wide.
$200–250 *DOR*

A shower head, with pull tap and chain, c1950, 18in (45.5cm) high.
$200–250 *HEM*

A Victorian white lavatory pan, 15in (38cm) wide.
$400–500 *WRe*

A vitrified salt-glazed fire clay lavatory pan, entitled 'The Vitrifyde', c1920, 16in (40.5cm) high.
$720–800 *POSH*

Bricks & Tiles

A quantity of handmade bricks, 18thC.
$70 per 100   *WEL*

A quantity of curved Victorian yellow stock bricks, 9 x 4in (23 x 10cm).
$1.50–3 each   *RECL*

A quantity of Victorian slate floor tiles, 10in (25.5cm) wide.
$65–80 per sq yd   *RECL*

r. A set of 4 late Victorian encaustic floor tiles, 8in (20cm) square.
$13–15   *RECL*

A quantity of black and red quarry tiles, c1890, 6in (15cm) wide.
$65–80 per sq yd   *DOR*

Chimney Pots

A Georgian panelled chimney pot, 23in (58cm) high.
$100–130   *DOR*

l. A crown chimney pot, c1860, 30in (76cm) high.
$100–130   *DOR*

A Victorian chimney pot, embossed 'R. Spencer, Sturminster Newton', 22in (56cm) high.
$140–160   *DOR*

A Victorian terracotta chimney pot, unglazed, 24½in (62cm) high.
$55–65   *ACA*

Doors & Door Furniture

A pine plank and
ledge door, c1800,
67in (170cm) high.
$140–160 *DOR*

An oak four-panelled
door, 19thC,
79½in (202cm) high.
$400–500 *WEL*

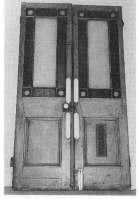

A pair of Bristol star
glazed painted pine
doors, c1850,
82in (208cm) high.
$650–800 *DOR*

A Victorian pine
four-panelled door,
80in (203cm) high.
$95–115 *DOR*

r. A pair of Art
Deco brass pull
handles, and a
pair of matching
push plates, 14in
(35.5cm) high.
$200–250 *HEM*

l. A pair of brass
door knobs, c1920,
2in (5cm) diam.
$55–70 *HEM*

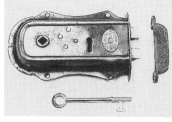

A silvered cast iron door
knocker, 17thC,
9in (23cm) wide.
$880–960 *DOR*

An Art Nouveau brass
door handle and finger
plate, cast in relief with
flora and curving tendrils,
c1900, 21in (53.5cm) high.
$600–650 *P*

l. A rimlock,
key and keep,
c1895, 6½in
(16.5cm) wide.
$100–120 *HEM*

A pair of brass finger plates, c1880, 11in (28cm) high.
$140–160 *DRU*

Fireplaces

A Regency steel and brass D-shaped fender, the pierced frieze cast with stylised elongated anthemions, the plinth applied with a band of similar stylised anthemions, 52½in (133.5cm) wide.
$600–650 *C(S)*

An Art Nouveau brass fender, c1899, 55in (140cm) wide.
$480–520 *DRU*

A Wealden cast iron fireback, cast in high relief with badges, fleurs-de-lys, trefoils and other motifs, 17thC, 46in (117cm) wide.
$2,700–3,200 *CSK*

A cast iron fireback, depicting the story of Susanna and the Elders, with cherubs, late 17thC, 39¾in (101cm) high.
$750–800 *P*

A cast iron fireback, with an arcaded design surmounted by a sun and leaves decorated with tulips, probably by Coalbrookdale Furnace, Berks County, Pennsylvania, dated '1764', 21in (53.5cm) wide.
$880–960 *S(NY)*

l. An American cast iron fireback, with the Great Seal of the United States, traces of gilt decoration, early 19thC, 17¾in (45cm) wide.
$3,200–3,500 *S(NY)*

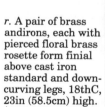

r. A pair of brass andirons, each with pierced floral brass rosette form finial above cast iron standard and down-curving legs, 18thC, 23in (58.5cm) high.
$600–720 *LHA*

A pair of Louis XVI style bronze and brass chenets, each surmounted by a draped cherub, on toupie feet, late 19thC, 14½in (37cm) high.
$1,700–1,900 *RIT*

A set of Victorian brass fire
irons, the leaf and berry cast
waisted grips with bud
pommels, 28¼in (71.5cm) long.
$1,000–1,200 *CSK*

A polished steel fire grate, the
pierced serpentine frieze flanked by
urns on tapering cylindrical columns,
late 18thC, 28in (70cm) wide.
$650–800 *P*

A neo-classical style pine and
polychrome fire surround, the
overhanging cornice above a
garland-moulded panel, raised
on corinthian columns, 19thC,
60in (152.5cm) wide.
$160–200 *SLN*

A reeded limestone fire surround,
c1850, 50in (127cm) wide.
$1,400–1,600 *DOR*

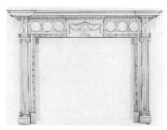

A George III carved pine fire
surround, with beaded and key
pattern inverted breakfront shelf,
the jambs with fluted Ionic columns
headed by urns, 74in (188cm) wide.
$800–900 *AH*

A pine and composite gesso fire
surround, the reverse breakfront
with frieze of festoon and
egg-and-dart moulding, ribbon
tied swags and central panel with
thistles and roses, late 18thC,
69in (175cm) wide.
$1,200–1,400 *P(Sc)*

r. A George III steel and iron
fire grate, the sides with
reeded columns headed by
urns, c1815, 39in (99cm) wide.
$3,800–4,200 *DRU*

A Victorian walnut fire surround,
the frieze carved with foliage,
fruits and mythological beasts
flanked by carved corbels, the
stiles with tapering columns and
Ionic capitals, 64in (163cm) wide.
$2,200–2,400 *P*

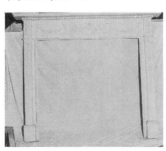

A Georgian style painted pine
fire surround, 19thC,
70in (178cm) wide.
$1,300–1,500 *WRe*

A Federal white-painted pine fire
surround, the central tablet once
fitted with an ornament, c1810,
81in (205.5cm) wide.
$680–800 *S(NY)*

A Regency dove grey marble fire
surround, 74in (188cm) wide.
$2,400–2,700 *WRe*

A Victorian rosewood fire surround
and overmantel, the upper section
with carved bird and floral
surmount, satinwood and bone inlay
depicting masks and scrollwork, the
fire surround with carved floral
swags, inlaid musical trophies and
figures, 75in (190.5cm) wide.
$8,800–9,600 *RBB*

An Irish pine fire surround,
c1880, 56in (142cm) wide.
$200–250 *TAN*

A late Victorian marble fire
surround, with mid-Victorian
horseshoe grate and 2 trivets,
72in (183cm) wide.
**Fire surround $1,100–1,300
Grate $650–800** *WRe*

An oak fire surround,
the moulded
pediment with
lunette and arcaded
panels below,
flanked on either
side by square
pilasters, c1900,
58in (147cm) high.
$720–800 *GAK*

l. A cast iron fire
surround, with
original tiled
insert depicting
irises, c1926,
36in (91.5cm) wide.
$800–1,000 *DOR*

A late Victorian St Anne's marble
fire surround, c1880, with inset
cast iron register grate, c1840,
72in (183cm) wide overall.
**Fire surround $2,400–3,200
Grate $1,900–2,200** *NOST*

A carved oak fire surround, c1880,
with brass canopy dog grate, early
20thC, 83in (211cm) wide overall.
**Fire surround $4,400–4,800
Grate $3,200–3,500** *NOST*

r. A cast iron range, c1860,
54in (137cm) wide.
$2,700–3,000 *DRU*

*This range came from the
Bank of England, London.*

Don't Forget!

*If in doubt
please refer to
the 'How to Use'
section at the
beginning of
this book.*

A Georgian cast iron
duck's nest grate,
24⅜in (63cm) high.
$600–650 *DOR*

A cast iron bedroom fire
surround, with a set of 12 Minton
tiles depicting animals, c1900,
37½in (95cm) high.
$1,200–1,400 *DRU*

METALWARE
Brass

A decorative brass alms dish, Nuremburg, c1580, 12in (30.5cm) diam.
$720–800 *KEY*

A pair of brass seamed candlesticks, early 18thC, 7½in (19cm) high.
$560–640 *KEY*

A Georgian brass coffee pot, possibly associated scrolled fruitwood handle with shell-carved top, cover damaged, c1735, 9in (23cm) high.
$2,200–2,700 *S(S)*

A Dinanderie brass figure of a female, probably from a candelabrum, early 16thC, 6¾in (17.5cm) high, on marble base.
$480–560 *Bea(E)*

Dinanderie is the term used for brass items originating from the Belgian town of Dinant, which was famous for its fine brass ware made in the Middle Ages.

A pair of French cast brass candlesticks, with chased anthemion and acanthus to the knops and urn-shaped candleholders, detachable nozzles, the bases with chased anthemion scrolls to the corners, traces of silver-plating, late 18thC, 11in (28cm) high.
$580–640 *WW*

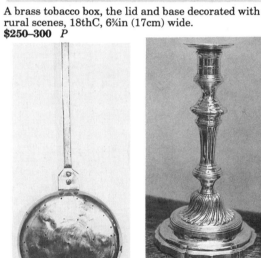

A brass tobacco box, the lid and base decorated with rural scenes, 18thC, 6¾in (17cm) wide.
$250–300 *P*

A brass warming pan, with wrought iron handle, hinged and domed lid pierced and chased in a floral pattern, 18thC, 42½in (108cm) long.
$320–400 *AH*

A pair of French brass swirl-based candlesticks, c1770, 11in (28cm) high.
$480–560 *KEY*

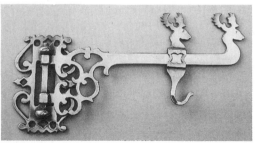

A brass bottle jack crane, decorated with 2 stags' heads, c1830, 14½in (37cm) long.
$130–150 *KEY*

This type of crane was screwed to the mantelpiece and a clockwork bottle jack suspended from it so that it hung in front of the fire. The jack incorporated hooks on which meat could be hung, and when it was wound-up it rotated first in one direction and then the other, ensuring that the food was properly cooked.

A brass topped trivet, on a cast iron tripod base, c1810, 13½in (34.5cm) high.
$400–500 *CPA*

l. A decorative brass doorstop, c1840, 15in (38cm) high.
$200–250 *SSW*

A brass toddy kettle, modelled as a melon, on ball feet, possibly Scottish, c1810, 11in (28cm) wide.
$800–900 *CAT*

Two cast brass doorstops, modelled as Punch and Judy, c1860, 12in (30.5cm) high.
$280–320 *SSW*

A brass picture frame, c1870, 14½in (37cm) high.
$170–200 *SSW*

A brass desk set, the 2 inkwells with paterae-cast lids and pineapple finials, with a letter rack, blotter and stand, late 19thC, 18¼in (46cm) wide.
$850–950 *P*

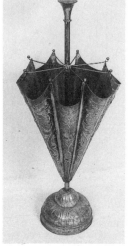

A brass umbrella stand, c1900, 39in (99cm) high.
$400–500 *SPU*

A pair of Georgian style brass candlesticks, late 19thC, 6in (15cm) high.
$200–250 *RIT*

An Edwardian brass and copper conical container, the domed cover with a finial, swing handle, 17in (43cm) high.
$80–100 *M*

A brass candlestick, 19thC, 11in (28cm) high.
$190–220 *SPU*

l. A brass stick stand, with fluted and bead-moulded leaf-cast sides, the base fitted with a drip tray, on bun feet, c1900, 26in (66cm) wide.
$11,500–13,000 *S*
This stand had rather more apertures than usual, and was a good quality piece.

A late Victorian brass baluster-shaped milk can, the strap handle initialled 'AVAD', 20in (51cm) high.
$85–100 *M*

A brass four-division magazine rack, on a tripod, late 19thC, 33in (84cm) high.
$400–450 *PCh*

A pair of brass reclining lion doorstops, late 19thC, 9in (23cm) wide.
$700–800 *PCh*

A Fabergé brass bowl, the interior embossed with the Imperial eagle and inscribed in Cyrillic 'War, 1914', 4½in (11cm) diam.
$1,700–2,200 *S(NY)*

Bronze

A bronze inkwell, in the form of Cupid seated on a cushion, by a follower of Niccolò Roccatagliata, 17thC, 7¾in (20cm) high.
$9,500–10,500 *C*

A bronze mortar, decorated with lions, c1680, 4½in (11cm) high.
$560–640 *KEY*

An Italian bronze inkwell, c1820, 6½in (16.5cm) high.
$480–520 *CAT*

A French bronze figure of Napoleon, on a stepped marble base, signed 'Pradier', 19thC, 11½in (29cm) high.
$1,300–1,500 *P*

A bronze figure of a forester, with an axe in his hand, the base inscribed 'Laporte', on a rouge marble base, 19thC, 28in (71cm) high.
$1,600–1,900 *P*

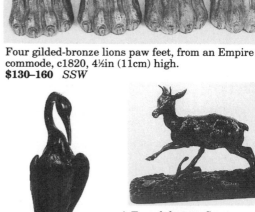

Four gilded-bronze lions paw feet, from an Empire commode, c1820, 4½in (11cm) high.
$130–160 *SSW*

An animalier bronze of a stork, c1860, 9in (23cm) high.
$1,100–1,200 *HEY*

A French bronze figure, entitled 'Chamois', by Pierre Jules Mêne, signed, c1860, 5in (12.5cm) long.
$950–1,200 *WeH*

Pierre Jules Mêne (1810–71) was born in Paris, the son of a metal turner. Largely self-taught, he opened his own foundry with his father in 1838, making his salon debut in the same year. He won a Second Class medal in 1848, First Class medals in 1852 and 1861 and was elected a member of the Légion d'Honneur in 1861. He exhibited at the Great Exhibitions of 1851 and 1862, many of his groups being designed for the English market.

A pair of gilt and patinated bronze ewers, each with a frieze of cherubs, the handles surmounted by a figure of Bacchus, 19thC, 22¾in (58cm) high.
$900–1,000 *CSK*

l. A pair of French bronze and marble urns, the scroll handles cast with masks, c1870, 26in (66cm) high.
$5,000–6,000 *S*

A pair of French bronze Marly horses, after Coustou, with attendants, on ebonised, tortoiseshell and cut-brass inlaid stands, with ormolu satyr masks, 19thC, 23in (58.5cm) high.
$5,000–5,500 *MCA*

A Viennese bronze squirrel, c1860, 7in (18cm) long.
$1,600–1,800 *SSW*

A patinated bronze model of a greyhound, c1870, 9in (23cm) high.
$1,400–1,600 *ANT*

A bronze urn and pedestal, after the Warwick vase, 19thC, 17¼in (44cm) high.
$1,000–1,200 *Bea(E)*

A pair of Victorian Gothic revival gilt-bronze wall appliqués, modelled in the form of winged mythical beasts, 15in (38cm) high.
$2,400–2,700 *CSK*

A bronze bust, 'Diane', by Emmanuele Villanis, signed, late 19thC, 5¼in (13cm) high, on a turned wooden plinth.
$370–450 *AH*

l. A bronze model of a crowing cockerel, by Emmanuel Fremiet, signed, stamped 'F. Barbedienne', c1880, 6in (15cm) high.
$430–480 *WeH*

The Parisian Emmanuel Fremiet (1824–1910) is particularly well-known for his equestrian statuary, as well as his sculpture of other animals and historical figures. He exhibited at the Paris Salon from 1843, became a member of the Royal Academy in 1892, and an honourary member in 1904. He was also Professor of Animal Drawing at the Natural History Museum.

A Renaissance style brass and ebony desk set, with a matching pair of candlesticks, the pierced support pen holder flanked by a pair of covered urns containing frosted insets, one marked 'Asprey & Sons, 166 Bond Street', late 19thC, 9½in (24cm) long.
$600–700 *RIT*

A pair of French bronze figures, each in the form of a classical maiden holding a vase on her shoulders, on red marble bases, late 19thC, 25in (63.5cm) high.
$2,000–2,500 *WDG*

An Italian bronze figure, after the antique of a Dancing Faun, on square base, 19thC, 31in (78.5cm) high.
$800–900 *CAG*

FURTHER READING
Eric Knowles, *Victoriana to Art Deco*, Miller's Publications, 1993.

r. A bronze portrait bust of a goddess, wearing a laurel wreath, the socle inscribed 'F. Halnon', on a fossilised marble plinth, late 19thC, 15¼in (39cm) high.
$1,400–1,600 *WW*

A gilt and bronze Bacchus ewer, cast with fruiting vines and a scene of cherubs, ram and reclining maiden on a chariot above raised gilt acanthus leaves, scroll handle cast with cherub and satyr mask terminal, late 19thC, 22½in (57cm) high.
$900–1,200 *WL*

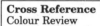

Cross Reference
Colour Review

A pair of Louis XVI style gilt-bronze urns, decorated with grape-leaf garlands flanked by 2 cornucopia-shaped handles, fitted for electricity, late 19thC, 32in (81.5cm) high.
$4,000–4,500 *LHA*

A pair of French gilt-bronze candelabra, each with 4 scroll leaf-cast branches, issuing from rams' masks, c1890, 20½in (52cm) high.
$8,500–9,500 *S*

A bronze model of an owl, c1890, 14in (35.5cm) high.
$850–950 *SUC*

A bronze model of a whippet, c1890, 8¾in (22cm) high.
$1,300–1,500 *ARE*

A Viennese cold-painted bronze figure of an Arab tribesman, mounted on a camel, stamped 'Bargman', c1890, 13in (33cm) high.
$6,400–7,200 *GAS*

An Italian bronze group, entitled 'Adieu', by C. Barbella, depicting a daughter parting from her mother, a young man at her side, signed and dated '1893', 26½in (67cm) high.
$3,200–3,500 *Bea(E)*

A bronze model of a chick and a snail, by Louis Edmond Masson, c1900, 4½in (11cm) long.
$720–800 *WeH*

Louis Edmond Masson (1838–1913) was born in Paris and studied under Santiago, Barve and Rouillard. Primarily an animalier, he exhibited at the Salon from 1867–81 and later at the Salon des Artistes Français, where he won an honourable mention for his work in 1890.

A bronze figure, by Gotthilf Jager, entitled 'Testing the Foil', on a marble base, signed, c1900, 11½in (29cm) high.
$600–700 *SLN*

A gilt-bronze and brass bird cage, the sides fitted with feeders, the base with a single drawer with liner, on bun feet, signed 'FR. OT. ST. Wien 28–3 1911', c1911, 43in (109cm) high.
$9,000–10,000 *S(NY)*

Cross Reference
Decorative Arts
Page 477.

l. A pair of French bronze urns, each cast with swan neck handles and with tendrils and flowerheads, above a frieze with classical dancing figures, c1910, 31in (79cm) high.
$10,000–12,000 *S*

A French bronze figure of Esmeralda, by Eugène Marioton, depicting a gypsy girl dancing with a goat, c1900, 34in (86cm) high.
$4,400–4,800 *S*

A gilt-bronze and alabaster bust of an Americas Princess, by Carl Kauba, with peacock headdress and wrapped in a puma's skin, its head and paws resting on pink veined marble base, early 20thC, 15in (38cm) high.
$1,400–1,600 *Oli*

Copper

A south German gilt-copper, brass and steel miniature casket, from the workshops of Michel Mann, the lid, sides and base incised with courtly figures, equestrian and hunting scenes, dated '1548', 2¾in (7cm) wide.
$2,800–3,200 *CSK*

A copper kettle and lid, with acorn finial, slight damage, 19thC, 13in (33cm) high.
$200–250 *MEG*

r. A copper jug, with a coin in the base, c1937, 1¼in (3cm) high.
$18–25 *No7*

A copper pan and lid, early 20thC, 14½in (37cm) diam.
$200–275 *MEG*

Iron

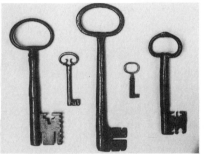

A selection of 5 iron keys, 17th & 18thC, largest 10¼in (26cm) long.
$40–50 smallest
$280–320 largest *KEY*

A tinder pistol or 'strike-a-light', 18thC, 7in (18cm) long.
$480–640 *KEY*

A wrought iron rush nip and candleholder, probably Irish, early 18thC, 11½in (29cm) high.
$400–500 *CSK*

A wrought iron pipe kiln, c1700, 13in (33cm) long.
$530–600 *RYA*

A wrought iron rush light holder, on a tripod base, c1780, 9½in (24cm) high.
$430–480 *RYA*

A wrought iron rush light holder, 18thC, 9½in (24cm) high.
$480–560 *SPU*

A wrought iron rush light holder, 18thC, 7in (18cm) high.
$400–500 *KEY*

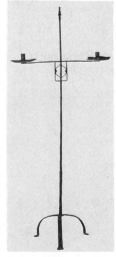

A wrought iron and brass double-arm candlestand, with drip pans, probably Pennsylvania, 18thC, 57¼in (145.5cm) high.
$8,000–9,000 *SK(B)*

A wrought iron rush nip and candleholder, 18thC, 12¼in (31cm) high.
$600–700 *CSK*

A wrought iron 'rat de cave', with fruitwood base, c1790, 8in (20.5cm) high.
$250–300 *RYA*

A pair of cast iron ornamental doorstops, c1840, 9in (23cm) high.
$600–700 *HEY*

A cast iron doorstop, modelled as a retriever, c1840, 15½in (39.5cm) long.
$200–250 *SSW*

A wrought iron rush light holder, on a tripod base and another on original turned wooden base, 18thC, 7in (18cm) high.
$350–450 each *KEY*

A cast iron miniature fireplace, with brass fire tools, c1820, 14in (35.5cm) high.
$130–160 *SSW*

Three iron keys, with quatrefoil and trefoil bows, c1850, largest 8in (20.5cm) long.
$65–80 each *KEY*

Locate the Source
The source of each illustration in Miller's can be found by checking the code letters below each caption with the Key to Illustrations.

An American cast iron doorstop, modelled as a Boston Terrier, c1870, 9in (23cm) high.
$135–150 *SSW*

A Victorian wrought iron baker's rack, with pierced scrolling floral supports joining slatted shelves, flanking baluster turned spindle base, 86¾in (220.5cm) high.
$950–1,200 *LHA*

A wrought iron stick stand, decorated with brass knobs, c1900, 21½in (54.5cm) high.
$160–200 *MEG*

Ormolu

A George III ormolu-mounted bluejohn pot pourri vase, attributed to Matthew Boulton, the beaded circular pierced top on a tapering body with acanthus leaves, lacking cover, 7in (18cm) high.
$4,400–4,800 *C*

A pair of north European ormolu and white marble cassolettes, each with a reversible nozzle surmounted by a foliate top and ball finial, late 18th/early 19thC, 9¼in (23.5cm) high.
$2,700–3,200 *C*

Cassolettes were used in wealthy households from the 18thC to burn scented pastilles as room fresheners.

A Regency ormolu bust of Bacchus, 7½in (19cm) high.
$4,800–5,400 *C*

A pair of Louis XV style ormolu urns, each fitted with a domed cover cast with flowerheads, the body flanked by asymmetrical rocaille handles, on a stepped circular white marble plinth, mid-19thC, 10in (25.5cm) high.
$1,700–1,900 *S(NY)*

A pair of decorative ormolu-mounted blue lapis coloured vases, 19thC, 10½in (26.5cm) high.
$2,000–2,400 *CAT*

A pair of Louis XVI style ormolu, gilt-metal and white marble two-branch candelabra, one modelled as a draped putto seated on a tree stump, the other as an infant satyr resting on a tree trunk, fitted for electricity, 19thC, 17in (43cm) high.
$2,000–2,500 *C(S)*

A pair of ormolu five-branch candelabra, each in the form of a tree, with 4 scrolling branches entwined by a serpent, the foliate base surrounded by dogs, 19thC, 17in (43cm) high.
$4,800–5,600 *C*

l. A pair of French ormolu and marble five-light candelabra, the curved foliate decorated candle arms centred by an ormolu turned finial, on scrolling leaf feet above a conforming plinth, repaired, 19thC, 24in (61cm) high.
$720–800 *RIT*

A pair of Louis XV style ormolu candlesticks, each in the form of a tree, one being climbed by a bear, the other by a panther, foliate cast bases with a pair of armorial shields, on scrolled feet, fitted for electricity, late 19thC, 18¼in (46.5cm) high.
$6,000–6,500 *C*

Pewter

I A pewter ball-knopped chalice, by maker R.F., touch in a beaded shield, c1650, 5in (12.5cm) high. **$3,200–3,500** *S(S)*

II A pewter knopped chalice, some restoration to bowl, mid-17thC, 5½in (14cm) high. **$1,300–1,600** *S(S)*

The very different prices realised by these two goblets at auction demonstrate very clearly how condition affects the value of a piece. *Item I* **was in almost perfect condition with a particularly pleasing foot with some wriggled decoration, while** *Item II* **had old restoration carried out to the bowl. Another feature of note is the rounded ball knop of** *Item I* **which is thought by many to be more stylistic than the disc knop of** *Item II.* *S(S)*

A pewter triple-reeded rimmed paten, the rim with ownership initials of 'A.P.' and 'S.K.', the reverse with the touch of the maker 'C.B.', dated '1670' in a circle, 6¾in (17.5cm) diam. **$1,300–1,450** *S(S)*

A pewter two-handled loving cup, c1770, 6¼in (16cm) high. **$560–640** *KEY*

A William & Mary capstan master pewter salt, with gadrooned top and foot, touch mark of 'R.D.' under base, c1690, 3in (9cm) high. **$2,500–3,000** *S(S)*

A pewter flat-lidded tankard, with wriggle decoration, the cover with a tulip and the owner's initials 'W.P.' within shield devices, lacking thumbpiece, the body possibly later decorated with an owl flanked by a tulip and rose, late 17thC, 5¼in (13cm) high. **$2,000–2,500** *CSK*

A set of 12 pewter plates, the underside of each with initials, London touch marks and crowned 'X', 18thC, 9in (23cm) diam. **$600–700** *P(B)*

A half pint pewter mug, 19thC, 3½in (9cm) high. **$55–65** *No7*

A pewter foot warmer, with iron handle, 19thC, 8in (20.5cm) diam. **$25–35** *No7*

Pewter

Pewter is an alloy of tin and lead – the higher the tin content the higher the quality. Sometimes a small quantity of antimony is added to harden the metal.

A French pewter tankard, marked Paqua, Bordeaux, 19thC, 7in (18cm) high. **$55–65** *No7*

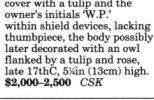

r. A pair of black-painted pewter chestnut vases and covers, applied with gilt lion masks to ring handles and with gilt decoration depicting a bird on a flowering branch, early 19thC, 12½in (32cm) high. **$650–750** *S(Am)*

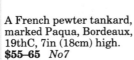

Spelter

A pair of Italian
spelter candle-
sticks, c1865,
15½in (39.5cm) high.
$640–720 *SSW*

A pair of Italian
spelter candle-
sticks, c1865,
16in (40.5cm) high.
$640–720 *SSW*

A gilded spelter paperweight,
modelled as a recumbent lion,
on a marble base, c1870,
6in (15cm) wide.
$50–65 *WAB*

A pair of French spelter Marly
horses, on replacement stands,
late 19thC, 4in (10cm) high.
$80–100 *MEG*

A polychrome spelter
figure of a Middle
Eastern woman, signed
'L. Hollot', late 19thC,
31in (78.5cm) high.
$4,500–5,000 *S(NY)*

A spelter figure of a
girl, holding a fan,
repair to arm,
late 19thC,
26¾in (68cm) high.
$160–200 *MEG*

A French spelter figure
of Cupid, standing on a
foliate ground, with a
plaque 'Printemps
Fleur', late 19thC,
19in (48cm) high.
$350–400 *CSK*

A pair of French
spelter figures of
Cupid, after models by
Auguste Moreau, with
plaques 'Badinage' and
'Alerte', late 19thC,
16½in (42cm) high.
$640–720 *CSK*

A pair of French spelter
figures, after Moreau,
modelled as a barefooted
youth with a dog, and his
female companion with a
sheep, late 19thC,
20in (51cm) high.
$500–560 *M*

A silvered-spelter model of a fox,
standing on a crystalline quartz
base, stamped 'NAPCO', c1900,
5in (12.5cm) long.
$160–200 *WeH*

A gilt-spelter novelty twin
inkwell, modelled as a
rhinoceros, c1900,
8½in (21.5cm) long.
$520–560 *WeH*

A spelter model of a horse and
rider, replacement feet to base,
c1900, 16in (40.5cm) high.
$130–160 *MEG*

ALABASTER

An alabaster relief-carved panel, depicting the Adoration of the Shepherds, with traces of gilt, within a contemporary giltwood and gesso frame, Malines, late 16th/early 17thC, 9 x 8in (23 x 20.5cm).
$1,600–1,800 *CSK*

An Italian alabaster statue of a fisherman, holding a fish in one hand, 19thC, 24½in (62cm) high.
$520–620 *P*

An alabaster figure of a nomadic huntsman, wearing robes and carrying a musket, on a rockwork marble plinth, 19thC, 22½in (57cm) high.
$570–640 *P*

An alabaster bust of Michelangelo, on a hardstone base, 19thC, 9¼in (23.5cm) high.
$560–620 *P*

l. An Italian alabaster figure of a female nude, by R. Gremigni, with drapery falling from her waist and hand raised to her chin, on a square base and plinth, signed, c1900, 28¼in (72cm) high.
$3,500–4,000 *C*

An Italian two-coloured alabaster figure of a child asleep on a chair, by Pugi, signed, c1900, 20¾in (52.5cm) high.
$5,000–5,600 *C*

MARBLE

A Derbyshire bluejohn urn-shaped vase, on an Ashford marble base, 18thC, 13¼in (33.5cm) high.
$4,800–5,600 *SPU*

l. A pair of French Directoire white marble and gilt-bronze vases, late 18thC, 11½in (29cm) high.
$5,000–5,600 *S(Z)*

A north European sculpted white marble relief-carved panel, depicting 7 martyrs shown as tonsured monks, probably 16thC, 29 x 17¾in (73.5 x 45cm).
$3,200–3,500 *CSK*

l. A marble bust, entitled 'America', depicting a woman in a native war bonnet as an allegory of America, early 19thC, 16in (40.5cm) high.
$950–1,000 *EL*

r. A white marble figure of a young girl kneeling, by Joseph Gott, dressed in a classical robe, on a stepped oval plinth base, signed, early 19thC, 11in (28cm) high.
$2,700–3,200 *DN*

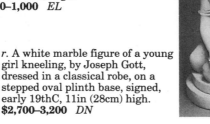

A white marble bust of Mary Clara Burmann, by Matthew Noble, on a circular socle, signed and dated '1867', 19½in (49.5cm) high.
$1,700–1,900 *S(S)*

A French white marble bust of Napoleon Bonaparte, after Antoine-Denis Chaudet, mid-19thC, 21in (53.5cm) high.
$2,500–2,800 *C*

A pair of *faux* marble pots with covers, supported by gilt dolphins, c1870, 5¾in (14.5cm) high.
$880–960 *CAT*

l. An Italian marble figure of Cupid, by A. Basetti, signed and dated '1876', 35¼in (89.5cm) high.
$3,200–3,500 *SLN*

TERRACOTTA

A white marble bust of a young woman, her head turned, on a waisted socle, late 19thC, 12½in (32cm) high.
$370–450 *P*

A European marble group of a winged cupid with putti, c1900, 29¼in (74cm) high.
$1,700–1,900 *FBG*

A terracotta hollow cast figure of a shepherdess, seated with a dog at her feet, damaged, faded paint, 19thC, 8¼in (21cm) high.
$350–400 *S(Am)*

A French terracotta bust of Rembrandt, by Albert-Ernest Carrier-Belleuse, on a turned wooden socle, signed, mid-19thC, 21¼in (54cm) high.
$2,400–2,700 *FBG*

> **Cross Reference**
> Colour Review

A terracotta bust of Liszt in old age, by Lucien Pallez, wearing a coat over a shirt and smock, on a cast socle, late 19thC, 34½in (87.5cm) high.
$1,900–2,200 *L*

Lucien Pallez was born in Paris in 1853, and exhibited at the Salon from 1873. He was awarded several prizes and a travelling scholarship both at the Salon and at the Expositions Universelles. He was made a Chevalier of the Légion d'Honneur in 1887. Pallez worked on several allegorical figures and monuments, but is most celebrated for his portrait busts.

A Goldscheider terracotta figure of a seated boy, playing the flute, late 19thC, 25½in (65cm) high.
$6,400–7,200 *AH*

A terracotta group of 2 black boys, one reading and the other writing, impressed 'J.M.' on base, c1900, 12in (30.5cm) high.
$1,900–2,200 *GAS*

LEATHER

A silver-mounted leather flagon, the loop handle with foliate terminal, later mounts and engraved oval cartouche, 17thC, 9in (23cm) high.
$2,500–3,000 *CSK*

A German leather and boar skin money belt, the pouch embroidered with stylised flowering vines and geometric borders surrounding inscription *'Ich Liebe'*, with compartmented interior, early 18thC, 39in (99cm) long.
$320–350 *LHA*

A Regency leather-covered workbox, with repoussé gilt-metal mounts and bracket feet, the lower drawer with a writing slope, fitted interior, 12in (30.5cm) wide.
$800–900 *CSK*

A leather flagon, with an angular side handle, c1700, 21in (53.5cm) high.
$2,400–2,700 *S(S)*

An American leather fire bucket, mid-19thC, 12in (30.5cm) high.
$1,900–2,200 *AWT*

TREEN

A laburnum goblet, c1750, 8in (20.5cm) high.
$1,200–1,400 *RYA*

A Scandinavian dipper cup, possibly birch, 18thC, 3¼in (8.5cm) diam.
$720–800 *AEF*

A George III fruitwood tea caddy, in the form of a melon, with traces of original green paint, the finial in the form of a stalk, 5¼in (13.5cm) high.
$4,000–4,500 *HOLL*

A pounce pot, c1760, 3¼in (8.5cm) high.
$650–700 *RYA*

l. A German fruitwood tea caddy, carved as a pineapple, 18thC, 7¾in (19.5cm) high.
$1,700–2,000 *P(S)*

A Welsh love spoon, carved with heart, diamond, club and spade motifs, c1820, 8in (20cm) long.
$850–900 *AEF*

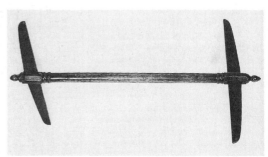

An oak 'niddy noddy', c1800, 25in (63.5cm) long.
$320–380 *CoA*

A 'niddy noddy' is a form of hand-held wool winder.

A wooden double container, the 2 compartments with hinged lids and central carrying handle, c1840, 9in (23cm) wide.
$550–625 *CoA*

A lignum vitae bilboquet game, c1820, 6in (15cm) high.
$480–560 *AEF*

A rosewood string barrel, with cutter, c1840, 10in (25.5cm) wide.
$160–180 *MB*

A rosewood and brass 'see me to bed', c1860, 3in (7.5cm) high.
$110–130 *BIL*

A match is inserted into the brass hole at the top, and burns for just long enough to light a person's way to bed.

A pair of Welsh nut crackers, mid-19thC, 6in (15cm) long.
$240–300 *SPU*

An elm kitchen bowl, 19thC, 15in (38cm) diam.
$580–640 *AEF*

A paperweight, with a view of Winchester Cathedral under glass, set in an oak base, 19thC, 5in (12.5cm) diam.
$65–80 *AAN*

A carved wood dog's head inkwell, c1880, 3¾in (9.5cm) high.
$900–1,000 *ARE*

A Swiss carved wood hook, in the form of a rabbit, c1890, 13in (33cm) high.
$1,400–1,600 *ARE*

A carved wood dog's head tobacco box, c1880, 7½in (19cm) high.
$2,200–2,700 *ARE*

An elm goblet, with knopped stem and circular foot, 19thC, 5in (13cm) high.
$180–200 *P*

Don't Forget!
If in doubt please refer to the 'How to Use' section at the beginning of this book.

FOLK ART

A bright-cut brass and turned maple bed warmer, decorated with fans and grapes centring a cartouche with a heart, crown and arrows, dated '1604', handle replaced, 51in (129.5cm) long.
$1,725–2,000 *S(NY)*

Warming pans filled with hot coals were used to air cold and damp beds. However, according to Dr Alexander Hamilton of Annapolis, people occasionally found more inventive uses for their design. He records in his 1744 diary a lengthy dinner where a dish of clams was kept warm in a warming pan.

Folk Art

Folk Art is a very broad term encompassing many collecting areas. For other examples in our Price Guide please refer to the sections on Kitchenware, Marine, Metalware, Treen, Boxes and Textiles.

An American carved wood sewing box, with spool rack, 19thC, 14in (35.5cm) high.
$260–300 *SK(B)*

An American carved birch and pine miniature secretaire bookcase, the top with a carved dog finial, opening to a fitted interior, 2 carved bookcase doors over a roll-top desk, 2 drawers, on paw feet, 19thC, 9in (23cm) wide.
$1,050–1,150 *SK(B)*

A Norwegian storage box, c1850, 10in (25.5cm) diam.
$450–500 *RYA*

A French boxwood comb, one side centred with a unicorn, the other with a cockerel, inscribed, c1500, 6¾in (17cm) wide.
$3,500–4,200 *S(NY)*

A Pennsylvanian Dutch sampler, with peacocks, hearts and flowering vines within a grain-painted frame, early 19thC.
$750–825 *LHA*

l. A mahogany, maple and pine inlaid games table top, early 20thC, 29½in (75cm) square.
$330–360 *EL*

Two canvas-backed wooden decoy ducks, by M. Madison Mitchell, Havre de Grace, MD, 1960s, 17in (43cm) long.
$500–550 *YAG*

A decoy duck, with original glass eyes and painted decoration, c1880, 12in (30.5cm) long.
$250–300 *RYA*

A hunting horn, engraved with animals, soldiers, shields, and a mermaid, signed 'William Wait 1792', possibly Canadian, 18thC, 15in (38cm) long.
$520–620 *EL*

Three turned and painted wood covered jars, probably Ohio, early 19thC, largest 7½in (19cm) high.
$1,500–1,800 *S(NY)*

A carved wood eagle, c1860, 28in (71cm) wide.
$250–300 *AWT*

An American carved and painted carousel horse, early 20thC, 60in (152.5cm) high.
$10,500–11,500 *SK(B)*

A Norwegian ale jug, c1780, 8in (20.5cm) high.
$720–800 *RYA*

An American tin lantern, the top inscribed 'H. Howard', pierced with geometric motifs, early 19thC, 20in (51cm) high.
$1,500–1,650 *S(NY)*

A carved pine model of a long-tailed bird, painted red, green and yellow on a cream ground, with wire legs, perched on a tree trunk, probably Pennsylvania, c1900, 13½in (34.5cm) high.
$2,300–2,500 *S(NY)*

An American silk needlework picture of George Washington and his family, after Edward Savage, with watercolour highlights, early 19thC, 18 x 24in (45.5 x 61cm).
$4,000–4,500 *SK(B)*

Don't Forget!
If in doubt please refer to the 'How to Use' section at the beginning of this book.

A needlework picture, worked in silk depicting flags, an eagle and a motto, c1890, 28½ x 33in (72.5 x 84cm), framed.
$375–425 *AWT*

A Quaker needlework sampler, by Mary Reed, aged 8 years, with a basket of fruit surrounded by foliate and animal devices and ribbon border, probably Pennsylvania, 1819, 19½ x 13¾in (49.5 x 35cm), framed.
$1,100–1,200 *SK(B)*

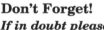

A cut-work picture, signed 'John Thomas & Louise Clark', painted cut paper, mica and dried flowers in a shadow box frame, American School, 19thC, 13½ x 11½in (34.5 x 29cm).
$2,500–2,750 *SK(B)*

A lithographed tin commemorative Francis Scott Key plate, by C. D. Kenny Co, c1914, 9½in (24cm) diam.
$60–70 *AWT*

A pieced and appliquéd cotton sampler quilt cover, by Eliza and Jane Vinal, Boston, Massachusetts, c1790, 86½ x 64in (219.5 x 162.5cm).
$3,200–3,500 *S(NY)*

An American pieced, appliquéd and embroidered cotton quilt, with star-shaped and hexagonal patterns, c1830, 95 x 72in (241.5 x 183cm).
$2,700–3,000 *S(NY)*

An American pieced silk and taffeta 'log cabin' quilt, with Barn Raising pattern, c1870, 72in (183cm) square.
$3,500–4,200 *S(NY)*

This quilt was found in Michigan.

A pieced and appliquéd cotton American eagle quilt, with central double star, Lebanon County, Pennsylvania, c1870, 79in (200.5cm) square.
$1,000–1,100 *S(NY)*

An American pieced and appliquéd cotton unicorn and horse quilt, with red and white patches in diamond panels, 19thC, 66 x 92in (167.5 x 234cm).
$1,850–2,000 *S(NY)*

A Grenfell wool mat, depicting a dog howling at the moon, early 20thC, 9½ x 7in (24 x 18cm).
$350–400 *AWT*

An Amish pieced wool quilt, the patches arranged in the Diamond in the Square pattern, Lancaster, Pennsylvania, c1921, 77 x 74in (195.5 x 188cm).
$4,600–5,000 *S(NY)*

A Portuguese horn snuff mull, in the form of a mother and child, c1700, 4in (10cm) high.
$2,000–2,300 *AEF*

l. A wooden trade sign, in the form of a razor, c1900, 16½in (42cm) long.
$35–40 *AWT*

A Scottish rushlight, on a lignum vitae socle, c1700, 15in (38cm) high.
$1,050–1,150 *SEL*

BOXES

A domed box, with gilt-metal lock and handles, covered in cream satin embroidered with stumpwork scenes of figures in landscapes, flowers, insects and birds, worked in coloured silks and coiled wire, with spangles, metal and glass beads, the edges bound with metal braid, late 17thC, 11in (28cm) wide. **$3,000–3,500** *DN*

A silver-mounted velvet-covered travelling casket, the hinged cover opening to a three-section pull-out shelf and 9 compartments, a drawer with ring handle, the interior lined with damask, on bun feet, c1740, 13in (33cm) wide. **$4,400–4,800** *Bon*

An inlaid satinwood tea caddy, c1790, 5in (12.5cm) high. **$1,400–1,600** *CAT*

An octagonal tea caddy, with gilt and blue floral quill work pattern, mounted with a silk embroidered monogrammed panel beneath glass, late 18thC, 6½in (16.5cm) wide. **$1,100–1,300** *LHA*

A zebrawood table snuff box, c1780, 9in (23cm) wide. **$320–370** *MB*

A mahogany and brass-bound letter box, the hinged top with brass letter slit above brass-inlaid front, side carrying handles, on carved paw feet, early 19thC, 15½in (39.5cm) wide. **$1,900–2,200** *P(Sc)*

A thuya wood sewing casket, with Palais Royale fittings, early 19thC, 9in (23cm) wide. **$720–880** *COT*

A William IV coromandel writing box, the fitted interior with a writing slope and ceramic insets, 16½in (42cm) wide. **$720–880** *WeH*

A late Georgian simulated coromandel needlework box, in the form of a miniature chest of drawers, with fitted interior, original blue paper lining, 2 drawers enclosed by 2 locking doors, lion mask ring-pull handles, on gilt-metal feet, 7in (18cm) wide. **$480–540** *TMA*

An early Victorian pewter-inlaid tortoiseshell-veneered tea caddy, the hinged cover with central brass plaque, ivory-veneered rims, the interior with tortoiseshell cover and mother-of-pearl handle, on ivory ball feet, 5¾in (14.5cm) wide.
$950–1,100 *B*

A walnut and brass-bound tea caddy, c1850, 9in (23cm) wide.
$350–400 *SSW*

A lady's rosewood and brass-bound vanity case, with inlaid brass pieces, interior mirror and electroplated fittings, 19thC, 12½in (32cm) wide, with leather carrying case.
$400–450 *AG*

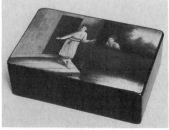

An Imperial Russian lacquered box, the lid with a picture of a girl on a step and a boy looking over a wall, by Vishnaichur, c1880, 5½in (14cm) wide.
$800–900 *SHa*

r. An Edwardian satinwood stationery box, 11½in (29cm) wide.
$160–240 *TMi*

A rosewood and brass-inlaid sewing box, by Thomas Lund, London, c1850, 11in (28cm) wide.
$350–450 *BIL*

A Fabergé bloodstone box, inlaid with gold and diamonds, c1860, 2in (5cm) wide.
$4,400–4,800 *SFL*

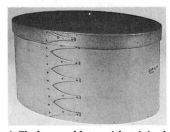

A Shaker oval box, with original pumpkin paint, remnants of paper label inscribed 'soap', probably New Lebanon, New York, 19thC, 15in (38cm) wide.
$8,000–9,000 *SK(B)*

A French fabric-covered hat box, c1880, 12½in (32cm) diam.
$90–100 *RYA*

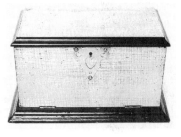

An Anglo-Indian sarcophagus-shaped micro-mosaic and ivory sewing box, with fitted interior, c1850, 13in (33cm) wide.
$1,300–1,500 *CORO*

A Victorian coromandel vanity case, with silver-mounted fittings, by Asprey, London, 12in (30.5cm) wide.
$5,700–6,400 *SUF*

A Victorian sewing box, with brass handle, 12in (30.5cm) wide.
$240–280 *SPU*

A burr walnut travelling dressing box, the velvet-lined interior with cut glass and silver monogrammed fittings, by H. Chapman Son & Co Ltd, London, c1870, 12in (30.5cm) wide.
$720–800 *RIT*

A pair of Charles X ormolu nine-light candelabra, each with baluster-shaped acanthus cast standard, mid-19thC, 20in (51cm) high.
$12,000–13,000 *S(NY)*

A pair of French gilt-bronze and marble four-light candelabra, early 19thC, 19in (48cm) high.
$9,500–10,500 *S(Z)*

A pair of French gilt-bronze four-light candelabra, 19thC, 22in (56cm) high.
$6,400–7,000 *S(Z)*

A pair French ormolu candelabra, each formed as a putto supporting cornucopiae issuing 6 stems terminating in flowerheads, on marble plinths, fitted for electricity, late 19thC, 50in (127cm) high.
$32,000–35,000 *C*

A pair of gilt-bronze and metal marble-mounted *épergnes*, in the form of palm trees supporting gilt-metal baskets, possibly Swedish, late 18thC, 36in (91cm) high.
$74,000–80,000 *S(Am)*

A late Victorian ormolu standard lamp, with frosted glass bowl, 54in (137cm) high.
$5,000–5,600 *C*

A Viennese cold-painted bronze lamp, Bergman vase stamp, late 19thC, 27½in (70cm) high.
$6,500–7,500 *P*

A Victorian brass oil lamp, with pink glass reservoir, 26in (66cm) high.
$200–250 *MEG*

A brass Corinthian column oil lamp, late 19thC, 28in (71cm) high.
$380–440 *MSW*

A pair of brass and painted spelter table lamps, c1910, 29in (73cm) high.
$880–1,000 *ML*

A silver Corinthian column table lamp, Sheffield 1911, 30in (76cm) high.
$1,400–1,600 *MSW*

A pair of painted spelter candle lights, 1920s, 29in (73cm) high.
$880–1,000 *ML*

An Italian rococo *tôle peinte* thirty-light chandelier, painted with multi-coloured flowerheads, mid-18thC, 50in (127cm) high.
$33,500–37,000 *S(NY)*

A French gilt-bronze and cut glass chandelier, stamped 'Baccarat', mid-19thC, 47in (120cm) high.
$6,400–7,200 *Bon*

A French ormolu chandelier fitted for electricity, c1900, 49in (124.5cm) high.
$13,500–15,000 *C*

A French neo-classical gilt-bronze chandelier, c1800, 27½in (70cm) high.
$7,000–8,000 *S(Am)*

A gilt-metal and cut glass chandelier, early 19thC, 49in (125cm) high.
$2,400–3,000 *S(Z)*

A French gilt-metal rock crystal and cut glass nine-light chandelier, 19thC, 31in (80cm) high.
$3,200–4,000 *S(Am)*

A gilt-metal and cut glass chandelier, 19thC, 60in (152cm) high.
$21,500–24,000 *C(S)*

An Italian carved wood and facetted crystal glass eight-light chandelier, 19thC, 43in (110cm) high.
$11,500–12,500 *S(Z)*

A French rococo gilt-bronze eight-light chandelier, late 19thC, 25in (63.5cm) high.
$1,600–1,900 *CSK*

A French ormolu six-light chandelier, fitted for electricity, c1900, 42in (106.5cm) high.
$4,800–5,600 *C*

A French gilt-bronze chandelier, late 19thC, 43½in (110.5cm) high.
$2,400–2,800 *CSK*

A wrought iron and gilt-metal lantern, c1900, 36in (92cm) high.
$13,500–15,500 *S*

A pair of cut glass and gilt-bronze chandeliers, c1910, 31in (79cm) high.
$4,800–5,600 *S*

A Victorian brass hanging lantern, c1870, 27in (39cm) high.
$3,200–3,600 *S*

A cut glass and brass chandelier, c1900, 43in (111cm) high.
$3,500–4,500 *S*

A European Turkish design carpet, c1870, 248in (630cm) long. **$11,000–12,500** *C*

A French *gros point* needlework carpet, with overall design of flowerheads and branches, late 19thC, 129 x 80in (327 x 204cm). **$13,000–14,500** *C*

A French needlepoint rug, c1875, 106in (269cm) long. **$6,500–7,500** *S(NY)*

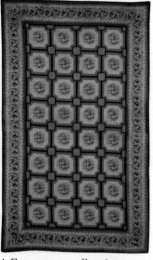

A European needlepoint carpet, minor colour runs, c1880, 222 x 131in (564 x 332cm). **$14,500–16,000** *S(NY)*

A Scandinavian pile runner, probably Finland, late 19thC, 139 x 52in (352 x 132cm). **$3,200–4,000** *C*

A Louis Philippe Aubusson carpet, small rewoven areas, mid-19thC, 186 x 155in (472 x 392cm). **$11,500–14,500** *S(NY)*

A Konya prayer rug, Turkey, early 19thC, 63 x 52in (160 x 132cm). **$5,000–5,500** *GH*

A Toussounian Hereke silk and metal thread rug, c1890, 79in (201cm) long. **$15,500–17,000** *C*

A Makri rug, the reserves with a stylised tree and medallions, Anatolia, late 19thC, 58 x 87in (147 x 221cm). **$4,800–5,600** *Dns*

A Mamluk style carpet, Turkey, partial end guard borders, repaired, c1900, 164 x 144in (417 x 365cm). **$9,000–10,000** *S(NY)*

A Ghiordes prayer rug, Turkey, 19thC, 66 x 47in (168 x 119cm). **$4,800–5,600** *GH*

A Konya prayer rug,
west Anatolia, 18thC,
57in (145cm) long.
$6,000–7,200 *C*

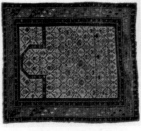

A Daghestan prayer rug,
north east Caucasus, 19thC,
42 x 47in (107 x 120cm).
$2,400–2,800 *Dns*

A Seychour khelleh,
north east Caucasus,
c1895, 195in (495cm) long.
$1,400–1,800 *P*

A Soumakh dragon carpet, east Caucasus,
late 19thC, 132 x 102in (335 x 259cm).
$15,200–16,800 *S(NY)*

A Shirvan rug, east Caucasus,
late 19thC, 72in (182cm) long.
$5,000–5,500 *SK(B)*

A Kashgai rug, the field with 2 linked
medallions, south west Persia, c1900,
46 x 78in (117 x 198cm).
$1,600–1,900 *Dns*

A Kazak Karatchop rug,
west Caucasus, late 19thC,
87in (221cm) long.
$11,500–13,500 *S*

A Sarouk Feraghan rug,
c1910, 79in (200cm) long.
$4,000–4,500 *KW*

An Afshar millefleurs rug, west Persia,
c1930, 91 x 61in (231 x 155cm).
$2,500–2,800 *AWH*

A Kashan silk rug,
central Persia, c1890,
82 x 52in (208 x 132cm).
$16,000–19,000 *KW*

A Feraghan rug,
west Persia, c1930,
104 x 50in (262 x 128cm).
$2,000–2,500 *AWH*

An Amritsar carpet,
north India, late 19thC,
129 x 85in (327.5 x 216cm).
$8,500–9,500 *C*

A Chinese pictorial rug,
with bird of paradise, c190?
92½ x 61in (235 x 155cm).
$7,200–8,000 *KW*

A sampler, by Ann Wane, aged 10, worked in cross stitch, c1820, 16½ x 12¼in (42 x 31cm).
$320–360 *TAR*

A sampler, by Frances Mary Harrison, with verse, dated '1839', 19 x 16in (48 x 40.5cm).
$720–800 *SPU*

A sampler, by Eleanor Warboys, aged 11 years, worked with verses, country scenes, vases of flowers and a floral border, c1805, 17 x 13in (43 x 33cm).
$1,200–1,400 *RA*

A sampler, worked in coloured silks with an Adam and Eve motif, family initials and spot motifs, inscribed 'At Cullodn Muer [Moor] Peter Law, dated '1746', 13 x 12in (33 x 30.5cm).
$14,500–16,000 *CSK*

A sampler, by Ann Higgins, with a verse, dated '1794', 21 x 13in (53 x 33cm).
$950–1,100 *GAZE*

A sampler, by Elizabeth Wood, dated '1847', 15 x 15½in (38 x 39.5cm), framed.
$550–650 *SPU*

A Berlin woolwork sampler, initialled 'P.T.', dated '1853', 13 x 8in (33 x 20.5cm).
$140–160 *JPr*

A sampler, by Jennet Black, worked with the Tree of Life, initials 'A.T.' and 'I.T.', short verse and a house, dated '1809', 17 x 13in (43 x 33cm).
$2,000–2,400 *RA*

A sampler, by Isabella Henderson, worked with a pheasant in a tree, dated '1837', 13¾ x 11in (35 x 28cm).
$720–800 *MRW*

A Berlin woolwork sampler, by Maria Terry, dated '1843', 18½ x 17½in (47 x 44.5cm).
$220–260 *JPr*

A sampler, by Margaret Williams, aged 7 years, c1861, 11½ x 9½in (29 x 24cm).
$260–300 *No7*

A Tournai Biblical tapestry, woven in
wools and silks, 15thC, 40in (102cm) high.
$28,000–32,000 *C*

A Flemish Biblical tapestry,
late 16thC, 122in (310cm) high.
$15,200–16,800 *Bon*

A Mortlake tapestry
fragment, late 17thC,
87in (221cm) high.
$10,500–11,500 *C*

A Flemish hunting tapestry, woven
in wool and silks, some repairs,
16thC, 192 x 120in (488 x 304cm).
$20,000–22,500 *Bon*

A Flemish tapestry, woven in silks
and wools, depicting a riding party
beside a country inn, c1700,
120 x 152in (305 x 386cm).
$23,000–25,500 *CSK*

A pair of Aubusson
tapestry panels, each
woven with a ribbon-
tied medallion, c1860,
130in (330cm) high.
$16,000–17,500 *S*

A French tapestry panel,
some wear, early
18thC, 59 x 64in
(150 x 163cm).
$5,000–5,500 *DN*

A French tapestry panel, woven in
wools, depicting a pastoral scene of
a shepherdess amidst classical ruins,
early 18thC, 80 x 109in (203 x 277cm).
$5,000–5,600 *P*

An Aubusson tapestry
panel, depicting a
parrot before an
exotic tree, 18thC,
110in (280cm) high.
$5,000–5,600 *S(Z)*

An Aubusson pastoral
tapestry, after a design
by Jean-Baptiste Huët
the elder, 18thC,
97in (247cm) high.
$11,200–12,800 *C*

An Aubusson armorial tapestry, woven in wools,
depicting the arms of Charles William Stewart-
Vane, 3rd Marquess of Londonderry, and his second
wife, early 19thC, 69 x 89in (175 x 226cm).
$16,000–17,500 *C*

A Swiss enamelled gold box, with 2 hinged vinaigrette compartments and a secret mechanism opening the lid of another compartment hidden in the base, probably Geneva, c1840, 3in (7.5cm) wide.
$5,600–6,400 *C(G)*

A Continental gold presentation box, with portrait miniature and coloured paste stones, maker's mark, signed by Y. B. Couvelet, dated '1821', 4in (10cm) wide.
$3,200–3,500 *Bon*

A Swiss gold and enamel snuff box, the hinged cover decorated with a quiver of arrows crossed with a bow, c1800, 3in (7.5cm) wide.
$8,800–9,600 *Bon*

An enamel writing box, the hinged cover printed and painted with figures, corded gilt-metal mounts, the interior with compartments and 2 glass bottles with enamel tops, c1770, 7in (17.5cm) wide.
$5,600–6,400 *C*

A Swiss enamelled gold snuff box, made for the Oriental market, the cover painted with trophies of music and flowers, Geneva, c1830, 3in (7.5cm) wide.
$13,800–15,200 *C(G)*

A Battersea enamel urn, with a rococo cartouche painted with a landscape, 18thC, 9in (23cm) high.
$1,000–1,200 *HYD*

A silver and enamel cigarette case, depicting a view of Windsor Castle, hallmarked London 1886, 3½in (9cm) wide.
$2,200–2,400 *SHa*

A Fabergé enamel card holder, with gold interior, signed by Henrik Wigström, early 20thC, 4¼in (11cm) high, with original box.
$8,000–8,800 *LHA*

A gold and enamel snuff box, engraved and decorated overall in opaque and translucent enamels, probably north Italian, c1840, 3¼in (8cm) wide.
$9,500–10,500 *S(G)*

A Fabergé *cloisonné* and silver-gilt *kovsch*, depicting birds within stylised floral decoration against a pale blue background, signed below Moscow Imperial double-headed eagle, late 19thC, 3in (7.5cm) wide.
$1,400–1,600 *Bon*

A gold, enamel and pearl needle case, the panels enamelled in translucent purple patterned with gold mullets and pellets within opaque white chain borders, beaded and topped by pearls, charge mark of Julien Alaterre, Geneva, c1785, 4¼in (11cm) long.
$1,900–2,200 *S(G)*

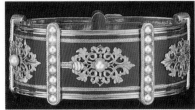

A French gold and enamel bangle, each panel with applied engraved foliate motif and half-pearl line divisions, 19thC, in a modern case stamped 'Boucheron'.
$4,000–4,500 *CSK*

A Fabergé gold, amethyst and diamond bangle, marked with initials of workmaster Knut Oskar Pihl, Moscow, c1890, 65mm wide.
$3,500–4,000 *S(NY)*

A Revivalist style coral, gold and enamel bracelet, brooch and pair of earrings, c1865, brooch 50mm wide.
$12,800–14,400 *C*

A gold brooch, set with an amethyst surrounded with pearls and turquoises, c1830, 32mm wide.
$1,200–1,400 *DIC*

A diamond Maltese cross brooch, mounted in silver and gold with detachable fittings, early 19thC, 40mm wide.
$5,000–5,500 *DN*

A late Victorian ruby and diamond hinged bangle, the flowerhead cluster with a single central diamond, mounted in silver and gold.
$4,000–4,500 *Bon*

A Victorian 15ct gold brooch, in the form of a fly, set with pearls, sapphires, rubies and diamonds, 35mm long.
$1,100–1,300 *GEM*

A star brooch, with a single pearl, sapphires, rubies and diamonds, mounted in silver and gold, c1890.
$2,800–3,500 *Bon*

A diamond and emerald cameo bar brooch, the cameo depicting a female bacchante, mounted in gold, c1880, 58mm wide.
$7,600–8,800 *C*

A Victorian 15ct gold brooch, set with seed pearls and diamonds, c1860, 50mm long.
$280–320 *PSA*

A gold and turquoise brooch, in the form of a spray of lilies of the valley, c1840, 50mm high.
$800–950 *DIC*

A diamond brooch, the flower-heads with diamond collet centres to pavé-set leaves and stems, c1935, 4in (10cm) high.
$12,800–14,400 *C*

A 15ct gold bracelet, the ovals set with amethysts and pearls, c1880, 7in (18cm) long.
$480–560 *PSA*

A Fabergé silver and translucent enamel buckle, initials for workmaster Henrik Wigström, c1900, 70mm wide.
$3,500–4,000 *S(NY)*

A Victorian cameo brooch, featuring a hand holding a bunch of flowers, set in a scrolled mount.
$250–300 *P(NW)*

A shell cameo, with the figure of Aquarius, in a gold Etruscan style pendant mount, 19thC.
$1,900–2,200 *CSK*

A Victorian cameo brooch, featuring 2 classical figures in a landscape, c1880, 60mm wide.
$550–625 *GEM*

A pair of ruby and diamond earrings, the drops with ruby centres within diamond scroll surrounds, mounted in silver and gold, c1860.
$7,200–8,000 *Bon*

An aquamarine and diamond pendant, suspended from a diamond-set bow, with a chain, c1910.
$3,200–3,600 *Bon*

A chalcedony cameo brooch pendant, the gold surround with enamel and diamond rim, in a half-pearl border, c1880.
$4,000–4,500 *CSK*

A French 18ct gold locket, inset with rubies and pearls, with hinged inner frames, c1900, 50mm high.
$720–800 *PSA*

r. A gold, half-pearl and peridot necklace, c1900.
$1,900–2,200 *DIC*

A Renaissance style gold and enamel 'pelican in her piety' pendant, with a pearl drop, c1890.
$7,300–8,000 *C*

A gold and enamel pendant, set with a central amethyst, the suspension ring with a pearl, c1900, 25mm high.
$800–950 *DIC*

A diamond and enamel pendant, picked out in diamonds with an arcaded garden, sunrise and swan below a bridge, c1900, 60mm high.
$37,000–40,000 *C*

A Chinese canopy bed, with latticework back and sides, on incurved legs with hoof feet, 18thC, 86in (218.5cm) wide.
$10,400–11,200 *S(NY)*

A Chinese horseshoe-back armchair, the splat carved with a cloud medallion, 17thC.
$5,500–6,500 *S(NY)*

A Korean red-lacquered wood storage chest, with openwork iron hinges, Choson Dynasty, 35½in (90cm) wide.
$2,500–3,000 *S(NY)*

A pair of Chinese tapered cabinets, with panelled doors, the interior with 2 shelves and a pair of short drawers, restored, 17thC, 28in (71cm) wide.
$32,000–35,000 *S(NY)*

A Japanese parquetry chest of 11 drawers, with geometric patterns, late 19thC, 32in (81cm) wide.
$1,100–1,300 *E*

A Chinese carved padouk wood table, with marble top, c1870, 22in (56cm) diam.
$950–1,100 *GBr*

A Chinese bamboo table, with black lacquer top and everted ends above a latticework apron, c1800, 84in (213cm) wide.
$6,500–8,000 *S(NY)*

A Chinese coromandel and black lacquer screen, one side with a palace garden scene, the reverse with flowers and birds, 19thC, 136in (345cm) wide.
$5,500–6,500 *S(NY)*

A Chinese table, the top inset with a *cloisonné* panel depicting a pheasant, 19thC, 37½in (95.5cm) wide.
$11,200–12,200 *HOLL*

A Chinese bamboo screen, the upper panels open, above latticework, c1800, 84in (213cm) wide.
$6,500–8,000 *S(NY)*

A Chinese elm table, with everted ends above pierced foliate carved cloud spandrels, recessed beaded legs joined by *ruyi* and cloud-decorated pierced panels, c1800, 82in (208cm) wide.
$4,400–4,800 *S(NY)*

A Chinese *cloisonné* enamel archaistic bowl, the C-scroll handles issuing from gilt dragons' heads, 16thC, 10¼in (26cm) wide.
$4,400–4,800 *C*

A Chinese enamel stem cup, the yellow ground decorated with flowers and butterflies, c1880, 8¼in (21cm) high.
$560–640 *DAN*

A Chinese Canton enamel *zhadou*, with white enamelled interior, 18thC, 4in (10cm) high.
$2,500–3,000 *S(NY)*

A Chinese painted Canton enamel censer, with double upright gilt loop handles, on tripod feet, Yongzheng seal mark and of the period, 2¾in (7cm) high.
$9,000–10,000 *S(NY)*

A Chinese *cloisonné* enamel censer, Qianlong period, 16in (40.5cm) high.
$3,200–3,600 *Wai*

A Chinese painted enamel sweetmeat tray and cover, the interior with a central dish surrounded by 8 small dishes, c1800, 14½in (37cm) diam.
$2,200–2,700 *CNY*

A Chinese *cloisonné* enamel and gilt-bronze figure-form support, Kangxi period, 11½in (29cm) high.
$7,200–8,800 *S(NY)*

A Chinese enamel hexagonal vase, decorated with flowers and birds on a blue ground, 19thC, 10¼in (26cm) high.
$560–640 *DAN*

A Japanese flask, decorated in lacquer and pottery, with a seed ojime and flask-form netsuke, 19thC, 4¾in (12cm) high.
$2,200–2,700 *S(NY)*

A Chinese pink and white overlay Peking glass lotus-form vase, with overlapping graduated finely veined petals, the base carved as a curling leaf and stem, 18thC, 4¼in (11cm) high.
$6,500–8,000 *S(NY)*

A Chinese reverse-painted and gilt glass picture, depicting an interior and 3 ladies with an old man, 19thC, in a later giltwood frame, 34¼ x 25½in (87 x 65cm).
$5,500–6,500 *C*

A Chinese coral bottle, carved with bats and emblems over waves and rocks, Qianlong period, 58mm high.
$8,800–9,600 *S*

A Chinese Canton enamel bottle, enamelled with a stylised lotus scroll, mark and period of Qianlong, 69mm high.
$8,000–9,000 *S*

A Chinese three-colour overlay glass bottle, carved with lotus flowers and foliage rising from stylised waves, 18thC, 58mm high.
$3,200–3,600 *S*

A Chinese red overlay glass bottle, carved with peony above lotus, and symbols, 1780–1860, 67mm high.
$5,000–5,600 *S*

A Chinese glass bottle, carved with continuous lotus leaves, on a foot in the form of a leaf, 1750–1860, 38mm high.
$7,300–8,000 *S*

A Chinese overlay glass bottle, carved with fish and lotus on a snowstorm ground, 19thC, 71mm high.
$1,000–1,100 *CNY*

A Chinese overlay snowstorm glass bottle, with fixed ring handles, 19thC, 67mm high.
$2,800–3,200 *CNY*

A Japanese two-case inro, by Kanshosai Toyo, with a stained ivory bowl and iron plate, carved and inlaid with a court musician, 19thC, inro 63mm high.
$5,600–6,200 *S*

A Chinese glass snuff bottle, the snowflake body overlaid with the image of a watch, small chips, Daoguang period, 46mm high.
$4,000–4,500 *S(NY)*

A Chinese single overlay snuff bottle, carved with a stag under a pine tree and a crane, Qianlong period, 65mm high.
$4,800–5,400 *S(NY)*

A Japanese four-case eggshell ground inro, decorated with a group of fish, eyes inlaid with horn, and a netsuke, c1800, 3¼in (8cm) long.
$11,500–13,000 *C*

A Chinese gilt-silver mounted white jade snuff bottle, embellished with precious stones, 19thC, 59mm high.
$950–1,100 *S(NY)*

A Japanese Somada style four-case inro, decorated with a Chinese sage and attendants, with gold and silver details, early 19thC, 74mm high.
$3,500–4,000 *S*

A Japanese lacquered three-case inro, decorated in gold, signed 'Shoho Saku' at the age of 80, with seal, and an agate ojime, unsigned, 19thC, 3½in (9cm) high.
$9,500–10,500 *S(NY)*

A Chinese celadon jade lotus-head stem cup, carved with 3 layers of petals, Ming Dynasty, 4in (10cm) high.
$7,500–8,000 *C*

A pair of Chinese archaistic jadeite ewers and covers, the tongue-form spouts extending from the mouths of mythical beasts, the covers set with 2 loops and stylised phoenix knops, 19thC, 6½in (16.5cm) wide.
$21,500–24,000 *S(NY)*

A Chinese white and brown jade carving of an old man and boy, on pierced rockwork, c1700, 4in (10cm) high.
$4,800–5,400 *C*

A Chinese jade dragon and vase group, the cover with a phoenix knop, 18thC, 5in (12.5cm) high.
$2,500–3,000 *S(NY)*

A Chinese white jade hanging pendant, with 3 rows of 'Eight Daoist Emblems', 17thC, 13½in (34.5cm) long.
$2,200–2,700 *S(NY)*

A Chinese jade group, one fish in grey stone, one in celadon stone, 18thC, 5½in (14cm) high.
$5,600–6,400 *S*

A Chinese woven panel, depicting boys at play, on a fine metallic ground, 17thC, 27 x 12½in (68.5 x 32cm).
$12,000–13,500 *S(NY)*

A Chinese embroidered silk woman's jacket, worked in gold threads, late Qing Dynasty.
$1,600–1,800 *CNY*

A rank badge, probably from a Chinese army general's robe, late 19thC.
$800–1,000 *Wai*

A Chinese jadeite figure of Guanyin, wearing a beaded necklace, 19thC, 16in (40.6cm) high.
$8,500–9,500 *S(NY)*

The back of a Chinese Daoist priest's robe, woven with dragons and a pagoda, flanked by the moon hare and sun bird interspersed with cranes, c1600, 47 x 69in (119.5 x 175cm).
$550–725 *S(NY)*

A Chinese embroidered silk lady's jacket, the cuffs worked with gold and silver threads, late 19thC, 35½in (90cm) long.
$1,700–2,000 *CNY*

A Chinese embroidered silk lady's coat, with Daoist and Buddhistic emblems, late 19thC, 45½in (115.5cm) long.
$2,800–3,500 *CNY*

A group of 4 Chinese gilt-bronze figures of Daoist warrior Immortals, each standing on rockwork bases, wearing armour and robes, traces of lacquer and gilt on each, minor casting faults, Ming Dynasty, 7¼in (18.5cm) high.
$4,400–4,800 *CNY*

A pair of Chinese gilt-bronze candle holders, in the form of elephants wearing elaborate bridles and straps, the saddle blankets incised with scrolling lotus, restored and regilded, 18thC, 7in (18cm) high.
$4,800–5,400 *C*

A Japanese silver vase, carved with flowers highlighted in gilt, with flowerspray handles, Taisho period, 10in (25.5cm) high.
$11,200–12,200 *S(NY)*

A Japanese bronze figure of an elephant, on a hardwood stand, signed, 19thC, 13in (33cm) wide.
$1,100–1,300 *SPU*

A Japanese lacquered wood and ivory okimono, signed 'Saneaki', late 19thC, 11in (28cm) high.
$5,000–5,500 *S(NY)*

A Chinese export lacquered tea caddy, the top and sides decorated with panels depicting landscape scenes, c1830, 10in (25.5cm) wide.
$850–950 *SSW*

A Japanese gilt-bronze group, signed 'Miyao', late 19thC, 14½in (37cm) high.
$21,500–24,000 *S(NY)*

A Chinese bronze censer, with stylised beast handles, marked, 17thC, 5in (12.5cm) high.
$6,500–7,500 *C(HK)*

A Chinese export lacquered box, c1820, 4in (10cm) long.
$120–140 *SSW*

A Japanese bronze censer, decorated with archaistic motifs, signed 'Miyao', late 19thC, 54½in (138cm) high.
$26,500–29,000 *S(NY)*

A Kashan lustre pottery bowl, the centre painted with a deer, Persia, c1200, 8½in (22cm) diam.
$7,300–8,000 *S*

A Kashan bowl, with opaque crackled glaze, Persia, early 13thC, 9¾in (25cm) diam.
$1,600–2,000 *C*

A Mamluk pottery dish, with a short central foot, repaired, Syria, 14thC, 12½in (32cm) diam.
$3,600–4,400 *C*

A Kubachi pottery dish, with a sloping bracketed rim, Persia, repaired, early 16thC, 14in (35.5cm) diam.
$7,800–8,400 *Bon*

An Iznik pottery dish, with sloping rim, Ottoman Turkey, c1620, 10½in (26.5cm) diam.
$2,200–2,700 *C*

An Iznik pottery dish, Ottoman Turkey, c1650, 11½in (29cm) diam.
$7,500–8,500 *C*

A Kütahya pottery lemon squeezer, with floral decoration, Turkey, 18thC, 5½in (14cm) diam.
$13,500–15,000 *Bon*

A Turkish glass chalice, the foot hung with lustres, 19thC, 12in (31cm) high.
$2,800–3,200 *S*

A Berber enamelled silver diadem, with 3 hinged elements, Algeria, c1900, 7¼in (18.5cm) diam.
$3,600–4,000 *S*

A manuscript leaf with illumination, depicting The Death of Bahrum Gur, gouache heightened with gold, Persia, c1340, 8½ x 12in (21.5 x 30.5cm).
$3,600–4,400 *C*

A polychrome enamelled and copper-gilt covered dish, Turkey, c1800, 6½in (16.5cm) diam.
$12,000–13,500 *S*

A Seljuk inset gold, hardstone and white metal bracelet, some stones replaced, Persia, 12thC.
$10,200–11,200 *C*

A pair of Qajar wooden doors, painted with birds and plants, Persia, 19thC, 69½in (176.5cm) high.
$9,400–10,200 *S*

An embroidered linen wrapping cloth, worked in silk, Ottoman Empire, 17thC, 44 x 38in (112 x 96.5cm).
$16,800–18,400 *S*

An Herat picture of a palace interior, mid-15thC, 13 x 10½in (33 x 26.5cm).
$1,700–1,900 *C*

An Ottoman embroidered silk taffeta lady's court kaftan, with silver metal threads, c1800.
$6,000–6,500 *S*

A pair of pine arched doors,
with black metal hinges,
c1880, 102in (259cm) high.
$880–960 *AL*

A copper weathervane,
in the form of a
cockerel, early 20thC,
58in (147cm) high.
$1,000–1,200 *P*

A bronze group of 2 wood
nymphs feeding a faun,
by F. V. Blundstone, dated
'1935', 35in (89cm) high.
$16,000–17,500 *S(S)*

A Victorian chimney
pot, now converted
to a flowerpot,
29½in (75cm) high.
$55–65 *ACA*

A copper sundial, on a
limestone column, 19thC,
38in (96.5cm) high.
$1,000–1,200 *MSW*

A pair of Portland stone Gothic style gargoyles, each
beast sitting on a winged lion, c1860, 26in (66cm) high.
$10,200–11,200 *S(S)*

A white marble figure
of the young Bacchus,
by Giovanni Maria
Benzoni, c1870,
40in (101.5cm) high.
$21,500–24,000 *S(S)*

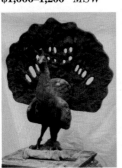

A pair of lead models of
peacocks, early 19thC,
23½in (59.5cm) high.
$5,000–6,000 *DRU*

A marble bust, possibly
Ferdinand de Lessepps,
19thC, 35in (89cm) high.
$4,000–4,500 *DRU*

A cast porcelain head,
depicting a river god,
1920s, 24in (61cm) high.
$1,300–1,600 *RECL*

A pair of Coade stone
columns, c1840,
43in (109cm) high.
$16,000–17,500 *S(S)*

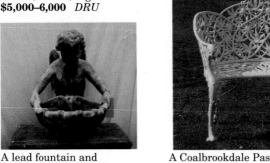

A lead fountain and
birdbath, early 19thC,
22in (56cm) high.
$2,800–3,500 *DRU*

A Coalbrookdale Passionflower pattern cast
iron seat, of scrolling curved form with pierced
seat, stamped, c1870, 42in (107cm) wide.
$16,000–17,500 *S(S)*

A George III painted and parcel-gilt 'jewelled' fireplace surround, with inverted breakfront top, 66in (167.5cm) wide.
$3,500–4,500 *C*

A late Victorian fireplace, the tiles decorated with flowers, 61in (155cm) wide.
$720–800 *WRe*

A cast iron fireplace, the tiled insert on each side decorated with flowers, early 20thC, 45in (114.5cm) wide.
$800–950 *WRe*

A Carolean carved oak overmantel, c1615, 70in (178cm) wide.
$6,500–8,000 *RECL*

A George III brass and steel basket grate, c1775, fireback earlier and repaired, 30in (76cm) wide.
$6,500–7,500 *S*

A cast iron hob fire grate, late 18thC, 32in (81.5cm) wide.
$950–1,100 *WRe*

An Irish pine fire surround and mantelpiece, carved with geometric panels, c1870, 62in (157.5cm) wide.
$200–250 *TAN*

A set of 3 polished steel and gilt-brass fire irons, mid-19thC.
$1,400–1,600 *CSK*

An Irish pine fire surround, carved with heart-shaped patterns, ribbed central panel, and inset sunburst corner pieces, c1800, 56in (142cm) wide.
$350–400 *TAN*

A pair of brass and iron andirons, the engraved obelisks with turned finials and bun feet, 19thC, 24in (61cm) high.
$2,500–3,000 *S*

A pair of brass andirons, each sphere surmounted by a flaming urn finial, with cast iron brackets, 19thC, 28¾in (73cm) high.
$2,200–2,600 *C(S)*

A Regency gilt-brass and bronze extending fire curb, in the form of a double-ended classical staff, on an inverted breakfront moulded base, c1810, 49in (124.5cm) wide extended.
$1,400–1,700 *S*

A French bronze figure
of a seated vestal virgin,
by Eugène Aizelin,
signed, early 19thC,
26¾in (68cm) high.
$4,500–5,500 *S*

A bronze classical figural
group, by Clodion, c1850,
16in (50cm) high.
$1,400–1,600 *SSW*

A pair of bronze and
ormolu candlesticks,
fitted for electricity,
19thC, 23½in (60cm) high.
$4,600–5,400 *C*

A bronze figure, by
Jean Baptiste Carpeaux,
signed, 19thC,
13in (33cm) high.
$6,500–7,500 *P*

A gilt-bronze and lapis lazuli centrepiece,
the border with reclining female figures with
flowering pitchers and 2 youths, by Cardeilhac,
Paris, c1890, 26½in (67cm) wide.
$25,500–32,000 *S*

A Belle Epoque gilt
bronze platter, by
A. Marionnet, c1910,
18in (45.5cm) wide.
$640–720 *RIT*

A French bronze and parcel
gilt bust of Helen of Troy,
cast from the model by
Jean-Baptiste Clésinger, late
19thC, 30½in (77.5cm) high.
$13,800–15,200 *C*

A pair of gilded
bronze vases, with
mask handles, c1875,
9¾in (25cm) high.
$800–900 *SSW*

A pair of bronze figures
of African women, by
C. Cumberworth, late
19thC, 25¾in (65cm) high.
$10,200–11,200 *S*

A bronze figure of a
clown, by Bernard-
Adrien Steüer, late
19thC, 22in (56cm) high.
$5,000–6,000 *S*

A bronze figure of Hebe,
by C. Buhot, seated on Zeus
disguised as an eagle, late
19thC, 27in (69.5cm) high.
$3,500–4,000 *E*

A pair of gilt-bronze and
marble candelabra,
signed 'A. Carrier',
c1870, 48in (123cm) high.
$20,000–21,500 *S*

A bronze figure, 'Girl
Tying Her Sandal', by
Sir Hamo Thornycroft,
c1918, 17in (43cm) high.
$7,000–8,000 *C*

A bronze figure,
by Charles Levy,
late 19thC,
31in (79cm) high.
$4,200–4,800 *C*

A George III brass tea urn, with original liner, with gadrooned rim, handles and shell-shaped feet, 17in (43cm) high.
$400–500 *MEG*

A Dutch brass ash bucket, with gadrooned rim, mask handles, raised on lions' paw feet, c1850, 13½in (34cm) high.
$350–400 *CAT*

A brass coal urn, the lid with leaf-cast finial, on splayed legs with claw feet, early 20thC, 24in (60cm) high.
$1,900–2,400 *S*

A Regency ormolu and white marble inkstand, the hinged shell enclosing a fitted interior, 7in (17.5cm) high.
$3,600–4,000 *C*

A polychrome spelter figure of a child looking over a wall, by E. Villanis, c1900, 7½in (19cm) high.
$370–420 *SUC*

A pair of brass jardinières or wall pockets, decorated with cherubs around an urn, c1880, 9½in (24cm) high.
$550–580 *CAT*

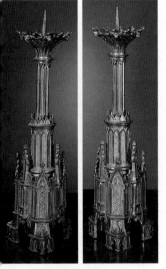

A pair of late Victorian gilt-brass altar pricket candlesticks, in neo-Gothic style, cast with tracery ornament, 23in (58cm) high.
$1,600–1,800 *C*

A Russian brass tea urn, of tapering form, complete with burner, with scrolled handles, on paw feet, early 20thC, 18in (45.5cm) high.
$320–400 *AWH*

A Louis Philippe ormolu centrepiece, the shallow bowl with vine cast underside, supported on 3 Bacchic putti, on stepped triform base, 23in (58.5cm) high.
$5,800–7,200 *C*

An alabaster urn-on-stand, carved with classical figures, mid-19thC, 74in (188cm) high.
$25,500–30,000 *S*

An Italian white marble group of 2 putto, after Pierre-Philippe Thomire, late 19thC, 24in (61cm) high.
$7,000–8,000 *C*

An alabaster model of a cockatiel, with glass eyes, mid-19thC, 19in (48cm) high.
$3,200–3,600 *CAT*

An Italian alabaster and parcel-gilt figure of a maiden, c1900, 39in (98.5cm) high.
$7,300–8,000 *C*

An Italian white marble figure of Venus, after the Antique, late 19thC, 34½in (87.5cm) high.
$7,300–8,000 *C*

An Italian white marble figure, by Antonio Tantardini, late 19thC, 49in (124.5cm) high.
$4,800–5,600 *C*

A marble sculpture, inscribed 'J. Warrington-Wood', dated '1869', 28½in (72.5cm) high.
$4,000–5,000 *SPU*

A white marble figure of Venus Italica, after Antonio Canova, late 19thC, 51in (129.5cm) high.
$14,200–15,200 *CSK*

An alabaster female figure, c1900, 36in (91.5cm) high.
$3,600–4,000 *C*

A terracotta group of the infant Christ and St John, possibly 19thC, 19½in (50cm) high.
$4,000–4,500 *S(Z)*

A pair of French griotte marble and brass-mounted urns, with stepped bases, late 19thC, 26½in (67.5cm) high.
$5,400–6,200 *S(S)*

A terracotta group of a nymph and 2 putti, after Joseph-Charles Marin, early 19thC, 13½in (34cm) high.
$7,300–8,000 *S*

An Italian terracotta allegorical group of 2 putti, emblematic of Spring, standing by a tree stump, 19thC, 66in (167.5cm) high.
$35,000–40,000 *C*

A pair of Italian walnut panels, carved with lions' masks, each with boldly modelled manes, 17thC, 11in (30cm) high, on later bronzed metal stands.
$6,400–7,200 *DBA*

A pair of walnut wall carvings, the figures entwined with snakes, late 17thC, 8¼in (21cm) high.
$750–900 *CAT*

A polychrome and gilt-wood relief of a male attendant, early 16thC, 11½in (29cm) high.
$4,800–5,400 *S*

A carved ivory and wood group of a man and a woman dancing, each wearing 18thC dress, late 19thC, 6½in (16.5cm) high.
$7,000–8,000 *C*

A Norwegian wooden ale jug, carved from the solid, c1889, 9in (23cm) high.
$1,300–1,400 *RYA*

A hand-painted papier mâché powder bowl, 1930s, 4in (10cm) diam.
$50–60 *SUS*

A Swiss boxwood nutcracker, with turned decoration, used for cob nuts or hazel nuts, 17th/18thC, 5in (12.5cm) long.
$950–1,100 *AEF*

A chip-carved layette tray, for the presentation of clothes for a newborn child, Friesland, 18thC, 14 x 22in (35.5 x 56cm) wide.
$1,200–1,400 *AEF*

A papier mâché letter box, with hinged lid and lock, mid-19thC, 6¾in (17cm) wide.
$240–270 *SPU*

A Dutch wooden table snuff shoe box, with lift-off lid, c1800, 5in (12.5cm) long.
$1,000–1,100 *AEF*

A George III papier mâché tea caddy, painted with a central floral basket, the interior with subsidiary cover, 6in (15cm) wide.
$2,000–2,400 *C*

A carved oak tea caddy,
with ivory knob and brass feet,
mid-18thC, 9in (23cm) wide.
$520–560 *BIL*

A brass-inlaid sewing
box, dated '1820',
10in (25.5cm) wide.
$600–700 *SPU*

A Georgian tortoiseshell, gold
and silver inlaid snuff box,
c1780, 2½in (6.5cm) diam.
$520–560 *MB*

An ebony and porcupine
quill work box, with lift-out
tray, Ceylon, c1820,
14in (35.5cm) wide.
$2,800–3,200 *CORO*

A Georgian mahogany
travelling writing box,
12in (30.5cm) wide.
$640–780 *SPU*

An Indian sandalwood dressing box,
with silver mounts and secret drawer,
c1800, 16in (40.5cm) wide.
$2,800–3,200 *CORO*

A Norwegian bentwood storage box,
with original painted decoration,
c1840, 5in (12.5cm) wide.
$400–500 *RYA*

A mahogany and silver-
mounted cutlery box,
containing 18 pieces
of cutlery, c1760,
15in (38cm) high.
$4,800–5,400 *S*

A brass-bound coromandel
work box, with ivory inlaid
inner lid, Ceylon, c1830,
16in (40.5cm) wide.
$1,400–1,900 *CORO*

A Regency rosewood sewing
box, with brass inlay,
9¾in (24.5cm) wide.
$280–320 *BIL*

A Dutch rosewood tea caddy, with
brass handle and mounts, c1780,
9½in (24.5cm) wide.
$560–640 *SSW*

A Regency lacquer box, with
chinoiserie decoration, c1820,
10¾in (27.5cm) wide.
$430–480 *SSW*

A coromandel tea caddy,
with brass mounts, c1840,
6½in (16.5cm) wide.
$320–360 *SPU*

A Tunbridge Ware octagonal card box, with a banding of roses and a spray of roses on the lid, c1840, 10½in (27cm) wide.
$720–880 *BAD*

A Tunbridge Ware games box, with composite veneer resembling marbling and a parquetry starburst, c1840, 10½in (26.5cm) wide.
$1,900–2,200 *BAD*

A coromandel inkstand, with cut glass ink bottles and fitted paper holders, c1860, 13in (33cm) wide.
$1,700–1,900 *ARE*

A coromandel stationary box, with gilt-bronze mounted Wedgwood plaques, c1860, 9½in (24cm) wide.
$3,200–3,500 *MB*

A Tunbridge Ware inlaid rosewood box, with central floral panel and stylised flower border, with lock, c1850, 13in (33cm) wide.
$160–200 *MB*

A figured walnut brass-bound tea caddy, with domed top, mid-19thC, 9in (23cm) wide.
$160–180 *PCh*

An ivory, horn and porcupine quill work box, with fitted interior, Vizagapatam, India, c1860, 13in (33cm) wide.
$2,800–3,200 *CORO*

A Victorian brass-mounted ebonised vanity case, by Abraham and Jane Brownett, 15in (38cm) wide.
$4,500–5,500 *C(S)*

A rosewood box, with silver mounts, by W. F. Williams, 1906, 5in (12.5cm) high.
$1,600–1,800 *THOM*

A walnut and mother-of-pearl inlaid work box, with original sewing implements, 19thC, 11¾in (30cm) wide.
$360–440 *MEG*

A porcupine quill and wood box, the quills arranged in a geometric pattern, inlaid with bone, 19thC, 8½in (21.5cm) wide.
$85–100 *SSW*

An Italian silver-mounted pen nib box, with Sorrento ware marquetry, c1880, 8in (20.5cm) long.
$80–100 *BIL*

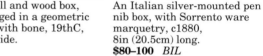

MUSIC
Cylinder Musical Boxes

A Swiss musical box, playing 10 airs as listed on the tune sheet, with 13in (33cm) cylinder, contained in an ebonised and grained case, with marquetry-inlaid lid and gilt-metal carrying handles, inscribed 'Pap Leon & Co, Paris, 1261A', 19thC, 25½in (65cm) wide.
$3,000–3,500 *AH*

A Swiss sublime harmony musical box, playing 8 mainly operatic airs, contained in a crossbanded walnut case with stringing, label inscribed 'Geo Baker & Co, Manufacturers, Geneva, No. 15935', 19thC, 25in (63.5cm) wide.
$3,500–4,000 *MCA*

A musical box, with 13in (33cm) cylinder playing 6 airs, contained in a grained case, with inlaid coloured floral spray to the front and rosewood-veneered banded lid, c1900, 25in (63.5cm) wide.
$2,000–2,300 *WW*

r. A Multiphone Manivelle musical box, each of the 5 interchangeable 1¾in (4.5cm) cylinders playing one tune operated by a hand-cranked mechanism, contained in a stained beech case with original winding handle, Swiss, late 19thC, 6½in (16cm) wide.
$650–800 *S*

A brass cylinder musical box, contained in a tulip wood cabinet with a floral marquetry oval panel, 19thC, 18in (45.5cm) wide.
$800–900 *MSL*

A Ducommun Girod organ Celeste musical box, the 11in (28cm) cylinder playing 6 airs on 2 combs, contained in a walnut-veneered case, with brass carrying handles, Swiss, c1870, 24in (61cm) wide.
$5,600–6,200 *S*

A Swiss musical box, No. 25054, with 6in (15cm) cylinder playing 8 airs, contained in a simulated rosewood case with inlaid decoration to the lid, late 19thC, 15¾in (40cm) wide.
$650–800 *DDM*

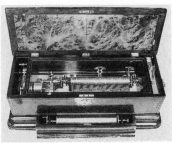

A cylinder musical box, by C. Paillard and Co, with 13in (33cm) comb and interchangeable cylinder movement each playing 6 airs, contained in a burr walnut, ebonised and string-inlaid case with brass foliate carrying handles, frieze drawer with spare cylinder, 19thC, 40in (101.5cm) wide.
$3,500–4,000 *AH*

A Oiseau Mechanique Sons Medaillon musical box, probably by Greiner, No. 16908, the 13in (33cm) cylinder playing 6 airs, with central organ operating a moving singing bird visible through the front of the case with an oil painting of Château Chillon on Lake Geneva and blind fretwork covering the organ, contained in a crossbanded and inlaid case, Swiss, c1880, 27¼in (69cm) wide.
$8,000–9,500 *Bon(C)*

A Swiss bells-in-sight musical box, No. 28302, with 6in (15cm) comb accompanied by 3 saucer-shaped bells with ball strikers, contained in an inlaid, crossbanded and transferred case, late 19thC, 16¼in (41cm) wide.
$880–960 *Bon(C)*

Disc Musical Boxes

The Alexandra disc musical box, by B. H. Abrahams, with 9in (23cm) discs, contained in a walnut-veneered case, Swiss, c1905, 27½in (70cm) wide, together with winding handle and 12 discs.
$2,000–2,500 *Bon(C)*

A Polyphon 11in (28cm) disc musical box, the movement with 2 combs, contained in walnut-veneered case with marquetry-inlaid lid, inset with a decorative print of putti, German, c1900, 15⅝in (40cm) wide, together with 34 discs.
$1,100–1,300 *Bea(E)*

A Polyphon musical box, the periphery driven disc playing 2 combs, German, c1900, 27¼in (69cm) wide, and one metal disc.
$3,200–3,500 *S(Am)*

A Symphonion table 11¾in (30cm) disc musical box, the periphery driven movement with sublime harmony comb arrangement, contained in a walnut-veneered case with winding handle and marquetry-inlaid lid, German, c1900, 19⅝in (50cm) wide, together with 36 metal discs.
$3,500–4,000 *S*

A Symphonion rococo musical box, the movement with 2 combs and playing 11¾in (30cm) discs, German, c1900, 18½in (47cm) wide, together with 10 discs.
$5,000–5,600 *Bea(E)*

A Symphonion 13½in (34.5cm) disc table musical box, the periphery driven movement playing on a single comb, German, c1900, 21in (53cm) wide, together with 6 maker's discs.
$2,500–3,200 *S*

A Symphonion musical savings bank, the 7½in (19cm) discs playing on a single comb with central drive, contained in an oak case with winding handle at the side and coin chute, the base with door to coin compartment, German, c1900, 16½in (42cm) high, together with Symphonion album containing 11 metal discs.
$6,000–7,200 *S*

A Polyphon 8in (20.5cm) disc table musical box, the lever wind movement contained in a walnut-veneered case, colour print applied to lid interior, German, c1910, 10in (25.5cm) wide, together with 11 discs.
$640–720 *S*

A Polyphon 15½in (39.5cm) disc table musical box, the periphery driven movement playing on 2 combs, German, c1910, 20¾in (53cm) wide, with 10 metal discs.
$5,000–5,600 *S*

Mechanical Music

A Victorian 22 key portable barrel pianoforte, by Henry Distin, with 7 tune barrel, the rosewood case with marquetry inlay, the upper panel filled with brocaded and watered silk, c1850, 27½in (70cm) high.
$1,400–1,550 *WW*

Phonographs

A Lorelei phonograph, with green and gilt oxidised finish, a floating reproducer, green and gilt horn, German, c1900, 7in (18cm) long.
$4,000–4,500 *P(Ba)*

Lorelei was a legendary siren who sat on the rocks high above the River Rhine and combed her long blonde hair whilst playing a lyre. Many boatmen were so transfixed by her music and beauty that they lost control of their ships which were wrecked on the jagged rocks.

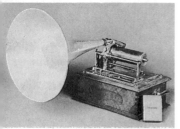

A Pathé Coquet phonograph, with composition reproducer, nickel-plated mechanism, original aluminium horn, c1902, 9in (23cm) wide.
$450–500 *P(Ba)*

A Bruguier silver-gilt singing bird box, the lid enamelled with an Alpine scene, the case decorated with flowerheads and geometric designs, Geneva, c1840, 4in (10cm) wide.
$14,500–17,000 *S*

An Edison Standard phonograph, No. 636723, with aluminium horn suspended by a crane, with handle and cover, American, c1905, 37½in (95cm) high.
$675–800 *Bon(C)*

An Italian piano melodico, by G. Racca, the 48 key movement contained in a shaped wooden case, with winding handle at the side and hinged housing covering the tracker bar, late 19thC, 48in (122cm) long.
$4,800–5,400 *S*

> **Miller's is a price GUIDE not a price LIST**

l. A Continental singing bird musical box, in the form of a book, with inset painted oval miniature and amethyst glass studs on a chased ground, stamped '925', London import mark, 1926, 4¼in (11cm) wide.
$4,000–4,500 *AH*

An Edison Standard phonograph, No. S250129, with black and brass horn and cover, American, c1903, 21¾in (55cm) high.
$675–800 *Bon(C)*

l. A Thomas Edison fireside phonograph, Model A, No. 26648, with K reproducer, combination gearing, oak case, maroon 19in (48cm) two-piece horn with crane, American, early 20thC, 20in (51cm) wide, with 12 cylindrical records and 2 spare containers.
$750–850 *MSL*

Gramophones

A Columbia coin-operated gramophone, No. AS501707, in an oak case, with winding handle at the side and ornamental top flash, American, late 1890s, 16½in (42cm) wide, together with a fitted box containing 12 cylinders and 3 others.
$3,300–3,800 *Bon(C)*

A Zonophone oak horn gramophone, Code No. HAO, with single spring worm-drive motor, on gooseneck tone arm, and an oak case with smooth oak horn, c1915, 17½in (44cm) diam.
$1,700–1,900 *CSK*

A cabinet gramophone, by The Masters Gramophone Co, 1920s, 40in (101.5cm) high.
$200–250 *OTA*

A Columbia gramophone, with brass horn and folding support, contained in an oak case, horn damaged, American, early 20thC, 19¼in (49cm) wide.
$1,200–1,400 *Bea(E)*

An Algraphone gilt electric gramophone, painted in the Adam style with scrolls and flowers, on turned leaf-carved supports, with shaped undertier, 1920s, 20½in (52cm) wide, with 5 volumes of 78 rpm records.
$1,300–1,450 *HOLL*

An His Master's Voice Model 163 floor standing gramophone, with exponential horn, 5A soundbox, in an oak case, c1927, 39¾in (101cm) high.
$1,200–1,400 *BTA*

A Columbia disc gramophone, with an oak case, single spring motor, soundbox, 9¾in (25cm) diameter turntable and an oak horn, American, c1904, 13½in (34cm) wide, together with a variety of spare parts and 10 discs.
$1,900–2,200 *S*

An HMV Model 460 gramophone, with pleated diaphragm and veneered case, with brush, mid-1920s, 39in (100cm) wide.
$2,400–2,700 *Bon(C)*

This gramophone attracted keen bidding because it was in unusually good condition, with the paper sound board undamaged. It also came with its original small brush.

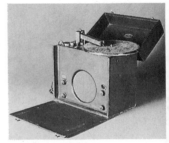

An Ansley Dynaphone portable radio and gramophone combination, the front opening to reveal the combination, with detachable turntable on top, electric pick-up and manual aerial concealed in brown leather case, 1930s, 15in (38cm) wide.
$280–320 *P(Ba)*

The Ansley Dynaphone was an expensive accessory for worldly travellers during the 1930s.

Musical Instruments

A cocuswood three-piece nickel-mounted clarinet, c1904, 23½in (60cm) long without mouthpiece, in fitted case.
$250–300 *P*

This was presented in 1904 by the Proprietors of the British Bandsman at the Crystal Palace Band Festival.

A fretless banjo, with 5 strings, abalone inlay and foliate carved heel, stamped 'S.S. Stewart, Phila PA', c1890, 11¾in (30cm) diam, with original leather case.
$1,300–1,450 *CSK*

A Paramount Style E tenor banjo, by William L. Lange, New York, rosewood neck and resonator with decorative wood inlay, the fingerboard with pearl inlay, c1927, 11¼in (28.5cm) diam.
$1,700–1,900 *SK*

Don't Forget!

If in doubt please refer to the 'How to Use' section at the beginning of this book.

A concertina, by C. Jeffries, inscribed, in a mahogany case, c1870, 6¼in (16cm) wide.
$4,300–4,800 *GH*

The original Jeffries concertina was named after a famous concertina-playing Cockney rag and bone man. This example was produced by an enterprising manufacturer of the same name.

A double bass, the flat two-piece back of faint narrow curl ascending from the joint, the ribs of similar curl, brass machine heads, early 19thC, length of back 43½in (110cm).
$14,000–16,000 *S*

A French double bass, labelled 'Rènè Cune Mirecourt … 1955', string length 41in (104cm).
$3,600–4,000 *CSK*

An American guitar, by Christian Frederick Martin, Nazareth, the two-piece Brazilian rosewood back with decorative centre strip, the sides similar with decorative inlay on the end block, the body bound in rosewood, the cedar neck with ebony fingerboard, c1856, length of back 17¾in (45cm) wide, with wooden case.
$2,000–2,300 *SK*

An American hollow body electric guitar, by Gibson Incorporated, Kalamazoo, with figured maple neck, bound ebony fingerboard with pearl block inlay, c1959, length of back 21in (53.5cm), with Magnatone tube amplifier.
$3,500–4,000 *SK*

A rosewood and silver-mounted transverse patent flute, by Monzani & Co, London No. 2760, with 7 silver keys and one later nickel key, mounted on integral wooden blocks, c1825, 26½in (67.5cm) long, in case.
$650–800 *P*

A George III mahogany square piano, by Riarr, Edinburgh, with string inlay, on square tapering legs with brass casters, joined by an undershelf, stamped 'No. 79', 62in (157.5cm) wide.
$1,400–1,600 *AH*

A Victorian walnut cottage organ, with ornamental shelved top, bevelled glass mirror, fretwork music rest, restored by Mason & Hamlin, 75in (190.5cm) high.
$560–640 *JAA*

An Austrian mahogany, ivory and ebonised harpsichord, decorated with neo-classical penwork, the lower frieze drawer fitted with inkwells, signed 'Ant. Mart Thymvienne, No. 99', early 19thC, 34¼in (87cm) wide.
$4,800–5,600 *S(NY)*

r. An American inlaid and ormolu-mounted mahogany upright piano, the case with drapery inset, flanked by turned columns, inscribed 'Loud & Brothers/Philadelphia', late 19thC, 52in (132cm) wide.
$2,800–3,500 *SLN*

l. A mahogany square piano, with chequer stringing, on a trestle support, the satinwood nameboard inscribed 'Thomas Haxby, York 1792', 52½in (133cm) wide.
$2,800–3,200 *CSK*

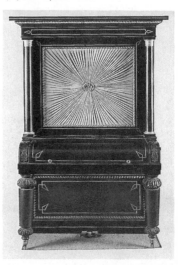

A Steinway ebonised upright piano, with engraved front panel, candle holders, rebuilt, c1891, 59½in (151cm) wide.
$9,500–11,000 *SI*

l. A Steinway upright piano, the ebonised case with floral marquetry front panels between fluted pilasters, with turned and fluted front legs, 1894, 72in (183cm) wide.
$1,100–1,500 *CSK*

An Edwardian painted satinwood baby grand piano, decorated with swags of flowers within a leaf border, signed Dochtenstein, c1895, 57in (145cm) wide.
$21,000–24,000 *S*

A Blüthner ebonised grand piano, c1900, legs later addition, 58in (147.5cm) wide.
$1,900–2,200 *C*

A grand piano, by Ernst Kaps, Dresden, c1901, 72in (183cm) wide.
$3,200–3,700 *SI*

A Klingmann walnut overstrung upright piano, restored, c1905, 59in (150cm) wide.
$1,600–2,400 *MOP*

A Collard & Collard rosewood and marquetry grand piano, decorated with palmettes and scrolling acanthus tendrils, on tapered legs with brass caps and casters, c1910, 71in (180cm) long.
$10,000–11,500 *CSK*

A Gaveau grand piano, original cream paint with gilding, c1905, 72in (183cm) wide.
$3,200–4,800 *PEx*

r. A Broadwood rosewood grand piano, reconditioned, c1911, 60in (152cm) wide.
$6,400–7,200 *SI*

A Collard & Collard rosewood grand piano, with fluted legs, repolished and reconditioned, c1910, 62in (157.5cm) wide.
$5,600–6,200 *SI*

A Steinway rosewood upright piano, c1920, 61½in (156cm) wide.
$11,500–13,500 *SI*

A Steck reproducing piano, incorporating the duo-art system, c1930, 58in (147cm) wide.
$8,800–10,400 *PIA*

A Barnes oak upright piano, straight-strung and over damped, reconditioned, c1932, 55in (140cm) wide.
$1,300–1,400 *SI*

Don't Forget!
If in doubt please refer to the 'How to Use' section at the beginning of this book.

An Austral Minstrelle walnut upright piano, reconditioned, c1935, 54¾in (139cm) wide.
$1,400–1,700 *SI*

r. A Weber mahogany grand piano, by The Aelian Co Ltd, c1935, 59in (150cm) wide.
$8,000–9,500 *SI*

An oak miniature piano, reconditioned, 1950s, 51in (159cm) wide.
$720–880 *SI*

l. A Challen mahogany upright desk piano, restored, c1960, 53½in (136cm) wide.
$1,400–1,700 *SI*

A Welmar mahogany upright piano, repolished and rebuilt, c1960, 58¼in (148cm) wide.
$4,500–5,500 *SI*

A mahogany spinet, by William Smith, with ebony naturals and ivory accidentals, with pierced brass hinges, on a trestle stand, early 18thC, 69¼in (175.5cm) wide.
$17,000–18,500 *CSK*

A Venetian red and gilt-japanned spinet, decorated with Chinese garden landscapes with figures making music, the hinged lid above a frieze with outset keyboard, mid-18thC, decoration later, 67in (170cm) wide.
$2,500–3,000 *C*

A brass tenor saxophone, No. 64614, engraved 'Henri Selmer/Paris' on the bell, c1956, 30in (76cm) long.
$2,200–2,600 *CSK*

l. A violin, by Richard Duke, London, after Jacobus Stainer, the one-piece back of medium curl, the ribs and scroll similar, the table of medium to fine grain, unlabelled, c1770, length of back 14in (35.5cm).
$9,600–11,200 *Bon*

An Italian viola, by Giuseppe Rossi, the two-piece back of faint medium curl with purfled arabesques, the ribs and scroll similar, 1918, length of back 16¼in (41.5cm).
$6,500–8,000 *CSK*

Cross Reference
Colour Review

A German viola, the two-piece back with medium grain, the ribs, table and head of a similar wood, with ebony turners and fingerboard, 19thC, length of back 17in (43cm), with bow, in a leather case.
$1,100–1,400 *AH*

r. A French violin, after Vuillaume, the two-piece back, ribs and scroll of bold medium curl, table of narrow to medium grain, labelled and attributed to 'Justin Audinot Luthier Mirecourt (Vosges)', c1890, length of back 14¼in (36cm).
$1,900–2,400 *P*

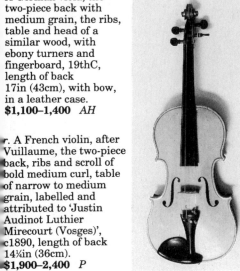

An American violin, No. 139, by Henry Richard Knopf, New York, the two-piece back of strong medium curl, the ribs and scroll similar, the top of medium grain, 1904, length of back 14in (35.5cm).
$2,500–3,000 *SK*

l. A violin, minor scroll restoration, c1900, length of back 7in (18cm).
$720–800 *P*

A French violin,
designed by T. Earle,
Hesketh, Manchester,
with one-piece back,
labelled and dated
'1929', length of back
14in (35.5cm),
the bow stamped
'N. Lambert', in a case.
$1,600–1,900 *CDC*

A French violoncello, by
Léopold Renaudin, the one-
piece back cut on the slab,
irregular medium curl,
ribs of similar curl, head
of narrow curl, the table
of fine grain in the centre
opening out towards the
flanks, c1790, length of
back 29½in (74.5cm),
in case.
$13,000–15,000 *S*

A French three-quarter
size violoncello, the two-
piece back of medium curl,
ribs and scroll plainer, the
table of medium grain,
Mirecourt, c1880, length
of back 27¼in (69cm).
$780–840 *Bon*

A German violoncello,
labelled 'Rocca',
c1880, length of back
29¾in (75.5cm).
$4,000–4,500 *CSK*

A French viola bow, the ebony frog and silver
adjuster both with pearl eyes, c1820, 69g.
$2,800–3,200 *SK*

A violin bow, by W. E. Hill & Sons, the
tortoiseshell frog inlaid with silver
fleur-de-lys, silver
overlaid ebony adjuster,
London 1931, 58g.
$4,400–4,800 *S*

A French violoncello,
by Prosper Colas, Paris,
the two-piece back of
medium to narrow curl,
the ribs and scroll
similar, the table of
medium to broad grain,
labelled, 1911,
length of back
30in (76cm).
$10,500–13,000 *Bon*

An early Victorian
walnut duet stand, the
foliate and scroll pierced
lyre-shaped music rests
above an adjustable
shaft, on a ring-turned
and reeded baluster-
shaped support and
tripod base.
$1,300–1,600 *CSK*

r. A rosewood duet
music stand, the stem
surmounted by a brass
pineapple finial, adjustable
within a column decorated
with foliate carving and
fluting, on a circular
base with 3 lions' paw
feet, mid-19thC.
$3,200–3,500 *S*

A rosewood music stand,
with twin-angled
sections, on a tripod
base, late 19thC,
48in (122cm) high.
$2,200–2,400 *L&E*

ICONS

A Russian icon of The Holy
Trinity, Moscow, 16thC,
10½ x 8¾in (27.5 x 22cm).
$13,500–16,000 *S*

A Greek icon of the Transfiguration,
some re-painting, 17thC,
14 x 9¾in (35.5 x 25cm).
$1,350–1,600 *P*

A Greek icon of St George slaying
the Dragon, the warrior saint
mounted on a rearing charger, the
young George seated behind him,
painted on a gold ground, 17thC,
13½ x 11½in (34.5 x 29cm).
$6,400–7,200 *S*

A Russian icon of the Vladimir
Mother of God, overlaid with
repoussé silvered-metal oklad
and applied halos, 17thC,
12½ x 10½in (32 x 27cm).
$1,450–1,600 *P*

A Macedonian triptych, the Mother
of God, Hodegetria and Saints, egg
tempera on wood, late 17thC,
11½ x 15in (29 x 38cm).
$5,600–6,400 *RKa*

A Greek icon of St George
slaying the Dragon, c1700,
24½ x 17¼in (62 x 44cm).
$5,600–6,400 *S*

A Russian icon of the
Prophet Zephaniah, c1700,
23½ x 16¼in (59.5 x 41.5cm).
$2,200–2,600 *S(NY)*

r. A Russian icon panel, painted with
Saints Floros and Loros, flanking
Archangel Michael holding 2 horses
by their bridles, with 3 Cappadocian
grooms driving a herd of horses to
water in the foreground, c1700,
23 x 35in (58 x 90cm).
$6,500–8,000 *S*

A Russian icon of the
Presentation in the Temple,
St Simeon depicted holding the
infant Christ in his arms, 18thC,
28½ x 21in (72.5 x 53.5cm).
$2,000–2,200 *S(NY)*

An east European carved
giltwood Gothic framed icon,
painted with a Madonna and
Child, 18thC, 12in (30.5cm) high.
$400–450 *TMA*

A Greek icon, the Mother of God
of the Life Bearing Font,
tempera on wood panel,
19thC, 19 x 15in (48 x 38cm).
$1,900–2,200 *JAA*

A Greek icon, Saint Kharlampry,
tempera on wood panel, signed,
19thC, 18 x 14in (45.5 x 35.5cm).
$480–560 *JAA*

A Russian icon of St George
and the Dragon, the
background of stylised
mountains and classical
architecture, the border
decorated with the
Archangels Michael and
Gabriel and 2 saints, 19thC,
14¼ x 12¼in (36 x 31cm).
$1,400–1,550 *P*

A Russian icon of the Presentation
of the Infant Mother of God in
the Temple, painted against an
architectural ground, 19thC,
13¾ x 14¼in (35 x 31cm).
$1,000–1,200 *P*

A Russian icon of Saints
Gregory, Vasili and John, the
Saviour depicted above clouds
at the top of the panel, 19thC,
34½ x 19in (87.5 x 48.5cm).
$2,000–2,500 *S(NY)*

A Russian icon, Vatopedskaya
Mother of God, tempera on
wood panel, in a silvered metal
frame, 19thC, 12 x 10in
(30.5 x 25.5cm).
$1,100–1,250 *JAA*

Don't Forget!

*If in doubt please
refer to the 'How
to Use' section at
the beginning of
this book.*

A Russian icon, late 19thC,
7½ x 5½in (19 x 14cm).
$880–960 *DaD*

A Russian icon of Christ
Pantocrator, standing on a grey
tiled floor against a gold ground,
19thC, 14¼ x 9¾in (36 x 24.5cm).
$480–560 *P*

A Russian silver and shaded
enamel icon of the Iverskaya
Mother of God, the oklad
repoussé and chased with
scrolling foliage, shaded enamel
haloes and corner plaques, the
Virgin's cheek painted with a
wound in commemoration of the
stabbing inflicted on the
prototype by an unbeliever,
maker's mark 'O.S.', Moscow,
1908–17, 12½ x 10½in (32 x 27cm).
$3,500–4,000 *S*

PORTRAIT MINIATURES & SILHOUETTES

A portrait miniature of a gentleman, by Thomas Flatman, with a landscape background, signed with monogram, c1660, 2½in (66mm) diam, in a silver-gilt frame.
$7,300–8,800 *S*

A portrait miniature of a lady, wearing a red dress with a blue shawl, by Susan Penelope Rosse, c1690, 2⅜in (61mm) diam, in a fitted fishskin case.
$560–680 *S*

A portrait miniature of Thomas Howard, 4th Duke of Norfolk, from the studio of Hans Holbein, blue background within a gold border, vellum laid down on card, mid-16thC, 1½in (40mm) diam, in a gilt-metal frame.
$1,400–1,800 *C*

A surprise miniature of a young lady, Italian School, with foliate and landscape background, 2½in (64mm) wide, in a gilt-metal frame.
$1,700–1,900 *C*

The reverse of this miniature contains a lever releasing a mechanism allowing the movement of the lady's right arm to hide her face with the mask.

A portrait miniature depicting a self-portrait of the artist, Richard Crosse, with sky background, signed on the reverse, mid-18thC, 2¼in (56mm) high, in a turned wood frame.
$1,600–1,800 *C*

A portrait miniature of a seaman, in the manner of John Gammage, in a gold-plated frame and hair mount, c1770, 3in (76mm) high.
$600–700 *WeH*

A portrait miniature of Mr Ridley, by John Smart, c1775, 1¾in (44mm) high, in a silver-gilt frame, blue glass reverse.
$5,000–5,500 *S*

A portrait miniature of a lady, by Andrew Plimer, the reverse with a gold monogram on plaited hair within a gold mount and blue glass border, in a gold frame, c1790, 2¾in (73mm) high.
$2,000–2,500 *Bon*

A portrait miniature of a gentleman, with a powdered wig and green jacket, English School, in a gold frame, c1790, 2½in (64mm) high.
$560–640 *WeH*

A portrait miniature of Warren Hastings, in a brown coat with gold-coloured buttons, by Thomas Hazlehurst, signed with initials, c1790, 2in (54mm) high.
$1,600–1,900 *Bon*

A portrait miniature of a young lady, her hair tied back and wearing a coral-coloured necklace and earrings, by Henry Burch, in a gold locket frame, c1800, 3in (76mm) high.
$2,400–2,700 *BHa*

A portrait miniature of Mr Oakden Parry, by George Engleheart, the reverse with added gold monogram 'J.F.W.' on plaited hair, c1800, 3½in (86mm) high.
$1,600–1,900 *Bon*

A portrait miniature of a young gentleman, by James Peale, signed with initials and dated '1800', 2¾in (73mm) high, in a silver-gilt frame.
$1,600–1,900 *C*

Cross Reference
Colour Review

A carved slate plaque of Sir John Jervis, Earl St Vincent, c1800, 4in (10cm) high.
$950–1,000 *TVM*

A portrait miniature of an officer, English School, c1800, 2in (50mm) high, in a gilt locket frame.
$720–800 *WeH*

A portrait miniature on ivory, of 2 boys wearing pale blue costume, in an elaborate gilt acanthus-carved frame, c1800, 3¼in (85mm) high.
$950–1,000 *WL*

A portrait miniature of a lady, wearing a white dress and turban, by Richard Cosway, in a gold-coloured frame, c1810, 2½in (63mm) high.
$3,200–3,500 *Bon*

A portrait miniature of a gentleman, by Jacob Spornberg, signed and dated, in a black papier mâché frame, c1810, 3¼in (86mm) high.
$1,200–1,300 *Bon*

A silhouette of a gentleman, by Alfred Darbyshire, dated '1841', 15 x 11in (38 x 28cm).
$160–200 *PSA*

A portrait miniature of a young lady, wearing a white dress, her hair tied with a bandeau, attributed to John Hazlitt, in a gold locket frame with hair behind, c1815, 4in (10cm) high.
$2,200–2,700 *BHa*

l. A silhouette of John Sheen, by John Field, painted on plaster in sepia and bronzed gold frame, inscribed with sitter's dates, c1820, 3in (76mm) high, in a red leather case.
$875–1,000 *Bon*

A portrait miniature of an officer of the 89th Foot (the Royal Irish Rangers), by Charles Buncombe, the reverse with an officer of the 64th Regiment of Foot (North Staffordshire), painted on card, in a gilded wood frame with lambs-tongue sight edge, c1816, 4½in (11.5cm) high.
$3,200–4,000 *Bon*

r. A portrait miniature of a lady, wearing a white floral bonnet and black dress, English School, c1840, 3in (76mm) high.
$880–960 *WeH*

A silhouette of Nathan Mayer Rochschild, holding 4 keys, signed, with a black border, in a maple wood frame, c1836, 10¼in (26cm) high.
$950–1,000 *Bon*

A portrait miniature of a young boy, by John Jules Nimmo, signed and dated '1857', 2in (50mm) high, in a gilt-metal frame with pierced ribbon cresting.
$1,600–1,800 *Bon*

A pair of portrait miniatures of a gentleman and his wife, by Dupré, signed, watercolour heightened with bodycolour, late 19thC, 3½ x 2½in (8.5 x 6.5cm), in ivory frames.
$775–875 *P(NE)*

ANTIQUITIES

A British Lower Paleolithic early
Acheulian hand axe, circa
300,000 BC, 3¼in (8cm) long.
$70–80 *ANG*

*This item was found
in Bournemouth.*

A Sumerian cream stone
amulet, in the form of the
head of a bull-man with
short horns, the eyes deeply
recessed for inlays, now
missing, late Uruk/Jemdet
Nasr Period, 3200–2900 BC,
¾in (18mm) high.
$4,000–5,000 *Bon*

A Mesopotamian terracotta votive
model of a house, the borders and
wall edges all decorated with a
chevroned moulding, incised cross-
hatched design flanking the doors,
with twin applied discs above each
door and window, each surmounted
by an animal in profile, circa
2900–2300 BC, 16¼in (41.5cm) long.
$11,500–13,500 *C*

A Nubian painted wooden funerary
panel, with the face of a bearded
man, a falcon perched on his left
shoulder and an Apis bull on his
right shoulder, repaired, Meroitic
Period, circa 2nd century AD,
12¼in (31cm) high.
$2,000–2,500 *C*

*Meroe was a city in Nubia which
flourished from 740 BC to AD 350.
Its court was greatly influenced
by Egypt and became very
powerful with the latter's decline.*

A Luristan bronze
Master of Animals
finial, 2 small
repairs, circa 1000 BC,
8½in (21.5cm) high.
$1,300–1,600 *HEL*

A Luristan bronze
mace-head, circa 800 BC,
5in (12.5cm) high.
$240–320 *HEL*

An Egyptian blue
ushabti figure,
with a single column
of hieroglyphics,
Third Intermediate
Period, circa 1000 BC,
6in (15cm) high.
$800–950 *HEL*

Cross Reference
Colour Review

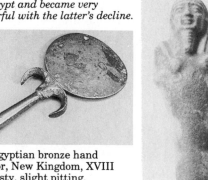

An Egyptian bronze hand
mirror, New Kingdom, XVIII
Dynasty, slight pitting,
corrosion, circa 1500–1100 BC,
7¾in (20cm) long.
$9,500–10,500 *SK*

   r. A composition ushabti
figure, Late Period, 8th–6th
century BC, 4¾in (12.5cm) high.
$130–150 *ANG*

An Egyptian bronze
figure of Amun,
wearing a pleated royal
kilt and jewelled collar
and armlets, right
leg and crown missing,
XXVI Dynasty, circa
664–525 BC,
5½in (14cm) high.
$3,200–3,500 *S*

An Egyptian carved
black basalt torso of
a man, with a column of
hieroglyphics down the
back, Late Period, circa
600 BC, 6¼in (16cm) high.
$1,700–1,900 *SK*

A Cypriot bichrome pottery vase, decorated with darker concentric bands on a buff ground, wear and encrustation to the surface, circa 1000–900 BC, 14in (35.5cm) high.
$650–800 *WW*

A grey Minyan ware kandila, small areas of restoration, Middle Helladic Period, 20th–16th century BC, 6in (15cm) high.
$1,300–1,600 *HEL*

Minyan ware is grey or yellow wheel-made pottery which first appeared around the 20th century BC in Greece and Troy, and may indicate a movement of new people into the region.

r. An Attic black-glazed trefoil oinochoe, the body with vertical ribbing, with high arched handle, a garland of leaves around the neck, traces of gilding, 5th–4th century BC, 6½in (16.5cm) high.
$6,000–6,500 *S*

A Daunian pottery krater, with geometric decoration, south Italy, 5th–4th century BC, 7in (18cm) high.
$480–640 *HEL*

An Apulian pottery bell krater, attributed to the Early Como Group, one side with a bearded satyr and a maenad, the other with 2 draped youths, laurel leaves around the exterior rim, circa 325 BC, 15½in (39cm) high.
$3,200–4,000 *S*

A Greek red-figure oinochoe, with a nude male carrying a situla, 4th century BC, 8¾in (22cm) high.
$880–960 *B&L*

A Gnathian pottery circular pyxis and cover, with 4 small containers inside, the lid with a pair of embracing lovers, Eros before them, the decoration enriched with white paint, circa early 3rd century BC, 9in (23cm) diam.
$3,200–4,000 *S*

An Etruscan biscuit-coloured hollow terracotta head of a female, the eyes with incised pupils, circa 4th–3rd century BC, 8in (20cm) high.
$2,000–2,500 *Bon*

Two Greek pottery female heads, with elaborate hairstyles, repaired, 3rd–2nd century BC, 2in (50mm) high.
$80–160 each *HEL*

A Hellenistic glass bead, in the shape of a stylised face, 4th–3rd century BC, 1in (25mm) high.
$1,300–1,600 *HEL*

r. A Gnathian pottery jug, decorated with grapes and vine tendrils, south Italy, 3rd century BC, 4in (10cm) high.
$250–300 *HEL*

An Etruscan Volterra alabaster funerary urn cover, in the form of a reclining male figure, his left arm resting on 2 cushions, his right hand holding a ribbed bowl, 2nd–1st century BC, 21½in (55cm) wide.
$4,300–4,800 *S(Am)*

Two Roman bronze ladles, with animal head terminals, 2nd–3rd century AD, largest 11in (28cm) long.
$240–280 each *HEL*

Three Roman glass tapering flasks, 2nd–3rd century AD, largest 7in (18cm) high.
$160–220 each *HEL*

A Roman pottery oil lamp, with central decoration of Helios, 2nd–3rd century AD, 3½in (9cm) wide.
$160–200 *HEL*

A Roman dark blue glass amphoriskos, mould-blown with encircling ribs, applied twin handles, circa 1st century AD, 4in (10cm) high.
$5,500–6,500 *Bon*

A Roman green glass shouldered vase, with flaring lip, 2nd–3rd century AD, 7in (18cm) high.
$480–560 *HEL*

A Roman green glass beaker, with incised grape cluster decoration, small chip to rim, 3rd–4th century AD, 3½in (9cm) high.
$480–640 *HEL*

A European brooch, early Iron Age, 4th–3rd century BC, 1in (25mm) long.
$110–120 *ANG*

A Roman bronze dish, in the form of a shell, with twin arched handles, the base with raised concentric ribs, 1st–2nd century AD, 8¼in (21cm) diam.
$1,600–1,900 *S*

A Roman bronze lamp, in the form of a legionnaire's sandalled foot, the opening supported by the slightly raised big toe, a double hinge on the back of the rim to support the lid, now missing, circa 4th–5th century AD, 4in (10cm) long.
$4,200–4,800 *Bon*

A Roman red slipware vessel, moulded as the head of a child, with a wreath on the thick hair, 3rd–4th century AD, 5¾in (14.5cm) high.
$480–560 *Bon*

> **Miller's is a price GUIDE not a price LIST**

l. A Romano-Celtic bronze mount for a leather miliitary belt or apron, with stylised Celtic war trumpet motif, 2 rear fixing studs, 1st–2nd century AD, 1¼in (33mm) long.
$50–60 *ANG*

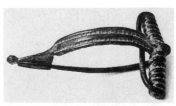

A Romano-British bronze votive reclining hound, 2nd century AD, 1¼in (35mm) long.
$160–200 *ANG*

l. A Romano-British bronze figure of Mercury, 1st–2nd century AD, 2¼in (60mm) high.
$400–500 *ANG*

A Romano-British bronze brooch, found in southern England, decorated and complete, 2nd–3rd century AD, 2½in (63mm) long.
$90–110 *ANG*

An Anglo-Saxon silver D-shaped buckle, with pin and elongated triangular-shaped plate, 6th century AD, 1½in (40mm) long.
$90–110 *ANG*

An Anglo-Saxon bronze cruciform brooch, the animal head terminal with protruding eyes and realistically shaped nostrils, iron pin missing, found in Kent, 5th–6th century AD, 3in (75mm) long.
$200–250 *ANG*

An Anglo-Saxon bronze cruciform brooch, 6th century AD, 2½in (65mm) long.
$160–200 *ANG*

An Anglo-Saxon gold pendant, with a central cabochon garnet set in a collar of twisted wire, decorated with applied filigree, suspension loop attached to the disc, found in Thanet, Kent, mid–late 7th century AD, 1¼in (30mm) diam.
$12,000–13,500 *S*

An Anglo-Scandinavian gold broad band ring, the surface decorated with 20 rows of undulating lines, alternating with 2 small impressed circles on the outer bends to give the impression of animal masks, circa 10th century AD, 9in (23mm) diam.
$4,000–4,500 *Bon*

r. A pewter pendant badge, depicting St Margaret of Antioch, on the reverse Christ crucified between Mary and St John, East Anglia, 15th century AD, ¾in (22mm) diam.
$70–80 *ANG*

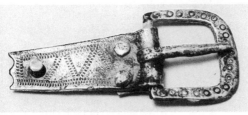

A late medieval silver buckle, with annulet decoration, the plate with 3 domed rivets, the typical wavy line decoration forming a capital letter 'M' for Our Lady, with pin, found in Dorset, 15th century AD, 1¾in (45mm) long.
$130–160 *ANG*

TRIBAL ART

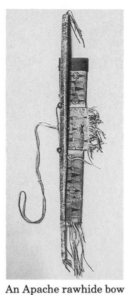

A Blackfoot hide knife case, made of aged commercial leather, the side and top decorated with rows of hemispherical brass tacks, Native America, 11¾in (30cm) long.
$2,000–2,400 *S(NY)*

An Apache rawhide bow case and quiver, the quiver decorated with medallions and bisected lozenge motifs, black, red, blue and yellow ink, and mineral pigments, Native America, 40½in (103cm) long.
$4,200–4,800 *S(NY)*

A Cheyenne toy cradle, made from a hide hood, lined with printed calico, decorated on the top with a column of triangles, sinew sewn against a white beaded ground, the lower section of printed cotton flannel, Native America, 16¼in (41.5cm) long.
$2,500–2,800 *S(NY)*

A Hopi cottonwood Kachina doll, wearing a kilt and sash, with red and yellow body paint, large case mask with protruding snout and blossom ears, Native America, 15½in (39.5cm) high.
$2,200–2,500 *S(NY)*

An American Navaho Indian rug, c1920, 36 x 68in (91.5 x 173cm).
$1,000–1,200 *YAG*

Miller's is a price GUIDE not a price LIST

Two Hopi carved and painted leather masks, one with a stylised face painted brick red, with 2 feathers on a string, probably Navajo, c1935, 7½in (19cm) high.
$1,200–1,300 *S(NY)*

l. A pair of American Plains Indian buckskin leggings, decorated with fringes and panels of white, yellow and black beadwork, the bottoms bound with strips of red trade blanket.
$540–600 *ASB*

A beaded cloth bag, decorated with an eagle above 2 songbirds flanking a spotted frog, and scrolled flowers, on a brown and black ground, Native America, late 19thC, 16½in (42cm) long.
$720–780 *EL*

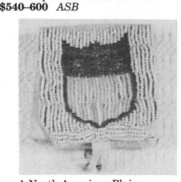

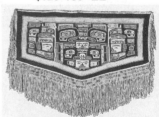

A Pima basket, decorated with geometric design, some damage, Native America, c1870, 16in (40.5cm) diam.
$380–450 *EL*

A North American Plains Indian buckskin cartridge pouch, the flap decorated with the US shield in white, red, blue and black beadwork, 3in (7.5cm) square.
$280–320 *ASB*

A Tlingit ceremonial dance blanket, finger woven in ivory, black, pale yellow and khaki wool, with a classic stylised heraldic crest pattern, composed of typical totemic devices, attributed to Mary Abbits Hunt, (1823–1919), Chilkat, Native America, 63in (160cm) wide.
$9,600–10,400 *S(NY)*

A carved wood face mask, with a pair of flat curved horns, the forehead with a scarification mark, remains of black and cream pigments, small side hole, on a metal stand, Ivory Coast, 16½in (42cm) high.
$1,400–1,600 *S(NY)*

A Guro Meddle pulley, the suspension lug carved with an antelope head, front panel with incised zig-zag band, side restored, north west Africa, 6¾in (17cm) high.
$480–560 *Bon*

A piece of copper and bronze Manilla currency, Ivory Coast, 5in (13cm) long.
$320–400 *LHB*

r. A Bambara double bowl container, the lower bowl supported by a horse and 2 figures, and 3 couples seated on stools, the lid with 2 figures holding a second bowl, the lid topped with 2 more figures, Mali, 46in (117cm) high.
$1,200–1,300 *SLN*

A Bamana hyena mask, of hollowed form with open mouth, inset metal teeth, pierced eyes, 14½in (37cm) high.
$9,400–10,000 *S(NY)*
This was collected in Segou, Mali, in 1956.

A Kuba-Pyaang helmet mask, scorched and painted decoration to the cheeks and nose, probably unfinished, central Africa, 17¾in (45cm) high.
$1,100–1,300 *Bon*

An Ibo people carved wood ancestor figure of a woman, Nigeria, 40½in (103cm) high.
$480–560 *LHA*

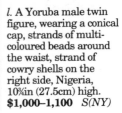

A Bambara vertical antelope headdress, metal sheeting on face and body, large lattice carving, Koutiala region, Mali Chi Wara, 46½in (118cm) high.
$600–640 *SLN*

A Kurumba wooden gazelle head, black, white and red pigment, ears damaged, Mali, early 20thC, 13¼in (34cm) high.
$720–800 *LHB*

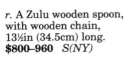

r. A Zulu wooden spoon, with wooden chain, 13½in (34.5cm) long.
$800–960 *S(NY)*

l. A Yoruba male twin figure, wearing a conical cap, strands of multi-coloured beads around the waist, strand of cowry shells on the right side, Nigeria, 10¾in (27.5cm) high.
$1,000–1,100 *S(NY)*

A Batak wood and iron container, with traces of red, black and white pigment, Sumatra, probably early 20thC, 9½in (24cm) high.
$160–200 *LHB*

A Kayan-Kenyah Dayak Hudoc mask, with 4 curled tusks, butterfly ears with tusk-like projections, painted with curvilinear motifs in black, white and orange, Asia, 12in (30.5cm) high.
$380–480 *Bon*

Masks such as these are used in dances connected with rice planting ceremonies and fertility rites.

r. A Timor wooden guardian post, probably early 20thC, 52½in (133.5cm) high.
$800–880 *LHB*

A Batak wooden panel, with red, black and white pigment, Sumatra, early–mid 20thC, 22¼ x 12½in (56.5 x 32cm).
$480–520 *LHB*

Miller's is a price GUIDE not a price LIST

An Easter Island figure, with asymmetrical bent legs, distinct rib cage encircling the torso, and a forward-thrusting neck surmounted by an oversized head with exaggerated features, rich dark brown patina, 22½in (57cm) high.
$4,000–4,800 *S(NY)*

An Aborigine phallocrypt, the oval shell incised with a zig-zag band around the perimeter, infilled with ochre pigment, twisted hair belt, Kimberley, Western Australia, 6½in (16.5cm) high.
$350–400 *Bon*

A whale tooth necklace, creamy patina, strung on twisted sennit string, Fiji, 12in (30.5cm) wide.
$4,200–4,800 *Bon*

These necklaces were made for chiefs and men of high rank. Although used in Tonga and Samoa, they were most popular in Fiji. The large teeth of the lower jaw were split into 6 or more sections, and then ground and polished into their present shape.

A Tongan ceremonial dance paddle, 25¼in (64cm) long.
$21,600–24,000 *S(NY)*

Collected on a mission to the South Pacific by Brigadier John Wesley in 1850.

MILLER'S COMPARES . . .

I An Aborigine parrying shield, the front faces with horizontal incised parallel zig-zags above and below a plain band of linked lozenges, nutty brown patina, Australia, 29½in (75cm) high.
$6,400–7,000 *Bon*

II An Aborigine parrying shield, the faces deeply incised with square sections of parallel chevrons and zig-zags, nutty brown patina, Australia, 30in (76cm) long.
$1,300–1,400 *Bon*

Aboriginal artefacts of quality are hard to find these days, and are mostly sold in Britain as a result of museums reducing their stocks, or the private collections of 19thC travellers being sold by their descendents. *Item I* achieved an exceptional price because of its rare shape and unusual central undecorated band. The decoration also provides a clue to the date of the shield, as the zig-zags appear to have been carved with the tooth of a marsupial. This is typical of pieces dating from the mid-19thC and any indication of a possible date will increase the value considerably. *Item II* was carved with a steel tool and was, therefore, probably made this century. *Bon*

BOOKS & BOOK ILLUSTRATIONS

SENSE
AND
SENSIBILITY:

A NOVEL.

IN THREE VOLUMES.

BY A LADY.

VOL. II.

London:
PRINTED FOR THE AUTHOR,
By C. Roworth, Bell-yard, Temple-bar,
AND PUBLISHED BY T. EGERTON, WHITEHALL.
1811.

Jane Austen, *Sense and Sensibility*, published by T. Egerton, Whitehall, 1811, first edition, 3 vols, 8°, half-titles, contemporary calf, gilt panelled spines, morocco labels, damaged.
$7,200–8,400 *P*

FURTHER READING
Catherine Porter, *Miller's Collecting Books*, Miller's Publications, 1995.

Sir James Bruce of Kinnaird, *Travels to Discover the Source of the Nile*, Edinburgh, 1790, first edition, 5 vols, 4°, titles with engraved vignettes 58 engraved plates and plans, 19thC morocco-backed boards.
$2,000–2,400 *P*

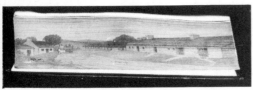

Robert Burns, *Poetical Works*, William Smith, London, 1847, 12°, green gilt tooled leather with double fore-edge depicting both the birthplace of Burns and Denure Castle.
$680–780 *LHA*

Helen Bannerman, *The Story of Little Black Sambo*, London, Grant Richards, 1899, 16°, first edition, illustrations by the author coloured from woodblocks by Edmund Evans, disbound in original green decorated cloth.
$3,600–4,000 *CSK*

Geoffrey Chaucer, *Troilus and Criseyde*, illustrated by Eric Gill, Golden Cockerel Press, Waltham St Lawrence, 1927, tall 8°, limited to 225 copies, one of 219 on Kelmscott handmade paper, printed in black, red and blue, wood-engraved plates, original morocco-backed boards gilt by Sangorski & Sutcliffe.
$2,200–2,700 *CSK*

Francis Bacon, *The Works*, edited by James Spedding, Robert Leslie Ellis and Douglas Denon Heath, London, published by Longmans, 1879, 14 vols, 8°, engraved or lithographed frontispieces to 5 volumes, brown half morocco gilt.
$2,200–2,500 *CSK*

J. M. Barrie, *Peter Pan in Kensington Gardens*, signed and illustrated by Arthur Rackham, 1906, 4°, limited to 500 copies.
$2,200–2,400 *HAM*

Johann Elert Bode, *Vorstellung der Gestirne auf XXXIV Kupfertafeln*, 1782, oblong 4°, plates only, 1 engraved title, 34 engraved plates of constellations.
$880–960 *DW*

Book Sizes
The size or format of a book is expressed by the number of times a single sheet of paper is folded into the sections which, when gathered and sewn, make up the finished volume.
Shown below are some of the usual descriptions of sizes:

Folio:	1 fold	2 leaves	Fo or 2°
Quarto:	2 folds	4 leaves	4to or 4°
Octavo:	3 folds	8 leaves	8vo or 8°
Duodecimo:	4 folds	12 leaves	12mo or 12°
Sextodecimo:	5 folds	16 leaves	16mo or 16°
Vicesimo-quarto:	6 folds	24 leaves	24mo or 24°
Tricesimo-secundo:	7 folds	32 leaves	32mo or 32°

Daniel Defoe, *The Novels and Miscellaneous Works*, edited by Sir Walter Scott, Oxford, printed by D. A. Talboys, 1840–41, 20 volumes, 12°, title page facsimiles, contemporary half vellum over marbled boards, flat-backed gilt spines with blue morocco lettering-pieces.
$5,800–6,400 *CSK*

Charles Dickens, *A Christmas Carol*, illustrated by John Leech, first edition, first issue, 1843, small 8°, half-title and title verso printed in blue, title printed in red and blue, 'Stave I' as first chapter heading, uncorrected text, original blind stamped cloth gilt.
$7,500–8,500 *DW*

John Dinsdale, *Random Drawings of Darlingtonian Doings*, 1879, 2°, 13 plates, one folding, original blue paper covers, damaged.
$160–180 *DN*

William Dugdale, *The Antiquities of Warwickshire*, edited by William Thomas, Coventry edition, 2 vols, 2°, 1730, 21 folding plates and plates in the text.
$1,100–1,300 *WL*

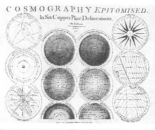

Samuel Dunn, *A New Atlas of the Mundane System 1796*, 4th edition, folio complete with 8 double plates, 42 hand-coloured folding maps, boards detached and cover board missing.
$2,000–2,200 *HOLL*

The East India Register, printed by J. L. Cox, London 1829, 8°, crimson gilt tooled leather with fore-edge painting depicting Leadenhall Street.
$480–560 *LHA*

Charles Dickens, *The Works*, Chapman & Hall, London, 1906, 21 vols, 8°, illustrations by 'Phiz' and others, contemporary red half calf, spines gilt, marbled boards with matching end papers.
$980–1,100 *CSK*

John Gerarde, *The Herball or Generall Historie of Plantes*, 1636, 2°, engraved title, old hand-colour to some engravings, old gilt-panelled calf, gilt decorated spine, damaged.
$1,300–1,500 *DW*

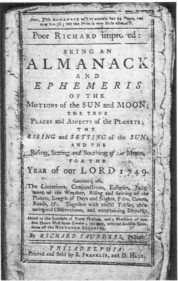

Benjamin Franklin, under the pseudonym Richard Saunders, *Poor Richard Improved: Being an Almanack and Ephemeris ... for the year 1749*, printed and sold by B. Franklin and D. Hall, Philadelphia, 1748, damaged, 6¾ x 4in (17 x 10cm).
$2,800–3,200 *SK*

Ian Fleming, *Casino Royale*, Jonathan Cape, London, 1953, 8°, first edition, original black cloth with red heart motif on upper cover, dust jacket.
$2,800–3,200 *CSK*

Graham Greene, *Brighton Rock*, published by The Viking Press, New York, first edition, original brick red and black cloth stamped in silver, 8°, 1938.
$1,100–1,200 *S*

The American edition was published in June 1938, one month before the English edition.

Graham Greene, *Our Man in Havana*, published by William Heinemann, first edition, presentation copy inscribed to his mistress Dorothy Glover, slightly foxed, original blue cloth dust jacket, 8°, 1958.
$1,500–1,600 *S*

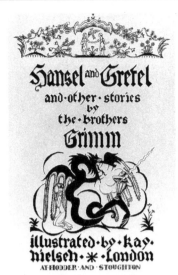

Brothers Grimm, *Hansel and Gretel and Other Stories*, illustrated by Kay Nielsen, 1925, 4°, original gilt decoration, limited signed edition of 600.
$2,200–2,500 *DW*

Oliver Goldsmith, *Poetical Works*, published by Longman, Brown, Green and Longmans, 1846, 8°, gilt tooled leather with fore-edge depicting Haymarket and Italian Opera House.
$480–560 *LHA*

The Fairy Tales of the Brothers Grimm, illustrated by Arthur Rackham, translated by Mrs Edgar Lucas, published by Constable & Co Ltd, London, 1909, 4°, 42 coloured plates, original gilt decorated vellum, badly soiled, limited signed edition, 238 of 750.
$700–780 *DW*

John Mason, *Self-Knowledge, A Treatise*, third edition, small 8°, 1748, contemporary red tooled goatskin, gilt panelled spine, Dutch floral endpapers, restored.
$600–720 *P*

ULYSSES

by

JAMES JOYCE

PUBLISHED FOR THE
EGOIST PRESS, LONDON
BY JOHN RODKER, PARIS
1922

James Joyce, *Ulysses*, published by John Rodker, Paris, for the Egoist Press, London, 1922, 4°, first English edition, limited to 2,000 copies, contemporary black morocco-backed cloth, worn, original blue wrappers bound in.
$600–720 *CSK*

r. Sir Thomas Malory, *Le Morte Darthur*, illustrated by Aubrey Beardsley, published by J. M. Dent & Co, 2 vols, 4°, 1894, photogravure frontispiece to each, black and white illustrations and decorations, later buckram retaining original printed wrapper to upper cover, one of 1,500 copies.
$520–560 *DW*

Camillo Mapei, *Italy, Classical, Historical and Picturesque*, 1847, 2°, half title, engravings, contemporary half calf gilt.
$1,600–2,000 *DW*

Beatrix Potter, *The Tailor of Gloucester*, published by Frederick Warne & Co, 1903, 16°, first Warne edition, first printing, coloured frontispiece, 26 plates by Potter, original dark green paper boards.
$1,200–1,300 *CSK*

Anthony Powell, *Venusberg*, published by Duckworth, London, 1932, 8°, first edition, presentation copy, inscribed by the author, original beige cloth.
$4,000–4,400 *CSK*

This was the author's second book, and is now very scarce.

'Running Title', pencil, pen and black ink and watercolour, by Ronald William Fordham Searle, illustration from *Slightly Foxed – but still desirable*, published by Souvenir Press, London, 1989, 12 x 9½in (30.5 x 24cm).
$1,600–2,000 *CSK*

'Molesworth: Down with Skool!', pencil, pen and black ink, watercolour and coloured chalks, by Ronald William Fordham Searle, cover design for paperback edition, published by Pavilion Books, London, 1992.
$5,000–5,600 *CSK*

'After a short interval [Rat] reappeared staggering under a fat, wicker luncheon-basket ...' pencil, pen and black ink and watercolour heightened with white, an illustration by Ernest Howard Shepard, for *The Wind in the Willows*, published by Methuen & Co Ltd, London, 1931, 9 x 7in (23 x 18cm).
$18,400–20,800 *CSK*

Captain John Smith, *The Generall Historie of Virginia, New England and the Summer Isles*, by J. Dawson and J. Haviland for Edward Blackmore, London, 1632, small 2°.
$40,000–45,000 *FBG*

Robert Southey, *The Life of Nelson*, illustrated by Frank Brangwyn, published by Gibbings & Co, London, c1912, limited to 100 copies signed by the artist, 10¼ x 7⅛in (26 x 18.5cm).
$320–400 *HB*

Jonathan Swift, *Gulliver's Travels*, illustrated by Rex Whistler, published by The Cresset Press, London, 1930, 2 vols, large 8° in 4s, limited to 195 copies.
$2,500–2,800 *CSK*

P. G. Wodehouse, *St Austin's*, published by Adam & Charles Black, London, 1903, 8°, first edition, first issue, 8 illustrations by Whitwell, Pocock and Skinner.
$1,300–1,400 *CSK*

This was P. G. Wodehouse's third novel, and is now scarce.

DOLLS

If you are a committed collector of dolls you will already be aware of the pitfalls and delights that accompany this collecting area. There is little more frustrating than to find a high quality doll, completely original in every respect, only to have it snatched from under your nose at auction; or to purchase a fine doll and then find a hairline crack in the bisque. On the other hand, dolls can become a wonderful obsession: you will want more and more, and finer and finer quality.

Having been interested in dolls for nearly 30 years, I am convinced that the finest examples are works of art, and the masterpieces are French *bébés* made from c1880 to 1900, and the German character dolls made from c1909 to 1913. Both types had bisque heads and wood and composition jointed bodies, or kid bodies with bisque arms. The heads are usually so finely coloured and painted that they look human – an exceptional achievement considering that the painter of a partly fired doll's head, unlike the painter of a portrait on canvas, cannot go over the details again.

From 1970, when the major auction houses first included dolls in their sales, there has been a dramatic rise in values: a doll which made $320 then would now be worth $19,200. And, of course, the number of collectors has increased worldwide, including those in Japan who, in the mid- and late 1980s, had an influential effect on prices. In recent years prices have levelled out but the continuing strength of the market can be shown by the fact that a recent sale of a major collection at Sotheby's took over $5.6 million. Recent fluctuations in the respective values of the currencies of doll-collecting countries have meant that UK prices have eased back a little, offering the discerning collector the chance to buy while the market is slightly down.

You should buy what pleases you, bearing in mind that a damaged head can reduce the value of a doll considerably, whereas minor damage to the body can be repaired with little if any effect on value. French *bébés* made between 1880 and 1900 have remained consistently popular with collectors and proved good value. So too have character dolls. Launched in 1908, they were modelled on actual rather than idealised children. However, they were not an immediate commercial success; they cost more to produce and many little girls found them too lifelike to play with.

In the 1970s and 1980s many collectors were keen on wax, early glazed china and early papier-mâché dolls. Their popularity waned to an extent from 1990, and as a result these dolls have fallen in value in recent years. They would now be a very sensible purchase (if they please you) and have the added advantage that many still have their original clothes. They were well cared for and, if stored properly, represent a unique piece of history. Dolls' houses, dolls' house furniture and miniature dolls have been steadily increasing in value over the last few years, seemingly unaffected by the economic factors that have depressed the antiques trade generally.

The following pages show a varied selection of dolls. Armand Marseille was the most prolific of the German makers and consequently his dolls will be found most often. His model 390 was one of the most popular dolls ever made. Model 1894 – first produced in that year and for many more subsequently – is far less common and usually of finer quality. The example shown on page 659 is 22½in (57cm) tall and usually would have a value of $640. This one has a price guide of $1,150–1,300 because she is completely original and is accompanied not only by the most delightful clothes but also a photo of her original owner. However, Kämmer & Reinhardt and J. D. Kestner were probably the two top quality German manufacturers. The Kämmer & Reinhardt girl dolls on page 657 have the characteristic sweet expressions. Wax dolls have suffered little with the passage of time. They often have the most exquisite clothes, (see pages 652–653), and are particularly good investments at the moment.

The Steiner Bourgoin model on page 660 is an example of an early French doll. She also has the added advantage of her original dress. She is charming, with a typical Victorian face, and would be a marvellous addition to a collection. So, too, would the Emile Jumeau *bébé* on page 655. This model has one of Jumeau's best faces, with a realistic profile and bulbous, paperweight eyes. Jumeau dolls will cost from $2,000 upwards; minor French makers are much less expensive.

Some very rare German character dolls have reached over $80,000, but only about one a year reaches the market. Much more obtainable and easier on the pocket is the Kämmer & Reinhardt model 121 on page 657 – a real little boy with a permanent smile.

Good collecting!

David Barrington

Selected Compositions

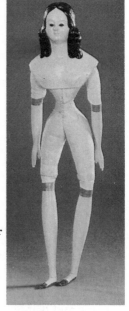

A Grödnertal wooden pedlar doll, with painted features, black painted hair, the peg-jointed wooden body with red painted slippers, in original red striped dress and straw bonnet, carrying a basket of her wares, German, c1820, 8¼in (21cm) high.
$2,400–2,700 *S*

A German carved wooden jointed lady doll, modelled on the 'Old Woman who lived in a Shoe', c1850, 10in (25.5cm) long.
$800–960 *YC*

r. A German shoulder-headed papier mâché doll, with painted closed mouth and rouged cheeks, fixed pupil-less glass eyes, black moulded hair, kid body with wooden lower limbs, c1830, 13¾in (35cm) high.
$2,000–2,200 *S*

r. A poured wax child doll, with inset blue eyes, blonde mohair and stuffed body with wax limbs, dressed in embroidered blue wool frock and hat, c1860, 30in (76cm) high.
$2,000–2,200 *CSK*

Dolls' Heads

Shoulder Heads
Many of the earliest dolls have shoulder heads where the shoulders, neck and head are moulded in one piece and the shoulderplate reaches the top of the arms. The head could be set into a kid body or sewn onto a cloth body.

Solid Domed
The few bisque-headed dolls with solid domed heads are called Belton heads. They can be socket heads, a later form of swivel head, or shoulder-plate heads. Wigs are stuck with glue. Sometimes the head has holes with the wig held in place with string.

Swivel Heads
On a swivel-headed doll the head and shoulder-plate are separate. The head fits into a cup on the shoulder-plate, which may be lined with kid, enabling the head to swivel.

Socket Head
The most common head type on the majority of French and German dolls and babies is the socket head. The base of the neck is rounded so that the head fits into a cup-shape at the top of the body.

l. A Pierotti poured wax shoulder-headed doll, with inserted blue glass eyes, finely painted eyebrows and lashes and moulded ears, mouth and tongue, inserted blonde hair, on a cloth body with poured wax lower limb, wearing a white christening gown, cream lace and silk bonnet and cloak, ends of 2 fingers and both thumbs missing, signed on back of neck, c1870, 28in (71cm) high.
$2,500–2,800
r. A poured wax shoulder-headed child doll, possibly by Meech, with fixed dark blue eyes, painted mouth, inserted blonde mohair wig, on a cloth body with poured wax lower limbs, moulded hands and fingers, wearing a white cotton dress, bonnet, underclothes, shoes and socks, c1860, 26in (66cm) high.
$900–1,200 *Bon(C)*

A German wax over papier mâché doll, with moulded bonnet, c1870, 13¾in (35cm) high.
$320–400 *YC*

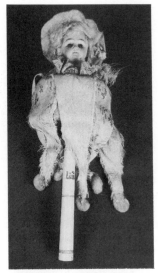

A Victorian china-headed spinning musical doll, 11½in (29cm) high.
$530–580 *SPU*

An American composition and fabric Shaker doll, dressed in a red cape and dress, c1900, 15in (38cm) high.
$800–960 *YAG*

A Lehmann tinplate walking sailor doll, early 20thC, 12in (30.5cm) high.
$240–280 *AAV*

A French pressed bisque swivel-headed doll, with closed mouth, fixed glass eyes, blonde real hair wig over cork pate, fingers missing, stamped 'Peronne', c1865, 18in (46cm) high.
$3,500–4,000 *S*

A French swivel-headed bisque fashion doll, with closed mouth, fixed blue glass eyes, blonde mohair wig over cork pate and gusseted kid body with separately stitched fingers, in original underclothes, c1880, 12in (30.5cm) high.
$900–1,000 *S(S)*

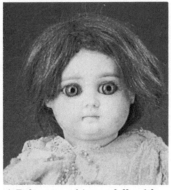

A Belton-type bisque doll, with fixed blue paperweight eyes, wood and composition body with ball joints, in original clothes, one leg detached, impressed '8', French, c1900, 15½in (39cm) high.
$1,400–1,600 *S(S)*

A Belton-type bisque doll, with closed mouth, fixed blue glass eyes, in original costume and hat, impressed '3', German, c1880, 11½in (29cm) high.
$900–1,000 *S(S)*

A German bisque doll, probably by Kestner, with open mouth, weighted blue eyes, jointed wood and composition body, replacement wig, impressed '355', c1900, 24in (61cm) high.
$740–840 *S(S)*

Selected Makers

A Bähr & Pröschild bisque-headed character doll, marked 'B&P 585', c1920, 19¾in (50cm) high.
$720–800 *YC*

An E. Barrois pressed bisque swivel-headed doll, with closed mouth, fixed blue spiral glass eyes, pierced ears, blonde mohair wig over cork pate, the gusseted kid body with separately stitched fingers, in a pink satin and black lace dress, impressed 'E 4 B' on the breastplate, c1870, 17in (43cm) high, with a box.
$3,000–3,200 *S*

l. A François Gaultier pressed bisque swivel-headed doll, with closed mouth, fixed blue glass eyes, pierced ears, brown real hair wig over original cork pate, the kid gusseted body with separately stitched fingers, in black and white striped shirt and tartan skirt with black edging, impressed '2' on head and 'FG' on shoulder, c1870, 15in (38cm) high.
$1,600–1,900 *S*

A Danel et Cie moulded bisque doll, with open/closed mouth, fixed blue glass paperweight eyes, blonde mohair wig, jointed wood and composition body, stamped 'Paris-Bébé Tête Déposé 5', c1889, 15in (38cm) high.
$4,800–5,600 *S*

A Cuno & Otto Dressel bisque-headed character doll, incised 'Jutta 1914', c1914, 24½in (62cm) high.
$800–960 *YC*

A Heinrich Handwerck bisque-headed doll, marked '99', c1910, 15¾in (40cm) high.
$800–960 *YC*

A Goss bisque shoulder-headed doll, with brown moulded hair, painted features, open/closed mouth with teeth, on a filled cloth body with bisque lower arms, dressed in WWI uniform, impressed 'G7', c1914, 13in (33cm) high.
$600–640 *P(Ba)*

r. A Heinrich Handwerck & Halbig bisque-headed doll, with sleeping eyes, open mouth, original wig, dressed in pantaloons, lawn petticoat and cotton nightdress, damaged, early 20thC, 12in (30.5cm) high.
$440–520 *MEG*

A Gebrüder Heubach bisque-headed character boy doll, incised '7602', c1910, 18in (46cm) high.
$1,600–1,900 *YC*

An Ernst Heubach bisque-headed doll, incised 'Germany 399', c1920, 12¼in (31cm) high.
$560–640 *YC*

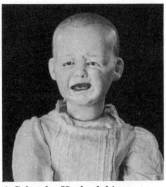

A Gebrüder Heubach bisque character doll, the crying face with open/closed mouth and simulated tongue, intaglio eyes and brush-stroke moulded hair, the ball-jointed wood and composition body in original costume, c1912, 13¾in (35cm) high.
$900–1,100 *S(S)*

r. A Jumeau moulded bisque doll, with open/closed mouth, fixed blue glass paperweight eyes, pierced ears, brown real hair wig, jointed wood and composition body with straight wrists, in original dress trimmed with lace, matching bonnet and brown leather shoes, body paint worn, incised 'Simonet' and with red check mark, c1880, 9in (23cm) high.
$3,000–3,500 *S*

An Ernst Heubach bisque-headed Oriental baby doll, marked 'Germany', c1920, 15in (38cm) high.
$800–960 *YC*

l. An Emile Jumeau bisque-headed doll, with fixed blue paperweight eyes, closed mouth, pierced ears, blonde mohair wig over cork pate, straight wrists, jointed wood and composition body, wearing a white cotton dress, with original dress and matching hat, stamped, incised 'Déposé E 10 J' and with red check marks, c1880, 21½in (54.5cm) high.
$9,600–10,400 *S(NY)*

A Gebrüder Heubach character doll, with closed watermelon mouth, weighted blue eyes, blonde wig and five-piece wood and composition body, in original costume, impressed '9573 3/0', c1914, 7⅞in (20cm) high, together with a wooden trunk containing doll's clothes.
$1,500–1,800 *S(S)*

A Jumeau portrait bisque-headed *bébé* doll, with fixed blue paperweight eyes, closed mouth, original blonde skin wig over cork pate, pierced ears, jointed body stamped, straight wrists, in original chemise and cotton pantaloons, limb stringing loose, incised '3' at neck socket, c1885, 13½in (34cm) high.
$3,800–4,000 *S(NY)*

A bisque swivel-headed Parisienne fashion doll, probably by Jumeau, with closed mouth, the eyes with large pupils, pierced ears, a cork pate with fine blonde wig, white kid gusseted body with stitched fingers and toes, dressed in contemporary black and gold costume with train and underwear, original kid boots, impressed '4' and remains of red mark to head, c1880, 19in (48cm) high.
$4,000–4,800   WW

A Tête Jumeau bisque doll, with closed mouth, fixed brown glass eyes, pierced ears, replacement blonde wig over cork pate, jointed wood and composition body, stamped in red 'Déposé Tête Jumeau Bte SGDG', c1890, 15in (38cm) high.
$2,400–2,700   S(S)

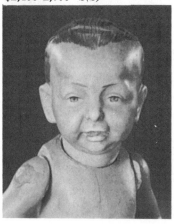

A Jumeau bisque-headed doll, with light brown paperweight eyes, stamped mark on head and body, original blonde mohair wig, fully jointed composition body, some restoration, late 19thC, 23½in (59.5cm) high.
$3,500–4,000   SK(B)

A Tête Jumeau moulded bisque doll, with open/closed mouth, fixed blue glass paperweight eyes, blonde real hair wig over cork pate and jointed wood and composition body, in bridal gown, stamped in red 'Déposé Tête Jumeau Bte SGDG 12', c1890, 27in (68.5cm) high.
$5,000–5,800   S

l. A Kämmer & Reinhardt, Simon & Halbig mulatto Kaiser Baby bisque doll, with open/closed mouth, painted brown eyes, brush-stroke hair and curved limb composition body, impressed '100 28', c1909, 10¾in (27cm) high.
$900–1,100   S(S)

Kaiser Baby dolls were said to have been modelled on the Emperor's son, who had polio as a child and was left with a deformed hand. Kaiser dolls have one arm bent inwards with the hand held upwards.

A Tête Jumeau bisque doll, with open/closed mouth, fixed brown glass eyes, pierced ears, mohair wig over cork pate and jointed wood and composition body, in original costume, stamped in red 'Déposé Tête Jumeau Bte SGDG 5', c1890, 14¼in (36cm) high.
$3,600–4,000   S(S)

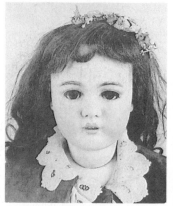

A Kämmer & Reinhardt, Simon & Halbig bisque-headed doll, with weighted brown glass eyes, eyelashes, open mouth, 4 upper teeth, brown real hair wig, on a wood and composition jointed body, original clothes and shoes, incised, c1900, 35½in (90cm) high.
$2,400–2,700   Bon(C)

A Kämmer & Reinhardt bisque character Kaiser Baby doll, with open/closed mouth, dimple and double chin, painted blue eyes, moulded blonde hair, composition body, c1909, 15in (38cm) high.
$900–1,000   S

A Kämmer & Reinhardt, Simon & Halbig bisque-headed doll, impressed, c1910, 21in (52cm) high.
$880–1,000 *YC*

A Kämmer & Reinhardt, Simon & Halbig, bisque-headed doll, with open mouth, in a floral dress and white cotton bonnet, incised 'S&H, K*R', c1910, 27½in (70cm) high.
$900–1,100 *YC*

Kämmer & Reinhardt (1886–c1940)

The company was founded in Waltershausen in 1886 by Ernst Kämmer, a designer and model maker, and Franz Reinhardt, an entrepreneur. The company produced some of the most highly prized and collectable German dolls. Ernst Kämmer died in 1901 but the company's success continued to grow. Character dolls were first registered in 1909 and from this date, until the advent of WWI, many of the most desirable character children were produced. After WWI the style changed and never achieved the same high quality again. This firm also produced celluloid composition and rubber dolls.

l. A Kämmer & Reinhardt bisque-headed character doll, mould mark '121', c1912, 15⅜in (40cm) high.
$1,100–1,300 *YC*

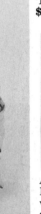

A Kämmer & Reinhardt, Simon & Halbig Mein Neuer Liebling doll, with weighted blue glass eyes, open mouth, 4 upper teeth, brown mohair wig, on a jointed wood and composition body, dressed in original white dress, underwear and shoes, incised '117n', c1920, 18in (46cm) high, in original box.
$2,000–2,400 *Bon(C)*

A Käthe Kruse cloth doll, with painted features and brush-stroked hair, cloth body with separately stitched thumbs, c1928, 17in (43cm) high.
$1,300–1,400 *S*

Käthe Kruse

Käthe Kruse founded her company at Bad Kosen in 1912, producing dolls that were safe, unbreakable, washable and attractive to children. After 1945 they were made at Donauwörth, and the company is still in existence today.

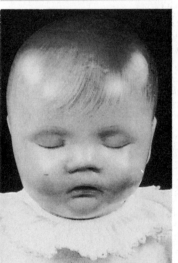

A Käthe Kruse plastic 'Traumerchen' doll, the sleeping painted head on stockinette-covered body probably filled with sand, with navel, c1982, 19in (48cm) high.
$1,100–1,300 *S*

A Kestner character doll, with blue moving eyes, red lips, open mouth, tongue, 2 teeth, composition body, wearing a pink silk dress and white bonnet, impressed '262.50', c1910, 19¾in (50cm) high.
$640–760 *GAK*

A Kestner bisque-headed doll, marked 'JDK 211', c1912, 14¼in (36cm) high.
$900–1,000 *YC*

A Kestner bisque-headed character baby doll, with painted eyes, incised 'JDK 14', c1912, 19¼in (50cm) high.
$800–960 *YC*

A Kestner bisque-headed character doll, incised 'JDK 260', c1910, 20½in (52cm) high.
$1,100–1,300 *YC*

A Kestner bisque-headed Bye-Lo baby doll, incised 'Grace Storey Putnam, Germany', c1925, 14½in (37cm) high.
$560–640 *YC*

A Gebrüder Kühnlenz bisque-headed black girl doll, with weighted brown eyes, open mouth with full lips, 4 upper teeth, black mohair wig, fully jointed wood and composition body, incised '34-29', c1900, 20in (51cm) high.
$2,500–2,800 *Bon(C)*

An early Lenci Spanish dancer doll, with painted brown side-glancing eyes, black curls, in original red felt frock, shawl, mantilla, with painted fan, hair comb and pendant, original paper label, 1920s, 25in (63.5cm) high.
$370–400 *CSK*

l. A Lenci pressed felt girl doll, with painted features, brown eyes looking to the left, fair mohair stitched wig, swivel joints at the neck, shoulders and hips, the 2 middle fingers stitched together, in original clothes, c1930, 17in (43cm) high.
$1,500–1,800 *S*

A Lenci felt doll, c1930, 24½in (62cm) high.
$800–960 *YC*

A Lenci pressed felt doll, with painted features, brown eyes looking to the left, plaited wig, jointed at neck, shoulders and hips, the two middle fingers stitched together, in original felt skirt and blouse, impressed 'G' on right foot, c1920, 16½in (42cm) high.
$780–880 *S(S)*

A Lenci felt doll, marked, c1930, 19in (48cm) high.
$900–1,100 *YC*

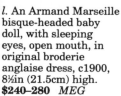

l. An Armand Marseille bisque-headed baby doll, with sleeping eyes, open mouth, in original broderie anglaise dress, c1900, 8½in (21.5cm) high.
$240–280 *MEG*

An Armand Marseille doll, in original cream dress, socks and brown boots, 2 fingers missing from left hand, 19thC, 23in (58.5cm) high.
$320–400 *SPU*

An Armand Marseille bisque doll, with open mouth, weighted blue eyes, blonde wig and ball-jointed wood and composition body, in original whitework costume, impressed '1894 AM DEP 4½', c1909, 22½in (57cm) high, and a photograph of her original owner.
$1,100–1,300 *S(S)*

An Armand Marseille bisque-headed googly eyed doll, incised '253 Nobbikids', c1920, 9¾in (25cm) high.
$1,400–1,600 *YC*

An Armand Marseille character bisque doll, with closed smiling mouth, weighted flirty eyes and five-piece composition body, impressed '323 M2/0M', c1914, 12¼in (31cm) high.
$1,200–1,300 *S(S)*

FURTHER READING
Sue Pearson, *Dolls & Teddy Bears Antiques Checklist* Miller's Publications 1992.

r. A May Frères et Cie bisque *bébé mascotte* doll, with closed mouth, brown paperweight eyes, blonde wig over cork pate, jointed wood and composition body, impressed 'Mascotte G', c1890, 17in (43cm) high.
$4,500–5,000 *S(S)*

A Montanari wax doll, c1870, 23in (58cm) high.
$900–1,100 *YC*

r. A Petit et Dumoutier pressed bisque doll, with closed mouth, fixed blue glass paperweight eyes, pierced ears, blonde real hair wig, jointed wood and composition body with metal hands, impressed 'P3D', c1880, 20½in (52cm) high.
$8,500–9,600 *S*

A Pierotti poured wax shoulder doll, with closed mouth, fixed brown eyes, inserted mohair wig, with poured wax lower limbs, in original costume, stamped 'Hamleys', one foot missing, c1880, 17¼in (44cm) high.
$370–400 *S(S)*

A Schoenau & Hoffmeister bisque-headed character doll, incised 'Hanna', c1920, 7¾in (20cm) high.
$480–560 *YC*

A Franz Schmidt bisque-headed character doll, mould No. '1295', c1912, 23½in (60cm) high.
$800–960 *YC*

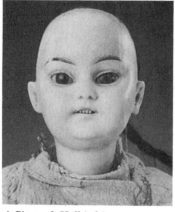

A Simon & Halbig bisque Oriental doll, with open mouth, weighted brown glass eyes, pierced ears, jointed wood and composition body, impressed '1199 DEP 3½', c1898, 11in (28cm) high.
$850–900 *S(S)*

A Simon & Halbig bisque-headed character doll, dressed as Father Christmas, c1900, 12in (30.5cm) high.
$1,300–1,600 *YC*

Simon & Halbig (active c1869–c1930)

Simon & Halbig were one of Germany's earliest and most prolific bisque head manufacturers, making dolls' heads for other German and French companies. The firm first produced shoulder-heads up to 1880, followed by socket-heads, and character heads were produced after 1900. Sleeping eyes and real hair eyelashes were introduced on some dolls from 1895 onwards. Almost all heads have a mould number, which is particularly important to look for when collecting these dolls as they can be identified and dated by the numbers.

A Simon & Halbig bisque-headed girl doll, incised 'S&H 1339', c1900, 12½in (32cm) high.
$800–960 *YC*

A Simon & Halbig bisque Oriental doll, with open mouth, fixed brown glass eyes, pierced ears, black real hair wig, five-piece composition body, in original costume, damaged, impressed '1329 4', c1910, 14½in (37cm) high, in original wooden box.
$1,200–1,300 *S(S)*

A Simon & Halbig bisque-headed girl doll, with weighted blue glass eyes, open mouth, 4 upper teeth, raised eyebrows, dark brown real hair wig, fully jointed wood and composition body, incised 'S&H 1079', c1905, 29½in (75cm) high.
$1,100–1,300 *Bon(C)*

A Simon & Halbig baby doll, replacement wig, c1910, 11½in (29cm) high.
$320–360 *AnS*

r. A Steiner Bourgoin bisque-headed doll, with lever-operated blue eyes, closed mouth, original blonde skin wig over paper pate, jointed wood and composition body with straight wrists, in original clothing, incised 'Sie C 3/0', c1885, 10½in (26.5cm) high.
$6,400–7,200 *S(NY)*

DOLLS' HOUSES & SHOPS

A painted pine dolls' house, divided into 6 rooms, with original blue finish, early 19thC, 24in (61cm) high.
$1,600–1,900 *SWN*

A stained wood dolls' house, with 4 rooms each with fireplace, the kitchen with an oven, all with elaborate wallpapers and papered floors, fully furnished, c1840, 34½in (87.5cm) high.
$8,500–9,500 *S*

This dolls' house is known as the Bisham Abbey Vansittart Dolls' house and once belonged to Henrietta Vansittart.

A Victorian painted wood double-fronted three-tier dolls' house, with 6 windows to the upper tiers and 2 bay windows below, the interior with 6 rooms, staircase and landing, with papered walls, carpeted floors and fully furnished, 38in (96.5cm) wide.
$1,900–2,200 *CAG*

r. A European painted wood shop, the *faux* tortoiseshell columns and fitted shelves with merchandise, slight damage, late 19thC, 20¾in (52.5cm) wide.
$1,900–2,100 *SK(B)*

A carved and painted dolls' house, the front and sides with brick effect, the middle with stepped Doric column porch leading to solid wooden door with brass door handle, mid-19thC, 44in (112cm) high.
$3,000–3,500 *Bon(C)*

A white painted dolls' house with a mansard roof, comprising 3 stories with 2 rooms on each floor, front opening, original wallpapers and paper *faux* parquet floor, roof lifts off, some interior paper damage, late 19thC, 26½in (67.5cm) wide.
$2,000–2,500 *SK(B)*

A Victorian yew wood and oak dolls' house, with hipped roof surmounted by a rooster finial, the hinged façade pierced with 5 graduated windows and a door, opening to reveal 3 floors, formerly a miniature blanket chest, 40in (102cm) high.
$2,200–2,600 *S(NY)*

A fishmonger's shop, the façade painted cream and the sides with papered brickwork, the interior with tile effect paper, cream painted shelves and counters, laden with wooden crates and wicker baskets of assorted fish, oysters, eels and shells, one counter with metal water tank and basin, c1890, 10¼in (26cm) high.
$880–1,000 *S*

A Moritz Gottschalk dolls' house, with lithographed paper exterior, verandah and sloping roof, dormer window in pitched 'tiled' roof, 2 chimneys and steps to front door, original wallpapers and flooring, wired for lighting, slight damage, German, c1910, 15in (38cm) wide, together with small quantity of wooden and plastic furniture.
$1,300–1,500 *S(S)*

A French grocery store, with yellow, red and blue façade, the interior painted pink, with shelves and drawers containing jars of bonbons, ginger and baskets of vegetables and fruit, a central desk with weighing scale and Parian doll assistant with kid body, c1890, 15in (38cm) high.
$1,900–2,200 *S*

TEDDY BEARS

A Bing teddy bear, with golden mohair, black shoe button eyes, pronounced clipped snout, black horizontally stitched nose, mouth and claws, swivel head, jointed shaped limbs and felt pads, worn, c1910, 9in (23cm) high.
$600–700 *CSK*

A Bing clockwork teddy bear, with cinnamon mohair, black shoe button eyes, pronounced clipped snout, black stitched nose, black stitched mouth and claws, swivel head, jointed limbs, felt pads, c1910, 9in (23cm) high.
$1,500–1,700 *CSK*

Two Chad Valley teddy bears, each with golden mohair, deep amber and black glass eyes, black stitched nose, mouth and claws, each with label to right foot, slight wear, *l.* 1930s, *r.* 1950s, largest 14in (35.5cm) high.
$320–370 each *CSK*

A Chad Valley teddy bear, with curly mohair, label on foot, c1950, 17in (43cm) high.
$480–600 *CMF*

A Chad Valley teddy bear, with label, c1950, 14in (35.5cm) high.
$280–320 *B&F*

An Eduard Crämer teddy bear, with short blond mohair, pronounced snout, brown and black glass eyes, brown stitched nose, mouth and claws, swivel head, jointed shaped limbs, felt pads and hump, growler broken, c1920, 14in (35.5cm) high.
$2,800–3,200 *CSK*

A Chiltern teddy bear, with pale golden mohair, deep amber and black glass eyes, pronounced clipped snout, black stitched nose, mouth and claws, swivel head, jointed shaped limbs and cardboard lined feet, pads recovered, growler broken, slight wear, c1930, 25in (63.5cm) high.
$420–480 *CSK*

> **Cross Reference**
> Colour Review

A Chiltern teddy bear, dressed as an Eton schoolboy, paws and pads replaced, c1930, 21in (53cm) high.
$400–500 *CMF*

A Chiltern teddy bear, with golden mohair, deep amber and black glass eyes, pronounced clipped snout, swivel head, jointed shaped limbs, velvet pads and large cardboard lined feet, worn, c1930, 24in (61cm) high.
$750–850 *CSK*

A Chiltern teddy bear, with mohair, straw and kapok filling, c1940, 16in (40.5cm) high.
$200–250 *CMF*

A Chiltern musical Hugmee bear, with squeeze box, c1940, 18in (45.5cm) high.
$480–560 *CMF*

A Chiltern Hugmee teddy bear, with mohair, c1950, 20in (51cm) high.
$320–400 *CMF*

A Dean's pink teddy bear, with clear and black glass eyes, clipped snout, black stitched nose and mouth, swivel head, jointed limbs, brown linen pads and button in left ear, slight wear, c1920, 12in (30.5cm) high.
$1,200–1,400 *CSK*

A Farnell teddy bear, with golden mohair, c1915, 21in (53cm) high.
$1,200–1,400 *CMF*

A Dean's 'Tru-To-Life' teddy bear, with blond mohair, brown and black glass eyes cut into internal rubber face mask with rubber eye sockets, wide apart eyes, clipped snout, black rubber nose and mouth, unjointed, stuffed with wood-wool, pink rubber feet pads, paws and claws, slight damage and wear, c1950, 20in (51cm) high.
$1,300–1,450 *CSK*

This realistic bear was the creation of Sylvia R. Wilgoss, chief designer for Dean's from the 1950s. The bear was created after extensive studies of real grizzly bears.

A Farnell teddy bear, with golden mohair, worn, c1920, 21in (53cm) high.
$3,500–4,000 *CMF*

r. A teddy bear cub, with golden mohair, deep amber and black glass eyes, clipped snout, black stitched nose and mouth, swivel head, jointed limbs and rexine pads, possibly Farnell, slight wear, c1930, 10½in (26.5cm) high.
$520–600 *CSK*

A Farnell teddy bear, c1920, 19in (48cm) high.
$640–720 *CMF*

J. K. Farnell & Co

Farnell & Co was founded by J. K. Farnell and his sister, Agnes, in 1897 and was based in West London. Along with other manufacturers the company claims to have been the inventor of teddy bears. Farnell supplied teddy bears to Harrods department store during the 1920s and the bear which inspired A. A. Milne to write *Winnie the Pooh* is thought to have been a Farnell bear bought by the author for his son Christopher. Farnell's factory was destroyed by fire in 1934 and bombed in 1940, but they continued production until 1968.

A Farnell teddy bear, with white mohair, deep amber and black glass eyes, pronounced square snout, pink stitched nose, mouth and claws, swivel head, large cupped ears, long jointed shaped limbs and rexine pads, repaired and worn, c1930, 28in (71cm) high.
$950–1,000 *CSK*

A Hermann mohair bear, c1950, 11in (28cm) high.
$190–220 *B&F*

A musical teddy bear, with long pale blond mohair, ears set wide apart, clear and black glass eyes painted on reverse, clipped snout, pink stitched nose, swivel head, jointed limbs, black stitched claws, long shaped feet, velvet pads and concertina musical movement in tummy, possibly a Glockenspiel bear by Helvetic, slight wear, c1920, 12in (30.5cm) high.
$1,900–2,200 *CSK*

FURTHER READING

Alison Beckett, *Collecting Teddy Bears & Dolls*, Miller's Publications, 1996

A Merrythought teddy bear, with golden mohair, pronounced clipped snout, amber and black glass eyes, black stitched nose, mouth and claws, swivel head, jointed limbs and brown felt pads, pads and paw claws replaced, worn, c1930, 23in (58.5cm) high.
$750–850 *CSK*

A Merrythought teddy bear, c1940, 14in (35.5cm) high.
$110–130 *PSA*

A Schuco 'Yes/No' teddy bear, with dark blue short mohair, black boot button eyes, pronounced clipped snout, black stitched nose and mouth, swivel head, jointed shaped limbs, cream linen pads, tail operating 'Yes/No' head movement and original swing tag, worn, c1926, 14in (36cm) high.
$18,500–21,000 *CSK*

A Schuco miniature compact teddy bear, with green short-pile mohair plush, black metal bead eyes and jointed limbs, the hinged torso opening to reveal compact, mirror, powder puff and lipstick holder with lipstick, slight wear, c1930, 3½in (9cm) high.
$880–960 *S(S)*

A pair of Steiff blond plush teddy bears, with sealing wax noses and boot button eyes, wide apart small rounded ears, swivel and metal rod jointed, with excelsior stuffing and felt pads, worn, c1904, largest 18½in (47cm) high.
$19,500–24,000 *S*

By 1904, Steiff bears were widely successful but there was still room for improvement, especially regarding their awkward limbs. The arms and legs would hang loosely after only very little play. Twisted wire was then used and eventually improved to a metal rod. However, the expense of this method led to the eventual disc-jointing of bear's limbs. Rod-jointed bears are extremely scarce due to their short production run and to find a pair is very unusual.

A Steiff teddy bear, with boot button eyes, long plush coat, stud in left ear, early 20thC, 23¾in (78cm) high.
$6,000–7,000 *DN*

A Steiff teddy bear, with golden curly mohair, boot button eyes, pronounced snout, black stitched nose, mouth and claws, elongated jointed shaped limbs, large spoon-shaped paws and feet, felt pads and hump, worn, c1905, 25in (63.5cm) high.
$9,500–10,500 *CSK*

A Steiff gold teddy bear, with black stitched, centre seamed snout, boot button eyes, wide apart rounded ears, back hump, swivel joints, excelsior stuffed, growler broken, c1908, 29in (74cm) high.
$13,000–14,500 *S*

A Steiff white teddy bear, with black boot button eyes, pronounced clipped snout, beige stitched nose, mouth and claws, swivel head, elongated jointed shaped limbs, cream felt pads, hump and button in ear, slight wear, c1910, 16in (41cm) high.
$3,200–4,000 *CSK*

MILLER'S COMPARES . . .

I A Steiff teddy bear, with golden curly mohair, black boot button eyes, pronounced clipped snout, black stitched nose, mouth and claws, swivel head, long jointed shaped limbs, spoon-shaped paws and feet, felt pads, hump, growler and button in ear, slight wear, c1910, 24in (61cm) high.
$6,000–7,000 *CSK*

II A Steiff teddy bear, with golden mohair, black boot button eyes, pronounced clipped snout, black stitched nose, mouth and claws, swivel head, elongated jointed shaped limbs and felt pads, pads recovered, slight wear, c1910, 13in (33cm) high.
$1,600–1,900 *CSK*

Pictured side by side in an auction catalogue, it might not be obvious why these two bears were expected to realise very different prices. They both date from the same period and appear to be in very similar condition. However, careful reading of the catalogue entry will reveal that *Item I* **is twice the size of** *Item II***, and it consequently realised nearly four times as much as** *Item II* **at auction.** *CSK*

A Steiff Record teddy bear, with golden mohair, black shoe button eyes, pronounced clipped snout, black stitched nose, mouth and claws, swivel head, jointed limbs, felt pads, hump, seated on a metal framed cart, losses and wear, c1913, 10in (25.5cm) high.
$2,200–2,600 *CSK*

Steiff Record animals were first introduced in 1912 with a monkey, Record Peter. The popular Record series was produced in a variety of animals, the most desirable of all being the teddy bear, introduced in 1913. When pulled, the teddy bear moves backwards and forwards creating the appearance that the bear is steering himself.

r. A Steiff teddy bear, with white plush, brown stitched snout, brown and black glass eyes, small pricked ears, swivel joints, excelsior stuffed and with growler, button in ear and remains of yellow label, c1920, 19½in (49.5cm) high.
$1,900–2,200 *S*

A Steiff teddy bear, with pale blond mohair, black boot button eyes, pronounced clipped snout, black horizontally stitched nose, mouth and claws, swivel head, elongated jointed shaped limbs, felt pads, hump and button in ear, c1910, 13in (33cm) high.
$4,800–5,600 *CSK*

A Steiff teddy bear, with golden mohair, brown and black glass eyes, pronounced snout, black stitched nose, mouth and claws, swivel head, jointed shaped limbs, cream felt pads, growler, hump and button in ear, repaired, slight wear, c1920, 17in (43cm) high.
$4,800–5,600 *CSK*

A Steiff teddy bear, with dark brown mohair, brown and black glass eyes, pronounced snout, black stitched nose, mouth and claws, swivel head, jointed shaped limbs, cream felt pads, hump, growler and button in ear, slight wear, c1920, 16in (41cm) high.
$1,500–1,800 *CSK*

A Steiff gold plush teddy bear, with black stitched snout, brown glass eyes, pricked ears and excelsior stuffed body with growler, swivel joints and felt pads, button in ear and remains of yellow label, c1925, 17in (43cm) high.
$3,000–3,500 *S*

A Steiff apricot wool plush teddy baby, with open felt-lined mouth, brown stitched snout, brown glass eyes, pricked ears, swivel joints, beige felt pads, button in ear and red textile label on the studded collar printed 'Teddy Baby ges.gesch Steiff marke', c1935, 13in (33cm) high.
$5,000–6,000 *S*

A Steiff blond silk plush teddy bear, with brown and black glass eyes, pronounced snout, black stitched nose, mouth and claws, swivel head, long jointed shaped limbs, felt pads, hump and button in ear, c1940, 19in (48.5cm) high.
$8,800–10,400 *CSK*

A Steiff teddy bear, with beige curly mohair, brown and black glass eyes, pronounced square snout, brown stitched nose, mouth and claws, swivel head, jointed shaped limbs, cream felt pads and growler, c1950, 25in (63.5cm) high.
$2,800–3,200 *CSK*

A Steiff teddy bear, with blond mohair and button in ear, c1960, 17in (43cm) high.
$720–800 *CMF*

A Steiff teddy bear, with golden curly mohair, brown and black glass eyes, pronounced square snout, black stitched nose, mouth and claws, swivel head, long jointed shaped limbs, hump, growler and button in ear, with yellow label intact, c1950, 30in (76cm) high.
$6,000–6,500 *CSK*

A Gebruder Sussenguth 'Peter' bear, with cream tipped black mohair, black and white glass googly eyes, open mouth, carved and painted wooden teeth and tongue, swivel head, jointed shaped limbs, beige felt pads, original ribbon and chest swing tag, growler broken, slight wear, c1925, 13in (33cm) high.
$3,200–3,800 *CSK*

Miscellaneous

A white long plush teddy bear, with blond stitched snout, brown and black glass eyes, pricked ears, excelsior stuffed, jointed and with press growler, beige velvet pads, probably German, c1920, 18in (46cm) high.
$1,500–1,700 *S*

A silk plush teddy bear, c1930, 30in (76cm) high.
$310–340 *CMF*

A dual plush covered teddy bear, with brown and black glass eyes, pronounced snout, black stitched nose, mouth and claws, swivel head, jointed limbs, felt pads, cardboard lined feet and growler, slight wear, c1930, 27in (68.5cm) high.
$1,100–1,300 *CSK*

A French mohair teddy bear, with replacement paws, c1920, 17in (43cm) high.
$560–640 *CMF*

A green teddy bear, with artificial silk plush, clear and black glass eyes painted on reverse, pronounced clipped snout, black stitched nose, mouth and claws, swivel head, jointed shaped limbs, cream felt pads and squeaker, c1930, 13in (33cm) high.
$780–880 *CSK*

A teddy bear, with blond mohair, c1930, 22in (56cm) high.
$480–560 *CMF*

r. A golden plush covered teddy bear, with brown and black glass eyes, pronounced snout, black stitched nose, mouth and claws, swivel head, jointed shaped limbs, felt pads and shaped cardboard lined feet, growler broken, repaired, slight wear, c1930, 30in (76cm) high.
$320–400 *CSK*

A German teddy bear, with original clothes, c1914, 18in (45.5cm) high.
$560–640 *CMF*

A German bear, with mohair, c1920, 14in, (35.5cm) high.
$560–640 *CMF*

A blue cotton silk plush teddy bear, c1930, 25in (53.5cm) high.
$240–270 *CMF*

SOFT TOYS

A pair of Dean's rag book Mickey and Minnie mouse soft toys, velvet covered with wide toothy grins, black button eyes, yellow hands, feet and tails, Mickey with green shorts, Minnie with red spotted skirt and felt hat, both with metal button, c1935, 6¼in (16cm) high.
$780–880 *S(S)*

Two Lenci Laurel and Hardy figures, each with pressed felt painted face, cut felt hair, swivel head and legs at the hips, one in black, the other in navy felt outfit, with tricorn hats edged in cream felt, c1935, 10¼in (26cm) high.
$1,500–2,000 *S*

A Steiff rabbit on wheels, with cream and beige mohair, black shoe button eyes backed with red felt, lead weighted floppy ears, original ribbon and bell, wooden wheels stamped, button in ear with remains of white label, c1913, 10in (25cm) long.
$440–520 *CSK*

A Winnie the Pooh soft toy, with label, made in Japan for Gund, USA, 1964, 6½in (16cm) high.
$80–100 *TED*

Seven Steiff velvet covered rabbit skittles, with black shoe button eyes, standing on turned wooden base, incomplete set, c1900, 8in (20cm) high.
$3,200–3,500 *CSK*

A Steiff giraffe, with printed mohair plush, felt ears and mouth, glass eyes, ear button and tag, mid-20thC, 98in (249cm) high.
$1,000–1,150 *SK(B)*

l. Two Steiff seated dogs, with pale blond mohair, brown and black glass eyes, remains of black stitched noses, swivel heads, original bells and one with button in ear, c1926, 4in (10cm) high.
$640–720 *CSK*

A cloth Krazy Cat, by the Knickerbocker Toy Co, USA, with black velveteen, black felt ears, white face and hands and yellow felt boots, printed information on soles of boots, c1930, 10½in (26.5cm) high.
$1,200–1,450 *SK(B)*

A Steiff cow on wheels, with brown and white mohair, boot button eyes backed with white felt, leather horns, leather and felt feet, original Steiff leather collar with bell and button in ear, on 4 wheels, voice mechanism broken, worn, c1910, 20in (51cm) high.
$850–950 *CSK*

A Strunz elephant, burlap-covered, with black boot button eyes, white felt tusks, rod and metal button jointing, black embroidered claws and card reinforced feet, repaired and worn, c1903, 14in (36cm) high.
$720–800 *CSK*

Wilhelm Strunz's Nuremberg-based factory was clearly influenced by Steiff, producing copies of Steiff products at a lower cost. It is interesting to see how this elephant closely resembles the earlier ones produced by Steiff.

TOYS
Boats

A Bassett-Lowke clockwork wooden model of a tug boat, the carved hull finished in black with red beneath water line, the deck with raised wheelhouse and lifeboats, on a stand, c1930, 23in (58.5cm) long.
$800–900 *S(S)*

A Bing clockwork three-funnel liner, painted in dark blue, ivory and red, main and promenade decks in sand yellow, with 4 card funnel inserts and cork, lacks 2 masts, flags and part railings, c1924, 32¾in (83cm) long.
$5,600–6,200 *CSK*

A Hornby 900 *Alcyon* battery-operated speed boat, French, c1960, 14in (35cm) long.
$110–130 *RAR*

A Bing 1st Series spirit-fired steam gunboat, with single cylinder oscillating engine and flat bottom boiler, repainted in black, green and pale yellow, with original wheeled trolley, some repairs and replacements, c1904, 22½in (57cm) long, and a later handmade wooden base for boat and trolley.
$3,200–3,500 *CSK*

A Bing 3rd Series clockwork liner, the red and black painted tinplate with white superstructure and tan decks, with davits for 4 lifeboats, original masts and lifeboats missing, c1920, 19¾in (50cm) long.
$1,450–1,700 *CSK*

A Pop-Pop tinplate steam boat, by Japan Alps Toy Co, c1930, 5in (13cm) long.
$80–90 *MSB*

A Bing tinplate and clockwork three-funnel liner, finished in black with white superstructure, red beneath water line and ochre funnels, 3 decks with perforated sheet handrails, 6 lifeboats, 2 anchors, restored, c1920, 25in (63.5cm) long.
$1,500–1,700 *S(S)*

A Falk tinplate clockwork three-funnel ocean liner, hand-painted in red and cream, the deck finished in orange, with 2 masts, 4 lifeboats, German, c1905, 16in (41cm) long.
$4,000–5,000 *S*

A Schönner tinplate clockwork gunboat, with cream hand-painted hull lined in red with gilt band, 2 masts, 3 funnels finished in orange and black, lifeboats, cannons, tiller wheel and adjustable rudder, c1900, 18½in (47cm) long, in original card box.
$3,200–3,500 *S(S)*

Trains

A 3¼in gauge four-wheel First Class passenger coach, with lined lake and cream painted wood, hinged doors, external and interior detail, correct leaf springing to axles and buffers, mid-19thC, 14½in (37cm) long.
$1,700–1,900 *CSK*

A 2½in gauge live steam LMS 4F tender locomotive, possibly by Bassett-Lowke, the spirit-fired boiler with water gauge, cab controls, early 20thC.
$1,500–1,600 *AH*

l. A Bassett-Lowke 0 gauge tinplate clockwork 'Prince Charles' locomotive, No. 62078, in blue livery, c1951, with original green box.
$600–675 *Mit*

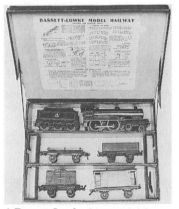

A Bassett-Lowke 0 gauge 4-4-0 'Prince Charles' train set, with locomotive and tender in BR green, black and white lining, running No. 62453, and 4 goods wagons in original yellow and brown box, after 1945, 15 x 18in (38 x 45.5cm).
$600–675 *WAL*

A Bing tinplate Continental station, with painted
two-storey design and arched canopy to the side,
on green base, c1912, 14¼in (36.5cm) wide.
$1,700–2,200 *S*

A Buco 20 volt SBB CFF electric outline
locomotive, lithographed in green, with two
coaches, red dining car and luggage van,
1945–52, coaches 11¾in (30cm) long.
$800–900 *CSK*

An Exley GWR sleeping car, in mint condition,
c1938, 17in (43cm) long.
$400–450 *HOB*

A Hornby 0 gauge No. 2 Pullman
car and dining saloon, both
finished in cream and green
livery with gold lining, fixed
doors, brass buffers and original
celluloid window inserts, c1921.
$350–380 *Bon(C)*

A Hornby 1st Series lattice girder
bridge, c1922, 22in (56cm) wide.
$320–400 *HOB*

A Bing 0-4-0 locomotive, with matching tender,
finished in green LNER livery, c1937,
26in (66cm) overall, boxed.
$160–190 *HOB*

An Elettren 0 gauge 'Wagon Lits' Pullman
brake van, with luggage containers, c1970,
15¾in (40cm) long.
$240–270 *RAR*

An Exley Southern Railway six-wheel spot
carriage, with green Southern livery, c1950,
9½in (24cm) long.
$380–430 *HOB*

A Hornby National Benzole Mixture
tank, c1925, 14in (35.5cm) long,
with original buff box.
$160–190 *HOB*

A set of 6 Hornby-Dublo railway
staff, in original box, together with
6 D passengers, pre-1939, unboxed.
$240–270 *CSK*

A Hornby 0 gauge 1st Series E320 20 volt electric
4-4-2 Flying Scotsman locomotive, and No. 2
Special LNER tender, painted in green,
slight damage, c1936, box for tender.
$600–650 *CSK*

A Hornby 0 gauge No. 3C clockwork 4-4-2 Flying
Scotsman locomotive, and a No. 2 Special LNER
tender, painted in green, tested label and leaflets,
slight damage, c1937, with boxes.
$880–960 *CSK*

A Hornby-Dublo LNER EDL7 tank goods set, 2nd issue, finished in black livery, with horseshoe magnet, elongated pick-ups, gold label and large windows, in original box, c1948.
$800–950 *CSK*

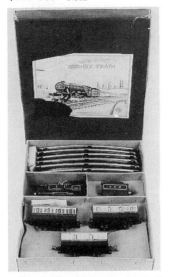

A Hornby No. 501 passenger train set, with 0-4-0 GW locomotive 9319, tender, two 1st coaches, brake van and track, boxed, c1950 18 x 16in (45.5 x 40.5cm).
$1,300–1,450 *P(Ba)*

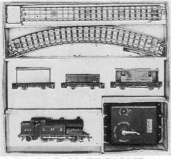

A Hornby-Dublo EDG7 LMS goods set, with LMS 0-6-2 locomotive No. 6917, 3 wagons, oval of track and controller, box with Royal Scot label, c1950, 15 x 18in (38 x 45.5cm).
$100–120 *WAL*

Hornby-Dublo Trains

The Hornby-Dublo range dominated the toy train market in Britian in the early post-WWII period. The most interesting and collectable trains are those made between 1945 and 1953, when Hornby produced a wide range of locomotives and accessories.

Although the railways were nationalised in Britain in 1948, Hornby did not produce trains in BR livery until 1953. As a result, some pre-1952 locomotives in the liveries of the 4 major British railway companies are very collectable today, particularly when they are still in their original boxes.

A major development in the company's history took place in 1957, when they upgraded their toy trains to a two-rail system and redesigned all their locomotives and stock. They continued to use diecast metal for most of the bodies, but they changed to a high-quality plastic for freight stock and used both plastic and tinplate for passenger stock. The end product was beautifully made but too highly priced for the marketplace resulting in a take-over by the highly successful Triang company in 1964.

A Hornby-Dublo EDP12 BR 'Duchess of Montrose' passenger train set, with glossy locomotive, early LMS pattern coach bogies, dated '10.53', in mid-blue box.
$640–720 *CSK*

A Hornby-Dublo EDP11 'Silver King' passenger train set, with glossy locomotive, spanner, 6 keeps and cover strip, c1954.
$750–800 *CSK*

A Jep 20 volt electric SNCF articulated two-unit rail car, with cloth bellows connection, painted in red and cream, c1936, 26¾in (68cm) overall.
$1,100–1,200 *CSK*

A Lionel 0 gauge girl's train set, with a pink locomotive, shell-blue caboose, lilac hopper car, pink gondola and tender, a yellow and a shell-blue box car, c1957, in original boxes except locomotive.
$1,600–1,800 *S(NY)*

It is unusual to find a train set made specifically for girls, which is why this set sold for approximately double its pre-sale estimate.

A gauge one 4-4-0 clockwork locomotive, freelance design, possibly by Märklin, hand-painted in green with red and black lining, battery-operated lamp fitted to smoke box, late 19thC.
$780–880 *AH*

Vehicles

An Arnold friction-powered Chrysler convertible, the red and cream painted tinplate with grey lithographed interior, composition driver and passenger, c1955, 11in (28cm) long.
$600–650 *CSK*

A Bing clockwork hand-painted two-seater open tourer, finished in green with yellow lining, gold radiator surround and red seats, yellow wheels with rubber tyres and metal handbrake lever, c1912, 9¾in (25cm) long.
$1,300–1,450 *Bon(C)*

MILLER'S COMPARES . . .

I A CIJ painted tinplate Alfa Romeo P2 racing car, No. 2, finished in red with cloverleaf emblem, treaded Michelin tyres, handbrake, adjustable suspension, starting handle, spoked wheels, drum brakes and spring motor, French, some losses, late 1920s, 21in (54cm) long.
$2,000–2,500 *S*

II A CIJ painted tinplate Alfa Romeo P2 racing car, No. 2, finished in silver with clover-leaf emblem, treaded Michelin tyres, handbrake, spoked wheels, bonnet straps, key and spring motor, repaired, French, c1920, 21in (54cm) long.
$1,300–1,450 *S*

Item I **sold for a higher price than** *Item II* **at auction because it had its original paint, and although it was lacking one or two parts, there were no repairs. The driver is often lacking, and the price would have been substantially higher if it had been present.** *Item II,* **ironically, is a scarcer piece than** *Item I* **because of its metallic paint, but its condition was the downfall as it had been repaired and repainted and also had patches of rust. Silver is the commonest of the metallic paints – these cars can occasionally be found in metallic red and blue, and the latter can fetch as much as $9,600 at auction.** *S*

A Budgie Toys AA Mobile Traffic Control Unit, No. 218, c1960, 6¾in (17cm) long.
$120–140 *RAR*

A Hoge tin traffic cycle-car delivery van, with wind-up motorcycle, rubber wheels, and driver, c1930, 10¼in (26cm) long.
$3,200–3,500 *SK(B)*

A Distler clockwork tinplate open two-seater tourer, with gear shift, finished in metallic green and red with chrome trim, c1940, 9½in (24cm) long, boxed.
$700–800 *P(Ba)*

A Solido Vanwall Formula 1 racing car, in mint condition, c1960, 4in (10cm) long, boxed.
$100–120 *OTS*

A Dinky Toys 943 Leyland Octopus 'Esso' tanker, c1960, 7in (18cm) long.
$480–540 *RAR*

A Japanese friction-driven tinplate London bus, with trademark 'H', c1962, 11¾in (30cm) long.
$65–75 *RAR*

A Moko orange prime mover, with grey diecast wheels, green detachable engine shields, light blue six-wheeled lowload trailer, original diecast drawbar, with bulldozer load, c1950, 12in (30.5cm) long overall, with original box.
$730–800 *WAL*

A Sturditoy No. 20 US Army truck, with khaki pressed steel body and original canvas cover, c1928, 27in (68.5cm) long.
$950–1,000 *SK(B)*

Aeroplanes

A Dinky aluminium 749 Avro Vulcan Delta-wing bomber, c1955, wingspan 6in (15.5cm). **$850–950** *CSK*

This was one of the biggest Dinky aircraft ever made and was for export to Canada only.

An Oro-Werke high wing passenger monoplane, the light green lithographed clockwork tinplate body with red and white details, c1933, 14¼in (36cm) wingspan. **$320–400** *CSK*

A Britains biplane and hanger, No. 1521, with diecast fuselage, 6 cylinder radial engine and wing support struts, tinplate wings, tailplane and rudder, finished in silver, two-wheel rubber-tyred undercarriage, seated pilot, the base of original card box folds out to form a hanger, c1930, wingspan 9in (23cm) wide. **$2,000–2,300** *WAL*

r. A TippCo battery-operated Lockheed Super-G Constellation aircraft, in KLM 'The Flying Dutchman' colours, slight wear, c1965, 18in (45.5cm) long. **$400–500** *P(Ba)*

Soldiers

A set of wax soldiers, by Bell of London, standing to attention in uniform with helmets and guns, over-painted in brown, 19thC, each 3in (75mm) high, boxed. **$190–220** *BIG*

A Heinrichsen set of toy soldiers, and a set of hand-painted, flat, cast tin soldiers, equipment and landscape pieces, 6 cloth tents with cardboard bases, c1865, 1¼in (30mm) scale. **$5,500–6,500** *LHA*

The German firm of Heinrichsen flourished from 1839 until WWII. Their style of flat tin models, noted for realistic poses and uniforms, dominated European and American toy markets and were also widely imitated.

An A. Theroude clockwork papier mâche infantry soldier, with painted features, wired arms, holding a musket, in original military uniform, on a three-wheeled platform with keywind mechanism causing him to turn his head, raise his right arm and fire, French, c1860, 9in (23cm) high. **$1,500–1,800** *S*

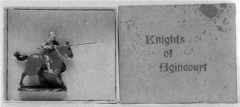

A Britains set No. 113 East Yorkshire Regiment, 8 soldiers standing to attention, pre-1939, in original box. **$130–160** *WAL*

A Britains set No. 1554 Royal Canadian Mounted Police, comprising a mounted officer and 6 men, 2nd type, in summer dress, pre-1939, in original box. **$120–140** *WAL*

A Britains Knights of Agincourt figure, in mint condition, c1954, 4in (10cm) high, with original box. **$160–200** *OTS*

A Britains set No. 429 Scots Greys and 1st Lifeguards, in winter dress, comprising 13 pieces, c1950, in original box with card insert. **$190–220** *WAL*

Mechanical Toys

A Martin 'Swimming Ondine' clockwork doll, the François Gaultier head with closed mouth, fixed blue glass eyes, blonde real hair wig, the torso housing the keywind mechanism causing the wooden legs and bisque hands to swim, French, c1870, 13in (33cm) long.
$1,600–1,800 *S*

A black and white fur-covered clockwork goat, his legs moving when the mechanism is wound, pulling a red and black painted tinplate open carriage with basketwork seat upholstered in buttoned sky-blue silk satin, in original box stamped 'Au Nain Bleu', French, c1900, 21¼in (54cm) long.
$1,900–2,200 *S*

A Leopold Lambert automaton of a Chinese tea drinker, the bisque head with brown glass eyes and bisque arms, wearing original yellow satin and gold embroidered coat, mounted on a red velvet base containing clockwork and musical movements playing a single air, French, c1890, 19in (48cm) high.
$6,500–7,500 *Bon(C)*

A Schoenau & Hoffmeister bisque-headed mechanical clown, c1900, 11¾in (30cm) high.
$1,100–1,300 *YC*

r. A German tinplate clockwork dockyard worker, made in US zone, c1950, 4¼in (11cm) long.
$110–130 *RAR*

A Schuco model of Donald Duck, with clockwork mechanism, painted body, felt hat and jacket, c1936, 6in (15cm) high.
$350–400 *HCC*

A Triang Minic clockwork elephant and howdah, c1950, 7in (18cm) long.
$135–155 *RAR*

An American tinplate wind-up pelican toy, by J. Chein, 1950s, 4¾in (12cm) high.
$120–140 *MSB*

A battery-operated Burger Chef toy, No. 212, c1960, 10in (25.5cm) high.
$110–130 *HCH*

Money Banks

A cast iron Punch and Judy show money bank, Buffalo, New York, c1884, 6½in (16.5cm) wide.
$1,000–1,200 *AWT*

A J. & E. Stevens 'I always did 'spise a mule' cast iron money bank, designed by James H. Bowen, c1879, 10in (25.5cm) long.
$1,700–2,200 *S*

As the lever below the mule is pushed, causing it to bolt, the seated figure is kicked backwards and the coin placed to the rear of the bench falls into the coin trap.

Money Banks

Although mechanical and 'still' (without mechanism) money banks had existed for centuries, their heyday was in America between 1869 and 1910, when most of the finest designs were made from cast iron.

Following the American Civil War, between 1861 and 1865, there was a shortage of coinage and an understandable desire for thrift. As a result, money banks became a popular way in which to encourage children to save money.

As well as having this serious side banks are often humourous, as can be seen in the examples in this section.

A J. & E. Stevens painted cast iron mechanical bank, in the form of a mule entering a barn, c1880, 8½in (21.5cm) long.
$520–560 *SK(B)*

A metal donkey money box, repaired, 19thC, 5¼in (13.5cm) long.
$110–130 *PCh*

A J. & E. Stevens 'Bad Accident' painted mechanical money bank, c1900, 10in (25.5cm) long.
$2,800–3,200 *EL*

Rocking Horses

A mid-Victorian rocking horse, with leather saddle and bridle, on bow-shaped rockers, the rockers reinforced at base, 50in (127cm) high.
$2,400–2,800 *LAY*

A dappled grey rocking horse, saddlecloth damaged, c1880, 37in (94cm) high.
$350–450 *PEN*

An F. H. Ayres rocking horse, on a spring safety stand, c1916, 50in (127cm) high.
Unrestored **$1,900–2,400**
Restored   **$4,000–5,000**
STE

Miscellaneous Toys & Games

A Wallis's revolving alphabet, hand-coloured lithograph on wood, with a picture of a father pointing out to his son the mirror on the wall which shows the alphabet, operated by a knob in the centre, c1850, 7¼in (18cm) square.
$1,100–1,200 *CSK*

A mid-Victorian calamander games compendium, brass bound and set with cabochon agates, the satinwood-lined fitted interior with a drawer below, containing an ivory chess set of Staunton pattern, draughts, whist markers, dice and shakers, and a calamander and satinwood chess and backgammon board, the lock engraved 'G. T. Dimmock, Norwich', 13in (33cm) wide.
$2,500–3,000 *P(O)*

A *Jeu de Course* platform horse racing game, by M. J. & Co, France, with circular track around which 6 cast racers spin by lever mechanism, with lid and box base covered in black textured paper, c1880, 9¾in (25cm) wide.
$160–200 *AG*

A Parker Brothers 'Duck Shooting' game, c1900, 13½in (34.5cm) wide.
$100–120 *AWT*

A Milton Bradley & Co game of Fish-Pond, with 12 fish and 2 fishing rods, c1890, 15in (38cm) wide.
$80–100 *AWT*

A doll's pram, with folding hood, worn, late 19thC, 20in (51cm) long.
$50–60 *PCh*

A McLoughlin Bros Home Baseball game, with playing field on box bottom, teetotum and 14 wooden disc tokens, c1897, 10½in (26.5cm) wide.
$2,000–2,500 *SK(B)*

A thuyawood veneered Royal Cabinet of Games compendium, the front and top opening with 2 lift-out trays, 2 leather-inlaid playing boards, cribbage board, set of chess and draughts pieces, dominoes and 6 dice, bezique markers, 2 packs of cards, 6 painted lead racehorses, jockeys and 3 jumps, late 19thC, 12¾in (32.5cm) wide.
$2,000–2,500 *WW*

A Victorian doll's wooden and canvas buggy, with stencilled patterns, c1880, 42in (106.5cm) long.
$280–320 *AWT*

EPHEMERA

The dictionary definition of ephemera is 'anything short-lived or transitory'. This term has become synonymous with different types of printed paper: magazine inserts, greetings cards, postcards, scrapbooks, cigarette cards, letters and billheads, menus, advertising material, packaging and other items which do not readily fall into such specific collecting categories as stamps or books.

Recent years have seen an increase both in the number of collectors and prices. Thematic collecting is popular, whether by type or by subject, such as sport, railway, transport, tobacco, alcohol and military subjects. These are especially sought-after.

There is a growing interest in packaging, ranging from printed labels (golfers on tins of tomatoes, feathered cricketers on poultry food) to designs on cheese labels. Trade catalogues, especially those examples that give an insight into how we lived before the two World Wars, are now much sought-after.

Over the years much of this type of material has been thrown away, but it can still be found in the cellars and filing cabinets of older companies or hidden away in family attics. Indeed the family postcard album has now become an investment for future generations rather than a plaything for the present one.

The stronger market for ephemera is confirmed by such items as the 1930 Mickey Mouse book on page 678 worth $2,200–2,400, a postcard (see page 679) by Pablo Picasso and sent by him to a friend in Paris now worth $700–800, an attractive set of 50 Player's cigarette cards showing butterfly girls now worth between $175–200, and a 1938 Republic one-sheet poster of the Lone Ranger (see page 681) valued at $4,500–5,500.

The auction market for ephemera varies greatly in terms of price and recognition of items, since it is being based upon the relative knowledge of the auctioneers who sell it. It is, of course, a huge and specialised field, and while certain salerooms handle thousands of lots, it is unusual for a valuable and important collection to be seen on the market. Some reproductions are, unfortunately, passed off as originals, and early printed illustrated ephemera should be inspected carefully. Condition is of paramount importance, so when deciding to collect ephemera, serious thought should be given to how the collection will be stored and displayed. Albums or frames are the best options.

A vast panorama of domestic, industrial and social history is available to the collector of these humble, printed items; and the fact that many of them date back two or three centuries means that the dictionary definition of ephemera as it relates to antiques and collectables is not entirely correct.

T. Vennett-Smith

Annuals, Books & Comics

The Magic Fun Book, D. C. Thomson, Dundee, 1942. **$450–520** *CBP*

This was the second of only 2 annuals for Magic Comic before wartime shortage of pulp and dyestuffs forced amalgamation with The Beano *the following year, becoming* The Magic-Beano Book.

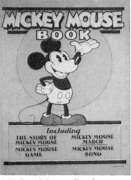

Mickey Mouse Book, Bibo and Lang, cover art by UB Iwerks, 1930. **$2,200–2,400** *CNY*

This was the first Disney book, and the first appearance of Mickey and Minnie Mouse.

The Hotspur 1, D. C. Thomson, first issue with the Swooping Vengeance and Buffalo Bill's Schooldays, 1933. **$200–250** *CBP*

Green Lantern No. 23, National Periodical Publications, 1946. **$80–90** *CBP*

Cross Reference
Colour Review

r. Donald Duck, in The Terror of the River, No 108, comic book, four colour, Dell Publishing, 1946. **$1,100–1,350** *CNY*

The Magic-Beano Book, D. C. Thomson, Dundee, 1949. **$350–400** *CBP*

The Incredible Hulk, No. 1, Marvel Comics Group, 1962. **$580–640** *CBP*

Autographs

Pablo Picasso, a signed postcard of Naples, written in French, 1917.
$700–800 *VS*

Winston Churchill arriving at the Mansion House after receiving the Freedom of the City of London, a signed black and white photograph, 1943, framed and glazed, 12 x 6in (30.5 x 15cm).
$1,000–1,200 *Bon*

A letter written in 1762 by George Washington to his brother-in-law, Colonel Burwell Bassett.
$33,500–37,000 *HAM*

This letter was written by Washington approximately 27 years before he became first President of the United States, and was sold by direct descendents of Betty Washington, George's only sister to survive to adulthood.

Prince Charles and Diana, Princess of Wales, a signed Christmas card, c1985.
$1,200–1,300 *VS*

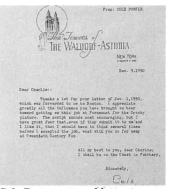

Cole Porter, a typed letter to Charles Brackett thanking him for his assistance in getting him a job on a Crosby film, dated 'Dec 9, 1950'.
$400–500 *SLN*

Marilyn Monroe, a signed black and white photograph, advertising the film *Baby Doll*, 1956, 9¼ x 7½in (23.5 x 19cm).
$7,500–8,000 *S*

Cigarette Cards

Franklyn Davey, Types of Smokers, set of 10, 1898.
$520–580 *VS*

Allen & Ginter, Wild Animals of the World, set of 50, 1888.
$430–480 *VS*

Godfrey Phillips, Cricketers, set of 192, c1924.
$15–25 each *ACC*

Adkin & Sons, Character Sketches, set of 12, 1900.
$80–90 *VS*

W. D. & H. O. Wills, Birds of Australasia, set of 100, 1912.
$100–120 *VS*

John Player & Sons, Fire Fighting Appliances, set of 50, c1930.
$110–220 *ACC*

Hignett's Ships and Flags, and Cap Badges, 2nd series, set of 25, 1927.
$130–200 *ACC*

Millhoff, Men of Genius, set of 25, 1924.
$120–140 *VS*

John Player & Sons, Butterfly Girls, set of 50, 1928.
$175–200 *VS*

John Player & Sons, Cricketers, set of 50, 1938.
$90–110 *ACC*

Postcards

A postcard showing vignettes of Washington DC, the White House, the Capitol, George Washington's House, Library of Congress and Treasury Building, published by Wilhelm Knorr, Germany, c1898.
$40–50 *PIn*

A postcard showing vignettes of Boston, the Public Park, Longfellow's House, Art Museum, Bunker Hill Monument, Massachusetts State House and Faneuil Hall, published by Wilhelm Knorr, Germany, c1898.
$40–50 *PIn*

Olympic Games, published in Switzerland to commemorate the 20th anniversary of the reintroduction of the Olympic Games, unused, 1914.
$50–60 *SpP*

A postcard showing Nuneaton Charter Day Procession, Warwickshire, 1907.
$30–40 *VS*

A Wiener Werkstätte postcard, The Meat Market, Old Roofs, design No. 540, unused, c1908.
$110–120 *SpP*

A postcard showing Whitby Town Crier, Yorkshire, 1904.
$45–50 *VS*

A postcard showing High Street, Stoney Stratford, Buckinghamshire, with 3 motor buses, 1913.
$30–35 *VS*

Posters

A poster depicting Mary Pickford, in *Coquette*, United Artists, US, paper-backed, 1929, 41 x 27in (104 x 68.5cm). **$400–500** *CSK*

A poster depicting The Lone Ranger, Republic Pictures, 1938, 41 x 27in (104 x 68.5cm). **$4,500–5,500** *C(LA)*

A poster depicting Popeye the Sailor in *Shakespearian Spinach*, Paramount, 1940, linen-backed, 41 x 27in (104 x 68.5cm). **$3,200–3,500** *S(NY)*

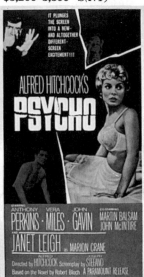

An LNER poster, printed by Baynard, July 1946, 40 x 81½in (102 x 207cm). **$480–560** *ONS*

A poster depicting Ronald Reagan in *Law and Order*, Universal, 1953, 30 x 40in (76 x 101.5cm). **$180–200** *CSK*

A poster depicting *The Rocky Horror Show*, tissue-backed, British, 1975, 30 x 40in (76 x 101.5cm). **$520–620** *S*

A poster depicting Alfred Hitchcock's *Psycho*, Paramount, linen-backed, 1960, 81 x 41in (206 x 104cm). **$1,250–1,350** *S(LA)*

A poster depicting Olivia Newton-John and John Travolta in *Grease*, 1978, 23½ x 15¾in (60 x 40cm). **$1,100–1,300** *C(LA)*

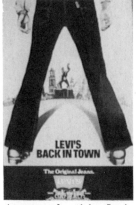

r. A poster depicting George Reeves in *Superman Flies Again*, Eros Films, 1954, 41 x 27in (104 x 68.5cm). **$160–200** *Bon*

A poster advertising Levi jeans, c1975, 45½ x 32½in (116 x 83cm). **$110–130** *VSP*

ROCK & POP

A silkscreen and flatbed lithograph on French rag, depicting The Beatles on a freight train, Hamburg, by Astrid Kircherr, October 1960, printed later, 20½ x 25in (52 x 63.5cm).
$1,400–1,600 *Bon*

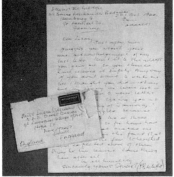

A handwritten letter by Stuart Sutcliffe to Susan Williams, 21st October, 1960.
$1,400–1,550 *S(NY)*

The Beatles, 'With The Beatles', with gold Parlophone label, 12in LP, Australian, 1960s.
$320–400 *CTO*

A signed colour photograph of Paul McCartney, with guitar, 8 x 5½in (20.5 x 21.5cm).
$270–300 *VS*

Paul McCartney's original birth certificate, No. DC 004399, 1942, 6¼ x 14in (16 x 35.5cm).
$73,000–80,000 *Bon*

John Lennon's fawn cotton stage suit, the pockets trimmed with black silk, rope-trimmed collar and fastenings, lined in gold satin, with label, and letter of authenticity from the tailor, 1963.
$35,000–40,000 *Bon*

A Bassett's Liquorice Allsorts mock-up box, signed on the lid in blue ballpoint by The Beatles with dedication by Paul, with illustration and musical note pattern in watercolour, probably 1963.
$9,500–11,000 *S*

This box appears to have been a design prototype for a line of confectionery planned by Bassett's, possibly as a result of The Beatles being pelted with jelly babies following George Harrison's chance remark about his liking for them.

r. A handwritten poem by Eric Clapton, titled on the top 'No. 2', initialled 'EC', c1980, 18 x 14in (45.5 x 35.5cm).
$1,400–1,600 *S(NY)*

This was one of 5 poems sent by Eric Clapton to a friend who was in prison in 1980.

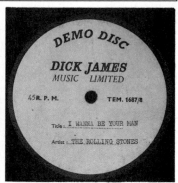

A single-sided 7in Dick James Demo Disc acetate recording of 'I Wanna Be Your Man', by The Beatles, wrongly credited to the Rolling Stones, 1963.
$700–800 *S*

A pair of John Lennon's hiking boots, labelled 'Original Chippewa Shoe Company, USA', c1964, and a letter from John's cousin.
$2,700–3,000 *Bon*

A gold-coloured metal ring, set with an opal, given to Mitch Mitchell's mother by Jimi Hendrix as a keepsake, late 1960s.
$1,600–1,800 *S*

A Bon Jovi modified acoustic guitar, custom-built for Richie Sambora, used on Bon Jovi's first 2 studio albums and on their first 2 tours, 1984, and a letter of authenticity and photograph.
$2,800–3,200 *S(NY)*

A poster written in Spanish, depicting Michael Jackson in *Moonwalker*, signed in black felt tip pen, 1988.
$240–280 *Bon*

A black and white photograph of Grateful Dead, signed in blue, 1985, 10 x 8in (25.5 x 20.5cm).
$320–400 *Lel*

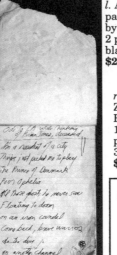

l. A handwritten seven-page poetry notebook, by Jim Morrison, with 2 pages of drawings, black pen and ink.
$25,500–29,000 *S(NY)*

r. A poster, Led Zeppelin at the Baths Hall, Ipswich, 16th November 1970, printed in blue and red, 30 x 20in (76 x 51cm).
$2,000–2,200 *S*

George Michael's 'Rockers Revenge' black leather jacket, featured in the video *Faith* and in *Freedom*, in which it was symbolically burned, the back with painted design, studs and rhinestones, fire damage to left arm, back and left front, requires re-stitching, and a copy of a letter of authenticity.
$2,800–3,200 *S*

A swatch of glazed cotton material produced for Ready Steady Go Goes Live, spring 1966, 36in (91.5cm) high.
$650–800 *CTO*

l. A limited edition of Brian May's Red Special guitar, signed in black marker and dated '95', and signed on the back by John Deacon and Roger Taylor, with letter from the Queen International Fan Club.
$1,700–2,000 *S*

SCIENTIFIC INSTRUMENTS
Dials

A boxwood Gunter quadrant, signed 'Antonius Thompson', with scales on both faces including hours, five stars with their right ascensions, calendar and degree scales, lacking sights and plumb bob mount, lateral crack on both faces, 1645–65, 15in (38cm) radius.
$12,500–13,500 *S*

A French brass Butterfield dial, signed 'Chapotot à Paris', with shaped gnomon and bird indicator, 3 engraved hour scales and compass rose, the reverse with decorated compass well and list of cities and their latitudes, mid-18thC, 2¾in (7cm) wide.
$1,700–1,900 *S*

A brass horizontal sundial, signed 'Tho Wright', the plate with engraved hour scale divided IIII–XII–VIII, calendar/month scales and settings for watch faster and slower, the centre with gnomon and compass rose with engraved latitude for 54°:15 minutes, c1730, 11in (28cm) diam.
$1,200–1,400 *S*

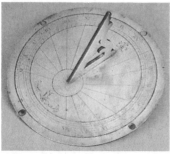

A brass horizontal garden sundial, signed 'Hill', engraved with foliate scrolls and Roman numerals, dated '1795', 8in (20.5cm) diam.
$480–560 *DN*

A brass horizontal sundial, with dials for Madrid, London, Paris, Vienna, Rome and Lisbon, the gnomon support fitted for string, the plate with inset compass, on a rosewood base, 18thC, 7in (18cm) wide.
$1,000–1,200 *CSK*

A brass Butterfield pattern dial, signed 'Chapotot à Paris', with hour scales for 40°, 45° and 50°, with folding bird gnomon, engraved for latitudes 40°–60°, inset compass, the underside engraved with the latitudes of 20 Continental cities and towns, late 18thC, 3in (7.5cm) wide, in original case.
$1,900–2,200 *CSK*

A brass universal equinoctial ring dial, signed 'Troughton and Simms London', the meridian ring with sliding suspension ring, engraved on one side with 2 quadrants, the other with declination scale, the equinoctial ring with twice I–XII hour scales, engraved with zodiac and calendar scales, early 19thC, 6¼in (16cm) diam.
$2,800–3,200 *CSK*

r. A pocket sundial, signed 'S. Porter, Magnetic Sun Dial', the hour ring enclosed by a serpent, late 19thC, 2¼in (5.5cm) diam, in turned ivory case.
$500–550 *CSK*

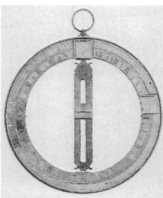

A brass universal equinoctial ring dial, the meridian ring with sliding suspension point, engraved on one side with 2 quadrants, the other with declination scale, the equinoctial ring with twice I–XII hour scale, engraved with calendar scale, 18thC, 6in (15cm) diam.
$1,900–2,200 *CSK*

A Braham brass universal equinoctial dial, signed 'Braham, Bristol', divided III–XII–VIII with folding spring loaded gnomon, engraved latitude arc with scale 0°–80° and inset compass rose, supported on 3 levelling screws, c1830, 4¼in (11cm) diam, in a mahogany case.
$2,400–2,700 *S*

Globes

A 2¼in (5.7cm) diam terrestrial globe, by C. C. Abel-Klinger, made-up of 12 coloured engraved paper gores, with brass axis pin, with a printed horizon ring incorporating a zodiac and calendar scale fitted in a simulated leather-covered card drum case, the lid with pictorial label depicting a family at a table studying globes, c1850, 2¾in (7cm) high.
$2,800–3,500 *CSK*

A pair of mahogany terrestrial and celestial library globe stands, the tripod legs with original brass casters, one with an 18in (45.5cm) diam Cary's new celestial globe, with one calibrated brass horizon and calibrated paper-ring, both missing base compass, early 19thC, 46in (116.5cm) high.
$9,500–10,500 *GH*

A 15in (38cm) diam terrestrial collapsing globe, by John Betts, London, printed in colours, mounted on a black enamelled brass umbrella type frame, c1860, carrying case 29½in (75cm) wide.
$680–800 *CSK*

A terrestrial floor globe, on a baluster-shaped stem with 3 cast iron foliate scrolled legs, with a cartouche inscribed 'S. Chedlers Terrestrial globe, Jersey City, New Jersey copyright 1889', restored, 40¼in (102cm) high.
$1,300–1,600 *S(NY)*

l. A 12in (30.5cm) diam terrestrial table globe, by Felix Delamarche, Paris, made-up of 12 lithographed gores depicting the routes of French voyages to the Pacific, metal axis, graduated brass meridian circle, hour-ring with printed horizon code, the globe mounted on a tripod stand, compass lacking, c1844, 24½in (62cm) high.
$6,000–6,500 *CSK*

A 12in (30.5cm) diam terrestrial table globe, by T. M. Bardin, on 4 ring-turned baluster legs joined by a cross-stretcher, c1820, the stretchers possibly later.
$5,000–5,500 *CSK*

A 15½in (39cm) diam celestial globe, by Columbus, Berlin, the 12 paper gores decorated in blue with yellow stars, their magnitude shown by size, aluminium meridian half-circle divided in 2 quadrants, on mahogany stand, c1910, 20in (51cm) high.
$1,100–1,300 *CSK*

A Kirkwood's 12in (30.5cm) diam terrestrial table globe, the hand-coloured engraved gores with brass hour and meridian circles and engraved horizon circle, on 4 turned ebonised supports, with stretchers, damaged, 19thC.
$1,900–2,200 *C(S)*

A 2in (5cm) diam terrestrial globe,
by Malby & Co, London, made-up of
12 coloured engraved paper gores, steel
axis pin, contained in a mahogany-lined
fruit-shaped case with hinged cover,
c1842, 3½in (9cm) high.
$2,800–3,200 *CSK*

An 18in (45.5cm) diam
celestial library globe,
by Malby & Co, London,
the sphere applied with
coloured gores, in a brass
meridian circle and coloured
horizontal circle, supported
on a mahogany stand with
3 scroll brass inlaid legs
joined by an undertier inset
with a compass, c1850.
$5,000–5,500 *B&L*

A 9in (23cm) diam terrestrial
globe-on-stand, by
A. C. Monfort, the sphere with
hand-coloured gores mounted
on papier mâché meridian,
within horizon ring applied
with print calendar and
zodiac scale, on fruitwood
base, 1825, 18½in (47cm) high.
$4,000–4,500 *S*

A pair of 5½in (14cm) diam
terrestrial and celestial globes,
by J. & W. Newton, each sphere
with hand-coloured gores, mounted
in brass meridian within wooden
ring applied with printed calendar
and zodiac scale, on 3 turned
mahogany legs with stretcher,
c1818, 9½in (24cm) high.
$14,000–15,000 *S*

*The size of these Newton globes is
very rare.*

A 3in (7.5cm) diam globe,
by Newton & Son, with
12 printed and hand-
coloured gores showing
the track of Cook's 3rd
voyage and Clark and
Gore's voyage of 1779,
damaged, c1840, mounted
in a turned wooden case.
$1,900–2,200 *Bon(C)*

A table-top globe, by Newton & Son,
with brass circumference, in turned
wooden tripod frame, linked by
stretchers, 1859, 20in (50.5cm) high.
$2,000–2,500 *WL*

A celestial table globe, by
J. Wilson & Sons, New York,
the papers corrected to 1826,
on a stand, 18in (45.5cm) high.
$6,500–7,000 *SK(B)*

*James Wilson (1763–1855), the
first commercial maker of globes
in the US, was self-taught in the
skills of geography and engraving.
However, both his terrestrial and
celestial globes are very accurate.*

A 12in (30.5cm) diam terrestrial
globe, by Phillips, late 19thC.
$350–400 *GAZE*

A 12in (30.5cm) diam Wrench
celestial globe, mounted in brass
meridian within horizontal ring
applied with calendar and zodiac
scales, on 4 ebonised wooden legs
with stretcher, mid-19thC,
16in (41cm) high.
$1,900–2,200 *S*

Medical & Dental

A George III mahogany apothecary chest, with fitted compartments, 10in (25.5cm) high.
$320–400 *TMi*

A mahogany apothecary's chest, the fitted interior with drawers, a baize-lined flap revealing rows of bottles, with a pair of hinged doors, sunken brass handles, early 19thC, 11in (28cm) high.
$1,800–2,200 *WW*

A mahogany travelling apothecary chest, the fitted interior with glass flasks and containers, the front section opening to reveal the inscription 'Prepared by J. Bigonet Philada Apothecary & Chemists No. 53 Seventh St', c1900, 21in (53.5cm) wide.
$3,500–4,000 *S(NY)*

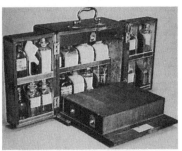

A mahogany household medicine chest, with 2 doors fitted for bottles, enclosing a fall containing drawers with glass pestle and mortar and a measure, further bottles and a drawer with compartments for scales, tin boxes and various handwritten remedies, labelled 'Savory, Moore & Co, London', 19thC, 11½in (29cm) wide.
$850–950 *DN*

A mahogany domestic medicine chest, divided into 2 sections, opening to reveal compartments of bottles behind walnut slides, with 7 drawers of various sizes below, 2 brass carrying handles and iron lock, early 19thC, 11¼in (28.5cm) high.
$2,000–2,500 *CSK*

A mahogany medicine chest, with brass carrying handles, hinged lid, drawer in the base fitted with glass bottles, flasks and pestle and mortar, incomplete, mid-19thC, 13in (33cm) wide.
$1,200–1,300 *S*

A mahogany domestic medicine chest, the lid with flush brass handle, enclosing a velvet-lined fitted interior containing 10 glass bottles, with drawer beneath containing brass and steel scales and drachm and grain weights, 19thC, 7in (18cm) high.
$1,100–1,250 *PF*

A mahogany domestic medicine chest, the hinged front opening to reveal compartments for 16 bottles, 2 drawers, the back with sliding cover for further bottles, inset brass handle, c1860, 8¾in (22cm) wide.
$600–720 *Bon(C)*

A Spanish walnut domestic medicine chest, bound with iron strapwork decoration, the front with 2 hinged compartments containing 16 bottles with tin lids, 5 tin canisters and 3 drawers, the lid with handwritten list of contents, mid-19thC, 10¼in (26cm) wide.
$1,500–1,700 *S*

l. A mahogany medicine chest, the plush-lined lid revealing compartments for 15 bottles, the double doors with compartments for 8 bottles and 4 short drawers, enclosing 2 accessory drawers below, 19thC, 8½in (21.5cm) wide.
$2,000–2,200 *C(Am)*

An oak medicine chest, the plush-lined lid revealing compartments for 20 bottles of 4 sizes, an accessory drawer with 4 creamware jars and covers, 5 bottles, a glass eye-rinsing cup, and a glass pestle and mortar, 19thC, 13½in (34cm) wide.
$1,400–1,600 *C(Am)*

A mahogany medicine chest, with 2 sliding covers revealing 2 compartments with 11 bottles, and 18 drawers containing glass jars, a glass pestle and creamware mortar, the rear also with 2 sliding covers revealing 2 compartments containing 9 bottles, 19thC, 11½in (29.5cm) wide.
$5,600–6,300 *C(Am)*

An iron surgical saw, with lead-weighted chequer-grip bone handle, 18thC, 11in (28cm) long.
$550–600 *CSK*

An iron bone-saw, the bow frame with tightening arrangement, the blade held between 2 jaws arranged to swivel, with pistol grip bone handle, early 19thC, 12in (30.5cm) long.
$650–800 *CSK*

A mahogany domestic medicine chest, the lid revealing compartments for 15 bottles, the drawer below with fitting for jars and bottles, containing glass eye bath, a pestle and mortar, with inset brass carrying handle, 19thC, 9in (23cm) wide.
$600–650 *CSK*

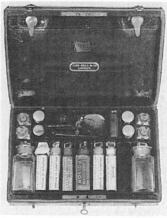

An embossed leather-covered apothecary's travelling case, the lid with prescription compartment and embossed in gilt 'John Bell & Co, London', containing 12 bottles and 4 jars, a brass balance with pans and weights and a measure, 19thC, 10in (25.5cm) wide.
$280–320 *CSK*

Don't Forget!

If in doubt please refer to the 'How to Use' section at the beginning of this book.

r. A part-set of surgical instruments, by Evans & Co, containing a bone-saw, 3 Liston knives, various scalpels, and other items, in plush-lined brass-bound mahogany case, late 19thC, 17½in (44.5cm) wide.
$1,600–1,900 *CSK*

An apothecary's chest, the front opening with 2 doors, the interior with bottles and 2 drawers, rear compartment enclosed by a slide enclosing 4 bottles, the top with flush brass handles, 19thC, 9in (23cm) wide.
$420–480 *E*

A trepanning set, with drill, 3 trephines, 3 scalpels and chisels, 2 perforators, a skull-screw, and other instruments, in chamois leather-lined leather case decorated with gilt tooling, 17thC, 16¾in (42.5cm) long.
$9,500–10,500 *CSK*

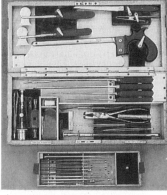

A surgeon's kit, by S. Maw Son & Thompson, with bone-saw, tourniquet, a collection of knives, scalpels and other items, in plush-lined brass-bound mahogany case, 19thC, 15½in (39.5cm) wide.
$2,500–2,800 *CSK*

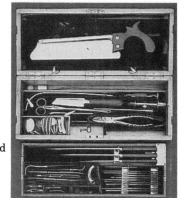

A treble concertina, by George Case, c1900, 8in (20.5cm) wide, in original rosewood hexagonal box. **$160–200** *P*

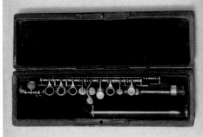

A cocuswood Boehm system piccolo, by Louis Lot, Paris, some modification, c1900, 12½in (31.5cm) long, in case. **$400–500** *P*

An Italian violin, by August de Planis, 1774, length of back 14in (35.5cm). **$35,000–40,000** *Bon*

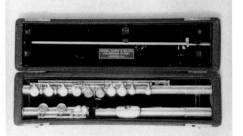

A silver Boehm system concert flute, The Romilly Coronet, c1900, 25¾in (65.5cm) long. **$480–540** *P*

A French silver-mounted violin bow, stamped 'Jerome Thibouville Lamy à Paris', 1920, 63g. **$750–900** *P*

A gold and tortoiseshell-mounted violin bow, attributed to François Tourte, frog and adjuster not original, c1800, 59g. **$9,500–11,000** *SK*

A French violin, workshop of J. B. Vuillaume, Paris, after Antonius Stradivarius, c1860, length of back 14in (35.5cm). **$21,000–24,000** *Bon*

A Mirecourt viola, c1900, length of back 16¾in (41.5cm). **$5,600–6,200** *P*

A French violin, by Georges Chanot, 1870, length of back 14in (35.5cm). **$22,500–25,500** *CSK*

A Scottish cello, by J. W. Briggs, 1925, length of back 29¾in (75.5cm). **$13,500–16,000** *Bon*

A Neapolitan violin, by Vincenzo Sanino, Naples, 1882, length of back 14in (35.5cm). **$17,500–19,000** *Bon*

A violoncello, attributed to Thomas Smith, London, c1760, length of back 29in (73.5cm). **$2,500–2,800** *P*

A Swiss Paillard Vaucher Fils musical box, c1880, 43in (109cm) wide.
$19,500–21,000 *S*

A Fortuna disc table musical box, German, c1900, 30in (76cm) wide.
$6,500–8,000 *S*

A Bontems birds automaton, French, restored, late 19thC, 22in (56cm) high.
$12,500–14,500 *S*

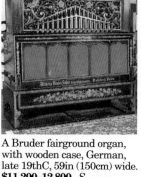

A Bruder fairground organ, with wooden case, German, late 19thC, 59in (150cm) wide.
$11,200–12,800 *S*

An Italian street barrel organ, c1870, 37⅜in (95cm) high.
$7,300–8,000 *S*

A George III mahogany square piano, by Wood & Co, Edinburgh, restored, c1800, 65in (165cm) wide.
$5,000–5,600 *S(Z)*

A German Symphonion 25¼in (64cm) disc musical box-on-stand, with coin-operated drive movement, c1900, 81in (207cm) high.
$12,500–13,000 *S*

A walnut inlaid piano, by John Brinsmead & Sons, London, c1890, 55½in (141cm) wide.
$1,150–1,300 *RPh*

A Bechstein golden rosewood inlaid upright piano, repolished and with reconditioned panel, c1897, 57½in (146cm) wide.
$4,400–4,800 *SI*

A marquetry, gilt-bronze, porcelain and lapis lazuli upright piano, by Declercq, Paris, originally with an Erard mechanism, c1865, 64⅝in (164cm) wide.
$70,000–80,000 *S*

A Murdoch mahogany upright overstrung piano, reconditioned, c1927, 52¾in (134cm) wide.
$1,300–1,450 *SI*

A Niendorf mahogany baby grand piano, repolished and reconditioned, c1932, 54in (137cm) wide.
$4,200–4,800 *SI*

A Broadwood satinwood and gilt-brass mounted grand piano, No. 46312, on square tapered legs with brass caps and casters, c1895, 72in (183cm) wide.
$3,200–3,500 *CSK*

PIANO-EXPORT

WHOLESALERS AND EXPORTERS OF QUALITY SECONDHAND PIANOS

Always 100-200 instruments in stock, including Grand Pianos by

STEINWAY ★ BECHSTEIN ★ BLUTHNER ★ BOSENDORFER
ERARD ★ PLEYEL ★ BROADWOOD

Many with highly decorated and inlaid cabinets

FULL PACKING AND SHIPPING ARRANGED WORLDWIDE AT VERY COMPETITIVE PRICES

Telephone or write to:
PIANO-EXPORT, Bridge Road, Kingswood, Bristol BS15 4PW, England
Tel: 0117 956 8300 · International: +44 117 956 8300

A portrait miniature, circle of Nicholas Hilliard, c1590, 1½in (36mm) high. **$3,200–3,500** *C*

A portrait miniature, by Isaac Oliver, on vellum, c1600, 2¼in (58mm) high. **$5,700–6,400** *C*

A portrait miniature, by Susan Penelope Rosse, of Mrs Elizabeth Rowe, c1695, 3in (76mm) high. **$1,300–1,600** *Bon*

A portrait miniature, by James Scouler, dated '1785', 2½ x 2in (64 x 50mm), in a cast gilt-metal mount. **$6,400–7,200** *C*

A portrait miniature, by Samuel Shelley, in a gold locket frame, c1790, 3in (76mm) high. **$1,400–1,600** *BHa*

A portrait miniature of a lady in a plumed hat, English School, c1785, 2in (50mm) high, in a gilt-metal frame. **$1,000–1,100** *WeH*

A portrait miniature, by Diana Hill, signed, c1787, 3in (76mm) high. **$6,400–7,200** *Bon*

A portrait miniature of a young lady, by George Engleheart, c1800, 2in (50mm) high. **$4,800–5,400** *BHa*

A portrait miniature, by William Wood, depicting Mary Russell, c1800, 3in (76mm) high. **$1,600–1,800** *Bon*

A portrait miniature, Continental School, 19thC, 3¼in (83mm) high. **$400–450** *WeH*

A portrait miniature, by John Wright, of James Arthur Murray, 1804, 2¾in (70mm) high. **$4,800–5,400** *Bea(E)*

A portrait miniature, by Louis Antoine Collas, signed, c1805, 2⅛in (64mm) high. **$6,000–6,500** *S*

A portrait miniature, by Andrew Plimer, of an officer of the Light Dragoons, 1815, 3¼in (84mm) high. **$4,800–5,400** *Bon*

A portrait miniature, by Marie Virginie Boquet, c1840, 3in (80mm) high. **$1,200–1,350** *Bon*

A Balkan icon, The Deisis and the Twelve Apostles, 17thC, 19¼ x 14⅛in (49 x 37cm).
$3,200–3,500 *C*

A Greek icon, the Descent from the Cross, on a gold ground, 17thC, 19½ x 23in (49.5 x 58.5cm).
$10,500–12,000 *S*

A Greek icon, St John the Baptist, 17thC, 67 x 35½in (170 x 90cm).
$11,200–12,800 *C*

A Russian icon, the Appearance of the Mother of God to St Sergei of Radonezh, Moscow, 16thC, 11½ x 9½in (29 x 24cm).
$4,800–5,600 *S*

An Italo-Cretan icon of the Virgin and Child, c1700, 14 x 17¾in (35.5 x 45cm).
$3,600–4,000 *S(NY)*

A Romanian icon of the Hodegitria Mother of God, c1700, 32½ x 22½in (82.5 x 57cm).
$3,500–4,000 *S(NY)*

A north Russian icon, The Holy Trinity, 17thC, 21½ x 16½in (54.5 x 42cm).
$13,000–14,500 *S*

A Russian icon of the Mother of God of Vladimir, egg tempera on wood panel, late 17thC, 22in (56.5cm) high.
$7,200–8,000 *RKa*

A Russian icon of the Council of Archangel Michael, c1800, 33½ x 26¼in (85 x 66.5cm).
$2,800–3,200 *S(NY)*

A Russian icon of Christ Pantocrator, maker's mark of A. Liubavin, St Petersburg, c1895, 8¾ x 7in (22 x 18cm).
$7,200–8,800 *C*

A Russian icon of St Gregory Palamas, egg tempera on wood panel, 19thC, 12¾ x 4¼in (32.5 x 11cm).
$1,300–1,450 *RKa*

A Russian icon of the Mother of God of Kazan, painted on copper, c1900, 28½ x 28in (72.5 x 71cm).
$5,600–6,400 *C*

A Mycenaean buff-ware
chalice, circa 1400–1375 BC,
7½in (19cm) high.
$6,400–7,200 *S(NY)*

A Cypriot bichrome-ware
storage jar, circa 1000–800 BC,
10½in (26.5cm) high.
$640–720 *HEL*

A composition statue
of Tueris, circa
664–525 BC,
4½in (11.5cm) high.
$7,000–8,000 *C*

An Egyptian bronze head
of a cat, with gold inlay,
1069–656 BC, 2¾in (7cm)
high, mounted.
$7,300–8,000 *Bon*

A Romano-Egyptian gold and glass bead necklace, circa
1st century AD, with modern clasp, 16¾in (42.5cm) long.
$3,200–3,500 *C*

An Egyptian bronze
mummiform figure
of Osiris, original gold
inlay, 664–525 BC,
8in (20.5cm) high.
$8,500–9,500 *Bon*

A Greek south Italian
pottery trefoil-lipped
oinochoe, 4th century BC,
5½in (14cm) high.
$800–1,000 *HEL*

A Canosan terracotta
female figure, with
traces of paint,
circa 3rd century BC,
15in (38cm) high.
$7,200–8,800 *S*

An Egyptian painted plaster
bust, 1st–2nd century AD,
17¼in (44cm) high.
$7,300–8,000 *S*

A Greek south Italian
fish plate, 4th century BC,
8¾in (22cm) diam.
$3,200–3,500 *C*

A Roman glass bottle,
early 1st century AD,
2¾in (7cm) high.
$1,700–1,900 *Bon*

A Greek bronze trefoil
oinochoe, with faceted
handle and mask of a
maenad, 4th century BC,
8¼in (21cm) high.
$13,500–15,000 *S(NY)*

A Roman engraved glass jar,
with engraved decoration,
crack above base,
4th century AD,
4½in (11.5cm) high.
$6,400–8,000 *C*

A Roman mould-blown
glass twin-handled
vessel, moulded
with rosettes, circa
1st–2nd century AD,
4in (10cm) high.
$5,500–6,500 *Bon*

A Hellenistic bronze
figure of Hermes, with
silver-inlaid eyes,
1st century BC,
10in (25.5cm) high.
$11,200–12,800 *S(NY)*

A Roman lead-glazed
skyphos, the interor
glazed amber yellow,
circa 1st century BC,
6¼in (16cm) wide.
$6,400–7,200 *S(NY)*

An African wood and brass grain measure, c1860, 8½in (21.5cm) high.
$320–350 *SSW*

An African Baga bird figure, with pierced handle, surmounted by a boat, 23½in (59.5cm) high.
$8,500–9,500 *S(NY)*

An African Baga wood and leather funeral drum, 49in (124.5cm) high.
$1,300–1,450 *LHB*

A Dogon figure, Mali, 25in (63.5cm) high.
$1,300–1,400 *LHB*

A Jola wood and hemp dance mask, Senegal, 22in (56cm) high.
$200–250 *LHB*

A Dogon wooden stool, Mali, 10in (25.5cm) high.
$320–380 *LHB*

A Yoruba female twin figure, Nigeria, 12in (30.5cm) high.
$4,400–4,800 *S(NY)*

Two Yoruba tribe bronze figures, Nigeria, c1840, 20in (51cm) high.
$2,200–2,700 *FHA*

A Yoruba colonial figure, Nigeria, legs damaged, c1930, 13½in (34.5cm) high.
$320–350 *LHB*

A Batac Singa wooden wall panel, Sumatra, 70in (178cm) high.
$1,600–1,900 *LHB*

A Native American hide pouch, 15¾in (40cm) high.
$21,000–24,000 *S(NY)*

An Aboriginal bark painting, 25½in (65cm) high.
$4,500–5,500 *S(NY)*

A Sioux beaded whitetail deer skull, overlaid with hide panel, Native America, 13in (33cm) long.
$8,000–9,000 *S(NY)*

A New Caledonian mask, pierced for attachment, 16¼in (41.5cm) high.
$4,800–5,400 *Bon*

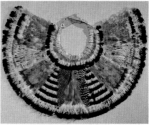

A Hawaiian feather cape, one side with white down, mid-19thC, 29in (73.5cm) diam.
$4,000–4,500 *S(NY)*

A French pressed bisque swivel-head fashion doll, with leather-covered wooden body and disc joints, closed mouth, fixed blue glass eyes, pierced ears, white mohair wig over cork pate, c1870, 19in (48.5cm) high.
$50,000–56,000 *S*

A Bru pressed bisque swivel-head doll, c1875, 14in (35.5cm) high.
$18,500–20,000 *S*

A Bru Jeune pressed bisque swivel-head doll with kid body, c1880, 36½in (92.5cm) high.
$13,000–14,500 *S*

A Limoges bisque doll, with lace trimmed bonnet and dress, clothes replaced, c1900, 27in (68.5cm) high.
$950–1,000 *AnS*

A French bisque-headed doll, by Belton, c1895, 15¾in (40cm) high.
$1,900–2,400 *YC*

An Ernst Descamps bisque-headed *bébé* doll, impressed mark, c1900, 22½in (57cm) high
$1,900–2,200 *YC*

A Ferdinand Gaultier bisque-headed fashion doll, incised, c1885, 17in (43cm) high.
$3,200–4,000 *YC*

A Grödnertal gesso covered wooden doll, with peg-jointed body, c1820, 13in (33cm) high.
$880–1,000 *P(Ba)*

A Gebrüder Heubach bisque-headed character doll, impressed mark, c1910, 18in (46cm) high.
$1,600–1,900 *YC*

A Tête Jumeau doll, c1885, 19in (48cm) high. $5,000–5,600 *S(S)*

A Käthe Kruse doll, c1922, 13in (33cm) high. $1,500–1,700 *Bon(C)*

A Jumeau Triste pressed bisque doll, c1875, 28in (71cm) high. $13,500–16,000 *S*

A Kämmer and Reinhardt bisque-headed doll, c1910, 15½in (39cm) high. $4,000–4,800 *YC*

A J. D. Kestner doll, c1900, 11in (28cm) high. $560–720 *MEG*

A Petit et Dumoutier pressed bisque doll, c1880, 22¾in (58cm) high. $9,500–11,000 *S*

A König & Wernicke doll, c1910, 14in (35.5cm) high. $1,900–2,200 *YC*

A J. D. Kestner bisque doll, c1912, 17in (43cm) high. $3,200–3,500 *YC*

A J. D. Kestner doll, c1910, 18in (46cm) high. $3,200–3,700 *YC*

A Bruno Schmidt doll, c1912, 20½in (52cm) high. $2,500–2,800 *YC*

An Emile Jumeau doll, c1885, 15in (38cm) high. $4,800–5,600 *YC*

An SFBJ bisque-headed pouty doll, c1912, 17in (43cm) high. $2,400–2,800 *YC*

An SFBJ bisque-headed doll, jointed body, c1900, 23in (58.5cm) high. $950–1,000 *PSA*

A Kämmer and Reinhardt bisque-headed doll, c1910, 15¼in (39cm) high. $4,000–5,000 *YC*

A Simon & Halbig bisque-headed boy doll, c1912, 16¼in (42cm) high. $2,800–3,200 *YC*

A Steiff teddy bear, with white mohair and boot button eyes, button in left ear, c1910, 19in (48.5cm) high.
$4,400–4,800 *CMF*

A Steiff teddy bear, with button in left ear, both arms restored, c1915, 20in (51cm) high.
$1,900–2,400 *CMF*

A Chad Valley mohair teddy bear, with glass eyes and stitched nose, straw filled, 1920s, 16in (40.5cm) high.
$200–225 *AnS*

A Steiff teddy bear, with gold mohair plush, amber glass eyes, swivel joints, large pads and growler, 1920s, 21in (53.5cm) high.
$1,100–1,300 *P(Ba)*

A Dean's plush mohair teddy bear, with glass eyes, growler operative, kapok filled, c1950, 16in (40.5cm) high.
$100–115 *PSA*

A Farnell gold mohair teddy bear, with glass eyes and stitched nose, replacement pads and paws, 1930s, 21in (53.5cm) high.
$3,500–4,000 *CMF*

A plush mohair teddy bear, c1950s, 14in (35.5cm) high.
$100–115 *PSA*

A Schuco teddy bear, with growler, 20in (51cm) high.
$240–280 *TED*

A Chiltern teddy bear, c1956, 18in (45.5cm) high.
$480–560 *B&F*

A Steiff teddy bear, with swivel jointed body, repaired, c1908, 26½in (67cm) high.
$2,000–2,500 *S(S)*

A Bing plush teddy bear, with metal label to side, repaired, c1910, 12in (31cm) high.
$1,200–1,350 *S(S)*

A teddy bear, c1920, 5in (12.5cm) high.
$80–100 *PSA*

A mohair jointed teddy bear, 1940s, 11½in (29cm) high.
$200–230 *B&F*

A Chad Valley teddy bear, with label, 1950s, 16in (40.5cm) high.
$200–250 *B&F*

A Merrythought teddy bear, with bells in its ears, designed 1957, 13in (33cm) high.
$320–360 *CMF*

A Chad Valley mohair teddy bear, with label, 1950s, 10in (25.5cm) high.
$200–250 *B&F*

A late Victorian children's Royal
Dairy milk float, 22in (56cm) long.
$950–1,100 *SMI*

A Lütz tinplate horse-drawn
omnibus, the interior with side
facing seats with papier mâché
horses, c1890, 23½in (60cm) long.
$14,500–16,000 *S*

A French wooden horse-drawn gig,
c1900, 31½in (80cm) long.
$1,700–1,900 *S*

A Günthermann roll-top limousine, with canvas
roof and tin driver, mid-1930, 17in (43cm) long.
$4,800–5,400 *P(Ba)*

A Distler limousine, with glass windscreen, tin driver,
and rear luggage rack, c1920, 14in (35.5cm) long.
$2,500–2,800 *P(Ba)*

An Arcade cast iron removal van, with opening rear doors,
nickel-plated wheels and driver, c1929, 13in (33cm) long.
$13,000–14,500 *SK(B)*

A Minic mechanical horse and pantechnicon,
c1937, 7½in (19cm) long, boxed.
$2,500–2,800 *RAR*

A Dinky Supertoys No. 905 Foden Flat Truck,
with chains, c1954, 7½in (19cm) long, boxed.
$550–600 *OTS*

A Dinky Supertoys No. 934 Leyland Octopus
Wagon, c1960, 7in (18cm) long, boxed.
$3,200–3,500 *RAR*

A Märklin lithographed and hand-painted
submarine, with stand, 1930s, 22in (56cm) long.
$3,500–4,000 *P(Ba)*

A Tippco Corvair 240 airliner, with retractable
undercarriage, c1965, 11in (28cm) long.
$370–400 *P(Ba)*

A Bing for Bassett-Lowke gauge 1 electric locomotive, 'George V', No. 2663, 1920s, 22½in (57cm) long.
$1,600–1,800 *RAR*

A Hornby No. 2 Pullman carriage, c1931, 13¼in (33.5cm) long, with original box.
$120–140 *HOB*

A Hornby No. 2 'Verona' Pullman carriage, c1938, 13¾in (35cm) long, with original box.
$550–600 *HOB*

A Graham Farish 00 Merchant Navy type locomotive, with 'Golden Arrow' flags, 1950s, 10½in (26.5cm) long.
$480–560 *RAR*

A Märklin locomotive No. 3005, and tender, c1957, with original box, 9½in (24cm) long.
$120–150 *OTS*

A Märklin six-wheeled dining car, in LMS maroon livery, c1927, 14in (35.5cm) long.
$280–320 *HOB*

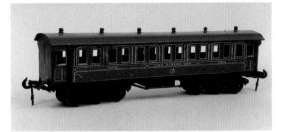

A Hornby No. 1SP 20 volt electric locomotive, in LMS maroon livery, No. 4312, c1935, 12¼in (31cm) long.
$320–400 *HOB*

A Märklin No. 346/3 DSG Schlafwagen, with red paintwork, c1951, 8in (20.5cm) long, with original box.
$130–160 *OTS*

A Märklin 'Orient Express' Wagon Lits dining car, No. 346/2J, c1951, 8in (20.5cm) long.
$200–250 *OTS*

An Aster gauge 1 live steam DB 4–6–4T locomotive, c1980, 18in (46cm) long.
$1,600–1,800 *RAR*

An Aster gauge 1 live steam locomotive, 'Sir Balin', Southern Railway 'King Arthur' class, 1980s, 23½in (60cm) long.
$3,000–3,300 *RAR*

A plush covered Felix the Cat,
early 20thC, 14½in (37cm) high.
$640–720 *Mit*

A fox, in hunting clothes,
1940s, 28in (71cm) high.
$225–250 *PSA*

A Roullet et Decamps musical
automaton, with Jumeau
head, restored, stamped mark,
c1880, 25in (63.5cm) high.
$12,000–14,500 *S*

A Gustave Vichy musical
automaton of a fruit seller,
c1870, 26in (66cm) high.
$24,000–26,500 *S*

A Roullet et Decamps musical
automaton of a butterfly catcher,
c1875, 23½in (60cm) high.
$15,000–17,500 *S*

A Nomura Remote Control Musical
Drummer Robot, 1950s, 8½in (21cm) high.
$17,500–19,000 *S(NY)*

A Britains set of Salvation
Army bandsmen, c1934.
$5,600–6,200 *S(S)*

A pull-along windmill, with
bisque-headed doll, c1900,
19¾in (50cm) high.
$2,800–3,200 *YC*

A carved and painted model of Noah's
Ark, with animal figures, late 19thC,
ark 27in (68.5cm) wide.
$7,200–8,000 *CNY*

A Schönhut articulated wooden
clown on a circus horse, c1900,
9½in (24cm) long.
$320–400 each *MEG*

A Kobi figure of a drummer,
with moving limbs and head,
c1915, 4in (10cm) long.
$400–450 *P(Ba)*

An F. H. Ayres rocking horse,
c1920, 50in (127cm) long.
Unrestored: $800–950
Restored: $2,400–2,700 *STE*

A postcard of RMS *Titanic,* signed
W. Fred Mitchell, Salmon No. 2956, 1912.
$80–90 *SpP*

John Player & Sons, Bygone Beauties,
set of 25, 1914.
$25–50 *MUR*

A woven postcard of Edward VII,
published by Grant.
$40–50 *SpP*

A linen poster, *Blaupunkt,*
by Louis Gaigg, c1939,
33 x 46½in (84 x 118cm).
$1,700–1,900 *VSP*

A lobby card, depicting *The Wizard of Oz,*
MGM, 1939, 11 x 14in (28 x 35.5cm).
$1,700–1,900 *S(LA)*

A linen-backed poster, depicting
Gone with the Wind, MGM,
1939, 41 x 27in (104 x 68.5cm).
$14,500–16,000 *S(LA)*

A New Zealand postcard, with
embroidered patriotic design,
unused, c1914.
$18–25 *SpP*

A linen-backed poster,
Anatomy of a Murder, 1959,
41 by 27in (104 x 68.5 cm).
$640–720 *S(LA)*

A linen poster, *Le Tueur à
Gages,* printed by
L. & H. Verstegen, c1946,
36½ x 52½in (92.5 x 133.5cm).
$800–900 *VSP*

A poster, *High Noon,*
printed by J. Lichtert
& Fils, c1953,
35 x 53in (89 x134.5cm).
$160–200 *VSP*

A poster, depicting
Charles Trenet,
Columbia, c1965,
30½ x 47¼in (77 x 120cm).
$720–800 *VSP*

An Italian linen poster,
Blow-up, MGM,
1966, 78 x 55in
(198 x 140cm).
$800–900 *S(LA)*

A Bloud type ivory azimuth diptych dial, c1700, 3¼in (8.5cm) wide.
$2,200–2,400 *CSK*

A Royal presentation pocket globe, by Joseph Moxon, with monograms for William & Mary, in a silver-mounted case, c1690, 3in (7.5cm) diam.
$98,000–110,000 *S*

A 2¾in (6.4cm) diam terrestrial pocket globe, by John Newton and William Palmer, London, 1783.
$5,000–5,600 *CSK*

A pair of 12in (30.5cm) diam globes, by Nicholas Bion, 1791, 21in (53.5cm) high.
$24,000–26,500 *S*

A celestial library globe, by Newton & Son, 1830, 20in (51cm) diam.
$6,500–8,000 *CSK*

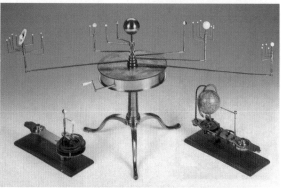

A brass planetarium, with tellurium and lunarium, the top with silvered brass compass rose signed 'W. & S. Jones, London', c1800, 16½in (42cm) high.
$60,000–64,000 *S*

A terrestrial clock globe, with French mechanism in the base, late 19thC, 16in (40.5cm) high.
$4,000–4,500 *CSK*

A French brass and mahogany planetarium, on a mahogany stand, c1840, 30in (76cm) high.
$35,000–40,000 *S*

A Culpeper type compound monocular microscope, late 18thC, 16½in (41cm) high.
$19,000–21,000 *S*

A medicine chest, with 6 glass bottles with stoppers, brass locking plate, early 19thC, 10in (20.5cm) wide.
$530–580 *BIL*

A mahogany medicine chest, with pestle, mortar, scales and bottles, mid-19thC, 11in (28cm) wide.
$1,700–2,000 *WeH*

A Victorian electronic wind direction indicator, by Apps, London, c1890, 14in (35.5cm) wide.
$1,300–1,600 *RTw*

A sunshine recorder, by Casella, mid-20thC, 7in (18cm) wide.
$1,350–1,450 *RTw*

A Nuremberg monocular microscope, early 19thC, 13in (33cm) high.
$1,400–1,600 *TMA*

A brass mater and rete of a signed astrolabe, made in Fez, c1345.
$30,000–32,000 *CSK*

A brass Holland circle, late 16thC, 8¾in (22cm) diam.
$3,200–3,500 *CSK*

A brass astrological astrolabe, c1600, 3¼in (8cm) diam.
$16,000–17,500

CSK

A brass horary quadrant, the recto face engraved and dated 'M. L. 1729', verso signed 'M. Lenetin', 5in (12.5cm) diam.
$4,000–4,500 *C(Am)*

A Muhammad Muqîm brass planespheric astrolabe, signed, 1691, 5in (12.5cm) diam.
$25,500–28,500 *S*

A Persian brass astrolabe, late 19th/20thC, 4½in (11.5cm) diam.
$2,000–2,500 *CSK*

A brass 4in (10cm) diam reflecting telescope, possibly Dutch, c1800, 24½in (62cm) long.
$2,800–3,500 *CSK*

A French brass and steel drawing set, 18thC, signed 'Diebolt', 8½in (21.5cm) wide.
$2,800–3,200 *CSK*

A Francis Watkins brass 5in (12.5cm) diam reflecting telescope-on-stand, c1770, length of tube 32in (81cm).
$16,000–17,500 *S*

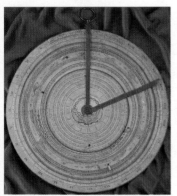

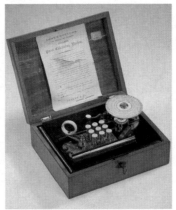

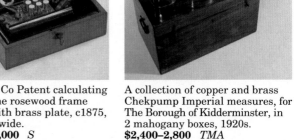

A manuscript lunar computer, with volvelle cardboard base plate, unsigned, c1800, 18½in (47cm) diam.
$5,000–5,600 *CSK*

A Pullen & Co Patent calculating machine, the rosewood frame mounted with brass plate, c1875, 9in (23cm) wide.
$11,200–12,000 *S*

A collection of copper and brass Chekpump Imperial measures, for The Borough of Kidderminster, in 2 mahogany boxes, 1920s.
$2,400–2,800 *TMA*

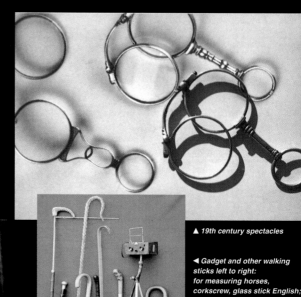

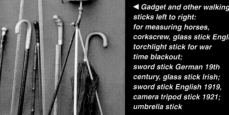

World Wide Web: **www.presence.co.uk/earlytech**

"Historic Televisions & Video Recorders. second edition"
International encyclopaedia of early televisions and historical facts, access free

A Dutch carved oak demi-lune taffrail,
18thC, 32⅜in (83cm) wide.
$2,800–3,200 *C(Am)*

A Siebe Gorman copper and
brass diver's helmet, c1950,
20in (51cm) high.
$2,700–3,200 *GWA*

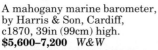

A mahogany marine barometer,
by Harris & Son, Cardiff,
c1870, 39in (99cm) high.
$5,600–7,200 *W&W*

A French prisoner-of-war bone
model of a 98 gun ship-of-the-line,
early 19thC, 10½in (27cm) wide.
$14,500–16,000 *S*

A shellwork 'sailor's favour', by Thomas
Stewart, in a glazed mahogany box,
19thC, 12¼in (31cm) square.
$2,000–2,500 *CAG*

A marine chronometer, by
Hamilton Watch Co, c1940,
7½in (19cm) square.
$1,600–2,400 *TMe*

A ship's bell, engraved 'NGUVU
1925', 8in (20.5cm) high.
$160–200 *GWA*

A Scandinavian shipbuilder's model of the cargo ship MS *Tasco*,
dated '1949', 50in (127cm) long, in a glazed display case.
$4,000–5,000 *S*

A Charles D. Holmes & Co Ltd engine
room telegraph, with enamel dial,
early 20thC, 13in (33cm) diam.
$700–800 *GWA*

A sailor's woolwork picture, depicting a fully rigged sailing
ship, and 'Forget Me Not', a crown and 6 flags, 19thC,
17 x 22in (43 x 56cm), framed and glazed.
$800–1,000 *CAG*

A 16 bore flintlock holster pistol, lock engraved Manton, 1770s, barrel 7½in (19cm) long.
$1,100–1,300 *WAL*

An Irish turnabout pistol, by William and John Rigby, Dublin, c1850, 6in (15cm) long.
$850–950 *HYD*

A military presentation sword, by Ames Manufacturing Co, Massachusetts, mid-19thC, 38¼in (97cm) long.
$1,400–1,550 *SK(B)*

A silver-mounted plug bayonet, restored, maker's mark 'WK', hallmarked London 1693, rayskin scabbard later, 18½in (47cm) long.
$5,000–5,600 *S(S)*

A flintlock blunderbuss, by Ketland & Co, c1800, barrel 15¼in (38.5cm) long.
$1,600–1,800 *ASB*

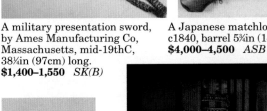

A Japanese matchlock pistol, c1840, barrel 5¾in (14.5cm) long.
$4,000–4,500 *ASB*

A pair of silver-mounted persussion holster pistols, by Jover, converted by Hollis, fullstocked, with foliate engraved locks, 1770s, barrels 9½in (24cm) long.
$4,200–4,800 *WAL*

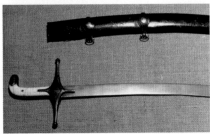

A Persian shamshir, with a curved single-edged blade, steel crossguard and pommel decorated with gold, bone grips, early 19thC, 36in (91.5cm) long.
$1,200–1,400 *GV*

An Indian Mutiny VC group of medals, awarded to Lt Col T. B. Hackett, late 19thC.
$95,000–105,000 *S(S)*

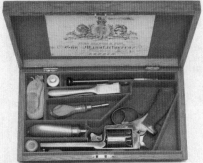

A 5 shot 54 bore Beaumont Adams double-action percussion revolver, c1880, 11½in (29cm) long, in an oak case.
$4,000–4,500 *WAL*

A South African presentation bowie knife, c1880, blade 8in (20.5cm) long.
$2,400–2,700 *WAL*

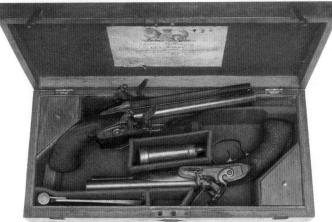

A pair of 20 bore double-barrelled flintlock holster pistols, by James Wilkinson, with steel trigger guards engraved with musical trophies, 1750s, barrels 8in (20.5cm) long.
$9,000–10,000 *WAL*

An officer's dirk, with gilt-metal mounts, late 19thC, blade 8¼in (21cmn) long.
$200–250 *HYD*

A 7in Frogback walnut sea reel, with ventilated face and drum core, early 20thC.
$240–280 *OTB*

An Edward Vom Hofe 3in multiplying reel, with nickel-silver rims, c1900.
$950–1,000 *RTh*

An Eaton & Deller leather-covered salmon fly wallet, c1910, 5½ x 9in (14 x 23cm).
$800–875 *RTh*

A carved wood salmon, inscribed 'Helmspace, weighs 25lbs, May 1913', 42in (106.5cm) wide.
$3,200–3,500 *GHA*

A Houghton Hardy wicker creel, with a metal plate to the reverse side, c1910, 14in (35.5cm) high.
$880–960 *RTh*

A photograph album of King George V's visit to the match between Chelsea v. Leicester City, 21 February 1920.
$200–250 *P(C)*

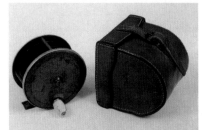

A C. Farlow & Co 3⅜in brass platewind salmon reel, in original black leather case, c1890.
$160–220 *OTB*

A Welsh International velvet cap, with 'F.A.W.' emblem, dated '1910'.
$2,400–2,700 *P(C)*

r. A smooth gutty golf ball mould, by Morris, c1850, 15in (38cm) high.
$10,500–12,000 *MUL*

A pottery jug, depicting a footballer and a golfer, 1950s, 6in (15cm) high.
$140–160 *P(C)*

A pair of Victorian brown leather lady's golf boots, by Royal.
$1,700–2,000 *MUL*

A silver-plated inkwell, with figure of a golfer and well in the form of a ball, c1895, 6½in (16.5cm) high.
$480–640 *MSh*

A smooth face lofting iron, with dished face, c1885, 38in (96.5cm) long.
$400–500 *MSh*

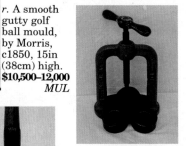

A Royal Doulton tankard, commemorating the Grand National 1937, 5¼in (13.5cm) high.
$100–110 *P(C)*

A white metal figure of a golfer, by W. Zwick, c1920, 12½in (32cm) high.
$650–800 *MSh*

A set of billiard room rules for billiards, life pool and pyramid pool, by Cox and Yeman, in original mahogany frames, 1872, 26 x 14in (66 x 35.5cm).
$1,400–1,600 *BRA*

An oak combined billiard/dining table, by E. J. Riley, with dual height mechanism, c1900, 72 x 36in (183 x 91.5cm).
$4,000–5,000 *BRA*

A billiard scoreboard, c1900, 21 x 38in (53.5 x 96.5cm).
$800–1,000 *SPU*

A box of billiard bowls, by Burroughes & Watts, London, c1900, 19½in (49.5cm) wide.
$250–300 *SPU*

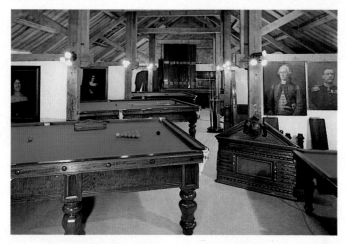

A set of oak Victorian jockey scales, by W. & T. Avery, with gilt-painted weighing machine, 35in (89cm) wide.
$4,200–4,800 *AP*

An iron and brass pétanque ball, 19thC, 4in (10cm) diam.
$50–60 *SSW*

A .450 C quality hammer sporting rifle, by J. Purdey & Sons, 1889, barrels 27in (68.5cm) long, in oak and leather case.
$7,300–8,000 *S*

A Welsh International goalkeeper's jersey, worn by Neville Southall during 1996–97 season.
$160–240 *P(C)*

A programme for Cardiff Arms Park Australia v. Wales rugby match, 1908.
$280–320 *P(C)*

A Copeland spirit flask, with rugby players in relief, late 19thC, 8¼in (21cm) high.
$950–1,000 *P(C)*

An American steel-stringed tennis racket, 1930s, 26⅛in (67.5cm) long.
$120–140 *WAB*

A leather and oak magazine case, by Cogswell & Harrison, London, fitted to take 600 cartridges, c1910, 16in (40.5cm) wide.
$800–1,000 *RTh*

A boxed set of 6 silver set of coffee spoons, with tennis motifs, Birmingham 1931, 3½in (9cm) long.
$120–140 *MSh*

A Harrow size Gilbert Parkhouse cricket bat, by Nicolls, signed with 73 signatures, c1960.
$160–200 *P(C)*

A stained glass panel, painted with an Edwardian tennis player, c1900, 12 x 20in (30.5 x 51cm).
$350–400 *MUL*

A ceramic jar and cover, the light blue ground baluster-shaped jar with dark blue handles, inscribed 'Leeches' in gilt scrolling, restored, mid-19thC, 13½in (34cm) high.
$5,500–6,500 *S*
Leech jars were kept on display by the pharmacist and had pierced lids to allow the leeches to breathe.

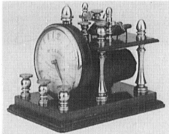

An electro-medical machine, the dial inscribed 'Mr W. H. Halse, Professor of Medical Galvanism, Kensington, London', and with the Prince of Wales' feathers, Roman numerals, mounted on an oak plinth base, with brass terminals and magnet, 19thC, 7¼in (18.5cm) long.
$770–850 *CSK*

A Regency carved ivory eye bath, supported on a tapering pillar, the plinth base with shell decoration, 3½in (9cm) high.
$3,600–4,000 *CSK*

A part-set of surgical instruments, by Arnold & Son, with 3 Liston knives, finger and skull-saws, and other items, in brass-bound mahogany case, late 19thC, 17in (43cm) wide.
$1,000–1,100 *CSK*

A cupping set, by Cluley, with lacquered brass 10 blade scarificator, 6 cupping glasses of various shapes, in a plush-lined mahogany case, 19thC, 11in (28cm) wide.
$580–720 *CSK*

A brass electro-medical shock machine, the hinged case fitted with resistance coil covered with velvet and an amp meter dial, lamp and 2 brass conductors on stands, the front with voltage select dial, mounted on 4 gilt-brass lion paw feet, late 19thC, 11in (28cm) wide.
$950–1,000 *S*

r. A pair of Nuremberg pattern copper grooved spectacles, with single wire nose, one lens cracked, late 17thC.
$1,500–2,000 *CSK*

A cupping set, with lacquered brass scarificator, syringe and nozzles to the 5 cupping glasses, arranged in a plush-lined mahogany case, 19thC, 7in (18cm) wide.
$1,400–1,550 *CSK*

A dental chisel, carved with the the face of a bewildered-looking patient, late 17thC, 2¾in (7cm) long.
$950–1,000 *CSK*

Meteorological

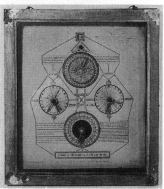

A weather prognosticator, paper-backed, by Henry Troake, Topsham, 19thC, 16 x 17½in (40.5 x 44.5cm), gilt framed and glazed.
$520–560 *TMA*

This was designed and improved upon the system of the astronomer Sir William Herschel.

A sunshine recorder, by J. Hicks, on slate base, c1910, 9in (23cm) square.
$1,000–1,100 *RTw*

A sunshine recorder, by Negretti & Zambra, the cast iron frame with glass sphere and bracket stamped with 'latitude 51° 39', c1910, 9in (23cm) wide.
$740–880 *S*

r. A brass sunshine recorder, by L. Casella, London, with fixed latitude, on slate base, c1890, 7in (18cm) square.
$1,000–1,100 *RTw*

l. A Victorian rosewood thermometer, by William Callaghan & Co, London, late 19thC, 8in (20.5cm) high.
$350–400 *JIL*

A Meteorological Office anemometer, with 4 brass cups, on cast iron base, dated '1930', 15in (38cm) high.
$400–500 *RTw*

Microscopes
Signed

A brass presentation dissecting microscope, by R. & J. Beck, the lens with focusing by rack-and-pinion above circular stage, on 4 brass columns above concave reflector and mahogany base, in mahogany case with 2 lenses, 1867, 7½in (19cm) wide.
$560–640 *S*

A brass cuff type monocular microscope, signed 'Dollond, London', the body tube supported on an upright limb with slide-bar and fine-screw focusing, mounted on a base with drawer and accessories, in a tapered mahogany case, late 18thC, 16in (41cm) high.
$2,800–3,500 *S*

A lacquered-brass compound monocular microscope, signed by the retailer 'James How, London', with rack-and-pinion focusing and fine adjustment, shaped stage and concave mirror, in a mahogany case, with additional eyepieces and bull's-eye condenser, late 19thC, 15½in (39cm) high.
$380–480 *P(NW)*

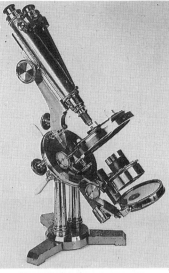

An International lacquered-brass binocular microscope, signed 'R. & J. Beck Ltd London 2056', with a rotating plate enframed 0–360°, the binocular body tube with rackwork to adjust interocular distance, rack focus, micrometer fine focus, substage condenser on rackwork, large plano-concave mirror, 1890s, 18½in (47cm) high, and a fitted case of accessories, in a mahogany carrying case with swing handle.
$8,000–9,000 *Bon(C)*

A brass compound monocular microscope, by William Harris & Co, with rack-and-pinion focusing, various accessories, on mahogany base with fitted drawer, early 19thC, 15in (38cm) high.
$2,800–3,200 *S*

r. A brass solar microscope, signed 'Dollond, London', the shutter plate with 2 wing nuts for adjustment to the mirror, spring barrel tube and condensing lens tube, in fitted mahogany case with accessories, late 18thC, the case 12in (30.5cm) long.
$2,000–2,400 *S*

A Culpeper type compound monocular microscope, signed 'Bleuler, London', with rack-and-pinion focusing, the plinth case with drawer of accessories, contained in a pyramid and plinth base mahogany case with 2 additional drawers, early 19thC, 23in (58.5cm) high.
$4,400–4,800 *CSK*

> **Miller's is a price GUIDE not a price LIST**

A lacquered-brass compound monocular microscope, signed 'W. & S. Jones, London', the stage with rack-and-pinion adjustment from the square section pillar incorporating the substage condenser and plano-concave mirror, with accessories, in fitted mahogany case with brass carrying handle, early 19thC, 12in (30.5cm) wide.
$4,000–4,500 *CSK*

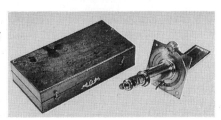

A brass lantern projection microscope, signed 'Newton & Co, London', with large condensing lens, circular rotating stage and projection lens with rack-and-pinion focusing, late 19thC, 22in (56cm) long.
$1,000–1,100 *S*

A brass Culpeper type compound monocular microscope, signed 'Silberrad, Aldgate, London', with rack-and-pinion focusing to the stage, on 3 supports above a plano-concave mirror on a wooden stand with accessory drawer, in a pyramidal-shaped mahogany case with drawer containing various accessories, early 19thC, 15in (38cm) high.
$2,700–3,200 *S*

A lacquered-brass microscope, signed 'Jas Smith, London, No. 36', draw-tube from 0–6in, the lower end with a thread for an erector lens, nosepiece lever fine focus, the knob divided from 0–100, large plano-concave mirror on a sliding collar, c1840, 18½in (47cm) high, with accessories, in a mahogany case with 12 drawers.
$8,000–9,000 *Bon(C)*

A brass Culpeper type compound microscope, signed 'Nairne & Blunt', with draw-tube focusing, circular stage with plano-concave reflector, mahogany base with drawer containing accessories, in mahogany pillar case with drawer fitted with 6 objectives, large format specimen slides and other accessories, c1800, 15¼in (38.5cm) high.
$3,200–3,500 *S*

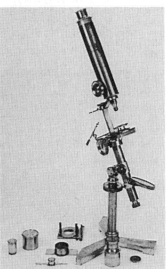

A lacquered-brass compound and simple monocular microscope, signed 'Andrew Pritchard, London', mounted on an arm on a triangular section rack-and-pinion limb with mechanical stage and concave mirror, mid-19thC, 20½in (52cm) high, in mahogany case, with contemporary handwritten Table of Powers and other accessories.
$1,600–1,800 *P*

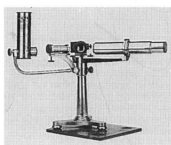

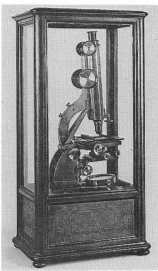

A lacquered-brass monocular microscope, signed 'M. Pillischer London No. 640', rack focus, rack adjustment to the eyepiece via a wheel with engraved positions 1–5, nosepiece long-lever fine focus, rotating mechanical substage on rackwork, large plano-concave mirror on a sliding collar, 1850s, 18in (46cm) high, together with various accessories in 3 drawers, in a glazed display case.
$3,500–4,000 *Bon(C)*

A brass Wenham's binocular microscope, by Ross, London, No. 4148, with rack-and-pinion coarse and micrometer fine focusing, with mechanical stage, substage with rack adjustment, and plano-concave mirror, with 2 objectives, condenser missing, 19thC, 13½in (34cm) high.
$1,100–1,300 *CSK*

l. A lacquered-brass spectroscope, signed 'Stienheil, München', with sighting-tube, adjustable slit, prism table, adjustable eyepiece with illuminated lamp, in mahogany case with accessory drawer, prism missing, 19thC, 16in 40.5cm) high.
$640–720 *CSK*

A lacquered and oxidised-brass Van Heurck type compound monocular microscope, by W. Watson & Sons, London, with rack-and-pinion coarse and micrometer fine focusing, mechanical circuit stage with slide holder adjusted by worm gear, substage Abbe condenser, iris diaphragm, the lower limb with plano-concave mirror, with a range of accessories, in fitted mahogany case, late 19thC, 16½in (42cm) high.
$2,000–2,500 *CSK*

A brass binocular dissecting microscope, by Watson & Sons, London, with rack-and-pinion focusing electric illuminant, mechanical stage, 1930s, 14in (36cm), in mahogany case with 2 oculars.
$650–800 *S*

A lacquered-brass and black-enamelled compound monocular microscope, signed 'Carl Zeiss Jena No. 4347', with fine-screw vernier adjustment, substage condenser, plano-concave mirror, with various accessories, 19thC, 13¾in (34.5cm) wide, in fitted iron-bound mahogany carrying case, and a microscope lamp, 12in (30.5cm) high.
$700–800 *CSK*

Unsigned

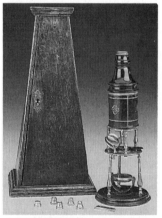

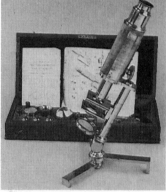

A Gould type botanical microscope, the lacquered-brass tapering pillar with objective mounted on a sliding arm, the stage with forceps and glass and swivel mirror, with 2 objectives, in plush-lined fishskin case, late 18thC, 4¾in (12cm) wide.
$1,200–1,300 *CSK*

A lacquered-brass Culpeper type microscope, the vellum-covered draw-tube with gilt tooling and inscribed bands with graduations to correspond with 5 objectives, with lignum vitae mount, in brass-mounted leather-covered gilt tooled outer body-tube, in tapering oak carrying case, late 18thC, 18in (47.5cm) high.
$6,500–8,000 *CSK*

A lacquered-brass Improved Compound Microscope, with rack-and-pinion focusing, tilting column support, sprung stage, and concave mirror on a folding flat tripod stand, early 19thC, 16¼in (41cm) high, in a fitted mahogany box with accessories, and contemporary pamphlet and diagram.
$1,000–1,200 *P*

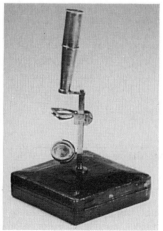

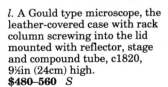

l. A Gould type microscope, the leather-covered case with rack column screwing into the lid mounted with reflector, stage and compound tube, c1820, 9½in (24cm) high.
$480–560 *S*

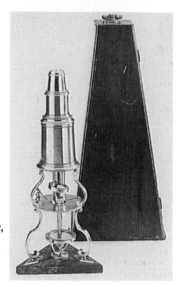

r. A Culpeper type monocular microscope, with sliding draw-tube focusing, the stage with specimen probe and frame for mirror or bull's-eye condenser, the base with swivel plano mirror, in pyramid-shaped mahogany case, possibly Continental, 19thC, 17¾in (45cm) high.
$1,500–1,700 *CSK*

Surveying & Drawing

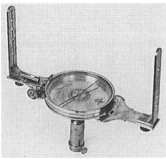

An American pattern brass surveyor's compass dial, signed 'B. Pike & Sons, New York', the horizontal circle divided in 4 quadrants, the shaped limb with bubble-level, azimuth scale divided 25°–0°–25°, with vernier scale, adjustment and twin fixed sights, 19thC, 15¾in (40cm) long.
$650–800 *CSK*

A surveying combined compass and cross staff, with pivot needle and silvered dial, 19thC, 3½in (9cm) high, with original tin case.
$200–250 *BSA*

A French rangefinder, by Ponthus & Therrode, the split lens telescope mounted with side drum and operating handle, in original fitted mahogany case with printed instructions, early 20thC, 10in (25.5cm) wide.
$750–900 *S*

A surveyor's cross head, with combined compass, c1860, 3in (7.5cm) high.
$120–140 *GWA*

A set of drawing instruments, in a shagreen case with hinged cover, including brass compasses and dividers, a 6in ivory sector, and scale rule, early 19thC, 7in (18cm) long.
$480–540 *DN*

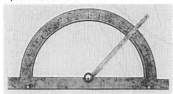

A brass protractor and rule, with engraved scales and swinging arm, 18thC, base 18¾in (47.5cm) wide.
$600–650 *CSK*

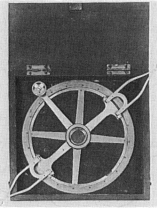

A lacquered-brass swinging-arm protractor, with rack adjustment, the centre glass with engraved graticule, in mahogany case, 19thC, 7½in (19.5cm) wide.
$320–350 *CSK*

A set of silver drawing instruments, signed 'P. Dollond, London', the silver-mounted shagreen covered case fitted with ivory sector, scale rule, dividers, compass and other accessories, c1760, 5in (12.5cm) long.
$4,400–4,800 *S*

This set realised a high price because it was made by Peter Dollond.

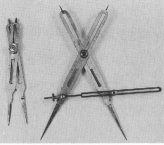

Two pairs of nickel silver proportional dividers, by W. F. Stanley, c1870, largest 9½in (24cm) long.
l. **$25–35**
r. **$70–100** *MRT*

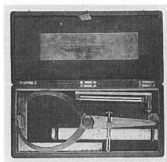

A set of Continental railway gauge instruments, in a leather-lined case, 19thC, 12¾in (32.5cm) wide.
$560–620 *CSK*

A brass scale rule, signed 'T. Wright', engraved with various scales including protractor and linear, with wheat ear decoration, 18thC, 6in (15cm) long.
$320–350 *CSK*

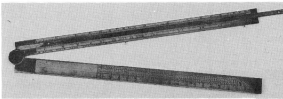

A two-fold boxwood and brass rule, by F. B. Cox, Birmingham, with Gunter's scale slide and timber load table, c1830, 24in (61cm) long.
$80–110 *MRT*

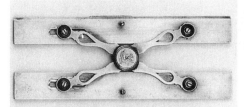

An electrum parallel rule, the articulated arms with pierced decoration, the centre hinge pin engraved with a crest, 19thC, 6½in (16.5cm) long.
$320–400 *CSK*

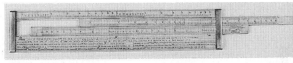

A boxwood and brass 2 slide rule, by James Noble, late 19thC, 12½in (32cm) long.
$160–200 *MRT*

Cross Reference
Colour Review

A brass sector, engraved on one face with chords, the reverse with combined scale rule, 17thC, 12in (30.5cm) long.
$250–280 *Bon(C)*

An American surveying compass, signed 'James Hain Jun, Philadelphia', the silvered dial with foliate decoration, the limb with 2 fixed sights, with cover, late 18thC, 14in (35.5cm) long.
$3,600–4,000 *CNY*

A lacquered-brass surveying level and alidade, signed 'Brander & Höschel, Augsburg', mounted on the vertical arc with bubble-level, adjusted by rack-and-pinion gear, the arc engraved in 2 quadrants with scales, inscribed with scale 'Pied de Giesen', and another fine scale, mounted on a tripod attachment, with folding legs, 18thC, alidade rule 18¼in (46cm) long.
$5,000–5,600 *CSK*

An American surveying compass, signed 'W. & L. E. Gurley, New York', the limb with 2 sights, level, vernier fine adjustment and tripod mounting, in fitted case with maker's trade label, 19thC, 16in (40.5cm) wide.
$800–950 *CNY*

An oxidised and lacquered-brass transit theodolite, signed 'W. & L. E. Gurley', the telescope with rack-and-pinion focusing, graduated bubble-level with axis mounted on turn A-frames over the compass box, the horizontal plate with level and cross-bubble enclosed silvered circle with viewing window, on tripod attachment, in fitted case, late 19thC, 13in (33cm) high.
$950–1,100 *CNY*

r. A lacquered-brass theodolite, signed 'J. Perfler, Wien, No. 14', the telescope with rack-and-pinion focusing and graduated bubble, with fine-screw adjustment, on tripod attachment, 19thC, 10¼in (26cm) high.
$800–880 *CSK*

A brass theodolite, by Troughton & Simms, the telescope with rack-and-pinion focusing, mounted in a trunion above a vertical semi-circle of degrees with silvered scale divided 90°–0°–70° and a horizontal circle of degrees with twin bubble levels and clamp, contained in a wooden case, late 19thC, 10½in (25.5cm) high.
$650–800 *S*

A black-enamelled and lacquered-brass transit theodolite, signed 'F. W. Breithaupt & Sohn, Hesse-Cassel, No. 3341, the telescope with rack-and-pinion focusing, graduated bubble-level, silvered scale, twin verniers and magnifiers, the shaped support with universal bubble-level, enclosed chamfered silver scale with 2 verniers and magnifiers, on tripod attachment, late 19thC, 15½in (39.5cm) high.
$1,300–1,400 *CSK*

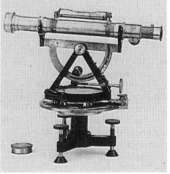

Telescopes

A mid-Victorian six-draw telescope, by Charles Baker, London, with whalebone covering to outer tube, engraved, late 19thC, 16in (40.5cm) long.
$530–580 *JIL*

A marbled-paper card brass-mounted 1in (2.5cm) four-draw telescope, with simulated fishskin-covered outer body-tube, the eyepiece stamped 'S. Patent April 24th 1906, Germany', the outer tube body-tube with label, 33¼in (84.5cm) long extended.
$160–200 *CSK*

A gilt five-draw monocular, with dyed ivory base, c1810, 3½in (9cm) high.
$640–720 *JIL*

A silver-plated six-draw monocular, with red-enamelled base, in leather carrying box, c1810, 2in (5cm) high.
$640–720 *JIL*

A brass 1½in (4cm) four-draw telescope, signed 'Thos Rubergall Optn to HRH the Duke of Clarence, London', with mahogany-covered outer body-tube, early 19thC, 20¾in (53cm) long extended.
$560–640 *CSK*

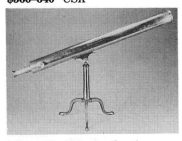

A brass 3in (7.5cm) refracting astronomical telescope, rack-and-pinion and draw-tube focusing with 2 eyepieces, on a turned tapering column with 3 green painted iron legs, with a painted pine box, 19thC, tube 37in (94cm) long.
$880–960 *DN*

A 2¾in (7cm) reflecting telescope, signed 'Nairne & Blunt, London', with milled nut, rod and screw focus to the secondary reflector, on a knuckle joint to a turned cylindrical pillar with folding tripod feet, early 19thC, 17¾in (45cm) long.
$950–1,100 *Bon (C)*

r. A 3½in (9cm) reflecting telescope, signed 'Nairne & Blunt, London', the tube with focusing to the secondary reflector by long shank and screw, supported by a bracket above a tapering column and folding tripod base, c1780, tube 19in (48cm) long.
$2,800–3,200 *S*

A brass 4in (10cm) astronomical refracting telescope, signed 'T. Cooke & Sons, York', the japanned body tube with rack-and-pinion focusing star-finder, 2 telescopic, steadying rods, mounted on a wooden tripod stand, in a wooden case containing various accessories, c1910, 58¾in (149cm) long.
$3,200–3,500 *S*

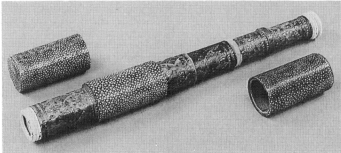

A ⅞in (20mm) telescope, body-tube with central shagreen covered band and 3 green and gilt decorated draws, with turned ivory eyepiece and lens mount, with 2 shagreen covers, 18thC, 8¾in (22cm) long.
$4,000–4,500 *P*

Weights & Measures

A steel balance, by Abraham Kruse, with brass pans and quantity of weights, with maker's trade label and proof marks, in a fruitwood case, late 18thC, 5¼in (13cm) wide.
$200–250 *CSK*

A steel balance, with brass pans and suspension straps, in a mahogany case, early 19thC, 18in (45.5cm) wide.
$130–200 *CSK*

A balance, the ivory beam scale signed 'W. C. Bloor', incised with various scales for lbs per gross, the beam with stamped scale for ounces, with adjustable poise and pan, on a wooden plinth base, 19thC, 16¼in (41cm) wide.
$280–320 *CSK*

A French brass chrondrometer, signed 'Rondony à Marseille', with steel beam, sliding brass weight, grain bucket, hopper and leveller, mounted and contained in a stained wooden case, early 19thC, 19¾in (50cm) wide.
$550–650 *S*

A chrondrometer was used for weighing grain.

A set of brass imperial measures, made for the County Borough of Bury, by W. & T. Avery, Birmingham, c1891.
$6,500–7,200 *DaD*

Miscellaneous

A electrostatic friction generator, with mahogany frame, wire brushes, glass and brass fittings, 19thC, 35½in (90cm) high.
$700–800 *Bon(C)*

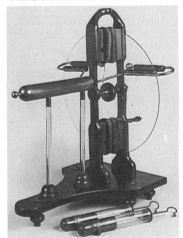

A Brunsviga Dupla calculator, the 2 mechanical calculating machines mounted in parallel with clearing and operating handles at the sides, German, c1925, 18½in (47cm) wide.
$400–500 *S*

A Gamages morse code signaller, c1915, 6in (15cm) wide.
$130–160 *GWA*

An Enigma enciphering machine, the Wehrmacht type with 3 rotors and standard keyboard, lampboard with 3 numbered 1-26 wheels and switching gear, in a black metal case within oak carrying case, the interior stamped with German Third Reich eagle and emblem, c1940, 13¼in (34cm) long.
$22,500–25,500 *S*

The Enigma was a machine solely for enciphering and deciphering messages by entering clear text on the keyboard, the enciphered text appearing letter by letter on the illuminated display. The Enigma machine was first patented in 1919 and developed by the German engineer Arthur Scherbuis for commercial codes and improved by the Kriegsmarine in 1926, Wehrmacht in 1928 and the Luftwaffe in 1935. Early types were unsuccessful and it was not until the late 1920s that the machine was refined by members of the Polish Cipher Bureau. Polish machines were sent to Britain and France in 1939, unknown to the German High Command, who had developed their own machines for the military forces. The German machines were made throughout WWII, with additional rotors added to further complicate the encoding and enciphering.

By the summer of 1940, with most of Western Europe under German occupation, Allied Intelligence operations were centred at Bletchley Park, Bucks. Here a highly secret group of code breakers were handling 4,000 German signals daily, with slightly lesser numbers of Japanese and Italian signals. The code breakers, or Ultra, worked 24 hours a day breaking the constantly changing codes. Its greatest test came during the Battle of Britain, July–September 1940, when much of the German cipher traffic relating to operation Sealord was being read at Bletchley and the information relayed to the British government and military commanders.

MARINE

Since the early 1970s I have noticed a steady increase in the number of replicas of marine and scientific instruments appearing on the market. These are now being sold, perhaps unwittingly, as originals, so for the benefit of both sellers and buyers alike, here are a few pointers on how to differentiate between a replica and an original.

Woolwork pictures were normally portraits of ships, produced by sailors using remnants of wool from their own clothing and stitched on old canvas sailcloth. The frames, normally bird's-eye maple, were bought ashore. The value of a good original will be in excess of $3,000. Copies may use synthetic wool with over-sophisticated portraits. Check the back to make sure the canvas is sailcloth and the frame original; rusty hand-cut nails may be reproductions but modern wire ones are definitely suspicious. Check too for a characteristic musty, aged smell. But beware: all these pointers can be replicated.

Original compasses are usually filled with liquid alcohol, bear a maker's name and have gimbals to keep them steady in all conditions. Materials used are brass and glass, with aluminium for the diaphragm and lead for the base. Replicas of the high quality British-made Sestrel ship's compass often have modern Phillips screws attaching the top glass to the bowl, over-clean fluid, and a bowl with a crystal-white interior.

Scrimshaw is the art practiced by sailors, who engraved whales' teeth to make objects to use for bartering or gifts for a sweetheart. An original tooth feels cold and is the colour of mellow oak; size varies from 2in to 8in (5cm to 20cm). Resin copies are warm and feel greasy when held for a short period. Pointers useful for spotting a new engraving on an original tooth are the colour of the tooth: ivory white when first prepared for engraving but turning to mellow oak over the years. If aged with a stain the roof of the tooth will be evenly coloured; an original will have uneven colouring.

Diving helmet replicas are purely ornamental and are easily identified as the inlet pipes and windows are only screwed to the helmet (originals will be braised and riveted); the corselette is stamped US Mark V. Recently a good copy of the British-made diver's helmet, called Siebe Gorman, has appeared on the market. It has rivets showing on the centre circular window, butterfly screws for the studs and the studs for holding chest weights are the wrong shape. All Siebe Gorman helmets are numbered (page 708), with matching numbers for helmet and corselette that should be visible internally on their respective coupling rings. There are many other collectable divers helmets available which may look like replicas but are actually used for pearl diving.

John Jefferies

Barometers

A mahogany marine barometer, the ivory plate signed L. Hughes, fitted for gimbal mounting, brass cistern and thermometer, 19thC, 37¼in (94.5cm) high.
$2,800–3,200 *C(Am)*

l. A rosewood marine barometer, the engraved bone scale signed L. Casella, with adjustable vernier, trunk set thermometer, brass gimbals and cistern, c1850, 37in (94cm) high.
$1,400–1,800 *Bon*

A marine barometer, with cast iron base and ceramic dial, c1880, 6in (15cm) diam.
$160–190 *RTw*

l. A rosewood marine barometer, the bone scales signed H. Wehmann Vegesack, with concealed mercury tube, vernier behind bowed glass, mercury thermometer, brass cistern cover and mounted in gimbals, c1880, 38in (96.5cm) high.
$6,000–6,500 *S*

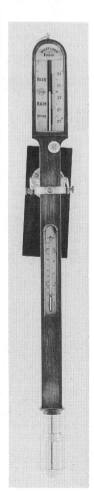

r. A mahogany marine barometer, by Lilley & Son, London, with ivory scales, replaced gimbals, c1870, 38in (96.5cm) high.
$3,200–4,000 *W&W*

Chronometers

An American two-day Elgin Model 600 marine chronometer, the frosted silver dial signed and numbered, with Earnshaw escapement, gimballed in a three-tier brass-bound mahogany box, c1943, 4in (10cm) diam.
$2,200–2,600 *C*

A two-day marine chronometer, by Rich. Hornby, Liverpool, with fusee, spring detent escapement and cut bimetallic balance with round compensation weights, silvered dial signed and numbered 837, gimbal-mounted in a mahogany and brass-bound three-section box, early 19thC, dial 3¾in (9.5cm) diam.
$4,000–4,500 *DN*

r. A Canadian two-day marine chronometer, the silvered dial signed A. B. Smalley & Son, with unrecorded auxiliary, Earnshaw escapement, cut bimetallic balance, cylindrical heat compensation weights, brass bowl and gimbal, three-tier mahogany box with brass stringing, c1912, dial 4in (10cm) diam.
$2,500–2,800 *C*

A French deck chronometer, by E. Delépine, with signed and numbered full plate spotted keywind revered fusee movement, Harrison's maintaining power, fully adjustable stud for the freesprung steel helical hairspring, Earnshaw spring detent escapement, c1840, 2½in (6.5cm) diam.
$5,000–5,600 *PT*

A Royal Observatory two-day marine chronometer, the silvered dial signed Victor Kullberg, reversed fusee, Earnshaw escapement, cut bimetallic balance, brass bowl, gimballed in plain three-tier mahogany box, c1917, dial 4in (10cm) diam.
$3,200–4,000 *C*

A two-day marine chronometer, the silvered dial signed Charles Frodsham, London, with Earnshaw escapement, cut bimetallic balance with segmental heat compensation weights, brass bowl and gimbal, three-tier brass-bound rosewood box, c1855, dial 4in (10cm) diam.
$3,500–4,000 *C*

A French 36-hour marine chronometer, the frosted silver dial signed Leroy, Earnshaw escapement, cut bimetallic balance, circular heat compensation weights with top screws, in brass drum case, plain three-tier mahogany deck watch style box, c1870, dial 2¾in (7cm) diam.
$2,400–2,800 *C*

An American two-day marine chronometer, the silvered dial signed and numbered H. H. Heinrich, New York, with Earnshaw escapement, cut bimetallic balance with brass bowl gimballed in three-tier brass-bound rosewood box, c1880, dial 4in (10cm) diam.
$4,000–4,500 *C*

A two-day marine chronometer, the silvered dial signed John Poole, Earnshaw escapement, cut bimetallic balance, cylindrical heat compensation weights, brass bowl, gimballed in brass-bound three-tier mahogany box, c1865, box 7in (18cm) square.
$4,500–5,000 *C(Am)*

Apparently this chronometer was captured during a daring action in the Boxer revolt of 1900, from a Chinese destroyer by Lieut Roger Keys, later Admiral of the Fleet Lord Keyes of Zeebrugge and Dover.

l. A mahogany two-day marine chronometer, the silvered dial signed S. Smith & Son, with Earnshaw escapement, Palladium helical balance spring, brass gimbal and bowl, in a brass-bound mahogany box, c1900, dial 4¼in (10.5cm) diam.
$3,200–3,500 *C*

Model Ships

A fully rigged model of the Dutch 18 gun frigate *De Onderneming*, with standing and running rigging, the planked hull finished in black and green, mid-19thC, 74in (188cm) long.
$13,000–16,000 *C(Am)*

A French bone prisoner-of-war model of a 42 gun frigate, the pinned and planked hull with standing and running rigging, carved stern decorated with rope motif, carved figurehead of a warrior, 3 ship's boats, on an ivory base, early 19thC, 19½in (49.5cm) long.
$10,000–11,000 *Bon*

A planked model of a sailing barge, with masts, booms, full suit of sails, standing and running rigging, the hull with 2 side swords, cockpit and cabin, c1850, 32¼in (82cm) long, with stand.
$7,200–8,000 *C(Am)*

A sailing model of a lugger-rigged fishing schooner, with masts, bowsprit, stern boom, stitched tan sails, the hull with hatch and finished in black, white and varnish, rudder missing, late 19thC, 53in (134.5cm) long.
$1,400–1,550 *CSK*

> *r.* A carved and painted wooden model of a three-masted ship, late 19thC, damaged, late 19thC, 49½in (125.5cm) long.
> **$1,100–1,200** *SK(B)*

A bone prisoner-of-war model of a ship, in a mirrored case, 19thC, 18¼in (46.5cm) long.
$4,400–4,800 *SK(B)*

A frigger crystal glass model of a frigate ship, with blue glass masts with rigging, blue glass sailors, coloured flags, blue anchor, ruby glass deck rail, with 3 pilot ships, a lighthouse, St Helen's, Lancashire, c1880, on a fibre-glass base, 21in (53.5cm) long.
$700–800 *GH*

A painted wood and metal waterline model of the steam yacht *Alexandria*, mounted on simulated sea against a painted marine background, late 19thC, in a glazed case, 33in (84cm) wide.
$2,800–3,200 *S*

An American shadowbox model of a three-masted ship under full sail, 19thC, 43in (109cm) long.
$2,000–2,500 *SK(B)*

A model of a tug, with laid-up hull, engine missing, 19thC, 27in (68.5cm) long, on a later base.
$430–480 *EL*

A planked and framed model of a steam Windermere style launch, with fore and aft decks, glazed engine room cover and saloon, gas-fired copper cross tube boiler by Bassett-Lowke, lagged steam line to Stuart BB single vertical cylinder engine, restored, late 19thC, 40½in (103cm) long.
$1,700–1,900 *CSK*

A carved pine half-hull model of a barque, on a mahogany wall mount, late 19thC, 49½in (125.5cm) long.
$2,200–2,700 *S(NY)*

A sailing model of a schooner, with top mast, damaged, late 19th/early 20thC, 45in (114cm) long.
$320–400 *SK(B)*

A George V silver model of a submarine, No. B1020, maker's mark JWB, on ebonised plinth, 16in (40.5cm) long.
$4,400–4,800 *MSL*

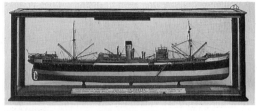

A builder's model of the SS *Cairnross*, by the Sunderland Shipbuilding Co Ltd, the shaped and painted hull with deck details, on wooden base, c1921, case 61½in (156cm) wide.
$10,500–12,000 *Bon*

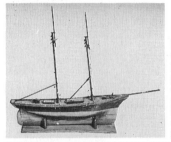

l. A pond yacht, the painted wooden hull finished in green and black with gold lining, gaff-rigged twin masts, late 19thC, 48in (122cm) long.
$1,100–1,300 *S*

Nautical Handicrafts

l. A horn snuff mull, carved in the form of a lady wearing a peaked bonnet and waisted dress, carrying a basket in one hand and a fish in the other, on a silver-mounted base with hinged lid, late 18thC, 4in (10cm) high.
$1,600–1,800 *S*

l. A walking stick, commemorating the Battle of Erie of 1813, the walnut shaft applied with silver plaques engraved 'Flagship Lawrence, Commodore O. H. Perry, We have met the enemy and they are ours, Sept 10th 1813', 19thC, 35in (89cm) long.
$2,000–2,500 *S*

Oliver Perry was ordered to build a fleet during the war of 1812 on Lake Erie to prevent a British advance into the USA. By August 1813 he had completed 2 brigs, USS Lawrence and Niagra, and several armed sloop. On the 10th September Perry engaged the British fleet commanded by Robert Barclay, and defeated him after a long bombardment during which the Lawrence and many of his men were lost.

r. A partially polychromed scrimshaw whale's tooth, the tooth decorated with a scene of a French and English frigate involved in an engagement, the reverse with scene of a French fort with an English corvette off the coast, and side with a view of tropical islands, early 19thC, 8in (20cm) long.
$8,500–9,500 *S*

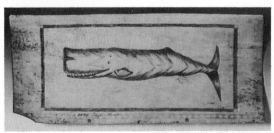

A scrimshaw whale panbone, engraved with whaling scene, heighted in red, the reverse with a portrait of a whale and indistinctly signed, '... 1835 Phip Breton', 13½in (34cm) long.
$5,000–5,600 *S*

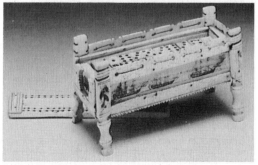

A French prisoner-of-war polychromed bone games casket, with painted floral decoration, the sides with scenes of naval engagements, with sliding lid, containing a set of dominoes, c1800, 6½in (16cm) wide.
$950–1,000 *S*

A scrimshaw whale's tooth, with a three-quarter rear view of a woman in blue on one side, the reverse with a woman's head and a heart, early 20thC, 6in (15cm) long. **$270–320** *EL*

l. A polychromed whalebone busk, with a floral spray above a heart, stars in the lobes, a sailor and his girl over 2 pierced hearts, floral circles and a flower, 19thC, 14in (35.5cm) long. **$1,600–1,800** *EL*

A scrimshaw whale's tooth, with polychrome floral decoration, 19thC, 6in (15cm) long. **$230–260** *EL*

A woolwork ship picture, depicting a three-masted steam and sailing ship, 19thC, 35¼in (89.5cm) wide. **$2,200–2,600** *SK(B)*

A woolwork picture, depicting ships of the Royal Navy including *Liverpool*, *Edgar*, *Minotaur* and *Racoon*, 19thC, 26¾in (68cm) wide, framed and glazed. **$2,800–3,200** *Bon*

l. A woolwork maritime picture, depicting a three-masted 102 gun naval vessel under full sail, a clipper and another ship, with silk detailing, early 19thC, 26in (66cm) wide, mounted. **$1,700–1,900** *CSK*

A sewing box, the lid with marquetry portrait of a steam and sail ship, the front similarly decorated with 2 ships, the red velvet-lined interior with pincushion and 5 compartments with mahogany lids, c1880, 12½in (32cm) wide. **$2,400–2,700** *S*

MILLER'S COMPARES . . .

I A sailorwork picture of a three-masted ship under full sail in the Solent, flying the red ensign, on a deep blue calm sea, with the 2 forts and 5 smaller yachts in the foreground, late 19thC, 17in (43cm) wide, framed and glazed. **$4,500–5,500** *S(S)*

II A sailorwork picture of a three-masted frigate under full sail on a choppy blue sea, flying the white ensign, late 19thC, 22in (56cm) wide. **$480–560** *S(S)*

The subject matter is very important when comparing works of art such as those pictured above. *Item I* is of great interest because it is of a known location, with the two Napoleonic forts in the Solent, which are still there today, and the small sailing boats in the foreground. Furthermore, *Item I* is worked in split stitch, a finer stitch than the plain running stitch of *Item II*. This indicates that it probably dates from c1860–70, whereas *Item II* is later, c1880–1900. *S(S)*

A sailorwork picture of the steam yacht SS *Osborne*, the Royal yacht, flying the Royal Standard, the red ensign on the stern and Union flag at bow and stern masts, late 19thC, 23¼in (59cm) wide, glazed and in maple frame. **$2,400–2,700** *S(S)*

Navigational Instruments

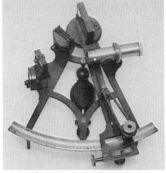

A compass dividing engine, the table with degree punch marks, the frame with articulated arm, with marker, 5 brass plates, compass card, on a wooden base, early 19thC, 14¼in (36cm) diam.
$3,200–3,500 *CSK*

l. A simple sextant, the light alloy frame with 2 arms mounted with peephole eyepiece, horizon glass and mirror, in blue velvet-lined mahogany case, late 19thC, 7¼in (18.5cm) radius.
$1,100–1,300 *S*

Sextants such as this are rarely seen.

A ship's binnacle and compass, the dial signed 'Castle and Company, Hull', the brass cover with oil lamp housing and flanked by Kelvin spheres, on hardwood column support, early 20thC, 57in (145cm) high, in mahogany box.
$1,600–1,900 *LAY*

r. A brass sextant, by J. Coombes, No. 5777, the triple circle frame with silvered scale and magnifier, 2 sets of coloured filters, boxwood handle, late 19thC, 6½in (16.5cm) radius, in fitted mahogany case with telescope and Kew Observatory certificate dated '1898'.
$680–740 *Bea(E)*

A brass oxtant, signed 'Graham & Parkes, Liverpool', with silver scale, magnifier, 2 sets of coloured filters and rosewood handle, c1830, 8in (20cm) radius, in a mahogany case with 3 telescopes.
$850–950 *S*

Miscellaneous

A whaling log of the ship *Mayflower*, of New Bedford, which Captain Joseph P. Chase kept from October 14, 1834 to April 28, 1838, and a report of one man lost overboard, description of whales taken, a call at Honolulu, and whale stamps.
$2,400–2,800 *EL*

A ship's brass oil lamp, c1869, 25½in (65cm) high.
$1,200–1,400 *DRU*

r. A marine steam engine, by Allen & Simmonds, restored by R. H. Pinnock, with boiler, late 19thC, 31½in (80cm) high.
$3,200–3,500 *ELA*

CAMERAS

An Alba camera No. 64, by Albini, Italy, the black enamelled body with an Albini Double Anastigmat f/5.5 100mm lens No. 5380, c1914.
$100–120 *CSK*

A Corfield Periflex 3 camera, c1959.
$90–115 *VCL*

An Ermanox Reflex camera No. M99919, by Ernemann, Germany, with an Ernemann Ernostar f/1.8 10.5cm lens No. 917079 and 3 single metal plate holders, in maker's fitted leather case, c1929.
$6,400–7,200 *CSK*

A Foth Derby camera, with 24 x 36mm format on 127 film, Germany, c1930.
$120–140 *ARP*

A Stereo Hawkeye Model 1 camera, by Blair Camera Co, Rochester, New York, rollfilm with red leather bellows, and a pair of Rapid Rectilinear lenses, c1904.
$320–350 *CSK*

A Crystar camera, Japan, c1950.
$60–70 *VCL*

A Tropical Klapp camera No. 923084, by Ernemann-Werke AG, Dresden, with polished teak body, lacquered brass fittings, tan leather bellows, and a Carl Zeiss, Jena Tessar f/4.5 15cm lens No. 569438 and 4 tropical double darkslides, c1925.
$1,400–1,550 *CSK*

A Fujimoto Semi Prince camera, 4.5 x 6cm format on 120 film, Japan, c1935.
$50–65 *ARP*

A Butcher quarter plate Cameo camera, c1900.
$80–100 *ARP*

An Ensign Selfix 820 camera, c1954.
$40–50 *VCL*

An Esaflex reflex camera, by Ernemann-Werke AG, Germany, with top-mounted reflex finder, later rear-mounted rollfilm back, and an Ernemann Ernostar f/1.8 10.5cm lens No. 224901.
$2,200–2,700 *CSK*

This camera was designed as a 120 rollfilm reflex camera using an Ernoflex body in 1950.

An Exakta Varex IIA camera, c1958.
$110–130 *VCL*

A tailboard camera, by
R. A. Goldmann, Wien, with
polished wooden body, lacquered
brass fittings and an Auzoux &
Cie Grand Angulaire No. C lens
No. 13474 with wheel stops, c1897.
$270–320 *CSK*

A Kodak vest pocket camera,
with 8 pictures on 127 film, the
first model with square cornered
bellows, without autographic
feature, Rochester, USA, c1912.
$160–200 *ARP*

A Kodak Brownie No. 2
camera, c1917.
$6–10 *VCL*

FURTHER READING
John Hedgecoe, *Workbook
of Photo Techniques,*
Mitchell Beazley, 1997.

A Baby Brownie Special plastic
camera, by Eastman Kodak,
Rochester, New York, c1930.
$40–50 *REN*

A Kodak Six-16 Junior rollfilm
camera, Rochester, USA, c1937.
$40–50 *ARP*

A Kodak Retina IIC camera, c1958.
$80–100 *VCL*

A Simplex camera, by Dr. R.
Krügener, Germany, with polished
mahogany body, with internally-
contained spring viewfinder and
lens, lacks focusing back, c1912.
$750–800 *CSK*

A Rover hand camera, by
J. Lancaster & Son, Birmingham,
the wooden body with Rectilinear
lens, in maker's leather case, c1891.
$520–560 *CSK*

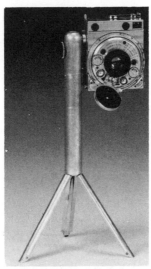

A Le Coultre Co Compass
35mm subminiature camera,
No. 1289, with a CCL3B
Anastigmat lens and a
folding sliding magnifier
fitted to camera back,
together with Compass
camera tripod, c1950.
$2,400–2,700 *S*

A Leica 1a black camera No. 42580,
with a Leitz Elmar 1:3, 5 f/50mm
lens, with lens cap, in maker's ever-
ready case, FIBY in maker's box
and lens hood, c1931.
$700–800 *P(Ba)*

A quarter plate lady's purse-style
camera, by J. Lancaster, the
embossed leather case with mahogany
interior, Achromatic lens with
iris diaphragm, Lancaster patent
'See-saw' shutter and Stone's patent
pneumatic cable release, c1894.
$2,500–3,000 *S*

A Leica III 35mm chrome camera
No. 138466, by Ernst Leitz,
Wetzlar, with Summar fl.25cm
lens, lens caps and ever-ready
case, c1934.
$200–250 *Bon(C)*

A London Stereoscopic Co Tropical
camera, The King's Own, with
polished teak body, brass binding
and fitting, leather bellows, and a
Goerz Doppel Anastigmat
f9/180mm lens, No. 243487, in a
Koilos pneumatic shutter, c1905.
$2,500–2,800 *P(Ba)*

**Miller's is a price GUIDE
not a price LIST**

A MPP Mark 7 micro technical
camera, c1960.
$200–250 *VCL*

A Nikon F2-S Photomic
black camera, No. 7381855,
with instructions and
maker's box, c1962.
$1,000–1,100 *CSK*

A Tropical Challenge camera
No. 374A, by J. Lizars, Glasgow,
with red leather bellows and a
Bauch & Lomb Rapid Rectilinear
lens in a pneumatic shutter,
in a leather case, c1905.
$560–680 *CSK*

A collapsible camera No. 12592,
by H. Mackenstein, Paris,
with polished mahogany body,
lacquered brass fittings,
removable viewfinder, red leather
bellows and a lens with built-in
sprung shutter, c1890.
$480–560 *CSK*

A Nikon F camera, c1962.
$110–130 *VCL*

A Photoret camera, in the form
of a watch, the nickel-plated
body with Meniscus lens and
revolving shutter, in maker's
wooden box with instructions
and unopened tin of magazine
film, American, c1894.
$1,400–1,600 *S*

A Holland field camera, by
Loman & Co, Amsterdam, with
mahogany body, red bellows, rear
roller blind shutter, damaged,
and a brass bound Loman & Co
No. 3 lens, c1900.
$280–320 *CSK*

A Beaumont's Patent brass
and mahogany quarter plate
camera, by Marion & Co,
London, with a Marion brass
bound lens No. 1106, c1933.
$520–560 *CSK*

A Peggy camera, with a
Carl Zeiss Tessar
f3.5/5cm lens and compur
shutter, German, c1930.
$600–650 *S*

A Retina IIa type 150 camera, c1939.
$110–130 *VCL*

A Rolleiflex 2.8F camera, c1970.
$560–640 *VCL*

A twin-lens quarter plate reflex camera, by Ross, London, with black leather-covered body, and a pair of brass-bound London Stereoscopic Co. Carlton lenses No. 19925, c1890.
$850–900 *CSK*

A Speed Graphic camera, c1946.
$110–130 *VCL*

An Una 6 x 9cm folding plate camera, the leather-covered wooden body with polished mahogany interior and brass fittings, black leather bellows with a Ross f4.5/5½in lens and compur shutter, contained in maker's leather case, c1905.
$560–640 *S*

A Steky subminiature camera, the nickel-plated body with a Stekinar f3.5/25mm lens, in maker's case and wooden box with instructions, Japanese, c1947.
$850–900 *S*

An Underwood Instanto mahogany and brass tailboard half-plate camera, Birmingham, c1836.
$400–500 *ARP*

A Zeiss Ikon Tenax camera, 24 x 24mm format on 35mm film, German, c1930.
$80–100 *ARP*

A wet-plate 5 x 5in sliding box camera, the wooden body with removable ground-glass screen and a brass-bound V & A lens No. 19426, c1860.
$1,100–1,300 *CSK*

A Voigtländer Bessa 6 x 9cm 120 size rollfilm camera, Braunschweig, Germany, c1931.
$65–80 *ARP*

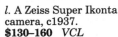

A tailboard camera, by P. Zigliara & Co, Geneva, with a brass-bound Planastigmat lens and double darkslides, in a leather case, c1865.
$320–350 *CSK*

A Contax 1(e) 35mm camera, by Zeiss Ikon, Stuttgart, with Sonnar f2/5cm lens and ever-ready case.
$110–140 *Bon(C)*

l. A Zeiss Super Ikonta camera, c1937.
$130–160 *VCL*

ARMS & ARMOUR
Armour

A German fluted breastplate, with turned and roped moveable gussets at the arms and associated waistplate carrying a skirt of 3 fluted lames, c1520, 17¼in (43.5cm) high.
$2,800–3,200 *S(NY)*

A pikeman's half suit of armour, the cabasset with brass rosettes, the peascod breastplate with articulated tassets, c1600, 30in (76cm) high.
$3,800–4,400 *WSA*

A German fluted close helmet for the field, decorated on both sides over the rear with 3 groups of flutes, the lower edge of the bevor and the 3 neck lames restored, probably Innsbruck, c1510, 10¾in (27.5cm) high.
$22,500–25,500 *S(S)*

This helmet almost certainly formed part of a distinctive group of fluted close helmets which were deposited as booty in the Imperial Arsenal of St Irene in Istanbul, probably taken from the Knights of St John at Rhodes when it fell to the Ottoman Turkish forces of Suleyman the Magnificent in 1522.

A suit of Infantry armour, the burgonet with high comb and hinged cheek pieces, the breastplate with heavy roped border, c1560, 45in (114.5cm) high.
$14,500–16,000 *WSA*

A pair of south German mitten gauntlets, with hinged pointed short cuffs, fitted with a single articulation, one with original thumbplate, mid-16thC, 13in (33cm) long.
$2,000–2,500 *S(NY)*

A three-quarter cuirassier armour, comprising close helmet, breastplate, backplate, arm defences, articulated gauntlets and tassets, complete with a half estoc, north German or Scandinavian, c1640.
$25,500–30,000 *ASB*

This is an exceptionally good example of this type of horseman's armour, particularly with its articulated arm defences. Armour of this type was worn by heavy cavalry during the Thirty Years War and also during the early part of the English civil wars.

A siege engineer's pot helmet, with heavy skull forged from a single piece of iron, the hinged visor with three-bar face guard, mid-17thC.
$2,300–2,700 *ASB*

Heavy duty helmets such as this were worn by engineer officers and others engaged in siege works where they were in danger from enemy sharp shooters.

r. A lobster tail helmet, the skull with raised crest, a single nasal bar and neck piece with artificially articulated lames and ear flaps, c1645, 10in (25.5cm) high.
$1,700–2,000 *WSA*

A cabasset, formed in one piece, with pear stalk finial to crown, brass rosettes around base, brim struck with armourer's mark of a shield, c1600.
$280–320 *WAL*

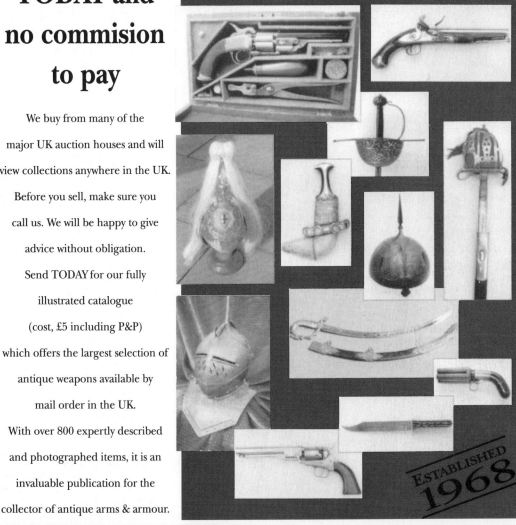

Daggers

A Scottish Highland dirk, with gilt-brass pommel, hardwood grip carved with thistles and traditional Celtic basket-weave pattern, decorated with small brass-headed nails, the straight double-edged blade probably cut down from an old sword blade, the ricasso struck with 2 armourer's marks, c1790, blade 15¼in (38.5cm) long.
$2,000–2,250 *ASB*

An African dagger, the double-edged blade of hand-forged native iron, the central portion decorated by an area of carved lines, probably from the Congo area, 19thC, blade 12in (30.5cm) long.
$200–225 *ASB*

> **Cross Reference**
> Colour Review

r. A nickel-silver and mother-of-pearl dirk, the double-edged blade marked 'Rodgers Cutlers to Her Majesty', in original brown leather sheath with nickel-silver mounts, c1870, blade 4in (10cm) long.
$1,100–1,200 *ASB*

A German left-hand dagger, with tapering double-edge blade of flattened diamond section, iron hilt, strongly fluted ovoid pommel with baluster finial, and wooden grip bound with iron wire, c1600, 16¼in (41.5cm) long.
$1,400–1,600 *S(S)*

Firearms
Blunderbusses

A flintlock blunderbuss, probably for ship's use, the iron barrel with flared muzzle and London proof marks to the breech, the lock of musket size, full length walnut stock and brass furniture, dated '1761', barrel 22in (56cm) long.
$1,700–2,000 *ASB*

A brass-barrelled flintlock blunderbuss, the 13½in (34cm) barrel with multi-faceted breech and strawberry leaf engraving, banana-shaped lockplate similarly engraved and signed 'G. Fisher', walnut fullstock with engraved brass furniture, c1680, re-stocked in mid-18thC.
$4,400–4,800 *WSA*

A flintlock blunderbuss, by Steele, with 9¾in (25cm) flared brass barrel, London proofs, engraved at breech, banana-shaped lockplate, with early bridle on pan, signed 'Stelle' (*sic*), walnut stock with engraved brass mounts, barrel lock and sideplate, c1710, remainder 1760.
$2,500–2,800 *WSA*

A brass-barrelled flintlock blunderbuss, by Hunt, the two-stage 13in (33cm) barrel with steel tang, full stocked, with wooden ramrod and engraved steel butt cap, c1780.
$720–800 *EP*

A flintlock coaching blunderbuss, with brass barrel, London proof marks and inscriptions to the breech 'Red Cross Street Southwark', walnut stock, the brass furniture comprising ramrod pipe, guard with leaf finial, engraved solid side plate, Brown Bess style escutcheon to wrist and large butt plate with long tang, repaired, c1790, barrel 16in (40.5cm) long.
$1,700–2,200 *ASB*

A flintlock blunderbuss, the 14in (35.5cm) brass cannon barrel with octagonal breech and proof marks, hinged spring bayonet released by a sliding catch, walnut full stock with ramrod, engraved brass trigger guard with acorn terminal, the steel lock signed 'Whittern', late 18th/early 19thC, 29½in (75cm) long excluding bayonet.
$1,800–2,000 *DN*

A brass-barrelled flintlock blunderbuss, with spring bayonet, the lock signed 'Clark, Dublin', early 19thC, 30¼in (77cm) long.
$880–960 *J&L*

Carbines

A 12 bore double-barrelled sealed pattern Lovell's flintlock cape carbine, browned twist barrels, 26in (66cm) swivel ramrod, plain locks engraved with crowned 'GR' cyphers and Tower, half-stocked with brass furniture, c1822.
$6,000–6,500 *S(S)*

A 22 bore Irish full stocked flintlock pistol carbine, signed 'Clarke, Dublin', the octagonal barrel with blade foresight, trigger of the single set type, steel furniture comprising 2 ramrod pipes, grip cap and spur trigger guard with pineapple finial, detachable steel-mounted walnut butt stock, c1810, barrel 10in (25.5cm) long.
$2,800–3,200 *ASB*

Fewer than 300 of these carbines were made between 1821–24. A nearly identical example is preserved in the Tower of London.

This pistol may have been made for an officer of Wellington's cavalry during the Napoleonic wars.

A 14 bore English convict guard percussion carbine, the round barrel with Birmingham proof marks and block form foresight, the 1842 pattern lockplate marked 'Birmingham Borough Goal' (*sic*), walnut stock, brass furniture, with its original iron ramrod, c1840, barrel 16in (40.5cm) long.
$950–1,100 *ASB*

A .685 calibre British Paget rifled percussion cavalry carbine, the round barrel rifled with 4 shallow grooves, fitted with a folding rear sight graduated to 300 yards, the lock marked 'VR' and 'Tower', walnut stock, brass furniture, the butt stock with ordnance store keeper's stamps including one for Enfield dated 1840.
$1,100–1,300 *ASB*

Muskets

This is one of the rarest types of British percussion cavalry carbine.

A flintlock musket, with plain iron barrel, octagonal at the breech, stained walnut half-stock, the butt with applied silver plaque inscribed 'Found on Falkirk Battlefield, 18th Jany', ramrod lacking, c1746, 55in (140cm) long.
$1,600–1,800 *C(S)*

A deactivated .303 Martini Enfield artillery carbine, the brown barrel with blade foresight and folding tangent rear sight, the action body with cocking indicator to left-hand side, the fore-end with bayonet bar and walnut stock, c1900, barrel 21in (53.5cm) long.
$400–450 *ASB*

An 11 bore British Honourable East India Company Brown Bess flintlock musket, made by Memory and dated '1791', the round barrel with bayonet stud/foresight to muzzle, the lock with large swan-necked cock and bearing the East India Company heart-shaped mark to its tail, walnut stock and brass furniture, barrel 39in (99cm) long.
$1,300–1,450 *ASB*

Michael Memory of Tower Hill was a contractor to the ordnance from 1756–1793 and to the East India Company from 1772 to the year of his death in 1798.

A .700 calibre Imperial Russian model three-band percussion infantry musket, manufactured at the Tula arsenal in 1840 as a flintlock and converted to percussion after 1844, the round iron barrel with brass foresight and notch rear sight, the lock with large French style hammer and remaining section of original priming pan, brass furniture, the tang bearing the doubled-headed eagle of the Imperial Romanov family, 1839–44, barrel 41½in (105.5cm) long.
$720–800 *ASB*

The M1844 musket conversion was used extensively by Russian troops during the Crimean War.

Pistols

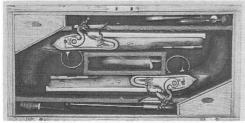

A pair of 16 bore flintlock duelling pistols, by Essex of London, with octagonal barrels, Tower private proofs, top flats engraved 'London', locks engraved 'Essex', roller bearing frizzen springs, in an oak case with flask, mould, cleaning rod and powder measure, 1750s, barrels 9in (23cm) long.
$2,700–3,200 *WAL*

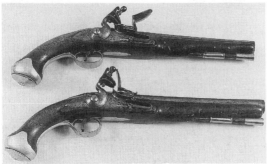

A pair of Light Dragoon flintlock pistols, each with brass mounts, engraved lockplates, marked 'Grice' and 'G.R.', dated '1760'.
$2,000–2,500 *BWe*

A 80 bore four-barrelled flintlock duck's foot pistol, signed 'Barker, Newark', the 4 barrels of cannon type, with grooved muzzles for loading key, with grip, inlaid with silver wire, c1790.
$4,400–4,800 *ASB*

Care and attention

Although the corrosive effect of gunpowder ignition is responsible for most of the pitting on antique firearms, many fine pieces have been spoilt by finger rust. Hastily put away after inspection, steel quickly acquires a reddish hue. Firearms should be wiped carefully after handling. Some collectors wear cotton gloves when picking up a gun. For long term storage a good-quality furniture wax is preferred to heavy oiling, which can stain woodwork. Never leave an antique weapon with any mechanical part under strain, such as the hammer cocked.

A percussion double-barrelled pistol, inscribed 'Collins', the circular tapering barrels above a ramrod, on a mahogany stock, c1870, 13in (33cm) long.
$560–680 *HYD*

A flintlock pocket pistol, by John Dafte, with 3½in (9cm) turn-off barrel, walnut half-stock with engraved iron mounts, signed, c1680.
$3,200–3,800 *WSA*

A pair of flintlock boxlock Queen Anne style pistols, engraved 'Haynes, London', with 3½in (9cm) turn-off cannon barrels and one-piece butts, wire inlaid with butt caps, in a wooden case with key, copper pistol flask and turnscrew, c1780.
$1,200–1,300 *EP*

A Turkish flintlock blunderbuss pistol, the flared steel barrel inlaid with silver, full-stocked with steel furniture and carved and silver wire inlaid, early 19thC, barrel 12¼in (31cm) long.
$480–540 *Bri*

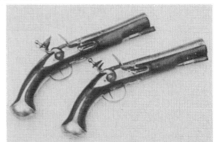

A pair of flintlock holster pistols, with brass barrels and furniture, full walnut stocks with later ramrods, some damage and repair, 18thC, 12½in (32cm) long.
$720–800 *Bea(E)*

A flintlock Tower-style pistol, with brass butt, trigger guard and mounts, the stock stamped 'T. Cook', and the barrel engraved 'Warminster', maker recorded, c1830, 15in (38cm) long.
$380–420 *CoH*

Revolvers

A five-shot 120 bore Tranter percussion revolver, 3¾in (9.5cm) blued octagonal barrel signed 'T. Richardson & Sons, Cork', engraved No. 16318T, one-piece chequered wood grips, in baize-lined mahogany case with accessories, c1850.
$1,900–2,200 *Gle*

A five-shot 120 bore Adams revolver, the 4¾in (11cm) octagonal barrel engraved 'Dooley, Liverpool', the scroll-engraved frame with side safety, engraved 'Adams patent No. 30435B', chequered walnut butt with horn butt cap, 1852.
$1,200–1,300 *WSA*

Rifles

A cased air rifle, by Joseph Wood, Lewes, with re-browned octagonal sighted rifled barrel signed at the breech, case-hardened scroll engraved action, shagreen-covered butt reservoir, walnut fore-end, horn fore-end cap and wooden ramrod, with original re-browned two-stage smooth bore barrel and accessories, early 19thC, barrel 30in (76cm) long, in original oak case.
$1,700–1,900 *CSK*

A .451 Alexander Henry Patent percussion military style match rifle, with browned twist match weight barrel with full-length sighting flat, engraved breech-tang fitted with raised bed for an adjustable Vernier sight, figured walnut full stock, chequered pistol-grip with engraved steel trap for spare nipples, original steel ramrod with bronze tip, c1865, barrel 33in (84cm) long.
$5,000–5,500 *S(S)*

A deactivated W. W. Greener Martini Henry rifle, the barrel with blade foresight and folding tangent rear sight, the action with cocking indicator to the right hand side, walnut stock, bayonet bar to front barrel band, Enfield, 1872, barrel 30in (76cm) long.
$450–520 *ASB*

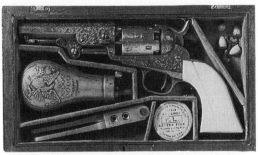

A cased .31 calibre Colt model 1849 percussion pocket revolver, factory engraved, No. 117841 for 1856, the cylinder with engraved hold-up scene, patinated ivory grip, with scroll engraving throughout, in fitted case, with original embossed Colt flask and brass bullet mould, 8¾in (22cm) long.
$5,600–6,400 *S(NY)*

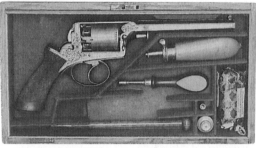

A five-shot 54 bore Adams self-cocking percussion revolver, engraved on top flat 'I. Purdey, London', the frame engraved 'Adams Patent No. 13,666R', and decorated with scrollwork, chequered walnut butt, in a fitted oak case with accessories, 1850s, 12in (30.5cm) overall.
$3,600–4,000 *WAL*

Swords

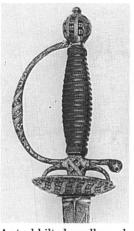

A mortuary sword, the blade signed 'Clemens Woller Me Fecit Solingen', steel hilt with scrolling side bars chiselled with foliage, grotesque masks and portrait busts, chiselled pommel, wood grip, mid-17thC, 33¾in (86cm) long. **$1,400–1,600** *Gle*

The mortuary sword is a popular name – and misnomer – for this type of sword. They are so-called because the side bars were chiselled with portraits of King Charles I and his Queen, Henrietta Maria, who were executed in 1649. Many of these swords, however, were made and used prior to their deaths.

A basket-hilted backsword, with straight single-edged German blade with a pair of fullers on each side, stamped, iron hilt decorated on the shell and knuckle-guard with incised grotesque masks, brass pommel cast and chased in relief as a monster head, original natural staghorn grip with an iron ferrule at the base, c1635, 35¾in (90.5cm) long. **$2,700–3,000** *S(S)*

A steel-hilted smallsword, the triangular section blade engraved with scrolls and strapwork, the hilt chiselled and pierced with scrolls and flowerheads between gilded bands, wire and ribbon-bound grip with Turks' heads, c1750, 34¼in (87cm) long. **$950–1,100** *Gle*

A Scottish regimental backsword, the single-edged blade with back fuller, the basket hilt of military type with replaced wooden grip, c1770, 36½in (93cm) long. **$1,400–1,600** *WSA*

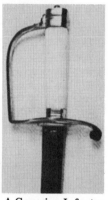

A Georgian Infantry officer's spadroon, the stirrup hilt with eight-sided pommel, knuckle bow, quillon, side bar and reeded ivory grip, the straight double-edged blade with spear point and fuller, c1790, later chromium plated blade, 32½in (82.5cm) long. **$560–620** *ASB*

An 1857 pattern Engineer Officer's Sword, blade by Joseph Starkey, profusely scroll-etched with Royal cypher & 'The Engineer & Railway Staff Corps', the scrolled gilt brass hilt with fishskin grip and plated scabbard, c1895, 38½in (98cm) long. **$560–640** *WSA*

An American War of Independence English Light Cavalry Trooper's sword, the straight blade with spear point, the brass D-shaped hilt of regulation pattern, with fishskin grip, no scabbard, c1780, 40½in (103cm) long. **$720–800** *WSA*

A Georgian Yeoman Warder's sword, with straight double-edged blade, brass hilt with up-turned shell-guard cast and chiselled with the horse of Hanover, pommel chiselled with a crown on either side, late 18thC, 29¾in (75.5cm) long. **$400–450** *S(S)*

l. A Victorian Light Infantry officer's sword, by Henry Wilkinson of London, the hilt with a non-standard brass knuckle bow and quillon, the slightly curved single-edged blade with spear point and fuller, etched with flowers, foliage, the Royal cypher and the Light Infantry bugle horn, blade 32in (81.5cm) long. **$350–380** *ASB*

The knuckle bow and quillon appears to be contemporary with the sword and may have been the result of a previous owner's personal preference for a different hilt.

Care and attention

Blades should be wiped after handling. Rust spots can be cleaned by rubbing the edge of a copper coin over the affected area, although this will not remove the stain. Blades should be waxed after cleaning – oil attracts dust and fluff. Treat leather scabbards and sheaths with leather oil. Never grasp a leather scabbard too tightly when drawing as weakened scabbards can result in cut fingers.

Garth Vincent
Antique Arms and Armour

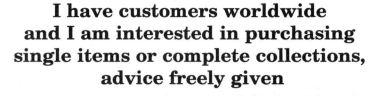

**I have customers worldwide
and I am interested in purchasing
single items or complete collections,
advice freely given**

**Dealer in antique and reproduction
arms and armour for the collector,
investor and interior decorator
Commission buying at auction**

Access & Visa accepted

Brochure available

The Old Manor House,
Allington, Nr Grantham,
Lincolnshire NG32 2DH
Telephone: 01400 281358

A SELECTION OF PRICES REALISED IN A 1997 AUCTION

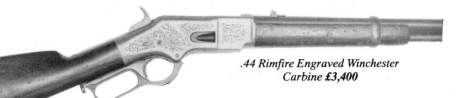

.44 Rimfire Engraved Winchester Carbine £3,400

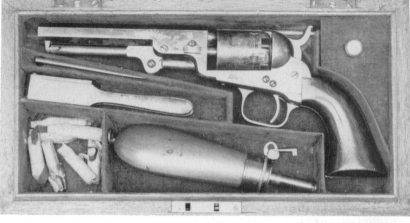

Cased 5-shot .31 Colt Model 1849 Pocket Percussion Revolver. London address £4,200

Military Cross Group given to Lieutenant H. A. Somerville, Royal Flying Corps, who shot down German Flying Ace Max Muller £4,750

Silver Inlaid Swept Hilt Continental Rapier c.1620 £2,900

English Civil War Sword, Hounslow Blade £2,100

Georgian Officer's Sabretache 18th Dragoons £2,500

INTERNATIONALLY YOURS

WALLIS & WALLIS

**WEST STREET AUCTION GALLERIES
LEWES, EAST SUSSEX, ENGLAND
TEL: 01273 480208   FAX: 01273 476562**

Elizabeth II Sidedrum of the Coldstream Guards £450

MILITARIA
Autographs

John Churchill, 1st Duke of Marlborough, an autographed letter, written to acknowledge congratulations following the Battle of Ramillies, to an unnamed peer, Rousselaer, 17/28 June 1706, 1 page.
$520–560 *P*

The Duke of Marlborough had won his famous victory on 23rd May 1706.

Field-Marshal Montgomery, a black and white original photograph, inscribed 'Rommel's white Arab stallion captured by me in Germany April 1945, Montgomery of Alamein', mounted, framed and glazed, 16 x 17in (40.5 x 43cm).
$640–720 *Bon*

Florence Nightingale, an autographed letter written from the Barrack Hospital, Scutari, to Mrs Allen, Red Cross and St John's sale stamp, 28 February 1856, 4 pages.
$1,100–1,200 *P*

A wartime autograph book, signed by a number of Dambusters and other bomber command aircrew, including one page inscribed 'The Dam(n) Boys May 30, 1943'.
$1,900–2,200 *S(S)*

These signatures were collected by Mary Pycroft, who worked at the Saracen's Head Hotel, Lincoln. The hotel was obviously a regular watering-hole for the many bomber squadrons based in Lincolnshire.

Costume

l. An officer's full dress tunic of the Royal Berkshire Militia, with both full dress and levee dress trousers, and a chain-link chinstrap, pre-1881.
$200–250 *DN*

An Irvin jacket of a Battle of Britain pilot, the late Air Commodore R. G. Dutton, CBE, DSO, DFC, 2 small repairs, with a letter from Dutton's widow, confirming that it was used 'in combat during The Battle of Britain'.
$2,800–3,400 *S(S)*

MILLER'S COMPARES . . .

I A WWII US Army Air Force A2 leather flying jacket, with artwork on back, inscribed 'Hell's Angels Group' with bombs.
$3,200–3,500 *CSK*

II A WWII US Army Air Force A2 leather flying jacket, with artwork on back, inscribed 'To Hell with Hitler', 10 bombs, and a caricature of Hitler surrounded by flames.
$680–800 *CSK*

These two very fine examples of painted flying jackets are in excellent condition despite being over 50 years old. The bomb designs on the backs are thought to denote the number of bombing raids participated in by the original owner. The 'To Hell With Hitler' design of *Item II* is extremely interesting because of its contemporary caricature of Hitler, but it was nevertheless *Item I* which really took off in the saleroom, realising four times its pre-sale estimate. This was because it is a jacket of the original Hell's Angels, who after the war went on to form the famous motorcycle group. *CSK*

A Georgian officer's rifle green jacket of the Montreal Rifles, padded ornaments to waist behind, 23 braided loops to chest with 3 lines of domed silver-plated buttons bearing 'GR' cypher within beaded title circles inscribed 'Montreal Rifles', c1810.
$1,600–1,800 *WAL*

Helmets

An Imperial Prussian artilleryman's pickelhaube, with brass helmet plate, ball top and mounts, leather-backed brass chinscales, both cockades, good condition, inside of neck guard stamped '1915.1910.IIA', c1910.
$430–480 *WAL*

An Imperial German non-commissioned officer's helmet of The Garde Reiter Regiment, the Tombak skull with silvered rayed star bearing Saxony arms, neck guard with silvered lion parade crest, good condition, c1910.
$3,500–4,000 *WAL*

A Victorian officer's blue cloth helmet of the 2nd Volunteer Battalion Norfolk Regiment, by Hawkes & Co, with silk lining, in japanned case.
$730–800 *S(S)*

A post-1902 officer's green cloth spiked helmet of The Durham Light Infantry, with gilt mounts, velvet-backed chin chain and ear rosettes, gilt and silver-plated helmet plate, leather and silk lining, in japanned tin case, very good condition.
$1,100–1,300 *WAL*

A Victorian officer's Lance Cap of the 12th (Prince of Wales Royal) Lancers, by J. B. Johnstone, patent leather skull with red felt top, quartered with bullion cord and embroidered peak, gilded and silvered plate struck with battle honours, with horsehair plume, silk lining, in japanned case.
$4,800–5,500 *S(S)*

r. A Victorian 6th Dragoon's trooper's helmet, brass skull decorated with band of laurel, oak leaves and acorns, the top spike with white horsehair parade plume, with original liner and brass chin scales attached by rose head bosses.
$1,100–1,200 *ASB*

Medals

A group of 3 medals awarded to Corporal James Button, 7th Royal Fusiliers, comprising: DCM Victorian issue, Crimea 1854 3 bars, and Turkish Crimea British issue, together with regimental account book, discharge certificate dated 'February 1857', testimonial letters, and a framed photograph.
$1,600–1,800 *WAL*

An MGS medal, 1793–1814, 6 bars, awarded to J. Lane, 3rd Foot Guards.
$1,000–1,100 *WAL*

A group of 6 medals awarded to Brigade Surgeon E. C. Markey, Army Medical Staff, comprising: Order of the Bath, CB breast badge; Afghanistan 1878–80 2 bars, Ahmed Khel, Kandahar, Kabul to Kandahar Star; Egypt, one bar 1884–85; IGS 1854 one bar, Chin Lushai 1889–90; Khedives 1884–6 Star.
$3,200–3,500 *Gle*

A group of orders and medals awarded to
C. W. Craven Bt., consisting of Baronet's
badge, Knights Bachelor's badge, OBE,
Queen's South Africa (NB), 1914–15 Trio,
1911 and 1937 Coronation, and miniatures.
$1,700–1,900 *MSL*

A group of 8 medals awarded to Lieutenant Colonel
F. W. Richey, RGA and Wing Commander, RFC,
comprising: DSO, GVR; OBE Military 1st type;
1914–15 Star; British War and Victory Medals, MID;
IGS 1908–35, one clasp; Waziristan 1921–24, MID;
Russia, Order of St Anne, 3rd class.
$1,900–2,200 *DNW*

A group of 8 medals, awarded to Major Percy
Pilkington, Lancashire Fusiliers, comprising: MBE
Military 1st type; Distinguished Conduct Medal,
E.VII.R; British South Africa Company Medal
1890–97, reverse Rhodesia 1896; Queen's South
Africa 1899–1902, 5 clasps; 1914–15 Star Trio;
Army LS & GC, E.VII.R.
$2,500–2,800 *DNW*

*Percy Pilkington took part in the famous Jameson Raid,
an unsuccessful attempt led by Sir Leander Jameson
to overthrow the Boer regime in the Transvaal.*

A group of 6 medals awarded to Corporal Frank
Palmer, 2/5th, Lancashire Fusiliers, comprising:
Distinguished Conduct Medal, GVR; Military Medal,
GVR, with 2nd award bar; 1914–15 Star Trio;
Médaille Militaire.
$2,200–2,700 *DNW*

A German group of 8 medals comprising: Prussia Iron
Cross 1914, 2nd Class; Saxony Order of the White
Falcon; Oldenburg War Merit Cross 1914; Hamburg
War Cross 1914; 1914–18 War Cross; Landwehr
Medal 2nd class; Prussia 100 year Anniversary
medal; Austria Order of Merit.
$600–650 *Gle*

A group of 9 medals awarded to Group Captain
B. D. Hobbs, RNAS, RCAF, comprising: Distinguished
Service Order, GVR; OBE; Distinguished Service
Cross, GVR, with 2nd award bar; British War and
Victory Medals, 1939–45, Star, Atlantic Star;
Canadian Voluntary Service war medal.
$9,600–10,400 *Gle*

Miscellaneous

An ammunition pouch, made of
sheets of leather sandwiched
together and decorated with brass
and iron plates cut in geometric
patterns, 18thC, 6in (15cm) square.
$250–300 *ASB*

A Mk III WWII army marching
compass, 1945.
$350–400 *GWA*

l. A watercolour heightened with
white and pencil, by Sandy Bertram,
depicting a fight over the Western
Front, Albatros and Sopwith
machines above a lone Harry Tate
RE8 observer biplane, signed and
dated '1919', 14 x 10in (36 x 26cm).
$1,200–1,300 *CSK*

SPORT

For many sports memorabilia collectors, recent market activity could be described as 'back to basics'. We have noticed a trend away from the high ticket items (over $10,000) towards the more affordable. It seems that a good number of buyers are now more concerned with the aesthetics of an item rather than its worth ten years down the road. Rather than buying a card to stick away in a dresser drawer, collectors are buying display items that can be hung on their walls for all to enjoy.

Baseball is still the number one in sport collecting, supported by two big transactions which took place during the year. First, Eddie Murray's 500th home run baseball was sold to a private collector for $500,000 by the young man who caught the ball. Although this seems a enormous sum to pay, the transaction did put the current sports collectables market in the international headlines. Secondly, a New York auction house sold the finest known example (in near mint condition) of the famous 1909 T206 Honus Wagner card for $640,500. This was the highest price ever realised for a single piece of sports memorabilia. Unfortunately, this was by far the height of the card market for the year.

New York City has always been a hot spot for sports collectables. The fact that the hometown Yankees won the World Series for the first time in almost 20 years created a frenzy for their memorabilia. Team signed baseballs were selling for $1,500 when they could be found.

The Championship also sparked interest in the old guard such as Babe Ruth, Lou Gehrig, Mickey Mantle and Joe DiMaggio.

Other sports such as American football, hockey, basketball, golf, horse racing and soccer are being bought with regularity. There is interest in both the historical and modern aspects of these areas.

The collectability of hockey and basketball were evident when the remaining contents of the Boston Garden, the old home of the Bruins and Celtics was sold. The two-day auction/sale grossed close to $1,000,000 and everything from old seats ($500–5,000) to a Bobby Orr game-used jersey ($15,000) was sold. Michael Jordan, the current basketball mega-legend is the most desired name in the field. His authentic game-used jerseys have topped the $20,000 mark.

Golfing memorabilia is the rising star of the collectables field. Rare vintage clubs and balls top the want list of many collectors. The year has seen many of these items sell in the $1,000–5,000 bracket. Current stars such as Tiger Woods are helping to improve the visibility of this sometimes overlooked sport.

The sports collectables field offers so much enjoyment for those that have a love for the games and history of them. It is important to treat collecting as a hobby and something to have fun with. If an item increases in value over the years, it is an added bonus. Happy collecting to all.

Mike Heffner

Baseball

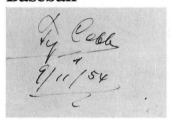

Ty Cobb's autograph, in ink, dated '9/11/54', 4 x 6in (10 x 15cm).
$350–400 *HALL*

A Topps No. 311 Mickey Mantle baseball card, c1952.
$2,500–3,000 *HALL*

A New York Yankees autographed baseball, signed on sweet spot by Babe Ruth, with 14 players' signatures, c1927.
$3,500–4,000 *HALL*

A H & B D29L bat manufactured for Joe DiMaggio while he was batting coach for the Yankees, 1960–64, 35in (89cm) long.
$3,500–4,000 *CNY*

A handwritten letter on Hotel Rennert stationery, by Joe Kelley, dated 'May 4th, '34'.
$5,000–5,500 *Lel*

l. A metal and fabric open vision catcher's mask, c1920, 10in (25.5cm) high.
$50–60 *YAG*

A pair of New York Yankees pin-striped pants, signed by Mickey Mantle, label on waistband 'Mantle–7–66–26 inches–Set 1, 1966', box-framed, 1966.
$5,750–6,250 *CNY*

A silver print photograph of Louis Sockalexis, and members of the Plattsburgh and Holy Cross baseball teams, 1896, 8 x 10in (20.5 x 25.5cm).
$2,000–2,200 *CNY*

A photograph of the New York Giant's, in the Old Polo Grounds, with original frame, 1892, 18 x 24in (45.5 x 62cm).
$2,400–2,700 *Lel*

> **Miller's is a price GUIDE not a price LIST**

l. Karl Spooner's 1955 Dodgers Championship ring, with his name on the side panel.
$21,000–23,000 *CNY*

The most important year in the history of the Brooklyn Dodgers was 1955, their only World Championship. Championship rings from that team are rarely available to collectors.

A photograph of Joe DiMaggio, taken after his last ever regular season game, signed and dated '10/3/51'.
$880–960 *Lel*

Champions 1912, a Red Sox World's Series programme.
$1,300–1,500 *HALL*

An All Star game programme, for the Major League Baseball All Star Game, 1936.
$1,350–1,550 *CNY*

Basketball

l. A World Championship 1983–4 Boston Celtics basketball, with 12 signatures including Bird, McHale, Jones, Ainge, Parish, Maxwell and Wedman.
$1,350–1,550 *Lel*

l. Jerry West's Lakers away-game worn basketball jersey, signed, c1973.
$4,500–5,500 *CNY*

A 1959–60 World Champion Boston Celtics presentation clock, the glass face framed by basketballs with 12 facsimile signatures, available only to players and dignitaries, 9in (23cm) wide.
$320–360 *Lel*

A 1985 All-Star basketball, signed by 22 members of the team, including Michael Jordan, Magic Johnson, and Larry Bird.
$3,500–4,000 *CNY*

A Harlem Globetrotters 78rpm record of Sweet Georgia Brown, signed by 9 members, including Marcus Haynes and Goose Tatum, 1950s.
$480–540 *CNY*

Billiards

A roll-over billiard/dining table, by George Edwards, c1875, 84 x 42in (213.5 x 106.5cm).
$6,500–8,000 *WBB*

A Maharajah's ornately carved and decorated billiard table, by George Wright, c1888, 144 x 72in (366 x 183cm).
$96,000–112,000 *WBB*

A mahogany billiard table, by Riley, c1890, 108 x 54in (274.5 x 137cm).
$4,300–4,800 *BRA*

An oak billiard/dining table, by Riley, on turned and twisted supports, c1920, 96 x 48in (244 x 122cm).
$6,400–7,200 *ABC*

A mahogany billiard table, by Thurston, on 6 fluted legs, c1890, 96 x 48in (244 x 122cm).
$4,800–5,600 *ABC*

A mahogany billiard table, by Thurston, on 8 turned and fluted legs, c1890, 144 x 72in (366 x 183cm).
$8,800–9,600 *ABC*

l. An oak swivel-action billiard/dining table, by George Edwards, on reeded legs, c1885, 84 x 48in (213.5 x 122cm).
$5,600–6,400 *ABC*

A carved oak billiard table, by Orme & Sons, c1900, 144 x 72in (366 x 183cm).
$12,000–13,500 *CBC*

A mahogany non-revolving cue stand, with 18 spring clips for cues, c1890, 40in (101.5cm) high.
$880–960 *ABC*

A mahogany freestanding billiard cue stand, to hold 14 cues/rests, late 19thC, 46in (117cm) wide.
$650–800 *BRA*

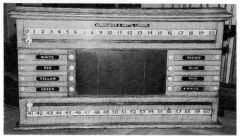

A wooden mace, a spider, and a rest, each with shaft, c1890, 58in (147.5cm) long.
$400–500 *BRA*

An oak billiard/life pool scoreboard, by Burroughes & Watts, with roller numbering, ivory markers and pointers, c1880, 36in (91.5cm) wide.
$1,600–1,900 *ABC*

A mahogany billiard scoreboard, by Burroughes & Watts, London, c1900, 39¼in (100cm) wide.
$400–500 *BRA*

An oak billiard scoreboard, by E. J. Riley, c1900, 27¼in (69cm) wide.
$200–250 *BRA*

A mahogany slider type billiard/snooker scoreboard, by Burroughes & Watts, with gold leaf lettering and wooden pointers, c1890, 30in (76cm) wide.
$480–560 *ABC*

A mahogany billiard and snooker scoreboard, by Burroughes & Watts, c1920, 39¼in (100cm) wide.
$320–400 *BRA*

A snooker scoreboard, c1920, 19in (48.5cm) wide.
$55–75 *SPU*

A brass gasolier, the ornate central section flanked by simple sweeping supports, with original shades, converted to electricity, c1875, 108in (274.5cm) wide.
$3,500–4,000 *BRA*

> **Cross Reference**
> Colour Review

r. An oak cabinet, with twin swivel revolving cue racks, marker, swivel mirror/slate, fitted ball boxes and drinks cabinet, c1885, 60in (152.5cm).
$9,500–11,000 *WBB*

Boxing

Harris Furniss, editor, *Famous Fights, Past and Present*, vols. 5–8, Nos. 53–104, bound as one, numerous illustrations of boxers and fights, contemporary cloth gilt, c1902–3.
$220–240 *DW*

A programme and ticket for Rocky Marciano v. Ezzard Charles, 1954.
$190–220 *HALL*

A signed and inscribed colour photograph of Mike Tyson, with 3 title belts, c1987, 10 x 8in (25.5 x 20.5cm).
$330–370 *VS*

An unused ticket for James Jeffries v. Jack Johnson, Reno, July 4th, 1910.
$880–960 *Lel*

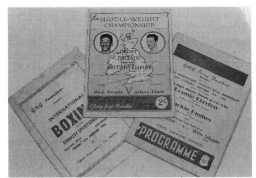

Three boxing programmes for 1949, 1950 and 1955.
$40–60 *MUL*

Cricket

A Dave Brown yellow cricket ball, for the 1996 Hong Kong Sixes, signed by Donald and Cronje, South Africa.
$120–140 *VS*

A Vizianagram team white wool blazer, which belonged to Sir Vijay Anand the Rajkumar of Vizianagram, the breast pocket embroidered in coloured wools with crest and brass buttons, c1936.
$560–620 *CSK*

A great patron of Indian cricket, Vizianagram captained the 1936 Indian side to England, leading his country in the 3 tests. He also organised his own team, which played first class cricket.

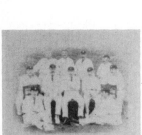

Surrey, a sepia photograph by Hawkins, laid down to printed mount, showing the team of 1891.
$175–200 *VS*

Cross Reference
Colour Review

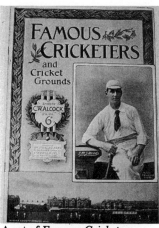

A set of *Famous Cricketers* magazines, edited by C. W. Alcock, published by Hudson & Kearns and the *News of the World*.
$130–160 *MUL*

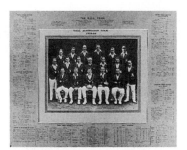

A signed photograph of the MCC touring team to Australia, 1928/9, with 17 signatures including Chapman, Hobbs, Sutcliffe, Larwood, Hammond, Leyland, Mead, Tate, with printed details of the 5 test matches and averages, with Chapman's name written in pencil to reverse, possibly his copy, 24 x 28in (61 x 71cm).
$530–580 *VS*

Thomas Henwood, *Cricket in the Dripping Pan, Lewes*, pencil, pen and black ink and wash drawing, inscribed in pen, 'T. Henwood, delt. 1833', framed and glazed, 3¾ x 5½in (9.5 x 14cm).
$560–620 *CSK*

Fishing

A Hardy nickel-silver spring balance, c1920, 6in (15cm) long.
$100–120 *RTh*

An oval-cased salmon, inscribed 'Tay N.B., Lower Stanley, Pitlochry Pool, Feb 7th, 1911, Weight 42lbs, length 51in, Girth 25½in, Killed by P. A. Scott', signed 'P. D. Malloch, Perth'.
$5,400–6,000 *C(Sc)*

A carved wood square tail rainbow trout, mounted, 1930s, 18in (45.5cm) long.
$560–640 *YAG*

A bowfronted glazed case, containing a trout, inscribed in gilt 'Trout 7lbs, caught by P. B. Kittel at Barford, R. Stour, 20th May, 1939', paper label 'J. Cooper & Sons, London', 13¼in (33.5cm) wide.
$1,300–1,500 *DN*

A Continental fishing barrel casket/seat, the hinged lid with applied fish motif, front with a medallion depicting a competition, lion mask ring handles, 19thC, 12in (30.5cm) high.
$1,700–2,000 *C(Sc)*

A bowfronted case, containing
2 perch, by Rowland Ward Ltd,
inscribed 'Perch, 1½lbs each,
caught River Kennet,
Thatcham, 3rd Jan, 1950,
by Julian Venables, aged 11',
20½in (52cm) wide.
$750–800   *C(Sc)*

A fly fishing line dryer, c1860,
15in (38cm) high.
$215–240   *RYA*

Two wood and iron handpainted fish
decoys, c1900, 8½in (21.5cm) long.
$200–225   *AWT*

Cross Reference
Colour Review

A crocodile skin fly wallet, with
brass lock and selection of sea-
front flies, c1890, 4in (10cm) wide.
$520–560   *RTh*

A Hardy brass three-draw gaff, with turned
handle, c1880, 44¼in (112.5cm) extended.
$880–960   *EP*

A Hardy 'Jim Vincent Broads Spoon' pike lure,
c1950, 5¼in (13cm) long.
$25–35   *OTB*

A fisherman's pine line rig, with drawer containing lead
weights, and set-up end tackle, 1930s, 7in (18cm) wide.
$25–35   *AnS*

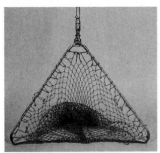

A Hardy folding landing net, with bronze and aluminium fittings, 1930s, 26½in (67cm) long.
$65–75 *WAB*

A Hardy 3in brass reel, with crank handle, c1880.
$720–800 *RTh*

A Eaton & Deller 2¾in trout fly reel, with raised check housing to brass face, ebonite handle, backplate and faceplate rim, c1880.
$130–160 *OTB*

A Hardy 3¾in 1896 pattern Perfect all-brass salmon fly reel, with shaded rod-and-hand trademark, enclosed oval log, strapped tension screw, dished drum with perforations and central locking screw, brass ball bearings in open race, brass rim with nickel silver pillars and ivorine handles.
$1,900–2,200 *EP*

A Hardy 3¾in 1891 Patent fly reel, with 4 column line guide, regulator with guard, ventilated drum, plate with rod-and-hand mark, foot stamped. .
$3,500–4,000 *S(S)*

This rare issue fly reel is in excellent original condition.

A Hardy Nottingham 4½in reel, the wooden drum with alloy backplate, twin ivorine handles, brass optional check button, Bickerdyke line guide and brass foot, c1890, in wooden case.
$2,800–3,200 *EP*

A Hardy Silex 4in reel, with leather case, c1905.
$400–450 *RTh*

A Hardy St George 3¾in trout fly reel, with knurled drum locking nut, strapped rim regulator screw, agate line guide, ivorine handle and brass foot, c1911.
$3,200–3,500 *EP*

A 2⅛in brass crankwind trout fly reel, embossed with angling scenes, late 19thC.
$220–280 *OTB*

This reel is possibly American, though this type was also known to have been made by Heaton of Birmingham in the 1880s.

A Malloch 4in brass side casting reel, with black leather case, c1905.
$530–600 *RTh*

A Malloch's Patent 3¾in alloy side casting reel, with reversible drum latch, faceplate engraved, c1930.
$110–140 *OTB*

A Scarborough 7½in mahogany and brass perforated fishing reel, c1910.
$450–520 *RTh*

r. A Slater Nottingham 4in reel, with Starback centre pin, c1900.
$70–90 *AnS*

A Pownall's Patent Drag Oilin Scarborough style 4½in wood and brass sea reel, with self-oiling mechanism, c1930.
$80–110 *OTB*

A Nottingham Starback 4in wood and brass reel, with Slater catch mechanism, c1920.
$50–65 *WAB*

An Edward vom Hofe 4¼in multiplying salt water reel, American, c1880.
$530–600 *RTh*

A Wilkes Osprey Brand 5¾in wooden Scarborough reel, with Slater latch, 1950s.
$80–90 *EP*

Football

An autographed football, bearing signatures of the Notre Dame team, including K. K. Rockne and others, late 1920s.
$2,200–2,400 *Lel*

An autographed football, bearing 33 signatures of the Baltimore Colts Superbowl Football World Champions, including Unitas, Morral and B. Smith, 1970.
$800–900 *Lel*

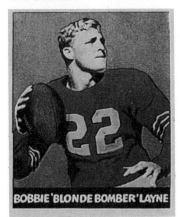

A set of 96 Leaf football cards, 1948.
$2,800–3,200 *CNY*

A leather and canvas flat top football helmet, with air holes at top, ear holes to hear the calls, c1900.
$950–1,100 *Lel*

A Reach football helmet, with earflaps, banded circular headpiece, matching backpiece, inner padding and incised logo, 1920s.
$550–600 *Lel*

A programme of the Superbowl II 1968 World Championship game, Greenbay v. Oakland.
$260–300 *HALL*

Golf

A feather-filled golf ball, c1840.
$4,500–5,500 *C(Sc)*

A hand-cut gutta percha golf ball, damaged, c1850.
$520–620 *C(Sc)*

A silver-plated golf candlestick, by Mappin & Webb, with 3 crossed clubs, mesh pattern ball and winner's wreath, c1910, 7in (18cm) high.
$320–370 *MSh*

Bernard Darwin, *The Golf Courses of the British Isles,* illustrated by Harry Rowntree, 1910, 4°, first edition, with 64 coloured plates, original gilt.
$580–640 *DW*

A long-nosed scared-head driver, by Tom Morris, St Andrews, the head stamped, sole with ram's horn inset, shaft with leather grip, c1870.
$2,400–2,800 *C(Sc)*

A rut iron golf club, marked, c1880, 40in (101.5cm) long.
$400–500 *MSh*

A scared-head spoon driver, by Anderson & Sons, Edinburgh, with brass sole plate, c1880.
$2,800–3,200 *MUL*

A silver-plated bronze figure, of a golfer, on a marble base, c1890, 6¼in (16cm) high.
$450–550 *MSh*

A black and white photograph of Bobby Jones and Roger Wethered, c1930, 12 x 8in (30.5 x 20.5cm).
$220–260 *MUL*

Satomi Munesugu, *Golf*, printed by IDL Graphics, lithograph in colours, backed on linen, c1935, 39½ x 28in (100 x 71cm).
$560–640 *C(Sc)*

A silver spirit flask, enamelled with a golfer, hallmarked Chester 1933, 3in (7.5cm) high.
$400–450 *GAK*

A silver golfing trophy, with gilt interior, cast as a rosebowl with acanthus decoration, on 4 golf ball supports and wooden plinth, inscribed 'Kodogaya Country Club, presented by The HCC Keiro-kai, 1858', 5½in (14cm) high.
$700–800 *C(Sc)*

A Victorian silver salver, with engraved foliate scroll decoration, the centre inscribed 'Dedicated to Henry Cotton MBE, on the occasion of his winning the Open Championship, 1948, from the Members of Royal Mid-Surrey Golf Club', 18in (46cm) diam.
$2,800–3,200 *C(Sc)*

Hockey

A Bruins 1928–29 Championship team photograph, signed by all 15 members including Art Ross, Eddie Shore, Dit Clapper and Harry Oliver, 13 x 19in (33 x 48.5cm).
$2,300–2,800 *Lel*

Phil Esposito's 1970 Stanley Cup winning jersey, with yellow 'A' on the front above Bruins shield.
$7,500–8,250 *Lel*

Bobby Orr's game-used 1972–3 jersey, with Bruins shield on front, captain's 'A' below left shoulder, autographed in black, 'Boston Bruins 50th Anniversary' patch on sleeve '4'.
$17,250–19,000 *Lel*

A Boston Bruins scrapbook, with 24 signatures including Lynn Patrick, Milt Schmidt, and Woody Dumart, 1949–50 and 1950–51.
$900–1,000 *Lel*

r. Celtics Time Out horn, 1950s, 20in (51cm) long.
$2,500–2,750 *Lel*

The 110 volt horn was first installed on the scorer's table in the 1950s. It was removed several years ago but, due to popular demand, was put back into action during the 1990s.

Sporting Guns

A 15 bore percussion double-barrelled shotgun, by Thomas Boss, ramrod with brass extractor and cover, 1849, damascus barrels 30in (76cm) long, in a mahogany case with accessories.
$1,000–1,200 *EP*

A percussion revolving sporting rifle, the rebrowned octagonal barrel engraved 'Samuel Nock, London', with long spur hammer, figured walnut full stock with patchbox, c1855, barrel 28in (71cm) long.
$2,500–2,800 *WSA*

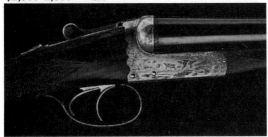

A flintlock fowling piece with left-hand lock, by Nock, Jover & Green, London, with twist barrel of Spanish style, inlaid with silver 'spider' foresight and gold-lined vent, engraved breech-tang, signed flat bevelled lock, figured walnut half-stock with pineapple chequered grip, engraved iron butt-plate, trigger-guard with acorn finial, horn fore-end cap, and original wooden ramrod, c1775, barrel 37¼in (94.5cm) long.
$1,300–1,450 *S(S)*

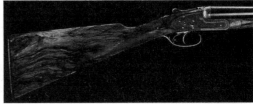

A 12 bore self-opening side-lock non-ejector gun, by J. Purdey & Sons, No. 12342, mid-extension, engraved frame and locks with bouquet and scroll c1886, Whitworth steel barrels 30in (76cm) long.
$9,600–10,400 *S*

l. A lightweight kell engraved 12 bore game model boxlock ejector gun, by John Wilkes, No. 14041, the with engraved scroll-backed frame, 1937, barrels 26½in (67cm) long.
$2,000–2,600 *S(S)*

Tennis

A set of ladies' tennis clothing, 1950s.
$90–115 *MUL*

A silver-plated tennis racket inkwell, c1900, 5in (12.5cm) long.
$250–280 *MUL*

A Hagenauer bronze figure of a male tennis player, c1925, 3½in (9cm) high.
$2,000–2,500 *CSK*

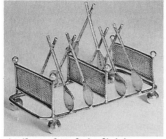

A silver-plated six-division novelty toastrack, c1902, 5¾in (14.5cm) long.
$1,400–1,600 *CSK*

r. A silver trophy, by Mappin Bros, London, inscribed '1863 Wimbledon, won by de Gendre', hallmarked, 8¼in (21cm) high.
$2,200–2,600 *CNY*

An oak free-standing 48 racket tennis press, with individually sprung spacing for each racket and circular wooden handles at either end for tension, c1910, 57in (145cm) long.
$5,600–6,400 *CSK*

GLOSSARY

We have defined here some of the terms that you will come across in this book. If there are any terms or technicalities you would like explained or you feel should be included in future, please let us know.

abalone: A marine snail whose shell is used for ornament or decoration.

abrash: Tone differences within the colour of a rug, normally due to variations in the dyes.

acid engraving: Technique of decorating glass by coating it in resin, incising a design and exposing the revealed areas to hydrochloric acid fumes.

acid-gilding: 19thC technique for decorating pottery whereby the surface is etched with hydrofluoric acid and the low-relief pattern gilded.

acorn knop: Wine glass stem in the shape of an upturned acorn – the cup uppermost.

agate ware: 18thC pottery, veined or marbled to resemble the mineral agate.

air-beaded: Glass containing bubbles of air, like strings of beads.

air-twist: Helical decoration in the stem of wine glasses, developed 1740-70, in which an air bubble in the glass is drawn out and twisted to form complex spirals.

albarello: A pottery vessel, sometimes of hour-glass shape, used for storing pharmaceutical ingredients.

ale glass: Drinking glass with tall stem and tall narrow bowl, capacity 3-4 fluid ounces, used for strong beer, sometimes decorated with barley ears and hops, 18thC.

all-bisque doll: One with body and limbs as well as head of biscuit-fired ceramic.

amboyna: Yellowish-brown burred wood imported from the West Indies and used as a veneer.

American Victorian: The period from 1830-1900 that incorporates several styles of furniture: Victorian, Gothic, Victorian rococo, Victorian renaissance and Eastlake.

Americana: Antiques and collectables that reflect the growth and character of American culture.

Amish: Followers of Jacob Amman who made up a religious sect that settled in Pennsylvania during the 1700s. They produce quilts and other simply designed handicrafts that are highly prized.

anchor escapement: Said to have been invented c1670 by Robert Hooke or William Clement. A type of escape mechanism shaped like an anchor, which engages at precise intervals with the toothed escape wheel. The anchor permits the use of a pendulum (either long or short) and gives greater accuracy than was possible with the verge escapement (qv).

arabesque: Scrolling foliate decoration.

architect's table: Table or desk, the top of which adjusts to provide an angled working area.

Arita: Name of a district in Hizen province on the island of Kyushu in south-west Japan, famous for its porcelain manufacture. Generic term for blue and white or polychrome porcelain produced for the Japanese home market.

armoire: A large French cupboard or wardrobe, usually of monumental character.

associated: Term used in antiques, in which one part of an item is of the same design but not originally made for it. *See marriage.*

astrolabe: Ancient instrument used to calculate the position of the stars and other measurements.

Aubusson: French town, centre of production of tapestries and tapestry-weave carpets since 17thC although formal workshops were not established until c1743.

automaton: Any moving toy or decorative object, usually powered by a clockwork mechanism.

ball-jointed doll: One with ball-jointed limbs, able to swivel in all directions, as opposed to stiff jointed.

baluster stem: Glass with a swelling stem, like an architectural baluster: 'true' if the thicker swelling is beneath, 'inverted' if above. From late 17thC.

barley-twist: Form of turning, popular in the late 17thC which resembles a spiral of traditional barley sugar.

basalt(es): Black stoneware with a smooth, stone-like finish; perfected by Josiah Wedgwood.

Bauhaus: An influential art school established in Germany in 1919. The name is now synonymous with design style.

bébé: Type of French doll made by Bru and others in the latter half 19thC, modelled on idealised children of 8-12 years of age.

bezel: The ring, usually brass, surrounding the dial of a clock and securing the glass dial cover.

bianco-sopra-bianco: Literally white on white, used in ceramics to describe an opaque white pattern painted on an off-white background.

bisque: French term for biscuit ware, or unglazed porcelain.

bladed knop: Knop with a concave outward curve, culminating in a sharp edge.

bluejohn: A blue or purple variety of fluorspar mined in Derbyshire, used for vases, tazze, small ornaments etc.

bombé: Outswelling, curving or bulging. Term used to describe a chest with a bulging front. In fashion from Louis XV period.

bonheur du jour: Small French writing table of delicate proportions with a raised back comprising a cabinet or shelves.

boteh: A stylised floral bush similar to a Paisley design found on rugs.

bowfront: An outwardly curving front.

bracket clock: Originally a 17thC clock which had to be set high up on a bracket because of the length of the weights; now sometimes applied to any mantel or table clock.

buffet: A piece of furniture comprising a number of open shelves.

bureau bookcase: Bureau with a glazed-fronted bookcase fitted above it.

bureau cabinet: Bureau with a solid-doored or mirrored cabinet fitted above it, often containing further fitted cupboards and drawers.

bureau de dame: Writing desk of delicate appearance and designed for use by ladies. Usually raised above slender cabriole legs and with one or two external drawers.

bureau-plat: French writing table with a flat top and drawers in the frieze.

cabaret set: A tea set on a tray for three or more people.

caddy: A container for tea, usually silver but also ceramic, wood or enamel. Wooden caddies are usually fitted with two compartments and contain a spoon and glass bowl for blending two types of leaf.

calamander: A hardwood, imported from Sri Lanka (of the same family as ebony), used in the Regency period for making small articles of furniture, as a veneer and for crossbanding.

camaieu: Porcelain decoration using different tones of a single colour.

cameo glass: Two or more layers of coloured glass in which the top layer/s are then cut or etched away to create a multi-coloured design in relief. An ancient technique popular with Art Nouveau glassmakers in the early 20thC.

candle slide: Small wooden slide designed to carry a candlestick.

Carlton House desk: A distinct type of writing desk which has a raised back with drawers extending forward at the sides to create an 'enclosed' central writing area. Named after the Prince Regent's London home.

carousel figures: Horses and other animals from fairground carousels or roundabouts, usually classified as either 'jumpers' or 'standers'.

cartouche: An ornate tablet or shield surrounded by scrollwork and foliage, often bearing an inscription, monogram or coat-of-arms.

caryatid: Strictly a female figure used as a support in place of a column, but frequently used to describe a figure of either sex. *See term.*

cased glass: One layer of glass, often coloured, sandwiched between two plain glass layers or vice versa, the outer layer engraved to create a decorative effect. An ancient technique revived in the 19thC. *See cameo glass and overlay.*

Castelli: Maiolica from the Abruzzi region of Italy, noted for delicate landscapes painted by members of the Grue family.

celadon: Chinese stonewares with an opaque grey-green glaze, first made in the Sung dynasty and still made today, principally in Korea.

cellaret: Lidded container on legs designed to hold wine. The interior is often divided into sections for individual bottles.

centrepiece: An ornament, usually decorative rather than functional, designed to occupy the centre of a dining table.

chaise longue: An elongated chair, the seat long enough to support the sitter's legs.

champlevé: Enamelling on copper or bronze, similar to *cloisonné*, in which a glass paste is applied to the hollowed-out design, fired and ground smooth.

chapter ring: The circular ring on a clock dial on which the hours and minutes are engraved, attached or painted.

character doll: One with a naturalistic face, especially laughing, crying, pouting etc.

character jug: 20thC earthenware jugs and sometimes mugs, depicting a popular character, such as a politician, general, jockey or actor. Developed from the Toby jug of the 19thC.

chesterfield: Type of large, overstuffed, button-backed sofa introduced in the late 19thC.

chiffonier: Generally a twin door cupboard with one or two drawers above and surmounted by shelves.

Chinese export porcelain: 16th–18thC wares made in China specifically for export and often to European designs.

Chinese Imari: Chinese imitations of Japanese blue, red and gold painted Imari wares, made from the early 18thC.

chinoiserie: The fashion, prevailing in the late 18thC, for Chinese-style ornamentation on porcelain, wallpapers and fabrics, furniture and garden architecture.

chryselephantine: Originally a combination of gold and ivory, but now a term used for Art Deco statues made of ivory and a metal, usually bronze.

cistern tube: A mercury tube fitted into stick barometers, the lower end of which is sealed into a boxwood cistern.

claw-and-ball foot: A carved foot, shaped like a ball held in a talon, or claw.

cleat: A strip of wood attached to the edge of a flat surface across the grain for neatness and extra strength.

clock garniture: A matching group of clock and vases or candelabra made for the mantel shelf. Often highly ornate.

cloisonné: Enamelling on metal with divisions in the design separated by lines of fine metal wire. A speciality of the Limoges region of France in the Middle Ages, and of Chinese craftsmen to the present day.

cocuswood: Wood from a tropical American tree, used for inlay, turning, musical instruments etc.

coffer: In strict definition a coffer is a travelling trunk which is banded with metalwork and covered with leather or other material. However, the word tends to be used quite freely to describe various kinds of chests without drawers.

coiffeuse: A French term for a dressing table.

Colonial: An American object made in the style of the period when the country consisted of 13 Colonies, usually of the 17thC or 18thC.

Commedia dell'Arte: Figures from traditional Italian theatre (Harlequin, Columbine, Scaramouche, Pantaloon) often depicted in 18thC porcelain groups.

cordial glass: Smaller version of a wine glass, with a thick stem, heavy foot and small bowl; evolved in the 17thC for strong drink.

coromandel: Imported wood from the Coromandel coast of India, of similar blackish appearance to calamander and used from c1780 for banding, and for small pieces of furniture.

country furniture: General term for furniture made by provincial craftsmen; cottage furniture and especially that made of pine, oak, elm and the fruitwoods.

countwheel: A wheel with segments cut out of the edge or with pins fitted to one face, which controls the striking of a clock. Also known as a locking plate.

credenza: Used today to describe a type of side cabinet which is highly decorated and shaped. Originally it was an Italian sideboard used as a serving table.

crested china: Porcelain decorated with colourful heraldic crests, first made by Goss but, by 1900, being produced in quantity by manufacturers throughout the UK and in Germany.

cup-and-cover: Carved decoration found on the bulbous turned legs of some Elizabethan furniture.

cut glass: Glass carved with revolving wheels and abrasive to create sharp-edged facets that reflect and refract light so as to sparkle and achieve a prismatic (rainbow) effect. Revived in Bohemia in the 17thC and common until superseded by pressed glass for utilitarian objects.

Cymric: The trade name used by Liberty & Co for a mass-produced range of silverware, inspired by Celtic art, introduced in 1899 and often incorporating enamelled pictorial plaques.

deadbeat escapement: A type of anchor escapement (qv) possibly invented by George Graham and used in precision pendulum clocks.

Delft: Dutch tin-glazed earthenwares named after the town of Delft, the principal production centre, from the 16thC onwards. Similar pottery made in England from the late 16thC is also termed 'delft' or 'delftware'.

Della Robbia: Florentine Renaissance sculptor who invented technique of applying vitreous glaze to terracotta; English art pottery made at Birkenhead, late 19thC, in imitation of his work.

Deutsche Blumen: Painted naturalistic flowers, single or in bunches, used as porcelain decoration at Meissen in the mid-18thC.

diaper: Surface decoration composed of repeated diamonds or squares, often carved in low relief.

die-stamping: Method of mass-producing a design on metal by machine which passes sheet metal between a steel die and a drop hammer. Used for forming toys as well as stamping cutlery etc.

drop-in seat: Upholstered chair seat which is supported on the seat rails but which can be lifted out independently.

écuelle: 17th and 18thC vessel, usually of silver, but also of ceramic, for serving soup. Has a shallow, circular bowl with two handles and a domed cover. It often comes complete with a stand.

electroplate: The process of using electrical current to coat a base metal or alloy with silver, invented 1830s and gradually superseding Sheffield plate.

enamel: Coloured glass, applied to metal, ceramic or glass in paste form and then fired for decorative effect.

entablature: The part of a structure which surmounts a column and rests on the capital; the cornice, frieze and architrave.

EPNS: Electroplated nickel silver; ie nickel alloy covered with a layer of silver using the electroplate process.

escapement: The means or device which regulates the release of the power of a timepiece to its pendulum or balance.

fairings: Mould-made figure groups in cheap porcelain, produced in great quantity in the 19th and 20thC, especially in Germany; often humorous or sentimental. So called because they were sold, or given as prizes, at fairs.

famille jaune: 'Yellow family'; Chinese porcelain vessels in which yellow is the predominant ground colour.

famille noire: 'Black family'; Chinese porcelain in which black is the predominant ground colour.

famille rose: 'Pink family'; Chinese porcelain decoration with prominent enamel of pink to purple tones.

famille verte: 'Green family'; Chinese porcelain with a green enamel overglaze, laid over yellows, blues, purples and iron red.

fauteuil: French open-armed drawing room chair.

fiddleback: Descriptive of a particular grain of mahogany veneer which resembles the back of a violin.

fielded panel: A panel with bevelled or chamfered edges.

filigree: Lacy openwork of silver or gold thread, produced in large quantities since end 19thC.

flag bottom chair: Chair made with a rush seat.

flatware (1): Collective name for flat pottery, such as plates, dishes and saucers, as opposed to cups, vases and bowls.

flatware (2): cutlery.

flow blue: A process used principally after 1840, in which flowing powder is added to the dye used in blue and white transferware so that the blue flows beyond the edges of the transfer, rendering the pattern less sharply defined. Items using this process were made primarily for the American market.

fluted: A border that resembles a scalloped edge, used as a decoration on furniture, glass, silver and porcelain items.

frigger: A decorative but impractical object created from 'end of day' glass to show off the glass blower's skill. Items include ships, pipes, hats, musical instruments etc.

frosted glass: Glass with a surface pattern made to resemble frost patterns or snow-crystals; common on pressed glass vessels for serving cold confections.

fusee: 18thC clockwork invention; a cone shaped drum, linked to the spring barrel by a length of gut or chain. The shape compensates for the declining strength of the mainspring thus ensuring constant timekeeping.

gadroon: A border or ornament comprising radiating lobes of either curved or straight form. Used from the late Elizabethan period.

gilding: Process of applying thin gold foil to a surface. There are two methods. Oil gilding involves the use of linseed oil and is applied directly onto the woodwork. Water gilding requires the wood to be painted with gesso. The term is also used in ceramics, glass etc.

girandole: A carved and gilt candle sconce incorporating a mirror, often of assymetrical design.

Glasgow School: A term used to describe the style developed in the late 19thC by Charles Rennie Mackintosh and his followers, a simplified linear form of Art Nouveau highly influential on Continental work of the period.

grisaille: Monochrome decoration, usually grey, used on ceramics and furniture during the 18th and 19thC.

guéridon: A small circular table designed to carry some form of lighting.

gul: From the Persian word for flower – usually used to describe a geometric flowerhead on a rug.

hallmark: Collective term for all the marks found on silver or gold consisting of assay office, quality, date and maker's marks; sometimes the term is used only of the assay office mark.

hand-pressed: Any glass object made in a hand-operated press instead of a machine press.

hard paste: True porcelain made of china stone (petuntse) and kaolin; the formula was long known to, and kept secret by, Chinese potters but only discovered in the 1720s in Meissen, Germany, from where it spread to the rest of Europe and the Americas. Recognized by its hard, glossy feel.

hardwood: One of two basic categories of timber. The hardwoods are the broad-leaved deciduous trees which replace their leaves every year. *See also softwood.*

harewood: Sycamore which has been stained a greenish colour. It is used mainly as an inlay and was known as silverwood in the 18thC.

Hausmaler: The German term for an independent painter or workshop specializing in the decoration of faience, porcelain or glass blanks.

herati: An overall repeating design of a flowerhead within a lozenge issuing small leaves. Used in descriptions of rugs.

Hirado: Japanese porcelain with figure and landscape painting in blue on a white body, often depicting boys at play, made exclusively for the Lords of Hirado, near Arita, mid-18th to mid-19thC.

Imari: Export Japanese porcelain of predominantly red, blue and gold decoration which, although made in Arita, is called Imari after the port from which it was shipped.

indianische Blumen: Indian flowers; painting on porcelain in the Oriental style, especially on mid-18thC Meissen.

intaglio: Incised gem-stone, often set in a ring, used in antiquity and during the Renaissance as a seal. Any incised decoration; the opposite of carving in relief.

ironstone: Stoneware, patented 1813 by Charles James Mason, containing ground glassy slag, a by-product of iron smelting, for extra strength.

Jacobite glass: Wine glasses engraved with symbols of the Jacobites (supporters of Prince Charles Edward Stuart's claim to the English throne). Genuine examples date from 1746 to 1788. Countless later copies and forgeries exist.

jadeite: A type of jade, normally the best and most desirable.

Jugendstil: German Art Nouveau style.

Kakiemon: Family of 17thC Japanese porcelain decorators who produced wares decorated with flowers and figures on a white ground in distinctive colours: azure, yellow, turquoise and soft red. Widely imitated in Europe.

kelim: Flat woven rugs lacking a pile; also the flat woven fringe used to finish off the ends of a pile carpet.

kiku mon: Japanese stylised chrysanthemum.

knop: Knob, protuberance or swelling in the stem of a wine glass, of various forms which can be used as an aid to dating and provenance.

kovsh: A Russian vessel used for measuring drink, often highly decorated for ornamental purposes from the late 18thC.

kraak porselein: A Dutch term for porcelain raided from Portuguese ships, used to describe the earliest Chinese export porcelain.

krater: An Ancient Greek vessel for mixing water and wine in which the mouth is always the widest part.

Kufic: Arabic angular script – used in rugs to refer to stylised geometric calligraphy.

lambing chair: Sturdy chair with a low seat frequently over a drawer or cupboard, traditionally used by shepherds at lambing time. It has tall enclosed sides for protection against draughts.

Laub und Bandelwerk: Literally 'leaf and strapwork – the German term for baroque cartouches that surround a pictorial reserve on porcelain pieces.

linenfold: Carved decoration which resembles folded linen.

lorgnette: A pair of opera glasses, or spectacles, mounted on a handle.

made up: A piece of furniture that has been put together from parts of other pieces of furniture. *See marriage.*

maiolica: Tin-glazed earthenware produced in Italy from the 15thC to the present day.

majolica: A heavily-potted, moulded earthenware covered in transparent glazes in distinctive, often sombre colours, developed by the Minton factory in the mid 19thC.

marriage: The joining together of two unrelated parts to form one piece of furniture. *See associated and made up.*

marvering: An ancient technique where hot threads of softened glass are rolled over a flat surface to smooth and fuse the glass and to fix trailed decoration.

mater: A thick round plate on an astrolabe (qv), with a shaped projection to take the suspension ring and which houses discs of brass engraved with scales.

mihrab: Prayer niche with a pointed arch; the motif which distinguishes a prayer rug from other types.

Meiping: Chinese for cherry blossom, used to describe a tall vase, with high shoulders, small neck and narrow mouth, used to display flowering branches.

millefiori: Multi-coloured, or mosaic, glass, made since antiquity by fusing a number of coloured glass rods into a cane and cutting off thin sections; much used to ornament paperweights.

netsuke: Japanese carved toggles made to secure sagemono ('hanging things') to the obi (waist belt) from a cord; usually of ivory, lacquer, silver or wood, from the 16thC.

niello: A black metal alloy or enamel used for filling in engraved designs on silverware.

nulling (knulling): Decorative carving in the form of irregular fluting which is usually found on early oak furniture.

oinochoe: In ancient times, a small jug with handles.

okimono: A small, finely carved Japanese ornament.

ormolu: Strictly, gilded bronze but sometimes used loosely for any yellow metal. Originally used for furniture handles and mounts but, from the 18thC, for inkstands, candlesticks, clock cases etc.

overlay: In cased glass, the top layer, usually engraved to reveal a different coloured layer beneath.

overmantel: Area above the shelf on a mantelpiece, often consisting of a mirror in an ornate frame, or some architectural feature in wood or stone.

overstuffed: Descriptive of upholstered furniture where the covering extends over the frame of the seat.

ovolo (1): Moulding of convex quarter-circle section. Sometimes found around the edges of drawers to form a small overlap onto the carcase.

ovolo (2): Small oval convex moulding chiefly used in repetition.

palmette: In rugs, a cross-section through a stylised flowerhead or fruit.

papier mâché: Moulded paper pulp, suitable for japanning and polishing, used for small articles such as trays, boxes, tea caddies and coasters.

Parisienne doll: French bisque head fashion doll with a stuffed kid leather body, made by various manufacturers between 1860 and 1890.

pate: Crown of a doll's head on to which the wig or hair is attached, usually of cork in the better quality dolls.

pâte-sur-pâte: 19thC Sèvres porcelain technique, much copied, of applying coloured clay decoration to the body before firing.

percussion lock: Early 19thC firearm, one of the first to be fired by the impact of a sharp-nosed hammer on the cartridge cap.

pewter: Alloy of tin and lead; the higher the tin content the higher the quality; sometimes with small quantities of antimony added to make it hard with a highly polished surface.

pier glass: Mirror designed to be fixed to the pier, or wall, between two tall window openings, often partnered by a matching pier table. Made from mid-17thC.

plate: Old fashioned term, still occasionally used, to describe gold and silver vessels; not to be confused with 'Sheffield plate', or plated vessels generally, in which silver is fused to a base metal alloy.

pole screen: Small adjustable screen mounted on a pole and designed to stand in front of an open fire to shield a lady's face from the heat.

portrait doll: One modelled on a well known figure.

poupard: Doll without legs, often mounted on a stick; popular in 19thC.

poured wax doll: One made by pouring molten wax into a mould.

powder flask: Device for measuring out a precise quantity of priming powder and made to be suspended from a musketeer's belt or bandolier and often ornately decorated. Sporting flasks are often made of antler and carved with hunting scenes.

powder horn: Cow horn hollowed out, blocked at the wide end with a wooden plug and fitted with a measuring device at the narrow end, used by musketeers for dispensing a precise quantity of priming powder.

pressed glass: Early 19thC invention, exploited rapidly in America, whereby mechanical pressure was used to form glassware in a mould.

puzzle jug: Type of jug made from the 17thC, especially in delft ware, with a syphon system and several spouts, none of which will pour unless the others are blocked.

pyx (pyxis): A small box used in ancient times to hold medicines.

quarter clock: A clock which strikes the quarter and half hours as well as the full hours.

quarter-veneered: Four consecutively cut, and therefore identical, pieces of veneer laid at opposite ends to each other to give a mirrored effect.

rack: Tall superstructure above a dresser.

register plate: The scale of a barometer against which the mercury level is read.

regulator: Clock of great accuracy, thus sometimes used for controlling or checking other timepieces.

rete: A skeletal brass disc which is placed over the plates of an astrolabe (qv) and which can be rotated to indicate the position of various stars.

rocaille: Shell and rock motifs found in rococo work.

rosette: A round floral design ornament.

roemer: Originally 16th/17thC German wide bowled wine glass on a thick stem, decorated with prunts, on a base of concentric glass coils, often in green glass (Waldglas). Widely copied throughout Europe in many forms.

sabre leg: Elegant curving leg associated with furniture of the Regency period but first appearing near the end of the 18thC. Also known as Trafalgar leg.

satinwood: A moderately hard, yellow or light brown wood, with a very close grain, found in central and southern India, Coromandel, Sri Lanka and the West Indies.

seal bottle: Wine bottles with an applied glass medallion or seal personalised with the owner's name, initials, coat-of-arms or a date. Produced from the early 17th to the mid-19thC when bottles were relatively expensive.

SFBJ: Société Française de Fabrication de Bébés et Jouets; association of doll makers founded 1899 by the merger of Jumeau, Bru and others.

shagreen: Skin of shark or ray fish, often used on sword grips and scabbards.

Sheraton revival: Descriptive of furniture produced in the style of Sheraton when his designs gained revived interest during the late Victorian and Edwardian period.

siphon tube: A U-shaped tube fitted into wheel barometers where the level of mercury in the short arm is used to record air pressure.

six-hour dial: One with only six divisions instead of twelve, often with the hours 1–6 in Roman numerals and 7–12 superimposed in Arabic numerals.

soft paste: An artificial porcelain made with the addition of ground glass, bone-ash or soapstone. Used by most European porcelain manufacturers during the 18thC. Recognized by its soft, soapy feel.

softwood: One of two basic categories of timber. The softwoods are conifers which generally have leaves in the form of needles, usually evergreen. *See hardwood.*

spandrel: Decoration in the corner of the field.

spelter: Zinc treated to look like bronze and much used as an inexpensive substitute in Art Nouveau appliqué ornament and Art Deco figures.

standish: Term for a pre-18thC silver inkstand.

stirrup cup: Silver cup, without handles, so-called because it was served, containing a suitable beverage, to huntsmen in the saddle, prior to their moving off. Often made in the shape of an animal's head.

sympiesometer: An instrument that uses a gas and coloured oil to record air pressure.

table ambulante: A small table which can be easily moved.

table clock: Early type of domestic clock, some say the predecessor of the watch, in which the dial is set horizontally: often of drum shape.

tallboy: An American term for a chest-on-chest.

tazza: Wide but shallow bowl on a stem with a foot; ceramic and metal tazzas were made in antiquity and the form was revived by Venetian glassmakers in 15thC. Also made in silver from 16thC.

tea kettle: Silver, or other metal, vessel intended for boiling water at the table. Designed to sit over a spirit lamp, it sometimes had a rounded base instead of flat.

teapoy: Piece of furniture in the form of a tea caddy on legs, with a hinged lid opening to reveal caddies, mixing bowl and other tea drinking accessories.

tear: Tear-drop shaped air bubble in the stem of an early 18thC wine glass, from which the air-twist evolved.

term: A pillar or pedestal terminating in a human head or torso, usually armless. *See caryatid.*

tester: Wooden canopy over a bedstead supported on either two or four posts. May extend fully over the bed, known as a full tester, or only over the bedhead half, known as a half tester.

tête à tête: A tea set for two people.

thuyawood: A reddish-brown wood with distinctive small 'bird's eye' markings, imported from Africa and used as a veneer.

tin glaze: Glassy opaque white glaze of tin oxide; re-introduced to Europe in 14thC by Moorish potters; the characteristic glaze of delftware, faience and maiolica.

touch: Maker's mark stamped on much, but not all, early English pewter. Their use was strictly controlled by the Pewterer's Company of London: early examples consist of initials, later ones are more elaborate and pictorial, sometimes including the maker's address.

transfer-printed: Ceramic decoration technique perfected mid-18thC and used widely thereafter for mass-produced wares. An engraved design is transferred onto a slab of glue or gelatin (a bat), which was then laid over the body of the vessel, leaving an outline. This was sometimes coloured in by hand.

trefoil: Three-cusped figure which resembles a symmetrical three-lobed leaf or flower.

tsuba: Guard of a Japanese sword, usually consisting of an ornamented plate.

Tudric: A range of Celtic-inspired Art Nouveau pewter of high quality, designed for mass-production by Archibald Knox and others, and retailed through Liberty & Co.

tulipwood: Yellow-brown wood with reddish stripe imported from Central and South America used as a veneer, inlay and crossbanding. Related to rosewood and kingwood.

tyg: A mug with three or more handles.

vargueño: A Spanish cabinet with a fall front enclosing drawers.

Venetian glass: Fine soda glass and coloured glass blown and pinched into highly ornamented vessels of intricate form, made in Venice, and widely copied from 15thC.

verge escapement: Oldest form of escapement, found on clocks as early as AD1300 and still in use in 1900. Consisting of a bar (the verge) with two flag-shaped pallets that rock in and out of the teeth of the crown or escape wheel to regulate the movement.

vernier scale: A short scale added to the traditional 3in(7.5cm) scale on stick barometers to give more precise readings than had previously been possible.

verre églomisé: Painting on glass. Often the reverse side of the glass is covered in gold or silver leaf through which a pattern is engraved and then painted black.

vesta case: Ornate flat case of silver or other metal for carrying vestas, an early form of match. From mid-19thC.

vitrine: French display cabinet which is often of bombé or serpentine outline and ornately decorated with marquetry and ormolu.

waxjack: A stand for holding a coil of sealing wax, first used mid-1700s.

WMF: Short for the German Württembergische Metallwarenfabrik, one of the principal producers of Art Nouveau silver and silver-plated objects, early 20thC.

wrythen: Twisted or plaited.

DIRECTORY OF SPECIALISTS

If you wish to be included in next year's directory, or if you have a change of address or telephone number, please advise Miller's Advertising Department by April 1998. We would advise readers to make contact by telephone before a visit, therefore avoiding a wasted journey.

ANTIQUITIES

Dorset

Ancient & Gothic,
PO Box 356,
Christchurch
BH23 2YD
Tel: 01202 478592

ARCHITECTURAL ANTIQUES

Cheshire

Nostalgia,
61 Shaw Heath,
Stockport
SK3 8BH
Tel: 0161 477 7706

Devon

Ashburton Marbles,
Grate Hall, North Street,
Ashburton TQ13 7QD
Tel: 01364 653189

Dorset

Dorset Reclamation,
Cow Drove, Bere Regis,
Wareham BH20 7JZ
Tel: 01929 472200

Kent

Posh Tubs,
Moriati's Workshop,
High Halden,
Ashford TN26 3LZ
Tel: 01233 850155

Lincolnshire

Britannia Brass Fittings,
Hemswell Antiques Centre,
Caenby Corner Estate,
Hemswell Cliff,
Gainsborough DN21 5TJ
Tel: 01482 227300

Surrey

Drummonds of Bramley,
Birtley Farm,
Horsham Road,
Bramley,
Guildford GU5 0LA
Tel: 01483 898766

ARMS & MILITARIA

Lincolnshire

Garth Vincent,
The Old Manor House,
Allington,
Nr Grantham
NG32 2DH
Tel: 01400 281358

Surrey

West Street Antiques,
63 West Street,
Dorking RH4 1BS
Tel: 01306 883487

Sussex

Wallis & Wallis,
West St Auction Galleries,
Lewes BN7 2NJ
Tel: 01273 480208

West Midlands

Weller & Dufty Ltd,
141 Bromsgrove Street,
Birmingham B5 6RQ
Tel: 0121 692 1414

Yorkshire

Andrew Spencer
Bottomley,
The Coach House,
Thongs Bridge,
Holmfirth HD7 2TT
Tel: 01484 685234

BAROGRAPHS

Somerset

Richard Twort,
Tel: 01934 641900

BAROMETERS

Berkshire

Walker & Walker,
Halfway Manor,
Halfway, Nr Newbury
RG20 8NR
Tel: 01488 658693

Devon

Atropos Antiques,
Watersmeet,
Lymebridge,
Hartland EX39 6EA
Tel: 01237 441205
Fax: 01237 441205
*Late of Sevenoaks,
Kent now trading from
Hartland, North Devon.
Tel: 01237 441205*

West Yorkshire

Kym S. Walker,
Foster Clough,
Hebden Bridge
HX7 5QZ
Tel: 01422 882808

Wiltshire

P. A. Oxley,
The Old Rectory,
Cherhill,
Nr Calne SN11 8UX
Tel: 01249 816227

BEDS

Hereford & Worcester

S. W. Antiques,
Abbey Showrooms,
Newlands,
Pershore WR10 1BP
Tel: 01386 555580

Wales

Seventh Heaven,
Chirk Mill, Chirk,
Wrexham County
Borough LL14 5BU
Tel: 01691 772622/773563

BOOKS

Middlesex

John Ives,
5 Normanhurst Drive,
Twickenham
TW1 1NA
Tel: 0181 892 6265
Reference Books

BOXES & TREEN

Berkshire

Mostly Boxes,
93 High Street,
Eton SL4 6AF
Tel: 01753 858470

London

Coromandel,
PO Box 9772,
SW19 3ZG
Tel: 0181 543 9115

Oxfordshire

Otter Antiques,
The Oxford Antique
Trading Co,
40-41 Park End St,
Oxford OX1 1JD
Tel: 0860 263562
Tel/Fax: 01865 407396
*18th & 19th century
tea caddies, writing
boxes, sewing &
jewel boxes.*

Somerset

Alan Stacey,
Boxwood Antique
Restorers,
Appointment only
Tel: 01963 33988
Fax: 01963 32555
*Cabinet making,
polishing, carving and
specialists in tortoiseshell,
ivory and mother-of-pearl
on boxes, caddies and
furniture. See our main
advertisement in Boxes
(colour) section.*

BRITISH ANTIQUE FURNITURE RESTORERS' ASSOCIATION

Avon

M. & S. Bradbury,
The Barn,
Hanham Lane, Paulton,
Bristol BS18 5PF
Tel: 01761 418910

Bedfordshire

Duncan Michael Everitt,
DME Restorations Ltd,
11 Church Street,
Ampthill MK45 2PL
Tel: 01525 405819
Fax: 01525 405819

Berkshire

Graham Childs, Alpha
(Antique) Restorations,
High Street, Compton,
Newbury RG20 6NL
Tel: 01635 578245

Ben R. W. Norris,
Knowl Hill Farm,
Knowl Hill, Kingsclere,
Newbury RG20 4NY
Tel: 01635 297950
Fax: 01635 299851
*Gilding, carving &
architectural woodwork
(ie panelling).*

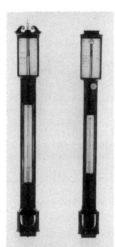

Buckinghamshire

David Hordern,
Restorations (Thame) Ltd,
8/9 Lea Lane, Thame
Road, Long Crendon,
Aylesbury HP18 9RN
Tel: 01844 202213
Fax: 01844 202214
All aspects of furniture restoration.

Cambridgeshire

Ludovic Potts,
Unit 1 & 1A, Haddenham
Business Pk, Station Rd,
Ely CB6 3XD
Tel: 01353 741537
Fax: 01353 741822
Cane and rushwork, gilding.

Robert Williams,
Osborn's Farm,
32 Church Street,
Willingham CB4 5HT
Tel: 01954 260972

Cornwall

Graham Henry Usher,
5 Rose Terrace, Mitchell,
Nr Newquay TR8 5AU
Tel: 01872 510551
*Furniture restoration,
French polishing, veneering,
marquetry – Tunbridge work*

Cumbria

Jeremy Hall,
of Peter Hall & Son,
Danes Road, Staveley,
Nr Kendal LA8 9PL
Tel: 01539 821633
Fax: 01539 821905

Derbyshire

Anthony Allen, Antique
Restorers & Conservators,
The Old Wharf Workshop,
Redmoor Lane, New Mills,
High Peak SK22 3JS
Tel: 01663 745274
*Boulle, marquetry, walnut,
oak, veneering, upholstery.*

Devonshire

Tony Vernon,
15 Follett Road, Topsham,
Exeter EX3 0JP
Tel: 01392 874635

Dorset

Michael Barrington,
The Old Rectory,
Warmwell,
Dorchester DT2 8HQ
Tel/Fax: 01305 852104
*18th & 19th century
furniture, gilding,
upholstery, antique metal
work. Organ case work
and pipe decoration,
mechanical models,
automata and toys.*

Richard Bolton,
Meadow Court,
Athelhampton House,
Dorchester DT2 7LG
Tel: 01305 848346
*All aspects of furniture
restoration. Courses
also available.*

Philip Hawkins,
Glebe Workshop, Semley,
Shaftesbury SP7 9AP
Tel: 01747 830830
Fax: 01747 830830
*Specialising in oak &
country furniture.*

Raymond Robertson,
Tolpuddle Antique
Restorers,
The Stables, Southover
House, Tolpuddle,
Dorchester DT2 7HF
Tel: 01305 848739

Spencer Robertson,
No 4 Burraton Yard,
Pondbury Village,
Dorchester DT1 3GR
Tel: 01305 257377
*Cabinet making, French
polishing. All aspects of
furniture restoration.*

Essex

Clive Beardall,
104B High Street
Maldon CM9 5ET
Tel: 01621 857890

Dick Patterson,
Forge Studio Workshop,
Stour Street,
Manningtree CO11 1BE
Tel: 01206 396222

Gloucestershire

BAFRA,
6 Tetbury Hill, Avening,
Tetbury GL8 8LT
Tel: 01453 835783

Keith Bawden,
Mews Workshops,
Montpelier Retreat,
Cheltenham GL20 2XG
Tel: 01242 230320

Alan Hessel,
The Old Town Workshop,
St George's Close,
Moreton-in-Marsh
GL56 0LP
Tel/Fax: 01608 650026

Stephen Hill,
5 Cirencester Workshops,
Brewery Court,
Cirencester GL7 1JH
Tel: 01285 658817
Fax: 01285 652554

Christian Macduff Hunt,
Hunt & Lomas,
Village Farm Workshops,
Preston Village,
Cirencester GL7 5PR
Tel: 01285 640111

Andrew Lelliott,
6 Tetbury Hill, Avening,
Tetbury GL8 8LT
Tel: 01453 835783
*Furniture and clock
cases, included on the
Conservation Unit
Register of the Museums
and Galleries Commission.*

Laurence Whitfield,
The Old School, Winstone,
Cirencester GL7 7JX
Tel: 01285 821342

Hampshire

Guy Bagshaw,
The Old Dairy,
Plain Farm, East Tisted,
Nr Alton GU34 3RT
Tel: 01420 588362
*Eclectic items, tutored
weekends.*

John Hartley,
The Old Forge,
Village Street, Sheet,
Petersfield GU32 2AQ
Tel: 01730 233792
Fax: 01730 233922

David C. E. Lewry,
Wychelms, 66 Gorran
Avenue, Rowner,
Gosport PO13 0NF
Tel: 01329 286901
Fax: 01329 289964
Furniture.

Hereford & Worcester

Jeremy J. Daffern,
55 The Hamlet,
Stoke Edith HR1 4HQ
Tel: 01432 890740

Hertfordshire

John B.Carr, Charles
Perry Restorations Ltd,
Praewood Farm,
Hemel Hempstead Road,
St Albans AL3 6AA
Tel: 01727 853487
Fax: 01727 846668

Kent

Timothy Akers,
The Forge,
39 Chancery Lane,
Beckenham BR3 6NR
Tel: 0181 650 9179
*Longcase and bracket
clocks, cabinet making,
French polishing.*

Benedict Clegg,
rear of 20 Camden Road,
Tunbridge Wells TN1 2PT
Tel: 01892 548095

Timothy Long Restoration,
St John's Church, London
Road, Dunton Green,
Sevenoaks TN13 2TE
Tel: 01732 743368
Fax: 01732 742206
*Cabinet restoration,
polishing, upholstery, brass
and steel cabinet fittings.*

Bruce Luckhurst, Little
Surrenden Workshops,
Ashford Road, Bethersden,
Ashford TN26 3BG
Tel: 01233 820589
1 year course available.

Lancashire

Eric Smith,
Antique Restorations
The Old Church, Park
Road, Darwen BB3 2LD
Tel: 01254 776222
*Furniture, vernacular
furniture, longcase clocks.
Registered with Museums
& Galleries Commission –
London.*

Lincolnshire

Michael E Czajkowski,
Czajkowski & Son,
96 Tor-o-Moor Road,
Woodhall Spa LN10 6SB
Tel: 01526 352895
*Restoration antique
furniture, clocks and
barometers. UKIC
registered with Museums
and Galleries Commission.*

London

Lucinda Compton,
Compton Hall Restoration,
Unit A 133 Riverside
Business Centre,
Haldane Place,
SW18 4UQ
Tel: 0181 874 0762
*Lacquer, gilding, painted
furniture.*

William Cook,
167 Battersea High Street,
SW11 3JS
Tel: 0171 736 5329

Marie Louise Crawley,
39 Wood Vale, SE23 3DS
Tel/Fax: 0181 516 0002
*Painted furniture, papier
mâché, tôle ware, lacquer
and gilding.*

Robert H. Crawley,
Aberdeen House,
75 St Mary's Road,
Ealing W5 5RH
Tel: 0181 566 5074

Sebastian Giles,
Sebastian Giles Furniture,
11 Junction Mews,
W2 1PN
Tel: 0171 402 1535
Comprehensive.

David Battle,
Phoenix Antique Furniture
Restoration Ltd, 96 Webber
Street, SE1 0QN
Tel: 0171 928 3624

Rodrigo Titian,
Titian Studio, 318 Kensal
Road, W10 5BN
Tel: 0181 960 6247
Fax: 0181 969 6126
*Carving, gilding, lacquer,
painted furniture and
French polishing.
Caning & rushing.*

Clifford Tracy Interiors
Ltd, 6-40 Durnford Street,
Seven Sisters Road,
N15 5NQ
Tel: 0181 800 4773

Andrew White,
16 Arminger Road,
W12 7BB
Tel/Fax: 0181 749 2576

Norfolk

David Bartram,
The Raveningham Centre,
Castell Farm, Beccles
Road, Raveningham
NR14 6NU
Tel: 01508 548721

Michael Dolling,
Church Farm Barns,
Glandford, Holt
NR25 7JR
Tel: 01263 741115

Roderick Nigel Larwood,
The Oaks, Station Road,
Larling, Norwich
NR16 2QS
Tel: 01953 717937

North Somerset

Robert P. Tandy,
Unit 5 Manor Workshops,
West End, Nailsea,
Bristol BS19 2DD
Tel: 01275 856378

Oxfordshire

Alistair Frayling-Cork,
2 Mill Lane,
Wallingford OX10 0DH
Tel: 01491 826221
*Furniture restoration,
stringed instruments,
clock cases and brass
fittings repaired.*

Clive Payne, Unit 4,
Mount Farm, Churchill,
Chipping Norton OX7 6NP
Tel/Fax: 01608 658856

Colin Piper,
Conservation & Restoration,
Highfield House,
The Greens, Leafield,
Witney OX8 5NP
Tel: 01993 878593
*Restoration and
conservation of fine
antique furniture, clocks
and barometers.*

Scotland

Jeremy Gow,
Gow Antique Restoration,
Pitscandly Farm, Forfar,
Angus DD8 3NZ
Tel: 01307 465342
Fax: 01307 462437
*17th & 18thC marquetry
English & Continental.*

William Trist,
135 St Leonard's Street,
Edinburgh EH8 9RB
Tel: 0131 667 7775
Fax: 0131 667 4333
*Furniture, clocks, barometers,
cane & rush seating.*

Shropshire

Richard A. Higgins,
The Old School, Longnor,
Nr Shrewsbury
SY5 7PP
Tel: 01743 718162
Fax: 01743 718022
*All fine furniture, clocks,
movements, dials and
cases, casting, plating,
boulle, gilding, lacquerwork,
carving, period upholstery.*

Somerset

Nicholas Bridges,
20 Newchester Cross,
Merriott TA16 5QJ
Tel: 01460 74672

Michael Durkee,
Castle House, Units 1 & 3,
Bennetts Field Estate,
Wincanton BA9 9DT
Tel: 01963 33884
Fax: 01963 31278
Antique furniture.

Alan Stacey,
Boxwood Antique Restorers,
Appointment only
Tel: 01963 33988
Fax: 01963 32555
*Cabinet making, polishing,
carving and specialists in
tortoiseshell, ivory and
mother-of-pearl on boxes,
caddies and furniture.
See our main advertisement
in Boxes (colour) section.*

Surrey

David J. Booth,
9 High Street, Ewell,
Epsom KT17 1PT
Tel/Fax: 0181 393 5245
*Comprehensive restoration
& large showrooms.*

Michael Hedgecoe,
21 Burrow Hill Green,
Chobham, Woking
GU24 8QS
Tel/Fax: 01276 858206

Stuart Dudley Hobbs,
Meath Paddock,
Meath Green Lane,
Horley RH6 8HZ
Tel: 01293 782349
*Furniture, clocks,
barometers.*

Simon Marsh,
The Old Butchers Shop,
High Street,
Bletchingly RH1 4PA
Tel: 01883 743350
Fax: 01883 744844

Timothy Morris,
Unit 4A, 19 St Peter's St,
South Croydon CR2 7DG
Tel: 0181 681 2992
Furniture & marquetry.

Timothy Naylor,
The Workshop,
2 Chertsey Road, Chobham,
Woking GU24 8NB
Tel: 01276 855122

David A. Sayer,
Courtlands Restoration
Courtlands, Park Road,
Banstead SM7 3EF
Tel: 01737 352429
Fax: 01737 373255

Sussex

William Maxwell Black,
Brookhouse Studios,
Novington Lane,
East Chiltington,
Lewes BN7 3AX
Tel: 01273 890175

Peter G. Casebow,
Pilgrims, Mill Lane,
Worthing BN13 3DE
Tel: 01903 264045
*Marquetry, parquetry,
metalwork.*

Simon Paterson,
74 Double Barn,
Chichester PO18 0RR
Tel: 01243 535393
*Boulle work, marquetry,
clock case & general
restoration & repair.*

Noel Pepperall, Dairy
Lane Cottage, Walberton,
Arundel BN18 0PT
Tel: 01243 551282
Gilding, painted furniture.

Albert Plumb,
31 Whyke Lane,
Chichester PO19 2JS
Tel: 01243 789100/771212
Fax: 01243 788468
Cabinet making, upholstery.

Wiltshire

William Cook,
High Trees House,
Savernake Forest,
Nr Marlborough SN8 4NE
Tel: 01672 513017
Fax: 01672 514455

Worcestershire

Jeffrey Hall,
Malvern Studios,
56 Cowleigh Road,
Malvern WR14 1QD
Tel: 01684 574913
Fax: 01684 569475

Phillip Slater,
93 Hewell Road, Barnt Gn,
Birmingham B45 8NL
Tel/Fax: 0121 445 4942
Inlay work, marquetry.

Yorkshire

Lucinda Compton,
Compton Hall Restoration,
Manor House, Marton-le-
Moor, Ripon HG4 5AT
Tel: 01423 324290
*Lacquer, gilding, painted
furniture.*

Rodney F. Kemble,
16 Crag Vale Terrace,
Glusburn, Nr Keighley
BD20 8QU
Tel: 01535 636954/633702
*Furniture and small
decorative items.*

T. L. Phelps,
Fine Furniture Restoration,
8 Mornington Terrace,
Harrogate HG1 5DH
Tel: 01423 524 604
*Specialist restoration &
conservation.*

CLOCKS & WATCHES

Cheshire

Coppelia Antiques,
Holford Lodge,
Plumley Moor Road,
Plumley WA16 9RS
Tel: 01565 722197
Fax: 01565 722744

Derbyshire

Dragon Antiques,
1 Tamworth Street,
Duffield,
Nr Derby DE56 4ER
Tel: 01332 842332

G. K. Hadfield,
Rock Farm, Chilcote,
Swadlincote DE12 8DQ
Tel: 01827 373466
Fax: 01827 373699

Essex

It's About Time,
863 London Road,
Westcliff-on-Sea SS0 9SZ
Tel/Fax: 01702 72574

Gloucestershire

Gerard Campbell,
Maple House, Market
Place, Lechlade GL7 3AB
Tel: 01367 252267

Jeffrey Formby,
Orchard Cottage,
East Street, Moreton-in-
Marsh GL56 0LQ
Tel: 01608 650558

The Grandfather Clock
Shop, Little House, Sheep
Street, Stow-on-the-Wold
GL54 1AA
Tel/Fax: 01451 830455

Hampshire

Bryan Clisby,
at Andwells Antiques,
High Street, Hartley
Wintney GU9 8DS
Tel: 01252 716436

Humberside

Time & Motion,
1 Beckside,
Beverley HU17 0PB
Tel: 01482 881574

Ireland

Jonathan Beech,
Westport
Tel: 00 353 98 28688

Kent

Gem Antiques,
28 London Road,
Sevenoaks TN13 1AP
Tel: 01732 743540

Gaby Gunst,
140 High Street,
Tenterden TN30 6HT
Tel: 01580 765818

Old Clock Shop,
63 High Street,
West Malling ME19 6NA
Tel: 01732 843246

Derek Roberts,
24-25 Shipbourne Road,
Tonbridge TN10 3DN
Tel: 01732 358986

Lincolnshire

Pinfold Antiques,
62 Rectory Road,
Ruskington NG34 9AD
Tel: 01526 832200

London

The Clock Clinic Ltd,
85 Lower Richmond Road,
SW15 1EU
Tel: 0181 788 1407

Jillings Antiques,
8 Halken Arcade,
Motcomb Street,
SW1X 8JT
Tel: 0171 235 8600
Fax: 0171 235 9898

Pendulum,
King House,
51 Maddox Street,
W1R 9LA
Tel: 0171 629 6606

Pieces of Time,
1-7 Davies Mews,
W1Y 1AR
Tel: 0171 629 2422

Roderick Antiques Clocks,
23 Vicarage Gate,
W8 4AA
Tel: 0171 937 8517

Norfolk

Keith Lawson, LBHI,
Scratby Garden Centre,
Beach Road, Scratby,
Gt Yarmouth NR29 3AJ
Tel: 01493 730950

Oxfordshire

Craig Barfoot,
Tudor House, East
Hagbourne OX11 9LR
Tel: 01235 818968

Scotland

John Mann, Antique
Clocks, Bruntshielbog,
Canonbie, Dumfries,
Galloway DG14 ORY
Tel/Fax: 013873 71827

Shropshire

The Curiosity Shop,
127 Old Street,
Ludlow SY8 1NU
Tel: 01584 875927

Suffolk

Edward Manson,
8 Market Hill,
Woodbridge IP12 4LU
Tel/Fax: 01394 380235

Surrey

Johann Bedingfeld,
1 West Street,
Dorking RH4 1BL
Tel/Fax: 01306 880022

The Clock Shop,
64 Church Street,
Weybridge KT13 8DL
Tel: 01932 840407

Horological Workshops,
204 Worplesdon Road,
Guildford GU2 6UY
Tel: 01483 576496

Sussex

Samuel Orr,
Antique Clocks,
36 High Street,
Hurstpierpoint,
Nr Brighton BN6 9RG
Tel: 01273 832081

USA

Old Timers,
Box 392, Camp Hill,
PA 17001-0392,
Tel: 001 717 761 1908
Fax: 001 717 761 7446

Wiltshire

P. A. Oxley,
The Old Rectory,
Cherhill,
Nr Calne SN11 8UX
Tel: 01249 816227

Allan Smith, Clocks,
Amity Cottage,
162 Beechcroft Road,
Upper Stratton,
Swindon SN2 6QE
Tel: 01793 822977

Yorkshire

Brian Loomes,
Calf Haugh Farm,
Pateley Bridge
HG3 5HW
Tel: 01423 711163

DECORATIVE ARTS

Greater Manchester

A. S. Antiques,
26 Broad Street,
Pendleton,
Salford M6 5BY
Tel: 0161 737 5938

Lincolnshire

Art Nouveau Originals,
Stamford Antiques Centre,
The Exchange Hall, Broad
St, Stamford PE9 1PX
Tel: 01780 762605

London

Artemis Decorative Arts
Ltd, 36 Kensington
Church Street, W8 4BX
Tel/Fax: 0171 376 0377

Cameo Gallery,
38 Kensington Church
Street, W8 4BX
Tel/Fax: 0171 938 4114

The Collector,
9 Church Street,
Marylebone NW8 8EE
Tel: 0171 706 4586
Fax: 0171 706 2948

Galerie Moderne,
10 Halkin Arcade, Motcomb
St, Belgravia SW1X 8JT
Tel: 0171 245 6907
Fax: 0171 245 6341

Pieter Oosthuizen,
c/o 23 Cale Street,
SW3 3QR
Tel: 0171 359 3322
Fax: 0171 376 3852

Rumours Decorative Arts,
10 The Mall, Upper St,
Camden Passage,
Islington N1 0PD
Tel/Fax: 01582 873561

Shapiro & Co,
Stand 380, Gray's Antique
Market, W1Y 1LB
Tel: 0171 491 2710

Wales

Paul Gibbs Antiques,
25 Castle Street, Conwy,
Gwynedd LL32 8AY
Tel: 01492 593429

Warwickshire

Rich Designs,
1 Shakespeare Street,
Stratford-upon-Avon
CV37 6RN
Tel: 01789 261612

Yorkshire

Muir Hewitt,
Halifax Antiques Centre,
Queens Road/ Gibbet St,
Halifax HX1 4LR
Tel: 01422 347377

DOLLS

London

Yesterday Child,
Angel Arcade,
118 Islington High Street,
N1 8EG
Tel: 0171 354 1601

EPHEMERA

Nottinghamshire

T. Vennett-Smith,
11 Nottingham Road,
Gotham NG11 0HE
Tel: 0115 983 0541
Fax: 0115 983 0114

EXHIBITION & FAIR ORGANISERS

Surrey

Cultural Exhibitions Ltd,
8 Meadrow,
Godalming GU7 3HN
Tel: 01483 422562

EXPORTERS

Devon

McBains of Exeter,
Exeter Airport,
Clyst Honiton,
Exeter EX5 2BA
Tel: 01392 366261
Fax: 01392 365572

Essex

F. G. Bruschweiler
(Antiques) Ltd,
41-67 Lower Lambricks,
Rayleigh SS6 7EN.
Tel: 01268 773761

Kent

Charles International
Antiques, The Poplars,
London Road (A20),
Wrotham TN15 7RR
Tel: 01732 823654

Merseyside

Kensington Tower Antiques,
Christchurch, Kensington,
Liverpool L7 2RJ
Tel: 0151 260 9466

Nottinghamshire

Antiques Across the World,
James Alexander Buildings,
London Road/Manvers St,
Nottingham NG2 3AE
Tel: 0115 979 9199
Fax: 0115 958 8314

Meadow Lane Antiques,
Meadow Lane,
Nottingham NG2 3HQ
Tel: 0115 986 7374
Fax: 0115 986 7375

Somerset

MGR Exports, Station
Road, Bruton BA10 0EH
Tel: 01749 812460
Fax: 01749 812882

Sussex

International Furniture
Exporters, The Old Cement
Works, South Heighton,
Newhaven BN9 0HS
Tel: 01273 611251
Fax: 01273 611574

Lloyd Williams Antiques,
Anglo Am Warehouse,
2A Beach Road,
Eastbourne BN22 7EX
Tel: 01323 648661
Fax: 01323 648658

The Old Mint House,
High Street, Pevensey,
Nr Eastbourne BN24 5LF
Tel/Fax: 01323 762337

Wiltshire

North Wilts Exporters,
Farm Hill House,
Brinkworth SN15 5AJ
Tel: 01666 510876

FURNITURE

Avon

Geoffrey Breeze Antiques,
6 George Street,
Bath BA1 2EH
Tel/Fax: 01225 466499

Berkshire

Country Furniture,
79 St Leonards Road,
Windsor SL4 3BZ
Tel/Fax: 01753 830154

Hill Farm Antiques,
Hill Farm, Shop Lane,
Leckhampstead,
Nr Newbury RG16 8QG
Tel: 01488 638541Fax:

The Old Malthouse,
Hungerford RG17 0EG
Tel: 01488 682209

Cumbria

Anthemion, Bridge Street,
Cartmel, Grange-over-
Sands LA11 7SH
Tel: 015395 36295

Derbyshire

Spurrier-Smith Antiques,
28, 30, 39 & 41 Church St,
Ashbourne DE6 1AJ
Tel: 01335 343669/
342198/344377
Fax: 01335 342198

Essex

Vic Hall, Junior Antiques,
41-67 Lower Lambricks,
Rayleigh SS6 7EN
Tel: 01277 624723
Specialising in bars.

France

Antiquites du Roy,
Z. A. de Bellevue,
35235 Thorigne Fouillard
Tel: 00 33 2 99 04 59 81/
Mobile 00 33 6 07 37 01 00
Fax: 00 33 2 99 14 59 47

Gloucestershire

Berry Antiques,
3 High Street, Moreton-
in-Marsh GL56 0AH
Tel: 01608 652929

Buxton

The 34th Buxton Antiques Fair
9th - 16th May 1998
The Pavilion Gardens,
Buxton, Derbyshire

Surrey

The 30th Surrey Antiques Fair
2nd - 5th October 1997
The Civic Hall, Guildford,
Surrey

Established Antiques Fairs
of distinction and high
repute offering pleasure to
both lovers and
collectors of craftsmanship
and fine works of art.
For further information and
complimentary tickets,
please contact:

CULTURAL EXHIBITIONS LTD.
8 Meadrow, Godalming, Surrey
Telephone: Godalming 01483 422562

Hertfordshire

Collins Antiques, Corner
House, Wheathampstead
AL4 8AP
Tel: 01582 833111

Kent

Douglas Bryan, The Old
Bakery, St Davids Bridge,
Cranbrook TN17 3HN
Tel: 01580 713103
Fax: 01580 712407
Oak & Country.

Flower House Antiques,
90 High Street,
Tenterden TN30 6JB
Tel: 01580 763764

Heirloom Antiques,
68 High Street,
Tenterden TN30 6AU
Tel: 01580 765535

Pantiles Spa Antiques,
4, 5, 6 Union House,
The Pantiles,
Tunbridge Wells TN4 8HE
Tel: 01892 541377

Sparks Antiques,
4 Manor Row,
Tenterden TN30 6HP
Tel: 01580 766696

Lincolnshire

Mitchell Simmons
Antiques Ltd,
Hopton Ironworks,
The Wong,
Horncastle LN9 6EB
Tel: 01507 523854
Fax: 01507 523855

Seaview Antiques,
Stanhope Road,
Horncastle LN9 5DG
Tel: 01507 524524
Fax: 01507 526946

London

Adams Rooms
Antiques & Interiors,
18-20 The Ridgeway,
Wimbledon Village
SW19 4QN
Tel: 0181 946 7047
Fax: 0181 946 4858

Butchoff Antiques,
233 Westbourne Grove,
W11 2SE
Tel: 0171 221 8174

Furniture Cave,
533 King's Road,
SW10 0TZ
Tel: 0171 352 4229

Oola Boola,
166 Tower Bridge Road,
SE1 3LS
Tel: 0171 403 0794
Fax: 0171 403 8405

Young, Robert Antiques,
68 Battersea Bridge Rd,
SW11 3AG
Tel: 0171 228 7847
Fax: 0171 585 0489

Middlesex

Phelps, Robert, Ltd,
133-135 St Margaret's Rd,
E Twickenham TW1 1RG
Tel: 0181 892 1778

Northamptonshire

Paul Hopwell,
30 High Street,
West Haddon NN6 7AP
Tel: 01788 510636
Oak & Country

Antiques Across The World,
James Alexander Buildings,
London Rd/Manvers St,
Nottingham NG2 3AE
Tel: 0115 979 9199

Oxfordshire

Key Antiques,
11 Horsefair,
Chipping Norton OX7 5AL
Tel: 01608 643777

Somerset

The Granary Galleries,
Court House, Ash Priors,
Nr Bishops Lydeard,
Taunton TA4 3NQ
Tel: 01823 432402/432816

Suffolk

Hubbard Antiques,
16 St Margaret's Green,
Ipswich IP4 2BS
Tel: 01473 226033
Fax: 01473 233034

Oswald Simpson,
Hall Street,
Long Melford
CO10 9JL
Tel: 01787 377523
Oak & Country.

Wrentham Antiques,
40-44 High Street,
Wrentham NR34 7HB
Tel: 01502 675583
Fax: 01502 675707

Surrey

Albany Antiques,
8-10 London Road,
Hindhead GU26 6AF
Tel: 01428 605528

Dorking Desk Shop,
41 West Street,
Dorking RH4 1BU
Tel: 01306 883327
Desks.

J. Hartley Antiques Ltd,
186 High Street,
Ripley GU23 6BB
Tel: 01483 224318

The Refectory,
38 West Street,
Dorking RH4 1BU
Tel: 01306 742111/
01483 729654
*Oak & Country, –
Refectory Table Specialist.*

Ripley Antiques,
67 High Street,
Ripley GU23 6AN
Tel: 01483 224981

The Chair Set,
84 Hill Rise,
Richmond TW10 6UB
Tel/Fax: 0181 332 6454

Anthony Welling,
Broadway Barn,
High Street, Ripley,
Woking GU23 6AQ
Tel/Fax: 01483 225384
Oak & Country.

Sussex

British Antique Replicas,
School Close,
Queen Elizabeth Avenue,
Burgess Hill RH15 9RX
Tel: 01444 245577

Dycheling Antiques,
34 High Street,
Ditchling BN6 8TA
Tel: 01273 842929
Chairs.

Stable Antiques,
98a High Street,
Lindfield RH16 2HP
Tel: 01444 483662

Wales

Country Antiques (Wales),
Castle Mill, Kidwelly,
Carms SA17 4UU
Tel: 01554 890534
Oak & Country.

Warwickshire

Apollo Antiques Ltd,
The Saltisford,
Birmingham Road,
Warwick CV34 4TD
Tel: 01926 494746
Fax: 01926 401477

Coleshill Antiques,
12-14 High Street,
Coleshill B46 1AZ
Tel: 01675 462931
Fax: 01675 467416
Furniture & Porcelain.

Don Spencer Antiques,
36A Market Place,
Warwick CV34 4SH
Tel: 01926 499857
Fax: 01564 775470
Desks.

West Midlands

Pierre of L.P. Furniture,
Short Acre Street,
Walsall WS2 8HW
Tel: 01922 746764

Martin Taylor Antiques,
140B Tettenhall Road,
Wolverhampton
WV6 0BQ
Tel: 01902 751166
Fax: 01902 746502

GLASS

Avon

Somervale Antiques,
6 Radstock Road,
Midsomer Norton,
Bath BA3 2AJ
Tel: 01761 412686

Norfolk

Brian Watson,
Antique Glass,
The Grange,
Norwich Rd, Wroxham,
Norwich NR12 8RX
Tel: 01603 784177
Fax: 01263 732519

West Midlands

David Hill,
96 Commonside,
Pensnett,
Brierly Hill DY5 4AJ
Tel: 01384 70523
*Reference books on
glass – mail order only.*

IVORY & TORTOISESHELL

Somerset

Alan Stacey,
Boxwood Antique Restorers,
Appointment only
Tel: 01963 33988
Fax: 01963 32555
*Cabinet making,
polishing, carving
and specialists in
tortoiseshell, ivory and
mother-of-pearl on boxes,
caddies and furniture.
See our advertisement
in Boxes section.*

KITCHENALIA

Lincolnshire

Janie Smithson,
Hemswell Antiques
Centre, Caenby Corner
Estate, Hemswell Cliff,
Gainsborough
DN21 5TJ
Tel: 01427 668389

Shropshire

No 7 Antiques,
7 Nantwich Road,
Woore CW3 9SA
Tel: 01630 647118

MARINE

Devon

Great Western Antiques,
Torre Station,
Newton Road,
Torquay
TQ2 5DD
Tel: 01803 200551
Fax: 01803 295115

MARKETS & CENTRES

Hampshire

Surrey & Hampshire
Antiques Ltd,
169 Fleet Road,
Fleet GU13 8PD
Tel: 01252 810833
Units available.

Lincolnshire

Hemswell Antique Centre,
Caenby Corner Estate,
Hemswell Cliff,
Gainsborough
DN21 5TJ
Tel: 01427 668389
Fax: 01427 668935

Shropshire

Old Mill Antiques Centre,
The Antique Dept Store,
Mill Street,
Low Town,
Bridgnorth
WV15 5AG
Tel: 01746 768778
Fax: 01746 768944

Sussex

Church Hill
Antiques Centre,
6 Station Road,
Lewes BN7 2DA
Tel: 01273 474842

MINIATURES

Gloucestershire

Judy & Brian Harden,
PO Box 14,
Bourton-on-the-Water,
Cheltenham
GL54 2YR
Tel/Fax: 01451 810684

MIRRORS

London

Overmantels,
66 Battersea Bridge Rd,
SW11 3AG
Tel: 0171 223 8151

MONEY BOXES

Yorkshire

John & Simon Haley,
89 Northgate,
Halifax
HX6 4NG
Tel: 01422 822148

ORIENTAL PORCELAIN

Devon

Mere Antiques,
13 Fore Street, Topsham,
Exeter EX3 0HF
Tel/Fax: 01392 874224

PACKERS & SHIPPERS

Avon

A. J. Williams, (Shipping),
607 Sixth Avenue,
Central Business Park,
Petherton Road,
Hengrove,
Bristol BS14 9BZ
Tel: 01275 892166
Fax: 01275 891333

Dorset

Alan Franklin Transport,
26 Blackmoor Road,
Verwood BH31 6BB
Tel: 01202 826539
Fax: 01202 827337

London

Featherston Shipping Ltd,
7 Ingate Place
SW8 3NS
Tel: 0171 720 0422
Fax: 0171 720 6330
Fine Art: 0171 720 0422
Moving: 0171 720 8041

Stephen Morris Shipping,
Barpart House,
Kings Cross Freight
Depot, York Way
N1 0UZ
Tel: 0171 713 0080
Fax: 0171 713 0151

Nottinghamshire

Meadow Lane Antiques,
Meadow Lane,
Nottingham NG2 3HQ
Tel: 0115 986 7374
Fax: 0115 986 7375

Sussex

British Antique Replicas,
School Close,
Queen Elizabeth Avenue,
Burgess Hill RH15 9RX
Tel: 01444 245577

Wales

Perpetual Antiques,
Marianne Prysau,
Caerwys, Nr Mold
Tel/Fax: 01352 721036

PAPERWEIGHTS

Cheshire

Sweetbriar Gallery,
Robin Hood Lane,
Helsby WA6 9NH
Tel: 01928 723851

PIANOS

Avon

Piano Export,
Bridge Road,
Kingswood,
Bristol BS15 4PW
Tel: 0117 956 8300

Kent

Period Piano Company,
Park Farm Oast,
Hareplain Road,
Biddenden,
Nr Ashford TN27 8LJ
Tel/Fax: 01580 291393
Specialist dealer and
restorer of period pianos.

Sussex

Sound Instruments,
Worth Farm,
Little Horsted,
Nr Uckfield TN22 5TT
Tel: 01825 750567
Fax: 01825 750566

West Midlands

Moseley Pianos,
Birmingham Piano
Warehouse,
Unit L, 68 Wirley Road,
Witton, Birmingham
B6 7BN
Tel/Fax: 0121 327 2701

PINE

Buckinghamshire

Jack Harness Antiques,
Westfield Farm,
Medmenham,
Nr Marlow SL7 2HE
Tel/Fax: 01491 410691

Cheshire

Mellor Country Pine,
219 Longhurst Lane,
Mellor,
Stockport SK6 5PN
Tel: 0161 426 0333
Fax: 0161 426 0149

Richmond Galleries,
Watergate Building,
New Crane Street,
Chester CH1 4JE
Tel: 01244 317602
Pine, country and
Spanish furniture.

Cleveland

European Pine Imports,
Riverside Park Industrial
Estate, Middlesborough
TS21 1QW
Tel: 01642 584351

Cumbria

Ben Eggleston Antiques,
The Dovecote, Long Marton,
Appleby CA16 6BJ
Tel/Fax: 01768 361849
Trade only

Derbyshire

Tanglewood Antiques,
Tanglewood Mill,
Coke Street,
Derby DE1 1NE
Tel: 01332 346005

Devon

Fine Pine,
Woodland Road,
Habertonford,
Nr Totnes TQ9 7SU
Tel: 01803 732465
Antique pine, country
furniture, decorative
antiques.

Essex

English Rose Antiques,
7 Church Street,
Coggeshall CO6 1TU
Tel: 01376 562683
Large selection of English
and Continental pine
furniture.

Gloucestershire

Amanda House,
The Barns,
Twigworth Court,
Twigworth GL2 9PG
Tel: 01452 731296

Hampshire

Pine Cellars,
39 Jewry Street,
Winchester SO23 8RY
Tel: 01962 777546

Ireland

Delvin Farm Antiques,
Gormonston,
Co Meath
Tel: 00 353 1 8412285
Fax: 00 353 1 841730

Honans Antiques,
Crowe Street,
Gort, County Galway
Tel: 00 353 91 631407

Old Court Pine,
Old Court, Collon,
Co Louth
Tel: 00 353 41 26270
Fax: 00 353 41 26455

Somerville Antiques &
Country Furniture Ltd,
Moysdale, Killanley,
Ballina, Co Mayo
Tel: 00 353 963 6275

Kent

Antique & Design,
The Old Oast,
Hollow Lane,
Canterbury CT1 3TG
Tel: 01227 762871
Fax: 01227 780970

Clive Cowell,
Glassenbury Timber Yard,
Iden Green, Goudhurst,
Cranbrook TN17 2PA
Tel: 01580 212022

The Old Mill,
High Street,
Lamberhurst
TN3 8EQ
Tel: 01892 891196

Up Country,
The Old Corn Stores,
68 St John's Road,
Tunbridge Wells
TN4 9PE
Tel: 01892 523341
Fax: 01892 530382

Lancashire

Enloc Antiques,
96 Keighley Road,
Colne BBH RPH
Tel: 01282 867101
Fax: 01282 867601

Northamptonshire

Country Pine Shop,
Northampton Road,
West Haddon NN6 7AS
Tel: 01788 510430

Weedon Bec Antiques,
66 High Street,
Weedon NN7 4QD
Tel: 01327 349910

Nottinghamshire

Harlequin Antiques,
79 Mansfield Road,
Daybrook,
Nottingham NG5 6BH
Tel: 0115 967 4590

Somerset

Gilbert & Dale,
The Old Chapel,
Church Street, Ilchester,
Nr Yeovil BA22 8LA
Tel: 01935 840464
Fax: 01935 841599
Painted pine.

Staffordshire

Johnsons,
120 Mill Street,
Leek ST13 8HA
Tel/Fax: 01538 386745
Specialists in English &
French, pine & fruitwood,
country furniture. Unique
objects & decorative
accessories. Most items
18th & 19th century.
Open 9–5 Mon to Sat.
Export trade welcome.

Surrey

Grayshott Pine,
Crossways Road,
Grayshott GU26 6HF
Tel: 01428 607478

Sussex

Bob Hoare,
Pine Antiques, Unit Q,
Phoenix Place, North St,
Lewes BN7 2DQ
Tel: 01273 480557

Ann Lingard,
Ropewalk Antiques,
Ropewalk,
Rye TN31 7NA
Tel: 01797 223486
Fax: 01797 224700

Graham Price,
Chaucer Trading Estate,
Dittons Road,
Polegate BN26 6JD
Tel: 01323 487167
Fax: 01323 483904

The Netherlands

Jacques Van Der Tol,
Antiek & Curiosa,
Antennestraat 34,
1322 A E Almere-Stad
Tel: 00 313 653 62050
Fax: 00 313 653 61993

Wales

Pot Board,
30 King Street,
Carmarthen,
Dyfed SA31 1BS
Tel: 01267 236623

Warwickshire

Cottage Pine Antiques,
19 Broad Street,
Brinklow,
Nr Rugby CV23 0LS
Tel: 01788 832673

Wiltshire

North Wilts Exporters,
Farm Hill House,
Brinkworth
SN15 5AJ
Tel: 01666 510876

Yorkshire

Eastburn Pine,
Unit 6, Eastburn Mills,
Eastburn,
Keighley BD20 7SJ
Tel: 01535 656297
Large stock of restored
and unrestored
English pine furniture
at trade prices.

PORCELAIN

Gloucestershire

Judy & Brian Harden,
PO Box 14
Bourton-on-the-Water,
Cheltenham GL54 2YR
Tel/Fax: 01451 810684

Gloucestershire

Clive & Lynne Jackson
Tel/Fax: 01242 254375
Mobile 0589 715275

Hampshire

Goss & Crested China Ltd,
62 Murray Road,
Horndean PO8 9JL
Tel: 01705 597446
Goss & Crested.

London

Marion Langham
Tel: 0171 730 1002
Fax: 0171 259 9266
Belleek.

Shropshire

Teme Valley Antiques,
1 The Bull Ring,
Ludlow SY8 1AD
Tel: 01584 874686

Warwickshire

Coleshill Antiques,
12-14 High Street,
Coleshill B46 1AZ
Tel: 01675 462931
Fax: 01675 467416
Furniture & porcelain.

Yorkshire

Crested China Co,
The Station House,
Driffield YO25 7PY
Tel: 01377 257042
Goss & crested china.

POTTERY

Avon

Andrew Dando,
4 Wood Street,
Queen Square,
Bath BA1 2JQ
Tel: 01225 422702
Fax: 01225 310717

Peter Scott,
Stand 39,
Bartlett Street
Antiques Centre,
Bath BA1 2QZ
Tel: 01225 310457
or 0117 986 8468
Mobile 0850 639770

Berkshire

Special Auction Services,
The Coach House,
Midgham Park,
Reading RG7 5UG
Tel: 0118 971 2949
Fax: 0118 971 2420

Buckinghamshire

Gillian Neale Antiques,
PO Box 247,
Aylesbury HP20 1JZ
Tel: 01296 23754
Fax: 01296 334601
Blue & white transferware.

Kent

Serendipity,
168 High Street,
Deal CT14 6BQ
Tel: 01304 369165
Staffordshire pottery.

Lancashire

Roy W Bunn Antiques,
34/36 Church Street,
Barnoldswick,
Colne BB8 5UT
Tel: 01282 813703
Fax: 01282 813703
Staffordshire Pottery.

London

Antiques Arcadia,
22 Richmond Hill,
TW10 6QX
Tel/Fax: 0181 940 2035
Staffordshire pottery.

Jonathan Horne
(Antiques) Ltd,
66C Kensington Church St,
W8 4BY
Tel: 0171 221 5658
Fax: 0171 792 3090

Valerie Howard,
2 Campden Street,
W8 7EP
Tel: 0171 792 9702
Masons & Quimper.

Jacqueline Oosthuizen,
23 Cale Street,
Chelsea SW3 3QR
Tel: 0171 352 6071
Fax: 0171 376 3852
Staffordshire pottery.

Rogers de Rin,
76 Royal Hospital Road,
SW3 4HN
Tel: 0171 352 9007
Wemyss.

Tyne & Wear

Ian Sharp Antiques,
23 Front Street,
Tynemouth NE30 4DX
Tel/Fax: 0191 296 0656

Wales

Islwyn Watkins,
1 High Street, Knighton,
Powys LD7 1AT
Tel: 01547 520145

Warwickshire

Janice Paull,
PO Box 100,
Kenilworth CV8 1YR
Tel: 01926 855253
Fax: 01926 863384

PUBLICATIONS

London

Antiques Trade Gazette,
17 Whitcomb Street,
WC2H 7PL
Tel: 0171 930 9958

West Midlands

Antiques Bulletin,
H.P. Publishing,
2 Hampton Court Road,
Harborne,
Birmingham B17 9AE
Tel: 0121 681 8000
Fax: 0121 681 8005

Restoration

Hertfordshire

Workshop Interiors,
6 Stanley Avenue,
Chiswell Green,
St Albans AL2 3AB.
Tel: 01727 840456
Fax: 01727 840822
*Furniture, restoration,
polishing, carving, turning,
gilding and upholstery.*

ROCK & POP

Cheshire

Collector's Corner,
Tudor House
29-31 Lower Bridge St,
Chester CH1 1RS.
Tel: 01260 270429
Fax: 01260 298996

**SCIENTIFIC
INSTRUMENTS**

Avon

Richard Twort
Tel: 01934 641900

Scotland

Early Technology,
84 West Bow,
Edinburgh EH1 2HH
Tel: 0131 226 1132
Fax: 0131 665 2839

SERVICES

Hampshire

Securikey Ltd,
P O Box 18,
Aldershot GU12 4SL
Tel: 01252 311888/9
Fax: 01252 343950
Security.

West Midlands

Retro Products,
Star Street, Lye,
Nr Stourbridge DY8 2RR
Tel: 01384 894042/
442065/373332
Fax: 01384 442065
Fittings & accessories.

SERVICES/HUMIDIFIERS

London

Air Improvement
Centre Ltd,
23 Denbigh Street,
SW1V 2HF
Tel: 0171 834 2834
Fax: 0171 630 8485
*Specialist suppliers of
hygrometers, humidifiers
& dehumidifiers.*

SILVER

London

The Silver Fund,
139A New Bond Street,
W1Y 9FB
Tel: 0171 499 8501
Fax: 0171 495 4789

Shropshire

Teme Valley Antiques,
1 The Bull Ring,
Ludlow SY8 1AD.
Tel: 01584 874686

SPORTS & GAMES

Berkshire

William Bentley Billiards,
Standen Manor Farm,
Hungerford RG17 0RB
Tel: 01488 681711
Fax: 01488 685197

Hampshire

Evans & Partridge,
Agriculture House,
High Street,
Stockbridge SO20 6HF
Tel: 01264 810702
Fax: 01264 810944

Kent

Old Tackle Box,
PO Box 55,
Cranbrook TN17 3ZU
Tel/Fax: 01580 713979

Lincolnshire

Cheshire Billiards Co,
Springwood Lodge,
Ermine Street,
Appleby DN15 0DD
Tel: 01724 852359

London

Angling Auctions,
P O Box 2095,
W12 8RU
Tel: 0181 749 4175
Fax: 0181 743 4855

The Reel Thing,
17 Royal Opera Arcade,
Pall Mall SW1Y 4UY
Tel: 0171 976 1830
Fishing tackle, sporting.

Nottinghamshire

T. Vennett-Smith,
11 Nottingham Road,
Gotham NG11 0HE
Tel: 0115 983 0541
Fax: 0115 983 0114

Shropshire

Mullock & Madeley,
The Old Shippon,
Wall-under-Heywood,
Church Stretton
SY6 7DS
Tel: 01694 771771
Fax: 01694 771772

Somerset

Billiard Room Antiques,
The Old School, Church
Lane, Chilcompton,
Bath BA3 4HP
Tel: 01761 232839

Surrey

Academy Billiard Co,
5 Camp Hill Industrial Est,
West Byfleet KT14 6EW
Tel: 01932 352067
Fax: 01932 353904

Scotland

Timeless Tackle,
1 Blackwood Crescent,
Edinburgh EH9 1QZ
Tel: 0131 667 1407
Fax: 0131 662 4215

TEDDY BEARS

Oxfordshire

Teddy Bears of Witney,
99 High Street,
Witney OX8 6LY
Tel: 01993 702616
Fax: 01993 702344

TOYS

Essex

Haddon Rocking Horses,
5 Telford Road,
Clacton-on-Sea
CO15 4LP
Tel: 01255 424745

Sussex

Wallis & Wallis,
West Street Auction Galls,
Lewes BN7 2NJ
Tel: 01273 480208
Fax: 01273 476562

Yorkshire

John & Simon Haley,
89 Northgate,
Halifax HX6 4NG
Tel: 01422 822148

WINE ANTIQUES

Buckinghamshire

Christopher Sykes,
The Old Parsonage,
Woburn, Milton Keynes
MK17 9QM
Tel: 01525 290259
Fax: 01525 290061

WALES

SOUTH EAST

SOUTH WEST

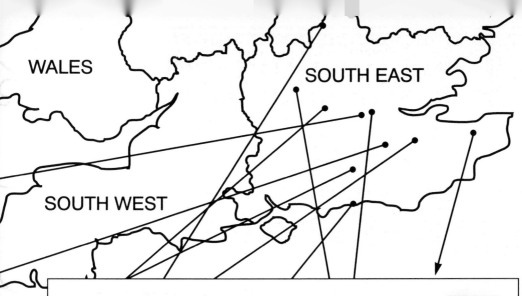

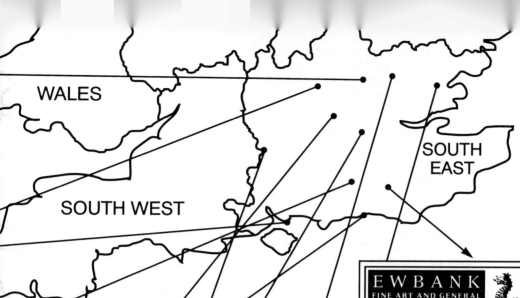

WALES

SOUTH EAST

SOUTH WEST

WALES

SOUTH EAST

SOUTH WEST

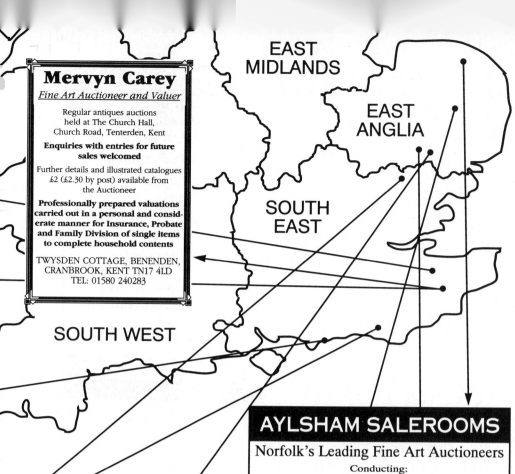

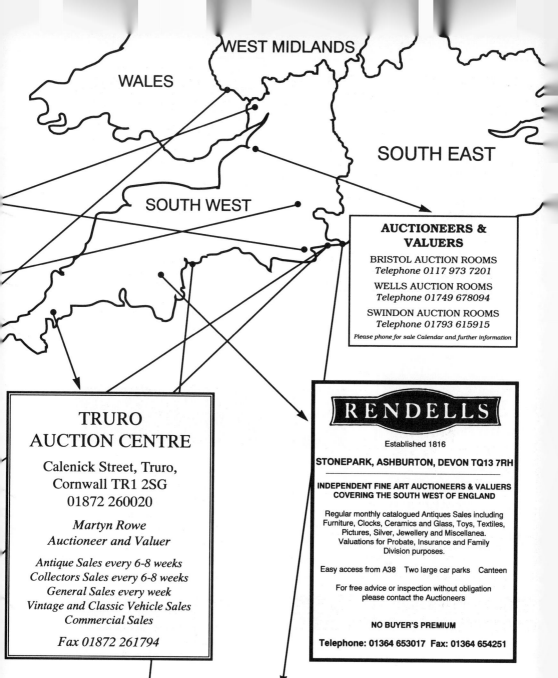

NORTH WEST

EAST MIDLANDS

WEST MIDLANDS

EAST ANGLIA

WALES

SOUTH EAST

SOUTH WEST

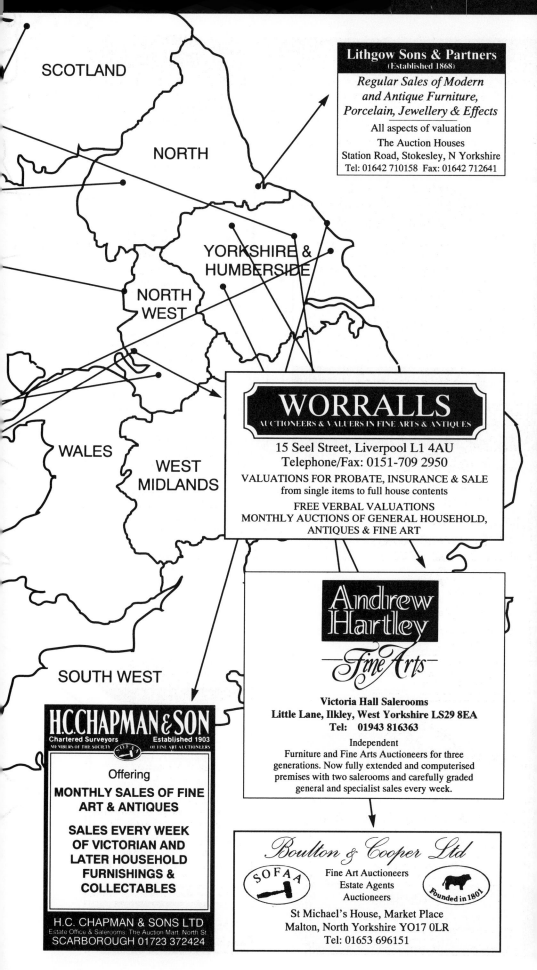

SCOTLAND

NORTH

YORKSHIRE &
HUMBERSIDE

NORTH
WEST

WALES

WEST
MIDLANDS

SOUTH WEST

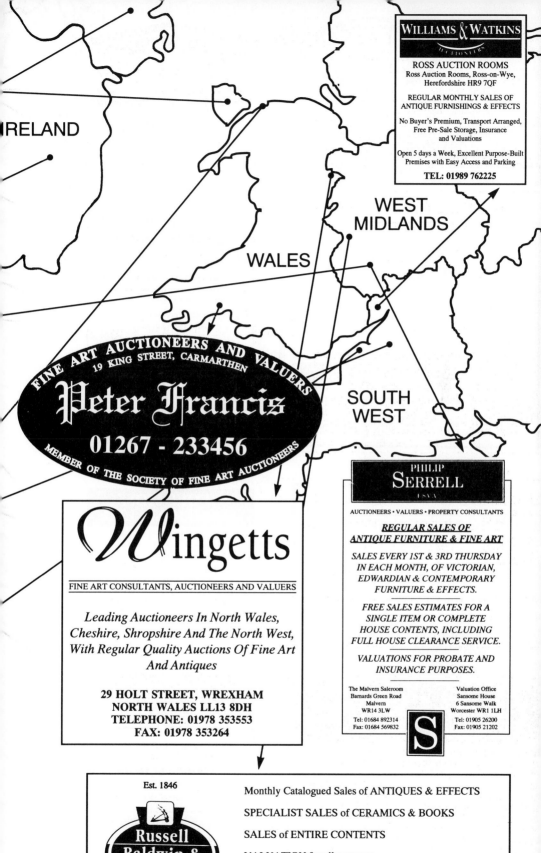

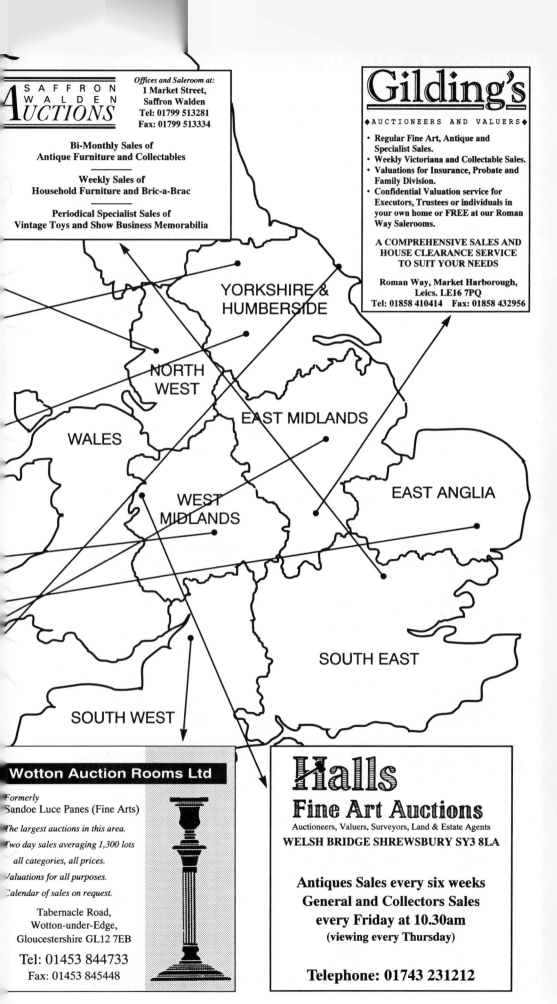

YORKSHIRE & HUMBERSIDE

NORTH WEST

WALES

EAST MIDLANDS

WEST MIDLANDS

EAST ANGLIA

SOUTH EAST

SOUTH WEST

DIRECTORY OF AUCTIONEERS

Auctioneers who hold frequent sales should contact us for inclusion in the next edition. Entries must be received by April 1998, and will be repeated in subsequent editions unless we are requested otherwise.

London

Academy Auctioneers
& Valuers,
Northcote House,
Northcote Avenue,
Ealing, W5 3UR
Tel: 0181 579 7466

Angling Auctions,
P O Box 2095,
W12 8RU
Tel: 0181 749 4175

Bloomsbury Book Auctions,
3/4 Hardwick Street,
Off Rosebery Avenue,
EC1R 4RY
Tel: 0171 833 2636

Bonhams,
Montpelier Street,
Knightsbridge,
SW7 1HH
Tel: 0171 393 3900

Bonhams,
65-69 Lots Road,
Chelsea, SW10 0RN
Tel: 0171 393 3900

Christie, Manson & Woods,
8 King Street,
St James's,
SW1Y 6QT
Tel: 0171 839 9060

Christie's South
Kensington Ltd,
85 Old Brompton Road,
SW7 3LD
Tel: 0171 581 7611

Comic Book Postal
Auctions Ltd,
40-42 Osnaburgh Street,
London, NW1 3ND
Tel: 0171 424 0007

Criterion Salerooms,
53 Essex Road,
Islington, N1 2BN
Tel: 0171 359 5707

Dix-Noonan-Webb,
1 Old Bond Street,
W1X 3TD
Tel: 0171 499 5022

Emerald Auctions,
212 High Road,
N2 9AY
Tel: 0181 883 0234

Forrest & Co,
17-31 Gibbins Road,
Stratford, E15 2HU
Tel: 0181 534 2931

Stanley Gibbons Auctions,
399 Strand,
WC2R 0LX
Tel: 0171 836 8444

Glendinings & Co,
101 New Bond Street,
W1Y 9LG
Tel: 0171 493 2445

Harmers of London,
91 New Bond Street,
W1Y 9LA
Tel: 0171 629 0218

Hornsey Auctions Ltd,
54/56 High Street,
Hornsey, N8 7NX
Tel: 0181 340 5334

Lloyds International
Auction Galleries,
118 Putney Bridge Road,
SW15 2NQ
Tel: 0181 788 7777

MacGregor Nash & Co,
Lodge House,
9-17 Lodge Lane,
North Finchley, N12 8JH
Tel: 0181 445 9000

Thomas Moore,
217-219 Greenwich High Rd,
SE10 8NB
Tel: 0181 858 7848

Onslow's,
The Old Depot,
The Gas Works,
off Michael Road,
SW6 2AD
Tel: 0171 371 0505

Phillips,
101 New Bond Street,
W1Y 0AS
Tel: 0171 629 6602

Phillips Bayswater,
10 Salem Road,
W2 4DL
Tel: 0171 229 9090

Proud Oriental Auctions,
Proud Galleries,
5 Buckingham St,
WC2N 6BP
Tel: 0171 839 4942

Rippon Boswell & Co,
The Arcade,
South Kensington Station,
SW7 2NA
Tel: 0171 589 4242

Rosebery's Fine Art Ltd,
Old Railway Booking Hall,
Crystal Palace Station
Road, SE19 2AZ
Tel: 0181 778 4024

Sotheby's,
34-35 New Bond Street,
W1A 2AA
Tel: 0171 493 8080

Southgate Auction Rooms,
55 High Street,
Southgate, N14 6LD
Tel: 0181 886 7888

Spink & Son Ltd,
5 Kings Street,
St James's,
SW1Y 6QS
Tel: 0171 930 7888

Town & Country House
Auctions,
42A Nightingale Grove,
SE13 6DY
Tel: 0181 852 3145/
0181 462 1735

Avon

Aldridges,
The Auction Galleries,
130-132 Walcot Street,
Bath, BA1 5BG
Tel: 01225 462830 &
462833

Auction Centres Bristol,
Prewett Street, Redcliffe,
Bristol, BS1 6TB
Tel: 0117 926 5996

Bristol Auction Rooms,
St John's Place,
Apsley Road, Clifton,
Bristol, BS8 2ST
Tel: 0117 973 7201

Clevedon Salerooms,
Herbert Road,
Clevedon, BS21 7ND
Tel: 01275 876699

Gardiner Houlgate,
The Old Malthouse,
Comfortable Place,
Upper Bristol Road,
Bath, BA1 3AJ
Tel: 01225 447933

Phillips,
1 Old King Street,
Bath, BA1 2JT
Tel: 01225 310609

Woodspring Auction Rooms,
Churchill Road,
Weston-super-Mare,
BS23 3HD
Tel: 01934 628419

Bedfordshire

Wilson Peacock,
The Auction Centre,
26 Newnham Street,
Bedford,
MK40 3JR
Tel: 01234 266366

Berkshire

Chancellors, R. Elliott,
32 High Street,
Ascot, SL5 7HG
Tel: 01344 872588

Dreweatt Neate,
Donnington Priory,
Donnington,
Newbury, RG13 2JE
Tel: 01635 31234

Martin & Pole,
12 Milton Road,
Wokingham, RG40 1DB
Tel: 0118 979 0460

Shiplake Fine Art,
31 Great Knollys Street,
Reading, RG1 7HU
Tel: 01734 594748

Special Auction Services,
The Coach House,
Midgham Park,
Reading, RG7 5UG
Tel: 0118 971 2949

Buckinghamshire

Amersham Auction Rooms,
125 Station Road,
Amersham, HP7 0AH
Tel: 01494 729292

Bourne End Auction Rooms,
Station Approach,
Bourne End, SL8 5QH
Tel: 01628 531500

Hamptons,
10 Burkes Parade,
Beaconsfield,
HP9 1PD
Tel: 01494 672969

Wigley's,
Winslow Saleroom,
Market Square,
Winslow, MK18 3AP
Tel: 01296 713011

Cambridgeshire

Cheffins Grain & Comins,
2 Clifton Road,
Cambridge,
CB2 4BW
Tel: 01223 358721/213343

Goldsmiths,
15 Market Place,
Oundle, PE8 4BA
Tel: 01832 272349

Grounds & Co,
2 Nene Quay,
Wisbech, PE13 1AG
Tel: 01945 585041

Maxey & Son,
1-3 South Brink,
Wisbech, PE13 1RD
Tel: 01945 584609

Cheshire

F. W. Allen & Son,
15/15a Station Road,
Cheadle Hulme, SK8 5AF
Tel: 0161 485 6069

David Dockree,
Cheadle Hulme Business
Centre, Clemence House,
Mellor Road,
Cheadle Hulme, SK7 1BD
Tel: 0161 485 1258

Highams Auctions,
Waterloo House,
Waterloo Road,
Staly Bridge, SK15 2AU
Tel: 0161 303 2924/
338 8698

Andrew Hilditch & Son,
Hanover House,
1a The Square,
Sandbach, CW11 0AP
Tel: 01270 762048/767246

Frank R. Marshall & Co,
Marshall House,
Church Hill, Knutsford,
WA16 6DH
Tel: 01565 653284

John Maxwell of Wilmslow,
133A Woodford Road,
Woodford, SK7 1QD
Tel: 0161 439 5182

Phillips North West,
New House,
150 Christleton Road,
Chester, CH3 5TD
Tel: 01244 313936

Peter Wilson,
Victoria Gallery,
Market Street,
Nantwich, CW5 5DG
Tel: 01270 623878

Wright Manley,
Beeston Castle Salerooms,
Tarporley, CW6 0DR
Tel: 01829 260318

County Durham

Denis Edkins,
Auckland Auction Room,
58 Kingsway,
Bishop Auckland,
DL14 7JF
Tel: 01388 603095

Thomas Watson & Son,
Northumberland Street,
Darlington, DL3 7HJ
Tel: 01325 462559/463485

Cornwall

Jeffery's,
5 Fore Street,
Lostwithiel, PL22 0BP
Tel: 01208 872245

Lambrays, incorporating
R. J. Hamm ASVA,
Polmorla Walk,
The Platt,
Wadebridge, PL27 7AE
Tel: 0120 881 3593

W. H. Lane & Son,
65 Morrab Road,
Penzance, TR18 2QT
Tel: 01736 361447

David Lay ASVA,
Auction House,
Alverton,
Penzance, TR18 4RE
Tel: 01736 361414

Phillips Cornwall,
Cornubia Hall,
Eastcliffe Road,
Par, PL24 2AQ
Tel: 0172 681 4047

Pooley and Rogers,
Regent Auction Rooms,
Abbey Street,
Penzance, TR18 4AR
Tel: 01736 368814

Martyn Rowe,
Truro Auction Centre,
Calenick Street,
Truro, TR1 2SG
Tel: 01872 260020

Cumbria

Cumbria Auction Rooms,
12 Lowther Street,
Carlisle, CA3 8DA
Tel: 01228 25259

Hackney & Leigh,
The Auction Centre,
Main Street,
Grange-over-Sands,
LE11 6AB
Tel: 015395 33316/33466

Mitchells,
Fairfield House,
Station Road,
Cockermouth, CA13 9PY
Tel: 01900 827800

Alfred Mossops & Co,
8 Victoria St,
Winderemere, LA23 1AB
Tel: 015394 88222

Penrith Farmers' & Kidd's,
Devonshire Chambers,
Devonshire Street,
Penrith, CA11 7SS
Tel: 01768 862135

Phillips Carlisle,
48 Cecil Street,
Carlisle, CA1 1NT
Tel: 01228 42422

James Thompson,
64 Main Street,
Kirkby Lonsdale, LA6 2AJ
Tel: 015242 71555

Thomson, Roddick & Laurie,
24 Lowther Street,
Carlisle, CA3 8DA
Tel: 01228 28939/39636

Derbyshire

Neales,
The Derby Saleroom,
Becket Street,
Derby, DE1 1HW
Tel: 01332 343286

Richardson & Linnell Ltd,
The Auction Office,
Cattle Market,
Chequers Road,
Derby, DE21 6EP
Tel: 01332 296369

Noel Wheatcroft,
Matlock Auction Gallery,
Old English Road,
Matlock, DE4 3LX
Tel: 01629 584591

Devon

Bearnes,
St Edmund's Court,
Exeter, EX4 1DU
Tel: 01392 422800

Bearnes,
1 Southernhay West,
Exeter, EX1 1JG
Tel: 01392 219040

Bearnes,
Avenue Road,
Torquay TQ2 5TG
Tel: 01803 296277

Bonhams West Country,
Devon Fine Art Auction Hse,
Dowell Street,
Honiton,
EX14 8LX
Tel: 01404 41872

Michael J. Bowman,
6 Haccombe House,
Netherton,
Newton Abbot,
TQ12 4SJ
Tel: 01626 872890

Eric Distin,
Chartered Surveyors,
2 Bretonside,
Plymouth, PL4 0BY
Tel: 01752 663046/664841

Eldreds,
13-15 Ridge Park Road,
Plympton,
Plymouth, PL7 2BS
Tel: 01752 340066

Robin A. Fine,
Fenner & Co,
Art & Antique Auctioneers,
The Stannary Gallery,
Drake Road,
Tavistock, PL19 0AX
Tel: 01822 617799/617800

Kingsbridge Auction Sales,
113 Fore Street,
Kingsbridge, TQ7 1BG
Tel: 01548 856829

Phillips,
Alphin Brook Road,
Alphington,
Exeter, EX2 8TH
Tel: 01392 439025

Potbury's, High Street,
Sidmouth, EX10 8LN
Tel: 01395 515555

Rendells,
Stone Park,
Ashburton, TQ13 7RH
Tel: 01364 653017

G. S. Shobrook & Co,
20 Western Approach,
Plymouth, PL1 1TG
Tel: 01752 663341

John Smale & Co,
11 High Street,
Barnstaple, EX31 1BG
Tel: 01271 42000/42916

Southwest Auctions,
South Street, Newport,
Barnstaple, EX32 9DT
Tel: 01837 810756

Martin Spencer-Thomas,
Bicton Street,
Exmouth, EX8 2SN
Tel: 01395 267403

Taylors,
Honiton Galleries,
205 High Street,
Honiton, EX14 8LF
Tel: 01404 42404

Ward & Chowen,
Tavistock Auction Rooms,
Market Road,
Tavistock, PL19 0BW
Tel: 01822 612603

Whitton & Laing,
32 Okehampton Street,
Exeter, EX4 1DY
Tel: 01392 52621

Dorset

Chapman, Moore & Mugford,
9 High Street,
Shaftesbury, SP7 8JB
Tel: 01747 852400

Cottees of Wareham,
The Market, East Street,
Wareham, BH20 4NR
Tel: 01929 552826

Dalkeith Auctions,
Dalkeith Hall,
Dalkeith Steps,
Rear of 81 Old
Christchurch Road,
Bournemouth, BH1 1EW
Tel: 01202 292905

H. Y. Duke & Son,
Dorchester Fine Art
Salerooms,
Dorchester, DT1 1QS
Tel: 01305 265080

House & Son,
Lansdowne House,
Christchurch Road,
Bournemouth, BH1 3JW
Tel: 01202 298044

William Morey & Sons,
The Saleroom,
St Michael's Lane,
Bridport, DT6 3RB
Tel: 01308 422078

Phillips Sherborne,
Long Street Salerooms,
Sherborne, DT9 3BS
Tel: 01935 815271

Riddetts of Bournemouth,
26 Richmond Hill,
The Square,
Bournemouth, BH2 6EJ
Tel: 01202 555686

Semley Auctioneers,
Station Road,
Semley,
Shaftesbury, SP7 9AN
Tel: 01747 855122

Southern Counties
Auctioneers,
Shaftesbury Livestock
Market, Christy's Lane,
Shaftesbury, SP7 8PH
Tel: 01747 851735

Michael Stainer Ltd,
St Andrew's Hall,
Wolverton Road, Boscombe,
Bournemouth, BH7 6HT
Tel: 01202 309999

Essex

Baytree Auctions,
23 Broomhills Ind. Estate,
Braintree, CM7 7RW
Tel: 01376 328228

Black Horse Agencies,
Ambrose,
149 High Road,
Loughton,
IG10 4LZ
Tel: 0181 502 3951

William H. Brown,
Paskell's Rooms,
11-14 East Hill,
Colchester,
CO1 2QX
Tel: 01206 868070

Cooper Hirst Auctions,
The Granary Saleroom,
Victoria Road,
Chelmsford,
CM2 6LH
Tel: 01245 260535

Grays Auction Rooms,
Ye Old Bake House,
Alfred Street,
Grays, RM17 6DZ
Tel: 01375 381181

Leigh Auction Rooms,
John Stacey & Sons,
88-90 Pall Mall,
Leigh-on-Sea,
SS9 1RG
Tel: 01702 77051

Saffron Walden Auctions,
1 Market Street,
Saffron Walden, CB10 1JB
Tel: 01799 513281

G. E. Sworder & Sons,
14 Cambridge Road,
Stansted Mountfitchet,
CM24 8BZ
Tel: 01279 817778

Trembath Welch,
The Old Town Hall,
Great Dunmow, CM6 1AU
Tel: 01371 873014

Gloucestershire

Bruton, Knowles & Co,
111 Eastgate Street,
Gloucester, GL1 1PZ
Tel: 01452 521267

Fraser Glennie & Partners,
The Old Rectory,
Siddington,
Nr Cirencester, GL7 6HL
Tel: 01285 659677

Hobbs & Chambers,
Market Place,
Cirencester, GL7 1QQ
Tel: 01285 654736

Hobbs & Chambers,
15 Royal Crescent,
Cheltenham, GL50 3DA
Tel: 01242 513722

Mallams,
26 Grosvenor Street,
Cheltenham, GL52 2SG
Tel: 01242 235712

Moore, Allen & Innocent,
33 Castle Street,
Cirencester, GL7 1QD
Tel: 01285 651831

Specialised Postcard
Auctions,
25 Gloucester Street,
Cirencester, GL7 2DJ
Tel: 01285 659057

Wotton Auction Rooms,
Tabernacle Road,
Wotton-under-Edge,
GL12 7EB
Tel: 01453 844733

Greater Manchester

Capes Dunn & Co,
The Auction Galleries,
38 Charles Street,
Off Princess Street,
M1 7DB
Tel: 0161 273 6060/1911

Hampshire

Andover Saleroom,
41A London Street,
Andover, SP10 2NY
Tel: 01264 364820

Basingstoke Auction Rooms,
82-84 Sarum Hill,
Basingstoke, RG21 1ST
Tel: 01256 840707

Bryan Clisby, at Andwells
Antiques, High Street,
Hartley Witney,
GU9 8DS
Tel: 01252 716436

Evans & Partridge,
Agriculture House,
High Street,
Stockbridge, SO20 6HF
Tel: 01264 810702

Farnham Auctions Ltd,
169 Fleet Rd,
Fleet, GU13 8PD
Tel: 01252 810844

Fox & Sons,
5 & 7 Salisbury Street,
Fordingbridge, SP6 1AD
Tel: 01425 652121

Jacobs & Hunt,
Lavant Street,
Petersfield, GU32 3EF
Tel: 01730 262744/5

George Kidner,
The Old School,
The Square, Pennington,
Lymington,
SO41 8GN
Tel: 01590 670070

May & Son,
18 Bridge Street,
Andover, SP10 1BH
Tel: 01264 323417

D. M. Nesbit & Co,
7 Clarendon Road,
Southsea, PO5 2ED
Tel: 01705 864321

Odiham Auction Sales,
The Eagle Works,
Rear of Hartley Wintney
Garages,
High Street,
Hartley Wintney,
RG27 8PU
Tel: 01252 844410

Phillips Fine Art Auctioneers,
54 Southampton Road,
Ringwood, BH24 1JD
Tel: 01425 473333

Phillips of Winchester,
The Red House,
Hyde Street,
Winchester, SO23 7DX
Tel: 01962 862515

Quay Auctions,
Fletchwood House,
Quayside Road,
Bitterne Manor,
Southampton,
SO18 1DP
Tel: 01703 211122

Romsey Auction Rooms,
86 The Hundred,
Romsey, SO51 8BX
Tel: 01794 513331

Hereford

Morris Bricknell,
Stuart House,
18 Gloucester Road,
Ross-on-Wye, HR9 5BU
Tel: 01989 768320

Russell, Baldwin & Bright,
Ryelands Road,
Leominster, HR6 8NZ
Tel: 01568 611122

Nigel Ward & Co,
The Border Property Centre,
Pontrilas, HR2 0EH
Tel: 01981 240140

Williams & Watkins,
Ross Auction Centre,
Overross,
Ross-on-Wye, HR9 7QF
Tel: 01989 762225

Hertfordshire

Brown & Merry,
Tring Market Auctions,
Brook Street,
Tring, HP23 5EF
Tel: 01442 826446

Hitchin Auctions Ltd,
The Corn Exchange,
Market Place,
Hitchin, SG5 1DY
Tel: 01462 442151

Andrew Pickford,
The Hertford Saleroom,
42 St Andrew Street,
Hertford,
SG14 1JA
Tel: 01992 583508

Humberside

Gilbert Baitson, FSVA,
The Edwardian Auction
Galleries, Wiltshire Road,
Hull, HU4 6PG
Tel: 01482 500500

Dickinson Davy & Markham,
Wrawby Street,
Brigg, DN20 8JJ
Tel: 01652 653666

H. Evans & Sons,
1 St James's Street,
Hessle Road,
Hull, HU3 3DH
Tel: 01482 23033

Isle of Wight

Watson Bull & Porter,
Isle of Wight Auction
Rooms, 79 Regent Street,
Shanklin, PO37 7AP
Tel: 01983 863441

Ways Auction House,
Garfield Road,
Ryde, PO33 2PT
Tel: 01983 562255

Kent

Albert Andrews
Auctions & Sales,
Maiden Lane,
Crayford, DA1 4LX
Tel: 01322 528868

Bracketts,
27-29 High Street,
Tunbridge Wells, TN1 1UU
Tel: 01892 533733

The Canterbury Auction
Galleries,
40 Station Road West,
Canterbury, Kent, CT2 8AN
Tel: 01227 76337

Mervyn Carey,
Twysden Cottage,
Benenden,
Cranbrook, TN17 4LD
Tel: 01580 240283

Halifax Property Services,
Fine Art Department,
53 High Street,
Tenterden, TN30 6BG
Tel: 01580 763200

Halifax Property Services,
15 Cattle Market,
Sandwich, CT13 9AW
Tel: 01304 614369

Edwin Hall,
Valley Antiques,
Lyminge,
Folkestone, CT18 8EJ
Tel: 01303 862134

Hobbs Parker,
Romney House,
Ashford Market,
Elwick Road,
Ashford, TN23 1PG
Tel: 01233 622222

Hogben Auctioneers,
St John's Street,
Folkestone, CT20 1JB
Tel: 01303 240808

Ibbett Mosely,
125 High Street,
Sevenoaks, TN13 1UT
Tel: 01732 452246

Lambert & Foster,
102 High Street,
Tenterden, TN30 6HT
Tel: 01580 762083/763233

B. J. Norris,
The Quest, West Street,
Harrietsham,
Maidstone, ME17 1JD
Tel: 01622 859515

Phillips Fine Art
Auctioneers,
49 London Road,
Sevenoaks, TN13 1AR
Tel: 01732 740310

Phillips Folkestone,
11 Bayle Parade,
Folkestone, CT20 1SG
Tel: 01303 245555

The Canterbury Auction
Galleries,
40 Station Road West,
Canterbury, CT2 8AN
Tel: 01227 763337

Town & Country House
Auctions, North House,
Oakley Rd, Bromley
Common, BR2 8HG
Tel: 0181 462 1735

Walter & Randall,
7-13 New Road,
Chatham, ME4 4QL
Tel: 01634 841233

Wealden Auction Galleries,
Desmond Judd,
23 Hendly Drive,
Cranbrook, TN17 3DY
Tel: 01580 714522

Peter S. Williams FSVA,
Orchard End,
Sutton Valence,
Maidstone, ME17 3LS
Tel: 01622 842350

Lancashire

Entwistle Green,
The Galleries,
Kingsway Ansdell,
Lytham St Annes,
FY8 1AB
Tel: 01253 735442

Robert Fairhurst & Son,
39 Mawdsley Street,
Bolton, BL1 1LR
Tel: 01204 528452/528453

Mills & Radcliffe incorp'ing
D. Murgatroyd & Son,
101 Union Street,
Oldham, OL1 1QH
Tel: 0161 624 1072

David Palamountain,
1-3 Osborne Grove,
Morecambe, LA4 4LP
Tel: 01524 423941

J. R. Parkinson & Son,
Hamer Auctions,
The Auction Rooms,
Rochdale Road,
Bury, BL9 7HH
Tel: 0161 761 1612/7372

Smythe's Son & Walker,
174 Victoria Road West,
Thornton Cleveleys,
FY5 3NE
Tel: 01253 852184

Tony & Sons,
4-8 Lynwood Road,
Blackburn, BB2 6HP
Tel: 01254 691748

Warren & Wignall Ltd,
The Mill, Earnshaw
Bridge, Leyland Lane,
Leyland, PR5 3PH
Tel: 01772 453252/451430

Leicestershire

William H. Brown,
Warner Auction Rooms,
16-18 Halford Street,
Leicester, LE1 6AS
Tel: 0116 255 9900

Churchgate Auctions,
66 Churchgate,
Leicester, LE1 4AL
Tel: 0116 262 1416

Gildings,
64 Roman Way,
Market Harborough,
LE16 7PQ
Tel: 01858 410414

Heathcote Ball & Co,
Castle Auction Rooms,
78 St Nicholas Circle,
Leicester, LE1 5NW
Tel: 0116 253 6789

David Stanley Auctions,
Stordon Grange,
Osgathorpe,
Loughborough, LE12 9SR
Tel: 01530 222320

Lincolnshire

A. E. Dowse & Son,
Foresters Galleries,
Falkland Way,
Barton-upon-Humber,
DN18 5RL
Tel: 01652 632335

Escritt & Barrell,
24 St Peter's Hill,
Grantham, NG31 6QF
Tel: 01476 65371

Goldings,
Grantham Auction Rooms,
Old Wharf Road,
Grantham, NG31 7AA
Tel: 01476 65118

Thomas Mawer & Son,
The Lincoln Saleroom,
63 Monks Road,
Lincoln, LN2 5HP
Tel: 01522 524984

Richardsons,
Bourne Auction Rooms,
Spalding Road,
Bourne, PE10 9LE
Tel: 01778 422686

Henry Spencer & Sons
(Phillips),
42 Silver Street,
Lincoln, LN2 1TA
Tel: 01522 536666

Marilyn Swain Auctions,
The Old Barracks,
Sandon Road,
Grantham, NG31 9AS
Tel: 01476 568861

John Taylor,
Cornmarket Chambers,
Louth, LN11 9PY
Tel: 01507 603648

Walter's,
No 1 Mint Lane,
Lincoln, LN1 1UD
Tel: 01522 525454

Merseyside

Cato Crane & Co,
Liverpool Auction Rooms,
6 Stanhope Street,
Liverpool, L8 5RF
Tel: 0151 709 5559

Hartley & Co,
12 & 14 Moss Street,
Liverpool, L6 1HF
Tel: 0151 263 6472/1865

Kingsley & Co,
3-5 The Quadrant,
Hoylake,
Wirral, L47 2EE
Tel: 0151 632 5821

Outhwaite & Litherland,
Kingsway Galleries,
Fontenoy Street,
Liverpool, L3 2BE
Tel: 0151 236 6561

Worralls,
13-15 Seel Street,
Liverpool, L1 4AU
Tel: 0151 709 2950

Norfolk

Ewings,
Market Place,
Reepham,
Norwich, NR10 4JJ
Tel: 01603 870473

Thomas Wm. Gaze & Son,
Diss Auction Rooms,
Roydon Road,
Diss, IP22 3LN
Tel: 01379 650306

Nigel F. Hedge,
28B Market Place,
North Walsham,
NR28 9BS
Tel: 01692 402881

G. A. Key,
Aylsham Salerooms,
8 Market Place,
Aylsham, NR11 6EH
Tel: 01263 733195

Northamptonshire

Corby & Co,
30-32 Brook Street,
Raunds, NN9 6LR
Tel: 01933 623722

Lowery's,
24 Bridge Street,
Northampton, NN1 1NT
Tel: 01604 21561

Merry's Auctioneers,
Northampton Auction &
Sales Centre,
Liliput Road,
Brackmills,
Northampton,
NN4 7BY
Tel: 01604 769990

Nationwide Surveyors,
28 High Street,
Daventry, NN11 4HU
Tel: 01327 312022

Southam & Sons,
Corn Exchange, Thrapston,
Kettering, NN14 4JJ
Tel: 01832 734486

H. Wilford Ltd,
Midland Road,
Wellingborough, NN8 1NB
Tel: 01933 222760

Northumberland

Louis Johnson Auctioneers,
63 Bridge Street,
Morpeth, NE61 1PQ
Tel: 01670 513025

Nottinghamshire

Arthur Johnson & Sons Ltd,
Nottingham Auction Centre,
Meadow Lane,
Nottingham, NG2 3GY
Tel: 0115 986 9128

Neales,
192-194 Mansfield Road,
Nottingham,
NG1 3HU
Tel: 0115 962 4141

C. B. Sheppard & Son,
The Auction Galleries,
Chatsworth Street,
Sutton-in-Ashfield,
NG17 4GG
Tel: 01773 872419

Henry Spencer & Sons
(Phillips),
20 The Square,
Retford, DN22 6XE
Tel: 01777 708633

T. Vennett-Smith,
11 Nottingham Road,
Gotham, NG11 0HE
Tel: 0115 983 0541

Oxfordshire

Dreweatt Neate Holloways,
49 Parsons Street,
Banbury, OX16 8PF
Tel: 01295 253197

Green & Co,
33 Market Place,
Wantage, OX12 8AH
Tel: 01235 763561/2

Mallams,
24 St Michael's Street,
Oxford, OX1 2EB
Tel: 01865 241358

Phillips,
39 Park End Street,
Oxford, OX1 1JD
Tel: 01865 723524

Simmons & Sons,
32 Bell Street,
Henley-on-Thames,
RG9 2BH
Tel: 01491 571111

Soames County Auctions,
Pinnocks Farm Estates,
Northmoor, OX8 1AY
Tel: 01865 300626

Shropshire

Halls Fine Art Auctions,
Welsh Bridge,
Shrewsbury,
SY3 8LA
Tel: 01743 231212

Ludlow Antique
Auctions Ltd,
29 Corve Street,
Ludlow, SY8 1DA
Tel: 01584 875157

McCartneys,
Ox Pasture,
Overture Road,
Ludlow, SY8 4AA
Tel: 01584 872251

Nock Deighton,
Livestock & Auction
Centre, Tasley,
Bridgnorth, WV16 4QR
Tel: 01746 762666

Perry & Phillips,
Newmarket Salerooms,
Newmarket Buildings,
Listley Street,
Bridgnorth, WV16 4AW
Tel: 01746 762248

Welsh Bridge Salerooms,
Welsh Bridge,
Shrewsbury, SY3 8LH
Tel: 01743 231212

Somerset

Black Horse Agencies,
Alder King,
25 Market Place,
Wells, BA5 2RG
Tel: 01749 673002

Cooper & Tanner,
Frome Auction Rooms,
Frome Market,
Standerwick,
Nr Frome, BA11 2PY
Tel: 01373 831010

Dores & Rees,
The Auction Mart,
Vicarage Street,
Frome, BA11 1PU
Tel: 01373 462257

John Fleming,
4 & 8 Fore Street,
Dulverton, TA22 9EX
Tel: 01398 23597

Gribble Booth & Taylor,
13 The Parade,
Minehead,
TA24 5NL
Tel: 01643 702281

Lawrence Fine Art
Auctioneers,
South Street,
Crewkerne, TA18 8AB
Tel: 01460 73041

Richards,
The Town Hall,
The Square,
Axbridge, BS26 2AR
Tel: 01934 732969

Wellington Salerooms,
Mantle Street,
Wellington,
TA21 8AR
Tel: 01823 664815

Wells Auction Rooms,
66/68 Southover,
Wells, BA5 1UH
Tel: 01749 678094

Staffordshire

Bagshaws,
17 High Street,
Uttoxeter, ST14 7HP
Tel: 01889 562811

Hall & Lloyd,
South Street Auction Rooms,
Stafford, ST16 2DZ
Tel: 01785 258176

Louis Taylor Auctioneers &
Valuers,
Britannia House,
10 Town Road, Hanley,
Stoke on Trent, ST1 2QG
Tel: 01782 214111

Wintertons Ltd,
Lichfield Auction Centre,
Wood End Lane, Fradley,
Lichfield, WS13 8NF
Tel: 01543 263256

Suffolk

Abbotts Auction Rooms,
Campsea Ashe,
Woodbridge, IP13 0PS
Tel: 01728 746323

Boardman Fine Art
Auctioneers,
Station Road Corner,
Haverhill,
Suffolk, CB9 0EY
Tel: 01440 730414

William H. Brown,
Ashford House,
Saxmundham, IP17 1AB
Tel: 01728 603232

Diamond Mills & Co,
117 Hamilton Road,
Felixstowe, IP11 7BL
Tel: 01394 282281

Lacy Scott,
Fine Art Department,
Auction Centre,
10 Risbygate Street,
Bury St Edmunds,
IP33 3AA
Tel: 01284 763531

Geoff Moss Auctions Ltd,
The Stables, Pettaugh
Road, Stonham Aspal,
Stowmarket, IP14 6AU
Tel: 01473 890823

Neal Sons & Fletcher,
26 Church Street,
Woodbridge, IP12 1DP
Tel: 01394 382263

Olivers,
Olivers Rooms,
Burkitts Lane,
Sudbury, CO10 6HB
Tel: 01787 880305

Phillips,
32 Boss Hall Road,
Ipswich, IP1 59J
Tel: 01473 740494

Suffolk Sales,
Half Moon House,
High Street,
Clare, CO10 8NY
Tel: 01787 277993

Surrey

Barbers Ltd,
Mayford Centre,
Smarts Heath Road,
Woking, GU22 0PP
Tel: 01483 728939

Chancellors,
74 London Road,
Kingston-upon-Thames,
KT2 6PX
Tel: 0181 541 4139

Clarke Gammon,
The Guildford Auction
Rooms, Bedford Road,
Guildford, GU1 4SJ
Tel: 01483 566458

Crows Auction Gallery,
Rear of Dorking Halls,
Reigate Road,
Dorking, RH4 1SG
Tel: 01306 740382

Ewbanks,
Burnt Common Auction
Rooms, London Road,
Send, Woking, GU23 7LN
Tel: 01483 223101

Hamptons Antique & Fine
Art Auctioneers,
93 High Street,
Godalming, GU7 1AL
Tel: 01483 423567

Lawrences Auctioneers,
Norfolk House,
80 High Street,
Bletchingley, RH1 4PA
Tel: 01883 743323

John Nicholson,
The Auction Rooms,
Longfield, Midhurst Road,
Fernhurst, GU27 3HA
Tel: 01428 653727

Parkins,
18 Malden Road,
Cheam, SM3 8SD
Tel: 0181 644 6633/6127

Phillips Fine Art
Auctioneers,
Millmead,
Guildford, GU2 5BE
Tel: 01483 504030

Richmond & Surrey
Auctions,
Richmond Station,
Kew Road, Old Railway
Parcels Depot,
Richmond,
TW9 2NA
Tel: 0181 948 6677

Wentworth Auction
Galleries,
21 Station Approach,
Virginia Water,
GU25 4DW
Tel: 01344 843711

P. F. Windibank,
The Dorking Halls,
Reigate Road,
Dorking, RH4 1SG
Tel: 01306 884556/876280

Sussex

Ascent Auction Galleries,
11-12 East Ascent,
St Leonards-on-Sea,
TN38 0DS
Tel: 01424 420275

John Bellman, Auctioneers,
New Pound Business Park,
Wisborough Green,
Billingshurst, RH14 0AY
Tel: 01403 700858

Burstow & Hewett,
Abbey Auction Galleries
and Granary Salerooms,
Lower Lake,
Battle, TN33 0AT
Tel: 01424 772374

Peter Cheney,
Western Road Auction
Rooms, Western Road,
Littlehampton, BN17 5NP
Tel: 01903 722264/713418

Clifford Dann Auction
Galleries,
20-21 High Street,
Lewes, BN7 2LN
Tel: 01273 480111

Denham's,
Horsham Auction
Galleries,
Warnham,
Horsham, RH12 3RZ
Tel: 01403 255699/253837

Eastbourne Auction
Rooms,
182-184 Seaside,
Eastbourne, BN22 7QR
Tel: 01323 431444

R. H. Ellis & Sons,
44-46 High Street,
Worthing, BN11 1LL
Tel: 01903 238999

Gorringes Auction
Galleries,
Terminus Road,
Bexhill-on-Sea,
TN39 3LR
Tel: 01424 212994

Gorringes Auction
Galleries,
15 North Street,
Lewes, BN7 2PD
Tel: 01273 472503

Graves, Son & Pilcher,
Hove Auction Rooms
Hove Street,
Hove, BN3 2GL
Tel: 01273 735266

Edgar Horn,
Fine Art Auctioneers,
46-50 South Street,
Eastbourne,
BN21 4XB
Tel: 01323 410419

Raymond P Inman,
The Auction Galleries,
35 & 40 Temple Street,
Brighton, BN1 3BH
Tel: 01273 774777

Lewes Auction Rooms
(Julian Dawson),
56 High Street,
Lewes, BN7 1XE
Tel: 01273 478221

Nationwide,
Midhurst Auction Rooms,
West Street,
Midhurst, GU29 9NG
Tel: 01730 812456

Phillips Fine Art
Auctioneers,
Baffins Hall, Baffins Lane,
Chichester, PO19 1UA
Tel: 01243 787548

Rye Auction Galleries,
Rock Channel,
Rye, TN31 7HL
Tel: 01797 222124

Sotheby's Sussex,
Summers Place,
Billingshurst, RH14 9AD
Tel: 01403 783933

Stride & Son,
Southdown House,
St John's Street,
Chichester, PO19 1XQ
Tel: 01243 780207

Sussex Auction Galleries,
59 Perrymount Road,
Haywards Heath,
RH16 3DR
Tel: 01444 414935

Rupert Toovey Auctioneers,
Star Road,
Partridge Green,
RH13 8RJ
Tel: 01403 711744

Wallis & Wallis,
West Street Auction
Galleries,
Lewes, BN7 2NJ
Tel: 01273 480208

Watsons,
Heathfield Furniture
Salerooms,
The Market,
Burwash Road,
Heathfield, TN21 8RA
Tel: 01435 862132

Worthing Auction Galleries,
Fleet House,
Teville Gate,
Worthing,
BN11 1UA
Tel: 01903 205565/203425

Tyne & Wear

Anderson & Garland
(Auctioneers),
Marlborough House,
Marlborough Crescent,
Newcastle-upon-Tyne,
NE1 4EE
Tel: 0191 232 6278

Boldon Auction Galleries,
24a Front Street,
East Boldon, NE36 0SJ
Tel: 0191 537 2630

Thomas N. Miller,
18-22 Gallowgate,
Newcastle-upon-Tyne,
NE1 4SN
Tel: 0191 232 5617

Phillips North East,
St Mary's, Oakwellgate,
Gateshead, NE8 2AX
Tel: 0191 477 6688

Sneddons,
Sunderland Auction
Rooms, 30 Villiers Street,
Sunderland, SR1 1EJ
Tel: 0191 514 5931

Worcester

Philip Laney,
Malvern Auction Centre,
Portland Road,
Malvern, WR14 2TA
Tel: 01684 893933

Philip Serrell,
The Malvern Saleroom,
Barnards Green Road,
Malvern, WR14 3LW
Tel: 01684 892314

Village Auctions,
Sychampton Community
Centre,
Ombersley, WR2 4BH
Tel: 01905 421007

Richard Williams,
2 High Street,
Pershore, WR10 1BG
Tel: 01386 554031

Andrew Grant,
St Mark's House,
St Mark's Close,
Worcester, WR5 3DJ
Tel: 01905 357547

Griffiths & Co,
57 Foregate Street,
Worcester, WR1 1DZ
Tel: 01905 26464

Phipps & Pritchard,
Bank Buildings,
Kidderminster, DY10 1BU
Tel: 01562 822244/6

Warwickshire

Bigwood Auctioneers Ltd,
The Old School,
Tiddington,
Stratford-upon-Avon,
CV37 7AW
Tel: 01789 269415

Locke & England,
Black Horse Agencies,
18 Guy Street,
Leamington Spa,
CV32 4RT
Tel: 01926 889100

West Midlands

Biddle and Webb Ltd,
Ladywood Middleway,
Birmingham, B16 0PP
Tel: 0121 455 8042

Cariss Residential,
20 High Street,
Kings Heath,
Birmingham, B14 7JU
Tel: 0121 444 0088

Ronald E. Clare,
Clare's Auction Rooms,
70 Park Street,
Birmingham, B5 5HZ
Tel: 0121 643 0226

Frank H. Fellows & Sons,
Augusta House,
19 Augusta Street, Hockley,
Birmingham, B18 6JA
Tel: 0121 212 2131

James & Lister Lea,
1741 Warwick Road,
Knowle,
Birmingham, B93 0LX
Tel: 01564 779187

Phillips,
The Old House,
Station Road, Knowle,
Solihull, B93 0HT
Tel: 01564 776151

K. Stuart Swash FSVA,
Stamford House,
2 Waterloo Road,
Wolverhampton,
WV1 4DJ
Tel: 01902 710626

Walker, Barnett & Hill,
Waterloo Road Salerooms,
Clarence Street,
Wolverhampton,
WV1 4JE
Tel: 01902 773531

Weller & Dufty Ltd,
141 Bromsgrove Street,
Birmingham, B5 6RQ
Tel: 0121 692 1414

Wiltshire

Henry Aldridge & Son,
Devizes Auction Rooms,
1 Wine Street,
Devizes, SN10 1AP
Tel: 01380 729199

Hamptons,
20 High Street,
Marlborough, SN8 1AA
Tel: 01672 516161

Kidson Trigg,
Friars Farm,
Sevenhampton,
Highworth,
Swindon, SN6 7PZ
Tel: 01793 861000/861072

Swindon Auction Rooms,
The Planks,
(off The Square),
Old Town,
Swindon, SN3 1QP
Tel: 01793 615915

Dominic Winter,
Book Auctions,
The Old School,
Maxwell Street,
Swindon, SN1 5DR
Tel: 01793 611340

Woolley & Wallis,
Salisbury Salerooms,
51-61 Castle Street,
Salisbury, SP1 3SU
Tel: 01722 424500

Yorkshire

Audsley's Auctions,
(C. R. Kemp BSc),
11 Morris Lane,
Kirkstall, Leeds, LS5 3JT
Tel: 0113 275 8787

Bairstow Eves,
West End Saleroom,
The Paddock,
Whitby, YO21 3AX
Tel: 01947 603433

Boulton & Cooper,
St Michaels House,
Market Place,
Malton, YO17 0LR
Tel: 01653 696151

H. C. Chapman & Son,
The Auction Mart,
North Street,
Scarborough, YO11 1DL
Tel: 01723 372424

Cundalls,
15 Market Place,
Malton, YO17 0LP
Tel: 01653 697820

M. W. Darwin & Sons,
The Dales Furniture Hall,
Bedale, DL8 2AH
Tel: 01677 422846

De Rome,
12 New John Street,
Westgate,
Bradford, BD1 2QY
Tel: 01274 734116

Dee, Atkinson & Harrison,
The Exchange Saleroom,
Driffield, YO25 7LJ
Tel: 01377 253151

David Duggleby,
The Vine St Salerooms,
Scarborough, YO11 1XN
Tel: 01723 507111

Eadon Lockwood & Riddle,
411 Petre Street,
Sheffield, S4 8LJ
Tel: 0114 261 8000

Eddisons,
Auction Rooms,
4-6 High Street,
Huddersfield, HD1 2LS
Tel: 01484 533151

Andrew Hartley,
Victoria Hall Salerooms,
Little Lane,
Ilkley, LS29 8EA
Tel: 01943 816363

Hutchinson Scott,
The Grange,
Marton-Le-Moor,
Ripon, HG4 5AT
Tel: 01423 324264

Lithgow Sons & Partners,
The Antique House,
Station Road,
Stokesley,
Middlesbrough, TS9 7AB
Tel: 01642 710158/710326

Malcolms No1 Auctioneers
& Valuers,
The Chestnuts,
16 Park Avenue,
Sherburn-in-Elmet,
Nr Leeds, LS25 6EF
Tel: 01977 684971

Christopher Matthews,
23 Mount Street,
Harrogate, HG2 8DQ
Tel: 01423 871756

Morphets,
6 Albert Street,
Harrogate, HG1 1JL
Tel: 01423 530030

Nationwide Fine Arts
& Furniture,
27 Flowergate,
Whitby, YO21 3BB
Tel: 01947 603433

Phillips Leeds,
17a East Parade,
Leeds, LS1 2BH
Tel: 0113 2448011

John H. Raby & Son,
The Sale Rooms,
21 St Mary's Road,
Bradford, BD8 7QL
Tel: 01274 491121

Henry Spencer & Sons Ltd
(Phillips),
1 St James' Row,
Sheffield, S1 1WZ
Tel: 0114 272 8728

Geoffrey Summersgill ASVA,
8 Front Street, Acomb,
York, YO2 3BZ
Tel: 01904 791131

Tennants,
The Auction Centre,
Harmby Road,
Leyburn, DL8 5SG
Tel: 01969 623780

Tennants,
34 Montpellier Parade,
Harrogate, HG1 2TG
Tel: 01423 531661

Thompson's Auctioneers,
Dales Saleroom, The Dale
Hall, Hampsthwaite,
Harrogate, HG3 2EG
Tel: 01423 770741

Tudor Auction Rooms,
28 High St, Carcroft,
Doncaster, DN6 8DW
Tel: 01302 725029

Ward Price,
Royal Auction Rooms,
Queen Street,
Scarborough,
YO11 1HA
Tel: 01723 353581

Wilby's,
6a Eastgate,
Barnsley, S70 2EP
Tel: 01226 299221

Wilkinson & Beighton
Auctioneers,
Woodhouse Green,
Thurcroft,
Rotherham,
SY3 8LA
Tel: 01709 700005

Windle & Co,
The Four Ashes,
541 Great Horton Road,
Bradford, BD7 4EG
Tel: 01274 57299

Ireland

James Adam & Sons,
26 St Stephen's Green,
Dublin 2
Tel: 00 3531 676 0261/
661 3655

Christie's Dublin,
52 Waterloo Road,
Dublin 4
Tel: 00 353 1 6680 585

Mealy's,
Chatsworth Street,
Castle Comer,
Co Kilkenny
Tel: 00 353 56 41229

Morgans Auctions Ltd,
Duncrue Crescent,
Duncrue Road,
Belfast, BT3 9BW
Tel: 01232 771552

Temple Auctions Limited,
133 Carryduff Road,
Temple,
Lisburn,
Co. Antrim, BT27 6YL
Tel: 01846 638777

N. Ireland

Anderson's Auctions,
28 Linenhall Street,
Belfast, BT2 8BG
Tel: 01232 321401

Scotland

Lindsay Burns & Co Ltd,
6 King Street,
Perth, PH2 8JA
Tel: 01738 633888

Christie's Scotland Ltd,
164-166 Bath Street,
Glasgow, G2 4TG
Tel: 0141 332 8134

Frasers Auctioneers,
8A Harbour Road,
Inverness, IV1 1SY
Tel: 01463 232395

William Hardie Ltd,
15a Blythswood Square,
Glasgow, G2 4EW
Tel: 0141 221 6780

J. & J. Howe,
24 Commercial Street,
Alyth,
Perthshire,
PH12 8UA
Tel: 01828 632594

Loves Auction Rooms,
The Auction Galleries,
52-54 Canal Street,
Perth, PH2 8LF
Tel: 01738 633337

M. D.'s Auction Co,
Unit 15-17 Smeaton
Industrial Estate
Hayfield Road,
Kirkcaldy,
Fife, KY1 2HE
Tel: 01592 640969

Robert McTear & Co
(Auctioneers & Valuers) Ltd,
Clydeway Business Centre,
8 Elliot Place,
Glasgow, G3 8EP
Tel: 0141 221 4456

John Milne,
9 North Silver Street,
Aberdeen, AB1 1RJ
Tel: 01224 639336

Robert Paterson & Son,
8 Orchard Street,
Paisley,
Renfrewshire, PA1 1UZ
Tel: 0141 889 2435

Phillips Scotland,
65 George Street,
Edinburgh, EH2 2JL
Tel: 0131 225 2266

Phillips Scotland,
207 Bath Street,
Glasgow, G2 4HD
Tel: 0141 221 8377

L. S. Smellie & Sons Ltd,
Within the Furniture
Market, Lower
Auchingramont Road,
Hamilton, ML10 6BE
Tel: 01698 282007

Sotheby's,
112 George Street,
Edinburgh, EH2 4LH
Tel: 0131 226 7201

Thomson, Roddick & Laurie,
20 Murray Street,
Annan, DG12 6EG
Tel: 01461 202575

West Perthshire Auctions,
Dundas Street,
Comrie,
Perthshire, PH6 2LN
Tel: 01764 670613

Whytock & Reid,
Sunbury House,
Belford Mews,
Edinburgh, EH4 3DN
Tel: 0131 226 4911

Wales

Dodds Property World,
Victoria Auction Galleries,
9 Chester Street,
Mold,
Clwyd, CH7 1EB
Tel: 01352 752552

E. H. Evans & Co,
Auction Sales Centre,
The Market Place,
Kilgetty,
Dyfed, SA68 0UG
Tel: 01834 812793/811151

Morgan Evans & Co Ltd,
28-30 Church Street,
Llangefni,
Anglesey,
Gwynedd, LL77 7DU
Tel: 01248 723303/421582

Peter Francis,
The Curiosity Saleroom,
19 King Street,
Carmarthen, SA31 1BH
Tel: 01267 233456

Morris Marshall & Poole,
10 Broad Street,
Newtown,
Powys, SY16 2LZ
Tel: 01686 625900

Phillips in Wales Fine Art
Auctioneers,
9-10 Westgate Street,
Cardiff,
Glamorgan, CF1 1DA
Tel: 01222 396453

Players Auction Mart,
Players Industrial Estate,
Clydach,
Swansea, SA6 5BQ
Tel: 01792 846241

Rennies,
87 Monnow Street,
Monmouth, NP5 3EW
Tel: 01600 712916

Rogers Jones & Co,
33 Abergele Road,
Colwyn Bay, LL29 7RU
Tel: 01492 532176

Wingett's Auction Gallery,
29 Holt Street,
Wrexham,
Clwyd, LL13 8DH
Tel: 01978 353553

Austria

Dorotheum Auctioneers,
1010 Vienna,
Dorotheergasse 17.
Tel: 0043 1/515 60-0

Australia

Phillips Sydney,
158 Queen Street,
Woollahra,
Sydney NSW 2025
Tel: 00 612 9326 1588

Canada

D. & J. Ritchie Inc,
Auctioneers & Appraisers
of Antiques & Fine Arts,
288 King Street East,
Toronto,
M5A 1K4
Tel: (416) 364 1864

Waddingtons,
189 Queen Street East,
Toronto,
Ontario, M5A 1SZ
Tel: (416) 362 1678

Channel Islands

Bonhams and Langlois,
Westaway Chambers,
39 Don Street,
St Helier, JE2 4TR
Tel: 01534 22441

Bonhams & Martel
Maides Ltd,
Allez St Auction Rooms,
29 High Street,
St Peter Port,
Guernsey, GY1 4NY
Tel: 01481 713463/722700

Hong Kong

Christie's Hong Kong,
2203-5 Alexandra House,
16-20 Chater Road,
Tel: 00 852 2521 5396

Sotheby's,
Li Po Chun Chambers,
18th Floor,
189 Des Vouex Road,
Hong Kong
Tel: 852 524 8121

Germany

Sotheby's Berlin,
Palais am Festungsgraben,
Unter den Linden,
Neue Wache, D-10117
Tel: 49 (30) 201 0521

Holland

Christies Amsterdam BV,
Cornelis Schuytstraat 57,
1071 JG Amsterdam.
Tel: (3120) 5755 255

Van Sabben Poster Auctions,
Oosteinde 30,
1678 HS Oostwoud,
Tel: 31 (0) 229 202589

Sotheby's Amsterdam,
Rokin 102,
Amsterdam, 1012 KZ
Tel: 31 (20) 550 2200

Italy

Christie's Rome,
Palazzo Massimo,
Lancellotti,
Piazza Navona 114,
Rome, 00186
Tel: 00 396 687 2787

Sotheby's Rome,
Piazza d'Espana 90,
00187, Rome
Tel: 39(6) 69941791/
6781798

Monaco

Christie's (Monaco),
SAM, Park Palace,
Monte Carlo 98000
Tel: 00 33 7 9325 1933

Sotheby's Monaco,
Le Sporting d'Hiver,
Place du Casino,
Monaco 98001 Cedex
Tel: 00 33 7 9330 8880

Singapore

Bonhams Singapore,
1 Cuscaden Road,
Business Centre,
The Regent Hotel,
249715
Tel: (65) 739 3092

Christie's,
Unit 3 Park Lane,
Goodwood Park Hotel,
22 Scotts Road
Tel: (65) 235 3828

Switzerland

Christie's (Int'l) SA,
8 Place de la Taconnerie,
1204 Geneva
Tel: 00 4122 319 1766

Phillips Geneva,
9 rue Ami-Levrier,
CH-1201 Geneva
Tel: 00 41 22 738 0707

Sotheby's,
13 Quai du Mont Blanc,
Geneva, CH-1201
Tel: 41 (22) 732 8585

Sotheby's,
20 Bleicherweg,
Zurich, GH-8002
Tel: 41 (1) 202 0011

USA

Frank H. Boos,
Frank H. Gallery,
420 Enterprise Court,
Bloomfield Hills,
Michigan, 48302
Tel: 00 1 810 332 1500

Butterfield & Butterfield,
220 San Bruno Avenue,
San Francisco, CA 94103
Tel: 00 1 415 861 7500

Christie's Los Angeles,
342 North Rodeo Drive,
Beverly Hills,
Calforina 90210
Tel: (310) 275 5534

Christie, Manson & Woods
International Inc,
502 Park Avenue,
New York, NY 10022
Tel: 00 1 212 546 1000

William Doyle Galleries,
175 East 87th Street,
New York, NY 10128
Tel: 00 1 212 427 2730

Eldred's,
Robert C Eldred Co Inc,
1475 Route 6A, East
Dennis, Mass 0796, 02641
Tel: 00 1 508 385 3116

Grogan & Co,
890 Commonwealth Ave,
Boston, MA 2215
Tel: 00 1 617 566 4100

Lesley Hindman Auctioneers,
215 West Ohio Street,
Chicago,Illinois, IL 60610
Tel: 00 1 312 670 0010

Leland's,
245 Fifth Avenue, Suite 902,
New York 10016
Tel: 00 1 212 545 0800

Louisiana Auction Exchange,
2031 Government Street,
Baton Rouge, LA 70806
Tel: 00 1 504 387 9777

Lubin Galleries,
30 West 26th Street,
New York, NY10010
Tel: 00 1 212 929 0909

Luper Auction Galleries,
Box 5143,
Richmond, VA 23220
Tel: 00 1 804 359 2493

Paul McInnis Inc Auction
Gallery,
Route 88, 356 Exeter Road,
Hampton Falls,
New Hampshire, 03844
Tel: 00 1 603 778 8989

John Moran Auctioneers,
3202 E Foothill Boulevard,
Pasadena, CA 91107
Tel: 00 1 818 793 1833

Mystic Fine Arts,
47 Holmes Street,
Mystic, CT6355
Tel: 00 1 203 572 8873

Phillips New York,
406 East 79th Street,
New York, NY10021
Tel: 00 1 212 570 4830

R. O. Schmitt Fine Arts,
85 Lake Street,
Salem, NH 03079
Tel: (603) 893 5915

Selkirk s,
4166 Olive Street,
St Louis, MO 63108
Tel: 00 1 314 533 1700

Skinner Inc,
357 Main Street,
Bolton, MA 01740
Tel: 00 1 508 779 6241

Skinner Inc,
The Heritage on
the Garden,
63 Park Plaza,
Boston, MA 02116
Tel: 00 1 617 350 5400

Sloan's,
C. G. Sloan & Company
Inc, 4920 Wyaconda Road,
North Bethesda,
MD 20852
Tel: 00 1 301 468 4911/
669 5066

Sotheby's,
1334 York Avenue,
New York, NY 10021
Tel: 00 1 212 606 7000

Sotheby's,
9665 Wilshire Boulevard,
Beverly Hills,
California, 90212
Tel: 00 1 310 274 0340

Adam A. Weschler & Son,
909 E Street NW,
Washington, DC 20004
Tel: 00 1 202 628 1281

Wolfs Gallery,
1239 W 6th Street,
Cleveland, OH 44113
Tel: 00 1 216 575 9653

INDEX TO DISPLAY ADVERTISEMENTS

INDEX

Italic page numbers denote color pages; **bold** numbers refer to information and pointer boxes